I was absolutely delighted when Tony asked me to contribute the foreword to this encyclopaedia of Manchester United, the world's most famous club with which I was fortunate and proud to serve over twelve years, loving every minute of the time spent in my adopted city. I can assure you that it does not come any better than captaining Manchester United and England.

Manchester United (now approaching its 125th birthday) is a club rich in history and tradition with so many great players having worn the famous red shirts. In the early days, Billy Meredith and Charlie Roberts set the trend, followed by the great post-war side with Johnny Carey and Jack Rowley; the 'Babes' with Duncan Edwards, Roger Byrne, Bobby Charlton, Tommy Taylor and Dennis Viollet; the team of the '60s with Denis Law, George Best and Nobby Stiles; right up to the all-conquering sides of the 1990s, with today's heroes. It is now a club capable of attracting the best players in the world.

I consider myself to have been so lucky to have taken my place in this pageant of great players, proud to be United's longest-serving club captain, leading the side to victory in three FA Cup Finals at Wembley and enjoying European success in Rotterdam before signing off my career in fine style by twice lifting the huge Premiership trophy in 1993 and 1994 with my successor Steve Bruce, then watching United's first 'double' so brilliantly completed. I knew as I left Old Trafford that the club's future was in good hands!

During my United career I had the honour of playing under two great managers, first Ron Atkinson, my former gaffer at West Bromwich Albion, then Alex Ferguson, men with differing styles, but sharing one common bond - a total commitment to making Manchester United the best club in the land, in Europe, in the world. This desire for excellence and success runs right through the club - from the manager himself, of course, via the chairman and directors, the players, the wonderful back-room staff, straight through to the marvellous laundry ladies and finally the massive, loyal support from all corners of the globe which helps ensure United's continued success.

You will find that this encyclopaedia has been wonderfully produced - it's one of the best I've ever seen on any one club. Whatever you want to know about Manchester United Football Club, or the people who have helped make it, through its long and glorious history, its ups and downs, its triumphs and tragedies, you should find it all within its many pages.

If you love Manchester United, if you love football, I heartily recommend it to you as an essential part of your football book collection.

Bryan Robson

Bryan Robson OBE

INTRODUCTION

If you are a Manchester United fan, and I know there are millions of you out there, then this is the ideal book for you. It should provide answers to most, if not all, of your questions about the world's best supported football club.

You should find everything here from the early pioneering days of Newton Heath when football was in 'black and white' right through to the glorious technicolour of today's brilliant side, playing at 'The Theatre of Dreams' against the world's top clubs. Whether you are young or old, this A-Z Encyclopaedia will fill a vital place on your bookshelf, always handy to check those important records of players and teams, past or present, vital or trivial.

I have attempted to make the 'A-Z Encyclopaedia & Statistical Record of Manchester United Football Club 1878-2002' as comprehensive as possible, utilising all the statistical information available which I have obtained from various sources over the past ten years.

I first started compiling this book, in a manner of speaking, at the same time I began putting together my '1945-85 Who's Who of Manchester United' in the 1980s.

The result of all these years of beavering is this bumper 300 plus page, 270,000 word 'Encyclopaedia' covering, in detail, the history of one of the biggest clubs in world football.

There is a complete Who's Who of each and every player who has represented the club in senior competitive football down the years...United's complete playing record at senior level is covered in depth with details of its Premiership/Football League, FA Cup and League Cup records given against each club United has opposed. United's European record is also given in full There is an international section listing the honours won by United players past and present, along with details of the club's top appearance-makers and champion goalscorers, attendance figures (home and away) and sendings-off.

There are also biographies on all the club's managers. There is a mini-history of Old Trafford, a section on substitutes, all the big-money and record-breaking transfers, players' nicknames, the club's chairmen and much, much more....

You can see that I have tried - with the help of lifelong United fan John Russell in particular - to cover everything there is to cover on Manchester United.

Over the past few years, I have liaised with many soccer statisticians (including United facts and figures man John Tuckett from Bristol), archivists, supporters and ex-players about Manchester United. I have gathered in sheet after sheet of information regarding the team and the club itself.

As a result literally thousands of facts and figures (some interesting, some not so interesting) have been driven into the computer, along with scores of fond memories, many points of view, some sobering thoughts and a great deal of general news and trivia appertaining to Manchester United FC.

Whether supplied verbally, by letter, by fax or e-mail, it has all been fed into the system and as a result I feel I have put together a bumper book, perhaps one of the best ever produced (statistically) on a major football club, certainly in the U.K.

As you can see, I have tried to cram as much into the book as I possibly could. I just hope I haven't missed too much, but if I have, I would dearly love to hear from you, so that my records can be updated and/or amended in readiness for the next 'big book' on Manchester United which hopefully will be an up-dated version of this elaborate 'Encyclopaedia'.

Manchester United as everyone in football knows (world-wide) is a big, big club with millions of supporters around the globe. Old Trafford is now one of the world's finest all-seater stadiums and when United are playing there, the support the fans generate is quite tremendous with an average turnout of 67,000 plus guaranteed every time - and rising!

There is plenty in this book to keep you occupied during the winter months and certainly enough information contained within the pages to enable you to get your friends and colleagues talking continuously about Manchester United down the pubs and clubs, in the stands, on the streets, anywhere in fact, where football - and United - is the major subject!

With so many facts and figures, statistics, listings and features contained in this publication, it is certain there will be a discrepancy, a small error, a spelling mistake, even a missing player or wrong word somewhere down the line. I am only human, like every one else, and even the great writers of the past made the odd mistake here and there, or missed out something which should have been included, got a year or a date wrong. Please accept my apologies if something is amiss. I have, with the assistance of several willing helpers, tried to ensure that everything in this book is factual, up-to-date and precise in every detail.

Statistical Information
The statistics shown at the end of each player's profile are for what are considered 'first-class' fixtures, viz:
•Premier League matches (1992-2002)
•Football League matches (1892-1992: Division 1 & 2)
•Football Alliance matches (1889-1892)
•FA Cup fixtures, both competition proper & qualifying rounds (1886-2002)
•Football League Cup fixtures, under various sponsorship (1960-2002)
•European competitions (between 1955 & 2002): Champions League, European Cup, European Cup-winners Cup, ICFC/UEFA Cup, European Super Cup.
•World Club Championship & Club World Championship.
•FA Charity Shield games
•Test Matches (1892-1897)
•Watney Cup (1970 & 1971)
•Anglo-Italian Tournament (1972-73)
•Screen Sport Super Cup (1985-86)

The club has been playing fixtures since 1878 (as Newton Heath L & YR, Newton Heath and as Manchester United since 1902). There are a lot of matches which have not been regarded as first-class. However, if a Newton Heath player appeared in at least one first-class fixture, details of 'other' appearances have been included (in brackets) at the end of his biography and 'other matches' include: Football Combination (1888-89), Manchester & District Challenge Cup, Lancashire Junior & Senior Cups, Palatine League, Manchester Senior Cup and friendly matches. Regrettably many of these early fixtures were not all that well documented, so the figures cannot be wholly accurate, yet give some indication of the players' involvement.
* Wartime appearances & goalscoring records are not included in the players' individual statistics, although some do appear under 'Appearances' and 'Goals & Goalscoring' sections.

This Book is dedicated to
Peter Crossley Thomson ... ace footballer and United fan

First Published in Great Britain by
Britespot Publishing Solutions Limited
Chester Road, Cradley Heath
West Midlands B64 4AB

September 2002

© Tony Matthews 2002

ISBN 1-904103-03-0

Cover design and layout
© Britespot Publishing Solutions Limited

Printed and Bound in Great Britain by
Cromwell Press Ltd
Aintree Avenue
White Horse Business Park
Trowbridge
Wiltshire
BA14 0XB

ACKNOWLEDGEMENTS

I must say a special big 'thank you' to John Russell, these days domiciled at Waterlooville in Hampshire, born and bred on the Stretford End, who has been tremendous in helping me compile this book.
I also acknowledge the assistance afforded to me by David Barber (from the Football Association), Haydn Parry (BBC Radio Sport), Manuel Tomas (FC Barcelona Museum curator), Sue O'Connell, John Tuckett (a United fan from Bristol), Bryan Horsnell (from Reading), Zoe Ward (FA Premier League) and Wayne Hathaway, a United supporter from Landscove, Devon.
Thank you, too - and 'sorry' darling for the inconvenience caused - to my loving wife Margaret who once again has had to put up without me for hours upon end whilst I've been sat thrashing away on the computer keyboard, thumbing through old reference books, matchday programmes and soccer magazines, checking and re-checking the thousands of statistics and stories as well as travelling up and down the country from sunny Devon.
And also a huge thank you to my good friend Bryan Robson for agreeing to write the foreword to this book.
Last but by no means least I must give a sincere thank you to everyone who has worked on the book at Britespot Publishing, especially to Roger Marshall, Paul Burns, Steve Parry, Chris Sweet and Chris Russell.
•The majority of old pictures used in this book have come from scrapbooks, photograph albums and certain programmes, owned by ex-players, United supporters and serious collectors of footballing memorabilia. We have been unable to establish clear copyright on some of these pictures and therefore the publishers would be pleased to hear from anyone whose copyright has been unintentionally infringed.

Bibliography

Both myself and John Russell have had to refer to several books to clarify certain relevant statistics, facts and figures, individual players' details and, indeed, stories and match reports from past seasons regarding Manchester United. There is some conflicting information in these sources and we have made judgement as to which is likely to be correct.

The list

Association Football & The Men Who Made It: 4 vols
AFS Who's Who: 1902, 1903, 1907 & 1909
Back Page United (S F Kelly)
The Encyclopaedia of Association Football (M Goldsworthy)
England v. Scotland (B James)
English Internationals Who's Who: 1872-1972 (D Lamming & M Farror)
FA Official Yearbooks
Football Grounds of Great Britain (S Inglis)
Football League Director: 1985-99
Footballers' Factfile (B Hugman/AFS) 1995-2002
Manchester United: A Complete Record 1878-1992 (I Morrison & A Shury)
Manchester United: Winners & Champions (A Shorrocks)
Manchester United (P M Young)
Manchester United Official Annual (various)
Rejected FC (D Twydell)
Rothmans Yearbook (Vols. 1-32)
The Definitive Newton Heath (A Shury & B Landamore) 2002
The United Alphabet (G Dykes)
Topical Times Who's Who of 2,000 Football Stars: 1933
Topical Times Who's Who 1938

Magazines

AFS Football Recollections
AFS Bulletins (various)
'Football Monthly' (1951-69)
'Goal' (1970s)
Manchester United 'home' programmes (various)
'Match' (1995-2002)
'Shoot' (1980s)
'Soccer Star' (1960s)
'World Soccer' (various)

We have also referred to several individual players/managers autobiographes and biographies for confirmation of various factual points.

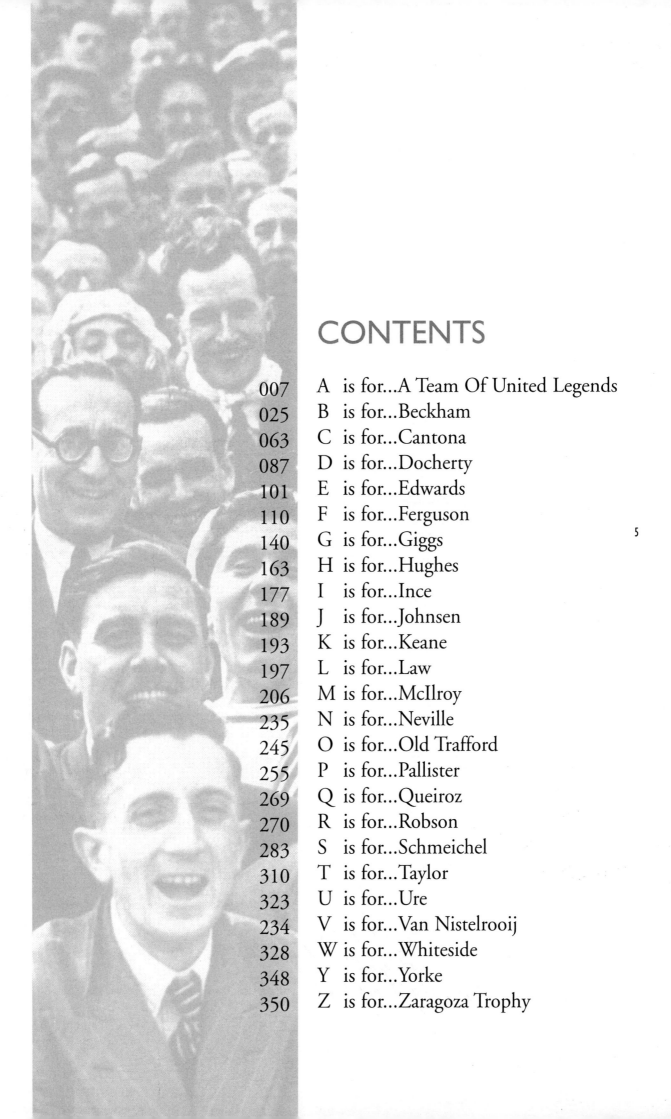

CONTENTS

5

European Champions Cup
Winners: 1968, 1999

European Cup-winners Cup
Winners: 1991

Football League Division One
Champions: 1908, 1911, 1952, 1956, 1957, 1965, 1967.
Runners-up: 1947, 1948, 1949, 1951, 1959, 1964, 1968, 1980, 1988, 1992

FA Premiership
Champions: 1993, 1994, 1996, 1997, 1999, 2000, 2001
Runners-up: 1995, 1998

Football League Division Two
Champions: 1936, 1975
Runners-up: 1897, 1906, 1925, 1938

FA Cup
Winners: 1909, 1948, 1963, 1977, 1983, 1985, 1990, 1994, 1996, 1999
Runners-up: 1957, 1958, 1976, 1979, 1995

Football League Cup
Winners: 1992
Runners-up: 1983, 1991, 1994

Inter-Continental Cup
Winners: 1999
Runners-up: 1968

UEFA Super Cup
Winners: 1991
Runners-up: 1999

FA Charity Shield
Winners: 1908, 1911, 1952, 1956, 1957, 1983, 1993, 1994, 1996, 1997
Joint holders: 1965, 1967, 1977, 1990
Runners-up: 1948, 1963, 1985, 1998

FA Youth Cup
Winners: 1953, 1954, 1955, 1956, 1957, 1964, 1992, 1995
Runners-up: 1982, 1986, 1993

UNITED'S
TROPHY CABINET

A for...

A TEAM OF
UNITED LEGENDS

To begin this unique encyclopaedia of the greatest football club in the world, I have selected a 'team' of United legends. With so many quality players having represented the club down the years, it was therefore difficult to leave out of the 'squad' of superstars so many brilliant players, but without reservation, this is my final choice of a 16-man squad, plus a 'management team.'

Danish international goalkeeper Peter Schmeichel; Republic of Ireland and United captain and right-back Johnny Carey; England's left-back Roger Byrne; dominant centre-halves Charlie Roberts and Bill Foulkes; the strong and purposeful Bryan Robson; French genius Eric Cantona; the formidable and the 'Only One' Duncan Edwards; dashing right-winger Billy Meredith; goal-machine Jack Rowley; ace marksmen Denis Law; the elegant and stylish Bobby Charlton; the brilliantly talented George Best; the resilient motivator Roy Keane; highly-skilled midfielder David Beckham and the dashing Ryan Giggs, with managers supreme Sir Matt Busby and Sir Alex Ferguson jointly in charge!

ABANDONED MATCHES

Like all major League clubs, United have had many competitive matches abandoned through various reasons, the weather being the main cause.

Here are details of some of United's abandoned fixtures:

Competition	Date	Opponents	Result	reason	replay score
League	Dec 1895	Leicester Fosse (h)	0-2 65 mins,	fog	lost 2-0
League	Dec 1903	Leicester Fosse (h)	2-1 78 mins,	fog	lost 5-2
FA Cup	March 1909	Burnley (a)	0-1+ 72 mins,	snow	won 3-2.
League	Aug 1960	Manchester City (a)	2-2 59 mins,	rain	won 3-1
League	Dec 1962	Arsenal (h)	1-0 57 mins,	fog	lost 3-2
League	April 1974	Manchester City (h)	0-1*82 mins,	pitch invasion.	

+ The referee in charge of the FA Cup-tie with Burnley at Turf Moor in 1909 was Herbert Bamlett, who later became manager at Old Trafford (1927-31). United made the most of the abandonment, going on to win their first ever FA Cup Final.

* Result made to stand after spectators ran onto the Old Trafford pitch following Denis Law's late back-heeler that gave City victory and condemned United to the Second Division for the first time since 1938.

AC MILAN

In the 1956-57 European Cup semi-final, United's patched-up post Munich side did well to earn a 2-1 first leg lead over Milan, Ernie Taylor (penalty) & Dennis Viollet the scorers. But in the San Siro they fell apart and lost 4-0, going out 5-2 on aggregate, proving no match for the skilled Italians. Milan then knocked United, the holders, out of the same competition at the semi-final stage in 1968-69. The Italians gained a distinct advantage by winning the first leg at home by 2-0 but despite a fine goal by Bobby Charlton, United couldn't claw back the deficit at Old Trafford and went down fighting, losing the tie 2-1 on aggregate. Denis Law, in fact, thought he had 'scored' a dramatic late equaliser but the referee (and linesman) failed to spot that the ball had crossed the line! TV replays suggested that United had been robbed of at least extra-time…but the score stood and the Reds went out.

ACCRINGTON

Heathens' League results v Accrington:

	Div	Home	Away
1892-93	1	D 3-3	D 2-2

Summary of League results:

	P	W	D	L	F	A
Division 1	2	0	2	0	5	5
Home	1	0	1	0	3	3
Away	1	0	1	0	2	2
Totals	2	0	2	0	5	5

Fact File:

Accrington FC was one of the twelve clubs which founded the Football League in 1888, being the only one not to have survived until the 21st century. In fact, the club survived only five seasons before resigning in 1893 rather than face the ignominy of relegation to Division Two. The final match of season 1892-93 (Newton Heath's first League season) saw the two clubs play out a 3-3 draw at North Road. This was Newton Heath's last League match at their original ground and also Accrington's last ever League match.

Formed as the Football Section of Accrington Cricket Club, they played all their League seasons at the cricket ground; the cricketers regarded them as a drain on their resources, whilst Accrington FC were denied the opportunity of building permanent stands, thus reducing their earning potential.

The club continued to play football, as amateurs, even moving to their own ground at Moorhead Park, but finally they wound up in 1896.

* Player with both clubs: T Hay

ACCRINGTON STANLEY

.FA Cup results v Stanley:

	Rd	Venue	Result
1902-03	3Q	Home	W 7-0
1945-46	3/1	Away	D 2-2
	3/2	Home	W 5-1

Fact File:

The clubs did not play each other in the Football League

This Lancashire club is not to be confused with Accrington FC (q.v.), being a distinctly separate club. Originally named 'Stanley Villa' they played local amateur football at the time Accrington FC was playing in the Football League. With the demise of Accrington in 1896, this club adopted the 'Accrington' prefix, considering themselves now the best side in the town.

To further the confusion, Accrington Stanley took over Accrington's ground at Moorhead Park, adopting their red shirts as well as their nickname 'owd Reds'. By 1921 they had progressed well enough to become founder members of the new Third Division (North), now playing at Peel Park.

They played 33 seasons in the Football League, mostly in the Third Division, finally resigning through financial problems during 1961-62, just four seasons after narrowly missing promotion to Division 2.

Players with both clubs include: A Ainsworth (Stanley WW2), C Briggs (United reserve & WW2), J Briscoe (United reserve), A Burrows (United WW2), T Chorlton, H Cockburn (Stanley WW2), AD Ferguson, G Glaister (United WW2), W Greenwood, J Hall; B Jones & W Keely (both United WW2), D Kerr (United reserve), J Lancaster; L Martindale & S Mercer (both United WW2), H Morgan, D Musgrave (United reserve), WJ Mutch (United reserve), W Porter and J Roach (both Stanley WW2), J Robinson (United WW2), HS Stafford & W Tyler (United reserves), J Walters, W Walton & JH Wilson (United reserves).

Also associated: J Hacking (United player, Stanley player-manager).

ADMISSION PRICES

When United gained entry into the Football League in 1892, the charge for admission to the 'ground' (the terraces) for a home game (depending on the context of the fixture) varied from 1d (1/2p) to 6d (2 1/2p).

When the club switched to Old Trafford (in 1910 - with an estimated capacity of around 80,000 -13,000 under cover) it was 6d (3p) admission to the terraces, 1s 6d (7 1/2p) and 2s (10p) to the covered sections and 5s (25p) for an unreserved seat in the main stand.

The 6d (2 1/2p) charge remained as a minimum entrance fee until after World War One (1919) when it was increased to one shilling (5p). For the next 23 years that shilling ('bob') admission price remained in force, giving rise to the phrase 'bob enders' for standing spectators on the popular side of the ground.

For the 1942-43 Wartime season it went up to 1s 3d (7 1/2p) and in 1946 rose to 1s 6d (7 1/2p).

Thereafter the entry fee went up gradually: 1952-53 to 1s 9d (9p); 1955-56 to 2s (10p); 1959-60 up to 2s 6d (12 1/2p); 1960-61 to 3s (15p); 1962-63 to 4s (20p); 1966-67 to 5s (25p); 1969-70 to 6s (30p); 1970-71 to 7s 6d (37 1/2p) and then upwards from 40p to 50p and on to £1 by 1978-79, rising after that to £1.30, £1.50, £2.00, £3.00, £5.00 and then £6.00 before the all-seater stadium ruling came into force.

The adult prices into Old Trafford over the last ten years have risen dramatically, due of course to Premiership football and United's great achievements on the field.

A ticket in 1992-93 cost between £8-£14, while a season ticket was priced between £228-£266

Come 1998 a 'cheap' adult was £13 and season tickets were costing almost £250 (cheapest).

In 2002, single match seat tickets at Old Trafford were priced between £21-£28, while seasons tickets cost some supporters upwards of £400.

* Reduced ticket prices are obtainable for children at all times.

Executive Boxes

Executive boxes at Old Trafford in 1992 were priced at £4,700, £4,950 & £14,950. A decade later prices had escalated to between £5,000 & £25,000 per season, depending on where they are situated inside the ground and the internal facilities they offer.

Complimentary Tickets

For 'League' matches, the visiting club can normally claim in the region of 40 complimentary tickets - 28 for use by players, manager and coach and 12 for the Directors. However, there is no set limit on how many complimentary tickets the home club can issue.

AGE

Oldest

The oldest player ever to appear for Manchester United in a League or major Cup game is Welsh international right-winger Billy Meredith, who was fast approaching his 47th birthday when he lined up against Derby County (at home) on 7 May 1921 in the First Division. Born on 30 July 1874, he was 46 years, 281 days old.

Goalkeeper Raimond van der Gouw - at the age of 39 years, 48 days - became the second oldest player in United's history to appear in a League game when he came on as a second-half substitute in the FA Premier League match at home to Charlton Athletic on 11 May 2002.

Three other players - Frank Mann (v. Sheffield Wednesday in November 1929), Tom Jones (v. Bradford Park Avenue in December 1937) and Jack Warner (v. Newcastle United in April 1950) were all over the age of 38 when they played their last games for United in the Football League.

A further seven players aged 37 and over have appeared at League level for the club - Bill Foulkes (1969), Jack Hacking (1935), Clarence Hilditch (1932), George Livingstone (1914), Teddy Partridge (1929), Bryan Robson (1994) and goalkeeper Andy Goram (2001).

David Robbie (born 6 October 1899) was 35 years, 11 months and 8 days old when he made his only League appearance for United against Southampton on 28 September 1935.

Youngest

Goalkeeper David Gaskell became the youngest player ever to appear in a first-class game for the club when he made his debut in the FA Charity Shield match against Manchester City on 24 October 1956. He was only 16 years and 19 days old when he came on as a substitute for Ray Wood at half-time, United having obtained the agreement of City and the referee - subs not having yet been legalised.

Wing-half Jeff Whitefoot was only 16 years, 105 days old when he made his League debut for United against Portsmouth (at home) on 15 April 1950, thus becoming United's youngest ever League debutant.

Duncan Edwards was 16 years, 185 days old when he played in his first League game for United against Cardiff City (at home) on 4 April 1953.

Two other players who made their first League appearance for United at the age of 16 were winger Willie Anderson v. Burnley at Old Trafford in December 1963 and Norman Whiteside away at Brighton in April 1982, as a substitute.

Sammy McIlroy and Roy Morton were both 16 years of age when they played for United in friendly matches against Bohemians (Ireland) in January 1972 and Mallorca in May 1972 respectively.

Arthur Rowley, as an amateur guest player from Wolverhampton Wanderers, made his debut in United's first team against Liverpool in a wartime game on 29 November 1941 at the age of 15 years and 222 days - possibly the youngest-ever player to don a United shirt at competitive level! Although Rowley's brother, Jack, would become a United legend, Arthur never played for the club in peacetime football, but achieved fame elsewhere, becoming the League's all-time greatest marksman with 434 goals in all.

9

Age Concern

Former United winger Billy Meredith was aged 49 years and nine months when he lined up in the 1924 FA Cup semi-final for Manchester City against Newcastle United - the oldest player ever to star in this competition. Meredith appeared in his last international match for Wales v. England, aged 45 in 1920.

Former United half-back Neil McBain (born 15 November 1895) was aged 51 years, 120 days when he took part in a Football League game for New Brighton at Hartlepools United (Division 3 North) on 15 March 1947. He was on the losing side 3-0. McBain was manager at the time, appearing in goal in an emergency, having not played League football since 1931. He thus became the oldest player ever to appear in the Football League.

Goalkeeper Les Sealey was 36 years, 179 days old when he lined up for United in the 1994 League Cup Final against Aston Villa.

Defender Allenby Chilton was aged 36 years, six months when he played his last League game for the club against Wolverhampton Wanderers in February 1955. He had made his England debut at the age of 32, in October 1950.

Scottish international winger Jimmy Delaney was some two months past his 36th birthday when he starred in his last League game for the club at Chelsea in November 1950.

Bobby Charlton (1973) and Steve Bruce (1996) were both past their 35th birthdays when they made their final appearances for the Reds.

Ex-United goalkeeper Pat Dunne was still playing non-League football in the mid-1990s at the age of 52. Likewise former Reds defender Paul Edwards was also 50 when he played in his last charity game in 1997-98.

John Sutcliffe, a United goalkeeper in the early 1900s, was almost 44 years of age when he ended his playing career in 1912 with Plymouth Argyle, while pre-WW1 outside-left George Wall was aged 42 when he retired from playing the game in 1927.

Jack Warner retired as a player in April 1953 at the age of 41. He was, for many years, United's oldest post WW2 player, lining up in his final game for the club in April 1950 (v. Newcastle) at the age of 38.

When goalkeeper Raimond van der Gouw came on as a substitute in the Worthington League Cup game v. Arsenal at Highbury in November 2001, he became United's oldest post WW2 player at 38 years, 227 days. He played his last game for the club in May 2002 at the age of 39 years, 48 days (see above).

Teddy Partridge played his last League game at the age of 40, for Crewe in 1931. Stan Pearson was also 40 when he last kicked a ball in earnest, for Chester in 1959.

Ex-players Frank Hodges and Arthur Potts both had long innings, dying aged 94 and 92 respectively.

Young Blood

Norman Whiteside became the youngest League Cup Final goalscorer when he netted for United in the Wembley showdown with Liverpool in March 1983 at the age of 17 years, 323 days. He then wrote himself into the record books by becoming also the youngest goalscorer in an FA Cup Final by netting in United's 4-0 replay win over Brighton two months later at the age of 18 years, 18 days.

In the summer of 1982, Whiteside became the youngest player ever to star in the Finals of the World Cup (he was aged 17 in Spain).

The average age of United's League side against West Bromwich Albion at Old Trafford early in the 1955-56 season (27 August) was 22 years, 106 days. Five years later when they played Bolton Wanderers in October 1960, the average age of the side was 22 years, 116 days.

For the 1958 FA Cup Final v. Bolton Wds, the average age of United's team was 23 years, six months.

United had six players under the age of 20 in their line-up against Port Vale in an away League Cup game in October 1994. The average age of the team that night was 22 years, 243 days.

The average age of United's European Cup winning side in 1968 was just 26 years. one month and 15 days - a competition record.

* See under international section for youngest and oldest capped players.

AGGREGATE SCORE

United's highest-ever aggregate victory in a two-legged match at senior level is 12-0 against RSC Anderlecht in a European Cup-tie in September 1956. United won the first leg 2-0 in Belgium and then went goal-crazy at Maine Road as they cantered through the return leg to win 10-0.

In the 1998-99 European Champions League competition (Group D) United beat Brondby IF 6-2 (a) and defeated them 5-0 (h) for an 11-2 aggregate victory.

In the Fairs Cup competition of 1964-65 United beat Borussia Dortmund 4-0 (h) and 6-1 (a) for a 10-1 aggregate win.

AINSWORTH, Alphonso

Born: Manchester on 31 July 1913. Died: Rochdale on 25 April 1975.

Career: Ashton United (1930), MANCHESTER UNITED (amateur 1933, professional February 1934), New Brighton (September 1935). Guested for Accrington Stanley, Bury, Oldham Athletic, Rochdale and Southport during the Second World War; then New Brighton (1946) and Congleton Town (1947).

'Alf' Ainsworth was a useful inside-forward who made the first of his two League appearances for the Reds against Bury a month after turning professional at Old Trafford. He scored over 50 goals in more than 200 League and Cup games for New Brighton either side of WW2.

Club record: 2 apps. 0 goal

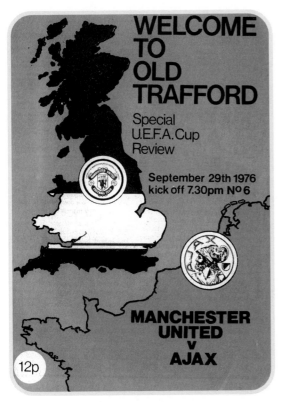

AITKEN, John

Born: Dumfries, Scotland, circa 1870.
Career: 5th King's Rifle Volunteers in Dumfries, NEWTON HEATH (July 1895-May 1896).
Left-winger John Aitken scored on his debut v. Crewe Alexandra, but played in only one more League game for the club before being released in the summer of 1896.
Club record: 2 apps. 1 goal (also one 'other' app)

AJAX AMSTERDAM

After going a goal behind in the first leg in Holland, United pulled back to win their opening round 1976-77 UEFA Cup encounter with Ajax thanks to goals by Sammy McIlroy and Lou Macari in the return fixture at Old Trafford.
Players with both clubs: J Cruyff, A Muhren, J Olsen, F Stapleton.
Also associated: J Rowley (United player, Ajax coach).

ALBINSON, George

Born: Prestwich, 14 February 1897. Died: Rochdale, April 1975.
Career: MANCHESTER UNITED (signed after a trial, May 1919), Manchester City (May 1921), Crewe Alexandra (1923-25), Witton Albion (late 1920s), Daily Herald FC (amateur, 1935).
Half-back George Albinson's only senior appearance for the club was against Liverpool in an FA Cup replay in January 1921. He gained a Cheshire League Championship medal with Crewe.
Club record: one app.

ALBISTON, Arthur Richard

Born: Edinburgh on 14 July 1957.
Career: Edinburgh & District schools, MANCHESTER UNITED (apprentice July 1972, professional July 1974), West Bromwich Albion (August 1988), Dundee (1989), Chesterfield (on loan, 1990), Chester City (1991), FC Molde of Norway (on loan). Retired in July 1993, later returned to Old Trafford as coach to United's junior players; Droylsden (manager 1996-97).
Left-back Arthur Albiston (19 at the time) made his FA Cup debut for United in the 1977 Final against Liverpool and celebrated by gaining a winners' medal. Three years earlier (in October 1974) he had made his senior debut for the club in a League Cup encounter against Manchester City in front of 55,000 fans at Old Trafford and his Football League baptism followed soon afterwards in a 0-0 draw with Portsmouth at Fratton Park.
A fine, steady defender with a splendid left-foot, he was a first team regular for nine years, from 1978 to 1987, he was the first United player ever to collect three FA Cup winners medals (his other two coming in 1983 and 1985).
Honoured by Scotland at schoolboy level, he went on to win 14 full caps for his country, appearing in the World Cup Finals in Mexico in 1986.
Club record: 487 apps. 7 goals

ALBUT, A H

Mr AH Albut was the first full-time official appointed by Newton Heath LYR. Hitherto, as part of the Lancashire & Yorkshire Railway Company, the football club had not been run as an adjunct of the Dining Room Committee. Now, in 1889-90 the club broke away from the railway, shortening its title to 'Newton Heath' and appointed Mr Albut as the club's first full-time secretary. He had previously served with no less a club than Aston Villa.
A terraced cottage at 33 Oldham Road, Newton Heath, was utilised as the club's office, at a weekly rent of six shillings (30p). The post of manager did not exist at this stage, so Mr Albut had responsibility for running all team affairs. He proved an inspired choice, always on the look-out for talented footballers to strengthen the team. He held the post for over ten years, until James West (q.v) took over the mantle in 1900.
It was Albut who was adament that Newton Heath should leave the totally unsuitable North Road goiund, recommending the move to Bank Street, Clayton.

ALDERSHOT

Fact File
United defeated the Shots 3-1 (away) in a 2nd round League Cup-tie in season 1970-71
Originally founded in 1926 as 'Aldershot Town' they made such rapid progress that they were elected to the Third Division (South) in 1932. Never progressing higher than this level, Aldershot were voted out of the League in 1991. Astonishingly the local fans refused to accept the club's winding up, forming another company of Aldershot Town (1992) Ltd, entering a team at the very bottom of the football pyramid system, continuing to use the Recreation Ground for their matches. Such has been the success of this brave enterprise that 'the Shots' now stand just two promotions away from the Football League.
In August 1982, United also played the Shots at The Recreation Ground in a match organised in aid of the South Atlantic Fund.
Players with both clubs include: P Coyne; J Greenwood, R Hampson & P O'Sullivan (United reserves), J Rowley (Shots WW2), T Sheringham, F Stapleton, N Tapken (Shots WW2).
Associated with Aldershot Town: J Grimwood.

11

ALLAN, John Thomas

Born: South Shields, February 1883.

Career: Bishop Auckland (1900), MANCHESTER UNITED (professional, May 1904), Bishop Auckland.(June 1906-08).

Inside-forward Jack Allan, appeared in two FA Amateur Cup Finals for the Bishops before joining the Reds. He was re-instated as an amateur when he rejoined the Bishops in 1906.

Club record: 36 apps. 22 goals

ALLEN, Reginald Arthur

Born: Marylebone, London, 3 May 1919.

Career: Corona FC, Bromley (1937), Queen's Park Rangers (1938), MANCHESTER UNITED (June 1950), Altrincham (May 1953-55).

Goalkeeper Reg Allen was a very capable goalkeeper, alert and courageous who made his United League debut against Fulham three months after joining the club prior to the start of the 1950-51 season.

He had made 251 competitive appearances for QPR, represented the FA XI, the Football League and helped United win the First Division title in season 1951-52.

Allen, serving as a Commando in WW2, spent almost four years as a prisoner-of-war after being captured by the Italians while serving in North Africa on 17 September 1941. He was also a keen cricketer and useful boxer.

Club record: 80 apps.

ALLMAN, Arthur

Born: Milton, Staffordshire 24 December 1890. Died: Milton, 22 December 1956.

Career: Smallthorne FC (Stoke-on-Trent), Shrewsbury Town (1910), Wolverhampton Wanderers (1912) Swansea Town (1913), MANCHESTER UNITED (£150, May 1914), Stoke (guest WW1), Millwall Athletic (May 1919), Port Vale (trialist, mid-1921), Aberaman (season 1921-22), Crewe Alexandra (1922), Aberaman (1924).

Arthur Allman was a strong-tackling full-back, very positive and fair, who made his senior debut for the Reds against Sheffield Wednesday (at home) in February 1915 when he stood in for John Hodge.

He served in the Army in France during WW1.

Club record: 12 apps.

AMATEURS

Over the years several excellent and experienced amateur footballers have played for Manchester United's first XI in League and/or Cup competitions and, indeed, some have represented their country at this level as well.

Sam Black was an amateur through his playing career. He served with Newton Heath during the pre-League era.

Among the many other amateurs who have been registered with Manchester United are forwards Jack Allan (ex-Bishop Auckland), Len Bradbury (Corinthians), school-teacher Warren Bradley (also a Bishop Auckland player), Harry Erentz (who was another Corinthian), outside-left Harold Hardman, who starred in the 1908 Olympic Games, winning a gold medal and later became Chairman of Manchester United, goalkeepers Les Olive and Mike Pinner (capped 51 times by England as an amateur) and another forward, John Walton, who also played for Great Britain in the Olympic Games of 1952.

Bradley, with Bob Hardisty and Derek Lewin, joined United from Bishop Auckland shortly after the Munich air disaster, primarily to help United's reserve team complete their fixture list. Only Bradley, who won two FA Amateur Cup medals with the Bishops (1956 & 1957), made United's first team.

Inside-forward Alan Gowling was registered as an amateur with United when he played for England amateurs in the late 1960s. He also represented Great Britain in the 1968 Olympic Games in Mexico.

United played an England Amateur XI at Old Trafford in September 1972.

* Technically all players under the age of 17 were in fact amateurs and some made their United debuts before becoming full-time professionals.

AMBLER, Alfred

Born: Manchester, autumn 1879

Career: Hawktown Juniors, Hyde United, NEWTON HEATH (August 1899), Colne FC (March 1900), Stockport County (1906), Exeter City (1908), Colne FC (1910).

Alf Ambler, an outside-left-cum-half-back, partnered Joe Cassidy on the left-wing when making his debut for the club in the 2-2 draw with Gainsborough Trinity on the opening day of the 1899-1900 season. His only goal was scored a week later in the 2-1 defeat at Bolton.

He had earlier helped Colne FC win the Lancashire Combination Second Division title (1906) and also played 56 Southern League games for Exeter.

Club record: 9 apps. one goal ((also 3 'other' apps, one goal)

ANDERLECHT (RSC)

United beat the Belgium League champions 12-0 on aggregate in a European Cup-tie in September 1956, winning the 1st leg 2-0 away and the return leg by 10-0 at Maine Road.

The game in Belgium was, in fact, United's first-ever European competitive match.

Twelve seasons later - in 1968-69 - United again defeated Anderlecht in the European Cup, this time ousting them in the 2nd round, 4-3 on aggregate with a 3-0 home win followed by a 3-1 defeat in Belgium.

The third time the teams met in the European Cup (Champions League) was in 2000-01, United winning 5-1 at Old Trafford and Anderlecht claiming a 2-1 victory in Belgium, both matches taking part at the Group stage in September/October.

ANDERSON, George Walter

Born: Cheetham, Manchester, circa February 1893.

Career: Broughton St James', Broughton Wellington, Salford United (1909), Bury (1910), MANCHESTER UNITED (£50, September 1911-17), Belfast United (guest, WW1).

George Anderson was a utility forward who averaged practically a goal every two games for United during the four seasons leading up to the Great War. Seemingly without permission, he played a few games for Belfast United during the hostilities and consequently a permanent move to the Irish club was cancelled by the club. Two years later Anderson was sent to prison for eight months - for his involvement in betting on football matches..

Club record: 86 apps. 39 goals

ANDERSON, John

Born: Salford, 11 October 1921.

Career: MANCHESTER UNITED (amateur, March 1938, professional December 1938), Plymouth Argyle (guest WW2), Nottingham Forest (August 1952), Peterborough United (1952). Retired June 1954 to become trainer-coach at London Road.

A competitive half-back, who represented Lancashire Schools as a teenager, John Anderson went off to war in the Royal Navy less than a year after becoming a full-time 'pro' with United. On returning to Old Trafford, he finally made his League debut against Middlesbrough at Maine Road on 20 December 1947, being given the daunting task of marking the legendary Wilf Mannion. So well did he perform that he kept his place for the rest of the season, gaining an FA Cup winners' medal in the process (when Blackpool were defeated 4-2 in the 1948 Final), Anderson sealing victory with his side's fourth goal in the 86th minute. He had played in only 16 League games prior to that Wembley triumph.

Club record: 40 apps. 2 goals

ANDERSON, Trevor

Born: Belfast, 3 March 1951.

Career: Portadown (1968), MANCHESTER UNITED (£20,000, October 1972), Swindon Town (November 1974), Peterborough United (1977) Linfield (1979). Later manager of the Irish League club.

Trevor Anderson was signed by United manager Frank O'Farrell as a possible replacement for George Best. Initially the sight of the slim, dark haired Irishman working his magic excited the Old Trafford faithful but alas, the arrival of new boss Tommy Docherty spelt danger for Anderson who was never really given a chance by the former Scottish international. He subsequently was transferred to Swindon Town. Capped 22 times by Northern Ireland (six gained as a United player) Anderson once scored a hat-trick of penalties when playing for Swindon against Walsall in April 1976. In later life he worked as a clerk for the Belfast City hospital

Club record: 22 apps. 2 goals

13

ANDERSON, Vivian Alexander

Born: Nottingham, 29 August 1956

Career: Nottinghamshire Schools, Nottingham Forest (professional 1974), Arsenal (£250,000, 1984), MANCHESTER UNITED (£250,000, July 1987), Sheffield Wednesday (January 1991), Barnsley (player-manager, 1993), Middlesbrough (assistant-manager, 1994).

Viv 'Spider' Anderson appeared in almost 600 League games during his first-class career. A skilful, attacking right full-back, he signed apprentice forms at The City Ground after representing Nottingham Schools. Over the next decade he amassed a fine record of some 450 games and 22 goals. The first black footballer to win a full England cap (v. Czechoslovakia in November 1978), he went on to star in 30 full internationals for his country, also gaining Under-21, 'B' and Football League honours. As a Forest player, he was a member of the League Championship-winning side, triumphed in two League Cup Finals and also celebrated two European Cup Final victories. After more than 150 outings for the Gunners he switched to Old Trafford, the fee being agreed by an independent tribunal. Approaching his 31st birthday, Anderson was Alex Ferguson's first signing for the club. And he certainly gave a good account of himself, before moving to Hillsborough. Two-and-a-half years later, having helped the Owls win promotion and reach two Cup Finals at Wembley, he became player-manager at Oakwell before his appointment as player/assistant-manager (to Bryan Robson) at Middlesbrough - remaining with the Riverside club for seven years during which they reached the Premiership.

Club record: 70 apps. 4 goals

ANDERSON, William John

Born: Liverpool, 24 January 1947.

Career: Liverpool & Merseyside Boys, MANCHESTER UNITED (junior, April 1962, professional, February 1964), Aston Villa (£20,000, January 1967), Cardiff City (£60,000, 1973), Portland Timbers (on loan 1975, signed again 1977). On retiring in 1982, he chose to live and work in the USA.

A fast raiding right (or left) winger, the possessor of remarkable dribbling skills, Willie Anderson suffered from George Best's ability to play on either flank, his first team appearances being limited to just 13 in five seasons. He had made his first senior appearance in 1963-64 whilst season 1965-66 saw him play in two major semi-finals, the FA Cup and European Cup as well as having the honour of being United's first ever 'official' substitute in the 1965 FA Charity Shield game. However, the arrival of England international John Connelly meant that Anderson moved to Villa Park early in 1967. Anderson won an FA Youth Cup winners medal with United and also gained England Youth international honours during his time at Old Trafford. He played for Villa in their 1971 League Cup Final defeat by Spurs and helped the Birmingham club win the Third Division Championship the following season. Quitting football in 1979, with career figures of over 400 senior appearances (57 goals) Anderson later became an Executive with a commercial radio station in Oregon, USA. Club record: 13 apps.

ANGLO-ITALIAN TOURNAMENT

United's record in the 1972-73 competition:

Venue	P	W	D	L	F	A
Home	2	1	1	0	4	2
Away	2	1	1	0	4	1
Totals	4	2	2	0	8	3

United played in Group One and despite being unbeaten, failed to qualify for the semi-finals after producing these results:

21 Feb	v. Fiorentina	(h)	drew 1-1 (Holton)	Att. 23,951
21 Mar	v. SS Lazio	(a)	drew 0-0	Att. 52,834
4 Apr	v. AS Bari	(h)	won 3-1 (Law, Storey-Moore, Martin)	Att. 14,302
2 May	v. Verona	(a)	won 4-1 (Charlton 2, Olney, Fletcher)	Att. 8,168

APPEARANCES

Listed here are the top appearance-makers for United in all first team competitions (totals include substitute appearances). Major first team competitions include: Premiership, Football League; Football Alliance, FA Cup, League Cup, European Champions Cup/League, UEFA Cup, Inter-Cities Fairs Cup, European Cup-winners Cup, European Super Cup, FIFA Club World Championship, FIFA World Club Championship, Screen Sport Super Cup, FA Charity Shield, Test Matches, Watney Cup & Anglo-Italian Tournaments.

Football League/Premiership
(qualification: 350 apps)

606	Bobby Charlton	(1956-73)
566	Bill Foulkes	(1952-70)
481	Joe Spence	(1919-33)
433	Alex Stepney	(1966-78)
423	Jack Silcock	(1919-34)
414	Tony Dunne	(1960-73)
380	Jack Rowley	(1937-55)
379	Arthur Albiston	(1974-88)
376	Martin Buchan	(1971-83)
368	Denis Irwin	(1990-2002)
361	George Best	(1963-74)
355	Brian McClair	(1987-98)
352	Allenby Chilton	(1939-55)

FA Cup (inc 3rd/4th play-off)
(qualification: 40 apps)

79	Bobby Charlton	(1956-73)
61	Bill Foulkes	(1952-70)
55	Tony Dunne	(1960-73)
46	George Best	(1963-74)
46	Mark Hughes	(1983-86/88-95)
46	Denis Law	(1962-73)
45	Brian McClair	(1987-98)
44	Alex Stepney	(1966-78)
43	Denis Irwin	(1990-2002)
43	Pat Crerand	(1962-71)
42	Jack Rowley	(1937-55)
41	Steve Bruce	(1987-96)
41	Peter Schmeichel	(1991-99)
40	Ryan Giggs	(1990-2002)

Football League Cup
(qualification: 30 apps)

51	Bryan Robson	(1981-94)
45	Brian McClair	(1987-98)
40	Arthur Albiston	(1974-88)
38	Mark Hughes	(1983-86/88-95)
36	Gary Pallister	(1989-98)
35	Alex Stepney	(1966-78)
34	Steve Bruce	(1987-96)
34	Mike Duxbury	(1980-90)
31	Denis Irwin	(1990-2002)
30	Martin Buchan	(1971-83)

European Competitions (inc. Super Cup)
(qualification: 40 apps)

75	Denis Irwin	(1990-2002)
72	Gary Neville	(1992-2002)
70	David Beckham	(1992-2002)
67	Ryan Giggs	(1990-2002)
65	Roy Keane	(1993-2002)
63	Paul Scholes	(1994-2002)
59	Ole G Solskjaer	(1996-2002)
58	Nicky Butt	(1994-2002)
50	Andy Cole	(1995-2001)
52	Bill Foulkes	(1956-69)

45	Bobby Charlton	(1956-73)
43	Peter Schmeichel	(1991-99)
41	Pat Crerard	(1963-71)
41	Gary Pallister	(1990-98)
40	Tony Dunne	(1963-73)
40	Philip Neville	(1994-2002)

Football Alliance
(qualification 30 apps)

62	Willie Stewart	
60	Alf Farman	
56	Roger Doughty	
52	Jack Owen	
41	J F Slater	
36	John Clements	
36	J Mitchell	

* Appearances made between 1890-92

All major first team competitions
(qualification: 450 apps)

766	Bobby Charlton	(1956-73)
688	Bill Foulkes	(1952-70)
545	Alex Stepney	(1966-78)
539	Tony Dunne	(1960-73)
529	Denis Irwin	(1990-2002)
510	Joe Spence	(1919-33)
487	Arthur Albiston	(1974-88)
485	Ryan Giggs	(1990-2002)
474	George Best	(1963-74)
473	Mark Hughes	(1983-86/88-95)
465	Bryan Robson	(1981-94)
459	Martin Buchan	(1971-83)

WW1 (1915-19)
(qualification: 50 apps)

132	Wilf Woodcock	
126	Jack Mew	
103	Jack Silcock	
101	Clarence Hilditch	
74	Ernie Ellis	
68	Tommy Meehan	
57	Cyril Barlow	
50	Tommy Forster	

WW2 (1939-46)
(not inc: '39-40 void League & '45-46 FA Cup games)
(qualification: 100 apps)

215	Jack Warner	
201	Jack Smith	
198	Johnny Carey	
188	Bert Whalley	
173	George Roughton	
171	Jack Breedon	
169	Billy Bryant	
131	Billy Porter	
110	Bill McKay	

GEORGE BEST

Consecutive Appearances

Steve Coppell, with 206, holds the United club record for most consecutive League appearances, achieved between 15 January 1977 (v. Coventry) and 7 November 1981 (v. Sunderland). He beat defender Allenby Chilton's record of 179, set between 10 March 1951 and 23 February 1955.

Arthur Albiston made 132 consecutive appearances for the club between 12 March 1980 and 23 April 1983, whilst goalkeeper Peter Schmeichel, with 94, has played the most consecutive League matches between the posts for United (1992-94).

Defender Bill Foulkes appeared in 61 consecutive FA Cup appearances for United beginning in January 1955 before injury kept him out of a 4th round clash with Norwich City in February 1967. He never played in another game in that competition. Foulkes played in all of United first 45 major European matches (1955-68) and he went on to appear in 52 out of a possible 58 ties during his time at Old Trafford.

Unchanged

Starting on 6 December 1975 and ending on 28 February 1976, United kept an unchanged starting line up in 13 consecutive League matches and five FA Cup games - a club record. The starting line-up was Stepney; Forsyth, Houston; Daly, B Greenhoff, Buchan; Coppell, McIlroy, Pearson, Macari and Hill. McCreery (8 times), Kelly, Nicholl and Coyne all came on as substitutes during this sequence.

United's first XI remained unchanged for the opening nine consecutive Football League games during both the 1956-57 and 1957-58 seasons. In the former campaign the side read: Wood; Foulkes, Byrne; Colman, Jones, Edwards; Berry, Whelan, Taylor, Viollet, Pegg, and in the latter it was the same line-up except that Blanchflower replaced Jones at centre-half.

Short Match Wonders

Listed here are the names of players who failed to compete the full 90 minutes of football in their only first-class game for Manchester United:

Peter Beardsley*	v. Bournemouth (h) League Cup, October 1982
Jon Clark	v. Sunderland (h) League, October 1976
Nick Culkin	v. Arsenal (a) PL, August 1999
Paul Jones	v. Fiorentina (h) Anglo-Italian Cup, February 1973
Jimmy Kelly	v. Wolves (h) League, December 1975
Pat McGibbon**	v. York City (h) League Cup, September 1996
Francis McGivern	v. Bari (h) Anglo-Italian Cup. April 1973
Colin McKee*	v. Coventry City (h) FPL, May 1994
Danny Nardiello	v. Arsenal (a) League Cup, November 2001
Alex Notman	v. Tottenham Hotspur (a) League Cup, December 1998
Patrick Olney	v. Verona (a) Anglo-Italian Cup, May 1973
Richard Wellens	v. Aston Villa (a) League Cup, October 1999
Anthony Whelan	v. Southampton (h) League, November 1980
Neil Whitworth*	v. Southampton (a) League, March 1991

* These players started the game in question but were substituted, the remainder appeared as substitutes.
**McGibbon was sent off in this match.

Late Sub

Goalkeeper Nick Culkin may well have had the shortest 'League career' as a United player. He replaced Raimond van der Gouw in the second minute of added time at the end of the away Premiership game with Arsenal in 1999. United won 2-1. As he went into goal after the 90th minute, no accurate estimate of his time on the field is possible but it was unlikely to have exceeded two minutes.

One Match Wonders

Apart from the players mentioned in the category 'short match wonders' here are details of other players who made only ONE senior appearance for the club (Newton Heath/Manchester United):

George Albinson (1921)	L Davies (1886)	William Longair (1895)	William Sarvis (1922)
Beau Asquith (1939)*	Donnelly (1890)	Longton (1886)	George Schofield (1920)
Bill Bainbridge (1946)	Jimmy Dyer (1905)	Pat McCarthy (1912)	Percy Schofield (1921)
Billy Behan (1934)	John Earp (1886)	Noel McFarlane (1954)	R Stephenson (1896)
Horace Blew (1906)	John Gourlay (1899)	David McFetteridge (1895)	Walter Taylor (1922)
Harold Bratt (1960)	William Gyves (1890)	Andrew Mitchell (1933)	Wilf Tranter (1964)
Albert Broome (1923)	Tony Hawksworth (1956)	Ben Morton (1935)	Turner (1890)
James Cairns (1895)	Edward Holt (1900)	George O'Brien (1902)	Sid Tyler (1923).
James Cairns (1898)	James Hopkins (1899)	T O'Shaughnessey (1890)	Dennis Walker (1963)
'Freddy' Capper (1912)	E Howells (1886)	W Owen (1898)	Walter Whitehurst (1955)
John Christie (1903)	Reg Hunter (1958)	John Prentice (1920)	Kerr Whiteside (1908)
Harry Cleaver (1903)	Sam Johnson (1901)	Albert Prince (1915)	John Whittle (1932)
Ted Dalton (1908)	David Jones (1937)	George Radcliffe (1899)	Neil Whitworth (1991)
	Peter Jones (1957)	Rattigan (1890)	Ian Wilkinson (1991)
	'Paddy' Kennedy (1954)	David Robbie (1935)	Tommy Wilson (1908)
	Joe Kinloch (1892)	Martyn Rogers (1977)	
	Albert Kinsey (1965)	'Josh' Rowe (1914)	

NB - In the abandoned 1939-40 season there were several others who appeared in only one League or Cup match, and others long before then who played in Football Alliance matches - not included in the list, therefore.

Most Appearances in a Season

Denis Irwin & Gary Pallister both appeared in 62 first-class matches for United in 1993-94.

15

Appearance Facts & Figures

Sir Bobby Charlton, OBE, made some 950 first-class appearances as a professional footballer with United, PNE, England & other internationals/representative sides (at various levels). His tallies of 604+2 League appearances and 764+2 outings in all competitions for United are both existing club records.

Billy Meredith appeared in 303 League games for United and 367 for Manchester City. The Welsh international winger claimed to have played in 1,584 games (various levels) and scored 470 goals during his career.

Joe Spence with 481, held the club's League appearance record for 33 years until his total was passed in 1966 by defender Bill Foulkes, who was subsequently overhauled by team-mate Bobby Charlton.

'Beau' Asquith made his Football League debut for United at Charlton on 2 September 1939 - the day before WW2 was declared. This was his only appearance for the club in a season when all records were expunged.

Paul Wratten made two 'sub' appearances for United for a combined total of 23 minutes on the field of play. The first was for the last six minutes of the League game v. Wimbledon (h) April 1991 and the second was the final 17 minutes against Crystal Palace (a) the following month.

Jack Rowley was in United's first team for a total of 17 years, 98 days - from 23 October 1937 (when he made his League debut v. Sheffield Wed) to 29 January 1955 when he turned out in the FA Cup-tie against rivals Manchester City.

Billy Toms appeared in all four Divisions of the Football League in the 1920s.

All-Rounders

In the days before squad numbers, a player's shirt number denoted his precise position on the field. For instance the player wearing the number 5 shirt was certainly the central defender/centre-half. Those donning numbers 7 and 11 were the right and left-wingers respectively and number 9 was the team's centre-forward, the main striker.

Since the introduction of squad numbers in 1993, the recording of all-rounders has been difficult to assess.

Over a decade (1984-94) the versatile Clayton Blackmore donned every outfield shirt for United in a competitive match (wearing numbers 2 to 14 inclusive at some time or another).

Between 1937 and 1953, Johnny Carey appeared in 10 different positions (including goal in one game) for the Reds. He never lined up at outside-left. He also represented his country (the Republic of Ireland) in six different positions.

Walter Cartwright also played in 10 different positions (except outside-right) for United's senior side between 1895 & 1904.

In 1889-90 Newton Heath entered the Football Alliance, the 'unofficial' Second Division. During that season Charlie Harrison played in nine matches covering four different positions. He had six outings in goal, one each at right and left back and another at centre-half.

APPLETON, Michael Anthony

Born Salford, 4 December 1975.

Career: MANCHESTER UNITED (apprentice 1972, professional, July 1974), Wimbledon (on loan, 1995), Lincoln City (on loan, 1995), Grimsby Town (on loan, 1997), Preston North End (£500,000, August 1997), West Bromwich Albion (£750,000, 2001).

Tough-tackling midfielder Michael Appleton's two senior outings for United were both in the League Cup. He later did well at Deepdale, playing in 140 games and helping PNE win the Division Two title in 1999-2000. He's since helped WBA reach the First Division Play-off semi-finals and then gain promotion to the Premiership in 2002..

Club record: 2 apps.

ARKESDEN, Thomas Arthur

Born: Warwick, March 1878. Died: Hulme, Manchester 25 June 1921.

Career: Burton Wanderers (1896), Derby County (1898), Burton United (1901), MANCHESTER UNITED (£150, February 1903), Gainsborough Trinity (July 1907). Retired from League football in June 1908.

Inside-forward Tommy Arkesden did exceedingly well during his four-and-a-half years with United, having two very good seasons, those of 1903-04 and 1904-05 when he partnered first Sandy Robertson and then the pacy Harry Williams on the left-wing.

He had previously played alongside the great Steve Bloomer for Derby in the 1899 FA Cup Final and seven years later helped United win promotion to the First Division, although appearing in only seven matches. During his Football League career (1895-1907) he scored 70 goals in 204 appearances (125 before joining United)..

Club record: 79 apps. 33 goals

ARSENAL
Summary of League/Premier results:

	P	W	D	L	F	A
Premier League	20	8	5	7	24	20
Division 1	126	51	28	47	194	187
Division 2	20	8	3	9	33	34
Home	83	46	23	14	157	75
Away	83	21	13	49	94	166
Total	166	67	36	63	251	241

Heathens/United's League results v. the Gunners:

Season	Div	Home	Away	Season	Div	Home	Away
1894-95	2	D 3-3	L 2-3	1957-58	1	W 4-2	W 5-4
1895-96	2	W 5-1	L 1-2	1958-59	1	D 1-1	L 2-3
1896-97	2	D 1-1	W 2-0	1959-60	1	W 4-2	L 2-5
1897-98	2	W 5-1	L 1-5	1960-61	1	D 1-1	L 1-2
1898-99	2	D 2-2	L 1-5	1961-62	1	L 2-3	L 1-5
1899-1900	2	W 2-0	L 1-2	1962-63	1	L 2-3	W 3-1
1900-01	2	W 1-0	L 1-2	1963-64	1	W 3-1	L 1-2
1901-02	2	L 0-1	L 0-2	1964-65	1	W 3-1	W 3-2
1902-03	2	W 3-0	W 1-0	1965-66	1	W 2-1	L 2-4
1903-04	2	W 1-0	L 0-4	1966-67	1	W 1-0	D 1-1
				1967-68	1	W 1-0	W 2-0
				1968-69	1	D 0-0	L 0-3
1906-07	1	W 1-0	L 0-4	1969-70	1	W 2-1	D 2-2
1907-08	1	W 4-2	L 0-1	1970-71	1	L 1-3	L 0-4
1908-09	1	L 1-4	W 1-0	1971-72	1	W 3-1*	L 0-3
1909-10	1	W 1-0	D 0-0	1972-73	1	D 0-0	L 1-3
1910-11	1	W 5-0	W 2-1	1973-74	1	D 1-1	L 0-3
1911-12	1	W 2-0	L 1-2				
1912-13	1	W 2-0	D 0-0	1975-76	1	W 3-1	L 1-3
				1976-77	1	W 3-2	L 1-3
1919-20	1	L 0-1	W 3-0	1977-78	1	L 1-2	L 1-3
1920-21	1	D 1-1	L 0-2	1978-79	1	L 0-2	L 1-1
1921-22	1	W 1-0	L 1-3	1979-80	1	W 3-0	D 0-0
				1980-81	1	D 0-0	L 1-2
				1981-82	1	D 0-0	D 0-0
1925-26	1	L 0-1	L 2-3	1982-83	1	D 0-0	L 0-3
1926-27	1	D 2-2	L 0-1	1983-84	1	W 4-0	W 3-2
1927-28	1	W 4-1	W 1-0	1984-85	1	W 4-2	W 1-0
1928-29	1	W 4-1	L 1-3	1985-86	1	L 0-1	W 2-1
1929-30	1	W 1-0	L 2-4	1986-87	1	W 2-0	L 0-1
1930-31	1	L 1-2	L 1-4	1987-88	1	D 0-0	W 2-1
				1988-89	1	D 1-1	L 1-2
				1989-90	1	W 4-1	L 0-1
1936-37	1	W 2-0	D 1-1	1990-91	1	L 0-1	L 1-3
				1991-92	1	D 1-1	D 1-1
1938-39	1	W 1-0	L 1-2	1992-93	PL	D 0-0	W 1-0
				1993-94	PL	W 1-0	D 2-2
1946-47	1	W 5-2	L 2-6	1994-95	PL	W 3-0	D 0-0
1947-48	1	D 1-1	L 1-2	1995-96	PL	W 1-0	L 0-1
1948-49	1	W 2-0	W 1-0	1996-97	PL	W 1-0	W 2-1
1949-50	1	W 2-0	D 0-0	1997-98	PL	L 0-1	L 2-3
1950-51	1	W 3-1	L 0-3	1998-99	PL	D 1-1	L 0-3
1951-52	1	W 6-1	W 3-1	1999-00	PL	D 1-1	W 2-1
1952-53	1	D 0-0	L 1-2	2000-01	PL	W 6-1	L 0-1
1953-54	1	D 2-2	L 1-3	2001-02	PL	L 0-1	L 1-3
1954-55	1	W 2-1	W 3-2				
1955-56	1	D 1-1	D 1-1				
1956-57	1	W 6-2	W 2-1				

* Game played at Anfield

FA Cup results v. the Gunners:

	Round	Venue	Result
1905-06	4	Home	L 2-3
1935-36	4	Away	L 0-5
1950-51	5	Home	W 1-0
1961-62	4	Home	W 1-0
1978-79	Final	Wembley	L 2-3
1982-83	S-final	Villa Park	W 2-1
1987-88	5	Away	L 1-2
1998-99	S-final	Villa Park	D 0-0 aet
	Replay	Villa Park	W 2-1 aet

League Cup results v the Gunners:

	Round	Venue	Result
1977-78	2	Away	L 2-3
1982-83	SF (1)	Away	W 4-2
	SF (2)	Home	W 2-1
1990-91	4	Away	W 6-2
2001-02	3	Away	L 0-4

FA Charity Shield

United have also met the Gunners four times in the annual FA Charity Shield game and their record reads:

Venue	P	W	D	L	F	A
Away	1	0	0	1	3	4
Neutral	3	0	1*	2	2	6
Summary	4	0	1	3	5	10

* United won 5-4 on penalties after a 1-1 draw.
The venue for the three games played on neutral ground was Wembley Stadium.

Mercantile Credit

Venue	P	W	D	L	F	A
Neutral	1	0	0	1	1	2

On 9 October 1988, a crowd of 22,182 saw Arsenal beat United 2-1 in the Mercantile Credit Trophy Final game at Villa Park. Clayton Blackmore scored for the Reds. In earlier rounds United had ousted Everton and Newcastle United, both at home.

Fact File

United have met Arsenal in 83 of the 99 seasons they have spent in League Football. Arsenal have been United's most frequent opponents; similarly United have been Arsenal's most frequent opponents - and a total of 110 of the 166 League meetings between the two clubs have taken place since World War Two.
In seven visits to Highbury over a period of seven years - 1971-78 - United played six League games and one League Cup-tie - and they conceded three goals every time they visited the ground!
In January 1948 United and Arsenal met at Maine Road before a league record crowd of 83,260. Featuring the best attack in the country v. the best defence, the match finished 1-1 after a titanic struggle.

On the last day of the 1951-52 season Arsenal arrived at Old Trafford needing to beat United by seven goals to win the League title! Seven goals were scored but six of them came from United who won 6-1 to take the crown ahead of the Gunners. On 1 February 1958 United played their last League game before the Munich air crash. They visited Highbury and beat Arsenal 5-4 in a thrill-a-minute contest in front of 63,578 spectators. United were 3-0 up before the Gunners came back to level things up at 3-3. The Reds then went into a 5-3 lead before the Gunners came again to reduce the deficit to one. David Herd, later to join United, scored one of Arsenal's goals.
In 1964-65 United clinched their first League title since 1957 when they beat Arsenal 3-1 at Old Trafford in the penultimate game of the season. Denis Law (2) and George Best scored the goals.
In 1977-78, the Gunners were explosive while United were the fall guys. Arsenal won both League games - the first on Guy Fawkes Night the second on April Fools' Day!
In October 1990, United had one League point deducted from their tally after a brawl involving several players during a home game against Arsenal (who had two points taken off their total). This was the first time in League history that two teams had received this type of punishment. Arsenal still won the title.
Only one player - full-back Viv Anderson - has been capped by England while serving both clubs. He won 16 caps with the Gunners and three with United. George Graham was capped eight times by Scotland whilst an Arsenal player and then appeared in four internationals when registered with United.
Frank Stapleton won the first of his 71 Republic of Ireland caps with Arsenal. He later added 23 more to his tally with the Gunners before appearing in 34 internationals as a United star. The others came with Ajax, Le Havre and Blackburn.
Both David Herd and Ian Ure were capped by Scotland during their time at Arsenal but neither was called into the national side in their years with United. On the other hand Brian Kidd was capped by England when with United but not as an Arsenal player.
On the way to winning the 'treble' in 1998-99 United met Arsenal in an epic FA Cup semi-final replay at Villa Park. In extra-time with United clinging on at 1-1 with ten men following Roy Keane's sending -off, Ryan Giggs scored a sensational winner following a 70-yard solo dribble. In the dying minutes of normal time Peter Schmeichel had saved a penalty taken by Dennis Bergkamp.
On 8 May 2002, Arsenal, having already won the FA Cup, went to Old Trafford and won 1-0 to clinch the double. They also took the Premiership title away from United and at the same time equalled the Reds' record of three Leaague and Cup 'doubles' (following earlier successes in 1970-71 & 1997-98). The Gunners also equalled United's 2000 Premiership record of 12 consecutive League victories…and they wernt on to beat that with a last-match of the season home game victory over Everton.
Arsenal also equalled United's record of 15 FA Cup Final appearances when they beat Chelsea in the 2002 showdown at the Millennium Stadium, Cardiff. At the same time Tony Adams emulated Bryan Robson's feat of captaining three FA Cup winning teams.
A crowd of 31,000 saw United lost a seven-goal thriller by 4-3 at Highbury against Arsenal in the 1948 FA Charity Shield game. Ronnie Burke, Jack Rowley and Lionel Smith (og) scored for United.
Players with both clubs include: V Anderson, T Baldwin, R Beale (Arsenal WW1), H Boyd, R Brocklebank (United WW2), W Campbell, A Cole, L Cunningham (Arsenal junior), G Fisher (United reserve), R Gaudie, G Graham (also Arsenal manager), R Halton (Arsenal WW2), D Herd, C Jenkyns, B Kidd (also United assistant-manager), F Knowles (Arsenal WW1), J Leighton (Arsenal loan), W McMillan (Arsenal trialist), J Moody, J Pennington (Villa trialist, United WW1), M Pinner (amateur), D Platt (United reserve), J Rimmer, J Sloan (United reserve & Arsenal WW2), F Stapleton, I Ure.
Also associated: T Docherty (Arsenal player, United manager), D Sexton (United manager, Arsenal assistant-manager/coach), S Houston (United player, Arsenal assistant-manager), B Whitehouse (coach/scout both clubs), G Wright (trainer/physio both clubs).

17

ASQUITH, Beaumont

Born: Painthorpe, 16 September 1910. Died: Barnsley, 12 April 1977
Career: Painthorpe Albion, Barnsley (1933), MANCHESTER UNITED (May 1939), guested for Barnsley, Blackburn Rovers, Bradford Park Avenue, Chesterfield, Doncaster Rovers Huddersfield Town, Leeds United and Rotherham United during WW2, then Barnsley (September 1945), Bradford City (1948), Scarborough (1950).
Inside/centre-forward 'Beau' Asquith made one League appearance for the Reds ...at the start of that ill-fated 1939-40 campaign v. Charlton (a) when all the records for that League 'season' were expunged.
Club record: one app.

ASSISTANT-MANAGERS

(See also under managers)
Jimmy Murphy was assistant-manager to Matt Busby for a number of years.
Archie Knox was succeeded as United's assistant-boss in 1991 by former player Brian Kidd who himself was replaced by Steve McClaren.
Carlos Queiroz is assistant-manager to Sir Alex Ferguson since summer 2002.

ASTLEY, Joseph Emmanuel

Born: Dudley, March 1899. Died: Manchester, autumn 1969.
Career: Cradley Heath, MANCHESTER UNITED (August 1924), Notts County (June 1928), Northwich Victoria (1929), Hyde United (1930).
Full-back Joe Astley made two only League appearances for United - taking over from Jack Silcock on both occasions (in March 1926 v. Bolton and April 1927 v. Sunderland). The second of these proved most unfortunate for Joe. He suffered a bad knee injury after just 12 minutes which necessitated a cartilage operation. He had played his last game for United!
Club record: 2 apps.

ASTON, John senior

Born: Prestwich, Manchester 3 September 1921.
Career: Ravensbury Street School, Crossley Lads' Club, Clayton Methodists, Mujacs FC, MANCHESTER UNITED (amateur, January 1938, professional December 1939), guested for Hamilton Academical, Hyde United, Plymouth Argyle and Portsmouth during WW2. Retired in May 1954 to become United's junior coach, later taking over as Chief Scout (1970-72).
John Aston, senior, played mainly as a full-back for United (but also turned out with some success as a centre-forward) and all told appeared in well over 280 senior games for the club, scoring 30 goals.
He began playing competitively during the war, appearing regularly as a guest with other clubs when free from his duties as a Royal Marine Commando. After the hostilities he returned to Old Trafford and remained with the club until 1972 (in various capacities) He gained 17 England caps and was a key member of United's FA Cup winning side of 1948 and League Championship side of 1952. Unfortunately the faithful John, who had always put United first, lost his job along with manager Frank O'Farrell as part of a mass 'clear out' in 1972.
United record: 284 apps. 30 goals

ASTON, John junior

Born: Manchester, 28 June 1947.
Career: MANCHESTER UNITED (apprentice, July 1962, professional July 1964), Luton Town (£30,000, July 1972), Mansfield Town (1977), Blackburn Rovers (1978-80).
John Aston junior (son of John, above) was a direct, out-and-out left-winger who represented both Manchester and Lancashire Schools before joining the Reds as an apprentice. He remained at Old Trafford for ten years before transferring to Luton Town. A Football League Championship winner with United in 1967, he produced a brilliant performance for the Reds in the European Cup Final victory over Benfica twelve months later and then helped the Hatters gain promotion to the First Division in 1974.
Club record: 187 apps. 27 goals

ASTON VILLA

FA Cup results v Villa:

	Round	Venue	Result
1905-06	3	Home	W 5-1
1907-08	3	Away	W 2-0
1910-11	2	Home	W 2-1
1919-20	2	Home	L 1-2
1947-48	3	Away	W 6-4
1956-57	Final	Wembley	L 1-2
1962-63	4	Home	W 1-0
1976-77	6	Home	W 2-1
2001-02	3	Away	W 3-2

League Cup result v. Villa:

	Round	Venue	Result
1970-71	S-final (1)	Home	D 1-1
	S-final (2)	Away	L 1-2
1975-76	3	Away	W 2-1
1992-93	3	Away	L 0-1
1993-94	Final	Wembley	L 1-3
1999-2000	3	Away	L 0-3

United's League/Premier record v. Villa:

Season	Div	Home	Away	Season	Div	Home	Away
1892-93	1	W 2-0	L 0-2	1957-58	1	W 4-1	L 2-3
1893-94	1	L 1-3	L 1-5	1958-59	1	W 2-1	W 2-0
1906-07	1	W 1-0	L 0-2	1960-61	1	D 1-1	L 1-3
1907-08	1	L 1-2	W 4-1	1961-62	1	W 2-0	D 1-1
1908-09	1	L 0-2	L 1-3	1962-63	1	D 2-2	W 2-1
1909-10	1	W 2-0	L 1-7	1963-64	1	W 1-0	L 0-4
1910-11	1	W 2-0	L 2-4	1964-65	1	W 7-0	L 1-2
1911-12	1	W 3-1	L 0-6	1965-66	1	W 6-1	D 1-1
1912-13	1	W 4-0	L 2-4	1966-67	1	W 3-1	L 1-2
1913-14	1	L 0-6	L 1-3				
1914-15	1	W 1-0	D 3-3	1974-75	2	W 2-1	L 0-2
				1975-76	1	W 2-0	L 1-2
1919-20	1	L 1-2	L 0-2	1976-77	1	W 2-0	L 2-3
1920-21	1	L 1-3	W 4-3	1977-78	1	D 1-1	L 1-2
1921-22	1	W 1-0	L 1-3	1978-79	1	D 1-1	D 2-2
				1979-80	1	W 2-1	W 3-0
1925-26	1	W 3-0	D 2-2	1980-81	1	D 3-3	D 3-3
1926-27	1	W 2-1	L 0-2	1981-82	1	W 4-1	D 1-1
1927-28	1	W 5-1	L 1-3	1982-83	1	W 3-1	L 1-2
1928-29	1	D 2-2	D 0-0	1983-84	1	L 1-2	W 3-0
1929-30	1	L 2-3	L 0-1	1984-85	1	W 4-0	L 0-3
1930-31	1	L 3-4	L 0-7	1985-86	1	W 4-0	W 3-1
				1986-87	1	W 3-1	D 3-3
1937-38	2	W 3-1	L 0-3				
1938-39	1	D 1-1	W 2-0	1988-89	1	D 1-1	D 0-0
				1989-90	1	W 2-0	L 0.3
1946-47	1	W 2-1	D 0-0	1990-91	1	D 1-1	D 1-1
1947-48	1	W 2-0	W 1-0	1991-92	1	W 1-0	W 1-0
1948-49	1	W 3-1	L 1-2	1992-93	PL	D 1-1	L 0-1
1949-50	1	W 7-0	W 4-0	1993-94	PL	W 3-1	W 2-1
1950-51	1	D 0-0	W 3-1	1994-95	PL	W 1-0	W 2-1
1951-52	1	D 1-1	W 5-2	1995-96	PL	D 0-0	L 1-3
1952-53	1	W 3-1	D 3-3	1996-97	PL	D 0-0	D 0-0
1953-54	1	W 1-0	D 2-2	1997-98	PL	W 1-0	W 2-0
1954-55	1	L 0-1	L 1-2	1998-99	PL	W 2-1	D 1-1
1955-56	1	W 1-0	D 4-4	1999-00	PL	W 3-0	W 1-0
1956-57	1	D 1-1	W 3-1	2000-01	PL	W 2-0	W 1-0
				2001-02	PL	W 1-0	D 1-1

Summary of League results:

	P	W	D	L	F	A
Premier League	20	12	6	2	25	11
Division 1	114	49	27	38	210	180
Division 2	4	2	0	2	5	7
Home	69	44	15	10	141	62
Away	69	19	18	32	99	136
Total	138	63	33	42	240	198

FA Charity Shield

A crowd of almost 28,000 saw United defeat Aston Villa 4-0 at Old Trafford in the 1957 FA Charity Shield game.

Fact file

On 27 December 1920 United played Villa at Old Trafford before a ground record crowd of 70,504 - never bettered for a club match. Villa won 3-1, having been beaten 4-3 by United at Villa Park on Christmas Day.

Villa have only won twice in League games at Old Trafford/Maine Road since the Second World War – a total of 47 matches; during this period Villa have also lost both FA Cup-ties on the former ground. When United lost 7-0 at Villa Park on 27 December 1930, it equalled the Reds' heaviest League defeat (previously handed out by Blackburn, also 7-0 winners in 1926).

When United secured their record 7-0 League win over Villa at Old Trafford on 8 March 1950, left-winger Charlie Mitten scored four times, three of them penalties. As Mitten prepared to take his third spot-kick, the Villa goalkeeper Joe Rutherford enquired: "Which corner is this one going in, Charlie?" Mitten coolly replied: "Same one as the other two".....Rutherford still stood no chance! United won the return fixture that season by 4-0.

United were 3-0 up on Aston Villa in their home League game on 30 August 1930. But they failed to acknowledge the fact that hot-shot Tom 'Pongo' Waring was around and he scored four times for the Midland club who stormed back to win a rip-roaring contest 4-3.

Villa's George Edwards scored one of the fastest FA Cup goals on record when he found the United net after just 13 seconds in a 3rd round tie at Villa Park in January 1948. United hit back strongly after that. They led 5-1 at half-time and went on to win a thrilling contest by 6-4.

In another third round tie in January 2002, United trailed 2-0 at Villa Park with 13 minutes remaining, but three exciting goals (two from Ruud van Nistelrooy) in a magical five minute spell saw United through, 3-2.

Twelve goals were scored in the two First Division clashes between the clubs in 1980-81 - both ended in 3-3 draws.

Players with both clubs include: W Anderson, F Barson, M Bosnich, H Bourne (United reserve), F Brett (Villa reserve), F Buckley, R Chester, A Comyn (United 'A' team), S Cooke (United School of Excellence Villa junior), S Crowther, J Cunningham (Villa reserve), M Delaney (United junior), D Dublin, A Farman (Villa reserve), G Fellows (United junior), J Fisher (Villa reserve), R Gaudie, C Gibson, J Gidman, G Graham, H Green, P Hall, H Halse, T Homer (Villa amateur), G Hunter, R Johnsen, P McGrath, A McLoughlin (United reserve), F Mann (Villa amateur), M Pinner, D Platt (United reserve), J Rimmer, L Sealey, P Schmeichel, W Thompson (Villa reserve), J Travers, J Walters (United reserve), J Warner, J Whitehouse, T Wilson, W Yates (Villa reserve).

Also associated: R Atkinson and T Docherty (managers of both clubs), D Sexton (United manager, Villa coach), M Musgrove (assistant-manager/coach at both clubs), B Whitehouse (coach at both clubs, scout with United), AH Albut (Villa committee member, United secretary).

ATHLETIC BILBAO

United lost the 1st leg of their European Cup quarter-final clash with Athletic Bilbao by 5-3 in front of 60,000 fans in Spain in mid-January 1957. But the Reds produced a terrific performance to win the return game by 3-0 before some 70,000 spectators at Maine Road and so powered through to the semi-finals with a splendid 6-5 aggregate victory.

Dennis Viollet and Tommy Taylor scored in both matches but the two crucial goals in the tie came from Liam Whelan and Johnny Berry. With United 5-2 down on a mud-bath of a pitch in Bilbao, following a blizzard, Whelan scored an amazing individualist goal to give United a glimmer of hope in the second leg. Berry hit the winner at Maine Road to send the huge crowd wild with delight.

ATHINAIKOS

United had to battle all the way to beat the Greek side Athinaikos in the 1st rd of the 1991-92 European Cup-winners Cup competition. Mark Hughes & Brian McClair scored the goals at Old Trafford for a 2-0 win while the away clash ended 0-0.

ATLETICO MADRID

United crashed out of the Cup-winners Cup in the 1st round in 1991-92, beaten 4-1 on aggregate by Atletico Madrid. Mark Hughes scored United's second leg goal at Old Trafford (1-1) following a 3-0 defeat in Spain.

Player with both clubs: Quinton Fortune.

Also associated: Ron Atkinson (manager of both clubs), Pat O'Connell (United player, Atletico coach/manager).

ATTENDANCES

Manchester United have not always played at Old Trafford! When the club began as Newton Heath (LYR) the team played at North Road, near to the carriage and wagon sheds where most of the players worked as railwaymen. Attendances were estimated in those days but it would seem that the biggest crowd ever to assemble at North Road was probably around 15,000, set for the visit of Sunderland in a Football League game on 4 March 1893. By the end of that season, Newton Heath, who by now had lost their railway connection, were elected to the Football League as runners-up to Forest in the Alliance - the Football League's unofficial Second Division.

Despite a poor start to their first campaign of Football League soccer, the club decided to move to bigger premises at Bank Street in Clayton, just a couple of miles away. Gradually Bank Street was built up and Newton Heath were still playing there when the momentous occasion of the club's liquidation occurred in 1902, rising 'phoenix-like' to re-emerge as Manchester United FC. The Bank Street ground had only held 20,000 spectators previously, but investment in the new club enabled extensions to be carried out so that 40,000 crowds were possible. Eventually the attendance record swelled to 50,000 in 1908 when United won their first League Championship.

By now it had become apparent that United had outgrown their Clayton ground and the club sought a better site that could attract support from all over Manchester and its surrounding district. Thanks to the generosity of the club's great benefactor, John H Davies, a brewery owner, the club had a purpose built stadium erected at Old Trafford by the leading stadium designer of that era, Archibald Leitch. The new stadium could house 80,000 spectators in relative luxury!

In 1941 the ground was devastated by enemy bombers in a raid on the industrial complex of Trafford Park. The club was forced to share grounds with its great rivals Manchester City at Maine Road until 1949 when they were able to return to Old Trafford.

The stadium has gradually been re-developed over the years to the present level as a superb 68,000 all-seater complex. Most of United's attendance records were set at Maine Road which had an 84,000 plus capacity in the heady post-war years when people flocked to football grounds, relieved that the country was at peace again. United have continued to attract vast crowds wherever they have played (especially since 1958).

Home Attendances

United's average home League attendances since the WW2, with the first three seasons at Maine Road:

League Division 1		**League Division 1**	
1946-47 43,615	1961-62 33,490	1975-76 54,750	1990-91 43,242
1947-48 53,660	1962-63 40,317	1976-77 53,710	1991-92 44,892
1948-49 46,023	1963-64 43,753	1977-78 51,938	
1949-50 41,455	1964-65 45,831	1978-79 46,430	**Premiership**
1950-51 37,159	1965-66 38,768	1979-80 51,566	1992-93 35,132
1951-52 41,030	1966-67 53,895	1980-81 45,071	1993-94 44,244
1952-53 35,737	1967-68 57,759*	1981-82 44,570	1994-95 43,681
1953-54 33,637	1968-69 51,121	1982-83 41,573	1995-96 41,700
1954-55 34,077	1969-70 51,115	1983-84 44,546	1996-97 55,080
1955-56 38,893	1970-71 44,754	1984-85 45,074	1997-98 55,164
1956-57 45,407	1971-72 45,999	1985-86 43,880	1998-99 55,188
1957-58 45,583	1972-73 48,623	1986-87 40,627	1999-00 58,017*
1958-59 53,258	1973-74 42,712	1987-88 39,105	2000-01 67,544*
1959-60 47,288		1988-89 36,473	2001-02 67,586*
1960-61 37,807	**League Division 2**	1989-90 39,003	* New League record
	1974-75 48,388		

Top attendances for United games at Old Trafford:
(in all major competitions: 67,550 and above):
70,504	v. Aston Villa (League)	27.12.1920
67,683	v. Middlesbrough (Premiership)	23.03.2002
67,651	v. Leicester City (Premiership)	17.11.2001
67,646	v. Newcastle United (Premiership)	02.01.2002
67,638	v. Southampton (Premiership)	22.12.2001
67,637	v. Coventry City (Premiership)	14.04.2001
67,603	v. West Ham United (Premiership)	01.01.2001
67,599	v. Liverpool (Premiership)	22.01.2002
67,599	v. Tottenham Hotspur (Premiership)	06.03.2002
67,597	v. Ipswich Town (Premiership)	23.12.2000
67,592	v. Aston Villa (Premiership)	23.02.2002
67,587	v. Sunderland (Premiership)	02.02.2002
67,583	v. Tottenham Hotspur (Premiership)	02.12.2000
67,582	v. West Ham United (Premiership)	08.12.2001
67,581	v. Southampton (Premiership)	28.10.2000
67,580	v. Arsenal (Premiership)	08.05.2002
67,577	v. Derby County (Premiership)	12.12.2001
67,576	v. Middlesbrough (Premiership)	11.11.2000
67,571	v. Charlton Athletic (Premiership)	11.05.2002
67,568	v. Chelsea (Premiership)	23.09.2000
67,559	v. Bolton Wanderers (Premiership)	20.10.2001
67,555	v. Leeds United (Premiership)	27.10.2001
67,552	v. Blackburn Rovers (Premiership)	19.01.2002
67,551	v. Ipswich Town (Premiership)	22.09.2001

Top 10 'home' crowds at Maine Road
83,260	v. Arsenal (League)	17.01.1948
82,771	v. Bradford Park Avenue (FA Cup)	29.01.1949
81,565	v. Yeovil Town (FA Cup Rd 5)	12.02.1949
75,598	v. Borussia Dortmund (Euro Cup)	17.10.1956
74,213	v. Preston North End (FA Cup)	28.02.1948
71,690	v. Manchester City (League)	07.04.1948
71,623	v. Bolton Wanderers (League)	26.03.1948
70,787	v. Newcastle United (League)	04.12.1948
70,453	v. Athletic Bilbao (European Cup)	06.02.1957
70,434	v. Bradford PA (FA Cup Rd 4, 2 rep)	07.02.1949

Lowest Attendances for United Away Games
2,750	v. Nelson (at Seedhill) Div 2	01.03.1924
6,537	v. Djurgaarden (in Holland) ICFC	23.09.1964
8,966	v. Oxford United (Manor Grnd) Div 1	02.05.1988
9,968	v. Accrington Stanley (Peel P) FAC	05.01.1946
11,788	v. Stoke City (at Anfield) FAC	19.01.1931

Other attendances of 80,000 and over that United have played to
135,000	v. Real Madrid (away) European Cup	11.04.1957
125,000	v. Real Madrid (away) European Cup	15.05.1968
114,432	v. Barcelona (away) European Cup	02.11.1994
105,000	v. Gornik Zabrze (away) European Cup	13.03.1968
99,882	v. Benfica (Wembley) European Cup Final	29.05.1968
99,842	v. Blackpool (Wembley) FA Cup Final	24.04.1948
99,756	v. Bolton Wands (Wembley) FA Cup Final	03.05.1958
99,604	v. Leicester City (Wembley) FA Cup Final	25.05.1963
99,445	v. Everton (Wembley) FA Cup Final	18.05.1985
99,304	v. Liverpool (Wembley) League Cup Final	26.03.1983
99,252	v. Liverpool (Wembley) FA Cup Final	21.05.1977
99,225	v. Aston Villa (Wembley) FA Cup Final	04.05.1957
99,219	v. Arsenal (Wembley) FA Cup Final	12.05.1979
99,115	v. Southampton (Wembley) FA Cup Final	01.05.1976
99,059	v. Brighton & HA (Wembley) FA Cup Final	21.05.1983
91,956	v. Liverpool (Wembley) FA Charity Shield	20.08.1983
91,534	v. Brighton & HA (W) FA Cup Final replay	26.05.1983
89,954	v. Bayern Munich (Barcelona) E Cup Final	26.05.1999
81,775	v. Liverpool (Wembley) FA Charity Shield	13.08.1977
81,639	v. Everton (Wembley) FA Charity Shield	10.05.1985
80,000	v. AC Milan (away) European Cup	14.05.1958

* It is always stated in the national press and certain reference books that FA Cup Final attendances from 1949 to 1980 were all rounded off at 100,000 (the number of tickets printed - not sold). Sources have revealed that there was never a full-house at the Empire Stadium.

How the Old Trafford attendance record has been broken down the years:
45,000*	United v. Liverpool	League	19.02.1910
50,000	United v. Bristol City	League	25.03.1910
60,000	United v. Manchester City	League	17.09.1910
65,101	United v. Aston Villa	FA Cup	04.02.1911
70,504	United v. Aston Villa	League	27.12.1920
71,779	Bolton Wds v. Sheffield Utd	FA Cup sf	24.03.1923
76,962	Wolves v. Grimsby Town	FA Cup sf	25.03.1939

* A further 5,000 spectators entered the ground without paying

"It's bloody tough being a legend."
'Big Ron'

ATKINSON, Ronald Frederick

Born: Liverpool, 18 March 1939
Career: Lea Village School (Stechford, Birmingham), BSA Works team, Aston Villa (signed as a professional in 1956), Wolverhampton Wanderers (trialist), Headington United/later Oxford United (from 1959-71), Witney Town (briefly as a player), Kettering Town (manager, 1971), Cambridge United (manager, 1974), West Bromwich Albion (manager, 1978), MANCHESTER UNITED (manager, June 1981-November 1986), West Bromwich Albion (manager for a second time, 1987-88), Atletico Madrid (manager 1988-89), Sheffield Wednesday (manager, 1989-91), Aston Villa (manager, 1991-94), Coventry City (manager, 1995-96, later Director of Football at Highfield Road), Sheffield Wednesday (manager again, 1997-98), Nottingham Forest (manager, 1999). He left The City Ground following Forest's demotion from the Premiership in June 1999.

When 'Big Ron' Atkinson arrived at Old Trafford in June 1981 to replace Dave Sexton the difference in style could not have been more marked. Atkinson, a larger than life 'Scouser', brash, opinionated, with a love for jewellery and a champagne lifestyle was different in all respects to the introvert Sexton. However, his reputation for getting his team to play attractive, attacking football appealed to the United following. Instantly he got work, signing Frank Stapleton to replace the departed Joe Jordan. Then he raided his former employers West Brom to recruit a ready made midfield as Bryan Robson and Remi Moses were signed in a £2.5 million package deal. With John Gidman adding experience to the defence, this was a much stronger United team to attempt to win the Championship again.

Results certainly improved with the side, as expected, playing with great style and panache. Garry Birtles started to score and with the precocious Norman Whiteside

arriving from 'nowhere' with rich promise, the team went on to reach two Cup Finals in 1982-83, losing unluckily to Liverpool in the League Cup but beating Brighton & Hove Albion in the FA Cup, albeit rather fortunately after a replay!

Two years later with young Mark Hughes leading the attack brilliantly, United won the FA Cup again, famously against the favourites Everton 1-0 after extra-time with only ten men (following Kevin Moran's dismissal), Whiteside's fabulous goal being rated as one of the best ever in a Wembley final.

Yet, despite further acquisitions of 'United type' players - Brazil, Graham, Muhren, Olsen & Strachan - the Championship remained tantalisingly out of reach as the two Merseyside clubs played 'ducks and drakes' with the trophy! Then, in 1985-86, came the apparent breakthrough as United brilliantly won their first 10 League matches (27 goals scored), unbeaten in 15 - surely the title must be theirs. But alas, the team faded badly, finishing a disappointing fourth, a massive 14 points being a rampant Liverpool side.

The following season began badly, this time the first 15 matches yielded only three wins and therefore over a 12-month period United's record read: P42 W12 D13 L17 Pts 49. The departure of the brilliant Mark Hughes, sold for £2.5 million to Barcelona, was viewed with dismay, which, following Ray Wilkins' transfer to AC Milan for £1.5 million in 1984, left the feeling that the club were not really serious about their intentions.

A dismal 4-1 thrashing at Southampton in the League Cup was the last straw, as Atkinson sadly left. In retrospect, finishes of 3, 3, 4, 4, 4 in his first five seasons (plus two FA Cup wins) were nothing to be ashamed of, and indeed, the club had begun playing in the true United style once more after seasons of dull mediocrity. 'Big Ron' would have his moments again, as Sheffield Wednesday beat United 1-0 in the 1991 League Cup Final, thus denying the Reds a 'domestic' Cup double. Then in 1992-93, as boss of Aston Villa, he ran United to the wire in the inaugural Premiership season before another League Cup triumph (with Villa) in 1994 again at United's expense, preventing them achieving a 'domestic whitewash'.

Atkinson will have his place in United's pantheon of great managers, starting a process which Sir Alex Ferguson would complete.

As a player, Atkinson amassed over 500 senior appearances with Oxford United, whom he helped gain Football league status and win the Fourth Division title. As boss of Kettering, he guided them to the titles of both the Southern League North and Premier Divisions, and came within a single vote of getting the non-League team into the Football League! He then assembled a very competent side at Cambridge - good enough to win promotion from the Fourth Division in 1977. Indeed, they were well on their way to winning promotion to the Second Division when he took over at The Hawthorns in 1978. Atkinson then guided the Baggies into the semi-finals of the FA Cup and the quarter-finals of the UEFA Cup.

NB: Atkinson was voted Manager of the Month 44 days after taking over the reins at Coventry City.

21

All-Seater Records

Since the all-seater ground regulations came into force, United have set existing attendance records at the following stadiums (all in the Premiership):

Reebok Stadium	v. Bolton Wanderers	27,350*	29.01.2002
The 'New' Valley	v. Charlton Athletic	26,475*	10.02.2002
Highfield Road	v. Coventry City	23,344	22.11.1995
Goodison Park	v. Everton	40,479	27.08.1997
Elland Road	v. Leeds United	40,255	25.04.1999
Filbert Street	v. Leicester City	22,170	18.03.2000
Anfield	v. Liverpool	44,929	11.09.1999
St James' Park	v. Newcastle United	52,134	30.12.2000
The City Ground	v. Nottingham Forest	30,025	06.02.1999
Hillsborough	v. Sheffield Wed.	39,640	02.02.2000
Selhurst Park	v. Wimbledon	30,115	09.05.1993

* Since bettered

• United also set an attendance record at The Dell (Southampton) before Saints moved to their new home in 2001. It was 15,262 for the Premiership game there on 13 April 1996.

• The attendance of 67,683 at Old Trafford for the United v. Middlesbrough game on 23 February 2002 is a record for an all-seater stadium in the Premiership.

• The FA Cup semi-final between Arsenal and Tottenham Hotspur at Old Trafford on 8 April 2001, attracted a crowd of 63,541 - this being the highest for any match involving two club sides on a neutral ground in England (other than those competing in a major Cup Final).

Attendance Facts & Figures

Highest

The biggest ever attendance for a Football League game in England - 83,260 - saw Manchester United take on Arsenal at Maine Road on 17 January 1948 (Division One). Some reference books have given the attendance at this game as 82,950 and even 81,962, but this United Encyclopaedia is taking the one of 83,260 as being correct, as it included all season ticket holders.

The second largest crowd ever to watch a United 'home' game has been 82,771 v. Bradford Park Avenue at Maine Road in January 1949. There was a turnout of 70,434 at the second replay between the two clubs nine days later (on a Monday afternoon), and in fact, the three Cup tussles between United and Park Avenue that season attracted an overall total of 182,297 spectators (there were 29,092 at Bradford for the first replay).

The record attendance for a mid-week League game in England was set in September 1957 when 72,077 fans packed into Goodison Park to watch the Everton v. United First Division encounter,

A crowd of 76,962 attended Old Trafford to watch the 1939 FA Cup semi-final between Grimsby Town and Wolverhampton Wanderers - a record for the ground.

In season 1947-48, over 143,000 attended the two local First Division derbies between United and City at Maine Road - 71,364 when City were at 'home' and 71,690 for United's 'home' game.

81,565 fans assembled at Maine Road to witness United's 5th round clash with non-League Yeovil Town in 1949.

United's biggest home crowd for a Second Division match is 60,585 v. Sunderland in November 1974.

United's biggest home crowd for a League Cup game has been 63,418 v. Manchester City in the 2nd leg of the 1969-70 semi-final played on 13 December. A crowd of 55,799 saw the first leg at Maine Road 10 days earlier.

The biggest crowd ever to watch a United first team game is 135,000 (estimated) in the giant Bernabeu Stadium, Spain for their European Cup semi-final, 1st leg clash with Real Madrid on 2 April 1957.

A then Inter-Cities Fairs Cup record attendance of 67,400 saw United's play-off game with Ferencvaros in Budapest, Hungary on 16 June 1965.

A crowd of 66,646 saw the FA Cup Final replay between Bradford City and Newcastle United at Old Trafford in April 1911. Twelve years later there were almost 72,000 spectators present for the FA Cup semi-final showdown between Bolton Wanderers and Sheffield United; 69,260 watched the semi-final between Huddersfield and Sheffield United in March 1928 and 69,292 supporters witnessed the semi-final encounter between Huddersfield Town and Sheffield Wednesday in March 1930.

Around 63,000 fans saw the Everton-Leeds United FA Cup semi-final in April 1968 and there were 62,144 at the Everton-Liverpool semi-final clash three years later.

A crowd of 28,067 attended Highbury to watch a giant screen beaming back pictures of Arsenal's away game at Old Trafford on 3 March 1967. The attendance at Old Trafford was 63,363.

A huge crowd of 21,502 saw United's home Central League game with Leeds United at Old Trafford on 7 October 1995…this is believed to have been United's biggest-ever second XI crowd. The main attraction - Eric Cantona!

There were 25,563 spectators inside Old Trafford when United played Swindon Town in the FA Youth Cup Final on 30 April 1964.

The 1954 FA Youth Cup Final between United and Wolverhampton Wanderers at Molineux (played on 26 April) attracted a crowd of 28,651.

Smallest

The smallest on record at Old Trafford (for a United senior game) is believed to have been 3,507 when Southampton were the visitors for a Second Division game in September 1931.

The lowest since WW2 (competitive level) was that of 11,381 for the FA Charity Shield encounter with Newcastle United in September 1952.

United's lowest home League attendance since 1946 (at Old Trafford) is 11,968 v. Fulham (Division One) in April 1950.

The lowest post WW2 home crowd (at Maine Road) was 8,456 for the United v. Stoke City (League Division One) in February 1947. The game was played on a Wednesday afternoon in sub-arctic conditions!

Only 2,750 saw the Nelson v. United Second Division League encounter in March 1924.

Just 8,966 spectators witnessed the Oxford United v. United First Division League clash at The Manor Ground in May 1988 - the second lowest crowd for a Reds' League game (home or away) since World War Two.

On the European circuit, the smallest attendance for a United game has been that of 6,537 at Djurgaarden in Sweden for an Inter-Cities Fairs Cup clash in September 1964.

Aggregate Attendances

An aggregate of 1,126,860 spectators attended the 21 home League games played by United at Maine Road in season 1947-48 (average 53,660).

During the three seasons United used Manchester City's ground, over three million spectators saw the club's 63 'home' First Division matches staged there. The average crowd was 47,766.

The first time more than a million spectators attended Old Trafford for a complete programme of League football was in season 1967-68 - total 1,212,939, resulting in an average of 57,759. This bettered Newcastle United's all-time record average home crowd of 56,351 which was set at St James' Park 20 years earlier in 1947-48.

Home and away in 1967-68 United's 42 League games were attended by over two million spectators, with some three million watching all matches. And this was the case again in seasons 1999-2000 (with an aggregate of 1,108,323 for 19 home games alone), 2000-01 (revealing an aggregate Old Trafford attendance figure of 1,283.317) and 2001-02 (when United's home Premier League average was 67,586, thus beating the previous season's record by just 42) the aggregate was 1,284,134.

Average Attendances

The first season back at Old Trafford (1949-50) United's average home League crowd was 41,455 - some 6,300 fewer than the overall average at Maine Road. In fact, it was 4,568 below the average for United's last campaign on City soil. As several parts of the ground were deemed unsafe, the capacity was now only 54,000.

Only once have rivals Manchester City had a better post WW2 seasonal average home League crowd than United - in 1954-55 (34,964 against 34,077).

When United won the 2nd Division Championship in 1974-75, the average League attendance at Old Trafford (48,389) was 2,000 more than the best-supported team in the top flight (Liverpool).

Crowd Dossier

The record attendance at Newton Heath's North Road Ground, Newton Heath, was 15,000, set for the visit of Sunderland in a Football Leaugue game on 4 March 1893. The lowest for a major first team game was 1,000, recorded against Walsall Town Swifts in April 1890 and v. Small Heath in December 1890 - both in the Football Alliance.

The biggest crowd to watch the Heathens play at their Bank Street Ground, Clayton, was 50,000... for the visit of Newcastle United in a First Division encounter on 8 February 1908. The lowest turnout for a competitive game was just on 1,000, registered on three occasions in the 1895-96 season, against Burton Wanderers, Darwen and Leicester Fosse (all in the Football League).

On 7 May 1921, United played Derby County in a League game at Old Trafford in front of 10,000 spectators. Immediately after this match had finished, relegation-doomed Stockport County (whose ground at Edgeley Park had been closed as a result of crowd behaviour) took on Leicester Fosse in a Second Division game. As a result many spectators actually stayed on to watch the 'free match'. The attendance figure for the County-Fosse game is given in the record books as just 13 - the number of paying customers who came to watch the second encounter. Considering that the exit gates would have been opened 10-15 minutes before the end of the United fixture (to allow people out of the ground) this figure of 13 is surely a reflection of thirteen people's honesty in those days! More realistically the attendance figure was perhaps upwards of 1,500, even around the 2,000 mark.

On 1 March 1969, two FA Cup quarter-finals were staged in Manchester - United v. Everton and City v. Tottenham Hotspur. They were seen by a combined total of 112,336 spectators - an English record for aggregate crowds in one provincial city on the same day. There were 63,464 at Old Trafford and 48,872 at Maine Road.

Ground Records

United set attendance records at the following club grounds: Dean Court, Bournemouth (28,799, FA Cup, 1957), The Reebok Stadium, Bolton (25,045, Premiership, 1997 - since bettered), The Recreation Ground, Hartlepool United (17,426, FA Cup, 1957), Boothferry Park, Hull City (55,019, FA Cup, 1949), The City Ground, Nottingham Forest (49,946, League, 1967), The Dell, Southampton (31,044, League, 1969), Vicarage Road, Watford (34,099, FA Cup, 1969), Selhurst Park, Wimbledon (30,115, Premiership, 1993) and The Racecourse Ground, Wrexham (34,445, FA Cup, 1957).

AWARDS (Honours)

•Six United players have all won the Football Writers' Association (FWA) 'Footballer of the Year' award: Johnny Carey (1949), Bobby Charlton (1966), George Best (1968), Eric Cantona (1996), Roy Keane (2000) and Teddy Sheringham (2001). Best was the youngest to win the award at the age of 21. Gordon Strachan (ex-United) won the award in 1991 (as a Leeds player).

•The PFA (Professional Footballers' Association) 'Player of the Year' award has been won seven times by United players: Mark Hughes (1989 & 1991), Gary Pallister (1992), Eric Cantona (1994), Roy Keane (2000), Teddy Sheringham (2001) and Ruud van Nistelrooy (2002). Two ex-United players, David Platt (1990) and Paul McGrath (1993) also won the award.

•Hughes is the only player to have won the PFA 'Player of the Year' award twice, while Cantona was the first foreign-born player to receive the honour.

•David Beckham was voted BBC Sports Personality of the Year in 2001. On the same night Sir Alex Ferguson was presented with the BBC's achievement award.

•The PFA 'Young Player of the Year' award has gone to a United player on five occasions: Mark Hughes (1985),

23

Lee Sharpe (1991), Ryan Giggs (1992 & 1993) and David Beckham (1997). Giggs was the first player to win this award twice. Peter Barnes (later to play for United) won the award as a Manchester City player in 1976 and Andy Cole, as a Newcastle player, did likewise in 1994.

•The PFA 'Player of the Year' and 'Young Player of the Year' awards went to Mark Hughes and Lee Sharpe respectively in 1991 and to Gary Pallister and Ryan Giggs in 1992, while Roy Keane won both senior awards (the FWA and PFA) Footballer of the Year prizes in 2000 as did Teddy Sheringham in 2001.

•United players won the PFA 'Young Player of the Year' award three seasons running, 1991-92-93.

•Mark Hughes has won a total of three PFA awards (1985, 1989 & 1991).

•A total of six players who were all registered with the club in 1995 had between them won ten PFA awards: Cantona, Cole, Giggs, Hughes, Pallister and Sharpe. Surprisingly though, all six never lined up together in the same match wearing United colours.

•United full-back Tony Dunne was voted the Irish 'Footballer of the Year' in 1969.

•Three United players - Denis Law (1964), Bobby Charlton (1966) and George Best (1968) - each won the coveted European 'Footballer of the Year' award. Best, at the age of 22, was the youngest winner of the prize.

•The prestigious Football Merit Award has been presented to four ex-United personalities, namely: Bobby Charlton CBE (1974), Denis Law (1975), Sir Matt Busby (1980) and Gordon Strachan (1995). The 1968 Manchester United European Cup winning team received the award in 1993.

•United boss Alex Ferguson was voted 'Manager of the Year' in 1993, 1994, 1996, 1997, 1999, 2000 and 2001. Ferguson was given the 'Freedom of Manchester' on 28 February 2000. Matt Busby had received the same honour in 1967.

•North of the Border, the future United stars, Martin Buchan and Gordon Strachan (both with Aberdeen) and Brian McClair (of Celtic) all won the Scottish Footballer of the Year awards in 1971, 1980 and 1987 respectively. McClair also won the Scottish PFA 'Player of the Year' award in 1987.

•George Best was voted 'Player of the Century' at the Rothmans Yearbook Millennium Awards Night in 2000. Manchester United were voted 'Team of the Century'.

•Over the seasons several United bosses have been voted 'Manager of the Month.'

•Manchester United were voted 'World Team of the Year' for 2000 at the Laureas Sports Awards in Monaco.

•United player John Scott was awarded the Military medal during World War One.

See also under Honours - for Sir, CBE, MBE, OBE awards.

AWAY FROM HOME

This is United's all-time record in competitive 'away' games at first team level:

Competition	P	W	D	L	F	A
League/PL	1974	637	515	822	2764	3287
FA Cup	157	65	41	51	251	234
League Cup	66	25	15	26	91	93
European	93	29	33	31	122	114
World Club	1	0	0	1	0	1
F Alliance	33	9	5	19	53	86
Test Matches	2	0	0	2	0	4
Totals	2326	765	609	952	3281	3819 (45.98%)

NB - Matches played on a neutral ground are listed under 'Neutral Grounds'.

Away Days

Manchester United's best away win in the Football League/Premiership (in terms of goals scored/difference) has been 8-1 at Nottingham Forest on 6 February 1999. Their heaviest defeat has been that of 0-7 - suffered on three separate occasions: Blackburn Rovers in April 1926, v. Aston Villa in December 1930 and versus Wolverhampton Wanderers in December 1931.

United's best away win in the FA Cup is 8-2 at Northampton Town on 7 February 1970, whilst their heaviest defeat in the competition has been 7-1 at Burnley in February 1901.

In League Cup action, United beat Arsenal 6-2 at Highbury on 28 November 1990 to register their best win in this competition while their heaviest reverse was suffered at Bloomfield Road against Blackpool in September 1966 when they lost 5-1.

On the European scene, United won 6-0 at Shamrock Rovers in the European Cup in September 1957 but crashed to their heaviest defeat by losing 5-0 at Sporting Club (Lisbon) in the Cup-winners Cup in March 1964.

United played 17 away Premier League games without defeat between 5 December 1998 and 11 September 1999. This club record ended spectacularly with an 0-5 defeat at Chelsea on 3 October 1999.

In contrast they failed to win any of 26 away League matches between February 1930 and April 1931.

A total of seven successive away Premiership wins were claimed by United during 1993 ...at the end of the 1992-93 season and at the start of the 1993-94 campaign.

B for...

BECKHAM,
David Robert Joseph

Born: Leytonstone, 2 May 1975.
Career: Wellington Avenue School, Chingford; Chase Lane School, Ridgeway Rovers, Waltham Forest District and Essex Schoolboys, MANCHESTER UNITED (associated schoolboy, July 1989, trainee, June 1991, professional January 1993), Preston North End (on loan, February/March 1995).

David Beckham led England out in the 2002 World Cup Finals in Japan and South Korea, not only as his country's captain, but as their most influential player, as well as being possibly the most popular footballer in the UK! All this was in stark contrast with his position after the 1998 World Cup in France, when having been sensationally sent-off in the quarter-final tie with arch enemies Argentina, he was generally held responsible for England's subsequent dismissal, to be reviled throughout the land.

His ability to rise above the widespread abuse showed much for his character and attitude, as he won over the public's opinion with a series of quite staggering displays in England's World Cup qualifying campaign, culminating with his incredible last-gasp equalizing goal against Greece at Old Trafford of all places to guarantee England's place in the 2002 Finals …

although he nearly didn't make it through to those Finals after breaking his foot late in the season, playing against Deportivo La Coruna in the Champions League. Thankfully he recovered in time to lead his country in the Land of the Rising Sun.

Beckham, despite growing up in Leytonstone, has been a United fan for as long has he can remember, famously turning up at Tottenham's training ground for a coaching session wearing a United replica kit. After winning a Bobby Charlton skills competition as an 11 year-old, Beckham joined his beloved Manchester United at the age of 14, playing in two FA Youth Cup Finals, in 1992 (as a winner) and 1993 (runner-up). He made his first team debut as a substitute in a League Cup-tie at Brighton as early as September 1992, clearly earmarked as a future star. However, it was the 1995-96 season before he won a regular place in Ferguson's 'team of kids' which amazingly won the Premiership and the FA Cup, Beckham's winning goal in the Cup semi-final proving a crucial factor!

But it was on the opening day of the 1996-97 Premiership season at Wimbledon, where his glorious 57-yard chip beat Dons' goalkeeper Neil Sullivan, that Beckham's name became more widely known. Soon he was a member of Glenn Hoddle's England side as well as being a key member of United's all-conquering team, alongside his former Youth team colleagues at Old Trafford.

His marriage to 'Spice Girl' Victoria Adams added to his fame, not to mention off the field pressure as he became popular and a fashion icon, never missing from the pages of the glossy magazines. Remarkably Beckham managed to balance his life, remaining a committed athlete, despite

Club record:
342 apps, 74 goals

massive media coverage of his private life.

With United he has already won five Premiership titles, has collected two FA Cup winners' medals and gained a European Cup winners' prize. He has over 50 senior England caps to his credit, having earlier gained recognition at youth and Under-21 levels, making nine appearances in the latter category. He can justifiably be termed a 'legend in his own lifetime', regularly in contention for the 'European Footballer of the Year' crown. Perhaps his greatest deeds still lie in the future.

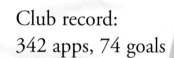

BAILEY, Gary Richard

Born: Ipswich, 9 August 1958.

Career: Witts University FC (South Africa), MANCHESTER UNITED (professional, January 1978), Kaizer Chiefs (S Africa, September 1987). Retired in 1990 followed by media work in South Africa.

Gary Bailey's father Roy was a goalkeeper with Ipswich Town in the 1960s - and it was he who guided his son to the top of his profession. Bailey junior - physically strong, who commanded his area with confidence, spent most of his younger days in South Africa (where his father was working). He was spotted 'keeping goal for Witts University by a former United star, Eddie Lewis. After a successful trial at Old Trafford he signed professional forms for the Reds, making his senior debut against his home-town club, Ipswich Town on 18 November that same year - the first of more than 375 competitive games for the club. At the end of his first season with United, Bailey collected an FA Cup runners-up medal, later gaining two winners' medals in the same competition - in 1983 and 1985 - as well as representing England in 14 Under-21 and two full internationals. A knee injury, suffered during the second-half of the 1985-86 campaign, effectively ended his United career, Bailey having his contract cancelled by the club early in 1987-88. He then spent a short time back in South Africa before retiring at the age of 31

Club record: 377 apps.

BAIN, David

Born: Rutherglen, Scotland, 5 August 1900

Career: Rutherglen Glencairn, MANCHESTER UNITED (initially a trialist, signed as a professional, May 1922), Everton (£1,200, June 1924), Bristol City (1928), Halifax Town (1930), Rochdale (1932). Quit League football in 1934.

Centre-forward Dave Bain, after impressing as a trialist, spent two seasons at Old Trafford. He gained Scotland junior international honours with his first club north of the border. A good striker of the ball, he was later converted into a half-back by Everton for whom he made 43 appearances, scoring three goals.

Club record: 23 apps. 9 goals

BAIN, James

Born: Dundee, 1878

Career: Dundee (1899), NEWTON HEATH (September 1899-May 1900). Returned to Scotland.

One of seven different centre-forwards used in 1899-1900, James Bain spent just one season with the club, when he was virtually a permanent reserve.

Club record: 2 apps. one goal

BAIN, James

Born: Rutherglen, 6 February 1902. Died: Polegate, Sussex, 22 December 1969.

Career: Rutherglen Glencairn, Glasgow Strathclyde, MANCHESTER UNITED(October 1922), Manchester Central (July 1928), Brentford (£250, late 1928). Later became assistant-manager of Brentford (1934) and then manager (1952-53)

Half-back Jimmy Bain was a Scottish junior international and younger brother of David (q.v.). He spent six years at Old Trafford but made only a handful of first team appearances during that time.

Club record: 4 apps.

BAINBRIDGE, William

Born: Gateshead, 9 March 1922

Career: Ashington, Hartlepools United (guest WW2), MANCHESTER UNITED (professional, December 1944), Bury (May 1946) Tranmere Rovers (1948). Left League football 1953.

Inside-forward Bill Bainbridge scored in his only senior outing for United, in a 3rd round, 2nd leg FA Cup tie against Accrington Stanley in January 1946 (won 5-1). That day he came in to partner Billy Wrigglesworth on the left-wing. He scored 63 goals in 168 League appearances for Tranmere.

Club record: one app. one goal

BAIRD, Henry C

Born: Belfast, 17 August 1913. Died: 22 May 1973.

Career: Bangor, Dunmurry FC, Linfield, MANCHESTER UNITED (January 1937), Huddersfield Town (September 1938), Ipswich Town (guest WW2), Ipswich Town (then full contract, 1946). Later 'A' team coach at Portman Road (1951-53)..

Harry Baird was a positive inside-forward who scored a goal every three games for United whom he served for just over 18 months prior to World War Two. He won an Irish Cup winners' medal with Linfield in 1936 and represented the Irish League in the same year before winning his only full cap in 1939. He made well over 200 appearances after leaving Old Trafford.

Club record: 53 apps. 18 goals

BALDWIN, Thomas

Born: Gateshead, 10 June 1945.

Career: Wrekenton Juniors, Arsenal (1962), Chelsea (1966), Millwall (1974), MANCHESTER UNITED (on loan,

27

January-February 1975), Seattle Sounders (1975), Gravesend & Northfleet (1976), Brentford (player-coach, 1977-80). Centre-forward Tommy Baldwin played in two FA Cup Finals with Chelsea, gaining a runners-up medal in 1967 and a winners' prize three years later. He also played in the London club's victorious 1971 European Cup-winners Cup team (v. Real Madrid) and in the 1972 League Cup Final defeat by Stoke City. He was capped twice by England at Under-21 level and in all he netted almost 100 goals in close on 250 competitive games for his senior clubs. He came to United as cover for Stuart Pearson halfway through the Second Division campaign of 1974-75.
Club record: 2 apps.

BALL, John
Born: Ince, Wigan, 13 March 1925
Career: Wigan Athletic, Gravesend (guest WW2), MANCHESTER UNITED (February 1948), Bolton Wanderers (September 1950 - deal included Harry McShane moving to United). Retired in 1958 and later became manager of Wigan Athletic (early 1960s).
Strong-tackling full-back John Ball appeared in more than 20 first-class games for United during his two-and-a-half years at Old Trafford. After that he appeared in over 200 games in eight seasons at Burnden Park. Capped by England 'B', he played for Bolton in the 1953 FA Cup Final defeat by Blackpool.
Club record: 23 apps.

BALL, John Thomas
Born: Southport, 13 September 1907. Died: Luton, 6 February 1976
Career: Banks Juniors, Croston FC, Southport (1924), Darwen (1927), Chorley (1928), MANCHESTER UNITED (May 1929), Sheffield Wed (£1,300, July 1930), MANCHESTER UNITED (December 1933), Luton Town (Oct 1934), Excelsior Roubaix, France (player-coach. 1936), Luton Town (mid-1936), Vauxhall Motors (player-coach, 1937), St Albans City (1938), Biggleswade (1940). Retired in WW2.
Centre-forward Jack Ball had two spells with United. After a decent spell with Darwen he scored 58 goals in one season for Chorley and then joined United for the first time at the end of the 1928-29 campaign, playing 24 matches (11 goals scored) the following year.
He spent three-and-a-half years at Hillsborough during which time the Owls finished in third place in the First Division three seasons running. He scored almost 100 goals in 135 games for the Yorkshire club before returning to United halfway through the 1933-34 campaign.
After that Ball went over to France for a month as player-coach of Excelsior Roubaix.
He had two claims to fame … in 1934 he played in all three Divisions of the Football League in a six-week period…and then in 1936 when unfit to play at centre-forward for Luton against Bristol Rovers, he sat in the stand and watched his deputy (converted from wing-half) Joe Payne rattle in no fewer than 10 goals in a 12-0 victory, to write his name in football history.
Club record: 50 apps. 18 goals

BALL, William Henry
Born: West Derby, Liverpool early 1876.
Career: Liverpool South End, Rock Ferry FC, Blackburn Rovers (1897), Everton (1898), Notts County (1899), Blackburn Rovers (1901), MANCHESTER UNITED (October 1902-May 1903).
A solidly built half-back, strong in his approach, Billy Ball was used predominantly as back up to cover for Downie, Griffiths and Cartwright, deputising in all three middle line positions. Prior to joining United, Ball had amassed almost a century of League & Cup appearances for his three other major clubs.
Club record: 4 apps.

BAMFORD, Thomas
Born: Port Talbot, 2 September 1905. Died: Queen's Park, Wrexham, 12 December 1967.
Career: Cardiff Docks XI, Cardiff Wednesday, Bridgend Town, Wrexham (1929), MANCHESTER UNITED (October 1934, signed with Billy Bryant/part-exchange for James Rice), Swansea Town (June 1938). Retired in 1946.
This 5ft 9in, brylcreem-haired figure of Tommy Bamford, a hard-shooting, bustling centre-forward of the 'old school' was a menace to both defenders and goalkeepers throughout his career. He had already netted 207 goals in 245 appearances for Wrexham (including a haul of 45 in 1930-31) before moving to Old Trafford where he continued hit the target on a regular basis, helping United win the Second Division Championship in 1935-36. United certainly got good value out of Bamford.
The greatest scorer in Wrexham's history, he won a Welsh Cup winners medal in 1931 and runners-up prizes in each of the next two seasons and followed up with two more Welsh Cup runners-up medals with Swansea in 1938 and 1940. Bamford was capped five times by Wales while with Wrexham, scoring once. He worked at a local steelworks during WW2.
Club record: 109 apps. 57 goals

BAMLETT, Herbert
Born: Gateshead, 1 March 1882. Died: October 1941.
Career: football referee, Oldham Athletic (manager, 1914-21), Wigan Borough (manager, 1921-23), Middlesbrough (manager, 1923-27), MANCHESTER UNITED (manager, April 1927-April 1931).
Herbert Bamlett was the youngest-ever referee (at the age of 32) to take charge of an FA Cup Final when he officiated in

the 1914 showdown between Burnley and Liverpool, the last to be staged at The Crystal Palace. He also took charge of several top-line Football League and other FA Cup matches and in fact, was regarded as one of the best referees in the country ..before turning to management.

Coincidentally he was in charge of the Burnley versus United FA Cup quarter-final clash at Turf Moor in 1909 which was called off with 18 minutes remaining due to heavy snow (see: Abandoned matches).

Bamlett held his position as United boss for four years, having moved into the 'hot seat' at Old Trafford when the Reds were struggling! In fact, he temporarily turned things round but after relegation was suffered in 1930-31 (when United lost all of their first 12 League games and eventually conceded 115 goals) his reign came to an unhappy end. Bamlett didn't figure in first-class football after leaving Old Trafford.

* Bamlett signed hot-shot centre-forward George Camsell for Middlesbrough. He scored 59 League goals for the Teeside club in 1926-27, a record that was beaten 12 months later by Dixie Dean's haul of 60 for Everton.

BANK STREET (ground)

Newton Heath FC had been virtually forced out of their North Road ground at the end of the club's inaugural Football League season (1892-93). In any event the ground was far from ideal for top level football, so no tears were shed on moving. Mr AH Albut, the club secretary, negotiated a two-year lease of the Bradford and Clayton Athletic Club Limited ground at Bank Lane (as it was then known) in Clayton, some two miles from North Road. Athletics was very popular at this time, so the ground already had a grandstand, running the length of the pitch with standing accommodation along the other side and behind each goal. Before the start of the 1893-94 campaign, the Newton Heath football club arranged for the other parts of the ground to be built up, whilst new dressing rooms and baths were put in place for the players. In all the club played for a little over 16 years at Bank Street before leaving for Old Trafford in February 1910, having become Manchester United in 1902.

Fact File

The playing surface at Bank Street left a lot to be desired and quite regularly spectators (and even the players) were distracted (and certainly disturbed and frustrated) by the thick smoke that bellowed out of nearby factory chimneys, often engulfing the ground. Occasionally matches were halted as the visibility was far from good.

The pitch was so poor that when Walsall Town Swifts turned up in 1895 for a Second Division match they were unwilling to play. However, the match went ahead, Newton Heath won 14-0 (a club record score) but the Football League ordered the fixture to be replayed after a Walsall protest - and this time the Heath won by just 9-0!

The first League game played on the ground by United (Newton Heath) was against Burnley on 2 September 1893 (Division 1). A crowd of 10,000 saw Alf Farman net a hat-trick in a 3-2 victory.

United's first defeat at Bank Street followed 4 November that same year when Darwen were triumphant by a goal to nil. The highest attendance recorded at Bank Street was that of 50,000 for the visit of Newcastle United for a First Division encounter on 8 February 1908. The lowest turnout for a competitive game was just on 1,000, registered on three occasions in the 1895-96 season against Burton Wanderers, Darwen and Leicester Fosse.

The last League game played by United at Bank Street was on 22 January 1910 when a crowd of 7,000 saw them destroy Tottenham Hotspur 5-0, Charlie Roberts (2) and Billy Meredith both getting on the scoresheet.

Within a week of moving out, the main stand was blown down in a storm, causing considerable damage to neighbouring houses.

Although the club was obviously glad to see the back of unloved Bank Street, it had been the ground which had seen the club's first major trophies, with the League Championship (1907-08) and FA Cup (1909) paraded there.

An idea of the conditions obtaining at Bank Street can be gathered from this extract from a contemporary newspaper report in 1907 as Southern League Portsmouth played an FA Cup replay there on a Wednesday afternoon: 'All the time the struggle was waging, the thirty Clayton chimneys smoked and gave forth their pungent odours, while the boilers behind (the) goal poured mists of steam over the ground.' (Manchester Guardian, 27 January 1907).

Manchester's famous Velodrome Stadium now stands a on a part of the site of United's former Bank Street ground.

The best piece of work within the ground was the 1,000-seater stand, made possible by a donation of £500 from John H Davies, the club's first major benefactor.

A representative match was staged at Bank Street on 4 April 1904 when the Football League side beat their counterparts from the Scottish League 2-1 in front of 5,000 spectators.

BANKRUPTCY (financial worries)

Early in 1902, Harry Stafford, the club's full-back and captain, and John Henry Davies, a local businessman, bailed Newton Heath out a financial crisis. The club was deep in debt, owing money here, there and everywhere (around £2,600 to be precise). As a result, on 9 January of that year, one of the many unhappy creditors, William Healey, the president of the club at the time, who was owed over £240 (big money in those days) went to the County Court in nearby Ashton-under-Lyne to seek a winding-up order. He succeeded....'Heath' were declared bankrupt and proceedings started in earnest to wind-up the club. The directors pleaded for more time, but in reality nothing would have saved them from folding. The receiver moved in to the Bank Street Ground, preparing to shut down the club... but then, just 24 hours from closure, the first of two life-savers, Stafford (who was the first appointed captain under their new name of Manchester United) came forward with some much-needed money. Soon afterwards John Davies produced some more and the club was saved. Mr Davies later became United's President.

Legend has it that Davies, out walking one evening, came across a St Bernard dog (belonging to Stafford). The dog had a money-collecting box strapped to its back and had 'escaped' from a club money-raising bazaar where it had been going amongst the spectators collecting money for club funds. Davies returned the dog to its rightful owner (Stafford) and

29

they became good friends…so much so they 'reformed the club' into Manchester United. Stafford - surely no other club ever had a more valuable captain - thus became arguably the most important player in the club's illustrious history! Some thirty years later (in the early 1930s) another wealthy businessman, this time a clothing manufacturer and ardent supporter of the club by the name of James W Gibson, saved Manchester United from another financial dilemma (albeit not quite on the same scale as the one in 1902). He later held the position of club Chairman for over 20 years. It was certainly Mr Gibson's generosity which kept the club afloat during the difficult 1930s and also during the war years, when the club was run from one of his offices in Cornbrook after the devastation of Old Trafford in 1941.

BANKS, John

Born: West Bromwich, 14 June 1875. Died: Barrow-in-Furness, January 1947.
Career: Christ Church School (West Bromwich), Stourbridge (1887), Oldbury Broadwell (1890), Oldbury Town (1892), West Bromwich Albion (1893), NEWTON HEATH (August 1901), Plymouth Argyle (May 1903), Leyton (1906), Exeter City (player 1907, coach and trainer 1910), Barrow (trainer 1912). Banks left football in 1922.
Hard-working wing-half or inside-forward Jack Banks made over 40 senior appearances for Newton Heath, having joined the club just after West Brom had been relegated from the First Division. He played in the 1895 FA Cup Final for the Throstles against Aston Villa and, in fact, appeared in over 130 first-class games before he moved to the Heathens. As their trainer he saw Carlisle elected to the new Third Division (North) in 1921. Banks was Exeter's first professional player.
Club record: 44 apps. one goal (also 6 'other' apps)

BANNISTER, James

Born: Leyland, 20 September 1880.
Career: Leyland Temperance, Leyland FC, Chorley, Manchester City (1902), MANCHESTER UNITED (December 1906), Preston North End (October 1909) Burslem Port Vale (briefly, 1912), Heywood (late 1912). Retired 1914.
Inside-forward Jimmy Bannister, a broad-speaking Lancastrian, was associated with Manchester City in 1906 when they were in turmoil with an inquiry unearthing possible illegal practices, resulting in five directors being dismissed and 17 players banned from playing for the club. All 17 players were put up for auction, but United stepped in early, signing Bannister along with Welsh wizard Billy Meredith, Sandy Turnbull and Herbert Burgess in a job lot! A shrewd piece of business by United manager Ernest Mangnall. He had netted 22 goals in 47 games for City and did a reasonable job for United before trying his luck at Deepdale. After the Great War, Bannister continued as landlord of the Ship Inn, Leyland, a position he had taken before the hostilities.
Club record: 63 apps. 8 goals

BANNED

In 1969, the Football Association found Manchester United guilty of making irregular payments and banned the club from playing friendlies against European teams at home or away.

BARBER, John

Born: Salford, 8 January 1901. Died: Manchester, 30 March 1961
Career: Salford Lads' Club, Clayton FC (1920), MANCHESTER UNITED (May 1922), Southport (May 1924), Halifax Town (1926), Rochdale (1927), Stockport County (1931), Hull City (trialist, 1932), Stockport (again late 1932), Bacup Borough (1933), later taking over as secretary of that club (1938).
Jack Barber, a reserve inside-forward, made only four first-class appearances for United during his two seasons with the club. He played in over 150 games for Rochdale and during a varied career he accumulated in excess of 250 appearances in League and Cup competitions (over 25 goals scored). On leaving football after WW2, he became a mill engineer, working in the area of Manchester.
Club record: 4 apps. 2 goals

BARCELONA (FC)

United have had some great matches against Barcelona, including two cracking 3-3 draws in the Group stage of the 1998-99 European Champions League when Dwight Yorke scored twice in the Nou Camp, with Brazilian genius Rivaldo in world-class form for Barca. The game at Old Trafford that season saw Luis Enrique and Giovaanni both score second-half penalties for the Spanish club.
Earlier, in the 1994-95 European Cup, United were held to a 2-2 draw by the Spanish champions but were then crushed 4-0 in sunny Barcelona - one of Alex Ferguson's few nightmare matches!
The team was suffering from the 'Four Foreigners' ruling in vogue at the time, thus preventing Alex Ferguson from fielding his strongest line-up. Eleven years before then, United had won a pulsating Cup-winners' Cup quarter-final contest against Barcelona, going through 3-2 on aggregate after clawing back from a 2-0 deficit in the Nou Camp. On an emotional night at Old Trafford, in front of 58,547 spectators, skipper Bryan Robson scored twice and Frank Stapleton once to send manager Ron Atkinson 'over the moon'!
In 1990-91 United embarked on a decade of unprecedented success by winning the European Cup-winners Cup for the first time. Two Mark Hughes goals earned them a 2-1 victory over Barcelona in Rotterdam to celebrate English clubs' return to Europe after the nightmares of Heysel.
United re-visited Barcelona's Nou Camp Stadium in May 1999 - to beat Bayern Munich 2-1 in the Champions League Cup Final!
Players with both clubs include: L Blanc, J Cruyff, M Hughes
Also associated: P O'Connell (United player, Barcelona manager/coach)

BARI

United played the Italian side Bari in a Group One game in the Anglo-Italian Tournament in April 1973. A crowd of 14,303 at Old Trafford witnessed United's 3-1 win, Denis Law, Ian Storey-Moore and Mick Martin scoring the Reds' goals.
David Platt was a reserve/Youth player with United who later assisted Bari in Italy's Serie 'A' (1991-92).

BARLOW, Cyril

Born: Newton Heath, 22 January 1889

Career: Newton Heath Parish Church, Northern Nomads, MANCHESTER UNITED (amateur, July 1914, professional December 1919), New Cross FC (later renamed Manchester North End, October 1922), MANCHESTER UNITED (January 1923). Versatile full-back Cyril Barlow played regularly for his local church team and also for Northern Nomads before joining United at the start of the last season before the Great War. Although he was recalled from New Mills during 1922-23 as cover against injury, he was not called up for first team duty.

Club record: 30 apps.

BARNES, Peter Simon

Born: Manchester, 10 June 1957.

Career: Chorlton Grammar School, Manchester & District Schools, Gatley Rangers (1971), Manchester City (1972), West Bromwich Albion (£650,000, 1979), Leeds United (£930,000, 1981), Real Betis (on loan 1982), Melbourne JUST, Australia (early 1984), MANCHESTER UNITED (on loan, May 1984), Coventry City (£65,000, late 1984), MANCHESTER UNITED (£50,000, July 1985), Manchester City (£30,000, January 1987), Bolton Wanderers (on loan, 1987), Port Vale (on loan, late 1987), Hull City (1988), Drogheda United (mid-1988), Sporting Farense, Portugal (autumn 1988), Bolton Wanderers (again, late 1988), Sunderland (early 1989), Tampa Bay Rowdies (mid 1990), Northwich Victoria (late 1990), Wrexham (non-contract, 1991), Radcliffe Borough (player & manager, mid-1991), Mossley (late summer 1991), Cliftonville, Ireland (1992), Norway (coach). Retired in 1993 and later worked with the Academy players at Maine Road (as well as some radio work).

Peter Barnes was a fast-raiding, tricky left-winger. The son of the former Manchester City half-back Ken Barnes, he had two spells at Old Trafford - the first on loan. Capped 22 times by England at full international level, he also played nine times for his country's Under-21 side and turned out for the Football League XI, having gained Youth recognition as a teenager. He was voted the PFA's ' Young Player of the Year' in 1976 (Source: PFA Annual 2000, see AWARDS, page 24.) and gained a League Cup winners medal with Manchester City twelve months later. During his nomadic career Barnes appeared in well over 300 Football League games and scored 47 goals. He later worked for Piccadilly Radio in Manchester.

Club record: 27 apps. 4 goals

BARNSLEY

United's League results v Barnsley:

Season	Div	Home	Away	Season	Div	Home	Away
1898-99	2	D 0-0	W 2-0	1923-24	2	L 1-2	L 0-1
1899-1900	2	W 3-0	D 0-0	1924-25	2	W 1-0	D 0-0
1900-01	2	W 1-0	L 2-6				
1901-02	2	W 1-0	L 2-3	1931-32	2	W 3-0	D 0-0
1902-03	2	W 2-1	D 0-0				
1903-04	2	W 4-0	W 2-0	1934-35	2	W 4-1	W 2-0
1904-05	2	W 4-0	D 0-0	1935-36	2	D 1-1	W 3-0
1905-06	2	W 5-1	W 3-0				
				1937-38	2	W 4-1	D 2-2
1922-23	2	W 1-0	D 2-2				
				1997-98	PL	W 7-0	W 2-0

United's FA Cup results v Barnsley:

	Round	Venue	Result
1937-38	4	Away	D 2-2
	Replay	Home	W 1-0
1963-64	5	Away	W 4-0
1997-98	5	Home	D 1-1
	Replay	Away	L 2-3

Summary of League results:

	P	W	D	L	F	A
Premier League	2	2	0	0	9	0
Division 2	30	17	9	4	55	21
Home	16	13	2	1	42	7
Away	16	6	7	3	22	14
Total	32	19	9	4	64	21

Fact File:

Players with both clubs include: V Anderson (Barnsley player-manager), B Asquith, F Barson, J Breedon, W Bullimore (United trainee), J Curtis, J Davie (United WW2), SC Davies (United trialist), J Dyer, A Goram, D Graham, E Hine (also Barnsley coach), G Holdcroft (United WW2), W Hunter, S Johnson, R Pegg, F Pepper, A Rammell (United reserve), E Round, G Stacey, T Taylor (signed by United for £29,999 in 1953), H Topping, J Travers, G Wall
Also associated: J McCartney (United player, Barnsley trainer/secretary-manager)

BARRETT, Francis

Born: Dundee, 2 August 1872. Died: Scotland, August 1907.

Career: Dundee Harp, Dundee (1893), NEWTON HEATH (September 1896), New Brighton Tower (May 1900), Arbroath (mid-1901), Manchester City (late 1901), Dundee (1902), Aberdeen (1903) .Retired 1905.

Frank Barrett, a shade on the small side for a goalkeeper, played with an air of confidence throughout his career. He was a fine shot-stopper and once saved two penalties in an away League game against Grimsby Town in April 1898, helping his side to a 3-1 victory. He gained two full caps for Scotland (v. Ireland and Wales in 1894 and 1895 respectively) and stood between the posts in Aberdeen's first-ever League game at Pittodrie in August 1903 when Stenhousemuir forced a 1-1 draw. He was only 35 when he died.

Club record: 136 apps. (also 38 'other' apps).

31

BARTHEZ, Fabien Alain

Born: Lavelanet, France, 28 June 1971.
Career: Toulouse (1991), Olympique Marseille (1992), AS Monaco (1995), MANCHESTER UNITED (£7.8 million, June 2000).

Goalkeeper Fabien Barthez - the man in black, sleeves rolled up - had an excellent first season with United, gaining a Premier League Championship medal after playing in 30 games, keeping 15 clean sheets in the process, as well as displaying extraordinary talent with the ball at his feet!

After helping his country win both the World Cup and European Championship in the space of two years - and despite an uneasy first game (in the FA Charity Shield v. Chelsea) - he certainly proved a worthy successor to Peter Schmeichel and produced some superb performances between the posts....although during his second season he did commit a few blunders, especially in a Champions League game against the Spanish club Deportivo La Coruna which ended in a 3-2 home defeat for the Reds. Barthez had now taken his total of full caps for France to near the 50 mark and was in his country's 2002 World Cup squad. He made over 100 League appearances for Marseille and more than 150 in League and Cup for AS Monaco. Barthez, in fact, played his first game for United in the defeat by Bayern Munich in the Germany City's Opel Masters tournament on 5 August 2000.

* His father, Alain Barthez, played international rugby for France.
Club record: 93 apps.

BARSON, Frank

Born: Grimethorpe, Sheffield 10 April 1891. Died: Winson Green, Birmingham 13 September 1968.

Career: Albion FC, Sheffield FC, Cammell Laird FC (Sheffield), Barnsley (1911), Aston Villa (£2,850, 1919), MANCHESTER UNITED (£5,000, August 1922), Watford (May 1928), Hartlepools United (as player/coach, 1929), Wigan Borough (late 1929), Rhyl Athletic (player-manager, 1931), Stourbridge (manager, 1935), Aston Villa (Youth team coach, then senior coach and later head trainer, 1935), Swansea Town (trainer, 1947-54), Lye Town (trainer, 1954-56). He retired from football, aged 65.

Centre-half Frank Barson's career took him all over the country. He started out with in his native Yorkshire, played in Birmingham, in Lancashire, Hertfordshire, North and South Wales, in the Black Country and in the North-east of England.

A real tough, rugged centre-half, the strongman in defence, Barson possessed a crunching tackle, was a vociferous captain. He was always a great inspiration to the rest of the team, being totally committed to the game, never shirking a tackle, bold, courageous and dedicated, a description befitting a man who was a blacksmith by trade!

Seven months after joining Aston Villa (from Barnsley) he was clutching an FA Cup winners medal after Huddersfield Town had been defeated 1-0 in the Final. He also won his solitary England cap that same season, against Wales at Highbury in March 1920. He went on to appear in over 100 first-class matches for Villa, scoring ten goals before moving to Manchester United in 1922 - after refusing to move from his Yorkshire home and live in Birmingham! He was adamant that he would never move to 'Brummagem' and often had heated words with the Villa Directors. On Boxing Day 1920, so determined was he to play for Villa, and due to a train derailment, he trudged seven miles through heavy snow to make sure he arrived in time for an away game at Old Trafford. He played out of his skin and helped Villa win 3-1 in front of a record crowd of 70,504.

With United, he perhaps performed even better than he did with Villa, going on to star in more than 150 games for the Reds in six years before switching south to Watford. A very controversial player, Barson was often in trouble with referees and during his career he was sent-off twelve times (not once with United). Indeed, his suspensions added up to more than a year, with one lengthy ban covering six months during his Watford days. He also received an eight-week suspension following an incident in the Manchester United v. Manchester City FA Cup semi-final at Sheffield in March 1926 when it was alleged he had fouled Sam Cowan, City's centre-half, who was knocked out!

Barson was promised a pub if he skippered Manchester United back to the First Division. He did just that and was handed the keys to a hotel in Ardwick Green. Scores of punters, full of flattery, turned up for the official opening but after 15 minutes Barson was so fed up that he handed the keys over to the head-waiter, walked out and never returned. He then quickly telegraphed his wife asking her to cancel the delivery of the furniture!

Club record: 152 apps. 4 goals

BAYER 04 LEVERKUSEN

United were paired with the strong and efficient German side in the two-legged semi-final of the 2001-02 European Champions League....and sadly they went out of the competition on the away goal rule, to the disappointment of skipper Roy Keane, and indeed to everyone associated with the club.

The first leg was staged at Old Trafford on 24 April and ended all square at 2-2, United being pegged back twice…but had England right-back Gary Neville stretchered off with a broken foot which serious jeopardised his chances of playing in the World Cup Finals that summer.

Zivkovic diverted Ole Gunnar Solskjaer's shot past 'keeper Butt on the half-hour mark to edge United in front. However, this opener was cancelled out by a 62nd strike from Michael Ballack. Dutchman Ruud van Nistelrooy then won and scored a 67th minute penalty to put United back in the driving seat before substitute Oliver Neuville levelled things up for a second time with a quarter-of-an-hour remaining. The attendance was 66,534.

Six days later in Germany, a crowd of 22,500 saw United take the lead in the 28th minute through Keane, but two minutes into added-time at the end of the first-half Neuville drilled in an equalizer for the home side and despite a few near misses, United couldn't get a second goal and went out of the competition despite not losing either of the two semi-final matches.

BAYERN MUNICH

United and Bayern met each other three times in the 1998-99 European Champions League competition. After two stage one draws, United did the business, albeit somewhat late, by winning the Final 2-1 in Barcelona (see under European Cup), the teams having drawn their two Group Stage matches 2-2 in Munich and 1-1 at Old Trafford.

However, the German champions gained sweet revenge by beating the Reds 3-1 on aggregate in the quarter-final tie of the same competition in 2000-01.

Amazingly it was a repeat prescription twelve months later when, after both clubs had progressed through from their respective groups in the 2001-02 European Champions League, United and Bayern were drawn together again in the second phase. Both matches ended in draws - 1-1 in the Olympic Stadium, Munich when 59,000 spectators saw Sergio grab an 87th minute equalizer for the German champions after Ruud van Nistelrooy had edged United in front with just over a quarter-of-an-hour remaining.

The game at Old Trafford attracted a crowd of 66,818, but it turned out to be a disappointing contest, ending in a 0-0 draw as both teams progressed through to the quarter-finals.

* United were beaten by Bayern in the pre-season Munich Opel Masters Tournament in August 2000.

Player with both clubs: M Hughes

BEADSWORTH, Arthur

Born: Leicester, autumn 1876.

Career: Hinckley Town, Leicester Fosse (1900), Preston North End (1902), MANCHESTER UNITED (October 1902), Swindon Town (May 1903) New Brompton (1905), Burton United (1906-07)..

Arthur Beadsworth, a reserve inside forward, scored on his debut for United at Woolwich Arsenal.

He did very well at both Swindon and during his 'League' career he amassed well over 100 appearances and scored 17 goals.

Club record: 12 apps. 2 goals

BEALE, Robert Hughes

Born: Maidstone, 8 January 1884. Died: Dymchurch near Folkestone, Kent 5 October 1950.

33

Career: Maidstone United, Brighton & Hove Albion (1905), Norwich City (1908), MANCHESTER UNITED (£275, May 1912), Arsenal (guest WW1), Gillingham (July 1919), MANCHESTER UNITED (September 1920-May 1921). Retired on leaving Old Trafford.

Goalkeeper Robert Beale, the son of a Maidstone councillor, had already appeared in over 100 Southern League games for Norwich before moving to Old Trafford. A cool, calm and reliable keeper, he took over the position immediately after both Hugh Edmonds and Harry Moger had been transfer-listed by the club. He represented the Football League against the Scottish League in 1913 and a year later played in an international trial, for the North v. England at Sunderland. He played only reserve team football during his second spell at Old Trafford.

Beale's son, Walter, also a goalkeeper, was on United's books in 1938-39. He failed to make the first XI.

Club record: 112 apps.

BEARDSLEY, Peter Andrew

Born: Longbenton, Newcastle-upon-Tyne, 18 January 1961.

Career: Wallsend Boys Club, Newcastle United (trialist 1977-78) Carlisle United (1979), Vancouver Whitecaps (1981), MANCHESTER UNITED (£300,000, September 1982 - signed on the recommendation of Jimmy Murphy and backed by ex-United star, Johnny Giles), Vancouver Whitecaps (May 1983), Newcastle United (£120,000, 1983), Liverpool (£1.9 million, 1987), Everton (£1 million, 1991), Newcastle United (£1.45 million, 1993), Bolton Wanderers (£450,000, 1997), Manchester City (on loan, early 1998), Fulham (1998), Hartlepool United (late 1998). Retired early 1999 and later returned to St James' Park as Newcastle's Academy coach (2000-01).

Inside-forward Peter Beardsley was a player 'lost' by United! He had just 45 minutes of football with the Reds, appearing in the first half of a second round League Cup fixture against Bournemouth at Old Trafford on 6 October 1982. After leaving Old Trafford, he drew up a magnificent club record, and eventually took his senior appearance tally at club and international level, to almost 1,000, scoring more than 275 goals. In English club football his record was impressive enough: 803 games and 250 goals. He also gained a total of 59 full caps for England and appeared in two 'B' internationals. He formed splendid strike-partnerships with Kevin Keegan at Newcastle (1983-87) and with Ian Rush at Liverpool. He also figured prominently alongside Gary Lineker in the England team. A member of two League Championship-winning sides at Anfield (1988 and 1990), as well as an FA Cup win in 1989, he played in two Charity Shield winning teams and then assisted Fulham in winning the Second Division title in 1999.

Club record: one app.

BEARDSMORE, Russell Peter

Born: Wigan, 28 September 1968.

Career: Wigan Schoolboys, MANCHESTER UNITED (apprentice June 1985, professional October 1986), Blackburn Rovers (on loan, December 1991), AFC Bournemouth (June 1993).

Utility player Russell Beardsmore represented England Schoolboys before joining United as an apprentice. He went on to win five Under-21 caps and helped the Reds win the European Super Cup in 1991. He found it difficult to hold down a regular place in the first XI at Old Trafford and after leaving the club he went on to appear in well over 200 appearances for the Cherries, up to May 1998, when he entered non-League football.

Club record: 72 apps. 5 goals

BECKETT, Robert

Born: Manchester, early 1867

Career: NEWTON HEATH (April 1886-May 1887)

Goalkeeper Bob Beckett's only senior appearance for the Heathens was in the FA Cup-tie against Fleetwood Rangers in October 1886. The tie, in fact, ended in controversy. With the scores level at 2-2 the Heathens refused to play extra-time. Rangers were awarded the game and they went on to meet Partick Thistle in the next round which they lost 7-0...did the Heathens know something?

A local lad Beckett was associated with the club for one season (1886-87).

Club record: one app. (also 25 'other' apps).

BECKHAM, David Robert Joseph

Refer to front of section.

BEDDOW, John Harry

Born: Burton-on-Trent, November 1885

Career: Trent Rovers (1902), Burton United (September 1904), MANCHESTER UNITED (February 1905), Burnley (July 1907). Retired circa 1911.

A fast-raiding right-winger or centre-forward, 'Clem' Beddow, a spectacular performer, spent two seasons with the club and scored virtually a goal every two games. He helped United win promotion to the First Division in 1906. He was struggling to overcome a knee injury during his last months at Old Trafford.

Club record: 34 apps. 15 goals

BEHAN, William

Born: Dublin, 3 August 1911. Died: Dublin, November 1991.
Career: Shelbourne (1929), MANCHESTER UNITED (September 1933), Shelbourne (May 1934), Shamrock Rovers (1934) Drumcondra (manager, 1935), later a United scout (1938-mid 1980s).
Reserve goalkeeper Billy Behan's only League appearance for United was against near-neighbours Bury in March 1934, when he replaced Jack Hall in a 2-1 victory. After his appointment as scout by the club he was responsible for 'finding' several great footballers (all from the Irish Republic) including Johnny Carey, Tony Dunne, Johnny Giles, Don Givens, Ashley Grimes, Kevin Moran, Paul McGrath and Liam 'Billy' Whelan....plus a few others!
For a one-match wonder his contribution to the club was truly immense!
Club record: one app.

BELL, Alexander

Born: Cape Town, South Africa, 1882. Died: Chorlton-cum-Hardy, 30 November 1934.
Career: Ayr Spring Vale, Ayr Westerlea, Ayr Parkhouse FC, MANCHESTER UNITED (£700, January 1903), Blackburn Rovers (£1,000, July 1913-15), Clackmannan FC (1921), Coventry City (trainer, 1922), Manchester City (trainer, 1925 until his death at the age of 42).
Born to Scottish parents, Alex Bell learnt his football as a centre-forward north of the border. He then became part of a formidable United half-back line that also included Charlie Roberts and Dick Duckworth and during his ten seasons with the Reds (up to 1912-13) he appeared in well over 300 first-class games. He helped the team win two League Championships (1908 and 1911), the FA Cup (1909) and promotion from Division Two. Capped by Scotland against Ireland in March 1912, Bell then helped Blackburn win the League title in his first season in 1914 and as trainer at Maine Road he saw City lose the 1926 FA Cup Final before winning the trophy in 1933.
Club record: 309 apps. 10 goals

BENEFIT, CHARITY & TESTIMONIAL MATCHES

Over the years Manchester United have sent out a team to play in scores of benefit, charity and/or testimonial matches for ex-players of the club, opposing players, even managers and coaches, relatives and officials. Sometimes the Reds have travelled abroad to fulfil a request, but have mainly played in the British Isles, always for a worthy cause.
Alf Farman was one of the first Heathens to receive a benefit from the club, rewarded with a game against rivals Ardwick in 1893.
Two years later Bob Donaldson received a benefit match when Newton Heath played Blackburn Rovers in April 1895, and in 1898 Fred Erentz was granted a testimonial by the club.
Jack Mew was the first United player to receive two benefits - 1920 and 1923.
On 10 September 1924, a combined Manchester United/Manchester City team played an Everton/Liverpool XI at Old Trafford in a testimonial/memorial match for former United manager Ernest Mangnall.
John Grimwood was rewarded with a benefit match in April 1925 after having served the club for six years prior to that.
In March 1928 United's home League game v. West Ham United was also a benefit match for Teddy Partridge.
United entertained Hibernian for a benefit match for Tom Curry on 30 September 1953.
Three years later, in April 1956, Johnny Aston was rewarded with a benefit match when United took on an All Star XI at Old Trafford.
In August 1968, a Drumcondra Select XI met Manchester United in a benefit match arranged on behalf of Liam 'Billy' Whelan's brother John. United wore an all-green strip in this game.
In November 1970, Manchester United met arch rivals City in a testimonial match at Old Trafford for long-serving defender Bill Foulkes. City won 3-0.
Alan Oakes' testimonial match at Maine Road ended Manchester City 1 United 3 in May 1972.
Bobby Charlton's testimonial match at Old Trafford (United v. Celtic) on 18 September 1972 attracted a crowd of 60,538 (the largest attendance at the time for such a game). The result was a goalless draw.
A month later, at Upton Park, West Ham defeated United 5-2 in Ronnie Boyce's testimonial game.
A year later (October 1973) United entertained Ajax Amsterdam in Denis Law's testimonial match. United won 1-0.
Shortly after this game United were in action again, in Tony Dunne's testimonial match. On this occasion they were beaten 2-1 at Old Trafford by rivals Manchester City.
The following month United travelled to Firhill and beat Partick Thistle 3-0 in Ron McKinnon's testimonial match.
Soon afterwards (12 December 1973) United played Stoke City at The Victoria Ground in a testimonial match for the former England World Cup goalkeeper Gordon Banks who had been forced to retire after losing an eye in a road accident. United won 2-1.
Chelsea were beaten 2-1 by United at Stamford Bridge in Eddie McCreadie's testimonial match in May 1974.
Manchester City defeated a United XI 3-2 at Maine Road in Mike Summerbee's testimonial match in September 1975.
Two months later (26 November 1975) a crowd of 36,646 attended Pat Crerand's testimonial match at Old Trafford when United '76' beat United's '68 European Cup-winning side by 7-2. David McCreery scored four goals.
On 9 December 1975, over 16,000 spectators saw United beat Plymouth Argyle 2-1 at Home Park in a testimonial match for Peter Middleton.
The Bobby Lennox/Jimmy Johnstone joint testimonial match at Parkhead between Celtic and United in May 1976 attracted a crowd of 48,000. Celtic won 4-0.

35

Close on 38,000 fans attended Alex Stepney's testimonial at Old Trafford in February 1977 when United beat their 1968 European Cup Final opponents Benfica 2-1.

A surprisingly low crowd of just 7,564 attended Glyn Pardoe's testimonial match at Maine Road in March 1977 when Manchester City beat United 4-2.

In April 1978 United played Preston North End at Deepdale in a testimonial match for one of their 1968 European Cup stars, David Sadler.

The following month United took a team to Loftus Road to play QPR in Dave Clement's testimonial match. Rangers won 4-2.

United played Chelsea at Stamford Bridge in Peter Bonetti's testimonial match in early September 1979. A crowd of 10,652 saw an eight-goal thriller go Chelsea's way 5-3.

Almost immediately in the same month (September) a combined Manchester City/United side beat a combined Everton/Liverpool side 2-1 at Maine Road in Colin Bell's testimonial match.

A crowd of 45,000 attended Danny McGrain's testimonial match - Celtic v. United - at Parkhead in August 1980. The Reds won 3-1 on penalties.

A crowd of 15,947 attended Sammy McIlroy's testimonial match at Old Trafford in November 1981 when United's '81 side drew 4-4 with the '77 FA Cup-winning side.

Former West Bromwich Albion striker Tony Brown had a testimonial whilst playing for Torquay United in December 1981. A crowd of 7,200 at Plainmoor saw the Gulls beat Manchester United 4-2.

Don Given's testimonial match on 10 August 1982 saw United beat a Republic of Ireland XI 4-2 at Dalymount Park, Dublin. The attendance was 17,000. Four days later Pat Nolan's testimonial match attracted 5,000 spectators as United beat Limerick 3-1.

Arthur Albiston's testimonial match between United and Celtic scheduled to take place at Old Trafford on 10 May 1983 was called off because the Scottish FA refused to give the Glasgow giants permission to play!

On 17 August 1983 United drew 2-2 with Aberdeen in Martin Buchan's testimonial match. Also in 1983, United beat Liverpool 4-3 at Windsor Park, Belfast in a benefit match for William Brennan and they also played St Patrick's United at Dalymount Park as part of the Paul McGrath transfer deal.

On 13 May 1974 Lou Macari had his testimonial match at Old Trafford when United played Celtic.

Ten goals were scored when United played Scunthorpe United in a benefit match for the England cricketer Ian Botham in December 1984. The scoreline finished level at 5-5.

United visited Shamrock Rovers (Dublin) to play a testimonial match for former player Shay Brennan on 14 August 1986. And in the very same month United took on the Spanish side Real Sociedad at Old Trafford in a testimonial match for Steve Coppell.

Jimmy Rimmer's testimonial match on 24 February 1987 saw United play Swansea City at The Vetch Field.

Celtic beat United 1-0 at Parkhead in Roy Aitken's testimonial match in March 1987.

United defeated an England XI 7-2 at Old Trafford in Gary Bailey's testimonial match in May 1987. Mark Hughes scored four goals as a 'United' guest!

Arthur Albiston's testimonial at Old Trafford on 8 May 1988 was between United and rivals Manchester City and three months later it was the same line-up (United v. City) for Kevin Moran's testimonial.

United met Hibernian at Easter Road for Scotsman George Rae's benefit match on 3 October 1988 and the following month they visited St Andrew's to play Birmingham City in a benefit game arranged for Blues' midfielder Ian Handysides.

Mike Duxbury's testimonial match - United v. Manchester City - was staged at Old Trafford on 13 August 1992.

Wilf McGuinness's testimonial match - Bury v. United at Gigg Lane on 1 August 1990 - attracted 7,162 spectators and ended goalless.

Also in 1990, on 20 November, an Old Trafford crowd of 41,658 attended Bryan Robson's testimonial when United lost 3-1 to Celtic.

A testimonial match for Sir Matt Busby was staged at Old Trafford in August 1991 when United played the Republic of Ireland national team. A crowd of 33,412 saw Eire win a very competitive match, 1-0.

Norman Whiteside had his testimonial on 3 May 1992 when United played 'his other club' Everton at Old Trafford and two years later, on 16 May 1994, Mark Hughes celebrated his testimonial when United played Celtic, also at Old Trafford. Three months after Hughes' big night, Clayton Blackmore had his testimonial when United visited Middlesbrough.

Brian McClair had his testimonial match on 15 April 1997 when Celtic once more visited Old Trafford to play a strong United side and six months later (5 October) United played Manchester City at Maine Road in a game for Paul Lake
In recent years the following have all had bumper testimonials at Old Trafford: Denis Irwin, Paul McGrath, Sir Alex Ferguson (v. World XI while United changed their 'name' to All Stars at half-time) and Ryan Giggs (v. Celtic) while United have also visited Parkhead to play Celtic in aid of Scottish international Tommy Boyd's tesimonial, Chesterfield (for John Duncan's benefit) and also Bournemouth....and no doubt there'll be plenty more testimonial/benefit matches in the years ahead!

BENFICA

United first met Benfica in the 1965-66 European Cup quarter-finals and they performed supremely well against Eusebio and Co. winning in style by 8-3 on aggregate. George Best was brilliant in Lisbon, scoring twice in a rampant United performance as they raced to an emphatic 5-1 victory, the first European game Benfica had lost at home!
Georgie Boy was at his 'Best' again at Wembley for the 1968 European Cup Final when again United pulled out all the stops to win the trophy for the first time with a 4-1 victory (See EUROPEAN CUP).

BENNION, Samuel Raymond

Born: Wrexham, 1 September 1896. Died: Burnley, 12 March 1968.
Career: Ragtimes FC, Chrichton's Athletic, Saltney (1919), MANCHESTER UNITED (April 1921), Burnley (November 1932, later coach, trainer and odd-job man at Turf Moor).

Welsh international right-half Ray Bennion - strong and combative - was capped 10 times at senior level and was also a member of the Welsh FA touring party to Canada in 1929. He made over 300 first-class appearances for United (286 in the Football League) during his eleven years at Old Trafford. He later served Burnley for 34 years, being present when the Clarets won promotion from Division Two and finish runners-up in the FA Cup in 1946-47.

He had earlier gained a Cheshire County Cup winners medal with Chrichton's Athletic (1921).

Bennion's son, John, played for Burnley, Hull City, Stockport County and Barrow.

Club record: 301 apps. 3 goals

BENT, Geoffrey

Born: Salford, 27 September 1932. Died: Munich, 6 February 1958.

Career: Salford Schoolboys, MANCHESTER UNITED (trialist 1948, amateur May 1949, professional April 1951 till his death).

Full-back Geoff Bent was a great competitor and excellent defender, as hard as nails, who had to live in the shadow of Roger Byrne, meaning his chances of first team football were limited. He sadly lost his life in the Munich air crash. He was only 25.

Club record: 12 apps.

BENTLEY, John James

Born in 1860 and a defender with Bolton Wanderers from 1877, he retired in 1885 to become secretary at Burnden Park, a position he held for 14 years, until 1897.

A qualified accountant, John Bentley was one of the Football League's early committee members, working arm in arm with its founder, William McGregor. He was also a well-respected referee and quality journalist who edited the Athletic News, a splendid sporty newspaper carrying excellent reports of football matches. Bentley was president of the Football League from 1893 to 1910 and in 1902 was named chairman.

Admired by many for the work he did for both club and country in 1912 Bentley took over the position of club secretary at MANCHESTER UNITED when Ernest Mangnall resigned. He stayed in this job until announcing his resignation in 1916. During seasons 1912-13 & 1913-14 he was also responsible for the team as there was no manager at that time - until Jack Robson was recruited in 1914. When Bentley quit in 1916 due to ill health, Robson assumed the dual role of manager-secretary.

John Bentley died on 2 September 1918, remembered as a man of equal stature to William McGregor, founder of the Football League

BERG, Henning

Born: Eidsvoll, Norway, 1 September 1969

Career: KFUM (1988), FC Valeringen (1991), SK Lillestrom (1995), VIF (1996), Blackburn Rovers, MANCHESTER UNITED (£5 million, August 1997-September 2000), Blackburn Rovers (£1.75 million).

Norwegian international defender Henning Berg, strong and positive, and who rarely lost out in physical encounters, was signed by United manager Alex Ferguson after making almost 200 appearances for the Ewood Park club. Whilst with the Reds he gained two more Premier Championship medals (1999 & 2000) to add to the one he had won earlier with Rovers (1995). After returning to Rovers he helped the Lancashire club regain Premiership status in his first season back at the club. Capped by his country at Under-21 level, Berg has now appeared in well over 80 senior internationals for Norway as well as more than 350 senior games in English football. Berg helped Blackburn win the League Cup in 2002.

Club record: 103 apps. 3 goals

BERRY, John James

Born: Aldershot, 1 June 1926. Died: Farnham, Hampshire, 1995.

Career: St Joseph's School (Aldershot), Aldershot YMCA, Birmingham City (1944), MANCHESTER UNITED (£15,000, August 1951). Retired from football after the Munich air disaster in February 1958.

A dashing wingman who can play on either flank - signed to replace Jimmy Delaney after some dazzling performances against United - Johnny Berry scored six goals in 114 first team outings during his time at St Andrew's, helping Blues win the Second Division title in 1948.

Only a small player, yet he was all heart. "No-one had more heart than Berry" said his colleague Dennis Viollet. He was a great footballer. Indeed, at Old Trafford, he was a star performer in the famous Busby Babes side and won three First Division Championship medals and an FA Cup runners-up medal in the space of five years. Extremely tricky, he brought vital experience to a young side, scoring some crucial goals, as well as laying on plenty more for his colleagues, especially Tommy Taylor and Dennis Viollet.

He also gained four full England caps and represented his country at 'B' team level as well as playing for the Football League side. After that tragic air crash in 1958 he returned to Aldershot to help run the family sports shop.

Berry's younger brother, Peter, also a winger, played for Crystal Palace and Ipswich Town.

Club record: 276 apps. 45 goals

BERRY, William Alexander

Born: Wearside (near Sunderland) 1882.

Career: Oakhill, Sunderland Royal Rovers (1902), Sunderland (1902) Tottenham Hotspur (1903), MANCHESTER UNITED (November 1906), Stockport County (February 1909), Sunderland Royal Rovers (1911). Retired in 1912.

Energetic utility forward Bill Berry occupied three different positions for United, including that of outside-right where he played until the legendary Billy Meredith returned after suspension. After that his first team appearances were considerably restricted.

Club record: 14 apps. one goal

"Best played in four
different countries
in the space of 10
days whilst a
Fulham player."

GEORGE BEST

Born: Royal Maternity Hospital, Belfast, 22 May 1946.
Career: Nettlefield Primary, Grosvenor High &
Lisnasharragh Intermediate Schools (Belfast),
MANCHESTER UNITED (junior June 1961,
professional May 1963), Toronto Indoor Soccer League,
Jewish Guild FC (South Africa), Dunstable Town (mid-
1974), Stockport County (1975), Los Angeles Aztecs,
Cork Celtic (1976), Los Angeles Aztecs (again), Fulham
(autumn 1976), Los Angeles Aztecs (third spell), Fulham
(second time), Los Angeles Aztecs (once more), Fulham
(again), Los Angeles Aztecs (fourth spell), Fort Lauderdale
Strikers (1978), Hibernian (1979), San Jose Earthquakes
(two separate spells, 1980 & 1981), AFC Bournemouth
(1983), then Brisbane Lions (mid 1983) & Golden Bay
FC (late 1983), both in Australia. Retiring in June 1984,
he has since suffered with his health, mainly due to drink.
He is now a television pundit.
After turning professional at Old Trafford, George Best
took to the footballing stage like a duck to water! He
made his United League debut on 14 September 1963

in a 1-0 home win over West Bromwich Albion and a little over three months later, on 28 December 1963, he scored his first League goal in an emphatic 5-1 home victory over Burnley. On 4 January 1964, he made his first appearance in the FA Cup against Southampton at The Dell and the very next month followed up with his first goal in that competition v. Barnsley. He also made his 'European' debut against Sporting Lisbon in the quarter-final of the Cup-winners Cup at Old Trafford.

Nicknamed 'El Beatle', he became a world-beater - a supreme master of all the football skills plus unlimited stamina and absolute bravery. Indeed, his skills were God-given, amazing balance coupled with speed off the mark made it difficult for defenders to man mark him. Anything was possible with Best in the team and he was a star in United's front-line, producing many outstanding performances and scoring and making plenty of goals (he was the First Division's top-scorer in 1967-68 with 28 goals, scoring 32 in all that season).

Capped 37 times by Northern Ireland, he made his international debut in April 1964 against Wales at Swansea (won 3-2) and played in his last game in October 1977 against Holland in Belfast.

An FA Youth Cup winner with United in 1964, he collected two League Championship medals in 1965 and 1967, and was voted Northern Ireland's 'Footballer of the Year' and the 'Texaco Superstar of the Year' at the same time.

In 1968, after scoring a fine individual goal in United's European Cup Final victory over Benfica, he was voted both PFA 'Footballer of the Year' and 'European Footballer of the Year', being the youngest recipient of the latter prestigious award.

He was sent-off for first time in his career against the South American club, Estudiantes de la Plata (at home) in a World Club Championship match in October 1968 (for fighting with Hugo Medina) before representing the Rest of the United Kingdom against Wales in July 1969.

In February 1970 he became only the second United player ever to score six goals in a senior game - obliging against Northampton Town (away) in an FA Cup-tie (won 8-2)…this was, in fact, his first match back after that four-week suspension.

After leaving Old Trafford in 1974, still only 27, his subsequent 'career' was of little significance although he did play in over 100 games in the NASL (scoring 37 goals). At club and international level, Best's record was excellent: 244 goals in 710 appearances.

Unfortunately he did have a temper and was sent-off five times during his career: once playing in a United game (at Chelsea in 1971), twice with Northern Ireland and once each with Fulham and Fort Lauderdale Strikers.

He was featured on the BBC TV programme 'This Is Your Life' (17 November 1971).

In July 2002, after a long wait, Best successfully underwent a 'difficult' ten-and-a-half hour liver transplant operation (by Professor Roger Williams) at London's Cromwell Hospital.

NB - Best played in four different countries in the space of 10 days whilst a Fulham player. He starred for the London club against Crystal Palace at Craven Cottage, played a League game in Wales against Cardiff City and a friendly in Scotland against St Johnstone, while also representing his country (Northern Ireland) in Belfast.

Club record: 474 apps. 181 goals

BETTING SCAM

In May 1915, an FA Commission decided unanimously that United's 2-0 League win over Liverpool a month earlier had been fixed! The score was allowed to stand but three United players - namely Sandy Turnbull, Enoch West and Arthur Whalley - were suspended from the game sine die, along with four Liverpool players. Turnbull & Whalley had their suspensions lifted at the end WW1, alas far too late for Turnbull who had been killed in action. West was not so lucky. He was not forgiven until 1945!

Prior to the game bookies had offered odds of 7-1 that the outcome of the game would be a 2-0 win for United! It was clear that the players did it purely for financial gain, rather than for football reasons.

With those two points being awarded to United, it meant that Chelsea were relegated from the First Division at the end of that season instead of the Reds. However, when football resumed after the hostilities in August 1919, the London club retained its First Division status after it had been extended from 20 to 22 clubs.

BIELBY, Paul Anthony

Born: Darlington, 24 November 1956

Career: MANCHESTER UNITED (apprentice July 1972, professional November 1973), Hartlepool United (initially on loan November 1975, signed December 1975), Huddersfield Town (1978-80).

Reserve left-winger Paul Bielby who was outstanding as a Youth player, made his League debut in the local derby against rivals City at Maine Road in March 1974 in front of more than 51,000 spectators. As a teenager he played in the same England Youth team as three future United players, Bryan Robson, Ray Wilkins and Peter Barnes, plus Glenn Hoddle. Whilst with Hartlepool, the Northern club had to seek re-election to the Football League on two occasions.

Club record: 4 apps

BIRCH, Brian

Born: Salford, 18 November 1931.

Career: Salford Schoolboys, MANCHESTER UNITED (amateur May 1946, professional May 1948), Wolverhampton Wanderers (£10,000, March 1952), Lincoln City (late 1952), Boston United (early 1956), Barrow (mid 1956), Exeter City (1958), Oldham Athletic (early 1960), Rochdale (1961), Boston United (1963), Mossley (mid 1963), Ellesmere Port (1964-67), Blackburn Rovers (junior coach, 1967-68). Also coached in Egypt, Sydney (Australia), the Phillipines, Turkey and Sweden during the 1960s.

Inside-forward Brian Birch was one of the first products of United's post-war Youth policy to emerge, making his debut as a 17 year-old. He served the club for six years as a junior player and then reserve, gaining England Youth international honours whilst at Old Trafford. However, with so many players to choose from he became surplus to requirements and after leaving the Reds went on to appear in well over 200 competitive games (over 60 goals scored) during his senior career.

Club record: 15 apps. 5 goals

BIRCHENOUGH, Herbert

Born: Crewe, June 1874.

Career: Crewe Alexandra (1892), Burlsem Port Vale (1898), Glossop (£250, 1900), MANCHESTER UNITED (October 1902), Crewe Alexandra (May 1903).

Excellent goalkeeper Herbert Birchenough, who played for the Football League against the Irish League in 1899, replaced Jimmy Whitehouse between the posts for United. It was surprising that he stayed at Old Trafford for just the one season before ending his senior career with Crewe.

Club record: 30 apps.

BIRKETT, Clifford

Born: Haydock, 17 September 1933. Died: January 1997.

Career: Newton-le-Willows Schoolboys, MANCHESTER UNITED (amateur September 1949, professional October 1950), Southport (June 1956) Compton's Recreationalists (1957), Wigan Rovers (summer 1959), Macclesfield Town (late 1959).

An England schoolboy international right-winger, alongside Dennis Viollet, Cliff Birkett made his League debut for United (in place of Tommy Bogan) against Newcastle in front of 34,502 fans at Old Trafford in December 1950. Along with Brian Birch (q.v) he was considered to be a future star in United's ranks, but could never quite make the final breakthrough, owing to the presence of Harry McShane and then Johnny Berry. He made only spasmodic first team appearances following his debut season when he played in nine senior matches.

Birkett's two brothers (Wilf and Ronnie) both played professional football.

Club record: 13 apps. 2 goals

BIRMINGHAM (CITY) (Small Heath)

Summary of League results

	P	W	D	L	F	A
Division 1	68	30	22	16	101	79
Division 2	12	3	1	8	12	17
Home	40	23	8	9	60	34
Away	40	10	15	15	53	62
Total	80	33	23	24	113	96

Heathen's/United's League results v Blues:

Season	Div	Home	Away	Season	Div	Home	Away
1896-97	2	D 1-1	L 0-1	1955-56	1	W 2-1	D 2-2
1897-98	2	W 3-1	L 1-2	1956-57	1	D 2-2	L 1-3
1898-99	2	W 2-0	L 1-4	1957-58	1	L 0-2	D 3-3
1899-1900	2	W 3-2	L 0-1	1958-59	1	W 1-0	W 4-0
1900-01	2	L 0-1	L 0-1	1959-60	1	W 2-1	D 1-1
				1960-61	1	W 4-1	L 1-3
1902-03	2	L 0-1	L 1-2	1961-62	1	L 0-2	D 1-1
				1962-63	1	W 2-0	L 1-2
1906-07	1	W 2-1	D 1-1	1963-64	1	L 1-2	D 1-1
1907-08	1	W 1-0	W 4-3	1964-65	1	D 1-1	W 4-2
1921-22	1	D 1-1	W 1-0	1972-73	1	W 1-0	L 1-3
				1973-74	1	W 1-0	L 0-1
1925-26	1	W 3-1	L 1-2				
1926-27	1	L 0-1	L 0-4	1975-76	1	W 3-1	W 2-0
1927-28	1	D 1-1	D 0-0	1976-77	1	D 2-2	W 3-2
1928-29	1	W 1-0	D 1-1	1977-78	1	L 1-2	W 4-1
1929-30	1	D 0-0	W 1-0	1978-79	1	W 1-0	L 1-5
1930-31	1	W 2-0	D 0-0				
				1980-81	1	W 2-0	D 0-0
1936-37	1	L 1-2	D 2-2	1981-82	1	D 1-1	W 1-0
				1982-83	1	W 3-0	W 2-1
1938-39	1	W 4-1	D 3-3	1983-84	1	W 1-0	D 2-2
1948-49	1	W 3-0	L 0-1	1985-86	1	W 1-0	D 1-1
1949-50	1	L 0-2	D 0-0				

Test Match record (Newton Heath v. Small Heath)

1892-93	D 1-1 (at Stoke)	W 5-2 (at Bramall Lane)

United's FA Cup results v Blues:

	Round	Venue	Result
1903-04	1	Home	D 1-1
	Replay	Away	D 1-1 aet
	2nd replay	Bramall Lane	D 1-1 aet
	3rd replay	Hyde Road	W 3-1
1927-28	5	Home	W 1-0
1950-51	6	Away	L 0-1
1956-57	Semi-final	Hillsborough	W 2-0
1968-69	5	Away	D 2-2
	Replay	Home	W 6-2

Fact File:

Players with both clubs include: J Berry, R Bonthron, S Bruce (also Blues manager), F Buckley, W Carrier (United reserve), T Cooke, A Coton (United reserve, later goalkeeping coach), C Craven, G Daly, SC Davies (United trialist), J Fall, R Gardner (amateur), W Garton, R Gibson, D Givens, J Greenhoff, GW Hicks (United reserve), F Hodges, G Hunter (Blues WW1), C Jenkyns, W Johnston (United trialist), F Jones, J Kirovski & D Kerr (United reserves), H Lappin, J Merrick (Blues & United reserve), RS Morton (United reserve), A Potts (Blues WW1), R Morton, W Rudd (United amateur), MC Russell & R Savage (United reserves), L Sealey (Blues trialist), L Sharpe (Blues associate schoolboy), S Sutton (United trialist), J Travers, D Wallace, J Wealands.
Also associated: F Goodwin & L Macari (United players, Blues managers), S Owen (United coach, Blues player & assistant-manager), B Fry (United reserve, Blues manager), R Brocklebank (United WW2 player, Blues manager), T Jones (United player, Blues assistant-trainer), R Duckworth jnr (United reserve, Blues scout).

BIRTLES, Garry

Born: Nottingham, 27 July 1956.
Career: Long Eaton Rovers, Long Eaton Rangers (1974), Nottingham Forest (1976), MANCHESTER UNITED (£1.25 million, October 1980), Nottingham Forest (£250,000, September 1982), Notts County (1987), Grimsby Town (1989-92), Gresley Rovers (manager, 1992).
Centre-forward Garry Birtles was signed from Forest by manager Dave Sexton and took quite some time to settle in at Old Trafford (failing to score in his first 25 League games for the club). He had arrived at the club seemingly on the verge of greatness, following a sensational time at Forest for whom he netted over 50 goals in more than 130 senior appearances under Brian Clough's management. Capped by England at Under-21 and 'B' team levels, he also played in three full internationals for his country and gained two European Cup winners' medals with Forest (1979 & 1980) while also collecting a League Cup winners medal and a runners-up prize in the same competition around that time. Birtles was undoubtedly grateful and relieved to get away from two years of misery and under achievement at Old Trafford. Later in his career he played as a defensive midfielder and then as a central defender.
Club record: 64 apps. 12 goals

BISSETT, George

Born: Cowdenbeath, 25 January 1897
Career: Glencraig Thistle, Third Lanark (season 1914-15), Army football (while serving in France) MANCHESTER UNITED (November 1919), Wolverhampton Wanderers (November 1921), Pontypridd (early 1924), Southend United (mid 1924). Retired in May 1926.
Scottish-born right-winger or inside-forward George Bissett spent two-and-a-half seasons with United. Fast and direct, he took over from John Hodge on the right-flank on arriving at Old Trafford but then lost his place to Billy Meredith and was 'out in the cold' when Billy Harrison arrived from Bissett's future club, Wolves in October 1920.
Club record: 42 apps. 10 goals

BLACK, Arthur Richard

Born: Glasgow, circa 1908
Career: Greenock Morton (1930), MANCHESTER UNITED (April 1932), St Mirren (November 1934).
Dick Black was a sprightly forward, who was seemingly more at home in the reserves than in the first XI; he scored over 30 goals for United's second string in 1932-33. Prior to moving to United he had claimed 38 goals in one season for Morton but unfortunately was not given a fair chance by manager Scott Duncan.
Club record: 8 apps 3 goals

BLACK, Samuel

Born: Burton-on-Trent, 27 February 1863
Career: NEWTON HEATH (summer 1878), Burton FC (May 1884).
Sam Black was the first captain of Newton Heath (LYR) when the club was formed in 1878 (he had come to Manchester to complete an apprenticeship). A great defender with a superb physique, Black's part in the early days of the club cannot be understated. His superhuman efforts both on and off the field, enabled the fledgling club to make

41

progress as one of the best in the area. He gave Newton Heath (LYR) six years stalwart service before returning to Burton in 1884. He did not play what we know as 'first-class football', Newton Heath (LYR) playing its first FA Cup-tie in 1886 and joining the Football Alliance in 1889, long after Black had left the club. Nevertheless, without the likes of Sam Black, there might not be a Manchester United today! Black - who remained an amateur throughout his career and won the club's first representative honour when playing for Manchester v. Bootle & Distriuct in 1884 - became a referee in later years.

NB: Although he did not play for the Heathens in a major competitive game, Black did score four goals in 45 'other' games for the club.

BLACKBURN ROVERS

United's League/Premier record v. Rovers:

Season	Div	Home	Away	Season	Div	Home	Away
1892-93	1	D 4-4	L 3-4	1937-38	2	W 2-1	D 1-1
1893-94	1	W 5-1	L 0-4				
				1946-47	1	W 4-0	L 1-2
1906-07	1	D 1-1	W 4-2	1947-48	1	W 4-1	D 1-1
1907-08	1	L 1-2	W 5-1				
1908-09	1	L 0-3	W 3-1	1958-59	1	W 6-1	W 3-1
1909-10	1	W 2-0	L 2-3	1959-60	1	W 1-0	D 1-1
1910-11	1	W 3-2	L 0-1	1960-61	1	L 1-3	W 2-1
1911-12	1	W 3-1	D 2-2	1961-62	1	W 6-1	L 0-3
1912-13	1	D 1-1	D 0-0	1962-63	1	L 0-3	D 2-2
1913-14	1	D 0-0	W 1-0	1963-64	1	D 2-2	D 3-1
1914-15	1	W 2-0	D 3-3	1964-65	1	W 3-0	W 5-0
				1965-66	1	D 2-2	W 4-1
1919-20	1	D 1-1	L 0-5				
1920-21	1	L 0-1	L 0-2	1992-93	PL	W 3-1	D 0-0
1921-22	1	L 0-1	L 0-3	1993-94	PL	D 1-1	L 0-2
				1994-95	PL	W 1-0	W 4-2
1925-26	1	W 2-0	L 0-7	1995-96	PL	W 1-0	W 2-1
1926-27	1	W 2-0	L 1-2	1996-97	PL	D 2-2	W 3-2
1927-28	1	D 1-1	L 0-3	1997-98	PL	W 4-0	W 3-1
1928-29	1	L 1-4	W 3-0	1998-99	PL	W 3-2	D 0-0
1929-30	1	W 1-0	L 4-5	2001-02	PL	W 2-1	D 2-2
1930-31	1	L 0-1	L 1-4				

Summary of League results:

	P	W	D	L	F	A
Premier League	16	10	5	1	31	17
Division 1	60	24	14	22	113	102
Division 2	2	1	1	0	3	2
Home	39	21	10	8	78	45
Away	39	14	10	15	69	76
Total	78	35	20	23	147	121

United's FA Cup results v Rovers:

	Round	Venue	Result
1892-93	1	Away	L 0-4
1893-94	2	Home	D 0-0 aet
	Replay	Away	L 1-5
1908-09	3	Home	W 6-1
1911-12	4	Home	D 1-1
	Replay	Away	L 2-4 aet
1927-28	6	Away	L 0-2
1984-85	5	Away	W 2-0

FA Charity Shield
A Wembley crowd of 60,402 saw United defeat Rovers 2-0 in the 1994 FA Charity Shield game.

Fact File:
United's first-ever Football League game was against Rovers on 3 September 1892 (Division 1). The venue was Ewood Park and Rovers won 4-3 in front of 8,000 spectators.
Rovers inflicted upon United their joint heaviest League defeat so far when beating them 7-0 at Ewood Park on 10 April 1926.
Five former United players - Henning Berg, Andy Cole (a goalscorer), John Curtis (as a substitute), Keith Gillespie and Mark Hughes all gained League Cup winners with Blackburn (v. Tottenham Hotspur) in February 2002.

Players with both clubs include: B Asquith (Rovers WW2), J Aston (junior), W Ball, R Beardsmore, A Bell, H Berg, T Bogan, P Bradshaw (United trialist), W Bryant, L Butt (United WW2), W Campbell, D Carter (United WW2), A Cole, A Comyn (United & Rovers 'A' teams), J Connelly, J Curtis, R Davies (Rovers trialist), W Dennis, R Donaldson, M Duxbury, K Gillespie, G Glaister (United WW2), W Goodwin, J Hall (Rovers WW2), R Haworth, M Hughes, R John (Rovers WW2), F Kennedy, P Kennedy, F Kopel, J Lowey (United reserve), H McShane, D May, K Moran, W Porter (Rovers WW2), J Smith, F Stapleton, E Thompson, D Yorke.
Also associated: J Carey (United player, Rovers manager & joint-manager), B Kidd (United player & assistant-manager, Rovers manager), B Birch (United player, Rovers junior coach).

BLACKMORE, Clayton Graham

Born: Neath, 23 September 1964
Career: Afan Nedd Schoolboys XI, MANCHESTER UNITED (apprentice June 1981, professional September 1982), Middlesbrough (May 1994), Bristol City (on loan, 1996), Barnsley (1999), Notts County (mid-1999), Leigh RMI (2001).
Midfielder Clayton Blackmore who could also perform with authority in the back four, made over 250 appearances for United. A Welshman, he joined the ranks at Old Trafford straight from school (after playing a bit of rugby) and made his League debut in May 1984 against Nottingham Forest. Over the next decade he performed well in the engine-room alongside many great players. Honoured by his country at schoolboy, Youth and Under-21 levels, Blackmore went on to win 39 full caps for Wales and was an FA Youth Cup finalist with United in 1982 before gaining an FA Cup winners medal (albeit as a 'sub') in 1990, a European Cup-winners Cup medal in 1991 and a Premiership Championship medal in 1993.
He donned every United shirt from number 2 to 14 (but not 13) before leaving Old Trafford for Middlesbrough in 1994. Under player-manager Bryan Robson, he helped the Teeside club win a place in the Premiership as First Division champions.
Club record: 251 apps. 27 goals.

BLACKMORE, Peter

Born: Gorton, Manchester, autumn 1879
Career: Ross Place Old Boys, NEWTON HEATH (October 1899-May 1900).
Local-born striker Peter Blackmore's only League appearance for the club was against New Brighton Tower in a Second Division League game in October 1899 when he became the fifth player tried in the centre-forward position that season!
He was not the answer.
Club record: 2 apps.

BLACKPOOL

United's League results v Blackpool:

Season	Div	Home	Away		Season	Div	Home	Away
1896-97	2	W 2-0	L 2-4		1946-47	1	W 3-0	L 1-3
1897-98	2	W 4-0	W 1-0		1947-48	1	D 1-1	L 0-1
1898-99	2	W 3-1	W 1-0		1948-49	1	L 3-4	W 3-0
					1949-50	1	L 1-2	D 3-3
1900-01	2	W 4-0	W 2-1		1950-51	1	W 1-0	D 1-1
1901-02	2	L 0-1	W 4-2		1951-52	1	W 3-1	D 2-2
1902-03	2	D 2-2	L 0-2		1952-53	1	W 2-1	D 0-0
1903-04	2	W 3-1	L 1-2		1953-54	1	W 4-1	L 0-2
1904-05	2	W 3-1	W 1-0		1954-55	1	W 4-1	W 4-2
1905-06	2	W 2-1	W 1-0		1955-56	1	W 2-1	D 0-0
					1956-57	1	L 0-2	D 2-2
1922-23	2	W 2-1	L 0-1		1957-58	1	L 1-2	W 4-1
1923-24	2	D 0-0	L 0-1		1958-59	1	W 3-1	L 1-2
1924-25	2	D 0-0	D 1-1		1959-60	1	W 3-1	W 6-0
					1960-61	1	W 2-0	L 0-2
1930-31	1	D 0-0	L 1-5		1961-62	1	L 0-1	W 3-2
					1962-63	1	D 1-1	D 2-2
1933-34	2	W 2-0	L 1-3		1963-64	1	W 3-0	L 0-1
1934-35	2	W 3-2	W 2-1		1964-65	1	W 2-0	W 2-1
1935-36	2	W 3-2	L 1-4		1965-66	1	W 2-1	W 2-1
					1966-67	1	W 4-0	W 2-1
1938-39	1	D 0-0	W 5-3					
					1970-71	1	D 1-1	D 1-1
					1974-75	2	W 4-0	W 3-0

Summary of League results:

	P	W	D	L	F	A
Division 1	48	23	13	12	91	60
Division 2	32	20	4	8	58	34
Home	40	26	8	6	83	34
Away	40	17	9	14	66	60
Total	80	43	17	20	149	94

United's FA Cup results v Blackpool:

	Round	Venue	Result
1891-92	4 (Qual)	Home	L 3-4
1896-97	5 (Qual)	Home	D 2-2
	Replay	Away	W 2-1
1907-08	1	Home	W 3-1
1910-11	1	Away	W 2-1
1947-48	Final	Wembley	W 4-2

United's League Cup results v Blackpool

	Round	Venue	Result
1966-67	2	Away	L 1-5

Fact File:

In the immediate post-war years matches between United and Blackpool produced some great football. The 1948 FA Cup Final was a prime example and is regarded by many critics as the best-ever (at Wembley). United, twice behind came back to win 4-2, despite the presence of the 'two Stans', Matthews and Mortensen.

When the teams met on 7 April 1956 at Old Trafford, the match was virtually a play-off for the First Division title. David Durie's early goal for the Seasiders set United's nerves jangling, but the young side finally got going and triumphed 2-1 with Tommy Taylor scoring the winning goal that gave the Busby Babes their first Championship success. The attendance was 62,277 - the best of the season and the biggest at Old Trafford for a League game since September 1936.

On 13 January 1962, Blackpool's League visit to Old Trafford resulted in a 1-0 win. United though played the entire game with only ten men. David Herd injured himself during the pre-match warm up and failed to take the field once the referee had signalled for the kick-off. Matt Busby had already handed in his team-sheet and with no substitutes allowed, it was 10 against 11 and the Seasiders just scraped home. Herd, although he never appeared in the game, is still credited with one appearance!

Players with both clubs include: W Buchan (United WW2), A Butterworth (United reserve), J Clarkin, W Davies; E Dodds & P Doherty (both United WW2), W Douglas, G Farrow (United WW2), J Grimwood, J Hacking, H Hardman (also United director & chairman), F Haydock, C Knowles (United amateur, 'Pool trialist), J Lydiate (United reserve), J McClelland, E MacDougall (also coach and assistant-manager of 'Pool), H McLenahan ('Pool trialist), S Matthews (United WW2), S Mercer ('Pool amateur, United WW2), I Moir, H Morgan, W Morgan, K Morton (United reserve), H O'Donnell (United WW2), J O'Kane, T O'Neil, R Parkinson, M Phelan, L Sealey, I Storey-Moore ('Pool trialist), E Taylor, A Whalley, R Wellens (United reserve), N Whitworth.

Also associated: F Buckley (United player, 'Pool manager), R Smith (United reserve, 'Pool coach), N Bailey (Blackpool player & also coach at both clubs).

43

BLACKSTOCK, Thomas

Born: Kirkcaldy, Fife, 1882. Died: Manchester, 8 April 1907.

Career: Dunniker Rangers, Bluebell FC, Raith Athletic, Leith Athletic, Cowdenbeath (1901) MANCHESTER UNITED (June 1903 until his death).

Full-back Tommy Blackstock, a rugged Scotsman, collapsed after heading the ball during United's Combination game against St Helens Recreationalists in April 1907. Sadly he died in the dressing room soon afterwards. He was only 25 years of age. Blackstock's coffin was sent home to Kirkcaldy by train, but not before a touching ceremony had taken place at Manchester railway station with the entire United team, club officials and several hundred supporters paying their last respects to a very popular player.

Club record: 38 apps.

BLANC, Laurent

Born: Ales, France, 19 November 1965

Career: Montpellier (1983), Napoli (1991), Nimes (1992), St Etienne (1993), Auxerre (1995), Barcelona (1996), Olympique Marseille (1997), Inter Milan (1999), MANCHESTER UNITED (September 2001).

Experienced French international centre-half, Laurent Blanc joined United as a straight replacement for the departed 'Jaap' Stam. Prior to his arrival at Old Trafford, the 35-year-old defender had already accumulated a fine playing record, appearing in well over 700 League, Cup and international matches since making his debut for Montpellier in the French First Division in 1983. Blanc has certainly enjoyed a distinguished international playing career with France, being a key member of his country's World Cup winning squad in 1998, but missing the Final against Brazil through suspension. He was then a winner, however, in Euro 2000 as Italy were defeated 2-1 in the Final in Rotterdam. Blanc has won a record 97 full caps for France, many as captain.

Club record: 46 apps, 3 goals

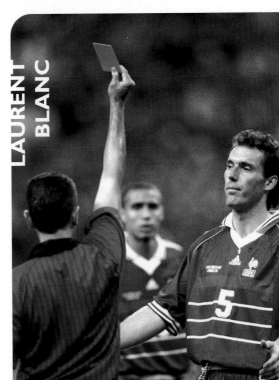

LAURENT BLANC

BLANCHFLOWER, John

Born: Belfast, 7 March 1933. Died: 2 September 1998

Career: Boyland FC, MANCHESTER UNITED (amateur May 1949, professional March 1950). Retired after Munich air crash (1958).

Dennis Viollet said: 'It was a magnificent feeling to know you had a guy like Jackie Blanchflower in your side. He did a tremendous job for United.'

Although a little short on pace, Blanchflower was a skilful, intelligent player, who started his career as an inside-forward before finding his niche in midfield, despite having to compete with Eddie Colman and Duncan Edwards. He later assumed the role of centre-half, the position he occupied in the 1957 FA Cup Final when, following an injury to Ray Wood, he took over in goal in his side's 2-1 defeat. His displays at the heart of the United defence were extraordinary as he brought a creative player's innate skills to a defensive berth. If he had been able to resume playing after Munich he would have probably revolutionised centre-half play.

A splendid footballer, Blanchflower had appeared in almost 120 first-class games for United before his playing days ended abruptly in February 1958. Thankfully he survived that ill-fated crash but he never regained full fitness, although he was retained as a member of staff at Old Trafford until June 1959.

Brother of Danny Blanchflower, the former Barnsley, Aston Villa and Tottenham Hotspur wing-half, Jackie Blanchflower made his League debut at right-half against Liverpool in November 1951, along with fellow debutant Roger Byrne. A member of two League Championship-winning sides (1956 & 1957), he only played in his debut match when the title was claimed in 1952.

Honoured by Northern Ireland at schoolboy level, he went on to gain 12 full caps for his country.

Club record: 117 apps. 27 goals

BLEW, Horace Elford

Born: Wrexham, 1878. Died, Wrexham, 1 February 1957.

Career: Grove Park School, Wrexham Old Boys (1895), Rhostyllen (season 1896-97), Wrexham (1897-1911), Druids (1903), Bury (1904), MANCHESTER UNITED (March 1906), Manchester City (September 1906), Brymbo FC (1910). Later served as a Wrexham director (1920s).

Welsh international full-back Horace Blew's only appearance for United was against Chelsea at Stamford Bridge in a Second Division League game in April 1906 in front of 60,000 spectators, helping secure promotion.

An amateur throughout his career, he remained with the club for just six months, switching across to neighbours City soon after the start of the 1906-07 season. In the late 1920s Blew was on the Board of Directors of Wrexham FC, a hotelier in the same town and also Mayor of Wrexham in 1923, receiving the Freedom of the Borough in 1948. Blew won 22 full caps for his country.

Club record: one app.

BLOMQVIST, Lars Jesper

Born: Tavelsjo, Sweden, 5 February 1974

Career: FC Tavelsjo IK (1990), Umea (1992), IFK Gothenburg (1993), AC Milan (1996), Parma (1997), MANCHESTER UNITED (£4.4 million, July 1998), Everton (December 2001-June 2002), Charlton (August 2002).

A Swedish international (eight caps won) he was a valuable member of United's treble-winning side in 1998-99. Voted Sweden's 'Player of the Year' in 1993, Jesper Blomqvist was recruited as back-up to Ryan Giggs. After receiving an injury on United's tour to Australia in the summer of 1999 Blomqvist saw out his contract, unable to play another game for the club. In the summer of 2001, his contract expired, he continued to assist the club, playing a few reserve team matches as he attempted to regain full fitness and, indeed, resurrect his career. He achieved his goal, joined Everton and duly made his debut for the Merseyside club on Boxing Day 2001 - against United.

Club record: 38 apps. one goal

BLOTT, Samuel Prince

Born: London, 1 January 1886. Died: Southend, March 1969.

Career: Southend United, Bradford Park Avenue (1907), Southend United (1908), MANCHESTER UNITED (May 1909), Plymouth Argyle (June 1913), Newport County (season 1920-21), having played for the British Army in Egypt during the Great War.

Reserve wing-half or utility-forward Sam Blott (known as 'Starting Price' from his initials) spent four years with the club, acting as cover for Alex Bell in his first season but thereafter was called up to deputise for various players. In fact, Blott appeared in six different positions for the Reds including that of outside-left.

His son, Cyril, was a player with Charlton Athletic (1937-39).

Club record: 19 apps. 2 goals

BOAVISTA

United met Boavista in Group 'A' of the 2001-02 European Champions League and they recorded two comprehensive victories on their way to the quarter-final stage. A crowd of 66,274 witnessed the first leg at Old Trafford when Ruud Van Nistelrooy (31 and 62 minutes), and Laurent Blanc (55) netted for United in a 3-0 win. The return contest at the Estadio de Bessa in Porto, was played in front of 13,223 spectators and Blanc (again), Ole Gunnar Solskjaer and David Beckham (with a penalty) found the net for the rampant Reds who as a result (another 3-0 victory) leapt to the top of their Group and earned a clash with the highly-respected Spanish champions, Deportivo La Coruna.

BOCA JUNIORS

United were scheduled to play a charity match against the Argentinan side Boca Juniors at Old Trafford in August 2002. The game, in aid of UNICEF - The United Nations Children's Fund - would raise money for children in the third world.

BOGAN, Thomas

Born: Glasgow, 18 May 1920. Died: Cheshire, 23 September 1993.

Career: Strathclyde (1937), Blantyre Celtic (1939), Renfrew (1943), Hibernian (autumn 1943), Celtic (early 1946), Preston North End (1948), MANCHESTER UNITED (August 1949), Aberdeen (March 1951), Southampton (1951), Blackburn Rovers (1953), Macclesfield Town (1954). Retired mid-1950s.

Inside-forward Tommy Bogan, clever on the ball, with a rare turn of speed, partnered another former Celtic player, Jimmy Delaney, on United's right-wing in several League matches during the 1949-50 season. He dropped out of favour following early promise and subsequently left the club to join Aberdeen.

Bogan had the misfortune to get injured and had to leave the field two minutes into Scotland's wartime international with England at Hampden Park in April 1945 - one of the shortest international careers on record! Three years later however, he returned to representative soccer when he lined up for the Scottish League against the Football League at St James' Park, Newcastle.

Bogan married Sir Matt Busby's niece.

Club record: 33 apps. 7 goals

BOLTON WANDERERS

United's League results v Wanderers:

Season	Div	Home	Away	Season	Div	Home	Away
1892-93	1	W 1-0	L 1-4	1936-37	1	W 1-0	W 4-0
1893-94	1	D 2-2	L 0-2				
				1938-39	1	D 2-2	D 0-0
1899-1900	2	L 1-2	L 1-2				
				1946-47	1	W 1-0	D 2-2
1903-04	2	D 0-0	D 0-0	1947-48	1	L 0-2	W 1-0
1904-05	2	L 1-2	W 4-2	1948-49	1	W 3-0	W 1-0
				1949-50	1	W 3-0	W 2-1
1906-07	1	L 1-2	W 1-0	1950-51	1	L 2-3	L 0-1
1907-08	1	W 2-1	D 2-2	1951-52	1	W 1-0	L 0-1
				1952-53	1	W 1-0	L 1-2
1909-10	1	W 5-0	W 3-2	1953-54	1	L 1-5	D 0-0
				1954-55	1	D 1-1	D 1-1
1911-12	1	W 2-0	D 1-1	1955-56	1	W 1-0	L 1-3
1912-13	1	W 2-1	L 1-2	1956-57	1	L 0-2	L 0-2
1913-14	1	L 0-1	L 1-6	1957-58	1	W 7-2	L 0-4
1914-15	1	W 4-1	L 0-3	1958-59	1	W 3-0	L 3-6
				1959-60	1	W 2-0	D 1-1
1919-20	1	D 1-1	W 5-3	1960-61	1	W 3-1	D 1-1
1920-21	1	L 2-3	D 1-1	1961-62	1	L 0-3	L 0-1
1921-22	1	L 0-1	L 0-1	1962-63	1	W 3-0	L 0-3
				1963-64	1	W 5-0	W 1-0
1925-26	1	W 2-1	L 1-3				
1926-27	1	D 0-0	L 0-4	1974-75	2	W 3-0	W 1-0
1927-28	1	W 2-1	L 2-3				
1928-29	1	D 1-1	D 1-1	1978-79	1	L 1-2	L 0-3
1929-30	1	D 1-1	L 1-4	1979-80	1	W 2-0	W 3-1
1930-31	1	D 1-1	L 1-3				
				1995-96	PL	W 3-0	W 6-0
1933-34	2	L 1-5	L 1-3				
1934-35	2	L 0-3	L 1-3	1997-98	PL	D 1-1	D 0-0
				2001-02	PL	L 1-2	W 4-0

Summary of League results:

	P	W	D	L	F	A
Premier League	6	3	2	1	15	3
Division 1	80	31	18	31	116	119
Division 2	12	3	2	7	14	22
Home	49	24	10	15	83	56
Away	49	13	12	24	62	88
Total	98	37	22	39	145	144

United's FA Cup results v Wanderers:

	Round	Venue	Result
1957-58	Final	Wembley	L 0-2
1961-62	3	Home	W 2-1
1990-91	4	Home	W 1-0

Fact File:

In the calendar year 1949 United were paired against Bolton four times in as many months, viz. 15/18 April 1949 (in 1948-49 season) and 24/31 August 1949 (in 1949-50 season) winning all four League matches. However, United failed to win at Bolton through 13 consecutive seasons: 1950-51 to 1962-63, drawing four losing nine, scoring only eight goals against 26 by Bolton.

Bolton are the only current club who have won more matches than they have lost against United!

Players with both clubs include: G Ainsley (United WW2), J Ball, P Barnes, P Beardsley, W Bradley, J Breedon (Bolton WW2), H Broomfield, B Cartman, W Davies, A Dunne (also Bolton player-coach), H Edmonds, A Farman, W Fielding (Bolton WW2), J Fitchett, B Fry (reserve), A Gowling, J Griffiths, J Hall (Bolton WW2), T Hamlett (United WW2), C Harrison, T Hay, D Healey (United reserve), R John (Bolton WW2), D Jones (Newton Heath reserve), B Kidd (also United assistant-manager), R Lawson, J Lydiate (United reserve), J McClelland, D McFetteridge, W McKay, H McShane, J Mitchell, H Morgan, W Morgan (1900s), W Morgan (1970s), J Morris (Bolton WW2), J Nuttall (United reserve), J O'Kane, T Poole (United junior), J Powell, R Smith, J Sutcliffe, H Whalley (Bolton WW2), P Wheatcroft, T Woodward (United WW2).

Also associated: W Ridding (United player, Bolton secretary-manager, trainer, manager), I Greaves (United player, Bolton assistant-manager & manager), E Mangnall (United manager, Bolton director), M Brown (assistant-manager both clubs).

BOND, James Ernest

Born: Preston, 4 May 1929

Career: Preston North End (1948), Leyland Motors, Army football, MANCHESTER UNITED (December 1950), Carlisle United (£5,000, September 1952), Cowdenbeath (1958-60).

A small, skilful left-winger, Ernie Bond waited eight months before making his United debut, coming into the team for the opening game of the 1951-52 season, away to West Bromwich Albion. He set up one of Jack Rowley's goals in the 3-3 draw.

He enjoyed his best spell in that Championship-winning campaign, netting three goals in consecutive matches, following an earlier strike versus Aston Villa in a 5-2 away win. With 19 appearances to his name he duly claimed his winners' medal.

Unfortunately he fell from favour the following year when David Pegg was introduced on the left-wing.

He made almost 200 League and Cup appearances for the Cumbrians after leaving Old Trafford.

Club record: 21 apps. 4 goals

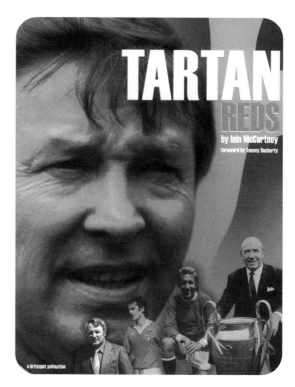

BONTHRON, Robert P

Born: Dundee, circa 1884.
Career: Raith Athletic, Raith Rovers (1900), Dundee (1902), MANCHESTER UNITED (May 1903), Sunderland (May 1907) Northampton Town (1908), Birmingham (1910), Leith Athletic (1912). Retired during WW1.
Right-back Bob Bonthron - a worthy successor to Harry Stafford - made well over 130 appearances for United whom he served for four years. A formidable defender, strong and reliable, he helped the team gain promotion to the First Division in 1906. He was replaced in the United side by Dick Holden.
Club record: 134 apps. 3 goals

BOOKS

Listed here are some of the many football books that have a direct reference to Manchester United FC. Some have been written by men who have been associated with the club....i.e players/managers.

Individual (s)
A Light In The North (Alex Ferguson)
Alex Ferguson - A Will To Win
Alex Ferguson - Managing My Life (My Autobiography)
Alex Stepney (Stepney) 1978
Anatomy Of A Football Star (David Meek on George Best)
Andy Cole - An Autobiography
Back At The Top (Bill Foulkes) 1965
Best Of Both Worlds (George Best) 1967
Bestie (Joe Lovejoy) 1998
Big Ron - A Different Ball Game (Ron Atkinson)
Blessed (George Best autobiography)
Captain of the Busby Babes (Roger Byrne) 1957
David Beckham - My World
Burchell on Beckham, 2001
Cantona (biography: Rob Wightman)
Cantona, Cantona - Eric Cantona
Captain Fantastic (Roy Keane) The Biography
Duncan Edwards - A Biography
Duncan Edwards - The Full Report (Ian McCartney) 2001
Dwight Yorke: Official Biography (Hunter Davies) 1999
Father Of Football: Matt Busby (David Miller)
Football Inside Out (Alan Gowling) 1977
Football Wizard - The Story of Billy Meredith (John Harding)
For Club & Country (Gary & Philip Neville: 1997-98)
Forward For England (Bobby Charlton) 1967
Genius At Work (Ryan Giggs)
George and Me (Angie Best, my autobiography)
George Best - Unseen Archives (Paragon Books) 2001
Head On: Jaap Stam (with Jeremy Butler) 2001
Heading For Victory (Steve Bruce) 1996-97
Heroes: Ryan Giggs (Alex Wilkins) 1997
In The Firing Line (Jim Leighton)
In Safe Keeping (Alex Stepney) 1969
Keane: The Autobiography (with Eamonn Dunphy) 2002
Denis Law - An Autobiography, 1979
Living For Kicks (Denis Law) 1963
Manchester United: My Team (Sammy McIlroy)
Manchester Unlimited (Mihir Bose) 1999
Matt...United...And Me (Jimmy Murphy) 1968
My Soccer Life (Bobby Charlton) 1964
My Story (Matt Busby) 1957
On Top Of The World (Pat Crerand) 1969
Ooh, Aah, Paul McGrath - The Black Pearl of Inchicore (Paul McGrath)
Roger Byrne - Captain of the Busby Babes
Ryan Giggs: Genius At Work,1996
Schmeichel: The Autobiography (with Elgon Balsby) 1999
Sir Matt Busby - A Tribute, 1994
Soccer At The Top (Matt Busby) 1973
Soccer My Battlefield (Nobby Stiles) 1968
Teddy Sheringham: My Autobiography, 1998
The Boss: The Many Sides of Alex Ferguson (Michael Crick) 2002
The Ferguson Effect: Alex Ferguson (Harry Harris)
The Good, The Bad, The Bubbly: George Best (R Benson, updated)
The Lawman - autobiography of Denis Law (Bernard Bale) 1999/2001
The Life Of A Legendary Goalscorer: Dennis Viollet (R Cavanagh, B Hughes MBE) 2001
This Game Of Soccer (Bobby Charlton) 1967
Tommy Taylor Story (The Smiling Executioner)
Touch and Go (Steve Coppell's autobiography).
United I Stand (Bryan Robson).
United We Stand (Noel Cantwell)

United To Win (Ron Atkinson)
United...We Shall Not Be Moved (Lou Macari)
View From The Dugout (Eric Harrison: autobiography) 2001
Wild About Football (Harry Gregg)

Historical/statistical/reference
A-Z Encyclopaedia & Statistical Record of Manchester United: 1878-2002 (Tony Matthews)
100 Great Players (Official Manchester United publication by Ivan Ponting)
Always In The Running (United's Dream Team, 1996)
Back Page United (Stephen F Kelly)
Barcelona To Brazil (Peters & Bostock) 2000
Champions Again: Manchester United (R Finn)
History of Manchester United (Alf Clarke) 1948
History of Manchester United (Tony Pullein) 1974
Irish Reds (Iain McCartney) 2002
Manchester United: Barson To Busby (E Thornton)
Manchester United (Alf Clarke) 1949 & 1951
Manchester United (Percy M Young)
Manchester United: A Complete Record 1878-1986 & 1878-1992 (Ian Morrison & Alan Shury)
Manchester United In Europe: The Complete Journey (1956-2001)
Manchester United Official Yearbook (annually, via the club)
Manchester United Who's Who: 1945-85 (Tony Matthews)
Manchester United (in old picture postcards)
Manchester United Story (D Hodgson)
Manchester United: 25 years: 1974-99 (John Robinson)
Manchester United Superstars
Manchester United: Tragedy, Destiny, History.
Manchester United: 25 years: 1974-99 (statistics)
Manchester United In The Sixties (Ian McColl) 1997
Manchester United: Winners & Champions (Alan Shorrocks)
Photographic History of Manchester United: Unseen Archives (Bellers, Absolom, Spinks) 1999 & 2001
Red & Raw: History of post-war United v. Liverpool Matches (Ivan Ponting) 1999
Red Dragons In Europe: A Complete Record (from 1956)
Red Voices (United From The Terraces)
Tartan Reds (Iain McCartney) 2002
The Day A Team Died (Frank Taylor)
The Definitive Newton Heath (Alan Shury & Brian Landamore) 2002
The Team That Wouldn't Die: Man Utd. (John Roberts) 1975 & 1998
The Illustrious History of Manchester United (David Meek & Tom Tyrrell) 2001
The Illustrated History of Manchester United: 1878-2001
The Irish Connection: United's Irishmen (Stephen McGarrigle)
The Official Manchester United Illustrated Encyclopaedia (various)
The Red Army (Manchester United)
The Unique Treble (Alex Ferguson's Inside Story: Match by Match) 1998-99
The Manchester United Alphabet (Garth Dykes) 1878-1994
There's Only One United (Geoffrey Green)
Three In A Row (Championship hat-trick: 2000-01)
United: Day By Day At Old Trafford (G Betts) 1998
United: The Busby Era (Mike Prestage) 2002

Varia
A-Z of Manchester Football (D Brandon) 1978
A Rough Guide to Man Utd (J White & A Mitten) 2001-02
Always In The Running (The Manchester United Dream Team) 1996
Beyond The Final Whistle (A Life of Football & Faith) John Boyers, Chaplain, MUFC
For Club And Country (Gary & Philip Neville) 1997-98

Manchester United Booklists (John White) 1988 & 1999
Manchester United Limited (The Rise of the World's Premier Club)
Official Man United Superstars (Rebecca Tow) 2002
Red Devils (Richard Kurg) 1998
Reds In The Hood (Terry Christian)
United! Despatches From Old Trafford
United In 2000 (Reds' Fans Review of the Season)
The Official Man Utd Superstars (Rebecca Tow) 2002
There's also been the Manchester United Football Book and in 2001-02, the 37th edition
was published..
The Charlton Brothers (Bobby & Jack)
Jack & Bobby (Charlton) (Leo McKinstry) 2002
Give A Little Whistle (G Hill/C Thomas)
Red Reviewed (United programme survey: 1946-58) by Roy Cavanagh

Other Publications by players (etc) with a United connection
Forward With Leeds (Johnny Giles)
In The Firing Line (Jim Leighton)
Only A Game (Eamonn Dunphy) 1976-87
My Life (Andy Goram)
* Dunphy also wrote 'Unforgettablee Fire - The Story of U2'

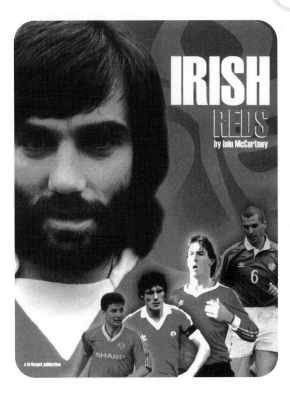

BOOTH, William

Born: Stockport, October 1880.
Career: Edge Lane FC, NEWTON HEATH (November 1900-May 1901).
Bill Booth, a reserve left-winger, replaced Jimmy Fisher for two League
games in December 1900, against Blackpool and Glossop, both of which
ended in victories, 4-0 and 3-0 respectively.
Club record: 2 apps.

BOOTLE

The clubs met in the Football Alliance (1889-92) the forerunner of the Football League's
2nd Division.
The Heathen's Alliance results v. Bootle:

Season	Home	Away
1889-90	W 3-0	L 1-4
1890-91	W 2-1	L 0-5
1891-92	W 4-0	D 1-1

FA Cup Record

	Round	Venue	Result
1890-91	2 (Qual)	Away	L 0-1

Fact File
Remarkably both clubs had first team fixtures in the Alliance on the day of their only FA Cup meeting, both fielding reserve teams for the Cup-tie.
Bootle entered the Football League in 1892 the same season as Newton Heath, but in Division Two, becoming Liverpool's second club alongside
Everton just as Liverpool AFC were being formed at Anfield Road, after Everton had moved to Goodison Park. Bootle only survived one season,
and even though the club finished 8th out of 12 they decided that the cost of running a League club was too much for their slender resources,
resigning from the League.

BORDEAUX

United capably 'doubled up' over the French team in the first stage of the 1999-2000 European Champions League - perhaps playing better
away than at home! They won 2-0 at Old Trafford and 2-1 in France
Players with both clubs: E Cantona, J Olsen, W Prunier.

BORUSSIA DORTMUND

United first met the Bundesliga side in their first season of European Cup football, 1956-57. Having disposed of RSC Anderlecht 10-0 three
weeks earlier, United raced into a 3-0 lead early in the first half (Dennis Viollet 2 & David Pegg the scorers). Expecting another rout, the 75,798
Maine Road crowd settled down for more of the same, but Dortmund stunned everyone (except their own fans) by outplaying United in the
second-half and in the end the home side were glad to hang on for a narrow 3-2 victory. A 0-0 draw in Germany saw United progress into the
next round, mightily relieved!
Dortmund beat United 1-0 in both legs of the 1996-97 European Cup semi-final.
Bobby Charlton scored five of United's 10 goals against the German side in their 10-1 aggregate Fairs Cup second round victory in 1964-65. He
netted a hat-trick in the 6-1 away win.
Player with both clubs: J. Kirovski.

BOSNICH, Mark John

Born: Fairfield, Sydney, Australia, 13 January 1972.
Career: Croatia Sydney, Liverpool (trialist, 1988-89), MANCHESTER UNITED (non-contract professional, June
1989), Croatia Sydney (June 1991), Aston Villa (1992), MANCHESTER UNITED (July 1999), Chelsea (January 2001).
Goalkeeper Mark Bosnich was brought up in the Croatian community of Sydney. He attended Manchester Polytechnic
as a student during his first spell at Old Trafford and made three first team appearances for the Reds before returning to
Australia. He replaced veteran 'keeper Nigel Spink at Villa Park and went on to appear in 228 matches for the Midland
club before returning to United.
Capped by his country at Youth and Under-23 levels, Bosnich has also played in 18 full internationals and starred for
Australia in the semi-final of the Olympic Games in Barcelona in 1992, but did not play for his 'host' country in the 2000 Games.
'Bozie' - who is adept at saving penalty kicks - gained two League Cup winners' medals with Villa (in 1994 and 1996)
and after helping United win the Premiership title in 2000, he suddenly found himself third choice at Old Trafford,
following the arrival of French World Cup star Fabien Barthez. In November 1999 he turned down the chance to join

47

the Scottish club, Celtic - preferring to fight for his place at United! However, he had second thoughts and two months later moved to Chelsea instead, having made less than 40 senior appearances for the Reds during his two spells with the club. He did not appear in the London club's first team until October 2001, having been relegated to third choice 'keeper at one point!

•Bosnich was fined £1,000 as well as receiving a stern warning from the FA for his 'Hitler-style' impression ('Sieg Heil') at White Hart Lane in October 1996.

Club record: 38 apps.

BOURNEMOUTH (AFC)

United's FA Cup results v Bournemouth:

	Round	Venue	Result
1948-49	3	Home	W 6-0
1956-57	6	Away	W 2-1
1983-84	3	Away	L 0-2
1984-85	3	Home	W 3-0
1988-89	5	Away	D 1-1
	Replay	Home	W 1-0

United's League Cup results v Bournemouth:

	Round	Venue	Result
1982-83	2 (1)	Home	W 2-0
	2 (2)	Away	D 2-2

Fact File

Although the clubs have never met in League action, two FA Cup-ties have been memorable.

In 1957 as United chased a 'treble' Bournemouth had shocked the football world by removing mighty Tottenham Hotspur in the 5th round at Dean Court - now they aimed to oust United! An upset was clearly on the cards as the Cherries led 1-0 at half-time. But United, having played with 10 men since early in the game when Mark Jones was stretchered off, stormed back with two second-half goals from Johnny Berry seeing them safely through to the Hillsborough semi-final after a thrilling tussle.

In 1984 Harry Redknapp's unfancied Third Division side caused one of the Cup's greatest upsets as United were dumped out at the third round stage, losing 2-0 at Dean Court. This was a famous victory for the Cherries.

Players with both clubs include: R Beardsmore, C Casper, G Farrow (United WW2), R Ferdinand, D Givens, E Green, G Haigh (United WW2), R Hampson (United reserve), G Hill (Bournemouth trialist), E MacDougall, J McDonald (United WW2), J O'Shea, M Rawlinson (United reserve), J Rowley, M Simmonds (United reserve), P Teather (United reserve), G Tomlinson, W Tyler (United reserve).
Also associated: M Busby (United manager, Bournemouth player as WW2 guest), D Williams (Bournemouth player, United coach)

BOYD, Henry

Born: Pollockshaws, Scotland, 1868.

Career: Sunderland Albion, Burnley (1892), West Bromwich Albion (£50, autumn 1892), Woolwich Arsenal (1894), NEWTON HEATH (£45, January 1897), Falkirk (August 1899).

Centre-forward Henry Boyd averaged a goal every two games for Newton Heath. He was the first player to notch 20 League goals in a season for the club, doing so in 1897-98 when he opened up by netting a hat-trick in each of the opening two matches against Lincoln City and Burton Swifts. He had earlier scored twice on his debut, in a 6-0 win over Loughborough in February 1897. A rough and ready inside or centre-forward, Boyd unfortunately had disciplinary problems and was suspended for a week for missing training and then received a fortnight's ban for going AWOL! On leaving the club in the summer of 1899, he returned to his native Scotland.

Club record: 60 apps. 32 goals (also 21 'other' apps, 10 goals)

BOYD, William Gillespie

Born: Cambuslang, Scotland, 27 November 1905. Died: Bristol, December 1967.

Career: Larkhall Thistle, Clyde (£2,250, 1930), Sheffield United (late 1933), MANCHESTER UNITED (February 1935), Workington (September 1935) Luton Town (1935), Southampton (1936), Weymouth (1937). Retired 1939.

Centre-forward Billy Boyd - a former shipyard worker - scored over 200 goals in three seasons for Larkhall Thistle before transferring to Clyde. He represented the Scottish League on three occasions and gained two full caps for his country, both in 1931. Despite only having a brief flourish with United, he drew up an excellent record in English and Scottish football, scoring 143 goals in 191 League games.

Club record: 6 apps. 4 goals

BOYLE, Thomas W

Born: Sheffield, 1897.

Career: Bullcroft Colliery FC, Sheffield United (1921), MANCHESTER UNITED (March 1929), Macclesfield (May 1930), Northampton Town (player-manager, 1930), Scarborough (manager, 1935).

Inside-forward Tommy Boyle, a rough and ready Yorkshireman who never really settled down at Old Trafford, gained an FA Cup winners medal with Sheffield United prior to joining the Reds in 1929. He played in well over 300 major competitive games and netted more than 80 goals during his career but did not figure in football after the Second World War. In later life was a publican on the outskirts of Middlesbrough.

Boyle's father also played for Sheffield United

Club record: 17 apps. 6 goals

48

BRADBURY, Leonard

Born: Northwich, 1914

Career: Manchester University, Northwich Victoria (season 1934-35), MANCHESTER UNITED (amateur forms, May 1935), Northwich Victoria (January 1937), Corinthians (& Birmingham University), MANCHESTER UNITED (August 1938). Retired in 1942.

Len Bradbury was an amateur footballer and student teacher at Altrincham Grammar School when he joined United second time round in 1938. A utility forward and England amateur international (capped against Ireland in 1936), he scored on his League debut for United against Chelsea in January 1939. He had earlier assisted the famous amateur side, Corinthians, while attending Birmingham University. He appeared for the Combined Universities team in 1937, starring in a 4-1 win over the FA Amateur XI at Exeter City's St James' Park ground..

Club record: 2 apps. One goal

BRADFORD (PARK AVENUE)

United's League results v Park Avenue:

Season	Div	Home	Away	Season	Div	Home	Away
1914-15	1	L 1-2	L 0-5	1932-33	2	W 2-1	D 1-1
				1933-34	2	L 0-4	L 1-6
1919-20	1	L 0-1	W 4-1	1934-35	2	W 2-0	W 2-1
1920-21	1	W 5-1	W 4-2	1935-36	2	W 4-0	L 0-1
1931-32	2	L 0-2	L 1-3	1937-38	2	W 3-1	L 0-4

Summary of League results:

	P	W	D	L	F	A
Division 1	6	3	0	3	14	12
Division 2	12	5	1	6	16	24
Home	9	5	0	4	17	12
Away	9	3	1	5	13	24
Total	18	8	1	9	30	36

United's FA Cup results v Park Avenue:

	Round	Venue	Result
1946-47	3	Away	W 3-0
1948-49	4	Home	D 1-1
	Replay	Away	D 1-1 aet
	2nd R	Home	W 5-0

Fact File

Bradford was elected to the Football League in 1908, five years after their city neighbours. They had a remarkable history: in April 1907 the professional rugby players of the Park Avenue club, seeing how well Bradford City were faring, decided to change codes. The rugby club had shared the Park Avenue CC ground; now with the aid of an affluent benefactor the players acquired an adjoining field hiring stadium specialist Archibald Leitch to build a Football Ground. The club immediately applied to the Football League for admission, but on refusal was astonishingly accepted into the Southern League despite their geographical position. The following season the fledgling club formed themselves into a Limited Company with benefactor Harry Briggs as chairman. Bradford was now immediately elected to the Football League in time for the 1908-09 season. For three seasons either side of the First World War, the city of Bradford, a rugby stronghold, had two First Division sides, Bradford played 51 seasons in the Football League before failing to gain re-election in 1970, replaced by Cambridge United.

The three 4th round FA Cup matches involving the two clubs in January/February 1949 attracted an astonishing 183,205 spectators in a ten day period. There were 82,771 present at Maine Road to witness a 1-1 draw. Some 30,000 fans saw the replay finish with the same scoreline at Park Avenue the following Saturday and then 70,434 assembled at Maine Road for the second replay on the Monday afternoon when United won 5-0. There were a record number of funerals taking place that day!!

Players with both clubs include: G Ainsley (United WW2), G Andrews (United reserve), B Asquith (Park Avenue WW2), J Brown, J Christie, G Crowther (United reserve), J Downie, J Dyer, G Gallon (United WW2), J Greenwood (United reserve), V Hayes, S Lynn, P McBride (United reserve), J McClelland, K McDonald, J Moody, J Myerscough, S Robertson, J Scott, T Spratt (United reserve), E Thompson (Park Avenue trialist), A Tonge (United reserve), H Topping, J Turnbull, A Turnbull, A Warburton (Park Avenue WW2), R White (United WW2).

Also associated: J Breedon and J Rowley (United players, Park Avenue managers),

BRADFORD CITY

United's League results v. City:

Season	Div	Home	Away	Season	Div	Home	Away
1903-04	2	W 3-1	D 3-3	1922-23	2	D 1-1	D 1-1
1904-05	2	W 7-0	D 1-1	1923-24	2	W 3-0	D 0-0
1905-06	2	D 0-0	W 5-1	1924-25	2	W 3-0	W 1-0
1908-09	1	W 2-0	L 0-1	1931-32	2	W 1-0	L 3-4
1909-10	1	W 1-0	W 2-0	1932-33	2	L 0-1	W 2-1
1910-11	1	W 1-0	L 0-1	1933-34	2	W 2-1	D 1-1
1911-12	1	L 0-1	W 1-0	1934-35	2	W 2-0	L 0-2
1912-13	1	W 2-0	L 0-1	1935-36	2	W 3-1	L 0-1
1913-14	1	D 1-1	D 1-1				
1914-15	1	W 1-0	L 2-4	1999-00	PL	W 4-0	W 4-0
1919-20	1	D 0-0	L 1-2	2000-01	PL	W 6-0	W 3-0
1920-21	1	D 1-1	D 1-1				
1921-22	1	D 1-1	L 1-2				

Summary of League results:

	P	W	D	L	F	A
Premier League	4	4	0	0	17	0
Division 1	20	7	6	7	19	17
Division 2	22	11	7	4	42	20
Home	23	15	6	2	45	9
Away	23	7	7	9	33	28
Total	46	22	13	11	78	37

United's League Cup results v City:

	Round	Venue	Result
1960-61	2	Away	L 1-2
1982-83	3	Away	D 0-0
	Replay	Home	W 4-1

United's FA Cup results v City:

	Round	Venue	Result
1922-23	1	Away	D 1-1
	Replay	Home	W 2-0

Players with both clubs include: B Asquith, S Barkas (United WW2), W Bryant, F Buckley, W Bullimore (United reserve), D Byrne, A Davies, A Dee (United reserve), S Dimond (United reserve), M Duxbury, D Ellis, J Gallon (United WW2), J Garvey, K Goddard (United reserve), E Goldthorpe, A Graham (also City coach & caretaker-manager), P Hall, H Hardman (also United director & chairman), W Heseltine (United reserve), W Jarvis, J O'Kane, F Potts (United reserve), L Sharpe, J Spence, F Stapleton (City player-manager), G Tomlinson, W Tyler (United reserve), G Walsh, A Westwood (United reserve), A Woodruff (United WW2).

Also associated: G Livingstone (United player, City trainer), J Sutcliffe (United player, City trainer), R Brocklebank (United WW2 player, City manager).

49

BRADLEY, Warren

Born: Hyde, 20 June 1933

Career: Durham City, Bolton Wanderers (amateur, 1954), Bishop Auckland (amateur 1955), MANCHESTER UNITED (amateur February 1958, professional November 1958), Bury (£40,000, March 1962), Northwich Victoria (1963), Macclesfield (late 1963), Bangor City (1964), Macclesfield (1966). Retired from competitive football in 1967

Right-winger Warren Bradley was only 5ft 5ins tall, but he was all heart, a positive footballer who loved a challenge. He turned in some great displays as an intelligent, sprightly winger who forged a telepathic partnership with Dennis Viollet, averaging a goal every three games for United (in League & FA Cup).

Another teacher/footballer, he played as an amateur for ten years before turning professional in 1958. He joined United in the aftermath of the Munich air disaster when a number of other Bishop Auckland players also volunteered to assist the club, mainly to allow the reserve side to complete its fixture list. Capped by England on three occasions at senior level, he also won two amateur caps and was twice an FA Amateur Cup winner with Bishop Auckland. Bradley, who remained a schoolteacher until his retirement, was the headmaster of a Manchester comprehensive school in the 1970s.

Club record: 66 apps. 21 goals

BRATT, Harold

Born: Salford, 8 October 1939

Career: Salford Schoolboys, Lancashire Schoolboys, MANCHESTER UNITED (amateur June 1955, professional November 1957), Doncaster Rovers (May 1961-63).

Half-back Harold Bratt's only senior game for United was in the 2nd round of the League Cup against Bradford City at Valley Parade in November 1960, a tie the Reds lost 2-1 in absolutely dreadful weather conditions. He represented England in Schoolboy internationals and gained an FA Youth Cup winners' medal in 1958.

Club record: one app.

BRAZIL, Alan Bernard

Born: Glasgow, 15 June 1959

Career: Celtic Boys' Club, Ipswich Town (1975) Detroit Express (on loan, 1978), Tottenham Hotspur (£450,000, 1983), MANCHESTER UNITED (£625,000, June 1984), Coventry City (January 1986), Queen's Park Rangers (1986-87), Whitham Town (early 1988), Chelmsford City (mid- 1988), FC Baden, Switzerland (season 1988-89), Chelmsford City (mid-1989), Southend Manor (1989), Bury Town (season 1989-90), Stambridge (1990), Chelmsford City (again, 1991), Wivenhoe Town (season 1991-92). Retired as a player in 1992.

Striker Alan Brazil holds the record for scoring most goals in a League game for Ipswich Town - five versus Southampton in February 1981. He also helped the Portman Road club win the UEFA Cup and finish runners-up on two occasions in the League. Brazil contributed reasonably well to United's cause (12 goals scored). A Scottish international at both Under-21 and senior levels (13 full caps gained), his senior career came to an early end in 1987 when he suffered a back injury. He still continued to play at a lower level, serving several non-League teams as well as having a spell in Switzerland. He is now a prominent soccer analyst on BBC Radio 5 (& local channels). It would not be unfair to say that Brazil's best footballing days were spent at Portman Rd, for he was a big disappointment at Old Trafford.

Club record: 44 apps. 12 goals

BRAZIL, Derek Michael

Born: Dublin, 14 December 1968

Career: St Kevin's Boys National School, Finglas Patrician College, Belvedere FC, Rivermount Boys' Club, trialist with West Ham United, Manchester City, Tottenham Hotspur and Chelsea, MANCHESTER UNITED (March 1986-August 1992). Served on loan with Oldham Athletic (1990), Swansea City (1991) and Cardiff City (1992) whilst at Old Trafford before joining Cardiff City permanently (mid 1992). Later assistant-manager and then manager of Notts County (2001-02).

Former Gaelic footballer Derek Brazil made two substitute League appearances in defence for United, his first against Everton in May 1989, his second versus Millwall in February 1990.

A Republic of Ireland international at Under-15, Under-18 and 'B' team levels, he helped Cardiff win the Third Division title in 1992-93 and went on to appear in almost 150 League and Cup games for the Welsh club before quitting top-class football in 1997.

Brazil's father played for Shamrock Rovers.

Club record: 2 apps.

BREEDON, John Norman

Born: South Hiendley near Barnsley, 29 December 1907,

Career: South Hiendley FC, Barnsley (1928), Sheffield Wednesday (1930), MANCHESTER UNITED (July 1935). Guested for Bolton Wanderers and Manchester City during WW2, then Burnley (October 1945), Halifax Town (manager, 1947-50), Bradford Park Avenue (manager, 1955), Leeds United (scout, 1960s). Retired from football in 1965-66..

Goalkeeper Jack Breedon, well built and a good shot-stopper, made 171 appearances for United during WW2. A Yorkshireman, he made his debut for United against Plymouth Argyle a month after joining the club and made his last appearance against Sheffield United in a wartime fixture in December 1944. On losing his place to Jack Crompton, he was transferred to Burnley in 1945.

Owing to his wife's reluctance to leave Leeds, Breedon declined the position of manager of New Brighton in 1946.

Club record: 38 apps.

BREEN, Thomas

Born: Belfast, 27 April 1917

Career: Drogheda United, Belfast Celtic, MANCHESTER UNITED (November 1936), Belfast Celtic (September 1939), Linfield (1944-47), Shamrock Rovers, Newry Town, Glentoran.

Irish-born goalkeeper Tommy Breen made over 70 senior appearances for United during the last three seasons before World War Two, helping the team gain promotion from Division Two in 1937-38 when making 33 League appearances. On the outbreak of war he moved back to Ireland to play for his former club Belfast Celtic and remained there until the end of his career. In all he won nine full caps for Northern Ireland as well as representing the League of Ireland (as a Shamrock Rovers player). He also appeared in five games for the Northern Ireland Regional team during the period 1942-46 and gained three Irish Cup winners' medals, the first with Belfast Celtic in 1941 and the last two with Linfield, in 1945 and 1946.

Club record: 71 apps.

BRENNAN, Seamus Anthony

Born: Manchester, 6 May 1937. Died: Waterford, 9 June 2000.

Career: Manchester Schoolboy football, MANCHESTER UNITED (groundstaff, 1954, professional April 1955), Waterford (player-manager, August 1970).

Originally a forward, Shay Brennan, after a spell in midfield, settled down at full-back, able to occupy both flanks confidently. A neat, intelligent footballer, he retained his forward skills, always being constructive in his distribution. An FA Youth Cup winner with United in 1955, he actually played at outside-left and scored twice on his senior debut against Sheffield Wednesday in the FA Cup-tie at Old Trafford in February 1958, the first game after the Munich air disaster. He failed to make United's team in two FA Cup Finals (1958 and 1963) but did play in the 1968 European Cup-winning side. He also figured in two League Championship-winning teams (1964-65 and 1966-67) and gained a total of 19 full caps for the Republic of Ireland, as well as appearing in two matches for the FA. In later life he ran his own parcel/package courier business near Waterford. However, after a minor heart attack from which he made a good recovery, he sadly died whilst on a golf course at Tramore, County Waterford in 2000, aged 63.

Club record: 359 apps. 6 goals

BRENTFORD

United's League results v. Brentford:

Season	Div	Home	Away
1933-34	2	L 1-3	W 4-3
1934-35	2	D 0-0	L 1-3
1936-37	1	L 1-3	L 0-4
1938-39	1	W 3-0	W 5-2
1946-47	1	W 4-1	D 0-0

United's FA Cup results v Brentford:

	Round	Venue	Result
1927-28	3	Home	W 7-1
1937-38	5	Away	L 0-2

United's League Cup results v the Bees:

	Round	Venue	Result
1975-76	2	Home	W 2-1

Summary of League results

	P	W	D	L	F	A
Division 1	6	3	1	2	13	10
Division 2	4	1	1	2	6	9
Home	5	2	1	2	9	7
Away	5	2	1	2	10	12
Total	10	4	2	4	19	19

Players with both clubs include: T Baldwin, J Brown, CJ Butler (United reserve), A Capper, J Christie, A Dawson, J Feehan, W Gorman (United WW2), W Grassam, V Hayes, S Houston, G Hunter (Bees WW1), T Manley, M Pollitt (United reserve), S Ratcliffe (United reserve), P Roche, W Spratt

Also associated: M Busby (United manager, Bees guest player WW2), S Coppell (United player, Bees manager), J Bain (United player, Bees assistant-manager & manager), T Cavanagh (United trainer/assistant-manager, Bees trainer & manager), F Blunstone (Bees manager & coach, United coach).

BRETT, Frank Bernard

Born: Kings Norton, Birmingham 10 March 1899. Died: Chichester, 21 July 1988.

Career: Redditch, Aston Villa (1920), MANCHESTER UNITED (£300, February 1921), Aston Villa (August 1922), Northampton Town (1923), Brighton & Hove Albion (1930), Tunbridge Wells Rangers (1935), Hove FC (re-instated as an amateur, 1936). He retired in 1937 to go into business in Sussex.

Frank Brett's career took him to various parts of the country. A resilient full-back, he failed to get an outing with Villa (first time round) and after signing for United, the matter was subsequently placed before the FA Committee. As a result United were fined ten guineas (£10.50p) for having registered Brett as one of their players before his transfer from Villa Park had actually been sanctioned.

51

Brett returned to Villa Park in 1922 and then made over 250 League appearances for Northampton Town. He later did just as well with Brighton (131 League games in five seasons). During his competitive career Brett amassed well over 400 League and Cup appearances.
Club record: 10 apps.

BRIBERY

During a League match at Villa Park on 29 April 1905, Billy Meredith, the Welsh international winger, later a Manchester United player, but then associated with Manchester City, was alleged to have bribed an Aston Villa player with £10. Thirteen weeks later, on 4 August, after the matter had been looked into by an FA Commission, it was announced that Meredith had been suspended for nine months (until the end of that 1905-06 season). However, more investigations followed after City officials reported Meredith to the FA for attempting to obtain wages without playing! At a second hearing Meredith produced a letter, written by a Manchester City Director, which clearly indicated that the original bribery attempt was made with the blessing of the club and that he (Meredith) would be looked after if anything went wrong. When the FA inspected City's books it was discovered that the club had been paying its players more than the mandatory maximum wage of £4 per week. As a result the FA fined City £250, the secretary and Chairman were both suspended from football for life and the club's other Directors were ordered to resign. Seventeen players were suspended until 1 January 1907 and forbidden ever to play for Manchester City again. Meredith, who categorically denied the charge of bribery, claiming he was made a scapegoat, was lucky not to be banned for life (he in fact had his life ban reduced until 31 December 1906). City's discomfort became United's windfall as manager Ernest Mangnall stepped in to purchase Meredith and four other City stars in a 'job lot'.

BRIGGS, William Ronald

Born: Belfast, 29 March 1943
Career: MANCHESTER UNITED (groundstaff, July 1958, professional March 1960), Swansea Town (May 1964), Bristol Rovers (1965). Retired from competitive football in 1968.
Goalkeeper Ronnie Briggs played in two Under-23 and two senior internationals for Northern Ireland. Reserve to fellow countryman Harry Gregg and Dave Gaskell, his outings were limited during his four years as a 'pro' at Old Trafford. He was, in fact, an inexperienced 17 year-old when called up to make his League debut against Leicester City in January 1961. With Gregg and Gaskell both sidelined with injuries, the unlucky Briggs conceded six goals. A week later he did far better as United held Sheffield Wednesday to a 1-1 draw in a third round FA Cup-tie at Hillsborough. Alas, the replay at Old Trafford was a disaster as the Owls hooted through to a convincing 7-2 victory with the hapless Briggs spellbound. At that point his confidence was at rock bottom. United quickly signed amateur international Mike Pinner, thus allowing Gregg, Gaskell, and poor Briggs, time to recover!
Club record: 11 apps.

BRIGHTON & HOVE ALBION (Brighton United)

United's League results v. Brighton:

Season	Div	Home	Away
1979-80	1	W 2-0	D 0-0
1980-81	1	W 2-1	W 4-1
1981-82	1	W 2-0	W 1-0
1982-83	1	D 1-1	L 0-1

Summary of League results

	P	W	D	L	F	A
Division 1	8	5	2	1	12	4
Home	4	3	1	0	7	2
Away	4	2	1	1	5	2
Total	8	5	2	1	12	4

Fact File
The most memorable match between the two clubs was at Wembley in the 1983 FA Cup Final. Brighton, then a top-flight club, albeit languishing in the bottom reaches of the table almost throughout the season, inspired by their flamboyant manager Jimmy Melia, shook United by taking an early lead.
It took United some time to find their feet but once they had they scored twice through Frank Stapleton and Ray Wilkins (who netted with a wonderful left-footed chip) to edge in front, only for Brighton to storm back and take the game into extra-time thanks to Gary Stevens' fine equaliser. As the match entered stoppage time Gordon Smith found himself with the goal at his mercy and a great chance to win the Cup for Brighton. He couldn't miss - but he did - shooting straight at 'keeper Gary Bailey from six yards out and United survived! Brighton's fanzine, bears the name - inspired by the commentator's words - '...and Smith must score!'
United, of course, comfortably won the replay 4-0 with Bryan Robson scoring twice.

United's FA Cup results v Albion:

	Round	Venue	Result
1908-09	1	Home	W 1-0
1980-81	3	Home	D 2-2
	Replay	Away	W 2-0
1982-83	Final	Wembley	D 2-2 Aet
	Replay	Wembley	W 4-0
1992-93	4	Home	W 1-0

League Cup Record

	Round	Venue	Result
1992-93	2 (1)	Away	D 1-1
	2 (2)	Home	W 1-0

Summary of League results:

	P	W	D	L	F	A
Division 1	18	9	6	3	25	16
Division 2	16	5	4	7	22	23
Home	17	9	3	5	30	18
Away	17	5	7	5	17	21
Total	34	14	10	10	47	39

Players with both clubs include: R Beale, F Brett, F Buckley, J Carolan, B Cartman (Albion trialist), A Chesters (Albion WW2), S Crowther, J Davie (United WW2), A Dawson, K Goodeve (United reserve), P Hall, H Haslam (Albion trialist, WW2), N Lawton, W Longair, G Nicol, P O'Sullivan (United reserve), SC Pearson (Albion WW2), W Pendergast & T Pirie (United amateur/reserves), J Pugh, A Ritchie, A Rowley (WW2 guest), RW Smith (United reserve), N Tapken (Albion WW2), M Thomas, W Tranter, R Turner, J Wassall (Albion WW2).
Also associated: J Robson (manager both clubs, also Albion assistant-manager), D Sexton (United manager, Albion player), F Goodwin (United player, Albion manager)

BRISTOL CITY

United's League results v City:

Season	Div	Home	Away	Season	Div	Home	Away
1901-02	2	W 1-0	L 0-4	1923-24	2	W 2-1	W 2-1
1902-03	2	L 1-2	L 1-3				
1903-04	2	D 2-2	D 1-1	1931-32	2	L 0-1	L 1-2
1904-05	2	W 4-1	D 1-1				
1905-06	2	W 5-1	D 1-1	1974-75	2	L 0-1	L 0-1
1906-07	1	D 0-0	W 2-1				
1907-08	1	W 2-1	D 1-1	1976-77	1	W 2-1	D 1-1
1908-09	1	L 0-1	D 0-0	1977-78	1	D 1-1	W 1-0
1909-10	1	W 2-1	L 1-2	1978-79	1	L 1-3	W 2-1
1910-11	1	W 3-1	W 1-0	1979-80	1	W 4-0	D 1-1

United's FA Cup results v City:

	Round	Venue	Result
1908-09	Final	Crystal Palace	W 1-0

Fact File:

In over a century of football, United's only Cup meeting with City was in the 1909 FA Cup Final.

Players with both clubs include: D Bain, A Cole, A Downie, S Goater (United reserve), W Higgins, J Jordan (also City assistant-manager & manager), S McGarvey, R Milne, MM Morgan (United reserve), T Parker, J Picken, E Thompson.

Also associated: T Cavanagh (United trainer & assistant-manager, City player).

BRISTOL ROVERS

United's League results v Rovers

Season	Div	Home	Away
1974-75	2	W 2-0	D 1-1

Summary of League results

	P	W	D	L	F	A
Division 2	2	1	1	0	3	1
Home	1	1	0	0	2	0
Away	1	0	1	0	1	1
Total	2	1	1	0	3	1

United's FA Cup results v Rovers:

	Round	Venue	Result
1934-35	3	Away	W 3-1
1955-56	3	Away	L 0-4
1963-64	4	Home	W 4-1

United's League Cup results v Rovers

	Round	Venue	Result
1972-73	3	Away	D 1-1
	Replay	Home	L 1-2

Fact File

The FA Cup third round tie at Eastville in January 1956 provided one of the great giant-killing acts in the history of the competition as Second Division Rovers hammered 'The Babes' 4-0 and even missed a penalty in the process! United, top of the League at the time, had no excuses, well beaten by a better side on the day. Now able to concentrate solely on the League, United duly went on to win the Championship

Players with both clubs include: P Bradshaw (United trialist), R Briggs, A Butterworth (United reserve), N Culkin, W Draycott, GW Hicks (United reserve), L Martin, J Norton, and W Pendergast, T Pirie & D Wilson (United amateur/reserves).

Also associated: D Williams (Rovers' player, United coach)

BRONDBY IF

United eased through their 1998-99 European Champions League stage one matches against Brondby without any fuss or bother. After two goals by Ryan Giggs had earned them a positive result in Scandinavia (6-2) they reproduced the style and panache to run up another convincing victory at Old Trafford (5-0) to take the tie 11-2 on aggregate.

Player with both clubs: P Schmeichel

BROOKS, William Henry

Born: Stalybridge, mid-1873

Career: Stalybridge Rovers, NEWTON HEATH (February 1896), Stalybridge Rovers (August 1897), NEWTON HEATH (May 1898), Stalybridge Rovers (June 1899).

Reserve centre-forward Billy Brookes scored twice on his League debut for Newton Heath against Loughborough Town in October 1898.

Club record: 3 apps. 3 goals (also 2 'other' apps)

BROOME, Albert Henry, BSc

Born: Unsworth, Lancashire, early 1900

Career: South Salford Lads' Club, Manchester University, Northern Nomads, Oldham Athletic (amateur, 1921), MANCHESTER UNITED (January 1923), Oldham Athletic (July 1924, reverting to a part-time professional), Welshpool (1925), Stockport County (1927), Mossley (1928). Retired in 1930 to concentrate on his work as a commercial traveller which he commenced in September 1924 as a Latics' player. Earlier in his life Broome obtained a BSc degree at University.

Reserve inside-forward Albert Broome's only League appearance for United was against Barnsley (away) in April 1923 (2-2 draw).

Broome's brother, Thomas, was also a professional footballer.

Club record: one app

BROOMFIELD, Herbert C

Born: Audlem near Nantwich, 11 December 1878

Career: Northwich Wednesday, Northwich Victoria (1899), Bolton Wanderers (1902), MANCHESTER UNITED (April 1907), Manchester City (July 1908), MANCHESTER UNITED (as an amateur, October 1910-April 1911).

Goalkeeper Herbert Broomfield had two spells with the club, his second as cover for the second XI custodian. He took over the duties from Harry Moger at the end of the 1907-08 season when United won the First Division title. Trained as a landscape gardener, he quit football in 1911 (following the arrival at the club of Hugh Edmonds) to a concentrate on his business as a painter and decorator. Broomfield was a key figure with the Players' Union, assuming the role of secretary for a time in 1908.

Club record: 9 apps

53

BROWN, James

Born: Scotland, circa 1870
Career: Dundee Our Boys, NEWTON HEATH (June 1892), Dundee (August 1893).
Left-back James Brown who was signed with Fred Erentz and Jimmy Coupar, appeared in the first six League games of Heathens' inaugural League season of 1892-93. He was then replaced by John Clements, for whom he deputised later in the campaign (v. Notts Co). Playing in a reserve fixture at Darwen in 1892, Brown was involved in a purely accidental collision, causing his opponent (Tommy Aspden) injury from which unfortunately he later died.
Club record: 7 apps. (also 13 'other' apps).

BROWN, James

Born: Kilmarnock, 31 December 1908. Died: New Jersey, USA 1995.
Career: Loans Athletic Juniors, Plainfield FC, then Bayonne Rovers of New Jersey, USA(1927), Newark Skeeters, USA (season 1928-29), New York Giants, USA (season 1929-30), Brooklyn Wanderers, USA (1930-31), MANCHESTER UNITED (September 1932), Brentford (May 1934) Tottenham Hotspur (1936), Guildford City (1937), Clydebank (1940). After serving in the war, he returned to America (1948) and was appointed coach at Greenwich High School in Connecticut (1950-51), later serving as a player and president of the Greenport United Soccer Club (1951-52). He was then senior coach at the Brunswick School and coached in Connecticut for 22 years (to 1975) and during his time there he also managed the Polish Falcon Soccer Club, albeit briefly during season 1957-58.
Versatile wingman Jimmy Brown - who scored for the United States in their 6-1 semi-final defeat by Argentina in the 1930 World Cup Finals - had a useful scoring record with United during his two seasons with the club. He spent a lot of his early football days playing - and scoring - in the American Soccer League and later returned to the States where he became a highly-respected football coach.
Three of his brothers played football while his son, George, was capped by the USA v. Mexico in 1957.
Club record: 41 apps. 17 goals

BROWN, James

Born: Leith, 1907
Career: Belhavenock FC, Maryhill Juniors, Wishaw YMCA, East Fife (season 1926-27), Burnley (1927), MANCHESTER UNITED (£1,000, June 1935), Bradford Park Avenue (February 1939) Retired during WW2.
Stylish half-back James Brown (no relation to the other two players of the same name but born into a family of six brothers) made well over 100 first-class appearances for United, helping the Reds win the Second Division Championship in his first season at Old Trafford. A former coalminer and Scottish junior international, he was a part-timer player with East Fife when they were runners-up in the Scottish Cup in 1927. He made 240 senior appearances as skipper of Burnley (before joining United).
Club record: 110 apps. one goal

BROWN Robert Beresford

Born: West Hartlepool, 6 September 1927
Career: MANCHESTER UNITED (amateur May 1946, professional August 1946 - played RAF football in season 1947-48), Doncaster Rovers (January 1949), Hartlepools United (1951). Retired from league football in 1956.
Goalkeeper 'Berry' Brown made only a handful of first team appearances for United during the late 1940s. He joined the Reds straight after WW2 (1946) and had to wait until January 1948 before making his League debut, taking over the green jersey from Jack Crompton. He then saved a penalty in a 2-1 defeat at Sheffield United. He later made over 130 League and Cup appearances for his home-town club, Hartlepools.
Club record: 4 apps.

BROWN, Wesley Michael

Born: Manchester, 13 October 1979
Career: MANCHESTER UNITED (apprentice, June 1995, professional November 1996).
A stylish defender, cool and efficient, Wes Brown won England Schoolboy and Youth caps as a teenager and then moved steadily up the ladder by playing eight times for the Under-21 side before claiming his first full cap in April 1999 in a friendly against Hungary in Budapest. He later suffered with knee ligament trouble before successfully recovering to star with club and country again. Unfortunately yet another injury caused him to miss practically all of the second half of the 2001-02 season but he came back just in time and was duly selected in Sven Goran Eriksson's World Cup squad in Japan and South Korea in the summer of 2002. Brown, confident and highly-regarded by many, remains one of United's most promising young players.
Club record: 88 apps.

54

"Bruce's 19 goals in 1990-91 are believed to be the most scored by a defender in a competitive League season."

STEPHEN ROGER BRUCE

Born: Corbridge, Northumberland, 31 December 1960
Career: Newcastle Boys, Northumberland County, Wallsend Lads' Club, Gillingham (1977), Norwich City (£135,000, 1984 - transfer fee agreed to be paid in stages), MANCHESTER UNITED (£825,000, December 1987), Birmingham City (June 1996), Sheffield United (player-manager, 1998), Huddersfield Town (manager 1999, later joining the Board of Directors at The Alfred McAlpine Stadium), Nottingham Forest (part-time coach, 2000), Wigan Athletic (manager, mid-2001), Crystal Palace (manager, summer 2001), Birmingham City (manager, winter 2001).

A former shipyard worker, centre-half Steve Bruce made well over 400 senior appearances for United and scored more than 50 goals…not a bad return for a defender! Earlier - as a strong, determined midfielder - he had lined up in 234 competitive games for Gillingham (winning eight England Youth caps in the process). Then, after being successfully converted into a defender at Carrow Road, he added a further 180 appearances to his tally with Norwich, being voted 'Man of the Match' when the Canaries won the 1985 Milk Cup Final and then starring for the Carrow Road club's Second Championship-winning campaign the following season.

During his nine-and-a-half years at Old Trafford (up to

the summer of 1996) Bruce served United magnificently, skippering the side many times and helping them collect trophies galore. Indeed, he was a key member of three Premiership, two League Cup, two FA Cup, a European Cup-winners Cup, Super Cup and two FA Charity Shield winning sides as well as claiming a handful of runners-up prizes into the bargain. It was a crying shame that he never won a full England cap, being recognised only with Youth and 'B' honours for all the effort he put in as a solid, reliable and totally committed defender who formed a great partnership with Gary Pallister. Bruce's 19 goals in 1990-91 are believed to be the most scored by a defender in a competitive League season.

He made 84 appearances for Birmingham City before entering the bottom rung of the managerial ladder, initially with Sheffield United in 1998, later returning as boss of Blues halfway through the 2001-02 season. He then successfully guided the St Andrew's club into the Premiership (after a 16-year exile from the top flight of Englissh football) via the First Division Play-off Final at Cardiff's Millennium Stadium when, ironically, his former cub, Norwich City, were defeated on penalties after a 1-1 draw. In all Bruce amassed a total of 907 appearances at club level (111 goals scored).
Club record: 414 apps. 51 goals

BROWN, William

Born: Cheshire circa 1873
Career: Stalybridge Rovers, Chester (1894), NEWTON HEATH (May 1896), Stockport County (December 1896), Hurst Ramblers (season 1898-99).
Reserve centre-forward 'Rimmer' Brown spent some 18 months with the club. After an early flourish, when he played alongside Bob Donaldson and James McNaught, he was given few opportunities in the first team after that and following the arrival at the club of Henry Boyd he drifted into obscurity.
Club record: 7 apps. 2 goals (also one 'other' app)

BRYANT, William

Born: Rotherham, autumn 1872
Career: Rotherham Town (1894), NEWTON HEATH (April 1896), Blackburn Rovers (£50, April 1900). Quit competitive League football in 1902.
Outside-right William Bryant was a positive footballer, keen and energetic who had four good seasons with the Heathens. He was the first Newton Heath player to gain Football League representative honours, doing so against the Irish League in 1897, when he lined up in the same forward-line as the great England goalscorer, Steve Bloomer.
Club record: 126 apps. 35 goals (also 36 'other' apps, 11 goals)

BRYANT, William

Born: Shildon, 26 November 1913. Died: County Durham, winter 1975.
Career: Timothy Huckworth School, Durham Schoolboys, Bishop Auckland Training Centre Juniors, Cockfield FC (1931), Wolverhampton Wanderers (late 1931), Wrexham (1933), MANCHESTER UNITED (October 1934). Guested for Chester during WW2, then Bradford City (November 1945), Altrincham, Stalybridge Celtic.
Outside-right Billy Bryant's record with United was excellent - a goal every four games. He joined the club in a joint deal involving Tommy Bamford, the Welsh international centre-forward and they did very well together, both being members of United's Second Division Championship-winning side in 1935-36. Bryant also played for the Reds in the League (North) Cup Final v. Bolton Wanderers in 1945. His departure in 1946, prior to the resumption of League football after WW2, forced United manager Matt Busby to sign Jimmy Delaney from Celtic.
Club record: 160 apps. 44 goals

BSKYB

In April 1999, the Department of Trade & Industry blocked a proposed move by BSkyB to buy out Manchester United Football Club for £623 million. The offer was initially made in September1998.

BUCHAN, George

Born: Aberdeen, 2 May 1960
Career: Aberdeen (1970), MANCHESTER UNITED (May 1973), Bury (August 1974), Motherwell (on loan, season 1975-76).
Younger brother of Martin (q.v), fair-haired winger George Buchan's four appearances for United were all as a substitute, coming off the bench for his debut against West Ham four months after moving to Old Trafford from Pittodrie. After leaving football in 1976, he concentrated on his teaching profession.
Buchan's father, Martin senior, was also a professional footballer with Aberdeen.
Club record: 4 apps.

BUCHAN, Martin McLean

Born: Aberdeen, 6 March 1949
Career: Banks o'Dee 'A' team, Aberdeen (1965), MANCHESTER UNITED (£125,000, March 1972), Oldham Athletic (August 1983). Retired through injury in October 1984, then Burnley (manager, for five months in 1985).
Defender Martin Buchan made well over 450 senior appearances for United. He had captained Aberdeen as a 20 year-old and a year later went up to collect the Scottish Cup after helping his side beat Celtic 3-1 in the Final. Voted Scottish 'Footballer of the Year' in 1971, he won the first of his 34 full international caps for his country that very same year before United boss Frank O'Farrell swooped to bring him south to Old Trafford for a record fee in 1972. Over the next eleven-and-a-half years Buchan - cool, calm and collected - gave United supreme service, marshalling the defence admirably, captaining the side to FA Cup glory over Liverpool in 1977, thus becoming the first player to skipper a Cup-winning team both north and south of the border. He also collected runners-up medals for defeats in the 1976 and 1979 FA Cup Finals besides winning a Second Division Championship medal in 1975.
On leaving Old Trafford he went to help the Latics stave off the threat of relegation, and then, after retiring with a hip injury, he had a brief spell in charge of Burnley before leaving football completely to concentrate on his job as promotions manager for the sportswear company Puma, based in Lancashire.
Club record: 459 apps. 4 goals

56

BUCKLE, Edward W

Born: Southwark, London, 28 October 1924

Career: Royal Navy football, MANCHESTER UNITED (amateur October 1945, professional, November 1945), Everton (November 1954), Exeter City (1955-57), Prestatyn FC (player-manager, summer 1957), Dolgellau (season 1961-62).

Ted Buckle served in the Royal Navy during WW2 before joining the Reds as an amateur inside-forward. He was thought to be too slight for the rigorous challenges in centre-field so he was switched to the wing and played on both flanks for United. He scored on his League debut v. Charlton Athletic in January 1947, having earlier netted against Leeds United when appearing for the Reds for the first time in a wartime game (November 1945).

Club record: 24 apps. 7 goals

BUCKLEY, Franklin Charles (Major Frank)

Born: Urmston, near Manchester, 9 November 1882. Died: Walsall, 22 December 1964

Career: Aston Villa (1905), Brighton & Hove Albion (mid-1905), MANCHESTER UNITED (August 1906), Manchester City (September 1907), Birmingham (1909), Derby County (1911), Bradford City (1914), The Footballers' Battalion, the Middlesex Wanderers during WW1 (attaining the rank of Major), Norwich City (player-manager, 1919-20), Blackpool (manager, 1923), Wolverhampton Wanderers (secretary-manager, 1927-44), Notts County (manager, 1944), Hull City (manager, 1946), Leeds United (manager, 1948), Walsall (manager, 1953). Left football in 1955..

Frank Buckley served in the Army for five years (1898-1903, participating in the Boer War) before becoming a professional footballer with Aston Villa. A solid, attack-minded centre-half who tackled hard but fair, he failed to make the grade at Villa Park and moved to Brighton (with his brother Chris). He made only three League appearances for United. Buckley gained one England cap v. Ireland in 1914 as a Derby player, having helped County win promotion to Division One two years earlier. He worked as a commercial traveller (1920-23) between his managerial appointments at Norwich & Blackpool.

Buckley the manager - known as the 'Iron Major' - was unequivocal, progressive, ambitious and voluble. His ideas were freely communicated to the local and national press. He was totally against the use of the white football and it was he who advocated the numbering of players' jerseys for the benefit of supporters. He transformed Wolves from a mediocre Second Division side into a positive First Division outfit, leading them to the Second Division Championship in 1932, the FA Cup Final in 1939 and Wartime League Cup success in 1942. He introduced many great players to Molineux, including Stan Cullis, Jimmy Mullen and Billy Wright and then brought the legendary John Charles into the game at Leeds United. He quit football at the age of 72 and was still enjoying the game when he died in Walsall aged 81. He was associated with football for 53 years. Between them Frank Buckley and his brother Chris, who became Chairman of Aston Villa, amassed over 400 League and Cup appearances.

Club record: 3 apps.

BULLOCK, James

Born: Gorton, Manchester, 25 March 1902. Died: Stockport, 9 March 1977.

Career: Gorton FC, Crewe Alexandra (amateur, 1919), Manchester City ('A' team, 1920), Crewe Alexandra (professional, 1921), Southampton (1924), Chesterfield (1929), MANCHESTER UNITED (£1,250, September 1930), Dundalk (£1,000, June 1931), Llanelli (1932), Hyde United (1933). Left football in 1935.

Inside/centre-forward Jimmy Bullock netted 30 goals (including four hat-tricks) in his only season with Chesterfield before joining United, earlier having netted a staggering total of 166 goals for Southampton's second XI. Unfortunately he failed to stamp his mark on the game during his stay at Old Trafford but after a spell in the Irish Free State League, he bounced back in style with Llanelli. In season 1932-33 he represented the Welsh League and also gained a Welsh League Championship medal when he netted 43 goals.

Club record: 10 apps. 3 goals

BUNCE, William

Born: Lancashire circa 1879.

Career: Rochdale Athletic (1898), Stockport County (1900), MANCHESTER UNITED (July 1902-April 1903).

Reserve full-back Bill Bunce made the second of his two senior appearances form United against his former club, Stockport.

Club record: 2 apps.

BURGESS, Herbert

Born: Openshaw, Manchester, winter 1883. Died: Manchester, summer 1954.

Career: Gorton St Francis, Openshaw United, Edge Lane FC, Mosside FC, Glossop (1900), Manchester City (£250, 1903), MANCHESTER UNITED (December 1906-June 1910). Retired and became a successful coach, holding positions in Austria, Denmark, Hungary, Italy, Spain and Sweden. He returned to Manchester in 1932 and two years later took over as manager of Ashton National FC.

Full-back Herbert Burgess - 'a Pocket Hercules' - made his League debut (for Glossop) at the age of 18. He played in an international trial match halfway through his first season with Manchester City and shortly afterwards won the first of his four full caps while also helping City beat Bolton to win the 1904 FA Cup Final. Burgess was one of four City players signed by United chief Ernest Mangnall in an auction following the illegal payment scandal.

He was a member of United's League Championship winning side in 1908 before his career ended with a damaged knee.

Club record: 54 apps.

57

BURKE, Ronald Stewart

Born: Dormanstown, Yorkshire, 13 August 1921
Career: St Albans City, Luton Town (amateur, 1941). Guested for Liverpool, Manchester City, and Rotherham United during WW2. MANCHESTER UNITED (amateur May 1946, professional August 1946), Huddersfield Town (£16,000, June 1949), Rotherham United (1953), Exeter City (1955), Tunbridge Wells Rangers (1957), Biggleswade Town (1959). Retired as a player in 1961. Later worked for Rolls Royce (Watford).
Powerfully built centre-forward Ronnie Burke served in the RAF during WW2 and was spotted playing forces football in Italy by Jimmy Murphy, who was soon to become United's assistant-boss under Matt Busby. Having turned down offers from Arsenal and Liverpool, he had to battle hard and long for a place in the first team at Old Trafford due to Jack Rowley's excellence, but certainly came up with the goods when selected for duty. He was in United's FA Cup Final squad in 1948 and led the front-line in that year's annual Charity Shield game against Arsenal. He went on to net over 50 goals in almost 80 first-class games for Rotherham and ended his League career with a record to his name of 170 appearances and 92 goals. He remained in football until he was 39 years of age, despite a suspect knee!
Club record: 35 apps. 22 goals

BURKE, Thomas

Born: Wrexham, 1862. Died: Prestwich, Manchester, February 1914.
Career: Wrexham Grosvenor, Wrexham February FC (1882), Wrexham Olympic (1884), Liverpool Cambrians (1885), NEWTON HEATH (August 1886), Wrexham Victoria (May 1890).
Half-back Tom Burke - who worked as a painter for L &YR - had already gained five caps for his country (Wales) before joining Newton Heath as a 23 year-old in 1886. He appeared in a further three internationals for his country before leaving Heath after four years service. Burke, who also won County representative honours with Denbighshire and gained a Welsh Cup winners' medal with Wrexham in 1883, died of lead poisoning.
Club record: 5 apps. (also 116 'other' apps, 12 goals)

BURNLEY

United's League results v Burnley:

Season	Div	Home	Away	Season	Div	Home	Away
1892-93	1	D 1-1	L 1-4	1947-48	1	W 5-0	D 0-0
1893-94	1	W 3-2	L 1-4	1948-49	1	D 1-1	W 2-0
				1949-50	1	W 3-2	L 0-1
1897-98	2	D 0-0	L 3-6	1950-51	1	D 1-1	W 2-1
				1951-52	1	W 6-1	D 1-1
1900-01	2	L 0-1	L 0-1	1952-53	1	L 1-3	L 1-2
1901-02	2	W 2-0	L 0-1	1953-54	1	L 1-2	L 0-2
1902-03	2	W 4-0	W 2-0	1954-55	1	W 1-0	W 4-2
1903-04	2	W 3-1	L 0-2	1955-56	1	W 2-0	D 0-0
1904-05	2	W 1-0	L 0-2	1956-57	1	W 2-0	W 3-1
1905-06	2	W 3-1	W 1-0	1957-58	1	W 1-0	L 0-3
				1958-59	1	L 1-3	L 2-4
				1959-60	1	L 1-2	W 4-1
1913-14	1	L 0-1	W 2-1	1960-61	1	W 6-0	L 3-5
1914-15	1	L 0-2	L 0-3	1961-62	1	L 1-4	W 3-1
				1962-63	1	L 2-5	W 1-0
1919-20	1	L 0-1	L 1-2	1963-64	1	W 5-1	L 1-6
1920-21	1	L 0-3	L 0-1	1964-65	1	W 3-2	D 0-0
1921-22	1	L 0-1	L 2-4	1965-66	1	W 4-2	L 0-3
				1966-67	1	W 4-1	D 1-1
1925-26	1	W 6-1	W 1-0	1967-68	1	D 2-2	L 1-2
1926-27	1	W 2-1	L 0-1	1968-69	1	W 2-0	L 0-1
1927-28	1	W 4-3	L 0-4	1969-70	1	D 3-3	D 1-1
1928-29	1	W 1-0	W 4-3	1970-71	1	D 1-1	W 2-0
1929-30	1	W 1-0	L 0-4				
				1973-74	1	D 3-3	D 0-0
1931-32	2	W 5-1	L 0-2				
1932-33	2	W 2-1	W 3-2	1975-76	1	W 2-1	W 1-0
1933-34	2	W 5-2	W 4-1				
1934-35	2	L 3-4	W 2-1				
1935-36	2	W 4-0	D 2-2				
1937-38	2	W 4-0	L 0-1				

Summary of League results

	P	W	D	L	F	A
Division 1	76	32	14	30	127	125
Division 2	26	15	2	9	53	32
Home	51	30	8	13	118	67
Away	51	17	8	26	62	90
Total	102	47	16	39	180	157

United's FA Cup results v Burnley:

Season	Round	Venue	Result
1900-01	1	Home	D 0-0
	Replay	Away	L 1-7
1908-09	4	Away	W 3-2
1909-10	1	Away	L 0-2
1953-54	3	Away	L 3-5
1964-65	5	Home	W 2-1

United's League Cup results v Burnley:

Season	Round	Venue	Result
1969-70	4	Away	D 0-0
	Replay	Home	W 1-0
1971-72	3	Home	D 1-1
	Replay	Away	W 1-0
1974-75	4	Home	W 3-2
1984-85	2 (1)	Home	W 4-0
	2 (2)	Away	W 3-0

Test Match record v. Burnley:

Venue	P	W	D	L	F	A
Home	1	1	0	0	2	0
Away	1	0	0	1	0	2
Totals	2	1	0	1	2	2

These two matches were played at the end of the 1896-97 season and as a result, Newton Heath failed to gain promotion!

Fact File:
United's first home League game was played on 10 September 1892 (Division 1) against Burnley. A crowd of 10,000 witnessed the 1-1 draw.
In 1909 Burnley, in the lower half of the Second Division met United, League champions two seasons earlier, in the Fourth Round of the FA Cup at Turf Moor. The match was played in early March in blizzard conditions. United were clearly knocked out of their stride as Burnley defended a 1-0 lead, but after 72 minutes with the lines invisible, the referee called a halt much to Burnley's annoyance. The match had to be replayed four days later, this time in more benign conditions, United winning 3-2 going on to win their first ever FA Cup beating Bristol City in the final at Crystal Palace. Burnley fans never forgot how United escaped and over 50 years later, should Burnley be losing to United, voices from the terrace would cry "Stop the game, its snowing!". (See 'Abandoned Matches').
Over the Christmas period in 1963, United lost 6-1 at Turf Moor but 48 hours later they turned the tables by beating the Clarets 5-1 at Old Trafford.
Players with both clubs include: J Beddow, G Beel (United reserve), R Bennion (also Burnley coach & trainer), H Boyd, J Breedon, R Brocklebank (United WW2), J Brown (half-back), J Connelly, J Cunningham, B Donaghy, G Haigh (United WW2), M Higgins (Burnley trialist), C Hillam, W Jackson, R John (Burnley WW2), D Johnson (United reserve), R Johnson (United WW2), S Jones (United reserve), FP Kippax (Burnley amateur, United WW2), W Longair, T Manns, W Morgan, T Morrison (also Burnley coach), G Nevin, R Newsome (WW2 both clubs), A Noone (United reserve), J O'Kane, L Page, S Parker, M Phelan (also United coach), J Picken, J Roach (Burnley WW2), B Robson (Burnley trialist, also United player & coach), J Smith (Burnley WW2), C Waldron, J Walton, A Warburton, A Woodruff (United WW2).
Also associated: M Buchan (United player, Burnley manager), G Clayton (United player, Burnley assistant-manager), J Doherty (United player, Burnley Chief Scout), N Bailey (Burnley player, United coach), E Mangnall (United manager, Burnley secretary), T Cavanagh (trainer/assistant-manager, both clubs).

58

BURNS, Francis S

Born: Glenboig, Lanarkshire 17 October 1948.

Career: St Augustine's School (Coatbridge), Lanarkshire Schoolboys, MANCHESTER UNITED (amateur June 1964, professional October 1965), Southampton (£5,000, June 1972), Preston North End (1973), Shamrock Rovers (1981). Emigrated to Australia in February 1987 and later managed the Western Australia club, Italia FC.

Defender Francis Burns - who could play as a full-back or wing-half - made over 150 first-class appearances for United. Captain of the Scottish Schoolboys side, he then gained Youth and Under-23 international honours before securing his only full cap for his country versus Austria in Vienna in 1969. In all he spent eight years with the Reds before transferring to Southampton. Burns later linked up with his former Old Trafford colleague Bobby Charlton at Deepdale before ending his playing days in the Republic of Ireland.

Club record: 157 apps. 7 goals

BURTON SWIFTS/UNITED

United's League results v Burton:

Season	Div	Home	Away	Season	Div	Home	Away
1894-95	2	W 5-1	W 2-1	1900-01	2	D 1-1	L 1-3
1895-96	2	W 5-0	L 1-4	1901-02	2	W 3-1	D 0-0
1896-97	2	D 1-1	W 5-3	1902-03	2	W 1-0	L 1-3
1897-98	2	W 4-0	W 4-0	1903-04	2	W 2-0	D 2-2
1898-99	2	D 2-2	L 1-5	1904-05	2	W 5-0	W 3-2
1899-1900	2	W 4-0	D 0-0	1905-06	2	W 6-0	W 2-0

Burton waived their right to play their FA Cup replay at Peel Croft in 1902-03, choosing instead to play at Bank Street Clayton (attendance 7,000).

Summary of League results

	P	W	D	L	F	A
Division 2	24	14	6	4	61	29
Home	12	9	3	0	39	6
Away	12	5	3	4	22	23
Total	24	14	6	4	61	29

United's FA Cup results v Burton:

	Round	Venue	Result
1902-03	1	Home	D 1-1
	Replay	Away*	W 3-1

Fact File:

There were two professional clubs in Burton-upon-Trent, Staffordshire, in the late 19th century, Burton Swifts and Burton Wanderers; for a three year period 1894-97 both clubs played in the Second Division of the Football League. The strain of such a small town trying to accommodate two League Clubs proved too great, however, the clubs merging as Burton United in 1901.

When the Football League was formed in 1888 comprising just 12 clubs, a further 12 clubs, disappointed at not being included, formed the Football Alliance. Amongst these clubs were Newton Heath (one of the founder members in 1889) and Burton Swifts (joining in 1891); when the Football League decided to form a Second Division in 1892, most of the Alliance clubs gained entry, Newton Heath in 2nd position allocated to Division One, Swifts, lower down, allocated to the Second. Burton Swifts (later Burton United) spent 15 consecutive seasons in the Second Division before failing the re-election process at the end of the season 1906-07, playing Newton Heath (later United) in twelve of those seasons.

Players with all clubs (Swifts, United & Heath) include: T Arkesden, A Beadsworth, J Beddow, T hay, T Leigh, A Mitchell.

BURTON WANDERERS

League record

Season	Div	Home	Away
1894-95	2	D 1-1	L 0-1
1895-96	2	L 1-2	L 1-5
1896-97	2	W 3-0	W 2-1

Summary of League results

	P	W	D	L	F	A
Division 2	6	2	1	3	8	10
Home	3	1	1	1	5	3
Away	3	1	0	2	3	7
Total	6	2	1	3	8	10

Fact file

Burton Wanderers were established as early as 1871; in the early years Wanderers were regarded as the strongest team in Burton upon Trent, so it was a great surprise when neighbours Swifts acquired League membership in 1892. However, a memorable FA Cup-tie with Notts County in 1894 attracted a 6,000 crowd to Burton's tiny Derby Turn ground and this persuaded Wanderers to apply for Football League membership. After all, Notts were the leaders in the Second Division at the time and went on to win the FA Cup that year. Wanderers were accepted and spent three seasons in the Second Division, before resigning, to return to the Midland League.

They had their moments, however, inflicting a 9-0 defeat on mighty Newcastle United in 1894-95, still the Magpies' record defeat, not to mention 8-0 over Manchester City (their joint worst defeat alongside 1-9 v. Everton).

The amalgamated club, Burton United, survived until 1909; Wanderers' old ground Derby Turn no longer exists whilst Swifts' ground Peel Croft is now a rugby ground. The present Burton club (Burton Albion) has no connection with these two clubs.

Player with both clubs: T Arkesden

BURY

United's League record against the Shakers:

Season	Div	Home	Away	Season	Div	Home	Away
1894-95	2	D 2-2	L 1-2	1925-26	1	L 0-1	W 3-1
				1926-27	1	L 1-2	W 3-0
1906-07	1	L 2-4	W 2-1	1927-28	1	L 0-1	L 3-4
1907-08	1	W 2-1	W1-0	1928-29	1	W 1-0	W 3-1
1908-09	1	W 2-1	D 2-2				
1909-10	1	W 2-0	D 1-1	1931-32	2	L 1-2	D 0-0
1910-11	1	W 3-2	W 3-0	1932-33	2	L 1-3	D 2-2
1911-12	1	D 0-0	W 1-0	1933-34	2	W 2-1	L 1-2
				1934-35	2	W 1-0	W 1-0
1922-23	2	L 0-1	D 2-2	1935-36	2	W 2-1	W 3-2
1923-24	2	L 0-1	L 0-2				
				1937-38	2	W 2-0	W 2-1

FA Cup Record

	Round	Venue	Result
1927-28	4	Away	D 1-1
	Replay	Home	W 1-0
1928-29	4	Home	L 0-1
1992-93	3	Home	W 2-0

League Cup Record

	Round	Venue	Result
1987-88	4	Away *	W 2-1
1998-99	3	Home	W 2-0 aet

* Tie played at Old Trafford at Bury's request

Summary of League results

	P	W	D	L	F	A
Division 1	20	12	3	5	35	22
Division 2	18	7	4	7	23	24
Home	19	9	2	8	24	23
Away	19	10	5	4	34	23
Total	38	19	7	12	58	46

Fact File:

For several seasons now. United's reserve and Youth teams have played their home matches at Gigg Lane, Bury.

Players with both clubs include: G Anderson, W Bainbridge, A Bellis (United WW2), H Blew, D Bradley (United reserve), W Bradley, G Buchan, D Carter (United WW2), G Clegg (United reserve), H Cockburn, J Connelly, E Connor; W Fairhurst, J Gallacher, J Gemmell, W Gorman, B Grayson (United reserve), G Griffiths & W Griffiths (all United WW2), R Halton, J Hanlon, M Higgins, A Hill (United reserve), P Hughes (United reserve), D Johnson (United reserve), D Jones & W Keely (United WW2), D Keough (United reserve), E Kilshaw (United WW2), J McCrae, S McIlroy, C McKee (United reserve), P McGuinness (United reserve), G McKee , L Martindale (United WW2), A Montgomery (also Bury manager), R Mountford (United reserve), G Mutch, J Nicholson, A Noone (United Youth), J O'Kane, SC Pearson, M Pollitt (United reserve), D Robbie (also Bury trainer), F Roberts & J Robinson (both United WW2), C Sagar, C Waldron, J Watton, M Whiteman (United reserve), HG Williams (United reserve), T Wyles (United WW2). Also associated: J Crompton (United player & trainer, Bury coach), I Greaves (United player, Bury coach), W McGuinness (United player & manager, Bury reserve team coach & physio), R Smith (United reserve, Bury coach & manager),

BUSBY, Sir Matthew, CBE

Born; Orbiston, near Belshill, Lanarkshire, 26 May 1909. Died: Manchester, 20 January 1994.

Career: Orbiston Village FC, Alpine Villa (1924), Denny Hibernian (1927), Manchester City (professional, February 1928), Liverpool (£8,000, 1936). Guested for Bournemouth, Brentford, Chelsea, Hibernian, Middlesbrough and Reading during WW2 before joining MANCHESTER UNITED as player-manager in February 1945, retiring as a player in October 1945. He remained in charge of team affairs at Old Trafford until June 1969 when he became administration-manager, taking over briefly as caretaker-manager from December 1970 until July 1971. He was appointed Director of the club in June 1971 and remained on the Board for more than eleven years, up to August 1982. He was elected President of United in March 1980 and retained that position until his death. He was also elected Vice-President of the Football League (1982), later becoming a life member.

Matt Busby's name is synonymous with Manchester United. All that the club has become is largely attributable to the great man's vision and genius. It is doubtful if any of the wonderful success achieved by the club during the 1990s and early 2000s would have been possible without the groundwork laid down by Busby from 1945 onwards.

When Company Sergeant Major Instructor Busby signed on as United's manager on 19 February 1945 the club was in dire straits. Heavily in debt, the ground utterly devastated by the War and with little idea of the strength of the club's playing staff, Busby faced a massive and daunting task. He astounded the players by joining them all on the training pitch in his track-suit, still a wonderful player, capable of passing on his vast knowledge at first hand, his astute managerial skills finely honed during his Army service.

He cleverly converted mediocre players in their declared positions into top-line footballers in the positions where he believed they would perform far better in the future. Gradually a top-class team emerged from the chaos, with home matches staged at Manchester City's Maine Road ground soon attracting huge crowds as news of United's unique fluency and flair spread.

His loyal players did not let him down, buying time while his younger players were developed in the 'United way' through the club's Youth policy hitherto unheard of in top-class football.

The team finished runners-up in four of the first five post-war League seasons, also winning the FA Cup magnificently in 1948. Young footballers around the country were attracted like magnets to Old Trafford (where the club duly returned in 1949) and after the League Championship was won in 1952, the 'old' team was broken up and the 'Busby Babes' were born.

The football world was staggered that such a young team could achieve so much. Further League titles were won in 1956 and 1957. And this guaranteed United entry into the prestigious European Cup competition...despite the Football League's reluctance, Busby's vision seeing this as the only way forward.

Then came the tragedy of Munich, the team decimated in that fatal air crash, Busby, fighting for his life as his patched-up team reached the FA Cup Final for the second year running. Busby would consider long and hard whether he could bring himself to build another team, but his wife's gentle persuasion saw him back at the helm in 1958-59.

SIR MATTHEW
BUSBY, CBE

Soon another great team was assembled with Charlton, Best, Law and Crerand the key players as the League title was won twice more, in 1965 and 1967, and the FA Cup in 1963. Then, gloriously, the coveted European Cup was claimed at Wembley in 1968 following United's famous 4-1 win over Benfica to crown a wonderful career.

During the fifties and sixties, United had reached the European Cup semi-finals on four other occasions (1956-57, 1957-58, 1965-66 and 1968-69). The team also won the FA Charity Shield outright three times while the teenagers lifted the FA Youth Cup a record six times (five triumphs in successive seasons: 1952-53 to 1956-57 inclusive).

Yet life could have been so different for Busby! Born in a two roomed miners' cottage, deep in the Lanarkshire coalfield, a poor family which would be shattered by the First World War when Busby lost his father and all his uncles. Rather than send young Matt down the pit, the family planned to emigrate to America where he would hopefully become a teacher. But before the official papers came through, an offer from Manchester City was received. Busby signed on the dotted line and the family stayed put!

After problems settling in at Maine Road, Busby prospered following a chance switch from inside-forward to wing-half.

Busby went on to play in 226 first-class games for City, appearing in two FA Cup Finals, gaining a loser's medal in 1933 and a winners' prize twelve months later, also gaining a Scottish cap (1934). Two years later he was transferred to Liverpool, playing in 125 League and Cup games for the Merseysiders up to 1939.

During WW2 he became virtually the manager of the British Army football side which contained most of the top internationals of the day and he gained further caps for his country in seven war-time matches.

Manchester had become Busby's home and he was honoured with the Freedom of the City in 1967. He was awarded the CBE in 1958, being knighted a decade later and in 1972 was made a Knight Commander of St Gregory the Great by the Pope, one of the highest civil awards in the Roman Catholic Church.

He was also a member of the Football League Management Committee (from June 1973), a Football League vice-president (from February-July 1982) and Scotland team manager for a short period during the 1958-59.season.

In 1949 he was offered the job as manager of Tottenham Hotspur and also as coach to the Italian national side. He refused both positions....to stay with United.

* Matt Busby's initial grounding in football was with his local side. They had a certain reputation in the area, Orbiston village, with only 32 houses, being known as 'Cannibal Island' where visiting teams were never in danger provided they lost! Rare away winners had to sprint from the pitch at the final whistle and come back a day later for their clothes and personal belongings.

61

"What matters above all things is that the game should be played in the right spirit with the utmost courage, with fair play and no favour, with every man playing as a member of his team without bitterness and conceit."

Sir Matt Busby (from his speech at Manchester Town Hall when he received The Freedom of the City of Manchester).

BUSBY BABES

The phrase, which incidentally the man himself abhorred, was originally coined by journalist Tom Jackson of the 'Manchester Evening News.' It came into common usage after Busby named his team for the League match at Huddersfield on 31 October 1953. The ageing side which had won the First Division title in 1952, was now producing disappointing results. Busby planned to introduce his young players gradually but after turning out an experimental team for a friendly at Kilmarnock, decided to make wholesale changes.

The team against Huddersfield included: Ray Wood, Bill Foulkes, Roger Byrne, Jeff Whitefoot, Duncan Edwards, Jackie Blanchflower, Tommy Taylor and Dennis Viollet alongside Johnny Berry, with veteran Allenby Chilton and Jack Rowley making up the eleven.

Such a young side had never been seen, but the rest is history!

The phrase 'Busby Babes' is now a convenient tag for the team which perished at Munich, including all those players from this date in 1953 when Busby's great experiment was unleashed.

Here are some other United players, affectionately known as the 'Busby Babes', who made the first team (listed in A-Z order): Geoff Bent, Shay Brennan, Joe Carolan, Bobby Charlton, Gordon Clayton, Eddie Colman, Ronnie Cope, Alex Dawson, John Doherty, David Gaskell, Fred Goodwin, Ian Greaves, Bobby Harrop, Tony Hawksworth, Mark Jones, Peter Jones, Paddy Kennedy, Nobby Lawton, Eddie Lewis, Noel McFarlane, Wilf McGuinness, Ken Morgans, Mark Pearson, David Pegg, Albert Scanlon, Jackie Scott, Colin Webster, Liam 'Billy' Whelan and Walter Whitehurst

And there are a few reserves as well, namely Beckett, Beswick, Bratt, English, Fidler, Fulton, Holland, Hunter, Littler, Madison, Queenan, Rhodes and Smith who also grew up with the above 'Babes'.

BUTT, Nicholas

Born: Manchester, 21 January 1975
Career: Boundary Park Juniors, MANCHESTER UNITED (apprentice, June 1991, professional January 1993)

An all-action, non-stop midfielder with an aggressive presence on the pitch, Nicky Butt developed through the junior ranks at Old Trafford to become an important member of Alex Ferguson's squad.

Recognised by England at schoolboy, Youth and Under-21 levels (seven appearances for the latter) he has now gained well over 20 senior caps for his country. He helped United win the Premiership trophy in 1996, 1997, 1999, 2000 and 2001, the FA Cup in 1996 (having been a finalist a year earlier), the European Cup in 1999, the FA Charity Shield in 1996 and 1997 and the FA Youth Cup in 1992.

Butt, who signed a seven-year contract with United in 2000, was named in England's World Cup squad in Japan/South Korea in the summer of 2002.

Club record: 324 apps. 24 goals

BYRNE, David

Born: Ringsend, Dublin, 28 April 1905
Career: St Brendan's FC (Dublin), Shamrock Rovers (1926), Bradford City (1927), Shelbourne (1928), Shamrock Rovers (1929), Sheffield United (1932), Shamrock Rovers (early 1933), MANCHESTER UNITED (May 1933), Coleraine (February 1934) Larne, Shamrock Rovers (1935), Hammond Lane FC (1936), Brideville FC (1937), Shelbourne (1938). Retired in 1940.

Winger David Byrne served the club for nine months, acting as reserve to Scotsmen James Brown and Neil Dewar. Capped twice by the Republic of Ireland before joining United, he later added a third to his tally in 1934. He netted on his League debut for United in a 2-1 defeat at Bury in October 1933.

Club record: 4 apps. 3 goals

BYRNE, Roger William

Born: Gorton, Manchester, 8 February 1929. Died: Munich, 6 February 1958.
Career: Abbey Hey Junior and Burnage Grammar Schools, Ryder Brow Youth Club (1947), MANCHESTER UNITED (junior 1948, professional March 1949 until his tragic death).

Roger Byrne was a class footballer and a terrific captain. He never used to plan his game and therefore play instinctively. He was utilised at outside-left for a time but developed into one of the finest left-backs in world football, amassing a fine set of statistics with United.

After RAF service, he made his Football League debut against Liverpool in November 1951 in a goalless draw at Anfield in front of more than 42,000 fans, establishing himself in the first XI that very same season, ending it as a goal-scoring left-winger as United clinched the First Division Championship.

He soon settled down, however, in the number three position and from there he went on to skipper both United and England. He won two more League Championship medals (1956 and 1957) and appeared in an FA Cup Final as well as gaining 33 consecutive international caps for England, playing also in three 'B' team matches and on six occasions for the Football League representative side. It was a body-blow to United and England when he sadly lost his life at Munich on 6 February 1958.

As a teenager Byrne played in the same forward-line for Ryder Brow Youth Club as the future Lancashire and England fast-bowler Brian Statham.

Club record: 280 apps. 20 goals

C for...   CANTONA, Eric

Born: Paris, France, 24 May 1966.
Career: Auxerre (amateur, 1981, professional summer, 1983), FC
Martigues (on loan, 1985), Olympique Marseille (£2.2 million,
1988), Bordeaux (on loan, early 1989), Montpellier (on loan
initially, then signed for £300,000, 1989), Olympique Marseille
(summer, 1990), Nimes FC (£1 million, 1991), Sheffield
Wednesday (trialist), Leeds United, (on loan, then signed
permanently for £900,000, 1992), MANCHESTER UNITED
(£1.2 million, November 1992-May 1997). Retired to become
Director of Football at Olympique Marseille, later French Beach
soccer team (player-manager). Cantona also became a film star and
after retiring (from competitive football) he made three films:
Mookie, Les Enfants du marais & Elizabeth. His first film role was
in Le Bonheur est dans le Pre in 1995.
Eric Cantona was undoubtedly a genius of a player, possessing rare
skills which inspired a generation of young United professionals to
aspire for such excellence. A multi-talented forward, deadly in front
of goal, he was equally skilled at bringing his colleagues into the
game with his wonderful vision and deft touch. For five glorious
seasons Cantona bestrode the 'Theatre of Dreams' like a colossus,
head always held high, trade-mark collar turned up, the darling of
the crowd who bellowed his name to the tune of the 'Marseillaise',

all eyes drawn to his magnetic presence. Perhaps no player in the history of the game aroused such extreme of passion in rival supporters!

Yet there was also a down side, a dark side to his nature which had led him into trouble with officialdom, team-mates and opponents throughout a tempestuous career.

It seemed it was not possible to have one without the other! Raised in Marseille, coached by his father, he made rapid progress, his precocious skills much sought after. His French career, however, was liberally riddled with astonishing outbursts against colleagues, match officials and even a disciplinary panel.

Despite successes on the field (the French Cup won with Montpellier in 1990, then the League title with Marseille in 1991, while also gaining 45 full caps for his country 19 goals scored) he had become the 'enfant terrible' of French football. Sensationally announcing his retirement at the age of 25.

Regretting his hasty decision, but seeing no future in French football, Cantona tried his luck in England, but there was no rush for his services.

He briefly joined Sheffield Wednesday before moving on to Leeds United, who were seeking inspiration to win the last First Division Championship before the introduction of the Premier League as the Reds sought to break their 25-year impasse. Cantona, used mainly as a substitute, did the trick as United froze in the latter stages. In the following season's FA Charity Shield he scored a sensational hat-trick against Liverpool at Wembley and immediately Leeds' fans were looking forward to their French 'ace' leading them to the inaugural Premiership title. Then, incredibly Cantona was sold by Leeds to Manchester United for what was to prove a bargain fee of just £1.2 million! Immediately Cantona became the catalyst for United's great leap forward as he brilliantly provided goals, but more importantly convinced his team-mates that they were capable of becoming champions.

Cantona was certainly good for United, but equally United were good for Cantona as he finally found his spiritual home (Old Trafford). United's training methods were rapidly updated to the great benefit of the entire team as the League title was confidently claimed, Sir Matt smiling benignly from the stands. The next season came the 'double', Cantona netting two penalties in the 4-0 FA Cup Final win over Chelsea, but sadly Cantona's disciplinary record on the field was poor as red cards continued to pile up (he was dismissed twice in five days in 1994 v. Swindon and Arsenal).

Then, notoriously in 1995 as United chased their third consecutive Premiership crown, Cantona was involved in a disgraceful incident with a Crystal Palace supporter at Selhurst Park, following yet another red card. The authorities threw the book at the Frenchman, handing him an eight month suspension. A civil action saw Cantona receive a prison sentence, later commuted to 120 hours of community service. In his absence the team stuttered along, losing the title on the last day of the season to Blackburn Rovers, missing their talisman's cool presence!

Three months into the following season (October 1995) Cantona returned to orchestrate another glorious 'double', arch-rivals Liverpool falling in the FA Cup Final to his last minute volley. Then in 1996-97, a fourth Premiership title, Cantona now captain, but the disappointment of losing a European Cup semi-final in which the great man was culpable of a number of glaring misses caused him to assess his future. Out of the blue he announced his retirement and suddenly he was gone for good!

His legacy as a United legend is immense as his influence lives on in United's young team. Cantona was, and is, 'Le Dieu' to the adoring fans who still sing his name. His fellow professionals (PFA) voted him 'Footballer of the Year' in 1994 and the football writers followed with their award in 1996. We shall probably never see his like again.

Club record: 185 apps. 82 goals

ERIC CANTONA

CAIRNS, James

Born: Manchester circa 1873

Career: Ardwick FC (March 1892), NEWTON HEATH (August 1894-May 1895).

Reserve full-back James Cairns' only League game for Newton Heath was against Bury in April 1895.

Club record: one app.

CAIRNS, James

Born: Scotland, circa 1874

Career: Stevenston Thistle (1895), Glossop North End (1896), Lincoln City (1897), NEWTON HEATH (April 1898), Berry's Association (November 1898-99).

Reserve inside-forward Jim Cairns was another player who made just a single League appearance for United, lining up against Burslem Port Vale in October 1898, six months after joining the club.

Club record: one app. (also 2 'other' apps)

CAMPBELL, William Cecil

Born: Inverness, 25 October 1865

Career: Woolwich Arsenal (reserves), Preston North End (1890), Middlesbrough (1891), Darwen (1892), Blackburn Rovers (1893), NEWTON HEATH (January 1894), Notts County (March 1894), Newark (1894). Retired circa 1896. Inside-forward Bill Campbell was a nomadic footballer whose career took him to eight different clubs. In May 1894, he was banned for two years by the FA for trying to persuade a former colleague of his at Blackburn to join him at Notts County. He later worked for a cigar/cigarette company

Club record: 5 apps. one goal (also 2 'other' apps)

CAMBRIDGE UNITED

League Cup Records

	Round	Venue	Result
1991-92	2 (1)	Home	W 3-0
	2 (2)	Away	D 1-1

Fact File:
There have been no League or FA Cup meetings between the two clubs as yet.
United's League Cup results v Cambridge:
Players associated with both clubs: G Brebner (Man U reserve), D Dublin, A Duncan (Man U reserve), G Maiorana (Cambridge trialist), N Mustoe (Man U reserve), TE Smith (Man U reserve), D Walker,
Also associated: R Atkinson (manager of both clubs), M Brown (Man U assistant-manager, player-coach at Cambridge).

CANTONA, Eric

Refer to front of section.

CANTWELL, Noel

Born: Cork, Ireland, 28 February 1932

Career: Western Rovers, Cork Athletic, West Ham United (full-time professional, 1952), MANCHESTER UNITED (£29.500, November 1960), Coventry City (manager, October 1967), Republic of Ireland (manager, during season 1967-68), New England Teamen (manager/coach, 1972), Peterborough United (manager, 1972-77), New England Teamen/Jacksonville Teamen (manager/coach, 1978-82), Peterborough United (manager, 1986-88, later Posh general manager, 1989-90). Also PFA Chairman from 1966 to October 1967.

After appearing in 263 competitive games for West Ham and also gaining a Second Division Championship medal (1958), left-back/centre-half/centre-forward Noel Cantwell joined the ranks at Old Trafford. He made his debut for the Reds during the month he joined the club and three years later skippered the side to victory over Leicester City in the 1963 FA Cup Final. Able to play equally as well in defence or attack, Cantwell was an inspirational footballer, totally committed who loved a challenge. He was widely expected to take over from Sir Matt Busby as manager of United but instead he left the club to become boss of Coventry. Cantwell won 36 caps for the Republic of Ireland (19 as a United player). Cantwell also represented Ireland at cricket and in later life became a publican in Peterborough.

Club record: 146 apps. 8 goals

CAPE, John

Born: Carlisle, 16 November 1911. Died: 1994

Career: St John's Council School (Carlisle), Penrith FC, Carlisle United (1929), Newcastle United (1930), MANCHESTER UNITED (£2,000, January 1934), Queen's Park Rangers (June 1937). Guested for Carlisle United during WW2, then Scarborough Town (1946), Carlisle (again, 1946-47). Retired to become reserve team coach/trainer at Brunton Park.

Outside-right/centre-forward Jack Cape, fast and direct with a powerful right-foot shot, gained a Second Division Championship medal with United in 1935-36. In May 1934 Cape scored possibly the most important goal in the club's history at Millwall as United avoided relegation to the Third Division on the season's last day. Cape sealed a 2-0 win having previously laid on the first goal for Tommy Manley.

A rugby and soccer player at school, he netted a hat-trick for Newcastle against United in a 7-4 victory for his side in September 1930.

Club record: 60 apps. 18 goals

CAPPER, Alfred

Born: Northwich, early 1891.

Career: Winnington Park School, Winnington Bible Class FC, Northwich Lads' Club, Northwich Victoria, MANCHESTER UNITED (amateur January 1911, professional August 1912), Witton Albion (April 1913), Sheffield Wednesday (1914), Brentford (1921). Retired from League football in 1924.

Reserve winger 'Freddy' Capper's only League appearance for United was against Liverpool in March 1912 when he deputised for George Wall in the 1-1 draw. He made well over 150 League appearances during his playing career.

Club record: one app.

CAPTAINS

Over the years several players have captained Newton Heath/Manchester United, some much longer than others. Here is an unofficial list of the recognised team skippers from 1882 to 2001:

1882-1900
Sam Black
Joe Cassidy
John McCartney
James McNaught
Jack Powell
Harry Stafford

1900-15
George Hunter
Jack Peddie
Charlie Roberts
George Stacey
Harry Stafford

1918-39
Frank Barson
Jimmy Brown
Clarence Hilditch
George McLachlan
Walter McMillen
Pat O'Connell
Louis Page
Jack Wilson

1940s
Johnny Carey
Stan Pearson

1950s
Roger Byrne
Allenby Chilton
Bill Foulkes

1960s
Noel Cantwell
Bobby Charlton
Bill Foulkes
Denis Law
Maurice Setters
Dennis Viollet

1970s
Martin Buchan
Gordon McQueen
Willie Morgan

1980s
Bryan Robson*
Ray Wilkins

1990s onwards
David Beckham
Steve Bruce
Eric Cantona
Ryan Giggs
Roy Keane
Gary Neville
Jaap Stam
* Also captain in the 1990s.

Other players who have led United periodically include: Arthur Albiston, Johnny Aston snr, Johnny Berry, Shay Brennan, Henry Cockburn, John Connolly, Steve Coppell, Pat Crerand, Tony Dunne, Mike Duxbury, Duncan Edwards, Brian Greenhoff, David Herd, Stewart Houston, Mark Hughes, Paul Ince, Denis Irwin, Lou Macari, Brian McClair, Wilf McGuinness, Sammy McIlroy, Hugh McLenahan, Charlie Mitten, Kevin Moran, Gary Pallister, Mike Phelan, Albert Quixall, Jack Rowley, David Sadler, Peter Schmeichel, Frank Stapleton, Nobby Stiles, Ernie Taylor, Ian Ure, Jack Warner, Neil Webb, Norman Whiteside and even goalkeeper Ray Wood.

Captain's Log

•When United won the FA Cup for the first time in 1909, Charlie Roberts skippered the side. Johnny Carey collected the FA Cup in 1948; Roger Byrne led the side in 1957, Noel Cantwell did likewise in 1963, Martin Buchan received the star prize in 1977 and Bryan Robson was team captain in 1983 and 1985. Buchan also captained United in two other FA Cup Finals - 1976 & 1979.

•In the 1990s, the League & Cup 'double' was achieved on three occasions with a different captain each time: 1994 (Bruce), 1996 (Cantona) & 1999 (Keane). Arsenal emulated United's feat of three doubles when they clinched their third success at Old Trafford in May 2002.

•A joyous and beaming Bobby Charlton lifted the European Cup at Wembley in 1968.

•Goalkeeper Peter Schmeichel skippered United to victory in the 1999 European Cup Final owing to a suspension imposed on Roy Keane.

•When United won the Premier League in 1993 & 1994, two captains simultaneously accepted the trophy - club captain Bryan Robson and team captain Steve Bruce.

•Bryan Robson took over the United captaincy from Ray Wilkins - one England international replacing another. Robson's reign of 12 years as skipper is a club record.

•The following players - all with a United connection - have captained England: Peter Beardsley, David Beckham, Bobby Charlton, Paul Ince, David Platt, Bryan Robson, Ray Wilkins.

•Peter Schmeichel (as a United player) led Denmark, Johnny Carey, Johnny Giles, Roy Keane, Noel Cantwell & Paul McGrath all captained the Republic of Ireland on the international front while Ryan Giggs skippered Wales in 2000-01. Full-back Carey also had the honour of skippering the Rest of The Europe side in 1947.

•When United changed its name from Newton Heath (1902) the first captain was Harry Stafford.

•Eddie McIlvenny (a United player, 1950-53) had skippered the USA in their surprise 1-0 victory over England at the 1950 World Cup in Belo Horizonte.

CARDIFF CITY

Summary of League results

	P	W	D	L	F	A
Division 1	24	11	7	6	45	37
Division 2	2	2	0	0	5	0
Home	13	5	6	2	28	19
Away	13	8	1	4	22	18
Total	26	13	7	6	50	37

FA Cup Record

	Round	Venue	Result
1921-22	1	Home	L 1-4

67

League record

Season	Div	Home	Away	Season	Div	Home	Away
1921-22	1	D 1-1	L 1-3	1954-55	1	W 5-2	L 0-3
				1955-56	1	D 1-1	W 1-0
1925-26	1	W 1-0	W 2-0	1956-57	1	W 3-1	W 3-2
1926-27	1	D 1-1	W 2-0				
1927-28	1	D 2-2	L 0-2	1960-61	1	D 3-3	L 0-3
1928-29	1	D 1-1	D 2-2	1961-62	1	W 3-0	W 2-1
1952-53	1	L 1-4	W 2-1	1974-75	2	W 4-0	W 1-0
1953-54	1	L 2-3	W 6-1				

Fact File

Duncan Edwards, aged 16 years, 185 days, made his Football League debut for United in the home against Cardiff on 4 April 1953.

Players with both clubs include: W Anderson, D Brazil, A Cashmore, A Chilton (City WW2), SC Davies (United trialist), M Delaney (United junior), S Evans, W Fielding, A Foggon, W Hullett (United reserve), D Jones, W Lievesey, K MacDonald, G McLachlan, M Martin, J Mellor, W Merry (United reserve), C Mitten (City WW2), G Moore, W Moyle (United reserve), W Owen (City WW2), T Pirie (United reserve), M Robinson, E Thompson, W Watson (United WW2), C Webster,

Also associated: F O'Farrell (manager of both clubs), R Smith (United reserve, City coach).

CAREY, John Joseph

Born: Dublin, 23 February 1919. Died: 1995

Career: Home Farm (Dublin), St James' Gate FC, MANCHESTER UNITED (£250, November 1936), Blackburn Rovers (manager, August 1953), Everton (manager, 1958), Leyton Orient (manager, 1961), Nottingham Forest (manager, 1963-68), Republic of Ireland (manager), Blackburn Rovers (joint-manager with Eddie Quigley, 1969-70), MANCHESTER UNITED (part-time coach 1980s). Also worked in the treasurer's office of Trafford Borough Council (based at Sale, Cheshire).

'Gentleman Johnny' Carey, United's right-back and captain during the immediate post-war year period, which saw him lead his side to FA Cup glory (in 1948) and the League Championship (in 1952), is revered as one of the club's greatest ever players, now firmly established as a United legend. A product of the famous Home Farm nursery, the eagle-eyed Louis Rocca spotted the young Carey, then a sprightly, intelligent inside-forward, playing with St James' Gate in Dublin. A £250 fee persuaded Carey to join United and he made his debut in September 1937, helping United to gain promotion from the Second Division that season and remaining a regular in the side until the outbreak of WW2.

When he resumed at Old Trafford in 1945, new manager Matt Busby soon realised that Carey's days as a forward were over, but recognising his leadership and organisational skills, decided his best place was at wing-half, where his skills could flourish. Quite soon, however, Carey - who had been nicknamed 'Cario' when he guested in Italy during WW2 - found himself at right-back, an inspired move, which allowed him to dictate United's strategy from a deep position which hitherto had only required brawn. With another converted forward, John Aston, at left-back, United's playing style was unique, the forwards relishing the quality passes supplied from the back.

Carey proved himself a most versatile defender, playing in every position including goalkeeper in an emergency at Sunderland after Jack Crompton had been taken ill prior to kick-off.

Carey was also a star at international level, making his debut for Eire (as the Republic of Ireland was known in those days) in the same season as he first played for United. In all, he played 29 times for Eire as well as lining up in seven internationals matches for Northern Ireland, being allowed 'dual citizenship' due to him volunteering to serve in the British Army.

In 1949 he captained Eire to a 2-0 victory over England at Goodison Park - the first ever home defeat by a country other than one from the United Kingdom. Three years earlier he had appeared in two matches against England over a period of three days for each of his countries!

In 1947, to celebrate the home countries' return to FIFA, a Great Britain side played the Rest of Europe at Hampden Park. Carey, captaining the European side in front of more than 135,000 spectators. At a celebratory meal after the game, a waitress congratulated Carey on his English - much to his obvious amusement.

In retiring in 1953, Carey as expected, became a much admired manager, first with Blackburn Rovers, steering them to promotion to Division One in 1958; then with Everton who reached their highest League position since the War (fifth in 1960-61); next at Leyton Orient whom he managed to lift into the top flight for the only time so far in the London club's history (1962) and then as boss of Nottingham Forest who he guided to the FA Cup semi-finals in 1967. He then returned to Ewood Park as joint-manager and finally ended his career in football by scouting for his beloved United.

John Carey certainly lived up to his name as a gentleman and a sportsman on the field. A man of disarming modesty and great humility, he never made a single enemy in a lifetime of football. When he was awarded the accolade of 'Footballer of the Year' in 1948 he commented that he was honoured to be mentioned in the same breath as the many great players who abounded in the First Division at that time, too modest to admit he was rightly judged as being the best.

Club record: 346 apps. 18 goals

CARLISLE UNITED

Fact File

There have been no League or League Cup meetings between the clubs as yet.

In fact, Carlisle have spent just one season in the 'top flight' (1974-75) and remarkably this was when United were in the Second Division!

Players with both clubs include: P Beardsley, E Bond, I Broadis (Man United WW2, Carlisle player & manager), J Cape, J Clark, A Davies, D Graham; S Jones & C Lynam (United reserves), D McCreery (Carlisle player-coach), S McGarvey, T Manns, T Parker, E Savage (Carlisle WW2), A Smith, E Sweeney, E Thompson, R Wallwork, GG Worrall (United reserve).

Also associated: H Gregg (United player & coach, Carlisle manager), A Asham (Carlisle player & manager, United scout), T Cavanagh (United trainer/assistant-manager, Carlisle player), T Curry (Carlisle player, United trainer).

FA Cup Record

	Round	Venue	Result
1977-78	3	Away	D 1-1
	Replay	Home	W 4-2

CARMAN, James

Born: Manchester, spring 1875
Career: Oldham County, NEWTON HEATH (November 1897-May 1898).
Reserve inside-forward Jim Carman scored his only League goal for the Heathens in a 4-0 home win against Burton Swifts on New Year's Day, 1898. He was not retained by the club after suffering an ankle injury.
Club record: 4 apps. 2 goals

CAROLAN, Joseph Francis

Born: Dublin, 8 September 1937
Career: Home Farm (Dublin), MANCHESTER UNITED (February 1956), Brighton & Hove Albion (December 1960), Tonbridge (1962), Canterbury City (1968).
Full-back Joe Carolan developed through the junior ranks at Old Trafford. He won two caps for the Republic of Ireland in 1959-60, but after more than 70 outings for the Reds he lost out to first Shay Brennan and then fellow countryman Noel Cantwell.
Club record: 71 apps.

CARROLL, Roy Eric

Born: Enniskillen, Northern Ireland, 30 September 1977,
Career: Hull City (trainee, July 1993, professional September 1995), Wigan Athletic (£350,000, April 1997), MANCHESTER UNITED (July 2001).
Goalkeeper Roy Carroll was signed by United as cover for Fabien Barthez. He made his Premiership debut against Aston Villa (away) in August 2001, his counterpart at the other end of the field being former Reds' star, Peter Schmeichel. He made exactly 50 first team appearances for the Tigers and 169 for Wigan, helping the latter club win the Auto-Windscreen Shield at Wembley in 1999. Carroll has been honoured by his country at three different levels, winning Youth, two Under-21 and eleven senior caps.
Club record: 10 apps.

CARSON, Adam

Born: Glasgow, Scotland, circa 1870.
Career: Glasgow Thistle, NEWTON HEATH (June 1892), Ardwick FC (March 1893), Liverpool (early 1894). Retired from League football in summer of 1894.
Reserve inside-forward Adam Carson represented the Scottish League v. the Scottish Alliance whilst with Glasgow Thistle and played in United's first-ever Football League game against Blackburn Rovers on 3 September 1892
Club record: 13 apps. 3 goals (also 7 'other' apps, one goal)

CARTMAN, Herbert Redvers

Born: Bolton, 28 February 1900
Career: Waterloo Temperance FC, Bolton Wanderers (1919), MANCHESTER UNITED (May 1922), Tranmere Rovers (June 1923), Brighton & Hove Albion (trialist, 1930), Stockport County (trialist, 1930), Chorley (summer 1930), Burscough Rangers (1931), Westhoughton Collieries (re-instated as an amateur, 1932). Retired in 1934.
All of Bert Cartman's three League appearances for United came in December 1922 - two of them against his future club Stockport. Basically an outside-right, he made well over 220 senior appearances for Tranmere (25 goals scored).
Club record: 3 apps.

CARTWRIGHT, Walter

Born: Nantwich, winter 1871
Career: Nantwich FC (1888), Heywood Central (1890), Crewe Alexandra (1893), NEWTON HEATH/MANCHESTER UNITED (June 1895-May 1905). Retired through injury. Later became a licensee and hotelier in Manchester (1920s).
A fine half-back, Walter Cartwright appeared in all eleven positions for the club, amassing well over 250 first-class appearances over a ten-year period, during which time he proved to be a wonderful servant.
On 7 March 1896 he kept goal for the Heath in an away game at Rotherham Town which ended in a 3-2 victory. Eleven days later he played the whole of the second half in goal when the Heathens lost 5-1 at Burton Wanderers. The scoreline at half-time had stood at 4-0!
It was said that had the club been able to field 'a team of Cartwrights' they could have beaten all comers!
During his time with Heywood Central, his team-mate was Jimmy Crabtree, later to play for Burnley, Aston Villa and England, while a colleague at Crewe was Harry Stafford (q.v).
Club record: 257 apps. 9 goals (also 44 'other' apps).

CASHMORE, Arthur

Born: Sparkbrook, Birmingham, 30 October 1893
Career: Sparkhill Avondale, Bromsgrove Rovers, Stourbridge, MANCHESTER UNITED (professional May 1913), Oldham Athletic (May 1914), Darlaston (1919), Cardiff City (late 1919), Notts County (late 1921), Nuneaton (1923) Shrewsbury Town (late 1923). Retired mid-1920s.
Reserve forward Arthur Cashmore's three League appearances for United in 1913-14 came in different positions: inside-right in the 1-0 defeat at home to Bolton Wanderers (his debut), inside-left in a 3-3 draw with Derby County at Old Trafford and centre-forward in the 1-1 draw at Bradford City. He helped Cardiff gain promotion to the First Division in his last season at Ninian Park.
Club record: 3 apps.

CASPER, Christopher Martin

Born: Burnley, 28 April 1975
Career: MANCHESTER UNITED (junior, June 1991, professional February 1993), AFC Bournemouth (on loan, 1996), Swindon Town (on loan, 1997), Reading (£300,000, September 1998).
Sturdy central-defender Chris Casper was an FA Youth Cup winner with United in 1992, and gained caps for England at Youth and Under-21 levels. He also played in the UEFA international Under-18 tournament in 1993. Casper broke his left fibula and tibia when playing for Reading against Cardiff City on Boxing Day 1999 - and after that his League career was effectively over! He was released by the Royals in June 2001.
Club record: 7 apps.

CASSIDY, Joseph

Born: Dalziel, Lanarkshire, 30 July 1872
Career: Motherwell Athletic, Blythe FC (1890), NEWTON HEATH (March 1893), Celtic (initially on loan, signed June 1893), NEWTON HEATH (March 1895), Manchester City (£250, April 1900), Middlesbrough (£75, 1901), Workington (player-coach, 1906).
Joe Cassidy netted exactly a century of goals during his two spells with Newton Heath. By far the club's first outstanding goalscorer, he was a nimble and very alert footballer. Defenders were often caught napping by his quick-silver actions and he acquired an excellent strike record, not only with the Heathens but throughout his career. He netted the first-ever League goal at Ayresome Park and went on to find the net 34 times in 135 League and Cup games for 'Boro - what a bargain!
Club record: 174 apps. 100 goals (also 49 'other' apps, 17 goals)

CASSIDY, Lawrence

Born: Manchester, 10 March 1923,
Career: Schoolboy and junior football (Manchester), MANCHESTER UNITED (amateur January 1947, part-time professional February 1947), Oldham Athletic (July 1956). Retired from League football in 1957.
No relation to Joe (q.v), Lawrie Cassidy - a schoolteacher by profession - was a reserve forward with United. He was snapped up from local junior football and developed quickly but with so many talented footballers registered with the club, found it difficult to get a look in at times, although he remained a loyal servant for some nine years, captaining the second XI for several seasons. A part-timer throughout his career, Cassidy, as headmaster of St Patrick's School, Collyhurst, was able to recommend one of his pupils to United - Brian Kidd. The school had previously produced Wilf McGuinness and Nobby Stiles.
Club record: 4 apps.

CELTIC

Bobby Charlton's testimonial match at Old Trafford (Manchester United against Celtic) on 18 September 1972 attracted a crowd of 60,538 (the largest attendance at the time for such a game).
Around 12,000 Bhoys' came south to Manchester to see Celtic beaten 1-0 by United in a friendly match in 1992-93. The attendance was 31,500 and Andrei Kanchelskis scored the only goal.
Players with both clubs include: T Bogan, J Cassidy, J Connachan, P Crerand, J Cunningham, J Delaney, T Docherty, AS Duncan, W Grassam, J Holton (junior), J Jordan, G Livingstone, B McClair, C McGillivray, L Macari (also Celtic manager), L Martin, T Morrison, H O'Donnell (United WW2). Also associated: A Grimes & M Martin (United players, Celtic coaches).

CENTENARY MATCHES

Manchester United FC celebrated its Centenary Year in August 1978 with a game at Old Trafford against Real Madrid. United won in style by 4-0. Sammy McIlroy (2) & Jimmy Greenhoff (2) shared the goals in front of 49,397 spectators.
In August 1982, a crowd of 19,000 saw United beat Glentoran 2-0 in a game arranged to celebrate the Irish club's centenary.
Tranmere Rovers celebrated their centenary with a friendly against United at Prenton Park in December 1982. A crowd of 5,164 saw Rovers win 2-0.
On 2 August 1990, to commemorate and celebrate a century of Irish football, a crowd of 10,037 at Windsor Park, Belfast saw United beat an Irish League XI 3-0. And three days later the Reds defeated Bohemians 3-0 before a crowd of 13,878 at the same venue.

CHADWICK, Luke Harry

Born: Cambridge, 18 November 1980
Career: MANCHESTER UNITED (apprentice, June 1997, professional February 1999), Royal Antwerp (on loan: two separate spells in 1998 & 1999).
An orthodox right-winger, Luke Chadwick - fast and tricky - who has been capped by England at Youth and Under-21 levels (playing in nine internationals in the latter category) had two successful loan spells in Belgium with Royal Antwerp (to gain experience and confidence). An extremely promising player, he duly returned to Old Trafford to collect a Premier League Championship medal in 2000-01, albeit when appearing mainly as a substitute.
Club record: 34 apps. 2 goals

CHAIRMEN

United's Chairmen in order of holding office:
1902 John H Davies (president)
1902-08 John J Bentley
1908-27 John H Davies
1927-32 George H Lawton
1932-51 James W Gibson
1951-65 Harold Hardman
1965-80 Louis Edwards
1980 to date Martin Edwards
* Professor Sir Roland Smith, a member of the Board of Directors, was Chairman of Manchester United Plc from 1997 to 2002, with Martin Edwards as Chairman/Chief Executive of the club itself. Sir Roy Gardner is now the Plc's non-Executive Chairman.

Chairman's Minutes

Father and son, Louis and Martin Edwards, have served as chairmen of United in succession for a total of 37 years.
Ian Donald, a United player (1968-73) later became a Director (1980), then vice-Chairman (1986) and finally Chairman (1994) of the Scottish League club, Aberdeen.

CHALMERS, William Stewart

Born: Glasgow, 5 March 1907
Career: Glasgow Schoolboys, Queen's Park (1924), Heart of Midlothian (1929), MANCHESTER UNITED (September 1932), Dunfermline Athletic (September 1934). He retired in June 1938.
Inside-forward Stewart Chalmers - an accountant by profession - spent two years with United, appearing in 22 League games in 1932-33 when he was paired (in the main) with James Brown on the right-wing. He was capped twice as an amateur by Scotland (as a Queen's Park player) and later gained a full cap (v. Ireland in February 1929 (whilst at Tynecastle).
Club record: 35 apps. one goal

CHAMPIONSHIPS (League)

United have won 16 League championships in all, 14 being 'top flight' trophies. Only Liverpool (with 22 in all and 18 in the top flight) have won more.
United won the old First Division seven times, the Premiership also on seven occasions, and the Second Division twice.
United's Championship-winning campaigns in detail:

Division One

Season	P	W	D	L	F	A	Pts
1907-08	38	23	6	9	81	48	52
1910-11	38	22	8	8	72	40	52
1951-52	42	23	11	8	95	52	57
1955-56	42	25	10	7	83	51	60
1956-57	42	28	8	6	103	54	64
1964-65	42	26	9	7	89	39	61
1966-67	42	24	12	6	84	45	60

Premiership

1992-93	42	24	12	6	67	31	84
1993-94	42	27	11	4	80	38	92
1995-96	38	25	7	6	73	35	82
1996-97	38	21	12	5	76	44	75
1998-99	38	22	13	3	80	37	79
1999-2000	38	28	7	3	97	45	91
2000-01	38	24	8	6	79	31	80
2001-02	38						

Division Two

1935-36	42	22	12	8	85	43	56
1974-75	42	26	9	7	66	30	61

* See under FOOTBALL LEAGUE for full details of all Championship triumphs:

CHAPMAN, John

When manager Jack Robson resigned in 1921 due to ill-health, the United board appointed 'Gentleman Jack Chapman, but retained Robson to act as his assistant. Chapman had previously had experience at Airdrieonians, but when he walked into Old Trafford in October 1921 he found the once great club in turmoil.
The 1921-22 season had begun badly for United with only one win in their first nine matches. Chapman was unable to halt the decline, United finishing bottom of Divsion One with only 28 points. It would take him three seasons to lift United back into the 'top flight' as runners-up to Leicester City in 1924-25. Chapman had signed such players as Frank Barson, Jimmy Hanson, Tom Jones, Frank McPherson and Frank Mann, not to mention the sensational negotiations which saw Albert Pape 'switch sides' when, expecting to play for Crystal Palace at Old Trafford, he suddenly found

71

himself in United's colours instead!

United fans started getting excited as, in 1925-26, although in mid-table back in Division One, the team reached the semi-final of the FA Cup, Wembley's twin towers at last in sight. Unfortunately Manchester City, of all people, spoilt the party, winning 3-0 at Bramall Lane. Then, part way through the 1926-27 campaign, the FA suspended Chapman 'from all involvement in football matters' due to alleged improper conduct. United had to wave farewell to Chapman forthwith, stalwart 'Lal' Hilditch stepping into the breach to see rge season out as player-manager. The details of Chapman's alleged misdemeanours were never made public.

CHAPMAN, William

Born: Murton, County Durham, 21 September 1902. Died: Murton, County Durham, 2 December 1967.
Career: Murton Council School, Murton Celtic, Murton PM, Hetton PM, Sunderland (trialist), Sheffield Wednesday (trialist, then professional, 1923), MANCHESTER UNITED (£250, May 1926), Watford (June 1928), Murton Colliery FC (1934). Retired in 1935.
Outside-right Billy Chapman played for several intermediate clubs before joining United with whom he spent two seasons before leaving the club (with two other players). Chapman, who made well over 250 League and Cup appearances during his career, including 210 in the League with Watford (22 goals).
Club record: 26 apps.

CHARLTON ATHLETIC

League record

Season	Div	Home	Away	Season	Div	Home	Away
1931-32	2	L 0-2	L 0-1	1952-53	1	W 3-2	D 2-2
1932-33	2	D 1-1	W 1-0	1953-54	1	W 2-0	L 0-1
				1954-55	1	W 3-1	D 1-1
1935-36	2	W 3-0	D 0-0	1955-56	1	W 5-1	L 0-3
1936-37	1	D 0-0	L 0-3	1956-57	1	W 4-2	W 5-1
1938-39	1	L 0-2	L 1-7	1986-87	1	L 0-1	D 0-0
				1987-88	1	D 0-0	W 3-1
1946-47	1	W 4-1	W 3-1	1988-89	1	W 3-0	L 0-1
1947-48	1	W 6-2	W 2-1	1989-90	1	W 1-0	L 0-2
1948-49	1	D 1-1	W 3-2				
1949-50	1	W 3-2	W 2-1	1998-99	PL	W 4-1	W 1-0
1950-51	1	W 3-0	W 2-1	2000-01	PL	W 2-1	D 3-3
1951-52	1	W 3-2	D 2-2	2001-02	PL	D 0-0	W 2-0

Summary of League results

	P	W	D	L	F	A
Premier League	6	4	2	0	12	5
Division 1	34	19	7	8	67	47
Division 2	6	2	2	2	5	4
Home	23	15	5	3	51	22
Away	23	10	6	7	33	34
Total	46	25	11	10	84	56

FA Cup Record

	Round	Venue	Result
1947-48	5	Home *	W 2-0
1993-94	6	Home	W 3-1

* Tie played at Leeds Road, Huddersfield.

League Cup Record

	Round	Venue	Result
1974-75	2	Home	W 5-1

Fact File
Charlton Athletic beat United 2-0 at the Valley on 2 September 1939 in the third League match of the 1939-40 season; the following day war was declared on Germany, the League was abandoned. When football resumed in 1946-47, the same fixture list was used, this time United winning 3-1.
The clubs have only met twice in the FA Cup - and both times United went on to win the trophy.

Players with both clubs include: A Chilton (Athletic WW2), G Crooks, A Davies, E Dunphy (United reserve), T Gibson, H Halse (Athletic WW1, also scout), C Hannaford, F Haydock, R Milne, G Moore, P 'O'Sullivan (United reserve), P Rachubka, M Setters, E Sweeney, A Whalley.
Also associated: M Musgrove (coach at both clubs, also United assistant-manager).

CHELSEA

Summary of League results

	P	W	D	L	F	A
Premier League	20	6	9	5	28	27
Division 1	96	45	24	27	175	120
Division 2	4	1	3	0	2	1
Home	60	23	21	16	95	62
Away	60	29	15	16	110	86
Total	120	52	36	32	205	148

United's League Cup results v Chelsea:

	Round	Venue	Result
1970-71	4	Home	W 2-1

United's FA Cup results v Chelsea:

	Round	Venue	Result
1907-08	2	Home	W 1-0
1949-50	6	Away	L 0-2
1962-63	5	Home	W 2-1
1978-79	3	Home	W 3-0
1987-88	4	Home	W 2-0
1993-94	Final	Wembley	W 4-0
1995-96	Semi-final	Villa Park	W 2-1
1997-98	3	Away	W 5-3
1998-99	6	Home	D 0-0
Replay		Away	W 2-0

FA Charity Shield
United have met Chelsea twice in the annual FA Charity Shield game, both encounters taking place at Wembley: in 1997 when United won 4-2 on penalties (after a 1-1 draw) and in 2000 when Chelsea won 2-0. The respective attendances were 73,636 and 65,148.

Fact File:
United have scored 107 League goals at Stamford Bridge in their 59 matches there, their highest total on any of their opponents' grounds.
Chelsea, League champions in 1954-55, were beaten 6-5 by United at Stamford Bridge in an 11-goal thriller in October in front of almost 56,000 fans. Dennis Viollet scored a hat-trick for the Reds.
Chelsea's league record at Old Trafford since 1966 is quite remarkable. In 27 matches they have lost only three times, winning 11 and drawing 13. This includes a run of 13 matches unbeaten between 1966 and 1987.
United's run of 37 home League games without defeat was ended by Chelsea when they won 3-1 at Old Trafford on 2 March 1968.
With only 90 seconds remaining of their home League game with Chelsea in November 1973, United trailed 2-0, but two late strikes by Jimmy Greenhoff and Tony Young earned the Reds an unexpected point

Players with both clubs include: T Baldwin, M Bosnich, D Brazil (Chelsea trialist), M Busby (Chelsea WW2), J Copeland (United reserve), S Crowther, M Donaghy, G Graham, H Halse, S Houston, G Hunter, B Jones (United WW2), J McCalliog, J McInnes (United WW2),

CHARLTON, Sir Robert, CBE

Born: Ashington, Northumberland 11 October 1937
Career: East Northumberland Schools,
MANCHESTER UNITED (amateur January 1953,
professional October 1954), Preston North End
(manager, May 1973, later serving as player-manager),
Waterford (early 1976), Wigan Athletic (director and
briefly caretaker-manager, 1982-83 season),
MANCHESTER UNITED (director from June 1984
to date).

One of Manchester United's greatest-ever players,
Bobby Charlton came from a football family, his
mother (a Milburn) had four brothers, all professional
footballers.

Charlton made his Football League debut for the
Reds, ironically against Charlton Athletic at Old
Trafford on 6 October 1956 and, wearing a pair of
Roger Byrne's old boots, scored twice in 4-2 win in
front of 41,439 spectators.

His first hat-trick for United was also in a League game
against Charlton - at The Valley on 18 February 1957!

He went on to score more than 250 goals in well over
750 senior appearances for the club (coming off the
bench only twice as a substitute, both in League
games) before going north to Preston in 1973, where
he became player-manager.

A player with tremendous shooting power, he won
three First Division Championship medals (in 1957,
1965 and 1967) and played in three FA Cup Finals
(those of 1957, 1958 and 1963) gaining a winners'
medal in the latter versus Leicester City. He also
skippered United to victory, scoring twice in the 1968
European Cup Final.

Originally an out and out striker, as his career
progressed he settled into the withdrawn centre-forward
role, pioneered by his hero, Alfredo Di Stefano.

In 1966, after helping England win the World Cup,
with his brother Jack, he was voted both European and

PFA 'Footballer of the Year.'

Capped a then record 106 times by England, Charlton
scored 49 international goals (still an England record)
including four hat-tricks. His final goal was claimed
against Colombia in Bogota in May 1970 and his last
appearance was against West Germany in Leon in the
World Cup quarter-final defeat the following month.

One of the original Busby Babes, Charlton won
Schoolboy international recognition before adding
Youth and Under-23 caps to his collection of honours
and he also represented the Football League.

He was a member of three of United's FA Youth Cup-
winning teams in the early 1950s and established
himself in the first XI at Old Trafford shortly before
the Munich air crash.

He played his last game in United's colours in April
1973 against Chelsea at Stamford Bridge.

In June 1994 he became only the second player
(behind Stanley Matthews) to be knighted for services
to football.

Charlton played in five major Cup Finals in the space
of 11 years: three in the FA Cup (1957, 1958, 1963),
the World Cup Final of 1966 and the European Cup
Final of 1968.

One of Charlton's close relatives was the former
Newcastle United and England legend Jackie Milburn.
Club record: 766 apps. 253 goals

United's League record against Chelsea:

Season	Div	Home	Away	Season	Div	Home	Away
1905-06	2	D 0-0	D 1-1	1960-61	1	W 6-0	W 2-1
				1961-62	1	W 3-2	L 0-2
1907-08	1	W 1-0	W 4-1				
1908-09	1	L 0-1	D 1-1	1963-64	1	D 1-1	D 1-1
1909-10	1	W 2-0	D 1-1	1964-65	1	W 4-0	W 2-0
				1965-66	1	W 4-1	L 0-2
1912-13	1	W 4-2	W 4-1	1966-67	1	D 1-1	W 3-1
1913-14	1	L 0-1	W 2-0	1967-68	1	L 1-3	D 1-1
1914-15	1	D 2-2	W 3-1	1968-69	1	L 0-4	L 2-3
				1969-70	1	L 0-2	L 1-2
1919-20	1	L 0-2	L 0-1	1970-71	1	D 0-0	W 2-1
1920-21	1	W 3-1	W 2-1	1971-72	1	L 0-1	W 3-2
1921-22	1	D 0-0	D 0-0	1972-73	1	D 0-0	L 0-1
				1973-74	1	D 2-2	W 3-1
1924-25	2	W 1-0	D 0-0				
				1977-78	1	L 0-1	D 2-2
1930-31	1	W 1-0	L 2-6	1978-79	1	D 1-1	W 1-0
1936-37	1	D 0-0	L 2-4	1984-85	1	D 1-1	W 3-1
				1985-86	1	L 1-2	W 2-1
1938-39	1	W 5-1	W 1-0	1986-87	1	L 0-1	D 1-1
				1987-88	1	W 3-1	W 2-1
1946-47	1	D 1-1	W 3-0				
1947-48	1	W 5-0	W 4-0	1989-90	1	D 0-0	L 0-1
1948-49	1	D 1-1	D 1-1	1990-91	1	L 2-3	L 2-3
1949-50	1	W 1-0	D 1-1	1991-92	1	D 1-1	W 3-1
1950-51	1	W 4-1	L 0-1	1992-93	PL	W 3-0	D 1-1
1951-52	1	W 3-0	L 2-4	1993-94	PL	L 0-1	L 0-1
1952-53	1	W 2-0	W 3-2	1994-95	PL	D 0-0	W 3-2
1953-54	1	D 1-1	L 1-3	1995-96	PL	D 1-1	W 4-1
1954-55	1	W 2-1	W 6-5	1996-97	PL	L 1-2	D 1-1
1955-56	1	W 3-0	W 4-2	1997-98	PL	D 2-2	W 1-0
1956-57	1	W 3-0	W 2-1	1998-99	PL	D 1-1	D 0-0
1957-58	1	L 0-1	L 1-2	1999-00	PL	W 3-2	L 0-5
1958-59	1	W 5-2	W 3-2	2000-01	PL	D 3-3	D 1-1
1959-60	1	L 0-1	W 6-3	2001-02	PL	L 0-3	W 3-0

T Meehan, C Mitten (Chelsea WW2), G Moore, P Parker, M Pinner, P Proudfoot, J Saunders, E Savage (WW2), A Stepney, M Thomas, J Turnbull, C Waldron.
Also associated: R Wilkins (United player, Chelsea player & assistant-manager/coach), N McBain (United player, Chelsea scout), T Docherty* (manager of both clubs, also player-coach at Chelsea), D Sexton (United manager of both clubs, also assistant & coach at Chelsea), F Blunstone (Chelsea player & coach, United coach & Youth manager).
* Docherty was manager of Chelsea when the London club reached three FA Cup semi-finals in successive seasons: 1965, 1966 & 1967. He then guided United to two successive semi-finals in the same competition - 1976 & 1977.

CHESTER (CITY)

United's FA Cup results v Chester:

Round	Venue	Result
1964-65	3	Home	W 2-1

Players with both clubs include: A Albiston, T Astbury (United WW2), G Barrett (United reserve), W Brown, W Bryant (Chester WW2), F Clempson, B Daniels (United reserve), R Davies, T Donnelly, R Duckworth jnr (United reserve), D Ferguson, W Goodwin, R Holland (United reserve), S Hopkinson, M Lane (United reserve), H Lappin, TH Lewis (United trialist), J Lowey (United reserve), P McCarthy, P McGuinness (United reserve), G McLachlan (Chester player-coach), J McMillan, I Moir, R Newsome (WW2 both clubs), SC Pearson (Chester player-manager), W Pendergast (United amateur/reserve), M Robinson, P Roche, G Scales (United WW2), T Sloan, RW Smith (United reserve), P Sutcliffe (United reserve), G Vose (Chester WW2), JA Walton.
Also associated: L Page (United player, Chester manager).

CHESTER, Reginald Alfred

Born: Long Eaton, Nottinghamshire, 21 November 1904. Died: Long Eaton, 24 April 1977.
Career: Long Eaton Rangers, Notts County (trialist, early 1920), Mansfield Town (trialist, early 1920), Peterborough & Fletton United (summer 1920), Stamford Town, Long Eaton Rangers (again), Aston Villa (1924), MANCHESTER UNITED (May 1935), Huddersfield Town (player-exchange involving Tommy Long, December 1935), Darlington (season 1937-38), Arnold Town (briefly), Woodborough United (summer 1938 until his retirement in May 1940).
Winger Reg Chester made his debut for Villa against Manchester United for whom he started the 1935-36 on the left wing, doing well before losing his place to Tom Manley. Chester top-scored for Darlington in their Third Division (North) campaign of 1937-38 with nine goals.
Club record: 13 apps. one goal

CHESTERFIELD (TOWN)

United's League record against Chesterfield:

Season	Div	Home	Away
1899-1900	2	W 2-1	L 1-2
1900-01	2	W 1-0	L 1-2
1901-02	2	W 2-0	L 0-3
1902-03	2	W 2-1	L 0-2
1903-04	2	W 3-1	W 2-0
1904-05	2	W 3-0	L 0-2
1905-06	2	W 4-1	L 0-1
1931-32	2	W 3-1	W 3-1
1932-33	2	W 2-1	D 1-1
1937-38	2	W 4-1	W 7-1

Summary of League results

	P	W	D	L	F	A
Division 2	20	13	1	6	41	22
Home	10	10	0	0	26	7
Away	10	3	1	6	15	15
Total	20	13	1	6	41	22

Fact File:
Although the clubs have never met in either of the two domestic Cup competitions, they did meet in May 1945 in the delightfully named 'League War Cup Knock-Out Competition' in a two legged semi-final.
The first leg, staged at Maine Road, resulted in a 1-1 draw. The second leg attracted a massive 32,013 crowd to Saltergate (the official record for the ground stands at 30,968 v. Newcastle United on 7 April 1939 for a Division Two fixture) as the last days of World War Two were played out. United won 1-0, their goal coming from inside left McDowell, a guest player who, as far as I can see, was appearing in his only game for the club.
Potentially Chesterfield's finest hour arrived in the FA Cup semi-final in 1996-97 played at Old Trafford when with the score at 2-1 to the Spire-ites, deep in the second-half, Jon Howard's shot off the underside of the bar being refused as a goal by the unmoved David Elleray. Oh, for a Russian linesman! The decision possibly deprived Chesterfield of being the first League club from outside the top two divisions to play in an FA Cup Final.
Players with both clubs include: A Albiston, B Asquith (Spire-ites WW2), G Beel (United reserve), A Bellis (United WW2), J Bullock, E Connor, R Duckworth jnr (United reserve), H Harrison (United WW2), M Dempsey, W Dennis, H Green (United reserve), P Hall, R Halton, L Lievesley, J Lowey (United reserve), S McAuley (United reserve), WS McMillen, J Moody, D Pierce (United Youths), M Pollitt (United reserve), P Robinson (United WW2), J Spence (also Spire-ites scout), WW Stevenson (United reserve), W Woodward (United reserve).
Also associated: R Brocklebank (United WW2 player, Chesterfield manager).

CHESTERS, Arthur

Born: Salford, 14 February 1910
Career: Sedgley Park, MANCHESTER UNITED (amateur 1928, professional November 1929), Exeter City (trialist July 1933, signed August 1933), Crystal Palace (Easter 1937). Guested for Brighton & Hove Albion, Fulham, Leicester City and Rochdale during WW2. Retired in 1946.
Goalkeeper Arthur Chesters - understudy at Old Trafford to Alf Steward and then Jack Moody - conceded no fewer than 30 goals in nine games for United, 22 in four outings early in the 1930-31 season. He helped Exeter with a Third Division South Cup medal in 1934, and was in the Palace goal when they won promotion from the Third Division South in 1938-39
Club record: 9 apps

CHILTON, Allenby C

Born: South Hylton, County Durham, 16 September 1918. Died: 1996.

Career: Ford Street School (South Hylton), Sunderland and Durham Schools, Seaham Colliery FC (1934), Liverpool (amateur, late 1938), MANCHESTER UNITED (professional, November 1938). Guested for Airdrieonians, Cardiff City, Charlton Athletic, Hartlepools United, Middlesbrough and Newcastle United during WW2. Grimsby Town (player-manager, March 1955, retired as a player in 1956), Wigan Athletic (manager, 1960), Hartlepools United (scout, 1961-62, then manager for season 1962-63 after which he quit football).

A rugged defender, Allenby Chilton hailed from the North-east and played in almost 400 first-class games for United, gaining an FA Cup winners medal in 1948 and being an ever-present in the League Championship-winning side of 1951-52. He had made his debut on the eve of WW2 at Charlton and would have to wait almost seven years for his second League appearance.

Chilton, who won two England caps at the age of 32, played a massive part in United's post-war success, utterly reliable at the hub of the defence, he missed only nine League matches in nine seasons. In his later years he acted as the father figure to the 'Busby Babes.' His place at centre-half went to Mark Jones. A League Cup (South) winner as a guest player with Charlton in 1944, he served with the Durham Light Infantry during WW2 and was twice wounded in battle, at Caen (France) and during the 'D' Day landings at Normandy.

Club record: 392 apps. 3 goals

CHISNALL, John Philip

Born: Stretford, Manchester 27 October 1942.

Career: MANCHESTER UNITED (amateur 1958, professional October 1959), Liverpool (£25,000, April 1964, Southend United (£12,000, 1967), Stockport County (1971). Left League football in 1972

An England Schoolboy international, Phil Chisnall's chances were limited at Old Trafford with so many other forwards eagerly wanting to play first team football. He won an England Under-23 cap before transferring to Anfield. Chisnall later scored 28 goals in 142 League games for Southend.

Club record: 47 apps. 10 goals

CHORLTON, Thomas

Born: Heaton Mersey, Cheshire, 1882.

Career: Heaton Mersey Juniors, All Saints FC, Northern FC, Stockport County (1900), Accrington Stanley (1902), Liverpool (1904), MANCHESTER UNITED (August 1912), Stalybridge Celtic (August 1914). Retired as player in November 1919, Manchester City (assistant-trainer 1919, then senior trainer at Maine Road until 1939).

Full-back Tom Chorlton was a member of Accrington Stanley's Lancashire Combination Championship winning side in 1903 and runners-up team the following year. A versatile defender, he then helped Liverpool take the Second Division crown in his first season at Anfield. He went on to appear in 122 senior games for the Merseyside club. He was subsequently a reserve at Old Trafford, deputising in four League games for John Hodge at right-back.

Club record: 4 apps.

CHRISTIE, David

Born: Scotland, 1885.

Career: Hurlford FC (1903), MANCHESTER UNITED (October 1907-May 1910). Later emigrated to Australia where he became coach to the Sydney-based club, Granville FC (mid 1920s).

Scottish-born forward David Christie was 22 when he joined United as reserve to the Turnbulls (Jimmy and Sandy) and consequently was given very few opportunities in the first XI. He loved to drive in long-distance shots and scored several goals from outside the penalty area for United's reserve side.

Club record: 2 apps.

CHRISTIE, John

Born: Manchester circa 1880.

Career: Sale Holmfield FC, MANCHESTER UNITED (September 1902), Manchester City (May 1904), Bradford City (1907), Croydon Common (1908), Brentford (1910). Retired in 1912.

Reserve full-back Jack Christie's only League game for United was against Doncaster Rovers in a Second Division game in February 1903, six months after joining the club. Whilst at Griffin Park Christie represented London against Paris in the annual challenge match.

Club record: one app.

CHRISTMAS DAY

United's last League game on Christmas Day was in 1957 v. Luton Town (h). Despite their being no public transport, a crowd of 39,444 saw the Hatters beaten 3-0.

75

In total United have played 39 League & Wartime games on 25 December....as follows:
Football League

1896 v. Manchester City (h)	won 2-1	18,000
1897 v. Manchester City (a)	won 1-0	16,000
1902 v. Manchester City (h)	drew 1-1	40,000
1903 v. Chesterfield (h)	won 3-1	15,000
1905 v. Chelsea (h)	drew 0-0	35,000
1906 v. Liverpool (h)	drew 0-0	20,000
1907 v. Bury (h)	won 2-1	45,000
1908 v. Newcastle United (a)	lost 1-2	35,000
1909 v. Sheffield Wed (h)	lost 0-3	25,000
1911 v. Bradford City (h)	lost 0-1	50,000
1912 v. Chelsea (a)	won 4-1	33,000
1913 v. Everton (h)	lost 0-1	25,000
1920 v. Aston Villa (a)	won 4-3	38,000
1922 v. West Ham Utd (h)	lost 1-2	17,500
1923 v. Barnsley (h)	lost 1-2	34,000
1924 v. Middlesbrough (a)	drew 1-1	18,500
1925 v. Bolton Wds (h)	won 2-1	38,503
1926 v. Tottenham Hot (a)	drew 1-1	37,287
1928 v. Sheffield Utd (h)	drew 1-1	22,202
1929 v. Birmingham (h)	drew 0-0	18,626
1930 v. Bolton Wds (a)	lost 1-3	22,662
1931 v. Wolverh'ton W (h)	won 3-2	33,123

1933 v. Grimsby Town (h)	lost 1-3	29,443
1934 v. Notts County (h)	won 2-1	32,965
1936 v. Bolton Wds (h)	won 1-0	47,658
1946 v. Bolton Wds (a)	drew 2-2	28,505
1947 v. Portsmouth (h)	won 3-2	42,776
1948 v. Liverpool (h)	drew 0-0	47,788
1950 v. Sunderland (a)	lost 1-2	41,215
1951 v. Fulham (h)	won 3-2	33,802
1952 v. Blackpool (a)	drew 0-0	27,778
1953 v. Sheffield Wed (h)	won 5-2*	27,123
1957 v. Luton Town (h)	won 3-0	39,444

*Tommy Taylor scored a hat-trick for United in this game

Wartime

1915 v. Manchester City (a)	lost 1-2	20,000
1940 v. Stockport Co (a)	won 3-1	1,500
1941 v. Manchester City (h)	drew 2-2	20,000
1942 v. Bolton Wds (h)	won 4-0	1,578
1943 v. Bolton Wds (a)	won 3-1	10,969
1945 v. Sheffield Utd (a)	lost 0-1	12,775

Summary of results

P	W	D	L	F	A
39	17	11	11	63	49

CLARK, Jonathan

Born: Swansea, 12 November 1958
Career: MANCHESTER UNITED (apprentice, March 1973, professional November 1975), Derby County (September 1978), Preston North End (1981also served as caretaker-manager at Deepdale, 1986), Bury (late 1986), Carlisle United (1987), Morecambe (early 1989), Rhyl (mid-1989). Retired early 1990s.
Midfielder Jonathan Clark made just one substitute appearance for United, taking over from Colin Waldron during the First Division League game with Sunderland at Old Trafford in November 1976.
He won Welsh schoolboy international honours before joining United. Clark ended his career with 227 League appearances to his name, and therefore was one that 'got away' from Old Trafford!
Club record: one app.

CLARK, Joseph

Born: Dundee, 1874
Career: Dundee (August 1896), NEWTON HEATH (September 1899-May 1900). Served in the army in South Africa from September 1900.
Joe Clark, an inside or centre-forward, partnered William Bryant in the right-wing in his only season with the Heathens. The club retained his registration papers when he enlisted in the army to fight in the Boer War.
Club record: 8 apps. (also 4 'other' apps)

CLARKIN, John

Born: Neilston, Renfrewshire, 1872.
Career: Glasgow Thistle, NEWTON HEATH (January 1894), Blackpool (June 1896). Left League football in May 1898.
John Clarkin was another Scottish-born player who accumulated a fine record during his two-and-a-half seasons with the club. A dashing outside-right, he came into the side thus allowing Alf Farman to switch inside. He had Bob Donaldson and Bill Kennedy as his partners over the next two seasons and did very well as the Heathens finished 3rd and 6th in the Second Division. Clarkin was transferred to Blackpool following the arrival of William Bryant from Rotherham Town.
Club record: 74 apps. 23 goals (also 25 'other' apps, 7 goals)

CLAYTON, Gordon

Born: Chadsmoor, Staffs 3 November 1936. Died: Stretford, Manchester 29 September 1991.
Career: Cannock & District Schoolboys, MANCHESTER UNITED (junior June 1952, professional in November 1953), Tranmere Rovers (£4,000, November 1959), GKN Sankey's (Wellington), Radcliffe Borough (1963), MANCHESTER UNITED (assistant to Chief Scout Norman Scholes in the early 1970s), Derby County (scout), Burnley (assistant-manager, 1983), Cheadle Town (manager), Northwich Victoria (assistant-manager, summer 1991 until his death).
Goalkeeper Gordon Clayton, an FA Youth Cup winner in 1953, made his only League appearances for United against the top two Midland clubs at that time, West Bromwich Albion and Wolves in 1957. With Ray Wood (and others) battling it out for a regular place in the first XI, Clayton moved down two Divisions to Tranmere in 1959. After leaving Prenton Park in 1961 he served briefly in the Police Force.
He sadly died whilst still in charge of non-League Northwich Victoria.
Club record: 2 apps.

CLEAVER, Harry

Born: Lancashire, circa 1880.
Career: Desborough, MANCHESTER UNITED (October 1902-May 1903).
Harry Cleaver's only League appearance for the Reds was against Burnley at home in April 1903 when he occupied the centre-forward berth in the absence of Dick Pegg and John Fitchett. He only spent one season with the club.
Club record: one app.

CLEGG, Michael Jaime

Born: Ashton-under-Lyne, 3 July 1977.
Career: MANCHESTER UNITED (trainee July 1993, professional July 1995), Ipswich Town (on loan, February 2000), Wigan Athletic (on loan, March-April 2000).
Defender Michael Clegg's tally of first team outings for United contains eight as a substitute. He gained two England Under-21 caps and collected an FA Youth Cup winners' medal during his time at Old Trafford.
Two other Clegg brothers, George and Steven, were also associated with United.
Club record: 24 apps.

CLEMENTS, John Ernest

Born: Nottinghamshire, circa 1876
Career: Nottingham St Saviours, Notts County (1889), NEWTON HEATH (June 1892), Rotherham Town (August 1894), Newcastle United (reserves, 1895). Retired 1896
Full-back John Clements played in United's first-ever Football League game at Blackburn (September 1892). He started out at right-back but later appeared on the opposite flank. He was transferred to Rotherham following the emergence of Fred Erentz. He failed to make the first XI at St James' Park.
In October 1893, Clements was one of a trio of Heathens' players who were suspended by the club for 14 days following alleged misconduct during a League game against Derby County earlier that month.
Club record: 79 apps. (also 53 'other' apps).

CLEMPSON, Frank

Born: Salford, 27 May 1930. Died: 1970.
Career: Aldelphi Lads' club, MANCHESTER UNITED (amateur March 1948, professional September 1948), Stockport County (February 1953), Chester (1959), Hyde United (player-manager, 1961). Left football in 1962
Utility forward Frank Clempson first came into United's first XI following an injury to Tommy Bogan. He helped the Reds win the League Championship in 1952 and after leaving Old Trafford was converted into a wing-half at Edgeley Park, going on to make well over 250 appearances for the Hatters.
Club record: 15 apps. 2 goals

COACHES

Over the years there have been scores of men (some ex-players) who have been employed as a coach (at various levels) by United. Prior to the Second World a 'coach' was, in fact, classified (in the main) as a trainer, and since 1960, a coach, besides being referred to as a trainer, has also been listed as the club's physiotherapist.
Here, listed in A-Z order, are some of United's coaches over the past 80 years (1922-2002): Arthur Albiston (juniors), Neil Bailey, Johnny Carey, Tony Coton (goalkeeping coach), Francisco Filo, Harry Gregg, Brian Kidd, Alan Hodgkinson (goalkeeping coach), Steve McClaren, Jimmy Murphy (also assistant-manager/acting manager), Carlos Queiroz, Jimmy Ryan, Nobby Stiles, Bert Whalley, Brian Whitehouse (also reserve team manager and scout), David Williams.

Coach's Clipboard
In the period following WW2, United used two training grounds, The Cliff (formerly the home of Broughton Rangers RLFC) and Littleton Road, both in the district of Salford.
These days the United training ground is the custom-built complex at Carrington.

COCKBURN, Henry

Born: Ashton-under-Lyne, 14 September 1923
Career: Goslings FC (season 1938-39), MANCHESTER UNITED (amateur, September 1943, professional in August 1944). Guested for Accrington Stanley in WW2. Then Bury (October 1954), Peterborough United (1956), Corby Town (1959), GKN Sankey, Wellington (1960), Oldham Athletic (assistant-trainer/coach, early 1961), Huddersfield Town (assistant-manager/coach 1964, then senior coach 1969-75).
Wing-half Henry Cockburn gave United ten years excellent service. Small, confident and totally committed, he gained 13 full caps for England at a time when there were several high quality wing-halves in the First Division. Despite his lack of inches (5ft 5ins and barely 10 stone in weight) Cockburn was a fiercely combative defender, being particularly strong in the air, capable of prodigious leaps, often winning out against the tallest of forwards.
He won an FA Cup winners medal with United in 1948 and followed up with a League Championship medal in 1952, before losing his place in the side to Duncan Edwards. Cockburn was the first United player to win a full England cap after the Second World War, helping his country beat Northern Ireland 7-2 in Belfast in September 1946, having played in only seven Football League matches prior to selection.
Cockburn was also a fine cricketer, playing regularly for Ashton in the Central Lancashire League.
Club record: 275 apps. 4 goals

77

COLCHESTER UNITED

FA Cup Record

	Round	Venue	Result
1978-79	5	Away	W 1-0

League Cup Record

	Round	Venue	Result
1983-84	3	Away	W 2-0

Players with both clubs include: K Goddard (United reserve), S Houston (Colchester player/coach), J McInally (Man Utd reserve), R Murray, W Pendergast (Man Utd amateur/reserve).

COLLINSON, Clifford

Born: Middlesbrough, 3 March 1920. Died: September 1990
Career: Urmston Boys Club, MANCHESTER UNITED (amateur May 1946, professional September 1946-May 1947)
Goalkeeper Cliff Collinson joined United at the age of 26. He was employed as deputy to Jack Crompton, before his release in the summer of 1947. He later resided in Bristol.
Club record: 7 apps

COLE, Andrew Alexander

Born: Nottingham, 15 October 1971
Career: Arsenal (apprentice 1987, professional 1989), Fulham (on loan, 1991), Bristol City (£500,000, 1992), Newcastle United (£1.75 million, 1993), MANCHESTER UNITED (£6 million, January 1995), Blackburn Rovers (£7.5 million, January 2002).

Striker Andy Cole scored five goals when Manchester United beat Ipswich Town 9-0 at Old Trafford in March 1995...a Premiership record. Prior to that, the striker had notched 34 goals in the 1993-94 season, with Newcastle United (also a Premiership record). This feat was equalled by Alan Shearer who was also playing for Newcastle twelve months later (1994-95). Cole, sharp and incisive, has always scored goals (he once netted eight in one game playing for Arsenal's junior team). The goals continued to flow thick and fast after he had left Highbury, netting 25 in 49 outings for Bristol City and 60 in only 84 first team appearances for Newcastle before Alex Ferguson secured his services for a then record fee of £6 million in 1995. Cole quickly made his mark with the Reds, scoring at will, while also topping up his collection of international caps for England, having previously represented his

country at schoolboy, Youth, Under-21 (eight appearances) and 'B' team levels. He went on to gain 13 senior caps as a United player.

A First Division Championship winner with Newcastle in 1993, he then added five Premiership winning medals to his tally with United (1996-97-99-2000-01) plus FA Cup success in 1996 and 1999 and European Cup glory, also in 1999 when, of course, he was a key member of the treble-winning side. He jumped at the chance of joining Blackburn Rovers early in 2001, after failing to hold down a regular place in United's forward-line following the arrival of Dutchman Ruud van Nistelrooy.

Cole is United's record scorer in the European Champions League (Cup) with 19 goals.

At Ewood Park, he linked up with another former United favourites Mark Hughes and winger Keith Gillespie, as well as defenders John Curtis and Henning Berg, and in his first half season with Rovers, scoring some vitally important goals including the winner in the Worthington League Cup Final victory over Tottenham Hotspur at Cardiff's Millennium Stadium.
Club record: 275 apps. 122 goals

COLLINSON, James

Born: Prestwich, early 1876

Career: NEWTON HEATH (August 1895-May 1901).

Jimmy Collinson spent six years with the club. Starting out as a full-back, he then had a decent run as an inside-forward before returning to the right-back berth. He found the net on his debut in a 5-5 draw with Lincoln City and also helped United win the Lancashire Senior Cup for the first time.

Replaced in the Heathens' defence by Harry Stafford, he later partnered William Bryant on the right-wing. His best season was in 1898-99 when he netted nine goals in 21 League games as the team finished 4th in Division 2.

Club record: 72 apps. 16 goals (also 27 'other' apps, 11 goals)

COLMAN, Edward

Born: Salford, 1 November 1936. Died: Munich, 6 February 1958

Career: Salford Schoolboys, Lancashire County Schools, MANCHESTER UNITED (amateur, June 1952, professional, November 1953 until his death).

Regarded as the creative genius of the Busby Babes team, Eddie Colman despite his lack of physique, was an aggressive tackler with a unique ability to carry the ball long distances, his 'shimmy' sending his opponents the wrong way, before delivering delicate defence-splitting passes to his forwards.

A tremendous player who looked certain to join his team-mate Duncan Edwards in the full England team...until he lost his life in tragic circumstances on the snow-covered Munich air-strip. He was captain of United's team that won the FA Youth Cup three seasons running (1953-55) and made his Football League debut in the Lancashire derby against Bolton in November 1955 - the first of more than 100 games for the club.

Club record: 108 apps. 2 goals

COLOURS

The colours of United (as Newton Heath) at the outset (like most of the other teams in the area, and indeed up and down the country) comprised generally plain shirts, either white or a shade of blue, with either black or white shorts. When they entered the Football League in 1892, and until 1894, they wore red and white quartered shirts with blue shorts.

For the next two seasons (up to 1896) the players donned green and gold halved shirts with black shorts, briefly revived in 1992-93 as a third strip.

However, for six years up to 1902, the club's kit comprised white shirts and blue shorts, but then with the club's change of name (to Manchester United) the now adopted famous red jersey with white shorts (very rarely black) became the club's first choice of colours, except for a five-year period in the 1920s (1922-27) when white shirts with a red 'V' back and front were used and for one season - 1933-34 - United's players were clad in maroon and white hooped jerseys with white shorts...in a desperate and unsuccessful attempt to avoid relegation.

Against Blackpool in the 1948 FA Cup Final at Wembley, v. Benfica in the 1968 European Cup Final and also in the 1992 League Cup Final against Nottingham Forest, United donned dark blue shirts. Against Aston Villa in the FA Cup Final of 1957 they turned out in an all-white kit.

United's change colours in recent years have been either black or white shorts, although occasionally they did appear in all white. However, following the introduction of Premiership football, United have worn a variety of alternative colours from black, to sky blue, to grey, to yellow and black to white (with black trimmings)... and even gold (with black facings),

At The Dell, for a Premiership game against Southampton in April 1996, United started off by wearing an all-grey strip. At half-time (and losing 3-0) they changed to a blue and white kit and reduced the deficit to 3-1. Grey seemed to be an unlucky colour for United... they never won a major League or Cup game when wearing it in season 1995-96.

Today the sale of replica kits is a massive business at the United Superstore, worn by supporters as a fashion item.

* United wore an all-green strip when they played a testimonial game in Ireland against a Drumcondra Select XI in August 1968.

COLVILLE, James

Born: Annbank, Ayrshire, circa 1869

Career: Annbank, NEWTON HEATH (October 1892), Fairfield FC (June 1893), Notts County (trialist), Annbank (1895). Retired circa 1898.

Outside-left Jimmy Colville was with the Heathens during their first season in the Football League. He took over the berth from Scotsman Bill Mathieson before giving way later in the campaign to Joe Cassidy.

Club record: 10 apps. one goal (also 7 'other' apps).

COMMERCIAL DEPARTMENT

Over the last 15 years or so, Danny McGregor has held the position of Commercial Manager at Old Trafford: He succeeded John Lillie in 1987.

CONNACHAN, James

Born: Glasgow, 29 August 1874.

Career: Glasgow Perthshire, Duntocher Hibernians, Celtic (1897), Airdrieonians (1898), NEWTON HEATH

(October 1898), Glossop North End (February 1899), Leicester Fosse (1900), Nottingham Forest (trialist, 1901), Morton (late 1901), Renton (1902) Britannia FC, Canada (1906), Dumbarton Harp (1907). Retired 1909.

A versatile player, James Connachan appeared in only a handful of games for the Heathens, occupying a different position each time. He made his debut at right-half in a 3-2 home win over Grimsby Town a week after joining the club, having spent only four days with Airdrie!

Club record: 4 apps. (also one 'other' apps)

CONNAUGHTON, John Patrick

Born: Wigan, 23 September 1949.

Career: MANCHESTER UNITED (apprentice May 1965, professional October 1966), Halifax Town (on loan, September 1969), Torquay United (on loan, October 1971- April 1972), Sheffield United (£15,000, October 1972), Port Vale (1974-80, Altrincham (1980-81).

England Youth international goalkeeper John Connaughton's three senior outings for United came within the space of eight days during April 1972 as he stood in for the injured Alex Stepney. His debut was away to Sheffield United, the club he joined later that year. He played in over 200 games for Port Vale and represented Altrincham in their 1982 FA Trophy Final defeat by Enfield at Wembley.

Club record: 3 apps.

CONNELL, Thomas Eugene

Born: Newry, Northern Ireland, 25 November 1957

Career: Newry Town (1975), Coleraine (1976), MANCHESTER UNITED (August 1978), Glentoran (£37,000, July 1982).

Reserve full-back Tom Connell's two League outings for United were in place of Stewart Houston either side of Christmas 1978 and each time he was on the losing side by 3-0, away to Bolton and at home against Liverpool. He represented Northern Ireland at both Under-21 and senior levels while serving with Coleraine.

Club record: 2 apps

CONNELLY, John Michael

Born: St Helens, 18 July 1938

Career: St Helens Town, Burnley (1956), MANCHESTER UNITED (£60,000, April 1964), Blackburn Rovers (£40,000, September 1966), Bury (1970). Retired in 1973.

Winger John Connelly had a fine career. A classy winger with two good feet and an eye for goal, his searing pace helped make United a force to be reckoned with.

He was initially an inside-right with St Helens Town before being converted into a right-winger by Burnley for whom he scored over 100 goals in 265 senior appearances, gaining a League Championship-medal in 1960, an FA Cup runners-up medal two years later and also appearing in two FA XI matches. During his two-and-a-half years at Old Trafford he netted on average a goal every three games for the Reds, collecting a second League Championship medal in 1965. An England Under-23 international (one cap), he represented the Football League on seven occasions and played in the opening game of the 1966 World Cup Finals (v. Uruguay). In all he won 20 senior caps for his country (10 with United) and scored seven international goals. He was on the losing side only three times. When he retired in 1973, his Football League record was very impressive: 573 appearances and 180 goals. After leaving the game he ran a successful fish and chip shop near Burnley.

Club record: 113 apps. 35 goals

CONNOR, Edward

Born: Liverpool, 1884. Died: January 1955.

Career: Eccles Borough, Walkden Central, MANCHESTER UNITED (May 1909), Sheffield United (£750, June 1911), Bury (1912), Exeter City (1919), Rochdale (1920), Chesterfield (autumn 1921) Saltney Athletic (late 1921). Retired in 1923.

Reserve outside-left Ted Connor deputised for George Wall in 13 of his 15 outings for the Reds. He later made almost 100 senior appearances for Bury. Connor returned to Old Trafford in the late 1920s as a scout and thereafter assisted the club for many years as an office worker.

Club record: 15 apps. 2 goals

COOKE, Terence John

Born: Birmingham, 5 August 1976.

Career: MANCHESTER UNITED (trainee, June 1992, professional July 1994), Sunderland (on loan, January-February 1996), Birmingham City (on loan, November-December 1996), Wrexham (on loan, October-November 1998), Manchester City (£1 million, January 1999), Wigan Athletic (on loan, early 2000), Sheffield Wednesday (two spells on loan, during first half of 2000-01 season), Grimsby Town (on loan, March-May 2002, signed July 2002).

Skilful right-winger who found it tough to gain first team football at Old Trafford. After leaving the Reds Terry Cooke failed to establish himself with any other club, making only 41 appearances for United's arch-rivals, City. He represented England at Youth team level before gaining four Under-21 caps, as well as helping United's youngsters win the 1995 FA Youth Cup, when he scored in both legs against Tottenham Hotspur.

Club record: 8 apps. one goal

COOKSON, Samuel Percy

Born: Bargoed, January or February 1891.

Career: Bargoed Town, MANCHESTER UNITED (as an amateur, signed for £50, February 1914, professional March 1914 to August 1919).

Half-back Sam Cookson remained a registered player with the club throughout the Great War but was transfer-listed in 1919. He didn't figure in League football after that.

Club record: 13 apps.

COPE, Ronald

Born: Crewe, 5 October 1934

Career: Crewe Schoolboys, MANCHESTER UNITED (groundstaff, June 1950, professional October 1951), Luton Town (£10,000, August 1961), Northwich Victoria (player in 1963, then caretaker-manager, 1965-66), Winsford United (1967-68), Northwich Victoria (again, as trainer-coach, 1969-70).

A well built, hard-tackling defender, Ronnie Cope spent ten years as a full-time professional with United and played in the 1958 FA Cup Final v. Bolton. A former England Schoolboy international, he was third choice at the heart of the defence before the tragedies of Munich and afterwards played very well at centre-half until losing his place to Bill Foulkes who moved across to allow Shay Brennan to fill the right-back berth.

Club record: 106 apps. 2 goals

COPPELL, Stephen James

Born: Croxteth, Liverpool, 9 July 1955.

Career: Liverpool University, Tranmere Rovers (1973, professional 1974), MANCHESTER UNITED (£60,000, February 1975-October 1983 when he retired). Crystal Palace (manager, then Technical Director at Selhurst Park, 1984-93), Manchester City (manager, 1996), Crystal Palace (two further spells as manager, 1997-98 & 1999-2000), Brentford (manager, 2001-June 2002).

Right-winger Steve Coppell made almost 400 first-class appearances for United, becoming a massive favourite of the fans.

He was playing for his University team when he joined Tranmere and within two years of having set foot inside Prenton Park he was starring in the First Division in front of 38,000 fans at Bolton when making his United debut, taking over from Scottish international Willie Morgan.

Fast, clever and direct, with a powerful right-foot shot, wonderfully self-motivated, he appeared in a club record 206 consecutive League games for United between 15 January 1977 and 7 November 1981. He won one England Under-21 cap and followed up with 42 senior international appearances, scoring seven times. He was an FA Cup winner with United in 1977 and a loser in both 1976 and 1979 as well as collecting a League Cup runners-up prize in 1983. He was forced to retire through injury in October 1983.

Chief Executive of the Football League Managers' Association and a former PFA chairman, Coppell was the Football League's youngest manager when he first took charge of Crystal Palace in 1984. He guided the Eagles to promotion from Division Two, albeit via the play-offs in 1989, and then took them to Wembley for the FA Cup Final (v. Manchester United) twelve months later. In 2002 he took Brentford to the Nationwide Division Two Play-offs where they lost to Reading. Soon afterwards he resigned.

Club record: 396 apps. 70 goals

COUPAR, James

Born: Dundee, 1869.

Career: Dundee Our Boys FC, MANCHESTER UNITED (June 1892), St Johnstone (May 1893), Rotherham Town (1894), Luton Town (1897), Swindon Town (season 1898-99), Linfield (early 1899-1900 season), Swindon Town (late 1899-1900 season), MANCHESTER UNITED (September 1901-May 1902).

Scotsman Jim Coupar averaged a goal every three games for United during his two spells at the club. A utility forward, he did very well with Luton and also with Swindon, but in 1905 he was re-instated as an amateur and possibly saw out the remainder of his career north of the border.

Coupar's brother Peter played for United's reserve side, Dundee and Stoke.

Club record: 34 apps. 10 goals (also 23 'other' apps, 4 goals)

COURT CASES

George Perrins, a Newton Heath player for four years (1892-96) was the centre of an article that appeared in the Birmingham Gazette in February 1894. The club sued the newspaper for £200 in damages after Perrins had been criticised for 'dirty play' during the League game against West Bromwich Albion in October 1893. At Manchester Assize Court, the verdict went in favour of the Heathens but the jury considered the damage encountered should be compensated by no more than one farthing (the lowest value coin of the realm at that time).

Eric Cantona appeared in court for his attack on a Crystal Palace supporter at Selhurst Park in January 1995. He was found guilty of the offence and was sentenced to two years imprisonment. This was later reduced (on appeal) to 120 hours of community service.

Former United and Welsh international midfield player Mickey Thomas was sentenced to prison after being found guilty of taking part in a counterfeit bank-note racket.

* See also Bribery

COVENTRY CITY

United's League record against the Sky Blues:

Season	Div	Home	Away	Season	Div	Home	Away
1922-23	2	W 2-1	L 0-2	1991-82	1	L 0-1	L 1-2
1923-24	2	L 1-2	D 1-1	1982-83	1	W 3-0	L 0-3
1924-25	2	W 5-1	L 0-1	1983-84	1	W 4-1	D 1-1
				1984-85	1	L 0-1	W 3-0
1937-38	2	D 2-2	L 0-1	1985-86	1	W 2-0	W 3-1
				1986-87	1	D 1-1	D 1-1
1967-68	1	W 4-0	L 0-2	1987-88	1	W 1-0	D 0-0
1968-69	1	W 1-0	L 1-2	1988-89	1	L 0-1	L 0-1
1969-70	1	D 1-1	W 2-1	1989-90	1	W 3-0	W 4-1
1970-71	1	W 2-0	L 1-2	1990-91	1	W 2-0	D 2-2
1971-72	1	D 2-2	W 3-2	1991-92	1	W 4-0	D 0-0
1972-73	1	L 0-1	D 1-1	1992-93	PL	W 5-0	W 1-0
1973-74	1	L 2-3	L 0-1	1993-94	PL	D 0-0	W 1-0
				1994-95	PL	W 2-0	W 3-2
1975-76	1	D 1-1	D 1-1	1995-96	PL	W 1-0	W 4-0
1976-77	1	W 2-0	W 2-0	1996-97	PL	W 3-1	W 2-0
1977-78	1	W 2-1	L 0-3	1997-98	PL	W 3-0	L 2-3
1978-79	1	D 0-0	L 3-4	1998-99	PL	W 2-0	W 1-0
1979-80	1	W 2-1	W 2-1	1999-00	PL	W 3-2	W 2-1
1980-81	1	D 0-0	W 2-0	2000-01	PL	W 4-2	W 2-1

Summary of League results

	P	W	D	L	F	A
Premier League	18	16	1	1	41	12
Division 1	48	21	13	14	72	47
Division 2	8	2	2	4	11	11
Home	37	23	8	6	72	26
Away	37	16	8	13	52	44
Total	74	39	16	19	124	70

United's FA Cup record against City:

	Round	Venue	Result
1911-12	2	Away	W 5-1
1912-13	1	Home	D 1-1
	Replay	Away	W 2-1
1962-63	6	Away	W 3-1
1984-85	4	Home	W 2-1
1986-87	4	Away	L 0-1

League Cup Record

	Round	Venue	Result
1980-81	2 (1)	Home	L 0-1
	2 (2)	Away	L 0-1

Fact File:
The Sky Blues had five players booked in the game against United on
Boxing Day 1971 - for not moving back the required distance when a free-kick had been awarded.
Coventry defender David Busst suffered a broken leg during the Premiership game between the two clubs at Old Trafford in April 1996. He never played again.

Players with both clubs include: P Barnes, P Bodak (United reserve), A Brazil, C Craven (City WW2 guest), G Daly, D Dublin, A Fitton, T Gibson, A Goram, A Grimes, J Holton, C Jenkyns, M Lane (United reserve), W McDonald, J Mitten (United trialist), R Newsome (United WW2), W Richards (Singers FC), B Robson (City trialist), L Sealey, M Setters, G Strachan (City player & manager), A Thomson, W Toms, E Toseland (United WW2), JA Walton.
Also associated: R Atkinson & D Sexton (managers of both clubs), N Cantwell (United player, City manager), A Bell (United player, City trainer).

COYNE, Peter David

Born: Hartlepool, 13 November 1958.
Career: MANCHESTER UNITED (amateur October 1973, professional November 1975), Ashton United (March 1977), Crewe Alexandra (1977), Hyde United (1981), Swindon Town (1984), Aldershot (on loan, 1989), Colne Dynamos (1990-91), Glossop, Radcliffe Borough.
A frequent and reliable marksman in United's junior sides, Peter Coyne netted one goal at senior level, in a 2-1 defeat at Leicester City in April 1976 when he deputised for Stuart Pearson. Capped seven times by England at schoolboy level, Coyne notched almost 100 goals in various competitions during his senior career, including 47 in 134 League games for Crewe.
His younger brother, Gerald, was on United's books in the mid-1970s.
Club record: 2 apps. one goal

CRAIG, Thomas (or Thomson)

Born: circa 1867
Career: NEWTON HEATH (professional, December 1889-April 1891).
The versatile Tom Craig made his debut for the Heathens in a Football Alliance game against Darwen shortly after joining the club, and then he scored in an FA Cup-tie against the holders Preston North End three weeks later. He occupied six different positions, four in the front-line, as a Heathens player.
Club record: 27 apps. 6 goals (also 29 'other' apps, 11 goals)

CRAVEN, Charles

Born: Boston, Lincolnshire 2 December 1909. Died: Solihull, 30 March 1972
Career: Boston Trinity, Boston Town, Boston United (1929), Grimsby Town (1930), MANCHESTER UNITED (£6,000, June 1938), Birmingham (December 1938), Tamworth (1939). Guested for Coventry City during WW2, Sutton Town (1951). Retired circa 1952-53.
Inside-forward Charlie 'Swerver' Craven was a ball-player who had a splendid bodyswerve (hence his nickname). He scored well over 100 goals in almost 300 games as a professional (256 in the League before joining United) and was named as reserve by England for the international against Holland in 1935.
Craven was also a good club cricketer and snooker player, once recording a break of 128.
Club record: 11 apps. 2 goals

CRERAND, Patrick Timothy

Born: Glasgow, 19 February 1939
Career: St Luke's Ballater Street and Holyrood Secondary Schools, Duntocher Hibernians, Celtic, MANCHESTER UNITED (£56,000, February 1963, later player-coach & assistant-manager to August 1976), Northampton Town (manager, during 1976-77). Also worked briefly as a publican (Park Hotel, Manchester)

Right-half Pat Crerand made over 400 appearances for United, becoming one of the club's finest ever half-backs. He was recruited by fellow Scot, Matt Busby, and settled into the United side immediately, collecting an FA Cup winners medal at the end of his first season when Leicester City were beaten 3-1 at Wembley. Crerand, an elegant, stylish footballer, went from strength to strength and besides performing superbly for United, he took his tally of Scottish caps to 16, having earlier represented his country at Under-23 level as well as playing for the Scottish League on seven occasions whilst at Parkhead. He was a loser with Celtic in the 1961 Scottish Cup Final but after succeeding with United two years later, he then collected two League Championship medals in 1965 and 1967 and a European Cup winning prize in 1968. Crerard was appointed player-coach at Old Trafford in August 1971, but halfway through the season he hung up his boots and was later promoted to assistant-manager. He left United in 1976 to spend six months in charge of Northampton Town
* Crerand's son, Danny, was associated with Rochdale in season 1967-68.
Club record: 401 apps. 15 goals

CREWE ALEXANDRA
United's League record against the 'Alex':

Season	Div	Home	Away
1894-95	2	W 6-1	W 2-0
1895-96	2	W 5-0	W 2-0

Summary of League results

	P	W	D	L	F	A
Division 2	4	4	0	0	15	1
Home	2	2	0	0	11	1
Away	2	2	0	0	4	0
Total	4	4	0	0	15	1

Players with both clubs include: P Abbott (United reserve), G Albinson, A Allman, I Ashworth (United reserve), H Birchenough, P Bodak (United reserve), W Bootle (United WW2), J Bottomly (United reserve), J Bullock, W Cartwright, P Coyne, D Cronin (United reserve), W Davies, A Downie (Alex player-coach), J Elms (United reserve), W Emmerson (United Youth), G Fellows (United junior), J Ford, J Greenhoff, T Harris, W Harrison, F Hodges, O James, A Kinsey, K Lewis (United junior), TH Lewis (United trialist), P McGuinness (United reserve), A Marshall, J Montgomery; H Morris & A Murphy (United reserves), E Partridge, W Pendergast (United amateur/reserve), D Platt (United junior), A Rice (United reserve), R Savage (United Youths), G Schofield, H Stafford, HS Stafford (United reserve), W Toms, A Waddington (United amateur, Alex player and manager), J Walters & R Ward (United reserves), A Westwood (United reserve), I Wilkinson, F Worrall (United WW2). Also associated: D Viollet (United player, Alex coach & manager), F Blunstone (Alex player, United Youth team manager), H Catterick (Alex manager, United WW2 player).

CRICKETING-FOOTBALLERS
Goalkeeper Andy Goram played 43 times for Scotland at football and he also represented his country in several cricket internationals. Eventually Rangers banned him from playing cricket, fearing injuries to his hands.
Arnie Sidebottom made over 20 first team appearances for United (1972-74). He was also a fast bowler with Yorkshire County Cricket Club and played in one Test Match for England v. Australia in 1985. His son also played for Yorkshire and England in 2000-01.
Freddie Goodwin, who played in 106 senior matches for United whom he served for seven years, 1953-60, was a very competent cricketer with Lancashire CCC.
Goalkeeper Alf Steward took 6-10 playing in the annual cricket match between Manchester United and rivals City in the early 1920s. Steward also played competitive cricket for Lancashire, Forfar and Perthshire.
Noel Cantwell, United's FA Cup winning captain in 1963, played football for the Republic of Ireland and cricket for Ireland.
United's David Sadler played football at senior level for England and represented his country and also Kent as a schoolboy cricketer.
The Essex and England all-rounder Trevor Bailey played for Walthamstow Avenue against United in the FA Cup replay in 1953.
Matt Busby, so impressed, offered the Lancashire and England fast bowler Brian Statham the opportunity to turn professional and play football for United in the late 1940s. He declined and chose to bowl over the Aussies instead!
Roger Byrne (Denton West CC), Henry Cockburn, Charlie Craven, Pat Crerand (Ashton CC), Ian Greaves (Crompton CC), Len Langford (a smart wicket-keeper), Gary Pallister, Bryan Robson, Jack Rowley (Yelverton CC, Devon), Alf Schofield (East Lancashire CC) and Jeff Whitefoot (Cheadle Heath CC) were all good club cricketers in their own right. Both natives of Shaw, near Oldham, defenders Ian Greaves and Paul Edwards were both considered potential County cricketers before choosing football.
David Herd, United's centre-forward in the 1960s, was also an excellent wicket-keeper/batsman at club level, and after his footballing days were over he represented Minor Counties side Cheshire.
Of the present United side, Phil Neville was an outstanding batsman in Lancashire CCC's Youth team before choosing the 'other'; Old Trafford to play his sport! Brother Gary is also a useful cricketer.
In the 1920s Billy Dennis played Minor Counties Cricket with Cheshire and in the Central Lancashire League as a professional with Milnrow. He was a fast bowler.
Bill Ridding, the former United player, was physiotherapist at Lancashire CCC (Old Trafford) 1969-71.
* The father of England and Lancashire captain Mike Atherton was once a junior on United's books.

CRICKMER, Walter
Walter Crickmer was one of the club's greatest servants. He was secretary of MANCHESTER UNITED for some 32 years, from 1926 until his tragic death in the Munich air disaster on 6 February 1958.
He acted as caretaker-manager for a season following the sacking of Herbert Bamlett at the end of the 1930-31 campaign. He, along with senior scout Louis Rocca, looked after team affairs until July 1932 when Scott Duncan was appointed as United's new boss. During the twelve months he was acting manager, Crickmer (totally dedicated to the club) carried on with his secretarial duties with great precision and he did likewise during the nine-year period from

November 1936 until 1945 when once again he acted as team manager.

During the war years Crickmer's efforts kept the club afloat, there is no doubting that. Supported all the way by the influential chairman James Gibson, Crickmer, in fact, took office in nearby Cornbrook following the bombing of Old Trafford in 1941. He did a remarkable job of running the club, selecting teams and arranging via local Army bases for guest players to be available when required.

It was Crickmer who appointed Matt Busby as United's manager - after Rocca had done the initial spadework by recommending the Scotsman to the club!

He was a little man in stature, but a giant in his influence on the club, a superb administrator with a computer-like brain. There were long periods in United's history when he virtually ran the club single-handedly.

* In 1938 Crickmer was largely responsible for the development and, indeed, the introduction of the Youth policy at Old Trafford, setting up the Manchester United Junior Athletic Club (known as 'the MUJAC').

CROATIA ZAGREB

Goals by David Beckham and Roy Keane gave United a 2-1 victory in Zagreb after a disappointing 0-0 draw at Old Trafford in the 1st stage of the 1999-2000 European Champions League competition.

* Croatia Zagreb are known as Dynamo Zagreb.

CROMPTON, John

Born: Newton Heath, 18 December 1921.

Career: Manchester Schools, Oldham Athletic (amateur, season 1942-43), Manchester City (amateur, early 1944), Stockport County (WW2 guest), MANCHESTER UNITED (groundstaff, June 1944, professional January 1945-June 1956), Luton Town (trainer, 1956-58), MANCHESTER UNITED (senior trainer, February 1958-June 1962), Luton Town (manager for one week, 1962), MANCHESTER UNITED (trainer, July 1962-May 1971), Barrow (coach, July 1971, then manager to 1972), Bury (assistant-manager/coach, 1972), Preston North End (assistant-manager, season 1973-74), MANCHESTER UNITED (reserve team trainer, June 1974-June 1981).

Retired six months short of his 60th birthday.

Goalkeeper Jack Crompton made well over 200 first-class appearances for United. He made his League debut against Grimsby Town in August 1946 and played his last senior game for the club against Huddersfield Town in October 1955. Reliable, daring and consistent, Crompton helped United win the FA Cup in 1948, but he never gained a League Championship medal, playing in only nine games in 1951-52 (as deputy to Reg Allen) and just one in 1955-56. Crompton had the reputation as a penalty-kick saver!

In 1958 he returned to United as senior trainer (after Munich) and in 1962 (after one week in office) he quit his position as manager at Kenilworth Road, choosing to stay with United instead. He served United for a total of 32 years, a wonderfully loyal servant to the club in a number of capacities.

In later life Crompton went over to Tenerife where, for a time, he coached at the island's Education Centre where he was also Governor.

Club record: 212 apps.

CROOKS, Garth Anthony, OBE

Born: Stoke-on-Trent, 10 March 1958.

Career: St Peter's FC (Penkhull, Staffs), Stoke Schoolboys, Stoke & Staffordshire Schools, Stoke City (1974, professional 1976), Tottenham Hotspur (£650,000, 1980), MANCHESTER UNITED (on loan, November 1983-January 1984), West Bromwich Albion (£100,000, 1985), Charlton Athletic (1987). Retired with a back injury, November 1990.

Striker Garth Crooks scored 53 goals in 264 competitive games for Stoke City before going on to net a further 105 in 238 outings for Spurs, moving to White Hart Lane after falling out with new boss Alan Durban. He gained two FA Cup winners medals with Spurs (in 1981 and 1982) and a League Cup runners-up medal. His loan with United was short and sweet, scoring in a 2-0 win at Ipswich and a 3-3 home draw with Notts County.

Capped four times by the England Under-21 side, he scored a hat-trick on his debut at this level against Bulgaria at Leicester in 1979. He retired with a fine record to his name - 168 goals in 468 club appearances.

Crooks was Chairman of the PFA in 1989-90. In later years he joined BBC TV as a soccer interviewer and summariser, a position he still retains today. He was awarded the OBE in June 1999.

Club record: 7 apps. 2 goals.

CROWD DISTURBANCES

At the start of the 1971-72 season Old Trafford was closed by the FA for two League games following an incident during a home game fixture the previous season when a knife was tossed onto the pitch. The two scheduled home fixtures - against Arsenal and West Bromwich Albion - were staged at Anfield and The Victoria Ground (Stoke) respectively - and United won them both by the same scoreline of 3-1.

CROWTHER, Stanley

Born: Bilston, Staffs, 3 September 1935.

Career: Stonefield Secondary Modern School, West Bromwich Albion (amateur 1950), Erdington Albion (1951), Bilston Town (mid-1952), Aston Villa (£750, 1955), MANCHESTER UNITED (£18,000, February 1958), Chelsea (£10,000, December 1958), Brighton & Hove Albion (1961), Rugby Town (1965) Hednesford Town (1967). Retired in 1969.

A wing-half, Stan Crowther left Villa Park to join United in one of the most dramatic transfers in the game's history! One hour and 16 minutes after signing for the Reds he stepped out in front of almost 60,000 fans inside the Old Trafford cauldron for a nervous FA Cup encounter against Sheffield Wednesday in the immediate aftermath of the Munich air disaster, a rare case of a player being allowed to appear for two clubs in the FA Cup during the same season. Crowther played in the Final against Bolton Wanderers, twelve months after appearing for Villa against United at the same stage of the competition.

Crowther, who was only acquired as a stop gap by United stand-in boss Jimmy Murphy, later made over 50 appearances for Chelsea. Orphaned at the age of 15, he won three England Under-23 caps and represented the Football League whilst at Villa Park. After quitting football Crowther became a senior foreman for Armitage Shanks in Wolverhampton. Club record: 20 apps.

CRUYFF, Jordi

Born: Amsterdam, 9 February 1974

Career: Ajax Amsterdam (1990), CF Barcelona (1992), MANCHESTER UNITED (£1.4 million, August 1996), Celta Vigo (on loan, 1999), Deportivo Alaves of Spain (May 2000).

Jordi Cruyff - son of the famous international Dutch striker Johan Cruyff - came off the subs' bench no fewer than 32 times as a United player!

He was at Old Trafford for four seasons, and despite several promising displays, never really held down a regular first team place. He played for FC Alaves in the UEFA Cup Final v. Liverpool in May 2001.

Cruyff has won nine caps for Holland and while with United played in two FA Charity Shield matches and won a Premiership medal in 1996-97.

NB: Dutch spelling of name is CRUIJFF.

Club career: 58 apps. 8 goals

85

CRYSTAL PALACE

United's League record against Palace:

Season	Div	Home	Away	Season	Div	Home	Away
1922-23	2	W 2-1	W 3-2	1989-90	1	L 1-2	D 1-1
1923-24	2	W 5-1	D 1-1	1990-91	1	W 2-0	L 0-3
1924-25	2	W 1-0	L 1-2	1991-92	1	W 2-0	W 3-1
				1992-93	PL	W 1-0	W 2-0
1969-70	1	D 1-1	D 2-2				
1970-71	1	L 0-1	W 5-3	1994-95	PL	W 3-0	D 1-1
1971-72	1	W 4-0	W 3-1				
1972-73	1	W 2-0	L 0-5	1997-98	PL	W 2-0	W 3-0
1979-80	1	D 1-1	W 2-0				
1980-81	1	W 1-0	L 0-1				

United's FA Cup record against Palace:

	Round	Venue	Result	
1989-90	Final	Wembley	D 3-3	Aet
	Replay	Wembley	W 1-0	
1994-95	SF	Villa Park	D 2-2	Aet
	Replay	Villa Park	W 2-0	

United's League Cup record against Palace:

	Round	Venue	Result
1970-71	5	Home	W 4-2
1985-86	2 (1)	Away	W 1-0
	2 (2)	Home	W 1-0
1987-88	3	Home	W 2-1

Summary of League results

	P	W	D	L	F	A
Premier League	6	5	1	0	12	1
Division 1	18	9	4	5	30	22
Division 2	6	4	1	1	13	7
Home	15	11	2	2	28	7
Away	15	7	4	4	27	23
Total	30	18	6	6	55	30

Players with both clubs include: K Ayres (United reserve), A Chesters, S Coppell (also Palace manager), W Davies, G Graham, A Hooper, J Kirovski (United reserve), L Lievesley; W Moyle & A Mycock (United reserves).

Also associated: JR Robson (manager of both clubs), S Bruce (United player, Palace manager), D Sexton (Palace player, United manager), B Whitehouse (Palace player, United coach & scout)

CULKIN, Nicholas James

Born: York, 6 July 1978

Career: York City juniors, MANCHESTER UNITED (£250,000, September 1995), Hull City (on loan, 1999) Bristol Rovers (on loan, 2000), Livingston (on loan, 2001), QPR (July 2002).

Goalkeeper Nick Culkin's only senior appearance for United - as a stoppage time substitute for Raimond van der Gouw - came

in the Premiership game against Arsenal at Highbury in August 1999. With Bristol Rovers he missed only one League game in 2000-01, but his excellent form failed to save the Pirates from relegation to Division Three. When on loan with Livingston, he helped the Scottish club reach the highest placing ever in the SPL (in only their seventh season as a League club)
Club record: one app.

CUNNINGHAM, John

Born: Glasgow, circa 1873.
Career: Benburb FC, Celtic (trialist, 1889), Burnley (late 1889), Glasgow Hibernian (late 1899), Celtic (1890), Partick Thistle (early 1892), Heart of Midlothian (autumn 1892), Glasgow Rangers (late 1892), Glasgow Thistle (1893), Preston North End (autumn 1893), Sheffield United (1897), Aston Villa (summer 1898), NEWTON HEATH (October 1898) Wigan County (March 1899), Barrow (1901). Retired circa 1902-03.
Scottish-born inside-forward and soccer journeyman, Johnny Cunningham spent just six months with the club. In all, Cunningham, short and stocky with a dapper moustache, was associated with 13 different football clubs, settling down best with Preston for whom he scored nine goals in 51 appearances.
Club record: 17 apps. 3 goals (also 5 'other' apps).

CUNNINGHAM, Laurence Paul

Born: St Mary's Archway, East London, 8 March 1956. Died: Madrid, 15 July 1989.
Career: South East Counties and North London Schools, Arsenal (junior), Leyton Orient (1972, professional 1974), West Bromwich Albion (£110,000, 1977), Real Madrid (£995,000, 1979), MANCHESTER UNITED (on loan, March-May 1983), Sporting Gijon (1983), Olympique Marseille, (1984), Leicester City (on loan, 1985-86), Rayo Vallecano (1986-87 season), FC Betis (trial, late summer 1987), FC Charleroi, Belgium (mid-1987)), Wimbledon (non-contract, early 1988) Rayo Vallecano (summer 1988 until his death).
Nicknamed 'El Negrito' in Spain, Laurie Cunningham helped Real win the Spanish League and Cup double and the following season collected a runners-up medal when his side lost to Liverpool in the final of the European Cup. His brief spell at Old Trafford failed to re-establish himself in English football.
He was the first Black player to represent his country in a major international when he lined up for the England Under-21 side against Scotland at Bramall Lane in April 1977. Speculation at the time was rife as to whether he would become the first Black footballer to win a full cap. He was, in fact, the second, behind future Manchester United full-back Viv Anderson.
Cunningham went on to win a further five caps at intermediate level as well as appearing in six full internationals and in one 'B' game.
On his day he was a brilliant footballer. He had pace, intricate footwork, fine finishing technique, power, expert reflexes, determination and wonderful balance. He enjoyed playing on the right-wing, but during his career occupied every forward position, always performing to an exceptionally high standard. He graced all the big stadiums in Europe and at times produced some wonderful performances.
Cunningham - who was sadly killed in a car crash on the outskirts of Madrid - appeared in almost 350 competitive games and scored over 50 goals.
Club record: 5 apps. one goal

CURRY, Joseph J

Born: Newcastle-upon-Tyne, early 1887
Career: Scotswood FC, MANCHESTER UNITED (February 1908), Southampton (April 1911, West Stanley (1913). Did not play after WW1. Strong-limbed defender Joe Curry spent three years with the club and struggled in get first team outings owing to the form of that great half-back trio of Duckworth, Roberts and Bell.
Club record: 14 apps.

CURRY, Thomas

Tom Curry, a quietly spoken Geordie, was first team trainer with MANCHESTER UNITED for almost 24 years. He sadly died in the Munich air crash on 6 February 1958.
Born in South Shields on 1 September 1894, he played for two local sides, South Shields St Michael's and South Shields Parkside before signing as a professional for Newcastle United in April 1912. A wing-half, he went on to make 248 senior appearances for the Magpies (five goals scored) up to January 1929 when he moved on a free transfer to Stockport County. He retired in July 1930 and became Carlisle United's trainer, taking a similar position at Old Trafford in June 1934. He represented the Football League in 1920 and whilst with Manchester United, he acted as trainer to the British Olympic team in 1948, the same year he 'trained' United's FA Cup-winning side under Matt Busby with whom he worked especially well. He certainly played a great part in bringing through the young players who would achieve fame as the 'Babes.'

CURTIS, John Charles

Born: Nuneaton, 3 September 1978
Career: MANCHESTER UNITED (apprentice August 1993, professional October 1995), Barnsley (on loan, late 1999), Blackburn Rovers (£2.25 million, June 2000).
An FA Youth Cup winner in 1995, full-back John Curtis made almost 20 first-class appearances for the Reds (10 as a substitute). Capped 16 times by the England Under 21s, he also represented his country at schoolboy, Youth and 'B' team levels. He has since established himself in Blackburn's Premiership side and was a non-appearing substitute when Rovers won the League Cup in 2002.
Club record: 19 apps.

D for...

DOCHERTY,
Thomas Henderson

Born: Pershaw, Glasgow, 24 August 1928.
Career: Schoolboy football in the Gorbals district of Glasgow,
Shettleston Juniors; served in the Highland Light Infantry (playing for
his regiment in Palestine), Celtic (July 1948), Preston North End
(£4,000, November 1949), Arsenal (£28,000, August 1958), Chelsea (
player/coach, February 1961, retired as player four months later and
then succeeded Ted Drake as manager, September 1961-October 1967),
Rotherham United (manager, November 1967 to November 1968),
Queen's Park Rangers (manager for just 29 days during November
1968), Aston Villa (manager, December 1968 to January 1970), FC
Porto (manager, February 1970 to June 1971), Hull City (assistant-
manager July-September 1971), Scotland (national team manager from
September 1971 to December 1972), MANCHESTER UNITED
(manager, December 1972 to July 1977), Derby County (manager,
September 1977 to May 1979), Queen's Park Rangers (May 1979 to
October 1980), Preston North End (manager, June-December 1981),
Sydney Olympic (manager, June 1982), South Melbourne (manager,
July-December 1982), Sydney Olympic (manager, January to July
1983), Wolverhampton Wanderers (manager, June 1984 to July 1985),
Altrincham (manager, October 1987 to February 1988). This was his
last appointment in the game and now he is employed as an after-dinner
speaking, travelling all over the world talking football and about his
eventful career.

Docherty certainly had a varied career in football. One could quite fill a dozen pages of this book talking about his soccer life. He was capped 25 times by Scotland, represented his country in one 'B' international and appeared in more than 450 League and Cup games north and south of the border. He gained a Second Division Championship medal and an FA Cup runners-up with Preston when he lined up behind Tom Finney.

When he took over as United manager in 1972, the club was certainly in need of 'The Doc.'

Although Best, Law and Charlton were still there, they had all seen better days. A new broom was needed badly and Docherty would prove to be the right man.

The much publicised Youth Policy had been allowed to decline, such had been the club's obsession of winning the European Cup. Now 'The Doc' had to restart virtually from scratch, yet the expectations were still sky high. Fellow Scots George Graham and Lou Macari were bought to prove stability and hopefully goals. Alex Forsyth and Jim Holton, two more Scots, arrived to bolster the defence. Relegation was narrowly avoided in the first season but was inevitable the next!

In a way relegation was not the disaster it first appeared, as Docherty now had a good clear out, replacing the dead wood with inspired signings of bright young players from unfashionable clubs, notably Steve Coppell (Tranmere Rovers) and Stuart Pearson (Hull City) whose vibrant brilliance enabling United to romp away with the Second Division title, returning to the top flight far stronger with a nucleus of some superb young players. Gerry Daly, Brian Greenhoff and Jimmy Nicholl emerged soon to be joined by the sparkling Gordon Hill from Millwall. United looked capable of an unlikely 'double' until the closing stages of the 1975-76, finally finishing an excellent third in the table while losing to Southampton 1-0 in the FA Cup Final after the young players 'froze' on the day! But United were on the move again, playing wonderful

football; then the following season the excellent Jimmy Greenhoff joined his brother to add another dimension to United's attack. Although 1976-77 never quite reached the heights of the previous season, United still finished sixth and won the FA Cup, beating arch rivals Liverpool 2-1 to deny the Merseysiders the glorious 'treble.'

The young stars of Old Trafford were now established internationals, Docherty having shaped a vibrant side in the true United tradition, the future seemingly bright.

Then came the bombshell of Docherty's alleged affair with Mary Brown, the wife of United's physiotherapist. The club was deeply embarrassed by the unwelcome publicity and asked Docherty to resign.

The fans were aghast - they had taken to Docherty and loved the way his young team played. Now he was gone.

In retrospect he would never be viewed alongside his fellow Scots, the two knights, but Docherty had played an important role in the history of Manchester United as the club finally remembered its proud traditions. The Stretford End never forgot 'The Doc', singing his name long after he had left.

Docherty would continue his journey from club to club, but after United 'everything is downhill!'

Prior to his association with United, Docherty had guided Chelsea into the First Division in 1963, guided them to League Cup success in 1965 and to the FA Cup Final in 1967. He broke Chelsea's transfer record four times during his time in charge at Stamford Bridge,

When in charge of FC Porto he narrowly missed out on winning the Portuguese League title and he certainly restored Scotland's pride on the international front.

The 'Doc' once said: "The ideal Board of Directors should be made up of three men, two dead and one dying." He also passed these comments about Ray Wilkins when he was at Old Trafford: "He can't run, he can't tackle and he can't head a ball. The only time he goes forward is to toss the coin."

DALE, Herbert

Born: Stoke-on-Trent, February 1867. Died: Ancoats, December 1925.

Career: Manchester FA, NEWTON HEATH (September 1887). Retired in 1892-93 to become a referee.

Reserve inside-forward Bert Dale's only game for the Heathens was in the FA Cup qualifying round against Bootle in October 1890.

His brother, George Dale, was a coach/trainer with Oldham Athletic during the 1920s.

Club record: one app. (also 2 'other' apps)

DALE, Joseph

Born: Northwich, 3 July 1921

Career: Witton Albion, MANCHESTER UNITED (June 1947), Port Vale (April 1948), Witton Albion (late 1948), Northwich Victoria (assistant-manager, 1959-60).

United's reserve outside-right Joe Dale deputised twice for Jimmy Delaney during his time at Old Trafford - against PNE and Stoke City on successive Saturdays in September/October 1947.

Club record: 2 apps.

DALE, William

Born: Manchester, 17 February 1905. Died: Manchester, June 1987.

Career: Sandbach Ramblers (1922), MANCHESTER UNITED (amateur April 1925, professional May 1926), Manchester City (£2,000, December 1931), Ipswich Town (1938), Norwich City (1940). Did not appear after WW2.

Full-back Billy Dale, a sound defender with good technique, made almost 70 first-class appearances for the Reds over a three-year period following his League debut v. Leicester City in August 1928. He won an FA Cup winners medal with Manchester City in 1933 and a League Championship medal four years later. He starred for Ipswich in their first League season of 1938-39.

Club record: 68 apps.

DALTON, Edward

Born: Manchester, circa 1888.

Career: Pendlebury FC (1903), MANCHESTER UNITED (amateur, September 1905, professional January 1906), Pendlebury FC (August 1908), St Helens Recreationalists (1909).

Ted Dalton, a reserve full-back, made just one League appearance for United, in a 7-1 defeat at the hands of Liverpool at Anfield in March 1908.

Club record: one app.

DALY, Gerard Anthony

Born: Cabra, Dublin, 30 April 1954.

Career: Bohemians, MANCHESTER UNITED (£20,000, April 1973), Derby County (£175,000, March 1977), New England Teamen (on loan, two separate spells, 1978 & 1979), Coventry City (1980), Leicester City (on loan, 1983), Birmingham City (1984), Shrewsbury Town (1985), Stoke City (1987), Doncaster Rovers (1988), Telford United (assistant player-manager 1989, then full-time manager 1990). Left football in 1993.

Republic of Ireland international Gerry Daly emerged as one of Tommy Docherty's bright young men, a brilliant, energetic midfielder whose skilful displays made him an instant hit with the fans.

Born in the same Dublin suburb as Johnny Giles, he spent almost four years at Old Trafford before joining Derby County. He helped United win back their First Division status in 1975 and played in the 1976 FA Cup Final defeat by Southampton. Daly, a fine penalty taker, missing only one in 17 at United, made well over 550 League and Cup appearances at club level, scoring almost 100 goals. In League action alone his record was 88 goals in 472 outings. Winner of 47 full caps for Eire, Daly also played once for his country's Under-21 side.

Club record: 144 apps. 32 goals

DARWEN

United's League record against Darwen:

Season	Div	Home	Away
1893-94	1	L 0-1	L 0-1
1894-95	2	D 1-1	D 1-1
1895-96	2	W 4-0	L 0-3
1896-97	2	W 3-1	W 2-0
1897-98	2	W 3-2	W 3-2
1898-99	2	W 9-0	D 1-1

Summary of League results

	P	W	D	L	F	A
Division 1	2	0	0	2	0	2
Division 2	10	6	3	1	27	11
Home	6	4	1	1	20	5
Away	6	2	2	2	7	8
Total	12	6	3	3	27	13

Fact File

Darwen, a small cotton mill town near Blackburn, played a very influential part in the establishment of professional football in the years before the formation of the Football League, being amongst the first clubs to pay players, against FA rulings. All the players in the early days were mill-workers who had to take time off work, even on Saturdays, in order to play. Without payment from the club, it would not have been possible to run the club on competitive lines.

Darwen's finest hour was against one of the strongest sides of the pre-League era, Old Etonians, in the FA Cup of 1879, travelling to London at great expense, forcing a 5-5 draw after trailing 1-5. The 'gentlemen' not only refused to play extra time but also refused to travel North for a replay, forcing the poor mill-workers to raise money from work-mates to make a second journey to London. Following another draw, Darwen again had to travel to London, a further collection necessary. Their gallant efforts forced the FA to change the rules of the competition. Darwen were elected to the Football League in 1891 as members of the Football Alliance, joining the single 'Division' of 14 clubs. Darwen spent just 8 seasons in the League, but the world had moved on since their gallant Cup battles, resigning in 1899 after a disastrous season gaining just nine points from 34 matches, two wins and 141 goals conceded. Nevertheless Darwen's place in English football history is secure.

Players with both clubs include: J Ball, C Briggs (United WW2), W Campbell, W Eaves (United reserve), G Haslam, J Howarth, A Pape (Darwen player-coach), E Thomson.

Also associated: C Knowles (United amateur, Darlington manager).

89

DAVENPORT, Peter

Born: Birkenhead, 24 March 1961

Career: Cammell Laird FC, Everton (amateur), Nottingham Forest (1982), MANCHESTER UNITED (£570,000, March 1986), Middlesbrough (November 1988), Sunderland (1990), Airdrieonians (1993), St Johnstone (1994) Stockport County (1995), Southport (player/assistant-manager 1996), Macclesfield Town (player-coach 1997, later manager, 2000)

Utility forward Peter Davenport scored a goal every four games for United whom he served for two-and-a-half years from March 1986. Signed as a replacement for Mark Hughes, he eventually moved on following Hughes' return. Davenport played in the 1992 FA Cup Final for Sunderland, was capped once by England at senior level v. Republic of Ireland in 1985 and he also played for his country's 'B' team. He took over from another former United player, Sammy McIlroy, as manager of the Silkmen in 2000, holding the position for barely four months.

All told (playing for clubs and country) Davenport appeared in almost 550 competitive games and scored more than 130 goals.

Club record: 109 apps. 26 goals

DAVIDSON, William R

Born: Annbank, Ayrshire, circa 1871.

Career: Annbank, NEWTON HEATH (July 1893-May 1895). Retired through injury.

Half-back Will Davidson was forced to retire two years after joining the Heathens (he was badly injured during a game at Crewe in November 1894). He later became the landlord of a public house in Manchester.

Club record: 44 apps. 2 goals (also 17 'other' apps, one goal)

DAVIES, Alan

Born: Manchester, 5 December 1961. Died: Gower, Swansea 4 February 1992.

Career: North Manchester High School, Mancunian Juniors, MANCHESTER UNITED (associate schoolboy September 1977, apprentice July 1978, professional December 1978), Newcastle United (£50,000, July 1985), Charlton Athletic (on loan, early 1986), Carlisle United (on loan, late 1986), Swansea City (1987), Bradford City (1989), Swansea City (1990 until his death).

Utility forward Alan Davies gained an FA Cup winners medal with United in 1983 (v. Brighton). He had made his League debut two years earlier against Southampton, but found his opportunities at Old Trafford limited.

Davies was capped on 13 occasions by Wales at senior level and appeared six times for the Under-21 side, having represented his country as a Youth team player prior to that. He was still registered with Swansea City when he committed suicide in 1992, aged 30.

Club record: 10 apps. one goal

DAVIES, John

Born: Lancashire, circa 1870

Career: NEWTON HEATH (July 1892-May 1893).

John Davies took over the Heathens' goalkeeping position during the latter stages of the 1892-93 season from Jimmy Warner.

Club record: 13 apps. (also 14 'other' apps).

DAVIES, Joseph Josiah

Born: Cefn Mawr near Ruabon, July 1865. Died: Cefn Mawr, 7 October 1943.

Career: Ruabon Welfare, Druids, NEWTON HEATH (July 1886), West Bromwich Albion (May 1890), Wolverhampton Wanderers (mid-1890), Kidderminster Olympic (briefly), Druids (1894). Retired: 1896.

Welsh half-back Joe Davies made just 23 senior appearances for the Heathens during his four seasons with the club although he did play in almost 140 'other' first team matches. He later worked as a farmer and ran a butcher's shop in the town of his birth.

Club record: 23 apps. 2 goals (also 138 'other' apps, 24 goals)

DAVIES, L

Born: Wales

Career: NEWTON HEATH (August 1886-May 1887).

Outside-left Davies made just one senior appearance for Newton Heath against Fleetwood Rangers in a 1st round FA Cup-tie in October 1886.

Club record: one app.

DAVIES, Ronald Tudor

Born: Ysgol Basing, Holywell, North Wales, 15 May 1942

Career: Flint Schools, Ysgol Dinas Basing FC, Blackburn Rovers (trialist), Chester (1959); Luton Town (£10,000, 1962), Norwich City (£35,000, 1963), Southampton (£55,000, 1966), Portsmouth (1973), MANCHESTER UNITED (£25,000, November 1974), Arcadia Shepherds of South Africa (March 1975), Millwall (on loan, late 1975), Los Angeles Aztecs (Easter 1976), Dorchester Town (late summer 1976), Los Angeles Aztecs (1977), Tulsa Roughnecks (1978), Seattle Sounders (1979), White Horse FC, Ampfield (1982), Totton FC (spring 1982). Retired mid-1980s, and later coached Orlando Lions FC

All of centre-forward Ron Davies' ten first-team appearances for United came as a substitute.
When he joined the club in 1974 he was in the twilight of an exceptionally fine career. He had already scored 275 League goals and had won 29 full caps for Wales, as well as lining up in three Under-23 internationals. One of the great marksmen of his time, Davies finally retired at the age of 41, having scored well over 320 goals in more than 700 competitive matches (for clubs and country). In the Football League alone his record was excellent - 275 goals in 549 appearances. Davies emigrated to California in the mid-1980s
Ron's younger brother, Paul, played for Arsenal and Charlton Athletic.
Club record: 10 apps.

DAVIES, Ronald Wyn

Born: Caernarfon, 20 March 1942
Career: Caernarfon Boys Club, Llanberis FC, Caernarfon Town (1959), Wrexham (1960), Bolton Wanderers (1962), Newcastle United (£80,000, 1966), Manchester City (1971), MANCHESTER UNITED (£25,000, September 1972), Blackpool (June 1973), Crystal Palace (on loan, late 1973), Stockport County (1975), Arcadia Shepherds (South Africa), Crewe Alexandra (1976), Bangor City, North Wales (1978). Retired 1980.
Centre-forward Wyn Davies - nicknamed 'Wyn the Leap' - like Ron (his fellow countryman, q.v) was well past his best when he joined the Reds in 1972.
Born just a couple of months before Ron (above), he was capped 34 times by Wales and also represented his country at Youth and Under-23 levels. In his professional career he scored in excess of 200 goals in more than 650 appearances, with his Football League record reading: 164 goals in 576 outings. Davies later ran a baker's shop in Bolton and now runs a smallholding near Caernafon
Club record: 17 apps. 4 goals

DAVIES, Simon Ithel

Born: Winsford, 23 April 1974
Career: MANCHESTER UNITED (apprentice June 1990, professional July 1992), Exeter City (on loan, 1993), Huddersfield Town (on loan, 1996), Luton Town (£175,000, August 1997), Macclesfield Town (late 1998).
Simon Davies - a strong, determined left-sided midfielder - has been capped once by Wales at senior level. He was an FA Youth Cup winner with United in 1992. Davies found opportunities limited on the left-wing with Ryan Giggs and Lee Sharpe ahead of him.
Club record: 20 apps. one goal

DAVIS, James

Born: Bromsgrove, 6 February 1982
Career: MANCHESTER UNITED (trainee 1999, professional 2001).
A striker, Jimmy Davis made his senior debut for United in their 4-0 League Cup defeat against Arsenal at Highbury on Bonfire Night, 2001. Davies represented England at Under-18 level five times during the 2000-01 season.
Club record: 1 app.

DAWSON, Alexander Downie

Born: Aberdeen, 21 February 1940,
Career: Hull Schools, MANCHESTER UNITED (junior, May 1955, professional, March 1957), Preston North End (October 1961), Bury (1967), Brighton & Hove Albion (1968), Brentford (on loan, 1970), Corby Town (1971-73). .
Centre-forward Alex Dawson - the son of a Grimsby-based trawlerman - was a fearless competitor, powerful and aggressive, a prolific goalscorer at every level with feet and head alike, finding the net on his League, FA Cup and League Cup debuts for the club. An England Schoolboy international, he helped United win the FA Youth Cup in 1956 and 1957 and played on the right-wing in the 1958 FA Cup final defeat by Bolton Wanderers, having bagged a hat-trick in the semi-final replay victory over Fulham when only 18 years, 33 days old - which made him the youngest post-war hat-trick hero at that time...and one of only a handful of players to claim a treble in a semi-final match. He lost his place in United's side to David Herd, his accelerated promotion after Munich adversely affecting his long term development. During his career he netted over 225 goals in more than 420 League and Cup appearances, gaining another FA Cup runners-up medal with Preston North End.
Club record: 93 apps. 54 goals

DEAN, Harold

Born: Hulme, Manchester, circa 1911
Career: Old Trafford FC (1929), MANCHESTER UNITED (amateur, September 1931), Mossley (December 1931).
Reserve centre-forward Harold Dean's two League games for United were against Chesterfield and Burnley in September/October 1931 when he deputised for Joe Spence.
Club record: 2 apps.

91

DEATHS

The Munich air disaster of 6 February 1958 claimed a total of eleven lives of people directly associated with the club(eight players and three officials). In all 22 people died in the crash, including eight journalists, one of them the former Manchester City and England goalkeeper Frank Swift.
(See under Munich).

Player	Age				
Frank Barrett	35	Mark Jones	24	John Scott	44
Geoff Bent	25	Les Lievesley	37	Les Sealey	43
Tom Blackstock	25	Oscar Linkson	28	Lawrie Smith	31
Roger Byrne	28	Pat McGuire	21	Tom Smith	33
Eddie Colman	21	Tom Meehan	28	Tommy Taylor	26
Laurie Cunningham	33	David Pegg	22	Sandy Turnbull	33
Alan Davies	30	Dick Pegg	37	Bert Whalley	45
Duncan Edwards	21	Billy Porter	40	Liam 'Billy' Whelan	22
Gilbert Godsmark	24	Charlie Radford	24	Walter Whittaker	38
Jim Holton	42	Hubert Redwood	30		
		Martyn Rogers	32		

Early Deaths

The following former Heath/United players all died at a relatively young age....

Fact File

Two Welshmen, Alan Davies (above) and Rees Williams both committed suicide; the former in Gower, Swansea in 1992 and the latter (aged 63) in the town of Abercanaid, near Merthyr in 1963.

Charlie Radford was killed in a motor cycling accident in 1924.

Hubert Redwood died of T.B. in 1943.

John Scott lost his life in tragic circumstances on a Manchester building site in June 1978.

Gilbert Godsmark died of a disease while serving in the Boer War in 1901.

Len Lievesey was coach of Turin when, along with several players and club officials, he was sadly killed in an air-crash in Superga, Italy in 1949.

Oscar Linkson, 'Sandy' Turnbull and Pat McGuire, a young amateur reserve with United, were all killed whilst on active service during WW1.

Former United player Aaron Hulme was 50 when he was killed in a motor cycling accident in 1933.

In January 1980, two Middlesbrough fans were killed when a wall collapsed at Ayresome Park as they made their way home after a League game against Manchester United whose own supporters were blamed for the incident!

92

DEBUTS

•Joe Spence scored four goals on his debut for United against Bury in a Lancashire Section match at Old Trafford in March 1919.

•United defender Allenby Chilton made his Football League debut for United in 1939, the day before WW2 was declared, had to wait seven years before appearing in his second match. Chilton was 32 when he made his England debut.

•The following players scored on their respective debuts for the club which also turned out to be their only senior appearance - Bob Stephenson v. Rotherham Town (League) in January, 1896, Billy Bambridge v. Accrington Stanley (FA Cup) in January 1946 and Albert Kinsey v. Chester (FA Cup) in January 1965.

•Alex Dawson scored on his Football League, FA Cup and League Cup debuts for United during the 1950s.

• On New Year's Day 1907, four players - Jimmy Bannister, Herbert Burgess, Billy Meredith and Sandy Turnbull - all made their debuts for United after being transferred from neighbouring Manchester City. Three years earlier they had all been found guilty of offences committed within the game (whilst associated with City) and all four had subsequently served a lengthy suspension which had expired.

•Tom Lowrie made his League debut for United in front of 71,000 fans at Maine Road in April 1948.

•On 7 February 1925, Albert Pape was ready to play for Clapton Orient against United in a League game at Old Trafford, but an hour or so before the scheduled 2pm kick-off he was transferred to the Reds and then turned out against his former club that afternoon. He celebrated the occasion by scoring in a 4-2 win.

•On 31 August 1946 United played their first League match in seven years, five players simultaneously making their League debuts for the club: Jack Crompton, Billy McGlen, Henry Cockburn, Jimmy Delaney and Charlie Mitten.

•Goalkeeper Alex Stepney made his League debut for United against rivals Manchester City in front of 62,085 spectators on 17 September 1966.

•Gary Neville (as a substitute) made his debut for United in the club's 100th European game against Torpedo Moscow in September 1992.

DEFEATS

An extended list of United's heaviest defeats at first-class level:

Home

1-7 v. Newcastle United (League)	10.09.1927
2-7 v. Sheffield Wed (FA Cup replay)	01.02.1961
4-7 v. Newcastle United (League)	13.09.1930
0-6 v. Aston Villa (League)	14.03.1914
0-6 v. Huddersfield Town (League)	10.09.1930

Away

0-7 v. Blackburn Rovers (League)	10.04.1926
0-7 v. Aston Villa (League)	27.12.1930
0-7 v. Wolverhampton W (League)	26.12.1931
1-7 v. Liverpool (League)	12.10.1895
1-7 v. Burnley (FA Cup replay)	13.02.1901

1-7 v. Aston Villa (League)	26.02.1910
1-7 v. Newcastle United (League)	10.09.1927
1-7 v. Charlton Athletic (League)	11.02.1939
2-7 v. Sheffield Wednesday (League)	16.11.1929
3-7 v. Grimsby Town (League)	26.12.1933
3-7 v. Newcastle United (League)	02.01.1960
4-7 v. Liverpool (League)	25.03.1908
0-6 v. Everton (League)	24.09.1892
0-6 v. Sunderland (League)	04.04.1893
0-6 v. Sheffield Wednesday (FA Cup)	20.02.1904
0-6 v. Aston Villa (League)	30.03.1912
0-6 v. Sunderland (League)	11.12.1926
0-6 v. Leicester City (League)	21.01.1961
0-6 v. Ipswich Town (League)	01.03.1980

Lost For Words

•United succumbed to 27 League defeats (in 42 games) in 1930-31. They were beaten nine times at home (21 starts) also in 1930-31 & suffered a similar fate in 1962-63.

• The most away defeats United has suffered in a League season has been 18 (out of 21 matches) in that disastrous 1930-31 campaign.

•The fewest League defeats suffered in a complete League season is three: in 1998-99, and 1999-2000 (both from 38-match programmes).

•On the road, the fewest defeats suffered by United has been two - in 1998-99.

• The fewest away defeats in a 21-match programme have been four in 1993-94. They also lost on four occasions (19 games) in 1905-06.

•United heaviest home defeat in the League Cup has been 3-0 - by lowly York City in 1995-96

•United's heaviest home defeat in a major European Competition is 3-2 by Real Madrid in 1999-2000 and by Deportivo La Coruna in 2001-02, having never lost by more than a single goal in a home tie.

DEFENSIVE RECORDS

•The fewest goals conceded by United in a complete League season has been 23 in 1924-25 (a record for Division 2 football).

•United did not concede a single goal in seven League games between 15 October and 3 December 1904. They repeated this sequence between 20 September & 1 November 1924.

•In the calendar year 1997, United went seven League games without conceding a goal (the last two of 1996-97, and the first five of 1997-98).

•Twice, in 1949-50 and 1981-82, United went six games without conceding a goal and they played through six competitive matches in each of seasons 1974-75, 1982-83 and 1992-93 without letting in a single goal.

•Over a period of some eight months - between April and December 1994 - United went a record 12 home League games without conceding a goal (almost 19 hours of playing time).

•During that same 1994-95 campaign, the Reds gave away only four Premiership goals at Old Trafford. They kept 18 clean sheets in the process.

•Peter Schmeichel did not concede a goal in his first four League outings for United (1991-92).

•The most clean sheets kept by United goalkeepers down the years has been 25 - in season 1924-25 (Alf Steward was the 'keeper). They had 24 'blanks' in 1993-94 when Peter Schmeichel and late on Gary Walsh commanded the number one position.

93

DELANEY, James

Born: Cleland, Lanarkshire 3 September 1914. Died: Cleland, Lanarkshire 26 September 1989.

Career: Cleland St Mary's FC (early 1933), Wishaw Juniors (trialist, summer 1933), Stoneyburn Juniors, Celtic (autumn 1933, MANCHESTER UNITED (£4,000, February 1946), Aberdeen (November 1950), Falkirk (late 1951), Derry City (1954), Cork Athletic (player-manager, season 1955-56), Elgin City (season 1956-57). Retired in April 1957.

Brittle-boned right-winger Jimmy Delaney won two Scottish League Championship medals with Celtic (1936 & 1938) and a Cup winners' medal in between times. He netted 79 goals in 178 senior appearances for the Glasgow club before his move to Old Trafford, Matt Busby having monitored his progress closely north of the border. Despite his fragile reputation, Delaney suffered no major injuries during his five years with United.

A member of United's FA Cup-winning team in 1948, Delaney was certainly an excellent capture, becoming a key member of United's famous forward-line.

After moving to Ireland he became the first player to collect three Cup winning medals in three different countries when Derry City lifted the Irish FA Cup in 1955, adding a FAI Cup runners-up medal to his tally with Cork soon afterwards. Capped 13 times by Scotland (four coming as a United player) Delaney also appeared in two Victory internationals and played six times for the Scottish League side. In the wartime encounter v. England in April 1946 he scored the game's only goal in front of 139,468 spectators at Hampden Park.

Club record: 184 apps. 28 goals

DEMPSEY, Mark James

Born: Manchester, 14 January 1964

Career: MANCHESTER UNITED (apprentice, May 1980, professional January 1982), Swindon Town (on loan, January-February 1985), Sheffield United (on loan, August 1985, then permanently September 1986)), Chesterfield (on loan, 1988), Rotherham United (autumn 1988), Macclesfield Town (1991). Retired mid-1990s.

Reserve midfielder Mark Dempsey made only a handful of senior appearances for United, his debut coming as a substitute in the European Cup-winners Cup encounter against Spartak Varna (home) in November 1983. It wasn't until December 1985 that he made his first League appearance for the club versus Ipswich Town.

Club record: 4 apps.

DENMAN, John

Born: Middlesbrough, circa 1870

Career: South Bank FC, NEWTON HEATH (March 1891-May 1892).

Reserve full-back Jack Denham spent just over a season with the club during which time he was unable to make an impact, leaving before the club entered the Football League.

Club record: 6 apps. (also 12 'other' apps)

DENNIS, William

Born: Mossley, 21 September 1896

Career: Ashton PSA, Army football (WW1). Guested for Birkenhead Comets FC & Tranmere Rovers (WW1), Stalybridge Celtic (1918), Blackburn Rovers (1919), Stalybridge Celtic (1920), MANCHESTER UNITED (May 1923), Chesterfield (February 1924), Wigan Borough (1928), Macclesfield (1930), Hurst FC (1931), Mossley's (trainer, 1934). Quit football during the late 1930s.

Billy Dennis, a reserve full-back, made only fleeting appearances during the 1923-24 season, his only one with the club. During his career he played in 312 League games. He had the distinction of serving in the British Army in both World Wars.

Club record: 3 apps.

DEPORTIVO LA CORUNA:

United met the Spanish champions in the Group stages of the 2001-02 European Champions League and in their away leg at the Riazor Stadium in front of 33,000 fans, they conceded two late goals to go down 2-1, having led 1-0 through a Paul Scholes strike five minutes before half-time.

A crowd of 65,585 attended the return match at Old Trafford and again United led - but a couple of horrific errors by goalkeeper Fabien Barthez gifted the Spaniards two goals for a 3-2 win. Ruud van Nistelrooy scored twice for United. Despite three defeats United still progressed to the next stage. Then after qualifying for the quarter-finals, United were ironically paired with the Spanish club again.

United played superbly well in the first leg in Spain, winning 2-0 before a 34,000 crowd thanks to a stunning 35-yard strike from David Beckham and a ninth European goal for Dutch ace van Nistelrooy. Unfortunately injuries to skipper Roy Keane in the first-half and Beckham late on (after an outrageous tackle by Diego Tristan who was shown only a yellow card), soured the evening.

This victory at La Coruna's stadium in April 2002 was United's first European success over a Spanish club in Spain. Their previous win in that country came in the 1999 European Cup Final v. Bayern Munich in Barcelona.

A crowd of 65,875 saw United, with goals by Ole Gunnar Solskjaer (2) and Ryan Giggs, take the return leg 3-2 at Old Trafford, but at a price! David Beckham suffered a broken foot following a reckless tackle by the Argentinian midfielder Aldo Duscher.

Thankfully he recovered in time to skipper England in the World Cup Finals that summer..

DERBIES (see also under Manchester City)

The first competitive match between the clubs took place North Road on 30 October 1891 when Newton Heath LYR beat Ardwick 5-1 in the first qualifying round of the FA Cup.

In all there have been 126 League 'derbies' (United have won 49 to City's 32) plus 10 more in Cup competitions (United 5 wins, City 4).

The first time United (as Newton Heath) and City opposed each other in League football was on 3 November 1894 in a League Division 2 game. United won 5-2 at Hyde Road, with Dick Smith scoring four times.

The first League game between the clubs after United had changed their name from Newton Heath, took place on 25 December 1902 and ended in a 1-1 draw at United's Bank Street ground, Clayton.

Bobby Charlton played in a club record 27 derbies for United against City. Alex Stepney starred in 24, Bill Foulkes in 23 and Martin Buchan 20.

DERBY COUNTY

United's League record against the Rams:

Season	Div	Home	Away	Season	Div	Home	Away
1892-93	1	W 7-1	L 1-5	1949-50	1	L 0-1	W 1-0
1893-94	1	L 2-6	L 0-2	1950-51	1	W 2-0	W 4-2
				1951-52	1	W 2-1	W 3-0
1906-07	1	D 1-1	D 2-2	1952-53	1	W 1-0	W 3-2
1912-13	1	W 4-0	L 1-2	1969-70	1	W 1-0	L 0-2
1913-14	1	D 3-3	L 2-4	1970-71	1	L 1-2	D 4-4
				1971-72	1	W 1-0	D 2-2
1919-20	1	L 0-2	D 1-1	1972-73	1	W 3-0	L 1-3
1920-21	1	W 3-0	D 1-1	1973-74	1	L 0-1	D 2-2
1922-23	2	D 0-0	D 1-1	1975-76	1	D 1-1	L 1-2
1923-24	2	D 0-0	L 0-3	1976-77	1	W 3-1	D 0-0
1924-25	2	D 1-1	L 0-1	1977-78	1	W 4-0	W 1-0
				1978-79	1	D 0-0	W 3-1
1926-27	1	D 2-2	D 2-2	1979-80	1	W 1-0	W 3-1
1927-28	1	W 5-0	L 0-5				
1928-29	1	L 0-1	L1-6	1987-88	1	W 4-1	W 2-1
1929-30	1	W 3-2	D 1-1	1988-89	1	L 0-2	D 2-2
1930-31	1	W 2-1	L 1-6	1989-90	1	L 1-2	L 0-2
				1990-91	1	W 3-1	D 0-0
1936-37	1	D 2-2	L 4-5				
				1996-97	PL	L 2-3	D 1-1
1938-39	1	D 1-1	L 1-5	1997-98	PL	W 2-0	D 2-2
				1998-99	PL	W 1-0	D 1-1
1946-47	1	W 4-1	L 3-4	1999-00	PL	W 3-1	W 2-1
1947-48	1	W 1-0	D 1-1	2000-01	PL	L 0-1	W 3-0
1948-49	1	L 1-2	W 3-1	2001-02	PL	W 5-0	D 2-2

Summary of League results:

	P	W	D	L	F	A
Premier League	12	6	4	2	24	12
Division 1	70	28	19	23	126	117
Division 2	6	0	4	2	2	6
Home	44	23	10	11	83	44
Away	44	11	17	16	69	91
Total	88	34	27	27	152	135

United's FA Cup record against County:

	Round	Venue	Result
1895-96	2	Home	D 1-1
	Replay	Away	L 1-5
1896-97	3	Away	L 0-2
1947-48	Semi-final	Hillsborough	W 3-1
1959-60	3	Away	W 4-2
1965-66	3	Away	W 5-2
1975-76	Semi-final	Hillsborough	W 2-0
1982-83	5	Away	W 1-0

United's League Cup record against County:

	Round	Venue	Result
1969-70	5	Away	D 0-0
	Replay	Home	W 1-0

Watney Cup

United met County in the Final of the 1970 Watney Cup and in front of 32,049 spectators at The Baseball Ground, they were defeated 4-1. George Best scored United's goal.

Fact File:

United first played County in season 1892-93, but did not beat them away from home until 1948-49 after 19 unsuccessful attempts (drawn 7, lost 12, goals 23 for 57 against). United have twice met County in the semi-final of the FA Cup at Hillsborough. In 1948 a Stan Pearson hat-trick saw United home 3-1 (going on to win the trophy) and in 1976 again it was another Pearson (Stuart) who helped the side win 2-0 thanks to two Gordon Hill goals.

Players with both clubs include: T Arkesden, F Buckley, J Clark, A Comyn (United 'A' team), G Daly, P Doherty (United WW2), W Douglas, E Green, J Griffiths (County WW2), W Halligan (United WW1), D Higginbotham, G Hill, T Leigh (County reserve), H Leonard, W Lievesley, P McGrath, H Mann, G Micklewhite (United reserve), R Milarvie, J Morris, R O'Brien, P Parker, F Stapleton, M Thomas, A Thomson (County trialist), G Vose (County WW2),

Also associated: T Docherty (manager of both clubs), S McClaren (United assistant-manager, County coach), F Blunstone (County assistant-manager, United Youth team manager), G Clayton (United player, County scout), A Ashman (United scout, Derby Chief Scout & assistant manager).

DEWAR, Neil Hamilton

Born: Lochgilphead, Argyllshire, 11 November 1908
Career: Lochgilphead United, Third Lanark (1929), MANCHESTER UNITED (£5,000, February 1933), Sheffield Wednesday (December 1933), Third Lanark (1937) Retired during the Second World War.
Centre-forward Neil Dewar drew up a useful scoring record with United. In 1931 he had helped Third Lanark win the Scottish Second Division title and also played in three full internationals for his country as well as representing the Scottish League. Dewar married the daughter of a Manchester United director (Councillor AE Thomson).
Club record: 36 apps. 14 goals

DIRECTORS

Over the years, several ex-players have served on the Board of Directors at Manchester United FC and they include Sir Bobby Charlton CBE, Harold Hardman, Les Olive and Harry Stafford.

Original Board of Directors (1902)

Mr John H Davies (Chairman), Mr J Brown of Denton, Mr W Davies of Manchester, Mr James Taylor of Sale and Harry Stafford.

Director's Minutes

In the early 1930s the United Board comprised: Mr J W Gibson (Chairman), Col. G Westcott, Mr M M Newton, Councillor A E Thomson and Mr Hugh Shaw.
In the first League season after WW2 (1946-47) seven men were on United's Board of Directors: Mr J W Gibson (Chairman), Mr Alan Gibson (Vice-Chairman), Mr H P Hardman, Dr W MacLean, Mr W H Petheridge and Mr G E Whittaker.

Other personnel who have served as members of the Old Trafford board (apart from those already named) include Mr Louis C Edwards, Mr C Martin Edwards (both also serving as Chairmen, the latter also Chief executive), Mr N Burrows, Sir Matt Busby, Mr G (Greg) Dyke, Mr J M Edelson, Mr R L Edwards, Mr D A Gill, Mr J G Gulliver, Mr D D Haroun, JP, Mr P F Kenyon, Mr M Knighton, Mr R P Launders, Mr A Midani, Mr E M Watkins Ll.M, Mr W A Young.
Ex-United player Eric Cantona and former manager Ron Atkinson both became Director of Football at Olympique Marseille and Coventry City respectively.
Steve Bruce was a short-time Director with Huddersfield Town, Bobby Charlton likewise with Wigan Athletic and Jeff Wealands with non-League side Altrincham.
Steve Coppell held the position of Technical Director with Crystal Palace; Johnny Giles was an Executive Director of the Irish club Shamrock Rivers and another former United player, Horace Blew, was a Director with Wrexham.
Jack Chapman, manager of United, became a Director of Plymouth Argyle; Sir Matt Busby CBE, initially signed as a player-manager by United, later held the position of Director at Old Trafford, while Ernest Mangnall, another ex-United manager, later served on the Board of Directors at Bolton Wanderers.
Neil Dewar, a player with the club in 1933, married the daughter of United director, Cllr AE Thomson.
And Ian Donald, a reserve full-back with United (1969-73) became a director, vice-Chairman and then Chairman of Aberdeen FC.

DISTURBANCES (Crowd)

•Following crowd trouble during their 1968 World Club Championship home game with Estudiantes de la Plata (see below) United were banned from European football for twelve months.
•United were banned from playing home games for three weeks at the start of the 1971-72 League season after crowd trouble at Old Trafford during the previous year. They played Arsenal at Anfield on 20 August and West Bromwich Albion at The Victoria Ground, Stoke three days later. United won both matches by 3-1.
•United were expelled from the 1977-78 European Cup Winners' Cup tournament after crowd trouble at an away match in France against St Etienne. The ban was later reduced....forcing United to play their 'home' leg 300 miles away at Home Park, Plymouth!
•United supporters were banned from travelling to away games on two separate occasions in the mid-1970s....and several clubs made their home games all-ticket when United were the visitors, also restricting the sale of matchday tickets to their own supporters after outbursts of hooliganism. (See also under Suspensions).

DJORDJIC, Bojan

Born: Belgrade, 6 February 1982
Career: Bromma Pojkarna (1990), MANCHESTER UNITED (£1 million, February 1999), Bromma Pojkarna (on loan, late 2000), Sheffield Wednesday (on loan, December 2001), AGF: Denmark (August 2002).
Midfielder Bojan Djordjic made his debut for United in season 2000-01, coming off the bench at Tottenham Hotspur on the final day of the campaign.
Bojan's father, Branko Djordjic was a Yugoslavian international with Red Star Belgrade
Club record: 2 apps.

95

DJURGAARDEN IF

In 1964, after earning a 1-1 draw in the first leg of a second round ICFC tie in Sweden before only 6,537 spectators, United came out on fire for the Old Trafford contest and won 6-1, Denis Law (3).Bobby Charlton (2) and George Best getting the goals.

DOCHERTY, Thomas Henderson

Refer to front of section.

DOHERTY, John Peter

Born: Manchester, 12 March 1935
Career: MANCHESTER UNITED (amateur, May 1950, professional March 1952), Leicester City (£6,500, October 1957, retired May 1958), Rugby Town (player-manager, summer 1958), Altrincham (player, autumn 1958) Hyde United (reserve team trainer, summer 1962). Employed as a scout for Burnley during the early 1980s while also working in insurance and finance.

Inside-forward John Doherty was at Old Trafford for seven years. He had to contest a first team place with so many class footballers, that despite his obvious ability. His senior appearances were rare. He had a troublesome knee which eventually forced his retirement from first-class football after a spell with Leicester City.

He was unlucky in that respect and also when he damaged his right knee (cartilage) playing for the RAF whilst completing his national service in 1954.

Club record: 26 apps. 7 goals

DONAGHY. Bernard

Born: Londonderry, Northern Ireland, circa 1881.
Career: Derry Celtic (1903), MANCHESTER UNITED (November 1905), Derry Celtic (May 1906), Burnley (summer 1907). Left League football in 1908.

Inside-forward Bernard Donaghy's three League appearances for the Reds came during the club's promotion-winning campaign of 1905-06. He twice represented the Irish League before joining United.

Club record: 3 apps.

DONAGHY, Malachy Martin

Born: Belfast, 13 September 1957
Career: Post Office SC (Belfast), Cromac Albion, Larne Town (1978), Luton Town (£20,000, summer 1978), MANCHESTER UNITED (£650,000, October 1988), Luton Town (on loan, mid 1989-90 season), Chelsea (£100,000, August 1992). Retired in May 1994.

Defender Mal Donaghy made almost 120 first-class appearances for the Reds. A steady, reliable defender with exceptional positional sense and awareness, he represented County Antrim at Gaelic football and played once for Northern Ireland at Under-21 level before going on to appear in 91 full internationals for his country, starring in both the 1982 and 1986 World Cup Finals. In fact, he skippered Northern Ireland at the age of 37. He also helped Luton win the Second Division title in 1982 and the League Cup in 1988 and made 415 League appearances during his two spells with the Hatters. He partnered Steve Bruce at the heart of the United defence before the arrival of Gary Pallister.

Club record: 119 apps.

DONALD, Ian Richard

Born: Aberdeen, 28 November 1951.
Career: Banks o'Dee 'A' Juveniles, MANCHESTER UNITED (apprentice June 1968, professional July 1969), Partick Thistle (January 1973), Arbroath (two seasons: 1973-75). Retired summer of 1976, later an Aberdeen director (appointed in 1980), becoming vice-Chairman (1986) then Chairman (1994) at Pittodrie, taking over the latter duties from his father, RM Donald, who 16 years earlier had given Alex Ferguson the manager's job at Aberdeen (June 1978). Serving under four different managers at Old Trafford and representing his country at Under-15, under-18 and Youth team levels, full-back Ian Donald was handed half-a-dozen first-team outings by United, his first against Portsmouth in a League Cup-tie in October 1970.

Club record: 6 apps.

DONALDSON, Robert

Born: Scotland, 1869
Career: Airdrieonians, Blackburn Rovers (albeit briefly in 1891), Airdrieonians, NEWTON HEATH (£50 down payment, May 1892), Luton Town (December 1897), Glossop North End (season 1898-99), Ashford (summer 1899). Retired in 1901. Later a trainer of a Manchester-based non-League club.

During his five-and-a-half years with the club, centre-forward Bob Donaldson scored virtually a goal every other game, including a haul of 56 in 131 League matches. An out-and-out striker, aggressive and hard-working, Donaldson netted on his debut against Burton Swifts in September 1891 (in the Football Alliance); he then scored against his former club (Blackburn) when making his Football League bow 12 months later, while simultaneously claiming United's first-ever goal in that competition. He also registered the club's first Football League hat-trick when he bagged a treble in a 10-1 home win over Wolves in October 1892. He was rewarded with a benefit match v. Blackburn in 1895.

Club record: 176 apps. 86 goals (also 76 'other' apps, 37 goals)

DONCASTER ROVERS

United's League record against Rovers:

Season	Div	Home	Away
1901-02	2	W 6-0	L 0-4
1902-03	2	W 4-0	D 2-2
1904-05	2	W 6-0	W 1-0
1935-36	2	D 0-0	D 0-0

Summary of League results

	P	W	D	L	F	A
Division 2	8	4	3	1	19	6
Home	4	3	1	0	16	0
Away	4	1	2	1	3	6
Total	8	4	3	1	19	6

Players with both clubs include: B Asquith (Rovers WW2), GE Bailey (United reserve), D Bradley (United reserve), H Bratt, R 'Berry' Brown, W Bullimore (United reserve), G Daly, VE Dodsworth (United reserve), P Doherty (United WW2, Rovers player & manager), J Dyer, G Gladwin, H Gregg, F Hopkin, L Lievesley, J Moody, G Moore, F Pepper, C Richards, E Vincent.
Also associated: M Setters (United player, Rovers manager), T Cavanagh (United assistant-manager/trainer, Rovers player), C Knowles (United amateur, Rovers coach).

DONNELLY
Born: Locally
Career: NEWTON HEATH (August 1890-May 1891).
Donnelly (first name unknown) was a reserve outside-left whose only game for the Heathens was against Bootle in the FA Cup in October 1890 in a match where both clubs fielded reserve sides owing to more important fixtures on the same day.
Club record: one app. (also one 'other' app)

DONNELLY, Anthony
Born: Middleton, early 1886. Died: Oldham, circa March 1947.
Career: Parkfield Lads' Club, Rhodes Church, Army football, Southampton (reserves), Norwich City (reserves), Heywood United (1907), MANCHESTER UNITED (July 1908), Heywood United (April 1912), Glentoran (1913), Heywood United (autumn 1913), Southampton (1919), Middleton Borough FC (late 1919). Retired early 1920s.
Full-back Tony Donnelly began his footballing career as a goalkeeper until his army service with the Royal Artillery.
Club record: 37 apps.

DOUBLE WINNERS
Manchester United have won the double (the Premiership title and FA Cup) on three occasions - an English record, shared by Arsenal. They were successful in seasons 1993-94, 1995-96 and again in 1998-99, completing the treble in the latter campaign, by winning the European Champions Cup.
Four players - Peter Schmeichel, Denis Irwin, Roy Keane and Ryan Giggs -all featured prominently in each of these three seasons.
The following players all figured in two double-winning campaigns: Steve Bruce, Gary Pallister, Paul Parker, Nicky Butt, David Beckham, Paul Scholes, David May, Eric Cantona, Andy Cole, Brian McClair, Gary Neville, Phil Neville, and Lee Sharpe.
Gary Neville and Butt also played (albeit only one match each) in 1993-94.
Earlier, in 1957, United travelled to Wembley hopeful of becoming the first club in the 20th century to complete the elusive 'double' having already won the league title by 11 points. Regrettably the early loss of goalkeeper Ray Wood meant United had to play the majority of the match with only 10 men, and an outfield player (Jackie Blanchflower) in goal. Aston Villa won 2-1 to dash United's hopes.

DOUGAN, Thomas
Born: Holytown, Lanarkshire, circa 1914,
Career: Tunbridge Wells Rangers, Plymouth Argyle (1936), MANCHESTER UNITED (professional, March 1939), Heart of Midlothian (September 1940), Kilmarnock (early 1946), Dunfermline Athletic (Easter 1946).. Did not play League football after 1948.
Reserve outside-right Tommy Dougan took over from Billy Bryant fairly late on during the 1938-39 season, making his debut against the champions-elect Everton.
Club record: 4 apps.

DOUGHTY, John
Born: Bilston, near Wolverhampton, winter, 1863. Died: Manchester, April 1937.
Career: Druids (1883), NEWTON HEATH (August 1886, professional 1887-May 1892), Hyde (season 1892-93), Fairfield.
Jack Doughty - the elder of two brothers who were deeply involved with Newton Heath during the early years - scored better than a goal every two games for the club (in senior and 'other' competitions).
Born to an Irish father and a Welsh mother, he was paid 10s (50p) a week (for a meal and train fare from Ruabon, North Wales) when he joined the Heathens from Druids. He was also fixed up with employment with the Lancashire & Yorkshire Railway Company, and later after turning 'pro', his wages rose to 30 shillings-a-week (£1.50). He made his Heathens debut against Fleetwood Rangers in the FA Cup in October 1886 when he claimed both goals in the 2-2 draw.
Doughty, who between 1886 and 1890 played eight times for Wales (winning seven of his caps as a Heathens player) and was once described as a 'crasher of the first order', scored four goals for the principality in an 11-0 win over Ireland in 1888, playing 'a rattling good game.' Four years later, in 1892 United played a selected Welsh international team in a benefit match for Doughty. Neither brother ever appeared in the Football League, but one suspects that they played together in many friendly matches prior to Newton Heath's entry in the League in 1892. Their club records refer to only first-class matches and give no indication of their importance to the early development of the club.
Doughty, the 'Warrior' as he was known, gained two Welsh Cup winners' medals (1885 & 1886) and two runners-up prizes with Druids and he also represented Denbighshire against Lancashire in 1885.
Club record: 31 apps. 14 goals (also 146 'other' apps, 97 goals)

97

DOUGHTY, Roger

Born: Cannock Chase, Staffs, 1867. Died: Prestwich, near Manchester, 19 December 1914.

Career: Druids (1884), NEWTON HEATH (July 1886), Fairfield FC (May 1892) West Manchester (1894), NEWTON HEATH (season 1896-97).

Wing-half Roger Doughty - younger brother of Jack (q.v) - had two spells with Newton Heath. He, too, was twice a Welsh Cup winner (1885 & 1886) and gained two full caps for his country (both in 1888) as well as playing in a tour game against the Canadians at Wrexham in 1891.

Doughty, who could play as a full-back, wing-half or inside-forward, was once a horse driver in a local colliery in his home county (Staffordshire). He wasn't regarded in the same class as brother John and was paid just £1-a-week after turning professional. Nevertheless he scored his fair share of goals - over 60 in more than 200 first-team outings. He also worked for the L & Y Railway Company.

Club record: 62 apps. 5 goals (also 146 'other' apps, 58 goals)

DOUGLAS, William

Born: Dundee circa 1872.

Career: Dundee Our Boys, Ardwick (1890), NEWTON HEATH (January 1894), Derby County (February 1896), Blackpool (1896) Warmley FC (1898-99), Dundee (1899). Did not play League football after 1902.

Goalkeeper Bill Douglas - who played in almost 50 consecutive games, commencing September 1894 - was suspended sine die by the club following the 'disgraceful beating' suffered by the team against Fairfield in a Manchester Cup-tie at Clayton in January 1896 (the Heathens lost 5-2).

Club record: 57 apps. (also 22 'other' apps).

DOW, John M

Born: Dundee, 1872

Career: Dundee Our Boys, Dundee FC, NEWTON HEATH (trialist January 1894, professional, February 1894), Fairfield FC (May 1897), Glossop North End (early 1898), Luton Town (1898), Middlesbrough (1900), West Ham United (season 1902-03), Luton Town (1903). Did not feature in League football after 1905.

Scottish full-back John Dow, strong and competent, also played for the Dundee Our Boys club (like Douglas, q.v), initially as a trialist. He spent just over three years with Newton Heath, leaving to join Fairfield in May 1897. At the age of 32 he was re-instated as an amateur and played regularly at non-League level for the next five years. When Dow arrived at the club for a trial, he was given the pseudonym of MJ Woods, but reverted to his proper name after being signed as a full-time professional.

Club record: 49 apps. 6 goals (also 19 'other' apps, 3 goals)

DOWNIE, Alexander Leek Brown

Born: Dunoon, circa 1876. Died: Withington, Manchester 9 December 1953.

Career: Glasgow Perthshire, Third Lanark (1898), Bristol City (season 1899-1900), Swindon Town (mid-1900), MANCHESTER UNITED (October 1902), Oldham Athletic (£600, October 1909), Crewe Alexandra (as player-coach, season 1911-12), Chorltonians FC (coach, 1913). Quit football in 1915.

Stylish wing-half Alex Downie - who scored on his United debut at Leicester Fosse in November 1902 - served the club for seven years, being a regular in the side alongside Charlie Roberts until December 1906 when Dick Duckworth came into the frame to bolster up the middle-line. However, Downie, a tremendous club man, bounced back again in 1907-08 and helped the Reds win the First Division title. He was rewarded with a benefit match in the next season.

Club record: 191 apps. 14 goals

DOWNIE, John Dennis

Born: Lanarkshire, 19 July 1925

Career: Lanark ATC, Bradford Park Avenue (1942, professional 1944), MANCHESTER UNITED (£18,000, March 1949), Luton Town (£10,000, August 1953), Hull City (1954) Kings Lynn (early 1958), Wisbech Town, Mansfield Town (1958-59 season), Darlington (1959-60 season), Hyde United (1960-61 season), Mossley (1961), Stalybridge Celtic (late in season 1961-62).. Left football in the mid-1960s.

Johnnie Downie worked as a 'Bevin Boy' at Castleford Colliery while learning the game at Bradford Park Avenue. He was signed by United, a club record buy at the time, having performed brilliantly in a series of cup-ties against United in 1948-49.

An inside-forward, clever on the ball with a good technique, he replaced the departed Johnny Morris in the first XI. He was the recipient of a League Championship medal in 1952 when he netted 11 goals in 31 First Division matches, partnering Ernie Bond on the left-wing most of the time..

Club record: 116 apps. 36 goals

DRAWS

5-5 has been United's highest-scoring draw in a major competition to date. They shared ten goals with Lincoln City at home on 16 October 1895 in a Second Division match.

United have also featured in seven 4-4 draws - all in the League. They have shared the spoils at home with Middlesbrough (in May 1931), Huddersfield Town (November 1947) and Newcastle United (January 1959). Away from home they have gained points from eight-goal thrillers with Liverpool (August 1953), Aston Villa (October 1955), Fulham (December 1960) and Derby County (December 1970).

United drew both their League Division One games with the champions Aston Villa in 1980-81 by 3-3, and they did likewise in their two European Champion's League Group 'D' encounters with Barcelona in 1998-99.

In the 1980-81 League season United drew a club record 18 games (11 at home, seven away).

United played out seven goalless draws in 1972-73 and they had three successive 0-0 scorelines in September 1921.

In 1893-94 United drew two of their 30 League matches. Their lowest number of draws in a 42-match programme is four, in 1934-35..

The team played out six successive League and Cup draws between mid-September and early October 1992.

United ran up six successive League draws between 30 October and 27 November 1988 whilst between 21 January and 22 April 1967 they conjured up a run of eight successive away draws.

There were four 1-1 scores for United in successive League games during September 1979 and the Reds drew their last four League games of the 1926-27 season.

The goalless draw with Chartlton Athletic on 11 may 2002 was United's first in the Premiership for three years - since their 0-0 encounter with Blackburn Rovers at Ewood Park on 12 May 1999.

DRAYCOTT, Levi William

Born: Newhall, near Derby, 15 February 1869

Career: Burslem Port Vale (briefly 1888), Stoke (1889), Burton Wanderers (1894), NEWTON HEATH (May 1896), Bedminster (May 1899), Bristol Rovers (1900), Wellingborough (1901), Luton Town (season 1902-03).

Half-back or right-winger Billy Draycott helped his first club, Port Vale, 'share' the Staffs Charity Cup in 1891. He had three excellent seasons with the Heathens, missing only one game in his initial campaign. After leaving the club he went on to appear in over 200 games before retiring in 1903.

Club record: 93 apps. 6 goals (also 30 'other' apps, one goal).

DUBLIN, Dion

Born: Leicester, 22 April 1969

Career: Oakham United, Norwich City (early 1988), Cambridge United (summer 1988), MANCHESTER UNITED (£1 million, August 1992), Coventry City (£2 million, September 1994), Aston Villa (£5.75 million, 1998), Millwall (on loan, March 2002).

Striker Dion Dublin was handed a free transfer by the Canaries in 1988. Ten years later he was valued at almost £6 million! The 6ft 2in striker was scoring plenty of goals for Third Division Cambridge (he hit a hat-trick on his League debut against Peterborough United) and his all-action displays were attracting many scouts and managers to The Abbey Stadium. After claiming 73 goals in just over 200 senior appearances for Cambridge (he was their top marksman three seasons running as well as helping them win the Third Division title in 1991) Dublin was swept away to Old Trafford by Alex Ferguson. Unfortunately - after scoring the winner on his full debut for the Reds - he suffered a broken leg and ankle ligament damage that effectively ruined the rest of that season...he was actually sidelined for five months without kicking a ball! He came back late on and scored seven goals in 13 Pontins League matches, but following the arrival of Frenchman Eric Cantona, he found himself technically a reserve forward and subsequently left the club for Highfield Road. After firing in 72 goals in 171 senior appearances for the Sky Blues, Dublin started off like a house on fire with Villa, hitting the net five times in his first two outings, and with the odd exception here and there he continued to do well with the Birmingham club. In December 1999 Dublin suffered a serious injury during the home game with Sheffield Wednesday. Fractured neck vertebrae were diagnosed and surgery was required to repair what could easily have been a life-threatening injury. Dublin was not expected to return that season but he defied all odds and helped Villa reach the FA Cup Final, scoring the deciding penalty in the semi-final shoot-out with Bolton Wanderers. A powerful, sometimes awkward looking player, exceptionally strong in the air and no mean performer on the ground, Dublin has so far earned four full England caps.

Club record: 17 apps. 3 goals

DUCKWORTH, Richard

Born: Collyhurst, Manchester, circa 1880.

Career: Smedley Road School, Harpurhey Wesleyan Juniors, Rossall Mission, Stretford FC, Newton Heath Athletic, MANCHESTER UNITED (October 1903, retired May 1915).

Half-back Dick Duckworth formed a tremendous middle-line alongside Alex Bell and Charlie Roberts. He gained two League Championship medals with United (1908 & 1911), an FA Cup winners medal (1909) and he also made five appearances for the Football League XI as well as touring South Africa with the selected FA party in 1910. Without doubt one of United's greatest pre-First World War players, Duckworth was solid in the tackle, positive in his movement and totally reliable. He never gave his opponent a moment's respite, always grafting in centre-field. A knee injury disrupted his career halfway through the 1913-14 season and although he remained a registered with player with the club until League football was suspended in 1915 owing to WW1, he was eventually forced to retire at the age of 35. He later became a licensee.

* Duckworth's son, Richard junior, who was on United's books in 1926, played for Rochdale, Oldham Athletic, Chesterfield, Southport, Chester, Rotherham United and York City, and he also managed Newark Town, York and Stockport County as well as scouting for both Birmingham City and Sheffield United.

Club record: 254 apps. 11 goals

DUKLA PRAGUE

United progressed through to the second round of the European Cup in 1957-58 with a relatively comfortable 3-1 aggregate victory over Dukla Prague, winning 3-0 (h) prior to a 1-0 defeat in Prague..

However, it was a different story as United battled to get through to the 2nd round of the 1983-84 European Cup-winners Cup competition. They managed it, just, on the away goal rule after being given a hard and testing time by a very professional and well-organised Prague side. The scores were 1-1 at Old Trafford and 2-2 in Czechoslovakia.

DUNCAN, Adam Scott Matthewson

Secretary/manager of MANCHESTER UNITED from June 1932 until September 1937, Scott Duncan was given a salary reported to be £800 per annum when he arrived at Old Trafford. He spent a great deal of money of new players during his five years with the club, including a fair few from Scotland, his home country. Unfortunately for the first three seasons in charge his efforts failed to produce the goods and, in fact, United were a moderate Second Division team, finishing 6th, 20th (just escaping from the claws of relegation to the Third Division in 1934) and 5th. However, in 1935-36 things improved ten-fold as the Reds won promotion as Division Two champions, only to fall straight back down the ladder the very next season. Soon afterwards Duncan departed to take over as boss of Southern League side, Ipswich Town. He stayed at Portman Road until 1958, acting as secretary for the last three years from August 1955. He steered the East Anglia club into the Football League and to promotion as Third Division (South) champions in 1954.

Born in Dumbarton on 2 November 1888, Duncan - an orthodox outside-right who represented the Anglo Scots against the Home Scots - played for Dumbarton Corinthians, Clydebank Juniors, Shettleston Juniors, Dumbarton, Newcastle United (with whom he won a First Division Championship medal in 1909) and Glasgow Rangers (signed for £600). Then as a wartime guest he served Manchester United (one game in November, 1918), Celtic and Partick Thistle before ending his playing days with Dumbarton (1919-20) and Cowdenbeath (from July 1920 until may 1922). He was then appointed secretary/manager of Hamilton Academical in July 1923. Two years later he took a similar position with his former club, Cowdenbeath, and then moved to Old Trafford after that. Duncan died in Helensburgh, Scotland on 3 October 1976, a month before his 88th birthday.

DUNDEE UNITED

United scraped into the 4th round of the 1984-85 UEFA Cup with a hard-earned victory over Dundee United. After a nail-biting 2-2 draw at Old Trafford in front of 48,278 spectators, United had to pull out all the stops to grab a 3-2 win at Tannadice where the turn-out was 21,821, an own-goal by the Dundee defender McGinnis proving a vital factor at the end of the night!

Players with both clubs include: F Kopel, C McGillivray (also Dundee United manager), R Milne.

DUNN, William

Born: Middlesbrough, circa 1877
Career: South Bank FC (1895), NEWTON HEATH (season 1897-98), Reading (1898).
Eight of Billy Dunn's first team appearances for the Heathens were on the left-wing as partner to Joe Cassidy. A versatile forward his other four were either as outside or inside-right.
Club record: 12 apps. (also 5 'other' apps).

DUNNE, Anthony Peter

Born: Dublin, 24 July 1941
Career: Shelbourne (1958), MANCHESTER UNITED (£5,000, April 1960), Bolton Wanderers (August 1973), Detroit Express (1979), Bolton Wanderers (coach, 1979-81), FC Stenjiker, Norway (coach, season 1982-83).
Full-back Tony Dunne amassed a fine record with United, appearing in almost 540 senior games. He gained an FAI Cup winners medal with Shelbourne prior to joining United and six months into his career at Old Trafford he made his Football League debut against Burnley.
A neat and tidy defender, small in size and build, he was never 'roasted' by his opposing winger due to his exceptional speed, comfortable in both full-back berths. In 1963 he gained an FA Cup winners' medal, added a League Championship winning prizes to his collection in 1965 and 1967 and then crowned it all by helping United win the European Cup in 1968, playing a 'blinder' in the Final.
Twelve months after that Wembley triumph Dunne was voted 'Irish Footballer of the Year'. He won 32 caps for the Republic of Ireland and also represented his country at amateur level, playing in the Olympic Games soccer tournament. He helped Bolton win the Second Division title and replaced his ex-colleague and former United defender Bill Foulkes as coach to the Norwegian club FC Stenjiker in 1982.
In his career Dunne amassed well over 750 appearances at club and international level. After football he ran a successful golf driving range in Altrincham.
Club record: 539 apps. 2 goals

DUNNE, Patrick Anthony Joseph

Born: Dublin, 9 February 1943
Career: Dublin City Boys, Everton (1959, professional 1960) Shamrock Rovers (1962), MANCHESTER UNITED (£10,500, May 1964), Plymouth Argyle (£5,000, February 1967), Shamrock Rovers (1970-71); thereafter Charity football.
Fearless Pat Dunne, who was one of six goalkeepers at Goodison Park in the early 1960s, made his debut for the Reds against his former club (Everton) in September 1964 when he replaced David Gaskell. He retained his place in the side and helped United win the First Division title, making 37 League appearances that season. Afterwards, Dunne contested the number one position with both Gaskell and Harry Gregg, finding it hard to hold down a first team spot. Then, following the arrival of Alex Stepney from Millwall, he departed to Plymouth, being voted 'Player of the Year' in his first season at Home Park. Dunne was capped five times by the Republic of Ireland in the 1960s. He was still an active player into his fifties.
Club record: 67 apps.

DUXBURY, Michael

Born: Accrington, 1 September 1959
Career: St Mary's College (Blackburn), Lancashire Schools, trialist with Arsenal, Everton, Leeds United and Liverpool, MANCHESTER UNITED (associated schoolboy May 1975, apprentice July 1976, professional October 1976), Blackburn Rovers (August 1990), Bradford City (on loan, then signed permanently, 1992).
A forward at school, Mike Duxbury developed into a versatile player, able to operate effectively in defence or midfield. Capped by England on seven occasions at Under-21 level and ten times by the full international side, he took over from John Gidman at right-back in United's first XI in 1982-83 - the season he gained the first of his two FA Cup winners' medals (his second followed in 1985). He was also in United's beaten League Cup Final side of 1983. On leaving Old Trafford he teamed up once more with his ex-team-mate Frank Stapleton at Ewood Park.
Duxbury's total of senior appearances for United included 299 in the Football League.
Club record: 382 apps. 7 goals

DYER, James Arthur

Born: Blacker Hill, nr Barnsley 24 August 1883.
Career: Wombwell FC, Barnsley (1901), Doncaster Rovers (season 1903-04), Ashton Town (season 1904-05), MANCHESTER UNITED (May 1905), West Ham United (May 1908), Bradford Park Avenue (season 1909-10), Wombwell FC (1910). Retired circa 1912.
Jimmy Dyer began his career as a centre-forward but ended it as a steady, reliable centre-half. His chances were limited at Old Trafford due to the presence of Charlie Sagar, Alex Menzies, 'Clem' Beddow and Jimmy Turnbull...hence his switch to the defence!
Club record: 1 app.

DYNAMO KIEV

Teddy Sheringham's goal (for a 1-0 win in front of 66,776) spared United's blushes in their 2000-01 Champions League home encounter against a tough, resilient Kiev side, following a workmanlike goalless draw on a heavy Kiev pitch earlier in the season.

E for...

EDWARDS, Duncan

Born: Dudley, West Midlands 1 October 1936. Died: Rechts der Isar Hospital, Munich, 21 February 1958. Career: Priory Road Junior and Wolverhampton Street Secondary Schools, Dudley Schoolboys, Worcestershire County XI, Birmingham & District Boys, MANCHESTER UNITED (amateur, June 1952, professional October 1953 until his death in 1958). Duncan Edwards was a colossus. There was only one Duncan. He was the greatest. So many people have said that - and it's true!

'Big Dunc' - as United and, indeed, England players (and supporters) knew him - was unique, the complete multi-purpose player, a talent for all seasons, yet with a gentle nature, quiet and unassuming.

Physically, he was remarkable - legs of elephant strength, oak-like thighs, a vast barrel chest, enormous shoulders and a solid frame to match anyone or anything! The red shirt of United or the white jersey of England often seemed to stretch to vast proportions to contain him! This physique, combined with great athleticism, made for an extraordinary player.

Allied to this asset was a brilliantly incisive footballing brain, plus a temperament which only the great possess - indifferent to occasion and unmoved by opposition, Edwards was brilliant.

He oozed confidence that allowed him to play as an inside-forward and score goals, to move back and defend like fury, or battle in midfield to cope with the artists of the mid-fifties.

Whichever role he filled he was fluid, distinctive and methodical. But it was as a left-half for which he will be best remembered.

There was an invincible quality about Edwards which spawned a string of anecdotes, many of them probably apocryphal.

Some years later Sir Matt Busby unveiled two stained glass windows in the church as a permanent memorial to the greatest of the Busby Babes. But perhaps the most memorable epitaph was spoken at his funeral by the Rev. A Dawson Catterell in his sermon: "Talent and even genius we shall see again. But there will be only one Duncan Edwards."

Around 1,000 people watched the unveiling of Duncan Edwards' statue in Dudley on 14 October 1999.

Club record: 177 apps. 21 goals

EARP, John

Born: Locally, circa 1864
Career: NEWTON HEATH (August 1884-April 1887)
During his three seasons with the club, Jack Earp played as a centre-forward, half-back and right-winger. His only senior appearance was in the FA Cup-tie against Fleetwood Rangers in October 1886.
Club record: one app. (also 64 'other' apps, 11 goals).

EDGE, Alfred

Born: Goldenhill, Stoke-on-Trent, winter 1864. Died: Stoke-on-Trent, April 1941.
Career: Goldenhill Wanderers, Stoke (1884), NEWTON HEATH (May 1889), Notts Jardines (May 1892), Stoke (autumn 1892), Macclesfield, Northwich Victoria (summer 1893), Ardwick (early 1894).
Inside-right Alf Edge had an excellent season with the Heathens, in the club's last campaign in the Football Alliance. He had been a member of Stoke's team against West Bromwich Albion in the club's first-ever Football League match in September 1888. After Stoke had been voted out of the League in 1890, he helped the Potters win the Football Alliance Championship in 1891, and represented the 'Alliance' against the Football League at Sheffield in April of that year. He chose to leave the Heathens in the summer of 1892 and signed for non-League side Notts Jardines. However, the transfer was not acceptable by the FA (as the Heathens knew nothing about the proposed move) and the player was suspended for a few months until he eventually agreed to return to his former club, Stoke. Edge was later rewarded with a gold medal for his service to Stoke for whom he holds the record of scoring most goals in an FA Cup-tie - five against Caernarfon Wanderers in October 1886.
Club record: 22 apps. 10 goals (also 20 'other' apps, 7 goals)

EDMONDS, Hugh

Born: Chryston, Ayrshire, 1884
Career: Hamilton Academical, Belfast Distillery (1907), Linfield (1908), Bolton Wanderers (1909), MANCHESTER UNITED (February 1911), Glenavon (player-manager, July 1912), Belfast Distillery (1913). Did not figure after WW1.
Goalkeeper Hugh Edmonds was languishing in Bolton's reserve side when signed by United in February 1911. Two months later he celebrated with a League Championship medal. He went on to make over 50 senior appearances in the first XI.
Club record: 51 apps.

EDWARDS, Duncan

Refer to front of section.

EDWARDS, Louis

Born in Salford in 1914, Louis Edwards was in the wholesale meat business when he joined the MANCHESTER UNITED board on 7 February 1958 (24 hours after the Munich air disaster). He was elected Chairman on 9 June 1965 and held that position for 15 years until handing over the mantle to his son, Martin, early in January 1980.
A former member of the Football League Management Committee, he gracefully stood down after Matt Busby had been nominated to sit on that same committee.
Edwards, who served United for a total of 22 years, died of a heart attack at his Cheshire home on 25 February 1980.

EDWARDS, Martin

Martin Edwards took over as Chairman of MANCHESTER UNITED (without hesitation) from his dedicated father at the club's Annual General Meeting in July 1980, having been unofficially appointed on 22 March of that year, a month after the death of his father, Louis (q.v). And he has been in office ever since, seeing the Reds win every honour in the game and, at the same time, become the world's richest football club, having been the driving force behind the club becoming a Plc.

EDWARDS, Paul Francis

Born: Shaw, near Oldham, 7 October 1947
Career: St Joseph's FC (Shaw), Chadderton Schoolboys, MANCHESTER UNITED (amateur December 1963, professional February 1965), Oldham Athletic (on loan, September 1972, then permanently, March 1973), Stockport County (1978-80), Ashton United (season 1980-81), Manchester United Old Boys. Retired from football in 1993.
Defender Paul Edwards had to wait six years before making his senior debut for United. He won England Under-23 honours during his time at Old Trafford, finally establishing himself in the League side during the second half of the 1968-69 season when he emerged as a useful right-back. His later appearances were at centre-half, but rarely appeared during Frank O'Farrell's reign as manager, seeming to lose confidence. Edwards was an excellent cricketer, considered a possible County player before choosing football.
Club record: 71 apps. 2 goals

ELLIS, David

Born: Kirkcaldy, 1900.

Career: Glasgow Ashfield, Airdrieonians (1920), Maidstone United (1922), MANCHESTER UNITED (£1,250, June 1923), St Johnstone (£500, September 1924), Bradford City (1926), Arthurlie FC (season 1928-29).

Winger David Ellis did not live up to expectations and struggled with his form at Old Trafford.

Club record: 11 apps.

ERENTZ, Fred C

Born: Broughty Ferry, March 1870. Died: Haughton Green, Denton 6 April 1938

Career: Dundee Our Boys, NEWTON HEATH (June 1892, retired May 1902).

Fred Erentz, a strong-tackling defender, appeared in well over 300 senior games during his ten years with the Heathens. Reliable, uncompromising, quick in recovery (he was a former quarter-mile champion in Scotland) Erentz was the team's penalty expert and initially formed a fine partnership in the Heathens half-back line with Billy Stewart, later accompanying Harry Stafford at full-back. A wonderfully consistent performer, Fred Erentz was a veritable giant in the club's early history. He was 16 stone in weight when he retired!

Club record: 310 apps. 10 goals (also 79 'other' apps, one goal).

ERENTZ, Harold Bernt

Born: Dundee, 17 September 1874. Died: Dundee, 19 July 1947

Career: Dundee (1895), Oldham County (1896), NEWTON HEATH (May 1897), Tottenham Hotspur (May 1898), Swindon Town (1904). Forced to retire after breaking his right leg in 1905. Later Corinthians trainer (pre WW1).

A Scotsman of Danish extraction and nicknamed 'Tiger', Harry Erentz (brother of Fred, q.v) was another hard-tackling defender who gave very little away. After failing to establish himself with the Heathens he went on to appear in more than 300 games for Spurs, helping them win the Southern League title in 1899-1900 and the FA Cup the following season.

Club record: 9 apps. (also 8 'other' apps)

ESTUDIANTES DE LA PLATA

United met the South American club champions over two legs in the 1968 World Club Championship.

The first game took place in Argentina on 25 September where United lost 1-0 in front of 55,000 spectators. The return leg at Old Trafford three weeks later (on 16 October) drew a crowd of 63,500 and ended level at 1-1, leaving Estudiantes the winners by 2-1 on aggregate, the crucial goal being scored by Juan Sebastian Veron's father! United, however, were banned from European football for one year after crowd trouble at their home game.

Player with both clubs: JS Veron

Associated: N McBain (United player, Estudiantes coach)

EURO '96

Three Group 'C' matches in Euro '96 were staged at Old Trafford. They were: Germany 2 Czech Republic 0; Russia 0 Germany 3 and Italy 0 Germany 0. A quarter-final showdown followed when Germany beat Croatia 2-0 before a semi-final contest saw the subsequent winners of the trophy France beat the Czech Republic 6-5 in a penalty shoot-out (after a 0-0 draw).

(See under OLD TRAFFORD).

EUROPEAN COMPETITIONS

United's full season-by-season record in the various European club competitions is:

Season	Competition	P	W	D	L	F	A	Rd	Manager
1956-57	EC	8	4	2	2	24	12	S/f	Matt Busby
1957-58	EC	8	5	1	2	19	12	S/f	Matt Busby
1963-64	ECWC	6	3	1	2	15	11	Q/f	Matt Busby
1964-65	ICFC	11	6	3	2	29	10	S/f	Matt Busby
1965-66	EC	8	7	0	1	23	8	S/f	Matt Busby
1967-68	EC	9	5	3	1	16	6	F (W)	Matt Busby
1968-69	EC	8	5	1	2	18	7	S/f	Matt Busby
1976-77	UEFA	4	2	0	2	3	4	2	Tommy Docherty
1977-78	ECWC	4	2	1	1	8	7	2	Dave Sexton
1980-81	UEFA	2	0	2	0	1	1	1	Dave Sexton
1982-83	UEFA	2	0	1	1	1	2	1	Ron Atkinson
1983-84	ECWC	8	3	3	2	12	9	S/f	Ron Atkinson
1984-85	UEFA	8	4	3	1	12	7	Q/f	Ron Atkinson
1990-91	ECWC	9	7	2	0	17	4	F (W)	Alex Ferguson
1990-91	ESC	1	1	0	0	1	0	F (W)	Alex Ferguson
1991-92	ECWC	4	1	2	1	3	4	2	Alex Ferguson
1992-93	UEFA	2	0	2	0	0	0	1	Alex Ferguson
1993-94	EC	4	2	2	0	8	6	2	Alex Ferguson
1994-95	EC	6	2	2	2	11	11	1st Gp	Alex Ferguson
1995-96	UEFA	2	0	2	0	2	2	1	Alex Ferguson
1996-97	EC	10	4	1	5	10	5	S/f	Alex Ferguson
1997-98	EC	8	5	2	1	15	6	Q/f	Alex Ferguson
1998-99	EC	13	6	7	0	31	16	F (W)	Alex Ferguson
1999-00	EC	14	8	3	3	21	11	Q/f	Alex Ferguson
1999-00	ESC	1	0	0	1	0	1	F (L)	Alex Ferguson
2000-01	EC	14	6	4	4	22	13	Q/f	Alex Ferguson
2001-02	EC	16	8	6	2	31	14	S.f	Alex Ferguson

European Summary:

Competition	Seasons	P	W	D	L	F	A	
EC/Champions Lge	13	126	67	34	25	249	127	(66.67%)
ICFC/UEFA	7	31	12	13	6	48	26	(59.68%)
ECWC	5	31	16	9	6	55	35	(66.13%)
E Super Cup		2	1	0	1	1	1	(50.00%)
Totals	25	190	96	56	38	353	189	(65.26%)

(Not including FIFA World Club championships etc).

Competition Summaries
European Cup/Champions League matches:

Venue	P	W	D	L	F	A	
Home	62	45	11	6	157	52	
Away	62	20	23	19	86	73	
Neutral	2	2	0	0	6	2	
Totals	126	67	34	25	249	127	(66.67%)

European Cup-winners Cup

Venue	P	W	D	L	F	A	
Home	15	10	5	0	38	10	
Away	15	5	4	6	15	24	
Neutral	1	1	0	0	2	1	
Totals	31	16	9	6	55	35	(66.13%)

ICFC/UEFA Cup

Venue	P	W	D	L	F	A	
Home	15	8	7	0	27	9	
Away	16	4	6	6	21	17	
Totals	31	12	13	6	48	26	(59.68%)

European Super Cup

Venue	P	W	D	L	F	A	
Home	1	1	0	0	1	0	
Neutral	1	0	0	1	0	1	
Totals	2	1	0	1	1	1	(50.00%)

Overall	P	W	D	L	F	A	
Home	93	64	23	6	223	71	
Away	93	29	33	31	122	114	
Neutral	4	3	0	1	8	4	
Totals	190	96	56	38	353	189	(64.63%)

Managers' 'European' records:

Manager	P	W	D	L	F	A
M Busby	58	35	11	12	144	66
T Docherty	4	2	0	2	3	4
D Sexton	6	2	3	1	9	8
R Atkinson	18	7	7	4	25	18
A Ferguson	104	50	35	19	172	93
(5 managers)	190	96	56	38	353	189

Competition Synopsis
European Cup/UEFA Champions League

As Football League champions, United first took part in this prestigious European competition in 1956-57 - the second season it had been held.

Their first opponents (and, indeed, the club's first-ever European opposition in a competitive match) were the Belgian champions, RSC Anderlecht. The game took place in Belgium on 12 September 1956 and in front of 35,000 spectators, goals by Dennis Viollet & Tommy Taylor earned United a 2-0 win.

The second-leg was staged at Maine Road and 40,000 fans saw a rather one-sided affair, United completely overwhelming the Belgian champions with a 10-0 victory with Viollet (4) & Taylor (3) leading the goal-rush.

After defeating Borussia Dortmund and then Athletic Bilbao, United succumbed in the semi-finals to the crack Spanish side Real Madrid, who went through 5-3 on aggregate.

A crowd of 135,000 (the biggest audience a United team has ever played to) saw the encounter in Spain which Real won 3-1.

The Italian giants AC Milan ended United's European Cup dreams twelve months later, winning the two-legged semi-final showdown 5-2 on aggregate, coming back from 2-1 down to win their home game in the San Siro 4-0 in front of almost 80,000 fans. Most of United's talented team, of course, had been killed on the snow-bound Munich runway only a month or so earlier.

It was disappointment again at the semi-final stage for United in 1965-66 when unfancied Partizan Belgrade went through to the Final with a 2-1 aggregate semi-final victory - after United had sensationally won 5-1 in Benfica in the previous round.

However, at long last, in 1967-68, United won the coveted European Cup (see below). En-route to the Final at

The first leg in Manchester United's match with Bilbao in the European Cup. At Bilbao the home team won 5-3 but in the second leg Manchester United won 3-0 and passed into the semi-final 6-5 aggregate score.

Wembley the Reds ousted Hibernians (Malta), FK Sarajevo (Yugoslavia), Gornik Zabrze (Poland) and Real Madrid (Spain), beating their Spanish foe 4-3 on aggregate after a marvellous 3-3 draw inside the majestic Bernabeu Stadium in the second-leg when 125,000 fans were present.

As holders United then went out of the competition, again at the semi-final stage, in 1968-69, losing once more to AC Milan, this time 2-1 on aggregate.

It would be another 25 years before United took part in the European Cup again. This time (1993-94) they went out in round 2, beaten by the Turkish side, Galatasaray on the away goals rule.

In 1994-95 United failed to progress beyond the first stage, winning two of their six matches, one being a convincing 4-0 home victory over Galatasaray!

On 30 October 1996, Fenerbahce, the Turkish champions, ended United's 40-year unbeaten home record in European competitions when they earned a 1-0 victory at Old Trafford in the Champions League.

It was semi-final agony again for Alex Ferguson's troops that season, beaten by Borussia Dortmund - their third home defeat of the campaign - this after United had impressed in the quarter-finals with a 4-0 win over FC Porto at Old Trafford.

Following defeat in the quarter-finals (to Monaco) in 1997-98, the European Cup found its way 'back' to Old Trafford the very next season - in sensational fashion (see match report).

After going through the various stages of the competition which included a qualifying victory over LKS Lodz, and a stage one triumph over Brondby, plus two 3-3 draws with Barcelona and a couple of stalemates with the arch enemy Bayern Munich, United found themselves in the quarter-finals. Here they disposed of the first of two Italian clubs, Inter Milan and then took out Juventus in the semis before meeting Bayern (again) in the Final in Barcelona. Amid great excitement the Reds scored twice in the dying seconds to snatch a famous victory in front of almost 90,000 spectators inside the ground and millions more watching on TV.

Their excursions in the 1999-2000, 2000-01 & 2001-02 European Champions League competitions were certainly entertaining and adventurous.

In the former United battled hard and long and reached the quarter-finals only to lose out to Real Madrid who came to Old Trafford and won 3-2, having been held to a 0-0 draw in the Bernabeu Stadium.

The following season again it was quarter-final disappointment for the Reds who again fell victims to their arch enemy from the German Bundesliga, Bayern Munich who won both legs, 1-0 at Old Trafford and 2-1 in Munich's Olympic Stadium.

Then in season 2001-02 - after a hard, sometimes uneasy passage, punctured with some excellent results both at home and away - United reached the semi-final stage. Unfortunately they fell victim of a very useful Bayer 04 Leverkusen side who, after drawing 2-2 at Old Trafford, were held 1-1 in the return leg in Germany, but United frustratingly went out on the away goal rule.

105

European Cup/Champions League Fact File

United reached the semi-final stage of the competition in each of their first five seasons of entering - 1956-57, 1957-58, 1965-66, 1967-68 & 1968-69.

United scored at least one goal in their first 26 home European Cup encounters. The run came to an end in October 1996 when they failed to break down a tight Fenerbahce defence and lost 1-0.

United's biggest European Cup win is 10-0 (v. Anderlecht in 1956) at Maine Road. Their biggest victory at Old Trafford has been 7-1 against the Irish club Waterford in October 1968.

Dennis Viollet (v. Anderlecht in 1956) and Denis Law (v. Waterford 1968) both scored four goals in a European Cup game.

Gary Neville has played in a record 70 European Cup/Champions League games for United, while Andy Cole has scored most goals, total 19.

1968 European Cup Final at Wembley Stadium
United 4 Benfica 1 (aet)

After three semi-final disappointments and having first played in the competition 12 years earlier, United at long last fulfilled Matt Busby's dream by winning the European Cup. And they did it in style, on English soil in front of almost 99,882 fans, with millions more watching world-wide on TV.

It was not a classic final by any means, but United, backed by 60,000 fans inside the stadium and with George Best and skipper Bobby Charlton in excellent form, had that extra fighting spirit when it mattered most.

After a hard fought and goalless first-half, United took the lead in the 53rd minute. David Sadler and Tony Dunne combined down the left and from Sadler's precise cross Charlton glanced a rare header wide of 'keeper Henrique.

The goal gave United confidence. John Aston started to make in-roads down the left; Sadler missed a golden opportunity of increasing the lead, Charlton fired wide, George Best came close but a second goal eluded them. Then against the run of play, and with only nine minutes remaining, Benfica equalised.

Eusebio broke free from Nobby Stiles' shackles, two passes were made before Garcia struck home a low drive past Alex Stepney.

Eusebio almost won it for the Portuguese champions soon afterwards, one on one with Stepney, but United's 'keeper somehow blocked the shot to keep United's hopes alive.

Two-and-a-half minutes into extra-time Best, weaving and darting through the middle, past two defenders, scored a terrific individual goal to edge in front at 2-1. Sixty seconds later, Brian Kidd - celebrating his 19th birthday - headed in number three and soon afterwards Charlton's right-footer made it 4-1. Game over... United were champions of Europe - at last! Watching on TV was poor Denis Law, in hospital, recovering from a knee operation, cruelly denied his rightful place in the club's history!

It was a night of celebration - especially for the three Munich survivors - Charlton, Bill Foulkes and manager Busby. It was one of football's most emotional nights - not only for United supporters and followers world-wide, but for England (and indeed British) football supporters in general.

Team: Stepney; Brennan, Dunne; Crerand, Foulkes, Stiles; Best, Kidd, Charlton, Sadler, Aston.

1999 European Cup Final in the Nou Camp Stadium
United 2 Bayern Munich 1

In front of 89,954 spectators - on what would have been Sir Matt Busby's 90th birthday - United sensationally won the European Champions Cup by scoring twice in stoppage time, after all had seemed lost in Barcelona!

The last 120 seconds of the 1999 Final were simply the most breathtaking in sporting history!

"The two minutes transcended sport" wrote the Daily Mail reporter, Jonathan Margolis, who added "It demeans the occasion to describe it merely as 'dramatic'...'sensational'...similarly sounds hollow. No, this was politics, it was history, it was art, it was destiny. It was an object lesson in life."

Around 200 million people world-wide saw this famous United victory. But until those dying moments Alex Ferguson's men had struggled to keep their game together. Perhaps the tension and nerves of going for the treble had got to the players. We shall never know (unless they tell you personally). But fight on they did and what a great finish they produced.

Bayern Munich, strong, determined and hugely confident, took the lead as early as the 6th minute through German international Mario Basler....United's defence was nowhere!

United tried desperately to break down the Munich mean-machine, to no avail...while at the same time a few hearts missed a beat or two as the Germans almost snatched a second goal which surely would have won them the Cup.

United were clearly missing their 'engine room' duo of Roy Keane and Paul Scholes, both cruelly suspended.

Then, with time almost up, United drove forward in numbers....even goalkeeper Schmeichel ventured up field. Beckham's corner on the left was headed on by United 'keeper to Dwight Yorke on the right hand side of the area. He headed the ball back into the danger-zone only for a Bayern defender to clear to safety. Or so he thought! Ryan Giggs returned the ball quickly and Sheringham, with just enough space, swivels to redirect it into the corner of the net with a low right-footer. Jubilation in the United ranks...and there was more to come.

Bayern launched an attack straight from restart. United held firm. The ball was lobbed upfield to substitute Ole Gunnar Solskjaer. As keen as a terrier he tried to wriggle past defender Kuffour who conceded a corner. Beckham again measured his left-wing flag-kick to perfection, curling the ball into the crowded penalty area (no Schmeichel this time - he was guarding his own goal). Sheringham leapt, got his head to the ball and succeeded in guiding it over to the right. In a flash Solskjaer pulled away from his marker (Kuffour), got his right boot to the ball and sent it flying into the top of the Bayern net to the 'keeper's left...time: 92 minutes, 17 seconds. United had done it. Schmeichel performed a somersault. Soon afterwards the referee (Collina of Italy) blew the final whistle. The United players and management celebrated, along with the fans all over the world. Manager Alex Ferguson had tears in his eyes, so too did most of the players.

Fergie said later: "I can't believe it. I can't believe it. Football - Bloody hell."

For Munich it must have been a nightmare, unable to believe what had happened.

Schmeichel, playing his last game for the Reds, was made captain for the night and what a proud man he was when he held aloft the massive European Champions League trophy

Team: Schmeichel; G Neville, Irwin, Johnsen, Stam, Butt, Beckham, Blomqvist (sub Sheringham, 66 mins), Cole (sub Solskjaer, 80), Yorke, Giggs.

Solskjaer asked about the winning goal, answered modestly: "Someone had to do it."

European Cup Winners' Cup

United's first opponents in the ECWC were the Dutch side Willem II whom they beat over two legs in the 1963-64 season. United drew 1-1 away (in Rotterdam) and won 6-1 at home for a comfortable 7-2 aggregate victory (their best to date in this competition).

United returned to Rotterdam to lift the same trophy in 1991.

Tottenham Hotspur's Dave Mackay unfortunately broke a leg during his side's Cup-winners Cup 2nd round 2nd leg encounter with United at Old Trafford in December 1963.

A last-ditch penalty kick fired home by Ray Wilkins earned United an equaliser against Dukla Prague in their home Cup-winners Cup encounter in September 1983.

Defender Graeme Hogg conceded an own-goal as United crashed to a 2-0 third round 1st leg defeat against CF Barcelona in the Nou Camp Stadium in March 1984.

United won the Cup-winners Cup in 1990-91 without losing a single match. They won five away from Old Trafford.

Skipper Steve Bruce scored four goals in that season's competition.

Mark Hughes appeared in a record 16 European Cup-winners Cup games for United, while Denis Law netted a record six goals.

1991 European Cup-winners Cup Final in Rotterdam
United 2 Barcelona 1

Mark Hughes was United's hero in Rotterdam - his two goals seeing off the Spanish Cup winners Barcelona in front of 48,000 spectators inside the Feyenoord Stadium.

Hughes, who had spent a disappointing time with Barcelona three years earlier, scored in the 67th and 74th minutes, his second from an acute angle. Ronald Koeman pulled a goal back for the Spanish club in the 80th minute, but with skipper Bryan Robson leading by example, Alex Ferguson's men held out for the tense closing stages to record a magnificent victory. Team: Sealey; Irwin, Blackmore; Bruce, Phelan, Pallister; Robson, Ince, McClair, Hughes, Sharpe. Subs (not used): Donaghy, Robins, Wallace, Walsh & Webb.

Fairs Cup/UEFA Cup
United's first opponents in the Fairs Cup were Djurgaarden of Sweden whom they met in the opening round in September/October 1964. The away leg ended level at 1-1 before United eased through the second leg at Old Trafford by 6-1, Denis Law netting a hat-trick in front of 38,437 fans.
United trounced the Bundesliga side Borussia Dortmund 10-1 on aggregate in the next round, winning 6-1 in Germany and 4-0 at Old Trafford. Bobby Charlton scored five of the goals including a hat-trick in the first leg.
In the Third Round Everton provided the opposition. After a 1-1 draw at Old Trafford a John Connelly goal saw United through at Goodison 3-2 on aggregate.
In the 4th round in 1964-65 (the quarter-final stage) United won 5-0 away to Racing Strasbourg, but were then held to a goalless draw at Old Trafford - enough to send United into the semis.
They met Ferencvaros (Hungary) in the two-legged semi-final in May/June 1965 and after winning 3-2 at home and losing 1-0 away, a replay was staged in Budapest which resulted in a 2-1 win for Ferencvaros in front of 60,000 fans, United seemingly having lost interest in this absurdly protracted competition.
After losing 1-0 to Ajax of Amsterdam in front of 30,000 fans in Holland in a 1st round 1st leg UEFA Cup encounter in September 1976, United came back to win 2-0 at Old Trafford with goals by Sammy McIlroy and Lou Macari. Almost 59,000 spectators attended the return leg. United lost to Juventus in the next round.
In 1980, United went out of the UEFA Cup in the opening round, defeated by Widzew Lodz who went through on the away goal rule after drawing 1-1 at Old Trafford and 0-0 in Poland.
United met two Hungarian clubs in 1984-85 - Raba Vasas ETO Gyor and Videoton.
After ousting Raba Vasas (5-2 overall), United then put out PSV Eindhoven 1-0 on aggregate in the 2nd round. They followed up with a 5-4 aggregate victory over the Scottish club Dundee United before going out of the competition 5-4 on penalties (after a 1-1 draw) to the other Magyar outfit, Videoton.
United failed to progress through either of their last outings in this competition in 1992-93 and 1995-96.
Arthur Albiston holds the record for most appearances in the ICFC/UEFA Cup for United - total 15. Bobby Charlton and Denis Law share the record for most goals in the competition for United - total 8.

European Super Cup
United defeated Red Star Belgrade 1-0 at Old Trafford to win the 1991 European Super Cup. A crowd of 22,110 saw Brian McClair net the all-important goal.
United travelled to the south of France (Monaco) to play the Italian side SS Lazio in the 1999 European Super Cup and in front of 14,461 spectators they were defeated 1-0.

European Talk-back
United have qualified to play in major European competitions on 25 occasions (second behind Liverpool).
United are the only British club side to have won both the European Champions Cup (1968 and 1999) and the European Cup-winners Cup (1991). And, in fact, they were the first English team to win the European Cup.
United have played competitive European football on ten different English, Irish, Scottish and Welsh grounds: Dublin Park/Showground (Shamrock Rovers), Goodison Park, Home Park (Plymouth), Maine Road, Old Trafford, Tannadice (Dundee United), Waterford FC, Wembley Stadium, White Hart Lane and Wrexham's Racecourse Ground.
The Reds have played European football against 69 different clubs in 31 countries: Austria, Belgium, Bulgaria, Croatia, Czech Republic, Czechoslovakia, East Germany, England, Finland, France, Germany (post unification), Greece, Hungary, Ireland (Republic), Italy, Malta, Monaco (principality of France), Netherlands, Northern Ireland, Poland, Portugal, Russia, Scotland, Slovakia, Spain, Sweden, Turkey, Ukraine, USSR, Wales, West Germany and Yugoslavia.
United had a run of 57 European games at 'home' (Maine Road, Old Trafford and Home Park) without defeat. The Turkish club Fenerbahce ended that sequence when they triumphed by a goal to nil in a Champions League encounter on 30 October 1996.
Over a period of 15 years (1965-80) United won 17 consecutive home matches in various European competitions. Between September 1957 and October 1993 United registered 17 straight European (Champions) Cup victories at Old Trafford. The sequence ended when the Turkish side Galatasaray forced a 3-3 draw.
Only once in their first 50 two-legged European games did United go through into the next round on the away goal rule. They drew 3-3 on aggregate with Dukla Prague in a 1st round ECWC tie in September 1983 and having shared the spoils at 2-2 away they went through after a 1-1 stalemate at Old Trafford.
United have been knocked out of European competitions twice via the penalty shoot-out. In March 1985 they lost 5-4 'from the spot' against Videoton (after a 1-1 aggregate score) and in September 1992, after two scoreless encounters, they failed 4-3 in their efforts from 12 yards against Torpedo Moscow. Both clashes were in the UEFA Cup.
Denis Irwin (75), Gary Neville (72), David Beckham (70), Ryan Giggs (67), Roy Keane (65), Paul Scholes (63) Ole Gunnar Solsjkaer (59), Nicky Butt (58), Bill Foulkes (52) and Andy Cole (50) are the top ten appearance-makers for United in European competitions.

Denis Law, with a total of 28 (in 33 appearances) has scored most 'European' goals for United. Bobby Charlton netted 22, followed by Andy Cole (19), Paul Scholes (17), Ryan Giggs (15), Ole Gunnar Solskjaer (15), David Herd (14), Roy Keane (14), Dennis Viollet (13) and David Beckham (12).

Beckman was named in the UEFA all-star international team for 2001.

NB: The venue for the 2002-03 European Champions League Cup Final will be Old Trafford, on 28 May 2003.

United's best 'European' victories have been:

10-0 v. RSC Anderlecht (h)	European Cup	September 1956	(12-0 on agg)
7-1 v. Waterford (h)	European Cup	October 1968	(10-2 on agg)
6-0 v. Shamrock Rovers (a)	European Cup	September 1957	(9-2 on agg)
6-0 v. HJK Helsinki (h)	European Cup	October 1965	(9-2 on agg)
6-1 v. Willem I (h)	ECWC	October 1963	(7-2 on agg)
6-1 v. Djurgaarden (h)	ICFC	October 1964	(7-2 on agg)
6-1 v. Borussia Dortmund (a)	ICFC	November 1964	(10-1 on agg)
6-2 v. IF Brondby (a)	European Cup	October 1998	(11-2 on agg)
5-0 v. RSC Strasborg (a)	ICFC	May 1965	(5-0 on agg)
5-0 v. IF Brondby (h)	European Cup	November 1998	(11-2 on agg)

United's heaviest 'European' defeats have been:

0-5 v. Sporting Club (a)	ECWC	March 1964	(4-6 on agg)
0-4 v. AC Milan (a)	European Cup	May 1957	(2-5 on agg)
0-4 v. FC Porto (a)	ECWC	October 1977	(5-6 on agg)
0-4 v. Barcelona (a)	European Cup	November 1994	(group match)
3-5 v. Athletic Bilbao (a)	European Cup	January 1957	(6-5 on agg)

United's biggest European draws

3-3 v. Red Star Belgrade (a)	European Cup	February 1958	(5-4 on agg)
3-3 v. Galatasaray (h)	European Cup	October 1993	(3-3 on agg)
3-3 v. Barcelona (h)	European Cup	September 1998	(Group match)
3-3 v. Barcelona (a)	European Cup	November 1998	(Group match)

EUROPEAN FOOTBALLER OF THE YEAR

Three United players - Denis Law (1964), Bobby Charlton (1966) and George Best (1968) - all received this coveted award during the 1960s.

EVANS, George

Born: Locally, circa 1869

Career: NEWTON HEATH (season 1890-91).

Centre-forward George Evans scored in four consecutive Football Alliance games for the Heathens during his only season with the club.

Club record: 13 apps. 4 goals (also 5 'other' apps, 3 goals)

EVANS, Sidney Thomas

Born: Darlaston, circa 1898

Career: Darlaston FC, Cardiff City (1920), MANCHESTER UNITED (May 1923), Pontypridd (August 1925).

Right-winger Sid Evans made only nine appearances for Cardiff City before joining United where he failed to gain regular first team football owing to the presence of David Ellis and Joe Spence

Club record: 6 apps. 2 goals

EVER PRESENTS

Here is a list of players who were ever-present in a full season of 'League' Football for the club:
(figures in brackets indicate number of games played that season)

Football Alliance
1889-90 (22) J Doughty
1890-91 (22) A Farman, R Milarvie,
  R Ramsey, J Slater
1891-92 (22) R Donaldson, W Stewart

Football League
1894-95 (30) W Douglas, J Peters
1896-97 (30) J McNaught
1897-98 (30) H Boyd, J Cassidy,
  J McNaught
1898-99 (34) F Barrett, J Cassidy
1899-00 (34) F Barrett, F Erentz
1900-01 (34) T Leigh
1906-07 (38) H Moger, G Wall
1919-20 (42) J Mew
1923-24 (42) C Moore
1924-25 (42) J Spence, A Steward
1926-27 (42) A Steward
1928-29 (42) J Hanson
1929-30 (42) J Spence
1930-31 (42) G McLachlan

1932-33 (42) J Moody
1935-36 (42) G Mutch, W Porter
1946-47 (42) SC Pearson
1947-48 (42) J Aston, snr
1948-49 (42) A Chilton, C Mitten
1949-50 (42) J Delaney, C Mitten
1951-52 (42) A Chilton
1952-53 (42) A Chilton
1953-54 (42) A Chilton
1955-56 (42) M Jones
1957-58 (42) W Foulkes
1958-59 (42) F Goodwin, A Scanlon
1959-60 (42) W Foulkes
1964-65 (42) S Brennan, J Connelly,
  A Dunne, W Foulkes
1966-67 (42) G Best, R Charlton
1970-71 (42) R Charlton
1972-73 (42) M Buchan
1973-74 (42) M Buchan, A Stepney
1974-75 (42) S McIlroy*
1975-76 (42) M Buchan, S Houston
1977-78 (42) S Coppell

1978-79 (42) S Coppell
1979-80 (42) G Bailey, M Buchan,
  S Coppell, J Nicholl
1980-81 (42) A Albiston, S Coppell
1981-82 (42) A Albiston, R Wilkins
1982-83 (42) M Duxbury
1983-84 (42) F Stapleton, R Wilkins
1987-88 (40) B McClair
1988-89 (38) S Bruce, M Hughes,
  J Leighton, B McClair
1989-90 (38) M Phelan
1991-92 (42) B McClair*

Premiership
1992-93 (42) S Bruce, B McClair*,
  G Pallister, P Schmeichel
1993-94 (42) D Irwin
* McIlroy made 41+1 'sub' appearance in 1974-75, likewise McClair in 1991-92 and 1992-93.

Fact File

Defenders Allenby Chilton and Martin Buchan with winger Steve Coppell, each with four, share the record for most ever-present campaigns for United, while Brian McClair also completed four League seasons although he did make two substitute appearances in that time. Coppell's were in four consecutive seasons (1977-81). He also made a club record 206 consecutive League appearances between 15 January 1977 and November 1981.

Owing to the rotating squad system, United have not had an ever-present since Denis Irwin back in 1993-94.

EVERTON

United's League record against Everton:

Season	Div	Home	Away	Season	Div	Home	Away
1892-93	1	L 3-4	L 0-6	1961-62	1	D 1-1	L 1-5
1893-94	1	L 0-3	L 0-2	1962-63	1	L 0-1	L 1-3
				1963-64	1	W 5-1	L 0-4
1906-07	1	W 3-0	L 0-3	1964-65	1	W 2-1	D 3-3
1907-08	1	W 4-3	W 3-1	1965-66	1	W 3-0	D 0-0
1908-09	1	D 2-2	L 2-3	1966-67	1	W 3-0	W 2-1
1909-10	1	W 3-2	D 3-3	1967-68	1	W 3-1	L 1-3
1910-11	1	D 2-2	W 1-0	1968-69	1	W 2-1	D 0-0
1911-12	1	W 2-1	L 0-4	1969-70	1	L 0-2	L 0-3
1912-13	1	W 2-0	L 1-4	1970-71	1	W 2-0	L 0-1
1913-14	1	L 0-1	L 0-5	1971-72	1	D 0-0	L 0-1
1914-15	1	L 1-2	L 2-4	1972-73	1	D 0-0	L 0-2
				1973-74	1	W 3-0	L 0-1
1919-20	1	W 1-0	D 0-0				
1920-21	1	L 1-2	L 0-2	1975-76	1	W 2-1	D 1-1
1921-22	1	W 2-1	L 0-5	1976-77	1	W 4-0	W 2-1
				1977-78	1	L 1-2	W 6-2
1925-26	1	D 0-0	W 3-1	1978-79	1	D 1-1	L 0-3
1926-27	1	W 2-1	D 0-0	1979-80	1	D 0-0	D 0-0
1927-28	1	W 1-0	L 2-5	1980-81	1	W 2-0	W 1-0
1928-29	1	D 1-1	W 4-2	1981-82	1	D 1-1	D 3-3
1929-30	1	D 3-3	D 0-0	1982-83	1	W 2-1	L 0-2
				1983-84	1	L 0-1	D 1-1
1936-37	1	W 2-1	W 3-2	1984-85	1	D 1-1	L 0-5
				1985-86	1	D 0-0	L 1-3
1938-39	1	L 0-2	L 0-3	1986-87	1	D 0-0	L 1-3
				1987-88	1	W 2-1	L 1-2
1946-47	1	W 3-0	D 2-2	1988-89	1	L 1-2	D 1-1
1947-48	1	D 2-2	L 0-2	1989-90	1	D 0-0	L 2-3
1948-49	1	W 2-0	L 0-2	1990-91	1	L 0-2	W 1-0
1949-50	1	D 1-1	D 0-0	1991-92	1	W 1-0	D 0-0
1950-51	1	W 3-0	W 4-1	1992-93	PL	L 0-3	W 2-0
				1993-94	PL	W 1-0	W 1-0
1954-55	1	L 1-2	L 2-4	1994-95	PL	W 2-0	L 0-1
1955-56	1	W 2-1	L 2-4	1995-96	PL	W 2-0	W 3-2
1956-57	1	L 2-5	W 2-1	1996-97	PL	D 2-2	W 2-0
1957-58	1	W 3-0	D 3-3	1997-98	PL	W 2-0	W 2-0
1958-59	1	W 2-1	L 2-3	1998-99	PL	W 3-1	W 4-1
1959-60	1	W 5-0	L 1-2	1999-00	PL	W 5-1	D 1-1
1960-61	1	W 4-0	L 0-4	2000-01	PL	W 1-0	W 3-1
				2001-02	PL	W 4-1	W 2-0

Summary of League results

	P	W	D	L	F	A
Premier League	20	16	2	2	42	14
Division 1	26	44	33	49	178	204
Home	73	40	18	15	129	72
Away	73	20	17	36	91	146
Total	146	60	35	51	220	218

FA Cup Record

	Round	Venue	Result
1902-03	2	Away	L 1-3
1908-09	2	Home	W 1-0
1952-53	5	Away	L 1-2
1956-57	5	Home	W 1-0
1965-66	Semi-final	Burnden Pk	L 0-1
1968-69	6	Home	L 0-1
1982-83	6	Home	W 1-0
1984-85	Final	Wembley	W 1-0 aet
1994-95	Final	Wembley	L 0-1

League Cup Record

	Round	Venue	Result
1976-77	5	Home	L 0-3
1984-85	3	Home	L 1-2
1993-94	4	Away	W 2-0

European Record

	Round	Venue	Result
Inter Cities Fairs Cup			
1964-65	3 (1)	Home	D 1-1
	3 (2)	Away	W 2-1

FA Charity Shield

United and Everton have met each other twice to decide the FA Charity Shield game. In 1963 United crashed 4-0 at Goodison Park in front of 54,840 spectators and in 1985 the Merseysiders won 2-0 at Wembley when the attendance was 81,639.

Screen Sport Super Cup

In season 1985-86 United played Everton twice in the Screen Sport sponsored Super Cup competition - arranged when English clubs had been banned from European competition following the Heysel Stadium disaster. The Merseysiders won both games, 4-2 at Old Trafford and 1-0 at Goodison Park.

Mercantile Credit Trophy

A goal by Gordon Strachan gave United victory over the Merseysiders at Old Trafford in the 1st round of this sponsored tournament in August 1988. United went on to lose to Arsenal in the Final.

Fact File

United & Everton have never met outside the 'Top Flight.' Their record of meeting in 73 of the 103 League seasons played by Everton (99 by United) is second only to United's games with Arsenal (82).

Players with both clubs include: D Bain, W Ball, P Beardsley, J Blomqvist, W Boyes (United WW2), J Broad (United reserve), E Buckle, G Burnett (United WW2), H Catterick (United WW2, also Everton manager), W Cresswell (United reserve), C Crossley (United WW1), P Davenport (Everton amateur), SC Davies (United trialist), E Dodds (United WW2), P Dunne, A Farmer (United reserve), T Gardner (United WW2), J Gidman, H Hardman, G Holdcroft (United WW2), M Higgins, M Hughes, W Hullett (United reserve), T Jackson, T Jones (Everton trialist), A Kanchelskis, F Kennedy, B Kidd, N McBain (also Everton scout), T Nuttall, G O'Brien, J O'Kane, A Schofield, M Thomas, T Wyles (United WW2). Also associated: J Carey (United player, Everton manager), A Knox (assistant-manager at both clubs), E Harrison (coach at both clubs).

EXETER CITY

Fact File

The clash with Exeter on 19 October 1960 at St James' Park was United's first ever Football League Cup-tie. The attendance was 14,494 and Alex Dawson scored United's first goal in this competition.

Players with both clubs include: A Ambler, J Banks (City player-coach & trainer), E Buckle, R Burke, A Chesters, E Connor, SI Davies, J Fitchett, B Fulton (United WW2), J Gallacher (United WW2), K Goddard (United reserve), W Goodwin, W Henderson, W Hunter, D Keough (United reserve), W Lievesley, J Mitten (United trialist), M Rawlinson (United reserve), G Roughton (City player-manager), M Setters, L Sharpe, N Whitworth, O Williams (United junior), W Woodward (United reserve). Also associated: A Stepney (United player, City scout), M Musgrove (also assistant-manager/coach at United, scout for both clubs & coach at Exeter).

United's FA Cup Record against the Grecians:

	Round	Venue	Result
1968-69	3	Away	W 3-1

And their League Cup Record:

	Round	Venue	Result
1960-61	1	Away	D 1-1
	Replay	Home	W 4-1

109

Born: Govan, Glasgow 31 December 1941. Career: player at Govan Senior School, for Scottish Schoolboys, Queen's Park (as an amateur, 1957), St Johnstone (season 1965-66), Dunfermline Athletic (part-time professional, 1966-67), Rangers (as a professional, £65,000, July 1967), Falkirk (£20,000, player-coach, November 1969), Ayr United.(May 1973, retired May 1974). Manager with East Stirling (July 1974), St Mirren (July 1975), Aberdeen (June 1978), MANCHESTER UNITED (November 1986 to date). Caretaker-manager of Scotland national side: September 1985 to June 1986, following Jock Stein's death. Sir Alex Ferguson is firmly established, not only as United's greatest ever manager, but the greatest manager in the history of English League football, his 16 trophies unsurpassed. In his time at Old Trafford he has transformed a 'sleeping giant' into the world's richest (and best known) club. As the 1986-87 season began in disappointing fashion under Ron Atkinson, chairman Martin Edwards looked to Aberdeen where Ferguson had done the seemingly impossible, successfully breaking the 'Old Firm' monopoly. Now Edwards challenged the ambitious Scotsman to come 'down south' and overturn the Merseyside monopoly.

On 5 November 1986, the challenge far too great for the former shipyard worker to refuse, Ferguson succeeded Atkinson as manager of MANCHESTER UNITED and since then the silverware has simply glittered in the Old Trafford boardroom!

F for...

FERGUSON, Sir Alex, CBE, OBE

When he set foot inside Old Trafford, Ferguson faced a massive challenge and success was not instant. By 1990 people were questioning Chairman Martin Edwards' wisdom and Ferguson's ability, but an FA Cup triumph turned the tables, followed next year by success in the European Cup-winners Cup, then in 1992 the League Cup. Yet the League Championship still evaded United's grasp as in 1991-92 the team choked in the home stretch, allowing Leeds to snatch the trophy at the death. The gap was now 26 years since United's last League success and again questions were being asked regarding United's ability. The signing of world class goalkeeper Peter Schmeichel and Eric Cantona finally persuaded the players that they were good enough, the newly inaugurated Premier League won in style, to set off a string of amazing successes.

Sir Alex Ferguson was knighted (for his services to Football, Manchester United of course) in July 1999 (following the club's European Champions Cup success which earned them the treble), having previously been awarded the OBE whilst with Aberdeen and the CBE with United.

In 2001, he became the first manager to win seven League titles (all in the Premiership) and the first to win the championship three seasons running. In addition there have been two European competitions won, four FA Cup Final victories (including three 'doubles'), a League Cup triumph and success in the Inter-Continental Cup and the European Super Cup. United fans were overjoyed when Sir Alex, early in 2002, reversed his decision to retire, signing a new three-year contract with the club.

As a player Ferguson was an aggressive centre-forward who was sent-off at least half-a-dozen times. He made a scoring debut with Queen's Park at Stranraer in 1958. He hit 15 goals in 31 appearances for the Scottish amateur club and later notched 31 goals in 32 games for St Johnstone in season 1965-66. He joined Glasgow Rangers in 1967 and scored 24 goals in 41 games during his time at Ibrox Park.. After four good seasons with Falkirk he moved to Ayr United, announcing his retirement as a player following a nasty injury received in his last match, ironically at Falkirk in April 1974. In all 'Fergie' scored 170 goals in 309 Scottish League games.

In the summer of 1974 he was appointed manager of East Stirlingshire - but parted company with the hard-up club before the end of that season. He immediately took over the reins of St Mirren (1975) and led the part-timers to promotion from the First Division to the Premiership in 1976-77. He was then dismissed by Saints in acrimonious circumstances and pursued a legal claim against the Scottish club for unfair dismissal.

Named manager of Aberdeen in 1978, he spent eight superb years at Pittodrie. In 1979-80 he guided the Dons to their first League title in 25 years (two further Premiership Divisions followed in 1983-84 and 1984-85). The Scottish Cup was won three times in succession: 1982, 1983 and 1984 and again in 1986 and in his last season Aberdeen also lifted the Scottish League Cup. But perhaps Fergie's greatest achievement 'north of the border' was when he proudly led the Dons to a 2-1 victory over the Spanish giants Real Madrid in the 1983 European Cup-winners Cup Final in Gothenburg in 1983.

In 1985-86 Fergie managed the Scottish national team, taking over in tragic circumstances following the sudden death of Jock Stein, who he had played against in an old firm derby. He successfully guided the Scots through to the final qualification stages of the World Cup after beating Australia 1-0 on aggregate. They were then placed in what was called the 'Group of Death' with Denmark, Uruguay and West Germany. They lost to both the Danes and the Germans and drew with the South Americans (after having a player sent-off). With only one point to show for their efforts, they were therefore eliminated.

Ferguson's son, Darren, was a player with Manchester United and Wolves before joining Wrexham while his youngest son, Jason, became a successful football agent.

* A keen and enthusiastic racegoer, Ferguson saw his co-owned horse - 9-1 shot The Rock of Gibralter, ridden by Johnny Murtagh and trained out of the matchless County Tipperary complex in Ireland by Aidan O'Brien - win the Sagitta 2,000 guineas at Newmarket in May 2002.

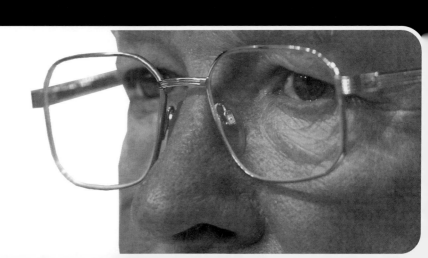

FAIR PLAY League

Manchester United won the Football League's Fair Play Award in successive seasons of 1975-76 & 1976-77. The Daily Mail newspaper and Vernons Pools sponsored the League between them in the late 1970s and the trophy was awarded for good behaviour on the field of play and presented to United at the end of those two campaigns.

FALL, Joseph William

Born: Miles Platting, Manchester, 1872
Career: Leigh Street FC, Middlesbrough Ironopolis (1891), NEWTON HEATH (August 1893), Small Heath (May 1895), Altrincham (season 1896-97).
Goalkeeper Joe Fall is believed to have been the first local-born player signed by Newton Heath after they had entered the Football League. He had one good season (his first) before being released following relegation at the end of the 1894-95 campaign. Became third choice 'keeper at Small Heath, making only two appearances for the club.
Club record: 27 apps. (also 11 'other' apps)

FAMILY CONNECTIONS

Brothers

The following sets of brothers have all been associated with Newton Heath/Manchester United, having played for the first team at competitive level.
Jack & Roger Doughty (1889-91); Fred & Harry Erentz (1892-1902); David & Thomas Fitzsimmons (1892-1900); Charles & Herbert Rothwell (1893-1903); James & John Hodge (1910-13); Brian & Jimmy Greenhoff (1968-80); George & Martin Buchan (1973-83) and Gary & Philip Neville (1991-2002)

Brotherly Love

•The Doughty brothers (Jack & Roger) played in the same United team together on 26 occasions. They started off in April 1890 (in the old Football Alliance).
•The Greenhoffs lined up together at senior level 80 times, while the Nevilles have been part and parcel of the United set-up for seven years and have also been in the same England side together. Indeed, in 1996 the Nevilles became the first set of brothers to win the 'double' since the Cowans of Aston Villa in 1897 and the first to gain League Championship medals since the Comptons (Denis and Les) of Arsenal in 1948. They also became thee ninth pair of brothers to play together for England and only the second (behind the Charltons, Bobby and Jack) during the 20th century.
•Both the Greenhoffs (in 1977) and the Nevilles (in 1996) gained FA Cup winners' medals with United.
•Brothers George (as a substitute) and Martin Buchan played in three League games together for United in September 1973, lining up against West Ham United, Leeds United and Liverpool.
•Brothers John and Bill Mathieson were registered together at Newton Heath in season 1892-93 (John did not play for the first team).
•Edward and Tom Howles were also players with the club at the same time in the mid-1880s.
•The Charlton brothers, Jack and Bobby, starred together in the same England team 28 times, winning the World Cup in 1966. They both became League club managers - Jack with Middlesbrough and Bobby with Preston - and they led their respective teams against each other in 1974. They also hold the respective League appearance records for United and Leeds.
•The Blanchflower brothers, Danny and Jackie, played in 12 internationals together for Northern Ireland.
•Danny Wallace had two brothers - Ray and Rod - and all three played in the same Southampton team in the mid-1980s.
•Brothers Bryan Robson and Gary Robson were both midfielders with West Bromwich Albion but never played in the same side together. Gary also played for Bradford City.
•Cyril Knowles, a United amateur, was the brother of Peter Knowles, ex-Wolves and now a Jehovah's Witness.
•Ernie Vincent's brother, Arthur, was registered with Durham City in the 1930s.
•Colin Waldron's brother, Alan, played for Blackpool, Bolton Wanderers, Bury and York City.
•George Wall's brother, Tom, joined United in 1908 but did not progress beyond the 2nd XI.
•Ernie Thomson and his brother George, both served with Darwen.
•John Sutcliffe's brother, Charlie (also a goalkeeper) played for Rotherham County.
•Tom Smith, a United player from 1924-27, was one of seven brothers, five of whom played League football. Two won England caps, Jack when with Portsmouth and Septimus with Leicester City.
•Billy Meredith's brother Sam played for Stoke and his nephew Jack for Everton.
•Tom Meehan's brother had an unsuccessful trial with United.
•James Coupar's brother Peter had a brief spell with United (as a reserve) before making his mark with Stoke and Dundee..
•Joe Lievesey (a goalkeeper who played for Arsenal and Sheffield United) and younger brother of Wilf were both registered with United in 1922-23. Another brother, Fred, played for Manchester City and Southend United while Les Lievesley, a United player in 1932-33, was the nephew of the three Lievesley brothers
•United's David Gwilym Jones was the younger brother of Bill Jones who played for Notts County and Newport County and also managed Cardiff City.
•Arthur Montgomery's brother John played for Notts County among others.
•George Mutch's brother, William, played for United's second XI and also for Accrington Stanley.

• Johnny Morris's brother, William, was a player with Rochdale. Johnny later managed Oswestry Town (1967-68) when his son was also a player with the non-League club.

• John Jones, a United player in the 1890s, was the brother of Richard, ex-Crewe Alexandra.

• Tom Chorlton's brother played for United's reserve team and also for Bury.

• Peter Coyne's brother, Gerald, was registered as a professional with United in season 1975-76.

• George Dale, the brother of former United player and referee Herbert Dale, was a coach at Oldham Athletic.

• Matt Gillespie's brother, Tom, played for Lincoln City and Manchester City and his nephew Robert served with Oldham Athletic, Luton Town, Port Vale, Wrexham and Barrow.

• Arthur Graham's brother, Tommy, was associated with Motherwell, Aston Villa, Barnsley, Halifax Town, Doncaster Rovers and Scarborough. A second brother, David, played for QPR, whilst a third, Jimmy, served with Bradford City and Rochdale.

• Frank Haydock's brother, Billy, played for Crewe Alexandra, Manchester City and Stockport County.

• Brothers James and John Hodge were registered players with United at the same time (before WW1) while their brother-in-law, Donny McLeod, a Scottish international, assisted Stenhousemuir, Celtic and Middlesbrough.

• Tom Nuttall's brother, Harry, made over 300 appearances for Bolton Wanderers and also won three England caps (1928 & 1929).

• Brothers John and William Owen were together at Newton Heath in 1887, but only John made the grade.

• The Jones brothers, John Owen and Richard, were both capped by Wales at senior level, both played for Bangor and Crewe Alexandra with 'JO' also assisting Newton Heath (1898-1900).

• Ernie Taylor's brother, Eddie, played for Willington FC in the 1950 FA Amateur Cup Final at Wembley.

• Ben Thornley's brother played for Altrincham and is a physiotherapist at Old Trafford.

• Ray Wilkins' brother, Graham, also played for Chelsea while another brother, Dean assisted Brighton, Leyton Orient and QPR.

• Jack Rowley, one of United's greatest marksmen (211 goals) had a younger brother, Arthur, who guested for United during WW2 as a 15 year-old. Arthur went on to set a Football League record, scoring 434 goals in the competition over a period of 20 years (1946-66) with West Bromwich Albion, Fulham, Leicester City and Shrewsbury Town. Their father had been a goalkeeper with Walsall.

• Cliff Birkett had two brothers who both played League football: Wilf was a goalkeeper with Southport and Shrewsbury Town and Ronnie a winger with Accrington Stanley, New Brighton and Oldham Athletic.

Like Father, Like Son:

• As a United player John Aston senior won an FA Cup winners' medal in 1948 and a League Championship medal in 1952. His son, John junior, gained a European Cup winners medal in 1968.

• Darren Ferguson and Paul McGuinness, the respective sons of United managers Sir Alex and Wilf, were both players at Old Trafford, the latter as a junior in 1992-93. Jason Ferguson, another son of Sir Alex, became a respected football agent.

• Peter Barnes' father, Ken, was a key member of Manchester City's half-back line during the 1950s.

• Two sons of Sandy Turnbull, Alex and Ronald, joined United's playing staff in August 1932 but both failed to make the required breakthrough.

• Joe Spence's son, Joe junior, made over 100 senior appearances for York City during the 1950s.

• Dick Duckworth's son, Richard (a junior at Old Trafford in 1926) played over 300 games as a half-back for seven different League clubs (including Chester, Chesterfield and York City) before going on to manage York City, Stockport County, Darlington and Scunthorpe United. He was also a scout for two major League clubs.

• Gary Bailey's father, Roy, was also a goalkeeper with Ipswich Town (1960s).

• Another goalkeeper with a 'goalie dad' was Andy Goram; Lewis (Lew) Goram played for Bury in the 1950s.

• Ryan Giggs' father, Danny Wilson, was a Welsh rugby international.

• Mark Higgins' father, John played defender with Bolton Wanderers and lined up against United in the 1958 FA Cup Final.

• Charlie Mitten's son, John Mitten, played for Newcastle United, Coventry City, Leicester City and Plymouth Argyle, among others, as well as having trials at Old Trafford in 1962-63 (along with Charlie senior, his elder son). Charlie's grandson (Paul) had a trial at Old Trafford in 1992-93.

• Tommy Docherty's son, Peter, also played for United and appeared in the 1982 FA Youth Cup Final, while his other son, Mick, played for Manchester City when 'dad' was boss at Old Trafford.

• Jimmy Murphy's son, Nick, was twice named as a United substitute in 1969, but never made it to the top. Neither did Sandy Busby, son of Sir Matt, who was a reserve at Ewood Park. He later became United's club shop manager.

• Danny Crerand, son of 1960s United favourite Paddy Crerand, was once a member of United's junior side while Johnny Giles' son, Michael, was a reserve team player with West Bromwich Albion.

• Goalkeeper Jack Hacking's son, John, was also a 'keeper with Accrington Stanley & Stockport Co..

• John Williamson's son, John jnr, played as an amateur for Oldham, Manchester City and Blackburn.

• Joe, the father of Leslie Lievesey, a United player in the 1930s, kept goal for Sheffield United and Arsenal and toured South Africa with the FA in 1910.

• Harry Gregg's son, John, was a midfielder with Barnsley and Nottingham Forest Under-18 sides.

• Danny Nardiello, the son of the former Coventry City and Welsh international winger Don Nardiello, played for United's senior side in season 2001-02, making his debut as a second-half substitute in the 4-0 League Cup defeat at Arsenal.

• Mick Martin's father, Con, played as a centre-half and goalkeeper for Aston Villa as well as winning caps for the Republic of Ireland.

• David Herd and his father, Alec, both played for Stockport County and they lined together for the Hatters in a League

113

game v. Hartlepool United in May 1951. David scored in a 2-0 win. Alec also assisted United as a guest during WW2.
•Sammy McIlroy's father played for United's reserve team while Gordon McQueen's father was a goalkeeper with Accrington Stanley (1930s).
•Stewart Houston's father played League football in Scotland with St Mirren.
•Arthur Thomson's father, Alex, played for both Middlesbrough and West Ham United.
•Jack Peddie's son played competitive League football in Canada.
•Jack Quin's father was registered as an amateur footballer with Edinburgh Hibernian. He was also a Scotland international trialist.
•Gordon Strachan's son, Gavin, also played for Coventry & Dundee (on loan) during the 1990s.
•Steve Bruce's son was once a junior at Old Trafford.
•Ray Wilkins' father (George) played for Brentford amongst others.
•George Nevin's father was a semi-professional footballer.
•Tom Nuttall's father, Jack, was a trainer with United before WW1.
•Diego Forlan's father was an international footballer with Uruguay, likewise the father of Jean Sebastion Veron, who played for Estudiantes against United in the World Club Championship of 1968, as well as representing his country, Argentina.

Family Album
•Rio Ferdinand's cousin is the former QPR & England striker Les Ferdinand, now with Spurs.
•Post WW2 United star Don Gibson was Matt Busby's son-in-law, marrying Matt's daughter, Sheena.
•Charlie Mitten was Albert Scanlon's uncle.
•Ray Westwood, the former Bolton Wanderers centre-forward, was the cousin of United's Teddy Partridge. Partridge's son, Teddy junior, was a junior at Old Trafford in the late 1950s.
•Bob McFarlane married the sister of the Doughty brothers who were at the club in the late 1800s.
•Nobby Stiles married Johnny Giles's sister.
•Tom Jones (b. 1899) was one of a family of 14 children (one brother, 12 sisters and himself).
•Paul Ince's cousin is champion boxer Nigel Benn.

FARMAN, Alfred H

Born: Kings Norton, Birmingham, 1869
Career: Birmingham Excelsior, Aston Villa (amateur, 1891), Bolton Wanderers (1892), NEWTON HEATH (initially signed September 1889, full-time professional June 1892), Bevoir FC (re-instated as an amateur, October 1895).
Hard-shooting outside-right Alf Farman made his debut for the Heathens against Long Eaton Rangers in a Football Alliance game in November 1889 and scored in a 3-0 win. He was an ever-present the following season and missed only one Alliance game in 1891-92. Farman then played in Newton Heath's first ever Football league game v. Blackburn Rovers in September 1892.
Clarkin then challenged him for his position and after losing out he moved inside before ending his career with the club after six years service, being rewarded with a benefit match (against near neighbours Ardwick) for his efforts.
Club record: 121 apps. 53 goals (also 97 'other' apps, 44 goals).

FEEHAN, John Ignatius

Born: Dublin, 17 September 1926. Died: 1995
Career: Bohemians (amateur, 1942), Waterford (1944), MANCHESTER UNITED (November 1948), Northampton Town (£525, August 1950), Brentford (1954). Retired from League football at end of the 1958-59 season.
'Sonny' Feehan played Gaelic football in his homeland before becoming a very useful goalkeeper. He acted as deputy to Jack Crompton at Old Trafford, getting limited call-ups. Following the arrival at Old Trafford of Reg Allen, Feehan moved to Northampton Town, making over 40 appearances for the Cobblers and a similar number for the Bees.
Club record: 14 apps.

FELTON, C

Born: Locally, circa 1865
Career: NEWTON HEATH (November 1887-April 1891).
A versatile player, Felton could play as a full-back, half-back or forward. He made his first senior appearance for the Heathens in season 1889-90. Basically a reserve he had the misfortune to finish up on the losing side in every major game he played (three in the Alliance, one in the FA Cup).
Club record: 4 apps. (also 30 'other' apps).

FENERBAHCE

United, after winning 2-0 in Turkey, surprisingly suffered their first-ever home defeat in 40 years of European competitions when Fenerbahce came to Old Trafford on 30 October 1996 and won 1-0 in the Group stage of the Champions League.

FERENCVAROS

United met Ferencvaros in the semi-final of the Inter Cities Fairs Cup in 1964-65. After David Herd had scored twice in the 1st leg at Old Trafford to edge United in front at 3-2, the Hungarian side grabbed a 1-0 win in Budapest and took the tie to a replay which was also staged in Hungary as late as 16 June. This time United failed to impress and lost 2-1.

FERGUSON, Sir Alex, CBE, OBE

Refer to front of section.

FERGUSON, Archibald Daniel

Born: Flint, North Wales, 25 January, 1903.
Career: Rhyl Athletic, MANCHESTER UNITED
(amateur, then professional March 1927), Reading (May
1928), Accrington Stanley (1929), Chester, (1932)
Halifax Town (1933), Stockport County (1935),
Macclesfield (1936). Retired in the late 1930s.
After leaving Old Trafford half-back or inside-forward
Danny Ferguson went on to take his tally of League and
Cup appearances during his ten seasons of competitive
football past the 250 mark, 120 with Accrington. His
four outings with United came towards the end of the
1927-28 season when the team was battling against
relegation. He later became a publican in Macclesfield.
Club record: 4 apps.

FERGUSON, Darren

Born: Glasgow, 9 February 1972
Career: Nottingham Forest (trialist), MANCHESTER
UNITED (apprentice, July 1988, professional July 1990),
Wolverhampton Wanderers (£250,000, January 1994),
Cosenza (trialist, late 1998), Sparta Rotterdam (on loan,
early 1999), Wrexham (free transfer, autumn 1999).
Sir Alex's son, Darren Ferguson, a competitive midfielder,
made almost 150 appearances for Wolves before joining
Wrexham for whom he has now played in well over 125
first-class matches. Capped by Scotland at Youth and
Under-21 levels (five caps won in the latter category) he
had Roy Keane, Mike Phelan, Bryan Robson and others
to contest a first team place with at Old Trafford.
Club record: 30 apps.

FERGUSON, John James

Born: Rowlands Gill, Newcastle-upon-Tyne, 1904.
Career: North-east football, Grimsby Town (1926),
Workington (1927), Spen Black & White FC (1928),
Wolverhampton Wanderers (early 1929), Watford (mid-
1929), Burton Town (1930), MANCHESTER UNITED
(May-December 1931), Derry City (1932), Gateshead
Utd (1934). Retired in the late 1930s.
Outside-right John Ferguson, well built with a good turn
of speed, scored his only goal for United in his second
League game - a 3-2 home defeat by Southampton in
September 1931.
Club record: 8 apps. one goal

FERRIER, Ronald Johnson

Born: Cleethorpes, 26 April 1914. Died: Cleethorpes, 11
October 1991
Career: Grimsby Wanderers, Grimsby Town (1933),
MANCHESTER UNITED (May 1935), Oldham
Athletic (£1,200, March 1938). Guested for Grimsby
Town, Reading and Southampton during WW2 while
serving with the RAF. Then played for Lincoln City
(1947), Grimsby Town (player & junior-coach, 1949),
Lysaghts Sports, Scunthorpe (player-coach, season 1950-51).
Ron Ferrier, an inside or centre-forward, was initially
reserve to Tom Bamford and George Mutch at Old

FERDINAND, Rio Gavin

Born: Peckham, London, 8 November 1978
Career: Camelot Primary School, Blackheath
Ditsrict Schools, West Ham United (trainee
1994, professional November 1995), AFC
Bournemouth (on loan, November 1996), Leeds
United (£18 million, November 2000),
MANCHESTER UNITED (£30 million, July 2002).
After weeks of speculation as to whether Rio
Ferdinand would or would not leave Elland
Road after the World Cup Finals in the Far East,
Alex Ferguson finally got his man when he
signed the Leeds United and England defender
for a club and British record fee of £30 million.
Ferdinand - the sixth most expensive footballer
in world soccer when he set foot inside Old
Trafford - had been one of the stars in Japan and
Korea and there is no doubt that the Leeds
Chairman Peter Risdale was bitterly
disappointed to lose such a class player. United,
though, were delighted to acquire the services of
the 23 year-old who had already been capped 19
times at senior level by his country as well as
appearing in a handful of youth and five Under-
21 internationals. Standing 6ft 2ins tall and
weighing over 13 stone, Ferdinand is rated as
one of the top six defenders in the game - and
he will get better. Fast over the ground, a firm
header of the ball, he reads the game superbly
well and his distribution is as good as any
midfield player. He played in almost 160 first-
class matches for West Ham, 11 on loan with
Bournemouth and a further 60 for Leeds before
his big-money switch to Old Trafford which
guaranteed him an initial weekly wage of
£70,000 (around £3.6 million-a-year).
* Rio's cousin is Les Ferdinand, the ex-QPR and
England striker who is now with Tottenham Hotspur.

Trafford, getting very little first team football during his three seasons with the club. He did however score seven goals in a Central League game against Bury reserves in March 1936. He netted 25 goals in 45 League games for the Latics before WW2 intervened.
Club record: 19 apps. 4 goals

FEYENOORD

United defeated the Dutch champions twice in the first Group stage of the 1997-98 European Champions League. Andy Cole scored a hat-trick in the 3-1 win in Rotterdam while the game at Old Trafford ended in a 2-1 victory for the Reds.

FIELDING, William J

Born: Broadhurst, nr Hyde, 17 June 1915
Career: Broadbottom YMCA, Hurst FC, Cardiff City (1936). Guested for Bolton Wanderers and Stockport County during WW2. Then Bolton Wanderers (1944), MANCHESTER UNITED (January 1947-June 1948). Retired.
Bill Fielding deputised for goalkeeper Jack Crompton during his 18-month stay at Old Trafford. He had helped Bolton won the Football League (North) Cup in 1945 and arrived at United in a player-exchange deal involving Billy Wrigglesworth.
Club record: 7 apps.

FIGHT BACKS

United have made a reputation, over the years, of conceding early goals only to recover late in the game to snatch a result. Here are just a few of their famous 'fight backs' down the years:
•In a League game at St James' Park in 1909-10, United found themselves 3-0 down at half-time against Newcastle. United, though, fought back brilliantly to draw level before 'Sandy' Turnbull scored a dramatic late winner.
•United, with a hat-trick from Tom Bamford, led Derby County 4-1 after 51 minutes in their away game in Septembner 1936. The Rams, though, stormed back to win the First Division encoiunter 5-4
•On 16 January 1957, United trailed Athletic Bilbao by 5-2 late on in their European Cup quarter-final tie at Estadio San Marnes when Liam 'Billy' Whelan scored a late goal to reduce the arrears. Three weeks later at Maine Road, United won the second-leg 3-0 (and the tie 6-5 on aggregate) to progress through to the semi-finals..
•In 1992-93 - and well into the second-half - United trailed Sheffield Wednesday 3-0 at Hillsborough in a Premiership game. However, three goals in the space of 17 minutes squared things up and then United came within a whisker of taking all three points with a late flourish.
•United trailed Tottenham Hotspur 3-0 at half-time in a Premiership game at White Hart Lane in October 2001. The final score, after a brilliant second-half display of attacking football by the Reds, was Spurs 3 United 5.
•In a 3rd round FA Cup-tie at Villa Park in January 2002, with less than a quarter of an hour remaining, United playing poorly, were 2-0 down - but they suddenly found their feet , scoring three times in five minutes to win the match 3-2.

FIORENTINA

United gained revenge for a 2-0 defeat in Italy by winning the return of their 1999-2000 Champions League 2nd stage encounter with Fiorentina by 3-1, Andy Cole, Roy Keane and Dwight Yorke the scorers at Old Trafford.
The Anglo-Italian Cup encounter was played at Old Trafford in February 1973 and just under 24,000 saw Jim Holton's goal earn United a share of the spoils at 1-1..

FIRSTS

•The first-ever Football League game played by Newton Heath was against Blackburn Rovers (a) on 3 September 1892 (Division 1). They lost a seven-goal thriller by 4-3.
•The first such game played by the club under the title Manchester United was on 6 September 1902 (also Division 2) at Gainsborough Trinity. United won 1-0, Charlie Richards having the pleasure of scoring the first 'United' goal!
•The first League game staged at Old Trafford was on 19 February 1910 when United lost 4-3 to Liverpool (Division 1).
•Newton Heath's first FA Cup-tie took place on 30 October 1886 when they drew 2-2 at Fleetwood Rangers. The game was awarded to Rangers after the Heathens refused to play extra-time!
•The first FA Cup-tie staged at Old Trafford was between United & Aston Villa on 4 February 1911 (rd. 2). A crowd of over 65,000 saw United win 2-1.
•The first League Cup-tie played by United was against Exeter City (a) on 19 October 1960. Almost 14,500 fans witnessed the 1-1 draw. The replay- on 26 October - was the first League Cup game at Old Trafford and in front of 15,662 fans, United won 4-1.
•United's first taste of European Cup football arrived on 12 September 1956 when they met the Belgian side RSC Anderlecht in the away leg of a preliminary round European Cup-tie. A crowd of 35,000 saw United won 2-0 with Dennis Viollet scoring the club's first 'European' goal. A fortnight later the return leg took place - United's first at 'home' in Europe - and although it was staged at Maine Road, some 40,000 fans saw the Reds sweep to an impressive 10-0 victory.
•United's first European encounter at Old Trafford took place on 25 April 1957, when 65,000 spectators saw mighty Real Madrid held to a 2-2 draw in the second-leg of the semi-final, under the newly-installed floodlights.
•The first floodlit match at Old Trafford had taken place on 25 March 1957 when Bolton Wanderers were the visitors for a League Division One game.
•The first Football League game ever to be played on a Saturday night (after 6pm) was that between Wolverhampton

Wanderers and Manchester United at Molineux on 4 October 1958. A crowd of 36,840 saw the Wolves win 4-0.
•The first black player to appear for United in a League game was Dennis Walker against Nottingham Forest (away) in May 1963.
•The first United player to be featured in Madame Tussauds was Nobby Stiles (with the World Cup).
•The first competitive indoor match in the U.K. was the FA Charity Shield game between Manchester United and Liverpool at the Millennium Stadium Cardiff, in August 2001.
NB - See also under other categories including substitutes.

FISHER, James
Born: Glasgow, June 1879.
Career: Caledonians, East Stirlingshire (1895), Edinburgh St Bernard's FC (1896), Aston Villa (1897), Kings Park FC (1898), NEWTON HEATH (October 1900-January 1902).
A utility forward who preferred the outside-left position, Jock Fisher's tally of 46 senior appearances for the Heathens contained a run of 34 consecutive League outings.
Club record: 46 apps. 4 goals (also 9 'other' apps, 2 goals)

FITCHETT, John
Born: Chorlton, winter 1874.
Career: Manchester Schoolboys, Talbot FC, Bolton Wanderers (1897), Southampton (1902), MANCHESTER UNITED (March 1903), Plymouth Argyle (May 1903), MANCHESTER UNITED (June 1904), Fulham (May 1905), Sale Holmfield (1906), Barrow (late 1906), Exeter City (1910). Quit League football in 1911.
The former captain of the Manchester Schoolboy team, full-back Jack Fitchett helped Bolton gain promotion to the First Division, twice represented the Football League and appeared for England in the unofficial international against Germany in 1901 during his five years at Burnden Park. He scored on his debut for United (v. Leicester Fosse shortly after joining the club in 1903). He made 11 League appearances (mainly as partner to Bob Bonthron) during his second spell.
Club record: 18 apps. One goal

FITTON, George Arthur
Born: Melton Mowbray, 30 May 1902. Died: Kinver, near Kidderminster September 1984.
Career: Melton Mowbray Schoolboys, Kinver Swifts, Kinver FC, Cookley St Peter's (1921), Kidderminster Harriers (1922), West Bromwich Albion (£400, autumn 1922), MANCHESTER UNITED (£1,000, May 1932), Preston North End (December 1932), Coventry City (1935-37, then third team coach at Highfield Road), Kidderminster Harriers (1938-39), West Bromwich Albion (assistant-trainer, 1948-50, then senior trainer until June 1956).
A smart, chunky left-winger, Arthur Fitton did very well with WBA, scoring 11 goals in 99 first team appearances during his 10 years at The Hawthorns where for most of the time he played in the reserve side, winning three Central League Championship medals in the 1920s.
He failed to make an impact at Old Trafford but later made 70 appearances for PNE and 59 (22 goals scored) for Coventry.
Club record: 12 apps. 2 goals

FITZPATRICK, John Herbert Norton
Born: Aberdeen, 18 August 1946
Career: Thistle Lads' Club (Aberdeen), MANCHESTER UNITED (groundstaff September 1961, apprentice July 1962, professional September 1963-July 1973). Retired with arthritis in knees. Returned home to Aberdeen where he became a wine dealer.
United's first-ever League substitute, replacing Denis Law in the away game against Tottenham Hotspur in October 1965, wing-half John Fitzpatrick had gained a Youth Cup winners medal with the Reds the previous year. A tireless worker, he fought earnestly for his place in the team despite the presence of Pat Crerand, Nobby Stiles and others, capable of playing in a number of defensive positions.
Club record: 150 apps. 10 goals

FITZSIMMONS, David
Born: Annbank, Ayrshire 1875
Career: Annbank FC, NEWTON HEATH (July 1895), Fairfield FC (August 1896), Chorley (season 1897-98), Wigan County (season 1898-99), NEWTON HEATH (August 1899-May 1900).
Half-back Dave Fitzsimmons, a strong, determined tackler, played very well during his first spell with the club but failed to make an impact second time round.
Club record: 32 apps. (also 10 'other' apps, 3 goals)

FITZSIMMONS, Thomas
Born: Annbank, Ayrshire 21 October 1870
Career: Annbank FC, Celtic (trialist, 1892), Annbank FC, NEWTON HEATH (November 1892), St Mirren (£75, May 1894), Annbank FC (1894), Fairfield FC (1895), Glossop North End (£50, 1897), Fairfield FC (summer 1897), Oldham County (late 1897), Chorley (early 1898). Wigan County (£25, summer 1898), Annbank FC (season 1899-1900).

Elder brother of David (q.v) Tom Fitzsimmons was a utility forward, fast and mobile who gave the club sound service
Club record: 30 apps. 6 goals (also 20 'other' apps, 9 goals)

FLEETWOOD RANGERS

The Heathens refused to play extra-time in their 1st round away tie against Rangers in the1886-87 FA Cup competition…So the referee awarded the game to Fleetwood. The scores had finished level at 2-2 after 90 minutes.

FLETCHER, Peter

Born: Manchester 2 December 1953
Career: Schoolboy football, MANCHESTER UNITED (apprentice August 1969, professional December 1970), Hull City (£30,000, plus Stuart Pearson, May 1973), Stockport County (1976), Huddersfield Town (1978-82).
Centre-forward, Peter Fletcher scored plenty of goals for United at Youth and reserve team level but his first team appearances were restricted owing to the abundance of forward power at Old Trafford. He went on to score 71 goals in 224 League and Cup games for his next three clubs including 45 in 115 outings for Huddersfield.
Club record: 10 apps. one goal

FLOODLIGHTS

Floodlights at Old Trafford were erected in 1957. And they were subsequently switched on for United's home League game against Bolton Wanderers on Monday evening, 25 March of that year when a crowd of almost 61,000 saw the visitors win 2-0.
In 1987 - after 30 years in use - the four main floodlight pylons were dismantled at Old Trafford and a brand new top-of-the range lighting system assembled. This has been updated since and the lights overlooking the playing pitch are second to none.

Rays of Light

The first floodlit football game played in the City of Manchester took place on 26 February 1889 at Belle Vue Gardens.
It was a charity match organised to raise money for the families of the victims involved in the Hyde Colliery explosion.
The teams taking part were Ardwick (Manchester City) and Newton Heath (United). £140 was raised and duly donated to the fund.
United travelled to Kilmarnock for a friendly in October 1953 - arranged to officially switch on the floodlights at Rugby Park. Manager Matt Busby experimented with a youthful team, so successfully the 'Babes' were born.

FOGGON, Alan

Born: West Pelton, County Durham 23 February 1950
Career: Newcastle United (apprentice 1965, professional 1967), Cardiff City (£25,000, 1971), Middlesbrough (£10,000, 1972), Rochester Lancers, USA (1976), Hartford Bi-centennials, USA (summer 1976), MANCHESTER UNITED (£40,000, July 1976), Sunderland (£25,000, September 1976), Southend United (1977), Hartlepool United (on loan, 1978), Consett, Whitley Bay.
A former England Youth international and Fairs Cup winner with Newcastle (1969), forward, Alan Foggon's three appearances for United were all as a 'sub' early in 1976-77. Signed by Tommy Docherty, he never fitted in at Old Trafford, yet during his career scored over 75 goals in more than 275 games.
Club record: 3 apps.

FOLEY, G

Born: Kent, circa 1875
Career: Ashford, NEWTON HEATH (February-June 1900).
A right-winger, Foley - signed on the recommendation of Bob Donladson (q.v); seemed to find it hard going at a higher level of football and left the Heathens after just four months service.
Club record: 7 apps. one goal

FA CHARITY SHIELD

United have competed for the Charity Shield on 20 occasions, the details of which are:

1908 United 1 Queen's Park Rangers 1	Att. 6,000
1908 United 4 Queen's Park Rangers 0 (replay)	Att. 45,000
1911 United 8 Swindon Town 4	Att. 10,000
1948 United 3 Arsenal 4	Att. 31,000
1952 United 4 Newcastle United 2	Att. 11,381
1956 United 1 Manchester City 0	Att. 30,495
1957 United 4 Aston Villa 0	Att. 27,923
1963 United 0 Everton 4	Att. 54,840
1965 United 2 Liverpool 2*	Att. 48,502
1967 United 3 Tottenham Hotspur 3*	Att. 54,106
1977 United 0 Liverpool 0*	Att. 81,775
1983 United 2 Liverpool 0	Att. 81,956
1985 United 0 Everton 2	Att. 81,639
1990 United 1 Liverpool 1*	Att. 66,558
1993 United 1 Arsenal 1+	Att. 66,519
1994 United 2 Blackburn Rovers 0	Att. 60,402
1996 United 4 Newcastle United 0	Att. 73,214
1997 United 1 Chelsea 1+	Att. 73,636
1998 United 0 Arsenal 3	Att. 67,342
1999 United 1 Arsenal 2	Att. 70,185
2000 United 0 Chelsea 2	Att. 65,148
2001 United 1 Liverpool 2	Att. 70,277

* Each club retained the shield for six months
+ United won on penalties, beating Arsenal 5-4 in a shoot-out in 1993 and Chelsea 4-2 in 1997.

Venues: 1908 and 1911 games staged at Stamford Bridge (against the Southern League Champions); 1948 fixture at Highbury; 1952, 1957, 1965 & 1967 all played at Old Trafford, 1956 at Maine Road; 1963 at Goodison Park, the eleven games between 1977 and 2000 were played at Wembley and the 2001 match at The Millennium Stadium, Cardiff.

Summary of Matches:

Venue	P	W	D	L	F	A
Home	4	2	2	0	13	7
Away	3	1	0	2	4	8
Neutral	4	2	1	1	14	7
Wembley	11	3	4*	4	12	12
Totals	22	8	7	7	43	34

* Include games that went to a penalty shoot-out.

Fact File

The 1908 replay with QPR (the first game was played in April) was carried over until August (at the start of the following season) and Jimmy Turnbull netted a hat-trick in United's 4-0 victory in front of some 45,000 spectators (recs. £1,275).

United's 8-4 Charity Shield win over Swindon Town in 1911 is a record for (a) the highest-scoring win in terms of goals for (by any team) and (b) the total of 12 goals is the biggest aggregate score for the annual event.Harold Halse was United's six-goal hero.

United's 4-0 win over Aston Villa in the 1957 game at Old Trafford was the first time the visitors had played a full game under floodlights. Tommy Taylor scored a hat-trick against Villa..

Spurs' 'keeper Pat Jennings netted one of his side's goals in the 3-3 draw at Old Trafford in 1967 - a game that also saw George Best and Bobby Charlton score spectacular efforts for United.

United appeared in six successive Charity Shield games: 1996-2001 inclusive, losing the last four.

The 2001 showdown between United and Liverpool at Cardiff's Millennium Stadium was the first competitive match ever played under cover in the U.K.

FA CUP (The Football Association Challenge Cup)

United first entered this competition in season 1886-87.

Their full record of FA Cup action (1886-2002) reads:

Venue	P	W	D	L	F	A
Home	170	109	33	28	352	154
Away	157	65	41	51	251	234
Neutral	56	28	14	14	93	63
Totals	383	202	88	93	696	451

Analysis	P	W	D	L	F	A
Competition Proper	358	189	81	88	639	425
Qualifying Rounds	25	13	7	5	57	26

NB - The 'home' ties include ten matches played during seasoins 1945-49: eight of them at Maine Road one each at Everton and Huddersfield.

United have appeared in 15 Finals (a record they share with Arsenal), winning the trophy a record 10 times. They have also appeared in 22 semi-finals (the same number as Arsenal) and bettered only by Everton (23). Their 14 Wembley Cup Finals (16 matches played including two replays) is also a record.

FA Cup Final Victories:

1909   United 1 Bristol City 0   The Crystal Palace

A crowd of 71,401 witnessed a disappointing contest. United generally had the best of the play against a City side who stood above them in the First Division table. United wore their change strip of all white with a red 'V'.

The difference between the sides was United's Welsh international wing wizard Billy Meredith. He caused plenty of problems, especially early on, but his fellow forwards failed to capitalise on his good work.

The only goal of the game came halfway through the first-half. Harold Halse struck the crossbar and Sandy Turnbull followed up to score from close range.

Skipper Charlie Roberts was rock solid at the back for United and he duly went up to collect the silver trophy with a broad smile on his face.

Team: Moger; Stacey, Hayes; Duckworth, Roberts, Bell; Meredith, Halse, J Turnbull, A. Turnbull, Wall.

1948   United 4 Blackpool 2   Wembley Stadium

Thirty-nine years to the day since their first FA Cup Final victory, United, playing in blue, this time produced a superb display against a Blackpool side that included the two Stans, Matthews & Mortensen, both England internationals, who could win matches single-handedly.

Close on 100,000 saw a six-goal thriller. 'Pool scored first in the 12th minute, full-back Eddie Shimwell blasting in a penalty under the diving Jack Crompton after Allenby Chilton had fouled Mortensen.

A mix-up between Eric Hayward and goalkeeper Joe Robinson allowed Jack Rowley to nip in an level the scores in the 28th minute, but seven minutes later it was 2-1 to the Seasiders. A chipped free-kick by Matthews from the right wing was headed on by Hugh Kelly for Mortensen to net from eight yards.

Early in the second-half United managed to nullify the dangerous wing play of Matthews and gradually took control of the game. They went on to claim a fine victory by scoring three times in just 15 minutes.

In the 69th minute, the lively Johnny Morris swung over a free-kick, the alert Rowley darting between two defenders to head firmly past Robinson in the Blackpool goal.

Shortly afterwards Crompton produced a blinding save from the dangerous Mortensen. His instant throw set up an attack from which Stan Pearson took Johnny Anderson's deft pass in his stride and gleefully glided it wide of the onrushing Robinson as he left his line.

United were in the driving seat and seven minutes from time Anderson's speculative long-range shot soared into the net to give United a two-goal margin...and ultimate victory, well deserved having beaten top-flight opposition in every round.

Full-back Johnny Carey proudly collected the Cup from King George VI.

Team; Crompton; Carey, Aston; Anderson, Chilton, Cockburn; Delaney, Morris, Rowley, Pearson, Mitten.

1963   United 3 Leicester City 1   Wembley Stadium

At the end of a relegation-threatened season United put their League worries behind them to record their third FA Cup Final triumph by beating a plucky Leicester side 3-1 in front of 99,604 spectators.

Although the underdogs, United played the better football throughout. And although the usually reliable Gordon Banks in the City goal made a couple of errors, victory was richly deserved.

United went ahead in the 29th minute. Pat Crerand's pass was collected by Denis Law who turned sharply and fired low into the net from just inside the area.

The second goal arrived in the 57th minute. Bobby Charlton's rocket being partially saved by Banks but David Herd, alert as ever, pounced to fire in the rebound.

Ken Keyworth dived in to head City momentarily back into the game with 10 minutes left but when Banks dropped Johnny Giles' right-wing cross into the path of Herd it was game, set and Cup to United.

Noel Cantwell held aloft the trophy - the second Irishman to skipper United to FA Cup glory.

Team: Gaskell; Dunne, Cantwell; Crerand, Foulkes, Setters; Giles, Quixall, Herd, Law, Charlton.

1977   United 2 Liverpool 1   Wembley Stadium

After losing to Southampton by a goal to nil twelve months previously United were much more resilient as they went in search of their fourth FA Cup Final victory. Liverpool, favourites before kick-off and on course for the double, had the better of the first-half exchanges. United defended stubbornly but looked weak in attack.

Early in the second-half things hotted up. On 50 minutes Liverpool were caught napping as Jimmy Greenhoff slotted a forward pass through to Stuart Pearson. He ran into the box and fired home hard and low past Ray Clemence at the near post.

United perked up - so did Liverpool - and two minutes later Jimmy Case, accepting Joey Jones' cross, turned smartly inside the box to fire a right-footer high past Alex Stepney's left-hand to level the scores.

But United hit back immediately and within two minutes had regained the lead.

Jimmy Greenhoff, full of running, seized on Tommy Smith's error and shot towards goal. The ball rebounded to Lou Macari who shot could have gone anywhere. Instead it struck Greenhoff as he followed through and Clemence was bemused as it flew into the net. Ray Kennedy, who rattled the woodwork in the first-half, hit a stanchion late on as Liverpool pressed for an equaliser that never came. Appropriately it was Martin Buchan who walked up the 39 steps to collect the silver prize.

Team: Stepney; Nicholl, Albiston; McIlroy, B Greenhoff, Buchan; Coppell, J Greenhoff, Pearson, Macari, Hill (sub. McCreery).

1983   United 4 Brighton & Hove Albion 0 (after a 2-2 draw) Wembley Stadium

There should never have been a replay in 1983! Brighton should have won at the first attempt! Gordon Smith missed a sitter late on to let United off the hook.

But such is football, it's so unpredictable - and United, at the second attempt, won in a canter by 4-0.

The initial game, played five days earlier in front of 99,059 fans, saw United come back from a goal down (scored by Smith) to lead 2-1 with strikes from Frank Stapleton & Ray Wilkins. But the Seagulls, battling hard, equalised through Gary Stevens, and then in extra-time so nearly snatched victory.

There were just over 91,500 fans present for the replay, Brighton having skipper Steve Foster available after missing the first game through suspension.

After a fairly even opening period of play, United scored twice in double-quick time. Arthur Albiston and Alan Davies set up skipper Bryan Robson for the opener on 14 minutes and then Davies nodded on Arnold Muhren's corner for Norman Whiteside to grab number two soon afterwards. This gave the Irishman the honour of becoming the first player to score in both the League Cup Final and FA Cup Final in the same season. He was also the youngest-ever FA Cup Final marksman at 18 years, 14 days.

Albion fought on bravely but after Robson had claimed his second goal a minute before the interval, it was only commonsense that they tried to keep the score within reasonable proportions.

Dutchman Muhren duly completed the scoring from the penalty spot after the influential Robson had been held up in the box by Stevens.

It was Robson himself who collected the trophy to celebrate a fifth FA Cup Final victory for the Reds.

Team (for both games): Bailey; Duxbury, Albiston; Wilkins, Moran, McQueen; Robson, Muhren, Stapleton, Whiteside, Davies. Sub. Grimes (not used).

1985   United 1 Everton 0   Wembley Stadium

For the first time ever in an FA Cup Final a player was sent-off - United's defender Kevin Moran was the unfortunate victim, banished by Policeman referee Peter Willis from County Durham for a 'professional foul' on Everton's Peter Reid with just 12 minutes of normal time remaining.

The game up to then hadn't been all that good. It certainly livened up after that red card situation and it was the ten men of United who finished the stronger, taking the game into extra-time. After a couple of near misses at both ends, it was Norman Whiteside who snatched a deserved winner for United, curling a terrific left-footer beyond Neville Southall with just 10 minutes of extra-time remaining. As in 1977, United had deprived a Merseyside team of the double!

For the first time in the club's history the same player - Bryan Robson - went up the Royal Box who collect the trophy - with a delighted Ron Atkinson looking on proudly.

Team: Bailey; Gidman, Albiston (sub Duxbury); Whiteside, McGrath, Moran; Robson, Strachan, Hughes, Stapleton, Olsen. The attendance was 99,445.

1990   United 1 Crystal Palace 0 (after a 3-3 draw) Wembley Stadium

A six-goal thriller had ended all-square to set up United's second FA Cup Final replay in seven years and again they came up with the goods, second time round!

A Wembley audience of just under 80,000 saw the first contest when United came back to equalise with a late Mark Hughes goal.

Gary O'Reilly scored first for the Eagles on 19 minutes…a goal that saw former United favourite Steve Coppell leap from the dug-out as Palace manager. Bryan Robson levelled things up ten minutes before half-time and then Mark Hughes pounced to edge United in front in the 62nd minute. Enter super-sub Ian Wright…who quickly equalised on 72 minutes to take the game went into extra-time. Within two minutes of the re-start Wright netted again to edge Palace 3-2 in front. But United had the last laugh when Hughes brought the scores level once more with his side's third goal in the 113th minute.

United's Scottish international goalkeeper Jim Leighton was partly blamed for all of Palace's goals in that game and he was subsequently replaced between the posts by Les Sealey for the replay.

There was a similar turnout for the mid-week replay which was decided by a spectacular goal scored by United's left-wing back Lee Martin in the 59th minute when he converted Neil Webb's astute diagonal ball into the box with a rising drive beyond Nigel Martyn.

Palace defended doggedly as Coppell adopted a more physical approach to the game. But United never really looked in trouble and for the third time a joyous Bryan Robson lifted the star prize.

First match: Leighton; Ince, Martin (Blackmore); Bruce, Phelan, Pallister (Robins); Robson, Webb, McClair, Hughes, Wallace.

Second match: Sealey in goal. Substitutes Blackmore and Robins (not used).

1994   United 4 Chelsea 0   Wembley Stadium

Having lost the two Premiership games to Chelsea by the same score of 1-0, United made it third time lucky in 1993-94 in clashes with the Londoners, beating them 4-0 in the FA Cup Final in front of 79,634 fans. The scoreline flattered United who were certainly the better side but not by four goals!

After a scoreless first-half when both 'keepers pulled off good saves, referee David Elleray awarded United two penalties in the space of five minutes. Both were converted by Eric Cantona …the first in the 59th minute after Eddie Newton was guilty of a foul on Denis Irwin and then in the 64th minute when Frank Sinclair was adjudged to have impeded the Ukrainian winger Andrei Kanchelskis.

In the 68th minute Mark Hughes netted number three and substitute Brian McClair completed the scoring with a fourth goal in the dying seconds. Skipper Steve Bruce beamed at the Royal Box as he collected the trophy to celebrate United's first 'double.'

Team: Schmeichel; Parker, Irwin (sub Sharpe); Bruce, Pallister, Ince; Kanchelskis (sub McClair), Keane, Cantona, Hughes, Giggs.

1996   United 1 Liverpool 0   Wembley Stadium

A sun-drenched crowd of 79,007 saw United win a disappointing Final by a single goal, scored four minutes from time by Eric Cantona. Victory gave the Reds the double for the second time.

From the start it was obvious that the contest would be defensively-minded with both teams showing too much respect for each other! If there was to be a result without the need of a replay it would be by a lone goal - and that went to United, albeit late on in the proceedings.

With only seven shots on target all afternoon (four by United) and with time fast running out, United won their fifth corner of the game in the 86th minute.

Liverpool's 'keeper David James - who pulled off three excellent saves early on - attempted to punch clear as the kick came over, but the ball deflected off his own striker Ian Rush and fell to the feet of Cantona on the edge of the penalty area. The Frenchman with his deadly right foot volleyed it back towards the goal through an ocean of green and white shirts and into the net past the unsighted James.

Cantona, United's captain and the first Frenchman ever to play in an FA Cup Final, went up to collect the star prize, United's ninth winning of the trophy, a new record.

Team: Schmeichel; Irwin, May, Pallister, P Neville; Beckham (sub G Neville), Keane, Butt, Giggs; Cantona, Cole (sub Scholes).

1999   **United 2 Newcastle United 0**   **Wembley Stadium**

A crowd of 79,101 saw this battle of the Uniteds, and it was the red & white of Manchester who came out on top, easing to a comfortable 2-0 victory, their 10th success in the competition. They also clinched the double (for the third time - a record) and were now within one match of capturing the unique treble.

Always in command, Alex Ferguson's men - despite losing skipper Roy Keane after nine minutes through injury - could and should have won by a far bigger margin. Substitute Teddy Sheringham, with his first real touch after coming onto the field for Keane, grabbed the first goal in the 11th minute following a decisive build-up through the centre of the Newcastle defence with Scholes. After several close shaves (around the Geordies' goal) Paul Scholes doubled the lead in the 53rd minute, converting an astute Sheringham lay-off, and he may well have scored again late on.

Keane hobbled up the steps to collect the Cup - and United celebrated once more!

Team (4-4-2): Schmeichel; G Neville, May, Johnsen, P Neville; Beckham, Keane (sub Sheringham), Scholes (sub Stam), Giggs; Cole (sub Yorke), Solskjaer.

FA Cup Final Defeats

1957   **Aston Villa 2 United 1**   **Wembley Stadium**

Two weeks before visiting Wembley in 1957, United were on course to complete a unique hat-trick of successes: the League Championship, European Cup & FA Cup. They deservedly won the League title, but disappointingly lost to Real Madrid in the semi-final of the European Cup and then, when still in with a great chance of doing the double, they were defeated narrowly by Aston Villa in the Cup Final.

After only six minutes United's goalkeeper Ray Wood was badly injured in a clash with the Villa left-winger, Peter McParland. Wood was stretchered off and Jackie Blanchflower took over between the posts. United reduced to 10 men (no substitutes).

This certainly disrupted United's plan but they remained the better side in a dull, goalless first-half, when they should have been awarded a penalty for a foul on Bobby Charlton.

United, playing in their all white change strip, continued to play well but Villa defended strongly and perhaps against the run of play McParland headed them in front. Five minutes later he cracked in a second. Wood returned to play on the wing. United pushed men forward and Tommy Taylor headed a late consolation goal. Villa held on and Johnny Dixon collected the Cup.

A crowd of 99,225 saw this United team in action: Wood; Foulkes, Byrne; Colman, Blanchflower, Edwards; Berry, Whelan, Taylor, Charlton, Pegg.

1958   **Bolton Wanderers 2 United 0**   **Wembley Stadium**

United, fielding a side assembled in what could only be described as 'tragic circumstances' following the Munich air disaster, were gunned down by Bolton's Nat Lofthouse! The 'Lion of Vienna' scored both his side's goals - the first as early as the third minute when he drove in a low shot from close in which eluded Harry Gregg's dive, and his second in the 55th minute when he shoulder-charged Gregg (and ball) over the line. To this day most spectators (& indeed TV. viewers) claimed the challenge was a foul. But Sheffield referee Jim Sherlock had other ideas and allowed the 'goal' to stand.

United were, in fact, outplayed for long periods by a forceful Bolton side who certainly made up for the disappointment they suffered five years earlier when they lost 4-3 to Blackpool after holding a 3-1 lead. As for United it was two successive FA Cup Final defeats under the Twin Towers - the first team to suffer such a fate! The supporters, however, were cheered to see Matt Busby, albeit looking very frail, watching from the touchline.

A crowd of 99,756 saw these eleven United players in action: Gregg; Foulkes, Greaves; Goodwin, Cope, Crowther; Dawson, E Taylor, Charlton, Viollet, Webster.

1976   **United 0 Southampton 1** **Wembley Stadium**

Few people gave Second Division Southampton a chance of winning the Cup in 1976. But we all know that football is a funny old game with surprises and shocks along the way! This was certainly a shock for Tommy Docherty and his young United team as they succumbed to a second-half goal by Bobby Stokes.

It was not a pretty Final by any means but Lawrie McMenemy's Saints side battled all down the line and certainly caused a major upset. The all-important goal was struck home in the 83rd minute. Jim McCalliog, a former United midfielder, threaded a smart ground pass through to Stokes who somehow found a way past 'keeper Alex Stepney with a not too well struck left-footer from just outside the area.

United's team in front 99,115 fans, was: Stepney; Forsyth, Houston; Daly, B Greenhoff, Buchan; Coppell, McIlroy, Pearson, Macari, Hill (sub McCreery)

1979   **Arsenal 3 United 2**   **Wembley Stadium**

Arsenal, two goals ahead with four minutes to play, were suddenly pegged back to all-square as United produced a powerhouse finish! But the Gunners had the last laugh, Alan Sunderland sliding home a late, late bullet to stun the United faithful, winning what would be known as the 'Five Minute Final.' Arsenal scored their first goal in the 12th minute, both Sunderland and Brian Talbot claiming to have touched David Price's cross before the ball entered the net. Talbot was later awarded the goal. Just before half-time Frank Stapleton, a future United player, put his side 2-0 up. And that's how it stood until the 87th minute when Gordon McQueen somehow scrambled the ball past Pat Jennings in a goalmouth melee (2-1). Less than two minutes later Sammy McIlroy danced through a labouring Arsenal defence to level the scores. Extra-time looked a certainty… that is until Liam Brady sent Graham Rix racing down the left-wing. His curling cross eluded Gary Bailey for the incoming Sunderland who had time and space to put the ball into the net to end United's dream! The attendance was 99,219 and United fielded: Bailey; Nicholl, Albiston; McIlroy, McQueen, Buchan; Coppell, J Greenhoff, Jordan, Macari, Thomas.

1995   **Everton 1 United 0**   **Wembley Stadium**

Paul Rideout's goal decided this Final in favour of the Merseysiders who in winning gained sweet revenge for that defeat by United ten years earlier.

A crowd of 79,592 witnessed a dogged contest, Rideout's goal coming on the half-hour mark from close range after a flurry of efforts had been thwarted by the United defence - and the woodwork! This in effect was United's second trophy loss in a week - the Reds having finished runner-up to Blackburn Rovers in the Premiership the previous Sunday!

Team: Schmeichel; G Neville, Irwin; Bruce (sub Giggs), Sharpe (sub Scholes), Pallister; Keane, Ince, McClair, Hughes, Butt.

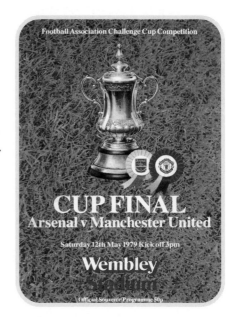

United's FA Cup Dossier

United have been involved in a record 10 semi-final replays, and they qualified for this stage of the competition five seasons running: 1962-63 to 1966-67, going through to Wembley just once in 1963.

In 1996 United reached their third successive FA Cup Final, thus becoming only the fifth club to achieve this feat behind Blackburn Rovers (who were the first in the 1880s), followed by West Bromwich Albion, then Arsenal and Everton.

United actually played in an FA Cup Final in each of six successive decades: 1948; 1957 & 1958; 1963; 1976, 1977 & 1979; 1983 & 1985; 1990, 1994, 1996 & 1999.

Bobby Charlton appeared in eight FA Cup semi-finals for United (taking in part in 12 games overall including replays): 1957, 1958 (two games), 1962, 1963, 1964, 1965 (two), 1966 & 1970 (three). This is an all-time record for the competition.

United have won each of the last ten FA Cup semi-finals they have played in: 1976, 1977, 1979, 1983, 1985, 1990, 1994, 1995, 1996 & 1999.

A crowd of just 17,987 saw United beat Crystal Palace in the 1995 FA Cup semi-final replay at Villa Park. This was the lowest attendance at this stage of the competition for 93 years - since March 1902 when 15,000 fans saw the Derby County-Sheffield United second replay.

As holders of the trophy, United did not take part in the 1999-2000 FA Cup competition, being obliged to play in FIFA's Club World Championship in the heat of Rio de Janeiro instead!

United have twice scored eight goals in an FA Cup game - beating Yeovil (home) 8-0 in February 1949 and Northampton Town 8-2 (away) in February 1970 (the day George Best scored a double hat-trick).

In January 1928 United defeated Brentford 7-1 at Old Trafford (their third biggest win) and in March 1963 they knocked out Huddersfield 5-0, also at home.

A 7-1 reverse at Burnley in February 1901 has been United's heaviest FA Cup defeat to date. They also lost 7-2 at home to Sheffield Wednesday in February 1961.

In February 1992, Southampton became the first team to knock a top-line club out of the FA Cup in a penalty shoot-out - beating United on spot-kicks at the end of a 4th round replay at Old Trafford.

Over a period of fifteen months (from January 1994 to April 1995) United were unbeaten in eleven successive FA Cup matches.

Stan Crowther played for two clubs in the 1957-58 FA Cup - Aston Villa first and then Manchester United. He also played in two Finals and was a winner with Villa v. United in 1957 and a loser with United v. Bolton Wanderers in 1958. (Crowther given special dispensation by the FA - post Munich).

Bryan Robson skippered United to victory in three FA Cup Finals (1983, 1985 and 1990) - the only player in history to achieve this feat.

Martin Buchan is the only player (so far) to have captained a team to victory in both the Scottish and English FA Cup Finals - Aberdeen in 1970 and United in 1977.

Along with Robson, six other players - Arthur Albiston (1977, 1983 & 1985), Mark Hughes and Gary Pallister (1990, 1994 & 1996) and Ryan Giggs, Roy Keane and Peter Schmeichel (all in 1994, 1996 & 1999) have gained three FA Cup winners' medals with United. And all of them played in one losing Final as well, although Giggs was, in fact, a substitute in 1995. Hughes later collected another winners' medal with Chelsea (1997).

Bobby Charlton played in three Finals (1957, 1958 and 1963), gaining a winner' medal in the latter.

Denis Irwin also played in three FA Cup Finals for the Reds, winning in 1994 and 1996, losing in 1995.

Striker Frank Stapleton won three FA Cup medals, one with Arsenal (v. United) in 1979 and two with United (1983 & 1985). He also collected two runners-up medals (1978 & 1980) and is the only player to have played and scored in Wembley Finals for two different teams (the Gunners & United).

Like Stapleton, fellow Irishman Johnny Giles also played in five FA Cup Finals (six games in total). He lined up for United in 1963 and then for Leeds in 1965, 1970, 1972 & 1973. The 1970 Final went to a replay. He was a winner in 1963 and 1972.

Harold Halse won the FA Cup with United in 1909 &Aston Villa in 1913 but was a loser with Chelsea in the 1915 Final.

Inside-forward Ernie Taylor played in three FA Cup Finals with three different clubs: Newcastle United in 1951, Blackpool in 1953 and United in 1958. He was a winner in his first two.

Billy Meredith won the FA Cup with both Manchester clubs - City in 1904 and United in 1909.

Arthur Albiston (1977 v. Liverpool), Alan Davies (1983 v. Brighton & Hove Albion) and Les Sealey (1990 v. Crystal Palace) all made their FA Cup debuts for United in Wembley Finals. Sealey was called up for the 1990 replay and became the only player to win an FA Cup winners' medal whilst on loan from another club (Luton). Davies had only appeared in three League games before his Wembley 'day out.'

United played every game of their 1990 FA Cup run (up to the semi-final) on a Sunday afternoon and the winning team (v. Crystal Palace) cost around £12 million to assemble, although the scorer of the winning goal in the replay - Lee Martin - was signed for nothing at all! And he was also the first left-back to score in a Final.

Manchester United have defeated Chelsea and Liverpool most times in the FA Cup (both eight). They have gained six against Aston Villa and Southampton, and five versus Derby County, Middlesbrough, Preston North End, Reading and Sheffield Wednesday.

Everton, Sheffield Wednesday and Tottenham Hotspur, all with five wins, have beaten United on most occasions in the competition. United met Wednesday four times in the tournament over a period of five seasons: 1957-58, 1959-60, 1960-61 & 1961-62.

United (also as Newton Heath) have met a total of 89 different clubs (with present-day names and former titles) in FA Cup football.

In 1964-65, United met Burnley, Stoke City and Wolverhampton Wanderers in First Division League games - and a week after playing each game they met again in the FA Cup competition.

United and Middlesbrough opposed each other three times in successive FA Cup campaigns: 1969-70, 1970-71 and 1971-72. Each time it took a replay to decide the issue, United winning the first and third encounters. Either side of these tussles United and 'Boro played against each other in the League Cup (1968-69 & 1972-73).

United and West Ham did battle against each other three times in the FA Cup over a period of four years: January 1983 to March 1986. United won 2-0 and 4-2 in the opening two encounters and then after a 1-1 draw, the Hammers gained revenge with a 2-0 replay victory in 1986.

Sheffield United and the Reds played against each other four times in five years in the early 1990s - and all clashes took place at Bramall Lane. The Blades were defeated in 1990, 1994 & 1995 and each time the Reds went all the way to the Final.

Bobby Charlton has made a record 79 FA Cup appearances for United (75 in succession between 1958 and 1973). He also made four in the competition for Preston North End and his total of 83 is the third highest in the competition behind Ian Callaghan (ex-Liverpool and Swansea City) and the great Sir Stanley Matthews (Blackpool & Stoke City).

Over a period of 13 years defender Bill Foulkes played in 61 consecutive FA Cup games for United (1954 to 1967).

Full-back Shay Brennan starred in four semi-finals for United (1958-62-65-66).

The player who has scored most FA Cup goals for United is Denis Law with a total of 34. Jack Rowley notched 26, George Best and Stan Pearson both netted 21 and Bobby Charlton claimed 19.

Charlton scored on his FA Cup debut for the Reds in the 2-0 semi-final win over Birmingham City at Hillsborough in 1957.

Norman Whiteside (at the age of 18 years, 18 days) became the youngest FA Cup Final scorer when he helped United win the trophy against Brighton after a replay in May 1983 (two months after scoring in the League Cup Final on the same ground).

Eric Cantona (with two penalties against Chelsea in 1994) became the first Frenchman to score in the FA Cup Final. He was also the first foreign-born player to lift the FA Cup and, indeed, was the first 'foreigner' to score in two FA Cup Finals - he got the winner against Liverpool in 1996.

The Greenhoff brothers (Brian and Jimmy) in 1977 and the Neville brothers (Gary and Phil) in 1996 and 1999, were members of successful United FA Cup winning sides.

United have scored four goals in an FA Cup Final game on three occasions: 1948 v. Blackpool, 1983 v. Brighton & Hove Albion (replay) and 1994 v. Chelsea. When they defeated Brighton 4-0, it was the biggest winning margin in a Final since Bury's 6-0 hammering of Derby County in 1903.

Stan Pearson (1948) and Alex Dawson (1958) join the elite band of players who've scored semi-final hat-tricks.

United's longest Cup-tie to date lasted for seven hours (four games including three replays, two going into extra-time). It was a first round encounter against Small Heath (Birmingham City) in 1903-04. United finally won through 3-1 at Hyde Road (Manchester).

Over a period of 15 years (either side of the WW2) United were drawn against non-League opposition on four occasions: Yeovil in 1938 and 1949, Weymouth in 1950 and Walthamstow Avenue in 1953. The Reds haven't met a team outside the 'League' since.

In 1945-46 United beat Preston North End 1-0 in an FA Cup game at Maine Road, but still went out of the competition after losing 3-1 at Deepdale! This was the only season whereby all rounds leading up to the semi-final stage were played over two legs.

United took on and defeated six fellow First Division teams, including the League Champions and FA Cup holders, on their way to FA Cup glory in 1948. With Old Trafford closed due to bomb damage, all their matches were played 'away' at Villa Park, Goodison Park, Leeds Road (Huddersfield), Maine Road, Hillsborough and Wembley, in that order.

The same thing happened in 1990 when United won 'away' at Nottingham Forest, Hereford United, Newcastle United, Sheffield United, Maine Road and Wembley.

Owing to the Arctic weather conditions which had gripped England, United won their 3rd, 4th, 5th and 6th round FA Cup ties in the space of 27 days during March 1963.

Tommy Docherty's last game as manager of United was the 1977 FA Cup Final against Liverpool. He resigned following the news of his alleged affair with Mary Brown, wife of the Old Trafford physiotherapist, Laurie Brown.

Alex Ferguson has won eight FA Cup Finals as a manager - four with Aberdeen (1982-83-84-86) and four with United (1990-94-96-99). And he became only the second man since WW2 to lift the trophy both north and south of the border.

FA Cup action against the Minnows

Since entering the Football League in 1892, Heathens/United have opposed the following non-League teams in the FA Cup:

1893-94	Middlesbrough (h) 4-0
1895-96	Kettering Town (h) 2-1
1896-97	West Manchester (h) 7-0, Nelson (h) 3-0, Kettering (h) 5-1, Southampton (a) 1-1, Southampton (h) 3-1
1898-99	Tottenham Hotspur (a) 1-1, Tottenham Hotspur (h) 3-5
1899-00	South Shore (a) 1-3
1900-01	Portsmouth (h) 3-0
1902-03	Accrington Stanley (h) 7-0, Oswaldtwistle R (h) 3-2, Southport Central (h) 4-1
1904-05	Fulham (h) 2-2, Fulham (a) 0-0, Fulham (Villa Park) 0-1
1905-06	Staple Hill (h) 7-2, Norwich City (h) 3-0
1906-07	Portsmouth (a) 2-2, Portsmouth (h) 1-2
1907-08	Fulham (a) 1-2
1908-09	Brighton Hove & Albion (h) 1-0
1910-11	West Ham United (a) 1-2
1911-12	Coventry City (a) 5-1, Reading (a) 1-1, Reading (h) 3-0
1912-13	Coventry City (h) 1-1, Coventry City (a) 2-1, Plymouth Argyle (a) 2-0
1913-14	Swindon Town (a) 0-1
1937-38	Yeovil Town (h) 3-0
1948-49	Yeovil Town (h) 8-0
1949-50	Weymouth (h) 4-0
1952-53	Walthamstow A (h) 1-1, Walthamstow A (a*) 5-2

* Played at Highbury.

Apart from the defeats indicated above, United have also been knocked out of the FA Cup competition from teams from a lower Division as follows:

1909-10	Burnley (a) 0-2
1926-27	Reading (Villa Park) 1-2
1929-30	Swindon Town (h) 0-2
1938-39	West Bromwich Albion (h) 1-5
1946-47	Nottingham Forest (h) 0-2
1950-51	Birmingham City (a) 0-1
1951-52	Hull City (h) 0-2
1952-53	Everton (a) 1-2
1955-56	Bristol Rovers (a) 0-4
1958-59	Norwich City (a) 0-3
1966-67	Norwich City (h) 1-2
1970-71	Middlesbrough (a) 1-2
1974-75	Walsall (a) 2-3*
1975-76	Southampton (n)+ 0-1
1981-82	Watford (a) 0-1
1983-84	Bournemouth (a) 0-2

* After a 0-0 draw
+ FA Cup Final at Wembley

FA YOUTH CUP

Manchester United have won the FA Youth Cup eight times, as follows:

1952-53

1st leg	United 7 Wolverhampton Wanderers 1	Att. 20,934
2nd leg	Wolverhampton Wanderers 2 United 2	Att. 14,290

1953-54

1st leg	United 4 Wolverhampton Wanderers 4	Att. 18,246
2nd leg	Wolverhampton Wanderers 0 United 1	Att. 28,651

1954-55

1st leg	United 4 West Bromwich Albion 1	Att.16,696
2nd leg	West Bromwich Albion 0 United 3	Att. 8,335

1955-56

1st leg	United 3 Chesterfield 2	Att. 25,544
2nd leg	Chesterfield 1 United 1	Att. 15,838

1956-57

1st leg	West Ham United 2 United 3	Att. 14,056
2nd leg	United 5 West Ham United 0	Att. 23,349

1963-64

1st leg	Swindon Town 1 United 1	Att. 16,899
2nd leg	United 4 Swindon Town 1	Att. 25,563

1991-92

1st leg	Crystal Palace 1 United 3	Att. 7,825
2nd leg	United 3 Crystal Palace 2	Att. 14,681

1994-95

1st leg	Tottenham Hotspur 2 United 1	Att. 8,213
2nd leg	United 1 Tottenham Hotspur 0	Att. 20.190

(score ended 3-3 on aggregate - United won 4-3 on penalties).

Youth Cup Fact File

Their biggest aggregate win in the Final is 9-3 v. Wolverhampton Wanderers in 1953. They defeated West Bromwich Albion 7-1 over two legs in 1954 and accounted for West Ham United by 8-2 in 1957.

United's heaviest defeat in the Final (over two legs) has been 7-6 on aggregate at the hands of Watford in 1986. They lost 4-1 over two legs against Leeds in 1993.

David Sadler scored a hat-trick in United's 4-1 second leg win over Swindon Town in the 1964 Final.

Eddie Colman and Duncan Edwards (1953-54-55), Bobby Charlton, Tony Hawksworth and Wilf McGuinness (1954-55-56) all gained three winners' medals apiece.

United never lost an FA Youth Cup game (home or away) for six years - between 1952 and 1958. The run finally ended when they went down to Wolves at Molineux in the 1958 semi-final

United's biggest win (one game) is 23-0 v. Nantwich Town (home) in season 1952-53.

Seven members of United's 1991-92 Youth team - David Beckham, Nicky Butt, Simon Davies, Ryan Giggs, Keith Gillespie, Gary Neville and Robbie Savage - all went on to become full internationals.

In May 1993, an aggregate crowd of 61,599 saw the two-legged Final between United & Leeds.

A record crowd of 35,949 the United v. Blackburn Rovers Youth Cup semi-final, 1st leg in April 1959.

FOOTBALL ALLIANCE

United's full record in the 'Alliance':

Venue	P	W	D	L	F	A	Pts
Home	33	19	7	7	93	47	45
Away	33	9	5	19	53	86	23
Totals	66	28	12	26	146	133	68

Manchester United (as Newton Heath) first entered this competition for the 1889-90 season. They had a disappointing campaign and finished in 8th position with just 20 points out of a possible 44. They won only nine of their 22 matches (seven at home) and lost 11. Their goal-average was 40-45. Their biggest victory was a 9-1 demolition of Small Heath (Birmingham City) on 7 April 1890 when Stewart (3) and J Doughty (2) led the goal-chase in front of 4,000 spectators. United's heaviest defeat was a 7-0 drubbing away at Grimsby Town on 8 February.

E Wilson scored United's first 'Alliance' goal in a 4-1 home win over Sunderland Albion on 21 September 1889. This was also United's first game in the competition and of course their first win!

In their second campaign of 1890-91 United floundered again to finish a place lower than before in ninth spot with only 17 points gained from seven wins and three draws. They were poor away from home, losing on nine occasions, their heaviest defeat coming at Nottingham Forest on 22 November where they crashed 8-2. A 6-3 triumph at home to Crewe Alexandra on 1 November was United's best win.

In 1891-92 they finally got it right and took the runners-up spot behind a forceful Nottingham Forest side. United ran up 31 points (from 12 wins & seven draws). Their biggest win was a 10-1 hammering of luckless Lincoln City at home while their worst defeat came away at Nottingham Forest by 3-0.

Bob Donaldson was top marksman with 20 of United's 69 goals, thus becoming the first player to net a score of goals for the club at 'League' level.

FOOTBALL COMBINATION

When the Football League was formed by the 12 founder members in 1888, there were several other clubs who failed the voting process and were desirous of playing League football.

As a result the Football Combination was formed to run along similar lines as the senior League, twenty clubs being initially accepted. It would have been impossible at the time for all the clubs to play each other on a home and away basis, so each club was left to its own device to arrange fixtures against, say, eight other clubs out of the members.

Newton Heath LYR were one of the members, choosing to play matches against Bootle, Burslem Port Vale, Darwen, Derby Midland, Halliwell, Leek Town and South Shore.

The remaining clubs in the Combination were Birmingham St George's, Blackburn Olympic, Crewe Alexandra, Derby Junction, Gainsborough Trinity, Grimsby Town, Lincoln City, Long Eaton Rangers, Northwich Victoria, Notts Rangers, Small Heath aand Walsall Town Swifts.

The rather haphazard nature of the competition failed to capture the publ;ic's imagination, no league tables were published and it folded in April 1889 with several matches left unplayed. Most of the clubs joined the Football Alliance (q.v) which exactly mirrored the Football League set-up. It was believed that Newton Heath had the best record in the Combination, but no trophy was presented!

FOOTBALL LEAGUE, FA PREMIER LEAGUE, PREMIERSHIP

Manchester United won the Football League championship seven times: 1907-08, 1910-11, 1951-52, 1955-56, 1956-57, 1964-65 & 1966-67 and they have so far lifted the Premiership title also on seven occasions: 1992-93, 1993-94, 1995-96, 1996-97, 1998-99, 1999-2000 and 2000-01.

The Second Division Championship has been won twice, in 1935-36 and 1975-75.

United have been 'Football League/Premiership' runners-up no fewer than 12 times, the last in 1997-98.

Newton Heath's/Manchester United's full 'League' record: 1892-2002 inclusive:

Divisions 1& 2 and the Premiership

Venue	P	W	D	L	F	A
Home	1974	1175	450	349	3981	1914
Away	1974	637	515	822	2764	3287
Totals	3948	1812	965	1171	6745	5201

Analysis
Premiership

Seasons	P	W	D	L	F	A
10	392	244	93	55	789	360

League Division One

Seasons	P	W	D	L	F	A
67	2740	1162	704	874	4523	3875

League Division Two

Seasons	P	W	D	L	F	A
22	816	406	168	242	1433	966

Synopsis of Season
United romped to their first ever League Championship trophy - finishing nine points clear of Aston Villa and Manchester City. Ernest Mangnall was now able to field the group of players acquired from neighbouring City, who were all under lengthy suspensions. His foresight was now realised as United, playing brilliant football, won 13 of their opening 14 matches, including a remarkable 6-1 win over the defending champions Newcastle on Tyneside. The title was practically sewn up by the New Year, so even though the team lost concentration during the second half of the season, the final winning margin amply demonstrated United's superiority.
Championship team (2-3-5 formation):
H Moger (29 apps); R Holden (26)/G Stacey (18), H Burgess (27); R Duckworth (35), C Roberts (32), A Bell (35); W Meredith (37), J Bannister (36), J Turnbull (26), A Turnbull (30), G Wall (36).
Others: A Downie (10), H Broomfield (9), J Picken (8), H Halse (6), A Menzies (6), W Berry (3), E Thompson (3), E Dalton, A Hulme, J McGillivray, K Whiteside, J Williams & T Wilson (all one each).
Goalscorers:
A Turnbull (25), Wall (19), Meredith (10), J Turnbull (10), Bannister (5), Halse (4), Roberts (2), Bell, Berry, Menzies & Stacey (all on each), own-goals (2)

Season 1910-11 (Manager: Ernest Mangnall)
League Division One

Venue	P	W	D	L	F	A	Pts
Home	19	14	4	1	47	18	32
Away	19	8	4	7	25	22	20
Totals	38	22	8	8	72	40	52

Average home attendance: 27,158
Top home attendance: 60,000 v. Manchester City
Biggest win: 5-0 v. Woolwich Arsenal (home), Preston North End (home)
Heaviest defeat: 2-4 v. Aston Villa (away)

Synopsis of Season
In 1907-08 it was Aston Villa who competed for the title, but this time the contest went to the last Saturday. Villa fans will always maintain that their team lost the Championship rather than United winning it! With two matches to play United travelled to Villa Park for the 'clincher', two points clear but Villa having a game in hand. On the day the Midland club were far superior, winning 4-2 to take over at the top on goal-average. Their game in hand was at Blackburn in mid-week, knowing a win would give them the title. With only minutes to go, the score standing at 0-0, Villa were awarded a penalty. The United contingent watching from the stands, held their breath as Charlie Wallace lined up the spot-kick. Amazingly he missed, goalkeeper Ashcroft saving. But the point seemed to have settled it in Villa's favour nevertheless. On the final Saturday United entertained Sunderland in front of a derisory crowd of around 10,000, indicating the supporters had given up hope! Villa travelled to Liverpool where they only required a draw. Despite conceding an early goal, United won 5-1, then news broke that Villa had been beaten 3-1 at Anfield...so the title came to Old Trafford for the first time!

Championship Team (2-3-5): H Moger (25 apps)/H Edmonds (13); A Donnelly (15), G Stacey (36); R Duckworth (22), C Roberts (33), A Bell (27); W Meredith (35), H Halse (23)/J Picken (14), E West (35), A Turnbull (35), G Wall (26).
Others: A Whalley (15), G Livingstone (10), L Hofton (9), R Holden (8), O Linkson (7), E Connor (7), T Homer (7), J Curry (5), J Sheldon (5), J Hodge (2), A Hooper (2), SP Blott & V Hayes (one each).
Goalscorers:
West (19), Turnbull (18), Halse (9), Homer (6), Meredith (5), Wall (5), Picken (4), Duckworth (2), Connor & Roberts (one each), own-goals (2)

Season 1935-36 (Manager: A Scott Duncan)
League Division Two

Venue	P	W	D	L	F	A	Pts
Home	21	16	3	2	55	16	35
Away	21	6	9	6	30	27	21
Totals	42	22	12	8	85	43	56

Average home attendance: 25,841
Top home attendance: 39,855 v. Burnley
Biggest win: 7-2 v. Port Vale (home)
Heaviest defeat: 1-4 v. Blackpool (away)

Championship Team (2-3-5):
J Hall (36 apps); J Griffiths (41), W Porter (42); J Brown (40), G Vose (41), W McKay (35); W Bryant (21)/J Cape (17), G Mutch (42), T Bamford (27), H Rowley (37), T Manley (31).
Others: R Chester (13), R Gardner (12), R Ferrier (7), T Lang (4), J Breedon (3), L Langford (3), W Owen (2), J Wassell (2), H Whalley (2), B Morton, H Redwood, D Robbie, W Robertson (all one each).
Goalscorers:
Mutch (21), Rowley (19), Bamford (16), Manley (14), Bryant (8), Cape (2), Chester , Gardner, Griffiths, Lang (all one each), own-goal (1)

Details of United's 'winning campaigns'..........
Season 1907-08 (Manager: Ernest Mangnall)
League Division One

Venue	P	W	D	L	F	A	Pts
Home	19	15	1	3	43	19	31
Away	19	8	5	6	38	29	21
Totals	38	23	6	9	81	48	52

Average home attendance: 23,368
Top home attendance: 50,000 v. Newcastle United
Biggest win: 6-1 v. Newcastle United (away)
Heaviest defeat: 4-7 v. Liverpool (away)

Synopsis of Season
United had fallen on hard times since those heady pre-WW1 days when the Championship had been won twice and the FA Cup once. In 1934 United had only escaped relegation to the Third Division with a desperate last match win at Millwall. This season, however, United had shown signs that they were slowly becoming a force again as they finished with a fine unbeaten run of 19 matches from January to the end of the campaign. Charlton Athletic, West Ham United and Sheffield United had all battled it out with United for promotion places. A splendid 2-1 win at West Ham set United up for a grand finale; then after a late 'double' over Bury, only Charlton could deny United the title. On the last Saturday of the season United, holding a slim one point lead, travelled across country to Hull and before a meagre crowd of just 4,540 were held to a 1-1 draw. This left the United supporters on tenterhooks, but luckily Charlton were also held to a draw, and so the Second Division Championship came to Old Trafford for the first time - and with it a return to the top flight.

125

Season 1951-52 (Manager: Matt Busby)
League Division One

Venue	P	W	D	L	F	A	Pts
Home	21	15	3	3	51	21	33
Away	21	8	8	5	44	31	24
Totals	42	23	11	8	95	52	57

Average home attendance: 41,030
Top home attendance: 54,245 v. Manchester City
Biggest win: 6-1 v. Arsenal (home) & Burnley (home)
Heaviest defeat: 2-4 v. Chelsea (away)

Synopsis of Season
Since WW2, Matt Busby had moulded United into one of the best, most attractive sides in the country; in the five post-war seasons United had finished 2, 2, 2, 4, 2, the title just evading them.
Now the pre-war players knew this could be their last chance. Ace marksman Jack Rowley started the season with 14 goals in the first seven matches (including three hat-tricks). As United again faltered towards the season's end , Busby switched young full-back Roger Byrne to the left-wing and his seven goals in the last six matches proved crucial as Liverpool and Burnley were beaten 4-0 and 6-1 in vital Easter encounters. On the final Saturday United led Arsenal by two points. The Gunners visited Old Trafford needing to win 7-0 to pip United for the title. In the event United eased to a comfortable 6-1 victory themselves, Rowley's hat-trick giving him the club scoring record of 30 League goals in a season. After their earlier near misses, no-one could deny United's Championship at last.

Championship Team (2-3-5):
R Allen (33); T McNulty (24), R Byrne (24)/W Redman (18); J Carey (38), A Chilton (42), H Cockburn (38); J Berry (36), SC Pearson (41), J Rowley (40), J Downie (31), E Bond (19).
Others: J Aston (18), D Gibson (17), H McShane (12), J Crompton (9), F Clempson (8), M Jones (3), J Whitefoot (3), B Birch (2), W McGlen (2), JA Walton (2), J Blanchflower & L Cassidy (one each).
Goalscorers: Rowley (30), Pearson (22), Downie (11), Byrne (7), Berry (6), Aston (4), Bond (4), Carey (3), Clempson (2), Cockburn (2), McShane (1), own goals (3).

Season 1955-56 (Manager: Matt Busby)
League Division One

Venue	P	W	D	L	F	A	Pts
Home	21	18	3	0	51	20	39
Away	21	7	7	7	32	31	21
Totals	42	25	10	7	83	51	60

Average home attendance: 38,893
Top home attendance: 62,277 v. Blackpool
Biggest win: 5-1 v. Charlton Athletic (home)
Heaviest defeats: 2-4 v. Everton (away), 0-3 v. Charlton Athletic (away)

Synopsis of Season
The 'Babes' really came of age this season as they romped to the Championship title by 11 points, breaking the magical '60 points' barrier in the process.
Of the side which had won the First Division in 1952 only Roger Byrne and Johnny Berry remained, Busby's exciting young team capturing the public's imagination with Tommy Taylor and Dennis Viollet the scourge of the country's defences, both topping 20 goals.
Yet, with three matches remaining, the title race was still in the balance as Blackpool, the only team capable of reaching United's points tally, visited Old Trafford for the crucial encounter. The Seasiders took an early lead and then held on tenaciously for a long time before late goals from Berry and Taylor settled the issue in United's favour with joy unconfined on the terraces. United remained unbeaten in their last 14 matches (10 wins). They only dropped three points at home (from three draws) and Busby's 'Youth policy' was completely vindicated, the future rosy.

Championship team (2-3-5): R Wood (41); W Foulkes (26)/I Greaves (15), R Byrne (39); E Colman (25)/J Whitefoot (15), M Jones (42), D Edwards (33); J Berry (34), J Blanchflower (18)/J Doherty (16), T Taylor (33), D Viollet (34), D Pegg (35).
Others: C Webster (15), L Whelan (13), F Goodwin (8), A Scanlon (6), G Bent (4), E Lewis (4), W McGuinness (3), J Crompton, J Scott and W Wehiturst (all one each).
Goalscorers: Taylor (25), Viollet (20), Pegg (9), Berry (4), Doherty (4), Webster (4), Whelan (4), Blanchflower (3), Byrne (3), Edwards (3), Jones, Lewis, McGuinness and Scanlon (all one each).

Season 1956-57 (Manager: Matt Busby)
League Division One

Venue	P	W	D	L	F	A	Pts
Home	21	14	4	3	55	25	32
Away	21	14	4	3	48	29	32
Totals	42	28	8	6	103	54	64

Average home attendance: 45,407
Top home attendance: 60,862 v. Bolton Wanderers*
Biggest win: 6-1 v. Newcastle United (home)
Heaviest defeat: 2-5 v. Everton (home)
* First floodlit game at Old Trafford.

Synopsis of Season
United retained their title in majestic style, amassing a club record 64 points, only two less than Arsenal's all-time League record. Remarkably their home and away records were identical with an incredible 14 matches won away. In an eventful season which saw United enter a major European Competition for the first time, the floodlights were finally installed at Old Trafford and at one stage a possible 'treble' was on the cards. United's young side simply got better and better. With Liam 'Billy' Whelan firmly bedded in at inside-right, the front-line was awesome with 100 goals topped for the first time by United, wing-halves Eddie Colman and Duncan Edwards ensuring that they saw plenty of quality ball.
Whelan and Taylor both reached the 30-goal mark (in all matches). Dennis Viollet wasn't too far behind with 25, while the young Bobby Charlton, an exciting natural goalscorer, ensured plenty of competition for places. United had opened the season in classical style, unbeaten in 12 matches (10 wins) to set the early pace. A surprise loss at the hands of Everton (2-5) ended a 31-match sequence of home League games without defeat, but this was a rare blemish in a near-perfect season.

Championship Team (2-3-5):
R Wood (39 apps); W Foulkes (39), R Byrne (36), E Colman (36), M Jones (29), D Edwards (34); J Berry (40), L Whelan (39), T Taylor (32), D Viollet (27), D Pegg (37).

126

Others: R Charlton (14), W McGuinness (13), J Blanchflower (11), G Bent (6), F Goodwin (6), A Scanlon (5), C Webster (5), A Dawson (3), J Doherty (3), I Greaves (3), G Clayton (2), R Cope (2), A Hawksworth (1).
Goalscorers:
Whelan (26), Taylor (22), Viollet (16), Charlton (10), Berry (8), Pegg (6), Edwards (5), Dawson (3), Webster (3), Scanlon (2), Colman (1), own-goal (1).

Season 1964-65 (Manager: Matt Busby)
League Division One

Venue	P	W	D	L	F	A	Pts
Home	21	16	4	1	52	13	36
Away	21	10	5	6	37	26	25
Totals	42	26	9	7	89	39	61

Average home attendance: 45,831

Top home attendance: 56,261 v. Chelsea

Biggest win: 7-0 v. Aston Villa (home)

Heaviest defeat: 1-3 v. West Ham United (away)

United won their first League 'crown' since the Munich air crash (1964-65)

Synopsis of Season
United won their first League 'crown' since the Munich air crash which had cruelly denied the brilliant young team of 1957-58 a chance of making history with a third consecutive title. Now only Foulkes and Charlton remained of that side, but with Denis Law and George Best in the forward-line, prompted by the subtleties of Paddy Crerand, this United team was one of the best ever. After suffering the disappointment of defeat in the semi-final of the FA Cup, United embarked on a title-winning run of seven consecutive wins, including a 5-0 victory at Blackburn to win the Championship from Leeds with a game to spare, both clubs incredibly on 61 points, United having a much better goal-average. Home matches with traditional rivals Liverpool (3-0) and Arsenal (3-1) were thrillingly won, allowing them the luxury of sustaining a defeat at Villa Park only hours after their celebration party had finished! Ironically Leeds would look back at their Cup success over United which perhaps took their eye off the ball in a crucial Championship decider at Elland Road in April which saw United win 1-0 through a John Connelly goal.

Championship Team (2-3-5):
P Dunne (39 apps); S Brennan (42), A Dunne (42); P Crerand (39), W Foulkes (42), N Stiles (41); J Connelly (42), R Charlton (41), D Herd (37), D Law (36), G Best (41).
Others: D Sadler (6), D Gaskell (5), M Setters (5), N Cantwell (2), J Fitzpatrick (2), J Aston jnr & I Moir (one each).
Goalscorers:
Law (28), Herd (20), Connelly (15), Best (10), Charlton (10), Crerand (3), Cantwell & Sadler (one each), own-goal (1).

Season 1966-67 (Manager: Matt Busby, later Sir Matt Busby, KCG, CBE)
League Division One

Venue	P	W	D	L	F	A	Pts
Home	21	17	4	0	51	13	38
Away	21	7	8	6	33	32	22
Totals	42	24	12	6	84	45	60

Average home attendance: 53,895

Top home attendance: 62,727 v. Nottingham Forest

Biggest win: 6-1 v. West Ham United (away), 5-0 v. Sunderland (home)

Heaviest defeat: 1-4 v. Nottingham Forest (away)

Synopsis of Season
The euphoria of England's World Cup triumph at Wembley carried over into the 1966-67 season, a wonderful campaign with five clubs vying for the title. Eventually United's remorseless consistency over the second-half of the season, 20 matches unbeaten (10 wins, 10 draws), up to the decisive game with a sensational 6-1 win at West Ham United which clinched the club's seventh Championship (and Busby's fifth).
At times United played breathtaking football. especially at home where they were unbeaten, dropping just four points. It was especially pleasing to see three locals boys - Nobby Stiles, Bobby Noble and John Aston junior - playing such a big part in the title success which would enable United to go on and lift the coveted European Cup the very next season.
Goalkeeper Alex Stepney had been signed from Chelsea and he would play a huge part in the club's success, not just this season but particularly in the European Cup triumph. United finished four points clear of runners-up Nottingham Forest who thrashed United at The City Ground by 4-1 in October. United drew record crowds to their matches, playing attractive football in the true Busby style.

Championship Team (2-3-5):
A Stepney (35 apps); A Dunne (40), R Noble (29); P Crerand (39), W Foulkes (33), N Stiles (37); G Best (42), D Law (36), R Charlton (42), D Herd (28), J Aston (26+4). D Sadler (35+1 apps) played in three different positions, centre-half, left-half & centre-forward with Charlton moving to inside-left.
Others: S Brennan (16), J Connelly (6), D Gaskell (5), N Cantwell (4), J Ryan (4+1), J Fitzpatrick (3), H Gregg (2), W Anderson (0+1).
Goalscorers:
Law (23), Herd (16), Charlton (12), Best (10), Aston (5), Sadler (5), Foulkes (4), Crerand (3), Stiles (3), Connelly (2), own-goal (1).

Season 1974-75 (Manager: Tommy Docherty)
League Division Two

Venue	P	W	D	L	F	A	Pts
Home	21	17	3	1	45	12	37
Away	21	9	6	6	21	18	24
Totals	42	26	9	7	66	30	61

Average home attendance: 48,388

Top home attendance: 60,585 v. Sunderland

Biggest win: 4-0 v. Blackpool, Cardiff City, Millwall, Oxford United (all at home)

Heaviest defeat: 0-2 Aston Villa, Hull City, Norwich City (all away)

Synopsis of Season

The shock to the system of United suffering the pain of relegation, just six years after being crowned European Champions, fortunately did not last long. Tommy Docherty's infectious enthusiasm produced another vibrant young United team. He had raided the lower Divisions, unearthing gems like Jim Holton, Stuart Pearson, Steve Coppell and Stewart Houston. Alongside home-grown products Brian Greenhoff, Sammy McIlroy and Gerry Daly, the side played some wonderful football, leading the Second Division from first to last, never 'headed'.

At Old Trafford, with attendances booming (higher than any in Division One) the team was practically unbeatable, only Bristol City leaving with both points. The crowd loved Docherty's youngsters, hopeful that the club was once again heading for the top. The 'Match of the Season' saw Sunderland visit Old Trafford in 30 November. The Wearsiders went into a 2-1 lead before the season's biggest crowd (over 60,500) before United fought back to register a famous victory by 3-2.

The title (and with it promotion) was sealed at Southampton in early April, Lou Macari crowning a fine first season as senior 'pro' with the all-important goal in a 1-0 win. During the last two home matches of the season the Stretford End faithful joyfully sang 'United Are Back, United Are Back.' And they were!

Championship Team (4-4-2):
A Stepney (40 apps); A Forsyth (39), J Holton (14)/S James (13)/A Sidebottom (12), M Buchan (41), S Houston (40); W Morgan (32+2), B Greenhoff (39+2), L Macari (36+2), G Daly (36+1); SJ Pearson (30+1), S McIlroy (41+1).
Others: J McCalliog (20), S Coppell (9+1), M Martin (7+1), A Young (7+8), A Albiston (2), T Baldwin (2), P Roche (2), R Davies (0+8), S McGarvey (0+2), G Graham (0+1), J Nicholl (0+1).
Goalscorers:
Pearson (17), Daly (11), Macari (11), McIlroy (7), Houston (6), Greenhoff (4), McCalliog (3), Morgan (3), Coppell (1), Forsyth (1), own-goals (2).

Season 1992-93 (Manager: Alex Ferguson)

FA Premier League

Venue	P	W	D	L	F	A	Pts
Home	21	14	5	2	39	14	47
Away	21	10	7	4	28	17	37
Totals	42	24	12	6	67	31	84

Average home attendance: 35,132 (due to ground redevelopment)

Top home attendance: 40,447 v. Blackburn Rovers

Biggest win: 5-0 v. Coventry City (home)

Heaviest defeat: 0-3 v. Everton (home)

Synopsis of Season

It had been a long wait - 26 years since the last League Championship had been won. There had been many false dawns along the way, the previous season (1991-92) the team had fatally 'choked' with the winning post in sight. Now with the advent of the brand new Premier League all-seater stadia, live Sky TV, United had done it at last, none more pleased than the Grand Old Man, Sir Matt Busby himself.

Manager Alex Ferguson's inspired signing of French 'enfant terrible' Eric Cantona was the catalyst for success as his inspirational play rubbed off on lesser mortals. Steve Bruce and Gary Pallister were rock-like in the centre of the defence with Peter Schmeichel nigh on unbeatable in between the posts. The goals did not come freely, but an unbeaten run of 10 matches in mid-season (eight wins) gave the team the belief that this was their year. Aston Villa pushed United all the way after early pacesetters Norwich City faded. In fact, a sensational 3-1 victory at Carrow Road ended the Canaries' hopes, sparking United into a seven-match string of wins to take the 'crown' in style. When the great day arrived it was strangely anti-climatic as Villa surprisingly lost at home to Oldham, gifting United the trophy. The wait had been worth it.

Championship Team (4-4-2):
P Schmeichel (42 apps); P Parker (31), S Bruce (42), G Pallister (42), D Irwin (40); R Giggs (40+1), P Ince (41), B McClair (41+1), L Sharpe (27); M Hughes (41), E Cantona (21+1).
Others: D Ferguson (15), A Kanchelskis (14+13), C Blackmore (12+2), M Phelan (5+6), B Robson (5+9), D Dublin (3+4), D Wallace (0+2), N Butt (0+1), N Webb (0+1).
Goalscorers:
Hughes (15), Cantona (9), Giggs (9), McClair (9), Ince (6), Bruce (5), Irwin (5), Kanchelskis (3), Dublin, Parker, Pallister, Robson & Sharpe (all one each), own-goal (1).

Season 1993-94 (Manager: Alex Ferguson)

FA Premier League

Venue	P	W	D	L	F	A	Pts
Home	21	14	6	1	39	13	48
Away	21	13	5	3	41	25	44
Totals	42	27	11	4	80	38	92

Average home attendance: 44,244

Top home attendance: 44,751 v. Liverpool

Biggest win: 5-0 v. Sheffield Wednesday (home)

Heaviest defeat: 0-2 v. Blackburn Rovers (away)

Synopsis of Season

United retained their Premier League crown in quite brilliant style after one of the best seasons in the club's illustrious history as all three domestic trophies were chased.

After 29 League matches, only one had been lost (at Chelsea) eight games being won in succession at one stage (September-November). Cantona was again the focal point, not only with crucial goals but in releasing Andrei Kanchelskis's blistering pace to deadly effect. But Blackburn could not be shaken off as they steadily overhauled United. When Chelsea completed a League 'double' at Old Trafford, the nerves were jangling, especially when Blackburn won at home with Cantona suspended. The title was up for grabs but United pulled themselves together as Rovers too began to feel the strain.

Four successive wins at the season's end including a hard-earned 2-0 victory at Leeds saw United closing in but after going a goal down at Ipswich and having Schmeichel carried off, the alarm bells began to ring - then up stepped Messrs Cantona and Giggs to score at a vital time to bring reward and ensure United's ninth 'top flight' title. This allowed United to enjoy a 'carnival day' in the final match of the campaign, the Championship won and the trophy duly presented.

Shortly after the League programme had ended, United went to Wembley, beat Chelsea in the FA Cup Final, and so clinched their first 'double'.

Championship Team (4-4-2):
P Schmeichel (40 apps); P Parker (39+1), S Bruce (41), G Pallister (41), D Irwin (42); A Kanchelskis (28+3), P Ince (39), R Keane (34+3), R Giggs (32+6)/L Sharpe (26+4); M Hughes (36), E Cantona (34).

Others: B McClair (12+14), B Robson (10+5), G Walsh (2+1), D Dublin (1+4), D Ferguson (1+2), C McKee (1), L Martin (1), G Neville (1), M Phelan (1+1), N Butt (0+1), B Thornley (0+1).
Goalscorers:
Cantona (18), Giggs (13), Hughes (11), Sharpe (9), Ince (8), Kanchelskis (6), Keane (5), Bruce (3), Irwin (2), Dublin, McClair, Pallister & Robson (all one each), own-goal (1).

Season 1995-96 (Manager: Alex Ferguson)
FA Premier League

Venue	P	W	D	L	F	A	Pts
Home	19	15	4	0	36	9	49
Away	19	10	3	6	37	26	33
Totals	38	25	7	6	73	35	82

Average home attendance: 41,700 (North Stand redeveloped for most of season)
Top home attendance: 53,926 v. Nottingham Forest
Biggest win: 6-0 v. Bolton Wanderers (away)
Heaviest defeat: 1-4 v. Tottenham Hotspur (away)

Synopsis of Season
This was one of the most incredible seasons in League history!
Newcastle, after heavy spending by manager Kevin Keegan, were setting the place on fire with some fantastic attacking football, 12 points clear going into the New Year, the Championship seemingly won with a flourish.
On the other hand manager Alex Ferguson had dismantled United's team with Kanchelskis, Ince and Hughes all sold and Cantona still suspended. Their replacements were another set of bright United 'kids', namely David Beckham, Paul Scholes, Nicky Butt and the Neville brothers, Gary and Philip.
Slowly Newcastle's enormous lead was whittled away as Cantona returned to inspire his fledglings to great deeds. Newcastle were beaten at Old Trafford over Christmas, but the crunch match was at St James' Park in early March. United HAD to win. The Magpies stormed the United goal throughout a torrid first-half but somehow Schmeichel could not and would not be beaten!
Then, soon after the interval, Cantona volleyed home. A deadly hush came over the ground. United held firm, the Tynesiders distraught!
Fergie's men were now just four points in arrears. They lost only one of their last nine matches while Newcastle lost three and drew two of their remaining ten. United proudly marched on to collect their second 'double'.
Cantona's goals proved crucial in the closing weeks, a single effort from the French ace earning three points on no less than six occasions.

Championship Team (4-4-2):
P Schmeichel (36 apps); G Neville (30+1), S Bruce (30), G Pallister (21), D Irwin (31)/P Neville (21+3); D Beckham (26+7), R Keane (29), N Butt (31+1), R Giggs (30+3); A Cole (32+2), E Cantona (30) & L Sharpe (21+10) in three different positions.
Others: P Scholes (16+10), B McClair (12+10), D May (11+5), P Parker (5+1), K Pilkington (2+1), W Prunier (2), T Cooke (1+3), S Davies (1+5), J O'Kane (0+1), B Thornley (0+1).
Goalscorers:
Cantona (14), Cole (11), Giggs (11), Scholes (10), Beckham (7), Keane (6), Sharpe (4), McClair (3), Butt (2), Bruce, Irwin, May & Pallister (all one each), own-goal (1).

Season 1996-97 (Manager: Alex Ferguson)
FA Premier League

Venue	P	W	D	L	F	A	Pts
Home	19	12	5	2	38	17	41
Away	19	9	7	3	38	27	34
Totals	38	21	12	5	76	44	75

Average home attendance: 55,080
Top home attendance: 55,314 v. Wimbledon
Biggest win: 5-0 v. Sunderland (home)
Heaviest defeat: 3-6 v. Southampton (away), also 0-5 v. Newcastle (away)

Synopsis of Season
After the thrills of Euro '96, the Premiership was awash with European stars, United having added their share, Karel Poborsky, Jordi Cruyff, Ronny Johnsen & Ole Gunnar Solskjaer joining the club.
United announced their intentions early on with a comprehensive 3-0 win away to Wimbledon, David Beckham's stunning 60-yard chip becoming the talk of football!
Just as it seemed United were easing their way to a fourth Premiership title, in October/November they stuttered alarmingly, losing three successive League matches, at Newcastle (by 5-0), at Southampton (6-3) and to Chelsea (2-1). Two single goal defeats in Europe suggested United were in crisis, but Alex Ferguson did not panic as the team went on a 16-match unbeaten run, recording 11 wins - one of them a crucial 2-1 victory at Arsenal.
United had found a new hero in Ole Gunnar Solskjaer who was leading marksman with 18 goals.
Liverpool had mounted a serious challenge, so when United visited Anfield with a six point lead with a game played more than Liverpool it took on the importance of a title decider. On the day centre-back Gary Pallister proved the key man with two stunning headed goals in the first half to virtually confirm a vital win and settle the Championship.
The final margin of victory was seven points with Newcastle, Arsenal and Liverpool all level on 68.

Championship Team (4-4-2/occasionally 4-3-3):
P Schmeichel (36); G Neville (30+1), R Johnsen (26+5)/D May (28+1), G Pallister (27), D Irwin (29+2); D Beckham (33+3), R Keane (21)/P Scholes (16+8), N Butt (24+2), R Giggs (25+1); O G Solskjaer (25+8), E Cantona (36).
Others: P Neville (15+3), K Poborsky (15+7), J Cruyff (11+5), A Cole (10+10), B McClair (4+15), M Clegg (3+1), R van der Gouw (2), J O'Kane (1), B Thornley (1+1), C Casper (0+2).
Goalscorers:
Solskjaer (18), Cantona (11), Beckham (8), Cole (7), Butt (5), Cruyff (3), Giggs (3), May (3), Pallister (3), Poborsky (3), Scholes (3), Keane (2), Irwin (1), G Neville (1), own-goals (5).

Season 1998-99
Ground: Old Trafford
Manager: Sir Alex Ferguson
FA Premier League

Venue	P	W	D	L	F	A	Pts
Home	19	14	4	1	45	18	46
Away	19	8	9	2	35	19	33
Totals	38	22	13	3	80	37	79

Average home attendance: 55,188
Top home attendance: 55,316 v. Southampton
Biggest win: 8-1 v. Nottingham Forest (away)
Heaviest defeat: 0-3 v. Arsenal (away)

Synopsis of season

This would be the greatest season in United's illustrious history - the Premiership title regained, the FA Cup and European Champions Cup all thrillingly won to complete an unprecedented 'treble'.

After the previous season's rather flat finish with Arsenal seemingly set to take over, manager Ferguson spent lavishly on striker Dwight Yorke, giant Dutch defender Jaap Stam and left-winger Jesper Blomqvist as cover for Giggs.

When Arsenal beat United 3-0 at Highbury in early September things looked ominous, but United battled on and kept in touch. Meanwhile in Europe, Yorke and Cole were terrifying defences with their telepathic understanding. A home defeat by Middlesbrough at Christmas hardly suggested what was to come but that would be their last set-back - 20 League matches, eight FA Cup games and five European fixtures would be successfully surmounted as United stormed on to take all three trophies in the space of eleven days. Playing the equivalent of three 'Cup Finals', they first accounted for Tottenham 2-1 on the Premiership's last Sunday to lift the title and so deny Arsenal's hopes of remaining champions; then they beat Newcastle 2-0 in the FA Cup Final at Wembley (Teddy Sheringham the hero) and finally overcame Bayern Munich 2-1 in Barcelona's Nou Camp Stadium to win the coveted European Cup after Sheringham and Solskjaer had pounced with two late goals to see off the Germans in a quite memorable encounter. It was certainly 'Glory, Glory Man United!'

Championship Team (mainly 4-4-2):
P Schmeichel (34); G Neville (34), R Johnsen (19+3), J Stam (30), D Irwin (26+3), P Neville (19+9);
D Beckham (33+1), R Keane (33+2), P Scholes (24+7)/N Butt (22+9), R Giggs (20+4)/J Blomqvist (20+5); A Cole (26+6), D Yorke (32).
Other Players: W Brown (11+3), H Berg (10+6), O G Solskjaer (9+10), T Sheringham (7+10), D May (4+2), R van der Gouw (4+1), J Curtis (1+3), J Cruyff (0+5), J Greening (0+3).
Goalscorers:
Yorke (18), Cole (17), Solskjaer (12), Beckham (6), Scholes (6), Giggs (3), Johnsen (3), Butt (2), Cruyff (2), Irwin (2), Keane (2), Sheringham (2), Blomqvist, G Neville & Stam (all one each), own goals (2).

Season 1999-2000 (Manager: Sir Alex Ferguson)

FA Premier League

Venue	P	W	D	L	F	A	Pts
Home	19	15	4	0	59	16	49
Away	19	13	3	3	38	29	42
Totals	38	28	7	3	97	45	91

Average home attendance: 58,017 (ground extensions partially complete)

Top home attendance: 61,629 v. Tottenham Hotspur

Biggest win: 7-1 v. West Ham United (home)

Heaviest defeat: 0-5 v. Chelsea (away)

Synopsis of Season

United retained the Premiership 'crown' in a most convincing manner with a record points tally for a 38-match programme. The winning margin over second-placed Arsenal was an incredible and quite unbelievable 18 points!

United began 1999-2000 just as they had ended the previous season, remaining unbeaten until October, thus taking their overall unbeaten League record (from December 1998) to 29 matches (45 in all competitions). Chelsea's astonishing 5-0 win at Stamford Bridge brought United down to earth as did a 3-1 defeat at White Hart Lane against Spurs two weeks later. However, only one further defeat would accrue all season and a blistering late run of 11 consecutive victories left everyone trailing, the title being sewn up at The Dell against Southampton with five games still to play! Dwight Yorke and Andy Cole, with almost 40 League goals between them, continued their remarkable partnership up front while Mark Bosnich ensured that Schmeichel was not missed too much in goal. As usual controversy surrounded United as FIFA invited them to take part in the inaugural Club World Championship in 'hot' Brazil in January which meant spending almost a month away in mid-season.

Surprisingly the leading clubs made little headway during United's enforced absence and when they returned to action suitably suntanned and relaxed, Ferguson's men soon got back on top of their game and went on the way to the Championship in some style.

Championship Team (4-4-2):
M Bosnich (23 apps); G Neville (22)/P Neville (25+4), M Silvestre (30+1)/H Berg (16+6), J Stam (33), D Irwin (25); D Beckham (30+1), R Keane (28+1), P Scholes (27+4)/N Butt (21+11), R Giggs (30); A Cole (23+5)/O G Solskjaer (15+13), D Yorke (29+3)/T Sheringham (15+12).
Other Players:
R van der Gouw (11+3), Q Fortune (4+2), M Taibi (4), D Higginbotham (2+1), R Johnsen (2+1), J Cruyff (1+2), J Greening (1+3), M Wilson (1+2), R Wallwork (0+5), M Clegg (0+2), N Culkin (0+1), J Curtis (0+1), D May (0+1).
Goalscorers:
Yorke (20), Cole (19), Solskjaer (12), Scholes (9), Beckham (6), Giggs (6), Keane (5), Sheringham (5), Butt (3), Cruyff (3), Irwin (3), Fortune (2), Berg (1), own-goals (3).

Season 2000-01 (Manager: Sir Alex Ferguson)

FA Premier League

Venue	P	W	D	L	F	A	Pts
Home	19	15	2	2	49	12	47
Away	19	9	6	4	30	19	33
Totals	38	24	8	6	79	31	80

Average home attendance: 67,544 (League record); ground extensions completed)

Top home attendance: 67,637 v. Coventry City

Biggest win: 6-0 v. Bradford City (home)

Heaviest defeat: 1-3 v. Tottenham Hotspur (away)

Synopsis of Season

United continued their consistent form to become the fourth English League side to win three successive Championships. Once again the margin of victory was comfortable - this time 10 points - although it should have been distinctly more as United carelessly lost their last three matches after the title was already safely under lock and key.

Defeats (both 1-0) at Arsenal in October and v. Liverpool at Old Trafford in December were the only 'blips' to a near perfect first-half performance as Teddy Sheringham played superbly and subsequently was rewarded with the two major 'Footballer of the Year' awards.

Wins of 6-0 & 5-0 over Bradford City and Southampton respectively hardly raised an eyebrow, but when in February Arsenal were thrashed 6-1 at Old Trafford (Dwight Yorke scoring a hat-trick) everyone knew the game was up and United would be declared worthy champions again. Unfortunately the ease of United's last two wins had an adverse effect on their European exploits. This season they went down to arch rivals Bayern Munich, losing both legs of a disappointing quarter-final clash.

Frenchman Fabien Barthez had won many friends with his occasionally eccentric goalkeeping and exceptional distribution, not to mention ball-juggling skills in his own area.

Championship Team (4-4-2):
F Barthez (30 apps); G Neville (32), W Brown (25+3), M Silvestre (25+5)/J Stam (15), P Neville (24+5)/D Irwin (20+1); D Beckham (29+2), R Keane (28), P Scholes (28+4))/N Butt (24+4), R Giggs (24+7); T Sheringham (23+6)/D Yorke (15+7), O G Solskjaer (19+12)/A Cole (15+4).
Other Players: R Johnsen (11), L Chadwick (6+10), Q Fortune (6+1), R van der Gouw (5+5), R Wallwork (4+8), J Greening (3+4), M Stewart (3), A Goram (2), D May (1+1), P Rachubka (1), H Berg (0+1), B Djordjic (0+1), D Healy (0+1).
Goalscorers:
Sheringham (15), Solskjaer (10), Beckham (9), Cole (9), Yorke (9), Scholes (6), Giggs (5), Butt (3), Chadwick (2), Fortune (2), Keane (2), Johnsen, G Neville, P Neville & Silvestre (all one each), own-goals (3).

Football League Fact File
Results from Newton Heath's first League season: 1892-93
Division One (position: 16th)

Opponents	H	A
Accrington	3-3	2-2
Aston Villa	2-0	0-2
Blackburn Rovers	4-4	3-4
Bolton Wanderers	1-0	1-4
Burnley	1-1	1-4
Derby County	7-1	1-5
Everton	3-4	0-6
Nottingham Forest	1-3	1-1
Notts County	1-3	0-4
Preston North End	2-1	1-2
Sheffield Wed	1-5	0-1
Stoke	1-0	1-7
Sunderland	0-5	0-6
West Brom Albion	2-4	0-0
Wolverhampton W	10-1	0-2

Summary:

Venue	P	W	D	L	F	A	Pts
Home	15	6	3	6	39	35	15
Away	15	0	3	12	11	50	3
Totals	30	6	6	18	50	85	18

Newton Heath pictured in 1893 minus their goalkeeper Davies.

Results from the first season in the Premiership
Season 1992-93 (position: champions)

Opponents	H	A
Arsenal	0-0	1-0
Aston Villa	1-1	0-1
Blackburn Rovers	3-1	0-0
Chelsea	3-0	1-1
Coventry City	5-0	1-0
Crystal Palace	1-0	2-0
Everton	0-3	2-0
Ipswich Town	1-1	1-2
Leeds United	2-0	0-0
Liverpool	2-2	2-1
Manchester City	2-1	1-1
Middlesbrough	3-0	1-1
Norwich City	1-0	3-1
Nottingham Forest	2-0	2-0
Oldham Athletic	3-0	0-1
Queen's Park Rgs	0-0	3-1
Sheffield United	2-1	1-2
Sheffield Wed.	2-1	3-3
Southampton	2-1	1-0
Tottenham Hotspur	4-1	1-1
Wimbledon	0-1	2-1

Summary of 1992-93 season's results:

Venue	P	W	D	L	F	A	Pts
Home	21	14	5	2	39	14	47
Away	21	10	7	4	28	17	37
Totals	42	24	12	6	67	31	84

Winning Sequences

United completed a run of 14 straight League wins in Division Two between mid-October 1904 and early January 1905.

The Reds won 18 successive home League matches in Division Two between 15 October 1904 and 23 September 1905.

Ten League wins on the trot were claimed over a period of eight weeks from September to November 1907 and this sequence was repeated (10 straight wins) at the start of the 1985-86 season (up to 28 September). This sequence contained five home wins and five away. In fact, the Reds were unbeaten in their opening 15 First Division fixtures, finally losing 1-0 away to Sheffield Wednesday on 9 November

United finished the 1980-81 season with a run of seven successive League victories (four of them at home). And at the end of the 1999-2000 campaign they recorded 11 straight Premiership wins on the bounce (five at home, six away) before adding a further victory to that tally at the start of the next season to make a combined run of 12 successive wins.

Between April and August 1993 United registered seven away wins on the trot in the Premiership.

Undefeated Sequences

United went 45 competitive games without defeat between 26 December 1998 and 29 September 1999. This superb sequence of results came to an end when they lost 5-0 to Chelsea at Stamford Bridge on 3 October 1999. The sequence of unbeaten matches comprised 29 in the Premiership, eight in the FA Cup and eight in the European Champions League (five in 1998-99, three in 1999-2000). In between times United did lose in the FA Charity Shield (to Arsenal) and European Super Cup, but these were one-off matches and do not count as 'competitive' in this category.

United remained unbeaten in all their 15 home Second Division League games in season 1894-95, recording nine wins and six draws. United also had an unbeaten home record in seasons 1896-97 (fifteen games), 1955-56 (21), 1966-67 (21), 1982-83 (21), 1995-96 (19) & 1999-2000 (19).

That 1894-95 sequence was extended to 26 games unbeaten when they played their first 11 home games without defeat the following season.

131

The Reds remained unbeaten in their opening 15 League games at the start of the 1985-86 season. The run came to an end when Sheffield Wednesday won 1-0 at Hillsborough on 9 November.

United were undefeated in 37 home League games between 27 April 1966 and 20 January 1968. Chelsea ended that run with a 3-1 victory on 2 March 1968.

United's undefeated sequence of League games between early February and mid-October 1956 reached 26 matches. They remained unbeaten away from home in 17 successive League matches between 5 December 1998 and 11 September 1999.

Winless Sequences

United went 26 away League games without a win between mid-February 1930 and early April 1931.

United failed to win any of 16 First Division matches played between 19 April and 25 October 1930.

Twice since WW2 United have had two sequences of 11 League games without a win: (a) from mid-December 1971 to early March 1972 and (b) from late November 1989 to early February 1990.

The first sequence (a) however, included three FA Cup wins; the second (b) two FA cup wins on the way to lifting the trophy at Wembley.

Sequences of Defeats

United lost 41 of their first 61 League games (commencing September 1892 to September 1894).

The Reds were defeated in 14 of their 15 away games during the 1893-94 League season and between 3 December 1892 and 8 September 1894 they lost 25 away games out of a possible 26.

United lost their opening 12 League games at the start of the 1930-31 campaign. They eventually won their first point after a 1-1 draw with Birmingham in October. This is a record for a top-flight team.

United lost 14 successive League matches during 1930 - commencing on 26 April when they were beaten 3-1 at Leeds and ending on 25 October when they went down 4-1 at Portsmouth.

United suffered six home League defeats on the trot at Old Trafford between the 3 May and 18 October 1930. They ended the run with a 2-0 win over Birmingham on 1 November.

United's worst away record has been 17 successive League defeats covering a period of 10 months between 26 April 1930 and 21 February 1931. This spell ended when they battled to earn a 0-0 draw at Birmingham on 7 March.

* For sequences of wins, draws and defeats - see under separate sections.

Football League Pot Pourri

Taking in all the Football League Divisions 1 & 2 and Premiership results as a complete package, United are now lying in second place (behind Liverpool) in terms of achieving most 'League' points. United's tally is 5,037 against Liverpool's 5,071. Arsenal with 4,851 points, Wolverhampton Wanderers 4,702, Aston Villa 4,680, Preston North End 4,669, Sunderland 4,644, Everton 4,633, Burnley 4,605 and West Bromwich Albion 4,557, make up the rest of the 'top ten' points winners in League football.

United are also lying second to Liverpool in the total number of wins in Football League/Premiership matches: 1,812 to 1,839.

Only Nationwide League Division One side Wolverhampton Wanderers, with 6,779 goals, have scored more than United who have so far netted 6,745.

United have met 79 different clubs in competitive League/Premiership football (including 13 no longer in the Football League).

United's first Football League game against Blackburn Rovers (away) took place on 3 September 1892 (Division One). They lost 4-3 in front of 8,000 spectators. Bob Donaldson had the honour of scoring the club's first League goal.

United ran up their first League win almost six weeks later on 15 September when they emphatically crushed Wolverhampton Wanderers 10-1, Donaldson & Willie Stewart both scoring hat-tricks in front of 4,000 fans. This victory still remains as United's best in both Football League and Premiership football.

United claimed runners-up spot in the old First Division in three successive seasons from 1946-47; finished fourth in 1949-50 and second again in 1950-51 before finally winning the title in 1951-52.

Promoted from Division Two as runners-up to Bristol City at the end of the 1905-06 campaign, United missed the Championship by four points despite scoring more goals: 90 to City's 83.

For their home First Division game against Burnley on 22 April 1957, United made NINE changes from the side that had played against Sunderland 48 hours earlier. They won both games 4-0 and 2-0 respectively! It should be appreciated that United would play Real Madrid in a European Cup semi-final just two days after the Burnley fixture.

United's first League game after the Munich tragedy, was at home against Nottingham Forest on 22 February 1958. A crowd of 66,124 witnessed the 1-1 draw. Two players who were on board that plane at Munich airport - Bill Foulkes and Harry Gregg - appeared in that game, having both starred in United's last European game against Red Star (Belgrade) and their first encounter after the crash (against Sheffield Wednesday in the FA Cup).

United started and finished their 1984-85 League programme with games against the same club - Watford.

On New Year's Eve 1892 United beat Derby 7-1 at home...a week later they lost 7-1 at Stoke.

In season 1897-98 United beat Arsenal 5-1 at home, but lost by the same score in London. That happened again in 1928-29 when United defeated Newcastle 5-0 at Old Trafford, but lost 5-0 at St James' Park and in December 1931, after beating Wolves 3-2 at home on Christmas Day, United lost 7-2 at Molineux 24 hours later.

In 1960-61 both the United v. Everton First Division games ended in 4-0 wins for the 'home' side.

On Boxing Day 1963 (when the goals flowed thick and fast all over the country) United crashed to a 6-1 defeat at

Burnley, but 48 hours later they won the return game at Old Trafford 5-1.

It was United 5 Spurs 1 and then Spurs 5 United 1 in the two League encounters in 1965-66.

Still To Play

Of the current clubs outside the Premiership, United have still to play the following at League level: AFC Bournemouth, Cambridge United, Carlisle United, Cheltenham Town, Colchester United, Darlington, Exeter City, Gillingham, Halifax Town. Hartlepool United, Kidderminster Harriers, Macclesfield Town, Mansfield Town, Peterborough United, Reading, Rochdale, Rushden & Diamonds, Scunthorpe United, Shrewsbury Town, Southend United, Torquay United, Tranmere Rovers, Wigan Athletic, Wrexham & Wycombe Wanderers.

Premiership Pot Pourri

United have never finished out of the top three in the Premiership. They have been declared champions a record seven times - in 1992-93, 1993-94, 1995-96, 1996-97, 1998-99, 1999-2000 & 2000-01 - and were runners-up in 1994-95 & 1997-98.

After the opening two League games at the start of the 1992-93 season, United were bottom of the table and the Daily Mirror sports-editor put out this headline in the national newspaper: 'Fergie's Bottom.'

When United won the Premiership in 1993, Aston Villa finished runners-up and Norwich City came third. These three teams finished in precisely the same positions in Division Two in 1974-75.

United's final points tally of 92 in 1993-94 is the highest for any season of top-flight English League football; their tally of 91 in 1999-2000 is the highest for a 38-match programme.

United finished runners-up to Blackburn Rovers in the Premiership in 1994-95, but if the 2 points-for-a-win rule had still been in force, then the outcome would have been different. United would have been declared champions on goal-difference after both teams had amassed 64 points.

FOOTBALL LEAGUE CUP

United entered this competition at the outset and this is their full record in the League Cup (1960-2002):

Venue	P	W	D	L	F	A
Home	66	47	10	9	137	55
Away	66	25	15	26	91	93
Neutral	4	1	0	3	3	6
Summary	136	73	25	38	231	154

133

Football League Cup Fact File

Manchester United entered the competition at the outset, their first opponents on 19 October 1960 being Exeter City at St James' Park. The game ended in a 1-1 draw and the replay, a week, later resulted in a 4-1 win for United.

Alex Dawson had the pleasure of scoring United's first League Cup goal at Exeter while Albert Quixall struck home United's first penalty in the return leg against the Grecians.

United's first defeat in the League Cup was suffered away at Bradford City on 2 November 1960, losing 2-1 in front of just 4,670 fans. Harold Bratt made his only first team appearance for United in this game at Valley Parade.

United did not enter the competition again until five years later when they were hammered 5-1 at Blackpool in a second round tie in September 1966, United's heaviest defeat in the tournament so far.

United were defeated 4-3 on aggregate by rivals Manchester City in the two-legged semi-final in 1969-70. A bumper crowd of 55,799 saw City win 2-1 at Maine Road and there were 63,418 present at Old Trafford to witness a 2-2 draw.

Twelve months later and United once more lost in the semi-final - this time to Third Division Aston Villa. United were held 1-1 at Old Trafford in front of 48,889 fans but were then defeated 2-1 in the return leg at Villa Park when the turnout was 58,667.

United met Stoke City three times in the 4th round of the League Cup in 1971-72. The Potters eventually made progress and they went on to beat Chelsea in the Final.

In season 1972-73, United were humiliated by another Third Division side, Bristol Rovers, who won 2-1 at Old Trafford in a 3rd round replay after a 1-1 draw at Eastville.

Arthur Albiston made his United debut in a 3rd round League Cup-tie against Manchester City (home) in October 1974, before 55,159 spectators.

United succumbed to their third semi-final defeat in 1974-75, this time losing out to Norwich City. The Canaries, managed by Ron Saunders, forced a 2-2 draw in front of 58,010 fans at Old Trafford before winning the return leg 1-0 at Carrow Road when the attendance was 31,621.

Gordon Hill netted a hat-trick in front of more than 52,000 fans when United slammed Newcastle United 7-2 at home in a 4th round tie in October 1976...this is United's biggest League Cup win to date, followed by their 6-2 triumph away at Arsenal in November 1990. This emphatic 4th round win was the Gunners' worst-ever defeat at Highbury (in League or Cup competition) since they moved there in 1913. The Reds led 3-0 at half-time with Lee Sharpe netting a hat-trick.

For each of their two League Cup clashes with Port Vale (home first and away second) played in September and October 1994, United made NINE changes from the side that had appeared in the previous League game. The Reds still won both matches against the Valiants.

United's heaviest home defeat in the League Cup is 3-0, suffered on three occasions, against Everton in December 1976, Tottenham Hotspur in October 1989 and York City in September 1995.

They lost 4-0 at Arsenal in season 2001-02.

United reached their first League Cup Final (now sponsored as the Milk Cup) in season 1982-83. En-route they dismissed AFC Bournemouth 4-2 on aggregate, Bradford City 4-1 after a replay, Southampton 2-0, Nottingham Forest 4-0 and Arsenal 6-3 on aggregate in the two-legged semi-final. At Wembley they lost 2-1 after extra-time to Liverpool in front of 98,664 spectators. Norman Whiteside scored United's goal. Paul McGrath made his United debut in the 3rd round clash at Bradford City and Peter Beardsley played his only game in a United shirt in the home clash with Bournemouth on 6 October (he was substituted by Whiteside).

Mark Hughes made his United debut as a substitute for Whiteside in the League Cup encounter with Port Vale in October 1983. Hughes scored his first League Cup hat-trick for United in a comprehensive 4-0 second round 1st leg victory over Burnley in September 1984. The Reds won the second leg 3-0 to clinch a comfortable 7-0 aggregate score (their biggest combined score in the competition).

United knocked two London clubs out of the League Cup in 1985-86 - Crystal Palace and West Ham.

After losing 4-1 to Southampton in a Littlewoods-sponsored League Cup 3rd round replay in November 1986, United dismissed their manager, Ron Atkinson.

When Halifax Town met United in a second round League Cup-tie in 1990-91 they were bottom of the Fourth Division without a single League goal to their name. Nevertheless, they scored in both legs against United before going out 5-2 on aggregate.

Bryan Robson has appeared in most League Cup games for the Reds - total 51. And striker Brian McClair is the leading scorer in League Cup football with 21 goals.

Eliminated By Lower Divisional Teams
United have been beaten in the League Cup on eight occasions by a team from a lower Division:

1960-61	Bradford City (Div 3) (a)	1-2	
1970-71	Aston Villa (Div 3) (a)	1-2	(2-3 on agg)
1972-73	Bristol Rovers (Div 3) (h)	1-2	
1973-74	Middlesbrough (Div 2) (h)	0-1	
1974-75	Norwich City (Div 2) s/f (a)	0-1	(2-3 on agg)
1978-79	Watford (Div 3) (h)	1-2	
1983-84	Oxford United (Div 3) (a)	1-2	
1990-91	Sheffield Wed (Div 2) (Final)	0-1	
1995-96	York City (Div 3) (h)	0-3	(3-4 on agg)

League Cup Final Victory
1992   United 1 Nottingham Forest 0   Wembley Stadium

Brian McClair's 15th minute goal was enough to bring United their only League Cup Final triumph...

A crowd of 76,810 saw Mike Phelan play a leading role in a rather disappointing contest. Paul Ince was unlucky on a couple of occasions late on as a desperate and tired Forest side defended in depth hoping for a breakaway equaliser. Both teams were without their inspirational captains, Bryan Robson and Stuart Pearce, which may have contributed to a poor quality Final. Forest included in their line-up two future United stars - Teddy Sheringham and Roy Keane.

Team: Schmeichel; Parker, Irwin; Bruce, Phelan, Pallister; Kanchelskis (sub Sharpe), Ince, McClair, Hughes, Giggs. Sub (not used): Webb.

League Cup Final defeats
1983   Liverpool 2 United 1 (aet)   Wembley Stadium

Ahead at half-time thanks to Norman Whiteside's 12th minute goal, United had the better of the exchanges in a tightly contested match and looked set for their first League Cup Final triumph until a defensive lapse let in left-back Alan Kennedy for a 75th minute equaliser. Even after that United may have stolen the glory but Bruce Grobbelaar, who led a charmed life in the Liverpool goal, kept his side in the game with two outstanding late saves. Eight minutes into extra time - after a few more near misses at both ends - the Merseysiders grabbed the winning goal through Ronnie Whelan, whose right-footed drive gave 'keeper Gary Bailey no chance. The attendance was 99,304.

Team: Bailey; Duxbury, Albiston; Moses, Moran (Macari), McQueen; Wilkins, Muhren, Stapleton, Whiteside, Coppell.

1991   United 0 Sheffield Wednesday 1   Wembley Stadium

With this victory in front of 77,612 spectators, Sheffield Wednesday became the first Second Division side to win the League (Rumbelows) Cup for 16 years - and they deserved it! In a rather dull encounter overall the Owls - managed of course of ex-United boss Ron Atkinson - generally had the better of the midfield exchanges and that is from where the winning goal came - scored in emphatic style by John Sheridan on 37 minutes. His thumping right foot half-volley sped past Les Sealey like a rocket - a strike good enough to win any game!

Despite constant United pressure during the second-half - some of it rather hectic - the Owls defence held firm with 'keeper Chris Turner, a former United player, producing some excellent saves.

Brian McClair and Lee Sharpe should have done better with the chances that came their way but on the day it was true Yorkshire grit that won the Battle of the Roses. Steve Bruce was outstanding at the heart of the United defence.

Team: Sealey; Irwin, Blackmore; Bruce, Webb (Phelan), Pallister; Robson, Ince, McClair, Hughes, Sharpe. Sub not used: Duxbury.

1994   Aston Villa 3 United 1   Wembley Stadium

Former United boss Ron Atkinson was manager of the Villa and in front of 77,231 spectators, his side pulled out all the stops, played well above their League form, and defeated the Reds 3-1. United were looking for a domestic 'treble'.

Ex-Villa 'keeper Les Sealey replaced the injured Peter Schmeichel in United's goal and he had to pick the ball out of the net on 25 minutes when Dalian Atkinson netted with his right shin. It was another 50 minutes before Villa struck again, Kevin Richardson's acutely-angled free-kick being converted by the lunging Dean Saunders. United hit back and in the 83rd minute Mark Hughes whipped in a heart-stopper to make it 2-1. Then Villa's 'keeper Mark Bosnich (ex-United and later to return to Old Trafford) pulled off a blinding save to thwart Hughes. With time running out, Andrei Kanchelskis handled Atkinson's shot on the line and was sent-off. Saunders clinched victory from the spot with the last kick of the game.

Team: Sealey; Parker, Irwin; Bruce, Pallister, Ince, Keane, Cantona, Kanchelskis; Hughes (sub McClair), Giggs (sub Sharpe). Sub (not used): Walsh.

FOOTBALL LEAGUE JUBILEE FUND

When the Football League celebrated its 50th birthday in 1938 a Jubilee fund was launched.

As part of this several local derbies were authorised to take place on the Saturday before the start of both the 1938-39 and 1939-40 seasons to raise money for the fund.

Appropriately United met rivals Manchester City, the results of which were:

20 August 1938	City 2 United 1	Att. 15,000
10 August 1939	United 1 City 1	Att. 20,000

FIFA CLUB WORLD CHAMPIONSHIP

In season 1999-2000, United, as European Champions, were invited to participate in the FIFA Club World Championship in Brazil. They were placed in Group 'B' along with Necaxa, Vasco Da Gama and South Melbourne and played each of their three matches in Rio during the month of January 2000.

The results were:

v. Necaxa	1-1 (Yorke)	Att. 26,000
v. Vasco Da Gama	1-3 (Butt)	Att. 10,000
v. South Melbourne	2-0 (Fortune 2)	Att. 25,000

United failed to qualify for the second phase.

Participation in this lengthy mid-season tournament meant that United were unable to fulfil their FA Cup obligations (even as holders) and were forced to pull out of the historic competition. FIFA have yet to hold another such competition.

United's record in the World Club Championship competition:

Venue	P	W	D	L	F	A
Neutral	3	1	1	1	4	4

FIFA WORLD CLUB CHAMPIONSHIP (Intercontinental)

After winning the 1968 European Cup, Manchester United met the South American champions, Estudiantes de la Plata in the World Club (Intercontinental) Championship, played over two legs in September/October 1968. A crowd of 55,000 saw United defeated 1-0 in Argentina while 63,500 fans saw the return leg at Old Trafford end in a 1-1 draw, United losing the contest 2-1 on aggregate. In the heated and often tense clashes, Nobby Stiles was sent-off in the away leg, while George Best received a similar fate at Old Trafford, dismissed along with Medina (for fighting).

United again participated in the World Club Championship in 1999, this time taking on Palmeiras in Tokyo on 30 November. A crowd of 53,372 saw Roy Keane score the only goal of a tight game to earn United a narrow 1-0 victory.

United's record in this competition:

Venue	P	W	D	L	F	A
Home	1	0	1	0	1	1
Away	1	0	0	1	0	1
Neutral	1	1	0	0	1	0
Totals	3	1	1	1	2	2

FORD, Joseph Bertram

Born: Northwich, 7 May 1886

Career: Witton Albion (1904), Crewe Alexandra (1905), MANCHESTER UNITED (October 1907), Nottingham Forest (June1910), Goole Town (1914). Did not figure after WW1.

Slim-looking left-winger, reserve to George Wall, Joe Ford did much better with Nottingham Forest for whom he made 104 senior appearances (12 goals).

Club record: 5 apps.

135

FOREIGN (OVERSEAS) BORN PLAYERS

Here is an unofficial list of foreign/overseas-born players (not including the Republic of Ireland) who have been associated with United at various levels, whether on trial, as a guest, on loan or as an amateur:

Fabien Barthez	France	Andrei Kanchelskis	USSR/Ukraine	Ole G. Solskjaer	Norway
Alex Bell	South Africa	Roy Killin	Canada	Jaap Stam	Netherlands
Henning Berg	Norway	Jovan Kirovski	USA	Massimo Taibi	Italy
Laurent Blanc	France	Charlie Mitten	Burma	Paul Teather	Holland
Jesper Blomqvist	Sweden	Arnoldus Muhren	Netherlands	John Thorrington	South Africa
Mark Bosnich	Australia	Erik Nevland	Norway	Ruud van Nistelrooy	Holland
Eric Cantona	France	Jimmy Nicholl	Canada	'Rai' van der Gouw	Netherlands
Jordi Cruyff	Netherlands	Jesper Olsen	Denmark	Juan Sebastian Veron	Argentina
Bojan Djordjic	Yugoslavia	Karel Poborsky	Czech Republic	Tom Wilcox	At sea
Wayne Emmerson	Canada	William Prunier	France	Dwight Yorke	Tobago (Canaan)
Diego Forlan	Uruguay	Paul Rachubka	USA	* Sartori was the first Italian to play for
Quinton Fortune	South Africa	Ricardo Lopez	Spain	United and, indeed, one of the first to appear
Shaun Goater	Bermuda	Carlo Sartori	Italy	in the Football League!
George Hunter	India	Peter Schmeichel	Denmark	** Chris Short joined United in May 1990,
Ronny Johnsen	Norway	Chris Short**	Germany	but four months later he moved to Notts
David Johnson	Jamaica	Mikael Silvestre	France	County after failing to appear in the first XI
Nikola Jovanovic	Yugoslavia	John Sivebaek	Denmark	at Old Trafford.

FOREIGN CONNECTION

The following United personnel (at various levels) have all been associated with 'foreign' clubs & countries either as a player, manager, coach, trainer, etc. Served as a player unless otherwise stated.

Arthur Albiston	FC Molde
Willie Anderson	Portland Timbers
Ron Atkinson	Atletico Madrid (manager)
Gary Bailey	Witts University FC, Kaiser Chiefs (S Africa).
Tommy Baldwin	Seattle Sounders
Jack Ball	Excelsior Roubaix, France (player-coach)
Peter Barnes	Real Betis, Melbourne JUST, Sporting Farense, Tampa Bay Rowdies, Norway (coach)
Fabien Barthez	Olympique Marseille, Toulouse, AS Monaco

Peter Beardsley	Vancouver Whitecaps
Henning Berg	KFUM, FC Valeringen, SK Lillestrom, VIF (Norway)
George Best	Los Angeles Aztecs, Fort Lauderdale Strikers, San Jose Earthquakes,
Brisbane Lions,	Golden Bay FC
Brian Birch	Phillipines (coach), Sydney, Australia (coach)
Laurent Blanc	Montpellier, Napoli, Nimes, St Etienne, Auxerre, Barcelona, Olympique Marseille, Inter Milan
Jesper Blomqvist	FC Tavelsjo IK, Umea, IFK Gothenburg, AC Milan, Parma
Frank Blunstone	FC Ethnikos & Aris Salonika (coach)
Peter Bodak	Royal Antwerp, Happy Valley FC (Hong Kong)
Mark Bosnich	Croatia Sydney
Roy Botham	Sydney Olympic
Paul Bradshaw	Vancouver Whitecaps
Alan Brazil	Detroit Express, FC Baden (Switzerland)
James Brown	Newark Skeeters, New York Giants, Brooklyn Wanderers, Greenport United (player-president), Connecticut (coach), Polish Falcons (manager)
Francis Burns	Manager of Italia FC (Australia)
Herbert Burgess	Coached in Austria, Denmark, Hungary, Italy, Spain and Sweden.
Eric Cantona	Auxerre, Bordeaux, Olympique Marseille, Montpellier, Nimes
Luke Chadwick	Royal Antwerp
David Christie	Granville FC, Sydney (coach)
James Connachan	Britannia FC (Canada)
Jordi Cruyff	Ajax Amsterdam & CF Barcelona, FC Deportivo Alaves & Celta Vigo (Spain)
Laurie Cunningham	Real Madrid, Olympique Marseille, Charleroi (Belgium), FC Betis, Rayo Vallecano
Gerry Daly	New England Teamen
Ron Davies	Arcadia Shepherds (S Africa), Los Angeles Aztecs, Tulsa Roughnecks, Seattle Sounders
Wyn Davies	Arcadia Shepherds (S Africa)
Bojan Djordjic	Bromma Pojkarna, AFG(Denmark)
Tommy Docherty	Manager of Sydney Olympic, FC Porto & South Melbourne
Tony Dunne	Detroit Express, Stenjker FC, Norway (player-coach)
Darren Ferguson	Cosena, Sparta Rotterdam
Alan Foggon	Hartford Bi-centennials, Rochester Lancers
Diego Forlan	Independiente de las Plata
Quinton Fortune	Kaiser Chiefs, RCD Mallorca, Atletico Madrid
Bill Foulkes	Coach to Chicago Sting, San Jose Earthquakes, Tulsa Roughnecks & Stenjker FC (Norway) and manager of Lillestrom, Viking Stavanger, FC Mazda (Hiroshima)
David Gaskell	Coach in Kuwait & South Africa
Johnny Giles	Vancouver Whitecaps (as player, manager & coach), Philadelphia Fury
Don Givens	Xamax Neuchatel (Switzerland)
Shaun Goater	North Village FC (Bermuda)
Freddie Goodwin	Manager of New York Generals & Minnesota Kicks
George Graham	California Surf
Brian Greenhoff	Hong Kong
Jimmy Greenhoff	Toronto Blizzard (player-coach)
Harry Gregg	Kitan Sports Club, Kuwait (manager-coach)
Clive Griffiths	Chicago Sting, Tulsa Roughnecks
Ashley Grimes	Osasuna (Spain)
Mickey Hamill	Fall River FC (Boston), Coats FC (Rhode Island), New York Giants (all in USA)
Frank Harris	USA football (1924-32)
Vince Hayes	CF Madrid (manager), Norway (coach), Weiner SV Austria (coach)
Danny Higginbotham	Royal Antwerp
Gordon Hill	Chicago Sting, Montreal Manic, New York Arrows, Kansas Comets, Tacoma Stars, HJK Helsinki, Twente Enschede, Nova Scotia, Palm Harbour (coach)
Jim Holton	Miami Toros, Detroit Express
Mark Hughes	Bayern Munich, CF Barcelona
Paul Ince	Inter Milan
Ronny Johnsen	Stokke FC, IF EIK-Tonsberg, Lyn Oslo, Lillestrom, Besiktas
Joe Jordan	AC Milan, Verona
Nicola Jovanovic	Red Star Belgrade, FC Buducnoet
Andrei Kanchelskis	Dynamo Kiev, Shakhytor Donestsk, Fiorentina
Jimmy Kelly	Chicago Sting, Los Angeles Aztecs, Tulsa Roughnecks, Toronto Blizzard
Fred Kennedy	Racing Club de Paris
Brian Kidd	Atlanta Chiefs, Fort Lauderdale Strikers, Minnesota Strikers
Roy Killin	Canadian football
Jovan Kirovski	Sporting Lisbon, Borussia Dortmund
Denis Law	Torino
Les Lievesley	Coached in Holland, Italy (Turin) and Spain
Eddie Lewis	Witts FC, South Africa (manager)
John Lowey	Chicago Sting, California FC

Neil McBain	Estudiantes de la Plata (coach)
Jim McCalliog	Chicago Sting, Norway (coach)
James McCrae	Egypt (coach)
David McCreery	Tulsa Roughnecks, Sundsvaal (Sweden)
Ted MacDougall	Detroit Express, Athena FC (Perth), South Africa (player-coach)
Scott McGarvey	Aris Limasol (Cyprus), FC Mazda (Japan)
Chris McGrath	Tulsa Roughnecks, South China FC
Wilf McGuinness	Aris Salonika (manager), Panachaiki Patras (manager)
Sammy McIlroy	Orgyte (Sweden), FC Modling
Eddie McIlvenny	Fairhill FC (USA), Philadelphia Nationals
George McLachlan	Le Havre (manager)
Gordon McQueen	FC Seiko, Japan (player-coach)
Mick Martin	Vancouver Whitecaps
Jack Mew	Lyra FC, Belgium (trainer-coach), Lima FC, Peru (coach)
Ralph Milne	Sing Tao FC (Hong Kong)
Charlie Mitten	Sante Fe (Bogota)
Ian Moir	South African football
Kevin Moran	Sporting Gijon (Spain)
Willie Morgan	Chicago Sting, Minnesota Kicks
Arnoldus Muhren	Ajax Amsterdam, FC Twente Enschede
David Musgrave	Johannesburg FC
Malcolm Musgrove	Coach to Connecticut Bi-centennials & Chicago Sting
Erik Nevland	IFK Gothenburg, Stavanger Viking
Jimmy Nicholl	Toronto Blizzard
Pat O'Connell	Manager/coach of Atletico Madrid, Barcelona, FC Sevilla, Racing Santander (two spells) & Real Betis (three times) & scout of FC Huelva
Frank O'Farrell	Coach in Iran (National team)
Jesper Olsen	FC Naestvedt, Ajax Amsterdam, Bordeaux, SM Caen (France).
John O'Shea	Royal Antwerp
Peter O'Sullivan	Hong Kong
Steve Paterson	Played in Australia, Hong Kong & Japan
Stuart Pearson	Played in North America and South Africa
Jock Peddie	American football
David Platt	Bari, Juventus, Sampdoria (player & coach)
Karel Poborsky	Cesko Budejovice, Viktoria Liskov, Slavia Prague, Benfica, SS Lazio, Sparta Prague
William Prunier	FC Auxerre, Olympique Marseille, Bordeaux, FC Copenhagen, Napoli, KV Kortrijk (Belgium)
Paul Rachubka	Royal Antwerp
Ricardo Lopez	Real Valladolid
Lance Richardson	Rowlands Gill FC (USA)
Jimmy Rimmer	Hamrun Sports Club (Malta)
Mark Robins	Panionios (Greece), Deportivo Orense (Spain)
Bryan Robson	Happy Valley (Hong Kong)
Jack Rowley	Ajax Amsterdam (coach)
Jimmy Ryan	Dallas Tornados
David Sadler	Miami Toros
Carlo Sartori	Bologna, FC Spal, Lecce, Rimini, FC Trento (all Italy)
Ted Savage	Holland (coach)
Peter Schmeichel	Brondby IF, Sporting Lisbon, Hvidovre (owner)
Lee Sharpe	Sampdoria
Mikael Silvestre	Rennes (France), Inter Milan
John Sivebaek	Vejle Boldklub, St Etienne, AS Monaco, Atalanta, Pescara
Paddy Sloan	Brescia, Milan, Turin, Udinese (United reserve & WW2)
Ole Gunnar Solskjaer	FC Clausenengen, FC Molde
Jaap Stam	FC Dos Kampen, FC Zwolle, Cambuur Leeuwarden FC, Willem II, PSV Eindhoven, SS Lazio
Frank Stapleton	Ajax Amsterdam, Le Havre
Alex Stepney	Dallas Tornados
Nobby Stiles	Vancouver Whitecaps (coach)
Ian Storey-Moore	Chicago Sting, South African football
John Sutcliffe	Arnhem (coach)
Massimo Taibi	Licata, Trento, Venezia, Como, Piacenza, AC Milan (2 spells), Reggiana, Atalanta (all in Italy)
Alan Tate	Royal Antwerp
Chris Taylor	Canadian football
Ernie Taylor	New Brighton FC, New Zealand (coach)
Mickey Thomas	Wichita Wings
Wilf Tranter	Baltimore Boys, St Louis Stars
Ian Ure	Coach in Iceland
Ruud van Nistelrooy	FC Den Bosch, FC Heerenveen, PSV Eindhoven
Rai van der Gouw	Go Ahead Eagles, Vitesse Arnhem
Juan Sebastian Veron	Estudiantes de la Plata, Boca Juniors, Sampdoria, Parma, SS Lazio
Dennis Viollet	Baltimore Bays, Washington Diplomats (coach), Jackson University (coach), Richmond, Virginia (coach)
Colin Waldron	Tulsa Roughnecks, Philadelphia Fury, Atlanta Chiefs
Danny Wallace	Saudi Arabia
Ronnie Wallwork	Royal Antwerp
Willie Watson	Miami Toros
Paul Wheatcroft	FC Fortuna
Neil Wood	Royal Antwerp
Ray Wood	Coach in Canada, Cyprus (also coach of the Cypriot natioonal team), Greece, Kuwait, Kenya, UAE, USA (Los Angeles Wolves) & Zambia.
Dwight Yorke	Signal Hill FC (Tobago)

FORMATION (FOUNDING) OF CLUB

Manchester United (Newton Heath) FC was formed in 1878 by railway workers at the carriage & wagon department of the LYR (Lancashire & Yorkshire Railway) and initially played under the name of Newton Heath (LYR) Cricket & Football Club, shortening the name to Newton Heath in 1885.

The club's first ground (used until 1893) was on North Road and two nearby public houses - the Three Crowns and Shears Hotel - were used as dressing/changing rooms for the respective teams. In their early days 'United' originally donned red and white quartered shirts and blue shorts, later switching to green and gold halved shirts with black shorts. In 1885 the club turned professional and applied unsuccessfully to join the newly-formed Football League in 1888. The following year 12 clubs, disappointed at not being able to join the Football League, formed the Football Alliance, Newton Heath being one of its founder members Entering the Football League in 1892, the club became known as Manchester United in 1902, after Newton Heath was declared bankrupt.

FORSTER, Thomas

Born: Northwich, spring 1894
Career: Northwich Victoria (1914), MANCHESTER UNITED (January 1916), Northwich Victoria (May 1922).
Sound-tackling half-back Tommy Forster had one excellent season with United (1920-21). It was said that if he had been a shade taller (he was only 5ft 6ins) he would have been a great player.
Club record: 36 apps.

FORSYTH, Alexander

Born: Swinton, Lanarkshire 5 February 1952
Career: Possil YMCA, Arsenal (junior, 1967), Partick Thistle (1968), MANCHESTER UNITED (£100,000, December 1972), Glasgow Rangers (on loan before signing permanently, August 1978), Motherwell (1982), Hamilton Academical (season 1983-84).
Clean-kicking, resourceful full-back, Alex Forsyth helped United win the Second Division Championship in 1975 and also played in the FA Cup Final twelve months later. Winner of one Under-23 and 10 senior caps for Scotland, he was a Scottish League Cup winner with Partick in 1972 and also represented the Scottish League side. Initially an outside-left, he netted 24 goals for Partick's reserve team in 1970-71. He was replaced in United's first XI by Jimmy Nicholl.
Club record: 121 apps. five goals

FORTUNE, Quinton

Born: Cape Town, South Africa, 21 May 1977
Career: Tottenham Hotspur (junior, season 1993-94), Kaiser Chiefs, RCD Mallorca (1995), Atletico Madrid (1996) MANCHESTER UNITED (£1.5 million, August 1999).
Fast-raiding left-winger Quinton Fortune was released by Spurs owing to a problem with his work permit. He represented his country at Under-23 level before establishing himself in the senior national side. He has over 40 caps to his name, and represented South Africa in the 2002 World Cup Finals in Japan and South Korea. Initially a fringe player and reserve to Ryan Giggs at Old Trafford, he had his best season in 2001-02, making almost 20 appearances.
Club record: 42 apps. 7 goals

FORLAN CORAZO, Diego

Born: Montevideo, Uruguay, 19 May 1979
Career: Independiente de las Plata (1996), MANCHESTER UNITED (£7.5 million, January 2002).
Long-haired striker, well built with good pace and strong shot, Diego Forlan joined United (in preference to Middlesbrough) on a five-year contract contract. His father was a Uruguayan international while young Diego won his first two caps soon after making his move to Old Trafford and then added more to his tally while on duty for his country in the 2002 World Cup Finals in Japan & South Korea, also scoring his first International goal.
Club record: 18 apps.

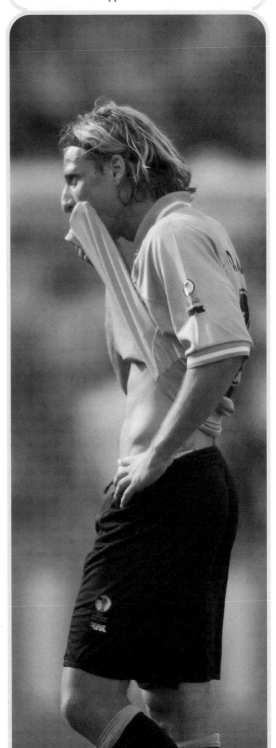

137

FOULKES, William Anthony

Born: St Helens, 5 January 1932

Career: Whiston Boys Club, MANCHESTER UNITED (amateur March 1950, professional August 1951-June 1970). Retired at the age of 38 to become Youth coach at Old Trafford until 1975. Later Chicago Sting (coach, 1975-77), Tulsa Roughnecks (coach, 1978), Witney Town (manager, 1979-80), San Jose Earthquakes (coach, 1980), FC Stenjker, Norway (manager, 1982-83), Lillestrom (manager, 1984), Viking Stavanger, Norway (manager, 1986), FC Mazda, Horishima, Japan (manager from 1988-92 when he quit football).

When the chips were down and there was a battle to be fought, Bill Foulkes was always in the thick of it. A teak-tough defender, able to play equally as well at right-back or centre-half, he survived the Munich air crash and gave United grand service (as a player) for a total of 20 years.

Although only an occasional scorer, his amazing goal (from open play) away at Real Madrid in the 1968 European Cup semi-final will remain a treasured memory for many of United's older fans.

A key figure in four of United's League Championship-winning sides - 1955-56, 1956-57, 1964-65 and 1966-67 - he was an FA Cup finalist in 1958 before gaining a winners medal in 1963, collecting a European Cup winners prize five years later. Despite being a first team regular for 18 years, he won only one England cap - but what a grand servant to the club. Club record: 688 apps. nine goals.

FRAME, Thomas

Born: Burnbank, Scotland, 5 September 1902. Died: Paisley, 17 January 1997.

Career: Burnbank Thistle, Cowdenbeath (1926), MANCHESTER UNITED (September 1932), Southport (July 1936), Rhyl Athletic (1937), Bridgnorth Town (1938-39). Did not play after WW2.

Tommy Frame was a strong, confident defender who started out as a right-back but finished as a solid centre-half. He also played as a wing-half and inside-forward and always gave a good account of himself. A broken leg, suffered in March 1934 (v. Blackpool) effectively ended his career with United, although he remained with the club for a further two seasons before transferring to Southport. Club record: 52 apps. 4 goals.

FRIENDLY MATCHES

Newton Heath first started to play friendly matches in 1878 - the year the club was formed. Before the formation of the Football League in 1888, the staple diet of football clubs was friendly and Cup matches. The club has continued to play friendlies ever since, although not too many since the 1970s, and very few since the introduction of the Premiership in 1992 - except of course for pre and end of season tours!

Friendly Banter

Newton Heath/United played rivals Manchester City (known as Ardwick until 1894) in friendly matches several times during the late 1800s, early 1900s. The first recorded friendly between the clubs was in January 1893 when Newton Heath won 5-3 at Hyde Road, although there had already been three matches in 1891 (FA Cup and Football Alliance). Three more friendlies between the clubs took place later that season, the Heathens winning two and City one (by 3-0).

A total of seven friendlies took place between United and City during WW1 (1915-19) and seven more took place between 1939-46, United winning 5-1 on City soil in August 1942.

United beat City 5-2 in a pre-season friendly at Old Trafford in August 1988, but a year later City gained revenge with a 2-0 win on the same ground.

After turning down UEFA's offer to play in the European Cup in 1958-59 (following the tragedy of Munich) United played two 'friendly' matches, home and away, against the crack Swiss side Young Boys of Berne. They won the contest 3-2 on aggregate.

A trip to Norway in August 1977 saw United beat Stromsgodset 9-0 in a pre-season friendly. Jimmy Greenhoff scored five of the goals.

In January 1980, United flew over to Yugoslavia to play Hadjuk Split in a friendly - they lost 6-0!

In August 1981, United, Aberdeen, Southampton and West Ham, competed in a four-club tournament at Pittodrie. United finished last!

In June 1983, United played Tottenham Hotspur in two 'friendly' matches in Swaziland.

United beat Naxar Lions 9-0 in a friendly in Malta at the end of the 1986-87 season.

In August 2001 United played two friendlies on the same day - both were regarded as first team matches v. Hereford United and Chester City.

In the pre-season of 2001-02 United fulfilled a total of nine friendly matches - all technically described as first-team fixtures as the squad players was evenly divided up with Messrs Yorke, Giggs and Butt all appearing for a so-called 2nd XI. United also played in a tournament in Holland pre-2002-03.

* See: Benefit/testimonial Matches

FULHAM

Summary of League results

	P	W	D	L	F	A
Premiership	2	2	0	0	6	4
Division 1	24	14	6	4	57	29
Division 2	18	9	4	5	21	18
Home	22	18	3	1	47	17
Away	22	7	7	8	37	34
Total	44	25	10	9	84	51

FA Cup results v. the Cottagers:

	Round	Venue	Result
1904-05	1	Home	D 2-2
	Replay	Away	D 0-0 aet
	2nd R	Villa Park	L 0-1
1907-08	4	Away	L 1-2
1925-26	6	Away	W 2-1
1957-58	SF	Villa Park	D 2-2
	Replay	Highbury	W 5-3
1978-79	4	Away	D 1-1
	Replay	Home	W 1-0
1998-99	5	Home	W 1-0
2000-01	3	Away	W 2-1

League results v. the Cottagers:

Season	Div	Home	Away	Season	Div	Home	Away
1922-23	2	D 1-1	D 0-0	1959-60	1	D 3-3	W 5-0
1923-24	2	D 0-0	L 1-3	1960-61	1	W 3-1	D 4-4
1924-25	2	W 2-0	L 0-1	1961-62	1	W 3-0	L 0-2
				1962-63	1	L 0-2	W 1-0
1932-33	2	W 4-3	L 1-3	1963-64	1	W 3-0	D 2-2
1933-34	2	W 1-0	W 2-0	1964-65	1	W 4-1	L 1-2
1934-35	2	W 1-0	L 1-3	1965-66	1	W 4-1	W 1-0
1935-36	2	W 1-0	D 2-2	1966-67	1	W 2-1	D 2-2
				1967-68	1	W 3-0	W 4-0
1937-38	2	W 1-0	L 0-1				
				1974-75	2	W 1-0	W 2-1
1949-50	1	W 3-0	L 0-1				
1950-51	1	W 1-0	D 2-2	2001-02	PL	W 3-2	W 3-2
1951-52	1	W 3-2	D 3-3				

Fact File

The most memorable matches between the clubs took place in the immediate aftermath of the Munich tragedy when Second Division Fulham, including Johnny Haynes (and Jimmy Hill) met the patched-up United side in the FA Cup semi-final. After an exciting 2-2 draw at Villa Park, highlighted by two Bobby Charlton 'specials' the teams replayed in mid-week with an afternoon kick-off at Highbury. United won a remarkable match 5-3 with Alex Dawson scoring a hat-trick.

Players with both clubs include: P Beardsley, G Best, A Chesters (Fulham WW2), A Cole, J Flitchett, R Halton (Fulham WW2), D Jones (Fulham trialist), J McDonald (United WW2), C Mitten, P O'Sullivan (United reserve), A Pape, P Parker, M Pearson, E 'Dick' Pegg, M Radcliffe (United WW2), A Rowley (United WW2), E Savage (Fulham WW2), A Stepney (Fulham trialist), W Tranter, R Turner, A Warburton. Also associated: D Sexton (United manager, Fulham coach), H Haslam (United trialist, WW2 player, Fulham Chief Scout)

GIGGS, Ryan Joseph

Born: (Ryan Wilson) Cardiff, 29 November 1973
Career: Salford Schools, MANCHESTER UNITED (trainee, July 1990, professional November 1990).
A direct winger with great technique, poise, pace, splendid bodyswerve and powerful shot, Ryan Giggs was voted PFA 'Young Player of the Year' at the end of his first season as a professional at Old Trafford, collected the same award in 1993 and has continued to win prizes ever since! Playing down the left flank, he was a key member of United's Premiership winning sides in 1993, 1994, 1996, 1997, 1999, 2000 and 2001. He also helped the Reds lift the FA Cup in 1994, 1996, 1997 and 1999 (and was a finalist in 1995), the League Cup in 1992, the European Champions Cup in 1999 and the European Super Cup in 1991. He also featured in five FA Charity Shield victories - and he won an FA Youth Cup winners' medal in 1992.
Raised in Salford after his father, Danny Wilson, a Welsh Rugby international, moved north to join Swinton, he starred for Salford and England Schools.
In recent seasons Giggs has become increasingly prone to a niggling hamstring problem, meaning that United boss Sir Alex Ferguson had to use him sparingly.
Capped almost 40 times by Wales at senior level, he also appeared in his country's Youth and Under-21 sides and his big disappointment is that he has not played in the World Cup Finals.

Giggs took his mother's maiden name when his parents separated. Anyone who ever saw Danny Wilson play rugby, will know from where Ryan inherited his pace!

There is no doubt that Ryan Giggs in full flow is one of the most exciting experiences in world football. His densational goaal in the FA Cup semi-final replay when he ran clean through the Arsenal's legendary water-tight defence to score the winner in extra-time will live forever in United's memory.

Club record: 485 apps. 99 goals

GAINSBOROUGH TRINITY

League results v. Trinity:

Season	Div	Home	Away
1896-97	2	W 2-0	L 0-2
1897-98	2	W 1-0	L 1-2
1898-99	2	W 6-1	W 2-0
1899-1900	2	D 2-2	W 1-0
1900-01	2	D 0-0	W 1-0
1901-02	2	W 3-0	D 1-1
1902-03	2	W 3-1	W 1-0
1903-04	2	W 4-2	W 1-0
1904-05	2	W 3-1	D 0-0
1905-06	2	W 2-0	D 2-2

Summary of League results

	P	W	D	L	F	A
Division 2	20	13	5	2	36	14
Home	10	8	2	0	26	7
Away	10	5	3	2	10	7
Total	20	13	5	2	36	14

Fact file

Trinity was elected to the Football League in 1896, taking its place in the Second Division, where it would play for 16 consecutive seasons before failing the re-election process in 1912. At the time of their election, the town was spelt 'Gainsbrough' the present spelling adopted around 1905.

The origins of the club were the local Trinity Church, which formed the 'Trinity Recreation Society' in 1872, first as a cricket team, adding football soon after. By 1877 the footballers had broken away from the church, now known as the 'Trinity Recreationalists'. By 1884 they had their own ground at Northolme, had turned professional, adding the town name to their title.

Trinity and Newton Heath (later United) were regular opponents between 1896 and 1906 when United at last gained promotion in 1906. Gainsborough Trinity these days play in the Unibond Premier League, its wonderful Supporters Club having raised the money to allow the club to buy the lease of its ground.

Players with both clubs: T Arkesden, VE Dodsworth (United reserve), A Henrys.

GALATASARAY

United were dumped out of the 1993-94 European Cup in the 2nd round by Galatasaray who went through courtesy of the away goal rule, scoring three times at Old Trafford to earn a 3-3 draw before a 0-0 scoreline in Turkey.

The following season United gained revenge - in a small way - by drawing 0-0 in Turkey and beating Galatasaray 4-0 at Old Trafford in the group stage.

GALLIMORE, Stanley Hugh

Born: Bucklow Hill, Cheshire, 14 April 1910.

Career: Witton Albion (1927), MANCHESTER UNITED (amateur September 1929, professional December 1929-May 1933, re-signed February 1934), Altrincham (June 1934), Northwich Victoria (1938-39). Did not feature after WW2.

Inside-forward Stan Gallimore was handed a free transfer by United at the end of the 1932-33 season after a long-term injury problem. He arranged to have a knee operation and successfully returned to Old Trafford after declaring himself fit to resume playing but was released again at the end of that season.

Club record: 76 apps. 20 goals

GAMES PLAYED

United played 63 first-class/competitive matches in both 1993-94 & 1998-99. In the calendar year 1990, United they part in 16 Cup games (FA, League Cup & ECWC), remaining unbeaten in them all. They even drew 1-1 with Liverpool in the Charity Shield game at Wembley.

Over a 72-hour period, covering the 7, 8 & 9 May 1988, United played three games at Old Trafford (a) Arthur Albiston's testimonial v. rivals Manchester City and two successive League games (b) v. Wimbledon and (c) v. Portsmouth.

United have played three League games on successive days over the Christmas period of the 25, 26 & 27 December on four separate occasions: in 1902, 1913, 1924 and 1930.

The Reds fulfilled four League fixtures in five days in mid-April 1909 and again in early April 1915 and in the latter month they actually played five matches in eight days.

United have met the same team in two different Cup competitions (namely the FA and League Cup) in the same season as follows: 1969-70 Manchester City and Middlesbrough; 1971-72 Stoke City, 1979-80 Tottenham Hotspur, 1982-83 Arsenal, 1984-85 Everton, 1985-86 West Ham United, 1991-92 Leeds United and 1992-93 Brighton & Hove Albion. Including the two League clashes, United met Stoke City five times in 1971-72.

United also played five games at Stoke's old Victoria Ground in the 1971-72 season. After beating WBA there in an early League game (owing to the closure of Old Trafford), they went on to meet the Potters in two League Cup replays, in a scheduled First Division match and also in an FA Cup replay.

United and Everton clashed five times in the space of 2 months in five different tournaments between October 1984 and September 1985. They did battle in a League Cup game, a First Division fixture, an FA Cup-tie, in the annual FA Charity Shield and also in the Screen Sport Super Cup. In all United and Everton have met in seven different competitions - the other two being the Inter-Cities Fairs Cup in 1964-65 and the Football League Centenary Trophy in 1988.

Longest Game

The longest 'games' involving Newton Heath/Manchester United have been those that went onto extra-time, covering at least 120 minutes in total, of which there have been many.

However, the longest 'game' (cup-tie) to complete was an Intermediate FA Cup-tie - United v. Small Heath - in season 1903-04 which went to a fourth game (a 3rd replay) before United won 3-1 at neutral Hyde Road. The total number of minutes played amounted to 420 (including two periods of extra-time).

Also there was the United-Southampton 4th round FA Cup replay in 1995-96 which went to a penalty shoot-out (although there was no actual open play other than the agreed 120 minutes of action).

GARDNER, Charles Richard

Born: Birmingham, early 1913
Career: Evesham Town (1930), Birmingham (amateur, 1932), Notts County (1933), Stourbridge (1935),
MANCHESTER UNITED (May 1935), Sheffield United (May 1937). Retired before WW2.
An inside-forward, Dick Gardner was rescued from non-League football by United and in his first season with the club helped them win the Second Division Championship.
Club record: 18 apps. One goal

GARTON, William Francis

Born: Salford, 15 March 1965
Career: Salford Schools, MANCHESTER UNITED (apprentice May 1981, professional March 1983), Birmingham City (on loan, March-April 1986), Salford City (player-manager, May 1990), Witton Albion (season 1993-94).
Centre-half Billy Garton was forced to quit competitive League football in 1980 due to injury (Achilles and back problems in the main).He was an FA Youth Cup winner with United in 1982 (v. Watford).
Club record: 52 apps.

GARVEY, James Patrick

Born: Hulme, Manchester, early 1878.
Career: Wigan Borough (1898), NEWTON HEATH (May 1900), Middleton FC (April 1901), Stalybridge Rovers, Southport Central (1902), Bradford City (1905). Retired through injury before the end of the 1905-06 season..
Goalkeeper James Garvey was reserve to Jimmy Whitehouse in season 1900-01. He later collected a Lancashire Senior Cup runners-up medal with Southport Central (1904).
Club record: 6 apps. (also one 'other' app)

GASKELL, John David

Born: Orrell, Lancs. 5 October 1940
Career: Lamberhead School, Wigan Schools, Lancashire Schoolboys, MANCHESTER UNITED (amateur June 1955, professional October 1957-June 1969), Wigan Athletic (on loan, July-August 1968), Orrell Rugby Union Club (albeit briefly, August 1969), Wrexham (1969).Retired 1972.
Goalkeeper Dave Gaskell represented England five times at schoolboy level before joining United. He made his debut in the 1956 FA Charity Shield match against Manchester City as a substitute and his Football League bow followed a year later against Tottenham Hotspur. Battling for a place in the side with Ray Wood and Harry Gregg, he was a first-class 'keeper who helped United win the FA Cup in 1963, replacing Gregg.
Club record: 120 apps.

143

GATE RECEIPTS

Details of how the gate receipts record has been broken at Old Trafford since United won the European Cup in 1968:

£63,438	United v. Estudiantes (World Club Championship)	25.09.1968
£88,495	Chelsea v. Leeds United, FA Cup Final replay	29.04.1970
£104,015	Leicester City v. Liverpool FA Cup semi-final	30.03.1974
£124,441	Liverpool v. Nottm Forest, League Cup Final replay	22.03.1978
£192,956	United v. Juventus, ECWC semi-final	11.04.1984
£232,174	United v. Nottingham Forest, FA Cup rd 6	18.03.1989
£432,346	United v. Legia Warsaw, ECWC semi-final	24.04.1991
£476,294	United v. Charlton Athletic, FA Cup rd 6	12.03.1994
£529,827	United v. Leeds United, FA Cup rd 5	19.02.1995
£576,494	United v. Southampton, FA Cup, rd 6	11.03.1996
£739,841	United v. Borussia Dortmund, Champions League	23.04.1997
£779,631	United v. Barnsley, FA Cup rd 5	15.02.1998
£850,289	United v. Liverpool, FA Cup rd 4	24.01.1999

Money Talk

The 43,143 crowd that assembled for the Sheffield Wednesday v. United League game at (Owlerton) Hillsborough on 30 November 1907 realised gate receipts of £1,100 - the first time the £1,000 mark had been reached for an Owls home game.
In 1914, an Old Trafford crowd of over 55,800 paid record receipts of £3,777 to see Burnley play Sheffield United in the FA Cup semi-final.
Seven years later (March 1923) the Bolton Wanderers v. Sheffield United FA Cup semi-final at Old Trafford realised record gate receipts for the competition of £7,600.
Eight years later, for the Everton-West Brom FA Cup semi-final, the gate receipts at Old Trafford were once again broken when £7,829 was taken at the turnstiles.
Record gate receipts of £327,124 were taken at the Crystal Palace v. United Premiership game at Selhurst Park in April 1993.
Record takings of £512,235 were banked from the Oldham Athletic v. United FA Cup semi-final encounter at Maine Road in April 1994.
And the Oldham v. United Premiership game at Boundary Park in December 1993 realised record gate receipts for the Latics of £138,680.

The following year - February 1994 - the QPR versus United Premiership game at Loftus Road produced record takings of £218,475. £336,702 created record gate receipts for Tottenham Hotspur when United visited White Hart Lane for a First Division game on 28 September 1991.

There were record takings at Bootham Crescent when United played York City there in a second round 2nd leg League Cup encounter on 3 October 1995.

The first time the £3 million barrier was broken for the annual Charity Shield game was in August 1998 when United lost 3-0 to Arsenal at Wembley.

Ten years ago (1992) on a League match-day at Old Trafford, the average income was around £500,000 (season tickets £240,000, gate receipts £160,000, exucutive boxes £20,000, programme sales £30,000, club shop takings £22,000, catering etc. £30,000). Nowadays (2002) a senior/competitive game at Old Trafford realizes takings of around £5.8 million.

GATESHEAD (Originally South Shields)

League results v. South Shields:

Season	Div	Home	Away
1922-23	2	W 3-0	W 3-0
1923-24	2	D 1-1	L 0-1
1924-25	2	W 1-0	W 2-1

Summary of League results

	P	W	D	L	F	A
Division 2	6	4	1	1	10	3
Home	3	2	1	0	5	1
Away	3	2	0	1	5	2
Total	6	4	1	1	10	3

Fact File

This club has a remarkable history, formed in 1899 as 'South Shields' they were elected to the Football League in 1919 prior to the formation of the regional Third Divisions, taking their place in Division Two as the League expanded from 40 clubs to 44. By 1928 South Shields were relegated to the Third Division (North) and due to their close proximity to both Newcastle and Sunderland their future was precarious.

In 1930, with Football League approval, the club left their Horsley Hill Road ground, decamping to Gateshead, taking over the Redheugh Park ground and adopting the town name. The club survived as a League outfit until the end of the 1959-60 season when they failed the re-election process, being replaced by FA Cup giant killers Peterborough United.

Gateshead survive today playing in the Unibond Premier League, just two promotions away from the Football League. As Gateshead they never met United in any competition.

Players with both clubs include: W Buchan & J Gallon (both Gateshead & United WW2 guests), R Clark (United reserve), W Cresswell (United reserve & S Shields), J Grimwood (S Shields), W Hunter (SS), S Jones (United reserve/Gateshead), L Richardson (SS), T Smith (SS), E Thompson (Gateshead), O Williams (United junior).

Also: J Ferguson (with Gateshead United).

GAUDIE, Ralph R.

Born: Guisborough, early 1876.

Career: South Bank FC (1895), Sheffield Saracens (1896), Sheffield United (1897), Aston Villa (1898), Woolwich Arsenal, (1899), MANCHESTER UNITED (August 1903), Darlaston (May 1904), Stourbridge (1906). Retired 1908. Ralph Gaudie was a left-half or inside-forward and he did well, especially with Woolwich Arsenal.

He was one of Ernest Mangnall's first signings at United, initially playing at outside-right, but once Alf Schofield took over, Gaudie days were numbered.

Club record: 8 apps..

GIBSON, Colin John

Born: Bridport, 6 April 1960

Career: Portsmouth Grammar School, West Sussex Schoolboys, Portsmouth (amateur, 1975), Aston Villa (1976), MANCHESTER UNITED (£275,000, November 1985), Port Vale (on loan, September-October 1990), Leicester City (£100,000, December 1990), Blackpool (summer 1994), Walsall (non-contract, autumn, 1994). Quit League football in 1996.

A competent left-back who also occupied a midfield position with no little skill, Colin Gibson had a fine career that spanned some 20 years. He was capped by England at Youth, Under-21 and 'B' team levels whilst at Villa Park and gained a First Division Championship medal in 1981 and a European Super Cup prize the following year. He scored 17 goals in 238 first team outings for Villa before switching his allegiance to Old Trafford. He spent a little over five years with United and later helped Leicester win promotion to the Premiership in 1994 (via the Play-offs). He appeared in a total of 364 League games.

Club record: 96 apps. 10 goals

GIBSON, James W

James Gibson, a local clothing manufacturing entrepreneur, came to United's rescue in one of its darkest hours! On the field United were in a parlous state with a string of poor results over several seasons. They were heavily in debt and the 1930s recession was biting deep in Manchester, as football was seen as a luxury which could not be afforded. At Christmas time 1931, Mr Gibson met the board and outlined a plan of recovery, investing £30,000 of his own money into the club, on condition he became president (Chairman) and was allowed to elect his own board members. The United directors had little choice and Mr Gibson took over.

It would be 1945 before his efforts bore fruit as he persuaded Matt Busby to take over as manager. During the war years, James Gibson kept the club afloat, the ground in ruins, just himself and faithful secretary Walter Crickmer (q.v) to keep things going. James Gibson must stand alongside John H Davies (q.v) as a saviour of Manchester United.

* Gibson was also credited with the creating of MANCHESTER UNITED'S Youth policy. Weary of watching United sides manned by journeymen professionals, he had a vision of a team filled with Manchester lads brought up in the club's ways. In or around 1938 he announced the formation of the MUJACs, a team which would recruit local boys to play in local Leagues. The fruits of this assisted Matt Busby greatly after the Second World War.

GIBSON, Richard Samuel

Born: Holborn, London, early 1889

Career: Sultan FC (1909), Birmingham (1911), Leicester Fosse (during WW1), MANCHESTER UNITED (£250, June 1921-April 1922). Prior to joining United, fast and clever right-winger Dick Gibson had done well with Birmingham for whom he scored 19 goals in 120 appearances, gaining a Second Division Championship medal in 1921. Signed as cover for the ageing Billy Harrison, he was released after just one season at Old Trafford.

Club record: 12 apps.

GIBSON, Terence Bradley

Born: Walthamstow, London, 23 December 1962

Career: Waltham Forest Schoolboys, Tottenham Hotspur (apprentice 1979, professional 1980), Gais FC, Sweden (on loan, 1981), Coventry City (£100,000, 1983), MANCHESTER UNITED (£600,000, January 1986), Wimbledon (£200,000, August 1987), Swindon Town (on loan, 1992), Charlton Athletic (trialist, 1993), Peterborough United (non-contract, late 1993), Barnet (early 1994). Then Youth team coach at Underhill before becoming Wycombe Wanderers assistant-manager/coach in 1999

Terry Gibson was a small, darting, stocky striker whose career realised over 80 goals in almost 300 games at club level. He gained both England schoolboy & Youth caps and when he joined United, Alan Brazil switched to Highfield Road as part of the deal. Sadly Gibson failed to produce the goods (goals) at Old Trafford and departed to Wimbledon after just one season with the Reds.

Club record: 27 apps. one goal

GIBSON, Thomas Richard Donald

Born: Manchester, 12 May 1929

Career: Weekend junior football, MANCHESTER UNITED (amateur November 1946, professional August 1947), Sheffield Wednesday (£8,000, June 1955), Leyton Orient (season 1960-61), Buxton Town (player-manager, early 1962-63).

A positive reliable half-back Don Gibson made well over 100 senior appearances for United during the first five years of the 1950s. After helping United finish runners-up in 1951, he gained a League Championship medal twelve months later and added a Second Division winners' medal to his collection with Wednesday in 1956. After his footballing days were over he ran a confectionery shop in Burnage. Don Gibson married Matt Busby's daughter, Sheena.

Club record: 115 apps.

GIDMAN, John

Born: Liverpool, 10 January 1954.

Career: Merseyside Schools, Liverpool (apprentice, 1969), Aston Villa (apprentice 1970, professional 1971), Everton (£650,000, 1979 - player exchange deal), Manchester United (£450,000, August 1981), Manchester City (free transfer, October 1988), Stoke City (1988), Darlington (player/assistant-manager, 1989), Kings Lynn (manager, 1993-94).

An attack-minded defender, John Gidman had an excellent career. He made 243 senior appearances (nine goals) for Aston Villa and won England caps at full, 'B' and Under-23 levels, having earlier represented his country as a Youth team player. He helped Villa win the FA Youth Cup in 1972 and the League Cup in 1977 but unfortunately missed the 1975 League Cup Final win over Norwich City after suffering an eye injury when a firework exploded in his face on Bonfire Night, 1974. Replacing Jimmy Nicholl at right-back, he helped United beat his former club Everton to win the FA Cup in 1985 but sadly a spate of niggling injuries interrupted his time at Old Trafford. After spells at Maine Road and The Victoria Ground, he ended his senior career with his former Villa team-mate Brian Little at Darlington in 1989. Gidman amassed 432 League appearances all told. He later ran a café/bar in Spain.

Club record: 123 apps. 4 goals

GIGGS, Ryan Joseph

Refer to front of section.

GILES, John Michael

Born: Cabra, Dublin, 6 November 1940

Career: Brunswick Street school (Dublin), St Colombus FC, Dublin Schools Select, Dublin City (later Munster Victoria), Stella Maris Boys, Leprechauns FC, Dublin (1954), Home Farm (1955), MANCHESTER UNITED (amateur, July 1956, professional November 1957), Leeds United (£37,500, August 1963), West Bromwich Albion (player-manager, 1975), Shamrock Rovers (player-manager & executive director of the club, 1977), Philadelphia Fury (1978), Vancouver Whitecaps (coach, 1980), West Bromwich Albion (manager, 1984-85).

Recovering well from a broken leg, suffered early on with United, Johnny Giles became a brilliant midfield schemer whose footballing career spanned almost 30 years. Unable to break into the team as an inside-forward, he switched to outside-right and won an FA Cup winners medal in that position with United in 1963. Then, perhaps surprisingly, he moved to Elland Road three months after that Wembley success, taking over from Bobby Collins and linking up in midfield with Billy Bremner. Over the next 12 years he won honours galore under Don Revie's management and scored

145

115 goals in 524 matches for Leeds before becoming West Bromwich Albion's first-ever player-manager, appointed in June 1975 in succession to Don Howe. He led Albion to promotion immediately.

Able to dictate play with intelligent passing, Giles was capped 60 times by the Republic of Ireland, whom he also managed for a short while in the late 1970s. He appeared in five FA Cup Finals, equalling the pre-war record set by Joe Hulme of Huddersfield Town and Arsenal.

Brother-in-law of Nobby Stiles, Giles became a soccer journalist and also worked for Irish television. His son, Michael, was briefly associated with West Brom.

Club record: 115 apps. 13 goals.

GILL, Anthony Dean
Born: Bradford, 6 March 1968
Career: Bradford & Keighley Schools, West Yorkshire Boys, MANCHESTER UNITED (apprentice June 1984, professional March 1986-December 1990).
Injuries, including a broken a leg, Achilles tendon and damaged ankle, ended defender Tony Gill's promising football career at the age of 22.
Club record: 14 apps. 2 goals

GILLESPIE, Keith Robert
Born: Bangor, Northern Ireland, 18 February 1975
Career: MANCHESTER UNITED (trainee July 1991, professional February 1993), Wigan Athletic (on loan, autumn 1993), Newcastle United (£1 million, early 1995 - in a deal involving Andy Cole), Blackburn Rovers (£2.25 million, January 1995), Wigan Athletic (on loan, early 2000).
Unable to establish himself in United's first team, winger Keith Gillespie moved to St James' Park as part of the deal that brought Andy Cole to Old Trafford. Fast, direct, good on the ball, he went on to make almost 150 appearances for Newcastle and followed up by helping Blackburn regain their Premiership status in 2001. Capped over 40 times by Northern Ireland, he had earlier been honoured by his country at schoolboy, Youth and Under-21 levels. He was an FA Youth Cup winner with United in 1992 and a League Cup winner with Blackburn ten years later.
Club record: 14 apps. 2 goals

GILLESPIE, Matthew
Born: Strathclyde, Scotland 24 December 1869.
Career: Strathclyde FC, Leith Athletic (1893), Lincoln City (1895), NEWTON HEATH (November 1896-May 1900).
A hat-trick hero in his first-ever game for the Heathens (a friendly against Fairfield FC), inside-forward Matt Gillespie went on to serve the club for four seasons and although occasionally his performances left a lot to be desired, he nevertheless drew up an excellent scoring record with the club.
Club record: 89 apps. 21 goals (also 24 'other' apps, 9 goals)

GIPPS, Thomas Savill
Born: Walthamstow, London, early 1888.
Career: Walthamstow FC, Tottenham Hotspur (professional 1907), Barrow (1910), MANCHESTER UNITED (May 1912-May 1920).
Half-back Tommy Gipps played intermittently for United during the three seasons leading up the First World War and although he was re-signed after the hostilities he failed to make the first XI and was given a free transfer.
Club record: 23 apps.

GIVENS, Daniel Joseph
Born: Dublin, 9 April 1949
Career: Dublin Rangers (1964), MANCHESTER UNITED (apprentice September 1965, professional December 1966), Luton Town (£15,000, April 1971), Queen's Park Rangers (£40,000, 1972), Birmingham City (£165,000, 1978), AFC Bournemouth (on loan, 1980), Sheffield United (1981), Xamax Neuchatel, Switzerland (summer 1981, retired in May 1987 to become coach).
A very useful striker, with good pace, 'Don' Givens was given very few opportunities to show off his talents at Old Trafford. However, after leaving the club he did very well, and went on to score more than 130 goals in close on 450 League and Cup appearances before moving abroad.
A League Championship winner with Xamax Neuchatel (1986-87), he stayed in Switzerland as a coach after retiring, before moving back to Ireland where he became manager of the Eire Under-21 side. Capped 56 times at senior international level (six coming as a United player) he actually appeared in his first game for the Republic of Ireland before he had made his debut for the Reds! Givens' father was a champion hurdler.
Club record: 9 apps. one goal

GLADWIN, George William E
Born: Chesterfield, 28 March 1907
Career: Worksop Town, Doncaster Rovers (1930), MANCHESTER UNITED (£3,000, February 1937). Guested for

Wrexham, Doncaster Rovers and West Ham United during WW2. Forced to retire during the hostilities after being wounded in France.

A tall, strong, adept player, George Gladwin performed as a wing-half or inside-forward and prior to joining United he had given Doncaster Rovers excellent service, appearing 226 League games and scoring 22 goals. He was a member of United's Second Division promotion-winning side in 1938, having just seven outings.

Club record: 28 apps. one goal

GLASGOW RANGERS

United beat Rangers to win the Coronation Cup in 1953.
A crowd of 31,818 saw United beat Rangers 1-0 in a friendly at Ibrox Park in August 1990. Four years later Eric Cantona was sent-off playing for United in a pre-season tournament v.Rangers at Ibrox Park.
Players with both clubs include: J Cunningham, A Forsyth, A Goram, A Kanchelskis, J McCartney, G McQueen (Rangers trialist), A Montgomery, J Nicholl (Rangers player-coach), J Turnbull, R Wilkins
Also associated: ASM Duncan & Sir A Ferguson (Rangers players, United managers), G Livingstone (United player, Rangers trainer)

GLOSSOP (North End)

Heathens/United's League results v. Glossop:

Season	Div	Home	Away
1898-99	2	W 3-0	W 2-1
1900-01	2	W 3-0	L 0-1
1901-02	2	W 1-0	D 0-0
1902-03	2	D 1-1	W 3-1
1903-04	2	W 3-1	W 5-0
1904-05	2	W 4-1	W 2-1
1905-06	2	W 5-2	W 2-1

Summary of League results

	P	W	D	L	F	A
Division 2	14	11	2	1	34	10
Home	7	6	1	0	20	5
Away	7	5	1	1	14	5
Total	14	11	2	1	34	10

Fact File

The town of Glossop has the distinction of being the smallest town to have housed a club playing in English football's 'top flight'. Formed in 1887 (thanks to the benevolence of Samuel Hill-Wood, later to be Chairman of Arsenal FC, beginning a Highbury dynasty lasting to this day), Glossop North End were elected to the Second Division of the Football League in 1898. Despite losing twice to Newton Heath they won the Second Division title in their first season. Their suffix 'North End' had been added to attract attention in their formative years; now the club was in the 'top flight' playing their heroes Preston North End, they saw no need to continue using their name, becoming 'Glossop'. They remained as a League Club, having been relegated back to Division Two after just one season, until 1915, resigning in 1919 before football was resumed after The Great War.

Players with both clubs include: H Birchenough, J Cairns, J Connachan, P Coyne, R Donaldson, J Dow, T Fitzsimmons, L Halton, T Knighton (United reserve), J Montgomery, H Rothwell, J Saunders.

147

GOALKEEPERS

In January 1893, United called on three outfield players to keep 'goal' in the game at Stoke after regular custodian Jimmy Warner had missed the train. Willie Stewart, Tom Fitzsimmons and John Clements all stood between the posts as the 10 men of United lost 7-1.

Sunderland used three different goalkeepers during the League game with United at Old Trafford in November 1966 - Jim Montgomery, Charlie Hurley and John Parke. David Herd still netted four goals in United's 5-0 victory.

Versatile half-back Walter Cartwright was asked to keep goal for United throughout the League games with Rotherham Town in March 1896 and Doncaster Rovers in February 1903. United won the first game 3-2 (away) and drew the second 2-2.

Defender Johnny Carey was United's goalkeeper throughout the First Division League game at Sunderland in February 1953. The result was a 2-2 draw.

Jackie Blanchflower kept goal for United in the friendly v. Helsingborg in May 1956 and a year later he took over from Ray Wood when he was injured as early as the 7th minute of the 1957 FA Cup Final against Aston Villa.

Several other 'outfield' players have donned the goalkeeper's jersey in an emergency for United.

They include Duncan Edwards in the 1956 FA Charity clash with Manchester City (he replaced Ray Wood during the first half); centre-forward Alex Dawson who replaced the injured Harry Gregg in the 2-0 home League win over double-chasing Spurs in January 1961; striker David Herd who donned the green jersey in two home League games against Liverpool in November 1963 and Blackburn Rovers in November 1965 (he too replaced the injured Gregg on both occasions); David Sadler who deputised for Alex Stepney at Arsenal in August 1970 and Brian Greenhoff who also stood in for Stepney in the away game at Birmingham City some two years later.

United's club secretary, Leslie Olive, was pressed into service during the 1952-53 season, keeping goal in two League matches when all three first team 'keepers (Wood, Crompton and Allen) were injured. He played at Newcastle United (won 2-1) and at Old Trafford against West Bromwich Albion (2-2 draw).

The unfortunate Tommy Breen conceded a goal after just 59 seconds of his League debut for United v. Leeds in November 1936. Fifteen months later the unlucky Breen conceded an own-goal (by touching a throw-in over the line) in United's FA Cup-tie at Barnsley in January 1938.

Early in 1961, Ronnie Briggs had 14 goals put past him in his first three games for United - six by Leicester, and eight by Sheffield Wednesday in two FA Cup encounters (1-1 draw and a 7-2 defeat).

One of the most remarkable goalkeeping performances for United was by Pat Dunne. He arrived at Old Trafford in May 1964 from Shamrock Rovers, aged 21, expecting to be the club's reserve 'keeper, Gaskell and Gregg vying with each other for the first team spot. After Gaskell had played in the first five matches of the 1964-65 season, injuries meant that Dunne had to play against Everton in a First Division match. Although the game ended in a 3-3 draw, Dunne played well and retained his place for the rest of the season, winning a League Championship medal in the process as well as playing in the semi-final of both the FA Cup and Inter Cities Fairs Cup. Dunne appeared in 37 League games that season and conceded just 29 goals, keeping 15 clean sheets. He also lined up in 21 Cup matches, yet played in only eight more games for the club before losing his place to Alex Stepney.

Dunne was not on the losing side in his first 19 games for United (8 September to 28 November 1964 inclusive (15 in the League and four in the Inter-Cities Fairs Cup).

Jimmy Rimmer was 12th man for United when they won the European Cup in 1968 and so collected a winners' medal. In 1981 he went off after just 10 minutes of Aston Villa's triumphant European Cup Final triumph over Bayern Munich and gained a second winners' medal in the process.

Gary Bailey saved three penalty kicks in United's 6-0 defeat by Ipswich Town at Portman Road in March 1980 (two were legitimate, the other was re-taken).

Goalkeeper Les Sealey played in only 56 senior games for United but still gained winners medals in the 1990 FA Cup Final and the 1991 European Cup-winners Cup Final as well as runners-up medals in two League Cup Finals (1991 and 1994).

Peter Schmeichel at 6ft 4ins is believed to have been United's tallest goalkeeper. He made 94 consecutive League appearances for the Reds from 14 March 1992 to 1 May 1994 - a club record for a 'keeper. He conceded only one goal in 17 matches at Old Trafford during the 1994-95 season. Between April 1994 and May 1995 the 'Great' Dane also managed 17 clean sheets in home games, keeping his fortress intact for almost 26 hours.

United utilised four different goalkeepers in four successive League games in two separate sequences during March 1896. They repeated the four-keeper act in February/March 1934 and did it again halfway through the year of 1991....playing four different custodians in successive matches. Those used in the latter year were Gary Walsh v. Crystal Palace (League), Les Sealey v. Barcelona (European Cup-winners Cup Final) and Mark Bosnich v. Tottenham Hotspur (League) in the last three fixtures of the 1990-91 season (all in May). The Aussie then handed over to Peter Schmeichel on the opening day of the 1991-92 season on 17 August v. Notts County (League).

United called up five different goalkeepers to their League side in 1952-53 - Reg Allen, Jack Crompton, Les Olive and Ray Wood plus defender Johnny Carey (mentioned earlier).

Five were also used in the calendar year of 1991 - Bosnich, Schmeichel, Sealey, Walsh and Ian Wilkinson. Jim Leighton was also at the club but wasn't called into first team action.

Three goalkeepers have all appeared in just one senior game for United - Billy Behan (1934), Tony Hawksworth (1956) and Ian Wilkinson (1991).

The oldest goalkeeper to appear in United's first XI (at senior level) is Raimond van der Gouw, aged 39 years 48 days, v. Charlton Athletic at Old Trafford on 11th May 2002. Jack Hacking was 37 years, 42 days old v. Norwich City in February 1935 and Andy Goram was 37 years, 31 days old when he played against Southampton in May 2001.

Sealey was 36 years, 179 days old when he played in the 1994 League Cup Final.

Dave Gaskell is United's youngest 'keeper at 16 years, 19 days v. Manchester City in the 1956 FA Charity Shield game at Maine Road. He made his League bow against Spurs in November 1957 at the age of 17 years, 56 days and was beaten by a Bobby Smith hat-trick as United went down 4-3 at Old Trafford.

Alex Stepney scored two League penalties for United in season 1973-74 v. Leicester City and Birmingham City (both at home). He also missed one against Wolves. In the build-up prior to that campaign Stepney had netted from the spot in a penalty shoot-out against Penarol in a friendly.

Peter Schmeichel headed United's last minute equaliser against Rotor Volgograd in a UEFA Cup clash at Old Trafford in September 1995. The game ended 2-2 but United still went on out the away goal rule.

Harry Gregg also scored a goal for United - doing so from the spot in a 10-1 friendly win over the Ukranian National side on tour in the USA in June 1960.

Pat Jennings, the Spurs 'keeper, clearing his lines, scored a goal from a distance of some 100 yards (the ball bounced over Alex Stepney's head) during the 1967 FA Charity Shield game at Old Trafford which ended in a 3-3 draw.

Mike Pinner won 51 caps for England at Amateur level and made his League debut for United in February 1961.

United used four different goalkeepers in League games in 1960-61 - Harry Gregg, David Gaskell, Ron Briggs and Mike Pinner.

Jimmy Rimmer appeared in both legs of the 1970-71 League Cup semi-final for Manchester United against Villa - his future club

United used three different goalkeepers during their 1965-66 European Cup campaign - Pat Dunne, David Gaskell & Harry Gregg.

In an emergency, Newton Heath goalkeeper Jimmy Whitehouse played at inside-left at Walsall in a League Division Two match in February 1901.

For a brief period during 1991 United were blessed with four international goalkeepers - Jim Leighton (Scotland), Mark Bosnich (Australia) and Peter Schmeichel (Denmark) at senior level and England Under-21 star Gary Walsh.

Since first entering the FA Cup competition in 1886, United have so far utilised a total of 85 different goalkeepers in major first team matches (45 before WW2 and 40 since 1945).

'Keeper Arthur Chesters conceded 22 goals in his four League outings for United in 1930-31.

Former United goalkeeper Jack Crompton became a coach in Tenerife after retiring.

148

Goalkeeping Appearance Records

Here is a list of United's top ten goalkeepers in terms of appearances made for the club:

Name	Seasons	League	Total
Alex Stepney	(1966-78)	433	539
Alf Steward	(1920-32)	309	326
Gary Bailey	(1978-87)	294	375
Peter Schmeichel	(1991-99)	292	398
Harry Moger	(1903-12)	242	266
Harry Gregg	(1957-67)	210	247
Jack Crompton	(1945-56)	191	212
Jack Mew	(1912-26)	186	199
Ray Wood	(1949-59)	178	208
Frank Barrett	(1896-1900)	118	136

* One other 'keeper, Robert Beale (1912-15) made 105 League appearances for the club (112 in all).

GOALS & GOALSCORERS

List of United's leading goalscorers in the various competitions.

All Senior Games (combined)
(qualification 100 goals)

253 Bobby Charlton
239 Denis Law
211 Jack Rowley
181 George Best
179 Dennis Viollet
168 Joe Spence
162 Mark Hughes
149 Stan Pearson
145 David Herd
131 Tommy Taylor
127 Brian McClair
122 Andy Cole
101 'Sandy' Turnbull
100 Joe Cassidy
100 Bryan Robson
100 Ole Gunnar Solskjaer
100 George Wall

Football League/Premiership
(qualification: 75 goals)

199 Bobby Charlton
182 Jack Rowley
171 Denis Law
159 Dennis Viollet
158 Joe Spence
137 George Best
127 Stan Pearson
119 Mark Hughes
114 David Herd
112 Tommy Taylor
94 Andy Cole
90 Joe Cassidy
90 'Sandy' Turnbull
89 George Wall
88 Brian McClair
78 Lou Macari
75 Ole Gunnar Solskjaer

FA Cup:
(qualification: 15 goals)

34 Denis Law
26 Jack Rowley
21 George Best
21 Stan Pearson
19 Bobby Charlton
17 Mark Hughes
15 David Herd

League Cup:
(qualification: 9 goals)

19 Brian McClair
16 Mark Hughes
10 Lou Macari
9 George Best
9 Steve Coppell
9 Lee Sharpe
9 Norman Whiteside

European Cups
(qualification: 12 goals)

28 Denis Law
22 Bobby Charlton
19 Andy Cole
17 Paul Scholes
15 Ryan Giggs
15 Ole Gunnar Solskjaer
14 David Herd
14 Roy Keane
13 Dennis Viollet
12 David Beckham

Football Alliance
(qualification 10 goals)

25 Alf Farman
20 Bob Donaldson
18 Willie Stewart
11 Jack Doughty

Wartime (1915-19)
(qualification: 12)

69 Wilf Woodcock
40 George Anderson
13 Ernie Ellis

Wartime (1939-46)
(Not inc. void League games + FA Cup-ties)
(Qualification: 25 goals)

160 Jack Smith
100 Jack Rowley
52 Johnny Carey
52 Stan Pearson
47 Billy Bryant
28 Johnny Morris

Own-Goals

In October 1923, playing against Manchester United in a League game at Boundary Park, the Oldham Athletic full-back Sam Wynne conceded two own-goals and also scored twice for his own club in a 3-2 win for the Latics. This was the first time this had ever happened in top-class football and it wasn't until 1977 that a player did it again. On this occasion it was Irish international Chris Nicholl of Aston Villa who 'scored four' times in the 2-2 draw with Leicester City at Filbert Street.

The unlucky FC Porto defender Alfredo Manuel Ferreira Murca conceded two own-goals against United in a European Cup Winners' Cup clash at Old Trafford in November 1977. United won the game 5-2 but went out 5-6 on aggregate.

United benefited from own-goals scored by the Tottenham Hotspur defender Phil Beal in League games in December 1965 and August 1968.

United received six own-goals in League football in 1975-76 (two in one game v. Newcastle).

Nobby Stiles scored an 'own-goal' for rivals Manchester City in the local derby at Old Trafford in September 1961 and he did likewise at Maine Road in January 1967. He also netted for United in that first League game.

Bryan Robson scored for both sides (United and Sheffield Wednesday) in a League game at Hillsborough in October 1987. The Reds won 4-2.

149

Debut Goals

Joe Spence grabbed four goals when making his first appearance for United - in a Lancashire Section game against Bury in March 1919.

Charlie Sagar celebrated his League debut for United with a hat-trick against Bristol City in a Second Division game in September 1905.

Harold Halse scored after just 30 seconds play when making his United League debut against Sheffield Wednesday in March 1908.

Denis Law (v. WBA, League, August 1962 and Huddersfield Town, FAC, March 1963), Tommy Taylor (two v. PNE, League, March 1953 and RSC Anderlecht EC, September 1956) both scored on their United debuts in the competitions stated.

Neil Webb scored on his debut for United in four different competitions....the Football League (v. Arsenal, at home, August 1989), FA Cup (v. Oldham Athletic, semi-final at Maine Road, April 1990), League Cup (v. Halifax Town at The Shay, September 1990) and in the European Cup-winners Cup (v. Pecsi Munkas, at Old Trafford, also in September 1990).

Centre-forward Alex Dawson scored on his League debut for the Reds against Burnley in April 1957, netted in his first FA Cup-tie v. Sheffield Wednesday in February 1958 and then hit another goal on his League Cup baptism versus Exeter City in October 1960.

David Herd scored on his United debut in the FA Cup, League Cup & European Cup-winners Cup but did not find the net on his League debut at West Ham; however he scored on his home debut four days later v. Chelsea.

Tommy Reid notched two goals when making his League debut for United v. West Ham in February 1929. He followed up, almost two years later, with a hat-trick on his FA Cup debut at Stoke City in January 1931.

Hat-trick Facts

The player who has scored most hat-tricks for United is Denis Law, with a total of 18 (including seven in the 1963-64 season). He also netted trebles in three European Cup competitions, including a hat-trick and a fourtimer in the first and second legs respectively of the 1st round European Cup tie against Waterford in September/October 1968.

Charlie Sagar celebrated his League debut for United with a hat-trick against Bristol City in a Second Division game in September 1905.

Teddy Sheringham was 34 years, 208 days old when he scored a hat-trick in a 5-0 win against Southampton on 28 October 2000 - the oldest United player to claim three goals in a game!

United's youngest hat-trick hero is Jack Rowley, aged 17 years 58 days v. Swansea Town (Division 2) in December 1937. He scored four goals in a 5-1 win - only his second League match for the club.

Alex Dawson became United's youngest post-war hat-trick hero at 18 years 35 days, when he struck home a treble in the 5-3 FA Cup semi-final replay win over Fulham at Highbury in 1958.

Two players have scored double hat-tricks (six goals) in a game for United - Harold Halse v. Swindon Town in the 1911 FA Charity Shield game (three goals in each half) and George Best in an 8-2 FA Cup win at Northampton in 1970.

A third player, Dick Smith, scored six times for Newton Heath v. Walsall Town Swifts in a League Division 2 match at Clayton in March 1895 (won 14-0). Unfortunately for the Heathens and Smith himself, both records were chalked off by the League who, after a protest from Walsall over of the state of the pitch, agreed to 'replay' the game which the Heathens won 9-0!

Jack Rowley fell one short of a double-treble with five goals for United against Yeovil in an FA Cup-tie at Old Trafford in February 1949 and Andy Cole hit a nap hand in a 9-0 Premiership defeat of Ipswich Town at Old Trafford in March 1995.

Denis Law and Jack Rowley both scored at least four goals in a game for United on four occasions. Rowley's tally included that fivetimer v. Yeovil (above), a feat Law never achieved.

Charlie Mitten bagged a fourtimer in United's 7-0 home League win Aston Villa at Old Trafford in March 1950; three of his goals came via the penalty spot.

Dennis Viollet hit a hat-trick for United in both League games against Burnley in the 1960-61 season.

United's inside-right George Mutch scored a hat-trick in the space of five minutes during a 4-1 home League win over Barnsley in September 1934.

Henry Boyd claimed hat-tricks in each of the first two Football League games at the start of the 1987-98 season v. Lincoln City and Burton Swifts.

Chris Taylor scored just six League goals for United (two hat-tricks) over a period of 10 days in April/May 1926 - the first v. Sunderland, the second v. West Bromwich Albion, both at Old Trafford.

Jack Rowley weighed in with three hat-tricks in quick succession at the start of the 1951-52 League campaign - the first two came in the opening matches against West Bromwich Albion (away) and Middlesbrough (home) and his third arrived in the seventh match against Stoke City at Old Trafford.

In 1948 Stan Pearson netted a sparkling hat-trick in United's semi-final win over Derby County at Hillsborough on the way to the first post-war FA Cup Final triumph.

Alex Dawson scored three hat-tricks in successive Central League games for United in season 1959-60.....a unique hat-trick of hat-tricks!

Andy Ritchie was also aged 18 when he netted a treble in United's 4-1 League success over Leeds (home) in March 1979. He was dropped for the next game!

Bob Donaldson and Willie Stewart both recorded trebles when United beat Wolves 10-1 in December 1892. Donaldson and Alf Farman notched hat-tricks in the 7-1 win over Derby County in December 1892; Billy Bryant and Joe Cassidy did likewise versus Darwen in December 1898 (won 9-0) and Sandy Turnbull & Jimmy Turnbull followed suit in the 6-1 FA Cup triumph over Blackburn in February 1909.

Dennis Viollet (with four goals) and Tommy Taylor (3) were hat-trick heroes in the 10-0 demolition job on RSC Anderlecht in the European Cup in September 1956 and Viollet and Albert Quixall netted three goals apiece in the 6-0 League victory over Burnley in April 1961.

Three players who scored hat-tricks to no avail for United were (a) Tommy Reid in the 7-4 home defeat by Newcastle in 1930-31 and (b) Jimmy Bullock v. Leicester City in the same season when United lost 5-4 at Filbert Street and (c) Dennis Viollet v. Burnley (a) in 1960-61 when United lost 5-3.

Jesper Olsen scored his only hat-trick for the Reds in the home League game with WBA on 22 February 1986 - past debutant Baggies' goalkeeper Stuart Naylor.

Ernie Goldthorpe scored a hat-trick in four minutes for United v. Notts County in February 1923. He struck between the 62nd and 66th minutes to finish with four goals in United's comprehensive 6-1 win.

Over the years United players have scored hat-tricks on five separate occasions in games at Leicester.

Denis Law netted a hat-trick against Ipswich Town at Portman Road two seasons running - in 1962-63 and 1963-64.

David Herd's fourtimer for United against Sunderland in November 1966 was scored past three different 'keepers. Those who donned the goalie's jersey for the Wearsiders were Jim Montgomery, Charlie Hurley and John Parke. United won the game 5-0.

Dick Smith is the only Heathens/United player to have netted four goals in a game against Manchester City - doing so in the very first Football League game between the clubs in November 1894. The Heathens won 5-2.

When United beat neighbours City 5-0 in a Premiership game at Old Trafford in November 1994. Winger Andrei Kanchelskis scored a hat-trick - becoming the first player to achieve that feat in a Manchester derby since City's Francis Lee in December 1970. The previous United player to net a treble in a Manchester derby had been Alex Dawson in December 1960, also at Old Trafford when City were defeated 5-1.

Bryan Robson scored a hat-trick for both West Bromwich Albion and England, but failed to claim a treble for United.

William 'Dixie' Dean (Everton) scored all his side's five goals against United at Goodison Park in October 1927.

Welsh ace Ron Davies, later to join United, scored all Southampton's goals in their 4-1 League win at Old Trafford in August 1969.

Almost 52,500 fans saw England international midfielder Martin Peters of Spurs also net a fourtimer when United lost 4-1 at Old Trafford in October 1972. His 1966 World Cup colleague Bobby Charlton scored in reply.

Dennis Bailey's hat-trick for QPR against United on New Year's Day 1992 was the last by a visiting player to Old Trafford (League or Cup).

Dwight Yorke scored a Premiership hat-trick for United in just 22 minutes against Arsenal at Old Trafford during the 2000-01 season. United won 6-1.

Five United players have scored hat-tricks at full international level for England - Bobby Charlton, Bryan Robson, Jack Rowley, Paul Scholes and Tommy Taylor. Rowley, in fact, scored a fourtimer against Northern Ireland in 1949; Charlton netted four trebles - against USA in 1959, Luxembourg 1960, Mexico 1961 and Switzerland 1963 - Robson scored three times against Turkey in 1984, Scholes likewise versus Poland in 1999, while Taylor grabbed two hat-tricks, the first against Denmark in 1956 and the second against the Republic of Ireland the following year.

Centre-forward Ted MacDougall, soon to join United, scored nine times for Bournemouth in their 11-0 FA Cup win over luckless Margate at Dean Court in November 1971.

Willie Stewart scored Newton Heath's first hat-trick in a Football Alliance game - against Small Heath in April 1890.

Former United player Wilf Lievesey scored a hat-trick of headers for Exeter City against Gillingham in April 1927. He also scored a fourth goal with his foot!

Consecutive Scoring

Liam 'Billy' Whelan sharess the record for United in terms of scoring goals in successive League games. He netted in each of eight consecutive First Division League matches covering a period of six weeks in 1956 - commencing on 5 September with the winner in a 2-1 victory at Chelsea and ending on 20 October with a strike in the 5-2 defeat by Everton at Old Trafford. Dutchman Ruud van Nistelrooy also scored in eight consecutive Premier/League games for United, commencing on 12 December 2001 with a goal in a 5-0 home romp over Derby County and ending with a penalty kick against Blackburn Rovers at Old Trafford on 10 January 2002 - a Premiership League record. The Dutchman scored 10 times in this sequence and during this same spell he also netted twice in a thrilling 3-2 FA Cup victory against Aston Villa, to set a United record of scoring in nine consecutive senior games.

George Best, Bobby Charlton and Dwight Yorke all scored in six successive League and/or Cup games for United.

Players who have scored 20 or more competitive goals in a season for United in Football Alliance, Football League, Premiership, FA Cup, League Cup, European, Charity Shield etc.

Season	Players
1891-92	Bob Donaldson (20), Alf Farman (20)
1894-95	Dick Smith (20)
1896-97	Joe Cassidy (25)
1897-98	Henry Boyd (22)
1898-99	Joe Cassidy (20)
1905-06	Jack Picken (25), Jack Peddie (20), Charlie Sagar (20)
1907-08	'Sandy' Turnbull (27), George Wall (22)
1908-09	Jimmy Turnbull (25)
1910-11	Enoch West (20)
1911-12	Enoch West (23)
1912-13	Enoch West (22)
1925-26	Frank McPherson (20)
1927-28	Joe Spence (24)
1928-29	Jimmy Hanson (20)
1930-31	Tommy Reid (20)
1935-36	George Mutch (23)
1946-47	Jack Rowley (28)
1947-48	Jack Rowley (28), Stan Pearson (26), Johnny Morris (21)
1948-49	Jack Rowley (30), Charlie Mitten (23)
1949-50	Jack Rowley (23)
1950-51	Stan Pearson (22)
1951-52	Jack Rowley (30), Stan Pearson (22)
1953-54	Tommy Taylor (23)
1954-55	Dennis Viollet (21), Tommy Taylor (20)
1955-56	Tommy Taylor (25), Dennis Viollet (20)

1956-57	Tommy Taylor (34), Liam Whelan (33), Dennis Viollet (26)
1957-58	Dennis Viollet (23), Tommy Taylor (22)
1958-59	Bobby Charlton (29), Dennis Viollet (21)
1959-60	Dennis Viollet (32), Bobby Charlton (21)
1960-61	Bobby Charlton (21), Alex Dawson (20)
1962-63	Denis Law (29), David Herd (21)
1063-64	Denis Law (46), David Herd (27)
1964-65	Denis Law (39), David Herd (28), John Connelly (20)
1965-66	David Herd (33), Denis Law (24)
1966-67	Denis Law (25)
1967-68	George Best (32)
1968-69	Denis Law (30), George Best (22)
1969-70	George Best (23), Brian Kidd (20)
1970-71	George Best (21)
1971-72	George Best (26)
1976-77	Gordon Hill (22)
1984-85	Mark Hughes (24)
1987-88	Brian McClair (31)
1990-91	Mark Hughes (21), Brian McClair (21)
1991-92	Brian McClair (25)
1993-94	Eric Cantona (25), Mark Hughes (21)
1997-98	Andy Cole (26)
1998-99	Dwight Yorke (29), Andy Cole (24)
1999-00	Dwight Yorke (23), Andy Cole (22)
2000-01	Teddy Sheringham (21)
2001-02	Ruud van Nistelrooy (36), Ole Gunnar Solskjaer (26)

Players with 20 or more League goals in a season

1891-92	Bob Donaldson (20)*
1897-98	Henry Boyd (22)*
1905-06	Jack Picken (20)
1907-08	'Sandy' Turnbull (25)*
1912-13	Enoch West (21)

1927-28	Joe Spence (22)
1935-36	George Mutch (21)
1946-47	Jack Rowley (26)*
1947-48	Jack Rowley (23)
1951-52	Jack Rowley (30)*
1953-54	Tommy Taylor (22)
1954-55	Tommy Taylor (20), Dennis Viollet (20)
1955-56	Tommy Taylor (25), Dennis Viollet (20)
1956-57	Liam Whelan (26), Tommy Taylor (22)
1958-59	Bobby Charlton (29), Dennis Viollet (21)
1959-60	Dennis Viollet (32)*
1960-61	Bobby Charlton (21)
1962-63	Denis Law (23)
1963-64	Denis Law (30), David Herd (20)
1964-65	Denis Law (28), David Herd (20)
1965-66	David Herd (24)
1966-67	Denis Law (23)
1967-68	George Best (28)
1987-88	Brian McClair (24)
1999-00	Dwight Yorke (20)
2001-02	Ruud van Nistelrooy (23)
	* New club record at the time

Players with 10 or more Cup* goals in a season

1956-57	Tommy Taylor (12)
1963-64	Denis Law (16)
1964-65	Denis Law (11)
1968-69	Denis Law (16)
1990-91	Mark Hughes (11)
1997-98	Andy Cole (10)
1998-99	Dwight Yorke (11)
2001-02	Ruud van Nistelrooy (13)
	* FA Cup, League Cup & all European Competitions

Goal-Talk

The most goals scored by a United player in a single season is 46 - by Denis Law in 1963-64. His tally comprised 30 in the Football League, 10 in the FA Cup and six in the European Cup-winners Cup.

Dennis Viollet's tally of 32 in the First Division in 1959-60, is a club record for most League goals in a campaign. Viollet was also the First Division's top marksman that season.

With 24 goals in only 33 League and FA Cup appearances for the club, Charlie Sagar had the best scoring ratio in terms of goals per game for United. His netted 20 goals in 30 League outings between 1905 and 1907.

Tommy Taylor had scored 131 goals in 191 first-class appearances for United before he lost his life on the Munich runway. He claimed 112 goals in 166 First Division matches to add to the 26 in 44 appearances for Barnsley.

Ronnie Burke hit 22 goals in his 35 senior appearances for the club (16 coming in 28 League games).

Two players have scored six goals in a competitive game for United - Harold Halse in the 8-4 FA Charity Shield win over Swindon Town in 1911 and George Best in an 8-2 FA Cup victory over Northampton Town in 1970.

Andy Cole (5) has netted most goals for United in a Premiership game v. Ipswich Town in March 1995, when the Reds won 9-0. Cole also netted four goals for United in a 5-1 Premiership win over Newcastle in August 1999.

Ole Gunnar Solskjaer scored four goals (after coming on as a substitute) in an 8-1 win at Nottingham Forest in February 1999, and followed up with another fourtimer against Everton in December 1999 (won 5-1), the only Premiership player so far to achieve the feat twice.

The most goals scored by a United player in a League game is 4 - and so far 15 players have achieved this feat. They are in A-Z order: Tom Bamford (v. Chesterfield, November 1937), Neil Dewar (v. Burnley, September 1933), Ernie Goldthorpe (v. Notts Co, February 1923), Alan Gowling (v. Southampton, February 1971), David Herd (v. Sunderland, November 1966), Denis Law (v. Ipswich, November 1962, v. Stoke C, December 1963 and Aston Villa, October 1964), Tom Manley (v. Port Vale, February 1936), Charlie Mitten (v. Aston Villa, March 1950), Jack Picken (v. Middlesbrough, April 1910), Jack Rowley (v. Swansea, December 1937, v. Charlton Ath, August 1947 and Huddersfield T, November 1947), Dick Smith (v. Manchester City, November 1894), Joe Spence (v. Crystal Pal, April 1924 and West Ham, February 1930), Tommy Taylor (v. Cardiff C, October 1954), Jimmy Turnbull (v. Middlesbrough, September 1908) and 'Sandy' Turnbull (v. W Arsenal, November 1907).

George Best (six v. Northampton T, February 1970), Jimmy Hanson (four v. Brentford, January 1928) and Jack Rowley (five v. Yeovil, February 1949) have scored most goals in an FA Cup-tie for United.

Dick Smith netted six goals & Joe Cassidy four in a 14-0 home League win over Walsall Town Swifts in March 1895. The game was 'replayed' after a protest and their scoring achievements counted for nothing.

Bryan Robson scored in each of 21 League seasons during his career (1974-95) starting off with West Bromwich Albion, then United and finally Middlesbrough.

United players (plus three opponents) between them netted a total of 103 goals in each of the 1956-57 and 1958-59 League seasons.

United, in fact, registered 143 competitive goals in 1956-57 (103 in the First Division, 15 in the FA Cup, 24 in the European Cup and one in the Charity Shield).

United scored thirteen goals in their four FA Cup games in January/February 1998, including ten in the first two. They beat Chelsea 5-3 away and Walsall 5-1 at home before succumbing in the fifth round to Barnsley, losing 3-2 at Oakwell after a 1-1 draw.

United's ace marksman Jack Rowley scored 14 goals (including three hat-tricks) in seven games at the start of the 1951-52 season.

Liam 'Billy' Whelan netted for United in eight successive League games during September & October 1956 (a club record).

Halfway through the 1961-62 season (between November and January) centre-forward David Herd scored in six successive competitive games for United (five League and one FAC).

Jack Rowley was United leading goalscorer (in League games and, indeed, in all competitions) in five of the first six post-war seasons (after WW2): He missed out to Stan Pearson in 1950-51.

Tommy Taylor scored most League goals for the club in 1953-54, 1955-56 & 1957-58 and shared the honour with Dennis Viollet in 1954-55.

Denis Law was chief marksman in 1962-63, 1963-64, 1964-65 & 1966-67 before George Best took over the mantle in 1967-68. Best remained as United's top League goalscorer in 1968-69, 1969-70, 1970-71 and 1971-72, thus holding top spot five seasons running, a club record.

Joe Cassidy top-scored for United in four out of five seasons between 1895-96 to 1899-1900. Joe Spence also headed the scoring charts on four occasions (1919-20, 1921-22, 1926-27 & 1927-28). He also shared top spot in 1920-21 & 1929-30.

Enoch West was United's leading marksman three seasons running: 1910-2 to 1912-13 inclusive.

Frank McPherson scored in each of United's first five League games at the start of the 1926-27 season.

Centre-back Steve Bruce bagged a total of 19 goals for United in the 1990-91 season (a record haul for a central defender in British football). His tally included 11 penalties and he was United's joint leading scorer in League matches with 13. Bruce ended his United career with a total of 79 goals to his credit - a record for a defender at any level.

Four players - George Best, Mark Hughes, Jack Rowley and Joe Spence - each topped United's scoring charts in five different seasons.

Rowley netted his first senior goals (four of them) for United on 4 December 1937 against Swansea Town in a Division Two game at Old Trafford. He claimed his last United goal 17 years, one month and eight days later against Reading in a 3rd round FA Cup replay on 12 January 1955, also at Old Trafford.

Welsh international winger Billy Meredith was 46 years and 197 days old when he scored his last senior goal for United against Everton (at home) on 12 February 1921 (Division 1). Bryan Robson was a little over 37 years and three months old when he netted his last goal for the Reds against Oldham Athletic in an FA Cup-tie in April 1994.

Three other United players who scored their last goal for the club after reaching the age 36, are Jimmy Delaney v. Charlton Athletic in September 1950, defender Bill Foulkes versus Real Madrid in the 1968 European Cup semi-final and Jack Warner in an FA Cup-tie against Charlton in February 1948.

The youngest goalscorer at League level for United has been Norman Whiteside, who was a week past his 17th birthday when he netted against Stoke City in May 1982.

United opened their 1905-06 League programme with a 5-1 home win over Bristol City and ended it with a 6-0 defeat of Burton United. Charlie Sagar scored a hat-trick in the first game and a brace in the last. United scored five or more goals on ten occasions this term (eight League, two FA Cup).

George Best headed the First Division scoring charts in 1967-68 with a future United player, Ron Davies (then of Southampton).

United scored at least one goal in each of 27 consecutive League games during the 1958-59 season (mid-October to early April).

Shay Brennan scored twice on his debut for United in an FA Cup tie against Sheffield Wednesday in February 1958 (the first game after Munich). He only netted four more goals in his next 354 senior appearances for the club.

Hugh McLenahan scored 12 goals in 116 appearances for United - but six of these came in five matches during April 1930.

Twenty different players (two of them opponents) found the net for United during the course of the 1899-1900 and 1994-95 seasons.

When United beat Wolves 10-1 in the League in 1892, six different players were on the scoresheet.

In season 1973-74, players wearing every shirt from 1-12, scored at last one goal for United that season (Alex Stepney was the goalkeeper). And in 1992-93 (the first season of Premiership football) goals were scored from players donning shirts numbered 2 to 11.

During the months of December and January in season 1992-93 (eleven matches played) eleven different United players scored goals at senior level.

United led Walsall Town Swifts 1-0 at half-time in their Second Division League game in April 1895. The final score was 9-0.

In the 1972-73 season United had on their books six players who had each netted over 100 League goals. They were George Best, Bobby Charlton, Wyn Davies, Denis Law, Ted MacDougall and Ian Storey-Moore.

United's last three League games of the 1959-60 yielded 20 goals with three fives! The Reds beat West Ham 5-3 at home, lost 5-2 at Arsenal and ended with a 5-0 win over Everton at Old Trafford.

Scottish international Ted MacDougall became the first player to finish up as leading scorer in three separate Divisions, doing so, in turn, with Bournemouth (Division 4) in 1970-71 and (Div. 3) in 1971-72 and Norwich City in 1975-76 (Div. 1). He played for United in 1972-73. MacDougall also holds the record for scoring most goals in an FA Cup-tie - nine for Bournemouth in an 11-0 victory over Margate in November 1971.

After Garry Birtles had joined United from Nottingham Forest in October 1980, it took him 30 games in Division One before he managed to secure his first League goal for the club - the winner against Swansea City (home) in September 1981, having made his League debut 11 months earlier. He did net in the FA Cup in between times!

Full-back Charlie Moore appeared in 328 first-class games for United (309 in the League) between 1919-30 and never scored a goal.

United have scored six or more goals in an away League game 16 times (more than any other club)..

In 1994 Eric Cantona became the first Frenchman to score in an FA Cup Final - netting two penalties for United in their 4-0 win over Chelsea.

Mark Hughes scored in four different matches for United at Wembley in 1993-94 - netting in the FA Charity Shield, the FA Cup semi-final, the League Cup Final and then the FA Cup Final.

United conceded a total of 19 goals in three successive League games during one week in September 1930. They lost 6-2 at Chelsea, 6-0 at home to Huddersfield Town and 7-4 at home to Newcastle United. During the entire month they conceded 30 goals in their seven League fixtures.

United conceded a club record total of 115 Football League goals in the 1930-31 season (37 at home, 78 away). They also let in six FA Cup goals.

In 1905-06, United's goal-scoring record in the League was 90 'for' and 28 'against' - a difference of 62.

In 1959-60 spectators certainly got good value for money when the 42 First Division matches involving the Reds produced 182 goals. United netted 102, while their opponents scored 80. The three FA Cup games played that season also produced a few goals - 11 of them.

In contrast, there were only 87 goals scored by United and their opponents in the 42 League fixtures in 1980-81 - a club record.

United blasted in 103 League goals in 1956-57 and again in 1958-59. In the first season Liam 'Billy' Whelan was top marksman with 26 goals followed by Tommy Taylor with 22 and Dennis Viollet 16. Bobby Charlton top-scored two seasons later with 29; Dennis Viollet netted 21 and Albert Scanlon 16.

The fewest League goals scored by United in a League season (since 1905) has been 38, in 1973-74 when they were relegated from the First Division.

United failed to score in 19 of their 42 League matches in that 1973-74 season.

United claimed only 14 goals in their 21 away League games in 1986-87.

United have gone five League games without a goal on three separate occasions (a) February-March 1902 (Division 2), (b) January-February 1924 (Division 2) and (c) February-March 1981 (Division 1). They also went six games (League and Cup) without scoring in January-February 1924.

United conceded only 23 goals in 42 Second Division matches in 1924-25.

In 1999-2000 United netted a record 97 goals in their Premiership programme of 38 matches.

United have scored a record 43 goals in FA Charity Shield matches and a record 31 in FA Cup Finals.

Denis Law, playing for arch-rivals Manchester City, once scored six goals in an abandoned FA Cup-tie against Luton Town in January 1961. His double hat-trick was scrubbed from the record books as City lost the 'replay' 3-1, Law again the scorer for City, making seven in all in a tie his team lost!

Billy Meredith scored 34 Division Two goals for Manchester City in 1898-99 - a record for a winger.

Prior to joining United Joe Spence hit 42 goals out of 49 for his school team Blucher Juniors in 1909-10.

Ole Gunnar Solskjaer has scored 100 goals in 253 games for United. He has netted 21 times in 104 'sub' outings and has hit 79 goals in his 149 starts.

Quick Scoring

Ryan Giggs found the net after just 15 seconds of United's Premiership game with Southampton in November 1995.

Ronnie Allen, the West Bromwich Albion and England centre-forward, put the Baggies 1-0 ahead after just 12 seconds of their League game at Old Trafford in December 1951. United hit back to win 5-1.

George Edwards of Aston Villa scored after only 13 seconds play when United visited Villa Park for a 3rd round FA Cup-tie in January 1948. The Reds went on to win 6-4.

Alan Ball of Arsenal also netted in the 13th second when United played the Gunners in a First Division game in November 1975.

In November 1938, Willie Hall (Spurs) scored a hat-trick for England against Ireland in an international match at Old Trafford inside three-and-a-minutes.

On the opening day of the 1966-67 season (20 August) United scored five goals in the first 23 minutes of their home game with West Bromwich Albion. The Baggies replied with three of their own later on as the Reds took the points with a 5-3 victory.

On 6 May 1967 United won 6-1 at West Ham. They were 3-0 ahead after 10 minutes and held a 4-0 advantage after 25 minutes.

On 13 October 1951 United trailed 2-1 away to Aston Villa at half-time in a League game. Within ten minutes of the restart United had scored four times to lead 5-2 which was the final result.

United were 3-0 up after just 23 minutes at Anfield in a Premiership game in January 1994. But Liverpool came back to earn a point at 3-3 with a 79th minute equaliser from Neil Ruddock.

Striker Ole Gunnar Solskjaer came off the bench to score four goals in the last 10 minutes of the Premiership game at Nottingham Forest in February 1999. United won 8-1.

In January 2002, United trailed Aston Villa 2-0 in a 3rd round FA Cup-tie. But three goals in a dramatic five-minute spell late in the game earned United victory.

Scoring Partnerships

'Sandy' Turnbull and Jimmy Turnbull were not related and were signed by the club from Manchester City and Leyton in December 1906 and May 1907 respectively.

During the three seasons of the Turnbulls, United also had Harold Halse in their attack and he scored 28 goals in total. Most of the goals were set up by wing-wizard Billy Meredith!

This was the Turnbull partnership

Season	Jimmy	Sandy	Totals
1907-08	11	27	38
1908-09	25	9	34
1909-10	9	13	22
Summary	45	49	94

After Jimmy had departed, Enoch 'Knocker' West (signed from Nottingham Forest) joined 'Sandy' Turnbull in United's attack. Between them they scored well over 100 goals for the club in three seasons.

Details of the red-hot Turnbull-West scoring partnership

Season	Turnbull	West	Totals
1910-11	20	20	40
1911-12	10	23	33
1912-13	10	22	32
Summary	40	65	105

United did not have two out and out goalscorers together during the inter-war years, Joe Spence carrying the work load on his shoulders for most of the time. Indeed, he netted 158 League goals for the club (in 481 matches) between 1919 and 1933.

Directly after WW2, Jack Rowley, who had arrived on the scene in the late 1930s, was joined in the United attack by Stan Pearson. The pair struck 312 goals in the first seven post-war seasons, Rowley hitting 170 & Pearson 142. Rowley (the 'Gunner') was the hard man, powerful with terrific shooting power; Pearson was more subtle, a great header of the ball, scoring by stealth rather than power, wonderfully two-footed.

A breakdown of the Rowley-Pearson double-act in the goalscoring stakes:

Season	Rowley	Pearson	Total
1946-47	28	19	47
1947-48	28	26	54
1948-49	30	17	47
1949-50	23	17	40
1950-51	15	23	38
1951-52	30	22	52
1952-53	16	18	34
Summary	170	142	312

Tommy Taylor, a great header of the ball, had tremendous acceleration making him the scourge of all defenders. Viollet, like Pearson before him, was a slick and smooth mover who could destroy defences with his lightning bursts and cool, deadly finishing. For just over five-and-a-half seasons (from August 1953 until the Munich air disaster in February 1958) when the League Championship was won twice (in succession) **Taylor and Viollet scored goals aplenty for United, their record for that time being:**

Season	Taylor	Viollet	Totals
1953-54	23	12	35
1954-55	20	21	41
1955-56	25	20	45
1956-57	34	26	60
1957-58	22	23	45
Summary	124	102	226

Viollet continued playing - and scoring for United - until January 1962 when he moved to Stoke City having netted 180 senior goals for the club.

155

This was the Charlton-Viollet partnership

Season	Charlton	Viollet	Totals
1958-59	29	21	50
1959-60	21	32	53
1960-61	21	16	37
Summary	71	69	140

For three whole seasons, 1958-59 to 1960-61, Viollet was partnered in the United attack by Bobby Charlton. They did remarkably well, scoring 140 goals. Viollet's haul of 32 (all in the League) in 1959-60 is still a club record.

From 1962 to 1967 two Scots, Denis Law and David Herd, terrorised defenders all over Europe as United won two League Championships and the FA Cup. Law was signed from Torino for £115,000. Herd was already at the club, having joined from Arsenal in 1961. The two internationals soon hit it off. Law's mercurial style earned him the title 'The King'. He had lightning reflexes and almost controlled aggression! Herd was noted for his powerful and accurate shooting.

Herd regrettably broke his leg at the end of the 1966-67 season, virtually ending his career. Law's cartilage problems meant that he never regained his former sharpness, eventually moving across to neighbouring Manchester City before retiring - where he scored THAT goal which sent United into the Second Division - the glory days a distant memory!

The Law-Herd combination:

Season	Law	Herd	Totals
1962-63	29	21	50
1963-64	46	27	73
1964-65	39	28	67
1965-66	24	33	57
1966-67	25	18	43
Summary	163	127	290

It would be 26 years before another League championship trophy was displayed in the Old Trafford boardroom after Alex Ferguson had gradually stamped his image on the 'sleeping giants' of English (and indeed European) football. Many strikers were tried in the intervening years but without notable success, although some individuals like Frank Stapleton and Norman Whiteside promised much. It would take Mark Hughes, a product of the Youth scheme, alongside Brian McClair to restore United's pride!

Hughes and McClair were scoring partners for five seasons during which time they netted 160 goals between them, helping United on their way to winning the Premiership title in its inaugural year.

This is the Hughes-McClair partnership

Season	Hughes	McClair	Totals
1988-89	16	16	32
1989-90	15	8	23
1990-91	21	21	42
1991-92	14	24	38
1992-93*	16	9	25
Summary	82	78	160

* Part season, McClair reverting to midfield on Cantona's arrival.

French genius Eric Cantona made a massive impact at Old Trafford, teaming up firstly with Mark Hughes and then with Andy Cole.

He and Welshman Hughes played together for two-and-a-half seasons and scored almost 100 goals.

This was their combined record:

Season	Cantona	Hughes	Totals
1992-93*	9	16	25
1993-94	25	21	46
1994-95*	14	12	26
Summary	48	49	97

* Part season

To replace Hughes, who would soon leave for Chelsea, United acquired the services of Andy Cole from Newcastle United and he quickly made his mark alongside Cantona. United were a force to be reckoned with and the Premiership crowns continued to roll in.

This was the record of the two 'C' men - crackshots in the United team:

Season	Cantona	Cole	Totals
1994-95*	14	12	26
1995-96	19	13	32
1996-97	15	7	22
Summary	48	32	80

Out of the blue, Cantona announced his retirement to the dismay of the United faithful. As a replacement Ferguson signed Teddy Sheringham from Tottenham Hotspur, but he took a time to settle into his new surroundings, Arsenal overtaking United to win the double in 1997-98. However, Ferguson, knew he needed a player of Cantona's qualities to play alongside Cole and he went out and signed Aston Villa striker Dwight Yorke for £12,5 million. His judgement paid off as Cole and Yorke forged a splendid partnership which culminated in the winning of the fabulous treble in 1998-99 - although as we know it was two other strikers, Sheringham and Ole Gunnar Solskjaer, who stole the limelight in Barcelona to win the European Cup! And they continued to assist Messrs Cole and Yorke up front, right through to the end of the 2000-01 season when Sheringham (scorer of 21 goals in his last season at Old Trafford) returned to White Hart Lane, replaced by Dutchman Ruud van Nistelrooy.

The Cole-Yorke partnership details

Season	Cole	Yorke	Totals
1998-99	24	29	53
1999-00	22	23	45
2000-01	13	12	25
Summary	59	64	123

The signing of Dutchman Ruud van Nistelrooy from PSV Eindhoven during the 2001 close season meant a change in the striking 'pecking order' as Cole, Yorke, Paul Scholes and finally 'super-sub' Solskjaer jostled for position. It would be Ole Gunnar Solskjaer, however, who would win the prize with Cole transferred to Blackburn, Yorke out of form and out of favour and Scholes returned to midfield. The 'Ruud and Ole show' was sensational with the promise of more to come!

The Van Nistelrooy-Solskjaer partnership details

Season	Nistelrooy	Solskjaer	Totals
2001-02	36	26	62

GODSMARK, Gilbert

Born: Derby, early 1877. Died from a disease while serving in the Boer War in South Africa, February 1901.
Career: Ashford FC (Kent), NEWTON HEATH (January-April 1900).
An inside-forward, quick and incisive with good skills, Gilbert Godsmark's promising career was cut short when he was called up as a reservist for the Boer War, where regrettably he died from a disease. He was another player recommended to the club by Bob Donaldson (q.v)...
Club record: 9 apps. 4 goals (also 2 'other' apps).

GOLDTHORPE, Ernest Holdroyd

Born: Middleton, near Leeds, 8 June 1898
Career: Yorkshire Schoolboys, Tottenham Hotspur (WW1 guest, 1917-19, whilst serving in the Army), Bradford City (1919), Leeds United (1920), Bradford City (1922), MANCHESTER UNITED (November 1922), Rotherham United (October 1925).
Centre-forward Ernie Goldthorpe had shown a lot of promise during his time with Leeds and Bradford City and he did well in his first season at Old Trafford, netting 13 goals in 22 League games, including a fourtimer in a resounding 6-1 win at Notts County. Injuries ruined his career, although he was a reasonably wealthy man, owning a number of farms in his native Yorkshire.
Goldthorpe's father was a quality Rugby League player.
Club record: 30 apps. 16 goals

GOODWIN, Frederick J

Born: Heywood near Bury, 28 June 1933
Career: Stockport Schoolboys, Cheshire & District Schoolboys, MANCHESTER UNITED (professional, October 1953), Leeds United (£10,000, March 1960), Scunthorpe United (player-manager, 1964), New York Generals (coach, 1966), Brighton & Hove Albion (manager, 1968), Birmingham City (Manager, 1970-75), Minnesota Kicks (coach, 1976).
Acting initially as a reserve to Eddie Colman and Duncan Edwards, Freddie Goodwin, a tall, intelligent, cultured wing-half, came into the first XI on a regular basis following the Munich air disaster and he played very well. He gained runners-up medals with United in both the League Championship and FA Cup and then helped Leeds win the Second Division title After retiring Goodwin became an excellent coach, always willing to try innovative ideas out on the pitch and off it (he once had his players doing yoga). It was he who developed Trevor Francis at Birmingham City, the club he guided to promotion from Division Two in 1972 and to two FA Cup semi-finals. He eventually retired to live in the States (his present home).
Goodwin was also a useful stock bowler on the cricket field, taking 27 wickets in 11 county matches for Lancashire CCC.
Quote from Goodwin during his managerial career: "It's tough at the top - it's hell anywhere else!"
Club record: 107 apps. 8 goals

GOODWIN, William

Born: Staveley, 1892
Career: Old Staveley Primitives, Chesterfield (1912), Blackburn Rovers (1913), Exeter City (1914), MANCHESTER UNITED (£650, June 1920), Southend United (August 1922), Dartford (1927). Retired 1928 and later ran a successful confectionery wholesale business in Southend.
Before moving to Old Trafford, reserve inside/centre-forward, Bill Goodwin netted 40 goals in 75 games for Exeter, breaking the Devon club's scoring record with 23 in 37 outings in 1914-15.
Club record: 7 apps. one goal

GORAM, Andrew Lewis

Born: Bury, 13 April 1964.
Career: West Bromwich Albion (1980), Oldham Athletic (1981), Hibernian (£325,000, 1987), Glasgow Rangers (£1 million, 1991), Notts County (1998), Sheffield United (1998), Motherwell (free transfer 1999), MANCHESTER UNITED (£100,000, March 2001), Barnsley (free transfer, May 2001), Coventry City (on loan, September 2001), Oldham Athletic (March 2002).
Andy Goram, a widely travelled, vastly experienced Scottish international goalkeeper was signed as a stop gap, following injuries to both first team custodians during 2000-01, making just two appearances before leaving for Barnsley.
Ron Atkinson was his manager at West Bromwich Albion and ex-United star Gordon Strachan at Coventry. He helped Rangers win five Premiership titles, two League Cup Finals and three Scottish FA Cup Finals, and gained 43 senior caps, plus one at Under-21 level. Goram made over 750 senior appearances at club and international level and is one of the very few sportsmen to have represented his country at both international football and cricket.
Club record: 2 apps.

GORNIK ZABRZE

United just about got the better of Gornik Zabrze in a real tough European Cup quarter-final battle in 1967-68. It was touch and go in Poland on a frozen pitch as United did extremely well to keep the home team down to a single goal advantage (0-1) after winning their home leg 2-0 when Brian Kidd and Florenski own-goal were the scorers.

GOTHENBURG (IFK)

It was honours even in the group stage of the 1994-95 European Champions League. Ryan Giggs scored twice in United's 4-2 home win while the Swedes won 3-1 in Gothenburg..
Players with both clubs include: E Nevland, J Blomqvist.

GOTHERIDGE, James

Born: Derby, 1863
Career: NEWTON HEATH (October 1884-April 1887), later West Manchester (season 1890-91).
A goalscoring left-winger, Jim Gotheridge spent three seasons with the Heathens, during which time he made close on 150 first-team appearances (and scored over 60 goals), the majority coming in 'other' competitions.
Club record: 6 apps. (143 'other' apps, 62 goals)

GOURLAY, John

Born: Scotland, 1879
Career: Annbank, NEWTON HEATH (February-May 1899)
A half-back, Jack Gourlay failed to impress during his only season with the club.
Club record: one app. (also one 'other' app).

157

GOWLING, Alan Edwin

Born: Stockport, 16 March 1949

Career: Stockport Schools, Cheshire Schools, MANCHESTER UNITED (amateur August 1965, professional August 1967), Huddersfield Town (£60,000, June 1972), Newcastle United (£70,000, 1975), Bolton Wanderers (£120,000, 1978), Preston North End (season 1982-83). Retired from competitive football in 1983.

A tall, angular striker, who had an awkward style which confounded defenders, Alan Gowling was converted into a highly effective attacking midfielder by manager Frank O'Farrell.

He joined United while studying for an economics degree at Manchester University. A member of the British soccer team in the Mexico Olympics he scored against Stoke on his League debut in March 1968, while still an amateur and went on to average a goal every four games for the Reds. Gowling later became Chairman of the PFA (November 1980) and was then deeply involved as general-manager of a Buxton-based chemical company.

Club record: 87 apps. 21 goals

GRADUATES (University)

The following, all Manchester United players at one time or another, graduated from University:

Gary Bailey	Physics (Witts University, South Africa)
Len Bradbury	Teacher-training (Manchester University)
Warren Bradley	General Studies (Durham University)
Albert Broome	Science (Victoria University)
Steve Coppell	Economics (Liverpool University)
Alan Gowling	Economics (Manchester University)
Harold Hardman	Law (Manchester University)
Brian McClair	Mathematics (Glasgow University)
Kevin Moran	Commerce (University College, Dublin)
Mike Pinner	Law (Cambridge University)
Nick Wood	Economics (Manchester University)

John Hanrahan also graduated from University College, Dublin but was only ever a Manchester United reserve and Youth team player.

GRAHAM, Arthur

Born: Castlemilk, Glasgow, 26 October 1952

Career: Cambuslang Rangers, Aberdeen (1969), Leeds United (£125,000, 1977), MANCHESTER UNITED (£45,000, August 1983), Bradford City (June 1985 as player, later reserve team & junior coach, then caretaker-manager at Valley Parade, 1989). Now working as a physiotherapist.

Winger Arthur Graham gained Scottish Cup and League Cup winners medals with Aberdeen. He also won Youth and Under-21 caps for his country while amassing 307 appearances for the Dons (46 goals scored) before moving to Elland Road in 1977. He spent six years with Leeds, notching another 44 goals in 257 games and collecting the first of his eventual tally of 10 full caps. A positive player with pace and ability, he once scored a hat-trick for Leeds in five-and-a-half minutes against Birmingham City in 1978.

Graham has seven brothers and three sisters. Three of the brothers, Tommy, David and Jimmy, all played professional football (see Family Connections).

Club record: 52 apps. 7 goals

GRAHAM, Deiniol William Thomas

Born: Cannock, Staffs, 4 October 1969

Career: Anglesey/Holyhead Grammar School, MANCHESTER UNITED (trainee July 1986, professional October 1987), Barnsley (£50,000, August 1991), Preston North End (on loan, 1992), Carlisle United (on loan, 1993), Stockport Co (1994), Scunthorpe Utd (1995), Emley FC (manager).

A Welsh schoolboy, Youth & Under-21 international, versatile forward Deiniol Graham was always struggling to gain first team football at Old Trafford.

Club record: 3 apps. one goal

GRAHAM, John

Born: Northumberland, 1873

Career: Blyth FC, Newton Heath (November 1893-May 1894)

A reserve centre-forward, Jack Graham deputised for Bob Donaldson during his only season with the Heathens.

Club record: 4 apps. (also 3 'other' apps, one goal)

GRASSAM, William

Born: Larbert, Stenhousemuir, 20 November 1878

Career: Redcliffe Thistle, Glasgow Maryhill (1897), Burslem Port Vale (1899), West Ham United (1900), Celtic (1903), MANCHESTER UNITED (September 1903), Leyton (June 1905), West Ham United (1905), Brentford (1909). Did not appear after WW1.

Before joining United, inside-forward Billy Grassam made over 100 appearances for Port Vale and West Ham, netting four times on his debut for the London club in their first-ever Southern League game against Gravesend in 1900. He did very well during his time at Old Trafford but did even better in his second spell at Upton Park, taking his Hammers' record to 68 goals in 179 outings. As a teenager Grassam represented both Glasgow and Scotland Juniors.

Club record: 37 apps. 14 goals

GREAVES, Ian Denzil

Born: Oldham, 26 May 1932

Career: St Joseph's FC, Buxton United (1951), MANCHESTER UNITED (May 1953), Lincoln City (December 1960), Oldham Athletic (1961), Altrincham (1963, announcing his retirement in May 1964). Then Huddersfield Town (coach 1964, manager, 1968), Bolton Wanderers (assistant-manager 1974, then manager late 1974-early 1980), Hereford United (assistant-manager, early 1980), Oxford United (manager, late 1980), Wolverhampton Wanderers (manager, for eight months in 1982), Mansfield Town (manager, 1983-89), Bury (coach), MANCHESTER UNITED (scout), Emley Town (manager, season 1991-92), Manchester City (scout).

Ian Greaves was a resilient full-back, hard and compact, who won a League Championship medal with United in 1956 and also played in the 1958 FA Cup Final against Bolton. As a manager, he saw Wolves suffer relegation to the Second Division in 1982, but he guided both Huddersfield (1970) and Bolton (1978) to the Second Division Championship. In 1985 he lifted Mansfield into the Third Division and two years later led the Stags to victory in the Freight Rover Trophy Final at Wembley. On four occasions Greaves was voted 'Manager of the Month' - once at Huddersfield and three times with Bolton.

Club record: 75 apps.

GREEN, Robert Edward

Born: Tewksbury, Gloucestershire, circa 1910. Died: Cheltenham.

Career: Bournemouth & Boscombe Athletic (professional 1929), Derby County 91931), MANCHESTER UNITED (1933), Stockport County (July 1934), Cheltenham Town (1936-37).

Inside-forward Eddie Green failed to make an impact at Old Trafford but later did well with Stockport, helping them won the Third Division (North) Cup in 1935.

Club record: 9 apps. 4 goals

GREENHOFF, Brian

Born: Barnsley, 28 April 1953

Career: Yorkshire Schoolboys, MANCHESTER UNITED (apprentice August 1968, professional June 1970), Leeds United (£350,000, August 1979), Hong Kong (on loan), Rochdale (1983-84 season), Chadderton FC (coach). Later became manager of a Manchester snooker centre.

Equally effective whether playing in central defence or in midfield where he could attack or defend, depending on the state of the game, Brian Greenhoff won a Second Division Championship medal with United in 1975, was an FA Cup loser in 1976, a winner in the same competition twelve months later, playing superbly well at the back when Liverpool were defeated 2-1. Capped 18 times by England at senior level, Greenhoff also represented his country at 'B' and Under-23 levels. He was at Old Trafford with his brother Jimmy (q.v) and on leaving United moved to Rochdale where his brother was then player-manager.

Club record: 271 apps. 17 goals

GRAHAM, George

Born: Bargeddie, Lanarkshire, 30 November 1944.

Career: Coatbridge Schools, Swinton FC (West Scotland), Coatbridge Boys, Aston Villa (1959, professional 1961), Chelsea (signed for £5,950, 1964), Arsenal (£50,000, plus Tommy Baldwin, 1966), MANCHESTER UNITED (£120,000, December 1972), Portsmouth (November 1974), Crystal Palace (1976), California Surf (on loan, 1978). Retired as a player in May 1980 and appointed Youth team coach/assistant-manager at Selhurst Park, later Queen's Park Rangers (coach, 1981), Millwall (manager, 1982), Arsenal (manager, 1986), Leeds United (manager, 1996), Tottenham Hotspur (manager, 1998). Left White Hart Lane in 2001 when Glenn Hoddle returned to take charge of the London club.

Nicknamed 'Stroller' inside-forward George Graham played in the losing 1963 League Cup Final for Aston Villa (v. Birmingham City). After that he went on to greater things - as a player, but more so as a manager. He formed a terrific striking partnership at Chelsea with Barry Bridges, netting 46 goals in 102 appearances for the Blues, gaining a League Cup winners' medal in 1965.

As a Gunner, he starred in 296 first-class matches and secured a further 77 goals, collecting both League Championship and FA Cup winning medals in 1971, earning a runners-up prize in the latter competition in 1972 and also helping Arsenal win the Fairs Cup in 1970, while receiving two losers' prizes in the League Cup Finals in the late 1960s. By this time he had settled into a midfield position.

Graham was the first player Tommy Docherty signed when he took over as boss at Old Trafford. He skippered a struggling side in 1973 and again the following year when they were relegated to the Second Division. He was with Portsmouth when they dropped into Division Three and then helped Palace gain promotion to the Second Division in 1977. In a fine league career, Graham made 455 appearances and notched 95 goals.

Capped as a schoolboy and Youth player by Scotland, Graham also represented his country twice at under 23 level and then went on to appear in a total of 12 senior internationals.

Moving into management with Millwall in 1982, his first success was to lead the Lions to victory over Lincoln City in the Final of the Football League Trophy (1983), guiding the Londoners to promotion from Division Three two years later. As boss of Arsenal, Graham saw two League titles won - in 1989 and 1991 - victory claimed in the League Cup Final of 1987 with a runners-up prize following in the same competition in 1988. He then tasted 'double' joy as the Gunners claimed both the FA Cup and League Cup in 1993. After leaving Highbury he took Leeds into Europe (1998) before moving back to North London to take charge of Arsenal's arch rivals Spurs!

He's one of the few men who've won the League title as a player & manager (both with Arsenal).

Club record: 49 apps. 2 goals

GREENHOFF, James

Born: Barnsley, 19 June 1946.

Career: Barnsley & Yorkshire Schoolboys, Leeds United (apprentice 1961, professional August 1963), Birmingham City (£70,000, 1968), Stoke City (£100,000, 1969), MANCHESTER UNITED (£120,000, November 1976), Crewe Alexandra (December 1980), Toronto Blizzard (player-coach, 1981), Port Vale (summer 1981), Rochdale (player-manager 1983-84), Port Vale (coach). Greenhoff later coached youngsters at a Butlins holiday centre and ran his own insurance business (Greenhoff Peutz & Co) before working for a Staffordshire-based paint company. He now lives in Alsager (North Staffs),

Inside-forward Jimmy Greenhoff was excellent at screening the ball (with back to goal and defenders behind him). A wonderfully skilful player, very talented, he packed a fierce shot in both feet, was also useful with his head and scored some cracking goals, a few of them terrific volleys. He became one of United's most popular players.

He netted United's fortuitous winner in the 1977 FA Cup Final (Lou Macari's effort rebounding off him and bouncing over the line) past a helpless Ray Clemence. However, two years later he was on the losing side as Arsenal pipped the Reds with a last-minute winner. Previously a League Cup and Fairs Cup winner with Leeds United (as well as being a runner-up in the latter competition during his time at Elland Road), he also helped Stoke City win the League Cup in 1972. The blond-haired Greenhoff represented the Football League and appeared in both 'B' and Under-23 internationals for England but a full cap eluded him, despite being consistently rated as one of the League's finest strikers.

* Greenhoff scored in two FA Cup semi-finals for different clubs on the same ground (Goodison Park). His first goal was for Stoke City against Arsenal in 1972 and his second for United v. Liverpool in 1979. He also netted in another semi-final for United versus Leeds at Hillsborough in 1977.

Club record: 123 apps. 36 goals

GREENING, Jonathan

Born: Scarborough, 2 January 1979

Career: York City (trainee, 1994, professional 1996), MANCHESTER UNITED (£500,000, March 1998), Middlesbrough (£2.5 million, July 2001).

Over half of midfielder Jonathan Greening's first-team appearances for United came as a substitute.

An England Youth international, he later added three Under-21 caps to his tally as a 'Reds' player and was a non-appearing substitute when United won the European Champions Cup in 1999. He quickly established himself in the first team at Middlesbrough and in May 2002 he added to his tally of intermediate caps.

Club record: 27 apps.

GREENWOOD, Wilson

Born: Padiham, Lancs. 1868. Died: Padiham, 1943.

Career: Blue Star FC (Burnley), Brierfield FC, Accrington (1893-95), Sheffield United (1895), Rossendale FC (1895), Rochdale Athletic (1896), Warmley (1897), Grimsby Town (1898), NEWTON HEATH (October 1900-May 1902).

All of reserve winger Wilson Greenwood's appearances for the Heathens were made in 1900-01 when he deputised twice for John Grundy and once for Alf Schofield.

Club record: 3 apps. (also 2 'other' apps).

GREGG, Henry, MBE

Born: Magherafelt, County Derry, Northern Ireland, 25 October 1932.

Career: Linfield Rangers, Linfield Swifts, Coleraine (1950), Doncaster Rovers (£2,000, 1952), MANCHESTER UNITED (£23,000, December 1957), Stoke City (December 1966), Shrewsbury Town (manager, 1968-72), Swansea City (manager, 1972-75), Crewe Alexandra (manager, 1975-78), Kitan Sports Club, Kuwait (manager-coach for five months in 1978), MANCHESTER UNITED (coach, November 1978-June 1981), Swansea City (coach, 1982), Swindon Town (assistant-manager, 1984-85), Carlisle United (manager, 1986-87).

A hero of the Munich air crash when he went back into the wreckage to help out his colleagues and surviving passengers, goalkeeper 'Harry' Gregg made almost 250 senior appearances for United before being replaced between the posts by David Gaskell. An agile, daring and courageous 'keeper, never afraid to dive in amongst flying boots, he is remembered as one of United's best ever goalkeepers.

Gregg played in the 1958 FA Cup Final defeat by Bolton when he was controversially bundled over the line by the England centre-forward Nat Lofthouse. An Irish schoolboy and amateur international, he also represented the Irish

League and went on to earn a total of 25 full caps for his country, appearing in the 1958 World Cup Finals in Sweden. He was working under former United star Lou Macari at Swindon, but left the County Ground after a clash of personalities! He later ran a hotel in his native Magherafelt (Ulster).

Gregg's son, John, was on Barnsley's books and was capped by Northern Ireland at Under-18 level.

Harry Gregg was born in the same town as Peter Doherty, another Irish legend.

Club record: 247 apps.

GRIFFITHS, Clive Leslie

Born: Pontypridd, 22 January 1955.

Career: Wales Schoolboys, MANCHESTER UNITED (amateur, then apprentice 1970, professional 1972), Plymouth Argyle (on loan, July-November 1974), Tranmere Rovers (on loan, October 1975-April 1976), Chicago Sting (April 1976), Tulsa Roughnecks (1980).

Versatile defender Clive Griffiths made all of his League appearances for United during the 1973-74 season when he deputised in the main for Jim Holton. He was as keen as anyone to take over the left-back berth but the arrival of Stewart Houston ended his dreams. Griffiths won two Under-23 caps for his country as a United reserve. He was at Chicago Sting with former United defender Bill Foulkes.

Club record: 7 apps.

GRIFFITHS, John

Born: Fenton, Stoke-on-Trent, 15 September 1909

Career: Shirebrook FC, Wolverhampton Wanderers (professional 1929), Bolton Wanderers (1932), MANCHESTER UNITED (March 1934). Guested for Derby County, Notts County, Port Vale, Stoke City & West Bromwich Albion during WW2. Hyde United (player-coach, 1946). Later became a masseur (physiotherapist) in Hyde.

Jack Griffiths was an impressive defender for United during the six seasons leading up WW2. A right-back perfectionist, he replaced Jack Silcock in the United side, helping them win the Second Division Championship in 1936.

Club record 176 apps. one goal

GRIFFITHS, William

Born: Manchester, winter 1876.

Career: Berry's Association FC, NEWTON HEATH/MANCHESTER UNITED (February 1899), Atherton Church House FC (June 1905).

Centre-half Billy Griffiths gave the club seven years excellent service. Quick off the mark, a strong tackler and neat passer of the ball, he succeeded James McNaught in the pivotal role and eventually handed over his duties to Charlie Roberts.

Club record: 175 apps. 30 goals (also 22 'other' apps, one goal)

GRIMES, Augustine Ashley

Born: Dublin, 2 August 1957.

Career: Stella Maris, Bohemians, MANCHESTER UNITED (trialist, August 1972), Bohemians (professional, 1975), MANCHESTER UNITED (£20,000, March 1977), Coventry City (August 1983), Luton Town (1984), Osasuna, Spain (1990), Stoke City (coach 1991, then player-coach, 1992), Celtic (coach, 1993-94), Stoke City (assistant-manager/coach 1994-95).

Almost one third of Ashley Grimes' first-team appearances for United were made as a substitute. A player with a useful left-foot, he was a hard-working midfielder who was sadly plagued by illness and injury during his time at Old Trafford. He appeared in successive League Cup Finals with Luton, gaining a winners' medal (v. Arsenal) in 1988 (as a substitute). He won 17 full caps for the Republic of Ireland and was also honoured by his country at Under-21 level.

Club record: 107 apps. 11 goals

GRIMSBY TOWN

Heathens/United's League results v. the Mariners:

Season	Div	Home	Away	Season	Div	Home	Away
1894-95	2	W 2-0	L 1-2	1929-30	1	L 2-5	D 2-2
1895-96	2	W 3-2	L 2-4	1930-31	1	L 0-2	L 1-2
1896-97	2	W 4-2	L 0-2				
1897-98	2	W 2-1	W 3-1	1932-33	2	D 1-1	D 1-1
1898-99	2	W 3-2	L 0-3	1933-34	2	L 1-3	L 3-7
1899-1900	2	W 1-0	W 7-0				
1900-01	2	W 1-0	L 0-2	1936-37	1	D 1-1	L 2-6
				1938-39	1	W 3-1	L 0-1
1903-04	2	W 2-0	L 1-3				
1904-05	2	W 2-1	W 1-0				
1905-06	2	W 5-0	W 1-0	1946-47	1	W 2-1	D 0-0
				1947-48	1	L 3-4	D 1-1

Summary of League results:

	P	W	D	L	F	A
Division 1	12	2	4	6	17	26
Division 2	24	14	2	8	47	37
Home	18	12	2	4	38	26
Away	18	4	4	10	26	37
Total	36	16	6	14	64	63

FA Cup Result

	Round	Venue	Result
1930-31	4	Away	L 0-1

Players with both clubs include: M Appleton, G Birtles, A Chilton (Town player-manager), T Cooke (United), C Craven, VE Dodsworth (United reserve), J Ferguson, R Ferrier (Town player-coach), D Fidler (United reserve), W Greenwood, W Higgins, H Lappin, H Leonard, S McGarvey, J Miller, J Quin, C Rennox, C Richards, T Ritchie (United reserve), C Roberts, M Rowbotham (United reserve), J Scott, L Sharpe (Town trialist), RW Smith (United reserve), W Tyler (United reserve), N Webb, J Whitefoot, J Whitehouse.

Also associated: C Spencer (United player, Town manager)

161

GRIMSHAW, Anthony

Born: Manchester, 8 December 1957.

Career: MANCHESTER UNITED (apprentice April 1974, professional December 1974-June 1979), Ballymena United (on loan, October-November 1978).

Both of Tony Grimshaw's appearances for United were as a substitute (one in the League, one in the League Cup) during the 1975-76 season. He broke his leg in a second XI game against Aston Villa in 1976 and never made a full recovery, being released at the end of the 1978-79 season.

Club record: 2 apps.

GRIMWOOD, John Barton

Born: Marsden, nr South Shields, 25 October 1898. Died: Childswickham, Worcs, 26 December 1977

Career: Marsden Schools, Marsden Rescue FC, South Shields, MANCHESTER UNITED (May 1919), Aldershot Town (June 1922), Blackpool, (£2,750, 1927), Altrincham (1928), Taylor Brothers FC, Trafford, Manchester (re-instated as an amateur, 1932). Later ran a successful milk company in the Manchester area.

Half-back John Grimwood could mix long, quick balls out of defence with a subtle pass either to his full-back or inside-forward. A strong header of the ball, he marshalled his defence and read the game superbly well, was always alert to what was happening around him and, indeed, all over the pitch. He made his debut for United in the local derby against Manchester City (away) in October 1919 in front of 30,000 fans.

Club record: 205 apps. 8 goals

GROUNDS

United have played 'home' League matches on the following grounds:

North Road, Newton Heath	1889-1893
Bank Street, Clayton	1893-1910
Old Trafford	1910-1941
Maine Road	1941-1949
Old Trafford	1949 to date
Anfield (Liverpool)	August 1971
Victoria Ground (Stoke)	August 1971

Ground Rules

North Road, close to the railway sheds where the early players worked, was the first 'ground' of Newton Heath (LYR) from 1878. The date 1889 (left) refers to the club's first League match in the Football Alliance on 21 September 1889 v. Sunderland Albion.

After Newton Heath had played one season of League Football at North Road, which was completely unsatisfactory, the club moved to Bank Street a couple of miles away. Although Bank Street was eventually built up to hold 50,000 spectators, the club (now Manchester United) needed somewhere more central, moving to Old Trafford in 1910 where they built a ground capable of housing up to 80,000.

Old Trafford was 'closed' due to war-damage following German bombing from 1941 until 1949, although reserve team football was played there from 1946.

During the 1947-48 season United also played 'home' FA Cup-ties at Goodison Park (Everton) and Leeds Road (Huddersfield), City requiring Maine Road for their home Cup-ties..

United played League matches against Arsenal at Anfield and West Bromwich Albion at The Victoria Ground, Stoke in August 1971...when the FA closed Old Trafford due to crowd disturbances the previous season.

United also played a 'home' European Cup-winners Cup first round, second leg game at Home Park, Plymouth in October 1977 v. St Etienne, again following crowd trouble at Old Trafford during the first leg of this tie in France.

GRUNDY, John

Born: Egerton, near Bolton, circa 1872.

Career: Wigan County, NEWTON HEATH (April 1895), Halliwell Rovers (1895), NEWTON HEATH (April 1900-May 1901).

Outside-left John Grundy failed to make the first team in his first spell at the club. He returned after a break of five years and scored on his debut against Chesterfield on 28 April 1900. He was named on the wing at the start of the 1900-01 season but lost his place following the arrival of Scotsman James Fisher.

Club record: 11 apps. 3 goals

GUEST PLAYERS

(See also: Wartime Football)

Several players guested for Manchester United during WW2, while many more had served in the same capacity during the 1915-19 period.

One of those recruited as a guest during WW2 was a well-built inside-left by the name of Arthur Rowley, younger brother of Jack Rowley. He was on Wolves' books at the time but later played for West Bromwich Albion, Fulham, Leicester City and Shrewsbury Town between 1946 and 1965 and who went on to score a record 434 League goals during an excellent career. Arthur made his bow in United's first team against Liverpool on 26 April 1941 at the age of 15 years and five days - possibly the youngest-ever player to don a United shirt at competitive level!

Also during WW2 United acquired the services of Peter Doherty, the Irish international inside-forward and Ernie Toseland, both from rivals Manchester City, who also provided Alex Herd, father of David.

They also had the pleasure of claiming the skills of (among many others) Ivor Broadis (later to play for Newcastle United, Manchester City and England), of ex-Burnley and Aston Villa star Bob Brocklebank (who was to become boss of Birmingham City); the former West Bromwich Albion, Everton and England left-winger Wally Boyes; Sunderland's goal-machine Eddie Burbanks; Blackburn Rovers' hardman Len Butt; Hugh O'Donnell (ex-Celtic, Preston North End and Blackpool), Harry Catterick (who went on to manage Everton); centre-forward Robbie Newsome of West Bromwich Albion; the versatile Duggie Reid of Portsmouth and Willie Watson, later to star for Sunderland and also for England against Australia in Test Match cricket..

Even the great Stanley Matthews (then of Stoke City) played as a guest for United v. Everton in 1940.

GYVES, William

Born: Manchester, summer 1867

Career: NEWTON HEATH (season 1890-91)

Second XI goalkeeper Bill Gyves' only appearance for the Heathens was in the FA Cup-tie against Bootle in October 1890, both sides fielding reserve teams due to 'more important' first team commitments on the same afternoon.

Club record: one app. (also 2 'other' apps)

H for...

HUGHES, Leslie Mark

Born: Wrexham, 1 November 1963

Career: Ysgol Rhiwabon, Rhos Aelwyd Boys (Under-16s), Wrexham Schoolboys, MANCHESTER UNITED (apprentice June 1980, professional November 1980), Barcelona (£2.5 million, August 1986), Bayern Munich (on loan, 1987), MANCHESTER UNITED (£1.5 million, July 1988), Chelsea (£1.5 million, July 1995), Southampton (£650,000, 1998), Everton (free transfer, March 2000), Blackburn Rovers (free transfer, October 2000 to May 2002). Also Welsh national team manager (2000 onwards).

In his two spells at Old Trafford, striker Mark Hughes scored a goal every three games for United.

He also helped the Reds win the FA Cup on three occasions (1985, 1990 & 1994), the European Cup-winners Cup (1991), the Football League Cup (1992), two Premier League Championships (in 1993 and 1994), the European Super Cup (1991) and the FA Charity Shield (1993 & 1994). After leaving Old Trafford he added another FA Cup Final medal to his collection with Chelsea (1997) and also helped the London club win both the Cup-winners Cup and League Cup (in 1998). His winning of four FA Cup winners' medals is a record. Capped 72 times by Wales, whom he also represented at schoolboy, Youth and Under-21 levels (gaining five caps in the latter category) in his prime Hughes was one of the best 'leaders of the attack' in the professional game. Able to hold the ball up and then lay it off to a colleague, he had strength, skill, could head a ball with great power and direction and possessed a powerful right-foot shot, with spectacular volleys a speciality. Nicknamed 'Sparky', he won the PFA Player of the Year award on two occasions (1989 and 1991) and is one of only a handful of players to have scored in the FA Cup, League Cup and European Cup-winners Cup Finals, his two goals seeing off Barcelona in the latter competition in 1991. He helped Blackburn Rovers regain their Premiership status in 2001, the same year he took his career appearance tally (in all major competitions, for clubs and country) past the 750 mark (230 goals scored). In February 2002, at the age of 38, Hughes returned home to Wales and helped Blackburn beat Tottenham Hotspur 2-1 to win the League Cup at the Millennium Stadium, Cardiff.

But no matter which club's shirt Hughes wore, he was always guaranteed a warm welcome back at Old Trafford.

Club record: 470 apps. 162 goals

HACKING, John

Born: Blackburn, 22 December 1897. Died: Accrington, 1 June 1955.

Career: Grimshaw Park Co-op FC (Blackburn), Blackpool (1919), Fleetwood (1925), Oldham Athletic (1926), MANCHESTER UNITED (May 1934), Accrington Stanley (player-manager, May 1935, retired as a player December 1935), Barrow (manager 1949 until his death)

Prior to joining United at the age of 36, experienced goalkeeper Jack Hacking had already amassed well over 250 League appearances (the majority with Oldham Athletic). He had also represented the Football League on two occasions and gained two full caps for England.

Hacking's son was also a goalkeeper with Accrington Stanley and Stockport County.

Club record: 34 apps.

HALIFAX TOWN

League Cup Results v. the Shaymen:

	Round	Venue	Result
1990-91	2 (1)	Away	W 3-1
	2 (2)	Home	W 2-1

Watney Cup

United were surprisingly knocked out of the 1971 Watney Cup competition by lowly Halifax in the 1st round. The Reds lost 2-1 at The Shay on 31 July in front of 19,765 fans. George Best netted for United.

Players with both clubs include: D Bain, J Barber, J Connaughton, J Coode (United reserve), J Copeland (United reserve), D Fidler (United reserve), I Fitzpatrick (United reserve), G Glaister & G Griffiths (both United WW2), K MacDonald, W Merry (United reserve), H O'Donnell (United WW2), T O'Neil, A Pape, E Partridge, M Pearson, P Roche, A Sidebottom, TW Stockdale (United reserve), C Taylor (United reserve), W Watson (United WW2).

Also associated: J Breedon (United player, Town manager), J McCalliog (United player, Town caretaker-manager & manager), E Harrison (United coach, Halifax player).

HALL, John

Born: Bolton, 1905

Career: Lincoln City (1923), Accrington Stanley (1924), MANCHESTER UNITED (May 1925-May 1927).

Reserve right-winger Jack Hall made all of his senior appearances for United in February 1926 when he deputised for Joe Spence. All three games ended in victories.

Club record: 3 apps.

HALL, John

Born: Failsworth, Lancs. 23 October 1912.

Career: Failsworth FC, Newton Heath Loco, MANCHESTER UNITED (September 1932), Tottenham Hotspur (June 1936). Guested for Blackburn Rovers, Bolton Wanderers, Hartlepools United, Nottingham Forest, Oldham Athletic, Rochdale and Stockport County during WW2. Stalybridge Celtic (1945), Runcorn (1946), Stalybridge Celtic (1947).

Competent goalkeeper Jack Hall made his senior debut (v. Oldham Athletic) twelve months after joining United. He went on to make 23 League appearances that season but managed only eight in 1934-35 before becoming first choice again the following campaign which proved to be his last, being replaced by Welshman 'Roy' John.

Club record: 73 apps.

HALL, Proctor

Born: Blackburn, early 1884

Career: Oswaldtwistle Rovers, MANCHESTER UNITED (September 1903), Brighton & Hove Albion (June 1905), Aston Villa (1906), Bradford City (late 1906), Luton Town (1907), Chesterfield (early 1908), Hyde (summer 1909), Newport County (1912), Mardy FC (1913-15).

Lightweight inside-forward Proctor Hall acted as a reserve at Old Trafford for two seasons, getting few opportunites in the senior side. He later starred in Newport's first ever season.

Club record: 8 apps. 2 goals

HALSE, Harold James

Born: Stratford, East London, 1 January 1886. Died: Colchester, 25 March 1949.

Career: Park Road School (Wanstead), Newportians FC (Leyton), Wanstead FC, Barking Town (1904), Clapton Orient (amateur 1905), Southend United (1906), MANCHESTER UNITED (£350, March 1908), Aston Villa (£1,200, July 1912), Chelsea (1913), Clapton Orient (guest WW1), Charlton Athletic (1921-23). Retired to become scout at The Valley, a position he held until 1925.

Harold Halse, an exceedingly fine marksman, scored over 200 goals in just two seasons for Southend before joining United. He then took just 45 seconds to find the net on his debut for the Reds.

When United beat Swindon Town 8-4 in the 1911 FA Charity Shield game, Halse scored six consecutive goals. He gained FA Cup winners' medals with both United and Villa and collected a runners-up medal in the same competition with Chelsea, a feat later equalled by another United player, Ernie Taylor who did it with Newcastle, Blackpool and the Reds in the 1950s. Small, rather slight in build, Halse had the knack of snapping up the half-chance - a real top-class opportunist. Capped once by England in June 1909 against Austria (two goals scored), he also played for the Football

League XI and won both First Division Championship and runners-up medals with United and Villa respectively in 1912 and 1913. Halse also netted a fivetimer for Aston Villa against Derby County in October 1912. Halse captained Charlton in their first season in the Football League (1921-22).
Club record: 125 apps. 56 goals

HALTON, Reginald Lloyd
Born: Buxton, Derbyshire 11 July 1916. Died: Buxton, March 1988.
Career: Cheddington Mental Hospital, MANCHESTER UNITED (October 1936), Notts County (June 1937), Bury (late 1937). Guested for Arsenal, Fulham, Portsmouth & Rochdale during WW2. Chesterfield (1948), Leicester City (1950), Scarborough Town (player-manager, 1953), Goole Town (season 1954-55).
Outside-left Reg Halton had four other players to contest a first team position with during his time at Old Trafford. He failed to make an impact, but later he did very well with his other clubs and amassed in excess of 260 League and Cup appearances before retiring. He was called up as a guest by Arsenal for their prestigious friendly against the crack Russian side Moscow Dynamo in 1945, alongside such luminaries as the two 'Stans', Matthews and Mortensen.
Club record: 4 apps. one goal

HAMILL, Michael
Born: Belfast, 19 January 1885. Died: 27 July 1943.
Career: St Paul's Swifts (Belfast), Belfast Rangers, Belfast Celtic, MANCHESTER UNITED (January 1911), Belfast Celtic (September 1920), Manchester City (£1,000, 1920), Fall River FC, Boston, USA (1924), Coats FC, Rhode Island, also New York Giants (1925), Belfast Celtic (1926), Belfast Distillery (manager), Belfast Celtic (manager).
Inside-forward (or wing-half) Mickey Hamill took time to settle in at Old Trafford but once he had sorted himself out he gave the club excellent service up until WW1. Capped by Ireland on seven occasions, he helped his country win the Home International Championship in 1913-14 for the first time in their history. He later made 128 first-class appearances for Manchester City
The fee of £1,000 paid by City for Hamill's signature in 1924 went to United who had retained his registration papers.
Club record: 60 apps. 2 goals

HANLON, John James
Born: Manchester, 12 October 1917.
Career: St Wilfred's School (Hulme), Manchester Schools, MANCHESTER UNITED (amateur November 1934, professional November 1935), Bury (October 1948), Northwich Victoria (1950), Rhyl (1953).
Inside or centre-forward John Hanlon was sharp and incisive and scored some fine goals. He had to wait until November 1938 (four years after joining the club) before he made his League debut, scoring in the 1-1 home draw with Huddersfield Town. Hanlon, serving with the Durham Light Infantry as a Sergeant, was a PoW in Stalag IVB Camp in September 1944 (after being captured by the Italians on the island of Crete). Unfortunately his wartime experiences took a lot out of Hanlon, his post-war appearances spasmodic as a result, demonstrating little of his pre-war promise.
Club record: 70 apps. 22 goals

HANNAFORD, Charles William
Born: Finsbury Park, London 19 November 1896. Died: Aylesbury, summer 1970.
Career: Belmont Road School (Tottenham), Page Green Old Boys, London Schools, Tufnell Park (1912), Maidstone United (1920), Millwall (1921), Charlton Athletic (1923), Clapton Orient (1924), MANCHESTER UNITED (December 1925-July 1927), Clapton Orient (season 1928-29).
Capped by England v. Wales at schoolboy level, inside-forward Charlie Hannaford had already appeared in 120 League games before joining United. Unfortunately he struggled to hold down a first team place at Old Trafford and asked for a transfer, subsequently joining his former club Clapton Orient.
He toured Australia with the FA party in 1925 (whilst with Orient), appearing in three Test Matches. He also gained an FA Amateur Cup runners-up medal with Tufnell Park in 1920. Hannaford was an excellent jazz pianist.
Club record: 12 apps.

HANSON, James
Born: Manchester, 6 November 1904.
Career: Holland Street and Birtley Street Schools, Manchester Schoolboys, Manchester YMCA, Bradford Parish FC (Cheshire League), Stalybridge Celtic, Manchester North End, MANCHESTER UNITED (trialist 1923-24 season, signed May 1924-May 1931). Retired through injury.
Centre-forward Jimmy Hanson was an outstanding schoolboy footballer who went on to give United supreme service during his seven years at Old Trafford. Sadly his career ended at the age of 27 after he failed to recover from a broken leg, suffered in the home game v. Birmingham on Christmas Day 1929. A hat-trick hero for United's second XI when on trial, he later scored a fivetimer and a double hat-trick (six goals) in reserve team games against Stoke City and Burnley in 1925-26 and 1926-27 respectively. His first team duties realised a goal every three games, and his haul of 20 in 1928-29 contained six penalties.
Club record: 147 apps. 52 goals

HARDMAN, Harold Payne

Born: Kirkmanshulme, Manchester 4 April 1882. Died: Sale, Cheshire 9 June 1965.

Career: South Shore High School (Blackpool), South Shore Choristers FC, Blackpool (1900), Everton (1903), MANCHESTER UNITED (August 1908), Bradford City (January 1909), Stoke (1910), MANCHESTER UNITED (September 1913-65).

Outside-left Harold Hardman - who chose to remain an amateur throughout his playing days - had a remarkable footballing career. An Olympic Games Gold medal winner in 1908 when England beat Denmark 2-0 in the Final, he went on to gain four full caps for his country, plus another 20 at amateur level. He helped Everton win the FA Cup in 1906 and finish runners-up twelve months later, and made four senior appearances for United in 1908, having made well over 200 prior to arriving at Old Trafford! He joined the Board of Directors at United in 1912 (whilst still a player with Stoke!) and he went on to serve the club almost continuously for the next 53 years, holding office as Chairman for the last 14 (from 1951 until his death in 1965).

Hardman was a remarkable man - a qualified solicitor he was able to withstand the rigours of professional football as a genuine amateur. In later years, still a solicitor and Chairman of United, this tiny, bird-like figure could be regularly found at the 'other' Old Trafford.

Club record: 4 apps.

HARRIS, Francis Edgar

Born: Urmston, Manchester 1 December 1899.

Career: Stretford & District Schools, Urmston Congregationalists, Army football (1917-19), Urmston Old Boys, MANCHESTER UNITED (February 1920, professional May 1920-May 1923), USA football (1924-32).

Wing-half Frank Harris teamed up with another former United player Mickey Hamill in the USA during seasons 1924-26. A well-built half-back, he scored on his League debut against Sunderland in 1920.

Club record: 49 apps. 2 goals

HARRIS, Thomas

Born: Ince-in-Makerfield, 18 September 1905.

Career: Skelmersdale United (1922), MANCHESTER UNITED (May 1926), Wigan Borough (July 1928), Rotherham United (1929), Crewe Alexandra (late 1929), Chorley (1931), Burton Town (1932), Prescot Cables FC (season 1933-34).

Tom Harris was a reserve inside-forward during his two seasons at Old Trafford, getting very few opportunities in the first XI. In season 1930-31 he netted well over 30 goals for Crewe's second team.

Club record: 4 apps. one goal

HARRISON, Charles

Born: Newton Heath 1862

Career: NEWTON HEATH (1886), Bolton Wanderers (1886), NEWTON HEATH (1889-90).

The versatile Charlie Harrison played for the Heathens as a goalkeeper, full-back, half-back and forward! He made his debut at inside-right in a 4-1 defeat at Darwen on 28 December 1889 and his first outing in goal was a 7-0 reverse at Grimsby Town on 8 February 1890. His eleven appearances were made in five different positions on the field.

Club record: 11 apps. (also 13 'other' apps)

HARRISON, William Ewart

Born: Wybunbury, 27 December 1886. Died: Wolverhampton, August 1948.

Career: Hough United, Crewe South End, Willaston White Star, Crewe Alexandra (1905), Wolverhampton Wanderers (£400, 1907), MANCHESTER UNITED (October 1920), Port Vale (September 1922), Wrexham (1923). Retired May 1924, but carried on playing in charity matches until well past his 40th birthday.

Dashing winger Billy Harrison gained an FA Cup winners medal in his first season with Wolves - scoring a fine individual goal in the Final against Newcastle United. Described as a 'master of the game' he could either use his tremendous pace to go past a full-back or tease the same defender with some mazy dribbling skills. Small in stature at 5ft 4in tall, he was never afraid to go in with the burliest defenders and took plenty of knocks during his career. He made almost 350 senior appearances and scored close on 50 goals for Wolves before his transfer to Old Trafford (secured to replace Billy Meredith). Harrison besides being a wonderful footballer, was also an excellent crown green bowler. He was landlord of the Rose and Crown public house in Tettenhall (Wolverhampton) for many years.

Club record: 46 apps. 5 goals

HARROP, Robert

Born: Manchester, 25 August 1936.

Career: Benchill Youth Club (Wythenshawe), MANCHESTER UNITED (amateur, June 1953, professional May 1954), Tranmere Rovers (£4,000, November 1959, jointly with Gordon Clayton), Ramsgate FC (season 1961-62).

An England Youth international half-back, Bobby Harrop who could also play as a forward, had to fight hard and long for a place in the side at Old Trafford. In fact, it was not until a month after the Munich air crash that he made his senior debut, lining up in front of more than 60,000 fans for the 6th round FA Cup-tie replay against West Bromwich Albion in March 1958.

Club record: 11 apps.

HARTLEPOOL UNITED (Hartlepools United, Hartlepool)

United's FA Cup result v 'Pool:

	Round	Venue	Result
1956-57	3	Away	W 4-3

Fact File

The 1957 FA Cup-tie, as United chased a major 'treble' across the grounds of Europe, is the only competitive match between the clubs. However, everyone of the 17,264 crowd who crushed into the tiny Victoria Park ground will never forget the day Hartlepools nearly brought off a famous victory against the illustrious 'Babes'. United were coasting at 3-0 in the first half, but 'Pool never gave up. They fought back bravely and the crowd went wild as a 65th minute equaliser raised hopes. Thankfully, from United's point of view, a late Liam 'Billy' Whelan goal ensured a safe passage into round 4...but the Reds would not face a harder match all season!

Players with both clubs include: P Abbott (Man Utd reserve), W Bainbridge ('Pool WW2), F Barson ('Pool player-coach), P Bielby, R 'Berry' Brown, A Chilton ('Pool WW2, later 'Pool scout & manager), G Crowther (Man Utd reserve), A Foggon, J Hall ('Pool WW2), F Knowles, S McAuley (United reserve), D McCreery ('Pool player & assistant-manager), H Morris (Man Utd reserve), A Pape, S Pears, J Shotton (Man Utd reserve), RW Smith (Man Utd reserve), P Wratten.
Also associated: C Turner (United player, 'Pool manager), C Knowles (United amateur, 'Pool manager), E Harrison ('Pool player, United coach).

HARTWELL, William

Born: 1885.
Career: Kettering Town, MANCHESTER UNITED (April 1904), Northampton Town (July 1905).
Left-winger Billy Hartwell was a slightly-built player who failed to make inroads during his time at Old Trafford, although all of his three League outings resulted in healthy victories!
Club record: 4 apps.

HASLAM, George

Born: Turton, Lancashire, spring 1898.
Career: Darwen, MANCHESTER UNITED (£750 with JT Howarth, May 1921), Portsmouth (£2,500, November 1927), Ashton National FC (1928), Whitchurch (late 1928), Lancaster Town (1929), Chorley (1930), Burscough Rangers (1931), Northwich Victoria (season 1931-32).
George 'Tiny' Haslam, a dogged centre-half, was a reliable performer during his six years at Old Trafford when he was first reserve to Frank Barson. He made his senior debut in 1922 and had his best season in 1925-26 (making 11 League and FA Cup appearances).
Club record: 27 apps.

HAWKSWORTH, Anthony

Born: Sheffield, 15 January 1938.
Career: Barnsley Schoolboys, MANCHESTER UNITED (amateur May 1953, professional April 1955-December 1958). Army football: 1956-57.
Goalkeeper Tony Hawksworth, capped four times by England Schoolboys before joining United, went to on to represent his country at Youth team level and also helped the Reds win the FA Youth Cup three seasons running: 1954-56. He managed only one League outing for the club, starring in a 2-2 draw at Blackpool in October 1956 after obtaining permission from the Royal Tank Regiment to replace the injured Ray Wood. Unfortunately he was released at the end of the 1957-58 season and never again appeared in first-class football.
Club record: one app.

HAWORTH, Ronald

Born: Lower Darwen, Lancashire, 10 March 1901. Died: Blackburn, autumn, 1973.
Career: Blackburn Rovers (1921), Hull City (1924), MANCHESTER UNITED (May 1926), Darwen (August 1927).
Inside-forward Ron Haworth was a United reserve in 1926-27, appearing in the opening two League games of the campaign against Liverpool and Sheffield United (both away).
Club record: 2 apps.

HAY, Thomas

Born: Staveley, Derbyshire, 1857.
Career: Staveley FC (1822), Bolton Wanderers (1883), Great Lever FC (1885), Halliwell FC (1886), Burslem FC (1887), NEWTON HEATH (September 1888), Accrington (1890), Burton Swifts (during season 1893-94).
Goalkeeper Tom Hay was a regular between the posts for the Heathens in their first season in the Football Alliance (1889-90), making 15 appearances. He also played in over 100 'other' matches for the club. Hay started out as a centre-forward before developing into an excellent 'last line of defence.' He twice represented the Lancashire County side, played for Sheffield District in annual games against Birmingham, Glasgow, Lancashire and London, but was often on the injured list, suffering a series of broken bones during his career.
Club record: 16 apps. (also 103 'other' apps)

HAYDOCK, Frank

Born: Eccles, 29 November 1940

Career: Clarendon County School (Eccles), Eccles & District Boys, Blackpool (amateur, 1956), MANCHESTER UNITED (amateur, early 1958, professional December 1959), Charlton Athletic (£10,000, August 1963), Portsmouth (£20,000, late 1965), Southend United (£8,000, early 1969). Later a hotelier in Blackpool (1980s).

Centre-half Frank Haydock joined United shortly before the Munich air disaster. He developed strongly through the club's nursery system but found it hard to get a game in the first team. Brave and determined, he accumulated well over 200 senior appearances as a professional, and actually made his debut for Charlton in a friendly against Manchester City in 1963, marking his older brother, Billy!

Club record: 6 apps.

HAYES, James Vincent

Born: Miles Platting, Manchester, spring 1879.

Career: Newton Heath Athletic, NEWTON HEATH (February 1901), Brentford (May 1907), MANCHESTER UNITED (June 1908), Bradford Park Avenue (November 1910), Norway Olympic team coach (1912), Wiener SV, Austria (coach, mid-1912), Rochdale (player-manager, 1913), Preston North End (secretary-manager, 1919-23), CF Madrid, Spain (manager, 1923-24).

Vince Hayes appeared in several positions during his career, but preferred the full-back role from where he gave the club splendid service during two useful spells, during which he won an FA Cup winners medal in 1909. He recovered from two broken legs to represent the Football League. He did a fine job as coach in Norway and in 1910 was appointed chairman of the Players' Union. In later life he was a publican in Stockport and ran a hotel in Prestwich.

Club record: 128 apps. 2 goals. (also 4 'other' apps, 2 goals)

HAYWOOD, Joseph H

Born: Wednesbury, circa 1893

Career: Hindley Central, MANCHESTER UNITED (£50, May 1913-May 1919). Quit football to play rugby.

Joe Haywood was a resolute half-back who was released by United at the end of the first post WW1 season and soon afterwards changed his sport from the round ball to the oval one!

Club record: 26 apps.

HEALY, David Jonathan

Born: Downpatrick, 5 August 1979

Career: MANCHESTER UNITED (trainee, July 1995, professional November 1997), Port Vale (on loan, February 2000), Preston North End (£1.5 million, December 2000)

Two of David Healy's senior outings for United were in the League Cup competition. He won seven caps for Northern Ireland as well as eight at Under-21 level and one for the 'B' team before joining Preston North End whom he helped reach the 2001 First Division Play-off Final (v. Bolton). He has since added to his collection of full caps, and with seven international goals already to his credit, he should soon become his country's leading scorer, overtaking Colin Clarke's total of 13.

Club record: 3 apps.

HEATHCOTE, Joseph

Born: Elton, autumn 1879

Career: Berry's Association, NEWTON HEATH (April 1899-May 1902).

Joe Heathcote was an inside-forward whose career came to a premature end when he suffered a compound fracture of the leg playing against Preston North End at Bank Street on New Year's Day 1902.

Club record: 8 apps. (also one 'other' app)

HEIGHT

Tallest

Three of the tallest players (at 6ft 4ins/1.93m) ever to appear in a first-class game for United are defenders Gordon McQueen and Gary Pallister along with goalkeeper Peter Schmeichel.

Goalkeepers Harry Moger (1903-12), Herbert Broomfield (1907-10) and Gary Walsh (1985-93) along with defender Jaap Stam were all 6ft 3ins tall.

Shortest

Among the shortest players to turn out at competitive level for the club (all standing at 5ft 4ins/1.63m) we have Bernie Donaghy (1905-06), Terry Gibson (1986-87) Billy Harrison (1920-22), Ernie Taylor (1958) and Billy Wrigglesworth (1937-47). Wingers Johnny Berry (1950s) and Warren Bradley (1958-62), Herbert Burgess (1906-10), 1950s wing-half Henry Cockburn and Bill Owen (1934-36) were around 5ft 5ins tall, whilst Billy Stewart and Gordon Strachan only a fraction taller.

HELSINKI (HJK)
After a 3-2 away win, United quickened the pace to see off the Finnish champions in the return leg of their preliminary round contest in the 1965-66 European Cup competition. John Connelly scored a hat-trick in the 6-0 romp at Old Trafford to give the Reds an emphatic 9-2 aggregate victory.

HENDERSON, William
Born: Edinburgh, 1898. Died: Rosyth, 1964.
Career: Edinburgh Schools, St Bernard's FC, Airdrieonians (1920), MANCHESTER UNITED (November 1921), Preston North End (January 1925), Clapton Orient, Heart of Midlothian (season 1926-27), Morton (1927-28), Torquay United (1928-29), Exeter City (1929-30).
Bustling centre-forward Bill Henderson scored on his League debut for United against Aston Villa only days after joining the club. He was top-scorer when he left the club for Preston during 1924-25.
Club record: 36 apps. 17 goals

HENDRY, James
Born: Scotland circa 1870.
Career: Alloa Athletic, NEWTON HEATH (September 1892-May 1893).
Reserve outside-left Jim Hendry was a Heathens player for one season, deputising in two matches for Willie Mathieson. He scored on his League debut in a record 10-1 win over Wolverhampton Wanderers.
Club record: 2 apps. one goal (also one 'other' app).

HENRYS, Arthur
Born: Newcastle 1870
Career: Gainsborough Trinity, NEWTON HEATH (season 1891-92), Notts Jardines*, NEWTON HEATH (October 1892), Leicester Fosse (March 1893), Notts Co (1896-97), Gainsborough Trinity..
A competent centre-half, Arthur Henrys was suspended temporarily in 1892 after his registration was not officially sanctioned by the FA. He helped Notts County win the Second Division Championship in his only season with the Magpies.
* Henrys transfer to Notts Jardines was suspended by the FA. Henrys remained a Newton Heath player; the Notts secretary was banned fron further management.
Club record: 28 apps. (also 28 'other' apps, one goal)

169

HERD, David George
Born: Hamilton, Lanarkshire, 15 April 1934.
Career: Princes Road School (Moss Side), Stockport County (amateur 1949, professional 1951), Arsenal (£10,000, 1954), MANCHESTER UNITED (£35,000, July 1961), Stoke City (July 1968), Waterford (1970), Lincoln City (manager, 1971-72).
Scottish international David Herd's father Alex (ex-Manchester City) was also a Stockport County player. They played together in the same League side in May 1951. Herd junior scored 109 goals in 185 games for Arsenal before joining United where he quickly established himself in the forward-line alongside Dennis Viollet with Bobby Charlton. He then drew up a fine partnership with Denis Law and top-scored in his first season at Old Trafford. In 1963 he netted twice in the FA Cup Final as United swept aside Leicester City. Powerful, alert, strong in the air, with a fierce shot, Herd went on to score almost 150 times for United, gaining two League Championship-winning medals in 1965 & 1967. He missed out on European glory in 1968, failing to regain his position in the side after fracturing his leg playing against Leicester in March of the previous year.
Playing in a team containing the brilliance of Best, Charlton, Crerand and Law, Herd's contribution is often overlooked. He was an uncomplicated player, doing the simple things extremely well; his goal ratio is sufficient testament to his undoubted abilities, enabling his name to be mentioned alongside Rowley, Taylor, Hughes and Cole as one of United's greatest centre-forwards.
Herd won five full caps for the country of his birth.
Club record: 265 apps. 145 goals

HEREFORD UNITED

FA Cup result v Town:

	Round	Venue	Result
1989-90	4	Away	W 1-0

Player with both clubs: K Goddard (United reserve), R Newsome (United WW2).
Associated with both clubs: R Smith (United reserve, Hereford assistant-manager), A Ashman (Bulls' assistant-manager, United scout).

HERON, Thomas Russell Ferrie

Born: Irvine, Ayrshire, 31 March 1936
Career: Royal Academy School (Scotland), Queen's Park, Kilmarnock, Portadown, MANCHESTER UNITED (March 1958), York City (May 1961), Altrincham (1966), Droylsden (1969-70).
Tommy Heron was a useful outside-left when he joined United but he was unable to get much action in the first XI and was switched to full-back where he acted as reserve to Shay Brennan and Joe Carolan.
Club record: 3 apps.

HEYWOOD

Heywood scratched from the 1891-92 FA Cup competition and as a result United went through from the 2nd qualifying round stage on default.

HEYWOOD, Herbert

Born: Little Hulton, Lancashire circa 1910.
Career: Turton FC, Oldham Athletic (amateur), Northwich Victoria, MANCHESTER UNITED (amateur April 1933, professional May 1933), Tranmere Rovers (December 1934), Altrincham (1935), Wigan Athletic, Astley &Tyldesley Colliery (re-instated as an amateur 1936-37).
Outside-right Herbert Heywood was reserve to James Brown during his time at Old Trafford. Both his goals came in a 4-1 home win over Hull City in October 1933.
Club record: 4 apps. 2 goals

HIBERNIANS (MALTA)

Two goals apiece by David Sadler and Denis Law gave United a comfortable 4-0 home victory over the Maltese part-timers in the first leg of a first round European Cup-tie in 1967-68. United eased up in the sun, drawing 0-0 to take the tie comfortably on aggregate.

HIGGINBOTHAM, Daniel John

Born: Manchester, 29 December 1978
Career: MANCHESTER UNITED (trainee, 1995, professional July 1997), Royal Antwerp (on loan, March-May 2000), Derby County (£2 million, July 2000).
Left-back Danny Higginbotham made only a handful of first-class appearances for United before being transferred to Derby. One of 'Fergie's Fledglings' he is 6ft 1in tall and weighs well over 12 stones - an excellent frame for defending! He is now successfully bedded in as a regular in the Rams' defence.
Club record: 7 apps.

HIGGINS, Mark Nicholas

Born: Buxton, 29 September 1958
Career: North West Derbyshire Schools, Everton (apprentice 1975, professional August 1976), MANCHESTER UNITED (£60,000, December 1985), Bury (on loan, January 1987, signing permanently for £10,000 the following month), Stoke City (£150,000, 1988-90), Burnley (trialist). Retired in 1991 with a back injury.
Central defender Mark Higgins initially announced his retirement (owing to a groin injury) at the end of the 1983-84 season, but he came back and continued to play until 1991, amassing a total of 260 League appearances. He covered for Kevin Moran and Billy Garton at Old Trafford.
His father John, also a central defender for Bolton Wanderers, made well over 200 appearances, lining up against United in the 1958 FA Cup Final.
Club record: 8 apps.

HIGGINS, William

Born: Smethwick, spring 1869
Career: Woodfield FC (Handsworth, Birmingham), Albion Swifts, Birmingham St George's, Grimsby Town (1892), Bristol City (1897), Newcastle United (1898), Middlesbrough (1900), NEWTON HEATH (October 1901-May 1902).
Half-back 'Sandy' Higgins had already played in more than 200 competitive games before joining the club from Middlesbrough. He failed to make an impression with the Heathens.
Club record: 10 apps.

HIGHER WALTON

Higher Walton were drawn at home against Newton Heath in the 1st qualifying round of the FA Cup competition in 1890-91 but waived the right to play in front of their own supporters and switched the tie to North Road where they lost 2-0 in front of a crowd of 3,000.

HIGSON, James

Born: Newton Heath
Career: Manchester Wednesday FC, NEWTON HEATH/MANCHESTER UNITED (late February-early May 1902).
Inside-forward 'Jamie' Higson was registered with United for barely three months - having been the first signing made by the 'new board' which was in place before the club's name change.
Club record: 5 apps. one goal

HILDITCH, Clarence George

Born: Hartford, Cheshire, 2 June 1894

Career: Hartford FC, Witton Albion, Altrincham, MANCHESTER UNITED (January 1916 as a trialist, signed almost immediately, then temporary player-manager from October 1926-April 1927, retiring as a player in 1932 to coach the younger players at Old Trafford for a season).

Half-back 'Lal' Hilditch spent seventeen years with United, developing from a utility forward into an quality wing-half, hard but fair, confident and dependable. He represented England against Wales in a Victory international in 1919 and toured South Africa with the FA party in 1920. He also played for the Football League XI.

Hilditch was well known for being one of the cleanest players ever to play the game; his contribution to United during a time when the club's fortunes were at their lowest ebb, was immense. He took over as United's only player-manager in October 1926 after Jack Chapman was suspended by the FA for alleged improper conduct. Hilditch saw out the season before returning to playing duties.

Club record: 322 apps. 7 goals

HILL, Gordon Alex

Born: Sunbury-on-Thames, 1 April 1954

Career: Ashford Youth Club (Kent), QPR (trialist), Southend United (trialist), Staines Town, Slough Town, Southall, Millwall (1973), Chicago Sting (on loan, 1975), MANCHESTER UNITED (November 1975 for £70,000, rising to £80,000 after international recognition), Derby County (£250,000, April 1978), QPR (£175,000, 1979), Montreal Manic (1981), Chicago Sting (1982), New York Arrows, Kansas Comets, Tacoma Stars, Helsinki, FC Twente Enschede, AFC Bournemouth (trialist), Northwich Victoria (1986, later caretaker-manager), Stafford Rangers (1987), Northwich Victoria (1988, later player-manager & player-coach), Radcliffe Borough (1990). Coached in Nova Scotia and latterly ran his own soccer school in Palm Harbor.

A fast, direct and tricky left-winger, Gordon Hill drew up an excellent scoring record with United. Nicknamed 'Merlin' he occasionally flickered in and out of the game, annoying his manager and fans alike, but on his day he was a fine footballer. He gained six full caps for England, and also represented his country at Youth, 'B' and Under-23 levels. He appeared in successive FA Cup Finals for United (1976 & 1977) being substituted in both, but he did collect a winners' medal in the latter (v. Liverpool).

Club record: 134 apps. 51 goals

HILLAM, Charles Emmanuel

Born: Burnley, 6 October 1908

Career: Clitheroe, Nelson (1930-31), Clitheroe, Burnley (1932), MANCHESTER UNITED (May 1933), Clapton Orient (May 1934), Southend United (1938), Chingford Town (WW2, later trainer 1948-49).

After just a moderate number of senior outings for United, goalkeeper Charlie Hillam went on to appear in 138 League games (116 in succession for Orient) after leaving Old Trafford.

Club record: 8 apps.

HINE, Ernest William

Born: Smithy Cross, near Barnsley 9 April 1901. Died: Huddersfield, April 1974

Career: New Mills FC, Staincross Station, Barnsley (amateur 1921, professional 1922), Leicester City (1926), Huddersfield Town (1932), MANCHESTER UNITED (£10,000, February 1933), Barnsley (December 1934-38, appointed coach at Leeds Road, 1939).

Inside-forward Ernie Hine had a tremendous League career. He scored goals galore - 127 in 291 games in two spells for Barnsley (including 123 in the League - still a club record), 148 in 247 outings for Leicester, four in 23 appearances for Huddersfield and another 12 goals in just over 50 outings for United. He possessed a tremendous right foot and often chose to shoot from outside the penalty area. He was into his thirties when he arrived at Old Trafford - what a pity!

Club record: 53 apps. 12 goals

HODGE, James

Born: Stenhousemuir, 5 July 1891. Died: Chorlton-cum-Hardy, 2 September 1970.

Career: Stenhousemuir, MANCHESTER UNITED (May 1910), Millwall Athletic (£1,500, December 1919), Norwich City (1922), Southend United (season 1923-24).

Wing-half/full-back James Hodge spent nine-and-a-half years with United. He was selected in nine different positions, even as an emergency goalkeeper, such was his willingness to get a game!

Club record: 86 apps. 2 goals

HODGE, John

Born: Stenhousemuir, circa 1894

Career: Stenhousemuir, MANCHESTER UNITED (June 1913-May 1919).

Defender John Hodge - the younger brother of James Hodge (q.v) - made all his appearances for United in the last two seasons before the Great War. He failed to re-appear in League football after leaving Old Trafford, having been placed on the transfer list at just £25.

Club record: 30 apps.

171

HODGES, Frank Charles

Born: Nechells Green, Birmingham, 26 January 1891. Died: Southport, 5 June 1985.
Career: Alum Rock All Souls FC (Birmingham), Birmingham City Gas Works FC, Birmingham (1912), St Mirren (WW1 guest), MANCHESTER UNITED (£100, August 1919), Wigan Borough (£100, June 1921), Crewe Alexandra (1922), Winsford United (1926).
A reserve inside-forward, Frank Hodges scored a goal every five games for United. He won a Scottish Victory Cup medal with St Mirren in 1919.
Club record: 20 apps. 4 goals

HOFTON, Leslie Brown

Born: Sheffield, early 1888
Career: Kiveton Park FC (Sheffield), Worksop Town, Denaby United, Glossop (1908), MANCHESTER UNITED (£1,000, July 1910-May 1913, re-signed after WW1 in September 1919), Denaby Main (February 1922).
Full-back Les Hofton had two spells with United either side of the Great War. Never a regular performer in the senior side, he skippered the second XI to the Central League Championship in 1920-21.
Club record: 19 apps.

HOGG, Graeme James

Born: Aberdeen, 17 June 1964
Career: Aberdeen & District Schools, MANCHESTER UNITED (apprentice, July 1980, professional June 1982), West Bromwich Albion (loan, November-December 1987), Portsmouth (August 1988), Heart of Midlothian (1991).
A central defender with a positive approach, Graeme Hogg took over from Gordon McQueen and was unlucky to miss the 1985 FA Cup Final v. Everton due to injury. Unfortunately, after looking a very promising prospect, once Paul McGrath and Kevin Moran had established themselves at the club, the unlucky Hogg became surplus to requirements.
Club record: 111 apps. one goal

HOLDEN, Richard

Born: Middleton, Lancashire, 12 June 1885.
Career: Parkfield Central (Oldham & District League), Tonge FC, MANCHESTER UNITED (amateur May 1904, professional September 1904-May 1914).
Dick Holden played his early football in the forward-line before converting into a sound tackling full-back who played in an England international trial in 1908. He missed out on a possible full cap through injury and then sat out the FA Cup Final the following year, also due to injury. He won a League Championship medal with United in 1907-08, but made only eight appearances in 1910-11 when then title was won for the second time. Holden served in WW1 with the RAF.
Club record: 117 apps.

HOLT, J Edward

Born: Newton Heath 1880
Career: Newton Heath Athletic, NEWTON HEATH (initially as a trialist, March 1899 to May 1900)
Right-winger Ted Holt's scoring debut for the Heathens was against Chesterfield (h) on 28 April 1900 when he deputised for Foley.
Club record: one app. one goal

HOLTON, James Allan

Born: Lesmahagow, Lanarkshire, 11 April 1951. Died: Baginton, near Coventry, 5 October 1993.
Career: Celtic (groundstaff), West Bromwich Albion (professional, 1968), Shrewsbury Town (1971), MANCHESTER UNITED (£80,000, May 1973), Miami Toros (on loan, summer, 1976), Sunderland (on loan, September 1976, signed permanently for £40,000, October 1976), Coventry City (1977), Detroit Express (on loan, 1980), Sheffield Wednesday (summer, 1981). Retired 1982.
Centre-half Jim Holton, released by West Bromwich Albion without ever making the first team, went on to win 15 caps for Scotland as a dominant, fearless and rugged defender. He sadly broke a leg playing against his future club, Sheffield Wednesday, in December 1974. He then broke the same leg in his comeback game (in the reserves) and at that juncture his United career was effectively over. A cult hero with the Stretford End supporters, and also a keen basketball player, he sadly died of a heart attack, aged only 42.
Club record: 72 apps. 6 goals

HOME FORM

This is United's 'home' record in all competitions:

North Road

Competition	P	W	D	L	F	A
League	15	6	3	6	39	35
FA Cup	4*	3*	0	1	10	5
F. Alliance	33	19	7	7	93	47
Totals	52	28	10	14	142	87 (63.46%)

* Includes one 'walkover' when opponents scratched and one match when opponents waived right to play at home, switching tie to North Road..

Old Trafford

Competition	P	W	D	L	F	A
League/PL	1613	936	383	294	3103	1548
FA Cup	122	77	24	21	217	108
League Cup	66	47	10	9	137	55
European	89*	60	23	6	205	69
World Club	1	0	1	0	1	1
Totals	1891	1120	441	330	3663	1781
						(70.89%)

* Includes one European Super Cup game

Maine Road

Competition	P	W	D	L	F	A
League	63	39	17	7	151	66
FA Cup	8	6	1	1	30	5
European	3	3	0	0	16	2
Totals	74	48	18	8	197	73 (77.02%)

Goodison Park (Everton)

Competition	P	W	D	L	F	A
FA Cup	1	1	0	0	3	0

Bank Street

Competition	P	W	D	L	F	A
League	281	192	47	42	682	263
FA Cup	35*	22*	8	5	92	36
Test Matches	2	1	1	0	3	1
Totals	318	215	56	47	777	300 (76.41%)

* Includes one match where opponents waived right to play replay at 'home' and switched to Bank Street.

Leeds Road (Huddersfield Town)

Competition	P	W	D	L	F	A
FA Cup	1	1	0	0	2	0

Anfield (Liverpool)

Competition	P	W	D	L	F	A
League	1	1	0	0	3	1

The Victoria Ground (Stoke City)

Competition	P	W	D	L	F	A
League	1	1	0	0	3	1

Home Park (Plymouth Argyle)

Competition	P	W	D	L	F	A
European	1	1	0	0	2	0

Overall Totals

Competition	P	W	D	L	F	A
League/PL	1974	1175	450	349	3981	1914
FA Cup	171	110	33	28	354	154
League Cup	66	47	10	9	137	55
European	93	64	23	6	223	71
World Club	1	0	1	0	1	1
F Alliance	33	19	7	7	93	47
Test matches	2	1	1	0	3	1
All Comps.	2340	1416	525	399	4792	2243 (71.73%)

Home From Home

Of all the teams who have played against the Reds in the Football League/Premiership, 22 have not won or did not win on United soil. They are Accrington FC, Brighton & Hove Albion, Bristol Rovers, Burton United/Swifts, Chesterfield (10 defeats out of 10), Crewe Alexandra, Doncaster Rovers, Gainsborough Trinity, Gateshead/South Shields, Glossop, Hull City, Leyton Orient, Loughborough, Millwall, Northampton Town, Oxford United, Rotherham Town/County/United, Stockport County, Swindon Town, Walsall/Town Swifts, Watford and York City..

HOMER, Thomas Percy

Born: Winson Green, Birmingham, early 1886.
Career: Dudley Road Council and City Road Schools (Winson Green), Birmingham Schools, Soho Caledonians (Handsworth & District League), Erdington FC, Aston Villa (amateur), Stourbridge (on loan), Kidderminster Harriers, MANCHESTER UNITED (October 1909-May 1912).
Centre-forward Tom Homer did well when called into action by United - his record proves that. He was 23 when he made his League debut against Woolwich Arsenal in October 1909 - and he then had the pleasure of netting one of the club's first-ever goals at Old Trafford, in the 4-3 defeat by Liverpool on 19 February 1910. His career was cut short by a knee injury. He later became a publican in Birmingham.
Club record: 25 apps. 14 goals

HONOURS

The following personnel received Birthday/New Year's Honours from HRH Queen Elizabeth II...
Sir Matt Busby, CBE
Sir Robert Charlton, CBE

Garth Crooks, OBE
Sir Alex Ferguson, CBE, OBE
Sir Roy Gardner (Plc Chairman)
Harry Gregg, MBE
Sammy McIlroy, MBE
Bryan Robson, OBE

Peter Schmeichel, MBE
Sir Roland Smith (Director)
Nobby Stiles, MBE
Gordon Strachan, OBE
Ray Wilkins, MBE
Sir Walter Winterbottom, CBE, OBE

HOOD, William

Born: Ashton-under-Lyne, early 1873.
Career: NEWTON HEATH (from season 1891-92), Stalybridge Rovers (May 1894)
The versatile Billy Hood occupied several positions during his time with the Heathens, appearing as a full-back, wing-half and utility forward. He possessed a neat touch.
Club record: 54 apps. 11 goals (also 44 'other' apps, 8 goals)

HOOPER, Arthur Henry

Born: Brierley Hill, West Midlands, early 1889

Career: Kidderminster Harriers, MANCHESTER UNITED (October 1909), Crystal Palace (June 1914-May 1915). Did not feature after WW1.

Arthur Hooper acted as a reliable reserve utility forward during his five years with the club, scoring on his debut v. Tottenham Hotspur.

Club record: 7 apps. one goal

HOPKIN, Fred

Born: Dewsbury, Yorkshire 23 September 1895 Died: Darlington, March 1970.

Career: Darlington, MANCHESTER UNITED and Tottenham Hotspur (WW1 guest), MANCHESTER UNITED (signed February 1919), Liverpool (May 1921), Darlington (season 1931-32), Redcar Borough FC (trainer, season 1933-34), Leeds United (assistant-trainer, late 1930s).

Balding Fred Hopkin was a fast and clever outside-left who enjoyed taking on his opponent, being a goal-maker rather than goal-scorer. After leaving Old Trafford he appeared in 359 competitive games for Liverpool, winning successive League Championship medals in his first two seasons at Anfield when he missed only two games out of 84. He also played in one international trial match whilst on Merseyside - the nearest he came to gaining a full England cap.

An interesting point - immediately Hopkin scored his first Liverpool goal (against Bolton in March 1923), a fire broke out in the main stand at Anfield and play was halted for some considerable time.

Club record: 74 apps. 8 goals

HOPKINS, James

Born: Manchester 1873.

Career: Berry's Association, NEWTON HEATH (March-May 1899).

Reserve inside-forward Jim Hopkins' only League appearance for United was against New Brighton Tower shortly after he had signed for the club.

Club record: one app.

HOPKINSON, Samuel

Born: Killamarsh, nr Sheffield, 9 February 1902.

Career: Killamarsh schoolboy football, North-east Derbyshire Schools, Rotherham County (1919), Shirebrook FC (1921), Valley Road BC, Sheffield (1922), Chesterfield (1924), Shirebrook FC (1927), Ashton National (1928), MANCHESTER UNITED (May 1929), Tranmere Rovers (May 1935).

Orthodox winger Sam Hopkinson - who won England schoolboy honours v. Scotland in 1917 - played his best football with Chesterfield. It looked as if his playing days had come to an end when he chose to enter non-League football in 1927, but he bounced back with United and served the club for six seasons, albeit mainly as a reserve during the first one and last three.

Club record: 53 apps. 12 goals

HOUSTON, Stewart Mackie

Born: Dunoon, Argyll, 20 August 1949

Career: Port Glasgow Rangers, Chelsea (1967), Brentford (£17,000, 1972), MANCHESTER UNITED (£55,000, December 1973), Sheffield United (July 1980), Colchester United (player-coach, 1983), Plymouth Argyle (coach), Arsenal (assistant-manager, 1990), Queen's Park Rangers (manager, 1996-97), Tottenham Hotspur (assistant-manager/coach, 1998-2000), Walsall (coach, August 2002).

Consistent full-back Stewart Houston was signed by manager Tommy Docherty twice - first for Chelsea and then Manchester United. He loved to over-lap and often acted as an extra attacker for the Reds. He won a Second Division championship in 1975 and appeared in the FA Cup Final defeat by Southampton twelve months later. Unfortunately he missed the 1977 Final through injury, his place being taken by Arthur Albiston who then generously offered Houston his winners' medal after the game! In 1982 Houston won another Second Division Championship medal with Sheffield United. Capped by Scotland in 1976, he also represented his country in two Under-23 internationals and was assistant to manager George Graham at Highbury. Houston's father played League football for St Mirren.

Club record: 250 apps. 16 goals

HOWARTH, John Thomas

Born: Darwen, Lancashire, 1899.

Career: Darwen, MANCHESTER UNITED (signed with George Haslam for £750, May 1921, left May 1923).

Reserve full-back John Howarth made all his League appearances for United in season 1921-22.

Club record: 4 apps.

HOWELLS, Edward

Born: Manchester, autumn 1862.

Career: NEWTON HEATH (883-87), Ten Acres FC (1887).

Half-back Edward Howells played in one FA Cup-tie for the Heathens, lining up against Fleetwood Rangers in October 1886. He was a prominent player in several 'other' matches for the club.

His name sometimes appeared as Howles.

His brother Thomas was also registered with Newton Heath at the same time.

Club record: one app. (also 33 'other' apps, 2 goals)

HUDDERSFIELD TOWN

United's League results v the Terriers:

Season	Div	Home	Away	Season	Div	Home	Away
1920-21	1	W 2-0	L 2-5	1946-47	1	W 5-2	D 2-2
1921-22	1	D 1-1	D 1-1	1947-48	1	D 4-4	W 2-0
				1948-49	1	W 4-1	L 1-2
1925-26	1	D 1-1	L 0-5	1949-50	1	W 6-0	L 1-3
1926-27	1	D 0-0	D 0-0	1950-51	1	W 6-0	W 3-2
1927-28	1	D 0-0	L 2-4	1951-52	1	D 1-1	L 2-3
1928-29	1	W 1-0	W 2-1				
1929-30	1	W 1-0	D 2-2	1953-54	1	W 3-1	D 0-0
1930-31	1	L 0-6	L 0-3	1954-55	1	D 1-1	W 3-1
				1955-56	1	W 3-0	W 2-0
1936-37	1	W 3-1	L 1-3				
				1970-71	1	D 1-1	W 2-1
1938-39	1	D 1-1	D 1-1	1971-72	1	W 2-0	W 3-0

Summary of League results

	P	W	D	L	F	A
Division 1	42	18	15	9	78	60
Home	21	11	9	1	46	21
Away	21	7	6	8	32	39
Total	42	18	15	9	78	60

FA Cup results v the Terriers:

	Round	Venue	Result
1911-12	1	Home	W 3-1
1923-24	2	Home	L 0-3
1962-63	3	Home	W 5-0

Fact File

When Huddersfield drew 4-4 at Maine Road in 1947-48, Jack Rowley scored all four of United's goals.

In 1949-50, when United beat the Terriers 6-0 at Old Trafford, visiting 'keeper Bob Hesford saved two penalties, both taken by Charlie Mitten, who later found the net with a 20-yard free-kick.

Players with both clubs include: B Asquith (Town WW2), H Baird, J Ball, P Bielby, H Bough (United reserve), R Burke, L Butt (United WW2), R Chester, G Crowther (United reserve), SI Davies, E Dodds & P Doherty (both United WW2), P Fletcher, A Gowling, E Hine, W Johnston, T Laing, D Law, H McShane, F Mann, L Martin, D May, J Nicholson, T Poole (United junior), G Roughton, A Sidebottom, J Smith, F Stapleton (Town player-coach), R Thomson (Town trialist), B Thornley, W Watson (1970s), W Watson (United WW2). Also associated: S Bruce. L Macari (United players, Town managers), I Greaves (United player, Town coach & manager), H Cockburn (United player, Town assistant-trainer/coach), J Jordan (United player, Town assistant-manager), T Cavanagh (Town player, United trainer/assistant-manager).

HUDSON, Edward Kearney

Born: Bolton, early 1887

Career: Walkden Central FC, MANCHESTER UNITED (January 1912), Stockport County (August 1919), Aberdare (season 1920-21).

Reserve defender Ted Hudson's first two senior outings for United were in each of the wing-half positions. He later played both as a right and left full-back.

Club record: 11 apps.

HUGHES, Leslie Mark

Refer to front of section.

HULL CITY

United's League results v the Tigers:

Season	Div	Home	Away
1905-06	2	W 5-0	W 1-0
1922-23	2	W 3-2	L 1-2
1923-24	2	D 1-1	D 1-1
1924-25	2	W 2-0	W 1-0
1933-34	2	W 4-1	L 1-4
1934-35	2	W 3-0	L 2-3
1935-36	2	W 2-0	D 1-1
1974-75	2	W 2-0	L 0-2

Summary of League results

	P	W	D	L	F	A
Div 2 Totals	16	9	3	4	30	17
Home	8	7	1	0	22	4
Away	8	2	2	4	8	13

FA Cup results v the Tigers:

	Round	Venue	Result
1948-49	6	Away	W 1-0
1951-52	3	Home	L 0-2

League Cup results v the Tigers:

	Round	Venue	Result
1987	2 (1)	Home	W 5-0
	2 (2)	Away	W 1-0

Watney Cup

Manchester United defeated Hull City 4-3 on penalties in the semi-final of the Watney Cup on 5 August 1970. A large Boothferry Park crowd of 34,007 witnessed the 1-1 draw after extra-time in normal play before the Reds squeezed through to meet Derby County in the Final.

Fact File

When Scond Division Hull City caused the FA Cup Third Round's biggest upset of 1952 by beating the League Champions-elect 2-0 at Old Trafford, it was a personal triumph for Hull's silver-haired player-manager, the legendary Raich Carter, who completely dominated the midfield, seemingly at walking pace!

Players with both clubs include: J Barber, P Barnes, D Brown (United reserve), W Buchan & E Burbanks (both United WW2), R Carroll, C Chadwick (United WW2), N Culkin, J Downie, P Fletcher, P Gibson (United reserve), W Halligan (United WW1), R Howarth, J Koffman (United reserve), A Mitchell, P O'Connell, S Pearson, J Wealands, J Whitehouse, N Whitworth, J Wood (United reserve). Also associated: T Docherty (United manager, City assistant-manager), F Buckley (United player, City manager), W McGuinness (United player & manager, City coach), S McClaren (Hull City player, United assistant-manager), T Cavanagh (United assistant-manager & trainer, City coach), S Owen (coach at both clubs, also United scout), M Brown (City player, United assistant-manager), R Brocklebank (United WW2 player, City manager).

175

HULME, Aaron

Born: Manchester, circa Easter 1883. Died: Failsworth, nr Manchester, November 1933.

Career: Newton Heath Athletic, Colne FC (summer 1904), Oldham Athletic (1904), MANCHESTER UNITED (May 1906), Nelson (July 1909), Hyde (1910), St Helens Recreationalists (1912), Newton Heath Athletic (1913-15). Did not play after WW1. Reserve full-back Aaron Hulme got very few opportunities in United's first XI. Sadly , he was killed in a road traffic accident.

Club record: 4 apps.

HUNTER, George C

Born: Peshawar, India, 16 August 1886. Died: London, February 1934.

Career: Intermediate football in Peshawar (arranged by his father), Maidstone, Croydon Common, Aston Villa (1908), Oldham Athletic (£1,200, early 1912), Chelsea (£1,000, 1913), MANCHESTER UNITED (£1,300, March 1914), guested for Croydon Common, Birmingham and Brentford during WW1, Portsmouth (August 1919). He announced his retirement in May 1922

A well-built, powerful half-back, noted for his tough and vigorous tackling, George 'Cocky' Hunter - a comedian in the dressing room - was rather reckless at times and often conceded free-kicks in dangerous positions while also giving away his fair share of penalties! Nevertheless, he was always a very competitive footballer with a fiery temper, made almost 100 appearances for Villa, with whom he won a League Championship medal in 1909-10 and twice represented the Football League in 1911. His manager and his colleagues could not control him at Chelsea but he was handed the captaincy at Old Trafford. He was in trouble however, with the United directorate in January 1915 and was suspended sine-die for failing to comply with training regulations, as the team's skipper it was thought he should have set a better example. Born into a military background within 10 miles of the Khyber Pass, Hunter served as a CSM in France and Gallipoli during WW1.

Club record: 23 apps. 2 goals

HUNTER, Reginald John

Born: Colwyn Bay, 25 October 1938

Career: Colwyn Bay, MANCHESTER UNITED (professional, November 1956), Wrexham (February 1960), Bangor City (1962-64).

Reserve winger Reg Hunter's only senior appearance for United was in a League game at Aston Villa in December 1958 when he deputised for Warren Bradley. He had earlier won an FA Youth Cup winners medal in 1957, and later collected a Welsh Cup winners medal with Bangor who beat his former club, Wrexham, after a replay in the 1962 Final.

Club record: one app.

HUNTER, William

Born: Sunderland, circa 1888.

Career: Sunderland West End (1906), Liverpool (1908), Sunderland (1909), Lincoln City (1ate 1909), Wingate Albion (1910), Airdrieonians, South Shields (1911-12), Barnsley (summer 1912), MANCHESTER UNITED (March 1913), Clapton Orient (July 1913), Exeter City (1914-15)..

William Hunter, a rough and ready centre-forward, deputised for George Anderson towards the end of the 1912-13 season and netted twice in a 3-0 home win over Newcastle in his second outing.

Club record: 3 apps. 2 goals

HURST, Daniel James

Born: Cockermouth, Lake District, autumn 1876

Career: Black Diamonds FC (Workington), Blackburn Rovers (1897), Workington (1900), Manchester City (1901), MANCHESTER UNITED (May 1902-May 1903).

Having spent a season with neighbours City, left-winger Danny Hurst made a useful start to his only campaign with the Reds, but he failed to hold his form and was released after just a year. He averaged a goal every four League games during his career (21 in 84 outings).

Club record: 21 apps. 4 goals

I for...
INCE, Paul Emerson Carlyle

Born: Ilford,
21 October 1967
Career: West Ham United
(apprentice, 1983,
professional 1985),
MANCHESTER
UNITED (£2.4 million,
September 1989), Inter
Milan (£8 million, July
1995), Liverpool (£4.2
million, 1997),
Middlesbrough (£1
million, August 1999),
Wolverhamton Wanderers
(August 2002).
The strong-running, hard-
working midfielder Paul
Ince helped United win
two FA Cup Finals (1990
& 1994), the European
Cup-winners Cup (1991),
the League Cup (1992)
and two Premiership titles
(1993 & 1994) as well as
gaining European Super
Cup and two FA Charity
Shield prizes. A
powerhouse of a
footballer with boundless
energy and no mean skill,
a ferocious tackle and grim
determination, he went on
to win 53 full caps for
England and was also
honoured by his country
at Youth, 'B' and Under-
21 levels. He skippered
United as well as England
and finished runner-up to
Paul McGrath in the PFA
'Player of the Year' poll in
1993. Ince made 72
League appearances for the
Hammers, 206 during his
six years at Old Trafford,
54 in Italy's Serie 'A', 65
for Liverpool and amassed
over 100 with
Middlesbrough. Ince is the
cousin of ex-champion
boxer, Nigel Benn.
Club record: 281 apps.
29 goals

IDDON, Richard

Born: Tarleton, Lancashire, 22 June 1901.

Career: Tarleton FC, Leyland (1920), Preston North End (for two seasons from 1921), Chorley (1923), MANCHESTER UNITED (May 1925), Chorley (July 1927), Morecambe (early 1928), New Brighton (mid-1928), Lancaster Town (late 1929), Horwich RMI (1931), Altrincham (1933-34).

Inside-forward Dick Iddon spent his two years at Old Trafford mainly in the reserves. His two senior games both ended in 1-0 defeats at West Ham (August 1925) and Burnley (February 1927). He helped Lancaster Town win the Lancashire Combination in 1929-30 by scoring 37 goals.

Club record: 2 apps.

INCE, Paul Emerson Carlyle

Refer to front of section.

INGLIS, William White

Born: Kirkcaldy, Fife, 2 March 1894. Died: Sale, Cheshire, 20 January 1968.

Career: Kirkcaldy United, Raith Rovers (1917), Sheffield Wednesday (1924), MANCHESTER UNITED (May 1925), Northampton Town (June 1930), MANCHESTER UNITED (assistant-trainer, August 1934, later coach, retired June 1961).

Along with Tom Curry and Bert Whalley, genial Scot Bill Inglis was mainly responsible for the development of so many young players at Old Trafford during the late 1940s and '50s. As a player he was named as reserve for Scotland on three occasions and also played for the Home Scots v. the Anglo Scots in an international trial in Glasgow. A full-back, he deputised initially for Charlie Moore in United's League side.

Club record: 14 apps. one goal

INJURIES & ILLNESS

David Beckham broke his foot early in 2002 and recovered in time to lead England in the World Cup Finals in Japan and South Korea that summer. Unfortunately his team-mate and good friend Gary Neville also fractured a bone in his foot but he sadly missed the finals in the Land of the Rising Sun.

Jack Wilson sadly broke both legs as a Newcastle player (1919-20) before joining United in 1926.

Bill Ridding's playing days ended in 1936 at the age of 24. He later became a successful manager with Bolton Wanderers.

Wilf McGuinness' playing career effectively came to an end when he broke a leg playing for United's second XI against Stoke City in 1959. He was only 22 at the time. He attempted a comeback and was named as a sub at Leicester in 1966, but never got the nod.

On the evening of 22 April 1967, Bobby Noble, United's 21 year-old former Youth team captain, was involved in a car crash on his way home after helping United earn a point from a goalless draw with Sunderland at Roker Park which virtually guaranteed them the League title. He received serious chest injuries and also broke his right knee-cap. He was forced to quit football in March 1969 after failing to regain full fitness.

Norman Whiteside was forced to retire through injury in 1991. He was only 26.

United's former England Youth international Nicky Wood was forced to quit the professional scene in January 1989 at the age of 23 (after suffering a spinal stress fracture).

Fellow England Youth team player Paul Wratten's career at Old Trafford ended in May 1992 when he failed to recover from two stress fractures in his legs.

Bryan Robson broke his leg three times in a year whilst a West Bromwich Albion player and Mark 'Pancho' Pearson suffered two broken legs in the mid-1960s. Both regained full fitness.

On 2 September 1992 Dion Dublin broke his leg while playing for Manchester United against Crystal Palace in only his sixth League game for the club.

Joe Heathcote's career ended at the age of 25 - after he had suffered a compound fracture of the right leg playing for Newton Heath against Preston North End on New Year's Day 1902.

Dave Busst, the Coventry City centre-back, broken his leg in the Premiership game with United at Old Trafford in April 1996. He never played again.

INTER MILAN

European Cup

Venue	P	W	D	L	F	A
Home	1	1	0	0	2	0
Away	1	0	1	0	1	1
Summary	2	1	1	0	3	1

Two goals by Dwight Yorke gave United a 2-0 home win over Inter in the 1998-99 Champions League quarter-final and then, holding on, Paul Scholes netted a decisive 'away' goal in the 1-1 draw in the San Siro Stadium to ease the nerves and take the Reds through on aggregate at 3-1. United's David Beckham and Milan's Diego Simeone opposed each other in these two encounters, having been involved the incident in the World Cup 2nd round tie in St Etienne, France on 30 June 1998 when Beckham was sent-off for 'aiming a kick' at the Argentinian midfielder. Players with both clubs include: L Blanc, P Ince, M Silvestre.

INTERNATIONAL & REPRESENTATIVE HONOURS

Details of United players who gained representative honours at various levels whilst with the club:

Full Caps

Argentina (1)   JS Veron (5*) 2001-02
Australia (1)   M Bosnich (1) 1999-2000
Czech Republic (1) K Poborsky (1) 1996-97
Denmark (3)   J Olsen (7) 1985-88, P Schmeichel (20) 1992-98, J Sivebaek (2) 1986-88
England (50)   V Anderson (3 caps) 1987-88, J Aston snr (17) 1947-51, G Bailey (2) 1984-85, D Beckham (54*) 1996-2002, J Berry (4) 1952-56, W Bradley (3) 1958-59, W Brown (6*) 1998-2002, N Butt (23*) 1996-2002, R Byrne (33) 1953-58, R Charlton (106) 1956-70, A Chilton (2) 1950-52, H Cockburn (13) 1946-52, A Cole (13) 1994-2001, J Connelly (10) 1965-66, S Coppell (42) 1977-83, M Duxbury (10) 1983-85, D Edwards (18) 1954-58, R.Ferdinand (1*) 2002, W Foulkes (1) 1954-55, B Greenhoff (17) 1975-78, H Halse (1) 1908-09, G Hill (6) 1975-78, P Ince (16) 1992-95, B Kidd (2) 1969-70, W McGuinness (2) 1958-59, J Mew (1) 1920-21, G Neville (52*) 1994-2002, P Neville (37*) 1995-2002, G Pallister (20) 1990-97, P Parker (3) 1991-94, SC Pearson (8) 1947-52, SJ Pearson (15) 1975-78, D Pegg (1) 1956-57, M Phelan (1) 1989-90, C Roberts (3) 1904-05, B Robson (77), 1981-92, J Rowley (6) 1948-52, D Sadler (4) 1967-71, P Scholes (49*) 1996-2002, L Sharpe (8) 1990-94, T Sheringham (13) 1997-2001, J Silcock (3) 1920-23, J Spence (2) 1925-27, A Stepney (1) 1967-68, N Stiles (28) 1964-70, T Taylor (19) 1952-58, D Viollet (2) 1959-62, G Wall (7) 1906-13, N Webb (8) 1989-92, R Wilkins (38) 1979-84, R Wood (3) 1954-56.
France (4)   F Barthez (5*) 2000-02, L Blanc (1) 2001-02, E Cantona (2), 1992-93, M Silvestre (3*) 2000-02
Holland (3)   J Cruyff (2) 1996-97, J Stam (8) 1997-2001, R van Nistelrooy (6*) 2001-02
Ireland (3)   W Crooks (1) 1921-22, M Hamill (3) 1911-14, D Lyner (1) 1922-23
Northern Ireland (24) T Anderson (6) 1973-75, G Best (32) 1963-74, J Blanchflower (12) 1953-58, T Breen (5) 1936-39), R Briggs (1) 1961-62, J Carey (7) 1946-49, R Carroll (2*) 2001-02, 1921-22, M Donaghy (18) 1988-92, K Gillespie (3) 1994-95, H Gregg (16) 1957-64, D Healy (7) 1999-2000, T Jackson (10) 1975-77, D McCreery (23) 1975-79, P McGibbon (5) 1994-97, C McGrath (16) 1976-79, S McIlroy (52) 1971-82, S McMillan (2) 1962-63, WS McMillen (3) 1933-37, P Mulryne (7) 1996-99, J Nicholl (41) 1975-82, J Nicholson (10) 1960-62, T Sloan (3) 1978-79, N Whiteside (36) 1981-88.
Norway (3)   H Berg (28) 1997-2000, R Johnsen (15*) 1996-2000, OG Solskjaer (36*) 1996-2002
Republic of Ireland (22) T Breen (2) 1936-37, S Brennan (16) 1965-70, N Cantwell (19) 1961-67, B Carey (2) 1992-93, J Carey (29) 1937-53, J Carolan (2) 1959-60, G Daly (9) 1973-77, A Dunne (24) 1962-71, P Dunne (5) 1964-67, J Giles (11) 1959-63, D Givens (6) 1969-70, A Grimes (14) 1978-83, D Irwin (56) 1990-2001, R Keane (45*) 1999-2002, P McGrath (31) 1985-89, M Martin (14) 1973-75, K Moran (38) 1980-88, L O'Brien (6) 1987-88, J O'Shea (2*) 2001-02, P Roche (7) 1974-75, F Stapleton (34) 1981-87, L Whelan (4) 1956-57
Scotland (20)   A Albiston (14) 1981-86, A Bell (1) 1911-12, M Buchan (32) 1972-77, F Burns (1) 1969-70, P Crerand (5) 1963-66, J Delaney (4) 1946-48, A Forsyth (6) 1973-76, G Graham (4) 1972-73, J Holton (15) 1972-75, S Houston (1) 1975-76, J Jordan (20) 1977-82, D Law (35) 1962-75, J Leighton (16) 1988-90, N McBain (1) 1922-23, B McClair (26) 1987-93, G McQueen (13) 1978-80, L Macari (18) 1973-78, T Miller (2) 1920-21, W Morgan (20) 1971-74, M.Stewart (3*) 2001-02, G Strachan (14) 1984-89
South Africa (1)   Q Fortune (10*) 1998-2002
Sweden (1)   J Blomqvist (3) 1998-2001
Trinidad/Tobago (1) D Yorke (7*) 1998-2002
Uruguay (1)   D Forlan (3*) 2001-02
USSR/CIS (1)   A Kanchelskis (4) 1991-95
Wales (24)   R Bennion (10) 1925-32, C Blackmore (38) 1985-94, T Burke (3) 1886-88, A Davies (7) 1983-85, J Davies (5) 1888-90, R Davies (3) 1972-73, S Davies (1) 1995-96, J Doughty (7) 1887-90, R Doughty (2) 1887-88, R Giggs (37*) 1991-2002, M Hughes (45) 1984-86/88-95, C Jenkyns (1) 1896-97, T Jones (4) 1926-30, W Meredith (26) 1907-20, G Moore (2) 1963-64, G Owen (2) 1888-89, J Owen (1) 1891-92, W Owen (4) 1888-89, J Powell (5) 1886-88, H Thomas (1) 1926-27, M Thomas (13) 1978-81, J Warner (1) 1938-39, C Webster (4) 1956-58, D Williams (2) 1928-29.
Yugoslavia (1) N Jovanovic (5) 1980-82

* Still adding to total as a United player.

NB - It should be noted that prior to 1924 there was an 'all' Ireland national team. Thereafter the country was divided into two different nations regarding football: the IFA (in the North) and the FAI (in the South). Two players - T Breen and J Carey - represented both the IFA and the FAI.

+ Roger Doughty played for Wales against Canada in an official international in September 1891.

REST OF THE WORLD (v. England)
D Law (1) 1963

REST OF EUROPE (v. Great Britain 1947, v. Scandinavia 1964)
J Carey (1) 1947, R Charlton (1) 1964, D Law (1) 1964

UNITED KINGDOM (v Wales)
G Best (1) 1969, R Charlton (1) 1969

WARTIME INTERNATIONALS
England - J Rowley (1) 1943-44

VICTORY INTERNATIONALS
England - C Hilditch (1) 1918-19
Ireland - J Carey (2) 1945-46, P O'Connell (1) 1918-19
Scotland - J Delaney (2) 1945-46
Wales - W Meredith (2) 1918-19, J Warner (1) 1945-46

INTERNATIONAL (v. Scotland, Burnden Park Disaster)
England - C Mitten (1) 1946-47, J Walton (1) 1946-47

'B' INTERNATIONALS
England - G Bailey (2) 1979-80, J Berry (1) 1951-52, R Byrne (3) 1953-54, H Cockburn (1) 1948-49, J Curtis (1) 1997-98, D Edwards (4) 1954-56, B Greenhoff (1) 1978-79, G Hill (1) 1977-78, P Ince (1) 1991-92, G Pallister (6) 1989-92, D Pegg (1) 1955-56, B Robson (1) 1990-91, J Rowley (1) 1948-49, L Sharpe (1) 1991-92, T Taylor (2) 1955-56, D Wallace (1) 1990-91, N Webb (4) 1990-92, R Wood (1) 1953-54.
Northern Ireland - J Nicholson (2) 1958-60, J Shiels (1) 1959-60
Republic of Ireland - D Brazil (2) 1989-90
Scotland - B McClair (1) 1989-90
Wales - C Lawton (1) 1991-92

UNDER-23 INTERNATIONALS

England - J Aston jnr (1) 1969-70, R Charlton (6) 1957-60, P Chisnall (4) 1963-64, S Coppell (1) 1975-76, D Edwards (6) 1953-57, P Edwards (3) 1969-70, W Foulkes (2) 1954-55, A Gowling (1) 1971-72, B Greenhoff (4) 1974-76, G Hill (1) 1975-76, B Kidd (10) 1966-70, W McGuinness (4) 1958-59, SJ Pearson (1) 1975-76, D Pegg (3) 1956-57, D Sadler (3) 1967-69, A Scanlon (5) 1958-59, M Setters (5) 1959-60, N Stiles (3) 1964-65, J Whitefoot (1) 1953-54, R Wood (1) 1953-54.
Northern Ireland - R Briggs (1) 1961-62, J Nicholson (3) 1961-64, N Whiteside (1) 1988-89
Republic of Ireland - D Brazil (2) 1988-90, P Dunne (1) 1965-66, F McEwen (1) 1965-66, R O'Brien (1) 1972-73
Scotland - F Burns (1) 1967-68, A Forsyth (1) 1973-74, J Holton (1) 1972-73, S Houston (2) 1974-75
Wales - C Griffiths (2) 1973-74, G Moore (3) 1962-64, K Morgans (2) 1957-59

UNDER-21 INTERNATIONALS

England - G Bailey (14) 1978-84, R Beardsmore (5) 1988-89, D Beckham (9) 1994-96, W Brown (8) 1998-2001, N Butt (7) 1994-97, C Casper (1) 1994-95, L Chadwick (10) 1999-2002, M Clegg (2) 1997-98, T Cooke (4) 1995-96, J Curtis (16) 1997-2000, M Duxbury (7) 1980-83, J Greening (11) 1998-2001, L Martin (2) 1988-89, R Moses (1) 1981-82, P Neville (7) 1994-97, M Robins (6) 1989-91, L Roche (1) 2000-01, L Sharpe (8) 1988-91, B Thornley (3) 1995-96, G Walsh (2) 1987-88, M Wilson (4) 2000-01
Northern Ireland - K Gillespie (1) 1993-94, D Healy (8) 1998-2000, D McCreery (1) 1977-78, P McGibbon (1) 1993-94, P Mulryne (3) 1998-99, J Nicholl (1) 1977-78
Republic of Ireland - D Brazil (7) 1986-89, B Carey (1) 1991-92, A Grimes (2) 1978-79, J O'Shea (9*) 2000-02, M Russell (3) 1986-87, R Teal (3) 1991-92, P.Tierney (2*) 2001-02, A Whelan (1) 1980-81
Scotland - A Albiston (5) 1976-78, G Brebner (8) 1996-98, D Ferguson (5) 1991-93, G Hogg (4) 1983-85, S McGarvey (4) 1981-84, A Notman (10) 1998-2001, M Stewart (5*) 1999-2002
Wales - C Blackmore (3) 1983-84, J Clark (1) 1977-79, A Davies (6) 1981-83, R Giggs (1) 1990-91, D Graham (1) 1990-91, C Griffiths (2) 1973-74, M Hughes (5) 1982-84, M Williams (2) 2000-01
*Still adding to his total as a United player.

UNOFFICIAL INTERNATIONALS

England - B Greenhoff (1) 1975-76, B Kidd (1) 1969-70, SJ Pearson (1) 1975-76, N Stiles (2) 1969-70
All-Ireland - M Martin (1) 1972-73

ENGLAND SELECT (v. Vejle)

R Charlton (1) 1960-61

THE THREE v THE SIX

R Charlton (1) 1973-74

FA OF IRELAND (wartime)

J Carey (1) 1945-46

ENGLAND XI (wartime)

J Rowley (1) 1943-44

IRELAND XI (wartime)

J Breen (2) 1943-45

ENGLAND (v Young England)

W Bradley (1) 1958-59, R Charlton (5) 1958-64, H Cockburn (1) 1953-54, N Stiles (1) 1964-65

YOUNG ENGLAND (v England)

R Byrne (1) 1953-54, D Edwards (1) 1953-54, W McGuinness (1) 1958-59, A Scanlon (1) 1958-59, D Viollet (1) 1953-54

INTERNATIONAL TRIALS

ENGLAND

R Beale (1) 1913-14, R Duckworth (2) 1907-12, J Griffiths (1) 1935-36, R Holden (1) 1907-08, J Mew (1) 1920-21, C Roberts (4) 1904-13, J Silcock (2) 1920-28, J Spence (1) 1926-27, G Stacey (1) 1911-12, G Vose (1) 1935-36, G Wall (3) 1906-11, A Whalley (1) 1913-14

SCOTLAND

N McBain (1) 1921-22, G Mutch (1) 1934-35, J Peddie (1) 1905-06, A Turnbull (1) 1909-10

OTHERS

FA XI

S Brennan (2) 1961-62, R Byrne (1) 1953-54, R Charlton (1) FA Charity Shield v. Spurs 1961-62, E Colman (1) 1956-57, J Morris (1) 1947-48, D Pegg (1) 1957-58, W Redman (1) 1951-52, J Rowley (1) 1947-48, A Scanlon (1) 1960-61, M Setters (1) 1960-61, T Taylor (2) 1954-56, D Viollet (1) 1954-55, J Walton (1) 1946-47, R Wood (1) 1957-58

FA XI (Wartime)

J Rowley (3) 1941-45, G Vose (1) 1941-42, W Winterbottom (2) 1941-42.

FA TOURS (to South Africa)

R Duckworth (1) 1910, C Hilditch (3) 1920, J Mew (1) 1920, G Wall (3) 1910, W Woodcock (2) 1920

IRISH TOUR (to Canada)

J Scott (4) 1953

WELSH TOUR (to Canada)

SR Bennion (3) 1929

FOOTBALL LEAGUE (wartime)
J Rowley (1) 1941-42

IRISH XI (wartime)
J Breen (1) 1942-43, J Carey (1) 1942-43

IRISH LEAGUE (wartime)
J Breen (2) 1942-45, J Rowley (1) 1942-43

FOOTBALL LEAGUE (Inter League)
R Allen (2) 1950-51, J Aston, snr (2) 1950, R Beale (1) 1913, J Berry (1) 1954, W Bryant (1) 1897, H Burgess (2) 1907-08, R Byrne (6) 1954-56, R Charlton (8) 1961-68, H Cockburn (1) 1950, J Connelly (1) 1966, R Duckworth (5) 1910-12, D Edwards (4) 1954-57, P Edwards (1) 1970, W Foulkes (2) 1954-55, C Gibson (1) 1987, H Halse (3) 1908-11, M Hamill (1)* 1913, C Hilditch (1)* 1910, V Hayes (1) 1910, L Hofton (2) 1911, B Kidd (1) 1970, P McGrath (1) 1987, W McGuinness (1) 1958, W Meredith (1)* 1913, J Mew (3)* 1919-22, C Moore (1)* 1927, J Morris (2) 1948, G Pallister (1) 1990, SC Pearson (1) 1952, A Quixall (1) 1958, C Roberts (8) 1905-12, B Robson (1) 1987, J Rowley (2) 1950-52, D Sadler (2) 1970-71, A Scanlon (1) 1959, J Silcock (4)* 1921-27, J Spence (1) 1926, A Stepney (2) 1968-70, N Stiles (3) 1965-68, J Sutcliffe (1) 1903, T Taylor (2) 1956, D Viollet (3) 1956-59, G Wall (5) 1909-12, E West (1) 1912, A Whalley (1) 1913, N Whiteside (1) 1987, R Wood (3) 1954-56.
* Total includes appearance in benefit match (Football League XI)

ALL BRITISH XI
J Breedon (1) 1940-41

NORTHERN COMMAND
J Bamford (3) 1942-44, C Webster (1) 1951-52

SOUTHERN COMMAND
SC Pearson (1) 1943-44

SOUTH EASTERN COMMAND
J Rowley (1) 1944-45

WESTERN COMMAND
A Chilton (1) 1941-42, G Hopkinson (1) 1941-42, H Redwood (2) 1941-42

COMBINED SERVICES
J Hanlon (1) 1944-45

ARMY
R Charlton (2) 1956-58, E Colman (1) 1956-57, D Edwards (2) 1955-57, W Foulkes (2) 1955-57

ARMY XI
J Carey (1) 1939-40, SC Pearson (2) 1942-43, J Rowley (4) 1943-45, JE Travers (3) 1914-17

RAF
J Griffiths (3) 1939-41, C Mitten (1) 1943-44, SC Pearson (1) 1943-44, G Savage (2) 1943-45, W Wrigglesworth (2) 1941-42, R Wood (1) 1953-54, J Whitefoot (1) 1953-54

COMBINED XI (Army/RAF)
J Rowley (1) 1946-47

CENTRAL LEAGUE XI
J Myerscough (1), 1920-21, A Steward (1) 1920-21

MANCHESTER (v. Bootle & District)
S Black (1) 1883-84

AMATEUR INTERNATIONALS
England - W Bradley (4) 1957-58, H Hardman (4) 1907-08, M Pinner (3) 1960-61, J Walton (3) 1951-52.

OLYMPIC GAMES
Great Britain - H Hardman (3) 1908, A Gowling (2) 1968

*See under 'Youth' for YOUTH INTERNATIONALS

CAPPED BEFORE AND/OR AFTER PLAYING FOR UNITED:

Here is an unofficial list of players who represented their country at senior level either (a) before joining United or (b) after leaving United. Wartime guests have not been included, neither have players who were released by the club, having had trials or had been registered on Schoolboy forms:

Argentina	JS Veron
Australia	S Ackerley, R Bartz, M Bosnich
Bermuda	S Goater
Cayman Isles	J Wood
Czech Rep.	K Poborsky

CIS/USSR	A Kanchelskis
Denmark	J Olsen, P Schmeichel, J Sivebaek
England	V Anderson, P Barnes, F Barson, P Beardsley, G Birtles, H Burgess, J Connelly, W Cresswell, L Cunningham, P Davenport, D Dublin, R Ferdinand, J Gidman, B Greenhoff, J Hacking, H Hardman, E Hine, P Ince, C Knowles, T Meehan, J Morris, L Page, G Pallister, P Parker, D Platt, A Quixall, W Rawlings, C Richards, J Rimmer, B Robson, C Sagar, T Sheringham, C Spencer, I Storey-Moore, J Sutcliffe, E Taylor, D Wallace, N Webb, R Wilkins, O Williams
France	E Cantona, F Barthez, L Blanc, W Prunier
Holland	J Cruyff, A Muhren, J Stam, R van Nistelrooy
Ireland	M Hamill, D Lyner, P O'Connell, J Peden
Jamaica	D Johnson
N. Ireland	T Anderson, H Baird, G Best, J Blanchflower, T Breen, R Briggs, R Carroll, T Connell, W Crooks, M Donaghy, K Gillespie, H Gregg, D Healy, P Hughes, T Jackson, D McCreery, P McGibbon, C McGrath, S McIlroy, WS McMillen, T Morrison, P Mulryne, C Murdock, J Nicholl, J Nicholson, J Scott, J Sloan, W Walsh (United amateur), N Whiteside
Norway	H Berg, R Johnsen, E Nevland, OG Solskjaer
Portugal	Ricardo Lopez
Rep of Ireland	T Breen, S Brennan, D Byrne, N Cantwell, B Carey, G Daly, A Dunne, E Dunphy, J Giles, D Givens, A Grimes, R Keane, P McGrath, A McLoughlin, M Martin, K Moran, L O'Brien, R O'Brien (United reserve), P Roche, J Sloan, F Stapleton.
Scotland	F Barrett, W Boyd, A Brazil, M Buchan, WS Chalmers, P Crerand, H Curran, J Delaney, N Dewar, A Forsyth, A Goram, A Graham, G Graham, D Herd, J Jordan, D Law, J Leighton, G Livingstone, W Longair, L Macari, E MacDougall, N McBain, J McCalliog, W McCartney, B McClair, J McCrae, G McQueen, A Menzies, T Miller, W Morgan, G Mutch, T Robertson, G Strachan, JF Ure.
South Africa	Q Fortune
Sweden	J Blomqvist
USA	J Kirovski, E McIlvenny
Trinidad/ Tobago	D Yorke
Wales	T Bamford, C Blackmore, H Blew, T Burke, A Davies, J Davies, R Davies, SC Davies (United trialist), W Davies, M Delaney, J Doughty, M Hughes, W Jackson, C Jenkyns, WR John, D Jones, TJ Jones, W Meredith, G Moore, P O'Sullivan (United reserve), GA Owen, W Owen, J Powell, R Savage, M Thomas, J Warner, DR Williams
Yugoslavia	N Jovanovic

The following players represented their country at Under-21 level prior to joining United:
England - V Anderson, P Barnes, G Birtles, A Cole, G Crooks, L Cunningham, C Gibson, P Ince, P Parker, B Robson, T Sheringham, D Wallace, N Webb, R Wilkins.
Northern Ireland - R Carroll, T Connell, M Donaghy
Scotland - A Brazil, A Goram, J Leighton, B McClair, G Strachan.
Wales - M Thomas

Players who gained Inter-League honours before joining or after leaving Newton Heath/United include:
J Ball, P Barnes, P Beardsley, S Bruce, J Greenhoff, J Hacking, H Hardman, E Hine, D Law, F Mann*, T Meehan, G Moore, A Pape*, W Roughton, C Sagar, I Storey-Moore, J Walton, N Webb, E West, R Wilkins.
* Appearance made in benefit match (Football League XI).

Other personnel associated with United who won full international caps during their respective careers:
England - Frank Blunstone, Syd Owen
Scotland - Matt Busby, Tommy Docherty, Frank O'Farrell
Wales - Jimmy Murphy

Cap That!

•Bobby Charlton's total of 106 full caps for England, gained between April 1958 and June 1970 was a record until beaten by his former skipper Bobby Moore in 1973. Charlton himself had passed Billy Wright's record of 105 caps when he played in his last international match against West Germany in the World Cup quarter-final in Brazil.

•Bryan Robson won 90 caps for England (13 with West Bromwich Albion, 77 with United). He lies fifth in the all-time list of most-capped England players, behind Peter Shilton with 125, Bobby Moore 108, Bobby Charlton 106 and Billy Wright 105..

•Denis Law won 55 Scottish caps (35 with United) between 1958-74. This was a record that stood for four years until Kenny Dalglish (then of Liverpool) took over the mantle in 1978. Dalglish went on to win 102. Other United players with a useful collection of Scottish caps are Jim Leighton (91), Joe Jordan (52), Gordon Strachan 50, Andy Goram (43), Martin Buchan (34) and both Gordon McQueen and Brian McClair (30). Ex-United manager Tommy Docherty won 25.

•Mal Donaghy gained a total of 91 caps for Northern Ireland; Sammy McIlroy collected 88 for the same country while Jimmy Nicholl (73), David McCreery (67), Jimmy Nicholson (41), Norman Whiteside (38), George Best (37), Keith Gillespie (36), and Tommy Jackson (35) follow on

•The most capped Welsh players with a United link are Mark Hughes (75), Mickey Thomas (51), Billy Meredith (48), Clayton Blackmore (39), Wyn Davies (34), Ryan Giggs (35 - still adding to his tally) and Ron Davies (29).

•Paul McGrath, with a total of 83 international appearances, is the Republic of Ireland's third most capped player (behind Steve Staunton and Tony Cascarino). Kevin Moran and Frank Stapleton both gained 71 caps, Denis Irwin (60), Johnny Giles (60), Don Givens (56), Mick Martin (52), Roy Keane (50 still playing), Gerry Daly (48), Alan McLoughlin (42), Noel Cantwell (36) and Tony Dunne (33). Cantwell scored 14 goals for his country (mainly as a centre-forward) and was leading marksman for many years before it was broken by two more United players (in turn), Don Givens and then Frank Stapleton.

•Giant goalkeeper Peter Schmeichel left United in 1999 with 110 Danish caps to his name (he later added more to his tally with Sporting Lisbon). Eric Cantona was capped 44 times by France (19 goals scored); Fabien Barthez is fast-approaching that total. Jaap Stam (30 caps and still playing), Arnold Muhren (23) and Ruud van Nistelrooy (also still playing) are United's top stars from Holland.

•United had at least one player capped at senior level by England in each of the first 25 post WW2 seasons: 1946-47 to 1971-72 inclusive.

•Neil Webb was the 1,000th player capped by England at full international level when he lined up against West Germany in September 1989.

Goal Nets

•Bobby Charlton with 49 goals is England's top-marksman in senior international football. Frank Stapleton was top-man for the Republic of Ireland with 20 (beaten by Niall Quinn) and Denis Law and Dalglish, each with a haul of 30, share the record for Scotland. Law claimed his total in 55 internationals, Dalglish in 102.

•Law twice netted fourtimers in a senior international match for Scotland - the first against Northern Ireland in November 1962, the second versus Norway a year later. Both games were played at Hampden Park. He also hit a hat-trick v. Austria in Bergen in June 1963.

•Charlton scored for England in 13 consecutive seasons. His senior international career spanned a total of 12 years, 56 days....from 19 April 1958 until 14 June 1970. Charlton also netted three penalties out of three for England.

•United's Doughty brothers, Jack with four and Roger with two, scored six goals between them when Wales beat Ireland 11-0 in 1888. They won two caps playing together.

•On 16 November 1949, when England beat Northern Ireland 9-2 at Maine Road; the United duo of Jack Rowley (4) and Stan Pearson (2) contributed six of their country's goals.

•Bryan Robson's 27-second goal against France in the 1982 World Cup Finals in Spain, was the fastest by an Englishman in this competition (first entered in 1950) and it was his country's second fastest at international level, behind Tommy Lawton's 17-second strike v. Portugal in 1947.

The Long Walk

•United's David Beckham was sent-off playing for England against Argentina in a vital World Cup game in St Etienne, France in June 1998.

•Twelve years earlier, in June 1986, ex-United midfielder Ray Wilkins was dismissed during England World Cup game against Morocco in Monterey, USA.

•United's Paul Scholes was sent-off playing against Sweden in a European Championship qualifier in June 1999, making him only the sixth player to be dismissed playing for England - but the first to take an early bath in a HOME game.

•United's Ryan Giggs has also been sent-off at senior international level, as captain of Wales v. Norway in Oslo in a World Cup qualifier in 2001.

Debutants

•Denis Law, at the age of 18 years, 236 days, became Scotland's youngest full international when he made his senior debut against Wales in October 1958. Norman Whiteside was Northern Ireland's youngest player when he lined up in his first international against Yugoslavia in June 1982, aged 17 years, 41 days. In October 1991, Ryan Giggs, aged 17 years, 321 days, became Wales' youngest debutant (as a substitute) v. Germany. And Johnny Giles, at the age of 18 years, 360 days, was the youngest player to don the green international jersey of The Republic of Ireland when he starred against Sweden in October 1959.

•Duncan Edwards aged 18 years, 183 days (v. Scotland in April 1955) was the second youngest England international player. Gary Neville became England's third youngest post Second World War international (behind Edwards and Joe Baker) when he made his debut at the age of 19 years, 123 days v. China in May 1996).

•Four United players - George Best, Sammy McIlroy, Jimmy Nicholson and Norman Whiteside - were all aged 17 when they won their first full caps for their country.

•Lee Sharpe was the youngest England Under-21 player when he was capped at that level against Greece in February 1989 at the age of 17 years, 252 days.

International Talk-Back

•Billy Meredith was aged 45 years, 229 days when he appeared in his last full international match for Wales against England in March 1920 (almost 25 years after his debut on 15 March 1895). Meredith made a record 20 full international appearances for Wales v. England.

•Johnny Giles' international career for the Republic of Ireland spanned 19 years, 210 days - from November 1959 to May 1979.

•Sammy McIlroy played for Northern Ireland in 12 full internationals against England.

•Two United players - goalkeeper Tommy Breen and full-back Johnny Carey - were both capped by the Republic of Ireland and Northern Ireland

•In the late 1990s, Jovan Kirovski, a junior at Old Trafford, won ten caps for the USA, but never got a single first team outing with the Reds.

•Brian Carey won two caps for Eire in 1992 whilst a regular in United's second team, and Pat McGibbon collected three for Northern Ireland in 1995 before he had been handed his United debut, likewise David Healy, also with Northern Ireland (2000-01).

•Don Givens was capped by the Republic of Ireland in May 1969 - three months before he made his first team debut for United.

•There were five United players in the Welsh team that took on Scotland in Edinburgh in 1888.

•Goalkeeper Mike Pinner won 51 caps as an amateur for England in the 1950s. Pinner, along with Len Bradbury, Warren Bradley, Harold Hardman and John Walton, all won England amateur caps while registered as players with United.

•Alan Gowling played for the Great Britain Olympic soccer team in 1968.

•David Sadler gained an England amateur cap at the age of 16 - the youngest player ever to do so.

183

International Squads

•Since the early 1970s (especially since 1972-73 when they had a total of 16), United have invariably had their first team squad packed full of international players. And following the introduction of Premiership football in 1992, manager Alex Ferguson has frequently named an entire squad of international players (at various levels). In 1998-99, when fit and available for selection, he fielded one of the strongest club sides in Europe, all full internationals. The 20 players used during the course of the season came from nine different countries - but only once (v. Juventus in the home leg of their European Champions League game) did he field a full team of internationals (and he also named another six on the subs' bench. The 20 players were: David Beckham, Wes Brown, Nicky Butt, Andy Cole, Gary Neville, Phil Neville, Paul Scholes and Teddy Sheringham (England); Peter Schmeichel (Denmark); Denis Irwin and Roy Keane (Republic of Ireland); Henning Berg, Ronny Johnsen and Ole Gunnar Solskjaer (Norway), Jordi Cruyff and Jaap Stam (Holland), Ryan Giggs (Wales), Phil Mulryne (Northern Ireland), Jesper Blomqvist (Sweden) and Dwight Yorke (Trinidad & Tobago). He also called in intermediate stars like Jonathan Greening and John Curtis. This trend continued the following season. Following Schmeichel's departure, in came Aussie international Mark Bosnich along with David Healy (Northern Ireland) and Quinton Fortune, the South African international. Then, in 2000-01, French 'keeper Fabien Barthez joined Mikael Silvestre, while in 2001-02 Juan Sebastian Veron (Argentina), Ruud van Nistelrooy (Holland) and Diego Forlan (Uruguay) added to the international class, while a few more Under-21 stars arrived on the scene as well!

•In October 1994 (v. Newcastle) United's Premiership team contained players who had represented eight different countries at full international level. They were: Schmeichel (Denmark); Irwin and Keane (Republic of Ireland), Gary Pallister and Ince (England), Brian McClair (Scotland), Eric Cantona (France), Andrei Kanchelskis (USSR) and Ryan Giggs and Mark Hughes (Wales). Skipper Steve Bruce was the only non-capped member of the starting line-up., Keith Gillespie (Northern Ireland) appearing as a substitute.

•In October 2000, at home to Southampton in the Premiership, United started off with EIGHT full England internationals in their line-up: Beckham, Brown, Butt, Cole, the Neville brothers, Scholes and Sheringham. The other three players were Frenchman Barthez, Irishman Irwin and Welsh ace Giggs…all internationals.

•In 2000-01 United again fielded (at times) a full 'international' team, with eight different countries represented. The players involved were Barthez (France); the two Nevilles (England), Irwin and Keane (Republic of Ireland); Wes Brown (England), Stam (Holland), Beckham, Scholes, and Butt (England); Giggs (Wales), Sheringham and Cole (England), Yorke (Trinidad & Tobago), Solskjaer (Norway) and Fortune (South Africa).

•Seven United players - David Beckham, Wes Brown, Nicky Butt, Andy Cole, Gary Neville, Paul Scholes and Teddy Sheringham all appeared for England against Albania in a World Cup qualifying match in March 2001.

•United's foursome of Roger Byrne, Duncan Edwards, David Pegg and Tommy Taylor played for England v. Eire in 1957 and 26 years later another four 'Reds' - Paul Ince, Gary Pallister, Paul Parker and Lee Sharpe played in the World Cup qualifying game against Holland. There were four United players in the England Under-23 side that played Hungary at Old Trafford on 23 March 1976 - Steve Coppell, Brian Greenhoff, Gordon Hill and Stuart Pearson.

•Six Newton Heath players were regulars in the Welsh international team during the 1889-90 season.

•For their First Division League game against West Ham at Old Trafford in January 1973, United fielded eight players who were past or future Scottish internationals: Martin Buchan, Alex Forsyth, George Graham, Jim Holton, Denis Law, Lou Macari, Ted MacDougall and Willie Morgan - all chosen by manager Tommy Docherty, himself a Scot!

•There were five United players who were regularly named in the Northern Ireland squad in season 1976-77 - Tommy Jackson, David McCreery, Chris McGrath, Sammy McIlroy and Jimmy Nicholl. Two ex-United players, George Best and Trevor Anderson, also figured for their country that season.

•Five United players - Alex Forsyth, Martin Buchan, Lou Macari, George Graham and Willie Morgan - were in the Scottish side that met England in the Centenary international at Hampden Park on 14 February 1973.

•There were 23 players with international honours (at various levels) on Manchester United's books in 1996 - 14 with full caps, 3 with 'B' caps and the other six with Under-21 recognition.

•Henry Cockburn was United's first post Second World War international, capped by England in 1946 - after having appeared in just seven Football League games for the club (although he had been prominent during WW2)..

•At the beginning of the 2001-02 season, United had 21 full capped players on the club's senior staff - Barthez, Beckham, Blomqvist, Brown, Butt, Carroll, Cole, Fortune, Giggs, Irwin, Johnsen, Keane, G Neville, P Neville, Scholes, Silvestre, Solskjaer, Stam, van Nistelrooy, Veron and Yorke. Stam was soon replaced by another international, Blanc, and later in the campaign Forlan arrived and was duly capped by Uruguay, while O'Shea was also capped at senior level. Blomqvist and Cole also left the club.

World Cup 'Reds'

•In the 2002 World Cup Finals in Japan & South Korea, United stars Beckham, Scholes, Butt and Brown were in the English squad, along with future 'Red' Rio Ferdinand. Barthez and Silvestre lined up for France, Keane was originally in the Eire party; Forlan played for Uruguay, Fortune for South Africa and Veron for Argentina. Ex-United star Sheringham was also in the England squad coached by ex-United man Steve McClaren.

•Five United stars - Alex Stepney, Bobby Charlton, Brian Kidd, Nobby Stiles and David Sadler - were named in England's World Cup squad for Mexico 1970 - but only Charlton played.

•Charlton made 14 appearances in World Cup matches for England..

•United's England duo of Bobby Charlton (1962, 1966 & 1970) and Bryan Robson (1982, 1986 & 1990) both appeared in three World Cups (as indicated). Scotland's Joe Jordan (1974, 1978 & 1982) also appeared in three World Cups, while with Leeds United and AC Milan respectively.

•Martin Buchan, Jim Holton and Willie Morgan were all in Scotland's 1978 World Cup squad.

•Viv. Anderson was named in the England World Cup squads of 1982 and 1986 but was never called into action.

Pot Pourri

•Anderson became the first black player to win a full England cap; another 'United' player to be, Laurie Cunningham, was the second.

•Ryan Giggs was an England schoolboy international (under the name of Ryan Wilson) before he was capped by Wales, having attended school in Salford!

•United's Shay Brennan was named in the England '40' for the 1962 World Cup Final campaign. He didn't make the last '22' and subsequently went on to win caps for the Republic of Ireland. Indeed, he became the first player to represent Eire at senior level who was not born in Ireland (he was born in Manchester of Irish parents).

•Charlie Mitten was named as 12th man by Scotland in 1946 (under the mistaken belief he was Scottish) for a game against England at Maine Road, arranged for the families of the victims of the Bolton-Stoke City FA Cup disaster at Burnden Park. In fact, England chose him for the same match!

•In June 1992, Peter Schmeichel became the first United player ever to win a European Championship medal when he kept goal for Denmark whose team also contained the former Reds' defender John Sivebaek.

•Another former United star - Arnold Muhren - gained a European Championship winning medal with Holland in June 1988 at the ripe old age of 37 years and 23 days - the oldest player to receive such a prize! In fact, midfielder Muhren was capped by his country before and after his time at Old Trafford but never received a call-up during his spell with the Reds.

•Roger Byrne, United's left-back and skipper, missed two penalties for England in 1956 - against Brazil and Yugoslavia. Byrne played in 33 consecutive internationals for England (1954-57) all at left-back.

•Gary Neville won his first England cap after just 19 Premiership games for the 'Reds.'

•Amateur international right-winger Warren Bradley was capped by England at senior level just six months after joining the club from Bishop Auckland.

•Peter Davenport's senior international career for England lasted for just 17 minutes - that was the length of time he was on the pitch as a second-half 'sub' against the Republic of Ireland in March 1985. Jimmy Rimmer kept goal for England in half a game (45 minutes) v. Italy in May 1976.

•Tommy Taylor netted two hat-tricks for England - against Denmark and the Republic of Ireland in 1956-57.

•Danny Wallace scored on his debut for England in January 1986 (v. Egypt). This was his only cap!

•Ray Wood, Bill Foulkes and Roger Byrne were 1-2-3 in England's defence against Northern Ireland in October 1954.

•The Blanchflower brothers, Danny and Jackie, appeared in 12 internationals together for Northern Ireland.

•Clayton Blackmore won his first three Welsh caps as a substitute.

•Welsh international Wyn Davies won full caps for his country with both United & Manchester City.

•Three Nottingham Forest players - Ian Storey-Moore, Garry Birtles & Peter Davenport - all later to join United, won full caps for England whilst at The City Ground, but were never called-up by their country during their time at Old Trafford.

•Colin Webster was United's first post WW2 Welsh international.

•Eight of Lou Macari's 24 caps for Scotland were gained as a playing substitute.

•Harry Gregg was beaten 21 times in six games when keeping goal for Northern Ireland against England.

•The Neville brothers (Gary and Phil) both played for United and England at senior level - in the European Championships, the World Cup Finals and in friendlies..

•Joe Davies, a United half-back in the late 1880s, was one of four brothers who played for Wales.

•Over a period of some 46 years (from 1946), United always seemed to have at least one player on their books who was a Northern Ireland international. This sequence came to an end when Mal Donaghy left Old Trafford in 1992.

•Eddie McIlvenny was captain of the USA when they sensationally beat England 1-0 in a World Cup encounter in Belo Horizonte in 1950. He played for United for three years up to 1953.

•In May 1991, when he lined up for the CIS (the former USSR) against Argentina, flying winger Andrei Kanchelskis became the first Manchester United player to make his international debut on his home club ground (Old Trafford).

•Former United midfielder Mick Martin scored both goals when the Republic of Ireland national team beat the Reds' 2-0 in a friendly match a Old Trafford in September 1974.

•United beat a Republic of Ireland XI 4-2 at Dalymount Park, Dublin in the 1992 (in Don Given's Testimonial match).

•David Beckham, Bobby Charlton, Bryan Robson and Ray Wilkins all skippered England whilst at Old Trafford. Paul Ince led England on many occasions in the late 1990s, being the first black player to achieve this honour. Two ex-United stars, Peter Beardsley and David Platt, have also skippered England, while Johnny Carey, Johnny Giles, Noel Cantwell, Roy Keane and Paul McGrath all led the Republic of Ireland on the international front. Carey was captain of the Rest of Europe in 1947. Ryan Giggs (Wales), Henning Berg (Norway) and Peter Schmeichel (Denmark) have all captained their country while serving as a 'Red Devil'.

•In January 1970, winger Ian Storey-Moore became the first double-barrelled-named footballer to play for England in a full international match (v. Holland) since 1898 when Charles Wreford-Brown played against Scotland.

•Steve Bruce was capped by England at Youth team level but nothing else came his way, and as a consequence, in 1993 manager Jack Charlton tried to tempt him to play for the Republic of Ireland - because of his Irish ancestry.

185

• To celebrate the British Trade Week in Tehran, United beat the Iran 'B' national side in a friendly match by 2-0 on 24 October 1977.

•Harry Haslam, who signed for United during WW2, was employed as an England scout in 1981-82.

•Teddy Sheringham is the third oldest player (behind Tom Finney and Stanley Matthews) to score in a full international match for England.

In Charge

•As well as 'managing' United the following have also been in charge of their respective countries... Sir Matt Busby (caretaker-boss of Scotland in 1958); Sir Alex Ferguson (Scotland boss in 1985-86 as well as being Jock Stein's assistant for 12 months prior to that); Jimmy Murphy (manager of Wales from 1956 to 1964, including the World Cup Finals of 1958) and Tommy Docherty (Scotland chief in 1971-72).

•Busby also managed the Great Britain Olympic soccer team in 1948.

•Walter Winterbottom, a United player in the late 1930s, managed England from 16 years, from 1946-62, taking in four World Cups (1950, 1954, 1958 & 1962).

•Dave Sexton was an England assistant-manager and coach as well as managing United.

Double Internationals

•John Sutcliffe, United's goalkeeper from 1903-05, was a double international, representing England at both soccer and rugby union. Noel Cantwell also represented the Republic of Ireland in two different sports - soccer and cricket.

•Another goalkeeper - Andy Goram - represented Scotland at both soccer and cricket.

•Tommy O'Neil represented England schoolboys at both soccer and rugby.

IPSWICH TOWN

League results v Town:

Season	Div	Home	Away	Season	Div	Home	Away
1961-62	1	W 5-0	L 1-4	1978-79	1	W 2-0	L 0-3
1962-63	1	L 0-1	W 5-3	1979-80	1	W 1-0	L 0-6
1963-64	1	W 2-0	W 7-2	1980-81	1	W 2-1	D 1-1
				1981-82	1	L 1-2	L 1-2
1968-69	1	D 0-0	L 0-1	1982-83	1	W 3-1	D 1-1
1969-70	1	W 2-1	W 1-0	1983-84	1	L 1-2	W 2-0
1970-71	1	W 3-2	L 0-4	1984-85	1	W 3-0	D 1-1
1971-72	1	W 1-0	D 0-0	1985-86	1	W 1-0	W 1-0
1972-73	1	L 1-2	L 1-4				
1973-74	1	W 2-0	L 1-2	1992-93	PL	D 1-1	L 1-2
				1993-94	PL	D 0-0	W 2-1
1975-76	1	W 1-0	L 0-3	1994-95	PL	W 9-0	L 2-3
1976-77	1	L 0-1	L 1-2				
1977-78	1	D 0-0	W 2-1	2000-01	PL	W 2-0	D 1-1
				2001-02	PL	W 4-0	W 1-0

Summary of League results

	P	W	D	L	F	A
Premier League	10	5	3	2	23	8
Division 1	40	19	6	15	57	53
Home	25	16	4	5	47	14
Away	25	8	5	12	33	47
Total	50	24	9	17	80	61

FA Cup results v Town:

	Round	Venue	Result
1957-58	4	Home	W 2-0
1969-70	3	Away	W 1-0
1973-74	4	Home	L 0-1
1987-88	3	Away	W 2-1

League Cup results v Town:

	Round	Venue	Result
1971-72	2	Away	W 3-1
1997-98	3	Away	L 0-2

Fact File:

In November 1962, under 18,500 fans saw Denis Law net four times in United's 5-3 League win at Portman Road. Ten months later there were over 28,000 spectators present to see United win 7-2 on the same ground, Law scoring a hat-trick on this occasion. Andy Cole scored five in United's 9-0 win in 1994-95, a Premier League record.

Players with both clubs include:

H Baird, A Brazil, M Clegg, W Dale, D Johnson (United reserve), T Laing, A Muhren
Also associated: A S Duncan (manager of both clubs).

IRISH CONNECTION

List of United personnel, including players (various levels), managers, coaches etc. who have been associated with clubs in Northern Ireland and the Republic of Ireland:

Players	Clubs
George Anderson	Belfast United
Trevor Anderson	Portadown, Linfield (player-manager)
Henry Baird	Linfield
Peter Barnes	Drogheda United, Cliftonville
Billy Behan	Shamrock Rovers, Shelbourne, Drumcondra (manager)
Harry Bird	Bangor City, Linfield, Dunmurry FC
Derek Brazil	Rivermount Boys Club (Dublin)
Tommy Breen	Drogheda United, Belfast Celtic, Linfield, Shamrock Rovers, Newry Town, Glentoran
Shay Brennan	Waterford (player-manager)
Jimmy Bullock	Dundalk
Francis Burns	Shamrock Rovers
David Byrne	Shamrock Rovers, St Brendan's FC (Dublin), Coleraine, Larne FC, Shelbourne, Brideville
Noel Cantwell	Cork Athletic
Brian Carey	Cork City
Johnny Carey	St James' Gate, Home Farm
Joe Carolan	Home Farm
Bobby Charlton	Waterford
Tommy Connell	Newry Town, Coleraine, Glentoran
James Coupar	Linfield
Willie Crooks	Belfast Celtic, Glentoran, Larne, St Gall's FC
Gerry Daly	Bohemians
Jimmy Delaney	Cork Athletic (player-manager), Derry City
Ephraim Dodds	Shamrock Rovers (United WW2)
Bernard Donaghy	Derry Celtic
Mal Donaghy	Larne Town
Tommy Donnelly	Glentoran
Pat Dunne	Shamrock Rovers
Tony Dunne	Shelbourne
Hugh Edmonds	Belfast Distillery, Linfield, Glenavon (player-manager)
'Sonny' Feehan	Bohemians, Waterford
John Ferguson	Derry City
Johnny Giles	Home Farm, Shamrock Rovers (player-manager), Dublin City, Stella Maris
Don Givens	Dublin Rangers
Haydn Green	Waterford (manager)
Harry Gregg	Linfield Rangers, Linfield Swifts, Coleraine
Ashley Grimes	Bohemians
Tony Grimshaw	Ballymena
Willie Halligan	Belfast Celtic (United WW1)
Mickey Hamill	Belfast Rangers, Belfast Celtic (also manager), Distillery (manager)
David Herd	Waterford
Tommy Heron	Portadown
Denis Irwin	Turner's Cross College FC (Cork)
Tommy Jackson	Glentoran, Waterford
Roy Keane	Cobh Rangers
Patrick Kennedy	Johnville FC (Dublin)
Oscar Linkson	Shelbourne

David Lyner	Owen O'Cork FC, Glentoran, Belfast Distillery	John O'Shea	Waterford
David McCreery	Coleraine	Louis Page	Glentoran (trainer-coach)
Kevin MacDonald	Coleraine	Jack Peden	Linfield, Belfast Distillery
Noel McFarlane	Waterford	Mike Pinner	Belfast Distillery
Scott McGarvey	Derry City (player-coach)	Tom Ritchie	Bangor City
Pat McGibbon	Portadown	Paddy Roche	Dublin Shelbourne
Chris McGrath	St Patrick's FC (Dublin)	Josh Rowe	Dublin Bohemians
Paul McGrath	St Patrick's Athletic	Arthur Rowley	Belfast Distillery (United WW2)
Eddie McIlvenny	Waterford (player-manager)	John Scott	Boyland FC, Ormond Star
Sammy McMillan	Ards (reserve), Linfield (amateur)	Jimmy Shiels	Ballymena, Dolphin FC, Belfast Celtic
Walter McMillen	Carrickfergus, Cliftonville and	Paddy Sloan	Glenavon (United reserve & WW2)
	Glentoran Linfield & Belfast Celtic (WW2)	Tommy Sloan	Ballymena United
James McNaught	Linfield	Frank Stapleton	St Martin's (Dublin), Bolton Athletic (Dublin)
Mick Martin	Bohemians, Home Farm	Norman Tapken	Shelbourne
William Merry	Drumcondra (United reserve)	Ernie Taylor	Derry City
Kevin Moran	Bohemians, Pegasus FC (Dublin)	Robert Turner	Glentoran
Tommy Morrison	Glentoran (also coach)	Dennis Viollet	Linfield (player-coach)
George Nicol	Glentoran	Liam 'Billy' Whelan	Home Farm
Ray O'Brien	Shelbourne	Tony Whelan	Bohemians, Shamrock Rovers, Bray Wanderers,
Liam O'Brien	Bohemians, Shamrock Rovers		Shelbourne
Pat O'Connell	Belfast Celtic	Managers	
Frank O'Farrell	Cork United (player)	Billy Behan	Drumcondra

Irish Blarney

The first Irish-born player to appear for Newton Heath in a Football League game was Jack Peden (from Belfast) v. Burnley in September 1893.

Tommy Morrison was the first Irishman to don a United shirt (after the club had changed its name), making his Football League debut in the home game with Manchester City on Christmas Day 1902. Twenty-four hours later Morrison became the first Irishman to score for United in a 2-2 draw with Blackpool (home).

Morrison also had the honour of being the first Irish-born player to score an FA Cup goal for the Reds, against Notts County in 1904.

In 1948, United's Johnny Carey became the first Irishman to captain a United FA Cup-winning side.

The following Irishmen all skippered United at one time or another: Carey, Noel Cantwell, Roy Keane, Sammy McIlroy and Norman Whiteside.

Among the Irish-born players who scored on their senior debut for United are: Pat O'Connell, David Byrne, Sammy McIlroy and Norman Whiteside.

In all major competitions, Irishmen between them have scored over 800 goals for Manchester United. George Best has registered the most - 178 in League and Cup.

Best, in fact, was the last Irishman to score a hat-trick in the FA Cup for United, achieving the feat in an 8-2 drubbing of Northampton Town in February 1970 (when he notched six goals - the most by an Irishman in a competitive game for the Reds).

Liam 'Billy' Whelan scored 33 goals (26 in the League) in 53 competitive games for United in season 1956-57 - the most for the club by an Irishman. George Best holds the record for scoring most League goals by an Irishman in a season, 28 in 1967-68. He weighed in with an overall tally of 32 (in 52 outings) that term.

Full-back Tony Dunne holds the record of being the top-man of all the Irish players to have appeared in most competitive matches for the club: 530.

When Frank Stapleton found the net for United in the 1983 FA Cup Final, he wrote himself in the record books by becoming the first player to score for two different clubs in FA Cup Finals at Wembley. He had netted for Arsenal (v. United) in the 1979 Final.

When Stapleton joined United from Arsenal in 1981 he became the club's most expensive Irishman at £900,000....and they could have signed him for nothing ten years earlier!

In season 1978-79, nine Irish-born players represented United at some time or another.

When Norman Whiteside came on as a substitute for United against Brighton on 24 April 1982, he became the youngest Irishman ever to appear for the club at senior level (aged 17 years, 351 days).

Also in 1982 Whiteside became the youngest player ever to appear in a the World Cup Finals (a record previously held by Pele).

In 1983 when he scored the winning goal for United against Liverpool, Whiteside became the youngest ever-goalscorer in League Cup Final at Wembley. And when he repeated that feat with the winning goal against Everton in 1985, he became the youngest player ever to net in an FA Cup Final.

Kevin Moran had the misfortune to become the first player to be sent-off in an FA Cup Final (v. Everton in 1985).

The Irishman who has won most full caps for his country whilst a United player has been Denis Irwin with a total of 56 for the Republic of Ireland. Sammy McIlroy gained 52 for Northern Ireland.

Dublin-born Billy Behan and Bob Bishop from Belfast, were United's 'chief' scouts in the Republic of Ireland and Northern Ireland respectively for many years after the Second World War (both retired in 1987). Bishop, appointed by Matt Busby, succeeded another Irishman, Bob Harper, going on to spot Best, McIlroy, David McCreery, Jimmy Nicholl and Whiteside, while Behan sent over Carey, Johnny Giles, Liam 'Billy' Whelan, Tony Dunne, Paul McGrath, Mick Martin and Kevin Moran, among others!

George Best and Jackie Blanchflower were both born in Belfast, the former in May 1946, the latter in March 1933.

Frank O'Farrell has been United's only Irish-born manager.

Sammy McIlroy (Northern Ireland) and Johnny Giles (Republic of Ireland) both managed their country.

Ex-United goalkeeper Ray Wood served as a coach with the Irish FA in Dublin (late 1960s).

United comfortably beat the Irish club Shelbourne 5-0 in a pre-szeason friendly in July 2002 - Roy Keane's first game back after his World Cup exit.

IRREGULARITIES

In July 1969, Manchester United FC was fined £7,000 and the team banned from playing friendly matches against foreign clubs after allegations of irregularities in the club's accounts involving payments to certain players were found proven.

187

IRWIN, Denis Joseph

Born: Cork, 31 October 1965

Career: Turner's Cross College (Cork), Leeds United (apprentice 1982, professional 1983), Oldham Athletic (free transfer, 1986), MANCHESTER UNITED (£625,000, June 1990, released May 2002), Wolverhampton Wanderers (one year contract from July 2002).

Full-back Denis Irwin - able to play on either the right or left side of the defence - has been a tremendously loyal servant to Manchester United and indeed to the Republic of Ireland. A steady, competent defender, with powerful right-foot shot (used mainly from dead-ball situations, especially penalty-kicks) he has never been given a roasting by a winger, always alert to danger, positive in his approach with superb positional sense. Winner of 56 caps for his native Eire, he has also represented his country at schoolboy, Youth, 'B', Under-21 and Under-23 levels. As a United player he was a member of seven Premier Championship winning sides (1993 & '94, '96 & '97, '99, 2000 & 01 (a record). He also gained a League Cup winners' prize (in '92), two FA Cup winners medals (in '94 & '96), a European Champions League medal (in '99), European Cup-winners Cup medal ('91) as well as three Charity Shield prizes and a Super Cup award.

After celebrating his 500th senior appearance for United on St Valentine's Day 2001, he subsequently lost his place to Frenchman Mikael Silvestre during the 2001-02 season but continued to be a valuable member of the squad, always there when required. A great club man, Irwin left Old Trafford after 12 years unstinting service, in the summer of 2002, joining the Nationwide League club Wolves on a one-year contract. Irwin, in fact, made his debut for United at Wembley... in the 1990 FA Charity Shield game against Liverpool.

Club record: 529 apps, 33 goals

JOHNSEN, Jean Ronny

JOHNSEN, Jean Ronny
Born: Sandefjord, Norway
10 June 1969.
Career: Stokke FC, IF EIK-
Tonsberg (1988), Lyn Oslo (1992),
Lillestrom (1994), Besiktas (1995),
MANCHESTER UNITED (£1.2
million, July 1996), Aston Villa
(August 2002).

Central defender Ronny
Johnsen, who at times has been
used in emergency as a midfielder,
had amassed almost 100 senior
appearances at club and
international level prior to joining
United. He had to battle hard and
long to hold onto a first team place
at Old Trafford, but was then
struck down by a series of niggling
injuries. Known to his colleagues as
the 'Ice Man' he is seemingly
permanently under treatment! A
treble winner with the Reds in
1999, he also starred in the
Premiership triumphs of in 1997
& 2001 and also collected a
Charity Shield prize in 1997. He
had taken his tally of Norwegian
caps (at senior level) to almost 50
at the end of the 2001-02 season
Club record: 150 apps. 9 goals

189

JACKSON, Thomas

Born: Belfast, 3 November 1946
Career: Glentoran, Everton (£10,000, 1968), Nottingham Forest (£150,000, player-exchange deal involving Henry Newton, 1970), MANCHESTER UNITED (£75,000, June 1975), Waterford (July 1978).
Midfielder Tommy Jackson won 35 caps for Northern Ireland (ten during his time at Old Trafford) and also represented his country at Under-23 level. He skippered United's second XI in his first season with the club, being unable to hold down a place in the first XI.
Club record: 23 apps.

JACKSON, William James

Born: Flint, 27 January 1876. Died: Flint, 25 March 1954.
Career: Flint (1894), Rhyl (season 1897-98), Flint (mid-1898), St Helens Recreationalists (early 1899), NEWTON HEATH (professional, July 1899), Barrow (season 1902-03), Burnley (summer 1903), Flint (re-instated as an amateur, 1905). Later managed Wigan County.
Welsh international Bill Jackson (capped once as a St Helens Rec. player) was the son of a Flint publican. A stockily built, hard-working inside-forward with a powerful shot, he once scored four goals in an FA Cup-tie for Burnley and gained a Lancashire Junior Cup winners medal with St Helens.
Jackson's son had a trial with Liverpool, but before he could be valued he sadly lost his life in WW1.
Club record: 64 apps. 13 goals (also 14 'other' apps, one goal)

JAMES, Steven Robert

Born: Coseley, nr Wolverhampton, 29 November 1949.
Career: MANCHESTER UNITED (apprentice, July 1965, professional December 1966), York City (January 1976), Kidderminster Harriers (1980), Tipton Town (1982-84).
Centre-half Steve James - an England Youth international - took over from Bill Foulkes at the heart of the United defence - and he did well initially before losing his place to Ian Ure. However when Frank O'Farrell took over as manager, James got back into the first XI and held his position for two seasons.
After that with Jim Holton wearing the No 5 shirt, his chances were restricted and he eventually left for Bootham Crescent.
James later became a publican in Tipton.
Club record: 164 apps. 4 goals

JAPAN SPORTS VISION

Early in 2002, Manchester United's push towards establishing a sound economic base in Asia continued with the news that the club had secured a merchandising and licensing agreement/deal with the Japanese Company, Japan Sports Vision (JSV).
United signed a five-year deal in order to establish its club brand in the lucrative Japanese market.
The club said that some 25 JSV Stores will all be carrying official Manchester United merchandise across Japan and other parts of Asia.

JENKYNS, Caesar Augustus Llewelyn

Born: Builth, Wales, 24 August 1866. Died: Birmingham, 23 July 1941
Career: Southfield FC, St Andrew's Sunday School team (Small Heath), Walsall Swifts, Small Heath (briefly, 1884), Unity Gas FC, Small Heath (professional, July 1888), Woolwich Arsenal (1895), NEWTON HEATH (May 1896), Walsall (November 1897), Coventry City (player-coach, season 1902-03), Unity Gas FC (1903-04), Saltney Wednesday (1904-05). Retired May 1905.
A big, burly footballer, Caesar Jenkyns was Small Heath's first-ever international, capped by Wales v. Ireland in 1892. A player with no little skill and a master of the shoulder charge - and more - he was reputed to have been fearsome on the field and often sent his opponent flying across the turf with a mighty challenge! He could head a ball - with power - up to 50 yards and once won a competition by kicking a dead ball 100 yards down field first bounce! Jenkyns, with his bone-shaking and muscle-bending tackles, was a great inspiration to the team. He skippered every club he served (and his country) but was often in trouble with referees and occasionally with spectators! Early in 1895, Small Heath decided to dispense with his services and suspended him for six weeks (until the end of the season) for brawling with a Derby County player and also for attempting to assault two spectators. A few months later, after transferring to Woolwich Arsenal, Jenkyns was sent-off but refused to leave the field. He walked eventually - but only after venting his opinion to players and officials alike. One report stated: 'Jenkyns is a heavyweight and it is possible that gives him a character as a foul player he does not deserve.'
He was immediately appointed skipper when he joined the Heathens in 1896 but was then sent-off (again) v. Notts County in December of that year. He returned and duly played his part in helping the team finish runners-up in the Second Division
In 1903 he was banned for taking part in an amateur match for Saltney whilst still holding professional status (with Coventry). The ban was lifted two years later when he joined Walsall - but his career was nearing an end by then.
With Small Heath, he gained a Second Division Championship medal in 1893 and won promotion to the First Division in 1894. On retiring he became a publican in Moxley, near Wednesbury and before the Great War joined the police force. His son, Octavius, had unsuccessful trials with Birmingham in 1912-13, while his brother, Plato, served in the City of Birmingham police force for a number of years.
Club record: 47 apps. 6 goals (also 9 'other' apps)

JOHN, William Ronald

Born: Briton Ferry, nr Neath, 29 January 1911. Died: Port Talbot, 12 July 1973.
Career: Neath Road Council School, Briton Ferry Schoolboys, Briton Ferry Athletic, Swansea Town (amateur, 1927), Walsall (1928), Stoke City (1932), Preston North End (1934), Sheffield United (late 1934), MANCHESTER UNITED (June 1936),

Newport County (May 1937), Swansea Town (summer 1937), guested for Blackburn Rovers, Bolton Wanderers, Burnley and Southport during WW2. Retired 1945.

Goalkeeper 'Roy' John - who started his playing career as a full-back - had already made 187 League appearances on joining United. A vastly experienced professional and established Welsh international, he conceded over two goals a game during his time at Old Trafford, being relieved of his duties by Tommy Breen. He had helped Stoke win the Second Division title in 1932.

Club record: 15 apps.

JOHNSEN, Jean Ronny

Refer to front of section.

JOHNSON, Samuel C

Born: Lancashire, circa 1880

Career: Tonge, NEWTON HEATH (January 1901), Barnsley (July 1901), Heywood (November 1902), Barnsley.

Inside-forward Sam Johnson was a member of a struggling Heathens 2nd XI during his time at the club.

Club record: one app.

JOHNSTON, William Gifford

Born: Edinburgh, 16 January 1901

Career: Edinburgh Schools, Dalkeith Thistle, Selby Town (1918), Huddersfield Town (1920), Stockport County (1924), MANCHESTER UNITED (October 1927), Macclesfield (June 1929), MANCHESTER UNITED (May 1931), Oldham Athletic (May 1932), Frickley Colliery (player-manager, 1935-36).

Inside-forward Billy Johnston had two spells with United and drew up an excellent scoring record. He captained the Edinburgh Boys team before representing Scotland Schools v. England and Wales at Hampden Park. He served in and played for the RFC (v the Army & Navy) before the end of WW1. Late in life he became a publican, initially in Salford and latterly in Abergele (North Wales). He was also an excellent golfer.

Club record: 77 apps. 27 goals

JONES, David Gwilym

Born: Ynysddu, Monmouth, 23 November 1914. Died: Swindon, 30 May 1988.

Career: Ynysddu FC, Tottenham Hotspur (1932), Northfleet (on loan), Cardiff City (1934), Fulham (trialist), Newport County (1935), Wigan Athletic (1936), MANCHESTER UNITED (December 1937), Swindon Town (June 1938), Cheltenham Town (season 1946-47).

Reserve centre-half Dave Jones' only senior game for United was against Bradford (away) in mid-December 1937 when he stood in for George Vose. United lost 4-0!

Club record: one app.

JONES, Ernest Peter

Born: Salford, 30 November 1937

Career: Wellington Street School (Salford), Lancashire & District Schools, MANCHESTER UNITED (junior, December 1952), Wolverhampton Wanderers (amateur, season 1953-54), MANCHESTER UNITED (amateur, July 1954, professional April 1955), Wrexham (March 1960), Stockport County (1966-68), Altrincham (1968-79).

Reserve full-back Peter Jones' only senior game for United was against Portsmouth in a First Division match in October 1957 (he deputised for Roger Byrne). He won two England Youth caps and an FA Youth Cup winners medal whilst with United. Later he helped Stockport win the Fourth Division title (1967) and was twice a Welsh Cup Finalist with Wrexham in 1962 & 1965.

Club record: one app.

JONES, Mark

Born: Barnsley, 15 June 1933. Died: Munich, 6 February 1958.

Career: Barnsley Schoolboys, MANCHESTER UNITED (amateur, June 1948, professional June 1950 until his tragic death in 1958).

As a gentle as a mouse off the field, centre-half Mark Jones was as hard as nails on it. Standing 6ft 2ins tall and weighing 14st 8lbs, he was a formidable defender whose only goal for the Reds was scored in the 2-1 home win over Birmingham City in December 1955. An England Schoolboy international (4 caps won), he was twice an FA Youth Cup winner with United (1955 & 1956) and he also helped the Reds win successive League Championships in 1956 & 1957 but missed the FA Cup Final in the latter year through injury. He was destined for full England honours before tragedy struck on that snowy runway in Munich.

Club record: 121 apps. one goal

JONES, Owen John

Born: Bangor, North Wales, 1869. Died: Crewe, September 1955.

Career: Bangor (1890-94), Crewe Alexandra (1894), Chorley (season 1897-98), NEWTON HEATH (May 1898), Bangor (December 1900), Earlstown FC (briefly in 1901), Stalybridge Rovers (1901-02).

John 'Chorley' Jones appeared in the Heathens' forward-line in the opening few League games at the start of the 1898-99 season. He was not considered again…after being suspended by the club for 'disobeying orders'. Later he was capped twice by Wales (as a Bangor player). He worked for the railway at Crewe for most of his life.

Club record: 3 apps. (also one 'other' app, one goal)

191

JONES, Paul Stanley

Born: Stockport, 10 September 1954

Career: Stockport Boys, MANCHESTER UNITED (apprentice 1968, professional December 1970), Mansfield Town (June 1973).

Reserve full-back Paul Jones made one first team appearance for United, coming on as a substitute for goalscorer Jim Holton during an Anglo-Italian Cup-tie v. Fiorentina at Old Trafford in February 1973.

Club record: one app.

JONES, Thomas

Born: Penycae, nr Wrexham, 6 December 1899. Died: Cefn, Wrexham, 20 February 1978.

Career: Acrefair FC, Druids, Everton (trialist), Oswestry Town (1922), MANCHESTER UNITED (April 1924, professional May 1924), Scunthorpe & Lindsey United (player-manager, July 1937-39), Chirk (during WW2), Druids (coach, early 1950s).

Full-back Tom Jones was signed as cover for Charlie Moore and Jack Silcock, but surprisingly made well over 120 senior appearances for the club before finally establishing himself as a regular in the side in 1933-34. A defender in the traditional mould, Jones was capped four times by Wales as a United player. Prior to his arrival at Old Trafford, he helped Oswestry win the North Wales Charity Cup and the Welsh National League. He was the eldest of a family of 14 children (12 of them sisters).

Club record: 200 apps.

JONES, Thomas John

Born: Tonypandy, Glamorgan, 6 December 1909. Died: 1995.

Career: Mid-Rhondda, Tranmere Rovers (1926), Sheffield Wednesday (1929), MANCHESTER UNITED (June 1934), Watford (£1,500, May 1935), Guildford City (1946), Tranmere Rovers (trainer-coach mid-1946), Workington (trainer-coach, 1953), Birmingham City (assistant-trainer, 1958), West Bromwich Albion (physiotherapist, 1966-68).

Inside or wing-forward Tommy Jones had already made 127 League appearances before joining United and was capped twice by Wales during his time at Hillsborough. He did well enough in his only season at Old Trafford and after WW2 he became a well-respected trainer/physio.

Club record: 22 apps. 4 goals.

JORDAN, Joseph

Born: Carluke, Lanarkshire, 15 December 1951.

Career: Blantyre Victoria, Morton (1968), Leeds United (£15,000, 1970), MANCHESTER UNITED (£350,000, January 1978), AC Milan (£325,000, July 1981), Verona (1983), Southampton (£100,000, 1984), Bristol City (player, early 1987, player/assistant-manager late 1987, manager 1988), Heart of Midlothian (manager, 1990), Celtic (assistant-manager, 1993), Stoke City (manager, 1993), Bristol City (manager, 1994-97), Huddersfield Town (assistant-manager to Lou Macari, 2000). Prior to linking up with Macari, Jordan worked as a soccer summariser on Channel 4's Football Italia.

Joe Jordan was a tall, robust and brave striker, strong in the air and on the ground who was capped by Scotland, gaining a League Championship with Leeds and appearing in two European Cup Finals before joining United. Nicknamed 'Smokin Joe' and 'Jaws', he went on to gain a total of 52 caps for his country (also playing for the Under-23 side) and became the first Scotsman to score in three World Cup Final tournaments: 1974, 1978 and 1982. An FA Cup finalist with United in 1979, he guided Bristol City to Freight Rover Trophy success in 1987.

Club record: 126 apps. 41 goals

JOVANOVIC, Nikola

Born: Cetinje, Yugoslavia, 18 September 1952

Career: Red Star Belgrade, MANCHESTER UNITED (£300,000, January 1980), FC Buducnoet (on loan, December 1981-July 1982, signed permanently December 1982 after United cancelled his contract).

A determined, resourceful defender, Nikki Jovanovic had already represented Yugoslavia at senior international level, gained a full coaching certificate and netted over 50 goals in almost 375 League and Cup games for Red Star before signing for United. He was basically a reserve (to Kevin Moran and Martin Buchan) and although he played in more than 20 League games he never really settled down at Old Trafford.

Club record: 26 apps. 4 goals

JUVENTUS

United's playing record against Juventus:
European Cup/ECWC/UEFA Cup

Venue	P	W	D	L	F	A
Home	5	2	2	1	6	5
Away	5	1	0	4	4	9
Summary	10	3	2	5	10	14

There have been ten pretty exciting contests between United and Juventus down the years and there is no doubt that the Italians have had the better of the exchanges…just!

Both teams have won semi-final clashes. United won 4-3 on aggregate to reach the 1998-99 European Champions League Final while Juventus won the 1983-84 Cup-winners Cup semi-final 3-2 on aggregate.

In 1998-99, the two semi-finals were both memorable matches. At Old Trafford, United had trailed 1-0, seemingly destined to go out of the tournament, but in injury-time Ryan Giggs scored to give his side a lifeline. Then in the Del Alpi Stadium in Turin, United again seemed to be heading for defeat as Inzaghi scored twice in the opening quarter, but skipper Roy Keane scored to inspire his men to a sensational 3-2 victory, Yorke and Cole notching the decisive goals to take United to Barcelona for the Final.

For their home game against Juventus in 1998-99, United's starting line-up contained 11 full internationals - and manager Alex Ferguson named another six on the subs' bench.

The first meetings took place in the second round of the Fairs Cup of 1976-77. Gordon Hill scored to give United a 1-0 home win. But Juventus were unstoppable in Turin and won 3-0.

Then came those 1984 Cup-winners Cup battles that ended 1-1 at Old Trafford and 2-1 to Juve in Italy.

The first two of the six European Cup encounters were played in 1996-97, Juventus winning both first stage matches by 1-0, Del Piero netting a 36th minute penalty to decide the issue at Old Trafford. In 1997-98 the clubs again met at the Group Stage of the Champions League, United winning 3-2 at Old Trafford but going down 1-0 at the Delle Alpi.

Players with both clubs: D Platt (United reserve).

K for...

KEANE, Roy Maurice

Born: Cork, 10 August 1971

Career: Cobh Ramblers, Nottingham Forest (1990), MANCHESTER UNITED (£3.75 million, July 1993).

Midfielder Roy Keane leads by example. Referred to as 'captain courageous' (for club and country - the Republic of Ireland) he has put his heart and soul into his performances for United since joining the club in 1993. A battler to the last, he never shirks a tackle, is totally committed and never accepts defeat. Hot-headed at times (he's suffered his fair share of sendings-off and ultimate suspensions) he has returned to the fray just as enthusiastic as ever. With Forest, he played in the 1991 FA Cup Final (beaten by Spurs) and a year later was a winner in the Zenith Data Systems Cup Final and played in the League Cup Final (beaten by his future club, United).

He has been a winner in 12 competitions for United: six Premiership titles, three FA Cup Final triumphs and three FA Charity Shield wins. He has yet to feature in a major European Final. Capped by Eire at schoolboy and Youth team levels, he has now reached the 58 mark in full international appearances as well as appearing in four Under-21 matches and in 2002 he was all set to lead the Republic of Ireland to the World Cup Finals in Japan and South Korea before being 'sent home' following a disagreement with boss Mike McCarthy!

Club record: 361 apps. 46 goals

KEANE, Roy Maurice

Refer to front of section.

KELLY, James William

Born: Carlisle, 2 May 1957
Career: MANCHESTER UNITED (amateur, April 1972, apprentice July 1972, professional May 1974), Chicago Sting (on loan, April-August 1976, signing permanently, April 1977), Los Angeles Aztecs (1978), Tulsa Roughnecks (1980), Toronto Blizzard (1981-82). Midfielder Jimmy Kelly - a Scottish Youth international trialist (via his parents' birthplace) - was a useful scorer in reserve team football for United, but was never a serious challenger for a regular first team spot at Old Trafford. He did very well, however, after deciding to try his luck in the NASL.
Club record: one app.

KENNEDY, Fred

Born: Bury, late 1902. Died: Failsworth, Lancashire, November 1963.
Career: Rossendale United (1920), MANCHESTER UNITED (May 1923), Everton (£2,000, March 1925), Middlesbrough (1927), Reading (1929), Oldham Athletic (1930), Rossendale United (1931), Northwich Victoria (late 1931), Racing Club de Paris (1932), Blackburn Rovers (1933), Racing Club de Paris (1934), Stockport County (1937-39). A lightweight inside-left, with good skills, Fred Kennedy went on to make over 120 appearances for his other clubs after leaving United, gaining both League and Cup winners medals with the Paris club.
He was awarded the Humane Society's Medal (for saving a young woman from drowning). In later life he became a champion crown green bowler.
Club record: 18 apps. 4 goals

KENNEDY, Patrick Anthony

Born: Dublin, 9 October 1934.
Career: Johnville FC (Dublin), MANCHESTER UNITED (amateur, February 1952, professional February 1953), Blackburn Rovers, (August 1956), Southampton (1959), Oldham Athletic (season 1960-61). Irish Schoolboy international Paddy Kennedy began his career as a centre-half but was converted into a full-back. He helped United win the FA Youth Cup in 1953 but was handed just one first team outing by Matt Busby - lining up in the First Division game against the reigning League champions Wolves in October 1954. He failed to make headway with any of the clubs he played for.
Club record: One app.

KENNEDY, William John

Born: Scotland
Career: Ayr Parkhouse, NEWTON HEATH (June 1895), Stockport County (December 1896), Greenock Morton (re-instated as an amateur, season 1899-1900). Inside-forward Billy Kennedy's goal-tally for the Heathens included a hat-trick in a 4-0 League win over Darwen in March 1896. Unfortunately he became surplus to requirements and left to join nearby Stockport County.
Club record: 33 apps. 12 goals (also 12 'other' apps, one goal)

KANCHELSKIS, Andrei

Born: Kirovograd, Ukraine, 23 January 1969.
Career: Dinamo Kiev, Shakhtar Donetsk, MANCHESTER UNITED (non-contract March 1991, signed for £650,000, May 1991), Everton (£5 million, August 1995), Fiorentina (£8 million, early 1997) Glasgow Rangers (£5.5 million, 1998-May 2002), Manchester City (on loan, early 2001), Southampton (August 2002).
An out-and-out winger, fast, tricky and direct, Andrei Kanchelskis accumulated a very useful scoring record with United. He spent a little over four years at Old Trafford, helping the Reds win the European Super Cup, the League Cup, the Premiership (twice), the FA Cup and the Charity Shield (twice) before transferring to Goodison Park. After 60 appearances for the Merseysiders he struggled at times in Italy's Serie 'A' before gaining two League, two Scottish Cup and League Cup winners medals with Rangers. He has 59 full international caps to his credit - 36 won awarded by Russia (five goals scored), six by the CIS and 17 by the USSR (three goals). Kanchelskis had amassed in excess of 450 senior appearances at club level (85 goals scored) before being released by Rangers aat the end of the 2001-02 season. He is the only player to have appeared in a Manchester, Liverpool and 'Old Firm' derby.
Club record: 161 apps. 36 goals

KANCHELSKIS, Andrei

194

KERR, Hugh

Born: Scotland, 1882
Career: Ayr FC, MANCHESTER UNITED (January-May 1904).
Reserve centre-forward Hugh Kerr deputised for Tom Morrison (v. Blackpool) and Billy Grassam (v. Grimsby Town) in two games in his brief spell with the club.
Club record: 2 apps.

KETTERING TOWN

Newton Heath played and defeated Kettering Town in two first round FA Cup-ties at their Bank Street ground. The first in 1895-96 ended in a 2-1 win and the second, a year, later, resulted in a 5-1 scoreline.
Associated with both clubs: R Atkinson (manager of United and Town).

KIDD, Brian

Born: Collyhurst, Manchester 29 May 1949
Career: St Patrick's School (Collyhurst), Manchester Schools, MANCHESTER UNITED (apprentice August 1964, professional June 1966), Arsenal (£110,000, August 1974), Manchester City (£100,000, 1976), Everton (£150,000, 1979), Bolton Wanderers (£110,000, 1980), Atlanta Chiefs (on loan, 1981), Fort Lauderdale Strikers (early 1982), Minnesota Strikers (1984), Barrow (manager, 1984), Swindon Town (assistant-manager, 1985), Preston North End (assistant-manager briefly, then manager 1986), MANCHESTER UNITED (junior coach and Director of School of Excellence, May 1988, Youth Development Officer, October 1990, assistant-manager to Alex Ferguson, 1995), Blackburn Rovers (manager, December 1998-November 1999), Leeds United (Director of Football, mid-2000, later assistant-manager/coach to David O'Leary)
Brian Kidd, who attended the same school as both Wilf McGuinness and Nobby Stiles, where his headmaster was the former Manchester United player Lawrence Cassidy (q.v) made his League debut for United in August 1967 against one of his future clubs, Everton....having impressed on the club's Australia summer tour. At the end of that season he celebrated his 19th birthday by scoring in United's European Cup Final victory over Benfica. A very skilful striker, hard-working with an appetite for the game, he represented England at Youth, Under-23 and senior levels (winning both his full caps as a United player). He also played for the Football League side.
Kidd, who was sacked as manager of Blackburn with two-and-a-half years of his contract still left, has done a tremendous job as Alex Ferguson's assistant at Old Trafford. He currently holds the same position with Leeds. In his League career in England he scored over 150 goals in more than 460 games.
Club record: 272 apps. 70 goals

KINLOCH, Joseph

Career: NEWTON HEATH (October 1892-June 1893).
Joe Kinloch was a reserve centre-forward who spent just nine months with the club.
Club record: one app.

195

KINSEY, Albert John

Born: Liverpool, 19 September 1945

Career: Liverpool & Merseyside Boys, MANCHESTER UNITED (apprentice June 1961, professional October 1962), Wrexham (March 1966), Crewe Alexandra (1973-74), Wigan Athletic (1974-75).

An England Schoolboy international in 1960 (v. Wales at Wembley in front of 90,000 spectators), Albert Kinsey deputised for Denis Law when making his United debut and he celebrated the occasion with a goal in the 2-1 FA Cup victory over Chester in January 1965. He was a player who 'got away' from Old Trafford as he went on to appear in 300 senior matches for Wrexham (99 goals).

Club record: one app. one goal

KISPEST HONVED

Roy Keane scored twice as United took a firm grip of their 1993-94 first round European Cup encounter with Kispest Honved by winning 3-2 in Budapest. And then it was Steve Bruce's turn at Old Trafford as he netted twice to steer United safely through (2-1) for an aggregate victory of 5-3.

KNIGHTON, Michael

Early in August 1989, Manchester United Chairman Martin Edwards publicly announced that property developer Michael Knighton was to purchase his majority share in the club in a £30 million deal, £20 million for the shares and a further £10 million to develop the Stretford End. However, three weeks later the deal was said to be 'off' as Knighton's backers decided to pull out at the last minute - although Knighton himself insisted that the proposed deal was still 'on.' However, a press statement later confirmed that Knighton had 'withdrawn from the agreement to buy Edwards' shares in exchange for a seat on the board at Old Trafford. Some years later Knighton became Chairman of Carlisle United. Knighton had gone out onto the Old Trafford pitch prior to the United v. Arsenal League game on 19 August 1989 to show off his ball-juggling skills!

As a young man he had been on the books of Coventry City but injury brought an abrupt end to his football career before it had really begun.

KNOWLES, Frank

196

Born: Hyde, Cheshire, early 1891

Career: Hyde FC, Stalybridge Celtic (summer 1911), MANCHESTER UNITED (December 1911), guested for Arsenal, Hyde & Oldham Athletic in WW1, Manchester City (October 1919), Stalybridge Celtic (early 1920), Ashington (1921), Stockport County (1922), Newport County (1923), Queen's Park Rangers (early 1924 to mid 1925), Ashton National (summer 1926), Macclesfield (late 1926-27).

Half-back Frank Knowles helped United's 2nd XI win the Central League in 1912. Mainly reserve to Charlie Roberts, hence his relatively low tally of senior outings over a four-year period to WW1.

Knowles was one of six passengers in a car that crashed in 1912. He survived but two other men died.

Club record: 47 apps.

KOPEL, Frank

Born: Falkirk, 28 March 1949

Career: Falkirk & District schoolboy football, MANCHESTER UNITED (amateur September 1964, professional April 1966), Blackburn Rovers (£25,000, March 1969), Dundee United (1972-82), Arbroath (assistant-manager 1982-83), later Forfar Athletic (assistant-manager, 1991-92).

A Scottish Schoolboy international right-half, Frank Kopel was converted into a very useful full-back. However, after failing to gain a regular place in United's first XI, went on to make over 300 League and Cup appearances for Dundee United, helping the Tayside club win the Scottish League Cup in successive seasons (1980 & 1981) and reach the domestic Cup Final in 1974 and 1981.

Club record: 12 apps.

KOSICE

United easily accounted for Slovakian champions Kosice during the first stage of the 1997-98 European Champions League explorations. Andy Cole scored in both matches which ended in two 3-0 wins for the Reds.

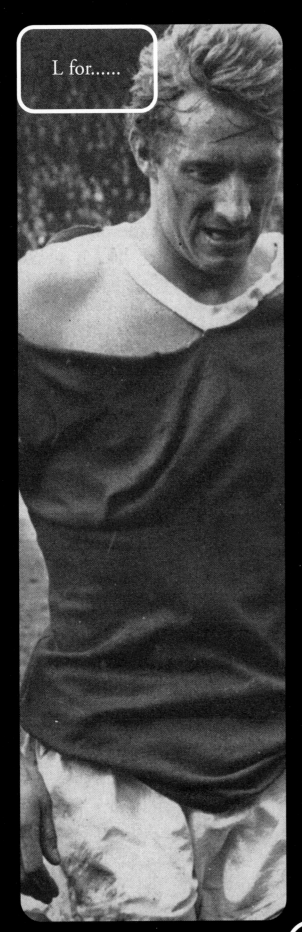

L for......

LAW, Denis

Born: Aberdeen, 24 February 1940.
Career: Hilton Primary, Kitty Brewster Junior, Powis
Secondary Modern School, Aberdeen Boys, Huddersfield
Town (amateur 1955, professional 1957), Manchester
City (£55,000, 1960), Torino (£125,000, 1961),
MANCHESTER UNITED (£115,000, August 1962),
Manchester City (July 1973). Retired after playing in the
1974 World Cup Finals for Scotland. Later became an
expert radio and TV summariser and after dinner speaker.
One of the greatest marksmen of his day, gifted with
balance, vision, alertness, control, deadly shot and superb
heading ability, Denis Law's tally of 239 goals for United
included 171 in the Football League, 34 in the FA Cup
and 28 in 33 European matches. He was 16 when he
played his first Football League game for Huddersfield
against Notts County at Meadow Lane on Christmas Eve
1956 and his last at the age of 34 for Manchester City
against United at Old Trafford on 27 April 1974....when
he netted his final goal - a cheeky back-heeler on 82
minutes which decided the contest and sent the Reds into
the Second Division!He had joined the Maine Road club
for a record fee (£10,000 more than the previous one).
He became the world's first £100,000 footballer when he
moved to the Italian club Torino. United secured his
services in 1962, thus becoming the first British club to
pay over £100,000 for a player (Jimmy Greaves having
cost Tottenham Hotspur £99,999).
Law won a total of 55 caps for Scotland, claiming a
record 30 goals. He also represented his country in three
Under-23 internationals and played for the Football
League. He scored for United in their 1963 FA Cup Final
win over Leicester City, was named European Footballer
of the Year in 1964, captured two League Championship
winning medals (1965 & 1967) but unfortunately missed
the European Cup Final of 1968 with a knee injury
(replaced by teenager Brian Kidd).
Despite the presence of all-time greats Best and Charlton
in the same forward-line, it is interesting to note that it
was Law whom the crowd dubbed 'The King'. Perhaps
only Eric Cantona has approached this level of hero
worship at Old Trafford.
In his senior career (in Britain) his record for his three
clubs and his country was superb - 637 appearances and
325 goals.

Club record: 409 apps. 239 goals

LANCASHIRE SENIOR CUP

Newton Heath/Manchester United participated in this local competition for many years, right up until the early 1970s. They appeared in 14 Finals and won the trophy outright on ten occasions, sharing it once (in 1920). Details of United's appearances in the Lancashire Senior Cup Final are as follows::

Fact File

United fulfilled 14 Lancashire Senior Cup encounters against their rivals Manchester City. The first took place in October 1900 which ended in a 2-0 defeat in round 2 and the last was played in November 1962 (round 1 replay) which United won 2-0.

1897-98	Newton Heath 2 Blackburn Rovers 1 (at Goodison Park)
1912-13	Blackburn Rovers 2 United 3 (at Bloomfield Road)
1913-14	Blackpool 0 United 1 (at Bloomfield Road)
1919-20	Liverpool 1 United 1 (at Anfield)
1928-29	United 2 Blackburn Rovers 1 (at Old Trafford)
1930-31	Liverpool 4 United 0 (at Anfield)
1937-38	Southport 0 United 1 (at Haig Avenue)
1940-41	United 1 Burnley 0 (at Old Trafford)
1942-43	Liverpool 1 United 3 (1st leg at Anfield)
1942-43	United 3 Liverpool 3 (2nd leg at Maine Road)
1945-46	United 1 Burnley 0 (at Maine Road)
1950-51	United 2 Bury 1 (at Old Trafford)
1959-60	Burnley 4 United 2 (at Turf Moor)
1968-69	United 1 Liverpool 0 (at Old Trafford)
1971-72	United 2 Burnley 2 (at Old Trafford)
1971-72 (rep)	Burnley 2 United 0 (at Turf Moor)

The two met in four semi-finals (1913-14, 1929-30, 1945-46 and 1950-51) and United won three of them, losing only in 1929-30.
A classic 1st round encounter in October 1958 ended United 5 City 4 at Old Trafford.
In seasons 1919-20, 1920-21 and 1921-22, the Football League games played between United and City counted towards qualification from the group stage in the Lancashire Senior Cup competition.
Blackburn Rovers (with 13) hold the record for most Lancashire Cup Final victories. Burnley achieved a total of 11.

LANCASTER, Joseph Gerard

Born: Stockport, 28 April 1926
Career: Heaton Norris Old Boys, MANCHESTER UNITED (amateur May 1949, professional February 1950), Accrington Stanley (November 1950), Northwich Victoria (1951-54).
With Jack Crompton injured, reserve goalkeepers Joe Lancaster, 'Sonny' Feehan & Ray Wood all deputised between the posts for United over a six-month period during 1949-50, Lancaster making his League bow in mid-January v. Chelsea in front of almost 47,000 fans at Old Trafford. Although on the small side for a 'keeper (5ft 10ins) he was extremely confident and an assured handler of the ball.
Club record: 4 apps.

LANG, Thomas

Born: Larkhall nr Motherwell, 3 April 1906. Died: 1988.
Career: Larkhall Thistle, Newcastle United (1926), Huddersfield Town (1934), MANCHESTER UNITED (in exchange for Reg Chester, December 1935), Swansea Town (April 1937), Queen of the South (1938), Burbank Thistle (WW2 guest), Ipswich Town (1946). Retired in 1947 to become trainer at Portman Road.
When United signed outside-left Tommy Lang, he was already a vastly experienced player, having already played in 249 League games (215 for Newcastle). He starred in the 1932 FA Cup Final when the Magpies beat Arsenal with that 'over the line' winning goal. Quick and neat in tight situations, he packed a powerful shot but found it hard going to hold down his first team place at Old Trafford.
Club record: 13 apps. one goal

LANGFORD, Leonard

Born: Sheffield, 30 May 1899. Died: Stockport, 26 December 1973.
Career: Sheffield Schoolboys, (Coldstream Guards, aged 15), Attercliffe Victory FC, Rossington Colliery, Nottingham Forest (1924), Manchester City (1930), MANCHESTER UNITED (June 1934-May 1937).
Goalkeeper Len Langford had 248 League games under his belt when he joined United from rivals City - signed as cover for Jack Hacking. He was an FA Cup finalist in 1933 before losing his place to Frank Swift at Maine Road.
Club record: 15 apps.

LAPPIN, Hubert Henry

Born: Manchester, early 1879. Died: Liverpool, May 1925.
Career: Springfield FC (Failsworth), Oldham Athletic (1900), NEWTON HEATH/MANCHESTER UNITED (trialist early 1901, signed as a professional April 1901), Grimsby Town (August 1903), Rossendale United (1904), Clapton Orient (1906), Chester (1907), Birmingham (1909), Chirk (1910), Hurst FC (1911), Macclesfield (1912).
Inside or outside-left Harry Lappin had a very good first full season with the Heathens but after the club had been renamed he lost his place in the team and eventually departed to Cleethorpes. He appeared as a losing finalist with Chester in the 1909 Welsh Cup Final.
Club record: 27 apps. 4 goals (also 7 'other' apps)

LAW, Denis

Refer to front of section.

LAWSON, Reginald Openshaw

Born: Halliwell, November 1880

Career: Halliwell St Paul's FC, Cheshire College, NEWTON HEATH (amateur, June 1900), Bolton Wanderers (amateur August 1901, professional September 1902), Southport Central (1903-04).

Utility forward Reg Lawson occupied all five front-line positions during his career. He appeared in the opening few games of the 1901-02 season for the Heathens, failing to make an impression. He later helped Southport Central win the Lancashire Combination and finish as runners-up in the Lancashire Cup Final.

Club record: 3 apps. (also one 'other' apps, one goal)

LAWTON, Norbert

Born: Newton Heath, Manchester, 25 March 1940

Career: St Gregory's Technical School, Manchester & Lancashire Schoolboys, MANCHESTER UNITED (amateur, 1956, professional April 1958), Preston North End (March 1963), Brighton & Hove Albion (1967), Lincoln City (1971). Retired through injury, summer 1972.

'Nobby' Lawton, a wing-half and occasional inside-left, scored a hat-trick for United in a 6-3 home League win over Nottingham Forest on Boxing Day 1961. He was a competent performer who lost his chance with the Reds following the arrival of Paddy Crerand from Celtic in late 1962. He played for PNE in the 1964 FA Cup Final defeat by West Ham. After football he became a sales director with an established export packaging company

Club record: 44 apps. 6 goals

LAZIO (SS)

United lost 1-0 to Lazio in the European Super Cup in Monaco in August 1999. The Italian side had the better of the exchanges on a well-grassed but sometimes difficult surface.

A crowd of 52,834 saw United earn a 0-0 draw in Rome against Lazio in the Anglo-Italian Tournament in March 1973.

Players with both clubs: K Poborsky, J Stam, JS Veron

LEE, Edwin

Born: Lymm, Cheshire, circa 1875

Career: Hurst Ramblers, NEWTON HEATH (May 1898-May 1900), later St George's FC (later coach, 1903-05).

Centre-forward 'Neddy' Lee had an eye for goal but was given few opportunities by the Heathens despite making a useful start to his League career.

Club record: 11 apps. 5 goals (also 2 'other' apps, one goal)

199

LEEDS CITY

Summary of League results

	P	W	D	L	F	A
Division 2	2	1	0	1	3	4
Home	1	0	0	1	0	3
Away	1	1	0	0	3	1
Total	2	1	0	1	3	4

United's League results v City:

Season	Div	Home	Away
1905-06	2	L 0-3	W 3-1

Fact File

Leeds City was formed in 1904 when a rugby club, Holbeck, packed with enthusiastic sportsmen and playing at Elland Road, decided it was time the City of Leeds had a football team. The area was predominantly a rugby stronghold, both League and Union, so the footballers faced a hard task attracting support. After just one season in the West Yorkshire League they surprisingly applied to the Football League, who, always anxious to make inroads into rugby territory, accepted their application.

In 1905-06 Leeds City played their first season of League football, finishing a creditable sixth in the Second Division but would never win promotion.

By 1915 the club was attracting average home gates of 15,000 to Elland Road, which had previously been known as the 'Old Peacock Ground' (after an adjacent public house) hence the club's nickname of 'The Peacocks'.

However after WW1 the FA demanded to see the club's accounts, alarmed at rumours of illegal payments to players. The club refused to co-operate, so the FA and Football League issued an order for the club to be wound up. After just eight matches of season 1919-20, Leeds City was dissolved, Port Vale being invited to complete Leeds' fixtures.

The people of Leeds were aghast at their city having no football team, so a public meeting was called, resulting in a new club being created named 'Leeds United' starting afresh with a new board of Directors. (see Leeds United).

Player with both clubs: S Cubberley (United reserve), W Halligan (United WW2), F Mann

LEEDS UNITED

Summary of League results

	P	W	D	L	F	A
Premier League	20	11	6	3	31	14
Division 1	62	21	23	18	82	74
Division 2	6	3	2	1	10	7
Home	44	20	16	8	67	35
Away	44	15	15	14	56	60
Total	88	35	31	22	123	95

League Cup results v Leeds:

	Round	Venue	Result
1990-91	Semi-final (1)	Home	W 2-1
	Semi-final (2)	Away	W 1-0
1991-92	5	Away	W 3-1

United's League results v Leeds United:

Season	Div	Home	Away	Season	Div	Home	Away
1922-23	2	D 0-0	W 1-0	1968-69	1	D 0-0	L 1-2
1923-24	2	W 3-1	D 0-0	1969-70	1	D 2-2	D 2-2
				1970-71	1	L 0-1	D 2-2
1925-26	1	W 2-1	L 0-2	1971-72	1	L 0-1	L 1-5
1926-27	1	D 2-2	W 3-2	1972-73	1	D 1-1	W 1-0
				1973-74	1	L 0-2	D 0-0
1928-29	1	L 1-2	L 2-3				
1929-30	1	W 3-1	L 1-3	1975-76	1	W 3-2	W 2-1
1930-31	1	D 0-0	L 0-5	1976-77	1	W 1-0	W 2-0
1931-32	2	L 2-5	W 4-1	1977-78	1	L 0-1	D 1-1
				1978-79	1	W 4-1	W 3-2
1936-37	1	D 0-0	L 1-2	1979-80	1	D 1-1	L 0-2
				1980-81	1	L 0-1	D 0-0
1938-39	1	D 0-0	L 1-3	1981-82	1	W 1-0	D 0-0
1946-47	1	W 3-1	W 2-0	1990-91	1	D 1-1	D 0-0
				1991-92	1	D 1-1	D 1-1
1956-57	1	W 3-2	W 2-1	1992-93	PL	W 2-0	D 0-0
1957-58	1	W 5-0	D 1-1	1993-94	PL	D 0-0	W 2-0
1958-59	1	W 4-0	W 2-1	1994-95	PL	D 0-0	L 1-2
1959-60	1	W 6-0	D 2-2	1995-96	PL	W 1-0	L 1-3
				1996-97	PL	W 1-0	W 4-0
1964-65	1	L 0-1	W 1-0	1997-98	PL	W 3-0	L 0-1
1965-66	1	D 1-1	D 1-1	1998-99	PL	W 3-2	D 1-1
1966-67	1	D 0-0	L 1-3	1999-00	PL	W 2-0	W 1-0
1967-68	1	W 1-0	L 0-1	2000-01	PL	W 3-0	D 1-1
				2001-02	PL	D 1-1	W 4-3

FA Cup results v Leeds:

	Round	Venue	Result	
1950-51	4	Home	W 4-0	
1964-65	SF	Hillsborough	D 0-0	
	Replay	City Ground	L 0-1	
1969-70	SF	Hillsborough	D 0-0	
	Replay	Villa Park	D 0-0	aet
	2nd R	Burnden Park	L 0-1	
1976-77	SF	Hillsborough	W 2-1	
1991-92	3	Away	W 1-0	
1994-95	5	Home	W 3-1	

League Cup results v Leeds:

	Round	Venue	Result
1990-91	SF(1)	Home	W2-1
	SF(2)	Away	W1-0
1991-92	5	Away	W3-1

Fact File

The section on Leeds City details the sad demise of Leeds' original football club. The club created in the aftermath in 1919 (Leeds United) could not take City's place in the Football League, Port Vale having been assigned to complete Leeds City's remaining fixtures. Fortunately the Midland League required a club to take over Leeds City reserves' fixtures, so Leeds United gratefully accepted the Midland League's offer.

In 1920 the Football League was creating a new Third Division as a way of assimilating the top teams of the Southern League. Aware that there had been widespread criticism of their heavy-handed disciplinary measures against Leeds City's alleged misdemeanours (never proven), the League now bent over backwards to accommodate Leeds United after Lincoln City resigned following the 1919-20 season.

Leeds United was elected directly into the Second Division, from which the new 'Peacocks' would gain the club's first ever promotion in 1924 as Second Division Champions.

In 1965 and 1970, the clubs twice met in the FA Cup semi-final, involving a total of five matches. Leeds won both contests by a single goal, United being unable to score in any of the five matches.

In season 1991-92 United and Leeds were locked in conflict for the League title. In January the two clubs were drawn against each other in both the domestic Cup competitions, Leeds having home advantage on each occasion. Thus Elland Road staged three 'showdowns' in 18 days, a League match (which ended 1-1), a League Cup-tie (won 3-1 by United) and an FA Cup-tie (also won by United 1-0). Leeds however, gained their revenge by going on to lift the League Championship trophy.

Players with both clubs include: G Ainsley (Man Utd WW2), B Asquith (Leeds United WW2), P Barnes; H Brook & E Burbanks (both Man Utd WW2), E Cantona, R Ferdinand, J Giles, E Goldthorpe, F Goodwin, A Graham, B Greenhoff, J Greenhoff, D Irwin, J Jordan, J McCalliog (Leeds amateur), G McQueen, A Ritchie (also Leeds Youth Academy Director), L Sharpe, G Strachan, C Turner.

Also associated: F Buckley & G Graham (United players, Leeds managers), S Houston (United player, Leeds assistant-manager), B Kidd (Man United player and assistant-manager of both clubs), J Breedon (United player, Leeds scout), F Hopkin (United player, Leeds assistant-trainer), S Owen (United coach & scout, Leeds Chief Scout), D Williams (coach at both clubs).

LEGIA WARSAW

United beat Legia 4-2 on aggregate in the semi-final of the 1990-91 Cup-winners Cup competition. Brian McClair, Mark Hughes and Steve Bruce scored in a brilliant 3-1 win in Warsaw while Lee Sharpe scored in the 1-1 draw at Old Trafford.

LEICESTER CITY (FOSSE)

League results v Leicester:

Season	Div	Home	Away	Season	Div	Home	Away
1894-95	2	D 2-2	W 3-2	1959-60	1	W 4-1	L 1-3
1895-96	2	W 2-0	L 0-3	1960-61	1	D 1-1	L 0-6
1896-97	2	W 2-1	L 0-1	1961-62	1	D 2-2	L 3-4
1897-98	2	W 2-0	D 1-1	1962-63	1	D 2-2	L 3-4
1898-99	2	D 2-2	L 0-1	1963-64	1	W 3-1	L 2-3
1899-1900	2	W 3-2	L 0-2	1964-65	1	W 1-0	D 2-2
1900-01	2	L 2-3	L 0-1	1965-66	1	L 1-2	W 5-0
1901-02	2	W 2-0	L 2-3	1966-67	1	W 5-2	L 2-3
1902-03	2	W 5-1	D 1-1	1967-68	1	D 1-1	D 2-2
1903-04	2	W 5-2	W 1-0	1968-69	1	W 3-2	L 1-2
1904-05	2	W 4-1	W 3-0				
1905-06	2	W 3-2	W 5-2	1971-72	1	W 3-2	L 0-2
				1972-73	1	D 1-1	D 2-2
1908-09	1	W 4-2	L 2-3	1973-74	1	L 1-2	L 0-1
1922-23	2	L 0-2	W 1-0	1975-76	1	D 0-0	L 1-2
1923-24	2	W 3-0	D 2-2	1976-77	1	D 1-1	D 1-1
1924-25	2	W 1-0	L 0-3	1977-78	1	W 3-1	W 3-2
1925-26	1	W 3-2	W 3-1				
1926-27	1	W 1-0	W 3-2	1980-81	1	W 5-0	L 0-1
1927-28	1	W 5-2	L 0-1				
1928-29	1	D 1-1	L 1-2	1983-84	1	W 2-0	D 1-1
1929-30	1	W 1-4		1984-85	1	W 2-1	W 3-2
1930-31	1	D 0-0	L 4-5	1985-86	1	W 4-0	L 0-3
				1986-87	1	W 2-0	D 1-1
1935-36	2	L 0-1	D 1-1				
				1994-95	PL	D 1-1	W 4-0
1938-39	1	W 3-0	D 1-1				
				1996-97	PL	W 3-1	D 2-2
1954-55	1	W 3-1	L 0-1	1997-98	PL	L 0-1	D 0-0
				1998-99	PL	D 2-2	W 6-2
1957-58	1	W 4-0	W 3-0	1999-00	PL	W 2-0	W 2-0
1958-59	1	W 4-1	L 1-2	2000-01	PL	W 2-0	W 3-0
				2001-02	PL	W 2-0	W 1-0

Summary of League results

	P	W	D	L	F	A
Premier League	14	9	4	1	30	9
Division 1	64	28	16	20	129	99
Division 2	32	16	6	10	58	42
Home	55	36	13	6	127	56
Away	55	17	13	25	90	94
Total	110	53	26	31	217	150

FA Cup results v Leicester:

	Round	Venue	Result
1962-63	Final	Wembley	W 3-1
1975-76	5	Away	W 2-1

League Cup results v Leicester:

	Round	Venue	Result
1993-94	3	Home	W 5-1
1996-97	4	Away	L 0-2

Players with both clubs include: A Beardsworth, B Carey (United reserve), A Chesters (City WW2), J Connachan, L Cunningham, G Daly, J Doherty, C Gibson, R Gibson (Fosse WW1), R Halton, A Henrys, E Hine, A Lochhead (also City manager), A Marshall, S Mercer (United WW2), FH Milnes (United reserve), J Mitten (United trialist), W Morgan, J Morris, J Norton (Fosse WW1), E Pegg, C Richards, M Robins, A Rowley (United WW2), MC Russell (United reserve), R Savage (United Youth), T Smith, J Travers.

Also associated: F O'Farrell and D Sexton (managers of both clubs), M Musgrove (assistant-manager/coach both clubs), L Page (United player, City scout).

LEIGH, Tom

Born: Derby, early 1875
Career: Derby County (reserves), Burton Swifts (1896), New Brighton Tower (1899), NEWTON HEATH (March 1900-May 1901).
A centre-forward possessing great pace, Tom Leigh scored a goal every three games for the Heathens during his two seasons with the club....having been top marksmen for Burton Swifts two seasons running. He was surprisingly released at the end of the 1900-01 campaign.
Club record: 46 apps. 16 goals (also 9 'other' apps, one goal)

LEIGHTON, James

Born: Johnstone, Renfrewshire, 24 July 1958
Career: Paisley & District Schoolboys, Dalry Thistle, Aberdeen (July 1977), Deveronvale (on loan, for season 1977-78), MANCHESTER UNITED (£450,000, June 1988), Arsenal (on loan, March-May 1991), Reading (on loan, November 1991-February 1992), Dundee (£200,000, February 1992), Sheffield United (on loan, March 1993), Hibernian (1993-98). Retired to become goalkeeping coach at Aberdeen.
Goalkeeper Jim Leighton was held responsible for United drawing the 1990 FA Cup Final with Crystal Palace (3-3). He was dropped for the replay! That apart, he was nevertheless a fine custodian, daring and agile, a fine shot-stopper with exceptional positional sense. He took over from Bobby Clark between the posts at Pittodrie and played under Alex Ferguson who duly signed him for United for a then British record transfer fee for a goalkeeper of almost half-a-million pounds. He was already an established international at the time and went on to win a total of 91 full caps for Scotland (a national record), also adding one at Under-21 level to his collection. He won medals galore with the Dons - in League, League Cup, Scottish Cup and European Cup-winners Cup and played in 376 senior games for the club.
Club record: 94 apps.

LEONARD, Harold Doxford

Born: Sunderland, summer 1886. Died: Derby, 3 November 1951
Career: Sunderland North End, Southwick FC, Newcastle United (1907), Grimsby Town (1908), Middlesbrough (1911), Derby County (late 1911), MANCHESTER UNITED (September 1920), Heanor Town (June 1921).
Centre-forward Harry Leonard had scored close on 100 goals in well over 220 League and Cup appearances before joining United. He was passed his best when he arrived at Old Trafford but still served the club well, acting mainly as a reserve striker. He helped Derby win the Second Division title in 1912 and 1915
Club record: 10 apps. 5 goals

201

LEWIS, Edward

Born: Manchester, 3 January 1935
Career: Goslings FC, MANCHESTER UNITED (amateur July 1949, professional January 1952), Preston North End (£10,000, December 1955), West Ham United (1956), Leyton Orient (1958), Folkestone Town (1964), Ford Sports FC, Dagenham (manager, 1965-66), Witts FC, South Africa (manager, late 1960s).
Centre-forward Eddie Lewis was only 17 years of age when he scored on his League debut for United against WBA in November 1952. His days, however, were numbered at Old Trafford when Tommy Taylor arrived from Barnsley and almost a year after leaving the Reds, Lewis linked up with West Ham, allowing future United manager Frank O'Farrell to move to Deepdale. He helped Orient win promotion to the First Division in 1962 and went on to appear in well over 170 senior games before entering non-League football in 1964.
Club record: 24 apps. 11 goals

LEYTON ORIENT (also Clapton Orient & Orient)

United's League results v 'Orient':

Season	Div	Home	Away
1905-06	2	W 4-0	W 1-0
1922-23	2	D 0-0	D 1-1
1923-24	2	D 2-2	L 0-1
1924-25	2	W 4-2	W 1-0
1962-63	1	W 3-1	L 0-1
1974-75	2	D 0-0	W 2-0

Summary of League results

	P	W	D	L	F	A
Division 1	2	1	0	1	3	2
Division 2	10	5	4	1	15	6
Home	6	3	3	0	13	5
Away	6	3	1	2	5	3
Total	12	6	4	2	18	8

Fact File
Leyton Orient started their Football League life in 1905 as 'Clapton Orient' playing at Millfields Road, Clapton. The club moved to Leyton FC's ground at Brisbane Road in 1937 after playing since 1931 at Lea Bridge Road. The original club was formed in 1881 as a part of Glyn Cricket Club. It's thought that several members of the team who worked for the Orient Shipping Line chose Orient as the team's name.
When Clapton Orient travelled to Old Trafford on 7 February 1925 they had a lively forward called Albert Pape (q.v.). A couple of hours before kick off, United negotiated Pape's transfer, getting details of the transfer to League Headquarters at Preston in time for Pape to line up for United against his former colleagues. United won 4-2, Pape one of the scorers as United headed for promotion.

Players with both clubs include: L Cunningham, B Fry (United reserve), D Gibson, H Halse, C Hannaford, H Haslam (United trialist, WW2), W Henderson, W Hunter, H Lappin, E Lewis, T Lucas (United trialist), T Manns, P O'Connell (Orient WW1), A Pape, P Proudfoot (reserve), M Pinner, C Rennox, F Roberts (United WW2), W Spratt, A Turnbull (both Orient WW1), C Turner, A Whalley (Orient WW1), O Williams (United reserve).
Also associated: D Sexton (Orient player & assistant-manager, United manager), J Carey (United player, Orient manager), N McBain (United player, Orient assistant-manager & manager), B Whitehouse (Orient player, United coach & scout).
* Players with Leyton FC & United: W Grassam, J Turnbull.

LIEVESLEY, Leslie

Born: Staveley, Derbyshire, summer 1911. Died: Superga, Italy, 4 May 1949

Career: Rossington Main Colliery, Doncaster Rovers (1919), MANCHESTER UNITED (February 1932), Chesterfield (March 1933), Torquay United (June 1933), Crystal Palace (1937-40). Later coached in Holland, Spain and Italy (Turin FC) from 1947 until his death.

Capable half-back Les Lievesley made 273 League appearances during his playing career but only two for United, deputising for Ray Bennion in games against Charlton and Oldham in March 1932. He was sadly killed in a plane crash - with several members (including international players) of Turin FC - just west of Turin in 1949.

Club record: 2 apps.

LIEVESLEY, Wilfred

Born: Netherthorpe, Staveley, 6 October 1902.

Career: Staveley Old Boys, Derby County (1920), MANCHESTER UNITED (October 1922), Exeter City (August 1923), Wigan Borough (1928), Cardiff City (season 1929-30).

Like his nephew Les (above q.v) the majority of outside-right Wilf Lievesley's career was spent elsewhere and in fact, he made 126 League appearances after leaving United.

He once scored a hat-trick of headers in a League game for Exeter against Gillingham in April 1927.

Two of Wilf Lievesley's brothers, Joe and Fred, played for Arsenal and Sheffield United and for Manchester City and Southend United respectively.

Club record: 3 apps.

LILLE

United met the French champions Lille in the 2001-02 European Champions League competition.
A late David Beckham goal saw United home 1-0 at Old Trafford in September and Ole Gunnar Solskjaer's effort earned a 1-1 draw in France a month later.

LIMITED COMPANY (plc)

Manchester United Football Club became a Limited Company in 1907 and was floated on the stock market in the summer of 1991. There are approximately 30,500 shareholders in possession of around 260 million shares in Manchester United plc. The majority shareholder (at present) is BSkyB with 9.9%; the Irish racehorse owners association (represented by JP McManus and John Magnier) also well represented with a total of 8.6%; Harry Dobson (a Scottish tycopon) owns just over £6.5%, the Royal Sun Alliance has 5% and Maurice Watkins is in possession of 1.5%.

In May 2002 United's Chief Executive Martin Edwards - who joined the United board in 1980 - sold his shares to Harry Dobson who has yet to set foot inside Old Trafford! The 54 year-old Scot spent £22 million buying Edwards' allocation and he said (from a base Finland): "It's an investment."

LINCOLN CITY

Heathens/United's League record v the Imps:

Season	Div	Home	Away
1894-95	2	W 3-0	L 0-3
1895-96	2	D 5-5	L 0-2
1896-97	2	W 3-1	W 3-1
1897-98	2	W 5-0	L 0-1
1898-99	2	W 1-0	L 0-2
1899-1900	2	W 1-0	L 0-1
1900-01	2	W 4-1	L 0-2
1901-02	2	D 0-0	L 0-2
1902-03	2	L 1-2	W 3-1
1903-04	2	W 2-0	D 0-0
1904-05	2	W 2-0	L 0-3
1905-06	2	W 2-1	W 3-2
1932-33	2	W 4-1	L 2-3
1933-34	2	D 1-1	L 1-5

Summary of League results

	P	W	D	L	F	A
Division 2	28	13	4	11	46	40
Home	14	10	3	1	34	12
Away	14	3	1	10	12	28
Total	28	13	4	11	46	40

FA Cup results v the Imps:

	Round	Venue	Result
1901-02	Int.	Home	L 1-2

Fact File:

The 5-5 draw with Lincoln City in 1895-96 represents United's highest scoring draw in League Football.

Players with both clubs include: M Appleton, G Beel (United reserve), B Birch, H Brook (United WW2), J Cairns, E Dodds (United WW2), R Flash (United reserve), JM Gibb (United reserve), M Gillespie, I Greaves, J Hall, W Hunter; F Jones, H Killin & T Knighton (Heathens/United reserves), N Lawton, J McCalliog (City player-coach), W McGlen (also City trainer), J McInally (United reserve), F Mann (City amateur), A Murphy (United reserve), G Nevin, M Pollitt, P Proudfoot (United reserves), A Rowley (WW2 guest with both clubs), J Saunders, E Savage, A Scanlon, C Turner, A Warburton (City WW2).

Also associated: D Herd (United player, City manager), M Brown (City player, United assistant-manager/coach), H Green (United player, City assistant-manager).

LINKSON, Oscar Horace S

Born: New Barnet, early 1888. Died: France, December 1916.

Career: Barnet & Alston FC, The Pirates FC (a touring amateur side), MANCHESTER UNITED (July 1908), Shelbourne, Ireland (August 1913), Queen's Park Rangers (season 1915-16).

Full-back Oscar Linkson was sadly killed whilst serving in France during WW1. United had spotted him during a continental tour while he was playing with another touring side, The Pirates. He proved a more than useful player during his five seasons with the club, appearing regularly during his last two campaigns before moving to Ireland.

Club record: 59 apps.

LIVERPOOL

Heathens/United's League results v Liverpool:

Season	Div	Home	Away	Season	Div	Home	Away
1895-96	2	W 5-2	L 1-7	1962-63	1	D 3-3	L 0-1
				1963-64	1	L 0-1	L 0-3
1904-05	2	W 3-1	L 0-4	1964-65	1	W 3-0	W 2-0
				1965-66	1	W 2-0	L 1-2
1906-07	1	D 0-0	W 1-0	1966-67	1	D 2-2	D 0-0
1907-08	1	W 4-0	L 4-7	1967-68	1	L 1-2	W 2-1
1908-09	1	W 3-2	L 1-3	1968-69	1	W 1-0	L 0-2
1909-10	1	L 3-4	L 2-3	1969-70	1	W 1-0	W 4-1
1910-11	1	W 2-0	L 2-3	1970-71	1	L 0-2	D 1-1
1911-12	1	D 1-1	L 2-3	1971-72	1	L 0-3	D 2-2
1912-13	1	W 3-1	W 2-0	1972-73	1	W 2-0	L 0-2
1913-14	1	W 3-0	W 2-1	1973-74	1	D 0-0	L 0-2
1914-15	1	W 2-0	D 1-1				
				1975-76	1	D 0-0	L 1-3
1919-20	1	D 0-0	D 0-0	1976-77	1	D 0-0	L 0-1
1920-21	1	D 1-1	L 0-2	1977-78	1	W 2-0	L 1-3
1921-22	1	D 0-0	L 1-2	1978-79	1	L 0-3	L 0-2
				1979-80	1	W 2-1	L 0-2
1925-26	1	D 3-3	L 0-5	1980-81	1	D 0-0	W 1-0
1926-27	1	L 0-1	L 2-4	1981-82	1	L 0-1	W 2-1
1927-28	1	W 6-1	L 0-2	1982-83	1	D 1-1	D 0-0
1928-29	1	D 2-2	W 3-2	1983-84	1	W 1-0	D 1-1
1929-30	1	L 1-2	L 0-1	1984-85	1	D 1-1	W 1-0
1930-31	1	W 4-1	D 1-1	1985-86	1	D 1-1	D 1-1
				1986-87	1	W 1-0	W 1-0
1936-37	1	L 2-5	L 0-2	1987-88	1	D 1-1	D 3-3
				1988-89	1	W 3-1	L 0-1
1938-39	1	W 2-0	L 0-1	1989-90	1	L 1-2	D 0-0
				1990-91	1	D 1-1	L 0-4
1946-47	1	W 5-0	L 0-1	1991-92	1	D 0-0	L 0-2
1947-48	1	W 2-0	D 2-2	1992-93	PL	D 2-2	W 2-1
1948-49	1	D 0-0	W 2-0	1993-94	PL	W 1-0	D 3-3
1949-50	1	D 0-0	D 1-1	1994-95	PL	W 2-0	L 0-2
1950-51	1	W 1-0	L 1-2	1995-96	PL	D 2-2	L 0-2
1951-52	1	W 4-0	D 0-0	1996-97	PL	W 1-0	W 3-1
1952-53	1	W 3-1	W 2-1	1997-98	PL	D 1-1	W 3-1
1953-54	1	W 5-1	D 4-4	1998-99	PL	W 2-0	D 2-2
				1999-00	PL	D 1-1	W 3-2
				2000-01	PL	L 0-1	L 0-2
				2001-02	PL	L 0-1	L 1-3

Summary of League results

	P	W	D	L	F	A
Premier League	20	8	6	6	29	27
Division 1	114	38	36	40	152	147
Division 2	4	2	0	2	9	14
Home	69	31	25	13	112	63
Away	69	17	17	35	78	125
Total	138	48	42	48	190	188

FA Cup results v Liverpool:

	Round	Venue	Result
1897-98	2	Home	D 0-0
	Replay	Away	L 1-2
1902-03	1	Home	W 2-1
1920-21	1	Away	D 1-1
	Replay	Home	L 1-2
1947-48	4	Home*	W 3-0
1959-60	4	Away	W 3-1
1976-77	Final	Wembley	W 2-1
1978-79	Semi-final	Maine Road	D 2-2
	Replay	Goodison Pk	W 1-0
1984-85	Semi-final	Goodison Pk	D 2-2
	Replay	Maine Road	W 2-1
1995-96	Final	Wembley	W 1-0
1998-99	4	Home	W 2-1

* Tie played at Goodison Park.

League Cup results v Liverpool:

	Round	Venue	Result
1982-83	Final	Wembley	L 1-2
1985-86	4	Away	L 1-2
1990-91	3	Home	W 3-1

Test Match Record
Season 1893-94 - Newton Heath 0 (bottom Div. 1) v. Liverpool 2 (top of Division 2) at Ewood Park, Blackburn (att. 3,000).

FA Charity Shield
United have met the Merseysiders five times in this annual pre-season encounter. So far both clubs have recorded one win apiece with three draws.
(See: Charity Shield)

Fact File
United have met Liverpool seven times in the FA Cup since the Second World War and have still to lose to them, their record includes two semi-finals (both replayed) and two Finals.
Liverpool were United's first League visitors when Old Trafford opened on 19 February 1910. They won 4-3.
A crowd of 70,277 assembled inside Cardiff's Millennium Stadium to see Liverpool beat United 2-0 in the 2001 Charity Shield game, the first indoor match in Britain. United's only 'Charity Shield' win arrived in 1983, when they triumphed 2-0 at Wembley.
When winning 1-0 at Old Trafford in January 2002, it was the first time the Merseysiders had registered four successive League victories over United since 1910, and also the first time they had recorded the League 'double' over the Reds for two seasons in succession.
Players with both clubs include: P Beardsley, R Burke ('Pool WW2), A Carson, A Chilton ('Pool amateur), P Chisnall, T Chorlton, W Fairhurst (United WW2), T Gardner (United WW2), J Gidman ('Pool apprentice), F Hopkin, W Hunter, P Ince, F Kippax ('Pool amateur, United WW2), T Knighton (United trialist), G Livingstone, N McBain, R MacDougall ('Pool reserve), T McNulty, G McQueen ('Pool trialist), T Miller, S Pears ('Pool reserve), T Reid, T Robertson, E Savage, J Sheldon, J Spence ('Pool reserve), H Whalley ('Pool WW2).
Also associated: M Busby ('Pool player, United manager).

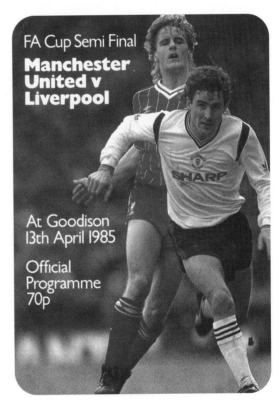

FA Cup Semi Final
Manchester United v Liverpool
At Goodison 13th April 1985
Official Programme 70p

LIVINGSTONE, George Turner

Born: Dumbarton, 5 May 1876. Died: Helensburgh, Dunbartonshire, 15 January 1950.
Career: Sinclair Swifts, Artizan Thistle, Heart of Midlothian (1896), Sunderland (1900), Celtic (1901), Liverpool (1902), Manchester City (1903), Glasgow Rangers (1906), MANCHESTER UNITED (January 1909 - appointed reserve team player-manager August 1911). Retired as a player during WW1; Dumbarton (manager, early 1919), Clydebank (manager, August 1919), Glasgow Rangers (trainer, 1920-27), Bradford City (trainer 1928-35).
Able to play as a wing-half or inside-forward, 'Geordie' Livingstone, vastly experienced, had made almost 250 League appearances prior to joining United in 1909. An FA Cup winner with Manchester City in 1904, he scored twice on his United debut (v. his former club City). He later represented Scotland in two internationals (both in 1906) and played for the Scottish League the following year after returning north of the border in 1906. Livingstone was banned for a time (with other Manchester City players) after an inquiry into illegal payments. He missed out on a second FA Cup winners medal with United in 1909, his place going to Harold Halse.
Club record: 47 apps. 4 goals

LOCHHEAD, Arthur William

Born: Busby, Lanarkshire, 8 December 1897.

Career: Army football (1915-18), Heart of Midlothian (1919), MANCHESTER UNITED (July 1921), Leicester City (£3,300, October 1925; appointed manager at Filbert Street, August 1934, resigned January 1936). Subsequently became a schoolteacher.

Arthur Lochhead, an aggressive inside-forward with a clever brain, splendid bodyswerve and deadly shot, gave United four years excellent service, averaging a goal every three games. An international trialist, he represented the Home Scots v. the Anglo Scots in 1920 and the Anglo Scots v. the Home Scots eight years later He went on to net 114 goals in 320 appearances for Leicester before taking over as manager at Filbert Street following the sudden death of his mentor, Peter Hodge.

Club record: 153 apps. 50 goals.

LOCOMOTIVE (Railway)

Over a period of seven years, between 1936 and 1943, British Rail built 23 steam locomotives each of which bore the name of a football club. 'Manchester United' was among those chosen for a B17 class locomotive, number 61662. The engine sadly went out of active service in 1960 as electrical/diesel trains took over the rails.

LODZ (LKS)

United had to work hard in Poland to earn a 0-0 draw, having eased home 2-0 at Old Trafford in their Champions League qualifying round matches against Lodz in 1998-99.

LONGAIR, William

Born: Dundee, 19 July 1870. Died: Scotland, 28 November 1926.

Career: Rockwell FC (Dundee), Dundee East End, Dundee (1893), NEWTON HEATH (February 1895), Dundee (June 1895), Burnley (November 1895), Sunderland (February 1896), Burnley (1897), Brighton United (1898), Dundee (May 1899; appointed trainer 1900-22 & then groundsman: 1924-26).

Reserve centre-half Bill 'Plum' Longair (who started out as a centre-forward) appeared once at senior level for the club - lining up against Notts County (home) in the final game of 1894-95 season. He went on to appear in more than 120 senior games after leaving the Heathens. He served Dundee (on and off) for well over 25 years.

Club record: one app.

LONG SERVICE

An unofficial list of personnel who have served Manchester United (Newton Heath) for 25 years or more:

60 years	Les Olive	Player, secretary, director
53 years	Harold Hardman	player, director, chairman
50 years	Billy Behan	player, Chief Scout
49 years	Sir Matt Busby	manager, caretaker-manager, director, president
47 years	Louis Rocca	player, Chief Scout
44 years	Jimmy Murphy	coach, assistant-manager, caretaker-manager, scout, consultant
38 years	Bobby Charlton CBE	player, director
34 years	John Aston, senior	player, junior coach, Chief Scout
32 years	Walter Crickmer	secretary, caretaker-manager
32 years	Jack Crompton	player, trainer
32 years	Bill Inglis	player, assistant-trainer
30 years	Martin Edwards	director, chairman
27 years	Bill Foulkes	player, coach

A special mention must be made to Tom Curry (trainer for almost 24 years) and Bert Whalley (player and coach also for close on 24 years) who both sadly died in the Munich air crash and would for sure have been included in the above list but for that fateful day in February 1958.

LONGEST SEASON

United's longest season was in 1964-65. It started on 22 August and finished nine months, 26 days later, on 16 June. The 1998-99 campaign opened on 9 August and ended on 26 May - a total of nine months, 17 days, likewise the 1967-68 season, from 12 August to 29 May. Two others covered a period of nine months and five days: the first in 1939-40 commenced on 26 August and ended on 1 June and the second was in 1970-71 which started the camaign on 1 August with a Watney Cup game and finished on 5 May with a First Division League game.

Other lengthy seasons were played in 1946-47 (31 August-26 May); 1962-63 (from 18 August-20 May) and 1971-72 (from 31 July-29 April).

LONGTON

Career: NEWTON HEATH (March 1885-April 1887).

An unknown inside-forward, Longton's only first-team appearance for United was against Fleetwood Rangers (a) in the 1st round of the FA Cup in October 1886, the club's first ever tie in this prestigious competition.

Club record: one app.

LOUGHBOROUGH

Heathens League results v 'Boro:

Season	Div	Home	Away
1895-96	2	W 2-0	D 3-3
1896-97	2	W 6-0	L 0-2
1897-98	2	W 5-1	D 0-0
1898-99	2	W 6-1	W 1-0
1899-1900	2	W 4-0	W 2-0

Summary of League results

	P	W	D	L	F	A
Division 2	10	7	2	1	29	7
Home	5	5	0	0	23	2
Away	5	2	2	1	6	5
Total	10	7	2	1	29	7

Fact file

Loughborough was elected to the Football League in 1895, playing just five seasons before failing the re-election process in 1900, having had to apply in three successive seasons. Supporters of the club referred to it as 'the Town' leading many to erroneously call the club 'Loughborough Town'.
During their brief career they beat Woolwich Arsenal 8-0 at their Athletic Ground in 1896-97; this remains Arsenal's heaviest defeat in their illustrious history.
Player with both clubs: E Pegg

LOWRIE, Thomas

Born: Glasgow, 14 January 1928
Career: Caledonian Road School (Perth), Glasgow YMCA, Troon Athletic, MANCHESTER UNITED (August 1947), Aberdeen (March 1951), Oldham Athletic (1952-55).
Wing-half Tommy Lowrie made his debut for United in the local derby against Manchester City in front of almost 71,000 fans at Maine Road in April 1948, when he replaced the injured Henry Cockburn. With three other excellent players able to occupy the same position as Lowrie his opportunities with the Reds were limited. He helped Oldham win the Third Division (N) title in 1953.
Club record: 14 apps.

LUTON TOWN

Heathens/United's League results v the Hatters:

Season	Div	Home	Away	Season	Div	Home	Away
1897-98	2	L 1-2	D 2-2	1982-83	1	W 3-0	D 1-1
1898-99	2	W 5-0	W 1-0	1983-84	1	W 2-0	W 5-0
1899-1900	2	W 5-0	W 1-0	1984-85	1	W 2-0	L 1-2
				1985-86	1	W 2-0	D 1-1
1937-38	2	W 4-2	L 0-1	1986-87	1	W 1-0	L 1-2
				1987-88	1	W 3-0	D 1-1
1955-56	1	W 3-1	W 2-0	1988-89	1	W 2-0	W 2-0
1956-57	1	W 3-1	W 2-0	1989-90	1	W 4-1	W 3-1
1957-58	1	W 3-0	D 2-2	1990-91	1	W 4-1	W 1-0
1958-59	1	W 2-1	D 0-0	1991-92	1	W 5-0	D 1-1
1959-60	1	W 4-1	W 3-2				

Summary of League results

	P	W	D	L	F	A
Division 1	30	22	6	2	69	19
Division 2	8	5	1	2	19	7
Home	19	18	0	1	58	10
Away	19	9	7	3	30	16
Total	38	27	7	4	88	26

FA Cup result v. the Hatters:

	Round	Venue	Result
1982-83	4	Away	W 2-0

Fact File

Newton Heath lost their first-ever home League game against the Hatters by 2-1 in September 1897. Thereafter, between 1898-99 and 1991-92, Luton were beaten in 18 consecutive League matches in Manchester - the best sequence of results the Heathens/United have achieved against any of their opponents.

Players with both clubs include: J Aston jnr, J Bell, W Boyd. R Burke, W Carrick (United reserve), R Cope, J Coupar, R Davies, S Davies, M Donaghy, R Donaldson, J Dow, J Downie, W Draycott, B Fry (United junior), D Givens, K Goodeve (United reserve), A Grimes, P Hall, J McCartney (also Town secretary-manager), A Menzies, R Parkinson, G Perrins, J Pugh (Luton WW1), D Robbie (United trialist), J Ryan (United player & coach), A Schofield, L Sealey, W Stewart, G Tomlinson.
Also associated: D Sexton (Luton player, United manager), S Owen (Luton player & manager, United coach & scout), J Crompton (United player & coach, Town trainer & manager, briefly), H Haslam (United trialist, WW2, Luton coach & manager), N McBain (United player, Hatters manager), B Whitehouse (Luton player, United coach & scout).

LYDON, George

Born: Newton Heath, Manchester, 24 April 1902. Died: Failsworth, 12 August 1953.
Career: Nelson United, Mossley, MANCHESTER UNITED (May 1928), Southport (January 1933), Burton Town (summer 1933), Hurst FC (1934), Great Harwood (1935-36).
Wing-half George Lydon's chances in United's first XI were restricted to just three owing to the form of Messrs Bennion, McLachlan, McLenahan, Vincent and Wilson. He did, however, make over 100 appearances for the reserves.
Club record: 3 apps.

LYNER, David

Born: Belfast, circa 1898.
Career: Owen O'Cork FC, Glentoran, Belfast Distillery, Glentoran, MANCHESTER UNITED (August 1922), Kilmarnock (December 1922). Queen's Island (1924), Clydebank (1925), Mid-Rhondda (in season 1925-26), New Brighton (season 1926-27).
An Irish international winger, David Lyner was a United player for barely four months, unable to gain a regular place in the side. He was twice an Irish Cup winner with Glentoran (in 1914 and 1917) and gained six full caps for his country as well as lining up in one Victory international (1919).
Club record: 3 apps.

LYNN, Samuel

Born: St Helens, 25 December 1920. Died: 1995.
Career: Lancashire schoolboys, Peasley Cross St Joseph's, MANCHESTER UNITED (amateur July 1935, professional January 1938), Bradford Park Avenue (February 1951-53).
Sammy Lynn was a resolute centre-half, who acted as reserve to Allenby Chilton at Old Trafford and rarely got a game with the seniors.
Club record: 13 apps.

LYONS, George

Born: Lancashire circa 1881.
Career: Black Lane Temperance FC, MANCHESTER UNITED (April 1904), Oldham Athletic (July 1906), Rossendale United (late 1906), Salford United (1907-08).
A reserve inside-forward, George Lyons played his first two League games for United at the end of the 1903-04 season (in place of Proctor Hall) but after that he hardly figured, appearing regularly though in the second XI.
Club record: 5 apps.

205

McILROY, Samuel Baxter, MBE

Born: Belfast, 2 August 1954

Career: Ashfield School (Belfast), MANCHESTER UNITED (apprentice August 1969, professional August 1971), Stoke City (£350,000, February 1982), Manchester City (1985), FC Orgyte, Sweden (on loan), Bury (1987), Modling (1988), Preston North End (player-coach 1990), Northwich Victoria (manager, 1991-92), Ashton United (manager, 1992-93), Macclesfield Town (manager, 1993-2000). Appointed manager of Northern Ireland (from February 2000).

Midfielder Sammy McIlroy represented Northern Ireland Schoolboys on four occasions as a 14 and 15 year-old before joining United. He developed quickly after that and made his League debut for the Reds as a striker against rivals Manchester City in front of 63,000 fans at Maine Road at the age of 17, scoring in a 3-3 draw. Soon afterwards he won the first of his 88 senior caps for his country while clocking up an excellent individual appearance record for United. A determined competitor with an eye for goal, McIlroy helped United win the Second Division Championship in 1975 and win the FA Cup in 1977, also playing in the two losing Cup Finals of 1976 and 1979. After leaving Old Trafford, following the arrival of Bryan Robson, he added a further 300 plus senior appearances to his tally, 276 in the Football League.

McIlroy's assistants at Northwich Victoria were first Gordon Clayton and then Norman Whiteside, and he was duly replaced s boss of Macclesfield by another former United player, Peter Davenport, following his appointment as team manager of Northern Ireland in 2000..

Club record: 419 apps. 71 goals

207

MUTV/MAN UTD RADIO/CLUB-CALL & MAN-U-MOBILE

MUTV is the club's United-dedicated TV channel. Initially it lost money (around £700,000 in 1999 and then £300,000 a year later) but things have picked up of late and with home and away first team matches being shown within 48 hours of the final whistle, there has been a steady increase in subscribers over the last two seasons - with more joining weekly!

* MUTV has its daily quota of phone-ins (mainly United-related) and the host is former player Paddy Crerand. Reserve team matches are covered 'live' and highlights are shown at various training sessions. There are also regular discussions about publications (mainly books) appertaining to Manchester United.

The subscription hotline number is: 0870 848 6888.

* Man Utd Radio is broadcast on 1413AM - but only within a five-mile radius of Old Trafford on a matchday. There is a match commentary with pre and post-match interviews

* The telephone number for Club-Call is 09068 121161. Unfortunately it lost its official status with the club in 2001. Calls cost 60p a minute at all times.

* Vodafone's Man-U-Mobile service replaced Club-Call as MUFC's official telephone call service - and to register you have to go onto the website at http://www.manumobile.com

Man-U-mobile text messages are charged at 24p and WAP cost 12p a minute at all times

McBAIN, Neil

Born: Campbeltown, Argyllshire, 15 November 1895. Died: 13 May 1974.

Career: Campbeltown Academicals, Hamilton Academical (trialist), Ayr United (1914), guested for Portsmouth and Southampton during WW1, MANCHESTER UNITED (November 1921), Everton (January 1923), St Johnstone (1926), Liverpool (1928), Watford (late 1928, then player-manager 1929-31, manager 1931-37), Luton Town (manager, 1938-39), New Brighton (secretary-manager 1946), Leyton Orient (assistant-manager 1948), Estudiantes de la Plata, Argentina (coach 1949), Ayr United (manager, 1955-56), Watford (manager 1956-59), Ayr United (manager 1963).

Half-back Neil McBain toured Canada and the USA with Scotland in the summer of 1921 prior to joining United. He made his debut for the club in a 1-0 home win over Aston Villa just 48 hours after signing and did very well during his first twelve months, despite relegation being suffered at the end of the 1921-22 campaign. Strong in the air and decisive and combative on the ground, he won his first full cap (v. England) whilst with United but after being played out of position (in the forward-line) he left the club to join Everton with whom he collected two more caps. On 15 March 1947, as New Brighton's secretary-manager, McBain came out of retirement to assist his club in an emergency, appearing in goal in a Third Division (N) game against Hartlepools United at the age of 51 years and four months - a Football League record which still stands. He had made his senior debut 32 years earlier with Ayr United and played during both World Wars.

Club record: 43 apps. 2 goals

McCALLIOG, James

Born: Glasgow, 23 September 1946.

Career: Glasgow Schools, Leeds United (mid-1963), Chelsea (professional autumn 1963), Sheffield Wednesday (£37,500, 1965), Wolverhampton Wanderers (£70,000, 1969), MANCHESTER UNITED (£60,000, March 1974), Southampton (£40,000, February 1975), Chicago Sting (mid-1977), Norwegian football (1977-78), Lincoln City (player-coach, 1978-79), Runcorn (player-manager, 1979-80), Halifax Town (caretaker-manager 1990, manager 1990-91).

Talented midfielder Jim McCalliog could not establish himself in Chelsea's first team and subsequently became Britain's costliest teenage footballer when he transferred to Hillsborough. His mother and father, three brothers and a sister moved to Yorkshire with him, all living in the same house! He made 174 appearances for the Owls, playing in the 1966 FA Cup Final against Everton, before signing for Wolves. He stayed at Molineux for almost five years, making 210 appearances, scoring 48 goals. After helping United regain their First Division status, he then set up the goal by which Southampton defeated the Reds 1-0 in the 1976 FA Cup Final.

His personal honours from the game included five full Scottish caps as well as Under-23 and Schoolboy caps. McCalliog became a publican in 1982 (when employed by Runcorn).

Club record: 38 apps. 7 goals

McCARTHY, Patrick

Born: 1888

Career: Chester, Skelmersdale United (1911), MANCHESTER UNITED (January 1912), Skelmersdale United (July 1912), Tranmere Rovers (autumn 1912), Chester (1913-15). Did not play after WW1.

Reserve centre-forward Pat McCarthy made only one League appearance for United, lining up in place of Enoch West in a 2-1 defeat against West Bromwich Albion soon after joining the club. He netted 39 goals for Tranmere in 1912-13.

Club record: one app.

McCARTNEY, W John

Born: Glasgow, 1866. Died: 18 January 1933.

Career: Cartvale FC (Renfrewshire), Thistle FC (Glasgow), Glasgow Rangers (1886), Cowlairs FC (Glasgow),

208

NEWTON HEATH (August 1894), Luton Town (April 1895), Barnsley (1898, then trainer 1900 and secretary-manager 1904), Heart of Midlothian (secretary-manager 1910-19), Portsmouth (secretary-manager 1920-27), Luton Town (secretary-manager 1927-29).

Broad-shouldered full-back John McCartney was a fine competitor who loved a challenge. He captained Luton for three seasons after leaving the Heathens and later became a football writer: 'The Story of the Scottish League: 1890-1930' being one of his best works.

Club record: 21 apps. one goal (also 9 'other' apps)

McCARTNEY, William

Born: Newmilns, Ayrshire, circa 1877.

Career: Rutherglen Glencairn FC, Ayr FC (1898), Hibernian (1900), MANCHESTER UNITED (May 1903), West Ham United (July 1904), Broxburn FC, Lochgelly (1905), Clyde (1906-08), Broxburn (1908-09), Clyde (1909-13).

Utility forward Bill McCartney arrived at United with a huge reputation but he failed to live up to expectations and left Old Trafford after just one season.

Club record: 13 apps. one goal

McCLAIR, Brian John

Born: Airdrie, 8 December 1963

Career: St Margaret's High School (Airdrie), Coatbridge FC, Aston Villa (apprentice 1980), Motherwell (professional, August 1981), Celtic (£100,000, summer - 1983), MANCHESTER UNITED (£850,000, July 1987), Motherwell (free transfer, June 1998). Soon after retiring in May 1999 he returned to Old Trafford as a coach and in 2001 was appointed reserve team coach.

Inside or centre-forward Brian McClair gave United tremendous service for 11 years. He was a grafter to the last, always giving 110 per-cent out on the pitch, working tirelessly for the team, a dedicated professional. In his later years McClair became a very effective midfield player. He won both Scottish Cup and Premier League Championship medals with Celtic for whom he scored 99 goals in 145 matches and followed up by helping United win the FA Cup in 1990 & 1994, the European Cup-winners Cup and European Super Cup in 1991, and League Cup in 1992 as well as Premiership titles in 1993, 1994, 1996 and 1997, also succeeding in the FA Charity Shield in 1994. He represented Scotland in 30 full internationals, also gaining caps at Youth, Under-21 and 'B' team levels, as well as being voted Scottish 'Footballer of the Year' in 1987.

Club record: 471 apps. 127 goals

McCLAIR, Brian John

McCLELLAND, James

Born: Dysart nr Kirkcaldy, Fife, 11 May 1902.

Career: Rossyln FC, Raith Rovers (1922), Southend United (1923), Middlesbrough (1925), Bolton Wanderers (1928), Preston North End (1929), Blackpool (1931), Bradford Park Avenue (1933), MANCHESTER UNITED (June 1936-May 1937).

Vastly experienced, wing-half or inside-forward Jimmy McClelland had already scored 168 goals and made 422 League appearances before joining United. He was well past his best but a valuable acquisition to the squad. He played in Middlesbrough's 1926-27 Second Division Championship-winning team when he aided and abetted the great George Camsell who netted 63 League and Cup goals in that campaign. McClelland then won an FA Cup winners' medal with Bolton (1929). His son, Charles, was also a professional footballer with Blackburn Rovers and Exeter City.

Club record: 5 apps. one goal

McCRAE, James

Born: Bridge of Weir, Strathclyde, 8 March 1897.

Career: Clyde (1914), (Scots Guards WW1), West Ham United (£100, 1919), Bury (£750, 1920), Wigan Borough (1923), New Brighton (1924), MANCHESTER UNITED (August 1925), Watford ((August 1926), Third Lanark (on loan, 1926-27). Retired circa 1928 and later coached in Egypt (said to be earning around £1,000-a-year)..

Wing-half Jimmy McCrae was a smart passer of the ball, whose best years were behind him when he joined United. He made almost 90 senior appearances for Bury and 50 for the Hammers.

McCrae's younger brother, David, was a Scottish international who served with St Mirren.

Club record: 13 apps.

McCREERY, David

Born: Belfast, 16 September 1957

Career: MANCHESTER UNITED (amateur, September 1972, apprentice April 1974, professional October 1974), Queen's Park Rangers (£200,000, August 1979), Tulsa Roughnecks (£125,000, 1981), Newcastle United (£75,000, 1982), Sundsvaal, Sweden (summer 1989), Heart of Midlothian (autumn 1989), Hartlepool United (player-coach 1991, assistant-manager, 1991-92), Carlisle United (trialist), Coleraine (briefly, autumn 1992), Carlisle United (player-coach/caretaker-manager, 1992-93), Hartlepool United (non-contract player/manager 1994-95), Barnet (scout, 1995), Blyth Spartans (football consultant 1995-96).

Midfielder David McCreery was capped by Northern Ireland as a schoolboy and as a 17 year-old helped United win the Second Division title in 1974-75. He added Youth, Under-21 and 67 senior caps to his collection as his game developed, being a tireless grafter in centre-field. He came on as a substitute (for Gordon Hill) in both the 1976 and 1977 FA Cup Finals, collecting a winners' medal in the latter. Nicknamed the 'Road-runner' McCreery made over 680 senior appearances at club and international level before retiring in the mid-90s. A half of his outings for United came as a substitute (53, with 39 coming in the Football League alone).

Club record: 110 apps. 9 goals

MacDONALD, Kenneth

Born: Llanrwst, nr Ruabon, Denbighshire, 24 April 1898.

Career: Inverness Citadel, Inverness Clachnacuddin, Aberdeen (1919), Caerau (mid-Wales), Cardiff City (1921), MANCHESTER UNITED (February 1923), Bradford Park Avenue (£1,500, with Joe Myerscough, October 1923), Hull City (1928), Halifax Town (1930), Coleraine (late 1930), Walker Celtic (early 1931), Spennymoor United (1931), Walker Celtic (late 1931), Blyth Spartans (1932-33).

Ken MacDonald, a centre-forward, achieved most of his success in the Third Division (North). Despite being born in Wales he started his career in Scotland where he was a prolific scorer in the Highland League before establishing himself with Aberdeen. Prior to joining United he had represented the Welsh League (v. the Southern League). He never really settled at Old Trafford yet after leaving the club he scored well over 150 goals in more than 200 first-class matches, including 135 in only 145 League games for Bradford (a club record 43 coming in 1925-26, another 28 the following season and 31 in 1927-28 when the Yorkshire club won the Division 3 (North) Championship). After quitting football MacDonald became a painter and decorator on Tyneside. One that got away? Definitely so.

* Some reference books list MacDonald as 'McDonald'.

Club record: 9 apps. 2 goals

McDONALD, William

Born: Coatbridge, Lanarkshire, circa 1903.

Career: Coatbridge FC, Dundee (season 1925-26), Broxburn United (summer 1926), Laws Scotia FC (1926-27), Airdrieonians (season 1927-28), MANCHESTER UNITED (with Richard Black, April 1932), Tranmere Rovers (August 1934), Coventry City (1936), Plymouth Argyle (summer 1939). Joined RAF but did not feature after WW2. Willie McDonald was a persistent inside-forward, hard-working who did far better after leaving United, amassing more than 170 League appearances and scoring 42 goals.

Club record: 27 apps. 4 goals

MacDOUGALL, Edward John

Born: Inverness, 8 January 1947

Career: ICI Recreationalists (Wigan), Liverpool (amateur 1964, professional 1966), York City (1867), Bournemouth & B Athletic (1969), MANCHESTER UNITED (£200,000 - later rising to £222,000 - September 1972), West Ham United (£170,000, March 1973), Norwich City (£140,000, late 1973), South African football (as a player-coach, summer 1975), Southampton (£50,000, 1976), AFC Bournemouth (1978), Detroit Express (1979), Blackpool (player-coach and assistant-manager, 1980), Salisbury (1981), Poole Town (late 1981), Gosport Borough, Athena FC, Perth, Australia (1982), Totton FC (autumn 1982), Andover FC (coach, later 1983). After running his own South Coast Sports Shops and working as a licensee, he emigrated to Canada in 1985 where he worked in property development, later becoming a millionaire living in Vancouver...He was willing to purchase his former club, AFC Bournemouth, for £1.2 million when they were in dire financial trouble.

Having done exceedingly well with York City and Bournemouth in Third Division circles (he netted a total of 137 goals in 230 games) centre-forward Ted MacDougall (signed by Frank O'Farrell) did not find favour with new manager Tommy Docherty and spent less than six months at Old Trafford. He was a League Cup finalist with Norwich City in 1975, gained seven full caps for Scotland (scoring on his debut in 1975 v. Sweden) and during his career scored over 300 goals, including 256 in the Football League - the first Scottish-born player since Denis Law to pass the double century mark. The highlight of MacDougall's interesting career was the day he scored nine goals (one a penalty) for Bournemouth in their 11-0 massacre of hapless Margate in a 1st round FA Cup-tie in November 1971. The previous season he had netted a club record 42 League goals for the Cherries.

Club record: 18 apps. 5 goals

McFARLANE, Noel William

Born: Bray, County Wicklow, 20 December 1934.
Career: MANCHESTER UNITED (April 1952), Waterford (June 1956).
A Republic of Ireland schoolboy international and FA Youth Cup winner with United in 1953, right-winger Noel McFarlane deputised for Johnny Berry in the First Division game against Tottenham Hotspur in February 1954 - his only appearance for the club.
Club record: one app.

McFARLANE, Robert

Born: Airdrie, circa 1866. Died: October 1898.
Career: Airdrieonians, Bootle (1888), Sunderland Albion (season 1890-91), NEWTON HEATH (season 1891-92), Airdrieonians (re-instated as an amateur, August 1892).
Tall, well-proportioned full-back Bob McFarlane had a useful season with the Heathens, helping them finish runners-up in the Football Alliance in 1892. He married a sister of the Doughty brothers who played for the Heathens and Wales (late 1880s/early '90s).
Club record: 21 apps. one goal (also 18 'other' apps)

McFETTERIDGE, David

Born: Lancashire
Career: Bolton Wanderers (1892), Cowlairs FC (1893), NEWTON HEATH (June 1894-May 1896), Stockport County (season 1896-97).
With defender Fred Erentz out injured for an away League game at Newcastle in April 1895, the Heathens team was shuffled somewhat allowing reserve Dave McFetteridge to make his only senior appearance for the club. He started off at inside-right but ended the match at right-back!
Club record: one app.

McGARVEY, Scott Thomas

Born: Glasgow, 22 April 1963.
Career: Celtic Boys Club (Glasgow), MANCHESTER UNITED (apprentice June 1979, professional April 1980), Wolverhampton Wanderers (on loan March-May 1984), Portsmouth (£100,000, July 1984), Carlisle United (on loan initially, signed permanently 1986), Grimsby Town (£30,000, 1987), Bristol City (1989), Oldham Athletic (mid-1989), Wigan Athletic (on loan, autumn 1989), Mazda, Japan (summer 1990), Aris Limassol (1992-93 season), Derry City (player-coach mid-1993), Witton Albion (early 1994), Barrow (season 1994-95), Redbridge Forest.
Capped four times by Scotland at Under-21 level, Scott McGarvey made over 200 appearances at senior level. He was a useful inside-forward with flair and commitment but never really made the most of his undoubted talents. McGarvey now owns his own company - Moneystone - which sells sand to sports clubs and agricultural concerns from a base at Levenseat Quarry near Glasgow.
Club record: 25 apps. 3 goals

McGIBBON, Patrick Colm

Born: Lurgan, 6 September 1973
Career: Portadown, MANCHESTER UNITED (£100,000, August 1992), Swansea City (on loan, September 1996), Wigan Athletic (£250,000, March 1977), Scunthorpe United (on loan, February 2002), Tranmere Rovers (August 2002)
A central defender, Pat McGibbon was sent-off in his only game for United, in a League Cup encounter against York City in September 1995. Recognised by his country at Schoolboy level, he went on to win seven full caps for Northern Ireland while also playing in five 'B' internationals and one Under-21 game. He has now made well over 225 senior appearances for Wigan, whom he helped win the Auto-Windscreen Shield at Wembley in 1999.
Club record: one app.

McGILLIVRAY, Charles

Born: East Whitburn, West Lothian, 5 July 1912. Died: 7 November 1986.
Career: Dreghorn Juniors (1927), Ayr United (1930), Celtic (1932), MANCHESTER UNITED (May 1933), Motherwell (April 1934), Dundee (1938), Heart of Midlothian, Albion Rovers, Morton, Dunfermline Athletic and Hibernian (in that order, all on loan between 1940-43), Dundee United (early 1944, later manager 1944-45), Stirling Albion (late 1945), Arbroath (1946), Downfield FC of Dundee (coach, 1947-48), LA Scots (1949-50).
Winger Charlie McGillivray - who won honours for Scotland at schoolboy level - did exceptionally well with Ayr early in his career but failed to make inroads at either Celtic or United. He later achieved a little more success back in his native Scotland, especially during WW2.
Club record: 9 apps.

McGILLIVRAY, John

Born: Broughton, Lancashire, circa 1890.
Career: Berry's Association, MANCHESTER UNITED (amateur January 1907, professional February 1907), Southport Central (July 1910), Stoke (1911), Dartford (1912).
Centre-half John McGillivray was reserve to Charlie Roberts at Old Trafford and consequently got very few opportunities in the first XI.
Club record: 4 apps.

McGIVERN, Francis

Born: Coatbridge, Scotland, 1952.
Career: Middlesbrough Schoolboys, Yorkshire Schools, MANCHESTER UNITED (apprentice, 1968, professional June 1970, released May 1972)...
A diminutive forward, Francis McGivern (standing just over 5ft 6ins tall and weighing under 10 stone) made one appearance for United's first XI, coming on as a second-half substitute for Ian Storey-Moore against Bari in the Anglo-Italian Cup competition on 4 April 1973. He did not figure in League football after leaving Old Trafford.
Club record: one app.

McGLEN, William

Born: Bedlington, 27 April 1921
Career: Blyth Spartans, (Services football in Italy), MANCHESTER UNITED (amateur January 1946, professional May 1946), Lincoln City (£8,000, July 1952), Oldham Athletic (early 1953), Lincoln City (trainer season 1956-57), Skegness Town (coach-manager, 1967-68).
Left-half Billy McGlen, a fierce tackling competitor who rejoiced in the nickname 'Killer', gave United splendid service for six years, able to play at left-back and even outside-left in the immediate aftermath of Charlie Mitten's sudden departure to Bogota. Later he helped Oldham win the Third Division (North) Championship (1953).
Club record: 122 apps. 2 goals.

212

McGRATH, Paul

Born: Ealing, London, 4 December 1959.
Career: St Patrick's Athletic (Dublin), MANCHESTER UNITED (£30,000, April 1982), Aston Villa (£450,000, August 1989), Derby County (£100,000, 1996), Sheffield United (1997). Announced his retirement in May 1998.
Centre-half Paul McGrath was 22 when Ron Atkinson signed him for Manchester United. A tall, commanding central defender, well built, he was cool, controlled and steady under pressure and went on to play in more than 200 first-class games during his seven years at Old Trafford, gaining an FA Cup winners medal in 1985. Despite his dodgy knees, McGrath continued to do the business for Aston Villa and he certainly paid back the near half-a-million pound transfer fee (with interest)! He helped Villa beat his old club (United) in the 1994 League Cup Final and added a second League Cup medal to his collection in 1996. As his career continued, so his performances got better and better! He went on win 83 full international caps for the Republic of Eire and starred in 323 senior games for Villa. He ended his playing days in 1998 with a magnificent club and international record under his belt of 648 appearances...despite being unable to train during the last two years!
Club record: 203 apps. 16 goals

McGRATH, Roland Christopher

Born: Belfast, 29 November 1954.

Career: Belfast & District Schools, Tottenham Hotspur (amateur 1970, professional 1972), Millwall (on loan 1976), MANCHESTER UNITED (£30,000, October 1976), Tulsa Roughnecks (February 1981), South China, Hong Kong (1982-83). Versatile forward Chris McGrath made his League debut for Spurs against Arsenal in the London derby in October 1973 and also played in the 1974 UEFA Cup Final. Capped by Northern Ireland at Schoolboy level, he went on to win a total of 21 full caps for his country. He was used mainly as a substitute by United, coming off the bench no fewer than 19 times.

Club record: 34 apps. one goal

McGUINNESS, Wilfred

Born: Manchester, 25 October 1937.

Career: St Patrick's School (Collyhurst), Manchester & Lancashire Schools, MANCHESTER UNITED (amateur January 1953, professional November 1954. Retired 1961 and appointed Youth team coach at Old Trafford, also acting as England Youth team manager (1963-64). Upgraded to United's senior coach in summer of 1969, then manager (June-December 1970). Demoted to reserve team coach (following the return to duty of Sir Matt Busby). Aris Salonika, Greece (manager: 1971-73), Panachaiki Patras, Greece (manager, season 1973-74), York City (manager, 1975-77), Hull City (coach, late 1970s), Bury reserve team coach & physiotherapist (1980-91). He retired in 1992 and became an established and much-respected after-dinner speaker.

Wing-half Wilf McGuinness, strong and a fierce competitor, was used, pre-Munich, as Duncan Edwards' deputy which allowed the young giant to play in other positions as required. After Munich, McGuinness took over Edwards' left-half berth for both United and England.

A schoolboy international at the age of 15, he made his League debut against Wolverhampton Wanderers two years later and won a First Division Championship medal in 1957. Captain of the England Youth team, he gained three FA Youth Cup winners medals (1953-54-55) and then won four Under-23 caps for his country, played in two full internationals (1958 & 1959), represented Young England and also played for the Football League. Unfortunately a broken leg, suffered at the age of 22 when playing in a Central League game v. Stoke City (at Old Trafford) virtually ended his career. He attempted a comeback (to no avail) and later became a very good coach, serving Bury in that capacity (and as a physio) for 11 years.

Club record: 85 apps. 2 goals

McILROY, Samuel Baxter, MBE

Refer to front of section.

McILVENNY, Edward

Born: Greenock, Refrewshire, 21 October 1924. Died: 1989

Career: Greenock Morton (before, during & after WW2), Wrexham (1947), Fairhill FC Inc, USA (1948), Philadelphia Nationals (1949), MANCHESTER UNITED (August 1950), Waterford (player-manager, July 1953).

Wing-half Eddie McIlvenny's claim to fame was when he skippered the USA to that famous 1-0 World Cup Finals victory over England at Belo Horizonte in 1950, being one of three non-American players in the team. He played in the opening two League games of the 1950-51 season (against Fulham and Liverpool) but thereafter was a permanent reserve to Don Gibson/Johnny Carey (and other half-backs) during his three years at Old Trafford.

Club record: 2 apps.

McKAY, William

Born: West Benhar, Lothian, 24 August (circa 1904 or 1905).

Career: Shotts Battlefield FC, East Stirlingshire (1925), Hamilton Academical (1927), Bolton Wanderers (1929), MANCHESTER UNITED (March 1932), guested for Stockport County & Port Vale during WW2, Stalybridge Celtic (season 1946-47).

Scottish-born wing-half or inside-forward Bill McKay made over 100 senior appearances north of the border and over 100 for Bolton Wanderers before joining United in 1932. A chatter-box on the field, he was a very capable, hard-working wing-half who gave the Reds splendid service before and during WW2, helping them win the Second Division Championship in 1936.

Club record: 184 apps. 15 goals

McKEE, Colin

Born: Glasgow, 22 August 1974

Career: Glasgow Boys, MANCHESTER UNITED (YTS June 1989, professional May 1992), Bury (on loan, January 1993), Kilmarnock (July 1994), Ross County (season 1994-95).

Colin McKee won Scottish Schoolboy honours and was 'Player of the Year' when United's reserve side won the Pontins League title in 1993-94 - the season he made his Premiership debut in midfield against Coventry City (May) in the final match of the season, marking Bryan Robson's departure. He then moved to Scotland in the close season..

Club record: one app.

213

McLACHLAN, George Herbert

Born: Glasgow, 21 September 1902

Career: Crosshill Amateurs. Parkhead Juniors, Clyde (1922-23), King's Park Strollers (on loan), Cardiff City (£2,000, 1925), MANCHESTER UNITED (December 1929), Chester (player-coach, June 1933), Le Havre, France (manager 1934), Queen of the South (manager, 1935-36).

Able to play as a wing-half or on the left wing (his preferred position) Scotsman George McLachlan spent three-and-a-half years at Old Trafford and during that time gave some sterling performances, being appointed captain in 1931-32. In 1925 he had played for Glasgow against Sheffield in the annual challenge match and also appeared in an international trial match in 1928 (for the Anglo Scots against the Home Scots).

Whilst at Ninian Park, he helped the Welsh club create footballing history as a member of Cardiff's side which took the FA Cup out of England for the only time, beating Arsenal 1-0. He scored 22 goals in 139 League games for the Bluebirds.

Club record: 116 apps. 4 goals

McLENAHAN, Hugh

Born: West Gorton, Manchester, 23 March 1909. Died: Macclesfield, May 1988.

Career: St Francis' School (Gorton), Manchester Schoolboys, Lancashire County Schools, Ambrose FC (Manchester), Longsight 'A' team (Lancs & Cheshire Amateur League), Ashton Brothers (Manchester), Stalybridge Celtic, Blackpool (trialist), Stockport County (1927), MANCHESTER UNITED (May 1927), Notts County (December 1936). Retired in 1939.

Half-back Hugh McLenahan - who was twice capped by England at schoolboy level - looked to be set for a lengthy run in the first team at Old Trafford, having made his debut as a part-timer when only 18. He sadly broke his leg in 1928 playing against Aston Villa, losing about a year's playing time before returning to duty. It was once thought that a freezer full of ice-cream, presented to Stockport County's bazaar committee, was part of the transfer deal that led to McLenahan joining United. But it later transpired that there was no official link - just a coincidence that both 'moves' took place simultaneously!

Club record 116 apps. 12 goals.

McLOUGHLIN, Alan Francis

Born: Manchester, 20 April 1967

Career: MANCHESTER UNITED (YTS, June 1983, professional April 1985), Swindon Town (free transfer, August 1986), Torquay United (on loan, March 1987), Southampton (£1 million, 1990), Aston Villa (on loan, 1991), Portsmouth (£400,000, early 1992), Wigan Athletic (£250,000, 1999).

Alan McLoughlin did not make a senior appearance for United! A Republic of Ireland international midfielder, capped 42 times by his country, he also played for Eire's 'B' team and when the 2001-02 season ended he had appeared in well over 550 League and Cup games as a professional. Certainly a player missed by United!

McMILLAN, Samuel Thomas

Born: Belfast, 29 September 1941

Career: Ashfield School, Ards FC (reserve team, 1956), Linfield (amateur), Boyland Youth Club (Belfast), MANCHESTER UNITED (amateur 1957, professional November 1959), Wrexham (£8,000, December 1963), Southend United (£6,000, 1967), Chester (late 1969), Stockport County (1970-72), Oswestry Town (1972-74), Lex XI, Wrexham (team coach).

Sammy McMillan helped Ashfield win the All-Ireland Schools Cup in 1955. He spent four years battling hard and long to secure a regular first team place at Old Trafford. Fast and tricky with a strong right-foot shot, he was capped twice by Northern Ireland whilst a United player and later netted 62 goals in 172 outings for Wrexham. During his career he scored over 100 first-class goals in some 355 League and Cup appearances. Another player 'missed' by United - despite scoring heavily for the reserves!

Club record: 15 apps. 6 goals

McMILLEN, Walter S

Born: Belfast, 24 November 1913.

Career: Carrickfergus FC, Cliftonville, Arsenal (trialist), MANCHESTER UNITED (August 1933), Chesterfield (December 1936), Millwall (1939), guested for Glentoran, Linfield & Belfast Celtic during WW2, Tonbridge FC (1950-51).

Northern Ireland international centre or wing-half Walter McMillen made 176 League appearances after leaving United. He had George Vose to contend with for a place in the first XI at Old Trafford, having done very well in the 1933-34 season. He won seven caps in total, three with United and four with Chesterfield, making him the joint record-holder (with Mark Williams) for most caps won by a Saltergate player!

Club record: 29 apps. 2 goals

McNAUGHT, James Rankin

Born: Dumbarton, 8 June 1870. Died: West Ham, London, March 1919.

Career: Dumbarton, Linfield, NEWTON HEATH (February 1893), Tottenham Hotspur (May 1898), Maidstone (1907). Retired 1909.

Scotsman James McNaught - 'The Little Wonder' - spent five excellent seasons with Newton Heath, initially as an inside-forward before settling in as a superb footballing centre-half, despite measuring only 5ft 6ins. A boilermaker by trade, he had joined the Heathens on a £4-a-week seasonal contract and after leaving the club he made over 250 senior appearances for Spurs, played for a Scotland XI versus an England XI and for the Anglo Scots against the Home Scots in an international trial, gained a Southern League Championship medal in 1899-1900 and was a keen and enthusiastic member of the Professional Players Union.

Club record: 163 apps. 12 goals (also 57 'other' apps, 9 goals)

McNULTY, Thomas

Born: Salford, 30 December 1929
Career: Salford Boys' Club, MANCHESTER UNITED (amateur May 1945, professional June 1947), Liverpool (February 1954 to summer 1958), Hyde United (1963-64).
Full-back Tommy McNulty helped United win the First Division Championship in 1951-52 when he played in over half of the League matches that season. Eventually he lost his place to Bill Foulkes and after leaving Old Trafford failed to establish himself in the first XI at Anfield, making only 36 League appearances in four years.
Club record: 60 apps.

McPHERSON, Francis Comber

Born: Barrow-in-Furness, Cumbria, 14 May 1901. Died: Davyhulme, Manchester, 5 March 1953.
Career: Barrow Shipbuilders FC, Partick Thistle (amateur, 1919), Chesterfield Municipal FC (late 1919), Barrow (1921), MANCHESTER UNITED (May 1922), Manchester Central (July 1928), Watford (£850, later in 1928), Reading (early 1930), Watford (summer 1933), Barrow (1937-39).
Frank McPherson was regarded as one of the fastest and cleverest forwards in the game during the 1920s. After helping Barrow win the Lancashire Combination Championship and gain election to the Third Division (North) he quickly established himself in United's second XI before taking up his position in the first team, playing superbly well alongside his inside partner Arthur Lochhead on the left flank, and then at centre-forward, being particularly successful following the change in the offside law (q.v) in 1925.
He went on to appear in 176 League games after leaving United (almost 100 goals scored).
Club record: 175 apps. 52 goals

McQUEEN, Gordon

Born: Kilbirnie, Strathclyde, 26 June 1952.
Career: Largs Thistle, Glasgow Rangers (trialist), Liverpool (trialist), St Mirren (1970), Leeds United (£30,000, 1972), MANCHESTER UNITED (£495,000, February 1978), FC Seiko, Hong Kong (player-coach, August 1985), Airdrieonians (manager, 1987-89), St Mirren (player-coach, 1989-91), Middlesbrough (reserve team coach, mid 1990s).
Centre-half Gordon McQueen scored some excellent goals for United - most of them powerful headers from set pieces! Once a junior goalkeeper, he developed into a formidable defender, strong and resilient, who never shirked a tackle, possessing a good turn of pace, was confident in his approach to the game and was always totally committed. He replaced England giant Jack Charlton at the heart of the Leeds' defence and then - following his record transfer from Elland Road - took over the No 5 shirt from Brian Greenhoff, going on to form an excellent partnership with fellow Scot, Martin Buchan. A beaten FA Cup finalist with United in 1979, McQueen was then a winner in 1983 (at Brighton's expense) and gained a second runners-up medal when Liverpool defeated United in the Football League Cup Final that same year. He won a total of 30 full caps for his country, 17 with Leeds, 13 with the Reds.
McQueen became seriously ill after contracting typhoid fever when playing in Hong Kong. Thankfully, he recovered his health (and fitness) and later - after a decent spell in Scotland - he was appointed reserve team coach at Middlesbrough (under the management of former United star, Bryan Robson).
His father, Tommy McQueen, was a goalkeeper with Accrington Stanley (late 1930s).
Club record: 229 apps. 26 goals

McSHANE, Henry

Born: Holytown, Strathclyde, 8 April 1920
Career: Bellshill Athletic, Blackburn Rovers (amateur, professional 1937), (RAF service WW2), Huddersfield Town (1946), Bolton Wanderers (1947), MANCHESTER UNITED (September 1950), Oldham Athletic (£750, February 1954), Chorley (player-coach, 1955-56), Wellington Town (season 1956-57), Droylsden (1958), Stalybridge Celtic (coach, 1961-62). Was the match-day PA Announcer and DJ at Old Trafford during the late 1960s, early '70s.
Winger Harry McShane had already played in 110 League games when he joined United. He could occupy either flank. He was sharp and incisive with a powerful shot and no mean skill! He replaced Charlie Mitten (in Bogota) on the left and then played on the right until Johnny Berry's arrival. He came to Old Trafford in a player-deal involving full-back John Ball. He helped United finish runners-up in the First Division in 1950-51 and then played in 12 matches when the League title was won the following season.
McShane is a founder member of the ex-United Players' Association. He is the is the father of the TV actor, Ian McShane (of Lovejoy fame) in which the Lovejoy character always drinks out of a 'United' mug in his workshop. Watch out for it!
Club record: 57 apps. 8 goals

MACKIE, Charles

Born: Scotland
Career: Aberdeen, MANCHESTER UNITED (May 1904), West Ham United (summer 1905), Aberdeen (late 1905), Lochgelly United (season 1906-07).
Centre-forward Charlie Mackie looked a promising acquisition when signed from Aberdeen but he was injured and sidelined when doing well and never regained his composure..
Club record: 7 apps. 4 goals

215

MACARI, Luigi

Born: Edinburgh, 4 June 1949.

Career: St Michael's Academy (Kilwinning), Kilwinning Amateurs, Celtic (professional, July 1966), MANCHESTER UNITED (£200,000, January 1973), Swindon Town (player-manager, July 1984), West Ham United (manager, 1989-90), Birmingham City (manager, 1991), Stoke City (manager mid-1991), Celtic (manager (1993-94), Stoke City (manager 1994-97), Sheffield United (Chief Scout 1998), Huddersfield Town (manager, autumn 2000, sacked June 2002).

Born to Italian parents, 'Lou' Macari was a busy little inside or centre-forward, always buzzing around the penalty area, menacing defenders and scoring his fair share of goals. He won a total of 24 caps for Scotland, also adding two more to his collection with the Under-23s as well as representing his country at both Schoolboy and Youth team levels. With the Bhoys he starred in two League Championship-winning sides (1970 & 1972), in two Scottish Cup winning teams (1971 & 1972) and in two victorious Scottish League Cup finals (1972 & 1973). He also collected a handful of League Cup runners-up medals, and above all he scored plenty of goals!

After seven years at Parkhead, Macari was one of several Scots signed by United manager Tommy Docherty shortly after he had taken over the reins at Old Trafford. He found it tough going for a time in the First Division, and at the end the 1973-74 season he tasted relegation for the first time in his career! United bounced back quickly, though, and in 1976 Macari played in the FA Cup Final defeat by Southampton. The following year he was a Cup Final winner after his shot was deflected into the net by Jimmy Greenhoff as Liverpool were beaten 2-1 but in 1979 he was a loser again, Arsenal winning in the last minute! Sacked as manager of Swindon after a row with his assistant and former Manchester United goalkeeper Harry Gregg, he was reinstated six days later, and then he took the Robins up from the Fourth to the Second Division in two seasons, the latter via the 1987 play-off final. Two years on and Swindon again reached the play-offs, but this time they lost to Crystal Palace. He held the manager's job at Upton Park for just 28 weeks, leaving after seeing his side hammered 6-0 by Oldham in a League Cup semi-final match. A month earlier the FA had charged Macari, and his former Swindon chairman, Brian Hillier, of unauthorised betting on a League game involving that club.

He succeeded Dave Mackay in the hot-seat at St Andrew's and guided Blues to victory in the Leyland DAF Final at Wembley but then surprisingly resigned, saying that the club lacked ambition! He subsequently saw Stoke win the Third Division play-offs in his first season in charge and later the Autoglass Trophy at Wembley as well as claiming the Second Division title.

Club record: 404 apps. 97 goals.

"Born to Italian parents, 'Lou' Macari was a busy little inside or centre-forward."

MAINE ROAD

Owing to Old Trafford being severely damaged by German bombs, Manchester United used Maine Road (headquarters of rivals Manchester City) from 1941 until 1949, playing three peacetime League seasons of home fixtures there (1946-49) plus five and a bit wartime seasons.

United's first League game at Maine Road was played on 31 August 1946 when a crowd of 41,025 saw them beat Grimsby Town 2-1 with goals by Charlie Mitten and Jack Rowley. Their last League game was against the champions-elect Portsmouth on 7 May 1949 when almost 50,000 fans saw United win a pulsating contest by 3-2, with Rowley (2) and Mitten the scorers once more.

On 17 January 1948, United met Arsenal at Maine Road before a massive audience of 83,260, a Football League record which could remain intact forever! The result was a thrilling 1-1 draw, Jack Rowley equalising Reg Lewis' early goal.

As United had no floodlights they were forced to play their first-ever home European Cup match at Maine Road, beating RSC Anderlecht 10-0 in the second leg of a preliminary round encounter on 26 September 1956. A crowd of 40,000 saw Dennis Viollet (4) and Tommy Taylor (3) lead the goal-rush.

In the next round United entertained Borussia Dortmund in the first leg and a massive crowd of 75,598 saw the Reds scrape through 3-2. There was another 70,000 audience for United's third European game v. Athletic Bilbao, which was won 3-0, overturning a two-goal deficit from the first-leg. United's Old Trafford floodlighting system was installed in time for the semi-final tie with Real Madrid.

Crowds of 82,771 and 81,565 packed into Maine Road to see United play Bradford (PA) and non-League Yeovil in 4th and 5th round FA Cup-ties in January & February 1949. There was a 70,434 turn out for the replay against Bradford, also at Maine Road, prior to that game against Yeovil.

NB: United paid their 'landlords' (City) £5,000 a season (a sizeable fee in those days) plus a share of the gate money for the use of their Maine Road ground. Despite this lucrative agreement, City asked United to leave at the end of the 1948-49 season. Therefore United had no option, despite the fact that their Old Trafford home was still far from suitable for League football (See under Old Trafford).

United's senior playing record at Maine Road:

Competition	P	W	D	L	F	A	Pts
League Div 1	63*	39	17	7	151	66	95 (75.4%)
FA Cup	8	6	1	1	30	5	-
European Cup	3	3	0	0	16	2	-
Summary	74	48	18	8	197	73	- (77%)

* These results include two 'home' League matches against Manchester City (both draws) but not two 'away' matches (also draws).

MAIORANA, Guiliano

Born: Cambridge, 18 April 1969

Career: Histon FC, Cambridge United (trialist), Norwich City (trialist), Watford (trialist), MANCHESTER UNITED (£30,000, December 1988-May 1994).

Six of 'Jules' Maiorana's senior appearances for United came as a substitute. A long-term knee injury subsequently ended the playing career of this exciting, if erratic, left wingman.

Club record: 8 apps.

MAJOR TITLES

Manchester United have so far won a total of 46 major football trophies:

7	Premiership
7	Football League Division 1
2	Football League Division 2
10	FA Cup
1	League Cup
2	European (Champions) Cup
1	European Cup-winners Cup
1	European Super Cup
1	Inter-Continental Cup
14*	FA Charity Shield

* Includes four times shared.

MANAGERS

The modern-day manager only came into vogue around the WW1 period. In the 19th century the secretary was responsible for the club in its entirety including the playing resources. In the early part of the 20th century, the secretary-manager came along.

Here are the respective details of the men responsible for Newton Heath/Manchester United's team affairs since the club first entered the Football Alliance in 1889 (those marked with an asterisk* were secretaries of the club). Only Alliance, Football League & Premiership, FA Cup, League Cup and all major European competitions haave been included in the tables.

Name	Term of Office					
A H Albut*	**September 1889 to June 1900**					
Competition	P	W	D	L	F	A
F Alliance	66	28	12	26	146	133
F League	248	114	39	95	480	397
FA Cup	29	12	6	11	54	50
Totals	343	154	57	132	680	580 (53.21%)

* Promotion gained from Alliance to Football League

James West*   July 1900 to July 1903

Competition	P	W	D	L	F	A
F League	102	40	18	44	133	49
FA Cup	11	6	2	3	26	18
Totals	113	46	20	47	159	67 (49.56%)

Ernest Mangnall September 1903 to September 1912

Competition	P	W	D	L	F	A
F League	334	181	66	87	614	424
FA Cup	36	19	9	8	73	47
Totals	370	200	75	95	687	471 (64.19%)

* Won two League championships, the FA Cup, and gained promotion (as runners-up) from Division 2.

John J Bentley September 1912 to December 1914

Competition	P	W	D	L	F	A
F League	76	34	14	28	121	105
FA Cup	6	2	2	2	6	5
Totals	82	36	16	30	127	110 (55.66%)

Jack Robson   December 1914 to October 1921

Competition	P	W	D	L	F	A
F League	134	40	41	53	179	201
FA Cup	5	1	1	3	4	6
Totals	139	41	42	56	183	207 (44.60%)

John Chapman October 1921 to October 1926

Competition	P	W	D	L	F	A
F League	210	81	55	74	271	253
FA Cup	14	6	3	5	19	26
Totals	224	87	58	79	290	279 (51.12%)

* Won promotion from Division 2 as runners-up

Clarence Hilditch October 1926 to April 1927

Competition	P	W	D	L	F	A
F League	30	9	11	10	33	29
FA Cup	3	0	2	1	4	5
Totals	33	9	13	11	37	34 (46.97%)

Herbert Bamlett April 1927 to May 1931

Competition	P	W	D	L	F	A
F League	168	52	36	80	258	359
FA Cup	12	5	3	4	20	13
Totals	180	57	39	84	278	372 (42.50%)

Walter Crickmer* May 1931 to June 1932

Competition	P	W	D	L	F	A
F League	42	17	8	17	71	72
FA Cup	1	0	0	1	1	4
Totals	43	17	8	18	72	76 (48.84%)

Archie Scott Duncan June 1932 to November 1937

Competition	P	W	D	L	F	A
F League	224	89	50	85	361	341
FA Cup	11	3	3	5	10	21
Totals	235	92	53	90	371	362 (50.42%)

* Won Second Division Championship

Walter Crickmer* November 1937 to February 1945

Competition	P	W	D	L	F	A
F League	70	28	22	20	124	103
FA Cup	6	2	2	2	7	9
Totals	76	30	24	22	131	112
(2 spells)	119	47	32	40	203	188 (52.94%)

* Won promotion from Division 2 as runners-up

Matt Busby   February 1945 to June 1969

Competition	P	W	D	L	F	A
F League	966	470	233	263	1913	1357
FA Cup	104	61	21	22	227	124
League Cup	4	1	1	2	7	8
Euro Comp	58	35	11	12	144	66
Totals	1132	567	266	299	2291	1555
						(61.84%) *

Won five League championships (7 times runners-up), two FA Cups (twice beaten finalists) and the European Cup.

Wilf McGuinness June 1969 to December 1970

Competition	P	W	D	L	F	A
F League	65	19	26	20	94	99
FA Cup	9	5	3	1	17	5
League Cup	14	8	4	2	20	11
Totals	88	32	33	23	131	115 (55.11%)

*Took United to three Cup semi-finals.

Sir Matt Busby December 1970 to June 1971

Competition	P	W	D	L	F	A
F League	19	11	2	6	37	28
FA Cup	2	0	1	1	1	2
Totals	21	11	3	7	38	30
* (2 spells)	1153	578	269	306	2329	1585
						(60.76%)

Frank O'Farrell June 1971 to December 1972

Competition	P	W	D	L	F	A
F League	64	24	16	24	89	95
FA Cup	7	3	3	1	12	5
League Cup	10	3	5	2	14	11
Totals	81	30	24	27	115	111 (51.85%)

Tommy Docherty December 1972 to July 1977

Competition	P	W	D	L	F	A
F League	188	84	49	55	267	208
FA Cup	19	12	3	4	28	18
League Cup	17	9	4	4	35	22
Euro Comps	4	2	0	2	3	4
Totals	228	107	56	65	333	252 (59.21%)

* Won Second Division championship and the FA Cup and also FA Cup finalist.

Dave Sexton   July 1977 to April 1981

Competition	P	W	D	L	F	A
F League	168	70	53	45	243	197
FA Cup	18	7	7	4	27	19
League Cup	7	2	0	5	9	13
Euro Comps	6	2	3	1	9	8
Totals	199	81	63	55	288	237 (56.53%)

Ron Atkinson June 1981 to November 1986

Competition	P	W	D	L	F	A
F League	223	108	63	52	349	207
FA Cup	21	14	4	3	36	15
League Cup	28	16	5	7	49	24
Euro Comps	18	7	7	4	25	18
Totals	290	145	79	66	459	264 (63.62%)

* Two FA Cup wins, also League Cup Finalists

Alex Ferguson November 1986 to end of 2001-02 season

Competition	P	W	D	L	F	A
F League/PL	617	341	163	113	1108	587
FA Cup	69	45	13	11	124	57
League Cup	55	34	6	15	95	60
Euro Comps	104	50	35	19	172	93
Totals	845	470	217	158	1499	797 (68.46%)

* Honours: seven Premiership titles (twice runners-up), four FA Cups (beaten finalist once), one League Cup (twice beaten finalists), one European Cup, one European Cup-winners Cup, one European Super Cup & one World Club championship.
(For career details of the above personnel, see under individual entries).

Managerial Notes:

Jimmy Murphy was appointed caretaker-manager at Old Trafford (from February 1958) whilst Matt Busby was recovering in a German hospital following the Munich air disaster. He continued to act as assistant-manager (to Busby) until June 1971. When United were without a manager from 1927-32 and 1937-45, club secretary Walter Crickmer looked after team affairs, virtually running the club single-handedly during the war years..

United Assistant-Managers
Listed in A-Z order: Mike Brown (to Ron Atkinson) Tommy Cavanagh (to Tommy Docherty). Brian Kidd, Archie Knox (1986-91) and Steve McClaren (to Alex Ferguson), Jimmy Murphy (to Matt Busby), Malcolm Musgrove (to Frank O'Farrell) and Jimmy Ryan (also to Sir Alex Ferguson).

United players (at various levels) who went on to become managers with other major clubs:

Trevor Anderson	Linfield
Billy Behan	Drumcondra
Derek Brazil	Notts County
Jack Breedon	Bradford Park Avenue, Halifax Town
Shay Brennan	Waterford (player-manager)
Steve Bruce	Birmingham City, Crystal Palace, Huddersfield Town, Sheffield United, Wigan Athletic
Martin Buchan	Burnley
Frank Buckley	Blackpool, Hull City, Leeds United, Notts County, Walsall, Wolverhampton Wanderers
Francis Burns	Italia FC (Australia)
Noel Cantwell	Coventry City, Jacksonville Teamen, New England Teamen, Peterborough United
Johnny Carey	Blackburn Rovers, Everton, Leyton Orient, Nottingham Forest
Bobby Charlton	Preston North End (player-manager)
Allenby Chilton	Grimsby Town (player-manager), Hartlepools United, Wigan Athletic
Jonathan Clark	Preston North End (caretaker-manager)
Steve Coppell	Brentford, Crystal Palace, Manchester City
Pat Crerand	Northampton Town
Jack Crompton	Barrow, Luton Town
Peter Davenport	Airdrieonians (player-manager), Macclesfield Town Bangor City
Jimmy Delaney	Cork Athletic (player-manager)
Tommy Doyle	Northampton Town (player-manager)
Hugh Edmonds	Glenavon (player-manager)
Bill Foulkes	Lillestrom, Mazda Horishima, Viking Stavanger, Stenjker (Norway)
Johnny Giles	Shamrock Rovers (player-manager), Vancouver Whitecaps, West Bromwich Albion
Freddie Goodwin	Birmingham City, Brighton & Hove Albion, Minnesota Kicks, New York Generals, Scunthorpe United (player-manager)
Arthur Graham	Bradford City (caretaker-manager)
George Graham	Arsenal, Leeds United, Millwall, Tottenham Hotspur
Ian Greaves	Bolton Wanderers, Huddersfield Town, Mansfield Town, Oxford United, Wolverhampton Wanderers
Haydn Green	Hull City, Swansea Town
Harry Gregg	Carlisle United, Crewe Alexandra, Kitan Sports Club (Kuwait), Shrewsbury Town, Swansea City
Jack Hacking	Accrington Stanley (player-manager), Barrow
Harry Haslam	Luton Town, Sheffield United
Vince Hayes	Madrid, Preston North End (secretary-manager), Rochdale (player-manager)
David Herd	Lincoln City
Tom Jones	Scunthorpe United
Joe Jordan	Bristol City, Heart of Midlothian, Stoke City
Cyril Knowles	Darlington, Hartlepool United, Torquay United
Eddie Lewis	Witts FC (South Africa)
Geordie Livingstone	Clydebank, Dumbarton
Arthur Lochhead	Leicester City
Brian Kidd	Blackburn Rovers, Preston North End
Wilf McGuinness	Aris Salonika, Panachaiki Pratas, York City
Neil McBain	Ayr United, Leyton Orient (also assistant-manager), Luton Town, New Brighton (secretary-manager), Watford (player-manager)
Jim McCalliog	Halifax Town (caretaker-manager & manager)
John McCartney	Barnsley, Heart of Midlothian, Luton Town, Portsmouth, St Mirren (all as secretary-manager)
David McCreery	Carlisle United (caretaker-manager), Hartlepool United (player-manager)
Sammy McIlroy	Macclesfield Town
Eddie McIlvenny	Waterford (player-manager)
George McLachlan	Le Havre, Queen of the South
Gordon McQueen	Airdrieonians
Lou Macari	Birmingham City, Celtic, Huddersfield Town, Swindon Town (player-manager), Stoke City, West Ham United
Charlie Mitten	Mansfield Town (player-manager), Newcastle United
Archie Montgomery	Bury, Albion Rovers
Jimmy Nicholl	Dunfermline Athletic (caretaker), Millwall, Raith Rovers (player-manager)
Pat O'Connell	Ashington, FC Barcelona
Louis Page	Chester, Newport County, Swindon Town
Steve Paterson	Inverness Caledonian Thistle
Stan Pearson	Chester (player-manager)
Stuart Pearson	Bradford City, West Bromwich Albion (caretaker-manager)
Bill Ridding	Bolton Wanderers, Tranmere Rovers
Andy Ritchie	Oldham Athletic
Charlie Roberts	Oldham Athletic
George Roughton	Exeter City (player-manager), Southampton
Arthur Rowley	Sheffield United, Shrewsbury Town (player-manager), Southend United
Jack Rowley	Ajax (coach/manager), Bradford Park Avenue, Oldham Athletic, Plymouth Argyle (player-manager), Wrexham
Bobby Smith	Swindon Town
Charlie Spencer	Grimsby Town
Frank Stapleton	Bradford City (player-manager)
Alf Steward	Torquay United
Nobby Stiles	Middlesbrough, West Bromwich Albion
Gordon Strachan	Coventry City (also player), Southampton
Chris Turner	Leyton Orient (joint-manager), Hartlepool United
Ian Ure	East Stirlingshire
Dennis Viollet	Crewe Alexandra
Tony Waddington*	Crewe Alexandra, Stoke City
Jack Warner	Rochdale (player-manager)

* An amateur with United in the 1940s.

United personnel who also managed at non-League level:

Arthur Albiston	Droylsden
Peter Barnes	Radcliffe Borough
Frank Barson	Stourbridge, Rhyl (player-manager)
Garry Birtles	Gresley Rovers
James Brown	Polish Falcons FC
Ted Buckle	Prestatyn FC
Eric Cantona	France Beach FC
Gordon Clayton	Cheadle Town
Frank Clempson	Hyde United (player-manager)
Ronnie Cope	Northwich Victoria (caretaker-manager)
Gerry Daly	Telford United
John Doherty	Rugby Town (player-manager)
Tommy Doyle	Scarborough*
Bill Foulkes	Witney Town
Billy Garton	Salford City (player-manager)
Don Gibson	Buxton (player-manager)
John Gidman	Kings Lynn
Deiniol Graham	Emley Town
Ian Greaves	Emley Town
Haydn Green	Bangor City, Ebbw Vale, Guildford
Reg Halton	Scarborough* (player-manager)
Harry Haslam	Barry Town, Tonbridge
Gordon Hill	Northwich Victoria (player-manager/coach)
Billy Johnston	Frickley Colliery (player-manager)
Brian Kidd	Barrow
Cyril Knowles	Hertford Town
Eddie Lewis	Ford Sports FC
Jim McCalliog	Runcorn (player-manager)
Billy McGlen	Skegness Town (manager-coach)
Sammy McIlroy	Ashton United, Macclesfield Town*, Northwich Victoria
Tommy Manley	Northwich Victoria
Charlie Mitten	Altrincham (player-manager)
Kenny Morgans	Cwmbran Town (player-manager)
Johnny Morris	Corby Town, Great Harwood, Kettering Town, Oswestry Town, Rugby Town
George Mutch	Banks o'Dee FC
Ray O'Brien	Arnold Town (joint-manager)
Pat O'Connell	Ashington* (player-manager)
Tommy O'Neil	Skelmersdale
Louis Page	Yeovil & Petters United
Steve Paterson	Elgin City (player-manager), Huntly FC (Scotland, manager)
Stuart Pearson	Northwich Victoria
Billy Porter	Hyde United (player-manager)
Arthur Rowley	Oswestry Town, Corby Town, Kettering Town (all as player-manager)
Harry Rowley	Burton Town (player-manager)
Ted Savage	South Liverpool
Charlie Spencer	Hastings United, Wigan Athletic* (player-manager)
Alf Steward	Altrincham, Manchester North End
Ian Storey-Moore	Shepshed Charterhouse & Burton Albion (both as player-manager)
Mickey Thomas	Portmadoc
Neil Webb	Reading Town
Jack Wilson	Leadgate Park FC (player-manager)

* Pre-Football League days

International Managers

The following all managed the country (named) at full international level and were also associated in some capacity with Manchester United FC:

(Sir) Matt Busby (Scotland)
Tommy Docherty (Scotland)
(Sir) Alex Ferguson (Scotland)
Johnny Giles (Republic of Ireland)
Mark Hughes (Wales)
Sammy McIlroy (Northern Ireland)
Jimmy Murphy (Wales)
(Sir) Walter Winterbottom (England)

219

Managerial Skill

When Matt Busby took over at United in 1945 he quickly became aware that his playing resources were not all that strong, even as pre-war players returned to the club. He knew that the club was deep in debt with the ground in ruins, so there was little likelihood of strengthening the side through the transfer market, coming to the conclusion that he would have to 'make do' with what he had. He studied his players closely, surprising them all by training with them in his track suit (pre-war managers were office-bound in suit and tie, seen only on Saturdays) but the players soon realised Busby was a superb player himself, capable of taking his place in the side if need be.

He decided to try certain players in different positions, coming up with a simple but extremely effective method of educating them in their new roles. Busby would talk with the player, telling him he thought he would make a great centre-half (or whatever); he then played them in the Tuesday practice match in their new position, Busby himself playing in direct opposition, talking the player through his duties in his new role throughout the game.

Thus Johnny Carey (an ageing inside-forward) became a cultured full-back; John Aston was also converted from an ordinary inside-forward into an international left-back; Allenby Chilton from a mediocre wing-half into an England centre-half; Henry Cockburn, another inside-forward who would never have made the grade in that position, into an international wing-half and John Anderson likewise.

He also convinced wingman Jack Rowley that his best position was centre-forward, a switch which brought sensational results. Jack Crompton, an amateur goalkeeper, became a top-class 'keeper; forwards Johnny Morris, Stan Pearson and Charlie Mitten were all pre-war professionals who had joined the club as youths, who prospered under Busby's methods. Only at outside-right did Busby fail to produce a top player, so he persuaded Chairman James Gibson to scrape together £4,000 to sign his old colleague Jimmy Delaney from Celtic; money well spent indeed.

These players, most of all, bought Busby time, winning both the League title and FA Cup in the process as United set the place alight with their brilliant football. As they aged, the 'Babes' came along to carry the torch and the rest is history.

Managerial Chit-Chat

Matt Busby was voted 'Manager of the Year' in 1968 and thereafter Alex Ferguson received the same award in 1993, 1994, 1996, 1997, 1999, 2000 & 2001.

Dave Sexton parted company with the club despite seven successive wins at the end of the 1980-81 season.

Tommy Docherty was United's manager when relegation was suffered to the Second Division at the end of the 1973-74 season.

Sexton followed Docherty as manager at three different clubs: Chelsea, QPR & United. He was employed by Aston Villa (another of Doc's old clubs) when Ron Atkinson was manager there. Atkinson himself had earlier followed Sexton into office at Old Trafford.

Geordie Livingstone was player-manager of United's reserve team.

Matt Busby (as manager of Scotland) selected Arsenal's Tommy Docherty for the national team in 1958.

Ernest Mangnall, United's manager for nine years from 1903, moved across the City to Hyde Road and was in charge of the 'Blues' for 12 years (1912-24). In his time he oversaw United's move to Old Trafford (1910) and City's move to Maine Road (1923).

The Charlton brothers, Bobby and Jack, managed Preston North End and Middlesbrough and came together for a Second Division match in 1973-74.

Ron Atkinson managed United in eight local derbies against City and was never on the losing side!

Clarence Hilditch has been United's only player-manager, holding office for seven months (in 1926-27).

Herbert Bamlett, who succeeded Hilditch in the 'hot seat' was formerly a senior referee and in 1914 he became the youngest official to take charge of an FA Cup Final (aged 32).

When Ian Ure took over as manager of East Stirlingshire in November 1974, he replaced Alex Ferguson.

Steve Coppell became the Football League's youngest manager when he took over as boss at Crystal Palace in June 1984 at the age of 38 years, 11 months.

Managerial Success

Sir Alex Ferguson is the most successful manager in United's history (appointed in November 1986). He so far has seven Premiership wins to his credit (1993, 1994, 1996, 1997. 1999, 2000 & 2001); four FA Cup wins (1990, 1994, 1996 & 1999); one League Cup triumph (1992), a European Cup victory (1999); success in the European Cup-winners Cup (1991); glory in the European Super Cup (1991) and Inter-Continental Cup (1999) and four FA Charity Shield wins (1993, 1994, 1996 & 1997). Ferguson also gained ten runners-up prizes. He is the first manager in English League history to manage a club to three successive League (Premiership) titles.

As a manager north of the border, Ferguson gained Scottish League, SFA Cup, League Cup and European Cup-winners Cup prizes with Aberdeen

Sir Matt Busby - the longest-serving manager in United's history: 25 years in total - won the League Championship five times (in 1952, 1956, 1957, 1965 & 1967); the FA Cup twice (in 1948 & 1963); the European Cup once (1968) and the FA Charity Shield outright on four occasions (1952, 1956, 1957 & 1965), sharing it with Tottenham Hotspur in 1967. Busby was also a runner-up in 12 competitions.

Ernest Mangnall was responsible for United's first League title success (1908) and their first FA Cup triumph (1909). He won another League championship in 1911 - to celebrate United's first full season at Old Trafford.

Apart from the above three, who have won just about all of United's trophies between them, the only other managers to win any major prizes have been Tommy Docherty (FA Cup in 1977) and Ron Atkinson (FA Cup in 1983 and 1985). The Second Division titkle was won by Scott Duncan in 1936 and Tommy Docherty in 1975..

United's reserve and Youth team managers:

Here are some of the men who have been employed as reserve and/or Youth team managers by United since the Second World War (listed in A-Z order): Eric Harrison, Brian McClair, Jimmy Murphy and Jimmy Ryan.

For many years, the person in charge of the club's second XI did not have a specific or official title; occasionally the senior player at the club (i.e. Gordon McQueen) would act as player-manager of the second team.

MANCHESTER & SALFORD CHARITY CUP (The Healey Cup)

Newton Heath challenged rivals Manchester City three times in the Final of this competition.

In April 1897, a crowd of 6,000 saw the Heathens beat City 5-2 at Hyde Road; a year later City won 4-2 at Bank Street in front of 3,000 spectators and in April 1899 the Heathens were beaten again, this time by 2-1, also at Bank Street before 1,500 onlookers.

MANCHESTER CITY (also Ardwick)

Heathens/United's League results v Ardwick/Manchester City:

Season	Div	Home	Away	Season	Div	Home	Away
1894-95	2	W 4-1	W 5-2	1956-57	1	W 2-0	W 4-2
1895-96	2	D 1-1	L 1-2	1957-58	1	W 4-1	D 2-2
1896-97	2	W 2-1	D 0-0	1958-59	1	W 4-1	D 1-1
1897-98	2	D 1-1	W 1-0	1959-60	1	D 0-0	L 0-3
1898-99	2	W 3-0	L 0-4	1960-61	1	W 5-1	W 3-1
				1961-62	1	W 3-2	W 2-0
1902-03	2	D 1-1	W 2-0	1962-63	1	L 2-3	D 1-1
1906-07	1	D 1-1	L 0-3	1966-67	1	W 1-0	D 1-1
1907-08	1	W 3-1	D 0-0	1967-68	1	L 1-3	W 2-1
1908-09	1	W 3-1	W 2-1	1968-69	1	L 0-1	D 0-0
				1969-70	1	L 1-2	L 0-4
1910-11	1	W 2-1	D 1-1	1970-71	1	L 1-4	W 4-3
1911-12	1	D 0-0	D 0-0	1971-72	1	L 1-3	D 3-3
1912-13	1	L 0-1	W 2-0	1972-73	1	D 0-0	L 0-3
1913-14	1	L 0-1	W 2-0	1973-74	1	L 0-1	D 0-0
1914-15	1	D 0-0	D 1-1				
				1975-76	1	W 2-0	D 2-2
1919-20	1	W 1-0	D 3-3	1976-77	1	W 3-1	W 3-1
1920-21	1	D 1-1	L 0-3	1977-78	1	D 2-2	L 1-3
1921-22	1	W 3-1	L 1-4	1978-79	1	W 1-0	W 3-0
				1979-80	1	W 1-0	L 0-2
1925-26	1	L 1-6	D 1-1	1980-81	1	D 2-2	L 0-1
				1981-82	1	D 1-1	D 0-0
1928-29	1	L 1-2	D 2-2	1982-83	1	D 2-2	W 2-1
1929-30	1	L 1-3	W 1-0				
1930-31	1	L 1-3	L 1-4	1985-86	1	D 2-2	W 3-0
				1986-87	1	W 2-0	D 1-1
1936-37	1	W 3-2	L 0-1				
				1989-90	1	D 1-1	L 1-5
1947-48	1	D 1-1	D 0-0	1990-91	1	W 1-0	D 3-3
1948-49	1	D 0-0	D 0-0	1991-92	1	D 1-1	D 0-0
1949-50	1	W 2-1	W 2-1	1992-93	PL	W 2-1	D 1-1
				1993-94	PL	W 2-0	W 3-2
1951-52	1	D 1-1	W 2-1	1994-95	PL	W 5-0	W 3-0
1952-53	1	D 1-1	L 1-2	1995-96	PL	W 1-0	W 3-2
1953-54	1	D 1-1	L 0-2				
1954-55	1	L 0-5	L 2-3	2000-01	PL	D 1-1	W 1-0
1955-56	1	W 2-1	L 0-1				

Summary of League results:

	P	W	D	L	F	A
Premier League	10	8	2	0	22	7
Division 1	104	35	39	30	141	147
Division 2	12	6	4	2	21	13
Home	63	27	22	14	98	76
Away	63	22	23	18	86	91
Total	126	49	45	32	184	167

FA Cup results v Ardwick/City:

	Round	Venue	Result
1891-92	1 (Qual)	Home	W 5-1
1925-26	Semi-final	Bramall Lane	L 0-3
1954-55	4	Away	L 0-2
1969-70	4	Home	W 3-0
1986-87	3	Home	W 1-0
1995-96	5	Home	W 2-1

League Cup results v City:

	Round	Venue	Result
1969-70	Semi-final (1)	Away	L 1-2
	Semi-final (2)	Home	D 2-2
1974-75	3	Home	W 1-0
1975-76	4	Away	L 0-4

221

FA Charity Shield
United defeated their near neighbours City 1-0 in the 1956 FA Charity game at Maine Road, Dennis Viollet's goal deciding the contest in front of 30,495 spectators.

Football League Jubilee Fund
United met City in successive seasons (August 1938 & August 1939) to raise funds for the Jubilee Fund authorised by the Football League.
In 1938 United lost 2-1 at Maine Road and the following year the teams fought out a 1-1 draw at Old Trafford.
* See: Football League Jubilee Fund
NB: Newton Heath also played City three times in the Manchester & Salford Charity Cup (q.v).

Fact File:
Possibly the first 'derby' played between the two 'Manchester clubs' took place on 12 November 1881 when Newton Heath LYR beat West Gorton St Mark's 3-0 in a friendly at North Road in front of 3,000 spectators. The West Gorton club later amalgamated with Gorton Athletic in 1884 to become Ardwick FC who then changed to Manchester City in 1894.
The first 'derby' against Ardwick was also played at North Road on 16 March 1889 when 2,000 spectators saw the Heathens win 4-1 in the second round of the Manchester & District Challenge Cup.
The first senior competitive'derby' took place on 3 October 1891 when Newton Heath met Ardwick at North Road in the 1st Qualifying Round of the FA Cup. The Heathens won 5-1, the crowd 11,000.
When the Reds beat City 5-1 at home on New Year's Eve, 1960, Alex Dawson scored a hat-trick.
United succumbed to five successive home League defeats at the hands of City: 1967-68 to 1971-72.
Sammy McIlroy scored on his League debut for United in a 3-3 draw with City in November 1971.
Paul Bielby made his United debut in front of more than 51,300 fans in the local derby with City at Maine Road on 13 March 1974. This game ended goalless and two players - Lou Macari and Mike Doyle - were sent-off for fisticuffs!
Denis Law's cheeky back-heeler sent United into the Second Division on 27 April 1974 - City winning the crucial derby game 1-0...although the fans invaded the pitch before full-time was called (see under abandoned matches).

Gordon Hill fired in two penalties for United in the 2-2 draw with City at Old Trafford in March 1978.

The 100th League derby between United and City took place at Old Trafford on 22 March 1980 and a crowd of 56,387 saw a Mickey Thomas goal give the Reds a 1-0 victory.

Six years later (September 1980) Mike Duxbury started his first game for the Reds, also against City (at home) when the crowd was almost 56,000.

Billy Meredith played in 29 'derby' matches at League level - 15 for United, 14 for City.

Bobby Charlton appeared in 27 (all of course for United) whilst Alex Stepney made 24 appearances, Bill Foulkes 23 and Martin Buchan 20.

Charlton also scored nine goals in League matches; Joe Spence claimed eight with Dennis Viollet and Eric Cantona both on seven.

Players with both clubs include: G Albinson, J Bannister, S Barkas (United WW2), P Barnes, F Barrett, P Beardsley, H Blew, P Bodak (United reserve), D Brazil (City trialist), J Breedon (City WW2); J Broad (reserve with both clubs), W Bootle & I Broadis (both United WW2), H Broomfield, F Buckley, J Bullock, H Burgess, R Burke (City WW2), J Cairns, A Carson, J Cassidy, J Christie, T Cooke, A Coton (United reserve and goalkeeping coach), J Crompton (United player & coach, City amateur), W Dale, B Daniels (United reserve), W Davies, P Doherty (United WW2), W Douglas, E Eastwood (United WW2), A Edge, A Emptage (United WW2), J Gidman, S Goater (United reserve), M Hamill, A Herd (United WW2), GW Hicks (United reserve), A Hill (United reserve), D Hurst, D Jones (Newton Heath reserve), A Kanchelskis, B Kidd, F Knowles, L Langford, D Law, G Livingstone, S McIlroy, J Macken (United reserve), W Meredith, R Milarvie, H Morgan, T Oakes (United amateur), W Porter (City WW2), A Potts (City reserve), J Quin, B Read, W Ridding, M Robins; J Robinson & P Robinson (both United WW2), H Rothwell, H Rowley, G Scales (City amateur, United WW2), P Schmeichel, W Smith, E Toseland (United WW2), A Turnbull, G Vose (City WW2); W Walsh & E Westwood (both United amateurs & WW2 guests), J Whitehouse, F Williams, W Woodcock, D Young (junior with both clubs)..

Also associated: E Mangnall (manager of both clubs), M Busby (City player, United manager), S Coppell (United player, City manager), A Bell (United player, City trainer), T Chorlton (United player, City assistant-trainer & trainer), A Stepney (United player, City goalkeeping coach), I Greaves (United player, City scout)

* Matt Busby won the FA Cup as a player with City and the same trophy as manager of United.

MANCHESTER & DISTRICT CHALLENGE CUP

As a club Newton Heath had its first successes in this competition which ran from 1884-85 to 1889-90 when the Manchester Senior Cup took over. It normally comprised two or three rounds, a semi-final on a neutral ground and a Final, also on a neutral ground.

Newton Heath reached the Final every season as shown:

Season	Opponents	Result	Venue	Attendance
1884-85	v. Hurst FC	lost 0-3	Whalley Range	3,500
1885-86	v. Manchester FC	won 2-1	Whalley Range	6,000
1886-87	v. West Manchester	lost 1-2	Whalley Range	4,000
1887-88	v. Denton	won 7-1	Whalley Range	8,000
1888-89	v. Hooley Hill	won 7-0	Whalley Range	4,000
1889-90	v. Royton	won 5-2	Brook's Bar	4,000

MANCHESTER SENIOR CUP

They entered this competition at the outset in 1885 and continued to compete right up until the mid-1960s, fielding a strong first XI well into the 1950s.

Over the years (1890s to mid-1960s) Newton Heath/United met Ardwick/Manchester City on 22 occasions in the **Manchester Senior Cup, their full record reading:**

P	W	D	L	F	A
22	11	3	8	51	38

The teams met each other in 10 Finals. Six were won by Newton Heath/United - 2-1 in April 1902, 3-0 in May 1924, 1-0 in May 1934, 3-1 in May 1935, 4-0 in April 1959 and 5-3 in May 1964

The four defeats against City were 4-0 in April 1901, 3-1 in December 1910, 4-2 in May 1928 & 2-0 in May 1933.

United's best Manchester Cup win over City is 9-1 - at Maine Road in the semi-final of November 1956.

There have also been six other semi-final clashes, in 1897-98, 1903-04, 1906-07, 1938-39, 1953-54 and 1956-57. City won the first three, United the last three.

City beat United 7-4 in a 3rd round replay at Maine Road in March 1925.

MANGNALL, J Ernest

Born in Bolton, Ernest Mangnall played as a goalkeeper played for the Bolton Grammar School team and in local football circles in his native Lancashire (representing his county on a couple of occasions). He was also a useful rugby player, a keen cyclist and excellent cross-country runner. Never quite good enough to become a professional footballer, he became secretary of Burnley in January 1900, a position he held for three years. He was then appointed secretary-manager of MANCHESTER UNITED in September 1903 and remained in office until August 1912 when he moved in the same capacity to neighbouring Manchester City. He spent 12 years in charge at Maine Road (up to July 1924). He later became a director of Bolton Wanderers.

He guided United to two League Championships (1908 & 1911), to promotion from Division Two in 1906 and FA Cup victory in 1909. He was awarded the Football League's long service medal in 1921.

Undoubtedly the first great manager employed by United, Mangnall, with the generous co-operation of Chairman John H Davies, helped transform United from a poverty-stricken club into an established, wealthy First Division side and took them to a new stadium (Old Trafford). He introduced many fine players to the club, among them Charlie Roberts, Dick Duckworth and goalkeeper Harry Moger, plus Welsh wing-wizard Billy Meredith and 'Sandy' Turnbull, both of whom were secured from his future club Manchester City when the Hyde Road club was hit by an illegal payments scandal.

After giving United supreme service he managed to keep Manchester City in the First Division and reach the FA Cup semi-finals in 1924 before his contract ran out.

Mangnall died in 1932.

MANLEY, Thomas

Born: Northwich, Cheshire, 7 October 1912. Died: 1988.

Career: Brunner Mods FC, Norley United, Northwich Victoria (spring 1930), MANCHESTER UNITED (amateur, September 1930, professional May 1931), Brentford (July 1939), MANCHESTER UNITED (WW2 guest), Northwich Victoria (manager, 1954).

Able to play as a wing-half, full-back and outside-left, Tom Manley was certainly a versatile footballer, as keen as mustard, who helped United win the Second Division Championship in 1936, giving United stalwart service in a difficult period for the club.

He made 116 League appearances for the Bees and after leaving Griffin Park in 1951 became a publican in Comberbatch.

Club record: 195 apps. 41 goals

MANN, Frank Drury

Born: Newark, 17 March 1891. Died: Nottingham, February 1959

Career: Newark Castle United (1905), Newark Castle Rovers (1906), Newark Town (1908), Leeds City (as an amateur, early 1909), Lincoln City (also as an amateur, 1909), Aston Villa (first as an amateur in late 1909, turning professional, summer 1911), Huddersfield Town (£1,000, summer 1912), MANCHESTER UNITED (£1,750, March 1923), Mossley (August 1930), Meltham Mills FC (late 1931, when he was re-instated as an amateur). He retired in 1932, aged 41.

An orthodox right-winger, Frank Mann made just one appearance for Villa before topping Huddersfield's scoring charts in his first two seasons at Leeds Road. He retained his goal touch after the War, netting 18 times in 43 games in 1919-20 when the Terriers came so close to completing the double (they finished runners-up in both the First Division Championship and FA Cup Final).

Mann gained an FA Cup winners' medal in 1922 and a year later, after notching 75 goals in 226 outings for Huddersfield, he was transferred to United. Amazingly after his departure from Leeds Road, the Yorkshire club went on to record three successive League Championship triumphs! Mann continued to play superbly well for the Reds who successfully converted him into a wing-half. He starred in the Old Trafford's Second Division promotion-winning side in 1924-25, being the important link between defence and attack. Nimble, fleet of foot, quick-thinking and remarkably consistent, Mann drifted into non-League football at the ripe old age of 39.

In total he made well over 400 League and FA Cup appearances and notched in excess of 80 goals.

Club record: 197 apps. 5 goals

MANN, Herbert Harry

Born: Nuneaton, Warwickshire, 30 December 1907.

Career: Griff Colliery FC (Nuneaton), Derby County (early 1926), Grantham Town (1929), MANCHESTER UNITED (May 1931), Ripley Town (November 1933).

All of right or left-winger Herbert Mann's senior outings for United came during the first half of the 1931-32 season. After giving up football he became a butcher in Derby.

Club record: 13 apps. 2 goals

MANNS, Thomas

Born: Rotherham, circa 1910

Career: Eastwood United WMC, Rotherham United (amateur, late 1930), Burnley (May 1931), MANCHESTER UNITED (June 1933 - with Charlie Hillam), Clapton Orient (June 1934), Carlisle United (summer 1935), Yeovil & Petters United (1936).

Tom Manns was a reserve right-half with United and came into the side for the Lancashire derbies away to Burnley and at home to Oldham Athletic in early February 1934. He won an East Lancashire Cup winners' medal with Burnley

Club record: 2 apps.

MARSHALL, Arthur George

Born: Liverpool, autumn, 1881.

Career: Crewe Alexandra, Leicester Fosse (1901), Stockport County (early 1902), MANCHESTER UNITED (May 1902), Portsmouth (season 1903-04).

Defender Arthur Marshall's only season with United was spent mainly in the reserves. All of his senior outings were in the right-back position, from early March to mid-April.

Club record: 6 apps.

MARTIN, Lee Andrew

Born: Hyde, Cheshire, 5 February 1968

Career: Tameside and Greater Manchester Schools, MANCHESTER UNITED (trainee June 1985, professional May 1986), Celtic (January 1994), Bristol Rovers (1996), Huddersfield Town (on loan, 1997). Forced to retire through injury in summer of 1999.

223

An attacking full-back, mainly down the left, Lee Martin had the pleasure - and honour - of scoring the winning goal for United in the FA Cup Final replay against Crystal Palace at Wembley in 1990. He had made his League debut two years earlier v. Wimbledon (as a substitute) and won two England Under-21 caps during his time at Old Trafford. United played Bristol Rovers in a benefit match for Martin in 2000.
Club record: 109 apps. 2 goals

MARTIN, Michael Paul

Born: Dublin, 9 July 1951
Career: Home Farm FC, Bohemians, MANCHESTER UNITED (£25,000, January 1973), West Bromwich Albion (£30,000, December 1975), Newcastle United (£100,000, late 1978), Vancouver Whitecaps (1984), Willingdon FC (mid 1984), Cardiff City (late 1984), Wolverhampton Wanderers (on loan), Peterborough United (early 1985), Rotherham United (1985), Preston North End (1985-86), Newcastle United (scout, assistant-manager, 1988), Celtic (coach, 1990-92).
Son of the former Aston Villa and Republic of Ireland goalkeeper/centre-half Con Martin , Mick Martin was a midfielder with flair, commitment and a big heart. He did very well with West Bromwich Albion and also with Newcastle United. Capped 51 times by the Republic of Ireland, Martin also represented his country at amateur and Under-21 levels and played for the League of Ireland (in 1972) and the All-Ireland team v. Brazil (in 1973). He helped West Brom gain promotion to the First Division in 1976. Unfortunately Martin is one of only a handful of players who have been sent-off in an FA Cup semi-final (1978). Nowadays Martin is deeply involved with the Ex-Players Association at Newcastle United.
Club record: 46 apps. 3 goals

MATHIESON, William

Born: Glasgow, 1870
Career: Clydesdale FC, Glasgow Thistle, South Shore, Clydesdale, NEWTON HEATH (June 1892), Rotherham Town (December 1895), Fairfield (1897), South Shore (1898).
Bill Mathieson played at outside-left in the Heathens' first ever Football League match in 1892. He did well initially but after a three-month flurry was thereafter basically a reserve, especially after the arrival of Jack Peden. He was unfortunate not to play on a winning side in any of his 10 League games.
Younger brother John played in two 'other' matches for the Heathens (1892-93).
Club record: 13 apps. 3 goals (also 15 'other' apps, 5 goals)

MAY, David

Born: Oldham, 24 June 1970
Career: Boundary Park Juniors, Blackburn Rovers (trainee 1986, professional 1988), MANCHESTER UNITED (£1.4 million, July 1994, released May 2002), Huddersfield Town (on loan, December 1999).
Reliable defender David May made over 150 senior appearances for Blackburn before transferring to Old Trafford in 1994. Over the next five years - when he played alongside a variety of centre-backs including Steve Bruce, Gary Pallister, Ronny Johnsen and Jaap Stam - he helped the Reds win three Premiership titles (1996, 1997 & 1999), the FA Cup twice (1996 & 1999), the European Cup (also in 1999) and the FA Charity Shield (1994). Unfortunately he spent the best part of twelve months on the injured list (from late 1999 to November 2000), only appearing occasionally in recent seasons.
Club record: 114 apps. 8 Goals

MEDAL WINNERS

Before his departure to Wolves, Denis Irwin won a record 19 medals with United: 7 Premiership, 3 FA Cup, one League Cup, one European Cup, one European Cup-winners Cup, one European Super Cup, one Inter-Continental Cup and 4 FA Charity Shields.
Ryan Giggs has so far won 18 senior medals with the club: 7 Premiership, 3 FA Cup, one European Cup, one League Cup, one European Super Cup, 4 FA Charity Shield, one Inter-Continental Cup. He was also an FA Youth Cup winner.
Gary Pallister gained eight individual medals with United (three Premiership, 3 FA Cup, one League Cup, one ECWC). He too, has also played in FA Charity Shield games. And Steve Bruce, Mark Hughes, Brian McClair and Lee Sharpe all collected seven medals during their United careers.
Eric Cantona became the first player to win English League Championship medals in successive seasons with different clubs, Leeds United and Manchester United, in 1991-92 and 1992-93 respectively. In all he won four Championship medals in consecutive seasons with Olympique Marseille in 1990-91, then Leeds (1991-92) and Manchester United (1992-93 and 1993-94). In 1995-96 he made it five Championship medals in six seasons.
Bill Foulkes won four League Championship medals with United as well as FA Cup and European Cup winners medals.
John Aston, senior in 1951-52 and his son John Aston, junior in 1966-67 are the only known father and son to have gained League Championship winning medals with the same club (United).
Gordon Strachan gained three FA Cup winners' medals north of the border with Aberdeen (1982-83-84) and followed up with a fourth with United in 1985.

With Celtic, winger Jimmy Delaney won two Scottish League Championship medals and a Scottish Cup winners' medal (in 1937) and followed up with an FA Cup winners medal with United in 1948 and an Irish Cup winners' medal with Derry City in 1954. Two years later he collected a FAI (Republic of Ireland) Cup runners-up medal with Cork City. Harold Halse was an FA Cup winner with both Manchester United and Aston Villa and a loser (in the Final) with Chelsea - all before WW1.

As a manager (Sir) Alex Ferguson has guided United to seven Premiership triumphs, European Cup and European Cup-winners Cup glory, four FA Cup Final victories, League Cup, Inter-Continental and European Super Cup successes and four FA Charity Shield wins - and during his time at Old Trafford United's youngsters have twice won the FA Youth Cup while the reserves have won the Pontins League Championship on three occasions.

He was the first manager to guide a team to three successive League titles and, indeed, the first to win seven League Championships.

MEEHAN, Thomas

Born: Harpurhey, Manchester, summer 1896. Died: St George's Hospital, SW London, 18 August 1924
Career: Newton FC, Walkden Central, Rochdale (early 1917), MANCHESTER UNITED (June 1917), Atherton (on loan), Rochdale (WW1 guest, then registered for League game in May 1919), Chelsea (£3,300, 1920-24).
Wing-half or inside-forward Tommy Meehan was a box-of-tricks and despite his small frame had great stamina. He twice represented the Football League, played for the Professionals v Amateurs in the 1923 FA Charity Shield game and was capped by England v. Ireland a year later. He died in hospital at the age of 28.
Club record: 53 apps. 6 goals

MEGASTORE (at Old Trafford)

In 1992 Edward Freedman took control of Manchester United's merchandising operation. Previously with Tottenham Hotspur (Commercial Department) he made rapid in-roads, opening a 5,000 sq.ft. supermarket (a Megastore) in a warehouse behind the Stretford End. Things have gone from strength to strength since then…..with fans from all four corners of the globe either calling in, writing, e-mailing of faxing for United merchandise.

MELLOR, John

Born: Oldham, Lancs, circa 1924
Career: Oldham Rugby Union Club, Greenacre Lads FC, Failsworth Trinity, Witton Albion, MANCHESTER UNITED (May 1929), Cardiff City (January 1937). Retired May 1938.
Jack Mellor was a strong, hard-tackling, durable full-back who gave United excellent service for almost eight years. He gained a Second Division Championship medal in 1936.
Club record: 122 apps.

MENZIES, Alexander William

Born: Blantyre, Lanarkshire, 15 November 1882.
Career: Blantyre Victoria, Heart of Midlothian (late 1902), Motherwell (on loan, 1903), Arthurlie (1904), Heart of Midlothian (1905), MANCHESTER UNITED (November 1906), Luton Town (September 1907), Dundee (season 1909-10).
In 1906 centre-forward Alex Menzies won a Scottish Cup winners' medal with Hearts and played for Scotland against England in the Home International tournament. He scored on his United debut against Sheffield Wednesday only days after joining the club but after that his form was variable and eventually lost his place to Jimmy Turnbull.
Club record: 25 apps. 4 goals

MERCANTILE CREDIT CENTENARY TROPHY

To celebrate the 100th birthday of the Football League, Arsenal, Everton, Liverpool, Manchester United, Newcastle United, Nottingham Forest, Queen's Park Rangers and Wimbledon were all invited to participate in a sponsored competition (the Mercantile Credit Centenary Trophy) during August/September/October 1988.

United defeated Everton 1-0 at home in their first game, Gordon Strachan the scorer in front of 16,439 fans. In the semi-final United, again at home, accounted for Newcastle United 2-0 after extra-time, Steve Bruce and Brian McClair the marksmen on this occasion before a crowd of 16,968.

Arsenal came through to meet United in the Final at Villa Park and it was the Gunners who took the honours, winning 2-1 in front of 22,182 spectators. Clayton Blackmore netting for the Reds while Paul Davis and Michael Thomas scored for the Londoners.

MEREDITH, William Henry

Born: Black Park, near Chirk, mid-Wales 30 July 1874. Died: Withington, Manchester 19 April 1958.
Career: Black Park FC (1890), Chirk (1891), Wrexham (briefly), Northwich Victoria (1892), Manchester City (amateur 1894, professional early 1895), MANCHESTER UNITED (October 1906), guested for Stalybridge Celtic and Celtic during WW1, Manchester City (player-coach,

July 1921-24), MANCHESTER UNITED (coach, September 1931-33).

Bandy-legged outside-right Billy Meredith had a superb career. With his trademark tooth-pick, he was certainly the star attraction at most grounds during the Edwardian period and represented both Manchester clubs and Wales, winning a total of 48 full caps, although he was actually selected for 60 internationals! Footballs first 'superstar' he was a deadly opponent, whether racing down the wing and whipping over decisive centres or cutting in to shoot at goal. He spent 15 years at Old Trafford and was one of the few players to appear for the club before, during and after World War One. One of the finest attacking wing-forwards of his day, Meredith was once described as 'the football wonder of all time.'

Lithe of foot and very awkward to tackle, he remained injury-free throughout his career and claimed to have played in 1,584 games (at various levels) scoring 470 goals. He appeared in 303 League games for United and 366 for Manchester City in the same competition. He helped City win two Second Division Championships (1899 & 1903) and also the 1904 FA Cup Final. Five years later he was a Cup Final winner again, this time with United over Bristol City in 1909, having helped United also win the First Division title in 1908, a prize he won again in 1911. He also collected a Welsh Cup winners' medal with Chirk in 1894 and represented Denbighshire v. Mid-Wales.

It was alleged that he once offered an Aston Villa player a £10 bribe to swing a match. As a result his contract was terminated by his club (Manchester City). Meredith was suspended by the FA until the end of March 1906 and thereafter a prolonged enquiry into other illegal payments led to another suspension. Before this ended however, Meredith joined United along with City team-mates Bannister, Burgess and 'Sandy' Turnbull but had to wait until 1 January 1907 before making his debut for the club - against Aston Villa! After leaving United - over a wages dispute - Meredith was almost 50 when he played his last competitive game for Manchester City in the 1924 FA Cup semi-final against Newcastle United.

He was a leading light in the fight to form a respected players' union and was always the champion when fighting for footballers' rights! After retiring from football in the 1930s, Meredith became a publican (having worked as a hotelier in 1915-16, taking over the Church Hotel in Manchester). He later worked at a cinema and ran a sports-outfitters shop. He was a frail-looking 83 years-old when he died in 1958.

Club record: 335 apps. 36 goals

MEW, John William

Born: Sunderland, 30 March 1889. Died: near Barton-on-Irwell, autumn, 1963.

Career: Marley Hill Council School, Church Choir FC, Marley Hill St Cuthbert's FC, Blaydon United, Marley Hill United, MANCHESTER UNITED (amateur July, professional September 1912), Barrow (September 1926), Lyra FC of Belgium(trainer-coach, 1927-28), Lima FC, Peru (coach, 1928-29).,

Goalkeeper Jack Mew was a safe handler, who seemingly always positioned himself centrally on the line. He was courageous and for a short man was very useful in the air, often punching the ball to safety.

Mew made his United debut in March 1913 (v. Middlesbrough) and that very same season gained a Central League Championship medal. He played once for the Football League, toured South Africa with the FA party in 1920, appeared in an international trial match the following year before winning his only senior cap for England against Ireland in October 1923.

Mew was rewarded with two benefits by United - the first player to be recognised in this way.

In 1924 at the age of 25, Mew went into business with Cecil Parkin, the Lancashire cricketer but two years later he moved from Old Trafford to Barrow before trying his luck as a coach in Belgium and then Peru.

Club record: 199 apps.

MIDDLESBROUGH

Heathens/United's League results v 'Boro:

Season	Div	Home	Away	Season	Div	Home	Away
1899-1900	2	W 2-1	L 0-2	1946-47	1	W 1-0	W 4-2
1900-01	2	W 4-0	W 2-1	1947-48	1	W 2-1	D 2-2
1901-02	2	L 1-2	L 0-5	1948-49	1	W 1-0	W 4-1
				1949-50	1	W 2-0	W 3-2
1906-07	1	W 3-1	L 0-2	1950-51	1	W 1-0	W 2-1
1907-08	1	W 2-1	L 1-2	1951-52	1	W 4-2	W 4-1
1908-09	1	W 6-3	L 0-5	1952-53	1	W 3-2	L 0-5
1909-10	1	W 4-1	W 2-1	1953-54	1	D 2-2	W 4-1
1910-11	1	L 1-2	D 2-2				
1911-12	1	L 3-4	L 0-3	1975-76	1	W 3-0	D 0-0
1912-13	1	L 2-3	L 2-3	1976-77	1	W 2-0	L 0-3
1913-14	1	L 0-1	L 1-3	1977-78	1	D 0-0	L 1-2
1914-15	1	D 2-2	D 1-1	1978-79	1	W 3-2	D 2-2
				1979-80	1	W 2-1	D 1-1
1919-20	1	D 1-1	D 1-1	1980-81	1	W 3-0	D 1-1
1920-21	1	L 0-1	W 4-2	1981-82	1	W 1-0	W 2-0
1921-22	1	L 3-5	L 0-2				
				1988-89	1	W 1-0	L 0-1
1924-25	2	W 2-0	D 1-1				
				1992-93	PL	W 3-0	D 1-1
1927-28	1	W 3-0	W 2-1				
				1995-96	PL	W 2-0	W 3-0
1929-30	1	L 0-3	W 3-2	1996-97	PL	D 3-3	D 2-2
1930-31	1	D 4-4	L 1-3				
				1998-99	PL	L 2-3	W 1-0
1936-37	1	W 2-1	L 2-3	1999-00	PL	W 1-0	W 4-3
				2000-01	PL	W 2-1	W 2-0
1938-39	1	D 1-1	L 1-3	2001-02	PL	L 0-1	W 1-0

Summary of League results

	P	W	D	L	F	A
Premier League	14	9	3	2	27	14
Division 1	66	31	14	21	121	108
Division 2	8	4	1	3	12	12
Home	44	27	7	10	90	55
Away	44	17	11	16	70	79
Total	88	44	18	26	160	134

FA Cup results v 'Boro:

	Round	Venue	Result
1893-94	1	Home	W 4-0
1932-33	3	Home	L 1-4
1960-61	3	Home	W 3-0
1969-70	6	Away	D 1-1
	Replay	Home	W 2-1
1970-71	3	Home	D 0-0
	Replay	Away	L 1-2
1971-72	5	Home	D 0-0
	Replay	Away	W 3-0
1998-99	3	Home	W 3-1
2001-02	4	Away	L 0-2

League Cup results v 'Boro

	Round	Venue	Result
1969-70	2	Home	W 1-0
1973-74	2	Home	L 0-1
1974-75	5	Away	D 0-0
	Replay	Home	W 3-0
1991-92	SF (1)	Away	D 0-0
	SF (2)	Home	W 2-1 aet

Fact File
Middlesbrough FC were not the first club from the town to play in the Football League. In 1893 Middlesbrough Ironopolis was elected into the Second Division at the same time as (Woolwich) Arsenal. Liverpool and Newcastle United. Middlesbrough were an amateur club for many years and it was some of their members who desired professional football who broke away to form 'Ironopolis' in 1889. At one stage Ironopolis invited Middlesbrough to amalgamate with them (to be known as 'Middlesbrough and Ironopolis') but Middlesbrough refused.
Ironopolis played just one season in the League at their delightfully named Paradise Ground, resigning despite finishing 11th out of 15. Following Ironopolis' demise, Middlesbrough turned professional in 1899, immediately elected to the Football League playing originally at Linthorpe Road (a cricket ground) before hiring the ubiquitous Archibald Leitch to build Ayresome Park partially built over the former Paradise Ground.
When Middlesbrough won at Old Trafford in 1998-99 it was their first League win there since 1929-30, a period encompassing 22 matches of which United won 17, five drawn.
The Brazilian Juninho missed a penalty for 'Boro in their 1-0 Premiership defeat (to a late David Beckham goal) in January 2000.
The second biggest crowd ever to assemble at Old Trafford - 67,683 - saw 'Boro beat United 1-0 in a Premiership game in March 2002.

Players with both clubs include: V Anderson (also 'Boro assistant-manager), C Blackmore, W Campbell, J Cassidy, C Chadwick (United WW2), A Chilton ('Boro WW2), P Davenport, J Dow, J Flanagan (United reserve), A Foggon, J Greening, W Higgins, P Ince, F Kennedy, C Knowles (United amateur, also 'Boro coach & assistant-manager), H Leonard, J McClelland, G Pallister, S Pears, A Robertson, B Robson (also 'Boro manager), A Rowley (WW2 guest for both clubs), MC Russell (United reserve), J Saunders, N Stiles, A Warburton ('Boro WW2), G Walsh, Osher Williams (United junior, 'Boro amateur), O Williams (United reserve), M Wilson, T Woodward (United WW2).
Also associated: H Bamlett (manager of both clubs), JR Robson ('Boro player, United manager), M Busby ('Boro WW2 player, United manager), S McClaren ('Boro manager, United assistant-manager).

MILARVIE, Robert

Born: Pollokshaws, Scotland, circa 1867. Died: Gorton, Manchester, November 1912.
Career: Pollokshields FC, Hibernian (briefly), Stoke (1888), Burslem Port Vale (1899), Derby County (1899), NEWTON HEATH (July 1890), Ardwick (May 1891-96).
Bob Milarvie was a very useful, combative inside-left who, as a Port Vale player, was the victim of a misdemeanour by the Potteries' club who fielded him illegally after failing to obtain his complete transfer from Stoke. He was an everpresent in the Heathens' Alliance League programme of 1890-91 when he partnered Bill Sharpe on the left-wing. He made 54 appearances in his five years with Ardwick (Manchester City), claiming 12 goals.
Club record: 23 apps. 4 goals (also 24 'other' apps, 13 goals)

MILLAR, George

Born: Scotland
Career: Glasgow Perthshire, NEWTON HEATH (December 1894), Chatham (season 1895-96).
A centre-forward with a good technique, George Millar spent only six months with the Heathens, scoring on his senior debut against Lincoln City three days before Christmas, 1894.
Club record: 7 apps. 5 goals (also 5 'other' apps)

MILLER, James

Born: Greenock, Scotland
Career: Port Glasgow Athletic, St Mirren (1918), Greenock Morton (1920), Grimsby Town (1921), MANCHESTER UNITED (March 1924), York City (June 1924), Boston Town (1925), Shirebrook FC (season 1927-28).
Inside-forward and Scottish international trialist 'Jock' Miller had already made over 100 League appearances prior to joining United. Unfortunately after a bright start to his Old Trafford career he faded from the scene and departed after spending barely three months with the club. He was top-scorer for York with 17 goals in the Midland League in 1924-25. Served with the Tank Corps during WW1.
Club record: 4 apps. one goal.

MILLER, Thomas

Born: Motherwell, 29 June 1890. Died: 3 September 1958.
Career: Larkhall Hearts, Glenview FC, Larkhall United, Hamilton Academical (1910), Liverpool (1912), MANCHESTER UNITED (September 1920), Heart of Midlothian (July 1921), Torquay United (1922-23), Hamilton Academical (from 1923), Raith Rovers (late 1926-27).
Inside or centre-forward Tom Miller scored 53 goals in 127 League games for Liverpool before joining United. He was at Old Trafford for just one season, finishing up as joint top-scorer in the League side, with only seven goals!
Club record: 27 apps. 8 goals

MILLWALL

United's League results v the Lions:

Season	Div	Home	Away
1931-32	2	W 2-0	D 1-1
1932-33	2	W 7-1	L 0-2
1933-34	2	D 1-1	W 2-0
1974-75	2	W 4-0	W 1-0
1988-89	1	W 3-0	D 0-0
1989-90	1	W 5-1	W 2-1

Summary of League results

	P	W	D	L	F	A
Division 1	4	3	1	0	10	2
Division 2	8	5	2	1	18	5
Home	6	5	1	0	22	3
Away	6	3	2	1	6	4
Total	12	8	3	1	28	7

FA Cup results v the Lions:

	Round	Venue	Result
1952-53	3	Away	W 1-0

227

Fact File

If there is one pivotal match in United's long history then arguably the match at Millwall on 5 May 1934 was it. The last Saturday of the season dawned with United next to the bottom of Division Two (32 pts) with Millwall one place higher (33 pts). A draw would not be enough to save United from the dreaded Division Three (North). On the day the whole team performed heroically, goals in either half from Tommy Manley and Jack Cape saving the famous club from ignominy. Had United taken the drop who knows what the future might have been. Even the best attendances were below 30,000, many as low as 10,000 so it is anybody's guess what might have happened in the Third (North). The entire history of the club could have changed markedly, perhaps they might have gone to the wall. Who knows?

In the event, promotion to Division One was achieved within two seasons, a Youth policy was begun which would stand them in good stead after the war when Matt Busby would take over the managerial reins. Thus the legend of United was born, one dreads to think what would have happened had Millwall won on that Saturday in May 1934.

Players with both clubs include: A Allman, T Baldwin, J Broad (United reserve), R Davies, D Dublin, E Dunphy and K Grogan (United reserves), C Hannaford, G Hill, J Hodge, C McGrath, WS McMillen, P Proudfoot (reserve), E Savage (Lions WW2), T Sheringham, A Stepney, W Stewart, J Sutcliffe, G Tomlinson, J Travers, S Tyler, D Wallace, J Walters (United reserve), A Whalley.

Also associated: G Graham & J Nicholl (United players, Lions managers)

MILNE, Ralph

Born: Dundee, 13 May 1961

Career: Dundee Celtic Boys Club, Aston Villa (trialist), Dundee United (professional 1977), Charlton Athletic (£125,000, 1987), Bristol City (on loan, then signed permanently for £70,000, early 1988), MANCHESTER UNITED (£175,000, November 1988-June 1991), West Ham United (on loan, early 1990), Sing Tao FC of Hong Kong (season 1991-92).

A very useful winger, Ralph Milne represented Scotland at Youth team level before gaining three Under-21 caps. He was an SFA Cup finalist with Dundee United in 1981 and two years later helped the Tannadice club win the Scottish League title, later collecting a League Cup runners-up medal (1984) and a second Scottish Cup runners-up medal in 1985. As a Charlton player he was in the Addicks team that lost the 1987 Full Members Cup Final to Blackburn at Wembley. He did a reasonable enough job at Old Trafford during a particularly bad time for injuries. During his professional career Milne amassed in excess of 400 League and Cup appearances.

Club record: 30 apps. 3 goals

MITCHELL, Andrew

Born: Scotland, 1870

Career: Airdrieonians, NEWTON HEATH (September 1892), Burton Swifts (June 1894-95).

Full-back Andrew Mitchell did very well during his two years with the club after taking over from skipper Bob McFarlane who ironically moved to Airdrie! A strong, clean kicker of the ball, he made almost 50 consecutive appearances for the Heathens before injury ended the run.

Club record: 61 apps. (also 27 'other' apps)

MITCHELL, Andrew

Born: Coxhoe, County Durham, 20 April 1907. Died: Blackburn, 3 December 1971

Career: Crook Town, Sunderland (late 1927), Notts County (season 1928-29), Darlington (summer 1929), MANCHESTER UNITED (£600, April 1932), Hull City (June 1933), Northampton Town (late 1933), Rossendale United (1934-35).

Nippy outside-right Andrew Mitchell made 127 League appearances before signing for United but unfortunately he failed to make an impact at Old Trafford and was given just one League outing - against Notts County in March 1933 when he partnered Bill Ridding on the right-wing.

Club record: one app.

MITCHELL, James

Born: Lancashire circa early 1860s.

Career: NEWTON HEATH (February 1885), Bolton Wanderers (July 1888), NEWTON HEATH (October 1888-May 1891).

During his two spells with the Heathens, full-back Jim Mitchell made almost 40 first-class appearances (36 coming in the Football Alliance) as well as playing in more than 160 'other' matches. He played in Bolton's first two games at the start of the inaugural Football League season of 1888-89.

Club record: 42 apps. (also 162 'other' apps, 3 goals)

MITTEN, Charles

Born: Rangoon, Burma, 17 January 1921. Died: Stockport, 2 January 2002.

Career: Dunblane Rovers, Strathallan Hawthorn, MANCHESTER UNITED (amateur, August 1936, professional January 1938), guested for Cardiff City, Chelsea, Southampton, Tranmere Rovers and Wolverhampton Wanderers during WW2, Sante Fe of Bogota (June 1950, remaining there until the summer of 1951), Fulham (January 1952), Mansfield Town (player-manager, early 1956), Newcastle United (manager, 1958-61), Altrincham (player-manager, 1962-63).

Born the son of a Sergeant Major in a Scottish regiment, serving in Burma, Charlie Mitten began playing serious football in Perthshire in 1935 (his family having moved initially to Glasgow in 1926). He was offered trials by both Glasgow Rangers and Hearts as a teenager but turned both clubs down to sign for United. After serving in the RAF during the War, he made his Football League debut in August 1946 v. Grimsby, going on to become one of United's star players in Matt Busby's post-war side. Although surprisingly he never won a full international cap, he played for England against Scotland at Maine Road in 1946 in aid of the Bolton Disaster Fund. Scotland, in fact, had already selected him as their 12th man, believing him to be a Scot!

A fast-raiding, hard-shooting left-winger, Mitten starred in United's FA Cup winning side of 1948 and in March 1950 he entered the record books by scoring a hat-trick of penalties in a four-goal haul which helped set a 7-0 win over Aston Villa. He appeared in only eleven more games for United after that - leaving (with a group of other players) to play in Bogota, Colombia, a country outside the jurisdiction of FIFA, but one offering far greater financial rewards for established footballers at that time! Mitten - dubbed the 'Bogota Bandit' after his exploits where he had given a good account of himself alongside some brilliant South American players, including Alfredo di Stefano.

He returned to England only to be suspended by the FA and fined £250. He later came back with Fulham and then took to management.

Mitten's sons, Charlie junior and John, were both on United's books as youngsters and later grandson Paul became a trainee at Old Trafford in 1992. His nephew, Albert Scanlon, was a 1950s United star.

Club record: 162 apps. 61 goals

MOGER, Henry Herbert

Born: Southampton, September 1879. Died: Manchester, June 1927.

Career: Forest Swifts, Freemantle FC (Hampshire), Southampton (1900), MANCHESTER UNITED (May 1903-June 1912).

Goalkeeper Harry Moger, 6ft 3ins tall and weighing almost 13 stones, served United for nine years. He took over the number one position in March 1904 from John Sutcliffe and remained first-choice between the posts until January 1911 when his place went to Scotsman Hugh Edmonds. He won two Football League Championship medals (1908 & 1911) and also starred in the 1909 FA Cup-winning team. A player who inspired confidence to the defenders in front of him, Moger unfortunately failed to win any representative honours despite being rated as one of the best 'keepers in both the south of England (as a Saints' player) and in the north (when he was with United).

Club record: 266 apps.

MOIR, Ian

Born: Aberdeen, 30 June 1943

Career: MANCHESTER UNITED (amateur, July 1958, professional July 1960), Blackpool (February 1965), Chester (£10,000, 1967), Wrexham (£10,000, 1968), Shrewsbury Town (1972), Wrexham (1973-75). Later played in South Africa,

A winger, with good pace and a direct approach. Ian Moir was spotted by United scout Archie Beattie. He had to fight for a place in the first team, his best season coming in 1963-64 when he helped United finish runners-up in the First Division. With George Best and John Connelly bedded in on the flanks he moved to Blackpool after seven years at Old Trafford, and later scored 24 goals in almost 200 League and Cup games (in two spells) for Wrexham, helping the Racecourse Ground club gain promotion to the Second Division in 1969-70 and reach the Final of the Welsh Cup the following season..

Club record: 45 apps. 5 goals

MONACO (AS)

Despite drawing both games against the French club (1-1 at home, 0-0 away), United went out of the 1997-98 Champions League in the quarter-finals on the away goal rule.

MONEY

Manchester United were the first club in England to announce a profit of more than £100,000 on a season. This happened in 1957-58 when their campaign was devastated by the Munich air crash.

More profit-making seasons followed over the next few years and in 1975-76, for the first time, the Old Trafford club revealed a healthy profit of well over £300,000....and it's gone up and up ever since. In the year 2001 Manchester United football club was said to be valued at £1 billion.

In the summer of 2002 it was revealed that United made an operating profit for the 2001-01 season of £31.1 million - Liverpool, in second place, made just over £10 million.

Also it was revealed that United's anticipated annual income for the forthcoming 2002-03 season would realise some £129.5 million, made up as follows:

Gate receipts	£46.6 million
TV Money	£31.1 million
Merchandising	£22 million
Conference/catering.	£7.8 million

MONTGOMERY, Archibald

Born: Chryston, Lanarkshire, 1871. Died: Lancashire, 5 January 1922.

Career: Chryston Athletic, Glasgow Rangers (1894), Bury (1895), MANCHESTER UNITED (May 1905), Bury (June 1906, later manager at Gigg Lane: 1907-14 and thereafter secretary-manager: 1914-15, then manager again, briefly in 1919-20 season), Albion Rovers (manager: 1920-22).

Goalkeeper Archie Montgomery made 210 League appearances for Bury before joining United. He was at Old Trafford for just one season, acting as reserve to Harry Moger. Starting out as a centre-forward before establishing himself as a 'keeper, Montgomery won junior international honours with Scotland and also captained the Scotland Junior side against Birmingham & District County Juniors. He was sent-off playing for Bury in a vital end-of-season Test Match against Liverpool, but still the Shakers won. He missed Bury's 1903 FA Cup Final triumph through injury.

Montgomery's brother John spent 13 years as a full-back with Notts County (1898-1911)

Club record: 3 apps.

MONTGOMERY, James

Born: Newfield, near Spennymoor, County Durham, circa 1890.

Career: Craghead FC, Glossop (early 1913), MANCHESTER UNITED (March 1915; retired as a player and became junior coach at Old Trafford, October 1921), Crewe Alexandra (June 1922-23).

Half-back Jim Montgomery's only goal for United came in a 5-1 romp over Preston North End (at home) in September 1919. A well-proportioned, strong-tackling defender, he suffered with injuries in season 1919-20 and was never the same player after that

Club record: 27 apps. one goal

MONTPELLIER

Defenders Clayton Blackmore and Steve Bruce came up with a goal apiece to earn United a 2-0 victory in France in their Cup-winners Cup quarter-final contest against Montpellier in 1990-91, after a disappointing 1-1 draw at Old Trafford had left all to do.
Players with both clubs: L Blanc, E Cantona

MOODY, John

Born: Heeley, Sheffield, 1 November 1903.

Career: St Wilfred's Roman Catholic School (Sheffield), Hathersage FC, Sheffield United (trialist), Arsenal (1925), Bradford (1928), Doncaster Rovers (1930), MANCHESTER UNITED (February 1932), Chesterfield (August 1933-September 1939).

Goalkeeper John Moody had gymnastic-like reflexes and at times was quite daring between the posts.

A top-class 'keeper, he was ever-present in 1932-33, making the decision to release him hard to fathom!

After leaving Old Trafford he added a further 186 League appearances to his tally with Chesterfield before WW2 disrupted his career. He gained a Third Division (North) Championship medal with the Saltergate club in 1935-36 when he was an ever-present.

Club record: 51 apps.

MOORE, Charles William

Born: Cheslyn Hay, near Cannock, Staffs, 3 June 1898.

Career: Hednesford Town (1915), MANCHESTER UNITED (May 1919. Released in June 1921 owing to injury, but he recovered full fitness and rejoined the club in September 1922, eventually retiring in the summer of 1931).

Full-back Charlie Moore thought his career might be over after suffering an ankle injury in 1921. But he made a full recovery and went on to amass well over 300 senior appearances for the club. Totally dependable and rated one of the best full-backs of his era, Moore was a sound tackler whose distribution was first-class. He was sorely missed in 1921-22 as United finished bottom of Division One. He returned to the fold and immediately drew up a superb partnership with Jack Silcock. Despite many outstanding performances Moore failed to win England recognition - due no doubt to the fact that he was with a struggling club!

Club record: 328 apps.

MOORE, Graham

Born: Cascade, near Hengoed, Glamorgan, 7 March 1941.

Career: Gilfach Primary and Bargoed Secondary Modern Schools, Bargoed YMCA, Cardiff City (groundstaff 1956, professional May 1958), Chelsea (£35,000, 1961), MANCHESTER UNITED (£35,000, November 1963), Northampton Town (£15,000, December 1965), Charlton Athletic (£6,000, 1967), Doncaster Rovers (£4,000, 1971. Retired 1974.

Inside-forward Graham Moore won Welsh Youth caps as a teenager before being regarded in 1961 as Cardiff City's 'greatest-ever discovery', his manager Bill Jones believing at the time that he would be better than John Charles! Sadly Moore broke a leg whilst at Ninian Park and a shin bone at Charlton and consequently never reached the dizzy heights expected of him, although during an interesting career he did score 61 goals in a total of 404 League appearances. After adding nine Under-23 caps to his collection, he went on to gain a total of 21 full caps for his country between 1960 and 1971, two as a United player under manager Matt Busby. Moore, an influential footballer and tireless worker, was also a very popular performer who represented the Football League in 1961 and won a Welsh Cup winners medal with Cardiff in 1959 and a runners-up medal with the same club a year later.

On quitting football Moore, who had been a coalminer in his Youth, took over pubs in York, Hemsworth and then Easingwold (in Yorkshire) in the late 1970/early 1980s before running a sub-post office in Scarborough.

Club record: 19 apps. 5 goals

MORAN, Kevin Bernard

Born: Dublin, 29 April 1956

Career: Bohemians, Pegasus (a Dublin college team), MANCHESTER UNITED (£2,000, February 1978), Sporting Gijon, Spain (August 1988), Blackburn Rovers (early 1990 to 1995).

Kevin Moran was an outstanding Gaelic footballer before signing professional forms for United in 1978. After that he developed into an extremely efficient, reliable and courageous centre-half who had the ability and capabilities of effectively stifling the natural ball skills of his opponents. He was certainly a brave competitor who quite often battled on with blood stains all over his shirt and face! It is said that Moran - dubbed 'Captain Blood' - received over 100 stitches to head wounds during his career.

Regarded as one of the most fearless footballers in the game, Moran - in his last season at Old Trafford - almost made the ultimate sacrifice when, after a clash of heads, he swallowed his tongue. But for the prompt action of United's physio Jim McGregor he would almost certainly have choked to death.

He was in fine form for United during the 1980s, helping the Reds win the FA Cup in 1983 (v. Brighton & Hove Albion) and technically in 1985 (v. Everton) despite the fact that he became the first player ever to be sent-off in an FA Cup Final, dismissed by policeman-referee Peter Willis for a professional foul on Peter Reid. He won 70 caps for the Republic of Ireland, being named in both the 1990 and 1994 World Cup Final squads by Eire manager Jack Charlton. Moran made 378 League appearances in total - 231 for United and 147 for Blackburn.

Club record: 290 apps. 24 goals

MORGAN, Hugh

Born: Lanarkshire circa 1873.

Career: Harthill Thistle, Airdrieonians (summer 1896), Sunderland (December 1896), Bolton Wanderers (early 1899), NEWTON HEATH (December 1900), Manchester City (July 1901), Accrington Stanley (summer 1902), Blackpool (May 1904).

Inside-forward Hugh Morgan had already made well over 100 senior appearances at club level before joining Newton Heath. A fair-haired, sprightly footballer, he was in fine form when Sunderland finished runners-up in the First Division in 1898, but failed to make much of an impression at Bolton or indeed with the Heathens.

Club record: 23 apps. four goals (also 4 'other' apps, one goal)

MORGAN, William

Born: Leigh, 1875

Career: Horwich FC, NEWTON HEATH (January 1897), Bolton Wanderers (March 1903), Watford (summer 1903), Leicester Fosse (summer, 1904), New Brompton (1906), Newton Heath Athletic (Easter 1910-11).

A well-balanced, utterly dependable wing-half, Billy Morgan - nicknamed the 'India Rubber Doll' - became something of a footballing nomad after leaving Manchester where his best days in League football were certainly spent, although his only reward was the winning of a Southern League Second Division Championship medal with Watford in 1904. He made well over 250 senior appearances as a professional.

Club record: 152 apps. 7 goals (also 30 'other' apps, 3 goals)

231

MORGAN, William

Born: Sauchie, near Alloa, 2 October 1944

Career: Alloa Schools, Fishcross Boys' Club, Burnley (amateur 1960, professional 1961), MANCHESTER UNITED (£100,000, August 1968), Burnley (June 1975), Bolton Wanderers (1976), Chicago Sting (on loan, 1977), Minnesota Kicks (on loan in 1978, 1979 & 1980), Blackpool (1980-82).

Willie Morgan, a direct, fast-running and clever ball-player, took over on the right-wing at Burnley in 1964 when John Connelly moved to Old Trafford. Four years later Morgan took the same path, recruited by the Reds following their European Cup triumph at Wembley. Already honoured by Scotland at Under-23 and senior levels, Morgan went on to take his tally of senior caps up to 21 with United, representing his country in the 1974 World Cup Finals. The following year he helped United regain their First Division status. A virtual replica of George Best, Morgan was positive in going forward, had a good turn of foot, could cross a ball with precision and speed and possessed a very useful right-footed shot. The sight of 'look-alike' Best and Morgan in the same forward-line must have scared opponents witless!

During his professional career (in Britain and the NASL) Morgan amassed in excess of 850 senior appearances, with 631 coming in the Football League - 196 with Burnley, 238 for United, 155 for Bolton and 42 for Blackpool).

Club record: 304 apps. 34 goals

MORGANS, Kenneth Godfrey

Born: Swansea, 16 March 1939

Career: Swansea Schools, MANCHESTER UNITED (groundstaff January 1955, professional August 1956), Swansea Town (£3,000, March 1961), Newport County (1964), Cwmbran Town (player-manager, 1967-70).

As a youngster outside-right Kenny Morgans, a member of United's 1956 and 1957 FA Youth Cup winning sides, had a great deal of confidence when he took the field. Sadly though, he was deeply affected by the Munich air crash from which he fortunately escaped serious injury, but never recovered his early promise. Capped twice by Wales at Under-23 level, he went on to play in 55 League games for Swansea and 125 for Newport. On retiring from the football scene he became a publican, based in Pontypool.

Club record: 23 apps.

MORRIS, John

Born: Radcliffe, Lancs. 27 September 1923.

Career: St John's School (Radcliffe), Mujacs FC, MANCHESTER UNITED (amateur, August 1939, professional March 1941), guested for Bolton Wanderers, Charlton Athletic & Wrexham during WW2, Derby County (£24,500, March 1949), Leicester City (£21,500, October 1952), Corby Town (player-manager, 1958), Kettering Town (player-manager, 1961), Rugby Town (manager, 1962), Great Harwood (manager, 1964), Oswestry Town (manager, 1967-69).

Originally a centre-half with the St John's school team, Johnny Morris saw action with the Royal Armoured Corps during the Second World War as tank crew whilst also gaining experience as a goalscoring inside-right with three League clubs as a guest player.

After establishing himself in United's senior side in 1946-47 (as partner to Jimmy Delaney), he won an FA Cup winners medal v. Blackpool in 1948 but less than a year later, after a disagreement with manager Matt Busby, he left for The Baseball Ground in a record transfer deal. During his time with Derby, Morris won three full caps for England, scoring on his international debut v. Norway. He also played for his country's 'B' team and represented the Football League on five occasions. Twice a Second Division Championship winner with Leicester (in 1954 and 1957) Morris gained a reputation as a brilliant ball playing inside-forward, later an inventive wing-half. Morris' record fee in March 1949 lasted only until December as Eddie Quigley moved from Sheffield Wednesday to Preston North End for £26,500. Remarkably, Quigley was Morris' uncle!
Club record: 93 apps. 35 goals

MORRISON, Thomas
Born: Belfast, 1874.
Career: Stormont FC (Belfast), Glentoran (1891), Burnley (1894), Glasgow Celtic (1895), Burnley (early 1897), MANCHESTER UNITED (December 1902), Colne FC (September 1904), Burnley (coach, 1905), Glentoran (coach, 1907-08). Tom Morrison had already amassed well over 200 League and Cup appearances and played for Ireland seven times at full international level prior to joining United.
Nicknamed 'Ching' he could play on the right-wing or as an inside-forward and at times looked very useful, especially during the first four months of his United career. He had excellent close control, was quick over short distances and packed a pretty strong right-foot shot. During his career he played in over 250 competitive games (for clubs and country).
Club record: 36 apps. 8 goals

MORTON, Benjamin Winston
Born: Sheffield, winter 1910
Career: Stourbridge FC, Wolverhampton Wanderers (early 1933), Stourbridge FC (1934), MANCHESTER UNITED (May 1935), Torquay United (May 1936), Swindon Town (autumn 1937), Stourbridge FC (1945-47).
Reserve centre-forward Ben Morton appeared in just one League game for United - against West Ham United at home in November 1935 when he deputised for Tommy Bamford in a 3-2 defeat. He headed Torquay's scoring charts in 1936-37 and 1937-38 and then did likewise with Swindon in 1937-38, also being the Third Division South's top marksman that season with 28 goals. He failed to make a first team appearance during his season at Molineux.
Club record: one app.

MOSCOW TORPEDO
After two goalless first round encounters in the 1992-93 UEFA Cup competition, it was the Russian players who held their nerve to win the ensuing penalty shoot-out 4-3 in Moscow.

MOSES, Remi Mark
Born: Miles Platting, Manchester, 14 November 1960
Career: Corpus Christi Boys' Club (Manchester), Manchester Schools, West Bromwich Albion (apprentice 1977, professional November 1978), MANCHESTER UNITED (£500,000, October 1981). Retired through injury, June 1988.
A strong-running, hard-tackling and resilient midfielder, Remi Moses joined United in the same deal which brought Bryan Robson to Old Trafford from West Bromwich Albion in a combined £2 million transfer deal in 1981. Capped eight times by England at Under-21 level, and recipient of a League Cup runners-up medal with United (v. Liverpool in 1983) he subsequently missed that year's FA Cup Final victory over Brighton & Hove Albion through suspension, then agonisingly missed out again in 1985, this time through injury, when United beat Everton 1-0 in the Final. A series of tediously painful ankle injuries (and operations) eventually ruined his career, causing Moses to hang up his boots, aged 27.
Club record: 199 apps. 13 goals

MUHREN, Arnoldus Johannus Hyacinthus
Born: Vollendam, Holland 2 June 1951
Career: Ajax Amsterdam (1967), FC Twente Enschede, Ipswich Town (1978), MANCHESTER UNITED (free transfer, July 1982), Ajax Amsterdam (June 1985-89); later coaching in Holland
Dutch midfielder Arnold Muhren helped Ipswich Town win the FA Cup (1978) and the UEFA Cup (1981) before joining United, signed by manager Ron Atkinson after his contract at Portman Road had expired. A real top-notch international (he won a total of 23 caps for his country - surprisingly none as a United player), Muhren had an educated left-foot....and at times seemed to make the ball talk. He celebrated his first season at Old Trafford by scoring from the penalty spot as United won the FA Cup Final v. Brighton...two months after walking off the Wembley turf a rather dejected man following Liverpool's League Cup victory over the Reds. Injured in March 1984, he failed to recover full fitness and returned to Ajax where he did remarkably well for a number of years, adding further caps to his tally, collected a European Cup-winners Cup winners medal in 1987 (v. Lokomotiv Leipzig) and a year later helped Holland beat Russia to win the European Championship Final in Germany. Muhren, one of the best left-footed players ever to don a United shirt - retired in 1989 with more than 500 competitive appearances under his belt...214 for Ipswich Town. Muhren now lives in Vollendam (Holland) and coaches youngsters while also workingfor a Dutch soccer magazine. He still plays for the ex-Ajax and ex-Holland teams in charity matches.
Club record: 98 apps. 18 goals

232

MULRYNE, Philip Patrick

Born: Belfast, 1 January 1978

Career: MANCHESTER UNITED (YTS June 1994, professional March 1995), Norwich City (£500,000, March 1999).

Since leaving Old Trafford for Carrow Road, midfielder Phil Mulryne has been honoured by his country at four different levels - Youth, 'B' (one cap), Under-21 (3 caps) and senior, winning over 12 full caps). Earlier he had helped United's youngsters win the FA Youth Cup in 1995. An excellent passer of the ball, he loves getting forward and is regarded as a set-piece specialist. With another ex-United player (Alex Notman) he helped Norwich City reach the First Division Play-off Final in 2002. Club record: 5 apps.

MUNICH AIR DISASTER

Pre Munich: (L to R) (back row) Eddie Colman, Ian Greaves, Ray Wood, Roger Byrne, Mark Jones, Duncan Edwards (front row) Dennis Viollet, John Berry, Tommy Taylor, John Doherty, David Pegg.

233

Having defeated Arsenal 5-4 in a thrilling First Division League encounter at Highbury on 1 February 1958, United then flew off to play the Yugoslavian champions Red Star Belgrade in a European Cup quarter final, second leg clash. United had won the first leg 2-1 and were confident of making progress in the competition - and they did an excellent job by earning a 3-3 draw to qualify for the semi-finals for the second season running by taking the tie 5-4 on aggregate, having led 3-0 at half-time.

Everyone associated with the club was delighted at the success achieved. But sadly on the return journey from Yugoslavia landing at Munich to refuel, the plane carrying the United party, plus reporters and colleagues, crashed on take-off from a frozen and snowbound Munich airport on 6 February.

A minute before half-past three, thousands of people in Britain tuned in to the BBC to hear the latest entry in Mrs Dale's Diary. They heard instead a one-minute news summary which told that disaster had struck the world famous football team.

Seven United players - Roger Byrne, Geoff Bent, Eddie Colman, Mark Jones, David Pegg, Tommy Taylor and Liam 'Billy' Whelan - were killed instantly. Johnny Berry, Jackie Blanchflower and Duncan Edwards, along with team manager Matt Busby were seriously injured. Edwards failed to pull through, but the others survived although Berry and Blanchflower never played football again.

Ken Morgans, Albert Scanlon, Dennis Viollet and Ray Wood were not too seriously injured, and Bobby Charlton, Bill Foulkes and Harry Gregg were able to walk away from the disaster, Gregg heroically finding time to go back into the plane to help with the rescue.

Others who died in the crash were: Walter Crickmer (United secretary) and trainers Tom Curry and Bert Whalley, plus eight journalists, Alf Clarke (Manchester Evening Chronicle), Don Davies (Manchester Guardian), George Follows (Daily Herald), Tom Jackson (Manchester Evening News), Archie Ledbrooke (Daily Mirror), Henry Rose (Daily Express), the former Manchester City and England goalkeeper Frank Swift (News of the World) and Eric Thompson (Daily Mail). Two members of the crew and two supporters also perished.

A total of 23 people lost their lives as a result of the dramatic crash. Three journalists, four crew members and four other passengers survived, along with the players and manager mentioned earlier.

Almost a fortnight after that tragic accident - on 19 February 1958 - close on 60,000 people packed into Old Trafford for the 5th round FA Cup-tie between United and Sheffield Wednesday. They were there to mourn the footballers ......the action on the pitch would be secondary - it was certainly not in their minds as they made their way sadly to the old ground. The programme that night showed eleven 'blank spaces' on the team-sheet.

Astonishingly Harry Gregg and Bill Foulkes were deemed fit enough to play. Respect having been beautifully observed, everyone seemed glad to get back to 'normal' again, the crowd roaring United on to a famous victory, but sympathy must go to the Wednesday team who must have found it difficult to raise their game on a night charged with immense emotion.

MURPHY, James Patrick

Born: Pentre, Glamorgan, 27 October 1910. Died: Manchester, 14 November 1989

Career: Ton Pentre Village School, Ton Pentre Boys, Treorchy Thursday FC, Treorchy Juniors, Mid-Rhondda United, West Bromwich Albion (1928), Swindon Town (1939), Morris Commercial FC (season 1939-40), MANCHESTER UNITED (coach, March 1945, assistant-manager 1955, later caretaker-manager, 1958, assistant-manager again, 1959-71. Thereafter employed by the club as a scout, and later as a consultant until his death in 1989).

Jimmy Murphy, Sir Matt Busby's right-hand man, took over the reins as team manager of Manchester United (the Busby Babes) immediately after the Munich air crash - and he did superb job, leading the club to the 1958 FA Cup Final.

A Schoolboy international, Jimmy 'Spud' Murphy - the son of Irish parents - was a vigorous attacking wing-half who played in 223 first-class games for WBA and won 15 caps for Wales before retiring in 1940 - to go to War! In fact, it was during his service with the Eighth Army that Murphy befriended Matt Busby. Consequently, when Busby took over as manager at Old Trafford, his first 'signing' (as senior coach) was Murphy. In later years Busby confirmed that it was his "most important signing!"

In October 1956, Murphy took an additional burden, that of the Welsh national team manager. He did a good job in that capacity, leading his country to the 1958 World Cup Finals in Sweden. However, it was fortunate, indeed, that Murphy did not travel on that fateful journey to Belgrade because of his involvement with the Welsh team.

But the pressure of holding two high-profile positions caught up with him and in 1964 he relinquished his position as boss of Wales. He continued as assistant-manager at Old Trafford until 1971 and then moved over to become a scout. Murphy was associated with United for some 44 years.

MURRAY, Robert D

Born: Edinburgh, 1914

Career: Newton Grange Star, Heart of Midlothian, MANCHESTER UNITED (£1,600, July 1937), Bath City (season 1938-39), Colchester United (registered season 1939-40).

Bob Murray played in the opening three League games at the start of the 1937-38 season and thereafter was regarded as a reserve inside-forward at Old Trafford.

Club record: 4 apps.

MUSEUM

234

Firmly bedded in to the North Stand at Old Trafford, the Manchester United museum is one of the biggest in the footballing world. Eye-catching, it is one of the main attractions for visitors (young and old) and is packed full of nostalgia, with photographs, shirts, medals, international caps, boots, footballs, programmes, newspaper-cuttings, scarves, rosettes and rattles etc. all placed neatly in secure cabinets, frames and files. The Munich air crash is remembered in newspaper-headlines of the day; there is also a section dedicated to Sir Matt Busby and of course there are the star players from every era.

The doors to the museum are open from 9.30am to 5pm Monday to Friday, except on a matchday when they close 30 minutes earlier. the admission prices are: £5.50 adults, £3.50 juniors and £15.10 for a family ticket (2 adults, 2 children). Under fives are admitted free.

For information, telephone 0161 868 8631.

MUTCH, George

Born: Aberdeen, 21 September 1912. Died: April 2001.

Career: Avondale FC, Banks o'Dee FC, Arbroath, MANCHESTER UNITED (£800, May 1934), Preston North End (£5,000, September 1937), Bury (autumn 1946), Southport (£1,000, player-trainer, 1947, retired as a player in 1948), Banks o'Dee (manager, 1950-52).

George Mutch was a forceful, hard-shooting and clever inside-forward and the player responsible for scoring a dramatic penalty winner for Preston against Huddersfield in the last minute of extra-time of the 1938 FA Cup Final. He won Schoolboy caps for Scotland as a teenager and later added a senior cap to his tally (starring against England in 1938). He was an ever-present and vital member of United's Second Division Championship-winning side in 1935-36 (top-scoring with 21 League goals) and in September 1934 he netted a hat-trick in five minutes for United in their 4-1 home League win over Barnsley. On retiring from football he set up a grocery business in Aberdeen and later became a PT instructor.

Club record: 120 apps. 49 goals

MYERSCOUGH, Joseph

Born: Galgate, Lancashire, 5 August 1893. Died: Seaforth, near Lancaster, 29 July 1975.

Career: Lancaster Town (spring 1913), MANCHESTER UNITED (May 1920), Bradford PA (£1,500 and Ken MacDonald, October 1923), Lancaster Town (1927), Rossendale United (season 1931-32), Morecambe (1932-33).

Inside-forward Joe Myerscough gained a Central League Championship medal at the end of his first season with United and was also selected to represent the Central League in the annual challenge match against the Lancashire Combination (1921). He started well with the Reds but faded out of the limelight. He later did very well at Bradford, scoring almost 50 goals in 131 senior appearances. He returned to Lancaster after hanging up his boots to become a painter and decorator.

Club record: 34 apps. 8 goals

Born: Bury, 18 February 1975
Career: Boundary Park Juniors, MANCHESTER UNITED (YTS, June 1991, professional January 1993). Able to play consistently well at right-back or centre-half, Gary Neville has been a vital ingredient in the Manchester United defence for over seven years, since establishing himself in the first XI in season 1994-95, having made his senior debut as a substitute v. Torpedo Moscow in the UEFA Cup in September 1992. Honoured by England at Youth team level, he has now gained over 50 senior caps, the majority in the right-back berth. Steady, reliable with sound positional sense, he was an FA Youth Cup winner with United in 1992 and since then has added five Premiership titles to his collection plus two FA Cup Final victories, a European Cup triumph and one FA Charity Shield success. Along with the French international Mikael Silvestre, Neville formed a fine 'full-back' pairing in 2001-02. Unfortunately he missed the 2002 World Cup finals through injury.
Club record: 349 apps. 3 goals

235

NAMES

Shortest

The players with the shortest surname (each with three letters) to have donned a first team shirt (at competitive level) for United have been: Dow (John), Hay (Tom), Law (Denis), Lee (Edwin), May (David), Mew (Jack) and Ure (Ian).

Longest

The player with the longest surname (taking the Dutch spelling) is Rutgerus Johannes van Nistelrooij which gives you 14 letters in his 'surname' (van Nistelrooij). Tom O'Shaughnessey (Tom) and Wrigglesworth (Billy) each have 13 letters in their surnames.

It is worth mentioning a United player from the 1980s - one Arnoldus Johannus Hyacinthus Muhren (known as Arnold) - who has no fewer than 32 letters in his full name. Van Nistelrooij has 30. In Newton Heath days the captain was Caesar Augustus Llewelyn Jenkyns (29 letters).

Same Name

The most players bearing the same surname who've appeared for United (seniors) are Davies (7) & Williams (7) with Brown, Jones & Smith (6). Strangely there have been no Smiths or Williams since WW2.

The Name Game

•It is commonly thought that Ian Ure has had the shortest name in professional football. Not so - he was christened John Francombe Ure.

•The player with the shortest overall name (six letters) who has served with Manchester United has been Tom Hay (possibly christened Tom and not Thomas). If he was called Thomas, then the shortest named players would be Denis Law, Tom Leigh and John Owen (each with eight letters). John Dow's middle name began with the letter M (perhaps comprising four or more letters) and Jack Mew's full name was John William Mew.

•John Dow made his debut for Newton Heath in March 1894 (v. Bolton Wanderers) under the name of MJ Woods.

•United changed its name from Newton Heath FC in 1902.

•Louis Rocca is the man who produced the name 'Manchester United'. Prior to this title being accepted other names were put forward like 'Manchester Celtic' and 'Manchester Central'. The Manchester Evening News of Saturday 26 April 1902 revealed the club's new name for the first time and commended it to its readers.

•Ryan Giggs was born Ryan Wilson but later adopted his mother's maiden name of Giggs.

•United signed three players - all named ROBERTSON - in the space of five days in May 1903, two named Alex. The first Alex ('Sandy') arrived from Middlesbrough, the other came from Hibernian while Tom was secured from Dundee.

•United have only ever had four players with surnames beginning with the letter 'I' - Iddon and Inglis both appeared in 1926-27, whilst Ince and Irwin appeared regularly together during the 1990s.

Unusual names

Several British-born players who have been associated with the club over the years have had unusual Christian names, include: Alphonso Ainsworth, J Emmanuel Astley, Beaumont Asquith, S Prince Blott, R Beresford Brown, H Redvers Cartman, Allenby Chilton, Malachy Donaghy, Levi W Draycott, H Bernt Erentz, J Ignatius Feehan, Augustine Ashley Grimes, T Savill Gipps, E Holdroyd Goldthorpe, Deiniol W T Graham, I Denzil Greaves, Proctor Hall, C Emmanuel Hillam, Aaron Hulme, P Emerson Carlyle Ince, H Doxford Leonard, Caesar Augustus Llewelyn Jenkyns, Norbert Lawton, R Openshaw Lawton, H Doxford Leonard, Oscar Horace Linkson, F Comber McPherson, Luigi 'Lou' Macari, Guiliano Maiorana, Remi Moses, Louis Antonio Page, S Clare Pearson, J Hope Peddie, Clatworthy Rennox, Lancelot Holliday Richardson, D Middleton Robbie, Elijah Round, Jocelyn A Rowe, H Bowater Rowley, Ezra J Royals, L Jesse Sealey, T Gable Smith, Joseph Waters Spence, Norbert P Stiles, B Lindsay Thornley, J Francombe Ure and Enoch J West.

Messrs Macari and Maiorana were both born of Italian parentage. The two Norberts, Lawton and Stiles, appeared in the same side.

Name Change

In June 2002, Marin Zdravkov, a Bulgarian living in the town of Shistov, won a two-year battle to change his name to 'Manchester United'.

NANTES ATLANTIQUE

A late, late Ruud van Nistelrooy penalty (awarded after Mario Yepes had handled inside the area and was subsequently sent-off) earned United a share of the spoils at 1-1 in the first game of the Group Two phase Champions League competition in Nantes in February 2002. The Romanian striker Viorel Moldovan had given the French side a 9th minute lead.

When the teams met at Old Trafford a week later, a crowd of almost 66,500 saw United overcome an early scare when the French side took the lead, to go on a register an impressive 5-1 victory, Ole Gunnar Solskjaer scoring twice while van Nistelrooy again converted a penalty for his 30th goal of the season. United's other goals came from a David Beckham trademark free-kick and Mikael Silvestre's header.

NARDIELLO, Daniel

Born: Coventry, 22 October 1982

Career: Wolverhampton Wanderers, MANCHESTER UNITED (apprentice, June 1998, October 2000).

Son of the former Coventry City and Welsh international winger of the 1970s, Donato Nardiello, Danny made his United debut in a 4-0 Worthington Cup defeat at Arsenal in November 2001. As a youngster and prepared to sign for Wolves, Nardiello was suddenly whisked away to Old Trafford, United having to pay a substantial fee in compensation for securing his services! He has already been rewarded with England Youth honours.

Club record: one app.

NECAXA

United entered the FIFA-arranged Club World Championship in Brazil in January 2000 and in their First Group game they drew 1-1 with the Mexican side Necaxa in Rio before a 26,000 crowd. Dwight Yorke scored United's equaliser with eight minutes left (having earlier missed a penalty).

NELSON

Summary of League results

	P	W	D	L	F	A
Division 2	2	1	0	1	2	1
Home	1	0	0	1	0	1
Away	1	1	0	0	2	0
Total	2	1	0	1	2	1

United's League results v Nelson:

Season	Div	Home	Away
1923-24	2	L 0-1	W 2-0

FA Cup result v. Nelson:

The Heathens defeated Nelson 3-0 at home in the 4th qualifying round of the FA Cup in season 1896-97.

Fact File

On a recent television 'phone in' a viewer rang from Nelson, "Where is Nelson?" asked the football 'personality' for that evening. He might well have asked. Nelson is a thriving former cotton mill town in East Lancashire, the next town after Burnley on the road 'over the top' to Yorkshire, having its heyday in the nineteenth century when 'cotton was king'. Nelson's cricket team boasted the world's finest all rounder, West Indian Learie Constantine; Nelson FC, established in 1881, shared their ground for a time before obtaining its own ground at Seedhill.
When the Football League created the Third Division (North) in 1921, Nelson was one of its founder members, winning the title in its second season, promoted to Division Two. United were also in this Division at the time, this season would be the only time the two clubs met in the League as Nelson were relegated after just one season. When they had achieved promotion in 1923, Nelson celebrated by arranging a tour of Spain where they recorded a win over Real Madrid.
However, in 1931, Nelson failed the re-election process after 10 seasons of League football. Nelson, as a football club, is still in existence, but playing lower down the League 'pyramid'. If you ever drive along the M65 and take the 'Nelson' exit, chances are you are driving over the old Seedhill ground, now buried under concrete, Nelson these days play at Victoria Park.

Players with both clubs include: J Flanagan (United reserve), W Halligan (United WW1), C Hillam, A Hulme, A Pape, J Quin, J Saunders, E Thomson, A Warburton.
* G Lydon (played for the Reds & Nelson Utd)

NEUTRAL GROUNDS

United have played several matches on a neutral ground, mainly Cup semi-finals and Finals.

Here is a list of such games:

Football League

20.08.1971	v. Arsenal	Div 1	won 3-1	Anfield
23.08.1971	v. W.B.Albion	Div 1	won 3-1	The Victoria Ground (Stoke)

These two fixtures were 'home' games - Old Trafford being closed due to incidents the previous season.

Test Matches

22.04.1893	v. Small Heath	drew 1-1	The Victoria Ground (Stoke)
27.04.1893	v. Small Heath	won 5-2	Bramall Lane (Sheffield)
28.04.1894	v. Liverpool	lost 0-2	Ewood Park (Blackburn)
27.04.1895	v. Stoke	lost 0-3	Athletic Ground (Burslem Port Vale)

FA Cup

21.12.1903	v. Small Heath	Int rd/2nd rep	drew 1-1	Bramall Lane
11.01.1904	v. Small Heath	Int rd/3rd rep	won 3-1	Hyde Road (Manchester)
23.01.1905	v. Fulham	Int rd/2nd rep	lost 0-1	Villa Park
27.03.1909	v. Newcastle Utd	semi-final	won 1-0	Bramall Lane
24.04.1909	v. Bristol City	Final	won 1-0	The Crystal Palace
27.03.1926	v. Manchester City	semi-final	lost 0-3	Bramall Lane
17.01.1927	v. Reading	3rd rd/2nd rep	lost 1-2	Villa Park
19.01.1931	v. Stoke City	3rd rd/2nd rep	won 4-2	Anfield
24.01.1948	v. Liverpool*	4th rd	won 3-0	Goodison Park
07.02.1948	v. Charlton Ath*	5th rd	won 2-0	Leeds Rd (Huddersfield)
13.03.1948	v. Derby County	semi-final	won 3-1	Hillsborough
24.04.1948	v. Blackpool	Final	won 4-2	Wembley
26.03.1949	v. Wolves	semi-final	drew 1-1	Hillsborough
02.04.1949	v. Wolves	s-final replay	lost 0-1	Goodison Park
05.02.1953	v. Walthamstow Ave	4th rd replay	won 5-2	Highbury
23.03.1957	v. Birmingham City	semi-final	won 2-0	Hillsborough
04.05.1957	v. Aston Villa	Final	lost 1-2	Wembley
22.03.1958	v. Fulham	semi-final	drew 2-2	Villa Park
26.03.1958	v. Fulham	s-final replay	won 5-3	Highbury
03.05.1958	v. Bolton Wands	Final	lost 0-2	Wembley
31.03.1962	v. Tottenham Hotspur	semi-final	lost 1-3	Hillsborough
27.04.1963	v. Southampton	semi-final	won 1-0	Villa Park
25.05.1963	v. Leicester City	Final	won 3-1	Wembley
09.03.1964	v. Sunderland	6th rd 2nd rep	won 5-1	Leeds Road
14.03.1964	v. West Ham Utd	semi-final	lost 1-3	Hillsborough
27.03.1965	v. Leeds United	semi-final	drew 0-0	Hillsborough
31.03.1965	v. Leeds United	s-final replay	lost 0-1	City Ground (Nottingham)
23.04.1966	v. Everton	semi-final	lost 0-1	Burnden Park (Bolton)
14.03.1970	v. Leeds United	semi-final	drew 0-0	Hillsborough
23.03.1970	v. Leeds United	s-final replay	drew 0-0	Villa Park
26.03.1970	v. Leeds United	sf 2nd replay	lost 0-1	Burnden Park
10.04.1970	v. Watford	3rd place p/off	won 2-0	Highbury
03.04.1976	v. Derby County	semi-final	won 2-0	Hillsborough
01.05.1976	v. Southampton	Final	lost 0-1	Wembley
23.04.1977	v. Leeds United	semi-final	won 2-1	Hillsborough
21.05.1977	v. Liverpool	Final	won 2-1	Wembley
31.03.1979	v. Liverpool	semi-final	drew 2-2	Maine Road

04.04.1979	v. Liverpool	s-final replay	won 1-0	Goodison Park
12.05.1979	v. Arsenal	Final	lost 2-3	Wembley
16.04.1983	v. Arsenal	semi-final	won 2-1	Villa Park
21.05.1983	v. Brighton & HA	Final	drew 2-2	Wembley
26.05.1983	v. Brighton & HA	Final replay	won 4-0	Wembley
13.04.1985	v. Liverpool	semi-final	drew 2-2	Goodison Park
17.04.1985	v. Liverpool	s-final replay	won 2-1	Maine Road
18.05.1985	v. Everton	Final	won 1-0	Wembley
08.04.1990	v. Oldham Athletic	semi-final	drew 3-3	Maine Road
11.04.1990	v. Oldham Athletic	s-final replay	won 2-1	Maine Road
12.05.1990	v. Crystal Palace	Final	drew 3-3	Wembley
17.05.1990	v. Crystal Palace	Final replay	won 1-0	Wembley
10.04.1994	v. Oldham Athletic	semi-final	drew 1-1	Wembley
13.04.1994	v. Oldham Athletic	s-final replay	won 4-1	Maine Road
14.05.1994	v. Chelsea	Final	won 4-0	Wembley
09.04.1995	v. Crystal Palace	semi-final	drew 2-2	Villa Park
17.04.1995	v. Crystal Palace	s-final replay	won 2-0	Villa Park
20.05.1995	v. Everton	Final	lost 0-1	Wembley
31.03.1996	v. Chelsea	semi-final	won 2-1	Villa Park
11.05.1996	v. Liverpool	Final	won 1-0	Wembley
11.04.1999	v. Arsenal	semi-final	drew 0-0	Villa Park
14.04.1999	v. Arsenal	s-final replay	won 2-1	Villa Park
22.05.1999	v. Newcastle Utd	Final	won 2-0	Wembley

* Technically 'home' matches - United played their home games at Maine Road at this time which was unavailable due to Manchester City also being drawn to play at home.

League Cup

26.03.1983	v. Liverpool	Final	lost 1-2	Wembley
21.04.1991	v. Sheffield Wed	Final	lost 0-1	Wembley
12.04.1992	v. Nottingham For	Final	won 1-0	Wembley
27.03.1994	v. Aston Villa	Final	lost 1-3	Wembley

European Cup

26.09.1956	v. Anderlecht*	Prel rd/2nd leg	won 10-0	Maine Road
17.10.1956	v. Borussia Dortm'd*	1st rd/1st leg	won 3-2	Maine Road
06.02.1957	v. Athletic Bilbao*	2nd rd/2nd leg	won 3-0	Maine Road
29.05.1968	v. Benfica	Final	won 4-1	Wembley
26.05.1999	v. Bayern Munich	Final	won 2-1	Nou Camp (Barcelona)

* Technically 'home' matches as there were no fllodlights installed at Old Trafford at that time.

European Cup-winners Cup

| 05.10.1977 | v. St Etienne* | 1st rd/2nd leg | won 2-0 | Home Park (Plymouth) |
| 15.05.1991 | v. Barcelona | Final | won 2-1 | Feyenoord St (Rotterdam) |

* Technically a 'home' match as United were banned from playing within 350 miles of Old Trafford.

FA Charity Shield

27.04.1908	v. QPR	drew 1-1	Stamford Bridge
29.08.1908	v. QPR, replay	won 4-0	Stamford Bridge
25.09.1911	v. Swindon Town	won 8-4	Stamford Bridge
13.08.1977	v. Liverpool	drew 0-0	Wembley
20.08.1983	v. Liverpool	won 2-0	Wembley
10.08.1985	v. Everton	lost 0-2	Wembley
19.08.1990	v. Liverpool	drew 1-1**	Wembley
07.08.1993	v. Arsenal	drew 1-1*	Wembley
14.08.1994	v. Blackburn Rovers	won 2-0	Wembley
11.08.1996	v. Newcastle Utd	won 4-0	Wembley
03.08.1997	v. Chelsea	drew 1-1+	Wembley
09.08.1998	v. Arsenal	lost 0-3	Wembley
01.08.1999	v. Arsenal	lost 1-2	Wembley
13.08.2000	v. Chelsea	lost 0-2	Wembley
12.08.2001	v. Liverpool	lost 1-2	Millennium Stadium (Cardiff)

** Each club held Shield for six months
* United won 5-4 on penalties
+ United won 4-2 on penalties

European Super Cup

| 27.08.1999 | v. SS Lazio | lost 0-1 | Monaco |

World Club Championship

| 30.11.1999 | v. Palmeiros | won 1-0 | Tokyo |

FIFA Club World Championship

06 01.2000	v. Necaxa	drew 1-1	Rio de Janeiro, Brazil
08.01.2000	v. Vasco Da Gama	lost 1-3	Rio de Janeiro, Brazil
11.01.2000	v. South Melbourne	won 2-0	Rio de Janeiro, Brazil

Mercantile Credit (Centenary)

| 09 10.1988 | v. Arsenal | Final | won 2-1 | Villa Park |

Lancashire Senior Cup

| 1897-98 | v. Blackburn Rovers | Final | won 2-1 | Goodison Park |
| 1912-13 | v. Blackburn Rovers | Final | lost 2-3 | Bloomfield Rd, Blackpool |

NB - During seasons 1946-47 to 1948-49 United used Maine Road for all their home Football League games. In season 1945-46 they played two 'home' FA Cup games at Maine Road and fulfilled one 'home' FA Cup tie at the same ground the following season, one in 1948 and four in 1949. The matches are regarded as 'home' games and not on neutral grounds in this section.

NEVILLE, Gary Alexander

Refer to front of section.

NEVILLE, Philip John

Born: Bury, 21 January 1977
Career: Boundary Park Juniors, MANCHESTER UNITED (YTS, June 1992, professional June 1994).
Younger brother of Gary (q.v) Phil Neville can also fill a variety of positions including those of full-back and midfield. Strong and competitive with good technique, he was also an FA Youth Cup winner with the Reds (1995) and then

proceeded to add five Premiership wins to his tally along with two FA Cup Final victories, two Charity Shield wins and European Cup glory in the treble winning season of 1998-99. Capped almost 40 times by England at senior level, Neville has also represented his country in Schoolboy, Youth and Under-21 internationals, collecting seven caps in the latter category. Neville made his senior debut for United in an FA Cup-tie v. Wrexham in January 1995. Before turning professional he was being groomed for cricket stardom at the 'other' Old Trafford. In earlier times he might have become a 'double' international.

Club record: 266 apps. 5 Goals

NEVIN, George William

Born: Lintz, County Durham, 16 December 1907. Died: Sheffield, early 1973.

Career: Dipton United, Lintz Colliery FC, Whitehead-le-Rangers, Newcastle United (late 1928), Sheffield Wednesday (mid-1930), MANCHESTER UNITED (January 1934), Sheffield Wednesday (March 1934), Burnley (mid-1935), Lincoln City (summer 1937), Rochdale (summer 1939).

Despite a nomadic career, burly full-back George Nevin seemed fated not to establish himself as a first-team footballer wherever he went. His brief United career lasted just a few weeks as manager Scott Duncan tried no less than 38 players during 1933-34 in narrowly avoiding relegation from Division Two. Nevin's 'career' comprised just 46 League appearances with six different clubs.

Club record: 5 apps.

NEVLAND, Erik

Born: Stavanger, Norway, 10 November 1977

Career: IFK Gothenburg, Viking Stavanger (on loan), MANCHESTER UNITED (July 1977), Viking Stavanger (August 2000).

Striker Erik Nevland, a Norwegian international (three caps won) was released by the club in the summer of 2000 after failing to establish himself in the first XI.

Club record: 6 apps. one goal

NEW BRIGHTON TOWER

Heathens' League results v the Tower:

Season	Div	Home	Away
1898-99	2	L 1-2	W 3-0
1899-1900	2	W 2-1	W 4-1
1900-01	2	W 1-0	L 0-2

Summary of League results

	P	W	D	L	F	A
Division 2	6	4	0	2	11	6
Home	3	2	0	1	4	3
Away	3	2	0	1	7	3
Total	6	4	0	2	11	6

Fact File:

New Brighton Tower has one of the most bizarre histories in English football. The town of New Brighton on The Wirral was a thriving Victorian seaside resort with a virtually identical tower to that at Blackpool. The Tower management, looking for out of season income, decided to form a football club to play at the Tower Ground. They applied to join the Football League in 1897 but, not surprisingly, were refused; then in 1898 their second application was successful despite having only one season in the Lancashire League, albeit as champions, to speak of. Spending was lavish on an array of professional footballers as New Brighton Tower made great efforts to reach the First Division where the big money lay. However, finishes of 5th, 10th and 4th failed to achieve the desired promotion, so, fearful of big losses, the management resigned from the League, never to be heard of again.

The club known as 'New Brighton' played in the Third Division (North) from 1923-51, but had no connection with the earlier side, although from 1946 they played at the Tower Ground, the tower itself having been dismantled during WW2 because of its close proximity to the port of Liverpool.

* Players with both clubs include: F Barrett, T Leigh, H Redwood.

NEW YORK YANKEES

On 7 February 2001, at the Sheraton Hotel in Manhattan, Manchester United joined forces with the American baseball giants New York Yankees (the Yankee-Nets) which also owns the New Jersey Jets basketball team.

The big-money super-deal was duly signed and approved by YankeeNets' Chairman Dr Harvey Schiller and United's Chief Executive Peter Kenyon with former player and Director Sir Bobby Charlton. It enabled United to sell its merchandise in the USA, initially in the Bronx district of New York and then in the giant Kite Town store in downtown Manhattan. In return United's official club shops at Old Trafford and elsewhere sold all the necessities appertaining to the Yankee's baseball (and possibly basketball) activities. .

NEWCASTLE UNITED

Summary of League results

	P	W	D	L	F	A
Premier League	18	8	7	3	26	20
Division 1	96	43	24	29	180	162
Division 2	14	7	1	6	23	16
Home	64	38	17	9	141	71
Away	64	20	15	29	88	127
Total	128	58	32	38	229	198

FA Cup results v the Magpies:

	Round	Venue	Result
1908-09	Semi-final	Bramall Lane	W 1-0
1989-90	5	Away	W 3-2
1998-99	Final	Wembley	W 2-0

Heathens/United's League results v the Magpies:

Season	Div	Home	Away	Season	Div	Home	Away
1894-95	2	W 5-1	L 0-3	1954-55	1	D 2-2	L 0-2
1895-96	2	W 2-1	L 1-2	1955-56	1	W 5-2	D 0-0
1896-97	2	W 4-0	L 0-2	1956-57	1	W 6-1	D 1-1
1897-98	2	L 0-1	L 0-2	1957-58	1	D 1-1	W 2-1
				1958-59	1	D 4-4	D 1-1
1906-07	1	L 1-3	L 0-5	1959-60	1	W 3-2	L 3-7
1907-08	1	D 1-1	W 6-1	1960-61	1	W 3-2	D 1-1
1908-09	1	W 1-0	L 1-2				
1909-10	1	D 1-1	W 4-3	1965-66	1	D 1-1	W 2-1
1910-11	1	W 2-0	W 1-0	1966-67	1	W 3-2	D 0-0
1911-12	1	L 0-2	W 3-2	1967-68	1	W 6-0	D 2-2
1912-13	1	W 3-0	W 3-1	1968-69	1	W 3-1	L 0-2
1913-14	1	D 2-2	W 1-0	1969-70	1	D 0-0	L 1-5
1914-15	1	W 1-0	L 0-2	1970-71	1	W 1-0	L 0-1
				1971-72	1	L 0-2	W 1-0
1919-20	1	W 2-1	L 1-2	1972-73	1	W 2-1	L 1-2
1920-21	1	W 2-0	L 3-6	1973-74	1	W 1-0	L 2-3
1921-22	1	L 0-1	L 0-3				
				1975-76	1	W 1-0	W 4-3
1925-26	1	W 2-1	L 1-4	1976-77	1	W 3-1	D 2-2
1926-27	1	W 3-1	L 2-4	1977-78	1	W 3-2	D 2-2
1927-28	1	L 1-7	L 1-4				
1928-29	1	W 5-0	L 0-5	1984-85	1	W 5-0	D 1-1
1929-30	1	W 5-0	L 1-4	1985-86	1	W 3-0	W 4-2
1930-31	1	L 4-7	L 3-4	1986-87	1	W 4-1	L 1-2
				1987-88	1	D 2-2	L 0-1
1934-35	2	L 0-1	W 1-0	1988-89	1	W 2-0	D 0-0
1935-36	2	W 3-1	W 2-0				
				1993-94	PL	D 1-1	D 1-1
1937-38	2	W 3-0	D 2-2	1994-95	PL	W 2-0	D 1-1
				1995-96	PL	W 2-0	W 1-0
1948-49	1	D 1-1	W 1-0	1996-97	PL	D 0-0	L 0-5
1949-50	1	D 1-1	L 1-2	1997-98	PL	D 1-1	W 1-0
1950-51	1	L 1-2	W 2-0	1998-99	PL	D 0-0	W 2-1
1951-52	1	W 2-1	D 2-2	1999-00	PL	W 5-1	L 0-3
1952-53	1	D 2-2	W 2-1	2000-01	PL	W 2-0	D 1-1
1953-54	1	D 1-1	W 2-1	2001-02	PL	W 3-1	L 3-4

League Cup results v the Magpies:

	Round	Venue	Result
1976-77	4	Home	W 7-2
1994-95	3	Away	L 0-2

FA Charity Shield

United have played the Magpies twice for the Charity Shield so far, winning both matches, 4-2 at Old Trafford and 4-0 at Wembley. (See: Charity Shield)

Mercantile Credit Trophy

A crowd of just under 15,000 saw United beat Newcastle 2-0 at Old Trafford in the semi-final of this sponsored competition in September 1988. The game went into extra-time before Steve Bruce and Brian McClair netted to take the Reds through to meet Arsenal in the Final (lost 2-1).

Fact File

United's FA Cup record against Newcastle Utd must be unique, having met them just three times in almost 100 seasons, won them all (none at Old Trafford) and won the FA Cup on each occasion. Since the Second World War, United have lost only twice at home to Newcastle Utd in a total of 39 matches (23 won 14 drawn). Either side of WW1 (1914 to 1931) United lost ten successive League games at Newcastle. United have conceded seven goals three times in League games against Newcastle. In September 1927, the Geordies won 7-1 at Old Trafford, in September 1930 they triumphed 7-4 also at Old Trafford and on 2 January 1960 United crashed 7-3 at St James' Park In between those two seven-goal hidings at Old Trafford, United twice recorded 5-0 home wins over the Geordies. Les Olive and Dennis Viollet made their League debuts for United against Newcastle at St James' Park on 2 April 1953. Sir Alex Ferguson celebrated his 600th game in charge as United beat the Magpies 3-1 at Old Trafford in a Premiership game in January 2001. Paul Scholes scored twice in this game - on his 300th appearance for the club, the first goal being his 50th in the Premiership.

Players with both clubs include: P Beardsley, I Broadis (Man United WW2), J Cape, A Chilton (Newcastle WW2), J Clements, A Cole, A Davies, W Davies, A Foggon, K Gillespie, A Gowling, W Higgins, T Lang, H Leonard, D McCreery, M Martin (also Newcastle assistant-manager, coach & scout), J Mitten (Man Utd trialist), G Nevin, L O'Brien, SC Pearson (Newcastle WW2), J Peddie, B Robson (Newcastle trialist), A Scanlon, C Spencer, N Tapken, E Taylor, W Woodward (reserve with both clubs). Also associated: C Mitten (United player, Newcastle manager), AS Duncan (United manager, Newcastle player), M Setters (United player, Newcastle Chief Scout), T Cavanagh (assistant-manager/trainer with both clubs), Tom Curry (Newcastle player, United trainer).

NEWTON, Percy

Born: Whitchurch, circa 1913

Career: Whitchurch FC, Chester (amateur 1932), Sandbach Ramblers (season 1932-33), MANCHESTER UNITED (£250, September 1933), Tranmere Rovers (May 1934 to June 1936).

Reserve centre-half Percy Newton played in just two League games for United during the 1933-34 season (against Burnley and Oldham Athletic in early February) deputising for the more established and experienced figure of Walter McMillen. When he was a Tranmere defender, he helped the Birkenhead side whip Oldham 13-4 in a League Division 3 (N) game on Boxing Day 1935.

Club record: 2 apps.

NEWTON HEATH

Newton Heath is a district of Manchester, about two miles north east of the city centre along the Oldham Road. In the second half of the 19th century, railways were spreading to all parts of the country, and at Newton Heath there was a large railway depot, the western end of the Lancashire and Yorkshire Railway (LYR) Company.

In 1878, the Dining Room Committee of the Company received a request from the Carriage and Wagon Works for permission and funds to form a cricket and football club to be known as Newton Heath (LYR). The committee granted permission, arranging for the football section to play at North Road near the works (q.v.).

The team quickly built up a strong reputation, originally in inter-departmental games with other railway depots, then with other local clubs. In 1886 the first tournament was won, the Manchester Cup, and as a professional club it was attracting players from Wales and Scotland. In the same year they entered the FA Cup for the first time. The railway authorities at Newton Heath had supported the club, welcoming the growing reputation of the club as a good thing for the railway company. Players were allowed time off to prepare for matches, concessionary travel on the train (which considerably reduced the club's travelling expenses) and the company would find jobs for new players from other parts of the country. Eventually the club would sever its railway links to become plain 'Newton Heath FC.'

In 1888 professional football took a massive step forward with the creation of the Football League. Newton Heath hoped to be in at the start, but could not raise enough votes. So successful was the League, however, that the following season a rival organisation was formed named the Football Alliance (q.v.) with Newton Heath one of the founder members.

The club now boasted its first paid official, Mr A H Albut, secretary, a former Aston Villa administrator, working out of the club 'office', a small terraced cottage at 33 Oldham Road, Newton Heath.

The third season of the Alliance (1891-92) saw Newton Heath finishing as runners-up to Nottingham Forest. During 1892 the Football League decided to expand, forming a Second Division with two extra places in the First Division. The Alliance filled up most of the Second Division places with Forest and the Heathens elected directly into the First Division.

Newton Heath now became a Limited Company with 2,000 £1 shares issued. Their first season was a disaster, the Heathens finishing bottom, but saved from relegation by the play-off (Test Match) system. The 1893-94 season saw them fare no better, this time relegated!

By 1902 the club was in dire straits, still in Division Two. Since 1893 the club had played at Bank Street (q.v) in neighbouring Clayton, but it was a poor ground with a bad pitch. Eventually the club was declared bankrupt (1902) but Manchester Breweries owner John H Davies (q.v) came to the rescue with a financial package which would enable them to continue playing. Having left Newton Heath long ago, he saw no reason for the club to continue under the name, desiring to attract a wider audience. At a public meeting, after the names 'Manchester Central' and 'Manchester Celtic' had been rejected, board member Louis Rocca proposed 'Manchester United' which was accepted. Newton Heath was dead and buried; a new club rose phoenix-like from the ashes, destined to become one of the biggest and most famous football clubs in the world.

* The district of Newton Heath has not forgotten its place in United's history, seven landmarks being named after victims of the Munich disaster: David Pegg Walk, Roger Byrne Close, Geoff Bent Walk, Eddie Colman Close, Mark Jones Walk, Tommy Taylor Close and Billy Whelan Walk. In nearby Salford, a block of flats has been named 'Duncan Edwards House.'

NICHOLL, James Michael

Born: Hamilton, Ontario, Canada, 28 February 1956
Career: Belfast Central School, MANCHESTER UNITED (amateur November 1971, apprentice October 1972, professional March 1974), Sunderland (on loan, December 1981-February 1982), Toronto Blizzard (£250,000, April 1983), Glasgow Rangers (on loan, 1983-84), Toronto Blizzard (mid 1984), West Bromwich Albion (late 1984), Glasgow Rangers (summer 1986 as reserve team player-coach), Dunfermline Athletic (summer 1989), Raith Rovers (player-manager, 1990-96), Millwall (manager, season 1996-97), Dunfermline Athletic (1999 as assistant-manager, also caretaker-manager), Jimmy Nicholl was born in Canada of Irish parents and in his early years at Old Trafford occupied the central defensive and sweeper positions before finally settling down at right-back where he became international class, winning a total of 73 full caps for Northern Ireland (41 as a United player) as well as one at Under-21 level, having earlier represented his country as a schoolboy. A steady, relaxed player, good on the ball with a useful turn of foot, he appeared in two FA Cup Finals with United, gaining a winners' medal in 1977 and a losers' in 1979 before losing his place to new signing John Gidman in 1981. He played in the 1983 NASL Soccer Bowl Final with Toronto Blizzard and then served the same club in the NASL Championship Series Final a year later, having returned to Canada following a loan spell at Ibrox Park. During his second spell with Rangers he gained both Skol Cup and Scottish League Championship winning medals. He played for his country in the 1982 and 1986 World Cup Finals and was named assistant-manager of the Northern Ireland national team in 1993….just as he was guiding Raith Rovers to the Scottish Second Division title. During his playing career Nicholl accumulated a very fine record, appearing well over 550 club and international matches over a period of 18 years.
Club record: 248 apps. 6 goals

241

NICHOLSON, James Joseph

Born: Belfast, 27 February 1943
Career: Methody College (Belfast), Boyland FC (Belfast), MANCHESTER UNITED (groundstaff June 1958, professional February 1960), Huddersfield Town £8,000, December 1964), Bury (late 1973), Mossley FC (1976), Stalybridge Celtic (1978).
Wing-half Jimmy Nicholson played both rugby and soccer as a youngster but always preferred the round ball game! Capped at Schoolboy, Youth, Under-23 and senior levels by Northern Ireland by the time he was 18, he went on to play in 41 full internationals as well as adding a 'B' cap to his collection as well.
He was only 17 when he made his United debut (v. Everton in August 1960) with his senior international debut following a year later. Compared at times with the great Duncan Edwards, he had to battle to get into the first XI at Old Trafford (remember Nobby Stiles and Maurice Setters were around at the time) but he did have one excellent season (1960-61) when he made 31 League appearances. He moved on (to Huddersfield) following the arrival of Pat Crerand, and went on to amass well over 300 senior appearances for the Terriers, skippering the Yorkshire club in 1969-70 when they won the Second Division title. During his career he made around 500 senior appearances, 422 in the Football League.
Club record: 68 apps. 6 goals.

NICKNAMES

Most footballers have a nickname - most of them conjured up by their colleagues, some attained from their personality, others carried on from their boyhood days. Here are some that have been attached to various United players:
Arthur 'Chips' Albiston, David 'Becks' & 'Golden-balls' Beckham, George 'El Beatle' Best, Laurent 'La Presidente' Blanc, Bill 'Rimmer' Brown, Eric 'King', 'Dieu' Cantona, Johnny 'Cario' Carey, Eddie 'Snake Hips' Colman,

Laurie 'The Black Pearl' Cunningham, Wyn ' The Leap' Davies, Alex 'The Black Prince' Dawson, Jack 'The Warrior' Doughty, Harry 'Tiger' Erentz, Ignatius 'Sonny' Feehan, Alex 'Bruce' Forsyth, Bill 'Cowboy' Foulkes, Daniel J 'Don' Givens, Shaun 'The Goat' Goater, Alan 'Bamber' Gowling, George 'Stroller' Graham, George 'Tiny' Haslam, Bill 'Sandy' Higgins, Clarence 'Lal' Hilditch, Gordon 'Merlin' Hill, Mark 'Sparky' Hughes, George 'Cocky' Hunter, Paul 'The Guv'nor' Ince, W Ronald 'Roy' John, OJ 'Chorley' Jones, Robert 'Curly' Jones, Joe 'Jaws' Jordan, Nicola 'Nikki' Jovanovic, Brian 'Kiddo' Kidd, Denis 'The King' Law, Edwin 'Neddy' Lee, GT 'Geordie' Livingstone, William 'Plum' Longair, David 'The Road-runner' McCreery, William 'Killer' McGlen, Jim 'The Little Wonder' McNaught, Lou 'The Judge' Macari, Paul 'the Black Pearl & Inchicore' McGrath, Charlie 'The Bogota Bandit' Mitten, Kevin 'Captain Blood' Moran, William 'The India Rubber Doll' Morgan, Tommy 'Ching' Morrison, Liam 'Stroller' O'Brien, Mark 'Pancho' Pearson, Stuart 'Pancho' Pearson, Ernest 'Dick' Pegg, Karel 'The Express Train' Poborsky; Clatworthy 'Charlie' Rennox, WA 'Bogie' Roberts, Alex 'Sandy' Robertson, Bryan 'Robbo' & 'Pop' Robson, Jocelyn 'Josh' Rowe, Jack 'Gunner' Rowley, Albert 'Scanny' Scanlon, Joe 'Ashton' Schofield, Lawrence 'Soldier' Smith, Billy 'Stock' Smith, Jakob 'Jaap' Stam, Norbert 'Nobby' & 'Happy' Stiles, Ernie 'Tom Thumb' Taylor,. JE 'George' Travers, Alex 'Sandy' Turnbull (also 'Turnbull The Terrible'), Juan Sebastian 'La Brujita', 'The Little Witch' & 'Seba' Veron, Ernie 'Ginger' Vincent, David Lloyd 'Danny' Wallace, Enoch 'Knocker' West, Anthony Gerard 'Anto' Whelan, Liam 'Billy' Whelan, Ray 'Butch' Wilkins, Harry 'Snowball' Wilkinson.

And there are the managers - 'Big Ron' Atkinson, 'Gentleman' Jack Chapman, Tommy 'The Doc' Docherty, Sir Alex 'Fergie' Ferguson and John 'Jack' Robson. And of course we have the team's nickname: 'The Red Devils', 'Busby Babes', 'United', 'The Reds', 'Man U' and prior to that it was Newton Heath as 'The Heathens' or 'The Heath'.

NICOL, George

Born: Saltcoats, Scotland, 1905.

Career: Ardrossan Winton Rovers, Kilwinning FC, Saltcoats Victoria (1927), MANCHESTER UNITED (January 1928), Brighton & Hove Albion (May 1929), Glenavon (briefly in 1932), Gillingham (three seasons: 1932-35) Centre-forward George Nicol, brave and strong, found it difficult to come to terms with senior football at Old Trafford, despite doing well in the reserves and, indeed, on his League debut against Leicester City in February 1928 when he scored twice. But after leaving United he went on to make well over 100 senior appearances for his next three clubs, scoring over 60 goals. Once a pork butcher in Scotland, he enjoyed fishing and a round of golf.

Club record: 7 apps. 2 goals

NOBLE, Robert

Born: Manchester, 18 December 1945.

Career: Stockport & District Boys, Cheshire County Schools, MANCHESTER UNITED (apprentice June 1961, professional December 1962, forced to retire in May 1969 due to head and neck injuries suffered in a road accident two years earlier). Full-back Bobby Noble won England Youth caps and skippered United's FA Youth Cup winning team of 1964 before making his Football League debut against Leicester City in April 1966. He was firmly bedded into United's first team (ready to collect a League Championship winners medal) when he was involved in a serious car crash in April 1967. He battled gamely to regain fitness and played for the 'A' team before he was told to quit the game because of double vision. A sad end to an extremely promising career, Bobby Noble being viewed as a future England full-back.

Club record: 33 apps.

NORTH ROAD

Newton Heath's first ground was at North Road, Newton Heath, near to the carriage and wagon works where the club was founded. They occupied the ground for some 13 years, from August 1880 until the summer of 1893. It was surrounded by typical Victorian buildings, set deep in an industrial part of Manchester. The playing surface left everything to be desired and in fact when the club entered the Football League in 1892, it was regarded as one of the worst in the country. It was often transformed (by the weather) from a rock hard, uneven surface into a mud-bath during the wettest part of the winter and then back again as the season came to a close. It was embarrassing to the club and more so because there were no dressing rooms, the players having to use the Three Crowns Public House which was half-a-mile away! The Heathens left North Road for Bank Street, Clayton, in the summer of 1893, playing their final Football League match there against Accrington FC, ironically that club's final League game!

Although crowd figuress were estimated in these early days, it is believed that the record attendance was 15,000 for the visit of Sunderland on 4 March 1893 in the club's last season at the ground.

These days nothing remains to give a clue that a football ground was there, even the road has changed its name to 'Northampton Road.'

NORTHAMPTON TOWN

Summary of League results

	P	W	D	L	F	A
Division 1	2	1	1	0	7	3
Home	1	1	0	0	6	2
Away	1	0	1	0	1	1
Total	2	1	1	0	7	3

United's League results v the Cobblers:

Season	Div	Home	Away
1965-66	1	W 6-2	D 1-1

FA Cup results v the Cobblers:

	Round	Venue	Result
1969-70	5	Away	W 8-2

Fact File
In the 1970 FA Cup-tie at Northampton, a crowd of 21,771 saw George Best score a club record six goals in United's emphatic 8-2 victory.
Players with both clubs include: R Bonthron, T Boyle (Town player-manager), F Brett, JI Feehan, W Hartwell, W Inglis, A Mitchell, G Moore, L Page, W Ridding, T Smith, J Wealands.
Also associated: P Crerand (United player, Town manager)

NORTON, Joseph Patrick

Born: Leicester, summer 1890.
Career: Leicester Imperial, Nuneaton Town, Stockport County (1910), Nuneaton Town, MANCHESTER UNITED (December 1913); guested for Leicester Fosse and Nottingham Forest during WW1; Leicester City (July 1919), Bristol Rovers (1920), Swindon Town (1922), Kettering Town (1923), Atherstone Town, Hinckley Athletic, Ashby Town.
Reserve winger Joe Norton happily turned out on either flank as well as acting as an emergency centre-forward when required. After leaving Old Trafford he helped Bristol Rovers register their first-ever win in the Football League by scoring a vital goal against Newport County in September 1920.
Club record: 37 apps. 3 goals

NORWICH CITY

United's League results v the Canaries:

Season	Div	Home	Away	Season	Div	Home	Away
1934-35	2	W 5-0	L 2-3	1982-83	1	W 3-0	D 1-1
1935-36	2	W 2-1	W 5-3	1983-84	1	D 0-0	D 3-3
				1984-85	1	W 2-0	W 1-0
1937-38	2	D 0-0	W 3-2				
				1986-87	1	L 0-1	D 0-0
1972-73	1	W 1-0	W 2-0	1987-88	1	W 2-1	L 0-1
1973-74	1	D 0-0	W 2-0	1988-89	1	L 1-2	L 1-2
1974-75	2	D 1-1	L 0-2	1989-90	1	L 0-2	L 0-2
1975-76	1	W 1-0	D 1-1	1990-91	1	W 3-0	W 3-0
1976-77	1	D 2-2	L 1-2	1991-92	1	W 3-0	W 3-1
1977-78	1	W 1-0	W 3-1	1992-93	PL	W 1-0	W 3-1
1978-79	1	W 1-0	D 2-2	1993-94	PL	D 2-2	W 2-0
1979-80	1	W 5-0	W 2-0	1994-95	PL	W 1-0	W 2-0
1980-81	1	W 1-0	D 2-2				

FA Cup results v the Canaries:

	Round	Venue	Result
1905-06	2	Home	W 3-0
1958-59	3	Away	L 0-3
1966-67	4	Home	L 1-2
1990-91	5	Away	L 1-2
1993-94	4	Away	W 2-0

League Cup results v the Canaries:

	Round	Venue	Result
1974-75	Semi-final (1)	Home	D 2-2
	Semi-final (2)	Away	L 0-1
1979-80	3	Away	L 1-4

Summary of League results

	P	W	D	L	F	A
Premier League	6	5	1	0	11	3
Division 1	34	18	9	7	53	26
Division 2	8	4	2	2	18	12
Home	24	15	6	3	38	12
Away	24	12	6	6	44	29
Total	48	27	12	9	82	41

Screen Sport Super Cup
United played City home and away in the Screen Sport Super Cup in 1985-86 - the season when English clubs were banned from European competition following the Heysel Stadium tragedy.
Both matches ended in 1-1 draws and were witnessed by crowds of 20,130 at Old Trafford and 15,449 at Carrow Road.

The last 'visiting' player to score a penalty at Old Trafford in a Premiership game was Ruel Fox, for Norwich City, in their 2-2 draw with United in season 1993-94. Several have been awarded since then, but none scored.

Players with both clubs include: R Beale, S Bruce, W Dale, R Davies, T Donnelly (City reserves), D Dublin, J Hodge, E MacDougall, G Maiorana (City trialist), FH Milnes (United reserve), P Mulryne, R Newsome (WW2 both clubs), A Notman, M Phelan (also City reserve team manager), S Ratcliffe (United reserve), M Robins, S Ratcliffe (United reserve), J Sloan (United reserve & WW2), T Smith, J Travers.
Also associated: F Buckley (United player, City manager)

NOTMAN, Alexander McKeachie

Born: Edinburgh, 10 December 1979
Career: MANCHESTER UNITED (YTS 1995, professional, December 1996), Aberdeen (on loan, February 1999), Sheffield United (on loan, January 2000), Norwich City (£250,000, November 2000).
Scottish striker Alex Notman was given just 19 minutes of action by United, sending him on as a second-half substitute at Tottenham Hotspur in a League Cup-tie in December 1998 when he replaced Nicky Butt in a 3-1 defeat. He represented Scotland at both Schoolboy and Youth team levels before going on to win four Under-21 caps after signing professional forms for United. He played (with another ex-United star, Paul Mulryne) for Norwich City in the 2002 First Division Play-off Final.
Club record: one app.

NOTTINGHAM FOREST

FA Cup results v the Forest:

	Round	Venue	Result
1934-35	4	Away	D 0-0
	Replay	Home	L 0-3
1946-47	4	Home*	L 0-2
1980-81	4	Away	L 0-1
1988-89	6	Away	L 0-1
1989-90	3	Away	W 1-0

* Played at Maine Road

Summary of League results

	P	W	D	L	F	A
Premier League	10	7	2	1	31	6
Division 1	72	30	17	25	115	100
Division 2	14	7	4	3	30	22
Home	48	28	11	9	105	57
Away	48	16	12	20	71	71
Total	96	44	23	29	176	128

243

Heathens/United's League results v the Forest:

Season	Div	Home	Away	Season	Div	Home	Away
1892-93	1	L 1-3	D 1-1	1970-71	1	W 2-0	W 2-1
1893-94	1	D 1-1	L 0-2	1971-72	1	W 3-2	D 0-0
1907-08	1	W 4-0	L 0-2	1974-75	2	D 2-2	W 1-0
1908-09	1	D 2-2	L 0-2				
1909-10	1	L 2-6	L 0-2	1977-78	1	L 0-4	L 1-2
1910-11	1	W 4-2	L 1-2	1978-79	1	D 1-1	D 1-1
				1979-80	1	W 3-0	L 0-2
1931-32	2	W 3-2	L 1-2	1980-81	1	D 1-1	W 2-1
1932-33	2	W 2-1	L 2-3	1981-82	1	D 0-0	W 1-0
1933-34	2	L 0-1	D 1-1	1982-83	1	W 2-0	W 3-0
1934-35	2	W 3-2	D 2-2	1983-84	1	L 1-2	L 0-2
1935-36	2	W 5-0	D 1-1	1984-85	1	W 2-0	L 2-3
				1985-86	1	L 2-3	W 3-1
1937-38	2	W 4-3	W 3-2	1986-87	1	W 2-0	D 1-1
				1987-88	1	D 2-2	D 0-0
1957-58	1	D 1-1	W 2-1	1988-89	1	W 2-0	L 0-2
1958-59	1	D 1-1	W 3-0	1989-90	1	W 1-0	L 0-4
1959-60	1	W 3-1	W 5-1	1990-91	1	L 0-1	D 1-1
1960-61	1	W 2-1	L 2-3	1991-92	1	L 1-2	L 0-1
1961-62	1	W 6-3	L 0-1	1992-93	PL	W 2-0	W 2-0
1962-63	1	W 5-1	L 2-3				
1963-64	1	W 3-1	W 2-1	1994-95	PL	L 1-2	D 1-1
1964-65	1	W 3-0	D 2-2	1995-96	PL	W 5-0	D 1-1
1965-66	1	D 0-0	L 2-4	1996-97	PL	W 4-1	W 4-0
1966-67	1	D 1-0	L 1-4				
1967-68	1	W 3-0	L 1-3	1998-99	PL	W 3-0	W 8-1
1968-69	1	W 3-1	W 1-0				
1969-70	1	D 1-1	W 2-1				

League Cup results v the Forest:

	Round	Venue	Result
1982-83	5	Home	W 4-0
1991-92	Final	Wembley	W 1-0
1998-99	4	Home	W 2-1

Fact File

United's 8-1 win at the City Ground in 1998-99 is the biggest away win and score in the club's history.

If United's win at Millwall (q.v.) at the end of the 1933-34 season (which saved them from relegation to Division Three, North) is regarded as the pivotal match in the club's entire history, then surely the FA Cup 3rd round tie of 1989-90 must run it a close second. Alex Ferguson's managerial tenure at Old Trafford seemed ever more fragile as yet another mediocre League season reached the halfway stage. His three years in the chair had certainly seen the club's revival, but Liverpool still seemed miles ahead, now a Cup run seemed unlikely, United never having beaten Forest in the FA Cup, never even scored a goal in five previous attempts, the most recent in the previous season's Sixth Round. A late Mark Robins goal gave United an unexpected reprieve beginning a Cup run which would see Mr Ferguson's job apparently on the line every round. The FA Cup Final win over Crystal Palace would prove the catalyst for a march of triumph through the 1990s.

In the 1983-84 season when Forest won 2-1 at Old Trafford and 2-0 at The City Ground, all their four goals were scored by players who were to have or already had United connections: Viv Anderson (2), Garry Birtles and Peter Davenport.

Players with both clubs include: J Anderson, V Anderson, G Birtles, J Connachan (Forest trialist), P Davenport, D Ferguson (Forest trialist), H Green, J Hall (Forest WW2), W Hullett (United reserve), T Jackson, D Johnson (United reserve), R Keane, L Langford, J Norton (Forest WW1), R Parkinson, D Platt (United reserve, Forest player-manager), C Richards, T Sheringham, I Storey-Moore, J Walters (United reserve), E West, J Whitefoot, N Webb.

Also associated: R Atkinson (manager of both clubs), J Carey (United player, Forest manager), T Cavanagh (United assistant-manager/trainer, Forest trainer/coach), A Asham (Forest WW2, United scout).

NOTTS COUNTY

Heathens/United's League results v County:

Season	Div	Home	Away	Season	Div	Home	Away
1892-93	1	L 1-3	L 0-4	1922-23	2	D 1-1	W 6-1
1894-95	2	D 3-3	D 1-1	1925-26	1	L 0-1	W 3-0
1895-96	2	W 3-0	W 2-0				
1896-97	2	D 1-1	L 0-3	1931-32	2	D 3-3	W 2-1
				1932-33	2	W 2-0	L 0-1
1906-07	1	D 0-0	L 0-3	1933-34	2	L 1-2	D 0-0
1907-08	1	L 0-1	D 1-1	1934-35	2	W 2-1	L 0-1
1908-09	1	W 4-3	W 1-0				
1909-10	1	W 2-1	L 2-3	1974-75	2	W 1-0	D 2-2
1910-11	1	D 0-0	L 0-1				
1911-12	1	W 2-0	W 1-0	1981-82	1	W 2-1	W 3-1
1912-13	1	W 2-1	W 2-1	1982-83	1	W 4-0	L 2-3
				1983-84	1	D 3-3	L 0-1
1914-15	1	D 2-2	L 2-4				
				1991-92	1	W 2-0	D 1-1
1919-20	1	D 0-0	W 2-0				

Summary of League results

	P	W	D	L	F	A
Division 1	30	13	7	10	44	39
Division 2	18	7	7	4	30	21
Home	24	11	9	4	41	27
Away	24	9	5	10	33	33
Total	48	20	14	14	74	60

FA Cup results v County:

	Round	Venue	Result
1903-04	1	Away	D 3-3
	Replay	Home	W 2-1

Fact File

United clinched their place back in the First Division (after one season in the Second) when they drew 2-2 with County at Meadow Lane on 19 April 1975.

County had nine players booked in the League game with United at Old Trafford on Boxing Day 1984 - including the entire seven man 'wall' at a free kick.

Players with both clubs include: J Astley, W Ball, G Birtles, C Blackmore, W Boyes (United WW2), W Campbell, A Cashmore, R Chester (County trialist), J Colville (County trialist), R Ford (United reserve), J Gallacher (United WW2, County coach), R Gardner, P Gibson (United reserve), S Goater (United reserve), A Goram, J Griffiths (County WW2), R Halton, A Henrys, H McLenahan, A Mitchell, R O'Brien, A Pape, M Pinner, M Pollitt (United reserve), C Richards, P Robinson (United WW2), R Walker.

Also associated: D Brazil & F Buckley (United players, County managers), A Ashman (scout for both clubs).

NURSERY CLUBS

Mujacs FC

In the late 1930s, Chairman James Gibson and secretary Walter Crickmer set up the Manchester United Juniors Athletic Club (MUJAC) to attract the best young talent from the Manchester area. Aimed at boys aged between 14-18, the teams played in local Leagues and were run by school teachers from Manchester, Salford, Stretford, Irlam and Flixton. This could be seen as the 'cradle' of the post-war Youth Scheme, so much favoured by Matt Busby. In the immediate post WW2 period, Johnny Morris, Johnny Aston, Charlie Mitten and Stan Pearson were all players who began with the Mujacs.

Goslings FC

Not an official 'nursery' but one much favoured by United who regarded it was an unofficial source of talent. Run by Mr A Gosling, a local wholesale greengrocer and fruiterer, Gosling's FC ran for many years, producing Jack Crompton and Henry Cockburn of the post-war side. During the War years when food was in short supply, Gosling's players would return home from matches having been 'paid' with fruit and veg. During WW2 when Walter Crickmer required a player to complete his United team of 'guest' players, Gosling's could always oblige.

Boundary Park Juniors

The Oldham-based junior club has provided several United players, including Nicky Butt, David May, Gary Neville, Phil Neville, Mark Robins and Paul Scholes. David Platt was also with the 'Juniors' club.

NUTTALL, Thomas Albert B

Born: Bolton, early 1889

Career: Heywood United (1908), MANCHESTER UNITED (May 1910), Everton (£250, May 1913), Stockport County (guest, during WW1), St Mirren (1919), Northwich Victoria (early 1920), Southend United (summer 1920), Leyland FC (1921) Northwich Victoria (1922-23). A smart, compact and positive inside-forward with an eye for goal, Tom Nuttall did far better for United's second XI than he did for the first team. But after leaving Old Trafford he appeared in well over 100 first-class matches, netting over 20 goals and helping Everton win the League title in 1915.

Nuttall's father, Jack, was United's assistant-trainer prior to WW1, and a younger brother, Harry, appeared in over 300 games for Bolton and gained three England caps in the late 1920s.

Club record: 16 apps. 4 goals

O for...

OLD TRAFFORD

John H Davies, United's president, had not merely saved the club
from extinction in 1902, he was now planning for the club to
become the finest in the land. On the field, United finally achieved
promotion in 1906, won their first League title in 1908, then their
first FA Cup in 1909. The club had a top class manager in Ernest
Mangnall and many leading players; now Mr Davies planned a
move to a ground in keeping with United's drive for excellence.
Mr Davies' brewery owned a piece of land at Old Trafford about
half a mile from the famous cricket ground. It lay on the border
between Manchester and Salford (the largest city never to have had
a League club), with large populations close at hand, excellent
communications and accessibility by rail, road and tramcar. There
would be ample room for expansion with no housing in the
immediate vicinity - in short, an ideal site. Although the new
ground would be five miles from the club's origins at Newton
Heath/Clayton, Davies was certain the club would quickly attract
new patrons.

He granted the club £60,000, hiring stadium expert Archibald Leitch to design a ground, capable of holding 100,000 spectators. However, costs far exceeded budget, so the ground was scaled down slightly to 80,000. In 1910 it was ready, boasting a gigantic main stand holding 12,000 people, with plush tip-up seats; the other three sides of the ground were all open terraces, but had plenty of gangways for the safe movement of spectators.

The ground officially opened on Saturday 19 February 1910 with the visit of Liverpool; trams and trains were packed, people from Salford walked to the ground, official estimates showing a 45,000 attendance with at least 5,000 more admitted as the gatemen, unable to cope with the masses, simply opened their turnstiles. 'Sandy' Turnbull had the honour of scoring the first goal on the ground, but Liverpool spoiled the party by winning 4-3. Nevertheless, the crowd were more than pleased, staggered at the scale of the ground and its bowling green of a pitch. At last Manchester boasted a stadium as good as any in the land. Soon FA Cup semi-finals, an FA Cup Final and a replay as well as internationals were allocated to Old Trafford.

Between the wars, however, United's fortunes took a dive, the team forever struggling with poor management and poor teams. The planned expansion of the ground could not be afforded; the only improvements being the covering of the two raised corner quadrants at either end of the main stand in the late 1920s, with the United Road terracing given a cover in 1936.

By 1939 the ground was in a sorry state of disrepair. Then in 1941, because if its close proximity to the Trafford Park Industrial Estate, busily engaged on munitions work, the ground became vulnerable to air-raids by German aircraft. Eventually the ground was hit by two massive bombs, one destroying the main stand, the other the terrace covering, the pitch being badly scorched by incendiaries. United had to play their matches at Maine Road, paying a hefty rental whilst granting their landlords a share of the gate.

In 1945. The War Damage Commission granted United £4,800 to clear the debris and £17,474 to rebuild the stands. Money itself could not solve the problem, building materials were scarce after the war, priority being given to housing and businesses. It would be 1949 before United could return to Old Trafford, although reserve team football had been possible there since 1945. The main stand could not be rebuilt, so when United entertained Bolton Wanderers on 24 August 1949, there were just a couple of thousand seats installed on an area of terrace which had survived the bombing where the stand had once stood, but open to the elements. The ground capacity was about 55,000. The following year the main stand was completed, very much a utility affair, but at least it had a roof and the cover on the United Road terrace had also been restored.

In 1957, the ground's first floodlights, on four large pylons, were installed.

The next improvement was the covering of the Stretford End in 1959, followed by the installation of seats at the top of the Stretford End terracing in 1962 which was extended upwards to the ground's perimeter wall. The capacity was now about 65,000.

In 1964 events took place which would enable Old Trafford to become the ground it is today.

The FA had chosen Old Trafford as one of the grounds to host the 1966 World Cup Finals. The club was allocated £40,000 for ground improvement, but with great foresight, Chairman Louis Edwards and his board decided to use this as a launching pad for the complete redevelopment of the ground. Although it would take about 25 years for the plan to reach final fruition, it meant that each stage was part of a master plan rather than merely piecemeal additions. The United Road terrace became the site of a massive cantilever stand, seating 10,000 with standing accommodation in front - the plan envisaged the ground eventually being completely enclosed by a single cantilever roof. In 1973 this was extended to cover the Scoreboard End, linking up with the corner stand, making three sides of the ground fully covered.

A feature of these stands was the inclusion of executive boxes, 80 in all at this stage. These have now become an essential part of all new grounds, but were revolutionary at the time.

Between 1978 and 1984, the Main Stand was completely revamped with a cantilever roof and many changes 'behind the scenes' with offices and restaurants a feature, with the corner stand at the City End also given a cantilever roof. Only the Stretford End now remained to complete the original plan.

Old Trafford had, thus, so far managed to satisfy the fans' desire to stand and watch the football with plenty of seats for those whose chose that method of spectating.

However, the Hillsborough disaster followed by Lord Justice Taylor's report put a stop to all that, so that when in 1993, a 10,164 all-seater stand was completed at the Stretford End, the ground plan was complete, but now the standing areas around the other three sides of the ground would need to be converted to seats. Thus the capacity of Old Trafford was now down to a mere 44,800, which clearly would not satisfy a club with United's massive support.

In 1995, plans were unveiled for a massive new stand on the United Road side of the ground to seat 25,300 fans, covered by the biggest cantilever roof in the world. The club needed to purchase some extra ground to accommodate this giant structure, but the 'North Stand' as it became known, was opened in 1996, the ground capacity now 56,000. Still this did not satisfy demand, so an additional tier was built on top of the Stretford End (West Stand) then the Scoreboard End (East Stand) bringing the capacity up to over 68,000, greater than when the ground was mainly standing.

Thus Old Trafford is now the envy of every club. Mr Davies' foresight almost a century ago has been fully vindicated even though there were detractors at the time who thought the move away from the old club's roots, would be a disaster. Now Old Trafford is a virtual shrine, known all over the world, visited by thousands every week just to marvel at the stadium, those lucky ones who have tickets, packing the ground, every home match a sell-out. The famous ground is once more favoured as a site for FA Cup semi-finals and England internationals.

FACT FILE

The first international match at Old Trafford saw Scotland beat England 1-0 in 1926.

England's 'B' team played the United States of America at Old Trafford in 1980.

The floodlights were switched on for the first time at Old Trafford for the United v. Bolton Wanderers League Division One game on 25 March 1957 (Mid-week match, 7.30pm k.o).

The first foreign club side to play at Old Trafford was Red Star, Belgrade on 12 May 1951 when they drew 1-1 with United in a Festival of Britain game.

A first at a British club ground opened at Old Trafford on 1 May 1986 - the Manchester United museum and visitors' centre.

Chelsea are the only team to contest two FA Cup Finals at Old Trafford (1915 & 1970).

The biggest League attendance ever recorded at Old Trafford was that of 70,504 for the United-Aston Villa First Division fixture on 27 December 1920.

The biggest crowd ever to assemble at the ground did so for the FA Cup semi-final encounter between Grimsby Town and Wolves in 1939. That day almost 77,000 fans paid to see Wolves win 5-0.

In July 1971, the Football League announced that Old Trafford would be officially closed for two weeks following a knife-throwing incident during United's home League game with Newcastle United the previous season. As a result United were forced to play two 'home' games on neutral grounds - against Arsenal at Anfield and West Bromwich Albion at The Victoria Ground, Stoke.

They won them both by the same score of 3-1. An aggregate of just under 51,000 spectators attended those matches and when United played their first game at Old Trafford that season, a crowd of 45,656 saw them beat Ipswich Town 1-0.

The Old Trafford pitch is 116 yards long by 76 yards wide.

United's record win on the ground is 9-0 v. Ipswich Town, Premier League, in March 1995. They also beat QPR 8-1 in March 1969.

The capacity of the ground in 2002 was officially 68,174, but several hundred seats are invariably left vacant to satisfy the principle of segregation.

In May 1987, for the first time, two Rugby League Premiership double-headers took place at Old Trafford: Wigan against Warrington and Hunslet versus Swinton.

Since then regular high-profile rugby matches have been staged at the ground including the first Rugby League international when Australia beat England 14-10 in front of 46,615 fans in November 1990.

The Lambert and Butler cricket competition was staged at Old Trafford in September 1981 (under floodlights). The four counties who took part were Derbyshire, Lancashire, Nottinghamshire and Yorkshire.

Several Jehovah's Witness conventions have also taken place at Old Trafford, plus a handful of rock and pop concerts, including 'The Vagabond Tour' featuring Rod Stewart, Status Quo and Joe Cocker in June 1991 when almost 40,000 fans turned up. Also singing at the ground have been Russell Watson and Simply Red with ardent United fan Mick Hucknall.

Other major matches staged at Old Trafford

Date	Competition	Match	Attendance
31.03.10	FA Cup sf replay	Barnsley 3 Everton 0	40,000
26.04.11	FA Cup Final replay	Bradford City 1 Newcastle United 0	66,646
28.03.14	FA Cup semi-final	Sheffield United 0 Burnley 0	55,812
24.04.15	FA Cup Final	Chelsea 0 Sheffield United 3	49,557
23.03.21	FA Cup sf replay	Wolverhampton W 3 Cardiff City 1	44,863
07.05.21	Division 2	Stockport County 0 Leicester Fosse 0	13*
14.05.21	Lancashire Cup Final	Manchester City 2 Bolton Wanderers 1	20,000
24.03.23	FA Cup semi-final	Bolton Wanderers 1 Sheffield United 0	71,779
11.02.24	FA Cup 2nd rd 2nd rep	Halifax Town 0 Manchester City 3	28,128
15.03.26	FA Cup rd 2, 2nd rep	Bolton Wds 1 Nottingham Forest 0	30,952
17.04.26	International	England 0 Scotland 1	55,000
06.12.26	FA Cup 1st rd 2nd rep	Rhyl 2 Stoke City 1	3,000
24.03.28	FA Cup semi-final	Sheffield United 2 Huddersfield T 2	69,260
12.05.28	Lancashire Cup Final	Manchester City 3 Bury 1	10,000
11.05.29	Lancashire Cup Final	Manchester United 2 Blackburn Rovers 1	18,000
22.03.30	FA Cup semi-final	Huddersfield Town 2 Sheffield Wed 1	69,292
14.03.31	FA Cup semi-final	Everton 0 West Brom Albion 1	69,241
10.02.36	FA Cup 4th rd 2nd rep	Bradford Park Avenue 2 WBA 0	11,685
30.01.39	FA Cup rd 4, 2nd rep	Sheffield Wednesday 2 Chester 0	15,321
25.03.39	FA Cup semi-final	Grimsby Town 0 Wolves 5	76,962
17.05.41	Lancashire Cup Final	United 1 Burnley 0	4,000
24.04.48	Schoolboy Intern'l	England 4 Northern Ireland 0	45,000
14.05.51	Lancashire Cup Final	United 2 Bury 1	6,000
24.01.55	FA Cup 3rd rd 4th rep	Bury 2 Stoke City 3	22,549
30.10.57	Representative match	FA XI 6. The Army 3	15,000
27.11.58	FA Cup 1st rd 2nd rep	Hartlepools Utd 2 Rochdale 1	4,000
02.05.61	FL Cup sf replay	Aston Villa 2 Burnley 1	7,953
26.02.62	FA Cup rd 5, 2nd rep	Preston North End 1 Liverpool 0	43,944
23.11.64	FA Cup rd 1, 2nd rep	Barrow 0 Grimsby Town 2	9,292
13.07.66	World Cup group 3	Portugal 3 Hungary 1	29,886
16.07.66	World Cup group 3	Portugal 3 Bulgaria 0	25,438
20.07.66	World Cup group 3	Hungary 3 Bulgaria 1	24,129
27.04.68	FA Cup semi-final	Everton 1 Leeds United 0	62,890
16.04.69	Lancashire Cup Final	United 1 Liverpool 0	3,500
20.04.70	FA Cup Final replay	Chelsea 2 Leeds United 1	62,078
21.12.70	FA Cup 2nd rd 2nd rep	Barnsley 0 Rhyl 2	3,296
08.02.71	FL Cup rd 4, 2nd rep	Huddersfield T 0 Stoke City 1	39,302
23.03.71	FA Cup semi-final	Everton 1 Liverpool 2	62,144
26.01.72	FL Cup sf 2nd replay	Stoke City 3 West Ham United 2	49,247
20.04.72	Lancashire Cup Final	United 2 Burnley 2	3,000
30.10.73	FL Cup 2nd rd replay	Manchester City 4 Walsall 0	13,646
30.03.74	FA Cup semi-final	Liverpool 0 Leicester City 0	59,897
03.01.75	FA Cup rd 3 replay	Altrincham 0 Everton 2	35,530
13.04.77	FL Cup Final 2nd rep	Aston Villa 3 Everton 2	54,749
09.11.77	FL Cup rd 3, 2nd rep	Manchester City 3 Luton Town 2	13,043
22.03.78	FL Cup Final replay	Liverpool 0 Nottingham Forest 1	54,290
09.11.78	FL Cup 3rd rd 2nd rep	Luton Town 2 Manchester City 3	13,043
14.10.80	'B' International	England 1 USA 0	7,176
07.05.89	FA Cup semi-final	Nottingham Forest 1 Liverpool 3	37,982
24.05.91	International	Argentina 1 Russia 1 (Rous Cup)	23,743
31.03.96	FA Cup semi-final	Liverpool 3 Aston Villa 0	39,021
09.06.96	Euro '96 group C	Germany 2 Czech Republic 0	37,300
16.06.96	Euro '96 group C	Russia 0 Germany 3	50,760
19.06.96	Euro '96 group C	Italy 0 Germany 0	53,740
23.06.96	Euro '96 quarter-final	Germany 2 Croatia 1	43,412
26.06.96	Euro '96 semi-final	France 0 Czech Rep 0 (CZ won 6-5 on pens)	43,877
13.04.97	FA Cup semi-final	Chesterfield 3 Middlesbrough 3	49,640
24.05.97	International	England 2 South Africa 1	52,676
05.04.98	FA Cup semi-final	Newcastle United 1 Sheffield United 0	53,452
11.04.99	FA Cup semi-final	Newcastle United 1 Tottenham Hotspur 0	53,609
08.04.01	FA Cup semi-final	Arsenal 2 Tottenham Hotspur 1	63,541
10.11.01	International	England 1 Sweden 1	64,413
14.04.02	FA Cup semi-final	Arsenal 1 Middlesbrough 0	61,168

* Only 13 spectators paid for admission to this game - although the actual attendance was given as 1,500 ...as some fans stayed behind after watching the United v. Derby County League game which had kicked off earlier in the afternoon. (see Attendances).

The European Champions League Final is scheduled to be played at Old Trafford in May 2003.

O'BRIEN, William Francis

Born: Dublin, 5 September 1964

Career: Stella Maris FC, Drumcondra (briefly), Bohemians, Shamrock Rovers, MANCHESTER UNITED (£50,000, October 1986), Newcastle United (£275,000, November 1988), Tranmere Rovers (£350,000, early 1994). Retired, June 1999.

A Republic of Ireland Schoolboy, Youth and Under-23 international and League of Ireland Championship winner with Shamrock Rovers before moving to Old Trafford (signed by Ron Atkinson) midfielder Liam O'Brien's tally of first team outings for the Reds included 19 as a substitute - his debut coming in December 1986 against Leicester City. Having failed to live up to expectations, he did much better at St James' Park, playing his part in Newcastle's Division One Championship-winning season of 1992-93, also gaining a total of 16 full caps for Eire. He scored 22 goals in 185 games for Newcastle and followed up by netting 12 times in 188 outings for Tranmere. Another player missed by United?

Club record: 36 apps. 2 goals

O'BRIEN, W George

Born: Lancshire, circa 1877

Career: Everton, NEWTON HEATH (March-April 1902)

Reserve winger George O'Brien, an amateur, was the last Everton player signed by the Heathens before the club changed its name to Manchester United.

Club record: one app.

O'CONNELL, Patrick

Born: Dublin, 8 March 1887. Died: London, 27 February 1959

Career: Belfast Celtic (1906), Sheffield Wednesday (1908), Hull City (1912), MANCHESTER UNITED (£1,000, May 1914), guested for Clapton Orient and Rochdale during WW1; Dumbarton (August 1919), Ashington (summer 1920, appointed player-manager for season 1921-22 - their first in the Football League), thereafter as manager/coach in Spain with Racing Santander (1922-29), possibly Atletico Madrid (1929-34), Real Betis, known then as Betis Balompie (1934-35), FC Barcelona (1935-38), Real Betis for a second time (1938-39), FC Sevilla (1940-45), Real Betis once more (1945-47) and Racing Santander again (1947-49). After retiring he chose to live in Spain, acting as a scout for Huelva (1949-58). He later returned to London where he died in poverty at the age of 71.

Half-back Pat O'Connell, despite winning five Irish caps during his spells with Sheffield Wednesday and Hull City, had made less than 90 senior appearances in six seasons with the two Yorkshire clubs. Nevertheless United splashed out £1,000 for this tough competitor, making him captain (Charlie Roberts having departed to Oldham Athletic)... and he gave some inspiring displays during the last season before WW1, going on to play in a Victory international (Ireland v. Scotland) in 1919. Two years later (as an Ashington player) he represented the North Eastern League against the Central League. His relatively modest playing career gave no inkling to his subsequent success in coaching over in Spain which included three excellent years in charge of FC Barcelona. Just as the Great War had blighted his playing career at Old Trafford, now the Spanish Civil War (1936-39) threatened to annihilate the Catalan champions. To escape the hostilities, O'Connell took the team to Mexico and the USA for a six month long 'tour' earning sufficient revenue to keep the club in business. On returning to Barcelona, the city was under the regime of Franco's fascist forces, but his Irish charm persuaded the occupying troops to retain the ground as a football stadium, despite having shot and killed the club president. O'Connell's name now enjoys legendary status at the famous old club. On his return to Britain in 1939, WW2 further hindered his football livelihood, so he decamped back to neutral Spain, coaching FC Sevilla throughout the hostilities. Even in the 1930s, when football managers were generally office-bound, O'Connell set the trend in Spain by training with the players in his football kit, eschewing the three-piece suit and buttonhole which was the uniform of the pre-WW2 manager.

As a manager/coach, he guided Real Betis to the Spanish League title for the first time in their history in 1935 and in successive seasons after that he saw Barcelona become champions of Catalonia in 1936 and the Mediterranean League twelve months later. He is still well-respected and admired by the Barcelona supporters

Club record: 35 apps. 2 goals.

O'FARRELL, Frank

Manager of MANCHESTER UNITED from June 1971 until December 1972, Frank O'Farrell's career in football spanned a total of more than 40 years. Born in Cork on 9 October 1927, he played initially for Cork United before joining West Ham United as a wing-half in January 1948. He moved from Upton Park to Preston North End in November 1956 but was forced to quit League soccer in 1961 due to injury. At that juncture he became player-manager of Weymouth and between 1965 and 1968 took charge of Torquay United, managing Leicester City from December 1968 until taking over the reins at Old Trafford. Almost a year after his departure from United, O'Farrell was appointed manager of Cardiff City (November 1972). He remained at Ninian Park until April 1974 when he became manager/coach of the Iranian national team, a position he held for a year or so prior to returning to the hot-seat at Torquay in November 1976, remaining there until March 1977. He went back for a third spell in June 1981 and stayed for a year before accepting the position of general manager at Plainmoor which he held until the summer of 1983 when he withdrew form serious football at the age of 56.

Capped by the Republic of Ireland nine times, O'Farrell played in more than 200 League and Cup games for the Hammers. As a manager he first took Weymouth to successive runners-up spots in the Southern League Cup as well as bringing the Southern League Championship to the south-coast club. He then successfully guided Torquay to promotion from Division Four in 1966 and took Leicester to the FA Cup Final in 1969 (beaten by Manchester City) and to the Second Division Championship in 1971. He found if difficult to follow in the footsteps of Sir Matt Busby at Old Trafford, United finishing a disappointing eighth at the end of his first season in charge, despite topping the table at the halfway stage. Unfortunately he and his assistant (Malcolm Musgrove) were sacked after only 18 months in office. He spent quite a bit of money whilst at the club, bringing in Ian Storey-Moore, Ted MacDougall and Martin Buchan (among others) with Buchan proving to be his best acquisition by far. O'Farrell now lives in retirement in Torquay...still checking out United's results!

OFFSIDE LAW

Until 1925 the offside rule had remained the same since the laws of the game had been revised in 1866: i.e that THREE players were required to render an attacking player on-side. After much pressure owing to certain teams ruthlessly exploiting this law with many matches being rendered farcical with as many as 40 'offsides', the International Board met in Paris, deciding that in future only TWO players would now be required; this is still the case today.

However, the 1925-26 season led to the total goals in League football increasing by a staggering 35% from 4,700 to 6,373. Huddersfield Town, in winning their third successive title, conceded 60 goals (still the best in the First Division as against only 28 the season before). Burnley and Manchester City both topped the century of goals against!

It is difficult to see how United coped in that first season of the 'new offside law' as they had won promotion the previous year.

In 1924-25, based in Division Two, they scored just 57 goals when finishing runners-up. Then in 1925-26, playing in Division One, they increased their tally to 66, finishing in ninth position.

Defensively in 1924-25 they conceded a mere 23 goals; in 1925-26 this figure increased to 73, but they were playing against better opposition.

Clearly the defence found more problems in adapting than the forwards. Most clubs adapted by moving their attacking centre-half back to a more defensive position between the two full-backs (a 'back three'). Frank Barson was United's centre-half before and after the change; Barson a 'hard man' would have had little difficulty in changing his role.

By the 1970s the average goals per match had returned to the pre-1925 levels.

O'KANE, John Andrew

Born: November, 15 November 1974

Career: MANCHESTER UNITED (trainee, 1991, professional January 1993), Wimbledon (on loan, June 1995), Bury (on loan, October 1996 & January 1997), Bradford City (on loan October 1997), Everton (£250,000+ January 1998), Burnley (on loan, October 1998), Bolton Wanderers (November 1999).

Full-back John O'Kane made just seven senior appearances for United (two as a substitute) before moving to Everton. He helped Bolton reach the Premiership in 2001.

Club record: 7 apps.

OLD TRAFFORD

Refer to front of section.

OLDHAM ATHLETIC

United's League results v the Latics:

Season	Div	Home	Away	Season	Div	Home	Away
1910-11	1	D 0-0	W 3-1	1931-32	2	W 5-1	W 5-1
1911-12	1	W 3-1	D 2-2	1932-33	2	W 2-0	D 1-1
1912-13	1	D 0-0	D 0-0	1933-34	2	L 2-3	L 0-2
1913-14	1	W 4-1	D 2-2	1934-35	2	W 4-0	L 1-3
1914-15	1	L 1-3	L 0-1				
				1974-75	2	W 3-2	L 0-1
1919-20	1	D 1-1	W 3-0				
1920-21	1	W 4-1	D 2-2	1991-92	1	W 1-0	W 6-3
1921-22	1	L 0-3	D 1-1	1992-93	PL	W 3-0	L 0-1
				1993-94	PL	W 3-2	W 5-2
1923-24	2	W 2-0	L 2-3				
1924-25	2	L 0-1	W 3-0				

FA Cup results v the Latics:

	Round	Venue	Result
1912-13	3	Away	D 0-0
	Replay	Home	L 1-2
1950-51	3	Home	W 4-1
1989-90	SF	Maine Road	D 3-3 aet
	Replay	Maine Road	W 2-1 aet
1993-94	SF	Wembley	D 1-1 aet
	Replay	Maine Road	W 4-1

League Cup results v the Latics:

	Round	Venue	Result
1991-92	4	Home	W 2-0

Summary of League results

	P	W	D	L	F	A
Premier League	4	3	0	1	11	5
Division 1	18	7	8	3	33	22
Division 2	14	7	1	6	30	18
Home	18	11	3	4	38	19
Away	18	6	6	6	36	26
Total	36	17	9	10	74	45

Fact File

Players with both clubs include: S Ackerley (United reserve), A Ainsworth (Latics WW1), B Birch, D Brazil, J Broad (United reserve), A Broome, M Buchan, G Burnett (United WW2), A Cashmore, L Cassidy, C Chadwick (United WW2), A Downie, R Duckworth jnr (United reserve), P Edwards, R Ferrier, T Fitzsimmons, A Goram, I Greaves, J Hacking, J Hall, (Latics WW2), W Halligan (United WW1), H Haslam (United trialist, WW2), W Heseltine (United reserve), H Heywood, A Hulme, G Hunter, D Irwin, A Jackson (United reserve), W Johnston, S Jones & T Jones (both United reserves), F Kennedy, P Kennedy, F Knowles (Latics WW1), J Koffman (United reserve), H Lappin, T Lowrie, G Lyons, S McGarvey, W McGlen, H McShane, M Pollitt (United reserve), W Porter, A Quixall, M Radcliffe (United WW2), T Reid, A Ritchie (also Latics manager), C Roberts (Latics player & manager), E Round, H Rowley, R Seddon (United trialist), J Silcock; W Snape, H Stock & H Tilling (both United WW2), W Toms, G Wall, G Walsh, J Walters (United reserve), J Warner (Latics player-coach), J Wealands, H Whalley (United WW2), F Worrall (United WW2).

Also associated: H Bamlett (manager of both clubs), J Rowley (United player, Latics manager: two spells), J Crompton (United player & coach, Latics manager), H Cockburn (United player, Latics assistant-manager/coach).

OLIVE, Robert Leslie

Born: Salford, 27 April 1928

Career: MANCHESTER UNITED (groundstaff, June 1942, registered as an amateur February 1952, retired February 1958).

Les Olive had a remarkable career at Old Trafford, although many supporters might not be familiar with his name. Initially signing for the club on schoolboy forms, he worked in the offices, helping over-worked secretary Walter Crickmer (q.v). He played regularly for United's junior sides without achieving much success. Indeed, he never looked like making it into League football.

His work in the offices gradually consumed more of his time, yet he always kept himself fit and made himself available (if required) for any 'A' or 'B' team matches, occasionally lining up for the reserves in a wide variety of positions.

He must have been amazed, however, when in April 1953, with United's three senior goalkeepers, Reg Allen, Jack Crompton and Ray Wood all injured, he was asked by manager Matt Busby to play between the posts for the first XI in a League game at Newcastle! He did well and helped United win 2-1, Tommy Taylor scoring twice in front of almost 39,000 fans. He played in the next match as well, a 2-2 home draw with West Bromwich Albion but then returned to the Old Trafford offices to continue his work behind a desk…and not a defence!

In 1955, Olive stepped up as Walter Crickmer's assistant and following the Munich air crash when sadly the faithful Crickmer was among those who lost their lives, Olive took over the reins from the great man. He held the position as secretary for the next 30 years, retiring in 1988. Later that year he was welcomed back to Old Trafford as a director, a position he holds to this day (2002).

In fact, he and Crickmer between them served as United's club secretary for a total of 62 years. Olive has taken his service with Manchester United FC to the 60-year mark. What an achievement.

Club record: 2 apps.

OLNEY, Patrick

Born: Cardiff, circa 1954

Career: MANCHESTER UNITED (trialist, March 1973, released May 1974).

Reserve forward Pat Olney made one substitute appearance for United, scoring in the process against Verona in an Anglo-Italian Cup-tie at home in May 1973. He replaced Willie Morgan in a 4-1 win. He did not play league football after leaving Old Trafford.

Club record: one app.

OLSEN, Jesper

Born: Fakse, Denmark, 20 March 1961

Career: FC Naestvedt (Denmark), Ajax Amsterdam (1981), MANCHESTER UNITED (£700,000, July 1984), Bordeaux (£400,000, November 1988), SM Caen, France (1990-92).

An enterprising winger, Jesper Olsen's tally of 24 goals for United included a hat-trick against WBA in a First Division game at Old Trafford in February 1986. A former bank clerk, he won two Dutch League championship medals and a Cup winning medal with Ajax, helped Denmark win the European Championships in 1984 and then did very well during his four years with United, gaining an FA Cup winners medal in 1985 while at the same time taking his total of full international caps past the 25 mark.

Club record: 178 apps. 24 goals

OLYMPIAKOS PIRAEUS

United met the Greek club Olympiakos in the European Champions League Group Stage in season 2001-02. After a 2-0 away win (Beckham and Cole on target) in front of more than 73,000 fans, the return fixture attracted 66,679 fans to Old Trafford as the Reds won 3-0 (with Van Nistelrooy, Solskjaer and Giggs the scorers).

OLYMPIQUE MARSEILLE

United met the French club Marseille at home and away in the 1st stage of the 1999-2000 European Champions League. Honours were even, with one win apiece: 2-1 to United at Old Trafford, 1-0 to Marseille in France.

Players with both clubs: F Barthez, L Blanc, E Cantona (also Director of Football at Marseille), L Cunningham, W Prunier.

O'NEIL, Thomas Patrick

Born: St Helens, Lancashire, 25 October 1952

Career: St Helens Schools, Lancashire Schoolboys, MANCHESTER UNITED (apprentice July 1968, professional November 1969), Blackpool (on loan, January-February 1973), Southport (August 1973), Tranmere Rovers (1978), Halifax Town (1980), Altrincham (summer 1982), Southport (autumn 1982), St Helens Town (1984), Warrington Town (1987), Irlam Town (assistant-manager, 1988), Skelmersdale United (manager, 199-92).

As a youngster, full-back Tommy O'Neil represented England Schoolboys at both rugby and soccer, captaining St Helens Boys and also Lancashire. A fighter to the last, never shirking a tackle, he made his League debut for United in the Manchester derby in May 1971. He eventually lost his place in the side (to Tony Young) following a change of manager. He broke his leg whilst a Halifax player but recovered and later captained St Helens Town at Wembley when they lifted the 1987 FA Vase.

Club record: 68 apps..

ONES THAT GOT AWAY!

Here are some of the many players released, sold or given away by United who went on to appear in 200 or so senior games and/or scored plenty of goals with other clubs (listed in A-Z order);

•After leaving United, inside-right 'Alf' Ainsworth played in over 200 games either side of WW2 for New Brighton (51 goals).

•David Bain made over 200 appearances for his four other clubs after leaving United in 1922 with only 23 senior games under his belt.

•James Bain, brother of David (q.v) made 191 League appearances alone after he departed from Old Trafford in 1928, having had just four outings for United..

•John Barber went on to make 214 League appearances and netted 22 goals after leaving United in 1924 with only four senior games under his belt.

•Thomas Andrew Barnett, released by United in 1928 without any senior games to his credit, went on to score 144 goals in 395 League games for Watford.

•Peter Beardsley made just one appearance for United (45 minutes of action) and then became an England international as well as making over 880 senior appearances for a variety of clubs including Everton, Liverpool and Newcastle. He scored more than 260 goals.

•George W Beel, a United trialist in 1919, failed to make an impression and was quickly released by the club. Over the next 14 years he amassed 458 League appearances and scored 243 goals while serving with Lincoln (twice), Merthyr Town, Chesterfield, Burnley and Rochdale in that order..

•Frank Brett made only ten appearances for United but thereafter he amassed well over 400 in the Football League for Northampton Town and Brighton.

•Jimmy Broad, a reserve with both Manchester City and United at the start of his career, went on to accumulate almost 200 senior appearances (over 90 goals scored) while assisting eight other clubs....

•Wayne Bullimore, released by United in 1991, went on to amass almost 200 senior appearances before dropping out of the Football League with Scarborough in 1999..

•Herbert R Cartman was handed just three senior appearances by United in 1922-23. He went on to score 33 goals in 215 League games for Tranmere Rovers (up to 1930).

•Brian Carey, capped by the Republic of Ireland whilst at Old Trafford, failed to get a single game in the first XI for United. He moved to Leicester in 1993 (after loan spells with Wrexham) and in 2002, following a permanent transfer to Wrexham, he passed the milestone of 250 senior games.

•William Chapman played in more than 200 senior games for Watford during the late 1920s/early '30s after making 26 appearances for United.

•Jonathan Clark, after one substitute outing for United, went on to amass 250 appearances for Derby County, Preston North End, Bury and Carlisle United.

•Full-back Warney Cresswell, a United reserve (no first XI outings) went on to become one of England's best ever players, winning seven full caps for England and made over 600 senior appearances after leaving Old Trafford in 1915..

•Welsh international centre-forward Stan Davies was a trialist with United in 1919 but was rejected as he was considered too frail! He went on to win 18 caps (in six different positions) and scored over 100 goals in 240 games with PNE, Everton, WBA, Birmingham, Cardiff, Rotherham & Barnsley.

•Goalkeeper Fraser Digby was sold to Swindon for £32,000 in 1986 having failed to get a first team game with the Reds. Over the next 13 years he made 417 League & 88 Cup appearances for the Robins. He also won five England Under-21 caps.

•Richard Duckworth junior was with United in 1926 but never made the first XI. After leaving Old Trafford he went on to make well over 300 senior appearances as a half-back while serving mainly with Chesterfield, Southport, Chester, Rotherham and York.

•Eamonn Dunphy left United in 1965 without ever playing in a senior game for the club. Over the next eleven years he amassed in excess of 500 League and Cup appearances while serving with York, Millwall, Charlton and Reading. He also won 23 caps for the Republic of Ireland..

•Dennis Fidler was an amateur with United before joining Manchester City in 1957. Over the next 21 years, playing also for Port Vale, Grimsby, Halifax and Darlington, he scored 68 goals in more than 250 League & Cup appearances as a professional.

•Peter Fletcher, a reserve with United in the early 1970s, had only a handful of senior outings for the Reds but after leaving the club he went on to appear in over 200 senior games (1974-81) while serving with Hull, Stockport and Huddersfield.

•Bryce Fulton failed to make United's first XI but after leaving Old Trafford in 1957 he went on to appear in over 200 League games for Exeter City and Plymouth Argyle.

•Right-winger Keith Gillespie, sold by United to Newcastle as part of the Andy Cole deal, made only 14 first team appearances during his time at Old Trafford, but since 1995 he's now taken his overall tally of first team outings to well past the 250 mark, while also establishing himself as a regular in the Northern Ireland side.

•Leaving Old Trafford in 1970 with only a nine senior outings to his name, Don Givens went on to amass an overall tally of 408 League appearances, scoring 113 goals, before moving to Switzerland in 1981. He also won a total of 56 full caps for the Republic of Ireland.

•By May 2002, striker Shaun Goater, released by United in 1989 without making the first team, had scored well over 200 goals at competitive level playing for Rotherham, Bristol City, Notts County and Manchester City - and had been capped 19 times by Bermuda.

251

•Reg Halton was allowed to leave United in 1937 after just four first XI appearances. He went on to play in a total of 244 League games for his other clubs (114 with Bury) up to 1953.

•Tom Heron, just three appearances for United, later starred in almost 200 games for York (1961-65).

•Andy Hill, capped by England at Youth level whilst with United, failed to make the first XI at Old Trafford, but after leaving the club he went on to accumulate 264 League appearances, including almost 100 with rivals Manchester City and 100 for Port Vale.

•David Jones was with Newton Heath in 1887-88 but was released without playing any senior games. He made 228 League appearances for Bolton (1887-98) & 115 for Manchester City (1898-1902).

•Peter Jones, given away by United, developed into a fine player and between 1959-68 amassed well over 300 senior appearances, including 226 in the League for Wrexham.

•Albert Kinsey made one FA Cup appearance for United (in 1965) and after leaving the club he later had 300 games for Wrexham, scoring almost 100 goals.

•Full-back Cyril Knowles was an amateir with Manchester United. He later became a full England international, made over 400 League appearances for Middlesbrough and Tottenham Hotspur.

•Defender Frank Kopel made only 12 senior appearances for United. He later moved to Scotland where he played over 300 games for Dundee United (1972-82).

•Defender Martin Lane, a United reserve in 1979-80, left Old Trafford without any senior appearances to his name. Over the next 12 years he was handed in excess of 300 League and Cup games while serving with Chester, Wrexham, Coventry and Walsall.

•Nobby Lawton made only 36 first-class appearances for United (1958-63) but after leaving the club he went on to add well over 300 more to his tally in major competitions.

•Eddie Lewis scored 11 goals in 24 League and FA Cup games for United in the early 1950s. After leaving Old Trafford in 1955 he went on to appear in well over 200 competitive matches for Leyton Orient, Preston and West Ham.

•John Lowey, a United reserve team player, left Old Trafford for Chicago without ever playing in the first team. After returning from the States he went on to make 217 appearances in the Football League (1977-88) while assisting Blackburn, Port Vale, Sheffield Wednesday, Wigan Athletic, Chesterfield, York and PNE.

•Sean McAuley, honoured by Scotland at Youth team level whilst with United, left Old Trafford without any first team games to his name, but thereafter he did well and over the next ten years (1992-2002) he appeared in over 300 competitive games while serving with St Johnstone, Chesterfield, Hartlepool, Scunthorpe, Scarborough & Rochdale.

•Ken McDonald left United in 1924 with only nine first team outings to his name. He later made over 200 League & Cup appearances up to 1930 with Bradford PA, Hull & Halifax (150 goals).

•Defender Pat McGibbon played once for United (sent-off) and after leaving the club became an established player, appearing in over 225 games for Wigan Athletic (1997-2002).

•Midfielder Alan McLoughlin left Old Trafford in 1986 without any first team outings to his name. Over the next 16 years he amassed over 560 senior appearances and won 42 caps for the Eire with Swindon, Torquay, Southampton, Aston Villa, Portsmouth, Wigan Athletic and Rochdale.

•Sammy McMillan scored 8 goals in 15 outings for United whom he served for six years (1957-63) before taking his career record to over 100 goals in more than 350 senior appearances

•Walter McMillen, capped three times by Northern Ireland as a United player, made less than 30 senior appearances for the club (1929-33) but afterwards he amassed almost 200 (176 in the Football League) while playing for Chesterfield and Millwall up to WW2.

•Jonathan Macken, capped by England at Youth team level but not given a senior outing by United, has gone on to score well over 70 goals for Preston North End (from 1997 before his £5 million transfer to Manchester City in March 2002..

•Midfielder Gary Micklewight left Old Trafford in 1979. Over the next 17 years he amassed well over 500 League and Cup appearances for QPR, Derby and Gillingham. He played in the 1982 FA Cup Final for QPR v. Spurs.

•Ian Moir, with 45 League games for United, went on to play in a further 276 after leaving the Reds.

•Jimmy Nicholson moved from United in 1964, having played in 58 League games. Over the next 12 years he added another 364 League appearances to his tally (with Huddersfield Town and Bury) and took his tally of full caps for Northern Ireland to 41.

•Midfielder Liam O'Brien made just 37 appearances for United (19 as a sub) before going on to accumulate a total of 373 with his two other clubs, Newcastle and Tranmere, also winning 16 full caps for Eire.

•Ray O'Brien, released by United in 1974 (following his arrival from Shelbourne), amassed 323 League and appearances for Notts Co, also assisted Derby, and won four full and two Under-23 caps for the Republic of Ireland over the next 10 years.

•Peter O'Sullivan left United as a 19 year-old in 1970 having failed to earn an outing in the first XI. Over the next 14 years, playing for Brighton, Fulham, Charlton, Reading & Aldershot (as well as in Hong Kong) he accumulated a fine record of 509 League appearances (435 for Albion). He was also capped by Wales at senior & Under-23 levels.

•Goalkeeper Stephen Pears made just five first team appearances for United and over 420 for Middlesbrough (1985-95)..

•David Platt was discarded by United in 1984. After that his career flourished, playing for Crewe, Aston Villa, in Italy, with Arsenal, Nottingham Forest (player-manager) and for England. He scored over 200 goals in 585 appearances in all competitions, netting 27 times in 62 full internationals. He is now coach of the England Under-21 side.

•Goalkeeper Mike Pollitt was released by United in 1991 without having a single outing in the first XI. Since then he has accumulated well over 350 senior appearances while assisting ten other clubs.

•Goalkeeper Terry Poole, a junior with United, was never given a senior outing by the club and after leaving Old Trafford in 1968, he went on to appear in over 200 League games for Huddersfield, while also assiting Bolton and Sheffield United.

•Striker Andy Rammell, after failing to make United's first XI, went on to score almost 90 goals in well over 400 competitive games for Barnsley, Southend, Walsall & Wrexham between 1990-2002.

•Simon Ratcliffe left United for Norwich City in 1987 with no first team outings to his name. He went on to appear in 214 League games for Brentford and over 100 for Gillingham.

•Goalkeeper Jimmy Rimmer did very well after leaving United for whom he made less than 50 senior appearances. He went on to amass in excess of 550 games in all competitions including 470 in the Football League. He won both First Division Championship & European Cup winners' medals with Aston Villa and gained a full England cap.

•Andy Ritchie spent three years at Old Trafford (1977-80) scoring 13 goals in 42 games. Over the next 22 years he added a further 197 goals to his tally in 619 first-class appearances.

•After leaving United Matt Robinson went on to make over 200 appearances for Barrow and Chester.

•Welsh international midfielder Robbie Savage failed to break into United's first XI and left Old Trafford on a free transfer to Crewe in 1994. He appeared in 95 senior games for the Gresty Road club before switching to Leicester for £400,000 in 1997. Over the next five years he starred for the Foxes in almost 200 competitive games, gaining a League Cup winners' medal in 2000, while also taking his tally of full caps past the 20 mark, having also represented his country at Youth and Under-21 levels. In May 2002 he joined Birmingham City for £2.5 million.

•John Scott, three games for United, went on to appear in 240 League matches for Grimsby Town (51 goals scored) and also served with York City after leaving Old Trafford in 1956.

•Robert W Smith spent four years as a professional at Old Trafford (1961-65) failing to get a senior outing. Over the next eight years (to 1973) he appeared in over 300 League and Cup games for Scunthorpe, Grimsby, Brighton, Chester and Hartlepool.

•Tommy Spratt, an England Youth international, failed to get a senior game with United but after leaving Old Trafford in 1961 he went on to appear in 468 League matches while serving with Bradford Park Avenue, Torquay (118 outings), Workington (144), York and Stockport.

•England Youth international winger Peter Sutcliffe, transferred by United in 1975 without playing in the senior side, went on to amass a fine record of 200 League outings while serving with Stockport County, Port Vale and Chester. He also played for Bangor City (Wales).

•James Thomson - just six games for United - went on to score over 80 goals in more than 350 League and Cup appearances in post-war football with St Mirren (1918-28)..

•Dennis Walker amassed over 200 League appearances after leaving United for whom he had just one senior game.

•Gary Walsh made just over 60 appearances for United (1985-88) but he has now passed the 200 mark with other clubs, having had two spells with Middlesbrough.

•Joe Walton (23 games for United) spent 14 years with PNE for whom he made 401 appearances.

•Ashley Westwood, an England Youth international left United in 1995. He's now played in more than 200 games for Crewe, Bradford City and Sheffield Wednesday.

•Eric Westwood, an amateur with United in 1937, later made 248 League appearances for Manchester City (1938-53) and also represented the Football League & England 'B'.

•Goalkeeper Walter Whittaker - just three League games for United - went on to make 425 appearances after leaving the club!

•Osher Williams, a junior player at Old Trafford, was released in 1977 and over the next 11 years appeared in well over 300 competitive games while serving in turn with Southampton, Gateshead, Exeter, Stockport, Port Vale and PNE.

•Bill Yates failed to impose himself at United who released him in 1906. Thereafter he went on to appear in 260 League & Cup games with Hearts, Portsmouth, Coventry over a period of seven years.

•England Youth international Eric Royston Young, a United reserve with no first team outings to his name, left Old Trafford in 1972 and over the next six years appeared in almost 200 competitive games for Peterborough, Walsall, Stockport and Darlington.

O'SHAUGHNESSEY, T

Born: Lancashire
Career: NEWTON HEATH (1890-92).
An unknown reserve inside or centre-forward who was recruited by the Heathens prior to the start of the 1890-91 season. His only senior game for the club was in the FA Cup against Bootle in October 1890. Three months later when playing in a friendly game against the Canadian tourists (in January 1891) he suffered a broken leg and it is understood he failed to make a full recovery and was released in the summer of 1892.
Club record: one app. (also 2 'other' apps)

O'SHEA, John Francis

Born: Waterford, 30 April 1981
Career: Waterford United (1996), MANCHESTER UNITED (professional, September 1998), AFC Bournemouth (on loan, January 2000), Royal Antwerp (on loan, season 2000-01).
Centre-half John O'Shea, capped by his country (Eire) at Youth, Under-21 and senior levels, made excellent progress via United's second and third teams before doing himself justice in the senior side. He gained valuable experience whilst playing in Belgium and during 2001-02 deputised for Laurent Blanc, Wes Brown and Ronny Johnsen at the heart of United's defence.
Club record: 16 apps.

OSWALDTWISTLE ROVERS

Manchester United accounted for Rovers by 3-2 in the 4th qualifying round of the 1902-03 FA Cup competition at Bank Street. The attendance was 5,000.

OWEN, George Alfred

Born: Chirk, Wales, 1865. Died: Chirk, 29 January 1922
Career: Chirk (1880), NEWTON HEATH (season 1889-90), West Manchester (season 1890-91), Chirk (1891-93), Druids (1893-95), Chirk (1895-96).
Inside-forward George Owen spent nine years with Chirk and was already a Welsh international when he joined the Heathens. He added two caps to his tally before moving across Manchester after just one season. He later gained a fourth cap (in 1893). A pupil teacher in his early Youth, he was described as a 'constructive' player, reliable and totally committed. He became a referee in local League football (in Wales) in the early 1900s.
Club record: 12 apps. 2 goals (also 41 'other' apps, 11 goals)

OWEN, John

Born: Chirk, 1865
Career: Chirk (1883-87), NEWTON HEATH (October 1887-May 1893).
Wing-half Jack Owen was a fine player, equally effective as a defender or attacker. He played most of his football at centre-half and possessed an exceptionally long throw, said to be able to propel the ball up to 50-60 yards from a standing position. He joined the Heathens at the age of 22 and gave the club good service for more than five years, gaining one full cap for Wales against Ireland in 1892. Earlier he was a Welsh Cup winner with Chirk (1887). An elder brother, William Owen, was registered with the Heathens in season 1887-88.
Club record: 61 apps. 3 goals (also 136 'other' apps, 9 goals)

OWEN, William

Born: mid-Wales circa 1875. Died: Chirk, 2 March 1946
Career: Holywell (1892), NEWTON HEATH (May 1898-May 1899).
Reserve winger Billy Owen - signed after appearing in Fred Erentz's testimonial match - spent just one season with the Heathens before leaving (perhaps returning to Wales).
Club record: one app. (also one 'other' app, 2 goals)

OWEN, William

Born: Northwich, Cheshire, 17 September 1906. Died: Newport, South Wales, 26 March 1981.
Career: Northwich Victoria, Macclesfield (1933), MANCHESTER UNITED (May 1934), Reading (January 1936), Exeter City (later 1936), Newport County (summer 1937, retired in 1947 to become trainer at Somerton Park, a position he held for two years); guested for Cardiff City & Mansfield Town during WW2.
Left-winger Bill Owen made an impressive start to his United career, scoring on his League debut against Norwich City in September 1934. That was his only goal for the club and although he produced some useful displays he was eventually replaced in the side by Reg Chester. He later gave 12 years service to Newport County.
Club record: 17 apps. one goal.

OXFORD UNITED

United's League results v the 'U's':

Season	Div	Home	Away
1974-75	2	W 4-0	L 0-1
1985-86	1	W 3-0	W 3-1
1986-87	1	W 3-2	L 0-2
1987-88	1	W 3-1	W 2-0

Summary of League results

	P	W	D	L	F	A
Division 1	6	5	0	1	14	6
Division 2	2	1	0	1	4	1
Home	4	4	0	0	13	3
Away	4	2	0	2	5	4
Total	8	6	0	2	18	7

FA Cup results v the 'U's':

	Round	Venue	Result
1975-76	3	Home	W 2-1
1988-89	4	Home	W 4-0

League Cup results v the 'U's':

	Round	Venue	Result
1972-73	2	Away	D 2-2
	Replay	Home	W 3-1
1983-84	4	Away	D 1-1
	Replay	Home	D 1-1
	2nd R	Away	L 1-2
1987-88	5	Away	L 0-2

Fact File:
United lost 2-0 at Oxford on 8 November 1986 - Alex Ferguson's first match in charge.
Associated with both clubs: I Greaves (United player, Oxford manager), R Atkinson (Oxford player, United manager), M Brown (Oxford coach & manager, United assistant-manager).

P for...

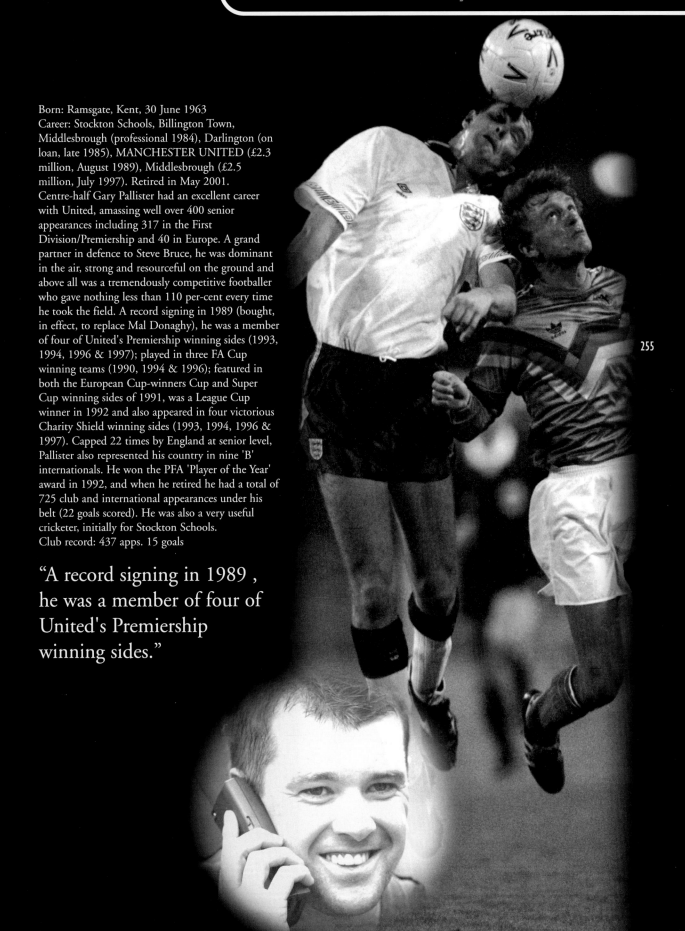

Born: Ramsgate, Kent, 30 June 1963
Career: Stockton Schools, Billington Town, Middlesbrough (professional 1984), Darlington (on loan, late 1985), MANCHESTER UNITED (£2.3 million, August 1989), Middlesbrough (£2.5 million, July 1997). Retired in May 2001.
Centre-half Gary Pallister had an excellent career with United, amassing well over 400 senior appearances including 317 in the First Division/Premiership and 40 in Europe. A grand partner in defence to Steve Bruce, he was dominant in the air, strong and resourceful on the ground and above all was a tremendously competitive footballer who gave nothing less than 110 per-cent every time he took the field. A record signing in 1989 (bought, in effect, to replace Mal Donaghy), he was a member of four of United's Premiership winning sides (1993, 1994, 1996 & 1997); played in three FA Cup winning teams (1990, 1994 & 1996); featured in both the European Cup-winners Cup and Super Cup winning sides of 1991, was a League Cup winner in 1992 and also appeared in four victorious Charity Shield winning sides (1993, 1994, 1996 & 1997). Capped 22 times by England at senior level, Pallister also represented his country in nine 'B' internationals. He won the PFA 'Player of the Year' award in 1992, and when he retired he had a total of 725 club and international appearances under his belt (22 goals scored). He was also a very useful cricketer, initially for Stockton Schools.
Club record: 437 apps. 15 goals

255

"A record signing in 1989 , he was a member of four of United's Premiership winning sides."

PSV EINDHOVEN

The clubs met in two European Cup Group matches in 2000-01. United had led after two minutes in Holland through a Paul Scholes penalty before going 3-1 down, but they made amends for that defeat with a similar scoreline at Old Trafford....helped by another goal from Scholes! Gordon Strachan's goal in extra-time (1-0) sent United through into the 3rd round of the UEFA Cup in 1984-85 following a 0-0 draw in Eindhoven.
Players with both clubs: J Stam, R van Nistelrooy

PAGE, Louis Antonio

Born: Kirkdale, Liverpool, 27 March 1899. Died: Birkenhead, 12 October 1959.
Career: St Alexander School (Liverpool), Sudley Schoolboys, Liverpool Schoolboys, Sudley Juniors, South Liverpool FC, Stoke (1919), Northampton Town (1922), Burnley (1925), MANCHESTER UNITED (£1,000, March 1932), Port Vale (October 1932), Yeovil & Petters United (player-manager, 1933-35), Newport County (manager, summer 1935-37), Glentoran (trainer-coach, late 1938), Carlton FC, Liverpool (manager, 1940-45), Swindon Town (manager, 1945-53), Chester (manager summer 1953-56), Leicester City (scout late '50s/early '60s).
Inside or outside-left Louis Page had already scored 134 goals in 380 League appearances prior to joining United, netting 115 times in 259 outings for Burnley.
He was a flying winger, elusive with a powerful shot who once scored six goals in one match for Burnley against Birmingham in April 1926. He was well past his best - and struggling with the odd injury - when he arrived at Old Trafford but was still made team captain! Capped seven times by England at full international level, he also represented the Football League on one occasion; as a manager Page guided Yeovil to the Southern League (Western Division) Championship and to the Southern League Cup Final in 1935. He won damages for wrongful dismissal by Newport County Serving in the Royal Navy during WW1, Page was torpedoed whilst on HMS Virginian.
His three brothers - John, Bill and Tommy - all played professional football with Merthyr, Northampton and Port Vale respectively....and they all (including Louis) represented England at baseball!
Club record: 12 apps.

PALATINE LEAGUE

A short-lived organisation which Newton Heath entered for two seasons: 1893-94 & 1894-95. In their first season (played in February and April 1894) the Heathens arranged home and away fixtures against Accrington, Bolton, Bury, Darwen and Everton. In fact, only eight matches were played, two were won, one drawn aand five lost.
The following year the Heathens met only Bury and Liverpool during January, February & March. One victory was claimed this time along with one draw and two defeats.
Normally, the first team was fielded on spare Saturdays in the Football League programme, but occasionally the reserves were asked to turn out instead.

PALLISTER, Gary Andrew

Refer to front of section.

PANATHINAIKOS

United met the Greek champions twice in the European Champions League 2nd stage in season 2000-01. Over 65,000 fans saw Paul Scholes score twice late on to give United a 3-1 home win and it was Scholes again, this time with a 90th minute equaliser, who salvaged a point in Athens (1-1).

PAPE, Albert Arthur

Born: Elsecar, near Wath-on-Dearne, 13 June 1897. Died: Doncaster, 18 November 1955.
Career: Wath Athletic, Army football, Bolton-upon-Dearne FC, Rotherham County (late 1919), Notts County (mid-1923), Clapton Orient (summer 1924), MANCHESTER UNITED (February 1925), Fulham (October 1925), Rhyl Athletic (1927), Hurst FC (1928), Darwen (player-coach, autumn 1928), Manchester Central (early 1929), Hartlepools United (summer 1929), Halifax Town (summer 1930), Burscough Rangers (1931), Horwich RMI (1932), Nelson (winter 1933).
Centre-forward Albert Pape joined the club in unusual circumstances. He was all set to play for Clapton Orient in a League game at Old Trafford but less than two hours before kick-off he was transferred to United and then went out and scored against his former club in a 4-2 win. He helped United win promotion that season but was then allowed to join Fulham, although he continued to train at Old Trafford. A very useful footballer, Pape scored well over 100 goals in almost 300 League and Cup games during his senior career.
Club record: 18 apps. 5 goals

PARKER, Paul Andrew

Born: West Ham, London , 4 April 1964
Career: Essex & Havering Schools, Fulham (apprentice)

1980, professional 1982), Queen's Park Rangers (£300,000, summer 1987), MANCHESTER UNITED (£2 million, August 1991), Derby County (free transfer, August 1996), Sheffield United (late 1996), Fulham (early 1997), Chelsea (Easter 1997), Heybridge Swifts (1998), Farnborough Town (1999), Chelmsford Town (assistant-manager, 2000-01). Right-back Paul Parker made over 180 appearances for Fulham and 160 for QPR before joining United. An adaptable, compact footballer, with exceptional positional sense, he enjoyed bringing the ball out of defence and setting up an attack rather than giving it a huge kick downfield, hoping to find a colleague.

He represented England at four different levels during a fine career, winning eight Under-21, three 'B' and 19 senior caps following his appearances for the Youth team. He was a League Cup winner in 1992, a Premiership winner in 1993 and 1994, also an FA Cup winner in the latter year as well as helping United win the Charity Shield in 1993.

Club record: 146 apps. 2 goals.

PARKER, Samuel

Born: Riccarton near Kilmarnock, 1872.
Career: Hurlford FC, NEWTON HEATH (January 1894), Burnley (October 1894), Southport Central (early 1895), Hurlford FC (summer 1895), Kilmarnock Athletic (1898-99).
Forward Sam Parker failed to bring much-needed strike-power to the Heathens' goal-shy front-line!
Club record: 11 apps. (also 4 'other' apps, one goal)

PARKER, Thomas Albert

Born: Eccles, Lancashire, 22 November 1906. Died: Manchester, 11 November 1964.
Career: MANCHESTER UNITED (amateur September 1930, professional October 1930), Bristol City (May 1932), Carlisle United (summer 1934), Stalybridge Celtic (season 1935-36).
Centre-half Tom Parker, a fine figure of a man, loved to drive forward from his defensive position. He failed to establish himself in United's first team and after leaving Old Trafford he made over 40 league appearances for Bristol City but struggled in a poor Carlisle side.
Club record: 17 apps.

PARKINSON, Robert

Born: Preston, 27 April 1873.
Career: Preston Ramblers, Preston Athletic, Fleetwood Rangers, Rotherham Town (1894), Luton Town (1895), Blackpool (1896), Warmley, Nottingham Forest (October 1898), NEWTON HEATH (November 1899), Watford (November 1900), Swindon Town (season 1901-02)..
Centre-forward Robert Parkinson had a good scoring record with the Heathens, including a run of five goals in consecutive matches. Unfortunately, along with William Bryant, he was suspended by the club for a misdemeanour and was released at the end of the 1899-1900 season.
Club record: 15 apps. 7 goals (also 7 'other' apps, one goal)

PARTIZAN BELGRADE

United met Partizan Belgrade in the semi-final of the European Cup in 1965-66 as favourites to lift the trophy, following their 5-1 win at Benfica. After losing the first leg 2-0 in Yugoslavia, George Best limping off with a knee injury, all they had to show for a lot of effort at Old Trafford was a single goal by Nobby Stiles. Sadly, it wasn't enough and they were out, beaten 2-1 on aggregate.

PARTRIDGE, Edward

Born: Lye, Worcestershire, 13 February 1891. Died: Manchester, circa 1973.
Career: Lye Schools, Stembermill St Mark's, to War with Welsh Regiment (1914-18), Ebbw Vale FC, MANCHESTER UNITED (£10, June 1920), Halifax Town (May 1929), Manchester Central (late 1929), Altrincham (1930), Crewe Alexandra (season 1930-31).
Diminutive ginger-topped inside or outside-left Teddy Partridge gave United nine years excellent service and was rewarded with a benefit match (v. West Ham in 1928) which guaranteed him £650. He established himself in the first XI immediately and had three excellent seasons before losing his place to Frank McPherson, regaining it in 1926-27. He played his last League game for Crewe at the age of 40.
Partridge's cousin was Ray Westwood who played for Bolton Wanderers and England whilst his son, David, was a junior on United's books in the 1950s.
Club record: 160 apps. 18 goals.

PATERSON, Steven William

Born: Mostodloch, Elgin, Scotland, 8 April 1958
Career: Nairn County, MANCHESTER UNITED (July 1974-July 1980)), Sheffield Wednesday (but failed a medical), played thereafter in Hong Kong, Japan and Australia, then registered with Forres Mechanics, Scotland (seasons 1986-88), Elgin City (player-manager, 1988-90), Huntly FC (manager, 1990-91), Inverness Caledonian Thistle (manager: 1995 onwards).
Defender Steve Paterson made half of his senior appearances for United as a substitute including outings against Ajax & Juventus in the UEFA Cup. A serious ankle injury caused him to leave Old Trafford.
Club record: 10 apps.

PAYNE, Ernest

Born: circa 1885.

Career: Worcester City, MANCHESTER UNITED (amateur, December 1908, left club, May 1909).

Reserve winger Ernie Payne stood in for Welsh wizard Billy Meredith in League games against Nottingham Forest and Sunderland in February/March 1909. His goal came in the 2-2 draw with Sunderland.

Club record: 2 apps. One goal

PEARS, Stephen

Born: Brandon, Durham, 22 January 1962

Career: Ushaw Moor Schools, Middlesbrough (trialist), MANCHESTER UNITED (apprentice July 1978, professional January 1979), Middlesbrough (on loan, November 1983, signed permanently for £80,000, July 1985), Liverpool (summer 1995), Hartlepools United (summer 1996). Retired May 1998.

Steve Pears was reserve goalkeeper (to Gary Bailey) at Old Trafford for four seasons before joining Middlesbrough, for whom he played in a total of 422 competitive matches. He failed to break into Liverpool's first team.

Club record: 5 apps..

PEARSON, Mark

Born: Ridgeway, Derbyshire, 28 October 1939.

Career: Ridgeway Village School, North East Derbyshire Schools, MANCHESTER UNITED (amateur, 1955, professional May 1957), Sheffield Wednesday (£20,000, October 1963), Fulham (summer 1965), Halifax Town (early 1968). Retired summer 1968.

Known affectionately as 'Pancho' (because of his long, bushy sideburns) inside-forward Mark Pearson won England Schoolboy honours as a 15 year-old before joining United. He quickly added a Youth cap to his collection and looked a very promising forward at times during his six-year professional career at Old Trafford. Later he suffered two broken legs and eventually quit competitive soccer at the age of 27.

Club record: 80 apps. 14 goals

PEARSON, Stanley Clare

Born: Salford, 11 January 1919. Died: 18, February 1997

Career: Adelphi Lads' Club, MANCHESTER UNITED (amateur, December 1935, professional May 1937); guested for Brighton & Hove Albion, Newcastle United and Queen's Park Rangers during WW2; Bury (£4,500, February 1954), Chester (player-manager autumn 1957, retired as a player summer 1957, resigned as manager late 1961), Prestbury FC (coach 1962-63).

A classy, two-footed inside-forward, willing to do his fair share of midfield foraging, Stan Pearson was a deadly finisher with feet or head. He was an integral part of the post WW2 side, scoring a hat-trick in the 1948 FA Cup semi-final. He had helped United win promotion from Division Two in 1937-38 and after the war, he scored in the 1948 FA Cup Final win over Blackpool and starred in the League Championship triumph in 1951-52, when he netted 22 goals, continuing a lethal scoring partnership with Jack Rowley. Capped by England on eight occasions, scoring five times (his first appearance coming against Scotland in 1948) Pearson also represented his country's 'B' team and the Football League, and in 1958 guided Chester to the Welsh Cup final. He later ran a newsagent's shop in Prestbury village.

Club record: 346 apps. 149 goals

PEARSON, Stuart James

Born: Hull, 21 June 1949

Career: East Riding Schools, Hull City (amateur 1966, professional 1968), MANCHESTER UNITED (£200,000, May 1974), West Ham United (£220,000, August 1979), Retired from League football in 1982 (through injury) but continued to play at a lower level, firstly in South Africa and the NASL; Sale (rugby club), Stockport County (coach, 1985-86), Northwich Victoria (manager, first half of 1986-87 season), West Bromwich Albion (coach/assistant-manager 1988-92, caretaker-manager at The Hawthorns, early 1991), Bradford City (assistant-manager, 1992-94).

An out-and-out striker with good pace and strong right-foot shot, Stuart Pearson headed Hull City's scoring charts for three seasons before moving to Old Trafford. He was United's leading marksman in 1974-75 when the Second Division Championship was won, and in 1976 he played in the FA Cup Final defeat by Southampton. He then scored the opening goal in the 1977 FA Cup triumph over treble-chasing Liverpool. Also nicknamed 'Pancho', Pearson was an FA Cup winner with the Hammers in 1980 and a League Cup finalist twelve months later (as a substitute). A knee injury (suffered in North America) ended his footballing career, although he did play a few games of rugby for Sale in 1985-86. Capped once by England at Under-23 level, Pearson went on to win a total of 15 full caps during 1976 & 1977, scoring 4 goals.

Club record: 180 apps. 66 goals

PECSI MUNKAS

United just got the better, overall, of the plucky Hungarian Cup holders in their 1st round Cup-winners Cup contest in 1990-91. The Reds won 2-0 at home and 1-0 away.

PEDDIE, John Hope

Born: Southside, Glasgow, 21 March 1877. Died: Detroit, USA, October 1928.
Career: Benburb FC, Third Lanark (summer 1895), Newcastle United (trialist early 1897, signed later that year), MANCHESTER UNITED (June 1902), Plymouth Argyle (May 1903), MANCHESTER UNITED (May 1904), Heart of Midlothian (early 1907 to May 1908), North American football (season 1908-09).
Before he joined United in 1902 centre or inside-forward Jack Peddie had already appeared in 174 League games. During his career he amassed over 350 in all competitions. A potent attacker, and neat dribbler, he possessed a powerful shot and often fired in long range efforts on goal. He had a casual manner and could be moody times, missing a few training sessions, bringing him into trouble with various managers and even directors! Many Geordie supporters bemoaned his transfer from Newcastle to United and likewise when he left Old Trafford first time round for Plymouth. He helped United gain promotion from Division Two during his second spell at the club.
Peddie's son became a star footballer in Canada
Club record: 121 apps. 58 goals

PEDEN, John

Born: Belfast, 11 March 1865
Career: Linfield (1886), NEWTON HEATH (February 1893), Sheffield United (July 1894), Belfast Distillery (1895), Linfield (1898-1903).
Jack Peden was the first Irish-born player to appear in a League game for the Heathens - making his debut against Burnley (at home) on 2 September 1893. Preferring the outside-left berth, Peden did very well during his eighteen-month stay with the Heathens, averaging a goal every four games. He won 24 caps for Ireland during his career, scoring seven goals. In 1902 he helped Linfield win the Irish Cup.
Club record: 32 apps. 8 goals (also 8 'other' apps, one goal)

PEGG, David

Born: Doncaster, 20 September 1935. Died: Munich, 6 February 1958
Career: Doncaster Schools, MANCHESTER UNITED (amateur, September 1950, professional September 1952 until his death in 1958).
A natural left-sided player, fast and direct, David Pegg was a great asset to the United team, creating a host of scoring opportunites for his colleagues. His finest hour was in the 10-0 thrashing of Belgian champions RSC Anderlecht in 1956 as his brilliant wing play laid on goal after goal for Taylor and Viollet, yet could not score himself!
He was capped five times by England at Schoolboy level before making his Football League debut as a 17 year-old against Middlesbrough in 1952. An FA Youth Cup winner with United in 1953 & 1954 (v. Wolves & WBA) he was regarded as a reserve until season 1955-56 when he came to the fore, producing some superb wing displays as United took the First Division Championship in style and then regained the trophy a year later with Pegg again in excellent form. A beaten Cup Finalist in 1957, Pegg had played in one full international for England as well as representing his country in three Under-23 matches and in one 'B' team game when he sadly lost his life in the Munich air crash. He was only 22.
Club record: 150 apps. 28 goals

PEGG, Ernest

Born: Leicester, summer 1878. Died: Leicester, 11 June 1916.
Career: Leicester Fosse (amateur, season 1895-96), Loughborough (1897), Kettering FC (1899-1900), Reading (season 1900-01), Preston North End (season 1901-02), MANCHESTER UNITED (June 1902), Fulham (May 1904), Barnsley (May 1905). Retired May 1906 through injury.
'Dick' Pegg was a very useful goalscoring inside-forward who made his debut for the club in the first League game played under the club's present name v. Gainsborough Trinity (away) on 6 September 1902. Before joining United he had helped Kettering win the Midland League title (1900). He was forced to retire early due to a knee injury. He was a licensee in Leicester at the time of his death.
Club record: 51 apps. 20 goals

PEGG, James Kenneth

Born: Salford, 4 January 1926

Career: Salford Youth football, MANCHESTER UNITED (amateur May 1945, professional November 1947), Torquay United (August 1949), York City (season 1950-51).

Capable reserve-team goalkeeper Ken Pegg played twice for United's first XI, in season 1947-48 when he replaced Jack Crompton in games against Derby County (away) and Everton (home) both of which ended in draws.

Club record: 2 apps.

PENALTY KICK

Firsts

The penalty kick was introduced to League and Cup football in England in September 1891.

It is thought that the first Newton Heath player to score from the penalty spot was Alf Farman in a friendly match against Blackpool on 5 September 1891.

The first reported penalty to be scored in a League game was by Joe Cassidy v. Grimsby Town at Bank Street on 1 January 1896 in front of 8,000 spectators. Cassidy completed a hat-trick that day.

Penalty Shoot-outs

The first penalty shoot-out United were involved in (at competitive level) came at the end of their Watney Cup semi-final tie against Hull City at Boothferry Park on 5 August 1970. Following a 1-1 draw (after extra-time) United went through to the Final with a 4-3 success from the spot.

The first FA Cup-tie to be decided on penalties was the 4th round replay between United and Southampton at Old Trafford in February 1992. The Saints triumphed in the end 4-2 after the scores had finished level at 2-2 in normal/extra playing time.

United have won two FA Charity Shield games at Wembley via a penalty shoot-out. They eclipsed Arsenal 5-4 in 1993 and Chelsea 4-2 in 1997.

Spot-kick Chit-chat

Charlie Mitten scored a hat-trick of penalties when United beat Aston Villa 7-0 in a League game at Old Trafford in March 1950. In this same game Villa's Billy Goffin missed from the spot.

Former United forward Trevor Anderson scored a hat-trick of penalties, playing for Swindon Town against Walsall in a League game in April 1976.

In the 1990-91 season United scored from 12 penalty kicks. Skipper Steve Bruce netted a new club record of 11 while Clayton Blackmore claimed the other one!

Six years earlier, in 1984-85, Gordon Strachan scored nine times from the spot for United with Arnold Muhren and Norman Whiteside each netting once. United had a total of 17 penalties awarded in their favour this term...a club record.

In season 1974-75 Gerry Daly put away four spot-kicks in the month of August. He finished up with a total of nine conversions while Jim McCalliog netted once.

Daly, in fact, missed only one penalty out of the 17 he took for United during the 1970s.

The honour of being the most successful spot-kick expert for United goes to Eric Cantona who had accumulated a record of 17 successful conversions out of a total of 20 spot-kicks. The Frenchman's three misses from 12-yards came against the Irish club Dundalk and Newcastle United in a pre-season tournament played at Ibrox Park, Glasgow in 1994 and against his former club, Leeds United, in a 4-0 win in 1996-97.

Albert Quixall scored 18 penalties for United and Steve Bruce 12. Each player had 22 attempts from the spot.

Dutch midfielder Arnold Muhren scored from the penalty spot in United's 1983 FA Cup Final replay victory over Brighton & Hove Albion.

The aforementioned Cantona became the first player to score two penalties in a Wembley FA Cup Final with his delightful strikes for United against Chelsea in 1994 (also a 4-0 win).

Cantona also netted a penalty in the FA Charity Shield game against Blackburn Rovers three months later (August 1994) to become the first player to score three penalties for the same club at Wembley.

During his career (to date) goalkeeper John Lukic has saved three penalties from United players. In December 1979 he stopped Ashley Grimes' effort when playing for Leeds; in December 1985, as an Arsenal player, he saved from Norman Whiteside and four years later, still a Gunner, he prevented Brian McClair from finding the net. McClair also fired a spot-kick over Lukic's crossbar when playing against Arsenal in February 1988.

Goalkeeper Alex Stepney netted from two penalty-kicks for United in season 1973-74 (v. Birmingham City and Leicester City). He missed a third spot-kick against Birmingham.

Hubert Redwood scored twice from the spot in United's 3-3 draw at Southampton (Division 2) in February 1938.

Winger David Pegg scored from the penalty spot in both legs of United's FA Youth Cup Final triumph over Wolves in April 1954.

United's reserve goalkeeper Alf Steward saved six penalties in Central League games during the 1923-24 season.

'Keeper Gary Bailey stopped two penalties during United's away League game at Ipswich Town in March 1980 - to no avail! The Reds still crashed to a 6-0 defeat!

The last visiting team to score a penalty in a Premiership/League game at Old Trafford was Norwich City - via Ruel Fox - in December 1993.

The Brazilian Juninho of Middlesbrough had his penalty saved by United's 'keeper Mark Bosnich in his side's 1-0 Premiership defeat at Old Trafford in January 2000.

The last 'visiting' player to miss a penalty in a Premiership game at Old Trafford was the Turkish international midfielder Muzzy Izzet of Leicester City who had his 12-yard kick saved by Fabien Barthez on 17 November 2001. Izzet, in fact, scored with his 'first' kick but referee Andy D'Urso ordered the penalty to be re-taken because Barthez had not been ready...he was cleaning mud off his studs standing by a goalpost. This time the Frenchman saved Izzet's anxious-looking 12-yard effort, much to the chagrin of the Leicester bench!

The last visiting team to score from the spot in any major competition at Old Trafford was Sturm Graz, via Vastic in the 87th minute of a European Champions League Group match in November 1999..

Barcelona netted with two second-half penalty kicks (converted by Luis Enrique and Giovanni past Peter Schmeichel) in their 3-3 European Cup draw at Old Trafford on 16 September 1998, and two years prior to that - on 20 Septermber 1996 - the Italian international Del Piero grabbed Juventus' 36th minute winner from the spot (1-0) in a European Cup clash, also against United at Old Trafford.

Ruud van Nistelrooy scored seven out of eight penalties for United in his first season at Old Trafford (2001-02).

There is an unconfirmed claim that Jack Crompton saved 10 consecutive penalties over a period of two seasons of wartime football with United. On 7 May 1949 (the last day of the season) United led champions-elect Portsmouth 3-2 at Maine Road, needing two points to cement their runners-up spot. In the very last minute Pompey were awarded a penalty. Crompton saved Duggie Reid's cannonball spot-kick at the expense of a broken wrist!

PEPPER, Francis
Born: Wortley, autumn 1875
Career: Greasborough FC, Sheffield United (1898), NEWTON HEATH (November 1898), Barnsley (June 1899), Doncaster Rovers (January 1902), South Kirkby (season 1902-03).
Reserve centre-half 'Frank' Pepper deputised for Billy Morgan in six successive League games halfway through the 1898-99 season.
Club record: 8 apps. (also 2 'other' apps)

PERRINS, George
Born: Birmingham, 24 February 1873
Career: Birmingham St George's, NEWTON HEATH (July 1892), Luton Town (May 1896), Chatham (1898), Stockport County (season 1901-02).
A wing-half, very reliable and forthright, George Perrins made two of his senior appearances for Newton Heath in goal. The first was in late February 1896 against Burton Wanderers at Bank Street (lost 2-1) and the second followed against the same opponents at their Derby Turn ground some 18 days later. At half-time in this second game United were 4-0 down when it was agreed that Walter Cartwright should play in goal in the second half. The final score was 5-1. As an outfield player, Perrins was a stern tackler, quick over short distances with strong defensive qualities.
Club record: 102 apps. (also 45 'other' apps, one goal)

PETERBOROUGH UNITED
FA Cup results v Posh:

	Round	Venue	Result
1975-76	4	Home	W 3-1

Fact File:
Players with both clubs include: T Anderson, P Bradshaw (Man Utd trialist), W Bullimore (Man Utd reserve), R Chester, H Cockburn, T Gibson, M Martin; J Sloan & L Steele (United reserves), GG Worrall (Man Utd reserve), T Wyles (Man Utd WW2), ER Young (Man Utd reserve).
Also associated: N Cantwell (United player, Posh manager: two spells), B Fry (United junior, Posh manager), J Anderson (United player, Posh trainer-coach).

PETERS, James
Born: Lancashire, circa 1870.
Career: Heywood Central, NEWTON HEATH (June 1894), New Brompton (1896), Sheppey United (for two seasons: 1897-99).
An 1890s winger, 'Jack' Peters' first season with the Heathens was excellent, appearing in all 30 League games. He held his form and position for two thirds of the following campaign before injury struck, forcing him to lose his place.
Club record: 50 apps. 14 goals (also 13 'other' apps, one goal)

PHELAN, Michael Christopher
Born: Nelson, Lancashire, 24 September 1962
Career: Barrowfield County Primary and Colne Park High Schools, Nelson & Colne Town, Lancashire Schools, Barrowfield Celtic Boys Club, Burnley (apprentice, 1979, professional summer 1980), Norwich City (summer 1985), MANCHESTER UNITED (£750,000, July 1989), West Bromwich Albion (May 1994), Norwich City (reserve team manager), Blackpool (non-contract), Stockport County (player-coach), MANCHESTER UNITED (coach, 2000-02).
Capped at Youth team level, hard-working midfielder Mike Phelan went on to play in one full international match for England, lining up against Italy in November 1989 (albeit as a second-half substitute). He helped Burnley win the Third Division Championship and reach the semi-final of the League Cup before moving to Carrow Road. He joined United on the same day as Neil Webb arrived from Nottingham Forest, both players making their League debuts for the Reds on the opening day of the 1989-90 season v. Arsenal.. An FA Cup winner with United (1990 v. Crystal Palace) Phelan then gained both a League Cup winners' and losers' medal plus a European Cup-winners Cup winning prize when United beat Barcelona 2-1 in Rotterdam in 1991. He also helped United win successive Premiership titles in 1993 and 1994 before being handed a free transfer; he later returned to Old Trafford in a coaching capacity.
Club record: 146 apps. 3 goals

261

PICKEN, John Barclay

Born: Hurlford, near Kilmarnock, 1880. Died: Plymouth, 31 July 1952

Career: Hurlford Thistle FC, Kilmarnock Shawbank, Bolton Wanderers (seasons 1899-1903), Plymouth Argyle (seasons 1903-05), MANCHESTER UNITED (May 1905), Burnley (December 1911), Bristol City (1913-15).

Jack Picken made over 150 League appearances before signing for United, and during his career he totalled well over 350 in League and Cup competitions. A fine Scottish footballer, he made his Football League debut for Bolton against Newton Heath and had the pleasure of scoring on his debut for United against Bristol City in September 1905. He helped United gain promotion to the First Division in 1906, but by the time the Football League title was won in 1908 he had lost his place in the side to Sandy Turnbull (making only eight senior appearances that season). Unfortunately he also missed out on an FA Cup medal in 1909 but made up for that by gaining a League Championship in 1911.In his last season at Old Trafford he shared a benefit with Dick Holden, each player receiving around £300.

Club record: 122 apps. 46 goals

PILKINGTON, Kevin William

Born: Hitchin, Herts, 8 March 1974

Career MANCHESTER UNITED (YTS June 1990, professional July 1992), Rochdale (on loan, February 1996), Rotherham United (on loan, January 1997), Port Vale (free transfer, July 1998), Macclesfield Town (trialist), Wigan Athletic (2000), Aberystwyth Town (briefly, 2001), Mansfield Town (summer 2001):

Goalkeeper Kevin Pilkington was reserve to Peter Schmeichel at Old Trafford and consequently got very few opportunities in the first team. Over a period of six seasons (from 1996-97) Pilkington made less than 100 League and Cup appearances at senior level, but he did help Mansfield gain promotion from the Nationwide League Division Three in 2001-02.

Club record: 8 apps.

PINNER, Michael John

Born: Boston, Lincolnshire 16 February 1934.

Career: Boston Grammar School, Wyberton Rangers, Notts County (1948), Cambridge University, Pegasus, Aston Villa (1954), Sheffield Wednesday (1957), Queen's Park Rangers (1959), MANCHESTER UNITED (February-March 1961), Middlesex Wanderers, Hendon, Chelsea Casuals, Chelsea (1961), Arsenal (late 1961), Swansea Town (1962), Leyton Orient (1962-85, turning professional in 1963), Belfast Distillery (1965-67). Retired to continue his work as a solicitor.

Goalkeeper Mike Pinner decided to turn professional at the age of 29 (in 1963), after having appeared in more than 250 competitive games as an amateur as well as winning more than 50 caps for his country at that same level. He played in the Olympic Games Soccer Tournaments in Melbourne (1956) and Rome (1960), represented the RAF on two occasions in the early 1960s (he was an officer in the forces) and played in four Varsity matches against Oxford University.

United briefly 'borrowed' this excellent amateur 'keeper in 1961, having both Harry Gregg and Dave Gaskell out injured and third choice custodian Briggs having conceded 13 goals in four matches!

Daring, agile and a fine shot-stopper, Pinner made a total of 110 Football League appearances.

Club record: 4 apps.

PLASTIC PITCHES

United have played only two teams on plastic/artificial surfaces in League football - Luton Town and Queen's Park Rangers and they achieved a fairly even record which reads:

Venue	P	W	D	L	F	A
Luton	3	0	2	1	3	4
QPR	5	2	2	1	7	4
Totals	8	2	4	2	10	8

United's first game was at Loftus Road against QPR on 13 January 1984 when a crowd of 16,308 saw Bryan Robson's goal earn the Reds a 1-1 draw.

United's first win on plastic followed on 11 May 1985 when they triumphed 3-1 at Loftus Road, Alan Brazil (2) and Gordon Strachan on target this time.

QPR inflicted upon United their first 'plastic' defeat, winning 1-0 on 15 March 1986.

United's first game at Kenilworth Road was played on 5 October 1985 when they drew 1-1 with Luton, Mark Hughes the scorer in front of 17,454 fans, breaking United's record opening sequence of 10 wins out of ten.

On 5 December 1987 United played their last League game on plastic at QPR, winning 2-0 with goals by Peter Davenport and Bryan Robson in front of 20,632 spectators.

Robson is the only player to have scored for United at both Luton and QPR and, in fact, he has netted most goals on plastic for United, total three.

PLAYERS

United called up a total of 38 players during the course of the 1933-34 season and over a period of three seasons (1931-34 inclusive) the club used no fewer than 62 players in League action alone.

In 1964-65, only 18 players were used as United took the First Division Championship,

Six players whose surname all began with the letter 'M' starred in United's first team in season 1974-75…Macari, McCalliog, McCreery, McIlroy, Martin & Morgan.

Black Players

Dennis Walker (born in Cheshire, 1944) was the first Black player to appear in a League game for United, doing so against Nottingham Forest in May 1963. This was his only outing for the first XI.

Others followed, namely Viv Anderson, Wes Brown, Andy Cole, Garth Crooks, Laurie Cunningham, Dion Dublin, Quinton Fortune, Paul Ince, Paul McGrath, Remi Moses, John O'Kane, Paul Parker, Mikael Silvestre, Danny Wallace, Tony Whelan and Dwight Yorke.

PLAYERS' UNION/PFA

The Players Union was formed in December 1907 following a meeting at the Imperial Hotel, Manchester, chaired by Billy Meredith and attended by some 500 footballers. Herbert Broomfield (United) was elected secretary. The chief complaints were regarding the maximum wage £4-a-week (which had been in force since 1901) and the injustices of the transfer system. The FA was not in favour of such an organisation, drawing up new contracts for players which included a clause disowning the Union.

Regrettably the bulk of the players caved in when faced with this dilemma and signed up; the Players' Union seemed to be doomed to failure. However, the Manchester United players, vigorously led by Charlie Roberts and Billy Meredith, stood their ground, virtually alone.

In August 1909, United's entire FA Cup winning team, were suspended, causing a sensation.

The players were banned from using United's facilities, but hired Fallowfield to train alone; they had received no pay throughout the summer.

They titled themselves 'The Outcasts FC' and had a 'team' photograph published.

The press took up United's brave fight as the new season approached. Gradually other players returned to the fold and after a number of desperate meetings, the FA backed down on the eve of the new campaign.

The United players had triumphed off the field, just as they had done on it, although the FA forced the Union out of their affiliation with the General Federation of Trade Unions.

The United players were heroes, but it would be another 50 years before the Union won any real rights...thanks to one Jimmy Hill!

It is no coincidence the PFA's head-quarters are still in Manchester.

The following all of whom played for United, held the position of PFA Chairman: Charlie Roberts (1919-21), Noel Cantwell (1966-67), Alan Gowling (1980-82), Steve Coppell (1982-84) and Garth Crooks (1988-90). Malcolm Musgrove, a United assistant-manager/coach & scout, was also chairman of the PFA in 1963-64.

263

PLAYING RECORD

United's full playing record at competitive level - to the end of the 2001-02 season:

Competition	P	W	D	L	F	A	
Premiership	392	244	93	55	789	360	
Division 1	2740	1162	704	874	4523	3875	
Division 2	816	406	168	242	1433	966	
FA Cup	383	202*	88	93**	696	451	
League Cup	136	73	25	38	231	154	
European CL/Cup	126	67	34	25	249	127	
ICFC/UEFA Cup	31	12	13	6	48	26	
ECWC	31	16	9	6	55	35	
European Super Cup	2	1	0	1	1	1	
Totals	4657	2183	1134	1340	8025	5995	(59.05%)

* Includes one match awarded when opponents scratched.
** Includes two matches drawn: one awarded as win for opponents after United refused to play extra-time and the others were won by opponents following penalty 'shoot-outs'

Other Competitions	P	W	D	L	F	A	
FA Charity Shield	22	8	7	7	42	43	
Screen Sport S Cup	4	0	2	2	4	7	
World Club Ch'ship	3	1	1	1	2	2	
Club World Ch'ship	3	1	1	1	4	4	
Watney Cup	4	1	1	2	6	9	
Test Matches	8	2	2	4	9	13	
Anglo-Italian Cup	4	2	2	0	8	3	
Mercantile Credit	3	2	0	1	4	2	
Football Alliance	66	28	12	26	146	133	
Totals	117	45	28	44	225	216	(50.43%)
Wartime (1/2)	260	140	49	71	699	427	

Overall Playing Record (at first team level):

Seasons	P	W	D	L	F	A	
1886-2002	4774	2228	1162	1384	8250	6221	(58.84%)

PLYMOUTH ARGYLE

FA Cup results v the Pilgrims:

	Round	Venue	Result
1912-13	2	Away	W 2-0
1923-24	1	Home	W 1-0
1931-32	3	Away	L 1-4
1973-74	3	Home	W 1-0

United's League record v. the Pilgrims:

Season	Div	Home	Away
1931-32	2	W 2-1	L 1-3
1932-33	2	W 4-0	W 3-2
1933-34	2	L 0-3	L 0-4
1934-35	2	W 3-1	W 2-0
1935-36	2	W 3-2	L 1-3
1937-38	2	D 0-0	D 1-1

Summary of League results

	P	W	D	L	F	A
Division 2	12	6	2	4	20	20
Home	6	4	1	1	12	7
Away	6	2	1	3	8	13
Total	12	6	2	4	20	20

Players with both clubs include: J Anderson & J Aston snr (both Argyle WW2), J Banks, G Barrett (United reserve), S Blott, T Dougan, P Dunne, J Flitchett, B Fulton (United reserve), C Griffiths, W Hullett (United reserve), W McDonald, J Mitten (United trialist), MM Morgan (United reserve), J Peddie, J Picken, D Robbie (Argyle player & coach), J Rowley (Argyle player-manager), L Sealey, J Sutcliffe, E Taylor (Argyle WW2), W Toms, J Walton.
Also associated: I Greaves & S Houston (United players, Argyle coaches), J Chapman (United manager, Argyle director), M Musgrove (assistant-manager/coach at United, Argyle coach/physio), A Ashman (scout for both clubs).

* United played St Etienne at Home Park, Plymouth, in a 1st round, 2nd leg European Cup-winners Cup 'home' encounter on 5 October 1977. United won 2-0 in front of 31,634 spectators.

POBORSKY, Karel

Born: Jindinchuv-Hradec, Czech Republic, 30 March 1972
Career: Ceske Budejovice, Viktoria Zizkov, Slavia Prague, Benfica, MANCHESTER UNITED (£3.5 million, August 1996), Benfica (£3 million, December 1998), SS Lazio (2000), Sparta Pargue (2002).
A Czech Republic international wide midfielder (wing-forward) with over 30 caps to his credit, Karel Poborsky helped United win the 1996 FA Charity Shield and Premiership title the following year. He was exciting to watch (when in top form and in full flow) and was dubbed 'The Express Train' when playing superbly well for his country in Euro '96. However, after some fine displays for United he then found himself on the bench, unable to hold down a regular first team place - hence his transfer to Benfica.
Club record: 48 apps. 6 goals

POINTS

The most points gained by United in a full Football League season (two points for a win in a 42-match programme) is 64, achieved in 1956-57.
They claimed a record total of 92 Premiership points (from 42 matches) in 1993-94 (three points for a win), then from only 38 games played in 1999-2000, the Reds acquired a total of 91 points.
The fewest number of points gained is 14 - in season 1893-94 (from 30 matches only).
The fewest number acquired (at three for win) has been 48 in season 1989-90
Just 22 points were banked from 42 First Division matches in 1930-31.

POLICE FORCE

Two United players - Caesar Jenkyns and Gordon Clayton - both served in the Police Force in various capacities. Referee Peter Willis, a Police-officer in Durham, sent off United defender Kevin Moran in the 1985 FA Cup Final v. Everton.

PORT VALE (Burslem)

Heathens/United's League results v the Valiants:

Season	Div	Home	Away	Season	Div	Home	Away
1894-95	2	W 3-0	W 5-2	1922-23	2	L 1-2	L 0-1
1895-96	2	W 2-1	L 0-3	1923-24	2	W 5-0	W 1-0
				1924-25	2	W 4-0	L 1-2
1898-99	2	W 2-1	L 0-1				
1899-1900	2	W 3-0	L 0-1	1931-32	2	W 2-0	W 2-1
1900-01	2	W 4-0	L 0-2	1932-33	2	D 1-1	D 3-3
1901-02	2	W 1-0	D 1-1	1933-34	2	W 2-0	W 3-2
1902-03	2	W 2-1	D 1-1	1934-35	2	W 2-1	L 2-3
1903-04	2	W 2-0	L 0-1	1935-36	2	W 7-2	W 3-0
1904-05	2	W 6-1	D 2-2				
1905-06	2	W 3-0	L 0-1				

Summary of League results

	P	W	D	L	F	A
Division 2	36	21	5	10	76	37
Home	18	16	1	1	52	10
Away	18	5	4	9	24	27
Total	36	21	5	10	76	37

FA Cup results v the Valiants:

	Round	Venue	Result
1919-20	1	Away	W 1-0
1925-26	3	Away	W 3-2
1928-29	3	Away	W 3-0

League Cup results v the Valiants:

	Round	Venue	Result
1983-84	2 (1)	Away	W 1-0
	2 (2)	Home	W 2-0
1986-87	2 (1)	Home	W 2-0
	2 (2)	Away	W 5-2
1994-95	2 (1)	Away	W 2-1
	2 (2)	Home	W 2-0

Players with both clubs include: A Allman (Vale trialist), J Bannister, P Barnes, A Bellis (United WW2), H Birchenough, J Connaughton, J Dale, A Dodd (United junior), L Draycott, E Eastwood (United WW2), D Fidler (United reserve), C Gibson, W Grassam, J Greenhoff (also Vale coach), J Griffiths (Vale WW2), T Hamlett (United WW2), W Harrison, D Healy, A Hill (United reserve), G Holdcroft (United WW2), F Jones (Newton Heath reserve), SF Jones (United reserve), W Keely (United WW2), C Lawton (United reserve), J Lowey (United reserve), W McKay (United WW2), R Milarvie, L Page, K Pilkington, R Ramsay, W Rawlings, D Ryan (United reserve), J Smith, P Sutcliffe (United reserve), M Twiss, D Webber (United reserve), O Williams (United junior).
Also associated: R Smith (Vale manager, United reserve), S Matthews (United WW2 player, Vale manager).

264

PORTER, William

Born: Fleetwood, Lancashire, July 1905. Died: Ashton-under-Lyne, 28 April 1946.

Career: Windsor Villa FC, Fleetwood FC, Oldham Athletic (summer 1926), MANCHESTER UNITED (January 1935); guested for Accrington Stanley, Blackburn Rovers, Manchester City & Oldham Athletic during WW2; Hyde United (player-manager, September 1944 until his death in April 1946).

Prior to joining United, resolute full-back Billy Porter had accumulated 274 League appearances for Oldham. Earlier he had helped Fleetwood win the Lancashire Combination Cup and when he moved to Old Trafford he took over the left-back berth from Welsh international Tom Jones. A fine positional player, he was an ever-present when United won the Second Division title in 1935-36 and later he skippered United during the early part of WW2. He took Hyde to the Final of the Cheshire Cup before his death at the age of 40.

Club record: 65 apps.

PORTO (FC)

United eased through to the 1996-97 European Champions League semi-finals with a 4-0 aggregate win over Porto (4-0 victors at home, 0-0 away), but 19 years earlier they had come unstuck against the Portuguese side, losing in the 2nd round of the Cup-winners Cup competition. United crashed to a 4-0 first leg defeat in Porto and although they battled hard to win the return leg 5-2 with Steve Coppell scoring twice (plus two own-goals) the visitors somehow netted twice and went through on aggregate after a great contest.

PORTSMOUTH

United's League results v Pompey:

Season	Div	Home	Away	Season	Div	Home	Away
1924-25	2	W 2-0	D 1-1	1949-50	1	L 0-2	D 0-0
				1950-51	1	D 0-0	D 0-0
1927-28	1	W 2-0	L 0-1	1951-52	1	L 1-3	L 0-1
1928-29	1	D 0-0	L 0-3	1952-53	1	W 1-0	L 0-2
1929-30	1	W 3-0	L 0-3	1953-54	1	W 2-0	D 1-1
1930-31	1	L 0-1	L 1-4	1954-55	1	L 1-3	D 0-0
				1955-56	1	W 1-0	L 2-3
1936-37	1	L 0-1	L 1-2	1956-57	1	W 3-0	W 3-1
				1957-58	1	L 0-3	D 3-3
1938-39	1	D 1-1	D 0-0	1958-59	1	W 6-1	W 3-1
1946-47	1	W 3-0	W 1-0	1974-75	2	W 2-1	D 0-0
1947-48	1	W 3-2	W 3-1				
1948-49	1	W 3-2	D 2-2	1987-88	1	W 4-1	W 2-1

Summary of League results

	P	W	D	L	F	A
Division 1	40	16	10	14	56	49
Division 2	4	2	2	0	5	2
Home	22	13	3	6	38	21
Away	22	5	9	8	23	30
Total	44	18	12	14	61	51

FA Cup results v. Pompey:

	Round	Venue	Result
1900-01	Supplementary	Home	W 3-0
1906-07	1	Away	D 2-2
	Replay	Home	L 1-2
1933-34	3	Home	D 1-1
	Replay	Away	L 1-4
1949-50	5	Home	D 3-3
	Replay	Away	W 3-1

League Cup results v Pompey:

	Round	Venue	Result
1970-71	3	Home	W 1-0
1989-90	2 (1)	Away	W 3-2
	2 (2)	Home	D 0-0
1991-92	3	Home	W 3-1
1993-94	5	Home	D 2-2
	Replay	Away	W 1-0

Players with both clubs include: J Aston, snr (Pompey WW2), R Davies, C Gibson (Pompey amateur), G Graham, R Halton (Pompey WW2), G Haslam, G Hogg, G Hunter, N McBain (Pompey WW1), S McGarvey, A McLoughlin (United reserve), J Mansell (United amateur), A Mitchell, D Reid (United WW2), N Webb, F Worrall (United WW2).
Also associated: J McCartney (United player, Pompey secretary-manager).

POTTS, Arthur Arnold

Born: Cannock, Staffs. 26 May 1888. Died: South Staffs. early 1981.

Career: Cannock Council School, Willenhall Swifts, Manchester City (briefly, mid 1913), MANCHESTER UNITED (September 1913), guested for Birmingham & Southport Central during WW1, Wolverhampton Wanderers (£100, June 1920), Walsall (autumn 1922), Bloxwich Strollers, Dudley Town (1924-25), Red White & Blue FC, Wolverhampton (as an amateur, briefly in 1931). Later became a publican in Wolverhampton.

After scoring 30 goals for Willenhall Swifts in 1912-13, inside-forward Arthur Potts had the briefest of spells at Manchester City before joining United. He made his League debut in a 5-0 defeat by Everton in late November 1913 and after that had to fight for a first team place with George Travers, finally getting a decent run in the side halfway through the 1914-15 campaign. He played in the 1921 FA Cup Final for Wolves who were beaten 1-0 by Spurs at Stamford Bridge.

Club record: 29 apps. 5 goals

NB: In some United record/reference books, for the FA Cup tie v. Sheffield Wednesday on 9 January 1915, the inside-right is listed as being the unknown player 'Fox'. This should read 'Potts'.

POWELL, John

Born: Ffrwd, near Wrexham, 25 March 1860. Died: Wrexham, 16 March 1947.

Career: Druids (1879), Bolton Wanderers (1883), NEWTON HEATH (1886, professional 1887 to May 1891).

Jack Powell who appeared as a full-back for the Heathens, is believed to have been the first Welsh-born footballer to sign as a professional for an English-based club. A strong header of the ball, he captained the Heathens and was a key member of the side in the first season in the Football Alliance (1889-90).

Club record: 25 apps. (also 140 'other' apps, 2 goals)

265

PREMIERSHIP (FA Premier League)

The FA Premier League was instigated in 1992, comprising the 'old' Football League's First Division of 22 clubs. In 1995 the present format of 20 clubs was adopted. United, despite losing their first-ever two matches, have dominated the Premier League; champions seven times, runners-up twice. Only Blackburn Rovers (1994-95) & Arsenal (1997-98 & 2001-02) have broken United's hold on the title.

This is United's impressive ten-year Premiership record:

P	W	D	L	F	A	Pts	
392	244	93	55	789	360	825	(74.11%)

United hold the following Premier League records:

- Biggest home win: 9-0 v. Ipswich Town 04.03.95
- Biggest away win: 8-1 v. Nottingham Forest 06.02.99
- Most goals in a season: 97 1999-2000 (38 matches)
- Most points in a season: 92 1993-94 (42 matches)
  - 91 1999-2000 (38 matches)
- Most wins in a season: 28 1999-2000 (38 matches)
- Fewest defeats in season: 3* 1998-99/1999-2000 (38 matches)
- Most points gained 825 1992-2002 inclusive (392 matches)
- Most wins achieved 244 1992-2002 (392 matches)
- Most goals scored 789 1992-2002 (392 matches)   (average 2.01 per match)
- Most titles won 7 1993, 94, 96, 97, 99, 2000, 2001
- Goals in game (player) 5** Andy Cole v. Ipswich Town 04.03.95
- Longest unbeaten run: 29 1998-99/1999-2000
- Best goalscoring sequence (individual): 8 matches (10 goals) Ruud van Nistelrooy (2001-02)
- Best average home attendance: 67,586 in 2001-02.
- Highest attendance: 67,683 v. Middlesbrough in 2001-02
- * Shared with Chelsea: 1998-99 & Arsenal 2001-02; ** Shared with Alan Shearer (Newcastle United).

Fact File

Ole Gunnar Solskjaer is the only Premier League player who has twice scored 4 goals in a game - v. Nottingham Forest (a) as a substitute, 1998-99 and v. Everton, 1999. Beside his five goals v. Ipswich Town in 1995, Andy Cole also scored four v. Newcastle United in 1999-2000.

Manchester United (1999-2000) and Arsenal (2001-02) share the record of 12 consecutive Premiership victories*.

In the summer of 2001 the Premier League presented United with the FA Carling Premiership trophy to retain in perpetuity in recognition of their three successive Championship wins: 1998-99, 1999-2000 & 2000-01.

When United first won the Premiership title in 1992-93, the 20 players used that season by manager Alex Ferguson cost the club almost £18.5 million....Ten years on the squad had cost around £100 million...and rising!

Since beaten by Arsenal in 2002-03

PRENTICE, John H

Born: Glasgow, circa 1900

Career: Manchester Amateur League football, MANCHESTER UNITED (amateur, then professional November 1919), Swansea Town (June 1920), Tranmere Rovers (late 1920), Hurst FC (1922-23).

Reserve left-winger John Prentice's only League appearance in United's colours was in the Roses battle against Bradford (PA) at home in April 1920, deputising for Fred Hopkin in a 1-0 defeat.

Club record: one app.

PRESIDENTS

William Healey, John H Davies, James W Gibson and Sir Matt Busby have all held the position of President of Manchester United (in that order).

Sir Matt Busby was appointed President of Manchester United FC on 22 March 1980. The board met to elect a new Chairman, Busby standing against Martin Edwards. Busby could not manage enough votes and as a result Edwards was duly elected, Busby himself being appointed President, a post which had been vacant since James Gibson died in 1951. Busby held the position until his death in January 1994.

Former Conservative Prime Minister Arthur Balfour, was a vice-President of Manchester United during the first part of the 20th century. John J Bentley (secretary of Manchester United from 1912-16) was President of the Football League from 1893 to 1910. And ex-United player, James Brown, later became player-President of the American club, Greenport United.

PRESTON, Stephen

Born: Gorton, Manchester, winter 1879

Career: Local junior football (in Manchester), NEWTON HEATH (April 1901), Stockport County (February 1903), MANCHESTER UNITED (September 1903 to May 1904).

Inside or centre-forward Steve Preston - small in stature - drew up an excellent record during his first full season with the club, top-scoring with 11 goals in 29 League games in 1901-02, netting twice on his debut against Gainsborough Trinity on 7 September. He was basically a reserve team player during his second spell.
Club record: 34 apps. 13 goals (also 7 'other' apps, 3 goals)

PRESTON NORTH END

Heathens/United's League results v North End:

Season	Div	Home	Away	Season	Div	Home	Away
1892-93	1	W 2-1	L 1-2	1936-37	1	D 1-1	L 1-3
1893-94	1	L 1-3	L 0-2				
				1938-39	1	D 1-1	D 1-1
1901-02	2	L 0-2	L 1-5				
1902-03	2	L 0-1	L 1-3	1946-47	1	D 1-1	D 1-1
1903-04	2	L 0-2	D 1-1	1947-48	1	D 1-1	L 1-2
				1948-49	1	D 2-2	W 6-1
1906-07	1	W 3-0	L 0-2				
1907-08	1	W 2-1	D 0-0	1951-52	1	L 1-2	W 2-1
1908-09	1	L 0-2	W 3-0	1952-53	1	W 5-2	W 5-0
1909-10	1	D 1-1	L 0-1	1953-54	1	W 1-0	W 3-1
1910-11	1	W 5-0	W 2-0	1954-55	1	W 2-1	W 2-0
1911-12	1	D 0-0	D 0-0	1955-56	1	W 3-2	L 1-3
				1956-57	1	W 3-2	W 3-1
1913-14	1	W 3-0	L 2-4	1957-58	1	D 0-0	D 1-1
				1958-59	1	L 0-2	W 4-3
1919-20	1	W 5-1	W 3-2	1959-60	1	D 1-1	L 0-4
1920-21	1	W 1-0	D 0-0	1960-61	1	W 1-0	W 4-2
1921-22	1	D 1-1	L 2-3				
1931-32	2	W 3-2	D 0-0				
1932-33	2	D 0-0	D 3-3				
1933-34	2	W 1-0	L 2-3				

* Played at Maine Road

Summary of League results

	P	W	D	L	F	A
Division 1	54	24	16	14	95	68
Division 2	12	2	4	6	12	22
Home	33	15	11	7	51	35
Away	33	11	9	13	56	55
Total	66	26	20	20	107	90

FA Cup results v North End:

Season	Round	Venue	Result
1889-90	1	Away	L 1-6
1945-46	4 (1)	Home*	W 1-0
	4 (2)	Away	L 1-3
1947-48	6	Home*	W 4-1
1961-62	6	Away	D 0-0
	Replay	Home	W 2-1
1965-66	6	Away	D 1-1
	Replay	Home	W 3-1
1971-72	4	Away	W 2-0

Players with both clubs include: M Appleton, J Bannister, A Beardsworth, D Beckham, T Bogan, E Bond, F Burns, A Butterworth (United reserve), W Campbell, R Charlton (PNE player & manager), J Clark (also caretaker-manager of PNE), J Cunningham, A Dainty (United WW2), S Davies (United trialist), A Dawson, A Fitton, A Gowling, D Graham, W Halligan (United WW1), D Healy, W Henderson, G Holdcroft (United WW2), R Iddon, R John, N Keen (United reserve), N Lawton, E Lewis, J Lowey (United reserve), J McClelland, S McIlroy (PNE player-coach), J Macken (United reserve), M Martin, C Murdock (United reserve), D Musgrave (United reserve), G Mutch, H O'Donnell (United WW2), E Pegg, D Sadler, G Sapsford, A Smith, J Turnbull, J Walton, W Watson (United WW2), O Williams (United junior). Also associated: F O'Farrell (PNE player, United manager), B Kidd (United player & assistant-manager, PNE manager), N Stiles (United player & coach, PNE chief coach & manager), V Hayes (United player, PNE secretary-manager), J Crompton (PNE assistant-manager), D Viollet (United player, PNE coach), T Cavanagh (PNE player, United assistant-manager/trainer), H Catterick (United WW2 player, PNE manager).

PRINCE, Albert J

Born: Staffordshire, circa 1892
Career: Stafford Rangers, MANCHESTER UNITED (amateur, February-May 1915).
Inside-left Albert Prince was a schoolmaster (in Stafford) who was handed his only first team outing (perhaps surprisingly) in the 2-1 home defeat by champions-elect Everton in February 1915.
Club record: one app.

PRINCE, D

Born: Lancashire, circa 1870
Career: NEWTON HEATH (August 1893 to May 1894).
Prince (possibly Douglas), an unknown reserve left-winger made his debut v. Darwen in November 1893, when the Heathens shuffled their forward-line following the suspension of three first team players.
Club record: 2 apps. (also 3 'other' apps, one goal)

PROFESSIONALISM

Professionalism in football was first seen as long ago as 1879 when Blackburn Rovers and Darwen recruited players from Scotland and covertly paid them wages. Over the next year or so Bolton Wanderers, Preston North End and several others followed suit, causing the clubs' suspension by the FA.
It wasn't until 20 July 1885 that professionalism was finally accepted into English soccer...an important step in the history of the game. United (then known as Newton Heath) were one of the first clubs to sign up as a professional organisation, doing so in August 1885.
The decision by the FA in 1885 was directly responsible for the formation of the first Football League three years later.
In fact, the FA had been forced to reverse their anti-professional stance by a group of Northern clubs led by Major William Sudell of PNE who threatened to leave the FA and form a British Association.

PROGRAMMES (Matchday)

In the early days of League football there were no programmes as such. Most clubs (including Newton Heath/Manchester United produced a single card (including the season's fixtures) which stated the date of the match, the names of the two clubs and the 22 players taking part, plus the referee for the day's action.

267

Programme Notes

For the first time in 1946, the front cover of United's official matchday programme - 'The United Review' - depicted a player shaking hands with a supporter. This remained as part of the style for a number of years and after a period when the programme was re-designed, it was re-introduced in the 1990s, the two figures being slightly altered over the years to reflect changing fashions!

During the three-day working week in January 1974, Plymouth Argyle - hoping for a replay - produced a full programme for the anticipated game with United at Home Park - before they had played the initial third round tie at Old Trafford. It was to no avail as United won 1-0. (This Argyle programme is now much sought-after by collectors).

A total of 74,680 official programmes were sold for United's 2nd leg encounter against Estudiantes in the World Club Championship at Old Trafford on 16 October 1968, -a record for any match except for a major Cup Final.

The previous record for the sale of United programmes (for one game) was for the First Division fixture with Arsenal at Old Trafford just a fortnight earlier, on 5 October 1968, when 64,772 copies of the matchday programme were sold (the attendance was 61,843). Previously 60,462 United programmes had been snapped up for their European Cup semi-final home clash with Real Madrid in April 1968.

Without confirmation, it is understood that during the calendar year of 1968 (incorporating that European Cup winning season), the printing company produced more than 800,000 home programmes for Manchester United FC.

It is believed that the Wembley authorities printed 275,000 programmes for the 1968 European Cup Final between United and Benfica, of which some 260,000 were actually sold.

And over 66,000 programmes were sold for the Chelsea v. Manchester United League game at Stamford Bridge in 1966 - a record for the London club.

During the 1950s and 1960s United's programme included a token which when pasted onto an official sheet could be used as proof of attendance when purchasing tickets for big matches. Unfortunately a 'black market' in these tokens began, leading to the mis-use of an enterprising (and initially) fair system. The practice was eventually discontinued.

PROMOTION

(See also under Football League).

Following relegation from the top flight of English football, United gained promotion from Division Two as follows: in 1905-06 (as runners-up), 1924-25 (as runners-up), 1935-36 (as champions), 1937-38 (as runners-up) and 1974-75 (as champions).

PRUNIER, William

Born: Montrueil, France 14 August 1967

Career: Auxerre (1985), Olympique Marseille (1988) Bordeaux (1990), MANCHESTER UNITED (on loan as a trialist, December 1995), FC Copenhagen (1996-97), Napoli, KV Kortrijk (Belgium).

French international centre-back William Prunier made only two Premier League appearances for United halfway through the 1995-96 season, alongside Gary Neville at the heart of the defence against QPR (home) and Tottenham Hotspur (away). owing to the absence of Steve Bruce. He was not retained.

Club record: 2 apps.

PUBLICANS

Several United footballers, after retiring, went into the licensing or hotel business. They include (among others): Horace Blew (hotelier), Pat Crerand, Will Davidson, Dick Duckworth, Fred Erentz, Harry Erentz, Danny Ferguson, Frank Haydock (hotelier), Vince Hayes (also a hotelier), Tom Homer, Steve James, Caesar Jenkyns, Jim McCalliog, Ted MacDougall, Francis McPherson, Tom Manley, Billy Meredith, Charlie Moore, Graham Moore, Kenny Morgans, Dick Pegg, Arthur Potts, Jack Powell, Bill Rawlings, George Sapsford, Ted Savage, Jack Silcock, Alex Stepney, Jeff Whitefoot, Jack Wilson, Tommy Wilson.

PUGH, James

Born: Swansea, circa 1896

Career: Hereford Thistle (1914), Luton Town (during WW1), Brighton & Hove Albion (1919), Abertillery (briefly), MANCHESTER UNITED (April 1922), Wrexham (July 1923-May 1925).

Reserve full-back Jimmy Pugh deputised for Jack Silcock in United's first team. He later made 41 first team appearances for Wrexham.

Club record: 2 apps.

Q for...

QUEEN'S PARK RANGERS

Summary of League results

	P	W	D	L	F	A
Premier League	8	6	2	0	16	8
Division 1	30	16	8	6	51	33
Home	19	15	3	1	39	13
Away	19	7	7	5	28	28
Total	38	22	10	6	67	41

FA Cup results v QPR:

	Round	Venue	Result
1976-77	4	Home	W 1-0
1988-89	3	Home	D 0-0
	Replay	Away	D 2-2 aet
	2nd R	Home	W 3-0
1990-91	3	Home	W 2-1
1994-95	6	Home	W 2-0

United's League results v QPR:

Season	Div	Home	Away	Season	Div	Home	Away
1968-69	1	W 8-1	W 3-2	1985-86	1	W 2-0	L 0-1
				1986-87	1	W 1-0	D 1-1
1973-74	1	W 2-1	L 0-3	1987-88	1	W 2-1	W 2-0
				1988-89	1	D 0-0	L 2-3
1975-76	1	W 2-1	L 0-1	1989-90	1	D 0-0	W 2-1
1976-77	1	W 1-0	L 0-4	1990-91	1	W 3-1	D 1-1
1977-78	1	W 3-1	D 2-2	1991-92	1	L 1-4	D 0-0
1978-79	1	W 2-0	D 1-1	1992-93	PL	D 0-0	W 3-1
				1993-94	PL	W 2-1	W 3-2
1983-84	1	W 3-1	D 1-1	1994-95	PL	W 2-0	W 3-2
1984-85	1	W 3-0	W 3-1	1995-96	PL	W 2-1	D 1-1

FA Charity Shield

United met QPR in the first ever FA Charity Shield game. The match between the respective League Champions of the Football League and the Southern League was held at Stamford Bridge on 27 April 1908 and ended in a 1-1 draw, Billy Meredith scoring for United. The match was replayed early next season, again at Stamford Bridge and on this occasion United won 4-0 with goals by Jimmy Turnbull (3) and George Wall. Although the first match attracted just 6,000 spectators, the replay had an audience of 45,000.

Fact File:

Rangers lost on each of their first twelve League and Cup visits to Old Trafford (starting in March 1969 when they crashed 8-1). They registered their first win on United soil on New Year's Day 1992, when they triumphed 4-1 with the help of a Dennis Bailey hat-trick.
Players with both clubs include: R Allen, A Brazil, J Cape, N Culkin, D Givens, G Hill, F Knowles, O Linkson (QPR WW1), D McCreery; J Merrick & G Micklewight (United reserves), P Parker, SC Pearson (QPR WW2), M Rogers, J Travers, E Vincent, A Warburton.
Also associated: T Docherty & D Sexton (managers of both clubs), S Houston (United player, QPR manager), G Graham (United player, QPR coach).

269

QUEIROZ, Carlos

Carlos Queiroz was appointed first-team coach by MANCHESTER UNITED in June 2002. Born in Mozambique in 1953, he took his first coaching job in football in 1978 and prior to taking up his duties at Old Trafford, he had worked at the highest level across Europe, in South America, in the Far East, in the USA and also in South Africa where he was that country's national team coach, having previously held a similar position with Portugal.

QUIN, William John Joseph

Born: Barrhead, Renfrewshire, 1890. Died: Leicester, 1957
Career: Manchester Xaverian College, Higher Broughton FC, Cheetham Hill FC, Manchester City (1907), MANCHESTER UNITED (June 1908), Nelson (June 1910), Chorley (later in season 1910-11), Eccles Borough FC (autumn 1911), Grimsby Town (summer 1912), Clyde (summer 1919), Ayr United (early 1921 to summer 1923). In July 1924 he was appointed linesman by the Scottish Football League.
Jack Quin was a schoolteacher before finally turning professional with Grimsby Town at the age of 22. Earlier he had failed to get a game with Manchester City and only made five League appearances after leaving Old Trafford (all with Grimsby).,
Club record: 2 apps.

QUIXALL, Albert

Born: Sheffield, 9 August 1933
Career: Sheffield Schools, Meynell Youth Club (Sheffield), Sheffield Wednesday (amateur 1948, professional August 1950), MANCHESTER UNITED (£45,000, September 1958), Oldham Athletic (£8,500, September 1964), Stockport County (summer 1966), Altrincham (winter 1967), Radcliffe Borough (1968-69).
United signed inside-forward Albert Quixall from Sheffield Wednesday for a British record fee in 1958. He had already represented England twice as a schoolboy, gained five full caps (his first in 1953 as a 20 year-old) and also starred in one Under-23 and three 'B' internationals while also playing four times for the Football League side as well as helping the Owls twice win the Second Division championship (1952 and 1956), scoring 65 goals in 260 games for the Hillsborough club. Wearing the shortest of shorts (when virtually all players donned much longer ones) Quixall was a clever, ball-player who was recruited to the Old Trafford ranks when the side was being rebuilt following the Munich air tragedy. He helped United win the FA Cup in 1963 before injuries started to affect his performances and after six years with the Reds he moved to nearby Boundary Park (after a very poor showing in the 1964 FA Charity game against Everton (which United lost 4-0). He netted 11 goals in 36 League games for the Latics. Soon after leaving football Quixall became a scrap metal dealer.
Club record: 184 apps. 56 goals

R for...

ROBSON, Bryan, OBE

Born: Witton Gilbert, Chester-le-Street, County Durham, 11 January 1957.

Career: Washington & Chester-le-Street Schools, trialist with Burnley, Coventry City & Newcastle United, West Bromwich Albion (apprentice 1972, professional August 1974), Happy Valley FC, Hong Kong (on loan, 1978), MANCHESTER UNITED (£1.5 million, October 1981), Middlesbrough (player-manager, May 1994, retiring as a player in 1997), MANCHESTER UNITED (part-time coach, 2001).

After making an impact in the Second Division and then starring in the top flight, and also in Europe, with West Bromwich Albion, the versatile Bryan Robson went on to greater things with Manchester United and England. He helped the Reds win successive Premiership titles (in 1993 & 1994) and skippered them to three FA Cup Final victories (in 1983 - when he scored twice in the replay win over Brighton, in 1985 (v. Everton) and in 1990 (v. Crystal Palace). He was a League Cup runner-up in 1991, but quickly made up for that disappointment by accepting a prized European medal when he lifted the Cup Winners Cup that same season as United beat Barcelona 2-1 in Rotterdam. He also led his country (England) on many occasions while taking his tally of senior caps to 90 (26 goals scored), thus becoming one of the finest midfield players in world soccer. He participated in three World Cups and his tally of international goals included a hat-trick against Turkey in 1984 and a strike after just 26 seconds in the World Cup game v. France in Spain, 1982....the tournament's second fastest goal at that time. Robson made his League debut for West Brom against York City in April 1975 and the following season helped the Baggies win promotion from the Second Division under player-manager Johnny Giles (a former United player).

Robson occupied the left-back, centre-half, wing-half and inside-forward positions during his time at The Hawthorns. He was an aggressive competitor with an endless supply of dynamic stamina. He had awareness, was creative, possessed excellent passing skills and powerful shot, was a superb header of the ball and had a penchant for hard work, being utterly fearless in the tackle, scoring 46 goals in almost 250 apperarances.

In October 1981 along with his Albion colleague Remi Moses, Robson was lured to Old Trafford by former boss Ron Atkinson in a deal worth £2 million, Robson being valued at £1.5 million.

Having achieved legendary status as 'Captain Marvel' with Manchester United, he became player-manager of Middlesbrough and guided the Teeside club into the Premiership at the end of his first season in charge. He retired as a player in May 1997 with an overall total of 832 competitive appearances under his belt (for club and country). He scored 172 goals.

His younger brother Gary was also associated with West Bromwich Albion (1981-93) and with Bradford City after that.

Club record: 465 apps. 100 goals

RABA VASAS ETO

Dutchmaan Arnold Muhren scored in both games for United as they eased through to the second round of the UEFA Cup in 1984-85. The Reds won 3-0 at home and drew 2-2 away for an aggregate 5-2 victory.

RACHUBKA, Paul Stephen

Born: St Louis, Opispo, California, USA, 21 May 1981

Career: MANCHESTER UNITED (YTS, June 1997, Pro July 1999), Royal Antwerp (on loan, season 2001-02), Charlton Athletic (trialist, April/May 2002, signed for £200,000, June 2002).

Third-string goalkeeper Paul Rachubka - an England Youth international (despite being born in the States) - played in just one Premiership game for United - a 2-0 home win over Leicester City in March 2001, when he was unexpectedly called off the bench as Fabien Barthez was injured in the pre-match warm-up. Earlier he had made his senior debut as a substitute in a Worthington Cup-tie v. Watford (following Raimond van der Gouw's sending-off).

Club record: three apps.

RACING STRASBOURG

A crowd of 30,000 saw two goals by Denis Law and further strikes from John Connelly, Bobby Charlton and David Herd give United a firm foot-hold at 5-0 in the away leg of their quarter-final 1964-65 Inter-Cities Cup encounter against Racing Strasbourg. The return clash at Old Trafford was an anti-climax to say the least - and 34,188 saw the disappointing contest that ended goalless!

RADFORD, James W Charles

Born: Walsall, 19 March 1900. Died: Wolverhampton, July 1924.

Career: Walsall Schools, Walsall (from 1916), MANCHESTER UNITED (May 1920 until his death).

An England schoolboy international (v. Scotland) in 1914, centre-forward Charlie Radford had scored 17 goals in 42 first team games for Walsall before joining United. However, there were already a handful of established goalscorers at Old Trafford, and as a result Radford was tried as a full-back where he developed into an exceptionally fine defender, going on to appear in almost 100 senior games for United, being a fine partner to Jack Silcock. He was only 24 when he was sadly killed in a motor cycling accident in Wolverhampton.

Club record: 96 apps. one goal

RAMSAY, David Robert

Born: Stoke-on-Trent, circa 1865.

Career: Burslem Port Vale (1886), Stoke (1888), NEWTON HEATH (July 1890), West Manchester (December 1891), Northwich Victoria (season 1892-93), Burslem Port Vale.(1893-94). Retired May 1894 (with knee injury).

Robert Ramsay was able to play as a full-back, wing-half or centre-half. An industrious footballer with great stamina, he was an ever-present at the heart of the Heathens' defence in their first season in the Football Alliance (1890-91). He made 90 first team appearances during his two spells with Port Vale but was eventually forced to give up the game after his right knee became disjointed!

Club record: 23 apps. 7 goals (also 28 'other' apps, 5 goals)

RAMSDEN, Charles William

Born: South Normanton, early 1903.

Career: South Normanton Colliery, Rotherham United (late 1925), MANCHESTER UNITED (May 1927), Stockport County (on loan, January-May 1928), Manchester North End (August 1932), Witton Albion (1934), Gresham & Craven FC (as an amateur 1935-36).

Winger Charlie Ramsden had played very well in United's reserve side and in two League games early in the 1927-28 season but then fell from favour following the arrival at Old Trafford of Welsh international Rees Williams. Thereafter Ramsden acted as cover for Williams (then converted Joe Spence) and despite a reasonable run in the first XI halfway through the 1930-31 campaign, he finally left the club in 1932.

Club record: 16 apps. 3 goals

RAPID VIENNA

United met the Austrian champions in both the 1968-69 & 1996-97 European Cup competitions. George Best scored twice and Willie Morgan once in United's 3-0 home win in the earlier tournament (which they took on aggregate with that same scoreline after a 0-0 draw). And in the latter tournament United won both matches by 2-0 in the first group stage matches. Ole Gunnar Solskjaer and David Beckham were on target at Old Trafford and Ryan Giggs and Eric Cantona found the net in Austria.

RATCLIFFE, George

Born: Lathom, autumn 1877

Career: NEWTON HEATH (trialist, November 1898-May 1899).

Outside-right George Ratcliffe deputised for the injured Billy Bryant in the third last League game of the 1898-99 season, doing well in a comprehensive 5-0 home win over Luton Town.

His name sometimes appeared as Radcliffe.

Club record: One app. (also one 'other' apps, one goal)

RATTIGAN, George

Born: Lancashire, circa 1868

Career: NEWTON HEATH (season 1890-91).

Reserve wing-half Rattigan made one FA Cup appearance for United, lining up against Bootle on 25 October 1890, both clubs turning out reserve sides.

Club record: one app.

RAWLINGS, William Edward

Born: Andover, Hampshire, 3 January 1896. Died: Chandlers Ford, 25 September 1972

Career: Andover FC, Army football (when serving in France with the 2nd/3rd Wessex Ambulance Corps), Southampton (amateur 1918, professional 1919), MANCHESTER UNITED (£4,000, March 1928), Port Vale (£1,200, November 1929), New Milton FC (1930), Newport IoW (season 1930-31). Later became a licensee in Southampton and also worked for the Admiralty, based in Portland.

Centre-forward Bill Rawlings scored almost 200 goals in close on 350 competitive games (156 goals coming in 294 League matches) for Southampton before joining United. Possessing a deadly shot (mainly in his right-foot) he was capped twice by England v. Wales and Scotland in 1922 and had an a big say in helping United pull clear of relegation with a flurry of important goals (10 in all) at the end of the 1927-28 season.

He awarded the 1914 Star and three Army football medals during the 1914-18 conflict.

Club record: 36 apps. 19 goals

READ, Thomas Herbert

Born: Manchester, circa 1879

Career: Stretford FC, Manchester City (summer 1895), MANCHESTER UNITED (August 1902 to May 1908). Retired after an ongoing knee injury.

Before joining United, Bert Read - a tough-tackling, thoughtful full-back - made 117 League appearances for Manchester City, helping them win the Second Division title in 1899. He had a sound first season with United but then injuries interfered with his game and he eventually became a permanent reserve, playing in only a handful of League games during his last four years with the club.

Club record: 42 apps.

READING

United's FA Cup record v the Royals:

	Round	Venue	Result
1911-12	3	Away	D 1-1
	Replay	Home	W 3-0
1926-27	3	Away	D 1-1
	Replay	Home	D 2-2 aet
	2nd R	Villa Pk	L 1-2
1935-36	3	Away	W 3-1
1936-37	3	Home	W 1-0
1954-55	3	Away	D 1-1
	Replay	Home	W 4-1
1995-96	4	Away	W 3-0

Watney Cup

United defeated Reading 3-2 at Elm Park in the 1st round of the 1970 Watney Cup. A crowd of 18,348 saw Bobby Charlton (2) and Paul Edwards find the net for United in a very competitive match.

Players with both clubs include: G Brebner (United reserve), C Casper, W Dunn, E Dunphy (United reserve), D Ferguson, R Ferrier (Reading WW2), H Green, R Hampson (United reserve), F Jones (Newton Heath reserve), F Kennedy, J Leighton, F McPherson; N Murphy & P O'Sullivan (United reserves), W Owen, E Pegg, L Richardson, T Ritchie (United reserve), W Robertson, M Robins, M Simmonds (United & Reading reserve), N Webb.

Also associated: M Busby (Reading WW2 player, United manager).

REAL MADRID

Venue	P	W	D	L	F	A
Home	3	1	1	1	5	5
Away	3	0	2	1	4	6
Summary	6	1	3	2	9	11

Real were United's first European Cup opponents at Old Trafford, playing there in the semi-final of the 1956-57 competition. Tommy Taylor scored in both legs of that semi-final against the Spanish champions, United losing 3-1 in Spain in front the club's biggest-ever 'live' audience - 135,000 - and being held to a 2-2 draw at home.

After the Munich air tragedy the two clubs were drawn together by mutual respect, Real generously playing a number of prestigious friendlies to help hasten United's return to the top.

When United won the European Cup in 1967-68, they knocked Real out at the semi-final stage. After George Best had edged United 1-0 ahead from the first leg, a spirited performance in front of 125,000 fans in the Bernabeu Stadium saw the Reds claim a tremendous 3-3 draw after trailing 3-1 at half-time. Defenders David Sadler and Bill Foulkes (with a late equaliser) were among the heroes that night.

In 1999-2000 Real gained revenge when they ousted United from the competition in the quarter-finals, winning 3-2 at Old Trafford after a goalless draw in Spain.

* In August 2000 United defeated Real 1-0 (Ole Gunnar Solskjaer the scorer) in Munich's Opel Masters tournament in Germany.

RED STAR BELGRADE

After a 2-1 home win in the first-leg of the 1957-58 European Cup semi-final United then travelled to Belgrade and forced a 3-3 draw to enter the semi-finals for the second year running. Sadly, as we all know, the team which had done the club proud and which was in line for a unique treble, was torn apart on the Munich air strip soon afterwards!

Brian McClair's goal at Old Trafford gave United the European Super Cup at Red Star's expense in 1991.

To celebrate the Festival of Britain, Red Star came to Old Trafford and drew 1-1 with United on 12 May 1951....thus becoming the first 'foreign' club side to visit the ground.

United also drew 4-4 with Red Star in a friendly match, also at Old Trafford, in August 1975.

REDMAN, William

Born: Manchester, 29 January 1928
Career: MANCHESTER UNITED (amateur, June 1944, professional November 1946), Bury (June 1954-1956),
Buxton FC (1956-57).
Billy Redman - who qualified as a draughtsman during his apprenticeship at Old Trafford - was a very useful left-back,
cool under pressure with a steady nerve. He looked good at times after taking over from converted forward Johnny
Aston early in 1951.. In fact, he played in the first 18 games of United's League Championship-winning season of 1951-
52 before losing his place to Roger Byrne.
Club record: 38 apps..

REDWOOD, Hubert

Born: St Helens, July 1913. Died: St Helens, October 1943
Career: Sherdley Albion (1930), MANCHESTER UNITED (amateur May 1933, professional August 1933). Had
guested for New Brighton during WW2 before contracting tuberculosis from which he died at the age of 30.
Hubert Redwood was a scrum-half on the rugby field at school as well as being a very efficient soccer full-back. He
gained a regular place in United's first team in 1936-37 and the following season played in 29 League games as the Reds
regained their First Division status.
Club record: 96 apps. 4 goals

REFEREES

Two former Newton Heath players - Herbert Dale (1887-93) and George Owen (1889-90) - both became referees after
retiring from the game, Dale in the Football League, Owen at non-League level (in Wales).
Herbert Bamlett (United's manager for four years: 1927-31), was the youngest referee ever to take charge of an FA Cup
Final when he officiated in the 1914 showdown between Burnley and Liverpool at Crystal Palace.
Bamlett was also the referee in charge of the Burnley v. Manchester United quarter-final FA Cup-tie at Turf Moor in
1909. He abandoned the game with just 18 minutes remaining with the Clarets 1-0 ahead. United went on to win the
re-arranged clash and ultimately won the Final against Bristol City.
John Bentley, United's club secretary from 1912-16, was a highly-respected former League referee.

REID, Thomas Joseph

Born: Motherwell, 15 August 1905. Died: Prescot, near Liverpool, 1972
Career: Blantyre Victoria (1922), Clydebank (1925), Liverpool (£1,000, 1926), MANCHESTER UNITED (February
1929), Oldham Athletic (on loan, March 1933, joining the Latics permanently for £400 three months later), Barrow
(season 1935-36), Rhyl Athletic (early 1938 - after being out of football for 18 months).
Overall Tommy Reid had an excellent career: scoring 145 goals in 245 League games.
An out-and-out centre-forward, well built, physically strong and robust his record with United was excellent. Taking
over from Billy Rawlings, he netted twice on his debut v. West Ham in February 1929 and at the end of that season he
had notched 14 goals in only 17 games - helping United pull clear from a possible relegation dog-fight. Injuries
interrupted his performances the following season but he bounced back in 1930-31 with another 17 League goals.
However, his efforts proved fruitless as relegation was suffered from the First Division. Read did well in 1931-32 and
again during the early stages of the following season before he joined cash-strapped Oldham (after a loan spell).
Club record: 101 apps. 67 goals

RELEGATION

Manchester United have suffered relegation from the top-flight of English football on five occasions.
In 1893-94 they finished 16th and bottom; in 1921-22 they again claimed last place (out of 22); in 1930-31 they took
the wooden spoon for a third time, conceding 115 goals in the process; in 1936-37 they went down in 21st position
after spending just one season back in Division One and finally in 1973-74 they slipped out of the limelight, again in
21st spot, after drawing one and losing three their last four matches.
In 1933-34 United escaped relegation to the Third Division by the narrowest of margins, beating Millwall 2-0 at The
Den to consign the Lions to relegation instead. Talk about too close for comfort - this was it!

RENNOX, Clatworthy

Born: Shotts, Lanarkshire, 25 February (possibly 1897).
Career: Dykehead FC, Clapton Orient (summer 1921), MANCHESTER UNITED (March 1925), Grimsby Town (season 1927-28).
Inside-forward 'Charlie' Rennox scored 24 goals in 101 League games for Orient before moving north to Old Trafford
to fill the gap left by the injured Tom Smith. He slotted in immediately and helped United gain promotion. The
following season he switched to the left to partner Harry Thomas and finished up as the club's second top-scorer with
18 goals as United reached the semi-finals of the FA Cup. Surprisingly he failed to make the first team at Grimsby.
Club record: 68 apps. 25 goals

RESERVES

In 1911-12 Manchester United were one of 17 founder members of the Central League, later renamed the Pontins League (Premier Division). In the late 1990s the FA Premier Reserve League (North) was introduced.

United were victorious in the Central/Pontins League competition nine times with their seasonal records reading:

Season	P	W	D	L	F	A	Pts
1912-13	38	22	11	5	79	30	55
1920-21	42	26	5	11	102	57	57
1938-39	42	24	6	12	93	60	54
1946-47	42	28	6	8	114	58	62
1955-56	42	30	8	4	117	33	68*
1959-60	42	26	8	8	114	69	60
1993-94	34	22	7	5	77	38	73
1995-96	34	22	5	7	71	35	71
1996-97	24	15	6	3	55	24	51

*United's first team also won the League Division One title.

United won the FA Premier Reserve League (North) in 2001-02 with this record:

Season	P	W	D	L	D	A	Pts
2001-02	24	12	7	5	47	28	43

Reserve XI Facts:

•United fielded SEVEN full internationals in their Central League side in December 1976 and quite frequently from 2000 to 2002 there were at least four or five senior internationals playing in the Reds' second XI.

•Ron Ferrier netted a record seven goals for United's second XI against Bury in March 1936.

•Albert Smith scored four goals for United's reserve side on two occasions in 1925-26.

•Jimmy Hanson was a prolific scorer throughout his career. He hit a hat-trick for United's 2nd XI v. Accrington Stanley whist on trial with the club in 1923-24. In 1925-26 he scored five goals against Stoke City reserves and followed up a year later with a double hat-trick (six goals) in a big win over Burnley's second string.

•When United won the Pontins League titles in 1993-94 and 1995-96, they finished 10 points clear of runners-up Aston Villa and Derby County respectively. Jovan Kirovski scored 20 of the team's 71 goals in 1995-96.

•United almost made it a hat-trick of Pontins League title triumphs in the 1990s, finishing third in the Premier Division in 1997-98, just one win (three points) behind the champions Sunderland and second-placed Liverpool.

• United's 'A' team won the Lancashire League Championship nine times in 12 years between 1987 and 1998. They finished runners-up twice. When winning in 1996-97 United lost only twice (in 28 games) and scored 108 goals.

•United's 'B' team won the Lancashire League Second Division title in 1989 and 1997 and were runners-up in on four other occasions between 1988 and 1996.

•United youngster Colin McKee was voted Pontins League 'Player of the Season' in 1992-93.

•Future United full-back Alex Forsyth top-scored for Partick Thistle reserves in 1970-71 with 24 goals.

•Charlie Ramsden was married on the morning of 2 March 1929 - in the afternoon he went out and netted twice for United's reserve side against Sheffield United at Old Trafford.

•Alf Steward represented the Central League v. the North-Eastern League in January 1921.

•In season 1923-24 Steward saved a total of six penalties in Central League games for United.

•On 22 April 1957 (Easter Monday) with a European Cup semi-final against Real Madrid due on the Wednesday, Matt Busby made NINE changes from Saturday's team that had played a League fixture against Sunderland. The predominantly reserve side beat Burnley 2-0 while the 'A' team (promoted to form the reserve side) won the Central League game at Burnley.

•United's reserve team (in recent years) has utilised Gigg Lane, Bury for their home games and they also played at Moss Lane, Altrincham.

•During the period 1946-49 with United sharing City's Maine Road stadium, the reserve teams of both clubs played their home matches at bombed out Old Trafford..

RICHARDS, Charles Henry
Born: Burton-on-Trent, Staffs, August 1875.
Career: Gresley Rovers, Notts County (summer, 1894), Nottingham Forest (early 1896), Grimsby Town (early 1898), Leicester Fosse (summer 1901), MANCHESTER UNITED (August 1902), Doncaster Rovers (March 1903).
Inside-forward Charlie Richards had already appeared in 180 League games by the time he signed for United. He was secured by the club as a reserve forward and failed to hold his place during the second half of season 1902-03. However, in his short time with the club, Charlie Richards wrote his name in United's history, scoring the first League goal under the club's new title of 'Manchester United' in a 1-0 win at Gainsborough Trinity.
Club record: 11 apps. 2 goals

RICHARDS, William
Born: West Bromwich, 6 October 1874. Died: 4 February 1926.
Career: Wordsley FC, Singers FC (Coventry), West Bromwich Standard, West Bromwich Albion (summer 1894), NEWTON HEATH (December 1901), Stourbridge (July 1902), Halesowen Town (season 1903-04).
For WBA, inside or centre-forward Billy Richards netted 32 goals in 122 League games and appeared in the 1895 FA Cup Final defeat by Aston Villa. He scored on his debut for United against Burslem Port Vale but he failed to recapture the form he had shown with the Throstles.
Club record: 9 apps. one goal

RICHARDSON, Lancelot Holliday

Born: Tow Law, County Durham, April 1899. Died: Cordoba, Argentina, 22 February 1958
Career: North Eastern County School football, Barnard Castle, Shildon Athletic, South Shields (summer 1923), MANCHESTER UNITED (£1,000, April 1926), Reading (summer 1929), Rowlands Gill FC (early in season 1932-33).
During his career, goalkeeper Lance Richardson made 174 League appearances. Having started out as a centre-forward, he was placed between the posts by chance and became a quality 'keeper. He replaced Jack Mew at Old Trafford, acting as deputy to Alf Steward. He made his United debut on the last day of the 1925-26 season (1 May) in a 3-2 win over West Bromwich Albion; spent the whole of the next season in the reserves and then made 32 League appearances in 1927-28 before finding himself back in the second XI for his final campaign with the Reds.
Club record: 42 apps.

RICHEST CLUB IN THE WORLD

In November 2001, a list compiled by Deloitte & Touche in conjunction with Sport Business Group declared Manchester United as the richest football club in the world with an annual turnover of £117 million during the 1999-2000 season. Real Madrid were second richest (£103.7 million) with Bayern Munich third (£91.6 million) and AC Milan fourth (£89.7 million). Bayern's total included transfer fees received!
*It was anticipated that United's turnover for 2002-03 would be over £150 million.

RIDDING, William

Born: Heswall, Cheshire, 4 April 1911. Died: Heaton, Bolton, 20 September 1981.
Career: Heswall PSA, Tranmere Rovers (autumn 1928), Manchester City (£3,000, early 1930), MANCHESTER UNITED (£2,000 plus Billy Dale and Harry Rowley, December 1931), Northampton Town (August 1934), Tranmere Rovers (mid-1935), Oldham Athletic (autumn 1935 - retiring May 1936), Tranmere Rovers ('A' team coach, 1938 to 1946, also acting as manager and trainer at Prenton Park during WW2), Bolton Wanderers (trainer 1946, temporary-manager 1950-51, secretary-manager early 1957, resigned summer of 1968).
Bill Ridding spent over 40 years in football. An inside-forward with neat touches, he played with 'Dixie' Dean and 'Pongo' Waring in his early days at Tranmere but injuries forced him to take early retirement at the age of 25. He became a qualified physiotherapist and in 1950 went as trainer with the England party to the World Cup Finals. In 1958 he guided Bolton Wanderers to FA Cup glory over Manchester United at Wembley. On leaving Burnden Park in 1968 he was appointed the physiotherapist of Lancashire CCC.
Club record: 44 apps. 14 goals

RIDGWAY, Joseph Arthur

Born: Chorlton-cum-Hardy, Manchester, Easter, 1873.
Career: West Manchester FC, NEWTON HEATH (July 1895), Rochdale Town (December 1901).
Goalkeeper Joe Ridgway was reserve to Billy Douglas during his early days with the Heathens. He was then injured, lost the chance of first team football on a regular basis and by the time he had regained full fitness, the club had recruited Scottish international Frank Barrett.
Club record: 17 apps. (also 2 'other' apps)

RIMMER, John James

Born: Southport, 10 February 1948
Career: Southport & Merseyside Schools, MANCHESTER UNITED (amateur, May 1963, apprentice, September 1963, professional May 1965), Swansea City (on loan October 1973 to February 1974), Arsenal (£40,000, February 1974), Aston Villa (£65,000, August 1977), Swansea City (August 1983), Hamrun Spartans of Malta (August 1986), Swansea City (coach, July 1987). He remained at The Vetch Field until May 1988 when he quit football to run a golf centre in Swansea.
A month after making his Football League debut for Manchester United against Fulham in April 1968, goalkeeper Jimmy Rimmer was named in United's squad for the European Cup Final at Wembley and the following season he appeared in both legs of the semi-final in the same competition against AC Milan.
He went on to make almost 50 senior appearances during his time at Old Trafford before transferring to Highbury. Agile and positive, he did not command his area with the sort of authority a manager would have liked - that finally arrived with experience some ten years after his United debut! And as a result - after gaining a full England cap against Italy in Milan in 1976 to go with the two he had already won at Under-23 level - he went on to give Villa excellent service during his six years at the club. He amassed 287 first team appearances, helping Villa win the League title in 1981, the European Cup (although he was only on the field for a few minutes before going off with a back injury) and the Super Cup in 1982. He was an ever-present for Villa on four occasions between the posts.
A real fitness fanatic, always on the bounce, Rimmer accumulated in excess of 550 appearances at club and international level (470 in the Football League).
Club record: 48 apps.

275

RITCHIE, Andrew Timothy

Born: Manchester, 28 November 1960

Career: Stockport Schools, MANCHESTER UNITED (apprentice, September 1977, professional, December 1977), Brighton & Hove Albion (£500,000, October 1980), Leeds United (£150,000, early 1983), Oldham Athletic (£50,000, summer 1987), Scarborough (free transfer, summer, 1995), Oldham Athletic (player-manager, summer 1998, retired as player, summer 1999, remained as manager until late 2001), Leeds United (Youth Academy Director, early 2002).

Striker Andy Ritchie scored 210 goals in 661 League and Cup games during his 25 years as a player, and was definitely one that 'got away' from Old Trafford!. Winner of eight caps for England at schoolboy level, Ritchie - strong and robust with an eye for goal - quickly added Youth and Under-21 honours to his collection and was regarded as an 'outstanding prospect' in the late 1970s, but he simply couldn't hold down a first team place with United - and that clearly mystified many supporters! He became a legend at Boundary Park, helping the Latics win promotion as Second Division champions in 1991 and then played in the first Premiership season of 1992-93, having been a key member of the Latics' team that reached the League Cup Final at Wembley in 1990. Ritchie later returned (as 'the Prodigal Son') to Boundary Park as manager and took his service with the Latics to eleven years.

Club record: 42 apps. 13 goals

ROACH, John E

Born: Lancashire, circa 1918

Career: MANCHESTER UNITED (amateur, October 1941, professional May 1944), guested for Accrington Stanley and Burnley during WW2. Retired in 1946.

Full-back John Roach (who made 43 appearances during the WW2 competitions) made two FA Cup appearances for United in the transitional season of 1945-46, lining up in both 3rd round games against Accrington Stanley (as partner to Bert Whalley).

Club record: 2 apps.

ROBBIE, David Middleton

Born: Motherwell, 6 October 1899. Died: Bury, 4 December 1978.

Career: Bathgate FC, Bury (summer 1921), Plymouth Argyle (summer 1935), MANCHESTER UNITED (trialist, September 1935), Margate (October 1935), Luton Town (early 1936), Plymouth Argyle (coach, summer 1936), Bury (trainer, season 1938-39).

David Robbie made 410 League appearances for Bury (101 goals scored) before joining United on a month's trial. In fact, he was almost 36 years of age when he was introduced against Southampton on 28 September 1935, making him possibly the oldest player ever to make his senior debut for United before Andy Gorams arrival in 2001.

Club record: one app.

ROBERTS, Charles

Born: Rise Carr, Darlington, 6 April 1883. Died: Manchester, 7 August 1939

Career: Rise Carr Rangers, Darlington St Augustine's, Sheffield United (trialist, 1900), Bishop Auckland (1901), Grimsby Town (1903), MANCHESTER UNITED (£600, April 1904), Oldham Athletic (£1,750, August 1913, retiring in 1919 through injury; manager of the Latics from January 1921-December 1922). Roberts was one of the founders of the Players' Union, acting as Chairman until September 1921.

Centre-half Charlie Roberts gave United supreme service for nine seasons, appearing in more than 300 senior games. Capped three times by England (fewer than his undoubted talents deserved), he also represented the Football League on nine occasions and skippered United to two League Championships (1908 & 1911) and to FA Cup glory in 1909. Many felt that he was victimised by the FA for his involvement with the Players' Union, hence his limited number of international honours. Tall, slim yet well built, he was a superb pivot, strong in the air and tackle, as well as being a fine reader of the game. He used to build up his stamina by working on East Coast trawlers as a fisherman during the summer months. He led Oldham to their highest-ever League position - runners-up to the First Division to Everton in 1915. He quit his job as manager at Boundary Park in 1922, confessing that he could not stand the strain of watching his club play! Roberts ran a successful wholesale tobacconist business in Manchester after leaving football, creating a distinctive cigar named 'Ducrobel' in honour of United's famous half-back line of Duckworth, Roberts and Bell.

Club record: 302 apps. 23 goals

ROBERTS, Robert H A

Born: Earlstown, Lancashire, circa 1892

Career: Altrincham, MANCHESTER UNITED (May 1912-May 1919).

Bob Roberts made two senior appearances as a reserve full-back for United, taking over the duties from George Stacey in League games against Sheffield Wednesday (home) and Bolton Wanderers (away) halfway through the 1913-14 season.

Club record: 2 apps.

ROBERTS, W A

Born: Lancashire, circa 1876

Career: NEWTON HEATH (April 1897-May 1899).

'Bogie' Roberts - a local-born winger - was fast, direct with plenty of pluck and endeavour, but unfortunately he was considered far too light for the rigours of competitive League and Cup football.

Club record: 10 apps. 2 goals (also 4 'other' apps, one goal)

ROBERTSON, Alexander

Born: Dundee, 1878

Career: Dundee Violet, Dundee (summer 1899), Middlesbrough (mid 1900), MANCHESTER UNITED (May 1903), Bradford Park Avenue (May 1907).

One of three Robertsons signed by United in May 1903, versatile forward 'Sandy' Robertson had helped Middlesbrough gain promotion to the First Division in 1901. He did well enough during his first season with United but then struggled with injuries and hardly figured at all over the next three years.

Club record: 34 apps. 10 goals

ROBERTSON, Alexander

Born: Scotland, circa 1882

Career: Hibernian, Fair City Athletic (on loan, early 1903), MANCHESTER UNITED (signed with Bill McCartney, May 1903-May 1907).

Half-back Alex Robertson played in over 100 League and Cup games for Hibs before joining United. He had been playing well before he was dismissed by United (along with fellow countryman Tom Robertson) for breaching club rules - only to be re-instated within a few days! He skippered the reserve side in 1905-06 after losing his place in the League side to Alex Bell.

Club record: 35 apps. one goal

ROBERTSON, Thomas

Born: Scotland, circa 1872

Career: East Benhar FC, Heatherbell FC, Motherwell, Fauldhouse FC, Heart of Midlothian (1896), Liverpool (£350, early 1898), Heart of Midlothian (mid 1902), Dundee (£200, autumn 1902), MANCHESTER UNITED (May-September 1903), Bathgate (season 1905-06).

Right or left-winger Tom Robertson won a Scottish League Championship medal with Hearts in 1897 and was capped by Scotland the following year. He went on to score 34 goals in 126 games for Liverpool, helping them win the League title in 1901. He played in the opening three League games of the 1903-04 season for United, but was then dismissed (initially with Alex Robertson, q.v) after turning up for a morning's training session, seemingly 'glassy-eyed' after a night out with his colleague.

Club record: 3 apps.

ROBERTSON, William S

Born: Falkirk, 20 April (circa 1904)

Career: Third Lanark (1921), Ayr United (1926), Stoke (£1,500, autumn 1929), MANCHESTER UNITED (March 1934), Reading (January 1936). Retired May 1937.

Compact wing-half Bill Robertson had already chalked up well over 250 League and Cup appearances as a professional (North and South of the border) before joining United. A sharp tackler, quick-witted with good positional sense, he won a Scottish League 'B' Championship medal with Ayr before going on to give Stoke five years excellent service, helping the Potters clinch the Second Division title in 1933. He replaced Hugh McLenahan in the United middle-line and was himself replaced by Jim Brown for the Second Division Championship season of 1935-36

Club record: 50 apps. one goal

ROBINS, Mark Gordon

Born: Ashton-under-Lyne, 22 December 1969

Career: North Chadderton Comprehensive School, Oldham Schools, Greater Manchester County FA, Boundary Park Juniors, Lilleshall School of Excellence, MANCHESTER UNITED (YTS, July 1986, professional September 1986), Norwich City (£800,000, August 1992), Leicester City (£1 million, early 1995), Reading (on loan, 1997), Deportivo Orense (early 1998), Panionios (Greece), Manchester City (free transfer, 1999), Walsall (free transfer, season 1999-2000), Rotherham United (summer 2000).

Forty-three of striker Mark Robins' first-class appearances for United were made as a substitute. The son of a policeman, he was considered 'a star of the future' as he banged in the goals for United's Youth and reserve teams and after making his full senior debut (in an FA Cup-tie v. QPR in January 1989) he established himself in the side during the second-half of the following season, gaining an FA Cup winners' medal in the process (after playing in the initial 3-3 draw with Crystal Palace) having scored crucial winning goals in the semi-final replay and at Forest in the 3rd round. Very useful coming off the bench, Robins, who won England recognition at Youth and Under-21 levels (six caps gained in the latter category), later helped Norwich qualify for the UEFA Cup and after recovering from a badly damaged right knee, he came back strongly, taking his appearance tally (in major competitions) past the 300 mark, while also pushing his total of goals towards 90, helping Rotherham gain promotion to the First Division in season 2000-01 by scoring 24 goals in 42 League games (his best seasonal return).

Club record: 70 apps. 17 goals

ROBINSON, James Wilson

Born: Belfast, 8 January 1898

Career: Belfast junior football, MANCHESTER UNITED (June 1919), Tranmere Rovers (free transfer, June 1932-May 1924).

Jim Robinson won Irish junior international honours as an outside-left before WW1. He was signed by United as cover for Fred Hopkin and although a very useful footballer, he eventually lost out to Teddy Partridge who joined United in June 1920.

Club record: 21 apps. 3 goals

ROBINSON, Matthew

Born: Felling, County Durham, circa 1904

Career: Pelaw FC, Cardiff City (early 1928), MANCHESTER UNITED (initially as a trialist, September 1931), Chester (March 1932), Barrow (for six seasons: 1932-38).

Matt Robinson preferred the outside-left berth but also played as an inside-left. A well-built footballer, he was signed as a reserve and played all his games for United in one stretch between late September and late November 1931 before losing his place. He made over 200 League appearances for Barrow (scoring 52 goals).

Club record: 10 apps.

ROBSON, Bryan, OBE

Refer to front of section

ROBSON, John R

The first man to hold the title of manager of MANCHESTER UNITED (he was in office from December 1914 until October 1921, also assuming the duties of secretary from 1916) Jack Robson had been a goalkeeper with Middlesbrough Swifts and Middlesbrough (from 1892-99). He then became secretary-manager of the Teeside club (May 1899) and held that position for six years, taking charge of Crystal Palace from May 1905 until April 1907. After that he managed Brighton & Hove Albion for six-and-a-half years (from March 1908) until taking the reins at Old Trafford. From October 1921 (after stepping down through ill-health) he acted as assistant-manager (to his successor Jack Chapman) until his death (of pneumonia) in Hull on 11 January 1922.

Born in Gainford, near Chester-le-Street, County Durham in the spring of 1854, he guided Middlesbrough (as the club's first official team manager) to promotion from Division Two in 1902 and eight years later took Brighton to the Southern League title in 1910. He was also Palace's first-ever manager. Although boss for seven years, he didn't have the greatest of times at Old Trafford, United finishing 18th in Division in 1914-15, 12th in 1919-20 and 13th in 1920-21.

* In 1902, Jack Robson was absolved of any responsibility when there was an illegal payments scandal at Middlesbrough FC.

ROCCA, Louis

Louis Rocca played an important part in the history of the club, his involvement stretching over half a century from the NEWTON HEATH days to the Matt Busby era.

His job description bore the unglamorous title of 'backroom staff' but within those words he fulfilled a whole variety of tasks which kept the club ticking over.

His first claim to UNITED fame came at the pivotal meeting in 1902 after John H Davies and his business colleagues had financially rescued Newton Heath by paying off its considerable debts. Now the club needed to move forward. The old 'Newton Heath' club was wound up and a new name was required. Everyone agreed that the club should bear the title 'Manchester' but Manchester FC was the name of the local rugby club, so therefore a suffix had be found!

'Central' was suggested, but that sounded too much like a railway station, 'Celtic' maybe...no, this might mean that the club had certain associations with Celtic organisations!

Then Louis Rocca stood up and suggested 'MANCHESTER UNITED' which was instantly agreed. And a change of colours was agreed as well, enter the famous red shirts!

At this point Rocca became involved with the running of the club 'from tea-boy to assistant manager' being the main scout for 48 years, signing (or finding) many great players for bargain prices, particularly during the inter-war years when very penny counted.

Rocca's second main claim to United immortality came in 1945 when he knew that the club was seeking a manager to lead the team into the post-war era. He knew Matt Busby well, once having had the chance to sign him from Manchester City for £150, but United could not raise the money at that time and he eventually went to Liverpool. Rocca contacted CSMI Busby by letter at the Royal Military Academy, Sandhurst, suggesting that United were interested in him. The rest is history!

Busby, in fact, was already considering an offer from Liverpool but the letter from his old friend Rocca settled the issue. United, under Busby's managerial genius, flourished as never before, creating a tradition for fine football played for sheer enjoyment of all concerned, players and supporters alike. The modern United fan has much to thank Busby...and indeed Louis Rocca...for.

Initially a junior player with the Heathens (signed originally in 1898), Rocca never made the first XI (only appearing in friendly matches). He remained a registered player with the club (as a part-time professional until his retirement in 1907). He died on 13 June 1950, aged 67.

ROCHDALE
United's FA Cup result v the 'Dale:

	Round	Venue	Result
1985-86	3	Home	W 2-0

Players with both clubs include: A Ainsworth ('Dale WW1), D Bain, J Barber, G Beel (United reserve), B Birch, A Chesters, E Connor, SC Davies (United trialist), SI Davies, R Duckworth jnr (United reserve), P Gibson (United reserve), B Greenhoff, J Greenhoff ('Dale player-manager), J Hall ('Dale WW2), R Halton ('Dale WW2), H Haslam (United trialist, WW2, 'Dale amateur), V Hayes ('Dale player-manager), W Keely (United WW2), S McAuley, JC McDermott, K McDowall, F McEwen & A McLoughlin (all United reserves), T Meehan, G Nevin, J Nuttall (United reserve), H O'Donnell (United WW2), P O'Connell ('Dale WW2), K Pilkington, M Radcliffe (United WW2), A Turnbull ('Dale WW2), C Waldron, G Wall, J Walters (United reserve), A Warburton ('Dale WW2), J Warner (player-manager)
Also associated: H Catterick ('Dale manager, United WW2 player), A Stepney (United player, 'Dale Commercial Dept).
* W Bunce & W Greenwood also played for Rochdale Athletic & J Ridgway for Rochdale Town.

ROCHE, Lee Paul

Born: Bolton, 28 October 1980
Career: MANCHESTER UNITED (apprentice 1997, professional February 1999), Wrexham (on loan, July 2000-May 2001).
Lee Roche made his United debut in the 4-0 League Cup defeat at Arsenal in November 2001. He appeared in 45 games for Wrexham during the 2000-01 season when he also gained an England Under-21 cap.
Club record: one app.

ROCHE, Patrick Joseph Christopher

Born: Dublin, 4 January 1951
Career: Dublin Shelbourne, MANCHESTER UNITED (£15,000, October 1973), Brentford (August 1982), Halifax Town (summer 1984), Chester City (late 1989-early 1990), Northwich Victoria (1991), Halifax Town (Football in the Community Officer).
Paddy Roche made over 50 appearances between the posts for United, deputising mainly for England international Alex Stepney. His best season at Old Trafford was in 1977-78 when he appeared in 19 League games (18 in succession). He later became understudy to Gary Bailey. Roche made 84 senior appearances for Brentford and followed up with well over 200 for Halifax. He was capped by the Republic of Ireland on eight occasions (seven as a United player) and he also represented his country in one Under-23 international.
Club record: 53 apps.

279

ROGERS, Martyn

Born: Nottingham, 26 January 1960. Died: Ringwood, Hampshire, March 1992.
Career: South Nottingham Schools, MANCHESTER UNITED (apprentice, May 1976, professional January 1977), Queen's Park Rangers (July 1979 to summer of 1981).
Capped nine times by England Schoolboys, full-back Martyn Rogers helped his country win the Under-15 international schools tournament in Germany in 1975. He never fulfilled the potential he had shown as a teenager and his only League game for United was against West Bromwich Albion at The Hawthorns in October 1977 when he stood in for the injured Arthur Albiston. His managers at QPR were Tommy Docherty and Terry Venables. He was only 32 years of age when he died in 1992.
Club record: one app.

ROTHERHAM UNITED (also County, Town)
Heathens/United's League results v Rotherham:

Season	Div	Home	Away
1894-95	2	W 3-2	L 1-2
1895-96	2	W 3-0	W 3-2
1922-23	2	W 3-0	D 1-1

Summary of League results

	P	W	D	L	F	A
Division 2	6	4	1	1	14	7
Home	3	3	0	0	9	2
Away	3	1	1	1	5	5
Total	6	4	1	1	14	7

FA Cup results v Rotherham:

	Round	Venue	Result
1965-66	4	Home	D 0-0
	Replay	Away	W 1-0 aet

League Cup results v Rotherham:

	Round	Venue	Result
1988-89	2 (1)	Away	W 1-0
	2 (2)	Home	W 5-0

Fact File
Rotherham United was formed in 1925 by the amalgamation of Rotherham Town and Rotherham County. Rotherham Town played in the Football League 1893-96, Rotherham County in 1919-25.
United have never played against Rotherham United in a League match.

Players with both clubs include: W Bryant, R Burke, J Clements, J Coupar, G Crowther (Man Utd reserve), S Davies (Man Utd trialist), M Dempsey, R Duckworth jnr (Man Utd reserve), S Goater (Man Utd reserve), E Goldthorpe, T Harris, GW Hicks (Man Utd reserve), S Hopkinson, R Jones (Man United reserve), T Manns, W Mathieson, R Mountford (Man Utd reserve), A Pape, R Parkinson, D Pierce (Man Utd Youths), K Pilkington, M Pollitt (Man Utd reserve), C Ramsden, M Robins, W Spratt, G Stacey, M Todd (Man Utd junior).
Also associated: M Setters (Man Utd player, Rotherham assistant-manager)

ROTHWELL, Charles

Born: Newton Heath, winter 1874

Career: NEWTON HEATH (amateur, season 1893-97).

An amateur and reserve team captain, inside-forward Charlie Rothwell, brother of Herbert (q.v) was a United player for four years, but made only three senior appearances. He scored twice when West Manchester were defeated 7-0 in an FA Cup-tie in December 1896..

Club record: 3 apps. 3 goals (also 10 'other' apps, 4 goals)

ROTHWELL, Herbert

Born: Newton Heath, spring 1877

Career: Newton Heath Athletic, NEWTON HEATH (briefly in 1897), Glossop North End, MANCHESTER UNITED (amateur, October 1902), Manchester City (amateur, December 1903), Newton Heath Athletic, Failsworth FC (late 1904).

An amateur full-back throughout his career, Bert Rothwell captained Glossop before joining United. He had one good season with the club, making 22 League appearances in 1902-03, mainly as partner to Bert Read who had played for Manchester City before joining United!

Club record: 28 apps.

ROTOR VOLGOGRAD

Although unbeaten in both games against Volgograd (2-2 at home, 0-0 away), United went out in the first round of the 1995-96 UEFA Cup competition on the away goal rule, despite Peter Schmeichel's sensational equaliser in the last minute at Old Trafford.

ROUGHTON, William George

Born: Manchester, 11 May 1909. Died: Southampton, 7 June 1989

Career: Lancashire & Manchester Schools, Droylsden FC, Huddersfield Town (late 1928), MANCHESTER UNITED (September 1936), Huddersfield Town (guest during WW2), Exeter City (player-manager, late 1945, retiring as a player after six months), Southampton (manager, 1952 to 1955 when he retired through ill-health).

Authoritative full-back George Roughton made 164 League appearances for Huddersfield Town before moving to Old Trafford. A former motor-factory worker (an apprentice engineer), he played for the Football League and toured Canada with the FA party in 1931, and was an international trialist (looking set for a full England cap) before an injury set him back halfway through the 1931-32 season. Three years earlier he was unlucky to miss the FA Cup Final (v. Arsenal). An instant success at Old Trafford, he still had the misfortune to go down with United, but then played his part in helping the club win promotion at the first attempt in 1938. He did a very good job at Exeter but admitted he failed at Southampton, due to limited resources. In fact, when he left The Dell, Saints were £60,000 in debt. He had a heart-by-pass operation in 1956.

Roughton, whose father was a famous runner, enjoyed lawn and table tennis besides his football.

Club record: 92 apps.

ROUND, Elijah

Born: Stoke-on-Trent, early, 1882

Career: Mexborough FC, Barnsley (mid 1904), Oldham Athletic (£1,000, Easter 1908), MANCHESTER UNITED (May 1909), Worksop Town (June 1910), Mexborough (season 1911-12...United retaining his registration papers until 1919, placing a £25 transfer fee on his head).

Goalkeeper Eli Round was reserve to Harry Moger during his one season with United. He made his League debut against the subsequent runners-up Liverpool in October with his other game, unluckily at eventual champions Aston Villa. He conceded 10 goals in his two games. Round, who suffered a serious hand injury while with Oldham, was a non-smoker and total abstainer, unusual at the time.

Club record: 2 apps.

ROWE, Jocelyn A

Born: Kingston-upon-Thames, circa 1880.

Career: Kingston Schools, Army football with the 2nd East Surrey Regiment (he served for fifteen years from 1899), Dublin Bohemians (as a guest, 1913), MANCHESTER UNITED (amateur, March 1914), Dublin Bohemians (1915), Kingstonian (1919-20).

'Josh' Rowe's only League appearance for United was against Preston North End (at Deepdale) in March 1914 when he stood in for full-back James Hodge. He represented the Irish League v. the Southern League in Dublin in 1913 and twelve months later was invalided out of the army after being wounded.

Club record: one app.

ROWLEY, Henry Bowater

Born: Bilston, near Wolverhampton, 23 January 1904

Career: Southend United (trialist), Shrewsbury Town (season 1927-28), MANCHESTER UNITED (£100, May 1928), Manchester City (with Billy Dale, December 1931), Oldham Athletic (on loan, February 1933, signed permanently by the Latics, August 1933), MANCHESTER UNITED (£1,375, December 1934), Burton Town (player-manager, July 1937), Gillingham (July 1938-39).

United secured the services of inside-left 'Harry' Rowley from Shrewsbury after he had netted 30 goals for the Shropshire club in 1927-28. Highly-rated, he eventually took over from Billy Johnston in United's forward-line and formed an excellent partnership on the left-wing with first Harry Thomas and later with George McLachlan. When he moved to Maine Road (with Dale) in 1931, Bill Ridding came to Old Trafford as part of the deal and when he returned to United his first job was to help the team regain its top Division status! A quality marksman, Rowley scored well over 100 goals for his major clubs.

Club record: 180 apps. 55 goals

ROWLEY, John Frederick

Born: Wolverhampton, 7 October 1920. Died: 26 June 1998.
Career: Dudley Old Boys, Wolverhampton Wanderers (late 1935), Cradley Heath (on loan), Bournemouth (early 1937), MANCHESTER UNITED (£3,500, October 1937); guested for Aldershot, Belfast Distillery, Folkestone, Shrewsbury Town, Tottenham Hotspur, Walsall and Wolves during WW2 when off duty from the South Staffs Regiment; Plymouth Argyle (player-manager, February 1955, retiring as a player in 1957), Oldham Athletic (manager, 1960-63), Ajax (coach, season 1963-64), Wrexham (manager, early 1966 to Easter 1967), Bradford Park Avenue (manager, Easter 1967 to Autumn 1968), Oldham Athletic (manager, autumn 1968 to Christmas 1969).

It was Major Frank Buckley who discovered Jack Rowley when he was manager of Wolves but somehow he escaped from the Molineux net and went on to give Manchester United excellent service, who signed the young winger from Bournemouth. In his second match for United, Rowley scored four goals against Swansea Town in 1937 at the age of 17 years, 58 days, becoming the club's youngest-ever hat-trick hero.

Capped six times by England at senior level, he netted four times in a 9-2 World Cup qualifying win over Northern Ireland at Maine Road in November 1949 and followed up with another goal in a 2-0 win over Italy a fortnight later. He also won one cap during WW2, lining up against Wales in 1944, starred in one 'B' international and represented the Football League. He won FA Cup (his two goals against Blackpool proving crucial) and First Division Championship winners medals with United in 1948 and 1952 respectively, having helped them win promotion from Division Two in 1938. Later he helped Plymouth Argyle win promotion from Division Three South in 1959 and then took Oldham to the Fourth Division title in 1963. When guesting for Wolves in November 1942, he scored all the Midland club's goals in an 8-1 wartime win over Derby County and in February 1944, as a guest with Spurs, he netted seven times in an 8-1 win over Luton, helping the London club win the League (South) title that season.

After the hostilities Rowley quickly re-established himself in United's front-line, now a powerful centre-forward, topping the scoring charts in five of the first six post-war seasons He had Stan Pearson as a striking-partner in these days and between them they terrorised defences all over the country as United finished runners-up in the First Division four times in five seasons before finally taking the Championship in 1952 when his haul of 30 League goals stood as a club record until Dennis Viollet surpassed it with 32 in 1959-60.

Rowley was a top-notch centre-forward. Naturally left-footed, nevertheless he had a 'cannonball' shot in both feet, being also a fine header of the ball. Nicknamed the 'Gunner' he was certainly the player full of fire and venom in United's potent attack of the immediate post-war era. Following the signing of centre-forward Tommy Taylor in March 1953, Rowley returned to his original left-wing position, his vast experience playing a great part in the 'Babes' development. Considering he lost seven years of his career to the War, Rowley's scoring record is staggering.

Always a competent cricketer, Rowley played for Yelverton CC when based in Devon (Plymouth). After leaving football, Rowley ran a newsagent's shop and sub post-office in Shaw near Oldham.

NB - On 22 October 1955, both Jack and his brother Arthur scored the 200th League goal of their respective careers - Jack for Plymouth Argyle against Barnsley and Arthur for Leicester City at Fulham - both in the Second Division. Arthur was first to reach the milestone by just 12 minutes and he went on to establish an all-time record of scoring 434 League goals while also serving with West Bromwich Albion, Fulham and Shrewsbury Town.

Club record: 424 apps. 211 goals

ROYALS, Ezra John

Born: Fenton, Stoke-on-Trent, early 1882.

Career: P.E.T (Stoke-based intermediate club), Chesterton White Star FC (late 1910), MANCHESTER UNITED (December 1911-May 1920), Northwich Victoria (early 1920s).

United's reserve goalkeeper Ezra Royals stepped into the breach on seven occasions during his time at Old Trafford, his best spell coming late in 1913-14 when he deputised in five successive League matches for Robert Beale, although his first three outings all ended in defeats!

In 1908-09 he played superbly well in the Midland Tramways Shield Final at St Andrew's Birmingham and was praised by William McGregor (founder of the Football League). Serving in the Territorial Army during WW1, he was based in France.

Club record: 7 apps..

RUGBY LEAGUE/UNION

•Goalkeeper, John Sutcliffe, was also a keen Rugby player with Bradford and Heckmondwike, winning an England cap v. New Zealand in 1889.

•Another former United goalkeeper David Gaskell played for Orrell Rugby League club in 1968-69 before signing for Wrexham.

•Tommy O'Neil represented England schoolboys as a rugby union player.

•John Mellor played for Oldham Rugby League club.

•United footballers Clayton Blackmore and Jack Cape were both competent rugby players at school.

•Stuart Pearson played briefly for Rugby Union side, Sale FC in 1985.

•Jimmy Nicholson and Hubert Redwood were both efficient rugby players at schoolboy level.

•Bob Valentine had two spells with Swindon rugby club. He was captain of the side.

•Gary Walsh, yet another United 'keeper, played competitive rugby in Wigan as a youngster.

•Neil Whitworth represented Leigh RLC.

•David Wilson captained Todmorden High School at rugby.

•United player Joe Haywood quit soccer to play rugby.

•Ernest Mangnall, the United manager, was a competent rugby player in his younger days.

•Fabien Barthez's father (Alain) and Ryan Giggs' father (Danny Wilson) both played international Rugby Union, for France and Wales respectively.

•Ernie Goldthorpe's father also played club rugby.

•United Chairman Martin Edwards played rugby in his younger days for Wilmslow RUFC.

•Rugby League ace Dennis Betts (Wigan) had trials with United as a teenager.

•Charlie Mitten attended Queen Victoria School, Dunblane in Scotland. This school is famous for its pipe band which has, for many years, played at all of Murrayfield's rugby internationals. Young Charlie, a piper, appeared several times at Scotland's international rugby ground pre WW2.

RYAN, James

Born: Stirling, 12 May 1945

Career: Corrie Hearts, MANCHESTER UNITED (apprentice, December 1962, professional January 1963), Luton Town (£35,000 plus players, April 1970), Dallas Tornados (on loan, 1976, signed permanently 1977), non-League football (1979-82), Luton Town (reserve team coach, early 1980s, later appointed manager early 1990, sacked in 1991), MANCHESTER UNITED (reserve team coach, summer 1991, later assistant-manager to Sir Alex Ferguson: summer 2001).

Jimmy Ryan, a promising right-winger, speedy with excellent footwork, gave some good displays, but the competition for wing players was too strong at the time and was converted into a very useful hard-working midfielder. He was involved in a four-man move when he left Old Trafford for Kenilworth Road, Don Givens among them. Ryan helped Luton finish runners-up in Division Two in 1973-74 and went on to appear in over 200 senior games for the Hatters (184 at League level). He was replaced by David Pleat in the manager's seat at Luton in 1991, and in 1993-94 guided United's second XI to their first Championship win (in the Pontins League) for 34 years. Since Steve McClaren's departure Ryan has taken over his role as assistant-manager to Sir Alex Ferguson.

Club record: 27 apps.. 4 goals

S for...

SCHMEICHEL,
Peter Boleslaw, MBE

Born: Gladsaxe, Denmark, 18 November 1963

Career: Hvidovre FC (1984), Brondby IF (1987), MANCHESTER UNITED (£550,000, August 1991), Sporting Lisbon (June 1999), Aston Villa (free transfer, July 2001), Manchester City (summer 2002).

Peter Schmeichel, the 'Great Dane', was United's greatest-ever goalkeeper. When he was in goal, the 'impossible' always seemed 'possible'.

His last appearance was as skipper of the victorious treble-winning team in the Final of the 1999 Champions League (v. Bayern Munich).

Schmeichel, with his massive frame, helped win a total of five Premiership titles with United plus one with both Brondby and Sporting Lisbon. He was also successful in two Danish Cup Finals (with Brondby) and in three FA Cup Finals, a League Cup Final, European Cup Final, European Super Cup and four FA Charity Shield matches with United. He also gained a European Championship winners medal with Denmark in 1992. A highly-influential figure between the posts, he had a great presence, was a tremendous shot-stopper, possessed exceptional aerial ability and was supremely confident in distribution with hand or foot.

He was capped 128 times by his country and was voted Danish 'Footballer of the Year' in 1990 while being voted the best goalkeeper in Europe in 1998. He has remarkably scored 10 goals in competitive football, his frequent forays upfield for set-pieces always exciting the crowd!

Schmeichel - who surprisingly joined promoted Manchester City for the 2002-03 season - was awarded the MBE (for services to football - and perhaps especially Manchester United) in December 2001.

* The Danish League club, Hvidovre, is wholly owned by Schmeichel.

Club record: 398 apps. One goal.

SADLER, David

Born: Yalding, Kent, 5 February 1946

Career: Kent County Schools, Maidstone United (Isthmian League), MANCHESTER UNITED (amateur, November 1962, professional February 1963), Miami Toros (on loan, May-August 1975), Preston North End (£25,000, November 1973). Retired through injury, 1977.

David Sadler was only 16 when he was capped by England at amateur level. As he developed he went on to gain Youth honours, three Under-23 caps, four senior caps (two in 1967, two in 1970) and twice played for the Football League - all as a central defender, his favoured position. He made his debut for United as a 17 year-old in the Roses battle against Sheffield Wednesday at Hillsborough in August 1963...replacing David Herd at centre-forward! That same season he helped the youngsters win the FA Youth Cup, scoring a superb hat-trick in the second leg of the Final against Swindon Town. As a 'cool, calm and collected' footballer, he gave very little away, regularly producing sound performances in any defensive position (even in midfield or attack when pushed forward). Generally his displays (at all levels) were considered to be solid and efficient. He won a League championship medal with United in 1966-67 and followed up a year later with a gritty display as the European Cup was won at Wembley, laying on the opening goal for Bobby Charlton. He made over 100 senior appearances for Preston, having been signed by his former United colleague Bobby Charlton. After leaving football Sadler worked as a branch manager for a Building Society.

Club record: 340 apps. 27 goals

SAGAR, Charles

Born: Daisy Hill, Edgworth, Lancashire, 28 March 1878. Died: Bolton, 4 December 1919.

Career: Turton Council School, Edgworth Rovers, Turton St Anne's (Bolton Sunday League), Turton Rovers (1896), Bury (1898), MANCHESTER UNITED (May 1905), Atherton FC (July 1907), Haslingden FC (Easter 1909).

Prior to becoming a United player, hard-shooting centre-forward Charlie Sagar had scored 73 goals in 174 League games for Bury - and he continued to be a dangerous striker during his two years with the club. Capped twice by England (against Ireland in 1900 and Wales in 1902), Sagar also represented the Football League on four occasions and was twice an FA Cup winner with Bury (in 1900 and 1903). He helped United win promotion to the First Division in his first season but a knee injury interrupted his flow and he failed to regain full fitness. He later went into business in Bolton.

Club record: 33 apps. 24 goals

ST ETIENNE

After a 1-1 draw in France, United had to play the return leg of their 1st round 1977-78 European Cup-winners Cup-tie against St Etienne at Plymouth Argyle's ground. They won 2-0, the Greenhoff brothers, Brian and Jimmy, making their only European appearance together.

United drew 0-0 with St Etienne in 1977-78 - the game arranged on behalf of the French Campaign For Cancer.

Players with both clubs: L Blanc, J Sivebaek

SAPSFORD, George Douglas

Born: Broughton, Manchester, 10 March 1896. Died: Abingdon, Oxfordshire, 17 October 1970

Career: South Salford Boys' Club, Clarendon FC (local league), MANCHESTER UNITED (amateur, April 1919, professional May 1920), Preston North End (£2,500, May 1922), Southport (£250, late summer 1925). Retired in summer of 1927 through injury.

A quick-witted, well-balanced footballer, inside-left George Sapsford helped United's second XI win the Central League title in 1921 before establishing himself in the League side at Old Trafford. He also represented the Central League select side (v. the Lancashire Combination) in the annual challenge match. After leaving United, Sapsford scored 31 goals in more than 100 League games for PNE and Southport...having played for the Deepdale club before his transfer papers had been officially sanctioned, Preston being fined five guineas for the misdemeanour. Sapsford was Southport's record signing when he moved to Haig Avenue from Deepdale. In later life he worked for BICC.

Club record: 53 apps. 17 goals

SARAJEVO (FK)

After a dogged but disciplined away performance that finished goalless, United went through to the 3rd round of the European Cup in 1967-68 with a 2-1 home victory over Sarajevo, George Best and John Aston the scorers.

SARTORI, Carlo Domenico

Born: Calderzone, Italy, 10 February 1948

Career: St Malachy's School (Collyhurst), Manchester Schools, Lancashire Schools, MANCHESTER UNITED (apprentice July 1963, professional February 1965), Bologna (£50,000, January 1973), then Spal FC, Lecce, Rimini FC & FC Trento (all in Italy) before retiring in 1984.

Carlo Sartori was the first Italian-born footballer to sign for United, having grown up in Manchester. His first two senior outings for the club were against top-line opposition (Tottenham Hotspur and Liverpool) in October 1968 when almost 100,000 fans watched the encounters at White Hart Lane and Anfield. A fiery, flame-haired midfielder, Sartori had two good seasons at Old Trafford (1968-70) before slipping into the reserves. Sartori was presented with an Italian Cup winners' medal by Bologna in 1974 despite not playing in the Final!

On returning to England in the mid 1980s, Sartori registered himself as a professional knife-sharpener.

Club record: 56 apps. 6 goals

SARVIS, William Isaac
Born: Merthyr Tydfil, summer 1898. Died: Llanelli, 22 March 1968.
Career: Merthyr Town (season 1921-22), MANCHESTER UNITED (May 1922), Bradford City (May 1925), Walsall (season 1926-27).
Billy Sarvis played once as an inside-right in United's League side - lining up against Coventry City (away) in September 1922 (in place of Arthur Lochhead). Soon afterwards he had the misfortune to suffer serious head injuries when he was knocked down by a car when crossing the road to board the team coach for an away reserve game. He spent some time in the Salford Royal Infirmary, with his life in danger. He then returned home to Wales, but after clearance from his doctor, he returned to Old Trafford early in 1924 to play on with the club.
Club record: one app.

SAUNDERS, James E
Born: Birmingham, circa 1879
Career: Glossop (1900), Middlesbrough (early 1901), NEWTON HEATH/MANCHESTER UNITED (August 1901), Nelson (season 1905-06), Lincoln City (autumn 1906), Chelsea (mid 1909), Watford (summer 1910), Lincoln Liberal Club FC (late 1910).
Reserve goalkeeper James Saunders spent four years with the club during which time he struggled to get into the first team while acting as deputy to first Jimmy Whitehouse and then Herbert Birchenough, John Sutcliffe and Harry Moger. He went on to appear in 65 League games for Lincoln City but was reserve at Nelson, Chelsea and Watford.
Club record: 13 apps. (also 2 'other' apps)

SAVAGE. Robert Edward
Born: Louth, Lincolnshire, early 1912. Died: Wallasey, Cheshire, 30 January 1964
Career: Louth Grammar School, Lincoln City (autumn 1928), Liverpool (mid 1931), MANCHESTER UNITED (January 1938), Wrexham (November 1938); guested for Carlisle United, Chelsea, Fulham, Millwall, Southport, West Ham United and York City during WW2. Retired in 1945, later coached in Holland before becoming manager of South Liverpool FC.
Half-back Ted Savage played in well over 200 senior games (196 in the Football League) before signing for United. A powerful player, he scored twice on his debut for Liverpool when playing as an inside-forward and joined United as a reserve, deputising for Jimmy Brown in each of his five senior outings (four League, one FA Cup) in January/February 1938.
Club record: 5 apps.

SAWYER, T
Born: Lancashire, circa 1878
Career: NEWTON HEATH (October 1899), Chorley (August 1901).
A short-stocky winger, Sawyer stood in for the injured William Bryant on the right flank in two games in season 1899-1900 and had another four outings right at the end of the following season.
Club record: 6 apps. (also 3 'other' apps)

SCANLON, Albert Joseph
Born: Manchester, 10 October 1935.
Career: St Wilfred's School, All Saints FC, Manchester Schools, MANCHESTER UNITED (amateur 1950, professional December 1952), Newcastle United (£18,000, November 1960), Lincoln City (£2,000, early 1962), Mansfield Town (Easter 1963), Belper Town (season 1966-67).
Albert 'Scanny' Scanlon was a great attacking, goalscoring winger with searing pace who could use either foot. He could run past defenders as if they were standing still. He was dangerous, a very unpredictable player and, like all wingers at Old Trafford, gave full-backs nightmares! He won two FA Youth Cup winning medals with United (1953 & 1954) but had to play second fiddle behind David Pegg in the pre-Munich days before getting his chance, on a regular footing, being an ever-present on the left-flank in 1958-59, after recovering from injuries sustained in the Munich air crash. Capped five times by England at Under-23 level, Scanlon played once for the Football League. He helped Mansfield win promotion from Division Four in 1963. He appeared in 177 League games (37 goals scored) after leaving Old Trafford. His uncle, Charlie Mitten (q.v) was a United player from 1936-50.
Club record: 127 apps. 35 goals.

SCHMEICHEL, Peter Boleslaw, MBE
Refer to front of section.

SCHOFIELD, Alfred John
Born: Liverpool, 1875.
Career: Liverpool junior football, Everton (summer 1895), NEWTON HEATH/MANCHESTER UNITED (August 1900-May 1907).
Outside-right Alf Schofield was fast and direct who had the knack of crossing the ball with precision when flying at pace down the wing. He starred in United's Second Division promotion winning team of 1905-06 before handing over his duties to Billy Meredith.
Schofield was also a very keen League cricketer.
Club record: 179 apps. 34 goals (also 13 'other' apps, 2 goals)

SCHOFIELD, George Willie

Born: Southport, 6 August 1896

Career: Southport junior football, MANCHESTER UNITED (August 1920), Crewe Alexandra (May 1922-May 1923), later with Altofts W R Colliery FC (re-instated as an amateur, Christmas 1927).

Reserve forward George Schofield played in only one League game for United ...at Bolton Wanderers in September 1920 when he took over from Billy Meredith on the right-wing. Slimly built, he had done reasonably well with Crewe before moving to United.

Club record: one app.

SCHOFIELD, Joseph

Born: Wigan, circa 1881

Career: Brynn Central FC, Ashton Town, MANCHESTER UNITED (with Charlie Wright, November 1903), Stockport County (June 1905), Luton Town (season 1906-07).

Reserve inside or outside-left Joe 'Ashton' Schofield lined up in two League games for United, both in March 1904, one against his future club Stockport County.

Club record: 2 apps.

SCHOFIELD, Percy

Born: Bolton, circa 1900

Career: Eccles Borough, MANCHESTER UNITED (May 1921), Eccles United (September 1922), Hurst FC (season 1923-24).

Utility forward Percy Schofield played in one League game for United, deputising for George Sapsford against Preston North End (home) in October 1921.

Club record: one app.

SCHOLES, Paul

Born: Salford, 16 November 1974

Career: Boundary Park Juniors, MANCHESTER UNITED (trainee, 1991, professional January 1993).

A workaholic in United's midfield engine-room, Paul Scholes is one of the first names manager Sir Alex Ferguson fills in on his team-sheet. Blessed with a terrific engine, determination, skill, commitment and powerful right-foot shot, Scholes certainly played his part in helping the Reds win five Premiership titles (1996, 1997, 1999, 2000 & 2001), two FA Cup Finals (1996 & 1999) and two FA Charity Shields (1996 & 1997). Unfortunately he missed out on European Cup glory in 1999 through suspension. Capped almost 50 times by England at full international level (and still adding to his total), he is as vital ingredient in Sven-Goran Eriksson's England plans as he is to United. The quiet man of the side, his face never seen in a glossy magazine, this little ex-striker, a product of Boundary Park Juniors, along with the Nevilles and Nicky Butt, Scholes is a vital part of United's most successful side. He played for England in the 1998 and 2002 World Cup Finals and also in the 2000 European Chaampionships.

Club record: 323 apps. 81 goals

SCOTT, John

Born: Motherwell, circa 1888

Career: Hamilton Academical, Bradford Park Avenue (autumn 1910), MANCHESTER UNITED (£750, June 1921), St Mirren (June 1922-23).

During his time with Park Avenue, half-back John Scott made well over 250 League and Cup appearances, helping the Yorkshire club win promotion to the First Division in 1913-14. An excellent ball-player, Scott was well past his best when he joined United, but he still gave 100 per-cent during his one season at Old Trafford, despite being involved with a relegation team for the second successive campaign.

Scott was awarded the Military Medal during the Great War.

Club record: 24 apps.

SCOTT, John

Born: Belfast, 22 December 1933. Died: Manchester, June 1978

Career: Boyland FC, Ormond Star FC, MANCHESTER UNITED (amateur, June 1950, professional October 1951), Grimsby Town (June 1956), York City (summer 1963), Margate (1964-65 season).

Spotted by United's Irish-based scout Bob Bishop, reserve winger Jackie Scott was handed just three League outings in the famous red shirt. He lined up in a 6-2 humiliation at the hands of Wolves (at Molineux) and against Stoke City in October 1952 (each time in place of Roger Byrne on the left flank) and away at Preston in January 1956, when he occupied the right-wing in the absence of Johnny Berry.

Scott was tragically killed when working on a Manchester building side. He was only 44.

Club record: 3 apps.

SCOTTISH CONNECTION

Here is a list of United personnel who were also associated with professional or semi-professional Scottish clubs, either as a player (at various levels), manager, assistant-manager, scout, coach etc.

Aberdeen   F Barrett, T Bogan, G Buchan, M Buchan, J Chapman, J Delaney, I Donald, A Graham, Sir A Ferguson (manager), A Knox (assistant-manager at both clubs), J Leighton, T Lowrie, K MacDonald, C Mackie, A Notman, T Pirie (United reserve), G Strachan, B Thornley

Airdrieonians   A Chilton, J Connachan, I Donald, R Donaldson, D Ellis, P Davenport, W Henderson, W Hunter, W McDonald, W McFarlane, G McQueen (manager), A Mitchell, H Morton, G Walsh

Albion Rovers   C McGillivray, A Montgomery (Rovers manager), J Rice (United reserve)

Alloa Athletic   J Hendry

Annbank   D Fitzsimmons, T Fitzsimmons, J Vance

Arbroath   F Barrett, F Kopel (assistant-manager), C McGillivray, G Mutch

Arthurlie   D Ellis, A Menzies

Artizan Thistle   G Livingstone

Avondale FC   G Mutch

Ayr FC   H Kerr

Ayr Albion   JF Ure

Ayr Parkhouse   A Bell, W Kennedy

Ayr United   Sir A Ferguson, N McBain (also manager), C McGillivray, J Quin, W Robertson, AC Smith

Ayr Westerlea   A Bell

Banks o'Dee   M Buchan, G Mutch (player & manager)

Bathgate   T Pirie (United reserve), D Robbie, T Robertson

Benburb FC   J Peddie

Blantyre Celtic   T Bogan, J Jordan, A Menzies, T Reid

Broxburn (Utd) FC   W McCartney, W McDonald

Campbeltown Acad.   N McBain

Cartvale FC   J McCartney

Celtic   T Bogan, W Buchan (United WW2), J Cassidy, J Connachan, P Crerand, J Cunningham, J Delaney, T Docherty, AS Duncan, W Grassam, A Grimes (coach), J Holton (junior), J Jordan, G Livingstone, B McClair, C McGillivray, L Macari (also manager), L Martin, M Martin (coach), T Morrison

Clackmannan   A Bell

Clyde   W Boyd, W McCartney, J McCrae, G McLachlan, J Quin

Clydebank   G Livingstone (manager), D Lyner, T Reid, J Thomson

Clydesdale   W Mathieson

Coatbridge BG   B McClair, W McDonald

Cowdenbeath   T Blackstock, AS Duncan, T Frame, W Stewart

Cowlairs FC   J McCartney

Cumnock FC   JF Ure

Dalry Thistle   J Leighton, JF Ure

Denny Hibernian   Sir M Busby

Deverondale   J Leighton

Dumbarton   AS Duncan, G Livingstone (manager), J McNaught, W Thompson

Dumbarton Harp   J Connachan, J Thomson

Dundee   A Albiston, J Bain, F Barrett, R Bonthron, J Brown, J Clark, P Coupar, W Douglas, J Dow, H Erentz, J Leighton, W Longair (also trainer & groundsman), W McDonald, C McGillivray, A Menzies, Sandy Robertson, T Robertson, W Stewart, G Strachan, J Turnbull

Dundee East End   W Longair

Dundee Harp   F Barrett,

Dundee United   F Kopel, C McGillivray (also manager), R Milne

Dundee Violet   A Robertson

Dunfermline Ath.   S Chambers, T Dougan, Sir A Ferguson, C McGillivray, J Nicholl (also assistant & caretaker-manager)

Dunocter Hibernian   J Connachan

East Fife   J Brown,

East Stirlingshire   J Fisher, Sir A Ferguson (manager), W McKay, J Turnbull, JF Ure

Elgin City   J Delaney, S Paterson (City player-manager)

Falkirk   H Boyd, J Delaney, Sir A Ferguson, J Turnbull

Forfar Athletic   A Knox (Forfar manager), F Kopel (Athletic assistant-manager)

Forres Mechanics   S Paterson

Glasgow Hibernian   J Cunningham

Glasgow Rangers   J Cunningham, AS Duncan, A Forsyth, A Goram, A Kanchelskis, G Livingstone (trainer), Sir A Ferguson, J McCartney, R McMorran (United reserve), G McQueen (Rangers trialist), A Montgomery, J Nicholl (Rangers player-coach), J Turnbull

Glasgow Thistle   A Carson, J Clarkin, J Cunningham, J McCartney, W Mathieson

Hamilton A.   J Aston snr, AS Duncan, H Edmonds, A Forsyth, A Herd (United WW2), N McBain (trialist), W McKay, T Miller, J Scott, G Wall

Heart of Bleath   A Herd (United WW2)

Heart of Midlothian   S Chambers, J Cunningham, T Dougan, W Henderson, G Hogg, J Jordan, G Livingstone, A Lochhead, J McCartney (Hearts secretary-manager), D McCreery, C McGillivray, A Menzies, T Miller, R Murray, J Peddie, T Robertson

Hibernian   G Best, G Brebner (United reserve), Sir M Busby (Hearts WW2 guest), T Bogan, W Cresswell, A Goram, J Leighton, W McCartney, C McGillivray, R Milarvie, A Robertson

Huntly FC   S Paterson (manager)

Hurlford   D Christie, S Parker

287

Hurlford Thistle	J Picken, A Turnbull
Inverness Cal. Thistle	S Paterson (manager)
Inverness Clach'n	K MacDonald
Kilmarnock	T Dougan, T Heron, D Lyner, C McKee, N Whitworth
Kilmarnock Athletic	S Parker
Kilmarnock Shawbank	J Picken
Kirkcaldy	W Inglis
Larkhall Thistle	W Boyd, T Lang
Law's Scotia FC	W McDonald
Leith Athletic	T Blackstock, R Bonthron, M Gillespie
Livingston	N Culkin, K Hilton
Lochgelly United	W McCartney, C Mackie
Morton (Greenock)	R Black, J Broad (United reserve), J Connachan, W Henderson, J Jordan, W Kennedy, E McIlvenny, C McGillivray, J McInnes (United WW2 guest), J Miller, P Roudfoot (reserve)
Motherwell	G Buchan, S Cosgrove, A Forsyth, A Goram, B McClair, C McGillivray, A Menzies, T Robertson, W Stewart, W Watson
Motherwell Athletic	J Cassidy
Nairn County	S Paterson
Queen of the South	T Lang, G McLachlan (Q of S manager), G Savage (United WW1 amateur)
Queen's Park	S Chambers, T Heron, T Pirie (United reserve), Sir A Ferguson
Partick Thistle	J Cunningham, I Donald, AS Duncan, K Fitzpatrick (United junior), A Forsyth, F McPherson
Pollockshields	R Milarvie
Port Glasgow Rangers	S Houston
Raith Athletic	R Bonthron
Raith Rovers	T Blackstock, R Bonthron, W Inglis, J McClelland, T Miller, J Nicholl (Rovers player & manager)
Renfrew	T Bogan
Renton	J Connachan, J Thomson
Rockwell (Dundee)	W Longair
Ross County	C McKee
Rosslyn FC	J McClelland
Rutherglen Glencairn	W McCartney
St Bernard's	J Fisher, W Henderson
St Johnstone	J Coupar, D Ellis, P Davenport, Sir A Ferguson, M Lynch, S McAuley, N McBain
St Mirren	R Black, T Fitzsimmons, F Hodges, Sir A Ferguson (manager), J McCartney (Saints secretary-manager), G McQueen (Saints player-coach), J Miller, T Nuttall, J Scott, J Thomson, JF Ure
Stenhousemuir	James Hodge, John Hodge
Stirling Albion	C McGillivray
Strathclyde	T Bogan, M Gillespie
Third Lanark	G Bissett, N Dewar, A Downie, J McCrae, J Peddie, W Robertson, J Whitehouse
Troon Athletic	T Lowrie
Walker Celtic	K MacDonald
Wishaw	P Proudfoot (reserve), C Rennox

Tartan Talk

In seson 1972-73 United had eight Scottish internationals on their books, plus another Scot in team manager Tommy Docherty

Sir Matt Busby, Tommy Docherty and Sir Alex Ferguson all managed the Scottish national team.

United, over the years, have played against several Scottish-based clubs (at various levels) and they include Aberdeen, Celtic, Dundee United, Heart of Midlothian, Hibernian, Kilmarnock, Partick Thistle, Rangers, St Johnstone, St Mirren.

SCOUTS

Among the many men who, down the years, have worked as a scout and/or Chief Scout for Manchester United football club, are the following: Johnny Aston, Archie Beattie (in Scotland), the Irish trio of Billy Behan (Ireland), Bob Bishop (Northern Ireland) and Johnny Carey; Gordon Clayton, Tony Collins*, Ted Connor, Ian Greaves, Bob Harpur (also based in Northern Ireland), Jimmy Murphy, Malcolm Musgrove, Syd Owen, Louis Rocca*, Norman Scales*, Eric Walker and Brian Whitehouse.

Finally, Joe Armstrong, a former GPO telephone engineer, who was responsible for bringing most of the 'Babes' to Old Trafford. He prepared the way by meeting the lads' parents, reassuring them that their offspring would be well cared for. 'Uncle Joe' as he was known to the young stars, played a great part in United's early post-war success.

NB - Harry Haslam, a United player in WW2, was appointed scout for England in the early 1980s.

* Chief Scout

SCREEN SPORT SUPER CUP

United's record in this 'consolation' competition was:

Venue	P	W	D	L	F	A
Home	2	0	1	1	3	5
Away	2	0	1	1	1	2
Totals	4	0	2	2	4	7

This competition was launched (as a one-off) in season 1985-86....in the aftermath of the Heysel Stadium disaster which resulted in a ban from the three major European competitions for the English clubs who had qualified - namely Everton, Liverpool, Manchester United, Norwich City, Southampton and Tottenham Hotspur. Liverpool beat Everton 7-2 on aggregate in the two-legged Final which was carried over until the following season.

United played four matches in the SSSC. They were defeated 4-2 at home by Everton on 18 September in front of 33,859 spectators; drew 1-1 with the Norwich City, also at home on 6 November (when 20,130 fans were present) and then shared the spoils, also 1-1, in the return game with the Canaries at Carrow Road on 2 December before an audience 15,449, seven days after losing 1-0 in the second game against Everton at Goodison Park where the turnout was 20,542.

Bryan Robson and Norman Whiteside, each with a penalty, Frank Stapleton and Colin Gibson, scored United's four goals. The unfortunate Stapleton conceded an own-goal for Everton's winner at Goodison.

SEALEY, Leslie Jesse

Born: Bethnal Green, London, 29 September 1957. Died: London, 19 August 2001

Career: Coventry City (apprentice, 1974, professional 1977), Luton Town (£120,000, summer 1983), Plymouth Argyle (on loan, autumn 1984), MANCHESTER UNITED (on loan, March-May 1990, signed on a free transfer, June 1990), Aston Villa (free transfer, July 1991), Coventry City (on loan, 1992), Birmingham City (on loan, autumn 1992), MANCHESTER UNITED (free transfer, January 1993), Blackpool (free transfer, July 1994), West Ham United (free transfer, late 1994), Leyton Orient (non-contract, summer 1996) and finally West Ham (on a non-contract, second half of season 1996-97). He remained as coach on a part-time basis at Upton Park until his sudden death from a heart attack in 2001.

Goalkeeper Les Sealey spent 25 years in the game (as player and coach).. During that time he served with nine different clubs and made a total of 568 League and Cup appearances. His last senior outing came as a West Ham substitute in an emotional farewell Premiership game against one of his former clubs, Manchester United, at Old Trafford in front of 55,249 spectators on 2 May 1997.

A real character, strong-willed, confident, aggressive, boisterous at times, even annoying and rather too vocal, Sealey was, without doubt, a very competent 'keeper. He was brought in by Alex Ferguson for the 1990 FA Cup Final replay against Crystal Palace after a poor first game showing by Jim Leighton and duly collected a winners' medal as United won 4-0. A year later he was on the losing side in the 1991 League Cup Final defeat by Sheffield Wednesday but soon afterwards gained a winners' medal when United won the European Cup-winners' Cup Final by beating Barcelona 2-1 in Rotterdam.

Sealey suffered another League Cup disappointment when Aston Villa beat United to lift the trophy in 1994. Earlier, as a Luton player, he had missed the 1988 League Cup Final through injury, but was then a loser as Nottingham Forest beat the Hatters in the Final of the same competition twelve months later. No international caps for Sealey, but plenty of highlights - and over 50 senior games between the posts for United.

Club record: 56 apps.

SECRETARIES

The men (listed in A-Z order) who have held the position of club secretary of Manchester United: A H Albut, J J Bentley, W Crickmer, J E Mangnall (as secretary-manager), K Merrett, L Olive, J T Wallworth, J West.

Secretary's Minutes

Walter Crickmer, who was sadly killed in the Munich air crash, was first appointed secretary at Old Trafford in 1926 and remained in office for 32 years.

Les Olive was secretary at Old Trafford for 30 years ...from 1958 until 1988.

289

SENDINGS-OFF

Here is an unofficial list of Manchester United players who have been sent-off at first team level:

Date	Player	Opposition	Competition
21.12.07	Sandy Turnbull	v. Manchester City (h)	League
24.05.08	Ernie Thomson	v. Ferencvaros (a)	Friendly
24.05.08	Dick Duckworth	v. Ferencvaros (a)	Friendly
16.01.09	Billy Meredith	v. Brighton & HA (h)	FA Cup
16.10.09	Sandy Turnbull	v. Aston Villa (h)	League
23.10.09	Sandy Turnbull	v. Sheffield United (a)	League
22.04.11	Enoch West	v. Aston Villa (a)	League
27.08.28	Jimmy Hanson	v. Aston Villa (a)	League
02.09.29	Charlie Moore	v. Leicester City (a)	League
29.10.32	Tommy Frame	v. Port Vale (a)	League
03.09.49	Henry Cockburn	v. Manchester City (h)	League
01.06.52	Roger Byrne	v. Atlas FC (a)	Friendly
29.01.55	Allenby Chilton	v. Manchester City (a)	FA Cup
15.03.58	Mark Pearson	v. Burnley (a)	League
08.08.59	Albert Quixall	v. Bayern Munich (a)	Friendly
08.08.59	Joe Carolan	v. Bayern Munich (a)	Friendly
13.08.63	Noel Cantwell	v. Eintracht Frankfurt (a)	Friendly
25.09.63	David Herd	v. Willem II (a)	ECWC
16.11.63	Denis Law	v. Aston Villa (a)	League
26.12.63	Pat Crerand	v. Burnley (a)	League
14.11.64	Denis Law	v. Blackpool (a)	League
05.06.65	Pat Crerand	v. Ferencvaros (a)	Friendly
06.11.65	Harry Gregg	v. Blackburn Rovers (h)	League
20.04.66	Pat Crerand	v. Partizan Belgrade (h)	Euro Cup
12.08.66	Nobby Stiles	v, FK Austria (a)	Friendly
27.06.67	Denis Law	v. Western Australia (a)	Friendly
07.10.67	Denis Law	v. Arsenal (a)	League
31.01.68	Brian Kidd	v. Tottenham Hotspur (a)	FA Cup
25.09.68	Nobby Stiles	v. Estudiantes (a)	WCC
16.10.68	George Best	v. Estudiantes (h)	WCC
23.04.69	John Fitzpatrick	v. AC Milan (a)	Euro Cup
01.05.71	Pat Crerand	v. Blackpool (a)	League
18.08.71	George Best	v. Chelsea (a)	League
04.02.73	Jim Holton	v. FC Porto (a)	Friendly
17.03.73	Jim Holton	v. Newcastle United (h)	League
08.08.73	Lou Macari	v. Penarol (a)	Friendly
13.03.74	Lou Macari	v. Manchester City (a)	League
07.08.75	Lou Macari	v. Holsterbro (a)	Friendly
07.01.78	Brian Greenhoff	v. Carlisle United (a)	FA Cup
30.08.78	Gordon McQueen	v. Stockport County (h)	FL Cup
01.08.79	Mickey Thomas	v. VF Bochum (a)	Friendly
02.04.80	Sammy McIlroy	v. Nottingham Forest (a)	League
30.10.82	Ashley Grimes	v. West Ham United (a)	League
02.05.83	Remi Moses	v. Arsenal (a)	League
24.11.84	Mark Hughes	v. Sunderland (a)	League
18.05.85	Kevin Moran	v. Everton (n)	FAC Final
26.10.85	Graeme Hogg	v. Chelsea (a)	League
25.01.86	Bryan Robson	v. Sunderland (a)	FA Cup
03.01.87	Liam O'Brien	v. Southampton (a)	League
04.04.88	Colin Gibson	v. Liverpool (a)	League
13.01.90	Steve Bruce	v. Derby County (h)	League
04.09.90	Steve Bruce	v. Luton Town (a)	League
06.10.91	Mark Hughes	v. Liverpool (h)	League
29.09.92	Mark Hughes	v. Moscow Torpedo (a)	UEFA Cup
25.07.93	Bryan Robson	v. Arsenal (n)	Friendly
03.11.93	Eric Cantona	v. Galatasaray (a)	Euro Cup*
09.01.94	Mark Hughes	v. Sheffield United (a)	FA Cup
12.03.94	Peter Schmeichel	v. Charlton Athletic (h)	FA Cup
19.03.94	Eric Cantona	v. Swindon Town (a)	Prem'ship
22.03.94	Eric Cantona	v. Arsenal (a)	Prem'ship
27.03.94	Andrei Kanchelskis	v. Aston Villa (n)	LC Final
06.08.94	Eric Cantona	v. G. Rangers (n)	Friendly
20.08.94	Paul Parker	v QPR (h)	Prem'ship
23.11.94	Paul Ince	v. Gothenburg (a)	Euro Cup
26.11.94	Mark Hughes	v. Arsenal (a)	Prem'ship
25.01.95	Eric Cantona	v. Crystal Palace (a)	Prem'ship
12.04.95	Roy Keane	v. Crystal Palace (n)	FAC S/f
28.08.95	Roy Keane	v. Blackburn Rovers (a)	Prem'ship
20.09.95	Pat McGibbon	v. York City (h)	FL Cup
28.10.95	Roy Keane	v. Middlesbrough (h)	Prem'ship
22.01.96	Nicky Butt	v. West Ham United (a)	Prem'ship
26.10.96	Roy Keane	v. Southampton (a)	Prem'ship
18.04.98	Ole Gunnar Solskjaer	v. Newcastle United (h)	Prem'ship
20.09.98	Nicky Butt	v. Arsenal (a)	Prem'ship
12.12.98	Gary Neville	v. Tottenham Hotspur (a)	Prem'ship
14.04.99	Roy Keane	v. Arsenal (n)	FAC SF
05.05.99	Denis Irwin	v. Liverpool (a)	Prem'ship
11.09.99	Andy Cole	v. Liverpool (a)	Prem'ship
03.10.99	Nicky Butt	v. Chelsea (a)	Prem'ship
06.01.00	David Beckham	v. Necaxa (n)	Club W Ch
12.02.00	Roy Keane	v. Newcastle United (a)	Prem'ship
29.04.00	Nicky Butt	v. Watford (a)	Prem'ship
13.08.00	Roy Keane	v. Chelsea (n)	FACS
31.10.00	Rai van der Gouw	v. Watford (a)	League Cup
28.11.00	Dwight Yorke	v. Sunderland (a)	League Cup
17.12.00	Luke Chadwick	v. Liverpool (h)	Prem'ship
31.01.01	Andy Cole	v. Sunderland (a)	Prem'ship
21.04.01	Roy Keane	v. Manchester City (h)	Prem'ship
15.09.01	Roy Keane	v. Newcastle United (a)	Prem'ship
31.08.02	Roy Keane	v. Sunderland (a)	Prem'ship

* Cantona was sent-off after the final whistle in this game.

Off The Cuff

•Although unconfirmed, it seems likely that the first United player to be sent-off in a competitive match was Sandy Turnbull - against Manchester City, 1907.

•Turnbull was ordered off in successive League matches in October 1909, and it was to be another 85 years before this happened again - Eric Cantona making the long walk in successive matches after dismissals against Swindon Town and Arsenal in the space of three days in March 1994.

•Cantona was actually sent-off five times over a period of 14 months between November 1993 and January 1995. He started off by taking the long walk at the end of United's European Cup clash with the Turkish champions Galatasaray in Istanbul. He took an early bath in a pre-season tournament match against Glasgow Rangers in August 1994 and was then banished from another Premiership encounter v. Crystal Palace at Selhurst Park early in 1995, in addition to the two mentioned above.

•George Best was sent-off at least six times during his career. He was dismissed twice as a United player - against Estudiantes in the World Club Championship in 1968 and versus Chelsea in a First Division game in August 1971...for arguing with his team-mate Willie Morgan, although he was later cleared of the offence by a committee at a personal hearing. He was banished once playing for Fulham (v. Southampton in October 1976); once for Fort Lauderdale Strikers (v. Toronto Metros in July 1978) and twice for Northern Ireland, against Scotland in April 1970 and versus Bulgaria in October 1976. Best's first dismissal came when playing for his country against Scotland in April 1970 - banished for throwing mud and spitting at English referee Eric Jennings.

•In May 1985, United defender Kevin Moran became the first player to be sent-off in an FA Cup Final when he was dismissed against Everton by policeman referee Peter Willis for committing a professional foul on Peter Reid.

•Nine years later, in the 1994 League Cup Final, Andrei Kanchelskis was red-carded for deliberate handball during the clash with Aston Villa...the first player to be sent-off in a League Cup Final.

•Henry Cockburn and Billy Linacre were sent-off together for fighting during the United-Manchester City derby in 1949. Twenty-five years later Lou Macari and City's Mike Doyle were dismissed in the derby at Maine Road. In fact, both players refused to 'walk' during this tough local encounter in 1974 and as a result strict referee, Clive Thomas, took all the players off the pitch until the matter was sorted. Eventually, after a five-minute delay, the game resumed with 10 players per side! Sandy Turnbull (1907), Allenby Chilton (1955, FA Cup) and Roy Keane (2001) were all banished in United games against City, while Neil Pointon (in 1992) is the only other City player to get himself sent-off in a local derby against United!

•Denis Law was sent-off along with future United centre-half Ian Ure at Highbury in 1967; Tottenham's Joe Kinnear accompanied Brian Kidd to the dressing room in an FA Cup-tie in 1968; Blackpool and England right-back Jimmy Armfield was dismissed with Pat Crerand during the League game at Bloomfield Road in 1971 and Liverpool's Gary Ablett took an early bath with United's Mark Hughes at Old Trafford in 1991.

•Pat McGibbon had the misfortune to be sent-off on his debut for United - against York City at Old Trafford in a League Cup match in September 1995. He didn't play for the club again!

•John Fitzpatrick's sending-off was in United's 1969 European Cup semi-final 1st leg encounter against AC Milan in Italy.

•Denis Law was sent-off following the fifth robust clash with Aston Villa's combative wing-half Alan Deakin during the League game in November 1963.

•Roy Keane has been ordered from the field ten times as a senior professional. His latest dismissal was against Newcastle United at St James' Park in September 2001 when United lost 4-3. He was sent-off three times in two seasons (1999-2001)... once against rivals Manchester City and also at Wembley in the FA Charity Shield game (United v. Chelsea). The fiery Irishman was shown the red card three times in 14 matches over a period of six months in 1995 (April, August & October).

•Scottish centre-half Jim Holton receiving two 'pointing fingers' over a six-week period in February/March 1973.

•Liam O'Brien was ordered off after just 85 seconds when playing for United against Southampton in January 1987.

•David Beckham became the first United player ever to be sent-off whilst representing England - dismissed in the World Cup encounter against Argentina in St Etienne in June 1998. Beckham was later sent-off, playing for United against Necaxa in the FIFA Club World Championship tournament in Rio De Janeiro in January 2000.

•Former United star Ray Wilkins was sent-off playing for England against Morocco in Monterey (World Cup) in June 1986.

•Respective 'Irish' internationals from north and south of the country, Harry Gregg and Noel Cantwell were sent-off playing for United's Central League side against Burnley in February 1965.

•United had ten players (at various levels) sent-off between August 1964 and June 1965. They suffered seven dismissals at first team level in 1993-94 and six the following season.

•Three visiting players were all sent-off at Old Trafford during the 1986-97 season - David Rocastle of Arsenal, Chris Fairclough of Nottingham Forest and Wimbledon's Brian Gayle.

•So far only three United goalkeepers have been sent-off in competitive matches: Harry Gregg v. Blackburn Rovers (in November 1965), Peter Schmeichel v. Charlton Athletic, FA Cup (in March 1994) and Raimond van der Gouw v. Watford, League Cup (October 2000).

•Former United centre-half Frank Barson is believed to have been sent-off at last a dozen times during his career, although none were with United, while Welsh international defender Caesar Jenkyns was also dismissed many times during the 1890s...once for fighting with spectators!

•Back in 1908, three United players were sent-off during a friendly with the Hungarian club side Ferencvaros in Budapest. But the referee was somehow made to change his mind and in the end only two went for an early bath - Dick

Duckworth and Ernie Thomson! George Stacey remained on the pitch.

•Left-half Jack Wilson was sent-off playing in a Central League game only days after joining the club from Newcastle in September 1926. He was subsequently suspended for two months!

•Charlie Moore, United's rugged full-back, was sent-off against Leicester City in September 1929 for retaliation.

•The usually quiet, baby-faced figure of Ole Gunnar Solskjaer was sent-off in the last minute of United's 1-1 Premiership draw with Newcastle in April 1998, following a professional foul to prevent a breakaway goal in the closing stages.

SEQUENCES

Winning Sequences

Taking in the part of two seasons, during an eight-month period from January to September 1951, United won 16 home matches in succession (13 League and three FA Cup).

In 1904-05 United won 14 League games in succession - the longest winning sequence in Division Two by any club in a season. They won six games on the road (all competitions) in 1985 and repeated that feat in January/February 1994 and January/March 1996. Between December 2001/February 2002 Uniuted won six successive Premiership away matches. In 2000, United set a new Premiership record of 12 successive wins, 11 at the end of the 1999-2000 season and one on first day of the following campaign.

Without A Win

United's worst run in the League without recording a victory is 16 games - achieved twice - firstly between 3 November 1928 and 9 February 1929 and secondly between 19 April and 25 October 1930. They suffered 14 defeats during the latter run. United did not win a single home match (in nine starts) during that spell in 1928-29.

Over a period of 14 months between 15 February 1930 and 3 April 1931, United went 28 League and Cup games without an away win. Between 30 September and 2 December 1961 United went 10 home and away games without a win, and over a period of two months early in 1978 (28 January to 29 March) United went eight home games without a win.

Defeats

United's worst-ever run of successive away defeats (continuous in all competitions) has been 15 - between 30 September 1893 and 8 September 1894.

At the start of season 1930-31, United lost all their first 12 League games. They had lost the last two League fixtures at the end of the previous campaign, making it 14 defeats in all - the club's worst ever losing sequence.

Undefeated Sequences

United's best-ever unbeaten run in competitive football was between 26 December 1998 and 25 September 1999. In that time they played 29 Premier League matches (a Premier League record), eight FA Cup games and eight European ties (45 matches in all). However, during this spell they did lose in the FA Charity Shield and the European Super Cup. The run of 29 unbeaten Premiership games equalled the record for 'top flight' football.

United's best-ever unbeaten run prior to 1998-99, spanned a total of 34 matches (in the Premiership and various Cup competitions) between 25 September 1993 and 2 March 1994.

United were unbeaten in 36 successive home games (all competitions) between 21 November 1992 and 13 February 1994.

The Reds registered a run of 20 away games (League and Cup) without defeat between 2 October 1993 and 22 March 1994.

United remained unbeaten in all of their 22 home matches (League, FA Cup & Test matches) in season 1896-97. They held firm again in each of their 21 home League games in 1955-56 and in all of their 29 home League and Cup encounters in 1982-83.

United remained unbeaten for 31 home League matches from 19 March (when Everton won 2-1 at Old Trafford) to 20 October 1956 (when Everton were again victors at Old Trafford, this time by 5-2).

After WW2 United remained unbeaten at home against London clubs for 11 seasons: from 1946-47 to 1956-57 inclusive. The first club from the 'capital city' to win at Old Trafford was Chelsea (1-0) in 1957-58. The sequence involved 48 unbeaten League and Cup matches.

United remained unbeaten at home in European competitions until 30 October 1996, when the Turkish side, Fenerbahce triumphed 1-0 at Old Trafford. The sequence comprised 57 matches in all major European tournaments.

* (For other sequences - see under respective Away from Home, League, FA Cup and League Cup categories).

SETTERS, Maurice Edgar

Born: Honiton, Devon, 16 December 1936,

Career: Honiton & Cullompton Schools, Exeter City (amateur, summer 1952, professional early 1954), West Bromwich Albion (£3,000, early 1955), MANCHESTER UNITED (£30,000, January 1960), Stoke City (November 1964), Coventry City (late 1967), Charlton Athletic (early 1970), Doncaster Rovers (manager, summer 1971, suspended late 1974 and subsequently dismissed from office), Sheffield Wednesday (coach, summer 1980), Rotherham United (assistant-manager 1982), Newcastle United (Chief Scout, 1984), Republic of Ireland (assistant-manager/coach under Jack Charlton 1986-95). Bandy-legged Maurice Setters was a tough-tackling, crew-cutted wing-half, who also filled in at full-back, centre-half and inside-right during a fine career which spanned 20 years. He gained England Schoolboy honours as a 15 year-old and went on to win one Youth cap and 16 at Under 23 level, also playing for the FA XI and Young England as well as making over 130 senior appearances for WBA before joining United. He helped the Reds win the FA Cup in 1963 and became a firm favourite with the supporters before losing his place effectively to Nobby Stiles. He had a long association with Jack Charlton at both Newcastle and with the Northern Ireland national team.

Setters, who received compensation to the value of £1,340 for unfair dismissal from his position as team manager of Doncaster, now lives in Bawtry near Doncaster and does some scouting around the Yorkshire area for various clubs.

Club record: 194 apps. 14 goals

SEXTON, David James

Dave Sexton was manager of MANCHESTER UNITED for a period of almost four years, from July 1977 until April 1981. Born in Islington, North London, on 6 April 1930, Sexton was an inside-forward with Newmarket Town, Chelmsford City, Luton Town (1951-52), West Ham United (1952-56), Leyton Orient (signed for £2,000, 1956-57), Brighton & Hove Albion (1957-59) and Crystal Palace (from 1959 until his retirement with cartilage trouble in 1962). He then became Chelsea's assistant-coach before taking over as manager of his former club Leyton Orient (January-December 1965). His next position saw him as coach at Fulham (early 1966) before he was named as Arsenal's assistant-manager/coach in the summer of 1966, moving back to Chelsea as team manager in October 1967. He remained at Stamford Bridge until October 1974 and for the next three years was in charge of Queen's Park Rangers. He replaced Tommy Docherty at Old Trafford and was then himself replaced by Ron Atkinson in 1981.

At this point Sexton, still eager to remain in football, took over the reins at Coventry City, holding office at Highfield Road for two years (1981-83). On leaving the Sky Blues he was enrolled by England, initially as assistant-manager to Bobby Robson and having a big say in the FA's School of Excellence at Lilleshall.

Since then he has worked in conjunction with several other former players and managers as the national team's senior coach (he is now on Sven-Goran Eriksson's coaching staff) while also assisting a handful of clubs as coach/scout, his main one being Aston Villa.

As a player Sexton turned out for the FA against the RAF in 1953 and represented the Football League (S) v. the FL (North) four years later. He was also a Third Division (South) Championship winner with Brighton in 1957-58. As a manager he guided Chelsea to victory in the 1970 FA Cup Final (when they beat Leeds United in a replay at Old Trafford) and followed up by seeing glory in the 1971 European Cup-winners Cup Final and as runners-up in the League Cup Final a year later before taking QPR into Europe (via the UEFA Cup) for the very first time. As United's boss, he led his players out for the Final of the 1979 FA Cup which ended in a last minute defeat by Arsenal. He also paid £825,000 for Ray Wilkins and £1 million for Garry Birtles before getting the sack!

A quiet man, Sexton has made a name for himself as one of the country's leading and most reliable coaches. Still going strong at over 70!

SHAMROCK ROVERS

This preliminary European Cup-tie was over after the first leg! United won in a canter in Ireland by 6-0 (Tommy Taylor and Liam 'Billy' Whelan both scoring twice) before tidying up at Old Trafford when Dennis Viollet bagged a couple of goals in a 3-2 victory..

Nobby Stiles played his first game for United against Rovers in a friendly in April 1960. His League debut followed six months later.

Players with both clubs include: W Behan, T Breen, F Burns, D Byrne, E Dodds (United WW2), P Dunne, J Giles (Rovers player-manager), L O'Brien, A Whelan.

SHARPE, Lee Stuart

Born: Halesowen, West Midlands, 27 May 1971

Career: Edgcliffe School (Kinver), Hagley High School (nr Kidderminster), Halesowen & Stourbridge Boys, Birmingham City (junior, 1986), Torquay United (trialist, then trainee 1987, professional 1988), MANCHESTER UNITED (£185,000, June 1988), Leeds United (£4.5 million, August 1996), Bradford City (£200,000, early 1999), Portsmouth (on loan early 2001), Grimsby Town (trials, July/August 2002), Exeter City (August 2002).

Playing mainly as an attacking winger, preferring the left-flank, Lee Sharpe was missed by the big Midlands clubs and snapped up by little Torquay as a teenager. He developed rapidly and became the Gull's youngest-ever player when he made his Football League debut at the age of 16 years, four months, seven days in the local derby against Exeter City on 3 October 1987. He was used as an emergency left wing-back during his early days with United before settling down as an orthodox winger. A strong, powerful runner, and excellent crosser of the ball, with an eye for goal, he helped the Reds win the European Cup-winners Cup Final in Rotterdam in 1991 and followed up with a League Cup winners medal in 1992 and three Premiership prizes (in 1993, 1994 and 1996) as well as FA Charity Shield success in 1994. Sharpe - who was sidelined with a severe bout of meningitis in 1992 - won eight full England caps and played in one 'B' and five Under-21 internationals during his eight seasons at Old Trafford. During his latter years with the club he was vying for his place with Ryan Giggs. After leaving United he struggled with injuries at both Elland Road and Valley Parade.

Club record: 263 apps. 36 goals

SHARPE, William H

Born: Lancashire, circa 1870

Career: NEWTON HEATH (1890-92), Wigan County (1896-97), Oldham Athletic (1897-1901).

Outside-left Bill Sharpe had one very good season with the Heathens, scoring six goals in 20 Football Alliance games in 1890-91. He seemed to be out of the game for quite a while after leaving the club before returning with Oldham County in 1896.

Club record: 27 apps. 6 goals (also 30 'other' apps, 6 goals)

SHEFFIELD UNITED

Heathens/United's League results v the Blades:

Season	Div	Home	Away	Season	Div	Home	Away
1893-94	1	L 0-2	L 1-3	1946-47	1	W 6-2	D 2-2
				1947-48	1	L 0-1	L 1-2
1906-07	1	W 2-0	W 2-0	1948-49	1	W 3-2	D 2-2
1907-08	1	W 2-1	L 0-2				
1908-09	1	W 2-1	D 0-0	1953-54	1	D 2-2	W 3-1
1909-10	1	W 1-0	W 1-0	1954-55	1	W 5-0	L 0-3
1910-11	1	D 1-1	L 0-2	1955-56	1	W 3-1	L 0-1
1911-12	1	W 1-0	L 1-6				
1912-13	1	W 4-0	L 1-2	1961-62	1	L 0-1	W 3-2
1913-14	1	W 2-1	L 0-2	1962-63	1	D 1-1	D 1-1
1914-15	1	L 1-2	L 1-3	1963-64	1	W 2-1	W 2-1
				1964-65	1	D 1-1	W 1-0
1919-20	1	W 3-0	D 2-2	1965-66	1	W 3-1	L 1-3
1920-21	1	W 2-1	D 0-0	1966-67	1	W 2-0	L 1-2
1921-22	1	W 3-2	L 0-3	1967-68	1	W 1-0	W 3-0
1925-26	1	L 1-2	L 0-2	1971-72	1	W 2-0	D 1-1
1926-27	1	W 5-0	D 2-2	1972-73	1	L 1-2	L 0-1
1927-28	1	L 2-3	L 1-2	1973-74	1	L 1-2	W 1-0
1928-29	1	D 1-1	L 1-6				
1929-30	1	L 1-5	L 1-3	1975-76	1	W 5-1	W 4-1
1930-31	1	L 1-2	L 1-3				
				1990-91	1	W 2-0	L 1-2
1934-35	2	D 3-3	L 2-3	1991-92	1	W 2-0	W 2-1
1935-36	2	W 3-1	D 1-1	1992-93	PL	W 2-1	L 1-2
				1993-94	PL	W 3-0	W 3-0
1937-38	2	L 0-1	W 2-1				

Summary of League results

	P	W	D	L	F	A
Premier League	4	3	0	1	9	3
Division 1	76	33	13	30	121	111
Division 2	6	2	2	2	11	10
Home	43	26	6	11	88	48
Away	43	12	9	22	53	76
Total	86	38	15	33	141	124

FA Cup results v the Blades:

	Round	Venue	Result
1989-90	6	Away	W 1-0
1992-93	5	Away	L 1-2
1993-94	3	Away	W 1-0
1994-95	3	Away	W 2-0

Fact File

United's first ever Premier League match was at Bramall Lane on 15 August 1992 when Sheffield United won 2-1.

After playing each other for almost a hundred years the two clubs finally met in the FA Cup in 1990; within five years they had met a further three times, coincidentally all four matches taking place at Bramall Lane.

Players with both clubs include: W Boyd, T Boyle, H Brook (Man Utd WW2), D Byrne, A Capper, J Connaughton, E Connor, J Cunningham, M Dempsey; E Dodds & G Farrow (both Man Utd WW2), R Gardner, D Givens, A Goram, W Greenwood, S Houston (also Blades coach & assistant-manager), R John, J Leighton (on loan to Blades), P McGrath, FH Milnes (Man Utd reserve), J Moody (Blades trialist), A Notman, P Parker, J Peden, F Pepper, T Poole (Man Utd junior), C Roberts (Blades trialist), J Sloan (Man Utd reserve & WW2), M Todd (Man Utd junior), M Twiss, E West.

Also associated: S Bruce (Blades manager), H Haslam (United trialist, WW2, Blades manager), A Rowley (United WW2 guest, Blades manager), L Macari (United player, Blades Chief Scout), A Hodgkinson (Blades' goalkeepr, United coach), R Duckworth jnr (United reserve, Blades scout)

SHEFFIELD WEDNESDAY (originally THE WEDNESDAY)

Heathens/United's League results v the Owls:

Season	Div	Home	Away	Season	Div	Home	Away
1892-93	1	L 1-5	L 0-1	1956-57	1	W 4-1	L 1-2
1893-94	1	L 1-2	W 1-0	1957-58	1	W 2-1	L 0-1
1899-1900	2	W 1-0	L 1-2	1959-60	1	W 3-1	L 2-4
				1960-61	1	D 0-0	L 1-5
1906-07	1	W 5-0	L 2-5	1961-62	1	D 1-1	L 1-3
1907-08	1	W 4-1	L 0-2	1962-63	1	L 1-3	L 0-1
1908-09	1	W 3-1	L 0-2	1963-64	1	W 3-1	D 3-3
1909-10	1	L 0-3	L 1-4	1964-65	1	W 1-0	L 0-1
1910-11	1	W 3-2	D 0-0	1965-66	1	W 1-0	D 0-0
1911-12	1	W 3-1	L 0-3	1966-67	1	W 2-0	D 2-2
1912-13	1	W 2-0	D 3-3	1967-68	1	W 4-2	D 1-1
1913-14	1	W 2-1	W 3-1	1968-69	1	W 1-0	L 4-5
1914-15	1	W 2-0	L 0-1	1969-70	1	D 2-2	W 3-1
1919-20	1	D 0-0	W 3-1	1974-75	2	W 2-0	D 4-4
1922-23	2	W 1-0	L 0-1	1984-85	1	L 1-2	L 0-1
1923-24	2	W 2-0	L 0-2	1985-86	1	L 0-2	L 0-1
1924-25	2	W 2-0	D 1-1	1986-87	1	W 3-1	L 0-1
				1987-88	1	W 4-1	W 4-2
1926-27	1	D 0-0	L 0-2	1988-89	1	D 1-1	W 2-0
1927-28	1	D 1-1	W 2-0	1989-90	1	D 0-0	L 0-1
1928-29	1	W 2-1	L 1-2				
1929-30	1	D 2-2	L 2-7	1991-92	1	D 1-1	L 2-3
1930-31	1	W 4-1	L 0-3	1992-93	PL	W 2-1	D 3-3
				1993-94	PL	W 5-0	W 3-2
1936-37	1	D 1-1	L 0-1	1994-95	PL	W 1-0	L 0-1
1937-38	2	W 1-0	W 3-1	1995-96	PL	D 2-2	D 0-0
				1996-97	PL	W 2-0	D 1-1
1950-51	1	W 3-1	W 4-0	1997-98	PL	W 6-1	L 0-2
				1998-99	PL	W 3-0	L 1-3
1952-53	1	D 1-1	D 0-0	1999-00	PL	W 4-0	W 1-0
1953-54	1	W 5-2	W 1-0				
1954-55	1	W 2-0	W 4-2				

Summary of League results

	P	W	D	L	F	A
Premier League	16	9	4	3	34	16
Division 1	84	34	19	31	135	124
Division 2	12	7	2	3	18	11
Home	56	37	13	6	116	50
Away	56	13	12	31	71	101
Total	112	50	25	37	187	151

FA Cup results v the Owls:

	Round	Venue	Result
1903-04	2	Away	L 0-6
1914-15	1	Away	L 0-1
1924-25	1	Away	L 0-2
1957-58	5	Home	W 3-0
1959-60	5	Home	L 0-1
1960-61	4	Away	D 1-1
	Replay	Home	L 2-7
1961-62	5	Home	D 0-0
	Replay	Away	W 2-0

League Cup results v the Owls:

	Round	Venue	Result
1990-91	Final	Wembley	L 0-1
1993-94	SF	Home	W 1-0
	SF(2)	Away	W 4-1

Fact File:
United have played Sheffield Wednesday four times in the FA Cup since WW2, and all four matches (plus two replays) were contained in a five year period (1958-62).
United beat the Owls on four occasions in season 1993-94 ...5-0 (h) and 3-2 (a) in the Premiership, 1-0 (home) and 4-1 (away) in the two-legged League Cup semi-final.
Players with both clubs include: V Anderson, J Bell, J Breedon, E Cantona (Owls trialist), T Cooke, N Dewar, B Djordjic, D Gibson, J Holton, W Inglis, E Kilshaw (United WW2), D Johnson (United reserve), T Jones, J Lowey (United reserve), J McCalliog, IL McKeown (United reserve), G Nevin, P O'Connell, M Pearson, M Pinner, A Quixall, G Stacey, E Toseland (United WW2), C Turner, A Westwood (United reserve).
Also associated: R Atkinson (manager of both clubs), M Setters (United player, Owls coach), F Blunstone (United Youth team manager, Owls caretaker-manager), H Catterick (Owls manager, United WW2 player).

SHELDON, John

Born: Clay Cross, Derbyshire, spring 1887. Died: Manchester, 19 March 1943
Career: Nuneaton FC, MANCHESTER UNITED (November 1909), Liverpool (November 1913). Retired through injury summer 1922.
After four seasons with United, during which his first team outings were restricted owing to the form and presence of Billy Meredith, wing-forward John Sheldon went on to make over 130 appearances (20 goals scored) in the first team at Liverpool for whom he played in the 1914 FA Cup Final v. Burnley. And on Good Friday 1915 he was named as one of the players involved in the betting scandal League match between United and Liverpool. In fact, Sheldon, who missed a penalty in that game, was suspended indefinitely but later had that quashed, thus allowing him to play for the Merseysiders after WW1. Club record: 26 apps. one goal.

SHERINGHAM, Edward Paul

Born: Highams Park, London, 2 April 1966
Career: Millwall (apprentice, 1982, professional early 1984), Aldershot (on loan, early 1985), Nottingham Forest (£2 million, summer 1991), Tottenham Hotspur (£2.1 million, summer 1992), MANCHESTER UNITED (£3.5 million, July 1997), Tottenham Hotspur (July 2001).
Once a goalscorer, always a goalscorer - and that simply sums up Teddy Sheringham.
He started bulging nets as a schoolboy, continued via Millwall's nursery, junior and intermediate sides, through the reserves and into the first team. He became the Lions' record marksman with 111 goals in 262 senior appearances before being transferred to Nottingham Forest. He continued to score regularly, notching a further 23 goals in only 62 outings for Forest. And still the goals flowed - another 98 coming with head and feet in 197 outings for Spurs before his switch to Old Trafford. Sheringham, in fact, was the Premiership's top marksman in 1992-93 with 22 goals and he also finished up as leading scorer in four of his five seasons at White Hart Lane, netting 75 goals in the Premiership (a record at that time).

During his four years at Old Trafford, Sheringham - superb at holding up play and bringing his midfielders and fellow forwards into the game - was adored by the fans as he rattled in almost 50 goals in just over 150 first-class matches....including that crucial equaliser in the European Champions League Final against Bayern Munich in 1999 - which led to that dramatic late goal by Ole Gunnar Solskjaer thus clinching the treble for the Reds (Premiership and FA Cup having been already won).
Sheringham gained a Second Division Championship medal with Millwall in 1988 and a Simod Cup winner's medal with Forest in 1992. And besides his treble success with United in 1999, he was also a member of two other Premiership-winning sides (2000 & 2001).
He was honoured by his country (England) at Youth team level and since then has added one Under-21 and 45 senior caps to his tally. He was also voted FWA and PFA Player of the Year for 2000-01 when he was United's top-scorer with 21 goals.
A League Cup finalist with Spurs in 2002, Sheringham, still eager to score goals and a player who certainly loves and enjoys his football to the full, was in Sven Goran Eriksson's World Cup squad in Japan & South Korea.
Club record: 153 apps. 46 goals

SIDEBOTTOM, Arnold

Born: Barnsley, 1 April 1954

Career: MANCHESTER UNITED (amateur January 1971, professional February 1972), Huddersfield Town (January 1976), Halifax Town (1978-79).

Long-haired Arnie Sidebottom was a well built reserve central defender, who stood in for Steve James initially and later broken leg victim Jim Holton, helping United win the Second Division Championship in 1975. One of the rare breed of cricketer-footballers, fast-bowler Sidebottom represented Yorkshire in the County Championship and England against Australia in 1985. His son also played cricket (as a bowler) for Yorkshire and England.

Club record: 20 apps.

SILCOCK, John

Born: New Springs, Wigan, 15 January 1898. Died: Ashton-under-Lyne, 28 June 1966.

Career: Aspull Juniors FC (a Wigan colliery team), Atherton FC (Lancashire Combination), MANCHESTER UNITED (amateur, April 1916, professional June 1917), Oldham Athletic (August 1934-35), Droylsden United (1936-37).

Jack Silcock, a rock-like full-back, gave United grand service immediately after WW1. He was spotted 'luckily' by manager Jack Robson who had, in fact, gone be watch another Atherton player (Tommy Lucas) but was so impressed by Silcock's defensive qualities that he signed him instead! Lucas went on to play 366 games for Liverpool while Silcock amassed almost 450 for United.

Regarded as one of the great names in United's history, Silcock was capped three times by England (it should have been more) and represented the Football League on three occasions as well appearing in two international trials. He and Charlie Moore formed a tremendous full-back partnership at Old Trafford (they played together more than 200 times for the club). Silcock also had other splendid partners at the back but he alone was the more classy defender, his clean-kicking, his tough and precise tackling and excellent positional sense being admired by many. After his footballing days were over, Silcock became a licensee of the Rob Roy Hotel, Stretford.

Club record: 449 apps. 2 goals

SILVESTRE, Mikael Samy

Born: Tours, France, 9 August 1977

Career: Rennes (1995), Inter Milan (1998), MANCHESTER UNITED (£4 million, September 1999).

Versatile defender Mikael Silvestre has proved to be a God-send to United! Able to play as an orthodox left-back, he often filled in as a central defender and gave excellent performances throughout. A strong, purposeful footballer, especially when driving forward from his left-back berth, Silvestre has won 12 senior caps for France following earlier honours at both Youth and Under-21 levels. He helped United win the Premiership title in successive seasons: 2000 and 2001 and , along with his Old Trafford team-mate Fabien Barthez, was in France's World Cup squad in Japan & South Korea in May/June 2002.

Club record: 136 apps. 2 goals

SIVEBAEK, John

Born: Vejle, Denmark, 26 October 1961

Career: Vejle Boldklub (1980), MANCHESTER UNITED (£285,000, February 1986), St Etienne (£220,000, August 1987), AS Monaco (1990), Atalanta (1992), Pecasri (1993-94). Later became a football agent (1999).

Strong-running full-back John Sivebaek failed a medical when United first wanted to sign him in 1985. After eventually arriving at the club he made his debut against Liverpool at Anfield in February 1986 but took time to settle in at Old Trafford. Then, following the arrival of Alex Ferguson, he fell from favour and was sold to St Etienne after barely 18 months with the Reds.

Club record: 34 apps. one goal.

SLATER, J F

Born: Lancashire circa 1869

Career: NEWTON HEATH (seasons 1890-93), Fairfield (August 1893).

Goalkeeper Slater was virtually an ever-present in the Heathens' Football Alliance campaigns of 1890-91 and 1891-92 but then lost his place to the former Aston Villa custodian Jimmy Warner when the club entered the Football League in 1892-93.

Club record: 44 apps (also 41 'other' apps)

SLOAN, Thomas

Born: Ballymena, 10 July 1959

Career: Ballymena United, MANCHESTER UNITED (£20,000, August 1978), Chester (1982-83).

Eight of reserve midfielder Tommy Sloan's senior outings for United came as a substitute. Capped by Northern Ireland at Under-21 level while with Ballymena, he went on to gain three full caps with United. He was in the Chester side that reached the semi-finals of the League Trophy in 1983.

Club record: 12 apps.

295

SMITH, Albert C

Born: Glasgow, circa 1900

Career: Peterhill FC (Glasgow), MANCHESTER UNITED (October 1925), Preston North End (July 1927), Dolphin FC, Ireland (season 1931-32), Carlisle United (season 1932-33), Ayr United (1933-34).

Albert Smith was a reserve centre-forward during his time at Old Trafford, making all his senior outings during the second half of the 1926-27 campaign. He later played over 40 times for both PNE and Carlisle before returning to Scotland.

Club record: 5 apps. one goal

SMITH, John

Born: Batley, 17 February 1915. Died: 1975

Career: Dewsbury Schools, Whitehall Printers FC (Leeds), Dewsbury Moor Welfare, Huddersfield Town (summer 1932), Newcastle United (£2,500, late summer 1934), MANCHESTER UNITED (£6,500, February 1938), Burnley (WW2 guest), Blackburn Rovers (March 1946), Port Vale (£1,200 season 1947-48), Macclesfield (1948-49).

Hard-shooting centre-forward Jack Smith, an England schoolboy international in 1929, had already scored 93 goals in 149 League games before joining United. He continued to find the net during his early months at Old Trafford, helping the Reds clinch promotion from Division Two in 1938. Unfortunately the War robbed him of six years of his career, although he did score over 20 more goals with his last two major clubs before entering non-League football in 1948. Although he made 201 appearances for United in Wartime football (scoring 160 goals) Smith never played in the post-War League side.

Club record: 42 apps. 15 goals

SMITH, Lawrence

Born: Manchester, 1881. Died: Garston, Liverpool, September 1912

Career: Army football, MANCHESTER UNITED (November 1902), New Brompton (June 1903), Earlstown FC (season 1904-05).

Lawrie 'Soldier' Smith was a tricky winger who perhaps lacked the build and power to make any real impact. He made his debut for United against Leicester Fosse (away) in November 1902 and then scored his only goal for the club against the same team in the return fixture in March 1903.

Club record: 10 apps. one goal

SMITH, Richard

Born: Halliwell, Lancashire, circa 1870

Career: Halliwell Rovers (1898), Heywood Central, NEWTON HEATH (June 1894-January 1898), Halliwell Rovers (briefly, 1899), Wigan County (also 1899), NEWTON HEATH (February 1900), Bolton Wanderers (January 1901), Wigan United (seasons 1901-03).

Inside-forward Dick Smith had a superb first season with the Heathens, scoring 20 goals in 30 League & FA Cup games as partner to Jimmy Peters, becoming the first player ever to score four times in a game for the club (in the 5-2 away win over rivals Manchester City in November 1894). In season 1895-96 Smith scored a 'club record' six goals in a 14-0 win over Walsall Town Swifts which would have stood had the Football League not declared the match null and void following Walsall's protest regarding the state of the pitch. Smith's six goals were therefore struck from the record books. When he returned to the club he was again used in a variety of positions, always giving a good, honest account of himself.

Club record: 104 apps. 36 goals (also 32 'other' apps, 9 goals)

SMITH, Thomas Gable

Born: Whitburn, County Durham, 18 October 1900. Died: Whitburn, 21 February 1934

Career: Marsden Villa, Whitburn FC, South Shields (1919), Leicester City (late 1919), MANCHESTER UNITED (January 1924), Northampton Town (£250, June 1927), Norwich City (summer 1930), Whitburn FC (early 1931).

Inside-forward Tom Smith did not look at home during the first few weeks of his association with United but afterwards he put in some very useful performances (mainly as partner to Joe Spence) and helped the team gain promotion from Division Two in 1925. During his career he appeared in over 300 competitive games and scored more than 50 goals, 47 coming in 274 League outings).

Smith was one of seven brothers, five of whom were professional footballers. Two of them won England recognition, Jack as a Portsmouth player and Septimus with Leicester City.

Club record: 90 apps. 16 goals

SMITH, William

Born: Cheshire, circa 1872

Career: Stockport County (briefly), Manchester City (mid 1897), Stockport County (season 1900-01), NEWTON HEATH (August 1901-May 1902).

Billy Smith - nicknamed 'Stockport' because there were two players sharing the same name at Manchester City - was a keen, enterprising utility forward who could also fill in as a half-back. He helped Manchester City win the Second Division title in 1898-99 when he had Billy Meredith as his partner on the right.

Club record: 17 apps. one goal ((also 4 'other' apps)

SNEDDON, John

Born: Lancashire, circa 1870
Career NEWTON HEATH (season 1891-92).
Inside-forward John Sneddon was an impressive
performer during the Heathens' Football Alliance
campaign of 1891-92. He had the pleasure (and honour)
of scoring the first-ever goal in a competitive Manchester
derby, against Ardwick in a 1st qualifying round FA Cup-
tie in October 1891, which the Heathens won
convincingly by 5-1. Three years later Ardwick would
become Manchester City.
Club record: 24 apps. 7 goals (also 21 'other' apps, 6 goals)

SOUTH MELBOURNE

On 2 January 2000, United beat the Australian side,
South Melbourne, 2-0 in the FIFA Club World
Championship in Rio de Janeiro, Brazil. The South
African international winger Quinton Fortune scored
both United's first-half goals in stifling heat in front of
25,000 spectators.
Associated with both clubs: Tommy Docherty (manager
at United and Melbourne).

SOUTHAMPTON (St Mary's)

United's League results v Saints:

Season	Div	Home	Away	Season	Div	Home	Away
1922-23	2	L 1-2	D 0-0	1978-79	1	D 1-1	D 1-1
1923-24	2	W 1-0	D 0-0	1979-80	1	W 1-0	D 1-1
1924-25	2	D 1-1	W 2-0	1980-81	1	D 1-1	L 0-1
				1981-82	1	W 1-0	L 2-3
1931-32	2	L 2-3	D 1-1	1982-83	1	D 1-1	W 1-0
1932-33	2	L 1-2	L 2-4	1983-84	1	W 3-2	L 0-3
1933-34	2	W 1-0	L 0-1	1984-85	1	D 0-0	D 0-0
1934-35	2	W 3-0	L 0-1	1985-86	1	W 1-0	L 0-1
1935-36	2	W 4-0	L 1-2	1986-87	1	W 5-1	D 1-1
				1987-88	1	L 0-2	D 2-2
1937-38	2	L 1-2	D 3-3	1988-89	1	D 2-2	L 1-2
				1989-90	1	W 2-1	W 2-0
1966-67	1	W 3-0	W 2-1	1990-91	1	W 3-2	D 1-1
1967-68	1	W 3-2	D 2-2	1991-92	1	W 1-0	W 1-0
1968-69	1	L 1-2	L 0-2	1992-93	PL	W 2-1	W 1-0
1969-70	1	L 1-4	W 3-0	1993-94	PL	W 2-0	W 3-1
1970-71	1	W 5-1	L 0-1	1994-95	PL	W 2-1	D 2-2
1971-72	1	W 3-2	W 5-2	1995-96	PL	W 4-1	L 1-3
1972-73	1	W 2-1	W 2-0	1996-97	PL	W 2-1	L 3-6
1973-74	1	D 0-0	D 1-1	1997-98	PL	W 1-0	L 0-1
1974-75	2	W 1-0	W 1-0	1998-99	PL	W 2-1	W 3-0
				1999-00	PL	D 3-3	W 3-1
				2000-01	PL	W 5-0	L 1-2
				2001-02	PL	W 6-1	W 3-1

Summary of League results

	P	W	D	L	F	A
Premier League	20	14	2	4	49	26
Division 1	44	20	14	10	68	50
Division 2	20	7	5	8	26	22
Home	42	27	8	7	85	44
Away	42	14	13	15	58	54
Total	84	41	21	22	143	98

FA Cup results v Saints:

	Round	Venue	Result
1896-97	2	Away	D 1-1
	Replay	Home	W 3-1
1962-63	Semi-final	Villa Park	W 1-0
1963-64	3	Away	W 3-2
1971-72	3	Away	D 1-1
	Replay	Home	W 4-1
1975-76	Final	Wembley	L 0-1
1976-77	5	Away	D 2-2
	Replay	Home	W 2-1
1991-92	4	Away	D 0-0
	Replay	Home	D 2-2 aet*
1995-96	6	Home	W 2-0

Note: * Lost on Penalty Kicks (2-4)

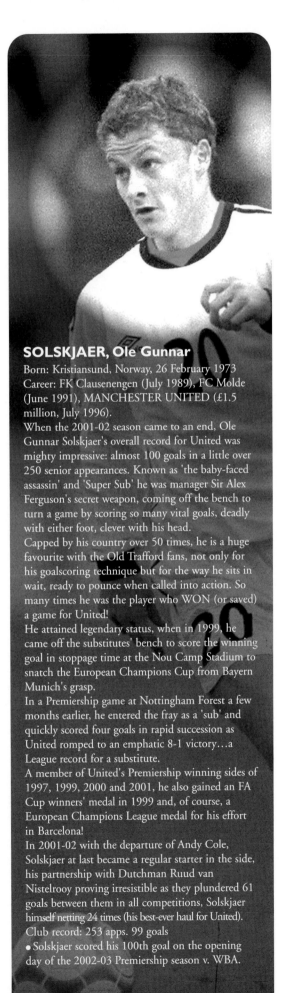

SOLSKJAER, Ole Gunnar

Born: Kristiansund, Norway, 26 February 1973
Career: FK Clausenengen (July 1989), FC Molde
(June 1991), MANCHESTER UNITED (£1.5
million, July 1996).
When the 2001-02 season came to an end, Ole
Gunnar Solskjaer's overall record for United was
mighty impressive: almost 100 goals in a little over
250 senior appearances. Known as 'the baby-faced
assassin' and 'Super Sub' he was manager Sir Alex
Ferguson's secret weapon, coming off the bench to
turn a game by scoring so many vital goals, deadly
with either foot, clever with his head.
Capped by his country over 50 times, he is a huge
favourite with the Old Trafford fans, not only for
his goalscoring technique but for the way he sits in
wait, ready to pounce when called into action. So
many times he was the player who WON (or saved)
a game for United!
He attained legendary status, when in 1999, he
came off the substitutes' bench to score the winning
goal in stoppage time at the Nou Camp Stadium to
snatch the European Champions Cup from Bayern
Munich's grasp.
In a Premiership game at Nottingham Forest a few
months earlier, he entered the fray as a 'sub' and
quickly scored four goals in rapid succession as
United romped to an emphatic 8-1 victory...a
League record for a substitute.
A member of United's Premiership winning sides of
1997, 1999, 2000 and 2001, he also gained an FA
Cup winners' medal in 1999 and, of course, a
European Champions League medal for his effort
in Barcelona!
In 2001-02 with the departure of Andy Cole,
Solskjaer at last became a regular starter in the side,
his partnership with Dutchman Ruud van
Nistelrooy proving irresistible as they plundered 61
goals between them in all competitions, Solskjaer
himself netting 24 times (his best-ever haul for United).
Club record: 253 apps. 99 goals
● Solskjaer scored his 100th goal on the opening
day of the 2002-03 Premiership season v. WBA.

297

League Cup results v Saints:

	Round	Venue	Result
1982-83	4	Home	W 2-0
1986-87	3	Home	D 0-0
	Replay	Away	L 1-4
1990-91	5	Away	D 1-1
	Replay	Home	W 3-2

Fact File:

Since 1969-70 United have played 29 home League matches against Southampton, losing only once in 1987-88, winning 21 drawing 7.

When United beat Saints 2-0 in a League game at The Dell in March 1990, Colin Gibson scored with his last kick before being substituted by Neil Webb. Later, striker Mark Robins then added a second goal with his first kick after replacing Mark Hughes.

Having not been drawn together in the FA Cup during the 20th century, the two clubs were coupled in successive draws: i.e. the semi-final of 1962-63 and the third round in 1963-64. United won both ties.

Players with both clubs: T Bogan, W Boyd, J Bullock, F Burns, J Curry, R Davies, A Donnelly, R Ferrier (Saints WW2), J Flitchett, M Hughes, J Jordan, A Kanchelskis, P Kennedy, N McBain (Saints WW1), J McCalliog, E MacDougall, J McDonald (United WW2), A McLoughlin (United reserve), C Mitten (Saints WW2), H Moger, W Rawlings, D Wallace, O Williams (United junior).

Also associated: G Roughton & G Strachan (United players, Saints managers), A Stepney (United player, Saints scout).

SOUTH SHORE (Blackpool)

United's FA Cup record against 'Shore':

Venue	P	W	D	L	F	A
Away	2	1	0	1	3	3

Both these Cup-ties took place in the 3rd qualifying round in seasons 1891-92 and 1899-1900 and both were staged at South Shore's Bloomfield Road ground; Newton Heath won 2-0 in the former competition while South Shore - later to amalgamate with Blackpool FC - won the second contest 3-1.

Player with both clubs: W Mathieson

(See also: Blackpool).

SOUTHPORT (Central)

Fact File

United defeated Southport Central 4-1 at home in the 4th qualifying round of the FA Cup in 1902-03.

When the Football League was launched in 1888, the people of Southport were concerned that the Lancashire seaside resort had no professional team. The Town Clerk called a meeting of all the town's clubs after which a professional team - Southport Central - was created, playing at the Athletic Ground on Sussex Road.

In 1905 the team switched to its Haig Avenue stadium and by the First World War the club was based in the powerful Central League, playing against the reserve teams of several major League clubs.

During that war the Vulcan Rubber Co adopted the team which became known as 'Southport Vulcan'. In 1919, as the club secretary completed the application form to enter the first post-war FA Cup, unsure whether a trade name would be acceptable to the FA, he entered the name 'Southport'. The club has been known by that name ever since. In 1921 it was elected to the Football League in the newly created Third Division (North). Southport played 50 consecutive seasons, never rising above Third Division level, before being voted out in 1978, to be replaced by Wigan Athletic. The club now plays in the Football (Nationwide) Conference.

Players with both clubs (Southport & Central) include: A Ainsworth (Southport WW1), J Ball, J Barber, C Birkett, C Briggs (United WW2), J Briscoe (United reserve), G Bissett, A Dainty (United WW2), P Davenport, R Duckworth jnr (United reserve), R English (United reserve), T Frame, J Garvey, J Gemmell (United WW2), R John (Southport WW2), P Latham (United reserve), R Lawton, G Lydon, P McBride (United reserve), J McGillivray, G Mutch (Southport player-trainer), D Musgrave (United reserve), T O'Neil, S Parker, A Potts (Central WW2), D Ryan (United reserve), G Sapsford, E Savage (Southport WW2), RH Scott (United reserve), R Seddon (United trialist), H Stafford, A Stapleton (United reserve), W Tyler (United reserve), A Warburton (Southport WW2), E Vincent, T Wyles (United WW2).

Also associated: E Harrison (Southport player, United coach).

Player with Southport Vulcan & United: W Toms

SPARTAK VARNA

After bringing home a 2-1 advantage from the away leg of their 2nd round European Cup-winners Cup encounter in 1983-84 with Spartak Varna, Frank Stapleton netted twice as United finished the job in style at Old Trafford, winning 2-0 for a 4-1 aggregate scoreline.

SPENCE, Joseph Waters

Born: Throckley, Northumberland, 15 December 1898. Died: 31 December 1966.

Career: Blucher Juniors, Throckley Celtic, Army football (from the age of 17 - serving with the Machine Gun Corps), Liverpool reserves (guest), Newburn FC, Scotswood (summer 1918), MANCHESTER UNITED (March 1919), Bradford City (June 1933), Chesterfield (mid 1933). Retired at the age of 40 in 1938, and later worked as a scout for Chesterfield.

Joe Spence was one of the undoubted heroes of United's dismal inter-war period, a wonderful servant, playing his heart out week after week in a struggling team. The cry from the terraces was invariably 'Give it to Joe' and Joe generally obliged!

An inside or centre-forward at school (he once bagged over 40 goals in a season) Spence helped his battalion win the Army Cup during WW1. He joined United after doing well with Newburn and Scotswood in the Northern League and made his senior debut at Derby in August 1919 - United's first game in the Football League since April 1915. He became a star performer, always the crowd's favourite, playing also on the right-wing where he was a clever, dangerous footballer. Injuries apart, Spence was a regular in the front-line for the next 13 years, being top-scorer or joint top-scorer in United's senior ranks on seven occasions. His tally of 481 League appearances remained a club record for some 33 years, until defender Billy Foulkes passed it in 1965-66. Awarded two benefits by United, Spence represented the Football League and won two full caps for England, lining up against Belgium and Ireland in 1926. Unfortunately he failed to win a single club medal whilst at Old Trafford, but in 1935-36 he helped Chesterfield clinch the Third Division (North) Championship. He went on to play in 613 League games (a record that stood for many years) with well over 200 goals scored. Spence's son,. Joe junior, was a Football League player, making well over 100 appearances as a defender for York City (1950-54).

Club record: 510 apps. 168 goals.

SPENCER, Charles William

Born: Washington, County Durham, 4 December 1899. Died: York, 9 February 1953.
Career: Glebe Rovers (1915), Royal Engineers Signals (WW1), Washington Chemical Works FC (1919), Newcastle United (autumn 1921), MANCHESTER UNITED (£3,250, July 1928), Tunbridge Wells Rangers (player-coach, May 1930), Wigan Athletic (player-manager, 1932-37), Grimsby Town (manager, 1937-51), Hastings United (manager, 1951-52), York City (manager, late 1952 until his demise in 1953).
Centre-half Charlie Spencer had already appeared in 161 League games before Manchester United signed him in 1928. Initially a creative half-back at St James' Park, he was transformed into a tough-tackling stopper centre-half after the advent of the new offside law in 1925 and developed into one of the best defenders in the country. In 1924 he played in two full internationals for England and then appeared in five unofficial test matches while touring Australia with the FA party in 1925. He later played in one international trial and captained the Football League side on two occasions in 1926 & 1928.. He helped Newcastle win the FA Cup in 1924 and the League Championship three years later. Spencer, who was dogged by serious illness late in his life, was a well-respected manager, especially at Blundell Park and whilst in charge of Tunbridge Wells he signed many established League players.
Club record: 48 apps.

SPONSORS (Sponsorship)

For many years the main sponsors for Manchester United were Sharp, the Japanese electronic giants, but on 2 February 2000 the club agreed a 4-year deal with Vodafone, worth upwards of £30 million.

SPORTING CLUB LISBON

United gave away a three goal advantage in the quarter-final of the 1963-64 European Cup-winners Cup competition. After leading 4-1 (from their home leg) and looking comfortable, they blew up in sunny Portugal in the second leg and crashed to a disastrous 5-0 defeat, their heaviest in a major European competition.
Player with both clubs: P Schmeichel.
Also associated: C Queiroz (coach with both clubs).

SPRATT, Walter

Born: Huddersfield, late 1892
Career: Rotherham Town (season 1910-11), Brentford (summer 1911), MANCHESTER UNITED (£175, February 1915), Clapton Orient (guest WW1), Brentford (1920-21), Sittingbourne, Elsecar Main FC Sheffield (1922-23)
Full-back Walter Spratt was a clean, precise tackler who gave nothing away. He represented London against Birmingham in 1914 and may well have made a name for himself had not the Great War intervened.. He was injured whilst playing as a guest for Orient during the hostilities and although he regained full fitness and played in United's reserve side, he was never the same player again!
Club record: 13 apps.

STACEY, George William

Born: Thorpe Hesley, near Rotherham, Easter 1887
Career: Thorpe Hesley FC, Sheffield Wednesday (1902), Thornhill United (1904-05), Barnsley (£100, summer 1905), MANCHESTER UNITED (£165, April 1907), Rotherham County (WW1 guest). Released on a free transfer from Old Trafford, May 1919.
A strong, aggressive ball-winner, with a bone-shaking tackle, full-back George Stacey replaced Dick Holden in United's ranks and gained a League Championship medal at the end of his first full season with the club, adding an FA Cup winners medal to his collection in 1909 and then claiming a second League Championship prize in 1911. An England trialist in 1912, Stacey was surprisingly never capped by his country but despite this he proved to be an excellent club man who gave United splendid service before the Great War. He ran a small business in Barnsley after retiring as a player and later went back to his first-ever job as a coal-miner.
Club record: 270 apps. 9 goals

STAFFORD, Harry

Born: Nantwich, winter, 1869
Career: Southport Central (1887), Crewe Alexandra (1890-91), NEWTON HEATH (March 1896-1902).Re-instated as an amateur June 1902 to become a MANCHESTER UNITED official, being a Director and groundsman at some stage while also playing an occasional game for Crewe Alexandra in season 1903-04. He later became a hotelier in Wrexham before emigrating to Australia and then moving to Montreal, Canada where he ran another hotel. Always keen on dogs, Stafford became a successful breeder and is understood that he kept a prize bull-dog, valued at $900 which never lost a show!
A right-back in his footballing days, Harry Stafford made 200 appearances for the club but scored only one - in a 3-0 home win over Portsmouth in a supplementary round of the FA Cup in January 1901 (this being his 147th outing for the club at senior level).
In fact, United owe Stafford (and his dog) an awful lot...for it was he (along with future President of Manchester United and local brewery owner John H Davies) who in 1902 bailed the club out of a financial crisis. Around £2,600 in debt,

the club's president at the time, William Healey, who was owed over £240 (a lot of money in those days) went to the County Court in Ashton-under-Lyne to seek a winding-up order on Newton Heath FC. He succeeded and the club was declared bankrupt- only for Stafford and Davies to come along and save the day. (See under BANKRUPTCY). Stafford, who captained the Heathens on many occasions, and was the re-born United's first skipper as well, thus became arguably the most important player in the club's illustrious history! He was a regular and consistent performer in the side for six seasons (1896-1902) and when he became ill in 1911, the board of directors handed him £50.
Club record: 200 apps. one goal (also 48 'other' apps)

STAM, Jakob

Born: Kampen, Holland, 17 July 1972.
Career: FC Dos Kampen (1990-92), Zwolle (season 1992-93), Cambuur Leeuwarden FC (summer 1993), Willem II (summer 1995), PSV Eindhoven (winter 1995), MANCHESTER UNITED (£10.75 million, July 1998), SS Lazio (£16.6 million, September 2001).
Rugged, no-nonsense centre-back 'Jaap' Stam, United's 6ft 3in, 14 stone shaven-headed rock solid defender, made over 200 senior appearances with five different clubs in the Netherlands before joining the professional ranks at Old Trafford in 1998. He helped United win the treble in 1999 and two more Premiership titles in 2000 and 2001, while also adding considerably to his collection of full international caps, which stood at 45 when he left United for SS Lazio in a shock transfer a week or so into the 2001-02 season, saying: "I had to leave England for the sake of my kids - although you'll probably never know the real truth!"
Manager Sir Alex Ferguson replaced Stam with the French international defender Laurent Blanc.
In October 2001 Stam was suspended from playing in Italian football after proving positive following a drugs test.
Club record: 127 apps. one goal

STAPLE HILL

United defeated Staple Hill 7-2 in a 1st round FA Cup-tie at their Bank Street ground, in mid-January 1906 in front of 7,560 fans. 'Clem' Beddow scored a hat-trick.

STAPLETON, Francis Anthony

Born: Dublin, 10 July 1956
Career: St Martin's FC (Dublin), Bolton Athletic (Dublin), MANCHESTER UNITED (trialist, early 1972), Wolverhampton Wanderers (trialist, also 1972), Arsenal (apprentice summer 1972, professional 1973), MANCHESTER UNITED (£900,000, August 1981), Ajax Amsterdam (August 1987), Derby County (on loan, early 1988), FC Le Havre, France (autumn 1988), Blackburn Rovers (summer 1989), Aldershot (non-contract, 1991), Huddersfield Town (player-coach, autumn, 1991), Bradford City (player-manager, late 1991 to summer 1994).
Having been capped by the Republic of Ireland at schoolboy level, centre-forward Frank Stapleton had an unsuccessful trial at Old Trafford only weeks before joining Arsenal - and then nine years later he moved from Highbury to United for a tribunal-fixed six-figure fee, signed by Ron Atkinson as a straight replacement for the departed Joe Jordan.
Adding Youth and full caps to his collection (he went on to play in 71 senior internationals for his country, scoring 20 goals - a record he held until 2001 when Niall Quinn took over the mantle) Stapleton helped Arsenal win the FA Cup in 1979 (scoring in a 3-2 win over United) and appeared in the European Cup-winners Cup Final a year later when Valencia took the trophy via a penalty shoot-out. After securing over 100 goals in almost 300 appearances for the Gunners, Stapleton moved to Old Trafford and immediately became a firm favourite with the fans. Although he didn't find the net as often as he or his manager would have liked, he still contributed greatly to United's cause and, in fact, headed the scoring charts in his first three seasons at the club, claiming 13, 19 and 19 goals respectively between 1981-84. Powerful in the air, smart and effective on the ground, he was the perfect partner for initially Garry Birtles, then Norman Whiteside and later Mark Hughes. Twice an FA Cup winner with United (v. Brighton in 1983 and v. Everton in 1985) he also played in the 1983 League Cup Final (beaten by Liverpool) and helped the Reds reach the semi-final of the European Cup-winners Cup in 1984. He also played in two FA Charity Shield matches (being a winner in 1983). When he scored against Brighton he became the first player to find the net in the FA Cup Final with different teams.
Following the arrival of Brian McClair, Stapleton left United in 1987 but he struggled with a back injury with Ajax and after a loan spell with Derby he joined Blackburn, finally entering management with Bradford City in 1991.
Club record: 291 apps. 79 goals

300

STEPHENSON, R

Born: Lancashire, circa 1873

Career: Talbot FC (Manchester), Owen's College (Manchester), NEWTON HEATH (amateur December 1895-April 1896), later with Northern Nomads (1905-06).

Reserve inside-left Stephenson scored once in his only League game for United - against Rotherham Town at home in January 1896 - when he replaced Dick Smith.

Club record: one app. one goal

STEPNEY, Alexander Cyril

Born: Mitcham, Surrey, 18 September 1942

Career: Surrey Schools, London Schools, Achilles FC (Surrey), Fulham (trialist), Tooting & Mitcham (Isthmian League, 1958-62), Millwall (amateur, then professional 1963), Chelsea (£50,000, summer 1966), MANCHESTER UNITED (£55,000, September 1966), Dallas Tornado (February 1979), Altrincham (player-coach, season 1979-80), Dallas Tornado (five months n 1980), later Manchester City goalkeeping coach, also worked for Stockport County & Rochdale FC Commercial Departments and acted as Northern-based scout for both Exeter City and Southampton while managing a car/van rental company in Rochdale where he also worked briefly as a publican.

Goalkeeper Alex Stepney made almost 550 senior appearances between the posts for United - and he scored two League goals, both penalties, against Leicester City and Birmingham City (both at home) in September/October 1973.

Before he joined Chelsea, Stepney helped Millwall win promotion from Divisions Four and Three in successive seasons (1965 & 1966), gained three England Under-23 caps and also played for Young England against England at Stamford Bridge. He spent barely four months with Chelsea before Matt Busby signed him to replace Dave Gaskell and veteran Harry Gregg. At the end of his first season Stepney (who made his debut in the local derby v. Manchester City in front of more than 62,000 fans) collected a League Championship medal and a year later proudly grasped his European Cup winners' medal as well as gaining his one and only full England cap (in a 3-1 win over Sweden at Wembley). In 1974-75 he missed only two League games as United won the Second Division title and then he appeared in successive FA Cup Finals, losing to Southampton in 1976 but then helping to beat Liverpool twelve months later.

An unspectacular goalkeeper, but reliable and consistent, with exceptional positional sense, Stepney sometimes made a difficult job look easy!

His remarkable point blank save from the brilliant Benfica inside-forward Eusebio, undoubtedly saved United from defeat in the European Cup Final in 1968, setting up that famous extra-time victory.

Club record: 545 apps. 2 goals

STEWARD, Alfred

Born: Manchester, 18 September circa 1896.

Career: Army football (Manchester Pals' Regiment: 1915-18), Stalybridge Celtic, MANCHESTER UNITED (amateur 1919), Heaton Park FC, MANCHESTER UNITED (professional January 1920), Manchester North End (player-manager, June 1932), Altrincham (player-manager 1933-34, then secretary-manager 1936-38), Torquay United (manager for two seasons: 1938-40).

Tall, brave and confident, with a safe pair of hands, possessing a good long kick, goalkeeper Alf Steward spent twelve years at Old Trafford. He took time to establish himself in the first XI at Old Trafford, finally claiming the number one position in season 1923-24, taking over from Jack Mew after some fine displays for the second XI when he saved no fewer than six penalties.

Earlier he had represented the pick of the Central League v. the North Eastern League early in 1921 and then won a Central League Championship medal at the end of that season. In 1924-25 - as an ever-present, he helped United gain promotion to the First Division, keeping a clean sheet on 25 occasions (a club record to this day) while also conceding a club record 23 goals!

Over a period of three-and-a-half years from April 1924 to September 1927, Steward only missed seven League games out of a possible 139 before losing his place to Lance Richardson. He regained his position in April 1928 and then went on to play in another 149 League games (out of 163) before handing over his gloves to John Moody in March 1932.

Steward, who was rewarded with two benefits by United, left Plainmoor shortly after the outbreak of WW2 (when the Devon club shut down), moving to the Birmingham area to work on munitions, later becoming group secretary of the BSA Recreation Centre in the city..

As well as being a fine goalkeeper, Steward was also a fine club cricketer and was on the books of Lancashire CCC for a short time. In 1922 he took 6 wickets for only 10 runs while playing for United against Manchester City in the annual cricket match between the two football clubs

Club record: 326 apps.

STEWART, Michael James

Born: Edinburgh, 26 February 1981

Career: MANCHESTER UNITED (apprentice, June 1997, professional March 1998),

Central midfield player Michael Stewart represented Scotland at Schoolboy level before joining United. He later added six Under-21 and three full caps to his collection as he strove to establish himself in the first team squad at Old Trafford.

Club record: 10 apps.

STILES, Norbert Peter, MBE

Born: Collyhurst, Manchester, 18 May 1942
Career: St Patrick's School (Collyhurst), Manchester
Schools, Lancashire Schools, MANCHESTER
UNITED (amateur September 1957, professional
June 1959), Middlesbrough (£20,000, May 1971),
Preston North End (£20,000, summer 1973 as a
player, appointed Chief Scout 1975, then manager
1977-81), Vancouver Whitecaps, Canada (coach,
1981-84), West Bromwich Albion (Youth team
manager, early 1984, then assistant-manager/coach,
spring 1984, manager autumn 1985 to early 1986,
then reserve/Youth team coach to 1989),
MANCHESTER UNITED (Youth team coach, July
1989 to summer, 1993).
'Nobby' Stiles was undoubtedly a great competitor
who became famous throughout the nation for his
toothless grin as he jigged round the pitch at Wembley
following England's World Cup triumph in 1966.
He gained two League Championship medals (in
1965 and 1967), a European Cup winners medal in
1968 when he worked overtime to shackle the skills of
Eusebio, and collected 28 full England caps (his first
in 1964), plus six at Youth level and three more with
the Under-23 side. He also represented the Football
League on three occasions. He missed the 1963 FA
Cup Final, Pat Crerand holding onto the No. 4 shirt -
but soon Stiles grabbed it and for the next five years
his was one of the first names   manager Matt Busby
marked on the team-sheet.
Rough, tough, as hard as iron, tireless, totally
committed, sometimes driving on when most of his
colleagues were flagging, Stiles was an inspiration in
many games and was certainly the United fans'
favourite son in a 14-year career. He joined former
colleague Bobby Charlton at Preston, having played
under his England team-mate and Bobby's brother
Jack Charlton at Middlesbrough. After a spell with his
brother-in-law, Johnny Giles, in the NASL with
Vancouver he then joined forces with Giles at West
Brom and after a spell as manager at The Hawthorns
he then worked as assistant to Ron Atkinson during
his second spell in charge of the Baggies.
In 1974, a modest and seemingly bewildered Stiles
was the subject of the BBC TV programme 'This Is
Your Life.' In June 2002, soon after helping promote
an England World Cup Who's Who book and
assisting in the launch of an anti-cholesterol
campaign, he suffered a mild heart attack.
Club record: 397 apps. 19 goals.

STEWART, William S

Born: Coupar Angus, Perthshire, 11 February 1870.
Died: Dundee, June 1945
Career: Dundee Our Boys, Warwick County, NEWTON
HEATH (May 1889), Luton Town (May 1895), Millwall
Athletic (season 1898-99), Luton Town (mid-1899), Thames
Ironworks (early 1900), Dundee (December 1900 to May 1901).
Willie Stewart was originally an inside-forward who later
converted into a centre-half, where he was outstanding in
the pivotal role. He was asked to keep goal in a League
game for Newton Heath on 7 January 1893 away at
Stoke after 'keeper Jimmy Warner had missed the train. The
Heathens played throughout the 90 minutes with only 10 men
and were beaten 7-1.
Scorer in the Heathens' first-ever Football Alliance game
against Sunderland Albion in September 1889, Stewart
then netted the club's first senior hat-trick against Small
Heath in the same Division in April 1890. A close-
dribbler with powerful shot, he missed only four of the
Heathens' 66 Alliance League matches and then starred in
76 out of the club's first 90 matches in the Football
League before going on to give Luton four years excellent
service, helping the Hatters claim their place in the
Football League.
Club record: 147 apps. 23 goals (also 96 'other' apps, 18 goals)

STEWART, William Todd

Born: Glasgow, circa 1911
Career: Church Boys Brigade (Glasgow), Shettlestone
Juniors, Cowdenbeath (summer 1931), MANCHESTER
UNITED (£2,350, November 1932), Motherwell (March
1934 to 1937).
Outside-left Billy Stewart was the first player signed by
manager Scott Duncan when he took over the reins at
Old Trafford (he had been Stewart's boss at
Cowdenbeath). A fleet-footed player with neat skills,
Stewart did well for close on two seasons before moving
back 'home' to Scotland with Charlie McGillivray.
Club record: 49 apps. 7 goals

STOCKPORT COUNTY

Heathens/United's League results v County:

Season	Div	Home	Away
1900-01	2	W 3-1	L 0-1
1901-02	2	D 3-3	L 0-1
1902-03	2	D 0-0	L 1-2
1903-04	2	W 3-1	W 3-0
1905-06	2	W 3-1	W 1-0
1922-23	2	W 1-0	L 0-1
1923-24	2	W 3-0	L 2-3
1924-25	2	W 2-0	L 1-2
1937-38	2	W 3-1	L 0-1

Summary of League results

	P	W	D	L	F	A
Division 2	18	9	2	7	29	18
Home	9	7	2	0	21	7
Away	9	2	0	7	8	11
Total	18	9	2	7	29	18

League Cup results v County:

	Round	Venue	Result
1978-79	2	Away *	W 3-2

* County waived their right to play at home – the match being
switched to Old Trafford where the attendance was 41,761.

Players with both clubs include: A Ambler, J Barber, C Barlow (United reserve), W Berry, G Best, G Brebner (United reserve), A Broome, W Brown, W Bunce; A Burrows & L Butt (both United WW2), A Cartman (County trialist), H Catterick (County amateur, United WW2), P Chisnall, T Chorlton, F Clempson, J Crompton (County WW2), D Cronin (United reserve), A Dainty (United WW2), B Daniels (United reserve), P Davenport, W Davies, J Dunkerley (United reserve), P Edwards; A Emptage & G Farrow (both United WW2), D Ferguson, W Fielding (County WW2), P Fletcher, D Graham, G Glaister (United WW2), E Green, J Hall (County WW2); H Harrison & A Herd (both United WW2), D Herd, E Hudson, W Johnson, EP Jones, F Kennedy, W Kennedy, F Knowles, D McFetteridge, W McKay (County WW2), H McLenahan, S McMillan, A Mallalieu (United reserve) A Marshall, J Norton, T Nuttall (County WW1), G Perrins, M Phelan, S Preston, P Proudfoot (reserve), A Quixall, C Ramsden, D Reid (United WW2), A Rice (United reserve), J Schofield, W Smith, T Spratt (United reserve), H Stock (United WW2), P Sutcliffe (United reserve), B Thornley, W Toms, P Tutty (United amateur), G Vose (County WW2), R Wallwork, J Wassall, H Whalley, O Williams (United reserve), W Woodward (United reserve), F Worrall (United WW2), ER Young (United reserve). Also associated: R Duckworth jnr (United reserve, County manager), SJ Pearson (United player, County coach), T Cavanagh (County player, United assistant-manager/trainer), T Curry (County player, United trainer), N Bailey (County player, United coach), A Stepney (United player, County's Commercial Dept).

STOKE CITY (originally STOKE)

Heathens/United's League results v the Potters:

Season	Div	Home	Away		Season	Div	Home	Away
1892-93	1	W 1-0	L 1-7		1963-64	1	W 5-2	L 1-3
1893-94	1	W 6-2	L 1-3		1964-65	1	D 1-1	W 2-1
					1965-66	1	D 1-1	D 2-2
1906-07	1	W 4-1	W 2-1		1966-67	1	D 0-0	L 0-3
					1967-68	1	W 1-0	W 4-2
1923-24	2	D 2-2	L 0-3		1968-69	1	D 1-1	D 0-0
1924-25	2	W 2-0	D 0-0		1969-70	1	D 1-1	D 2-2
					1970-71	1	D 2-2	W 2-1
1931-32	2	D 1-1	L 0-3		1971-72	1	W 3-0	D 1-1
1932-33	2	L 0-2	D 0-0		1972-73	1	L 0-2	D 2-2
					1973-74	1	W 1-0	L 0-1
1936-37	1	W 2-1	L 0-3					
					1975-76	1	L 0-1	W 1-0
1938-39	1	L 0-1	D 1-1		1976-77	1	W 3-0	D 3-3
1946-47	1	D 1-1	L 2-3		1979-80	1	W 4-0	D 1-1
1947-48	1	D 1-1	W 2-0		1980-81	1	D 2-2	W 2-1
1948-49	1	W 3-0	L 1-2		1981-82	1	W 2-0	W 3-0
1949-50	1	D 2-2	L 1-3		1982-83	1	W 1-0	L 0-1
1950-51	1	D 0-0	L 0-2		1983-84	1	W 1-0	W 1-0
1951-52	1	W 4-0	D 0-0		1984-85	1	W 5-0	L 1-2
1952-53	1	L 0-2	L 1-3					

Summary of League results

	P	W	D	L	F	A
Division 1	62	25	20	17	98	78
Division 2	8	1	4	3	5	11
Home	35	17	13	5	63	29
Away	35	9	11	15	40	60
Total	70	26	24	20	103	89

FA Cup results v the Potters:

	Round	Venue	Result
1894-95	1	Home	L 2-3
1930-31	3	Away	D 3-3
	Replay	Home	D 0-0 aet
	2nd R	Anfield	W 4-2
1935-36	4	Away	D 0-0
	Replay	Home	L 0-2
1964-65	4	Away	D 0-0
	Replay	Home	W 1-0
1966-67	3	Home	W 2-0
1971-72	6	Home	D 1-1
	Replay	Away	L 1-2 aet

League Cup records v. the Potters:

	Round	Venue	Result
1971-72	4	Home	D 1-1
	Replay	Away	D 0-0 aet
	2nd R	Away	L 1-2
1993-94	2 (1)	Away	L 1-2
	2 (2)	Home	W 2-0

Test Match
On 27 April 1895, Newton Heath were beaten 3-0 by Stoke at Burslem in front of 10,000 fans and as a result failed to gain promotion to the First Division.

Fact File
When Stoke beat United 7-1 at The Victoria Ground in a League in January 1893, the Reds fielded only 10 men. Goalkeeper Jimmy Warner missed the train and three different players stood between the posts during the course of the game - Willie Stewart, Tommy Fitzsimmons and John Clements.
The Potters knocked United out of both the League Cup and FA Cup competitions in season 1971-72.
The Potters were the only team to win a League game at Old Trafford in 1975-76 (1-0).

Players with both clubs include: A Allman (City WW1), H Bough (United reserve), P Coupar (United reserve), G Crooks, G Daly, W Draycott, A Edge, A Farmer (United reserve), J Gidman, J Greenhoff, H Gregg, J Griffiths (City WW2), A Grimes (also City coach), H Hardman (also United director & chairman), W Harrison (Stoke WW1), D Herd, F Hesham (United reserve), M Higgins, R John, K Lewis (United junior), J McGillivray, S McIlroy, S Matthews (United WW2), R Milarvie, J Owens (Heathens reserve), L Page, R Ramsay, W Robertson, M Setters, M Thomas, D Viollet.
Also associated: J Jordan & L Macari (United players, Stoke managers), A Waddington (United amateur, Stoke City manager), N Tapken (United player, City trainer).

STONE, Herbert Henry
Born: St Albans, Easter 1873
Career: NEWTON HEATH (July 1893), Ashton North End (July 1895).
Half-back Bert Stone was reserve to Willie Stewart, James McNaught and Will Davidson during his time with the Heathens and got very few chances in the first team..
Club record: 7 apps. (also 5 'other' apps)

STOREY-MOORE, Ian
Born: Ipswich, 17 January 1945
Career: Scunthorpe Schools, Scunthorpe United (trialist), Ashby Juniors (Scunthorpe), Blackpool (trialist), Nottingham Forest (amateur 1961, professional 1962), MANCHESTER UNITED (£200,000, March 1972, retired on medical advice, December 1973); later played for Burton Albion (player-manager from September 1974), Chicago Sting (making 14 appearances in 1975), Shepshed Charterhouse (player-manager 1976-77); also played in South Africa,
The first player with a 'double-barrelled' name to join United, winger Ian Storey-Moore had finished up as top scorer for Forest in five seasons (netting 118 goals in 272 first-class games) before moving to Old Trafford - a month after a transfer deal with Derby County had fallen through (which resulted in the Rams receiving a £5,000 fine and a fierce reprimand from the FA). Fast and direct with a powerful shot in both feet, the well-built figure of Storey-Moore certainly revived a struggling United side. Unfortunately things didn't work out for player or club when a medical examination revealed that Storey-Moore had a severely damaged ankle which sadly forced him to quit big-time football at the age of 28. Capped once by England at senior level (v. Holland in 1970), he played in two Under-23 internationals and represented the Football League twice. In the late 1980s he became a turf accountant with a betting office near to The City Ground, Nottingham and also figured regularly on local radio.
Club record: 44 apps. 13 goals

303

STRACHAN, Gordon David, OBE

Born: Edinburgh, 9 February 1957
Career: Craigroyston School, Edinburgh Schools, Dundee (autumn 1971), Aberdeen (£50,000, late 1977), MANCHESTER UNITED (£500,000, August 1984), Leeds United (£300,000, March 1989), Coventry City (free transfer, Easter, 1995, player-manager from November 1996, retired as a player, summer 1997), Southampton (manager, 2001-02).

Prior to joining United (as a replacement for Ray Wilkins) fiery red-haired inside-forward/midfielder Gordon Strachan won seven medals with Aberdeen - two Scottish Premierships (1980 & 1984), three Scottish Cups (1982-83-84), the European Cup-winners Cup (1983) and the European Super Cup (also 1983). With the Reds he added an FA Cup winners' medal to his collection in 1985 and then as a Leeds player gained both Second Division and First Division Championship medals (in 1990 & 1992 respectively) as well as victory in the FA Charity Shield, again in 1992. He also won 50 full caps for Scotland (1980-90) as well as appearing in one Under-21 international and earning honours for his country at both schoolboy and Youth team levels. Unfortunately he did not have the same success as a manager, seeing Coventry relegated from the Premiership in 2001 after 34 years in the top flight. However, his move to Southampton during the 2001-02 season signalled a vast improvement in the Saints' performances, steadily pulling out of the relegation zone and into mid-table.

He made a total of 883 club appearances and scored 188 goals - a wonderful return.

A precise passer of the ball, Strachan was also a clever dribbler. He was dogged on the ball and often brushed past tackles, twisting and turning and using the skilful change of direction to confuse his opponent(s). He packed a powerful right-foot shot (and was no slouch with his left either), he was re-united with former Pittodrie boss, Alex Ferguson in November 1986, but then surprisingly left Old Trafford for rivals Leeds barely two-and a-quarter years later. He was certainly an inspirational signing by Elland Road chief Howard Wilkinson as he was instrumental in bringing top-flight soccer back to the Yorkshire club and then crowning it all by helping them win the last League Championship before the introduction of the Premiership. Voted 'Footballer of the Year' and the FWA 'Player of the Year' in 1990-91, Strachan was awarded the OBE (for services to football both north and south of the border) in the New Year's Honours list in 1993.

Gordon's son, Gavin Strachan, also played for Coventry City and Dundee (on loan) during the 1990s.

Club record: 205 apps. 38 goals

STREET, Ernest

Born: Manchester, circa 1880
Career: Sale Holmfield FC, MANCHESTER UNITED (May 1902), Sale Holmfield (on loan, April-October 1903); released by United, April 1904.

Ernie Street was a reserve outside-right with United for two seasons. Two of his senior outings came in the FA Cup when he stood in for Alf Schofield in the ties against Liverpool and Everton in February 1903.

Club record: 3 apps.

STURM GRAZ

Roy Keane scored in both United's first stage wins over Graz in the 1999-2000 Champions League. The Reds won 2-1 at home - when Vastic netted an 87th minute penalty for the vistors - and 3-0 away. Twelve months later United made it four wins out of four with further victories of 3-0 at home and 2-0 away, this time in the second stage of the Champions League competition, Keane again on target in the home match.

SUBSTITUTES

For almost a hundred years, League, FA Cup and major international football was played without accepting the principle of using substitute players, even following serious injuries. For years the football authorities stubbornly resisted pressure for their introduction.

Eventually in 1965 the Football League tentatively introduced a regulation which allowed a single substitute to be nominated and then only introduced onto the field in the case of an injury to one of his colleagues.

Within a year the rule had been relaxed slightly, allowing the named substitute to be used for any reason. Gradually the rule has been extended to allow five nominated substitutes, including a specialised goalkeeper, three of whom can be used - and for some international matches as many as seven substitutes can be named on the team-sheet before kick-off, only three to be used.

As a measure of how the game has developed, it is worth noting that in the first season when substitutes were allowed (1965-66) Manchester United utilised only four players out of the 42 named for their respective League games. In 2000-01, a total of 92 were called off the bench in the 38 Premiership matches, substitutes now utilised tactically as well as to cover for injuries.

Substitute 'Firsts'

* Goalkeeper David Gaskell was the first substitute used by United in a competitive game. He came into the action against Manchester City in the FA Charity Shield game at Maine Road on 24 October 1956.

He came on at the start of the second-half to replace the injured Ray Wood after Duncan Edwards had donned the green jersey for a short while before the interval, leaving United with only 10 men. During the half-time break both managers agreed that the 16 year-old Gaskell (signed directly after playing for Wigan Schools) could take Wood's place for the remaining 45 minutes. In doing so Gaskell became the youngest player ever to appear for United in a competitive game.

For the record United won the game 1-0, Gaskell (wearing borrowed kit) pulling off several fine saves to deny the City forwards. Gaskell had attended the match purely as a spectator, having only recently joined the club!

•The first 'official' substitute named by Manchester United was winger Willie Anderson, for the Charity Shield game against Liverpool at Old Trafford on 14 August 1965. He replaced George Best in the 2-2 draw.

•United's first named substitute for a Football League game was Noel Cantwell v. Sheffield Wednesday (Division 1) on 21 August 1965. He was not called into action.

•The first 'sub' used by the Reds in a League match was John Fitzpatrick who came on for Denis Law during the away game against Tottenham Hotspur on 16 October 1965. United lost 5-1.

•The first 'sub' to score for United in the League was John Connelly (on for John Aston) against Leicester City (at Filbert Street) on 13 November 1965. United won 5-0.

•United's first FA Cup substitute called into action was David Sadler v. Exeter City (at St James' Park) in a 3rd round tie on 4 January 1969. He replaced George Best in a 3-1 win.

•United's first FA Cup scoring substitute was John Aston junior v. Southampton at Old Trafford in a 3rd round replay on 19 January 1972. He came on for Sammy McIlroy in the 4-1 victory (aet).

•Alan Gowling had the pleasure of being United's first substitute in a League Cup game. He came off the bench to replace Brian Kidd during the 2nd round clash with Middlesbrough at Old Trafford on 3 September 1969. United won 1-0.

•Sammy McIlroy was the first substitute to come on and score a League Cup goal for United - doing so against Bristol Rovers at Old Trafford in a 3rd round replay on 2 October 1972. He replaced Brian Kidd as United lost 2-1.

•In European football, goalkeeper Jimmy Rimmer had the honour of becoming United's first used substitute when he took over between the posts from Alex Stepney during the 1st round 1st leg European Cup encounter with Waterford at Lansdowne Road, Dublin on 18 September 1968. United won 3-1.

•Alan Davies became United's first European scoring substitute when he found the net against Juventus at Old Trafford in the European Cup-winners Cup semi-final 1st leg showdown with the Italians on 2 April 1984. He replaced John Gidman in the 1-1 draw.

•Goalkeeper Nick Culkin may well have had the shortest League 'career' as a United player. He replaced Raimond van der Gouw in the second minute of added time during the Premiership game at Highbury in 1999 and whilst on the field he pulled off an excellent save as United won 2-1. As he went into goal after the 90th minute, no accurate estimate of his time on the field is possible but it was unlikely to have exceeded two minutes.

•Another 'keeper, Raimond van der Gouw, played his last game as a substutute for United against Charlton Athletic in the FA Premier League at Old Trafford on 11 May 2002 at the age of 39 years and 48 days, making him the oldest post-war player for the club and the second oldest of all-time (See under Age).

United's Substitutes (playing a key role in the 1998-99 treble triumph)

•Ole Gunnar Solskjaer came off the bench in the Premiership game against Nottingham Forest at The City Ground on 6 February 1999, replacing Dwight Yorke in the 72nd minute. United were leading 4-1 at the time and then Solskjaer netted another four times to ensure an 8-1 victory. Solskjaer's haul of four goals is the most ever scored by a substitute.

•Solskjaer came off the bench (as one of a triple substitution) against Liverpool at Old Trafford in the 4th round FA Cup-tie when United were trailing 1-0. He helped set up Dwight Yorke's 88th minute equaliser and then scored a dramatic late winner in stoppage time when a replay at Anfield looked certain.

•Ryan Giggs was a substitute against Arsenal at Villa Park in the FA Cup semi-final replay on 14 April 1999. He was brought on in place of Jesper Blomqvist in the 62nd minute. In the 19th minute of extra-time, with United down to 10 men and clinging on at 1-1 following Roy Keane's sending-off, Giggs (after a mazy 70-yard dribble and vicious shot) scored what some pundits described as the 'goal of the century' to send United through to Wembley.

•In the FA Cup Final against Newcastle United at Wembley on 22 May 1999, striker Teddy Sheringham was brought on as a substitute for the injured Roy Keane after only nine minutes play. Within two minutes of his arrival he had given United the lead and in the second-half he set Paul Scholes up to seal victory and so complete the second part of the treble.

•Four days after that Wembley triumph, it was the dynamic duo of Solskjaer and Sheringham who won the European Champions League Cup Final for United in the Nou Camp Stadium, Barcelona against Bayern Munich. They both came off the bench (Solskjaer in the 67th minute and Sheringham in the 81st) as United, a goal down, pushed players forward in an effort to save the game. With the 90 minutes already up on the watch, United still trailed by that first-half goal. Then in a crowded penalty-area Sheringham swivelled to crack home a right-footed equaliser following David Beckham's corner, and finally, with added-time fast running out, Sheringham flicked on another Beckham flag-kick, for the alert Solskjaer to bang in the winner from close range. Never before or since could two substitutes have caused such a turn-around in a major match.

Super-sub

Ole Gunnar Solskjaer has acquired the dubious title as United's 'super-sub' for his uncanny ability to pick up the pace of the game, no matter how late his arrival into the action, and score important goals. His record with United (up to the end of the 2001-02 season) is quite unbelievable.

In his first five seasons with the club, he made 206 appearances (133 in the Premiership), scoring 74 goals (58 League). Of these appearances, 119 were in the United starting line-up (57 goals scored - giving him a 48 per-cent strike-record) while 87 were made as a substitute (17 goals scored). This tends to disprove the theory that Solskjaer is only effective coming off the bench, further underlined, it might be said, by his performances in 2001-02 when he finally became a permanent fixture, scoring 26 goals in 47 outings (lining up alongside Ruud van Nistelrooy in the main) of which just four were netted in a total of 17 substitute appearances.

Substitute Fact File

Top 10 substitute appearance-makers for United:

Player	Total	League	FAC	FLC	European	Others
Ole Gunnar Solskjaer	104	57	9	0	35	3
Brian McClair	73	59	7	1	6	0
Paul Scholes	71	52	7	2	10	0
Nicky Butt	61	47	2	0	12	0
Phil Neville	60	38	4	1	15	2
David McCreery	53	39	6	4	3	1
Teddy Sheringham	52	31	5	0	11	5
Lee Sharpe	50	33	7	8	2	0
Ryan Giggs	49	37	4	4	3	1
Andy Cole	44	34	2	0	7	1
Clayton Blackmore	44	36	6	2	0	0
Mark Robins	43	29	4	7	2	1

Top substitutes in League/Premiership
59 Brian McClair
57 Ole Gunnar Solskjaer
52 Paul Scholes
47 Nicky Butt
39 David McCreery
38 Phil Neville
37 Ryan Giggs

Top substitutes in League Cup
8 Lee Sharpe
7 Mark Robins
5 Mal Donaghy
5 Lou Macari
4 Ryan Giggs
4 David McCreery
4 Tony Young

Top substitutes in FA Cup
9 Ole Gunnar Solskjaer
7 Brian McClair
7 Paul Scholes
7 Lee Sharpe
6 Clayton Blackmore
6 David McCreery
5 Mike Duxbury
5 Teddy Sheringham
5 Dwight Yorke

Top substitutes in European Competitions
35 Ole Gunnar Solskjaer
15 Phil Neville
12 Nicky Butt
11 Teddy Sheringham
10 Paul Scholes

Bench Talk

David McCreery came on as a 'sub' for United in both the 1976 and 1977 FA Cup Finals, each time replacing winger Gordon Hill. McCreery, in fact, is the only teenager ever to appear in two FA Cup Finals.

Ron Davies was called upon as a substitute by United on 10 occasions in 1974-75, these being his only appearances for the club.

David Wilson had six games for the club and he too appeared each time as a substitute.

Frank Stapleton came on a substitute for United in six successive League games during March/April 1986.

Bobby Charlton made 767 appearances for United at senior level but only twice did he come on as a substitute - in League games against Chelsea (h) and Newcastle United (a) in season 1972-73.

During the latter stages of the first half of a friendly match between Eintracht Frankfurt and United in Los Angeles in May 1970, Francis Burns was replaced by substitute Steve James. Just after half-time Burns re-entered the action when he took over from Paul Edwards. Burns then departed again (replaced by full-back Willie Watson) but amazingly he came onto the pitch for a third time late on in place of Pat Crerand. All told Burns was on the field for just over 50 minutes.

Among the players who were named as a substitute by United for a competitive game but never saw any action on the pitch are: Brian Carey, Fraser Digby, David Johnson, Craig Lawton, Peter McBride, Nicky Murphy, Paul Sixsmith and Eric Young. Defender Carey went on to win full international honours for the Republic of Ireland as well as playing steadfastly for Wrexham and Leicester City. Goalkeeper Digby starred for England at Under-21 level and made over 500 appearances for Swindon Town and Johnson became a prolific goalscorer with Bury and then Ipswich Town and won an England 'B' call-up and was also capped by Jamaica.

Ole Gunnar Solskjaer has scored 21 goals in 104 substitute appearances for United (20.20%).

SUNDAY FOOTBALL

The first Sunday game at competitive level played by United was on 27 November 1983, away to West Ham United in a league Division One game. A crowd of 43,111 witnessed the 1-1 draw in which Ray Wilkins scored for the Reds.

Nowadays, Sunday matches are frequent throughout the season owing to live TV coverage on various channels.

SUNDERLAND

Heathens/United's League results v Sunderland:

Season	Div	Home	Away	Season	Div	Home	Away
1892-93	1	L 0-5	L 0-6	1956-57	1	W 4-0	W 3-1
1893-94	1	L 2-4	L 1-4	1957-58	1	D 2-2	W 2-1
1906-07	1	W 2-0	L 1-4	1964-65	1	W 1-0	L 0-1
1907-08	1	W 3-0	W 2-1	1965-66	1	D 1-1	W 3-2
1908-09	1	D 2-2	L 1-6	1966-67	1	W 5-0	D 0-0
1909-10	1	W 2-0	L 0-3	1967-68	1	L 1-2	D 1-1
1910-11	1	W 5-1	W 2-1	1968-69	1	W 4-1	D 1-1
1911-12	1	D 2-2	L 0-5	1969-70	1	W 3-1	D 1-1
1912-13	1	L 1-3	L 1-3				
1913-14	1	W 3-1	L 0-2	1974-75	2	W 3-2	D 0-0
1914-15	1	W 3-0	L 0-1				
				1976-77	1	D 3-3	L 1-2
1919-20	1	W 2-0	L 0-3				
1920-21	1	W 3-0	W 3-2	1980-81	1	D 1-1	L 0-2
1921-22	1	W 3-1	L 1-2	1981-82	1	D 0-0	W 5-1
				1982-83	1	D 0-0	D 0-0
1925-26	1	W 5-1	L 1-2	1983-84	1	W 2-1	W 1-0
1926-27	1	D 0-0	L 0-6	1984-85	1	D 2-2	L 2-3
1927-28	1	W 2-1	L 1-4				
1928-29	1	W 3-0	L 1-5	1990-91	1	W 3-0	L 1-2
1929-30	1	W 2-1	W 4-2				
1930-31	1	D 1-1	W 2-1	1996-97	PL	W 5-0	L 1-2
1936-37	1	W 2-1	D 1-1	1999-00	PL	W 4-0	D 2-2
				2000-01	PL	W 3-0	W 1-0
1938-39	1	L 0-1	L 2-5	2001-02	PL	W 4-1	W 3-1
1946-47	1	D 0-3	D 1-1				
1947-48	1	W 3-1	L 0-1				
1948-49	1	L 1-2	L 1-2				
1949-50	1	L 1-3	D 2-2				
1950-51	1	L 3-5	L 1-2				
1951-52	1	L 0-1	W 2-1				
1952-53	1	L 0-1	D 2-2				
1953-54	1	W 1-0	W 2-0				
1954-55	1	D 2-2	L 3-4				
1955-56	1	W 2-1	D 2-2				

Summary of League results

	P	W	D	L	F	A
Premier League	8	6	1	1	23	6
Division 1	94	36	22	36	154	162
Division 2	2	1	1	0	3	2
Home	52	29	12	11	112	61
Away	52	14	12	26	68	109
Total	104	43	24	37	180	170

FA Cup results v Sunderland:

	Round	Venue	Result
1925-26	5	Away	D 3-3
	Replay	Home	W 2-1
1963-64	6	Home	D 3-3
	Replay	Away	D 2-2 aet
	2nd R	Leeds Rd	W 5-1
1985-86	4	Away	D 0-0
	Replay	Home	W 3-0
1995-96	3	Home	D 2-2
	Replay	Away	W 2-1

League Cup results v Sunderland:

	Round	Venue	Result
1976-77	3	Home	D 2-2
	Replay	Away	D 2-2 aet
	2nd R	Home	W 1-0
2000-01	4	Away	L 1-2 aet

Test Matches
At the end of the 1896-97 season Newton Heath met Sunderland in two Test matches - to decide who would play in the First Division next season. After a 1-1 draw at Bank Street, Clayton, Sunderland won their home game at Newcastle Road 2-0 to retain their place in the top flight, leaving the Heathens in Division Two.

Fact File:
A record crowd of 16,000 at Bank Street saw the Newton Heath v. Sunderland Football League game on 4 March 1893.
After becoming the first club to be elected to the Football League after the founding twelve clubs in 1890, they were never relegated until 1958 by which time the club had won the League title six times, the last in 1935-36. Since then Sunderland have been relegated a further six times including once to the Third Division in 1987. During the 44 seasons since their first relegation (after 57 consecutive playing seasons in the 'top flight') Sunderland have spent only 17 in the 'top flight'.
Season 2000-01 was the club's 100th League season, only ten of the twelve founder members could exceed this, i.e. Aston Villa, Blackburn Rovers, Bolton Wanderers, Burnley, Derby County, Everton, (a record 98 seasons in the 'top flight' alone), Notts County, Preston North End, West Bromwich Albion, and Wolverhampton Wanderers each with 102 League seasons at that time.
In the first seven seasons after the Second World War, United lost at home to Sunderland six times, since then Sunderland have won at Old Trafford just once, in 1967-68 in a sequence of 23 matches.
United have been drawn four times against Sunderland in the FA Cup, United winning all four after at least one replay.
David Herd netted four goals past three different goalkeepers when United whipped Sunderland 5-0 at Old Trafford in November 1966.

Players with both clubs include: G Ainsley (United WW2), P Barnes, W Berry, R Bonthron, I Broadis (United WW2), E Burbanks (United WW2), W Chapman (Sunderland trialist), T Cooke, A Coton (United reserve & goalkeeping coach), C Crossley (United WW1), P Davenport, A Foggon, J Holton, W Hunter, G Livingstone, W Longair, A Mitchell, H Morgan, J Nicholl, M Pollitt (United and Sunderland reserve), N Tapken (Sunderland WW2), E Taylor, C Turner, W Watson (United WW2), O Williams (United reserve)..

SUNDERLAND ALBION

Heathen's Alliance results against Albion:

Season	Home	Away
1889-90	W 4-1	L 0-2
1890-91	L 1-5	L 1-2

Sunderland AFC (q.v) was formed in 1879 under the name 'Sunderland & District Teachers AFC', the leading light Jimmy Allan. By 1885 when professionalism was legalised, Sunderland AFC began to import many Scottish players. Soon the entire team comprised Scots. Jimmy Allan was not best pleased by the state of affairs, setting up a rival club, grandly named 'Sunderland Albion' having taken most of Sunderland's English players with him!
Albion eventually gained a place in the Football Alliance in its inaugural season of 1889-90, meeting Newton Heath and finishing third in the table
The next season (1890-91) Sunderland AFC were elected to the Football League and as a result Albion's attendances suffered, the club eventually folding in 1892.
Shortly afterwards most of the Alliance clubs were elected to the Football League, but it was too late for poor Albion.

Players with both clubs: H Boyd, R McFarlane

SUPPORTERS' CLUBS

Manchester United have supporters' clubs spreading right across the globe, in 24 different countries from New Zealand to Iceland, Malta to Malaysia, USA to Ireland, South Africa to Switzerland, Australia to the Far East (China, Hong Kong, Thailand)…and more are being formed right now!
Apart from those registered in the U.K, the Scandinavian branch (formed in 1981), has a membership in excess of 28,000 - and rising! The Maltese branch is well-established too.
The United's supporters' club magazine sells around 350,000 copies in Thailand every month - purchased obviously by United supporters or followers!

307

The first indication of a Manchester United supporters' club dates back to the 1920s, an unofficial organisation. However, in 1930 the club refused to meet with the Supporters' Club arguing that they were an unofficial body not recognised by the club and unrepresentative of the bulk of supporters.

At a public meeting comprising about 3,000 supporters of the club at the Hulme Town Hall in mid-October 1930, it was decided to boycott a League match between United and Arsenal at Old Trafford as a vote of 'no confidence' in the Board of Management. A crowd of 23,406 attended the game when around 50,000 was expected.

Former player Charlie Roberts was the Supporters Club's chief spokesman, being nominated for a place on the United board of directors. United lost all of their first 12 League games at the start of that season (1930-31) yet the board showed no inclination to turn matters round.

The unofficial body, which claimed to represent the bulk of the supporters, small though that number was, wanted a new manager, a recognised scouting system, money spent on quality signings, a new share issue to raise much-needed funds as well as wanting five shareholders to be co-opted on to the board. They had no success, although manager Herbert Bamlett was sacked at the end of the season, it would take the arrival of new chairman James W Gibson (q.v) to put the club back where it belonged.

In 1998, after BskyB's approach to United to buy the club for £623 million, chief spokesman Alan Walsh of IMUSA (the Independent Manchester United Supporters' Association - an unofficial organization) conducted a well-organised campaign against the takeover, supported by SUAM (Shareholders United Against Murdock). Some astute political lobbying led to the Department of Trade & Industry referring the matter to the Monoplies and Mergers Committee and the Office of Fair Trading

The proposed take-over did not take place, the collapse of the bid hailed as a victory for 'people power.'

Because football clubs had subscribed only £60 of the £300 required for a Duncan Edwards memorial window to be placed in St Francis' Church, Dudley, Manchester United supporter Sidney Terry donated the remainder. He had missed the ill-fated Munich air trip due to a cold.

NB - The Supporters Club membership office telephone number is: 0161 868 8450

SUSPENSIONS (& Fines)

Kevin Lewis, a United reserve team player, was give a five-match suspension in December 1971 for attacking a referee. He never played for United again but later appeared in Stoke City's first team and then went over to South Africa and won a League Championship medal with Cape Town Spurs.

In January 1995, Eric Cantona was suspended, initially for 14 days and later extended to eight months world-wide, until 30 September, for attacking a supporter at Selhurst Park as he walked along the touchline following his sending-off against Crystal Palace in a Premiership game. He jumped over the advertising hoarding and left fly with a two-footed attack on the fan and then waded in with his fists for good measure before being dragged away by his colleagues. The errant French star was immediately banned and given a fortnight to answer the FA's charges as the police received a complaint from the attacked supporter (Matthew Simmons) who, in turn, was banned from Selhurst Park for the rest of the season. As a result United also suspended Cantona for the remainder of that season's first team games (increased by the FA to the end of September 1995) and fined him two weeks' wages (amounting to around £20,000). He was later fined a further £10,000 by the FA. Cantona was stripped of the captaincy of his country.

With Cantona absent United - on course for the double at one stage - failed to win anything in 1994-95 and the media clearly blamed the Frenchman for this! However, the following season Cantona skippered United to their second double!

United, as a club, was fined £7,000 by the FA in 1969 for irregularities in the administration department at Old Trafford.

Three Newton Heath players - John Clements, Bob Donaldson and George Perrins - were all suspended for 14 days following misconduct during a League game against Derby County in October 1893.

Enoch 'Knocker' West was suspended 'for life' in April 1916...for his part in 'fixing' the result of the Manchester United-Liverpool League game in April 1915 (won 2-0 by United). However, the ban was lifted in December 1945 when West was aged 59.

'Sandy' Turnbull and Arthur Whalley along with four Liverpool players were also involved in the betting 'scam' (a 7-1 bet on a 2-0 win for United). They received life suspensions, but after the War (1919) the suspensions were lifted on the two United players, but too late for Turnbull who had sadly been killed in action.

George 'Cocky' Hunter was suspended sine-die by United's directors in 1914-15...for failing to comply with training regulations set down by the club. He later played for Portsmouth (1919-22).

SUTCLIFFE, John William

Born: Shibden, near Halifax, 14 April 1868. Died: Bradford, 7 July 1947

Career: Bradford (rugby club), Heckmondwike (rugby club), Bolton Wanderers (late summer, 1889), Millwall Athletic (£400, Easter 1902), MANCHESTER UNITED (May 1903), Plymouth Argyle (January 1905), Southend United (coach, summer 1912), Heckmondwike AFC (early 1913), Arnhem FC, Holland (coach, 1914-15), Bradford City (trainer, 1919-21), Goalkeeper John Sutcliffe made 364 League and FA Cup appearances for Bolton and another 57 for Millwall before joining United. He later starred in 208 senior matches for Plymouth.

Initially a talented Rugby Union three-quarter (he was capped by England in that position v. New Zealand in 1889) John Sutcliffe turned to soccer after his club, Heckmondwike was suspended for illegal professionalism!

He became a centre-forward at Bolton but was quickly placed in goal - and thereafter he blossomed in that position, going on to serve the club for almost thirteen years, being first-choice custodian (virtually unchallenged) from October 1890 until 1902. He was in the Wanderers' beaten FA Cup Final side of 1894 and in 1898 was said to be earning £5-a-week (healthy wages in those days). In March 1893 he won the first of his five England caps, and was always on the winning side for his country. He also played three times for the Football League. He was the first Bolton player to be sent-off at Burnden Park - dismissed for dissent during a League game against Sheffield Wednesday in January 1902. Joining United at the age of 35, he spent a season and a half with the club, being replaced by the emerging Harry Moger. He continued to keep goal until he was almost 44, playing his last League game for Plymouth in April 1912

Reported to be one of the fastest footballers in the game during the 1890s - Sutcliffe proved that during annual sports days when he entered the 120 and 440 yard races, winning both comfortably! He was also a fine club cricketer and once had the best batting average in a season for Great Lever CC.

Club record: 28 apps.

SWANSEA CITY (Town)

United's League results v the Swans:

Season	Div	Home	Away
1931-32	2	W 2-1	L 1-3
1932-33	2	D 1-1	L 1-2
1933-34	2	D 1-1	L 1-2
1934-35	2	W 3-1	L 0-1
1935-36	2	W 3-0	L 1-2
1937-38	2	W 5-1	D 2-2
1981-82	1	W 1-0	L 0-2
1982-83	1	W 2-1	D 0-0

Summary of League results

	P	W	D	L	F	A
Division 1	4	2	1	1	3	3
Division 2	12	4	3	5	21	17
Home	8	6	2	0	18	6
Away	8	0	2	6	6	14
Total	16	6	4	6	24	20

Players with both clubs include: P Abbott (United reserve), A Allman, T Bamford, A Bellis (United WW2), P Bodak (United reserve), D Brazil, R Briggs, S Cubberley (United reserve), A Davies, J Gallon (United WW2), H Green, R John, T Lang, P McGibbon, MM Morgan (United reserve), K Morgans, B Morton, W Moyle (United reserve), M Pinner, J Prentice, J Rimmer (also Swans' coach), H Thomas, J Warner, C Webster.
Also associated: H Gregg (United player & coach, Swans manager & coach), F Barson (United player, Swans trainer), R Smith (United reserve, Swans coach & assistant-manager)

309

SWEENEY, Eric E

Born: Rock Ferry, Birkenhead, 3 October 1905

Career: Flint Town, MANCHESTER UNITED (amateur April, professional, May 1925), Charlton Athletic (June 1930), Crewe Alexandra (season 1931-32), Carlisle United (1932-33).

Inside-forward Eric Sweeney was a Welsh FA Cup finalist for Flint Town v. Wrexham in April 1925 and after an impressive display he was signed by United! He had one good season at Old Trafford (1926-27) when he scored four times in 17 first-class matches. During his eight years in League football, Sweeney played in less than 100 games.

Club record: 32 apps. 7 goals

SWINDON TOWN

United's League results v the Robins:

Season	Div	Home	Away
1993-94	PL	W 4-2	D 2-2

Summary of League results

	P	W	D	L	F	A
Premier League	2	1	1	0	6	4
Home	1	1	0	0	4	2
Away	1	0	1	0	2	2
Total	2	1	1	0	6	4

FA Cup results v the Robins:

	Round	Venue	Result
1913-14	1	Away	L 0-1
1929-30	3	Home	L 0-2

League Cup results v the Robins:

	Round	Venue	Result
1996-97	3	Home	W 2-1

Fact File

United, the Football League champions, met Swindon Town, the Southern League champions, in the FA Charity Shield, at Stamford Bridge on 25 September 1911. United won 8-4, Harold Halse scoring six of their goals, a club record, later equalled by George Best, who scored six times at Northampton Town in the FA Cup in 1970.

Players with both clubs include: T Anderson, A Beardsworth, C Casper, J Coupar, P Coyne, C Crossley (United WW1), J Davis (United reserve), M Dempsey, F Digby (United reserve), A Downie, H Erentz, T Gibson, GW Hicks (United reserve), D Jones, A McLoughlin (United reserve), L Macari (also Town manager), B Morton, A Noone (United Youth), J Norton, R Parkinson, J Travers, N Webb, HG Williams (United reserve).
Also associated: L Page (United player, Town manager), R Smith (United reserve, Town manager), H Gregg (United player & coach, Town assistant-manager), B Kidd (United player & assistant-manager with United and Town)

TAYLOR, Thomas

Born: Smithies, Barnsley, 29 January 1932. Died: Munich, 6 February 1958

Career: Barnsley Schools, Smithies United (January 1948), Barnsley (amateur February 1948, professional, July 1949), (Army football whilst at Oakwell), MANCHESTER UNITED (£29,999, March 1953 until his death in 1958).

'Anyone who allowed Tommy Taylor free access into the penalty area was foolish' said United defender Bill Foulkes. Big, strong and brave, he was a great centre-forward who simply loved scoring goals, his incredible heading prowess never bettered in English football. When he was playing, the wingers in the side didn't bother looking if Taylor was in the box....they knew he would be there and duly swung over the ball, in the air or on the ground. A wonderful athlete, capable of prodigious leaps, coupled with perfect timing, he was a nightmare for defenders to face

The grandson of a Barnsley player, Taylor was discharged from the Army after suffering a knee injury. He didn't play football for almost a year but after regaining full fitness he joined Barnsley and went on to score 26 goals in 44 League games for the Tykes (netting a hat-trick in his second outing) before moving to Old Trafford where he became a sterling performer. Succeeding Jack Rowley in attack, Taylor scored twice on his debut against Preston in March 1953 and finished the season with seven goals to his name in only 11 starts.

Taylor, however, was not just a 'penalty box' centre-forward, his immense stamina enabling him to make unselfish runs, while his passing skills made him the perfect leader of the line.

Capped by England within two months of arriving at Old Trafford, he went on to appear in 19 full internationals, scoring 16 goals, including two hat-tricks v. Denmark and the Republic of Ireland in 1956-57. Taking over the centre-forward berth from Bolton's Nat Lofthouse, he also played for his country's 'B' team and twice represented the Football League. A League Championship winner with the Reds in 1956 and 1957, he scored in the FA Cup Final defeat by Aston Villa in the latter year before that cruel and devastating air crash took the life of one of United's greatest-ever marksmen, his goal ratio has rarely been bettered.

Matt Busby, not wanting the young Taylor to have a £30,000 price tag on his head, gave the spare £1 to the club's tea-lady!

Club record: 191 apps.

TAIBI, Massimo

Born: Palermo, Italy, 18 February 1970.

Career: Licata, Trento, AC Milan, Como, Piacenza, AC Milan, Venezia, MANCHESTER UNITED (£4.5 million, September 1999), Reggiana (£1 million, July 2000), Atalanta (season 2001-02)

Goalkeeper Massimo Taibi - reserve to Mark Bosnich with Raimond van der Gouw - made only four first team appearances for United in season 1999-2000 before returning to his native Italy.

Prior to his big-money move to Old Trafford, the 6ft 3in, 12st 13lb custodian had almost 300 appearances in Italian Serie 'A' and 'B' football. He didn't have the greatest of stays in England - although he was voted 'Man of the Match' on his debut in the Premiership when United beat 3-2 Liverpool at Anfield in September 1999.

Club record: 4 apps.

TAKEOVERS

In January 1984, Robert Maxwell failed in a bid to takeover Manchester United Football Club. Five years later (in August 1989) Michael Knighton, a local businessman, made a similar approach, offering to buy out Martin Edwards' majority shareholding for a seat on the board at Old Trafford. . And in 1999 BSkyB offered £623 million to buy out United! This was scuppered by the Department of Trade & Industry.

TAPKEN, Norman H

Born: Wallsend, Northumberland, 21 February 1914. Died: June 1996

Career: Wallsend Thermal Welfare FC, Newcastle United (summer 1933), MANCHESTER UNITED (December 1938), guested for Aldershot, Brighton & Hove Albion, Chester, Darlington, Newcastle United & Sunderland during WW2; Darlington (April 1947), Shelbourne (season 1948-49), Stoke City (assistant-trainer, 1952-60)..

Competent, unspectacular goalkeeper Norman Tapken made over 100 senior appearances prior to joining United halfway through the last full season before WW2, signed to replace the injured Jack Breedon. Later in life he helped Shelbourne finish runners-up in the League of Ireland Championship as well as gaining prizes for winning the League of Ireland Shield and the Leinster Cup and finish runners-up in the Irish Cup with the same club. In 1948-49 he also played twice for the League of Ireland representative side.

Club record: 16 apps.

TAYLOR, Christopher

Born: Small Heath, Birmingham, summer 1904

Career: Canadian football (15 months: 1920-21), Evesham Town (1922), Redditch FC (1923), MANCHESTER UNITED (£300, February 1924), Hyde United (September 1931). Retired with knee injury, 1932.

Inside-forward or centre-half Chris Taylor scored 20 goals for United's second XI in 1924-25 during that season, making his first team debut at Coventry City.. Out with cartilage trouble from October 1926, he struggled to regain full fitness and although he came back briefly, another knee injury ended his Old Trafford (and eventually his playing) career. He later returned to Birmingham and worked at the Perry Barr greyhound track.

Club record: 30 apps. 7 goals

TAYLOR, Ernest

Born: Sunderland, 2 September 1925. Died: Birkenhead, 9 April 1985

Career: Hylton Colliery Juniors, Newcastle United (£10, summer 1942), Plymouth Argyle (WW2 guest), Blackpool (£25,000, autumn, 1951), MANCHESTER UNITED (£8,000, February 1958), Sunderland (£7,500, December 1958), Altrincham (summer 1961), Derry City, Ireland (for four months, in mid 1961-62 season), Carshalton Athletic (1963), coach to New Brighton FC, Christchurch, New Zealand (1964-67), later Heswall FC (consultant).

Pint-sized inside-forward Ernie Taylor - known as 'Tom Thumb' and a former naval submariner - was only 5ft 4ins tall and weighed barely 10 stones. Wearing a size 4 boot, he was certainly a titch among giants, but what a fine player he turned out to be, possessing great passing skills, often causing havoc amongst opposing defenders! He scored 28 goals in 143 senior games for Newcastle, gaining an FA Cup winners medal in 1951, before joining Blackpool for whom he netted 55 goals in 242 outings. He starred alongside Stanley Matthews at Bloomfield Road and helped the Seasiders win the FA Cup in 1953. Signed by United as a stop-gap directly after the Munich air crash, he did a fine job in the forward-line and played in the 1958 FA Cup Final defeat by Bolton before leaving Old Trafford and returning to his homeland to sign for Sunderland. He added 71 more League and Cup appearances (3 goals) to his tally at Roker Park. Taylor won one full England cap, playing in that humiliating 6-3 home defeat by Hungary in 1953. He also appeared in one 'B' international for his country. After coaching in New Zealand he returned to England and later worked for the Ford Motor Company at Hooton in Cheshire. His brother, Eddie Taylor, played for Willington in the 1950 FA Amateur Cup Final.

Club record: 30 apps. 4 goals

TAYLOR, Thomas

Refer to front of section.

311

TAYLOR, Walter

Born: circa 1900.

Career: New Mills FC, MANCHESTER UNITED (£25, December 1921-April 1922, released on a free transfer). With both Richard Gibson and Billy Harrison out injured, reserve right-winger Walter Taylor was handed his only League appearance for the Reds in a 3-0 defeat by Sheffield United at Bramall Lane in January 1922.

Club record: one app.

TELEVISION

The first time Manchester United appeared 'live' on TV. was in 1948, then the BBC televised that season's FA Cup Final victory over Blackpool. However, precious few TV sets were in use at that time, transmission being limited to the London area.

ITV was the first company to cover a United home game on 25 April 1957 when they filmed the United v. Real Madrid European Cup semi-final 2nd leg from Old Trafford.

The first time pictures were shown of a United game from Old Trafford on BBC TV. (via their Sports Special programme) came four months later - from the League fixture with Leicester City in August 1957.

In 1971, United were the first club to call on television pictures to get a player - namely George Best - cleared of a sending-off mishap at Chelsea earlier that month. The club presented a tele-recording of the incident to the disciplinary committee.

Another 'first' for United was the introduction of closed-circuit screening at Old Trafford of the club's crucial First Division League encounter with Arsenal which was played at Highbury on a cold Friday night in early March 1967. A crowd of over 28,000 attended Old Trafford while 63,363 assembled at the Gunners' North London home to witness the 1-1 draw. United also utilised the closed-circuit network of cameras to beam pictures back to Old Trafford of their European matches against AC Milan in Italy in 1969 and St Etienne at Home Park, Plymouth in 1977.

TEST MATCHES

In the early days of the Football League there was no automatic promotion and relegation. A club's fate was decided by a series of Test Matches, played at the end of a season.

The bottom two clubs in Division One were paired with the winners and runner-ups in Division Two.

United, in their first season in the League (as Newton Heath), finished bottom of Division One and had to play Small Heath (champions of Division 2) to decide who played where the following season. The Heathens remained in the top flight by drawing 1-1 with Blues at Stoke and then beating them 5-2 in the second game at Bramall Lane, Alf Farman grabbing a smart hat-trick.

Unfortunately the following season it was not so good for the Heathens. They again finished bottom of the First Division, and were forced to play Liverpool in a Test Match at Ewood Park. They lost 2-0 and were relegated!

Newton Heath's next taste of Test Match football came in April 1895. They ended the season in third place in Division Two and had to play and beat Stoke (at Burslem) to gain promotion. They failed to beat the Potters, losing 3-0.

After taking second spot in Division Two in 1896-97 the Heathens were involved in their fourth Test Match showdown. This time they had to fulfil four matches, opposing both Burnley and Sunderland, at home and away.

They lost 2-0 at Turf Moor but won their home game by the same score. The Heathens then drew 1-1 at home with Sunderland yet lost the return fixture 2-0 on Wearside and as a result stayed in Division Two.

Summary of Newton Heath's Test Match action:

Venue	P	W	D	L	F	A
Home	2	1	1	0	3	1
Away	2	0	0	2	0	4
Neutral	4	1	1	2	6	8
Totals	8	2	2	4	9	13

THINGS THEY HAVE SAID

A few interesting funny one-liners, wise cracks, gaffes, blunders from those with a United connection:

•I met Mick Jagger when I was playing for Oxford United. Little did I know that one day he'd be almost as famous as me...Ron Atkinson (1984).

•It's bloody tough being a legend...Ron Atkinson (1983)

•No, I always thought I was good...Ron Atkinson, when asked if he thought he was a better manager for his unhappy experiences as boss of Atletico Madrid (1983).

•I've mastered the trick of pleasing the eight lads I have to leave out every Saturday...Alex Ferguson, (1998)

•We cheat, we tell lies, we con people - that's the only way to survive. It's the law of the land...ex-manager Tommy Docherty (1979) two years after leaving United.

•I hate losing - it stinks...Peter Schmeichel after the 1993 FA Cup Final defeat by Everton

•Money in the bank is no use to a football team. You have to put your money on the field where the public can see it...Matt Busby (1965).

•United will no longer be a football club; it will be a giant Old Trafford fruit machine...Tommy Docherty, 1998 on the proposed takeover of the club by BSkyB

•I have never been kissed so much in my life - especially by men...Wilf McGuinness (1971) when manager of Aris Salonika who finally won an away match!

•Peter Schmeichel got more passes from midfield than the players did...Alex Ferguson (1995) after a poor United away performance at Norwich

•We can only go up. If we get any lower, we'll fall off the pools coupon…Tommy Docherty (1973) during United's struggle against relegation

•He was as near perfection as man and player as it is possible to be…Matt Busby on Bobby Charlton, (1966).

•He's the greatest player of his age I have ever seen. Yet although he's soared up among the stars, his feet are still on the ground…Matt Busby on Duncan Edwards (1957).

•He needed five stitches - three in the first half, two at the interval after his brain started to seep through…Alex Ferguson after Steve Bruce had suffered a gashed head (1993).

•A little elf, so brilliant that there was nothing to teach him…Matt Busby talking about George Best (1982).

•Could start a row in an empty house…Alex Ferguson on Dennis Wise (1993).

•He's a big-time Charlie…Alex Ferguson on Paul Ince (1998)

•He's a cry baby when the going gets tough…Arsenal boss George Graham talking about Eric Cantona (1994)

•He's so mild-mannered when the volcano inside him isn't erupting…Alex Ferguson on Cantona (1994).

•Unless everyone gets six points for a win and United none, I don't think they will be caught…Ron Atkinson, Villa manager, during the title race of 1993

•It looks as though we are going to be happy just to stay on the same Ceefax page as Manchester United…Ron Atkinson (1994).

•It's hard when you have that useless player Bryan Robson and that not bad centre-half Pallister as subs…Sheffield United boss Dave Bassett on United's riches!

•When did I know the game was won? When I saw their team-sheet…Alex Ferguson after United's 5-3 FA Cup win over Chelsea (1998)

•They've obviously never been to a Glasgow wedding…Alex Ferguson after being warned as to what United can expect when they play Galatasaray in Instanbul (1993)

•You're welcome to my home phone number but don't ring me during the Sweeney…Ron Atkinson, (1981).

•Suddenly I was depicted as a champagne-swigging, cigar-smoking, Jack-the-Lad who could hardly move his body because it was weighted down by gold trinkets…Ron Atkinson, talking to the media in Birmingham's jewellery quarter (1984)

•The great thing about football management is you know when you sign a contract that the only thing missing is the date of your sacking…Tommy Docherty, 1981

•I've been punished for falling in love…Tommy Docherty on being sacked by United after his affair with Mary Brown, wife of the club's physio, Laurie Brown (1977).

•Preston - they're one of my clubs. Well I have had more clubs than Jack Nicklaus…Tommy Docherty, 1979

•When one door opens, another smashes you in the face…Tommy Docherty, 1981

•I've been forced to swap my Merc for a BMW, I'm down to my last 37 suits and I'm drinking non-vintage champagne…Ron Atkinson after his sacking by United (1986).

•I see Atletico (Madrid) just sacked another manager - before the season has even started. He must have had a bad photo-call…Ron Atkinson (1995).

•There can be few managers who have lost their job after seven consecutive victories…Dave Sexton after his sacking by United (1980)

•The ideal Board of Directors should be made up of three men, two dead and one dying…Tommy Docherty (1977).

•When I joined East Stirling I asked the Chairman if I could see the player file? I discovered he only had eight players! I said: 'Mr Chairman, you know you need eleven players to start a bloody game of football'…Alex Ferguson, from his book: A Year in the Life: The Manager's Diary (Virgin 1995)

•Kenny Dalglish has associates, but only a few friends. There's nothing wrong with that because, at the end of the day, you only need six people to carry your coffin…Alex Ferguson (1990s).

•I'll never be able to achieve what Tommy Docherty did - take Aston Villa into the Third Division and Manchester United into the Second…Ron Atkinson (1994).

•We learned a lot from United today - including how to count…Shrewsbury Town boss Kevin Ratcliffe, after United's 8-1 pre-season win at Gay Meadow in 2000.

•I'm pleased with the way my partnership with Teddy is going on the pitch, but it's fair to say we don't have Sunday lunch together. We are still not talking…Andy Cole on his feud with Teddy Sheringham (2000).

•Everyone knows that for us to get a penalty we need a certificate from the Pope and a personal letter from the Queen …Sir Alex Ferguson answering claims by Leeds United defender Lucas Radebe that referees favour the Old Trafford club (2000).

•If we win at Old Trafford next weekend then we will have two legs out…former United player Gordon Strachan talking about his next away game as boss of Coventry City (2001).

THIS IS YOUR LIFE

Three Manchester United players - George Best, Nobby Stiles and Bryan Robson, along with managers Sir Matt Busby & Sir Alex Ferguson - have all featured on the BBC TV programme 'This Is Your Life.'

Busby was approached by host Eamonn Andrews before the derby clash between United and Manchester City at Maine Road in May 1971.

313

THOMAS, Henry

Born: Swansea, 28 February 1901

Career: Swansea Town (season 1919-20), Porth FC (1920-22), MANCHESTER UNITED (April 1922), Merthyr Town (October 1930), Abercarn FC (1932-33).

Fleet-footed outside-left 'Harry' Thomas did very little at Swansea but became a huge hit with the Welsh non-League side Porth where he partnered international inside-forward Evan Jones. He helped Porth win their domestic League title (1922) before transferring to Old Trafford, where he took time to settle before establishing himself in the first team in 1925-26. Clever and diminutive, Thomas was not the most consistent of players but he was a fine crosser of the ball and was capped once by his country, against England in 1927. Facing stiff competition for the left wing berth, his United career is relatively modest for an eight year stay.

Club record: 135 apps. 13 goals

THOMAS, Michael Reginald

Born: Mochdre, near Colwyn Bay, North Wales, 7 July 1954

Career: Clwyd & Conwy Schools, North Wales Schools, Wrexham (amateur, 1969, professional 1972), MANCHESTER UNITED (£300,000, November 1978), Everton (August 1981 - in a £450,000 deal that also involved John Gidman), Brighton & Hove Albion (£350,000, late 1981), Stoke City (£200,000, summer 1982), Chelsea (£75,000, early 1984), West Bromwich Albion (£100,000, late summer 1985), Derby County (on loan, end of 1985-86 season), Wichita Wings, US Indoor Soccer League (£35,000, 1986-87), Shrewsbury Town (£5,000, season 1988-89), Leeds United (£10,000, summer 1989), Stoke City (on loan, end of 1989-90 season before signing permanently for the Potters on a free transfer), Wrexham (seasons 1991-93), Conwy United (briefly in 1993), Inter Cardiff (1995) & Portmadoc (Manager). Prior to joining Inter Cardiff, Thomas received an 18-month prison sentence in for handling counterfeit money. He later took to after dinner speaking and also acted as a part-time coach and is now a keen and enthusiastic presenter on Century Radio, MUTV and Sky TV

One of Wrexham's best-ever home-grown footballers, inside-forward/midfielder Mickey Thomas was a tireless competitor, sometimes controversial who encountered his fair share of problems on and off the field! He was, nevertheless, an exciting player, full of flair and commitment who thrilled supporters wherever he went. He helped Wrexham win the Welsh Cup on three occasions, gain promotion to the Second Division in 1978 and collected the first eleven of his 51 caps for Wales, also claiming two at Under-21 and two at Under-23 levels, before moving to Old Trafford, signed by Dave Sexton. An FA Cup Finalist with United in 1979, he succeeded Gordon Hill (in effect) on United's left-flank and there is no doubt he did well for the club, the fans loving his 100 per-cent commitment. He spent barely three months at Goodison Park before starting on his nomadic ways. He enjoyed some success at Stoke and Chelsea, helping the latter club win the Second Division title in 1984. He was 35 years of age when he joined Leeds and he kicked his last ball in earnest (in League football) with Wrexham in January 1993, six months short of his 40th birthday, having amassed in excess of senior 780 appearances at club and international level, scoring almost 100 goals.

Club record: 110 apps. 15 goals.

THOMPSON, John Ernest

Born: Newbiggin, Northumberland, summer 1909

Career: Benfieldside Council School, Stakeford United, Ashington (trialist), Bradford Park Avenue (trialist), Carlisle United (1928), Bristol City (1929), Bath City (1930), Blackburn Rovers (1931), MANCHESTER UNITED (£4,500, November 1936), Gateshead (March 1938), York City (1939-40).

Inside/centre-forward Ernie Thompson had helped Carlisle win the North-Eastern League in 1928-29 and scored 84 goals in 179 League and FA Cup games for Blackburn before joining United. The son of a former boxing champion, Thompson, who had suffered a fractured leg in 1933, scored on his debut for United at home to Liverpool only days after joining the club. He failed to make any real impact at Old Trafford and, after retiring during WW2, he became a successful businessman in the North-east.

Club record: 3 apps. one goal

THOMPSON, William

Born: Scotland, circa 1870.

Career: Dumbarton, Aston Villa (1892), NEWTON HEATH (March 1893-May 1894).

Inside-right Willie Thompson failed to make the first team at Aston Villa and was restricted to just three senior games with the Heathens, making his League debut as partner to another ex-Dumbarton player James McNaught at Burnley three weeks after joining the club in 1893.

Club record: 3 apps. (also one 'other' app)

THOMSON, Arthur

Born: West Stanley, summer 1903

Career: West Stanley FC (1925), Derby County (trialist), Morecambe FC (1927), Huddersfield Town (trialist, late 1927), MANCHESTER UNITED (May 1928), Southend United (August 1931), Coventry City (1932-33), Tranmere Rovers (1933-34).

Arthur Thomson, initially an outside-right, joined United as a reserve forward and made his debut on the left-wing in a home 4th round FA Cup-tie v. Bury in January 1929. deputising for Teddy Partridge.

Thomson's father Alex, played centre-forward for Middlesbrough and West Ham United.

Club record: 5 apps. One goal

THOMSON, Ernest

Born: Lancashire, circa 1882

Career: Darwen, MANCHESTER UNITED (May 1906), Nelson (May 1909), Cardiff City (season 1911-12), Nelson (1912-14).

Ernie Thomson was one of a handful of reserve half-backs at the club during the early 1900s and his first team outings were severely limited owing to the form of Duckworth, Roberts & Bell, among others!

Club record: 4 apps..

THOMSON, James

Born: Dumbarton, circa 1890

Career: Clydebank, Renton FC, MANCHESTER UNITED (May 1913-May 1914), Dumbarton Harp (during WW1), St Mirren (1918-28).

Left-winger Jim Thomson was reserve to George Wall during his one season at Old Trafford. He helped St Mirren win the Scottish Victory Cup in 1919 and seven years later collected a Scottish Cup winners medal when Saints beat Celtic 2-0 in front of 125,000 fans at Hampden Park. He made more than 350 League and Cup appearances in post-war Scottish football (over 80 goals scored)…and in the circumstances must go down as a player missed by United!

Club record: 6 apps. one goal

THORNLEY, Benjamin Lindsay

Born: Bury, Lancashire, 21 April 1975

Career: MANCHESTER UNITED (junior 1989, trainee July 1991, professional January 1993), Stockport County (on loan, November-December 1995), Huddersfield Town (on loan, February-March 1996, signed permanently for £175,000, March 1998), Aberdeen (July 2001).

An England Schoolboy international, left-winger Ben Thornley - a Tom Cruise look-alike - added three Under-21 caps to his tally before leaving Old Trafford. Overall, he scored eight goals in 126 senior appearances for Huddersfield Town (possibly another player missed by the Reds!). His brother is a masseur at Old Trafford as well as playing for Altrincham.

Club record: 14 apps.

TOKYO

United played their World Club Championship game against Palmeiras in Tokyo on 30 November 1999. A crowd of 53,372 saw Roy Keane net the only goal of a competitive encounter to earn his side a 1-0 win.

315

TOMLINSON, Graeme Murdoch

Born: Watford, 10 December 1975

Career: Bradford City (trainee, 1991, professional December 1993), MANCHESTER UNITED (£100,000, July 1994), Wimbledon (on loan June-August 1996), Luton Town (on loan, March-April 1996), AFC Bournemouth (on loan, August-September 1997), Millwall (on loan, March 1998), Macclesfield Town (free transfer, July 1998), Exeter City (free transfer, summer 2000).

Reserve striker Graeme Tomlinson's two outings for United were both as a substitute in the League Cup competition in 1994-95 (his debut coming against Port Vale). Over a period of 10 years (1992-2002) he managed only 150 senior appearances at senior level (57 with Macclesfield).

Club record: 2 apps.

TOMS, William Edward

Born: Manchester, 19 May 1896

Career: Altrincham, Eccles Borough (1914), Southport Vulcan (WW1 when serving as a Lieutenant in the Army)), MANCHESTER UNITED (amateur September, then professional, October 1919), Plymouth Argyle (£500, September 1920), Oldham Athletic (£250, summer 1921), Coventry City (£150, June 1922), Wrexham (autumn 1923), Crewe Alexandra (1924), Great Harwood (1925-26), Winsford United (1926-29), CWS Margarine Works FC, Manchester (re-instated as an amateur, 1929-30).

Stocky centre-forward Billy Toms never really got a chance to show his talents at Old Trafford but after leaving the club he netted over 50 goals in more than 150 senior games before drifting into non-League football in 1925. He was the first player signed by former United player Charlie Roberts when he became manager of Oldham Athletic.

Club record: 14 apps. 4 goals

TOPPING, Henry

Born: Manchester, October 1908

Career: Manchester Junior football, MANCHESTER UNITED (December 1932), Barnsley (May 1935), Macclesfield Town (season 1936-37)..

Full-back Harry Topping was reserve to Jack Silcock during his stay at Old Trafford and his first team sorties were limited to just 12 in two-and-a-half years.

* There were two other players by the name of H Topping in League football during the late 1930s, one with Manchester City (reserves), Exeter City and New Brighton and the other with Stockport County. Some reference books have got all three mixed up regarding personal statistics!

Club record: 12 apps. one goal

TORONTO CUP

In May 1970 United beat both Celtic and the Italian club AS Bari to lift the Toronto Cup in Canada.

TOTTENHAM HOTSPUR

Summary of League results

	P	W	D	L	F	A
Premier League	20	14	3	3	39	21
Division 1	102	45	28	29	165	144
Division 2	8	2	3	3	6	13
Home	65	43	12	10	126	62
Away	65	18	22	25	84	116
Total	130	61	34	35	210	178

FA Cup results v Spurs:

	Round	Venue	Result
1898-99	1	Away	D 1-1
	Replay	Home	L 3-5
1922-23	2	Away	L 0-4
1925-26	4	Away	D 2-2
	Replay	Home	W 2-0
1961-62	SF	Hillsborough	L 1-3
1967-68	3	Home	D 2-2
	Replay	Away	L 0-1 aet
1978-79	6	Away	D 1-1
	Replay	Home	W 2-0
1979-80	3	Away	D 1-1
	Replay	Home	L 0-1
1996-97	3	Home	W 2-0

League Cup results v Spurs:

	Round	Venue	Result
1979-80	2 (1)	Away	L 1-2
	2 (2)	Home	W 3-1
1980-81	2 (1)	Away	L 0-1
	2 (2)	Home	L 0-1
1989-90	3	Home	L 0-3
1998-99	5	Away	L 1-3

European Cup-winners' Cup record v. Spurs:

	Round	Venue	Result
1963-64	2 (1)	Away	L 0-2
	2 (2)	Home	W 4-1

United's League results v Spurs:

Season	Div	Home	Away	Season	Div	Home	Away
1909-10	1	W 5-0	D 2-2	1965-66	1	W 5-1	L 1-5
1910-11	1	W 3-2	D 2-2	1966-67	1	W 1-0	L 1-2
1911-12	1	L 1-2	D 1-1	1967-68	1	W 3-1	W 2-1
1912-13	1	W 2-0	D 1-1	1968-69	1	W 3-1	D 2-2
1913-14	1	W 3-1	L 1-2	1969-70	1	W 3-1	L 1-2
1914-15	1	D 1-1	L 0-2	1970-71	1	W 2-1	D 2-2
				1971-72	1	W 3-1	L 0-2
1920-21	1	L 0-1	L 1-4	1972-73	1	L 1-4	D 1-1
1921-22	1	W 2-1	D 2-2	1973-74	1	L 0-1	L 1-2
1925-26	1	D 0-0	W 1-0	1975-76	1	W 3-2	D 1-1
1926-27	1	W 2-1	D 1-1	1976-77	1	L 2-3	W 3-1
1927-28	1	W 3-0	L 1-4				
				1978-79	1	W 2-0	D 1-1
1931-32	2	D 1-1	L 1-4	1979-80	1	W 4-1	W 2-1
1932-33	2	W 2-1	L 1-6	1980-81	1	D 0-0	D 0-0
				1981-82	1	W 2-0	L 1-3
1935-36	2	D 0-0	D 0-0	1982-83	1	W 1-0	L 0-2
				1983-84	1	W 4-2	D 1-1
1937-38	2	L 0-1	W 1-0	1984-85	1	W 1-0	W 2-1
				1985-86	1	D 0-0	D 0-0
1950-51	1	W 2-1	L 0-1	1986-87	1	D 3-3	L 0-4
1951-52	1	W 2-0	L 0-2	1987-88	1	W 1-0	D 1-1
1952-53	1	W 3-2	W 2-1	1988-89	1	W 1-0	D 2-2
1953-54	1	W 2-0	D 1-1	1989-90	1	L 0-1	L 1-2
1954-55	1	W 2-1	W 2-0	1990-91	1	D 1-1	W 2-1
1955-56	1	D 2-2	W 2-1	1991-92	1	W 3-1	W 2-1
1956-57	1	D 0-0	D 2-2	1992-93	PL	W 4-1	D 1-1
1957-58	1	L 3-4	L 0-1	1993-94	PL	W 2-1	W 1-0
1958-59	1	D 2-2	W 3-1	1994-95	PL	D 0-0	W 1-0
1959-60	1	L 1-5	L 1-2	1995-96	PL	W 1-0	L 1-4
1960-61	1	W 2-0	L 1-4	1996-97	PL	W 2-0	W 2-1
1961-62	1	W 1-0	D 2-2	1997-98	PL	W 2-0	W 2-0
1962-63	1	L 0-2	L 2-6	1998-99	PL	W 2-1	D 2-2
1963-64	1	W 4-1	W 3-2	1999-00	PL	W 3-1	L 1-3
1964-65	1	W 4-1	L 0-1	2000-01	PL	W 2-0	L 1-3
				2001-02	PL	W 4-0	W 5-3

FA Charity Shield

United (the League champions) were held to a 3-3 draw at Old Trafford by Spurs (the FA Cup winners) in the 1967 FA Charity Shield game. Goalkeeper Pat Jennings was among the Spurs scorers! The attendance was 54,106.

Fact File

United and Spurs met each other three times (twice in the League, once in the FA Cup) over a period of eight days in late-January/early February 1968.

United came back from 2-0 down to beat Spurs 4-3 on aggregate in the 2nd round of the 1963-64 European Cup-winners' Cup competition. A crowd of 50,000 attended Old Trafford to see Bobby Charlton and David Herd both score twice to see off plucky Spurs who sadly had Dave Mackay carried off with a broken leg.

United beat Spurs 2-1 at home on 16 May 1999 to win their fifth Premiership title in seven seasons.

United were trailing 3-0 at half-time to Spurs in a Premiership game at White Hart Lane in September 2001, but a brilliant second-half performance saw the Reds storm back to register a terrific 5-3 victory.

In 1952 United and Spurs were on tour together in Canada & North America and played two exhibition matches in Toronto and New York. Spurs won 5-0 and 7-1 respectively - despite United being the reigning League champions!

United entered the Swaziland International Challenge Cup in June 1983. They met Spurs twice, winning 2-1 and losing 2-0 in front of crowds of 8,000 and 5,000 respectively.

Players with both clubs include: J Attwell (United trialist), W Berry, A Brazil, I Broadis (United WW2), J Brown, G Crooks, J Davie (United WW2), H Erentz, Q Fortune (Spurs junior), T Gibson, T Gipps, E Goldthorpe (Spurs WW1), A Hall (United WW1), J Hall, C Hannaford (Spurs WW1), F Hopkin (Spurs WW1), DG Jones (Spurs reserve), C Knowles (United amateur, also Spurs player & scout), C McGrath, J McNaught, T Manley (Spurs WW1), F Milnes, W Nicholson (United WW2, also Spurs manager), T Nuttall (Spurs WW1), J Rowley (Spurs WW2), T Sheringham, J Travers (Spurs WW1), R White (United WW2)..

Also associated: G Graham (United player, Spurs manager), S Houston (United player, Spurs assistant-manager/coach), C Knowles (United amateur, Gulls' manager).

* When guesting for Spurs in February 1944 United's Jack Rowley scored seven goals in an 8-1 win over Luton Town.

TOWNSEND THORESEN CUP

In August 1983, United beat Brighton & Hove Albion on penalties to win the Townsend Thoresen Cup.

TRAINERS (also masseurs & physiotherapists)

Here is an unofficial list of trainers/masseurs/physiotherapists who have served United down the years: F Bacon, Laurie Brown, Tommy Cavanagh, Jack Crompton, Tom Curry, Ted Dalton, Jim Headrige. Jim McGregor, A Nealmer, Jack Pullar, Rob Swire, George Timmins, Jack Timmons.

Jack Nuttall, whose son Tom played for United, was assistant-trainer at Old Trafford prior to WW1.

Bill Inglis was assistant-trainer at Old Trafford either side of WW2 (right up to 1961).

The brother of former United player Ben Thornley, was a physio/masseur at Old Trafford in 2001-02.

See also COACHES as certain appointments also involved 'training'.

TRANMERE ROVERS

United's League Cup result v Rovers:

	Round	Venue	Result
1976-77	2	Home	W 5-0

Players with both clubs include: W Bainbridge, H Cartman, G Clayton, S Coppell, G Crowther (United reserve), F Dawson (United reserve), W Dennis (Rovers WW1), J Flanagan (United reserve), K Gill (United reserve), C Griffiths, R Harrop, H Heywood, S Hopkinson, B Jones (United WW2), T Jones (also Rovers trainer & coach), P McCarthy, W McDonald, C Mitten (Rovers WW2), P Newton, L O'Brien, T O'Neil, J Prentice, W Rainford (United reserve), J Robinson, J Sloan (United reserve & WW2), A Thomson, W Toms, W Woodward (United reserve). Also associated: W Ridding (United player, Rovers trainer, coach & manager).

TRANSFERS

Players 'bought' for club record fees

Fee	Player	Signed from	Date
£600	Charlie Roberts	Grimsby Town	April 1904
£1,000	Les Hofton	Glossop NE	July 1910
£1,750	John Wood	Dumbarton	May 1922
£5,000	Frank Barson	Aston Villa	August 1922
£5,000	Neil Dewar	Third Lanark	February 1933
£6,500	Jack Smith	Newcastle United	February 1938
£18,000	John Downie	Bradford Park Avenue	March 1949
£29,999	Tommy Taylor	Barnsley	March 1953
£45,000	Albert Quixall	Sheffield Wednesday	September 1958
£115,000	Denis Law	Torino	August 1962
£125,000	Martin Buchan	Aberdeen	March 1972
£180,000	Ian Storey-Moore	Nottingham Forest	March 1972
£200,000	Ted MacDougall	Bournemouth	September 1972
£200,000	Lou Macari	Celtic	January 1973
£200,000	Stuart Pearson	Hull City	March 1974
£350,000	Joe Jordan	Leeds United	January 1978
£495,000	Gordon McQueen	Leeds United	February 1978
£825,000	Ray Wilkins	Chelsea	August 1979
£1.25 million	Gary Birtles	Nottingham Forest	October 1980
£1.5 million	Bryan Robson	West Bromwich Albion	October 1981
£1.5 million	Mark Hughes	Barcelona	July 1988
£2.3 million	Gary Pallister	Middlesbrough	August 1989
£4.2 million**	Paul Ince	West Ham United	September 1989
£7 million*	Andy Cole	Newcastle United	January 1995
£10.75 million	Jaap Stam	PSV. Eindhoven	May 1998
£12.6 million	Dwight Yorke	Aston Villa	August 1998
£19 million	Ruud van Nistelrooy	PSV. Eindhoven	April 2001
£28.1 million	Juan Sebastian Veron	SS Lazio	July 2001
£30 million+	Rio Ferdinand	Leeds United	July 2002

** Fee agreed to be paid in two installments.
* Deal involved Keith Gillespie (sold to Newcastle for £1 million)
+ A record fee involving two British clubs.

Other 'big money' signings (£1 million +)

Fee	Player	Signed from	Date
£7.8 million	Fabien Barthez	AS Monaco	June 2000
£7.5 million	Diego Forlan	Estudiantes de las Plata	Jan 2002
£5 million	Henning Berg	Blackburn Rovers	Aug 1997
£4.5 million	Massimo Taibi	Venezia	Sept 1999
£4.4 million	Jesper Blomqvist	Parma	July 1998
£4 million	Mikael Silvestre	Inter Milan	Sept 1999
£3.5 million	Karel Poborsky	Slavia Prague	Aug 1996
£3.5 million	Teddy Sheringham	Tottenham Hotspur	July 1997
£2.5 million	Roy Carroll	Wigan Athletic	July 2001
£2.5 million	Ricardo Lopez	Real Valladolid	Aug 2002
£2 million	Dion Dublin	Coventry City	Sept 1994
£1.7 million	Paul Parker	Queen's Park Rangers	Aug 1991
£1.5 million	Neil Webb	Nottingham Forest	July 1989
£1.5 million	Ole Gunnar Solskjaer	FC Molde	July 1996
£1.5 million	Quinton Fortune	Atletico Madrid	Aug 1999
£1.4 million	David May	Blackburn Rovers	July 1994
£1.4 million	Jordi Cruyff	Barcelona	Aug 1996
£1.3 million	Danny Wallace	Southampton	Sept 1989
£1.2 million	Eric Cantona	Leeds United	Nov 1992
£1.2 million	Ronny Johnsen	Besiktas	July 1996
£1 million	Jonathan Greening	York City	March 1998
£1 million	Bojan Djordjic	Brooma Pojkarna	Feb 1999

Back To Club

List of players/officials who had two spells with the club, some in different roles as the previous one:

Arthur Albiston	player/juniors coach
Jack Ball	player/player
Cyril Barlow	player/player
Peter Barnes	player/player
Robert Beale	player/player
Billy Behan	player/scout
Mark Bosnich	player/player
Len Bradbury	player/player
Bill Brooks	player/player
Herbert Broomfield	player/player
Johnny Carey	player/scout
Bobby Charlton	player/director
Gordon Clayton	player/asst to Chief Scout
Ted Connor	player/scout/office clerk
Tony Coton	player/gk coach
James Coupar	player/player
Jack Crompton	player/coach/trainer
Jack Fitchett	player/player
Dave Fitzsimmons	player/player
Stan Gallimore	player/player
Ian Greaves	player/scout
Harry Gregg	player/coach
John Grundy	player/player
Harold Hardman	player/player/director/chairman
Charlie Harrison	player/player
Vince Hayes	player/player
Arthur Henrys	player/player
Mark Hughes	player/player
Bill Inglis	player/assistant-trainer
Bill Johnston	player/player
Peter Jones	player amateur/professional
Brian Kidd	player/assistant-manager
Harry McShane	player/PA announcer
Brian McClair	player/coach
Tom Manley	player/player
Billy Meredith	player/coach
Jack Mitchell	player/player
Jack Peddie	player/player
Mike Phelan	player/coach
Steve Preston	player/player
Bryan Robson	player/coach
Herbert Rothwell	player/player
Jimmy Ryan	player/coach/asst-manager
Les Sealey	player/player
Dick Smith	player/player
Nobby Stiles	player/coach
Jimmy Turnbull	player/player
George Vose	player/player
Jack Whitney	player/player
Harry Wilkinson	player/player

Players 'sold' for record fees:

Fee	Player	Transferred to	Date
£3,300	Tom Meehan	Chelsea	Dec 1920
£5,000	George Mutch	Preston North End	Sept 1937
£10.000	Joe Walton	Preston North End	March 1948
£24,500	Johnny Morris	Derby County	March 1949
£37,500	Johnny Giles	Leeds United	Aug 1963
£40,000	John Connelly	Blackburn Rovers	Sept 1966
£50,000	Francis Burns	Southampton	June 1972
£60,000	Alan Gowling	Huddersfield Town	June 1972
£170,000	Ted MacDougall	West Ham United	March 1973
£275,000	Gordon Hill	Derby County	April 1978
£350,000	Brian Greenhoff	Leeds United	Aug 1979
£500,000	Andy Ritchie	Brighton & Hove Albion	Oct 1980
£800,000	Neil Webb	Nottingham Forest	Nov 1992
£1.5 million	Ray Wilkins	AC Milan	June 1984
£2.5 million	Mark Hughes	Barcelona	Aug 1986
£7 million	Paul Ince	Inter Milan	June 1995
£16.6 million	Jaap Stam	SS Lazio	Sept 2001

317

Other 'big money' sales (£1 million+)

Fee	Player	Transferred to	Date
£7.5 million	Andy Cole	Blackburn Rovers	December 2001
£5.5 million	Andrei Kanchelskis	Everton	August 1995
£4.5 million	Lee Sharpe	Leeds United	August 1996
£3 million	Karel Poborsky	Benfica	December 1998
£2.5 million	Gary Pallister	Middlesbrough	July 1998
£2.25 million	John Curtis	Blackburn Rovers	June 2000
£2 million	Danny Higginbotham	Derby County	July 2000
£2 million	Dwight Yorke	Blackburn Rovers	July 2002
£1.75 million	Henning Berg	Blackburn Rovers	December 2000
£1.5 million	Mark Hughes	Chelsea	June 1995
£1.5 million	David Healy	Preston North End	December 2000
£1.5 million	Jonathan Greening*	Middlesbrough	July 2001
£1 million	Keith Gillespie	Newcastle United	January 1995
£1 million	Massimo Taibi	Reggiana	July 2000
£1 million	Mark Wilson*	Middlesbrough	July 2001

* Two players involved in a joint deal worth £2.5 million

Loan Transfers

Several 'young, up and coming players' have been loaned out by United (to various clubs at all levels) to gain experience and they include David Beckham (to Preston North End) in February 1994.

However, we have to go back a long way to find the first loan deals involving United.

Ernie Street was loaned out to Sale Holmfield FC for six months, commencing in April 1903, possibly the first 'loan' deal arranged by the club.

Charlie Ramsden went to Stockport on loan for some four months: January to May 1928. Harry Rowley followed, pushed out to Oldham in 1933 and just after that Tommy Reid also went from Old Trafford to Boundary Park for a short spell on loan.

One the first players recruited by United when the 'loan transfer' was officially sanctioned by the Football League was Tommy Baldwin from Chelsea early in 1975. Later, England international Laurie Cunningham was signed from Real Madrid and Garth Crooks from Tottenham Hotspur (both in 1983) then Peter Barnes from Leeds in 1984. The latter trio all played for WBA during their respective careers.

Les Sealey arrived from Luton in 1990 (& played in the FA Cup Final) and in recent times United have signed Frenchman William Prunier from Bordeaux (1995-96).

Among those loaned to other clubs over a 25 year period during the 1970s, '80s & early '90s (apart from the many untried youngsters who were strategically placed elsewhere so that they could gain experience at competitive level) were David Gaskell to Wigan Athletic (1968), John Connaughton to Halifax (1969) & Torquay (1971-72), Willie Watson to Huddersfield (1970), Clive Griffiths to Plymouth & Tranmere (1970), Paul Edwards to Oldham Ath (1972), Tommy O'Neil to Blackpool (1973), Jimmy Rimmer to Swansea (1973-74), Paul Bielby to Hartlepools (1975), David Sadler to Miami Toros (1975), Jim Holton, also to Miami Toros & Sunderland (1976), Jimmy Kelly to Chicago Sting (1976), Colin Waldron to Sunderland (1977), Alex Forsyth to Glasgow Rangers (1978), Nikki Jovanovic to Buducnoet (1981-82), Jimmy Nicholl to Sunderland (1981-82), Stephen Pears to Middlesbrough (1983), Scott McGarvey to Wolves (1984), Jeff Wealands to Huddersfield (1984), Mark Dempsey to Sheffield United & Swindon (1985), Billy Garton to Birmingham (1986), Graeme Hogg to WBA (1987), Mark Higgins to Bury (1987), Derek Brazil to Oldham (1990), Mal Donaghy to Luton (1989-90), Colin Gibson to Port Vale (1990), Neil Whitworth to PNE (1992), Barnsley (1992), Rotherham (1993) and Blackpool (1993), Russell Beardsmore to Blackburn (1991), Jim Leighton to Arsenal & Reading (1991-92), Simon Davies to Exeter (1993), Danny Wallace to Millwall (1993) & Keith Gillespie to Wigan Athletic (also 1993).

Over the last decade loan deals have levelled themselves out and among those involving United have been Terry Cooke to Sunderland, Birmingham & Wrexham (between 1996-98), Jordi Cruyff to Celta Vigo (1999), Luke Chadwick two spells with Royal Antwerp (1999), Chris Casper to Bournemouth & Swindon (1996 & 1997), Ronnie Wallwork to Carlisle United, Stockport County & Royal Antwerp (1990s), Grant Brebner to Cambridge United (1998) and Hibernian (1999); Nick Culkin to Hull (1999), Bristol Rovers (2000-01) & Livingston (2001-02), Michael Clegg to Ipswich (2000), John O'Shea & Danny Higginbottom to Royal Antwerp (2001), Paul Rachubka to Charlton (2002) and Danny Webber to Watford (2002).

Transfer Spiral

Since the late 1930s, it has been United's policy to encourage their own youth development. However, as befits the best supported club in the land, they have never shied away from buying players to strengthen the squad, often breaking transfer records in the process. This section aims to demonstrate the inexorable rise of transfer prices by comparing the costs of three of Sir Matt Busby's great teams with the three of Sir Alex Ferguson's.

Busby's Triumphs:

•FA Cup Winners 1948: This side, the first of the great post-WW2 teams, contained two players bought pre-war: John Carey (£250 in 1936) & Jack Rowley (£3,.500 in 1937). Busby's only outlay was £4,000 for Jimmy Delaney in 1946..........Total outlay: £7,750

•The Pre-Munich 'Babes' League Champions 1956 & 1957: Busby's youth policy now provided him with the comfort of having two quality players for each position. The squad which had won two successive titles now sought a third, plus the European Cup. Still there from the 1952 Championship side were Ray Wood (£5,000 in 1949) & John Berry (£15,000 in 1951), the only additions necessary being Tommy Taylor (£29,999 in 1953) and Harry Gregg (£23,000 two months before 'Munich.'). The future looked extremely bright at this point in time..........Total outlay £73,000

•Champions 1965 and 1967, European Cup winners 1968: After Munich, Matt Busby realised that time was not on his side if United were to win the European Cup. He augmented his squad with Noel Cantwell (£29,500) and Tony Dunne (£5,000 both in 1960), David Herd (£35,000 in 1961), Denis Law (a record £115,000 in 1962), Pat Crerand (£56,000 in 1963), John Connelly (£60,000) and Pat Dunne (£10,500, both in 1964) and finally Alex Stepney (£55,000 in 1966). Survivors Charlton and Foulkes lifted the coveted European Cup..........Total outlay £366,000.

Ferguson's Triumphs:

•The first Premiership champions of 1992-93: When Alex Ferguson arrived late in 1986 he was lucky enough to inherit Bryan Robson (signed by Ron Atkinson for £1.5 million in 1981), around whom he gradually built his team. His first major signing was Brian McClair (£850,000 in 1987), followed by Steve Bruce (£825,000 in 1987), Mark Hughes (£1.5 million) and Lee Sharpe (£185,000, both in 1988), Gary Pallister (£2.3 million), Paul Ince (£4.2 million), Neil Webb (£1.5 million), Danny Wallace (£1.3 million) and Mike Phelan (£750,000, all in 1989), Denis Irwin (£625,000 in 1990), Peter Schmeichel (£500,000), Paul Parker (£1.7 million) and Andrei Kanchelskis (£650,000, all in 1991) and finally, the catalyst Eric Cantona (£1.2 million) along with Dion Dublin (£1 million, both in 1992). Supplemented by outstanding homegrown talents, this squad at last brought the League title back to Old Trafford after a gap of 26 years..........Total outlay £20.585,000

•The 'Treble' Winners of 1998-99: Sir Alex Ferguson's squad had been turned over remarkably since 1993, only Schmeichel and Irwin of the purchased players remaining. An exceptional crop of homegrown talent formed the 'spine' of the team, supplemented by several big money signings: Roy Keane (£3.75 million in 1993), David May (£1.4 million in 1994), Andy Cole (£7 million in 1995), Ronny Johnsen (£1.2 million), Ole Gunnar Solskjaer (£1.5 million), Jordi Cruyff (£1.4 million) and Raimond van der Gouw (£200,000, all in 1996), Teddy Sheringham (£3.5 million) and Henning Berg (£5 million, both in 1997), Dwight Yorke (£12.6 million), Jaap Stam (£10.25 million) and Jesper Blomqvist (£4.4 million, all in 1998)..........Total outlay £53,325,000

•The Team of 2001-02: Sir Alex Ferguson spent heavily in pre-season on two world class players whom he believed would bring the European Champions Cup back to Old Trafford. Still on the books from the 1999 'treble-winning' team were signings Irwin, Keane, May, Cole, Johnsen, Solskjaer, van der Gouw and Yorke. New arrivals since then had been Mikael Silvestre (£4 million) and Quinton Fortune (£1,5 million, both in 1999) and Fabien Barthez (£7.8 million in 2000). In April 2001 he recruited striker Ruud van Nistelrooy (£19 million) and during the close season the Argentinian midfielder Juan Sebastian Veron (£28.1 million) and Irish goalkeeper Roy Carroll (£2.5 million) were acquired, whilst the Uruguayan forward Diego Forlan (£7.5 million) and French defender Laurent Blanc (free) arrived during the season..........Total outlay £98,675,000.

Transfer Talk

* The fee of £4,000 paid by United for Southampton's Bill Rawlings in 1928 was agreed on the number of appearances he made for the club.

* The signing of Tommy Taylor from Barnsley in 1953 was set at £29,999 - because Matt Busby didn't want the player to have a £30,000 transfer tag on his head. The odd £1 was handed to the tea-lady!

* The signing of Reg Allen from QPR in June 1950 for £11,000 was a British record for a goalkeeper.

* When Sheffield Wednesday inside-forward Albert Quixall left Hillsborough for Old Trafford in 1958, the fee involved was a British record for any player at the time.

* Since 1958 Gordon McQueen's switch from Elland Road to Old Trafford in 1978, Bryan Robson's move from WBA in 1981, Gary Pallister's transfer from Middlesbrough in 1989, Roy Keane's move from Nottingham Forest in 1993, Andy Cole's diversion from Newcastle in 1995, Dwight Yorke's transfer from Villa Park in 1998, the signing of Dutchman Ruud van Nistelrooy in 2001, the capture of the Argentinian midfielder Juan Sebastian Veron, also in 2001 and the acquisition of England international defender Rio Ferdinand in 2002, were all record transfers at the time involving a British club. The transfers of Pallister, Stam and Ferdinand were records deals involving defenders.

* Future United centre-half Ian Ure's move from Dundee to Arsenal for £62,500 in 1963 was a record at the time between two British clubs.

* Alex Stepney's £55,000 move from Millwall to United in 1966 was a record for a 'keeper at that time.

* The £200,000 fee paid by United for centre-forward Ted MacDougall from Bournemouth in 1972 was a record for a Third Division player. United later paid an extra £22,000 to the Dean Court club following MacDougall's move to West Ham.

* Dion Dublin's £1 million transfer from Cambridge to United in 1992 was a record sale for the Abbey Stadium club. And when Dublin left Coventry for Villa Park for £5.75 million in 1998, the fee involved here was a record 'sale' for the Highfield Road side.

* Former United star Andrei Kanchelskis moved from Fiorentina to Glasgow Rangers for a record fee for the Ibrox Park club of £5.5 million in 1998.

* When United signed Lou Macari from Celtic for £200,000 in 1973, the fee created a record for a player leaving a Scottish club for an English League club.

* When United signed centre-forward Albert Pape from Clapton Orient in 1925, the deal took place in the Orient dressing room at Old Trafford just hours before a League game against United! The transfer was sealed and Pape went out and scored against his former colleagues in a 4-2 win.

* Denis Law's move from Italy to Old Trafford in 1962 was the first transfer from abroad of a British player for more than £100,000.

* When Neil Webb joined the Reds from Nottingham Forest in 1986, it was the first time a transfer fee of more than £1m had been set by a tribunal.

* When Joe Walton moved to Deepdale in 1948, the £10,000 fee paid by PNE was a record for a full-back at that time.

* Garry Birtles was bought for £1.25m and sold (back to Nottingham Forest) for £275,000...a deficit of £975,000.

* United 'lost' £200,000 on Terry Gibson....signed for £630,000 and sold for £430,000. In 2002 they lost over £10 million when DwightYorke moved to Ewood Park!

* Peter Beardsley left Old Trafford for Vancouver Whitecaps in a £250,000 deal in 1983; four years later he moved to Liverpool for almost £2m.
* In 1927, it was said that Hugh McLenahan's transfer to United from Stockport was clinched after Louis Rocca (United's scout) had agreed to hand over a freezer full of ice-cream to the Edgeley Park club to be used at the summer fete!
* Over a period of eight years - 1964-72 - United signed (from other clubs) just three players: Scotsmen Willie Morgan & Ian Ure and English-born 'keeper Alex Stepney.
* Matt Busby spent £100,000 on new players over two years: 1967-69; Wilf McGuinness's expenditure was £80,000 in 1969-70 while Frank O'Farrell spent half-a-million pounds on four new recruits.
* Tommy Docherty splashed out £1.2 million (1972-77); Dave Sexton spent £3.65 million (1977-81); Ron Atkinson doubled that by signing players to the value of £7.36 million (1981-86) and during his 16 years in charge (1986-2002) Alex Ferguson's outlay has been over £140 million, perhaps nearer £150 million (see Transfer Spiral).
* When Rio Ferdinand joined United in 2002 his transfer was the sixth most expesive in the history of football - behind Zinedine Zidane, £46.5 million (Juventus to Real Madrid); Luis Figo, £37 million (Barcelona to Real Madrid); Hernan Crespo, £35.7 million (Parma to Lazio); Gianluigi Buffon, £32 million (Parma to Juventus) & Christian Vieri £31 million (Lazio to Inter Milan).

TRANTER, Wilfred

Born: Pendlebury, Manchester, 5 March 1945
Career: St Gregory's (Pendlebury), Manchester Schools, Lancashire Schools, MANCHESTER UNITED (junior, summer 1961, professional April 1962), Brighton & Hove Albion (May 1966), Baltimore Bays (on loan, mid 1968), Fulham (early 1969), St Louis Stars (mid 1972).
Wilf Tranter's only appearance as a reserve centre-half for United was against West Ham United at Upton Park in March 1964 when he stood in for Billy Foulkes. United won 2-0. He was with Dennis Viollet during his time with Baltimore Stars in the NASL.
Club record: one app.

TRAVELLING MEN

There have been several nomadic footballers/managers/coaches who have travelled all over the country (& world) plying their trade. Here are a few 'wanderers' who have been associated with United:
•Winger Peter Barnes (q.v) played for 20 different clubs (various levels) during 21-year period. Among the League sides he represented (home & abroad) were: Manchester City (two spells), WBA, Leeds United, Real Betis, Melbourne JUST (Australia), Manchester United (two spells), Coventry, Bolton Wanderers (two spells), Port Vale, Hull, Drogheda United, Sporting Farense, Sunderland, Tampa Bay Rowdies, Northwich Victoria, Wrexham, Radcliffe Borough & Cliftonville, (Ireland).
•JE 'George' Travers (q.v) was a great soccer journeyman…appearing for 17 different clubs, 12 with Football League status, between 1904-31.
•Tommy Wilson (q.v) also assisted 17 clubs including spells with several bi clubs like Aston Villa, Blackburn, Bolton & Manchester United. He was later manager and then chairman of Rochdale.
•Billy Wrigglesworth served with 16 different clubs (various levels & WW2) between 1928-54.
•Tommy Docherty (q.v), as a player, coach and manager, was associated with no fewer than 16 different football clubs (worldwide) over a period of 40 years (1948-88)
•Player John Downie (q.v) played for 12 different clubs during his career (1940-62).
•Walter Whittaker (q.v) played for 14 clubs (senior & non-League) during his career (1893-1914).

TRAVERS, James Edward (George)

Born: Newtown, Birmingham, 2 November 1888. Died: Smethwick, 31 August 1946.
Career: Bilston United (1904-05), Rowley United (1905-06), Wolverhampton Wanderers (July 1906), Birmingham (August 1907), Aston Villa (December 1908), Queen's Park Rangers (May 1909), Leicester Fosse (August 1910), Barnsley (January 1911), Manchester United (February 1914), Swindon Town (July 1919), Millwall Athletic (June 1920), Norwich City (October 1920), Gillingham (June 1921), Nuneaton Town (September 1921), Cradley St Luke's (November 1922), Bilston United (August 1929 to May 1931, when he retired, aged 42). Travers, a wonderfully admired soccer nomad, guested for Tottenham Hotspur in WW1 when on leave from the Army (based in Salonika). A well-built, hard-shooting inside or centre-forward with good ability, Travers was something of a soccer nomad and never really settled down in one place, or indeed, with any one club, except Barnsley where he spent three years. He made over 80 appearances for the Tykes and gained an FA Cup winners medal v. WBA in 1912. For the Villa, he scored a hat-trick against Bury on Boxing Day 1908 when deputising for his personal idol, Harry Hampton. He helped Manchester United avoid relegation to the Second Division, appeared in Millwall's first League game v. Bristol Rovers in August 1920 and scored for Norwich when they recorded their first-ever League win a few months later. His career in the Football League, Southern League and in the FA Cup spanned 250 matches and he netted 75 goals.
Club record: 21 apps. 4 goals

TREBLE WINNING CAMPAIGN

In 1998-99, Manchester United became the first club to win the treble - lifting the three most prestigious trophies available to English clubs: the Premiership title, the FA Cup & the European Champions' Cup. It took them 59 matches to do it. They netted 123 goals and suffered only three defeats, all in the Premiership. The team ended the season with a run of 33 matches without defeat - one short of the club record set in 1993-94. United defeated every other Premiership team at least once, Arsenal & Chelsea in the FA Cup. And, in fact, the only team United played and did not beat at some time during the campaign was Barcelona (two 3-3 draws).

United's FA Cup Final triumph was their tenth, extending their record over Tottenham Hotspur who had achieved eight victories at that time.

Alex Ferguson was an FA Cup-winning manager for a record fourth time, while Ryan Giggs, Roy Keane & Peter Schmeichel joined the elite band of footballers who collected a third FA Cup winners' medal with the same club. It was also Keane's fifth FA Cup Final appearance (one with Nottingham Forest & four with United).

During 1998-99 United fielded 20 FULL internationals from nine different countries in all competitions (including the Worthington Cup). In the European Champions League home game with Juventus, United started off with a team comprising 11 full internationals and they had another six on the subs' bench!

United's League results in 1998-99:

Opposition	H	A
Arsenal	1-1	0-3
Aston Villa	2-1	1-1
Blackburn Rovers	3-2	0-0
Charlton Athletic	4-1	1-0
Chelsea	1-1	0-0
Coventry City	2-0	1-0
Derby County	1-0	1-1
Everton	3-1	4-1
Leeds United	3-2	1-1
Leicester City	2-2	6-2
Liverpool	2-0	2-2
Middlesbrough	2-3	1-0
Newcastle United	0-0	2-1
Nottingham Forest	3-0	8-1
Sheffield Wednesday	3-0	1-3
Southampton	2-1	3-0
Tottenham Hotspur	2-1	2-2
West Ham United	4-1	0-0
Wimbledon	5-1	1-1

Summary of the 38 League games:

Venue	P	W	D	L	F	A	Pts
Home	19	14	4	1	45	18	46
Away	19	8	9	2	35	19	33
Totals	38	22	13	3	80	37	79

FA Cup

Rd 3	Middlesbrough	(h)	3-1
Rd 4	Liverpool	(h)	2-1
Rd 5	Fulham	(h)	1-0
Rd 6	Chelsea	(h)	0-0
Rep	Chelsea	(a)	2-0
SF	Arsenal	(Villa Park)	0-0aet
Rep	Arsenal	(Villa Park)	2-1aet
Final	Newcastle United	(Wembley)	2-0

European Champions League (Cup)

Q2/1	LKS Lodz	(h)	2-0
Q2/2	LKS Lodz	(a)	0-0
Group	Barcelona	(h)	3-3
Group	Bayern Munich	(a)	2-2
Group	Brondby IF	(a)	6-2
Group	Brondby IF	(h)	5-0
Group	Barcelona	(a)	3-3
Group	Bayern Munich	(h)	1-1
QF1/1	Inter Milan	(h)	2-0
QF/2	Inter Milan	(a)	1-1
SF/1	Juventus	(h)	1-1
SF/2	Juventus	(a)	3-2
Final	Bayern Munich	(n)	2-1

Goalscorer
United used 23 players in winning the three trophies; the leading scorers were:

Player	PL	FAC	EC	Total
Dwight Yorke	18	3	8	29
Andy Cole	17	2	5	24
Ole Gunnar Solskjaer	12	1	2	15*
Paul Scholes	6	1	4	11
Ryan Giggs	3	2	5	10

* Solskjaer also scored three goals in the Worthington (League) Cup

•Only three others club (all before United) completed the treble (winning the European Cup and both major domestic League and FA Cup competitions): Celtic (1966-67), Ajax (1971-72) and PSV Eindhoven (1987-88). Ajax, in fact, added both the European Super Cup and World Club Championship to their list of successes in 1972.

•In 1993-94, the Reds became the first team to win the League (Premiership), FA Cup & FA Charity Shield in the same season...and they also lost to Aston Villa in the League Cup Final.

TURNBULL, Alexander

Born: Hurlford, near Kilmarnock, 1884. Died: Arras, France, 3 May 1917
Career: Hurlford Thistle, Manchester City (June 1902), MANCHESTER UNITED (December 1906), Clapton Orient & Rochdale (WW1 guest when free of army duties with the Footballers' Battalion).
'Sandy' Turnbull's career was cut short when he was tragically killed whilst on active service during WW1. He was 33. A quick-witted, brave and enormously talented inside-forward, Turnbull scored 60 goals in 119 games for Manchester City, helping them win the Second Division Championship in 1903 and the FA Cup twelve months later, before he was banned(with a number of other players) by the FA over an illegal payments scandal in 1906. When free from suspension Turnbull along with Billy Meredith, Herbert Burgess and Jimmy Bannister were all signed by United. He quickly bedded himself into the United side and in season 1907-08 was top-scorer with 27 League and Cup goals when the League Championship was won. He blotted his copybook by becoming the first United player to be sent-off in a Manchester derby - dismissed against his former club on 21 December 1907 after scoring twice in a 3-1 win.
In April 1909 Turnbull then netted the only goal of the game as United beat Bristol City to win the FA Cup Final and two years after that he added a second First Division Championship medal to his collection when he and Enoch West netted 37 League goals between them.

Granted a joint benefit with colleague George Stacey v. Manchester City in April 1914, Turnbull - who was nicknamed 'Turnbull The Terrible' being a big favourite with the supporters - was then sensationally banned for life in 1915 after betting irregularities. Following his death in action, the ban was 'posthumously' lifted by the football authorities.

In 1932, two of Turnbull's sons, Alex junior and Ronald, both signed as amateurs for United but neither made the grade.

* Turnbull was all set to sign for Bolton Wanderers in 1902 but before he could put pen to paper Manchester City came in with a better offer and he joined them instead of the Burnden Park club

Club record: 247 apps. 101 goals.

TURNBULL, James McLachlan

Born: East Plain, Bannockburn, Stirlingshire, 23 May 1884.

Career: East Stirlingshire FC (1900), Dundee (1901-03), Falkirk (1903-04), Glasgow Rangers (Easter 1904), Preston North End (early 1905), Leyton FC (summer 1906), MANCHESTER UNITED (May 1907), Bradford Park Avenue (September 1910), Chelsea (summer 1912), MANCHESTER UNITED (trialist, September 1914), Hurst FC (season 1914-15).

No relation to Sandy, centre-forward Jimmy Turnbull did extremely well in Scottish football before moving to Preston in 1905. He scored a fivetimer for Falkirk against Aberdeen in the Dewar Shield semi-final of 1904 and then made over 30 senior appearances for Rangers. He struggled to get into the first team at Deepdale but bounced back with 13 goals in 36 Southern League games for Leyton before joining United. A strong, forceful player, Turnbull helped United win the League title in 1908 & the FA Cup in 1909 before transferring to Bradford, replaced in the United side by Enoch West. He attempted a comeback with United in 1914 and later in life became a businessman, based in Chorlton, Manchester.

Club record: 78 apps. 45 goals.

TURNER (No.1)

Career: NEWTON HEATH (season 1890-91).

Turner, an unknown reserve centre-forward, made one senior appearance for United, against Bootle in an FA Cup-tie in October 1890, both teams having other fixtures that day, fielding their reserve sides.

Club record: one app.

TURNER (No.2)

One of nine players tried at centre-forward during the 1902-03 season, Turner's only first-team appeartance was against Oswaldtwistle Rovers in the qualifying round of the FA Cup.

Career: MANCHESTER UNITED (season 1902-03)

Club record: one app.

TURNER, Christopher Robert

Born: Sheffield, 15 September 1958

Career: Sheffield Wednesday (apprentice, summer 1975, professional 1976), Lincoln City (on loan, 1978), Sunderland (£80,000, summer 1979), MANCHESTER UNITED (£275,000, August 1985), Sheffield Wednesday (£175,000, September 1988), Leeds United (on loan, late 1989), Leyton Orient (autumn, 1991, retired as a player 1994, joint-manager at Brisbane Road, 1994-95), Hartlepool United (manager, March 1999).

During his playing career, goalkeeper Chris Turner, who was capped five times by England at Youth team level, amassed a total of 588 League and Cup appearances for his six clubs, including 205 during his two spells at Hillsborough and 223 for Sunderland for whom he played in the 1985 League Cup Final defeat by Norwich City. A very safe and competent 'keeper, he joined United as cover for Gary Bailey and after gaining a first team place (from February 1986) he held the number one position until Gary Walsh took over in 1987 and then was first choice again prior to the arrival of Jim Leighton a year later. In 1990-91 he was a League Cup Final winner at Wembley with Sheffield Wednesday against United and he also helped the Owls clinch promotion to the First Division that same season. In his first season with Orient he saw the London club win promotion from Division Three.

Club record: 81 apps.

TURNER, John

Born: circa 1876

Career: Gravesend United, NEWTON HEATH (September 1898-May 1899).

Reserve Jack Turner was one of eight different players who appeared in the centre-half position for the Heathens in season 1898-99. He failed to make an impact.

Club record: 3 apps. (also 2 'other' apps, one goal)

TURNER, Robert

Born: circa 1878

Career: NEWTON HEATH (May 1898), Brighton United (August 1899), Fulham (Christmas 1900), Glentoran (season 1901-02).

Young reserve defender Bob Turner deputised in the left-back and right-half positions of the Heathens during his only season with the club.

Club record: 2 apps. (also 3 'other' apps)

TWISS, Michael John

Born: Salford, 18 December 1977

Career: MANCHESTER UNITED (trainee, June 1993, professional July 1996), Sheffield United (on loan, August-September 1998), Port Vale (free transfer, July 2000), Leigh RMI (season 2001-02)

A full-back or left-sided midfielder, Michael Twiss made just two senior appearances before helping Port Vale win the LDV Van Trophy at Cardiff's Millennium Stadium in 2001.

Club record: 2 apps.

TYLER, Sidney

Born: Wolverhampton, 7 December 1904. Died: Walsall, 25 January 1971

Career: Stourbridge, MANCHESTER UNITED (May 1922), Wolverhampton Wanderers (May 1924), Gillingham (seasons 1927-29), Norwich City (trialist), Millwall (Easter 1929), Colwyn Bay United (seasons 1931-33), Chamberlain & Hookham (Birmingham Works League as an amateur: 1933-34).

Described as a 'polished full-back' Sid Tyler made 123 League appearances during his career - but only one for United (against Leicester City) in November 1923.

Club record: one app.

U for...

URE, John Francombe

UNITED HALT

As befits a club founded by railwaymen, Manchester United has its very own railway station (open on matchdays only), providing supporters with a fast journey from the centre of the city, straight to Old Trafford itself, passengers decanting on to the stadium concourse behind the main stand. This is not to be confused with the Metropolitan station at Old Trafford cricket ground.

UNITED ON THE NET

If you go to a computer and type the words 'Manchester United' into the search engine, around 750 (perhaps a few more) websites will appear on the screen!
They cover everything...from banners & flags to shareholders to opinions to talk-ins to archive information to features to interviews to supporters club news to the club shop etc. etc.
Manchester United's official club website - www.manutd.com was said to have been the most-visited website in China a couple of years ago! In fact, at the height of the dot-com frenzy, it is said that the plc's value reached the £1billion mark.

Born: Ayr, Scotland, 7 December 1939
Career: Ayr Academy, Scottish National Association of Boys Clubs XI, Ayr Albion FC, Dalry Thistle, Dundee (1958), Arsenal (£62,500, summer 1963), MANCHESTER UNITED (£80,000, August 1969), St Mirren (August 1972), Cummock FC (coach 1973-74), East Stirlingshire (manager, late 1974 to 1975). Later coached in Iceland 1976-77.
Before joining Arsenal, strong, resilient Scottish defender Ian Ure had amassed a fine appearance record with Dundee whom he helped win the First Division Championship and then reach the semi-finals of the European Cup in 1962-63. He was also capped by his country at Under-23 and senior levels as well as representing the Scottish League on four occasions. As an Arsenal player (signed initially for a record transfer fee between to British clubs by manager Billy Wright) he made 202 first-class appearances and during his six years at Highbury was sent-off four times, one dismissal earning him a six-week suspension after spitting at Denis Law...the player he teamed up with in 1969! With the Gunners he collected a Football League Cup runners-up medal (v. Swindon Town) in 1968 but a year later was a winner in the same competition (v. Leeds in 1969). He also added three more full caps to his tally (ending up with 11). Signed as cover for and eventually successor to Bill Foulkes by Wilf McGuinness, Ure had one good season at Old Trafford (his first) before struggling with his form.
After leaving football he was employed as a social worker in Kilmarnock and then at Glasgow's Low Moss Prison (1993 onwards)
Club record: 68 apps. one goal

V for...

VAN NISTELROOIJ,
Rutgerus Johannes

Born: Oss, Holland, 1 July 1976
Career: FC Den Bosch, FC Heerenveen (semi-professional, June 1995, professional August 1996), PSV Eindhoven (summer, 1998), MANCHESTER UNITED (£19 million, April 2001).

It took another 12 months, plus £1 million more than expected, but United boss Sir Alex Ferguson finally got his man - signing the Dutch international striker in readiness for the start of the 2001-02 season, making him the most expensive footballer in British soccer history, if only for a week or two!

Ruud van Nistelrooy (giving him his English spelling) should have signed for United in July 2000 but he failed a medical on a damaged knee. Then, while recovering from that set-back, he suffered cruciate ligament injury which delayed his transfer even longer. Thankfully, in the end, all was signed, sealed and delivered and the raven-haired striker set about his business of scoring goals for United - and what a great first season he had! He set a new club record of scoring in nine consecutive League and Cup games including a new Premier League record of finding the net in eight consecutive matches. He finished the

season as the club's top marksman with 36 goals (23 in the Premiership alone plus a record 10 in the European Champions League). Van Nistelrooy seems to possess all the attributes necessary to make a world-class striker and should prove a shrewd investment in years to come.

To celebrate his first season at Old Trafford he was voted PFA 'Footballer of the Year.' He has 20 Dutch caps to his credit with 8 goals scored.

Club record: 49 apps 36 goals

VALENCIA (CF)

Over 54,600 fans saw United beat Valencia 3-0 at Old Trafford in the 2nd stage of the 1999-2000 European Champions League before going to Spain and earning a 0-0 draw in front of more than 48,000 spectators. A season later, a Wes Brown own-goal three minutes from time gave Valencia a 1-1 draw in front of 66,715 fans at Old Trafford while the away 'leg' again finished level at 0-0.

Two UEFA Cup games were played in 1982-83. United were held 0-0 at home but lost 2-1 in Valencia.

VALENTINE, Robert

Born: Lancashire, circa 1880.

Career: Swinton Rugby League club (1900), MANCHESTER UNITED (May 1903), Swinton Rugby League Club (June 1907).

Bob Valentine captained the Swinton RL Club from the full-back position before changing codes and becoming a goalkeeper with United whom he served for four years, basically acting as reserve to first John Sutcliffe and then Harry Moger, eight of his senior outings coming during the 1905-06 season. He reverted to playing rugby after leaving United but suffered a serious knee injury in the winter of 1907.

Club record: 10 apps.

VAN DER GOUW, Raimond

Born: Oldenzaal, Holland, 24 March 1963

Career: Go Ahead (Deventer), Vitesse Arnhem, MANCHESTER UNITED (July 1996), West Ham United (June 2002).

Signed as cover for Peter Schmeichel, 6ft 3in goalkeeper Raimond Van der Gouw made only 60 first-class appearances in six seasons with the club. However, every time he stood between the posts, he regularly produced the goods, his saves often earning United a point and sometimes a crucial victory. He gained both FA Cup and European Cup winners medals in 1999 and followed up a year later by claiming his first Premiership winners' medal, adding a second to his collection in 2001 before reverting back to third choice 'keeper behind French international Fabien Barthez and new signing Roy Carroll, a Northern Ireland international.

When Van der Gouw appeared in the League Cup-tie at Arsenal on 5 November 2001, he became the oldest post WW2 United player at the age of 38 years, 227 days (taking over the mantle from Jack Warner). He then became the second oldest United player in the club's history to appear in a competitive match (behind the great Billy Meredith) when, at the age of 39 years and 48 days, he came on as a second-half substitute in the final Premiership game of the season v. Charlton Athletic at Old Trafford, on 11 May 2002. After being released by United, he turned down a move to Coventry City in favour of remaining in the Premiership with West Ham.

Prior to his transfer to Old Trafford back in 1996, Van der Gouw had appeared in 258 League games for Vitesse and over 100 first-class games for Go-Ahead.

Club record: 60 apps.

VAN NISTELROOIJ, Rutgerus Johannes ('Ruud')

Refer to front of section.

VANCE, James

Born: Stevenston, Ayrshire, 1876

Career: Annbank, NEWTON HEATH (January 1896), Fairfield FC (December 1896), Annbank (1897).

Inside or centre-forward Jimmy Vance was signed as reserve cover by the Heathens at a time when Joe Cassidy was out injured. He played the rest of that season as partner to Dick Smith on the left and did well. However, the following season he played only once before joining the Manchester club Fairfield.

Club record: 11 apps. one goal (also 6 'other' apps, 2 goals)

VASCO DA GAMA

United were beaten 3-1 by the Brazilian side Vasco da Gama in the FIFA Club World Championship in Brazil in January 2000. The group 'B' game was played in Rio and was attended by just 5,000 spectators. Nicky Butt scored United's consolation goal with nine minutes remaining. Internationals Romario (2) and Edmundo had earlier given their side a commanding 3-0 half-time lead

VERONA

United played Verona in a Group One game in the Anglo-Italian tournament in May 1973. A crowd of 8,168 in Italy saw United gain a 4-1 victory. Bobby Charlton (playing in his last United game) scored twice, Patrick Olney (on his debut) also found the net likewise Peter Fletcher, while Fagni grabbed a consolation goal for the Italians. Victory though wasn't enough to see the Reds qualify for the next stage.

VICTORIES (Wins)

United's biggest wins in all major competitions (6-0 minimum score)

Home

10-0	v. RSC Anderlecht (European Cup)	26.09.1956	7-0	v. Aston Villa (League)	08.03.1950
10-1	v. Wolverhampton Wanderers (League)	15.10.1892	7-0	v. Aston Villa (League)	24.10.1964
9-0	v. Walsall Town Swifts (League)	03.04.1895	7-0	v. West Bromwich Albion (League)	08.04.1970
9-0	v. Darwen (League)	24.12.1898	7-0	v, Barnsley (Premiership)	25.10.1997
9-0	v. Ipswich Town (Premiership)	04.03.1995	7-1	v. Derby County (League)	31.12.1892
8-0	v. Yeovil Town (FA Cup)	12.02.1949	7-1	v. Brentford (FA Cup)	14.01.1928
8-1	v. Queen's Park Rangers (League)	19.03.1969	7-1	v. Millwall (League)	22.10.1932
7-0	v. West Manchester (FA Cup)	12.12.1896	7-1	v. Waterford (European Cup)	02.10.1968
7-0	v. Accrington Stanley (FA Cup)	01.11.1902	7-1	v. West Ham United (Premiership)	01.04.2000
7-0	v. Bradford City (League)	02.01.1905	7-2	v. Staple Hill (FA Cup)	13.01.1906
			7-2	v. Port Vale (League)	08.02.1936

325

7-2	v. Bolton Wanderers (League)	18.01.1958
7-2	v. Newcastle United (League Cup)	27.10.1976
6-0	v. Loughborough (League)	06.02.1897
6-0	v. Walsall (League)	30.10.1897
6-0	v. Doncaster Rovers (League)	26.10.1901
6-0	v. Doncaster Rovers (League)	01.04.1905
6-0	v. Burton United (League)	28.04.1906
6-0	v. Bournemouth (FA Cup)	08.01.1949
6-0	v. Huddersfield Town (League)	05.11.1949
6-0	v. Huddersfield Town (League)	28.04.1951
6-0	v. Leeds United (League)	09.09.1959
6-0	v. Chelsea (League)	26.12.1960
6-0	v. Burnley (League)	12.04.1961
6-0	v. HJK Helsinki (European Cup)	06.10.1965
6-0	v. Newcastle United (League)	04.05.1968
6-0	v. Bradford City (Premiership)	05.09.2000

Away

8-1	v. Nottingham Forest (Premiership)	06.02.1999
8-2	v. Northampton Town (FA Cup)	07.02.1970
8-4	v. Swindon Town (FA Charity Shield)*	25.09.1911
7-0	v. Grimsby Town (League)	26.12.1899
7-1	v. Chesterfield (League)	13.11.1937
7-2	v. Ipswich Town (League)	03.09.1963
6-0	v. Shamrock Rovers (European Cup)	25.09.1957
6-0	v. Blackpool (League)	27.02.1960
6-0	v. Bolton Wanderers (Premiership)	25.02.1996

* Played at Stamford Bridge

Victory Salutes

Newton Heath's 10-1 win over Wolves was their first League victory of any kind and the first such scoreline in the Football League itself.

Newton Heath beat Walsall Town Swifts 14-0 at home in a Second Division League game in March 1895, but the Saddlers objected to the state of the pitch. This was upheld, the result declared null and void, and a replay ordered - which United won 9-0 (see above). If that score from the initial match had been allowed to stand, then it would have still been listed as the biggest League victory by any club playing in any Division.

United registered a club record 14 League wins in succession in season 1904-05 (Division 2).

The following season, in 1905-06, United registered a club record 28 League wins (out of 38 games) which was equalled in 1956-57 (from 42 matches when they were Division 1 champions) and again in 1999-2000 (from only 38 games when they won the Premiership title - again).

In season 1993-94 United claimed a club record total of 41 victories in all first-class matches (27 in the Premiership, six League Cup, six FA Cup, 2 European Cup).

United's tally of 39 domestic wins in that 1993-94 campaign is also a record.

United achieved a total of 22 away wins in 1993-94 (all games). Twenty came on opponents' soil, the other two on neutral grounds.

The fewest League wins registered by United in a complete season has been six (from 30 games) in 1892-93 and again in 1893-94 (also from 30 games). They won seven (from 42 starts) in 1930-31.

The fewest number of home League wins recorded in a season by the Reds has been 5 (out of 15) in 1893-94. They won only six times (in 21 starts) in 1919-20, 1930-31 and 1962-63.

United did not win a single away game in the 1892-93 League season; they managed just one in 1901-02, 1914-15, 1921-22, 1930-31 and 1986-87 (the latter at Liverpool).

VERON, Juan Sebastian

Born: La Plata, Argentina, 9 March 1975
Career: Estudiantes de la Plata (1993), Boca Juniors (1995), Sampdoria (£13 million, summer 1996), Parma (£20 million, summer 1998), SS Lazio (£20 million, summer 1999), MANCHESTER UNITED (£28.1 million, July 2001).

Shaven-headed Argentina midfielder 'Seba' Veron - nicknamed La Brujita (the Little Witch) - joined United from Italian Serie 'A' soccer for a British club record fee in the summer of 2001, agreeing an £80,000-a-week contract for his first season at Old Trafford. He was already an established professional before becoming a United star, having amassed almost 250 senior appearances, including 150 in Italy (23 goals scored). He was a silver medal winner (with Argentina) in the 1996 Olympic Games; won the Italian Serie 'A' title, the UEFA Cup and the European Super Cup (with Parma) in 1999 and followed up by gaining success with Lazio in Italy's Serie 'A', the Italian Cup and the Italian Super Cup, all in 2000. He was in Argentina's World Cup squad for the 2002 World Cup Finals in Japan & South Korea, bringing his tally of caps to 50.

* Veron's father, Ramon, also played for Estudiantes de la Plata and scored at Old Trafford when they beat United in the World Club Championship game in 1968.

Club record: 40 apps. 5 goals

VIDEOS

Over the last 20 years or so more than 250 different videos have been produced with a Manchester United connection (i.e the club, team, players and managers etc).

The History of The Club (produced by the BBC in 1988, later up-dated) has proved to be one of the best sellers.

Another important video was Munich Remembered, also released in 1988.

Videos covering each of United's Premiership campaigns (1992-93 to 2001-02) have also been excellent sellers, along with 'The Treble' of 1999; 'Champions of Europe' and 'Au Revior Cantona' and 'Eric The King' (Cantona) and the video entitled 'The Real David Beckham'. Other videos include: 'Manchester United - Beyond The Promised Land - the Movie'; 'Theatre of Dreams' (an insiders' Guide to Old Trafford); 'Magnificent 7's (50 Years of Genius); Peter Schmeichel (Definitely the Best Goalkeeper in the World); '300 United Premiership Goals'; 300 United All-time Greatest Goals; 'United In The 70s'; United In The 80s'; 'United In The 90s'; United's 'Munich Memorial Match'; 'A Knight To Remember' (A-Z of Sir Alex Ferguson); 'Ryan Giggs Revealed'; 'Ole Gunnar Solskjaer: Who Put the Ball in the German's Net'; 'The George Best Story'; 'George Best Genius Maverick Legend'; 'George Best - Genius'; 'Best Intentions' (George Best); 'A Tribute To Duncan Edwards'; 'The 1968 European Cup Final' (United 4 Benfica 1); 'Champions of Europe: 1998-99'; all the action from United's 1976, 1977, 1979, 1983 (both games), 1985, 1990 (both games), 1994 & 1996 Wembley FA Cup Finals; the 3-1 League win over Liverpool in 1989; 101 Great United Goals (2 tapes); 'The Official FA Cup History of Manchester United'.

* The Soccer Brilliance Series (via Bobby Charlton's School of Football) has released a coaching video by Gary Neville, entitled 'Defensive Heading.'

VIDEOTON

United met Videoton in the quarter-finals of the UEFA Cup in 1984-85 and after the scores had finished level, even after extra time in the second leg (after both side had won 1-0 at home) a disappointed United lost the penalty shoot-out 5-4 in Hungary.

VINCENT, Ernest

Born: Seaham Harbour, County Durham, 28 October 1907. Died: Bircotes, near Worksop, 2 June 1978.

Career: Durham County Schools, Dawdon Colliery (1923-25), Hyhope Colliery (season 1925-26), Seaham Harbour FC, Washington Colliery (1929-30), Southport (trialist, then signed summer 1930), MANCHESTER UNITED (£1,000, February 1932), QPR (June 1935), Doncaster Rovers (1937-38).

Ernie 'Ginger' Vincent was a very useful half-back; a powerful tackler, he enjoyed two good seasons in the Second Division with United (1931-33).

Club record: 65 apps. One goal

VIOLLET, Dennis Sydney

Born: Manchester, 20 September 1933. Died: USA, 6 March 1999.

Career: Manchester Schools, MANCHESTER UNITED (trialist, autumn 1947, amateur summer 1949, professional September 1950), Stoke City (£25,000, January 1962), Baltimore Bays (1967-68), Witton Albion (early 1969), Linfield (player-coach, season 1969-70), Preston North End (coach, 1970-71), Crewe Alexandra (coach, early 1971, manager for four months, late 1971), Washington Diplomats (coach 1974-77), later coach Jackson University and in Richmond, Virginia.

Inside-forward Dennis Viollet was quicksilver sharp, incisive, a wonderful chance-taker. He could read a situation seconds before a defender could…and that proved fatal to the opposition! Not only could he sniff out a goal, he could also create them with some wonderful, deft touches.

A superb partner to Tommy Taylor, his 20 League goals in 1955-56 helped United clinch the First Division Championship and his contribution of 16 the following season ensured that the title remained at Old Trafford. Thankfully he survived the Munich air crash in 1958 and went on to collect a runners-up medal in that season's FA Cup Final, having missed out on a Final appearance the year before through injury. In 1959-60 he broke United's seasonal scoring record with 32 goals in 36 First Division matches and at the end of that campaign he played in the first of two full internationals for England against Hungary (his second in 1961 was v. Luxembourg). He also played three times for the Football League. Quite why the selectors did not select him to partner Tommy Taylor is difficult to fathom. Viollet, positive in every aspect of attacking play, scored on average two goals every three games for United. His League figures were 159 strikes in 259 outings (all in Division One) and he also held United's scoring record for most goals in one European Cup campaign (nine in 1956-57) before Van Nistelrooy bettered it with ten in 2001-02. It remains a mystery why he was allowed to leave Old Trafford in 1962.

As a Stoke City player, teaming up with Stanley Matthews and Jackie Mudie, he helped the Potters win the Second Division title in 1963 and the following year he collected a League Cup runners-up prize when Stoke were beaten by Leicester City. He later won the Irish Cup with Linfield (1970). Viollet spent the last 25 years of his life in the United States as a much respected coach.

Club record: 293 apps. 179 goals

VORWAERTS (ASK)

United comfortably won through to the 2nd round of the 1965-66 European Cup competition with a 5-1 aggregate win over the East German side ASK Vorwaerts. David Herd scored a hat-trick in the 3-1 win at Old Trafford after Denis Law and John Connelly had prepared the way in 'cold war' East Berlin where United won 2-0..

VOSE, George

Born: St Helens, 4 October 1911. Died: Wigan, 20 June 1981.

Career: Peasley Cross Athletic, MANCHESTER UNITED (September 1932); guested for Chester, Derby County, Manchester City & Stockport County during WW2; MANCHESTER UNITED (re-signed January 1946), Runcorn (season 1946-47).

George Vose was a footballing centre-half with St Helens before becoming one of the stars of Manchester United. Establishing himself in the first XI at Old Trafford in 1933, he then became an integral part of the team and when United won the Second Division Championship in 1935-36, he appeared in 41 matches, forming a superb middle-line along with James Brown and Billy McKay. Following relegation he was then the lynchpin when the Reds regained their First Division status as runners-up in 1937-38, playing in 33 League games on this occasion when his senior defensive colleagues were again Messrs Brown and McKay. The fair-haired Vose, a delight to watch when in possession, unfortunately missed out on international recognition but he did play in one England trial match in 1939 before WW2. Although he re-signed with United after the hostilities, he quickly moved into non-League football without appearing in the first XI.

Club record: 211 apps. one goal

Born: Belfast, 7 May 1965

Career: West Belfast Schools, MANCHESTER UNITED (apprentice, June 1981, professional July 1962), Everton (£750,000, August 1989). Forced to retire with knee injury, summer 1991. Later assistant-manager of Northwich Victoria (1991-92).

Striker/midfielder Norman Whiteside- from Belfast's Crumlin Road - made his Football League debut for United as a 16 year-old against Brighton & Hove Albion in April 1982. Then, as a late 17th birthday present, he scored on his first full outing for the club at home to Stoke in mid-May.

Whiteside proved to be one of the great discoveries of the 1980s and his rise to the top was nothing less than meteoric - just like Roy of the Rovers!

He was spotted by United scout Bob Bishop in 1980 while playing at weekends in West Belfast and after scoring over 100 goals in one season of junior football he joined the ranks at Old Trafford (leaving Liverpool and a few others behind). He quickly stepped up a grade to professionalism and overtook George Best as the youngest-ever Irishman to don the famous red jersey.

Named in Billy Bingham's Northern Ireland squad for the 1982 World Cup Finals in Spain, Whiteside duly made his international bow against Yugoslavia in Zaragoza in June of that year to become the youngest player (at 17 years, 41 days) ever to figure in the World Cup Finals (taking over from Pele). He turned out to be one of the stars of the tournament.

He followed up in 1983 by scoring in the League Cup

Final as United lost to Liverpool (making him the youngest ever scorer in a major Wembley Final); he poached the winner against Arsenal in the FA Cup semi-final and then struck one of four goals that United put past Brighton to win the Cup Final replay.

Aged 19, he rattled in a hat-trick when West Ham were thumped in the quarter-final of the 1985 FA Cup competition and in the Final his sensational goal earned the ten men of United victory over Everton.

In 1986 Whiteside again appeared in the World Cup Finals and he went on to take his tally of international caps to 36 with United. After demanding a move following a rift with new boss Alex Ferguson, he was transferred to Everton with whom he added two more to his collection before injury forced him into retirement at the age of 26.

Whiteside certainly had a temper, a mean streak, which earned him the tag of 'Nasty Norman' by the press... for several brushes with officialdom after skirmishes on the pitch which saw him receive several red and yellow cards, resulting in a batch of suspensions..

He later became Sammy McIlroy's number two at Northwich Victoria (taking over the duties from another ex-United player, Gordon Clayton). He eventually quit football in 1992 to become a physiotherapist, concentrating, not unnaturally, on footballers' problems. Visitors enjoying United's hospitality at home matches, might well be greeted by Norman's disarming smile as he acts as host in the hospitality suites.

Club record: 278 apps. 68 goals

WALDRON, Colin

Born: Bristol, 22 June 1948

Career: Bury (apprentice, professional 1966), Chelsea (£25,000, mid-1967), Burnley (£25,000, late 1967), MANCHESTER UNITED (£20,000, May 1976), Sunderland (on loan, February-May 1977), Tulsa Roughnecks (April 1978), Philadelphia Fury (1978), Atlanta Chiefs (1979), Rochdale (1979-80).

Colin Waldron was a very capable defender who sadly failed to make his mark at Old Trafford, having previously appeared in over 300 League games for Burnley, helping then win the Second Division Championship in 1972-73 and reach the FA Cup semi-finals a year later. During his career the Bristolian played in well over 400 competitive games (in England and the NASL).

His younger brother Alan Waldron, played for Blackpool, Bolton, Bury and York City.

Club record: Four apps.

WALKER, Dennis Alan

Born: Northwich, Cheshire, 26 October 1944

Career: Cheshire & District Schools, MANCHESTER UNITED (apprentice, September 1960, professional November 1961), York City (April 1964), Cambridge United (1968-69), Poole Town.

A promising wing-half in the club's Youth team, Dennis Walker was the first black player to appear in United's first XI at competition level, occupying the left-wing berth against Nottingham Forest at The City Ground on the last day of the 1962-63 season when manager Matt Busby rested key players ahead of the FA Cup Final against Leicester City. He later gave York excellent service, playing in 169 senior games for the Bootham Crescent club (19 goals scored) and then helped Cambridge twice win the Southern League title and the Southern League Cup in the space of seasons: 1968-70.

Club record: One app.

WALKER, Robert

Born: Lancashire, circa 1879

Career: Notts County, NEWTON HEATH (trialist, one month: January 1899), Notts County.

Rugged defender Bob Walker appeared twice in the Heathens' first XI during his four-week trial period. He failed to impress in games against Glossop North End and Walsall.

Club record: 2 apps. (also one 'other' app)

329

WALL, George

Born: Boldon Colliery, nr Sunderland, County Durham, 20 February 1885. Died: Manchester, 1962

Career: Boldon Royal Rovers, Whitburn (1901), Jarrow (1903), Barnsley (late 1903), MANCHESTER UNITED (April 1906), Oldham Athletic (March 1919), Hamilton Academical (1921-22), Rochdale (1922-23), Ashton National FC (1923-26), Manchester Ship Canal FC (1926-27).

One of the finest left-wingers of the pre-First World war era, Wall was fast, clever, cheeky and a fine goalscorer who was brilliant at cutting inside his full-back and having a crack at goal whenever possible. He helped United win two League championships (1908 & 1911), the FA Cup in 1909 and the FA Charity Shield, also in 1908. Around this time he was outstanding and if there had been such a thing as the PFA 'Footballer of the Year Award' he would have carried off the star prize at least twice, despite Meredith's presence!

Wall scored exactly 100 goals for United...and laid on many more for his colleagues. He was capped seven times by England (1907-13) and scored twice in the 2-0 win over Scotland in 1909 that clinched the Home International championship that season. He also represented the Football League on four occasions, played his last League game for Rochdale at the age of 38 and kicked his last ball in earnest three years later. He made over 500 League appearances during an excellent career. During WW1, Wall, who donned the kilt of the famous Black Watch Regiment, attaining the rank of Sergeant, was spotted by Louis Rocca who in so many words, said: "He's a star." As usual, Louis was absolutely right!

Club record: 319 apps. 100 goals

WALLACE, David Lloyd

Born: Greenwich, London, 21 January 1964.

Career: West Greenwich School, Southampton (apprentice 1980, professional 1982), MANCHESTER UNITED (£1.3 million, September 1989), Millwall (on loan, March-April 1993), Birmingham City (£400,000, October 1993), Wycombe Wanderers (1995), Saudi Arabian football (1995-96).

Darting winger 'Danny' Wallace - and his two brothers, Rod and Ray - made Football League history when, in October 1988, they appeared together for Southampton against Sheffield Wednesday in a First Division match. Wallace (D) also became the youngest player ever to appear for Saints in a senior game - aged 16 years, 10 months against United in November 1980. He went on to appear in 310 first-class games during his nine years at the Dell (scoring 74 goals). He also scored on his Under-21 debut for England v. Greece in 1985 and followed up with another goal in his only full international outing - a 4-0 win over Egypt in January 1986.

He won an FA Cup winners medal at the end of his first season at Old Trafford and was in good form until injuries started to interfere with his performances. With Ryan Giggs ready to step forward, Wallace moved on to give Birmingham City two years' service before drifting slowly down the ladder (after Blues had suffered relegation).

Club record: 71 apps. 11 goals

WALLWORK, Ronald

Born: Manchester, 10 September 1977.

Career: MANCHESTER UNITED (apprentice June 1993, professional March 1995, out of contract May 2002), Carlisle United (on loan, December 1997-January 1998), Stockport County (on loan, March-April 1998), Royal Antwerp (on loan, late 1990s), West Bromwich Albion (free transfer, June 2002).

Defender Ronnie Wallwork - an England youth international - helped the club's youngsters lift the FA Youth Cup in 1995 and the seniors the Premiership in 2001. Eighteen of his senior outings were made as a substitute. Although his appearances have been spasmodic he has never let United down, whether playing in central defence or midfield.

Club record: 28 apps.

WALSALL (Town Swifts)

Heathens' League results v the Saddlers:

Season	Div	Home	Away
1894-95	2	W 9-0	W 2-1
1896-97	2	W 2-0	W 3-2
1897-98	2	W 6-0	D 1-1
1898-99	2	W 1-0	L 0-2
1899-00	2	W 5-0	D 0-0
1900-01	2	D 1-1	D 1-1

FA Cup results v the Saddlers:

	Round	Venue	Result
1897-98	1	Home	W 1-0
1974-75	3	Home	D 0-0
	Replay	Away	L 2-3 aet
1976-77	3	Home	W 1-0
1997-98	4	Home	W 5-1

Summary of League results

	P	W	D	L	F	A
Division 2	12	7	4	1	31	8
Home	6	5	1	0	24	1
Away	6	2	3	1	7	7
Total	12	7	4	1	31	8

Fact File

When Walsall Town Swifts lost 9-0 at Bank Street to Newton Heath on 3 April 1895 this was a replayed fixture by order of the Football League. When they had first turned up at Bank Street for the original fixture on 9 March 1895 they had been appalled by the state of the pitch. They complained to the referee before the start, but he insisted the match go ahead, although he registered the club's official complaint in his match report.

The game resulted in a 14-0 win for Newton Heath, this would have been a Football League record, never bettered in any division. However, Walsall Town Swifts continued to complain after the match, the League management committee noting their pre-match complaint, ordering the match to be replayed.

It is worth noting that the pitch in April was only marginally better than it had been in March. On a personal note, the Heathens' star forward Dick Smith scored six times which would still be a club record if only it had been allowed to stand. In the replayed match Smith scored twice. Walsall caused an FA Cup upset to match their famous 2-0 win over Arsenal in 1933, when they beat United 3-2 in a replayed tie in 1975.

Players with both clubs include: P Bodak (United reserve), C Crossley (United WW1), C Gibson, C Jenkyns, R John, M Lane (United reserve), R McMorran (United reserve), J Merrick (United reserve), R Newsome (WW2 player with both clubs), A Potts, C Radford, A Rammell (United reserve), M Robins, J Rowley (Saddlers WW2), W Sarvis, J Warner, ER Young (United reserve). Also associated: F Buckley (United player, Saddlers manager), S Houghton (United player/Walsall coach), A Ashman (Saddlers' manager & scout, United scout), P Bradshaw (United trialist, Saddlers' coach).

WALSH, Gary

Born: Wigan, 21 March 1968

Career: Wigan Schools, MANCHESTER UNITED (apprentice June 1983, professional April 1985), Airdrieonians (on loan, one month, August 1980), Oldham Athletic (on loan, November-December 1993), Middlesbrough (£500,000, August 1995), Bradford City (£500,000, autumn 1997), Middlesbrough (on loan, 2000).

Agile and courageous goalkeeper Gary Walsh won two England Under-21 caps during his time at Old Trafford where initially he was reserve to Gary Bailey, and then Chris Turner before finally getting his chance of regular first-team football during the 1986-87 season. He became second best again when Jim Leighton arrived on the scene in June 1988 and then played second fiddle to Peter Schmeichel before finally moving on to Middlesbrough after 12 years at Old Trafford, during which time he averaged barely five games a season! However, he was an European Cup-winners Cup and European Super Cup winner with United in 1991, also gaining an FA Cup winners prize in 1994. He then helped Bradford City reach the Premiership for the first time ever in season 1998-99, having played in the top flight with Middlesbrough prior to that (under the management of former United star Bryan Robson and his assistant Viv Anderson). When the 2001-02 season ended Walsh's total number of appearances at club level was slowly edging towards the 300 mark.

Club record: 63 apps.

WALTHAMSTOW AVENUE

After the wholehearted and brave amateurs of Walthamstow Avenue had battled hard and long to earn a superb 1-1 FA Cup draw at Old Trafford in front of 34,748 spectators on 31 January 1953, they chose to stage the 4th round replay at Highbury five days later. This time an audience of 49,119 saw United ease through 5-2 with Jack Rowley scoring twice. Playing for Avenue was England Test cricketer Trevor Bailey, a genuine all-rounder.

WALTON, John Andrew

Born: Horwich, 21 March 1928. Died: Lancashire, 1979

Career: Schoolboy football (in Horwich), Army football, Plymouth Argyle ('A' team), Saltash United, Bury (amateur summer 1949), MANCHESTER UNITED (amateur, July 1951), Bury (amateur July 1952, professional February

1954), Burnley (1954), Coventry City (autumn 1956), Kettering Town (1958), Chester (season 1959-60).
Stocky reserve inside-forward John Walton - who was a Sergeant in the Army Education Corps - won three caps for
England as an amateur during his one season at Old Trafford when he stood in for John Downie in two League games
(v. PNE & Derby County). After leaving the Reds, Walton took his tally of amateur caps to 19 and he also represented
Great Britain in the 1952 Olympic Games (v. Luxembourg). Later living in Chorley, he became a teacher, based at
Horwich Grammar School.
Club record: 2 apps.

WALTON, Joseph

Born: Manchester, 5 June 1925
Career: Manchester & District Schools, Lancashire Schools, MANCHESTER UNITED (amateur, April 1940),
Gosling's FC (on loan 1941-42), MANCHESTER UNITED (as professional October 1943), Preston North End
(£10,000, March 1948), Accrington Stanley (early 1962).
Joe Walton, a full-back, was loaned out to local amateur side, Gosling's FC, to gain experience during WW2. Reserve to
Messrs Carey and Aston, he represented the FA on three occasions during the hostilities and in August 1946 he played
for England against Scotland in aid of the Burnden Park Disaster Fund, also appearing in 36 Regional North League
games for United in 1945-46 and representing the Football League in 1948. When Walton moved to Deepdale it was
for a record fee for a full-back. Five years later he helped North End finish runners-up in Division One and twelve
months after that came second again, this time in the 1954 FA Cup Final. He made 401 League appearances for Preston
before moving to Accrington Stanley where he ended his career.
Club record: 23 apps.

WARBURTON, Arthur

Born: Whitefield, near Bury, 30 October 1903. Died: Bury, 21 April 1978
Career: Sedgley Park, MANCHESTER UNITED (amateur February, professional, May 1929), Burnley (December
1933), Nelson (mid-1934), Fulham (autumn 1934), Queen's Park Rangers (season 1938-39), guested for Bradford Park
Avenue, Lincoln City, Middlesbrough, Rochdale & Southport during WW2). Retired 1946.
Inside-forward Arthur Warburton's best season at Old Trafford was 1930-31 when, in a struggling side and as partner to
Joe Spence on the right-flank, he scored five goals in 24 League and Cup games He made over 90 League and Cup
appearances after leaving United.
Club record: 39 apps. 10 goals

WARNER, James

Born: Lozells, Birmingham, April 1865. Died: 1929
Career: Hampton Road School, Milton FC, Aston Villa (summer 1886), NEWTON HEATH (July 1892), Walsall
Town Swifts (September 1893). Retired 1894 with a back injury. Later Warner went to the USA to coach in Pittsburgh
(September 1907-1909).
A supple and shrewd goalkeeper, agile enough to reach the most difficult of shots, Jimmy Warner played in two FA Cup
Finals for Villa, both against West Bromwich Albion. He gained a winners' medal in the first in 1887, but rumours
abounded that he 'sold' the 1892 Final which Villa lost 3-0. As a result, his pub in Aston came in for a bit of a battering
from irate supporters! He later sold it under pressure. A 'keeper who preferred to punch the ball rather than catch it,
Warner then spent a season with the Heathens, infuriating the club directors by failing to turn up for a game at Stoke
which ended in a 7-1 defeat! He was suspended for 'carelessness' and played in only two more games afterwards..
Club record: 22 apps. (also 11 'other' apps)

WARNER, John

Born: Trealaw, Tonypandy, Glamorgan, 21 September 1911. Died: Tonypandy, Glamorgan, 4 October 1980.
Career: Trealaw Juniors, Trealaw Rangers, Treorchy Juniors (1930), Aberaman (1932), Swansea Town (early 1934),
MANCHESTER UNITED (June 1938), Oldham Athletic (player-coach, June 1951), Rochdale (player-manager, season 1952-53).
Wing-half 'Jack' Warner made his League debut for United against Aston Villa on 5 November 1938. He impressed all
and sundry and duly held his position in the team throughout that last pre-war campaign, appearing in 215 competitive
games for the Reds during the hostilities and then holding his position in 1946-47. A player who prided himself on his
physical fitness, he was a smart tackler and a fine passer of the ball. He very rarely headed the ball! A colleague and
friend of Welsh international Bryn Jones who was transferred from Wolves to Arsenal for a record fee of £14,000 in
1938, Warner and Jones played together for their country against England at Cardiff in 1936. Warner later added a
second full cap to his collection (v. France in 1939) and he also played in one wartime international. He was captain of
United's Central League side before moving to Boundary Park as player-coach in 1951 (signed by the former England
international full-back George Hardwick). He played his last game for Rochdale at the age of 42, having been 38 years,
seven months and one day old when he appeared in his last game for United against Newcastle on 22 April 1950,
making him at the time the second oldest player for the club and the oldest since WW2. Van der Gouw later took over
as United's oldest post-war player. After footbaall Warner ran a betting shop, just two miles from Old Trafford.
Club record: 119 apps. 2 goals

331

WARTIME FOOTBALL

United's playing record (first team level) during the two World War periods. Friendlies have not been included, nor have the three void League games of 1939-40 or the FA Cup matches played in 1945-46.

World War One

Season	P	W	D	L	F	A
1915-16	36	9	9	18	53	75
1916-17	36	17	6	13	63	63
1917-18	36	14	9	13	51	56
1918-19	36	13	5	18	60	64
Summary	144	53	29	62	227	258

World War Two

Season	P	W	D	L	F	A
1939-40	26	16	0	10	79	46
1940-41	37	15	8	14	85	69
1941-42	37	22	10	5	123	53
1942-43	39	24	6	9	116	56
1943-44	39	23	9	7	111	68
1944-45	40	21	5	14	87	73
1945-46	42	19	11	12	98	62
Summary	260	140	49	71	699	427

During WW2 United's seasons were played in the following sections:

1939-40 War Regional League (Western Division)
1940-41 North Regional League
1941-42 Football League Northern Section
1942-46 Football League North

War Cry

•When the Great War broke out in 1914, the Football authorities, controversially some say, allowed League football to continue for one extra season (1914-15). Despite massive public and media objections and some reservations by several clubs up and down the country, the League programme for that campaign was played out in full, with several games having very poor attendance figures.

•By May 1915 it had become all too obvious that initial forecasts stating 'it would be all over by Christmas (1914)' were woefully wide of the mark, so both the League and the FA Cup competitions were finally suspended.

•On advice of the War Office, regional tournaments were played as a way of maintaining morale throughout the country.

•United took part in the Lancashire Section (Principal Tournament) which ran until February or March of each season when a shorter tournament - the Lancashire Section Subsidiary (Southern) tournament - took its place.

•In 1918-19 the Subsidiary and Principal tournaments doubled up as a qualification to bring about the four Lancashire Senior Cup semi-finalists.

•United's best win (in terms of goals scored) during the Great War period was 6-1, at home to Blackburn in September 1917. United also beat Bolton Wanderers 6-3 at home in March 1917.

•The Reds' heaviest defeat during the 1915-19 wartime period was 7-1 - suffered away to Liverpool in April 1916 and by the same scoreline at Burnley in September of that same year.

•The biggest crowds United played to during the Great War period were 35,000 against Manchester City (both at home and away) in April 1919 (after the hostilities were officially over). The lowest turnout for a United wartime encounter was just 650 at Oldham in March 1916.

•United utilised over 150 players in a total of 144 games fulfilled during the 1915-19 period. Wilf Woodcock missed only 12 of these matches, appearing in 132. Jack Mew made 126 appearances, followed by Jack Silcock with 103 and 'Lal' Hilditch with 101. (See under APPEARANCES).

•Woodcock top-scored with 69 goals; George Anderson hit 40 (See under GOALS & GOALSCORERS)

•Towards the end of the last season of WW1, 20 year-old Joe Spence made his debut for United. Just out of the Army, having guested for Liverpool, he scored four times in his first game for the Reds v. Bury at Old Trafford in March 1919, and totalled six in four outings at the end of that campaign.

•Spence would prove United's best-ever wartime signing, playing in more than 500 League and Cup games for the club and scoring 168 goals before retiring in 1938 - a United legend at a time when the club was at its lowest ebb.

•The Old Trafford faithful (what few there were) were known then to say 'Give it to Joe!'

• The football authorities had learned their lessons of 1914 when World War Two was declared on 3 September 1939. This time the Football League programme (after just three matches had been fulfilled at the start of that 1939-40 season) was unhesitatingly abandoned.

•Almost immediately regionalised competitions (League and Cup) were formulated. Professional footballers were conscripted into the Armed Forces like all other physically fit young men, but most of them were generally enlisted into the Army Physical Training Corps or equivalent in the Royal Navy or RAF, or as Regimental PTIs.

•Both the Army and RAF were able to field powerful sides for the various representative matches that were arranged, while players guested for any club nearby to where they were stationed..

•United took their place in the War Regional League (Western Division), playing not only neighbours City and the likes of Everton and Liverpool, but also coming face to face with Wrexham, New Brighton, Crewe Alexandra, Port Vale and Chester etc.

• The competitions themselves ran on imaginative lines. For instance, the North Regional League of 1940-41 comprised 36 teams, each playing 35 matches. No points were awarded, the League placings being decided on goal-average (goals scored for divided by goals against).

•In 1940-41 United met Liverpool four times and Blackburn Rovers thrice, on one occasion at Stockport's ground as nearby Trafford Park was being blitzed by heavy bombing from enemy war planes! Blackburn were forced to recruit four spectators from the terraces to make up their match at Stockport. United won 9-0.

•Between 1942 and 1945 the Football League North competition comprised two separate tournaments, one in each half of the season with some of the scheduled matches in the second phase also counting towards Cup competitions. United's only major success during this three-year period came in 1941-42 when they won the Football League Northern Section (Second Championship).

•The players who did most of the hard work in capturing that Championship were: goalkeeper Breedon; defenders Roughton, Warner, Porter and Whalley and forwards Bryant, Smith, Morris, Catterick and Carey.

•On 2 March 1941, Old Trafford was devastated by enemy bombs which had obviously been meant to land on nearby Trafford Park! The main stand was flattened, thus leaving the corner stands and paddock unsafe. Thereafter United were forced to play all their home matches at Manchester City's Maine Road ground. They did not return to Old Trafford until August 1949, though reserve team football was possible from 1946.

•In May 1941 United won the 'annual' Lancashire Cup Final, beating Burnley 1-0 thanks to Johnny Carey's goal and Jack Breedon's penalty save from Bob Brocklebank,

•Throughout WW2 United was run almost single-handedly by club secretary Walter Crickmer, who also doubled up efficiently as team manager. After Old Trafford had been bombed, he operated from a temporary office in Chairman James Gibson's business premises based at Cornbrook.

•In October 1945, United recruited Company Sergeant Major Instructor Matthew Busby as its new manager. United beat Bolton 3-2 in his first game in charge. The rest, as they say, is history.

•The three First Division League games played at the start of the ill-fated 1939-40 season which were subsequently declared null and void, ended: United 4 Grimsby 0 (h), Chelsea 1 United 1 (a) and Charlton 2 United 0 (a). Allenby Chilton made his United debut at Charlton the day before WW2 was declared. He would have to wait almost seven years for his next 'real' League debut, having survived the D-Day landings.

•United's best win during WW2 was to give hapless New Brighton a competent 13-1 hiding at home in August 1941. Jack Rowley scored seven of his side's goals that day.

•United's worst defeat in WW2 was 6-0 - suffered surprisingly at the hands of New Brighton (away) in May 1940.

•United scored six goals in each of three successive home games in 1939-40 - beating Tranmere Rovers 6-1, Stockport 6-1 and New Brighton 6-0 in that order.

•United drew 5-5 at Blackburn in December 1940.

•United put 15 goals past Chester in eight days in October 1941, winning 7-0 away and 8-1 at home. Fourteen were fired past Wrexham in December 1941 (United winning 10-3 at home and 4-3 away).

•United netted a total of 20 goals in four games v. Crewe Alexandra in 1942-43. They won 7-0, 3-2, 4-1 and 6-0.

•A crowd of 57,395 saw the United-Bolton Wanderers League North Wartime Cup Final 2nd leg encounter at Maine Road in May 1945. It ended level at 2-2 when Bolton's Malcolm Barrass headed home a last minute equaliser to give his side an aggregate 3-2 victory following the Wanderers 1-0 first leg victory at Burnden Park when the turnout was 40,000.

• The biggest attendance for a United WW2 game was 62,144 at Maine Road for their 'home' game with Manchester City in April 1946. City won 4-1. This match took place long after the hostilities had ceased in 1945.

•The lowest attendance United played in front of during WW2 was a meagre 700, at home to Liverpool on 30 November 1940 at the height of the 'blitz.'

•During World War Two, United used more than 170 players in a total of 260 competitive games. Jack Warner appeared in 215 of them, Jack Smith in 201 and Johnny Carey in 198. Close behind came Bert Whalley with 188 appearances, George Roughton with 173, Jack Breedon on 171, Billy Bryant 169, Billy Porter 131 and Billy McKay 110. (See also under Appearances).

•Jack Smith finished up as United's top-scorer in WW2 with 160 goals. Jack Rowley claimed exactly 100 (in 79 games), Johnny Carey netted 52, Stan Pearson also 52 (in 75 starts) and Billy Bryant 47. (See under GOALS & GOALSCORERS).

•Jack Rowley scored in six successive games during April and May 1941. Jack Smith equalled that feat during March/April/May 1943 and repeated the sequence seven months later. Although prolific during WW2 soccer, Smith did not appear in post-war League football.

•Rowley also scored on his debut for the Football League v Scottish League at Blackpool in October 1941. A month later he netted five times for United against Tranmere Rovers; in November 1942 he scored all Wolves' goals in their 8-1 wartime win over Derby County and in February 1944, again playing as a guest, he claimed seven goals for Spurs in their 8-1 win over Luton Town.

•It is on record that only one United player lost his life during WW2. He was Ben Carpenter, killed on active service. Among those who were taken as POW was Johnny Hanlon (captured in Crete and later held in Stalag IVB in Germany). Allenby Chilton was wounded during the Normandy landings.

•Billy Dennis (a United player in 1923-24) was one of only a handful of professional footballers to serve in both World Wars.

WASSALL, John Victor

Born: Shrewsbury, 11 February 1917. Died: 1994

Career: Wellington Town (1933), MANCHESTER UNITED (February 1935), Brighton & Hove Albion (WW2 guest), Stockport County (October 1946 to May 1947).

Jackie Wassall helped Wellington Town win the Birmingham & District League in 1934. A ball-playing utility forward, he made his League debut against Swansea in November 1935, lining up on the right-flank, the position he held for the next game (v. West Ham). But after that he spent most of the next two seasons in the reserves before having a good run in 1938-39 when he scored four times in 27 First Division matches. Named one of the best 'Young Players of 1939' by the Topical Times magazine, Wassall was then denied his best footballing years by WW2.

Club record: 48 apps. 6 goals

333

WATERFORD

As holders of the trophy, United began their 1968-69 European Cup campaign with an emphatic 10-2 aggregate win over Waterford in the opening round. After a 3-1 win on the Emerald Isle when Denis Law slipped in a hat-trick, the Scottish international went to town at Old Trafford and whipped in a fourtimer as United raced to a comfortable 7-1 victory. Nobby Stiles, Francis Burns and Bobby Charlton also netted in the second leg.

Players with both clubs include: S Brennan (Waterford player-manager), R Charlton, J Feehan, D Herd, T Jackson, N McFarlane, E McIlvenny (Waterford player-manager), J O'Shea.

Also associated: H Green (United reserve, Waterford manager).

WATFORD

United's League results v the Hornets:

Season	Div	Home	Away
1982-83	1	W 2-0	W 1-0
1983-84	1	W 4-1	D 0-0
1984-85	1	D 1-1	L 1-5
1985-86	1	D 1-1	D 1-1
1986-87	1	W 3-1	L 0-1
1987-88	1	W 2-0	W 1-0
1999-2000	PL	W 4-1	W 3-2

Summary of League results

	P	W	D	L	F	A
Premier League	2	2	0	0	7	3
Division 1	12	6	4	2	17	11
Home	7	5	2	0	17	5
Away	7	3	2	2	7	9
Total	14	8	4	2	24	14

FA Cup results v the Hornets:

	Round	Venue	Result
1949-50	4	Away	W 1-0
1968-69	4	Home	D 1-1
	Replay	Away	W 2-0
1981-82	3	Away	L 0-1

FA Cup third place play-off v. the Hornets:

	Round	Venue	Result
1969-70	Play Off	Highbury	W 2-0

League Cup results v the Hornets:

	Round	Venue	Result
1978-79	3	Home	L 1-2
2000-01	3	Away	W 3-0

Players with both clubs include: A Barnett (United reserve), F Barson, J Broad (United reserve), W Chapman, A Coton (United reserve & goalkeeping coach), J Ferguson, R Flash (United reserve), K Goodeve (United reserve), G Haigh (United WW2), T Jones, N McBain (Watford player-manager & scout), J McCrae, G Maiorana (Watford trialist), F McPherson, W Morgan, R Parkinson, J Saunders, D Webber.

Also associated: H Green (United player, Watford manager), R Wilkins (United player, Watford assistant-manager),

WATNEY CUP

United's record in this sponsored competition was:

Venue	P	W	D	L	F	A
Away	4	1	1*	2	6	9

* United won 4-3 on penalties.

Fact File

The first time a competitive football match in Great Britain was decided with a penalty shoot-out featured Manchester United against Hull City in the semi-final of the Watney Cup at Boothferry Park in August 1970. United finally won 4-3 after a 1-1 draw when Denis Law netted in front of 34,007 sun-drenched spectators - an amazing turnout!

In the first round of that 1970 tournament, United beat Reading 3-2 at Elm Park with goals by Bobby Charlton (2) and Paul Edwards in front of 18,348 fans. But they lost 4-1 to Derby County in the Final at the Baseball Ground before 32,049 spectators. United fielded this team: Stepney; Edwards, Dunne; Crerand, Ure, Sadler; Morgan (Stiles), Law (Fitzpatrick), Charlton, Kidd & Best (the goalscorer).

The following season United didn't get past the first round, losing 2-1 at lowly Halifax Town. Best was again on target and the crowd at The Shay was almost 20,000 - another tremendous assembly for such a competition.

WATSON, William

Born: New Steventon, Motherwell, 4 December 1949

Career: MANCHESTER UNITED (amateur June 1965, professional December 1966), Huddersfield Town (on loan, March-April 1970), contract cancelled, April 1973; Miami Toros (May 1973), Burnley (trialist, mid-1973), Motherwell (season 1973-74).

Full-back Willie Watson represented Scotland at schoolboy level before joining the junior ranks at Old Trafford. Engaged in the first team at Old Trafford by Wilf McGuinness, Watson failed to make an impact and was eventually released by the club in 1973.

He was taken on loan to Huddersfield by Ian Greaves, the former United defender

Club record: 14 apps.

WEALANDS, Jeffrey Andrew

Born: Darlington, 26 August 1951

Career: Darlington Cleveland Bridge FC, Wolverhampton Wanderers (apprentice summer 1968 professional autumn 1968), Northampton Town (on loan, early 1970), Darlington (summer 1973), Hull City (£10,000, early 1972), Birmingham City (£30,000, summer 1979), MANCHESTER UNITED (on loan, February 1983 - signed permanently August 1983), Oldham Athletic (on loan, March-May 194), Preston North End (on loan, December 1984-January 1985), Altrincham (May 1985), Barrow (season 1987-88), Altrincham (1988-1992), also Director of latter club.

Goalkeeper Jeff Wealands was signed (initially on loan) from Birmingham City as cover for Gary Bailey. A safe-handler with good positional sense, he had an interesting career which spanned almost 25 years. He appeared in more than 400 League and Cup games, helped Birmingham win promotion to the First Division in 1980 and six years later returned to St Andrew's, playing his part in a major iant killing act as Altrincham knocked Blues out of the FA Cup. He then helped the non-League side beat Enfield in the FA Trophy Final at Wembley.

Club record: 8 apps.

WEATHER

The hottest weather a United team has played in has been 101 degrees - in the FIFA Club World Championships in Rio de Janeiro, Brazil in January 2000.

When the team visited Australia in 1968, they played in temperatures touching 98 degrees Fahrenheit.

WEBB, Neil John

Born: Reading, Berkshire, 30 July 1963
Career: Reading Schools and junior football, Reading (apprentice summer 1979, professional late 1980), Portsmouth (£87,500, summer 1982), Nottingham Forest (£250,000, summer 1985), MANCHESTER UNITED (£1.5 million, July 1989), Nottingham Forest (£800,000, November 1992), Swindon Town (on loan, autumn 1994), Grimsby Town (non-contract, 1996), Reading Town, Combined Counties League (manager, 2000-01).

Neil Webb was an attacking midfielder with wonderful ball and passing skills who was already an experienced professional by the time he joined United, having amassed almost 400 League and Cup appearances for his three previous clubs. He was only 19 when he moved to Fratton Park and just 22 when Forest's boss Brian Clough enticed him to The City Ground. A month or so after gaining a League Cup winners' medal with Forest in 1989 (scoring in a 3-1 victory over Luton) he moved to Old Trafford but a ruptured Achilles tendon forced to out of action early in the 1989-90 season. He recovered full fitness and at the end of that campaign helped United beat Crystal Palace in the FA Cup Final replay. Unfortunately he missed the following year's European Cup-winners Cup Final win over Barcelona and was substituted as United lost to Sheffield Wednesday in that season's League Cup Final. Nevertheless he earned his place in England's squad for the ill-fated European Championships in Sweden before returning to Forest in the winter of 1992, helping the East Midlands club regain its top flight status in 1994. He quit competitive football in 1996 with well over senior 700 appearances (at club and international level) under his belt (140 goals). His League record was 456 appearances and 114 goals. In fact, he scored on his debut for United in four different competitions: FL, LC, FAC and ECWC.

Capped initially by England as Youth player, Webb represented his country in 26 senior internationals and appeared in three Under-21 games, starred four times for the 'B' team and also played for the Football League side. He is married to Shelley, a sports journalist who appeared in the BBC TV programme 'Standing Room Only.'

Webb's father, Doug, was an inside-forward with Reading during the period: 1955-67. A third generation of footballing Webbs is emerging as Neil's two sons , Luke and Josh are at the Academies of Arsenal and Reading respectively.

Club record: 110 apps. 11 goals

WEBBER, Daniel Vaughn

Born: Manchester, 28 December 1981.
Career: Schoolboy football, MANCHESTER UNITED (trainee, June 1998, professional, January 1999), Port Vale (on loan November-December 2001), Watford (on loan March-May 2002 and August-September 2002).

Danny Webber made his United debut as a substitute, replacing Ronnie Wallwork during a League Cup-tie against Sunderland in November 2000. A very promising striker, he has been capped by England at Youth team level and was the squad for the 2002 summer Under-20 tournament in Toulouse, France.

Club record: 2 apps.

WEBSTER, Colin

Born: Cardiff, 17 July 1932. Died: Swansea, March 2001
Career: Windsor Clive & Ely Schools, Avenue Villa FC (Cardiff), Cardiff Nomads, Cardiff City (amateur 1949, professional summer 1950), MANCHESTER UNITED (May 1952), Swansea Town (£7,500, October 1958), Newport County (£3,500, Easter 1963), Worcester City (summer 1964), Merthyr Tydfil (1965), Portmadoc (season 1965-67).

Colin Webster joined Cardiff as an amateur but following National Service (when he played for the Northern Command side with Dennis Viollet) he was released on a free transfer. Snapped up by fellow Welshman Jimmy Murphy, United's assistant-manager (on Viollet's recommendation) he spent six years at Old Trafford, making his League debut against Portsmouth in November 1953. Robust and aggressive, a good tactician, he had speed, control and could deliver a fine pass as well as strong shot. Fortunately for him he was confined to bed with a bout of 'flu, otherwise he would have been involved in the Munich air crash in 1958!

He did however gain an unwarranted reputation as a dirty player when in effect he was simply a hard, fair competitor who enjoyed a challenge and went in where it hurt most! Webster became the first player since 1946 to have been sent-off four times!

An ideal squad player, adept in all forward positions, Webster was an utterly reliable reserve.

He helped United win the League title in 1956 and two years later was on the left-wing when the Reds lost 2-0 to Bolton in the FA Cup Final.

Capped four times by Wales (his first coming when he was a United reserve and the other three during the World Cup Finals in Sweden in 1958), Webster went on to gain a Welsh Cup winners medal with Swansea (1961). In later life Webster worked as a scaffolder and then as a park ranger in South Wales before his death in Swansea in 2001 after a two-year battle against lung cancer.

Club record 79 apps. 31 goals

WEDGE, Francis Edgar

Born: Dudley, summer 1876.

Career: Manchester Talbot FC, NEWTON HEATH (December 1896-May 1898), Chorlton-cum-Hardy FC (amateur club).

Reserve inside or centre-forward Frank Wedge scored on his League debut for the Heathens in the 1-1 draw with Leicester Fosse in November 1897 and then netted again in his next match, a 2-1 win over Grimsby Town a week later. He left the club at the end of that season and later became a prolific marksman in amateur football.

Club record: 2 apps. 2 goals.

WEIGHT

One of the lightest footballers ever to appear in a senior game for United is Ernie Taylor who tipped the scales at only 10st 2lbs in 1958. Ryan Giggs (initially at 9st 9lbs) and Billy Wrigglesworth (9st 7lbs) have been two other light-weight United forwards.

Of the heavy brigade, Fred Erentz was said to have weighed in at 16 stones when he decided to retire in 1902. Goalkeeper Gary Walsh was almost 15st in weight at one time during his United career (1985-93). Defender Caesar Jenkyns tipped the scales at 14st 4lbs and full-back John McCartney weighed in at 14 stone when they were on Newton Heath's books in the 1890s. Goalkeeper Peter Schmeichel and John Powell (late 1880s) also weighed in at around 14st.

WELLENS, Richard Paul

Born: Manchester, 26 February 1980

Career: MANCHESTER UNITED (professional, May 1997), Blackpool (March 2000)

Midfielder Richard Wellens - with a tigerish tackle - made just one substitute appearance for United, in a League Cup-tie against Aston Villa (away) in October 1999. An England youth international, he left the club for Blackpool but failed to save the Seasiders from relegation. However, he was instrumental a year later as the Bloomfield Road club regained their Second Division status via the Millennium Stadium Play-off Final against Leyton Orient.

Club record: one app.

WELSH CONNECTION

Here is a list of United personnel (players at various levels, managers, coaches etc) who have been associated with Welsh League clubs (not including Football League clubs - see separate cataegories):

Arthur Allman	Aberaman	David Jones	Chirk
Neil Bailey	Newport County (player)	Owen Jones	Bangor
Tom Bamford	Cardiff Wednesday, Bridgend Town	Tom Jones	Druids, Acrefair, Chirk (WW2)
Frank Barson	Rhyl Athletic (player-manager)	Tommy Jones	Mid-Rhondda
George Beel	Merthyr Town (United reserve)	Harry Lappin	Chirk
George Bissett	Pontypridd	Thomas H Lewis	Connah's Quay, Rhyl (United trialist)
Jimmy Broad	Caernarfon Town (United reserve)	David Lyner	Mid-Rhondda
Albert Broome	Welshpool	Ken MacDonald	Caerau
Ted Buckle	Prestatyn Town (manager), Dolgellau	Alan Mallalieu	Rhyl
Jimmy Bullock	Llanelli	Kenny Morgans	Cwmbran Town (manager)
Tom Burke	Wrexham Victoria, Wrexham Olympic	Walter Moyle	Barry Town, Merthyr Town (United reserve)
William Carrier	Merthyr Town	George Owen	Chirk, Druids
Jonathan Clark	Rhyl	John Owen	Chirk
Sam Cookson	Bargoed Town	Albert Pape	Rhyl Athletic
Charlie Crossley	Ebbw Vale (United WW1)	Ted Partridge	Ebbw Vale
Stan Cubberley	Swansea Town	Jack Powell	Druids
Joe Davies	Druids	Bill Pendergast	Rhyl (United reserve)
Wyn Davies	Caernarfon Town, Bangor City	Kevin Pilkington	Aberystwyth Town
Amos Dee	Merthyr Town	Jimmy Pugh	Abertillery
Mark Delaney	Carmarthen	Tommy Reid	Rhyl Athletic
John Doughty	Druids	William Sarvis	Merthyr Town
Horace Drew	Druids	Peter Sutcliffe	Bangor
Sid Evans	Pontypridd	Eric Sweeney	Flint Town
Billy Fairhurst	Rhyl Athletic (United WW2)	Harry Thomas	Merthyr Town, Abercarn, Porth FC
Danny Ferguson	Rhyl	Mickey Thomas	Conwy United, Inter Cardiff, Portmadoc (manager)
Tom Frame	Rhyl		
Haydn Green	Ebbw Vale (manager), Bangor City (manager)	Sid Tyler	Colwyn Bay United
Johnny Hanlon	Rhyl	Robert Ward	Rhyl Athletic (United reserve)
Harry Haslam	Barry Town (manager)	Jack Warner	Aberaman
Ted Hudson	Aberdare	Colin Webster	Merthyr Tydfil, Portmadoc, Cardiff Nomads
Bill Hullett	Merthyr Tydfil (United reserve)	Tony Young	Bangor City
Reg Hunter	Colwyn Bay, Bangor City	* Jackson had three separate spells with Flint.	
Bill Jackson	Flint Town*, Rhyl		

Dragon Talk

The first player to leave Wales to become a professional in the Football League is believed to have been Jack Powell, who left the Druids for Bolton Wanderers in October 1883, signing 'pro' forms two years later. He moved to Newton Heath in 1886. Mickey Thomas was capped by Wales at senior level when with seven different Football League clubs.

WEMBLEY STADIUM

United's playing record at the Empire Stadium:

Competition	P	W	D	L	F	A
FA Cup Finals	16	9	2	5	30	18
FA Cup semi-final	1	0	1	0	1	1
League Cup Finals	4	1	0	3	3	6
Charity Shield	11	3	4*	4	11	12
European Cup Final	1	1	0	0	4	1
Totals	33	14	7	12	49	38

* Two of these four Charity Shield games went to penalty shoot-outs (United winning both) while after the other two games each club retained the trophy for six months.

Wembley Fact File

United had to wait 25 years from the stadium opening to make their first ever appearance at The Empire Stadium, doing so in the 1948 FA Cup Final. They have certainly made up for that long wait since then!

Denis Law scored goals past Gordon Banks at Wembley on four different occasions in three separate competitions. He netted for United in the 1963 FA Cup Final v. Leicester City, for Scotland v. England in the home internationals of 1965 and 1967 and for the Rest of the World versus England in 1963.

United played at Wembley four times in 1993-94 - in the FA Charity Shield, the League Cup Final and the FA Cup semi-final and Final.

The Reds also played at the Empire Stadium on four occasions in the 1983 calendar year: League Cup Final, FA Cup Final and replay and FA Charity Shield.

WEST, Enoch James

Born: Hucknall Torkard, Nottinghamshire, 31 March 1886. Died: Manchester, circa 1970
Career: Sheffield United (late 1900), Hucknall Constitutionals (1904), Nottingham Forest (summer 1905), MANCHESTER UNITED (June 1910). Suspended sine die, from December 1915.

Enoch 'Knocker' West scored a century of goals in 169 League and 15 Cup games for Nottingham Forest before joining United. He helped the East Midland club win the Second Division championship in 1907 and was one of a trio of Forest players who scored hat-tricks in that joint record First Division win of 12-0 over Leicester Fosse in April 1909. Powerful in all aspects of forward play, he replaced Jimmy Turnbull in United's attack and netted 20 goals in 38 senior games in his first season with the club, gaining a League Championship medal in the process. He finished up as leading marksman in the next two campaigns. In April 1915 he was involved in a plot to 'fix' the result of the United v. Liverpool League game (a betting 'scam' on the 2-0 scoreline). As a result he was suspended for life (with seven other players). West's was the longest ban in football at that time. It was eventually lifted when he was approaching his 60th birthday - in November 1945 - after almost 30 years, having always protested his innocence. West played for the Football League v. the Southern League in 1912 - his only representative honour. He was also a fine billiards player...and could well have become a professional in that field.
Club record: 181 apps. 80 goals

WEST, James

James West was Newton Heath's second full-time secretary; there was still no 'football Manager' so it was the secretary who ran the club, lock, stock and barrel.

West took over in 1900 as A H Albut retired, overseeing the club's demise in 1902, to re-appear as 'Manchester United FC.' After just one season as 'United' Mr J Ernest Mangnall was appointed the club's first 'Secretary-Manager', West taking a back seat, joining forces with ex-skipper Harry Stafford (q.v) in organising the day-to-day running of the club itself.

In 1904 James West applied to the City Magistrates for a licence to sell drinks at the Bank Street ground; unfortunately for West (and Manchester United who lost a crucial source of income) the application was refused. He was later suspended from all aspects of professional football by the FA for making illegal payments to players.

WEST BROMWICH ALBION

Summary of League results

	P	W	D	L	F	A
Division 1	92	36	22	34	166	154
Division 2	8	3	2	3	8	9
Home	50	26	13	11	102	65
Away	50	13	11	26	72	98
Total	100	39	24	37	174	163

FA Cup results v Albion:

	Round	Venue	Result
1938-39	3	Away	D 0-0
	Replay	Home	L 1-5
1957-58	6	Away	D 2-2
	Replay	Home	W 1-0
1977-78	4	Home	D 1-1
	Replay	Away	L 2-3 aet

Heathens/United's League results v Albion:

Season	Div	Home	Away	Season	Div	Home	Away
1892-93	1	L 2-4	D 0-0	1957-58	1	L 0-4	L 3-4
1893-94	1	W 4-1	L 1-3	1958-59	1	L 1-2	W 3-1
				1959-60	1	L 2-3	L 2-3
1901-02	2	L 1-2	L 0-4	1960-61	1	W 3-0	D 1-1
				1961-62	1	W 4-1	D 1-1
1904-05	2	W 2-0	W 2-0	1962-63	1	D 2-2	L 0-3
1905-06	2	D 0-0	L 0-1	1963-64	1	W 1-0	W 4-1
				1964-65	1	D 2-2	D 1-1
1911-12	1	L 1-2	L 0-1	1965-66	1	D 1-1	D 3-3
1912-13	1	D 1-1	W 2-1	1966-67	1	W 5-3	W 4-3
1913-14	1	W 1-0	L 1-2	1967-68	1	W 2-1	L 3-6
1914-15	1	D 0-0	D 0-0	1968-69	1	W 2-1	L 1-3
				1969-70	1	W 7-0	L 1-2
1919-20	1	L 1-2	L 1-2	1970-71	1	W 2-1	L 3-4
1920-21	1	L 1-4	W 2-0	1971-72	1	W 3-1 *	L 1-2
1921-22	1	L 2-3	D 0-0	1972-73	1	W 2-1	D 2-2
1925-26	1	W 3-2	L 1-5	1974-75	2	W 2-1	D 1-1
1926-27	1	W 2-0	D 2-2				
				1976-77	1	D 2-2	L 0-4
1936-37	1	D 2-2	L 0-1	1977-78	1	D 1-1	L 0-4
				1978-79	1	L 3-5	L 0-1
1949-50	1	D 1-1	W 2-1	1979-80	1	W 2-0	L 0-2
1950-51	1	W 3-0	W 1-0	1980-81	1	W 2-1	L 1-3
1951-52	1	W 5-1	D 3-3	1981-82	1	W 1-0	W 3-0
1952-53	1	D 2-2	L 1-3	1982-83	1	D 0-0	L 1-3
1953-54	1	L 1-3	L 0-2	1983-84	1	W 3-0	L 0-2
1954-55	1	W 3-0	L 0-2	1984-85	1	W 2-0	W 2-1
1955-56	1	W 3-1	W 4-1	1985-86	1	W 3-0	W 5-1
1956-57	1	D 1-1	W 3-2				

* Played at The Victoria Ground (Stoke).

Fact File

Amongst the most memorable matches between the two clubs were the two dramatic 6th round FA Cup clashes in 1958 after the tragedy of Munich. Drawn at The Hawthorns, Albion were clear favourites to win, having already beaten United 4-3 in a thrilling League game on the same ground earlier in the season (when Tommy Taylor netted with two brilliant headers). Yet somehow the patched-up United side with Bobby Charlton playing his first match since the crash, earned a 2-2 draw, the 'Baggies' equalizing in the dying minutes. At Old Trafford the gates were locked an hour before kick-off and those present saw Colin Wenster's sensational goal in stoppage time put United in the semi-finals against all the odds. The 20,000 who coulddn't get into the ground listended to a radio commentary outside! A few days later Albion returned to Old Trafford and beat United 4-0 in the return League game.

Between 1960-61 and 1985-86 United played WBA 24 times at Old Trafford, losing just once, a sensational 5-3 scoreline in 1978-79. Jesper Olsen scored all United's goals when they completed the double over Albion with a 3-0 home win in February 1986 - having raced to an emphatic 5-1 victory at The Hawthorns earlier in the season.

Players with both clubs include: A Alliston, M Appleton, J Banks, P Barnes, H Boyd, W Boyes (United WW2), P Bradshaw (United trialist), A Comyn (United 'A' team), G Crooks, S Crowther (Albion amateur), L Cunningham, J Davies (Albion reserve), SC Davies (United trialist), A Fitton (also Albion trainer), J Giles, A Goram (Albion reserve), J Griffiths (Albion WW2), G Hogg, J Holton (Albion reserve), M Martin, R Moses, R Newsome (United WW2), J Nicholl, J Pennington (United WW1), M Phelan, W Richards, B Robson, A Rowley (United WW2), M Setters, A Smith (United reserve), J Stanton (Heath reserve), M Thomas, R Wallwork. Also associated: R Atkinson (manager of both clubs), N Stiles (United player & coach, Albion assistant-manager & manager), J Murphy (Albion player, United assistant-manager & caretaker-manager), SJ Pearson (United player, Albion assistant-manager & caretaker-manager), M Brown (assistant-manager/coach at both clubs), B Whitehouse (Albion player, United coach & scout), T Jones (United player, Albion trainer/physio), A Ashman (Albion manager, United scout), G Timmins (Albion player/United trainer).

WEST HAM UNITED

United's League results v the Hammers:

Season	Div	Home	Away	Season	Div	Home	Away
1922-23	2	L 1-2	W 2-0	1970-71	1	D 1-1	L 1-2
				1971-72	1	W 4-2	L 0-3
1925-26	1	W 2-1	L 0-1	1972-73	1	D 2-2	D 2-2
1926-27	1	L 0-3	L 0-4	1973-74	1	W 3-1	L 1-2
1927-28	1	D 1-1	W 2-1				
1928-29	1	L 2-3	L 1-3	1975-76	1	W 4-0	L 1-2
1929-30	1	W 4-2	L 1-2	1976-77	1	L 0-2	L 2-4
1930-31	1	W 1-0	L 1-5	1977-78	1	W 3-0	L 1-2
1932-33	2	L 1-2	L 1-3	1981-82	1	W 1-0	D 1-1
1933-34	2	L 0-1	L 1-2	1982-83	1	W 2-1	L 1-3
1934-35	2	W 3-1	D 0-0	1983-84	1	D 0-0	D 1-1
1935-36	2	L 2-3	W 2-1	1984-85	1	W 5-1	D 2-2
				1985-86	1	W 2-0	L 1-2
1937-38	2	W 4-0	L 0-1	1986-87	1	L 2-3	D 0-0
				1987-88	1	W 3-1	D 1-1
1958-59	1	W 4-1	L 2-3	1988-89	1	W 2-0	W 3-1
1959-60	1	W 5-3	L 1-2				
1960-61	1	W 6-1	L 1-2	1991-92	1	W 2-1	L 0-1
1961-62	1	L 1-2	D 1-1				
1962-63	1	W 3-1	L 1-3	1993-94	PL	W 3-0	D 2-2
1963-64	1	L 0-1	W 2-0	1994-95	PL	W 1-0	D 1-1
1964-65	1	W 3-1	L 1-3	1995-96	PL	W 2-1	W 1-0
1965-66	1	D 0-0	L 2-3	1996-97	PL	W 2-0	D 2-2
1966-67	1	W 3-0	W 6-1	1997-98	PL	W 2-1	D 1-1
1967-68	1	W 3-1	W 3-1	1998-99	PL	W 4-1	D 0-0
1968-69	1	D 1-1	D 0-0	1999-00	PL	W 7-1	W 4-2
1969-70	1	W 5-2	D 0-0	2000-01	PL	W 3-1	D 2-2
				2001-02	PL	L 0-1	W 5-3

Summary of League results

	P	W	D	L	F	A
Premier League	18	11	6	1	42	19
Division 1	68	27	15	26	123	103
Division 2	12	4	1	7	17	16
Home	49	32	6	11	115	54
Away	49	10	16	23	67	84
Total	98	42	22	34	182	138

FA Cup results v the Hammers:

	Round	Venue	Result
1910-11	3	Away	L 1-2
1963-64	SF	Hillsborough	L 1-3
1982-83	3	Home	W 2-0
1984-85	6	Home	W 4-2
1985-86	5	Away	D 1-1
	R	Home	L 0-2
2000-01	4	Home	L 0-1

League Cup result v the Hammers:

	Round	Venue	Result
1985-86	3	Home	W 1-0

Fact File

From 1987-88 to 2000-01 United won all eleven League matches at Old Trafford against West Ham.

On the other hand between 1968-69 and 1987-88 United played 16 matches at Upton Park without a win (8 draws, 8 defeats).

West ham enjoy nothing better than denying United...in 1991-92 with United and Leeds neck and neck for the title, the Hammers, already doomed to relegation, played the game of their lives to beat United 1-0, thus allowing Leeds to snatch the crown.

Then in 1994-95, United again visited Upton Park on the season's last day, two points adrift of Blackburn Rovers who visited Liverpool. United laid siege to the Hammers' goal throughout the second-half as the score stood at 1-1, but the home side's heroic resistance denied United time and again. So although Blackburn lost at Anfield (their supporters weeping at seemingly missing out on the Premiership title) suddenly it all changed as United's result was announced, Blackburn taking the title by a single point, as West Ham's fans 200 miles away celebrated as though they had won the League title themselves.

United have been drawn against West Ham six times in the FA Cup, winning only twice, yet both times United went on to win the trophy.

Players with both clubs include: D Brazil (WHU trialist), N Cantwell, J Copeland (Man Utd reserve), C Crossley (Man Utd WW1), G Crowther (Man Utd reserve), J Dow, J Dyer, R Ferdinand, G Gladwin (WHU WW2), W Grassam, P Ince, E Lewis, W McCartney, J McCrae, E MacDougall, C Mackie, R Milne, SJ Pearson, E Savage (WHU WW2), L Sealey (Hammers player & coach), W Stewart (Thames Ironworks), FH Milnes (Man Utd reserve)., R Van der Gouw, HG Williams (Man Utd reserve). Also associated: F O'Farrell & D Sexton (Hammers players, Man Utd managers), L Macari (Man Utd player, Hammers manager), M Musgrove (Hammers player, Man Utd assistant-manager/coach).

WEST MANCHESTER

This club played at Brook's Bar, about a mile from where Old Trafford stands today.
Newton Heath defeated their local rivals West Manchester 7-0 in the 3rd qualifying round of the FA Cup at their Bank Street ground in 1896-97. Cassidy, Gillespie and Rothwell each scored twice in front of 6,000 spectators.

WETHERELL, Joseph

Born: Oswaldtwistle, winter 1872
Career: NEWTON HEATH (season 1896-97)
Local-born goalkeeper Joe Wetherell made two League appearances for United, replacing Joe Ridgway who was out of action with a shoulder injury..
Club record: 2 apps.

WEYMOUTH

Weymouth, known as the 'Terras' due to their distinctive coloured shirts, visited Old Trafford for a 3rd round FA Cup-tie in January 1950. After a plucky fight, in front of 38,284 spectators, they finally succumbed 4-0 with United's Jack Rowley hitting two of his side's goals.
Player with both clubs: W Boyd.

WHALLEY, Arthur

Born: Rainford, near Prescot, 17 February 1886. Died: Wythenshawe, Manchester, 23 November 1952.
Career: Brynn Central FC (Wigan junior club), Blackpool (season 1908-09), MANCHESTER UNITED (£50, June 1909), Army football (Middlesex Regiment), Clapton Orient (WW1 guest), Southend United (£1,000, September 1920), Charlton Athletic (1921-24), Millwall (1924-26), Barrow (player/trainer-coach, later 1926 to1927).
Powerful centre-half (or wing-half) Arthur Whalley helped United win the First Division title in 1911. He remained a regular in the side until a knee injury severely disrupted his performances in 1914 - soon after appearing in an international trial match for England (North v. the South). A year earlier he had represented the Football League against the Irish League. He was caught up in the sensational betting scandal in 1915 (with Enoch West, q.v) but only received a short ban (plus a caution)reappearing in the first post-war seasons. He made almost 150 more senior appearances after leaving United (98 with Charlton). A Sergeant in the Army, he was seriously wounded at Passchendale but recovered full fitness to play on until he was over 40 years of age (his last League game was for Barrow in 1927). He later became a Manchester-based bookmaker's clerk and also changed his name to Arthur Booth. He suffered a tragic accidental death when his bedding caught fire at his home.
Club record: 106 apps. 6 goals

WHALLEY, Herbert

Born: Ashton-under-Lyne, 6 August 1912. Died: Munich, 6 February 1958
Career: Ferguson & Pailins FC, Stalybridge Celtic (late 1933), Stockport County (briefly - transfer not sanctioned), MANCHESTER UNITED (May 1934), guested for Bolton Wanderers, Liverpool & Oldham Athletic during WW2; re-engaged by UNITED (April 1946) as a coach after playing career cut short by an eye injury.
Bert Whalley was a very competent half-back whose career carried on during WW2 when he made a further 188 appearances for the club. Along with Tom Curry and Bill Inglis, he helped in the development of so many talented footballers at Old Trafford during the late 1940s, early '50s before sadly losing his life in the Munich air crash (when he took the flight in place of Jimmy Murphy).
Club record: 39 apps.

WHELAN, Anthony Gerard

Born: Dublin, 23 November 1959
Career: Bohemians (1976-80), MANCHESTER UNITED (£30,000, August 1980), Shamrock Rovers (July 1983), Manchester City (on loan), Rochdale (on loan), Fort Lauderdale Strikers (NASL), Atlanta Chiefs (NASL), Cork, Shelbourne, Shamrock Rovers, Bray Wanderers, Shelbourne, retired 1995.
Full-back 'Anto' Whelan made just one substitute League appearance for United, coming on for central defender and fellow countryman Kevin Moran against Southampton at Old Trafford in November 1980. Capped by the Republic of Ireland at Under-21 level v. England in 1981, he later made over 200 senior appearances in Irish League football
Club record: one app.

WHELAN, Liam Augustine

Born: Dublin, 1 April 1935. Died: Munich, 6 February 1958
Career: Home Farm FC (Dublin), MANCHESTER UNITED (professional, May 1953 until his death).
Inside-forward Liam 'Billy' Whelan scored on average a goal every two games for United. He scored in eight successive League games during September/October 1956 - a club record that stood for almost 46 years until equalled by Ruud van Nistelrooy in 2001-02. Although appearing slow and cumbersome when running, his speed of thought and reflexes were lightning sharp. A quiet, introspective young player, he needed convincing of his real worth.
Tremendous on-the-ball, he had a terrific engine and was running as hard at the end of the game as he was at the start. He got United going in midfield - as well as assisting prominently in attack. He was coolness itself near goal, his finishing

clinical even in the tightest of situations. His best season was in 1956-57 when he scored 33 goals (26 in the League).

A real ball-artist, he made his United League debut against PNE in March 1955 and his presence in the side the following season went a long way in helping the Reds win the First Division title in successive seasons, able to score and make goals with equal facility. He scored twice when United destroyed RSC Anderlecht 10-0 in their first home European Cup game, starring when - according to Matt Busby - the team gave one the 'purest, most flawless exhibitions of football' he had ever seen.

Whelan was the only non-Englishman in the side, several newspapers suggesting the United side be picked en-bloc for England! Whelan also played in the 1957 FA Cup Final defeat by Aston Villa and was capped four times by the Republic of Ireland at full international level.

When United's Youth team participated in the Youth tournament in Switzerland prior to the 1954 World Cup Finals, the watching Brazilians were so impressed by Whelan, they wanted to take him back with them to Rio, such was his skill! Unfortunately, although he was not in United's first XI at the time of the Munich tragedy (having lost his place to Bobby Charlton), he travelled with the party and sadly one of United's greatest ever players lost his life!

Club record: 98 apps. 52 goals

WHITEFOOT, Jeffrey

Born: Cheadle, Cheshire, 31 December 1933.

Career: Stockport & District Schools, MANCHESTER UNITED (junior, 1950, professional January 1951), Grimsby Town (November 1957), Nottingham Forest (summer 1958; retired 1968 through injury). Served in the RAF (1951-52). Later became a publican.

Jeff Whitefoot was only 16 years, 105 days old when he made his League debut for United against the reigning champions Portsmouth at Old Trafford on 14 April 1950....making him the youngest player ever to serve the club at senior level. Capped by England at Schoolboy level, and later by the Under-23s (v. Italy) wing-half Whitefoot gained a regular place in the first XI during the 1953-54 campaign and two years later collected a League Championship winning medal before losing his place to Eddie Colman. After a season at Blundell Park, he went on to appear in 285 League and Cup games for Nottingham Forest, helping Billy Walker's side win the 1959 FA Cup Final (v. Luton Town).

Club record: 95 apps.

WHITEHOUSE, James C

Born: Birmingham, 9 April 1873. Died: Birmingham, 7 February 1934.

Career: Albion Swifts, Birmingham St George's, Grimsby Town (1892), Aston Villa (£200, 1896), Bedminster (1898), Grimsby Town (1899), NEWTON HEATH/MANCHESTER UNITED (September 1900), Manchester City (February 1903), Third Lanark (September 1903), Hull City (July 1904), Southend United (seasons 1905-07).

A well built 'keeper, Jimmy Whitehouse was described as being 'a clean handler and reliable last line of defence' and in an emergency he also proved to be an above average inside-forward! A League and FA Cup 'double' winner with Villa in season 1896-97, he made 160 appearances in his two spells with Grimsby and in fact prior to joining the Heathens had already played in over 200 League & Cup games.

Club record: 64 apps. (also 13 'other' apps)

WHITEHURST, Walter

Born: Manchester, 7 June 1934.

Career: Ryder Brow Boys' Club, MANCHESTER UNITED (amateur, August 1950, professional May 1952), Chesterfield (November 1956), Crewe Alexandra (1960), Macclesfield Town, Chorley (1961-62).

Walter Whitehurst made only one League appearance for United, but made almost 100 in League and Cup for Chesterfield. Reserve to the likes of Colman and Whitefoot at Old Trafford, on moving to Saltergate he linked up again with several former United players.

Club record: one app.

WHITESIDE, Kerr D

Born: Scotland, 1887.

Career: Irvine Victoria FC, MANCHESTER UNITED (May 1907), Hurst FC (August 1910). Retired 1915.

A Scottish junior international (1905), wing-half Kerr Whiteside was a United reserve for three seasons, receiving only one first team call-up - for the League game against Sheffield United at Bramall Lane in January 1908. He became a popular captain of Hurst FC.

Club record: one app.

WHITESIDE, Norman

Refer to front of section.

WHITNEY, John Henry

Born: Newton Heath, spring 1874
Career: NEWTON HEATH (October 1895 to May 1896), non-League football (1896-1900... registration retained by club), NEWTON HEATH (August 1900 to May 1901).
Half-back/defender John Whitney had two spells with the club. A reserve all the while, he was sidelined with an injury for the majority of his first season at Clayton and played in only two games when he returned to the club for his second spell.
Club record: 3 apps.

WHITTAKER, Walter

Born: Manchester, 20 September 1878. Died: Swansea, 2 June 1917.
Career: Molyneaux FC, Buxton, NEWTON HEATH (February 1896), Fairfield FC (during season 1896-97), Grimsby Town (May 1897), Reading (1898), Blackburn Rovers (1900), Grimsby Town (1901), Derby County (1903), Brentford (1904), Reading (1906), Clapton Orient (1907), Exeter City (1910), Swansea Town (player-manager, 1912), Llanelli (also player-manager, June-November 1914).
Reserve goalkeeper Walter Whittaker deputised for Joe Ridgway during the closing stages of the 1895-96 season. making his debut against his future club, Grimsby Town. Certainly a player allowed to slip through the net by the Heathens, Whittaker went on to appear in well over 450 league and Cup games during his career, helping Blackburn win the Lancashire Cup in 1901. He died of pneumonia.
Club record: 3 apps. (also 3 'other' apps)

WHITTLE, John T

Born: Leigh, Lancashire, circa 1912
Career: Hindsford FC (Lancashire Alliance), MANCHESTER UNITED (amateur October, professional December 1919), Rossendale United (July 1932), Fleetwood, Hindsford FC (re-instated as an amateur, 1933-34).
John Whittle, a reserve left-winger, was given just one League outing by United, against Swansea Town (away) in January 1924 in place of Stanley Gallimore.
Club record: one app.

WHITWORTH, Neil Anthony

Born: Wigan, 12 April 1972
Career: Wigan Schools, Greater Manchester Schools, Wigan Athletic (trainee 1988-90), MANCHESTER UNITED (£45,000, June 1900), Preston North End (on loan, January 1992), Barnsley (on loan, February 1992), Rotherham United (on loan, August 1993), Blackpool (on loan, December 1993), Kilmarnock (£265,000, September 1994), Wigan Athletic (free transfer, early 1998), Hull City (free transfer summer 1998), Exeter City free transfer summer 2001).
A central defender, Neil Whitworth (the son of a former Rugby League player with Leigh RFC) made one League appearance for United, lining up against Southampton at The Dell in March 1991 at right-back. He spent seven full years in League football (1991-98) but made only 35 appearances in total.
Club record: one app.

WIDZEW LODZ

United went out of the UEFA Cup competition in the first round in 1980-81 to 'Lodz', beaten on the away goal rule. They were held 1-1 at Old Trafford and 0-0 in Poland.

WILCOX, Thomas Walter J

Born: On board the four-masted barque, the 'Grassendale' en-route to America, 1879. His birth was officially registered at St Stephens', Stepney, London in 1881 when he returned from the States. Died: Blackpool, September 1962.
Career: Millwall Athletic (reserve), Cray Wanderers (Ireland), Woolwich Arsenal (reserve), Norwich City (autumn 1905), Blackpool (1906-07 season), MANCHESTER UNITED (August 1907), Carlisle United (July 1909), Goole Town (summer 1912), Abergavenny FC (Wales).
Goalkeeper Tom Wilcox, the son of a sea captain, lined up in League games against Nottingham Forest (h) and Sheffield Wednesday (a) during the 1908-09 season when Harry Moger was absent. As a squad member he was rewarded with a special gold medal when United won their first League title in 1908.
Whilst in the USA (before the turn of the 20th century) he won the World Punchball Championship - putting him in good stead for his goalkeeping duties which were to follow later.
Whilst registered with United, Wilcox worked for the Zonophone Gramophone Company and after leaving the club he helped Carlisle win the local Cumbria Cup. He served with The Royal Welsh Fusiliers during WW1 and after the hostilities he ran two successful tobacconists' shops in Preston until 1938. He retired to Blackpool where he died at the age of 83.
Club record: 2 apps.

341

WILKINS, Raymond Colin, MBE

Born: Hillingdon, Middlesex, 14 September 1956
Career: Middlesex Schools, London Schools, Chelsea (apprentice 1971, professional 1973), MANCHESTER UNITED (£825,000, August 1979), AC Milan (£1.5 million, June 1984), Paris St Germain (summer 1987), Glasgow Rangers (winter 1987), Queen's Park Rangers (late 1989), Crystal Palace (summer 1994), Queen's Park Rangers (non-contract player 1994-96, then player-manager, briefly), Wycombe Wanderers (free transfer, 1996), Hibernian (free transfer), Millwall (free transfer), Leyton Orient (non-contract, early 1997), Chelsea (assistant-manager, 1998-2001), Watford (assistant-manager, summer 2001).

Ray Wilkins retired as a player in 1997 with more than 900 club and international appearances under his belt - 608 in the Football League alone. He scored more than 60 goals. Winner of 84 full England caps, he also represented his country at Schoolboy, Youth, Under-21 and Under-23 levels and was an FA Cup winner with United in 1983, scoring a superb goal in the first match against Brighton, and a Scottish Premiership and Skol League Cup winner with Rangers in 1988-89

A midfield play-maker, with superb passing ability, 'Butch' Wilkins was Chelsea's youngest-ever captain at the age of 18, leading the Blues to promotion from Division Two in 1976. He rejoined his former boss Dave Sexton at Old Trafford and went on to give United five seasons excellent service when he teamed up with initially his fellow England colleague Bryan Robson, Sammy McIlroy and the Dutchman Arnold Muhren before leaving to play in Italy. He was awarded the CBE in the Queen's Birthday Honours List in June 1993 for his services to the game of football.

Wilkins came from a footballing family, George, his father, playing for several League clubs in post-war football, whilst brothers Graham and Dean also enjoyed League careers.
Club record: 194 apps. 10 goals

WILKINSON, Henry

Born: Bury, 1883.
Career: St John's Sunday School (Bury), Newton Heath Athletic (in season 1902-03), MANCHESTER UNITED (amateur October, professional December 1903), Hull City (July 1904), West Ham United (May 1905), MANCHESTER UNITED (March 1906), Haslingden (June 1906), St Helens Recreationalists (Easter 1907), Bury (mid-1907), Oswaldtwistle Rovers (1908), Rochdale (late 1908).

Former iron factory worker Harry 'Snowball' Wilkinson, who was also an accomplished athlete (often taking part in sprint and quarter-mile races) joined United with Dick Duckworth. A short, stocky footballer, his best position was outside-left, where he played in eight League and one FA Cup-tie games between late December 1903 and mid-March 1904 in place of regular winger Dick Wombwell.
Club record: 9 apps.

WILKINSON, Ian Matthew

Born: Warrington, 2 July 1973
Career: MANCHESTER UNITED (trainee, June 1989, professional May 1991), Stockport County (non-contract, July 1993), Crewe Alexandra (autumn 1993-94).

Goalkeeper Ian Wilkinson was called up for first-team action just once by Alex Ferguson - for the League Cup encounter against Cambridge United in October 1991. He made just three League appearances for Crewe.
Club record: one app.

WILLEM II

After a European Cup-winners Cup 1st round, 1st leg 1-1 draw in Holland against Willem II, Denis Law scored a hat-trick as United turned the screw at Old Trafford to race to a comfortable 6-1 second leg victory.
Player with both clubs: J Stam

WILLIAMS, David Rees

Born: Abercanaid, near Merthyr Tydfil, 1900. Died: Abercanaid, 30 December 1963
Career: Pentrebach FC (near Merthyr), Merthyr Town (1919-22), Sheffield Wednesday (£1,000, 1922-27), MANCHESTER UNITED (signed, October 1927), Thames AFC (August 1929), Merthyr Town (1931-33), Glenavon (1933-34), Hoover FC (coach).

A Welsh Schoolboy international, winger Rees Williams had already appeared in 228 League games and gained six full caps for his country before joining United. Happy on either flank, he took over on the right from Billy Meredith for Wales and did well in his early internationals, prompting several leading clubs to run the rule over his ability to take on and beat defenders on the outside. United, Aston Villa and Sunderland all wanted to sign him but he decided to join Sheffield Wednesday whom he helped win the First Division title in 1927. He gave the Owls five years' excellent service before switching to Old Trafford. A trickster, he failed to produce the goods with United, losing his place on the right to Joe Spence in his first season and then to fellow countryman Harry Thomas on the left in his second, although he did win a further two caps. Williams once clocked 10.2 seconds for the 100 yards

Williams, whose parents kept a public house in Merthyr called the 'Rhysi' Tavern, committed suicide, aged 63, after being worried about his health after retiring from work at the Hoover factory in Merthyr.

Club record: 35 apps. 2 goals

WILLIAMS, Frank H

Born: Kearsley, Lancashire, 1908.

Career: Stalybridge Celtic, MANCHESTER UNITED (amateur trialist, April 1927), Stalybridge Celtic (June 1927), MANCHESTER UNITED (professional, May 1928 - re-instated as an amateur, September 1929), Altrincham (August 1931).

Reserve half-back Frank Williams deputised for Ray Bennion in each of the three League games he took part in during the 1930-31 season when United conceded 13 goals in losing 7-4 to Newcastle and 3-0 to both Huddersfield Town and Sheffield Wednesday in the space of eight days.

Club record: 3 apps.

WILLIAMS, Frederick

Born: Manchester, circa 1874

Career: Hanley Swifts, South Shore FC (Blackpool), Manchester City (winter 1896), MANCHESTER UNITED (June 1902 to May 1903).

Before joining United, well-built inside-forward Fred Williams made 124 League appearances for Manchester City, helping the win the Second Division Championship in 1899. All his four goals in United's colours were scored in the FA Cup, including a hat-trick in a 7-0 win over Accrington Stanley in November 1902 while partnering Daniel Hurst on the left-wing.

Club record: 10 apps. 4 goals

WILLIAMS, Harry

Born: Hucknall Torkard, Nottinghamshire, 1899.

Career: Hucknall Olympic FC, Sunderland (amateur then professional, 1920), Chesterfield (season 1921-22), MANCHESTER UNITED (May 1922), Brentford (September 1923 to May 1925).

Harry Williams scored for Chesterfield in their first League game at Saltergate v. Stalybridge Celtic in September 1921. He did well during his early months at Old Trafford but after losing his place in the side following the emergence of Joe Myerscough and Ernie Goldthorpe, he was placed on the transfer list and eventually moved south to Brentford.

Club record: 5 apps. 2 goals

WILLIAMS, Henry

Born: Farnworth, near Bolton, Lancashire, 1883.

Career: Bolton Sunday School League football, Walkden St Mary's (Manchester), Turton FC, NEWTON HEATH (briefly as an amateur, season 1899-1900), Bury (amateur, summer 1900), Bolton Wanderers (winter 1901), Burnley (summer 1903), MANCHESTER UNITED (May 1904), Leeds City (August 1908).

A well-proportioned winger, 'Harry' Williams was Burnley's joint leading scorer before joining United. (second time round). Scoring on his debut for the club against Bristol City in September 1904, he did reasonably well on the left flank before losing his place to new signing Dick Wombwell. He failed to make the first team with Leeds.

Club record: 36 apps. 8 goals

WILLIAMS, Joseph

Born: Cheshire circa 1883

Career: Macclesfield FC, MANCHESTER UNITED (November 1905 to May 1907).

Reserve inside-right Joe Williams - partnering Billy Meredith - scored on his League debut for United in a 2-0 home win over Sunderland in March 1907 when he deputised for Jack Picken. A year earlier had had scored a hat-trick for United's reserve side against Stalybridge Rovers. He was released on a free transfer at the end of the 1906-07 season.

Club record: 3 apps. one goal

WILLIAMS, William

Born: Lancashire, circa 1873

Career: Everton (early 1894), Blackburn Rovers (1898), Bristol Rovers (season 1900-01), NEWTON HEATH (August 1901-May 1902), Bristol Rovers (1902-03).

Reserve forward Bill Williams had four outings in United's League side - three at inside-right and one on the right-wing - during the first two months of the 1901-02 season. He netted five times in 24 games for Everton and followed up one strike in 31 outings for Blackburn and netted five times in 17 appearances for Bristol Rovers including a hat-trick in a 15-1 FA Cup win over Weymouth. Williams represented the Football League v. Irish League as an Everton player.

Club record: 4 apps. (also one 'other' app)

WILLIAMSON, John

Born: Manchester, circa 1892

Career: Wartime football (France) with Manchester Pals' Regiment, also guest appearances for St Mirren (1917-18), Ancoats Lads' Club, MANCHESTER UNITED (trialist, September 1919, professional October 1919), Bury (May 1921), Crewe Alexandra (season 1922-23), later with British Dyestuffs FC (as an amateur, 1927-28).

Reserve half-back John Williamson made his two League appearances for United in April 1920 against the same club, Blackburn Rovers - replacing the injured John Grimwood. He won a Central League championship medal in 1920-21 before moving to Gigg Lane.

Williamson's son, John junior, born in Newton Heath, played as an amateur for Oldham Athletic and a professional with both Blackburn Rovers and Manchester City.

Club record: 2 apps.

WILSON, David Graham

Born: Burnley, 10 March 1969

Career: Todmorden High School, Calderdale Schools, Yorkshire Schools, MANCHESTER UNITED (apprentice June 1985, professional March 1997), Lincoln City (on loan, October-November 1990), Charlton Athletic (on loan, March-May 1991), Bristol Rovers (July 1991-May 1993).

All of reserve central midfielder David Wilson's six first team appearances for United were made as a substitute during the 1988-89 season. He had skippered his school team at rugby and then earned himself nine caps for England Schoolboys at football as a 15 year-old in 1984. He played in the first leg of the 1986 FA Youth Cup Final against Manchester City and three years later led the club's Youth team to third place in the Blue Stars Zurich International Youth Tournament in Switzerland.

Club record: 6 apps.

WILSON, Edgar

Born: circa 1867

Career: NEWTON HEATH (season 1889-90).

An inside-forward, Wilson had an excellent strike record with the Heathens for whom he assisted for just the one season. He notched two goals in the first-ever Football Alliance game v. Sunderland Albion in September 1889 which was won by 4-1. Nothing further is known about Wilson's career.

Club record: 21 goals 7 goals (also 15 'other' apps, 5 goals)

WILSON, John Thomas

Born: Leadgate, County Durham 8 March 1897.

Career: Leadgate St Ives, Leadgate United, Newcastle United (summer 1919), Leadgate Park (player-manager, 1920), Durham City (early 1922), Stockport County (seasons 1922-26), MANCHESTER UNITED (£500, September 1926), Bristol City (June 1932-summer 1933).

Initially an inside or centre-forward Jack Wilson sadly broke both his legs during his time with Newcastle. Thankfully he recovered full fitness, was converted into a half-back and went on to make well over 150 League and Cup appearances before joining United. A strong, physical player who enjoyed a challenge, Wilson was suspended for two months after being sent-off during a Central League game. That misdemeanour over and dealt with, he gave United sterling service over a period of six years before being released on a free transfer with a handful of other players in 1932.

He became a licensee in Tynemouth after pulling out of football.

Club record: 140 apps. 3 goals

WILSON, Mark Antony

Born: Scunthorpe, 9 February 1979

Career: MANCHESTER UNITED (apprentice, June 1995, professional February 1996), Wrexham (on loan, February-March 1998), Middlesbrough (£2.5 million deal with Jonathan Greening, July 2001).

Reserve midfield player Mark Wilson won both Schoolboy and Youth team honours for England as a teenager His appearances for United were severely restricted, causing him to seek fame at Middlesbrough during the summer of 2001.

Club record: 10 apps.

WILSON, Thomas Carter

Born: Preston, 20 October 1877. Died: Blackpool, 30 August 1940.

Career: Fishwick Ramblers FC (Preston), Ashton-in-Makerfield FC, West Manchester FC, Ashton Town, Ashton North End, Oldham County (summer 1896), Swindon Town (season 1897-98), Blackburn Rovers (1898-99), Swindon Town (1899-1900), Millwall Athletic (1900-01), Aston Villa (1901-02), Queen's Park Rangers (1902-04), Bolton Wanderers (summer 1904), Leeds City (late 1906), MANCHESTER UNITED (February 1908), Chorley FC (manager, June 1912), Rochdale (chairman, autumn 1919, then manager from July 1922 to February 1923).

An England international trialist (playing for the South v. the North in 1901) outside-left Tommy Wilson made 173 League appearances before joining United at the age of 30. His only outing for the club was against one of his former employers, Blackburn, just after he had moved from Leeds City. He became a licensee after finishing playing, having married the daughter of a publican in 1897.

Club record: one app.

WIMBLEDON

United's League results v the Dons:

Season	Div	Home	Away	Season	Div	Home	Away
1986-87	1	L 0-1	L 0-1	1993-94	PL	W 3-1	L 0-1
1987-88	1	W 2-1	L 1-2	1994-95	PL	W 3-0	W 1-0
1988-89	1	W 1-0	D 1-1	1995-96	PL	W 3-1	W 4-2
1989-90	1	D 0-0	D 2-2	1996-97	PL	W 2-1	W 3-0
1990-91	1	W 2-1	W 3-1	1997-98	PL	W 2-0	W 5-2
1991-92	1	D 0-0	W 2-1	1998-99	PL	W 5-1	D 1-1
1992-93	PL	L 0-1	W 2-1	1999-00	PL	D 1-1	D 2-2

Summary of League results

	P	W	D	L	F	A
Premier League	16	11	3	2	37	15
Division 1	12	5	4	3	14	11
Total	28	16	7	5	51	26
Home	14	9	3	2	24	9
Away	14	7	4	3	27	17
Total	28	16	7	5	51	26

FA Cup results v the Dons:

	Round	Venue	Result
1993-94	5	Away	W 3-0
1996-97	4	Home	D 1-1
	Replay	Away	L 0-1

League Cup result v the Dons:

	Round	Venue	Result
1988-89	3	Away	L 1-2

Players with both clubs include: M Appleton, D Bradley (United reserve), L Cunningham, T Gibson (also Dons coach), W Moyle (United reserve), J O'Kane, G Tomlinson.

WINTERBOTTOM, Sir Walter, CBE, OBE

Born: Oldham, Lancashire, 31 March 1913. Died: Guildford, 16 February 2002.
Career: Royton Amateurs FC, Manchester City (amateur), Mossley FC, MANCHESTER UNITED (May 1936, retired through injury 1938, but re-appeared as a guest player with Chelsea during WW2), Mossley (player-manager, briefly 1944-45).
Walter Winterbottom, a schoolteacher by profession, was England manager for 16 years: 1946-62. During that time he took his country to four World Cup Finals (1950-54-58-62) before handing over the duties to Alf Ramsey. He was awarded the CBE (for services to football) in 1963 and knighted in 1978. He was also honorary vice-President of the FA Council, a position he first held in 1945.
An extremely promising amateur centre-half, his career was ended abruptly through a back injury in 1938. Winterbottom then turned his attention to the coaching side of the game. After leaving the RAF (having attained the rank of Wing Commander) he joined the FA as their Director of Coaching. His coaching manual was widely respected, becoming the coaches' 'bible' in this country and abroad. As Director of Coaching he was made responsible for the England team on the restart in 1946, his job title becoming 'manager' in 1947. During his time as national team manager, England fulfilled a total of 139 matches of which 78 were won, with 33 draws and only 28 defeats, two of them against the famous Hungarians - 6-3 at Wembley and 7-1 in Budapest in 1953-54.
Club record: 27 apps.

WOLVERHAMPTON WANDERERS

Heathens/United's League results v the Wolves:

Season	Div	Home	Away	Season	Div	Home	Away
1892-93	1	W 10-1	L 0-2	1958-59	1	W 2-1	L 0-4
1893-94	1	W 1-0	L 0-2	1959-60	1	L 0-2	L 2-3
				1960-61	1	L 1-3	L 1-2
1922-23	2	W 1-0	W 1-0	1961-62	1	L 0-2	D 2-2
				1962-63	1	W 2-1	W 3-2
1924-25	2	W 3-0	D 0-0	1963-64	1	D 2-2	L 0-2
				1964-65	1	W 3-0	W 4-2
1931-32	2	W 3-2	L 0-7				
				1967-68	1	W 4-0	W 3-2
1936-37	1	D 1-1	L 1-3	1968-69	1	W 2-0	D 2-2
				1969-70	1	D 0-0	D 0-0
1938-39	1	L 1-3	L 0-3	1970-71	1	W 1-0	L 2-3
				1971-72	1	L 1-3	D 1-1
1946-47	1	W 3-1	L 2-3	1972-73	1	W 2-1	L 0-2
1947-48	1	W 3-2	W 6-2	1973-74	1	D 0-0	L 1-2
1948-49	1	W 2-0	L 2-3				
1949-50	1	W 3-0	D 1-1	1975-76	1	W 1-0	W 2-0
1950-51	1	W 2-1	D 0-0				
1951-52	1	W 2-0	W 2-0	1977-78	1	W 3-1	L 1-2
1952-53	1	L 0-3	L 2-6	1978-79	1	W 3-2	W 4-2
1953-54	1	W 1-0	L 1-3	1979-80	1	L 0-1	L 1-3
1954-55	1	L 2-4	L 2-4	1980-81	1	D 0-0	L 0-1
1955-56	1	W 4-3	W 2-0	1981-82	1	W 5-0	W 1-0
1956-57	1	W 3-0	D 1-1				
1957-58	1	L 0-4	L 1-3	1983-84	1	W 3-0	D 1-1

Summary of League results

	P	W	D	L	F	A
Division 1	74	32	13	29	127	116
Division 2	6	4	1	1	8	9
Home	40	26	5	9	80	44
Away	40	10	9	21	55	81
Total	80	36	14	30	135	125

FA Cup results v the Wolves:

	Round	Venue	Result
1948-49	Semi-final	Hillsborough	D 1-1 aet
	Replay	Goodison Pk	L 0-1
1964-65	6	Away	W 5-3
1965-66	5	Away	W 4-2
1972-73	3	Away	L 0-1
1975-76	6	Home	D 1-1
	Replay	Away	W 3-2 aet

Fact File
United's first meeting with Wolves in their Newton Heath days, took place on 15 October 1892 at North Road, Newton Heath. It was Newton Heath's first season of the League Football, Wolves' fifth, having been one of the founder members of the Football League in 1888. Newton Heath's season had got off to a poor start, just two drawn matches, four defeats, seven goals scored 19 conceded. Wolves, on the other hand had won four out of their first six. Wolves had had to make four changes through injuries, and after 12 minutes lost one of their forwards. Newton Heath took full advantage of the visitors' disarray ramming in ten goals in a record win which has stood throughout the club's long history. Amazingly, Newton Heath would win only five more matches all season, finishing in bottom place.
When United crashed 7-0 at Molineux in a Second Division fixture on 26 December 1931, the scoreline equalled their heaviest in League football (shared with reverses at Villa Park in 1930 and Ewood Park in 1926). The day before United had beaten Wolves 3-2 at Old Trafford!

Players with both clubs include: A Allman (Wolves reserve), G Andrews (United reserve), B Birch, P Bradshaw (United trialist), W Bryant, J Davies, A Dee (reserve with both clubs), G Farrow (United WW2), D Ferguson, J Ferguson, R Flash (United reserve), J Griffiths, W Halligan (United WW1 guest), W Harrison, P Ince, D Irwin, P Jones (Wolves amateur), J McCalliog, J McDonald (United WW2), S McGarvey, M Martin (Wolves on loan), C Mitten (Wolves WW2), B Morton, D Nardiello (WW junior), R Newsome (WW2 both clubs), W Pendergast (Wolves reserve), A Potts, A Rowley (Wolves amateur, United WW2), J Rowley (Wolves reserve), F Stapleton (Wolves trialist), M Todd (United junior), J Travers, S Tyler, J Wealands, W Wrigglesworth.
Also associated: T Docherty (manager of both clubs), F Buckley & I Greaves (United players, Wolves managers), R Atkinson (Wolves trialist, United manager), G Fellows (United reserve, Wolves coach), C Turner (United player, Wolves coach).

WOMBWELL, Richard

Born: Nottingham, summer 1877

Career: Bulwell FC, Ilkeston Town (late 1898), Derby County (1899-1902), Bristol City (summer 1902), MANCHESTER UNITED (March 1905), Heart of Midlothian (January 1907), Brighton & Hove Albion (summer 1907), Blackburn Rovers (with two other players, £750 combined fee, early 1908), Ilkeston United (for season 1910-11).

Outside-left Dick Wombwell, clever on the ball with good pace and strong kick, replaced Harry Williams in United's line-up towards the end of the 1904-05 season. He had already made 175 League appearances prior to joining United from Bristol City whom he helped win promotion to the First Division in 1905. He was one of three United players who joined Hearts together and in 1907 he collected a runners-up medal when the Edinburgh club were beaten by Celtic in the Scottish Cup Final. He ended an interesting career with over 50 goals to his credit in well over 275 senior outings.

Club record: 51 apps. 3 goals

WOOD, John

Born: Leven, Fife, Scotland, circa 1892

Career: Leven Boys, Hibernian (1912 - served in the Army during WW1), Dunfermline Athletic (£300, 1920), Lochgelly United (1921), Dumbarton (1921-22), MANCHESTER UNITED (£1,750, May 1922), Lochgelly United (June 1923), St Mirren (later 1923), East Stirlingshire (season 1925-26).

Right-winger John Wood collected a Scottish Cup runners-up medal with Hibernian in 1914 (beaten in a replay by Celtic) and in season 1920-21 scored 25 goals in 36 outings with Dumbarton. He netted on his debut for United against Crystal Palace in August 1922 but that proved to be his only goal for the club. Failing to impress after making a useful start to his Old Trafford career, he later finished up as St Mirren's joint top-scorer with 13 goals in 1923-24.

Club record: 16 apps. one goal

WOOD, Nicholas Anthony

Born: Oldham, 11 January 1966

Career: Hulme Grammar School, Oldham & District Boys, Manchester University, MANCHESTER UNITED (apprentice, June 1981, professional May 1983). Retired with back injury, January 1989.

England Youth international striker Nicky Wood made four appearances for United's during the late-1980s before his career was terminated by injury. He gained an Economics Degree whilst at university.

Club record: 4 apps.

WOOD, Raymond

Born: Hebburn-on-Tyne, County Durham, 11 June 1931. Died: Bexhill, East Sussex, 7 July 2002.

Career: Newcastle United (amateur, summer 1948), Darlington (professional, late summer 1949), MANCHESTER UNITED (£5,000, December 1949), Huddersfield Town (£1,500, December 1958), Bradford City (autumn 1965), Barnsley (season 1966-67), Los Angeles Wolves (coach/manager, 1968), Later coached in Canada, Cyprus, Greece, Kenya, Kuwait, the UAE and Zambia. He also served the Irish FA in Dublin and between 1969-72 revitalised the previously disheartened Cypriot national team. After pulling out of football Wood ran a sportswear business in Bexhill, East Sussex prior to taking over a suit department in Hastings. Retiring in 1991, he lived in Sussex until his death at the age of 71.

"Goalkeeper Ray Wood had lightning reflexes and made many world-class saves. "It amazed many people why he didn't win more than the three international caps he received" said United defender Bill Foulkes.

Wood joined United as an 18 year-old (as cover for Jack Crompton) just six months into his professional career. He made his debut for the club against his boyhood heroes, Newcastle United, in a League game at Old Trafford in December 1949 in front of 30,000 fans....the first of more than 200 senior appearances for the Reds. He had to wait until the 1953-54 season before finally establishing himself in the first XI (owing to the arrival in the camp of Reg Allen from QPR). But once in, Wood stayed and performed brilliantly at times between the posts. He helped United win successive League Championships in 1956 and 1957, also appearing in the 1957 FA Cup Final when he was injured in a collision with Peter McParland and had to leave the field. He bravely returned late on but Aston Villa took the trophy 2-1. A survivor of the Munich air crash (he regained consciousness under the wheels of the plane, having suffered head, hip and leg injuries) Wood, who also represented England and 'B' and Under-23 levels as well as playing three games for the Football League, was replaced between the posts at Old Trafford by Irishman Harry Gregg, played in more than 200 games for Huddersfield (he was signed by Bill Shankly) and in 1962 qualified as an FA coach. After his spells at Valley Parade and Oakwell he travelled the world, coaching in numerous countries.

Club record: 208 apps..

WOODCOCK, Wilfred

Born: Ashton-under-Lyne, early 1892

Career: Abbey Hey FC, Stalybridge Celtic, MANCHESTER UNITED (May 1912), Manchester City (£1,000, May 1920), Stockport County (early 1922), Wigan Borough (season 1924-25).

Ball-playing inside-forward Walter Woodcock was a regular in United's senior side during WW1, being the team's top-scorer on three occasions. Indeed, he amassed a total of 132 appearances for the club and netted the most goals (69) during the hostilities. He toured South Africa with the FA party in 1920, playing in two Commonwealth internationals. He could not come to an agreement with the United directors over a benefit and this led to him leaving the club. Woodcock, who helped rivals City finish runners-up in the League Championship in 1921, was Stockport's leading marksmen in 1923-24, going on to add a further 105 League appearances to his overall tally.

Club record: 61 apps. 21 goals.

WORKINGTON

Fact File:

Workington, a club often erroneously referred to as 'Workington Town', played for 26 seasons in the Football League. Formed in 1884 by local steelworkers, the club moved to Borough Park in 1937 and when New Brighton resigned from the League in 1951, Workington took their place. At one time, the legendary Bill Shankly managed the club before moving on to greater things at Liverpool. Their only meeting with United came in season 1957-58 when United had to travel into Cumbria for a Third Round FA Cup-tie. In front of a record 21,000 crowd, anxious to see Busby's famous 'Babes', Workington led 1-0 at half time. Was there a famous 'giant killing' act on the cards? No - a Dennis Viollet 'hat trick' in the second half saw a relieved United home. Within a month, many of the famous team were dead at Munich - and Workington never forgot those boys who for 90 minutes graced their tiny ground.

Workington never played higher than the Third Division, but consecutive seasons when finishing 23rd, 23rd, 24th and 24th in the Fourth, saw them voted out of the League in 1977 to be replaced by Wimbledon.

For many seasons the club shared their Borough Park ground with the town's Rugby League side Workington Town (hence the confusion in the football club's title). On one remarkable Saturday afternoon, the club staged home matches for both codes in what must have been a logistical miracle, with goal posts and line markings changed while one crowd was cleared and the other allowed in.

Players with both clubs include: W Boyd, J Cassidy, J Ferguson, D Healy (United reserve), T Spratt (United reserve), A Woodruff (United WW2).
Also associated: T Jones (United player, Workington trainer/coach), A Ashman (Workington manager, united scout).

WORLD CUP (Finals)

Manchester United's Old Trafford ground staged three Group 3 World Cup matches in July 1966.

In the first game Portugal beat Hungary 3-1 before a crowd of 29,886 and then the Portuguese (including Eusebio) defeated Bulgaria 3-0 in front of 25,438 spectators. The third encounter saw Hungary get the better of Bulgaria by 3-1, watched by a crowd of 24,129. There was great disappointment in Manchester that Brazil, although allocated to the 'North West' group, played all their matches in Liverpool at Goodison Park. This perhaps goes some way to explaining the disappointing crowds.

WORRALL, Harold

Born: Northwich, 19 November 1918. Died: 1979
Career: Winsford United, MANCHESTER UNITED (October 1937), Swindon Town (£1,000, June 1948-May 1949).
Full-back Harry Worrall joined United a month before his 19th birthday but owing to WW2, he had to wait more than nine years before making his League debut, doing so at the age of 28 against Wolverhampton Wanderers at Molineux in November 1946 in front of 46,704 spectators. He went back to Molineux again twelve months later and this time helped United to a staggering 6-2 win. Unfortunately with a wealth of defensive cover available at Old Trafford, Worrall's first team opportunities were few and far between.
Club record: 6 apps.

WORST START (to a season)

The worst start to a League season by United was made in 1930-31 when, playing in the First Division, they lost all of their opening 12 matches, conceding a total of 49 goals. The won only one of their first 18 matches, had registered just three victories after 26 starts and when the season ended all they had to show for their efforts was a total of 22 points (out of 84) gained from seven wins and eight draws.

WRATTEN, Paul

Born: Middlesbrough, 29 November 1970
Career: Middlesbrough Schools, MANCHESTER UNITED (apprentice, June 1987, professional December 1988) Contract cancelled by club, May 1992.
An England schoolboy international midfielder (nine caps won), Paul Wratten made just two substitute appearances for United's League side - his debut coming against Wimbledon in April 1991. Unfortunately he suffered recurring stress fractures to both legs and this led to his contract being cancelled.
Club record: 2 apps.

347

WREXHAM

Fact File
Steve Bruce scored for United in both legs of their 2nd round European Cup-winners Cup encounter with Wrexham in 1990-91.
As if Wrexham did not face enough problems in these ties, they suffered badly from the 'four foreigners only' regulation in vogue at that time. As Welsh Cup winners they were expected to field a predominantly Welsh side, but the bulk of their squad was English! As a result several YTS players had to be drafted in by manager Brian Flynn.
Players with both clubs include: T Bamford, P Barnes, H Blew (also Wrexham director), W Bryant, T Burke, B Carey (United reserve), T Cooke, W Davies, D Ferguson, D Gaskell, W Harrison, R Holland (United reserve) R Hunter, P Jones, A Kinsey, M Lane (United reserve), E McIlvenny, S McMillan, I Moir, J Morris (Wrexham WW2), W Pendergast (United amateur/reserve), J Pugh, J Rice (United reserve), L Roche (United reserve), E Savage, M Thomas, W Toms, M Wilson.
Also associated: J Rowley (United player, Wrexham manager), B Whitehouse (Wrexham player, United coach & scout).

United's FA Cup results v Wrexham:

	Round	Venue	Result
1956-57	4	Away	W 5-0
1994-95	4	Home	W 5-2

League Cup result v Wrexham:

	Round	Venue	Result
1969-70	3	Home	W 2-0

European Cup-winners' Cup results v. Wrexham:

	Round	Venue	Result
1990-91	2 (1)	Home	W 3-0
	2 (2)	Away	W 2-0

WRIGGLESWORTH, William Herbert

Born: South Elmsall, Yorkshire, 12 November 1912. Died: 1980
Career: Frickley Colliery FC, Chesterfield (summer, 1932), Wolverhampton Wanderers (December 1934), MANCHESTER UNITED (January 1937), guested for Arsenal, Brentford, Cardiff City, Chelsea, Walsall and York City during WW2; Bolton Wanderers (January 1947), Southampton (autumn 1947), Reading (summer 1948), Burton Albion (player-manager briefly in 1949), Scarborough (late 1949 to summer 1950), schools football coach (1951-52), Accrington Stanley (trainer, 1952-54).
Diminutive outside-left Billy Wrigglesworth had made 84 League appearances prior to joining United and he added another 30 to his tally after leaving the club. Only 5ft 4ins tall and weighing under 10 stones, he nevertheless gave a good account of himself and was never afraid to 'mix it' with the hefty defenders who opposed him.
An exceptionally tricky player, possessing a remarkable shot for a small man, he scored regularly. During WW2 he netted 24 goals in 70 matches. He eventually joined Bolton Wanderers in exchange for goalkeeper Bill Fielding when Matt Busby faced a goalkeeping crisis prior to an FA cup-tie.
Club record: 37 apps. 10 goals

Y for...

YORKE, Dwight

Born: Canaan, Tobago, 3 November 1971

Career: Signal Hill FC, Aston Villa (£120,000, December 1989), MANCHESTER UNITED (£12.6 million, August 1998), Blackburn Rovers (£2 million, July 2002).

Striker Dwight Yorke spent almost nine years with Aston Villa for whom he scored 97 goals in 287 appearances before his then record transfer to Manchester United - a move that made him the 12th costliest footballer in the game's history and the second highest-priced player involved in a transfer between two British clubs. A buddy of the great West Indies Test cricketer Brian Lara, Yorke, in fact, came on as a substitute no fewer than 40 times for Villa - 36 in the League - a club record.

Clever on the ball with a smart turn of speed and sweet right-foot shot - Yorke claimed the fastest goal in a Premiership match when he scored after just 13 seconds for United against Coventry City on 30 September 1995...this record was beaten, however, by Ledley King's strike for Tottenham Hotspur against Bradford City in December 2000 (timed at 10 seconds).

A regular performer in the Trinidad & Tobago national team (he now has over 30 caps to his credit) Yorke gained a League Cup winners medal with Villa in 1996 and then helped United win three Premiership titles (1999, 2000 & 2001), the FA Cup and the European Cup when, of course, he was a member of Reds' famous treble-winning side. When the curtain came down on the 2001-02 season - and despite having had to battle for a first team place with new-signing Ruud van Nistelrooy and Ole Gunnar Solskjaer, rumours about a possible move increased and when ex-United star Mark Hughes announced his retirement as a player at Blackburn, Yorke was quickly signed by Rovers boss Graeme Souness for £2 million, thus re-uniting him with his former Old Trafford colleague Andy Cole.

Club record: 152 apps. 66 goals

YATES, William

Born: Birmingham, circa 1883
Career: Aston Villa (1903) Brighton & Hove Albion (1905-06), MANCHESTER UNITED (June 1906), Heart of Midlothian (January 1907), Portsmouth (1908), Coventry City (1911-14). Retired during WW1.
Inside-forward Bill Yates, a reserve at Villa Park, did very well in his one season at Brighton but failed to deliver the goods for United. He helped Hearts reach the Scottish Cup Final in his first season at Tynecastle, finishing on the losing side to Celtic (3-0) along with Dick Wombwell (q.v.). He then made over 100 appearances for Portsmouth and Coventry. Certainly a player missed by both Villa and United!
Club record: 3 apps.

YEOVIL TOWN

United first met the gallant non-League side, Yeovil Town (formerly Yeovil & Petters United) in the third round of the FA Cup in 1937-38 and in front of 49,004 fans at Old Trafford they went through 3-0.
The second meeting was a 5th round tie played at Maine Road in February 1949. This time United romped to a convincing 8-0 victory in front of a massive 81,565 crowd. Jack Rowley scored five times in the match. Yeovil had been the sensation of the season's FA Cup competition. On their notorious sloping pitch at The Huish, the Southern League side had completed 'giant-killing' acts over League opposition: Bury (in round 3), then Sunderland (in round four). Player-manager Alec Stock was in great demand afterwards, going on to manage several League sides in a glittering career.
Player with both clubs: T Manns (Y & P Utd).
Also associated: L Page (United player, Yeovil & P Utd manager).

YORK CITY

United's League results v the Minstermen:

Season	Div	Home	Away
1974-75	2	W 2-1	W 1-0

Summary of League results

	P	W	D	L	F	A
Division 2	2	2	0	0	3	1
Home	1	1	0	0	2	1
Away	1	1	0	0	1	0
Total	2	2	0	0	3	1

League Cup results v the Minstermen:

	Round	Venue	Result
1995-96	2 (1)	Home	L 0-3
	2 (2)	Away	W 3-1

Fact File
York City produced one of the greatest Cup upsets of all time by winning 3-0 at Old Trafford in the Coca-Cola (League) Cup. Although United fielded a much stronger side in the second leg at York, the Minstermen held on for a famous victory.

Players with both clubs include: H Bough (United reserve), L Butt (United WW2), N Culkin (City junior), R Duckworth jnr (United reserve and also York manager), E Dunphy (United reserve), J Greening, T Heron, S James, E MacDougall, J Miller, R Pegg, E Savage (City WW2), J Scott, J Sharples (United reserve), T Spratt (United reserve), E Thompson, D Walker.
Also associated: W McGuinness (United player & manager of both clubs)

YORKE, Dwight

Refer to front of section.

YOUNG, Arthur

Born: Scotland, circa 1883
Career: Hurlford Thistle, NEWTON HEATH (October-November 1906).
Arthur Young had a month's trial with the Heathens, hoping to take over on the right-wing from Alf Schofield. He failed to make an impression, was sent back home.
Club record: 2 apps.

YOUNG, Terence Anthony

Born: Urmston, Manchester, 24 December 1952
Career: Urmston Schools football, MANCHESTER UNITED (amateur, May 1968, apprentice August 1968, professional December 1969), Charlton Athletic (January 1976), York City (free transfer, 1976-78), Bangor City (early 1980-82).
'Tony' Young made his senior debut for United as a substitute against Ipswich Town in September 1970. His next outing followed in April 1972 (v. Liverpool). He gained a regular place in the side as a full-back in 1972-73 (under manager Tommy Docherty) before losing his place during the relegation campaign of 1973-74. He was on reserve most of the time when the Second Division championship was won at the first attempt. He was paid a loyalty bonus of £6,000 by Charlton...after failing to settle in London! Ex-United player and manager Wilf McGuinness signed Young when he was in charge of York City.
Club record: 101 apps. one goal.

YOUTH FOOTBALL

• Tom Curry, Bill Inglis and Bert Whalley - the last two ex-United players - were three men who had a great influence on the post Second World War career development of the United starlets. It is one thing signing a promising schoolboy, but another altogether is making him into a mature professional footballer. Remembering that most of these young boys were living away from home for the first time in their lives it was therefore vitally important they had the right up-bringing, the sort of 'uncle figure' to whom to turn. Messrs Curry, Inglis and Whalley, in their different ways, played a massive role in producing player after player from United's famous Youth academy.
•Jimmy Murphy, the former West Bromwich Albion and Welsh international wing-half, was the RSM, the 'iron hand' who kept the youngsters on the straight and narrow, but it was Whalley who would make sure they wrote home

regularly to their families. Curry would listen to their problems sympathetically whilst Inglis would ensure that they always looked on the bright side, even in difficult times!

•Regrettably Curry and Whalley were with the team on that fateful day - 6 February 1958 - when so may people perished on the snow covered Munich runway.

•Inglis soldiered on as best he could until retiring in 1961 at the age of 67, having been a fantastic servant to Manchester United Football Club for 32 years as a player, assistant-trainer and coach. He died at his home in Sale, Cheshire in January 1968.

•Eric Harrison was born in Hebden Bridge on 5 February 1938. In a modest, unspectacular career, which spanned 14 years (1957-71) he served as a midfielder with Halifax Town, Hartlepool United, Southport and Barrow, accumulating 513 League appearances and scoring 16 goals. He then turned his hand to coaching where his main talent lay, first at Everton as Youth team coach, progressing via the reserves to first team level. However, in 1981, after ten excellent years at Goodison Park, he was appointed Youth team coach by Manchester United where his great skills began to bear fruit. When Alex Ferguson arrived at Old Trafford he first turned his attentions to the Youth Academy and found in Eric Harrison, the right man to carry out his plans. Current stars such as the Neville brothers, Butt, Scholes, Beckham, Giggs, Brown and many others have much to thank Eric Harrison for. He officially retired at the age of 60 (in 1998) but was retained by the club as an advisor at United's Youth Academy at Carrington. Harrison might not have achieved stardom as a player, but as 'star-maker' he had few equals.

•As laid down by current FA guidelines, United's Youth Scheme, later renamed the School of Excellence, has, since 1998, become known as the Manchester United Academy, the first Director being Les Kershaw, assisted by Youth Development Officer, David Bushell.

NB - See also under: Curry, Inglis, Whalley and FA Youth Cup.

Youth Caps
Listed here are several United players who were capped at Youth team level by their country:

Bermuda	S Goater
England	D Beckham, P Bielby, B Birch, S Brightwell, W Brown, W Bullimore, N Butt, W Casper, L Chadwick, G Clayton, J Connaughton, T Cooke, J Curtis, J Davis, D Edwards, J Elms, I Fitzpatrick, D Fox, D Fraser, D Gaskell, J Greening, A Hawksworth, A Hill, D Hilton, S James, D Johnson, E Johnson, EP Jones, B Kidd, J Lawrence, W McGuinness, J Macken, K Mooniaruck, RS Morton, B Muirhead, A Murphy, D Nardiello, G Neville, P Neville, R Noble, M Pearson, G Poole, P Rachubka, A Ritchie, L Roche, M Rose, P Scholes, RW Smith, T Spratt, P Sutcliffe, M Szmid, A Taylor, K Taylor, J Walker, R Wallwork, D Webber, R Wellens, A Westwood, P Wheatcroft, N Wood, P Wratten, ER Young.
Northern Ireland	K Gillespie, D Healy, D McCreery, P Mulryne, C Murdock
Republic of Ireland	D Brazil
Scotland	D Ferguson, G Hogg, S McAuley, A Notman, M Stewart
Wales	C Blackmore, R Giggs, D Graham, M Hughes, C Lawton, R Savage
Great Britain Youth	R Harrop.

Z for...

ZALAEGERSZEI
Manchester United played the Hungarian club over two legs in the 3rd qualifying round of the Champions League in August 2002. (See LATE NEWS).

ZARAGOZA TROPHY (City of)
United beat the Hungarian side Honved 3-1 and the host club Real Zaragoza 5-3 (after extra time) to win The City of Zaragoza Trophy in August 1982.

LATE NEWS EXTRA

United' early matches at the start of the 2002-03 season:

European Champions League

Preliminary Round

14.08.2002 1st leg	v. Zalaegerszeg (a)	lost 0-1	Att. 35,850
27.08.2002 2nd leg	v. Zalaegerszeg (h)	won 5-0	Att. 66,814

Competition Proper (Group 'F')

18.09.2002	v. Maccabi Haifi (h)	won 5-2	Att. 63,439

Summary

A 90th minute strike by Koplarovic ruined United's trip to Hungary but the return at Old Trafford turned out to be a formality as goals by Ruud Van Nistelrooy (2, one penalty), David Beckham, Paul Scholes and Ole Gunnar Solsjkaer eased Ferguson's men into the competition proper. The visitors had ex-Charlton Athletic goalkeeper Sasa Ilic sent-off in the second-half.

Diego Forlan scored his first senior goal (a late penalty) against Haifi. In this same match Spanish goalkeeper Ricardo and 19 year-old Danny Pugh (born 19.10.82 in Mancester) made their United debuts.

When the champions League draw was made - on 29 August 2002 - United were confirmed in Group 'F' along with the German champions Bayer Leverkusen (who eliminated the Reds at the semi-final stage in 2001-02), Olympiakos (Greece) and Maccabi Haifa.

Start to the 2002-03 Premiership programme - United's 100th League season...

17.08.2002	v. W B Albion	(h) won 1-0	Att. 67,645
23.08.2002	v. Chelsea	(a) drew 2-2	Att. 41,541
31.08.2002	v. Sunderland	(a) drew 1-1	Att. 47,586
03.09.2002	v. Middlesbrough	(h) won 1-0	Att. 67,464
11.09.2002	v. Bolton Wds	(h) lost 0-1	Att. 67,623
14.09.2002	v. Leeds United	(a) lost 0-1	Att. 39,622
21.09.2002	v. Tottenham Hotspur	(h) Won 1-0	Att. 67,611

Super-sub Ole Gunner Solsjkaer came off the bench to score his 100th senior goal for United and earn all three points against newly-promoted WBA on the opening day of the season. His goal in the 78th minute came after the Baggies had lost skipper Derek McInnes, sent-off for a two-footed lunge at Paul Scholes.

United bounced back twice to earn a point at Stamford Bridge. Chelsea led on three minutes (via William Gallas); David Beckham equalised on 26 minutes; Dutchman Boudewijn Zenden gave the Blues the lead on the stroke of half-time and then Ryan Giggs emulated Solsjkaer's feat by reaching a century of goals for the Reds with another equaliser halfway through the second-half.

Roy Keane was sent-off for the tenth time as a United player in the 1-1 draw at The Stadium of Light. He was dismissed by referee Uriah Rennie for elbowing fellow Republic of Ireland international Jason McAteer in the face in the last minute of the game after Ryan Giggs' 7th minute goal had been cancelled out by Tore Andre Flo's close range effort with 20 minutes remaining.

A 28th minute penalty, struck home by Ruud Van Nistelrooy, gave United a hard-earned home win over plucky Middlesbrough.
Bolton recorded their second successive Premiership win at Old Trafford - and again it was Kevin Nolan, scorer of the winning goal in a 2-1 victory in October 2001, who claimed the all-important strike this time round.

Defeat at Leeds in mid-September (Harry Kewell's goal deciding the issue halfway through the second-half) meant that United had made their worst-ever start to a Premiership campaign (8 points gained from the first six matches). It also ended a run of 14 away Premiership games without defeat. Rio Ferdinand got a hostile reception on his return to Elland Road.

Pre-Season Matches
United's build-up to the 2002-03 season included the following fixtures:

20.07.2002	v. Shelbourne*	(a)	won 5-0
27.07.2002	v. Chesterfield **	(a)	won 5-0 (John Duncan's testimonial)
27.07.2002	v. Bournemouth	(a)	won 3-2 (Mel Machin's testimonial)
30.07.2002	v. Valarenga	(a)	won 2-1 (in Norway)
10.08.2002	v. Boca Juniors+	(h)	won 2-0 (Van Nistelrooy 2)

Notepad
17 year-old Kieron Richardson scored in the 5-0 win over Chesterfield at Saltergate.
The home game with Boca Juniors was In aid of UNICEF: The United Nations Children's Fund.

Amsterdam International Tournament

02.08.2002	v. Ajax	lost 1-2	(Scholes)
04.08.2002	v. Parma (Italy)	won 3-0	(Giggs, Veron, Solskjaer)

Transfer Trail
Bizarrely United signed goalkeeper Ricardo Lopez Felipe from the Spanish club Real Vallodolid on transfer deadline-day (31 August) for £1.5 million...after failing to sign Portuguese international Ricardo, another 'keeper, from the Portuguese side Boavista!

Defender Ronny Johnsen joined Aston Villa; Bojan Djordic signed for AGF Denmark and Danny Webber extended his loan spell with Watford. Three reserves - Kevin Grogan (to Millwall), Kirk Hilton (to Livingston) and Jimmy Davis (to Swindon Town) - also left Old Trafford.

Six former United players also found new clubs: Paul Ince signed for Wolves (from Middlesbrough), Jesper Blomqvist joined Charlton Athletic (from Everton), Southampton snapped up Andre Kanchelskis (from Rangers), Lee Sharpe left Bradford City for Exeter City but quit St James' Park after just 17 days; Jovan Kirovski switched from Crystal Palace to Birmingham City (after a loan spell with Borussia Dortmund) and Pat McGibbon joined Wigan Athletic from Tranmere Rovers on a monthly contract.

● Former United player Steve Coppell was appointed assistant-manager of Swindon Town in September 2002.